I0138945

CONCISE DICTIONARY ENGLISH-HINDI

A Perfect Reference tool for Writers, Educationist, Aspirants of Competitive Exams & Students

Prof. Shrikant Prasoon

Published by

F-2/16, Ansari Road, Daryaganj, New Delhi-110002
☎ 011-23240026, 011-23240027 • *Fax* 011-23240028
Email info@vspublishers.com • *Website* www.vspublishers.com

Regional Office Hyderabad
5-1-707/1, Brij Bhawan (Beside Central Bank of India Lane)
Bank Street, Koti, Hyderabad - 500 095
☎ 040-24737290
E-mail vspublishershyd@gmail.com

Branch Office Mumbai
☎ 022-22098268
E-mail vspublishersmum@gmail.com

ISBN 978-93-505713-6-1
Edition 2014

Printed at Param Offseters Okhla New Delhi-110020

Publisher's Note/प्रकाशकीय

A good response from dealers and commendable appreciation received from readers to our previously published dictionaries on science, commerce and language subjects has encouraged us to undertake yet another publication garnering high demand – An **English-Hindi-Dictionary**. The use of lexicographical techniques and latest compilation methods has further enhanced the utility of this dictionary. This edition will meet the requirements of students, researchers, travelers, scholars, translators, educationists, and writers. For better usefulness, 'Words or Terms' have been drawn from literature, science, geography, commerce & business etc. 'Terms' come tagged with explanatory meaning in Hindi alone but with a sentence in English, for clear understanding for use both in speaking and writing.

'Terms' have been serialized in alphabetical order, *i.e.,* A-Z for ease in searching. To the extent possible, 'Terms' used in common parlance have been included, avoiding less frequent ones.

In the Appendices section, body parts, common ailments, apparel, cereals, fruit & vegetables, herbs & spices, and household items etc have been included for additional reference making it even more comprehensive.

We hope hoped that this dictionary will prove useful for student community besides others such as, educationists, writers, translators and common man.

We would be happy to have your views and comments for improving the content and quality of the book.

विज्ञान एवं वाणिज्य विषयों पर हमारे द्वारा प्रकाशित शब्द कोशों को बाजार से प्राप्त सराहना के फलस्वरूप हमने इस शब्दकोश को तैयार किया है जिसकी माँग उत्तरोत्रर बढ़ती जा रही है

इस शब्दकोश को कोशविज्ञान के सिद्धातों और तकनीक को उपयोग में लाने के कारण यह शब्दकोश उपयोगिता में काफी व्यापक हो गया है। इस संस्करण से छात्रों, शिक्षाविदों, भ्रमणकारियों, शोधकर्ताओं, विद्वानों और लेखक की आवश्यकता की पूरी मदद मिलेगी। इस शब्दकोश में विभीन्न स्रोतों जैसे

अर्थशास्त्र, वाणिज्य, विज्ञान प्रोद्यौगिकी, प्रबंधन राजनीति भूगोल इत्यादि से आये शब्दों को भी शामिल किया गया है और साथ में उस शब्द के अर्थ को ठीक से समझने में मदद के लिये एक वाक्य भी दिया गया है अंग्रेजी भाषा में।

प्रत्येक अंग्रेजी शब्द या प्रविष्टि (एंट्री) का व्याकरण के साथ ही हिंदी और प्रविष्टियों को अल्फाबेटिकल (A – Z) रूप में प्रस्तुत किया गया है जिससे कि खोजना सरल एवं आसान है। केवल उन्ही प्रविष्टियों को शामिल किया गया है जो रोजमर्रा के बातचीत में प्रयोग में आती है। उपयोग में कम आने वाले शब्दों को विशेष रूप से सम्मिलित नहीं किया गया है।

पाठकों की सहूलियत हेतु शब्दकोश के अंत में अनेकों उपयोगी व अनिवार्य परिशिष्ट भी दिये गये हैं। शब्दकोश पर्यटकों, लेखकों, शिक्षाविदो और अनुवादों के लिये अत्यन्त उपयोगी साबित होगा।

हम पुस्तक की सामग्री और गुणवत्ता में सुधार लाने के लिये अपने विचारों और टिप्पणियों का स्वागत करेंगे।

Experiment Method/प्रयोग विधि

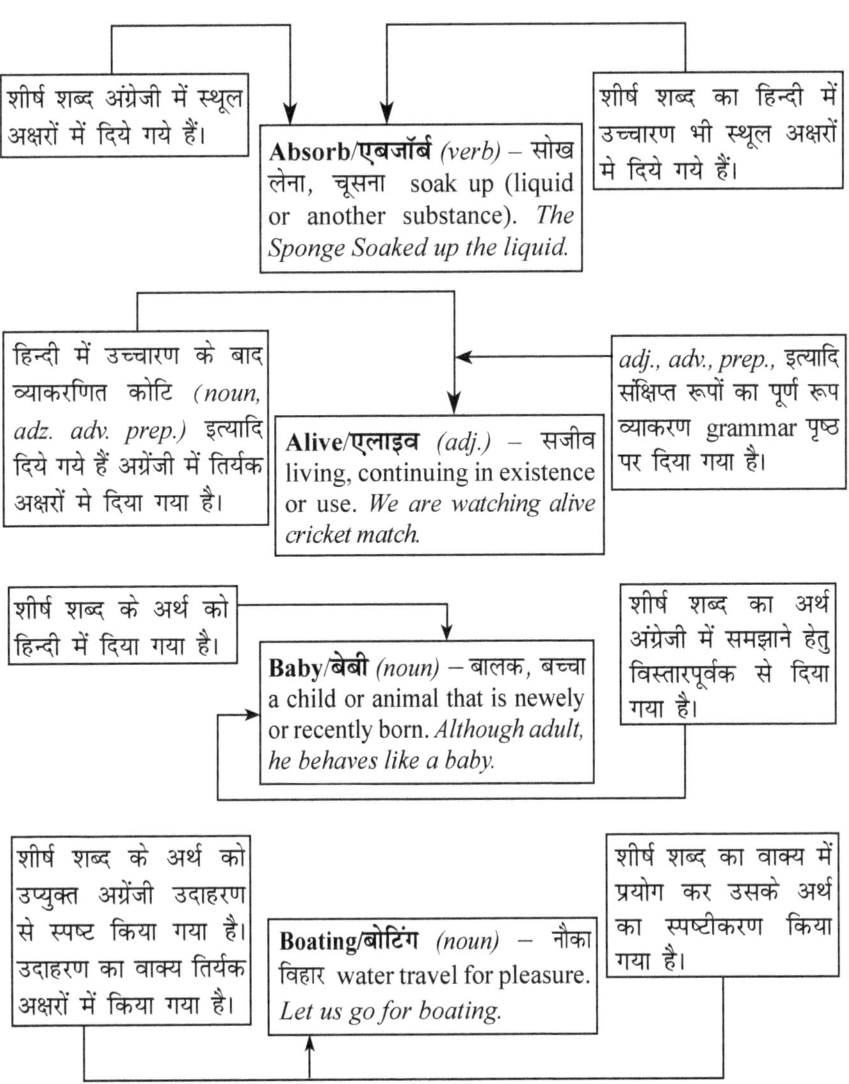

शीर्ष शब्द अंग्रेजी में स्थूल अक्षरों में दिये गये हैं।
शीर्ष शब्द का हिन्दी में उच्चारण भी स्थूल अक्षरों मे दिये गये हैं।
Absorb/एबजॉर्ब (verb) – सोख लेना, चूसना soak up (liquid or another substance). The Sponge Soaked up the liquid.
हिन्दी में उच्चारण के बाद व्याकरणित कोटि (noun, adz. adv. prep.) इत्यादि दिये गये हैं अग्रेंजी में तिर्यक अक्षरों मे दिया गया है।
adj., adv., prep., इत्यादि संक्षिप्त रूपों का पूर्ण रूप व्याकरण grammar पृष्ठ पर दिया गया है।
Alive/एलाइव (adj.) – सजीव living, continuing in existence or use. We are watching alive cricket match.
शीर्ष शब्द के अर्थ को हिन्दी में दिया गया है।
शीर्ष शब्द का अर्थ अंग्रेजी में समझाने हेतु विस्तारपूर्वक से दिया गया है।
Baby/बेबी (noun) – बालक, बच्चा a child or animal that is newely or recently born. Although adult, he behaves like a baby.
शीर्ष शब्द के अर्थ को उप्युक्त अग्रेंजी उदाहरण से स्पष्ट किया गया है। उदाहरण का वाक्य तिर्यक अक्षरों में किया गया है।
शीर्ष शब्द का वाक्य में प्रयोग कर उसके अर्थ का स्पष्टीकरण किया गया है।
Boating/बोटिंग (noun) – नौका विहार water travel for pleasure. Let us go for boating.

Label/लेबल

also	भी	*humorous*	हास्यकर
abbr.	संक्षिप्त रूप	*informal*	अनौपचारिक
chemistry	रसायन विज्ञान	*law*	कानूनी प्रयोग
compounds	यौगिक शब्द	*literary*	साहित्यिक
exclamation	विस्मयादिबोधक शब्द	*mathematics*	गणित
feminine	स्त्रीलिंग	*medical*	चिकित्सा
figurative	अलंकारिक	*music*	संगीत
formal	औपचारिक	*official*	आधिकारिक
geography	भूगोल	*philosophy*	दर्शन शास्त्र
geology	भूविज्ञान	*technical*	तकनीकी
geometry	रेखा गणित	*written*	लिखित
grammar	व्याकरण		

Grammar in Short/संक्षेप में व्याकरण

abbr.	abbreviation	संक्षिप्त
adv.	adverb	क्रियाविशेषण
adj.	adjective	विशेषण
conj.	conjunction	समुच्चयबोधक शब्द
det.	*determiner*	निर्धारक
excl.	exclamatory	विस्मयादिबोधक शब्द
noun	noun	संज्ञा
prep.	preposition	पूर्वसर्ग
pl.	plural	बहुवचन
verb	verb	क्रिया
[American English]	American English	अमेरिकन अंग्रेजी
[British English]	British English	ब्रिटिश अंग्रेजी

Table of Content/विषय-सूची

भूमिका 1
A.. 5
B.. 36
C.. 57
D.. 99
E.. 124
F.. 140
G.. 160
H.. 174
I.. 191
J.. 221
K.. 224
L.. 228
M.. 238
N.. 257
O.. 266
P.. 287
Q.. 326
R.. 329
S.. 352
T.. 397
U.. 418
V.. 428
W.. 436
X.. 443
Y.. 444
Z.. 446
Appendix-1 448
Appendix-2 450
Appendix-3 452
Appendix-4 455
Appendix-5 456
Appendix-6 461
Appendix-7 462
Appendix-8 465
Appendix-9 467
Appendix-10 469
Appendix-11 471
Appendix-12 473
Appendix-13 475
Appendix-14 478
Appendix-15 481
Appendix-16 483
Appendix-17 485
Appendix-18 489
Appendix-19 491
Appendix-20 493
Appendix-21 502
Appendix-22 504
Appendix-23 507

Appendix-24 509
Appendix-25 511
Appendix-26 512
Appendix-27 513
Appendix-28 528
Appendix-29 579
Appendix-30 591
Appendix-31 592
Appendix-32 594
Appendix-33 597

भूमिका

मैं पुस्तकों, शब्दकोशों के बीच उन्हीं के साथ बड़ा हुआ। जैसे-जैसे मैं बड़ा होता गया, मेरे पास शब्दकोशों की संख्या बढ़ती चली गयी। सत्तर के दशक में मैंने एक माह के अपने पूरे वेतन को देकर 'रीडर्स डायजेस्ट इन्साइक्लोपिडिक डिक्शनरी' मँगायी थी। वह आज भी है तथा इतना भारी है कि उसे मेज पर भी नहीं रखा जाता। वह अलमारी में ही स्थिर लेटा रहता है। कोई शब्द जब किसी अन्य शब्दकोश में नहीं मिलता तभी उसकी याद आती है और उसमें उसका विवरण प्राप्त हो जाता है।

कोई भी कह सकता है कि तब वेतन ही कितना था? जितना भी था, यथेष्ट था। आज रुपये का मूल्य ही नहीं है। अट्ठाइस हजार दीजिए तब एक तोला सोना मिलेगा। उस समय रुपये की खरीद-शक्ति बहुत अधिक थी। 250/- में एक भर सोना। आज के हिसाब से उस कोश की कीमत हुई बयालिस हजार रुपये। आश्चर्य है न? मगर यही सच है। मिट्टी और वस्तुओं की कीमत बढ़ी है, और रुपये और आदमी कीमत घटी है।

आज यह हिसाब बता पाना बहुत मेहनत का काम है कि मेरे पास कितने शब्दकोश है। अति लघु डेढ़ इंच गुणा ढाई इंच के शब्दकोश से लेकर बारह इंच गुणा पन्द्रह इंच तक के शब्दकोश है। कई भाषाओं में है, साहित्य कोश है समानार्थ और विपरीतार्थक कोश है किन्तु श्री वामन शिवराम आप्टे के 'संस्कृत हिन्दी शब्दकोश' की बराबरी करने वाला कोई दूसरा शब्दकोश नहीं है क्योंकि उन्होंने स्थान और पंक्ति उदाहरण में देकर यह बताया है कि किस स्थान पर किस कवि-महाकवि ने किस अर्थ में उस शब्द-विशेष का प्रयोग किया। है न आश्चर्यजनक? मगर सच है। माननीय आप्टे जी ने कितना पढ़ा और याद कर रखा था कि शब्दों के भिन्न-भिन्न अर्थों में प्रयोग के कई-कई उदाहरण दे दिये हैं। उन्हें मेरा सादर नमन है।

अगर मैं दूसरा जनम पा सका और इस जन्म के ज्ञान को बचा पाया तथा इतना भी और संचित कर सका तब मैं हिन्दी में वैसा ही एक शब्दकोश लिखूँगा। यह निवेदन भी मैं कर रहा हूँ कि जो वैसा ज्ञान रखते है वे उनके कोश को देखकर वैसा कोश तैयार करने का प्रयास करें। श्री गणेश और माँ सरस्वती उनकी सहायता करेंगे।

इतने शब्दकोशों के जमा होने के पीछे दो अन्य कारण भी थे। एक तो यह कि मेरे 'सोलोमन पब्लिक स्कूल' में जो शिक्षक कार्य करते थे उन्हें मैं कोश देखने के लिए प्रेरित और यदा-कदा मजबूर भी करता था। दूसरा कारण था, मेरे पढ़ने-लिखने के तीन स्थान का हो जाना। हर जगह मुझे कोशों की आवश्यकता पड़ती थी और कई-कई कोश

रहते थे। विद्यालय में अलग थे और मेरे छोटे से पुस्तकालय में भी जिसमें मेरे बैठने और पढ़ने-लिखने का स्थान कभी नहीं बन सका, उसमें कोश रखे रहते हैं।

उन पुराने और अब के नये शब्दकोशों को देखने से अनेक अन्तर स्पष्ट हो जाते है। अंग्रेजी हिन्दी शब्दकोशों को जानबूझकर अंग्रेजीमय कर दिया गया है जो एक षड़्यन्त्र की तरह लगता है कि भारतीयों को भारतीय शब्दों से बिलग कर दिया जाय ताकि वे हिन्दी शब्दों के बदले अंग्रेजी के शब्दों का प्रयोग करें और हिन्दी कभी राष्ट्रभाषा न बन सके। अपनी अस्मिता गवाँकर केवल हिंगलिश बनकर किसी कोने में दुबकी रहे और दूसरे यह चिल्लाकर कह सकें कि हिन्दी में शब्द ही नहीं हैं। पहले केवल वैज्ञानिक शब्दावली के सन्दर्भ में ऐसी उक्ति आती थी। अब अखबारों के हर लेख में, यहाँ तक कि शीर्षक और उपशीर्षक में भी अंग्रेजी शब्दों की भरमार रहती है। प्रचारों तक में भी यही स्थिति है। वस्त्रों पर भी सार्थक, निरर्थक अंग्रेजी लिखा मिलता है।

इस सन्दर्भ में निम्न बिन्दुओं पर विचार किया जाना चाहिए-

⇛ विदेशी प्रभाव में और हिन्दी को प्रभावहीन करने के उद्देश्य से अंग्रेजी हिन्दी जो नये शब्दकोश आये हैं, विशेषकर अंग्रेजी-हिन्दी कोश, उनमें अंग्रेजी के नब्बे प्रतिशत शब्दों का अंग्रेजी शब्द ही हिन्दी अर्थ के रूप में देवनागरी लिपि में दिया गया है। यानी हिन्दी में उस शब्द के लिए शब्द नहीं है।

⇛ अधिकांश शब्दों का हिन्दी अर्थ न देकर उस शब्द का अर्थ हिन्दी में समझाया गया है।

⇛ अगर हिन्दी अर्थ दिया भी गया है तब सबसे अन्त में कही एक से अधिक हिन्दी में अर्थ है तब भी प्रमुख अर्थ को अन्त में दिया गया है।

⇛ ऐसे बहुत कम शब्द है जहाँ सीधे और सही हिन्दी अर्थ दिया गया है। शायद उसे अन्य तरह से दे पाना सम्भव नहीं रहा हो।

⇛ अंग्रेजी अर्थ देने के बाद दूसरा स्थान उर्दू को दिया गया है और हिन्दी शब्दों को ध केलकर पीछे कर दिया गया है। तब नाम अंग्रेजी हिन्दी शब्दकोश देना चाहिए था।

⇛ शब्दों को जोड़कर कठिन करके संस्कृत को जनसमुदाय से दूर कर देने का एक सफल प्रयास जो मध्यकाल और ब्रिटिश युग में हुआ, हिन्दी शब्दों को जोड़कर कठिन करने का प्रयास इनमें भी किया गया है। यह सबको पता है कि अपभ्रंश के रूप में हिन्दी की उत्पत्ति ही इस या ऐसी कठिनाई के विरोध में हुई फिर हिन्दी को कठिन बनाने का प्रयास क्यों फिर हिन्दी को कठिन करने का अर्थ? कारण स्पष्ट है, इसे भारत की राष्ट्रभाषा कभी न बनने देना।

⇛ अंग्रेजी शब्दों का अर्थ भी भ्रम फैलाने के लिए किया गया है। कुछ अन्य शब्दों के साथ रहने पर जो अर्थ होता है बिना उन शब्दों के ही अस्सी प्रतिशत शब्दों का वही अर्थ दिया गया है जैसे 'प्रिवेण्ट' का अर्थ रोकना होता है, उसे घटित होने से रोकना बताया गया है तब क्या प्रवेश करने और सदस्य बनने से रोकने के लिए इस शब्द का प्रयोग नहीं होगा।

⇛ हिन्दी में उच्चारण लिखने में भी घपला है। आधे वर्णों का प्रयोग नहीं हुआ है जबकि हिन्दी बिना आधे वर्णों के लिखी ही नहीं जाती। हिन्दी की आत्मा को ही मार देने का यह निम्नस्तरीय प्रयास है।

⇛ हलन्तों की भरमार है, जैसे कि हिन्दी हलन्त से ही लिखी जाती है।

⇛ शब्दों के बीच में हलन्त का प्रयोग अति-विशिष्ट स्थान पर ही होता है जो सामान्य पाठक के लिए नहीं होता। हिन्दी में शब्द के अन्त में हलन्त का प्रयोग होता है इनमें लिखें उच्चारणों में हलन्त ही हलन्त है।

⇛ जहाँ किसी वर्ण का पूरा उच्चारण होता है यानी स्वर के साथ होता है वहाँ हलन्त का प्रयोग होता ही नहीं। हलन्त का प्रयोग वस्तुतः व्यंजन से स्वर को अलग करने के लिए किया जाता है।

⇛ उच्चारण लिखने में न आधे वर्णों का प्रयोग हुआ है और न रेफ का, जबकि ये हिन्दी भाषा के प्राण से है। ऐसे शब्दकोशों का प्रयोग करने वाले रेफ और आधे अक्षर भूला जायेंगे।

⇛ यहाँ तक कि जो दूसरे वर्णों के साथ र् लगाया जाता है जैसे क्रम, ग्राम या कृपा, मृत आदि उच्चारण लिखने में उनका प्रयोग है ही नहीं।

⇛ इनके अतिरिक्त उच्चारण लिखने नब्बे प्रतिशत उच्चारण में एक अतिरिक्त 'अ' जोड़ा गया है जो उच्चारण को सही होने ही नहीं देगा और हिन्दी पाठकों को भ्रमित कर देगा।

⇛ कहीं भी द्विगुणित 'अ' ध्वनि का चिह्न ऽ का प्रयोग नहीं है।

⇛ इन सबके कारण हिन्दी जानने वाले बच्चे कभी भी अंग्रेजी शब्दों को उच्चरित नहीं कर सकेंगे और अंग्रेजी से तो दूर रहेंगे ही, हिन्दी से भी दूर हो जायेंगे।

⇛ नुक्ते का मनमाना प्रयोग है जबकि हिन्दी में नुक्ता होता ही नहीं है और न वर्तनी आदि में इसे बताया या पढ़ाया ही जाता है।

⇛ जबकि यह नियम स्पष्ट है कि शब्द किसी भी भाषा के हों जब वे दूसरी भाषा में ग्रहण किये जाते हैं तब उन पर दूसरी भाषा के व्याकरण का शासन चलता है। रेल और स्टेशन अंग्रेजी भाषा के शब्द है किन्तु हिन्दी में इनका बहुवचन रेल्स या स्टेशन नहीं, रेलों, स्टेशनों होगा। इस नियम का भी खूब मजाक उड़ाया गया है।

⇛ एक षड्यन्त्र पहले ही से चल रहा था कि भारत से नौकरी या अध्ययन के लिए विदेश जाने वाले हर व्यक्ति को अंग्रेजी की अलग परीक्षा देनी पड़ती है या विदेश में जाकर फिर अंग्रेजी सीखना पड़ता है। पच्चीस वर्षों का उनका देश में किया गया प्रयास व्यर्थ कर दिया जाता है केवल एक छोटा-सा काम करके कि भारत में तो अंग्रेजी शब्दकोश आते है उन्हें ब्रिटेन में नहीं बेचा जाता और वहाँ जो कोश बेचा जाता है उसे भारत में नहीं आने दिया जाता।

⇛ पहले जो शब्दकोश भारत में बिकता था, नये कोश उससे भिन्न है। इसलिए यह आवश्यक हो गया कि पुराना शब्दकोश इस देश में रहे ही नहीं। इसलिए नया संस्करण देकर पुराना संस्करण वापस ले लिया गया किन्तु बड़े पैमाने पर वापसी के कार्य के बावजूद बहुत सारे लोगों ने अपनी प्रतियाँ नहीं दी और इसका प्रमाण रह ही गया।

⇛ जब अंग्रेजी एक ही है तब अलग-अलग शब्दकोश क्यों?

⇛ जब आप भारतीयों के लिए अलग शब्दकोश देते हैं तब उन्हें ब्रिटेन में प्रयुक्त अंग्रेजी भाषा की परीक्षा क्यों लेते हैं? इसलिए बहुत अच्छी अंग्रेजी जानने, लिखने, बोलने वाले भारतीयों को भी अन्त तक अंग्रेजी सीखते रहने के लिए बाध्य किया जाता है।

⇛ एक और भी कारण है-विदेशों में भारतीयों की अनुपम सफलता से भी ईर्ष्या है इसलिए अंकुश लगाने के लिए नये-नये नियम और आदेश आते रहते है।

इसलिए एक संक्षिप्त और एक वृहद् 'अंग्रेजी हिन्दी शब्दकोश' की आवश्यकता महसूस हुई। वृहद् कोश में अभी कुछ बिलम्ब होगा किन्तु यह संक्षिप्त कोश आपके हाथ में है।

⇛ इसमें अंग्रेजी शब्द है और देवनागरी में उनका प्रचलित उच्चारण है जिसमें किसी प्रकार के बनावटीपन को नहीं आने दिया गया है।

⇛ इस शब्दकोश में है हिन्दी में सभी मुख्य अर्थ। अधिकतर शब्दों के कई अर्थ होते है और चेष्टा यह रही है कि सभी अर्थ दिये जायें।

⇛ इस शब्दकोश को बहुत परिश्रम से सहज, सरल और पाठकों के लिए अति उपयोगी बनाया गया है। कोई तामझाम नहीं, कोई बनावट नहीं और निश्चित रूप से कोई षड़यन्त्र नहीं।

⇛ यह सब पाठकों के हित में और उन्हीं के लाभ के लिए है स्पष्ट है और सीधा है।

⇛ जो अंग्रेजी शब्दों के लिए हिन्दी चाहते है, उनके लिए यह अति उपयोगी शब्दकोश है।

Aa

A/ए - अंग्रेजी वर्णमाला का पहला अक्षर the first letter of the English alphabet

(1) First note in music.

(2) First known quantity in Algebra.

Aback/एबैक *(adv.)* - पीछे की ओर

The ship came into the harbour with all sails aback.

Abaction/एबैक्सन *(noun)* - एक साथ बहुत से पशुओं की चोरी

Police have registered a case of abaction.

Abandon/एबैंडॅन *(verb)* - त्यागना

We abandoned the old car in an empty parking lot.

Abase/एबेस *(verb)* - नीचा करना, मान घटाना

He was angry with his friend and abased him in public.

Abash/एबैश *(verb)* - घबड़ा देना, संकुचित करना

His father abashed him by criticizing him before his friends.

Abashment/एबैशमेंट *(noun)* - लज्जा से आयी हुई विकलता

I left abashment as it was my first time to perform on stage.

Abba/एब्बा *(noun)* - पिता, सबका पिता, ईश्वर

Abba will certainly listen to our prayers.

Abbess/एबेस *(noun)* - महन्तिन

He wanted the abbess to hear his confession.

Abbey/एबे *(noun)* - मठ, गुरुद्वारा a

Once there was an abbey here now the building is dilapidated and deserted.

Abbot/एबॉट *(noun)* - मठाधिकारी, गुरुद्वारे का महन्त

The abbot here is very popular he listen the grievances of all people.

Abbreviate/एब्रीवियेट *(verb)* - छोटा करना, संक्षिप्त करना

Etc. is an abbreviated form of etcetera.

Abdal/एबडल *(noun)* - दरवेश

He behaves like on abdal.

Abdiel/एबडियल *(noun)*- ईश्वर का अनुचर, देवदूत

I hope that on abdiel will come for our help.

Abdomen/एबडोमेन *(noun)* - मनुष्य का पेट या उदर

His abdomen is flat because he does a lot of exercise.

Abdominal/एबडोमिनल *(adj)* - उदर सम्बन्धी

We took our brother to doctor as he complained of severe abdominal pain.

Abduce/एबड्यूस *(verb)*- एक भाग से दूसरे को पृथक् करना

The problem was big but he soon abduced the conclusion.

Abduct/एबडक्ट *(verb)* - बहका ले जाना

Ashok's son has been abducted.

Abduction/एबडक्सन *(noun)* - फुसलाकर किसी का अपहरण करना

Abduction of children has increased and the police have become active.

Abecedarion/एबसेडेरियन *(noun)* - नवसिखुआ

He is an abecedarian learning the basics of computer.

Abed/एबेड *(adv.)* - बिछावन पर

He was so tired that he went abed at once and slept.

Aberrance/एबेरेन्स *(noun)* - धर्मनिष्ठा से विचलन

Aberrance from the right path usually occurs in young age.

Abet/एबेट *(verb)* - सहारा देना

His wife died and police have arrested him for abetment to suicide.

Abhor/एब्हॉर *(verb)* - घृणापूर्वक अविश्वास करना

I abhor scenes of crime and violence.

Abide/एबाइड *(verb)* - पालन करना

We must abide by the rules of traffic.

A

Ability/एबिलिटी *(noun)* – अधिकार, योग्यता
He has the ability of speaking five languages.

Abject/एबजेक्ट *(adj.)* – अधम, नीच
He lives in abject poverty on footpath.

Ablactate/एबलेक्टेट *(verb)* – छाती का दूध पिलाना
The mother got sick and the infant was ablactated.

Ablactation/एबलॉकटेशन *(noun)* – माता का दूध पिलाने की क्रिया
Ablacation is usually advised by doctors when babies can't get mother's milk.

Ablation/एब्लेशन *(noun)* – शरीर के क्लेशकर भाग का पृथक् करना
Exposed to strong winds over long periods even rocks undergo ablation.

Ablaze/एब्लेज *(adj.)* – जलता हुआ, प्रकाशपूर्ण
The bus was set ablaze by miscreants.

Able/एबल *(adj.)*– 'योग्य' अर्थ का प्रत्यय जो संज्ञा
He is able to lift such a heavy weight.

Ablepsy/एबलेप्सी *(noun)* – अन्धापन, दृष्टि शून्यता
He suffers from ablepsy.

Ablocate/एब्लोकेट *(verb)* – किराये पर देना
He has ablicated his premises to an embassy.

Abloom/एब्लूम *(adj)*– फूलने की अवस्था में
The whole garden is abloom with flowers.

Ablush/एब्लश *(adj)* – लज्जित होते हुए
She felt ablush when he expressed his love for her.

Ablution/एब्ल्यूशन *(noun)* – कोई धार्मिक कार्य करने से पहले शरीर इत्यादि को शुद्ध करना
Ablution is usually done by priests early in the morning.

Ably/एब्ली *(adj)* – योग्यता से, प्रवीणता से
He played ably and scared a centuary.

Abnegate/एब्निगेट *(verb)* – त्याग करना
Babar abnegated wine when Humayu was seriously sick.

Aboard/एबोर्ड *(adv. & prep.)* – जहाज की छत पर, समीप
He was aboard the ship in time.

Abode/एबोड *(noun)* – क्रिया के भूतकाल का रूप
Residence: their right of adobe in Britain. Himalaya is the abode of gods.

Aboil/एब्याल *(adv.)* – उबलता हुआ
The milk is aboil now put in rice.

Abolish/एबॉलिश *(verb)* – हटा देना, नाश करना
Sati pratha was abolished during the British rule.

Abolition/एबॉलिशन *(noun)* – घृणित, घिनौना
The credit to abolition of Sati pratha must go to Raja Ram Mohan Rai.

Abominate/एबॉमिनेट *(verb)* – अति घृणा करना, द्वेष करना
I abominate such rude behaviour.

Aboral/एबॉरल *(adj.)* – मुँह की दूसरी ओर करना
Remote from the mouth is called aboral.

Aboriginal/एबोरिजिनल *(adj.)* – स्वदेशीय, आदि देशवासी
Aboriginal rituals are fascinating.

Aborigines/एबओरिजिन्स *(noun)* – किसी देश के आदि निवासी
Aborigines of Australia are known all over the world.

Abort/एबॉर्ट *(verb)* – गर्भपात होना
She wanted to abort her child.

Abound/एबाउन्ड *(verb)* – उमड़ उठना, भरपूर होना
This pond abounds in fish.

About/एबाउट *(prep.&adv.)* – विषय में, निकट
I know nothing about him.

Above/एबव *(prep.&adv.)* – ऊपर, शिखर पर
High above the mountains a plane was flying.

Abracadabra/एब्राकाडाब्रा *(noun)* – जन्त्र-मन्त्र
The magician said Abracadabra and the lady disappeared.

Abrade/एब्रेड *(verb)* – खुरच देना, नष्ट करना
Strong winds abrade away the fertile earth.

Abreast/एब्रेस्ट *(adv.)* – छाती से छाती मिलाते हुए
While climbing over we found a huge rock abreast us.

Abridge/एब्रीज *(verb)* – कम करना, संक्षेप करना
This is the abridged edition of Mahabharata, you won't have to read the lengthy book now.

Abrogate/एब्रोगेट *(verb)* – रद्द करना, तोड़ना
I shall not abrogate this agreement.

Abrupt/एब्रप्ट *(adj.)* – अचानक, खुड़बुड़ी
Her abrupt speech shocked me.

Abruption/एब्रप्सन *(noun)* – एकाएक छूटने का कार्य

The sudden abruption of the rock from the mountain was shocking.

Abruptly/एब्रप्टली *(adj)* – एकाएक, तत्परता से

He left the room abruptly.

Abscess/एबसेश *(noun)* – व्रण, शरीर के किसी भाग में मवाद भर जाना

After the accident an abscess formed on his left leg.

Abscound /एब्सकॉन्ड *(verb)* – चुपके से भाग जाना

He absconded from the prison through a tunnel.

Absence/एबसेन्स *(noun)* – किसी स्थान से अनुपस्थिति

Her parents were worried because of the absence of their daughter from home.

Absent/एबसेन्ट *(adj.)* – अनुपस्थिति

Many students were absent from the class.

Absinth/एबसिन्थ *(noun)* – चिरायता

He became an addict to absinth.

Absolute/एबसल्यूट *(adj.)* – सम्पूर्ण

A dictator is an absolute ruler.

Absorb/एबजॉर्ब *(verb)* – सोख लेना, चूसना

The sponge soaked up the liquid.

Abstain/एब्सटेन *(verb)* – पृथक् रहना, बचे रहना

You are sick with an infection lungs so abstain from smoking.

Abstenious/एबसटेनियस *(adj.)* – अटपाहारी, संयमी

He is an abstenious man and never touches alcohol.

Abstention/एबसटेंशन *(noun)* – तटस्थ रहने की क्रिया

Abstention is my preference in such cases.

Absterge/एब्सटरेज *(verb)* – पापों को धो देना

I with to absterge now.

Abstinent/एब्सटिनेन्ट *(noun)* – उपवास करने वाला, संयमी

My friends is an abstinent and he would never drink a beverage which has even the least alcohol.

Abstract/एब्सट्रैक्ट *(adj.)* – भाववाचन, आदर्श

Love is an abstract idea.

Absurd/एबसर्ड *(adj.)* – मूर्खतापूर्ण, निरर्थक

It is an highly absurd theory nobody can make head or tail of it.

Abundance/एबनडेन्स *(noun)* – प्रचुरता

This garden is famous for its abundance of flowers.

Abuse/एब्यूज *(verb)* – गाली, दुर्व्यवहार

During a fight the man abused one another a lot.

Abut/एबट *(verb)* – मिलना

My and my friend's houses are abutting.

Acacia/अकासिया *(noun)* – गोंद उत्पन्न करने वाला बबूल का पेड़

The villages of India abound in Keeker (acacia) trees.

Academy/एकेडेमी *(noun)* – पाठशाला, ज्ञानसमाज

The academy of space of us is famous all over the world.

Acarpous/एकारपस *(noun)* – अनुपजाऊ, बाँझ

This plant is acarpous as it produces no flower or fruit.

Accelerate/एक्सीलरेट *(verb)* – जल्दी करना, चाल बढ़ाना

If you accelerate highly the car will rush madly.

Accentuation/एक्सेच्यूशन – अक्षरों पर दबाव डालकर उच्चारण

Proper accentuation helps a lot in correct pronunciation.

Accept/एक्सेप्ट *(verb)* – स्वीकार करना, सकारना

I'll accept this job offer.

Acceptation/एक्सेप्टेशन *(noun)* – कृपापूर्वक स्वागत

There is acceptation of many Hindi words into English language.

Access/एक्सेस *(noun)* – समीप में पहुँचना

I have direct access to the minister office.

Accession/एक्सेशन *(noun)* – राज्याभिषेक, चढ़ाव

He has gained accession to the rank of Admiral.

Accidented/एक्सीडेन्टेड *(verb)* – असमतल, ऊँचे-नीचे धरातल पर

The car accidented badly.

Accipitral/एक्सीपिट्रल *(adj)* – तीक्ष्ण दृष्टि वाला

Vulture is an accipitral bird.

Acclaim/एक्लेम *(verb)* – जय-जयकार करना

His efforts were acclaimed.

Acclamation/एक्लेमेशन *(noun)* – जय ध्वनि जय-जयकार

He received great acclamation for his speech.

A

Acclivity/एक्लीविटी *(noun)* – पहाड़ की चढ़ाई, चढ़ाव
In the way, we went through an acclivity.

Accommodate/एकोमोडेट *(verb)* – लोगों के कहीं बैठने या ठहरने की पर्याप्त सुविधा होना
Each apartment can accommodate up to six people.

Accompanier/एकॉमपेनियर – साथ देने वाला
My friend is my accompanier in this journey.

Accompany/एकॉमपेनी *(verb)* – साथ देना, सेवा करना
My father accompanied me to my school.

Accomplice/एकॉमप्लिस *(noun)* – अपराध में साथ देने वाला मनुष्य
He was my accomplice in the crime.

Accord/एकार्ड *(verb)* – मिलना, समान होना
His services have been accorded.

According/एकॉर्डिंग *(adv.)* – अनुरूप
According to an announcement by the government petrol will be cheaper by two rupees.

Accouncheur/एकाउन्सर *(noun)* – प्रसूति-वैद्य
He is an accouncheur.

Account/एकाउन्ट *(noun)* – गणना करना, हिसाब करना
Your application has been taken into account.

Accountship/एकॉउन्टशीप *(noun)* – मुनीम का पद या कार्य
I am interested in accountship.

Accredit/एक्रेडिट *(verb)* – विश्वास करना, मान्यता करना
He has been accredited with a lot of praise.

Accumulate/एक्यूमुलेट *(verb)* – ढेर लगाना, इकट्ठा करना
He accumulated a lot of wealth.

Accurate/एक्यूरेट *(adj.)* – अचूक, यथार्थ
Accurate shooting got him a gold in games

Accusatory/एक्यूसेटरी *(adj.)* – दोष या अभियोग लगाने वाला
Out of anger she gave me black accusatory looks.

Accuse/एक्यूज *(verb)* – अपराधी ठहराना
He was accused of murder. The court trial went on for 7 years.

Accustom/एकस्टम *(verb)* – परिचय कराना, अभ्यास डालना
I am not accustomed to waiting for such long hours.

Accentric/एक्सेन्ट्रीक *(adj.)* – केन्द्र में स्थित न रहने वाला
He was turned out of the meeting because of accentric behaviour.

Acephalous/एसेफेलस *(adj.)* – बिना सिर का, बिना चौधरी का
Worms who don't have a clear defined head are called acephalous.

Acerbate/एसरबेट *(verb)* – कड़वाहट और तीखा करना
Insult noted out to him made him acerbated.

Acerbic/एसरबिक *(adj.)* – खट्टा
He was acerbic in his speech which angered many people.

Acerbity/एसरबिटी *(noun)* – कटु वचन
Acerbity developed between two brothers on a land dispute.

Acervate/एसरवेट *(adj.)* – गुच्छों में उगने वाला
This acervate may have medicinal properties.

Acetic/एसेटिक *(adj.)* – सिरके के सदृश खट्टा
Thin object contains acetic acid let us give it a medical test.

Acetify/एसेटिफाइ *(verb)* – सिरका बनाना, खट्टा करना
This solution has been acetified let's take it to the laboratory.

Acetous/एसिटस *(adj.)* – खट्टा
Producing or resembling vinegar.

Achieve/एचिव *(verb)* – प्राप्त करना
He has achieved a lot in such a short time

Achromatic/एक्रोमेटिक *(adj.)* – बिना रंग का
These glass are achromatic.2. without colour. Water is achromatic, i.e. it has no colour.

Acid/एसिड *(noun)* – खट्टा, तीखा
Some rowdy boys threw acid over a girl, her skin was burnt away.

Acidification/एसेडिफिकेशन *(noun)* – अम्लीकरण
Acidification of this liquid has taken place.

Acidulate/एसिड्यूलेट *(verb)* – थोड़ा खट्टा करना
Don't worry this substance is only slightly acidulated.

Aciform/एसिफॉर्म *(adj)* - सूई की आकृति के समान
This aciform object is as sharp as a needle.

Acme/एक्मि *(noun)* - शिखर
He has become very rich and touched acme at last.

Acne/एक्नि *(noun)* - मुहाँसा, डोड़सा
In young age acne often appear on the face.

Aconite/एकोनाइट *(noun)* - कुचला
Aconite is a plant used in homeopathic medicines.

Acorn/एकॉर्न *(noun)* - शाहवलूत, जैतून के वृक्ष का फल
This fruit is used in Ayurvedic therapy.

Acoustic/एकॉस्टिक *(adj.)* - ध्वनि-सम्बन्धी
The acoustic system of the auditorium failed and there was no performance for a long time.

Acquaint/एक्वेन्ट *(verb)* - परिचित होना
Why should you talk to me? I am not acquainted with you.

Acquiesce/एक्विएज् *(verb)* - सन्तुष्ट होना, मौन, स्वीकार करना
I acquiesce to your suggestion.

Acquire/एक्वायर *(verb)* - प्राप्त करना, कमाना
She has acquired great skill in designing clothes.

Acquisition/एक्विजिशन *(noun)* - प्राप्ति, लाभ
A painting by Picasso is his latest acquisition.

Acquit/एक्विट *(verb)* - निर्दोष ठहराना
He has been acquitted from the charge of murder.

Acrid/एक्रिड *(adj.)* - तीखा
The food in this place smells acrid.

Acrobat/एक्रोबैट *(noun)* - नट, रस्से नाचने वाला
Acrobats in the circus gave stunning performance.

Acropolis/एक्रोपोलिस *(noun)* - दुर्ग
I visited an acropolis when I was in Greece.

Across/एक्रॉस *(prep. & adv.)* - एक ओर से दूसरी ओर
He went across the room and opened the door.

Act/एक्ट *(verb)* - कार्य करना
According to police the bomb explosion was an act of sabotage.

Acting/एक्टिंग *(noun)* - नाटक का अभिनय
His acting in the film was so powerful that it became an all time hit.

Action/एक्सन *(noun)* - कार्य, कृति
If you don't take action in time things may go out of control.

Actively/एक्टिवली *(adj)* - सक्रियता से
He actively helps the needy.

Active/एक्टिव *(adj.)* - चंचल, चपल
On account of his sharp mind and active imagination he has become a popular writer.

Actor/एक्टर *(noun)* - अभिनेता
He is a very fine actor he has always given powerful performances.

Actual/एक्चुअल *(adj.)* - वास्तविक
The actual damage to the car was not as great as we had feared.

Acuity/एक्वीटी *(noun)* - तीक्ष्णता, बुद्धि की परीक्षा
He has great acuity that is why he is considered an authority over history.

Acumen/एक्यूमेन *(noun)* - तेजी, बुद्धिकी सूक्ष्मता
He has great business acumen that is why he is so successful.

Acuminate/एक्यूमिनेट *(adj.)* - नुकीला
This acuminate plant has a sharp tapering point.

Adage/एडेज *(noun)* - सूत्र, कहावत
There is an adage that as you sow so shall you reap.

Adam/एडम *(noun)* - पुरुष, मनु
Adam ate the apple and sin entered his mind.

Adamant/एडामंट *(adj.)* - हीरा, वज्र
He is very adamant by nature and won't change his opinion about you.

Adapt/एडैप्ट *(verb)* - नई परिस्थिति के अनुरूप व्यवहार करना
Creatures who could not adapt to changing environment gradually died away.

Add/एड *(verb)* - जोड़ना, अधिक करना
If we add two and two it makes four.

Addict/एडिक्ट *(noun)* - निरत होना, व्यसन होना
He is addicted to drugs.

Addle/एडल *(adj.)* - सड़ा, बाँझ
His addled behaviour surprised all people.

Address/एड्रेस *(verb)* - निवेदन करना, अभिभाषण करना
The president is addressing a meeting, he can't meet you.

A

Adept/एडेप्ट *(adj.)* - प्रवीण, गुणी
He is adept at oil painting.

Adequate/एडिक्वेट *(adj.)* - योग्य, पर्याप्त
Children should be given adequate supply of milk.

Adhere/एडःहियर *(verb)* - मजबूती से चिपकना, दृढ़ होना
I'll adhere to my words no matter what comes

Adhesion/एडहीसन *(noun)* - चिपकने की प्रक्रिया
Adhesion to good habits always pays.

Adieu/एड्यू *(verb)* - नमस्कार, जाते समय का अभिवादन
When we had reached the airport I said adieu to my friend.

Adit/एडिट *(noun)* - खान में आने-जाने का मार्ग
We reached the mine through an adit.

Adjacent/एड्जेसन्ट *(adj.)* - निकट या बगल
My house is adjacent to my school.

Adjective/एडजेक्टिव *(noun)* - विशेषण, आश्रित
What adjective would you use to describe my home.

Adjoin/एडज्वाइन *(verb)* - जोड़ना, लगाना
These two pieces of wood are adjoined together with a strong adhesive.

Adjourn/एजर्न *(verb)* - विलम्ब करना, टालना
The court is adjourned for today.

Adjudge/एडजज *(verb)* - निर्णय करना
The witness was adjudged to be true

Adjunet/एडजंक्ट *(noun)* - मिला हुआ, जुड़ा हुआ
This person is my adjunct and will remain with me wherever I go.

Adjure/एज्यूर *(verb)* - शपथपूर्वक आज्ञा देना या कहना
He adjured to do sometime destructive

Adjust/एडजस्ट *(verb)* - अनुकूल बनना, व्यवस्था करना
I have adjusted to my new home.

Adjutant/एज्यूटेंट *(noun)* - बड़े अफसर का सहायक
He is an adjutant to the general.

Adjuvant/एज्यूवेंट *(noun)* - सहायक पुरुष
Adjuvant therapy has started and doctors are looking for complete recovery.

Administer/एडमिनिस्टर *(verb)* - प्रबन्ध करना, सहायता देना, प्रशासन चलाना, देखभाल करना
The chemist administered the drug to me.

Administrator/एडमिनिस्ट्रेटर *(noun)* - शासक, प्रबन्धन कर्ता
My father is a good administrator and ably handled a flourishing business.

Admirable/एडमायरेब्ल *(adj.)* - प्रशंसनीय-श्रेष्ठ
You have done admirable work.

Admissible/एडमिसिब्ल *(adj.)* - ग्राह्य, अंगीकार योग्य
I am a lifelong member of this club and hence admissible to it any time.

Admission/एडमिशन *(noun)* - स्कूल क्लास आदि में प्रवेश
These days it is very difficult to find admission in a good school.

Admissive/एडमिशिव *(adj.)* - स्वीकारी, मानने वाला
All children up to 14 are admissive to free education in government schools.

Admonish/एडमॉनिश *(verb)* - धीरे से झिड़कना, डाँटना, फटकारना
I admonished him for his rude behaviour.

Adnominal/एडनॉमिनल *(adj.)* - संज्ञा से जुड़ा हुआ

Ado/एडू *(noun)* - कष्ट, उपद्रव
It was much ado about nothing.

Adobe/एडोब *(noun)* - धूप में सुखाई हुई ईट
Hermits build their adobe in jungle.

Adolescence/एडोलसेंस *(noun)* - किशोरावस्था
The time period between adolescence (13-19 years) and adulthood is very critical from many angles.

Adolescent/एडोलसेंट *(adj.)* - 13-19 की उम्र का किशोर लड़का या लड़की
Adolescents often remain confused if not properly guided.

Adopt/एडॉप्ट *(verb)* - कानूनन गोद लेना
He adopted an attitude of innocence.

Adorable/एडोरेबल *(adj.)* - आराध्य, पूजनीय
My mother is very adorable.

Adore/एडोर *(verb)* - आराधना करना
I simply adore my English teacher.

Adown/एडाउन *(prep.)* - नीचे, नीचे की ओर
The liquid was poured adown his throat.

Adrift/एड्रिफ्ट *(adj.&adv.)* - इधर-उधर तैरते हुए
This boat was found adrift in the sea.

Adscript/एडस्क्रीप्ट *(adj. & noun)* – बाद मे लिखा हुआ, दास

In order to complete the book he adscripted another character.

Adult/ऐडल्ट *(noun)* – यौवन प्राप्त पुरुष, युवा

He is an adult and can take his own decision

Adulterant/एडल्टरन्ट *(noun)* – अपमिश्रक, मिलावट

Water is adulterant often mixed in milk.

Adust/एडस्ट *(adj.)* – जला हुआ, झुलसा हुआ

She looks adust.

Adultery/एडल्टरी *(noun)* – व्यभिचार, पर पुरुष या पर स्त्री के बीच यौन सम्बन्ध

Adultery is crime and severely punished in Muslim countries.

Advanced/एडवांस्ड *(adj)* – उन्नत

The work has completed before the advanced date.

Advantage/एडवांटेज *(noun)* – लाभ या फायदे की स्थिति, महत्त्व

His being elected as a party candidate is of advantage to me.

Adventure/एडवेन्चर *(noun)* – उत्तेजक, असाधारण

We have planned great adventure in the jungles of east Africa.

Adverb/एडवर्ब *(noun)* – क्रिया विशेषण

She walked slowly. In this sentence slowly is an adverb.

Adversary/एडवरसरी *(noun)* – प्रतिवादी, विरोधी

He is my adversary in estate business.

Adversative/एडवरजेटिव *(adj.)* – विरोध-सूचक

This adversative attitude upset me.

Adverse/एडवर्स *(adj.)* – विपरीत, प्रतिकूल

This medicine may have adverse effects.

Advert/एडवर्ट *(verb)* – ध्यान दिलाना, संकेत करना

There was an advert in the newspaper regarding sale of summer clothes.

Advertise/एडवर्टाइज *(verb)* – विज्ञापन देना, घोषित करना

If you want tenant, one way is to advertise in the newspaper.

Advisability/एडविजेबिलिटी *(adj)* – शीघ्र होने की योग्यता

The chairman questioned the advisability of our plan.

Advisable/एडवाइजेब्ल *(adj.)* – अनुमति योग्य, चतुर

It is an advisable step you took.

Advice/एडवाइस *(verb)* – परामर्श देना, सलाह करना

I advise you to leave this place at once.

Advocacy/एडवोकेसी *(noun)* – पक्ष का समर्थन, वकालत

This advocacy in the court was brilliant.

Advocate/एडवोकेट *(noun)* – दूसरे के लिये बहस करने वाला, सिफारिश करना

My father was a famous advocate.

Adynamia/एडायनामिया *(noun)* – किसी रोग के कारण उत्पन्न हुई कमी

Adynamia in him is the result of long disease from which he is recovering.

Adynamic/एडायनेमिक *(adj)* – शक्तिहीन, निर्बल

His adynamic speech thrilled everybody.

Aeon/एवोन *(noun)* – युग, कल्प

Such astrological wonders among planets happen in aeons.

Aeration/एअरेशन *(verb)* – वायु में मिलने का कार्य

Aeration of clothes makes them dry.

Aerial/एरियल *(noun)* – वायु सम्बन्धी, काल्पनिक, एंटिना

If the aerial is in right direction TV transmits good pictures.

Aeriferous/एरिफरस *(adj)* – वायु ले जाने वाला

Bronchial tubes are aeriferous.

Aeriform/एअरीफार्म *(adj.)* – वायु के समान, अवास्तविक

Water is not as aeriform as wind.

Aerify/एरीफाइ *(verb)* – भरना

This water has been aerified i.e. turned into gas.

Aero/एअरो *(combining form)* – 'वायु' अर्थ का उपसर्ग

Aerobics keep you physically fit.

Aesthetics/एस्थेटिक्स *(plural noun)* – सुन्दरता से सम्बन्धित, सौंदर्य शास्त्र

We should never lose sense of aesthetics.

Aether/एथर *(noun)* – तेजो वह तत्व, आकाश

Our earth is surrounded by aether.

Affable/एफबल *(adj.)* – सुशील, मिलनसार

He is very affable by nature always laughing mixing and socializing.

A

Affect/अफेक्ट *(verb)* – प्रभाव डालना, प्रेम करना
His words have affected me so much. I am going to apologize to him.

Affectation/एफेक्टेशन *(noun)* – अहंकार, आडम्बर, ढोंग, दिखावा
His speech shows a lot of affectation these can't be his genuine feelings.

Affected/अफेकटिड *(adj.)* – प्रभावित
His behaviour is clearly affected. He can't be gentle.

Affection/एफेक्सन *(noun)* – प्रेम, अनुराग
I have great affection for my granddaughter.

Affective/एफेक्टिव *(adj.)* – उत्तेजित करने वाला
His affective cheerfulness touched all people.

Affiance/एफियान्स *(noun)* – वरदान, विवाह के लिए वचन देना
She is affiance with her boyfriend.

Affidavit/एफिडेविट *(noun)* – शपथपत्र, हलफनामा
I had to produce an affidavit in police station to the effect that I had lost my ID.

Affiliate/एफिलिएट *(verb)* – गोद लेना, किसी बड़ी संस्था से मिलाना
This college is affiliated with Delhi University.

Affined/एफाइन्ड *(adj.)* – संयुक्त, सम्बद्ध
These two triangles are affined.

Affinity/एफिनिटि *(noun)* – आत्मीयता, आकर्षण समानता, सम्बन्ध
I enjoyed great affinity with her and consequently I married her.

Affirm/एफर्म *(verb)* – निश्चय के साथ कहना, दृढ़ता पूर्वक कहना
I publicly affirmed that I had never seen that man before.

Affirmative/एफर्मेटिव *(adj.)* – सकारात्मक स्वीकार या अंगीकार सूचक
Unlike interrogative and negative sentences affirmative sentences show consent.

Affix/एफिक्स *(verb)* – संयुक्त करना, जोड़ना
Affix this stamp on the envelope and drop it into a letterbox.

Afflict/एफ्लिक्ट *(verb)* – पीड़ा देना, कष्ट देना
He is afflicted with a terrible wound.

Affluence/एफ्लूएन्स *(adj)* – धन की समृद्धि, अधिकता
His affluence carried a lot of weight and he became the President of the club.

Affluent/एफ्लूएन्ट *(adj.)* – धनवान, परिपूर्ण, समृद्ध
He is an affluent person and owns a chain of malls.

Afford/एफोर्ड *(verb)* – कुछ करने या खरीद सकने के लिए पर्याप्त धन या समय निकाल सकना
I can't afford such a costly TV.

Afforest/एफॉरेस्ट *(verb)* – जंगल लगाना
The land mafia has afforested large chunks of land for commercial gain.

Affray/एफ्रे *(noun)* – कलह
Affray near the cinema hall caused the police to intervene.

Affright/एफ्राइट *(verb & noun)* – डराना, भय, ऊधम
The lonely jungle in the night affrighted.

Affront/अफ्रन्ट *(noun)* – सामना करना, अपमानित करना
It was an affront on his part to insult his senior.

Affuse/एफ्यूज *(verb)* – उड़ेलना, छिड़कना
I affused a lot of affection on her.

Afield/एफिल्ड *(adv.)* – खेत में, या खेत पर
He was afield for hunting.

Afire/एफायर *(adv.&adj.)* – जलती अवस्था में
The mob set afire the police jeep.

Aflame/एफ्लेम *(adv.& adj.)* – आगे जलते हुए, चमकते हुए
The aeroplane went down aflame as it hit a mountain.

Afloat/एफ्लोट *(adv.&adj.)* – बहता हुआ, जहाज पर
It must have been afloat for a long time.

Afraid/एफ्रेड *(adj.)* – डरा हुआ, त्रस्त
I am afraid that my father might not have another heart attack.

Afresh/एफ्रेश *(adv.)* – नये सिरे से
He started afresh even after total bankruptcy.

After/आफ्टर *(prep.)* – पीछे बाद मे, अनुसरण में
I entered the house after my father had gone.

Again/अगेन *(adv.)* – फिर, पुनः
Again he won the trophy.

Against/एगेन्स्ट *(prep.)* – प्रतिकूल
I am totally against this project.

Agamist/एगमिस्ट *(noun)* – विवाह-विरोधी
He is an agamist and will never marry nor will he encourage others to marry.

Agape/अगेप *(adv)* – आश्चर्य से मुहँ खोले हुए

The surprise news left him agape.

Agenda/एजेंडा *(noun)* – विषयों की सूची, कार्यसूची

The chairman was given the agenda as soon as the meeting started.

Agent/एजेंट *(noun)* – कार्यकर्ता, प्रतिनिधि, मुनीम

Travel and property agents are useful people.

Aggravate/एग्रेवेट *(verb)* – (स्थिति को) बिगाड़ देना अधिक गंभीर बनाना

His drunken behaviour has aggravated an already bad situation.

Aggregate/एग्रेगेट *(noun)* – एकत्रित करना, कुल जोड़

The aggregate of points gained by her in the match is very impressive.

Aggress/एग्रेस *(verb)* – पहले छेड़छाड़ करना, अतिक्रमण करना, चढ़ाई करना

The army aggressed and went on offensive.

Aggrieve/एग्रिव *(verb)* – दु:ख देना

As he was attacked upon he is the aggrieved party.

Aghast/एगास्ट *(adj.)* – भय से चकित, विस्मित

I felt aghast at his cheap behaviour.

Agile/एजाइल *(adj.)* – फूर्तिला, चपल, शीघ्र चलने वाला

Snake is an agile creature.

Agist/एजिस्ट *(verb)* – कुछ धन लेकर चराने के लिए दूसरे के पशु लेना

My profession was to agist the cattle.

Agitate/एजिटेट *(verb)* – आंदोलित करना, अशांति करना

The news of accident agitated them.

Agitation/एजिटेशन *(noun)* – व्याकुलता, घबराहट

In a state of agitation he attacked his opponent.

Aglet/एग्लेट *(noun)* – चेन के किनारे पर लगाने की धातु की नोक

The aglets of my shoes have become loose.

Aglow/एग्लो *(adv)* – गरम, चमकता हुआ

The palace was aglow with lights.

Agnate/एग्नेट *(adj.)* – सगोत्र, पूर्वज

We are agnate.

Agog/एगॉग *(adj.)* – गतिमान, आतुर

He was agog with excitement as he entered the movie hall.

Agonic/एगोनिक *(adj)* – कोण न बनाने वाला, कोण रहित

The needle is pointing to the North so it must be a point on the agonic.

Agonist/एगोनिस्ट *(noun)* – योद्धा, लड़ाका

He is an agonist in the field of boxing.

Agonize/एगोनाइज *(verb)* – पीड़ा देना, कष्ट सहना, किसी कठिन समस्या पर लंबे समय तक सोचना

I was agonized to hear about his accident.

Agony/एगोनी *(noun)* – यातना, अति शारीरिक पीड़ा, व्यथा

I am far away from my family and thus living in great agony.

Agoraphobia/एगोराफोबिया *(noun)* – भीड़ से डर लगना

He is afraid of vast open space. Doctors say it is a disease named agoraphobia.

Agrarion/एग्रेरियन *(adj.)* – कृषि या भूमि सम्बन्धी

Agrarian revolution in France is very famous.

Agree/एग्री *(verb)* – अनुकूल होना

I agree with you in this matter.

Agrestic/एग्रस्टिक *(adj)* – ग्रामीण, देहाती

Rural people have agrestic simplicity.

Agriculture/एग्रिकल्चर *(noun)* – खेती, कृषि धर्म

Agriculture forms an important part of a country's economy.

Aground/एग्राउण्ड *(adj.&adv.)* – अटका हुआ, धरती पर फंसा हुआ

The ship ran aground and was damaged.

Ahead/अहेड *(adv.)* – बढ़कर, आगे की ओर आगे

America is far ahead than any other country in space science.

Aheap/एहिप *(adj)* – ढेर में, डर से काँपता हुआ

The sheep felt panic and were aheap.

Ahem/एहेम *(exclamatory)* – आश्चर्य या अविश्वास सूचक अन्यय, ध्यान आकर्षित करने के लिए एक अव्यय

He didn't like the talks going on and to show his disagreement loudly said ahem.

Aid/एड *(verb)* – सहायता करना, सहारा देना

The aided me in times of crisis.

Ail/एल *(verb)* - पीड़ा या व्यथा का होना

The ailing from TB.

Aim/एम *(verb)* - लक्ष्य करना, प्रयत्न करना

I aimed my rifle at the wolf and shot him.

Air/एअर *(noun)* - वायु, हवा

Air surrounded earth if there were no air he won't be able to breathe and would die.

Aisle/एजल *(noun)* - गिरजाघर का एक ओर का भाग

I walked through the aisle in the church and reached the pulpit.

Ajar/एजार *(adj. & adv.)* - अधखुली दशा में

I left the door ajar to watch his activities.

Akin/एकिन *(adj.)* - सगोत्र, सम्बन्धी नातेदार

He being my brother is akin to me.

Alacrious/एलाक्रियस *(adj)* - प्रसन्न, खुश

His talk is so alacrious I enjoyed it greatly.

Alacrity/अलैक्रिटी *(noun)* - प्रसन्नता, खुशी, उत्साह

The alacrity in his nature makes him good companion.

Alolia/एलोलिया *(noun)* - बोली बन्द हो जाना

He is suffering from alolia and thus can't speak.

Alamort/एलामोर्ट *(adj)* - अधमरा, उत्साहहीन, उदास

Every living thing is alamort.

Alarm/एलार्म *(noun)* - संकेत, चेतावनी

The news has set alarm bells ringing in my mind.

Albeit/अलबीइट *(conj.)* - यद्यपि, ऐसा होते हुए भी, हालाँकि

He is poor albeit honest.

Albino/एल्विनो *(noun)* - रंगहीन मनुष्य, वर्णहीन मनुष्य, सूरजमुखी मनुष्य

A strong child was born to her having no colouring in eyes skin or hair it was an albino.

Album/अलबम *(noun)* - चित्र, टिकट रखने की जिल्द

This album consists all my pictures of childhood.

Albumen/एल्ब्यूमिन *(noun)* - गाढ़ा पदार्थ, अण्डे की सफेदी

Albumen in the egg has lots of proteins.

Alcohol/अल्कोहल *(noun)* - शराब, बीयर आदि मादक पेय

Alcohol is an active agent in liquor or brew.

Alcove/अल्कोव *(noun)* - घिरौची, मेहराबदार ताखा

I fitted my almirah in the alcove.

Alegar/एलेगर *(noun)* - खट्‌टी शराब

This alegar made of sour ale won't suit your taste.

Alert/एलर्ट *(noun)* - सावधान

This watchman is very alert you can't enter the compound without his permission.

Algebra/एल्जेब्रा *(noun)* - बीजगणित

So far mathematics is concerned he is very weak in algebra.

Algid/एल्जिड *(adj.)* - जड़ैया की शीत अवस्था का

In winter this room becomes very algid.

Alias/एलिअस *(noun)* - उपनाम, कटिपत नाम

Raj alias Raju was a notorious thug.

Alien/एलिअन *(adj.)* - अन्य देश का, अन्य ग्रह का

He hails from USA. He is an alien.

Alienate/एलिअनेट *(verb)* - चित्त हटाना, पराधीन करना

The father has legally alienated the rights of his property to his son.

Alienist/एलिअनिस्ट *(noun)* - उन्माद रोग का विशेष चिकित्सक

Alienists deal with mind.

Aliform/एलिफॉर्म *(adj.)* - पर के आकार का

An aliform kite flew in the sky.

Alight/एलाइट *(verb)* - उतरना, नीचे से आना

He alighted from the moving bus.

Alike/एलाइक *(adj.)* - सदृश, तुल्य

Both the brother are alike. They also behave alike.

Aliment/एलीमेंट *(noun)* - पोषण, आहार, आश्रय

The judge fixed the aliment for the divorced women.

Alimony/एलीमोनी *(noun)* - परित्यक्त पत्नी के भरण-पोषण का भत्ता, गुजारा, भरण-पोषण

After the divorce he was ordered to pay a huge amount as alimony to his divorced wife.

Aliquot/एलीक्योट *(noun)* - किसी पूर्ण विभाजक संख्या पर

When an aliquot of the river water was taken it was found to be contaminated.

Alive/एलाइव *(adj.)* - सजीव

We are watching alive cricket match.

Alkali/ऐलकलाइ *(noun)* - क्षार

This mixture seems to be alkaline.

Alkaloid/अल्कलॉइड *(noun)* - वनस्पतिओं का मूल तत्व

Alkaloid compounds of a plant act physiologically on humans.

Alkanet/एल्कानेट *(noun)* - रतनजोत

This blue flowered plant is called alkanet.

All/ऑल *(pronoun)* - पूरा, कुल, समूचा

In all only ten students are present.

Allay/एले *(verb)* - शांत करना, दमन करना, निराकरण करना

His talk allayed my fears.

Allegation/एलिगेशन *(noun)* - आरोप, इल्जाम

The allegation against him is that of murder.

Allege/अलेज *(verb)* - बिना प्रमाण के आरोप लगाना

It is alleged that he got drunk and hit his wife.

Allegiant/एलिजिएण्ट *(adj)* - राजभक्त

It is not possible to be allegiant to two masters.

Allegoric/एलगोरिकल *(adj.)* - लाक्षणिक, रूपकमय

In ancient times allegoric tales occupied an important place.

Allegro/एलेग्रो *(adj.&adv.)* - प्रसन्न, प्रफुल्ल, आनन्द से

The allegro movement on women's rights succeeded in the end.

Alleviate/एलीवियेट *(verb)* - छुटकारा देना, (पीड़ा को) कम करना

The doctor's treatment alleviated my pain.

Alley/एले *(noun)* - संकरी गली, उद्यानपथ

I saw two cats fighting in the alley.

All Fours/ऑल फोर्स *(noun)* - ताश का एक खेल

In the card game all fours is very popular in clubs.

Alliance/एलाइअन्स *(noun)* - नाता, रिश्ता, सन्धि

There is alliance between the two states to preserve wild life.

Alligate/एलिगेट *(verb)* - बाँधना या जोड़ना

The two ends of the rope were alligated together to form a circle.

Alligation/एलिगेशन *(noun)* - बन्धन की क्रिया

Allegation between the two lasted a long time.

Alligator/एलिगेटर *(noun)* - ग्राह, घड़ियाल

Alligator looks like crocodile but there is some difference.

Alliterate/एलिटरेट *(verb)* - एक ही अक्षरों से आरम्भ होने वाले शब्द का प्रयोग

Alliteration as a form of poetry.

Allocate/एलोकेट *(verb)* - भाग लगाना, हिस्से के रूप में बाँटना

All person were allocated their duties by the election officer.

Allocution/एलोक्यूशन *(noun)* - व्याख्यान

He was given an allocution before delivering the speech.

Allot/एलॉट *(verb)* - भाग देना, विभक्त करना, किसी काम के लिए समय तय करना

I have been allotted a flat by DDA.

Allotment/एलॉटमेंट *(noun)* - आवंटन, बाँटा गया, निर्धारित हिस्सा

Rupees one lakh was allotted by the centre to the flood hit areas.

Allottee/एलॉटी *(noun)* - वह व्यक्ति जिसको या जिसके प्रति भाग दिया गया हो

He is an allotte in the DDA lottery scheme.

Alloverishness/एलोवरीशनेश *(adj)* - अशक्तता, असुविधा

She is suffering from alloverishness.

Allow/अलाउ *(verb)* - कुछ करने की अनुमति देना

Photography is not allowed inside the court

Allowance/अलाउअन्स *(noun)* - अनुमोदन, वह मात्रा, राशि जिसे ले जाने की छूट मिली हो

You'll get an allowance of Rs. 2000/- p.m. to run the house.

Allspice/ऑलस्पाइस *(noun)* - एक प्रकार का मसाला, एक प्रकार का मसाला जिसमें लौंग दालचीनी, जायफल आदि की गंध होती है

While visiting Caribbean island I ate the fruit allspice. It was very nice.

Allude/एल्यूड *(verb)* - उद्देश्य करना, संकेत करना

While in restaurant I alluded at having an ice cream.

Alluvial/एलुविअल *(adj)* - जलोढ़ कछारी, नदी के बहाव या बाढ़ से बना हुआ

The alluvial soil is greatly fertile.

Alluvion/एलुवियन *(noun)* - कछारी भूमि, बाढ़ से जमी हुई मिट्टी

Formation of alluvion land by deposition the sea or river of sedimentation has made this piece of land very fertile.

A

Ally/एलाइ *(noun)* – मैत्री करना, जोड़ना
In 2nd World War America was an ally of France and UK.

Almanac/एल्मानक *(noun)* – मन्त्र, जन्त्री, पंचांग
Let me consult the almanac to find an auspicious date for marriage.

Almanographer/एल्मानोग्राफर *(noun)* – पंचांग बनाने वाला ज्योतिषी
Every year almanographers get busy in making the almanac.

Almighty/ऑलमाइटि *(adj.)* – सर्वशक्तिमान, परमेश्वर
God is almighty.

Almond/आल्मन्ड *(noun)* – बादाम फल, बादाम
It is said that five almonds in the morning everyday are greatly beneficial for health.

Almoner/एल्मोनर *(noun)* – भिक्षा, वितरक, भिक्षा बाँटने वाला अध्यक्ष
He is on the important part of almoner because he distributes alms.

Almost/ऑलमोस्ट *(adv.)* – प्राय:, लगभग
He almost died of malaria.

Alms/आल्म्स *(pl. noun)* – भिक्षा, धर्मदान
Alms have been distributed among the poor.

Aloe/एलो *(noun)* – बोल, मुसब्बर
This bitter juice is that of aloe drink it is a good laxative, you'll get rid of your constipation also.

Alone/एलोन *(adj.&adv.)* – एक, अकेला
Of all I alone supported him.

Along/अलांग *(prep.&adv.)* – बराबर, साथ-साथ, एक सिरे से दूसरे सिरे तक या की ओर
I went along the railing and soon reached the hall.

Alopecia/एलोपेसिया *(noun)* – बालों का गंजापन
He suffers from alopecia and has lost a lot of hair.

Aloud/एलाउड *(adv.)* – ऊँचे स्वर में, चिल्लाकर
Please speak aloud I can't hear you.

Alow/एलोव *(adv.)* – नीचे स्थान में
Alow there is a lake.

Alp/आल्प *(noun)* – ऊँचा पहाड़, पर्वत की चोटी
When in Europe I tried to climb alps.

Alpaca/ऐलपाका *(noun)* – एक प्रकार का चौपाया
When I went to South America I saw alpaca related to ilama.

Alpha/अल्फा *(noun)* – वर्णमाला, का पहला अक्षर
Both English and Greek alphabet have a, as their first letter.

Alphabet/अल्फाबेट *(noun)* – वर्णमाला, प्रथम सिद्धान्त
Without alphabet there can be no language.

Alpinist/अल्पिनिस्ट *(adj.)* – ऊँचे पहाड़ पर चढ़ने वाला
This plant grows on alps hence we can call it alpinist plant.

Already/ऑलरेडी *(adv.)* – पहले से, अभी
I have already finished the book.

Also/ऑल्सो *(adv.)* – और, सिवाय, भी
He is handsome and also intelligent.

Altar/अल्टार *(noun)* – पूजा का ऊँचा स्थान, वेदी
Wine and bread were put on the altar in the church.

Alter/ऑल्टर *(verb)* – बदलना
He completely altered his appearance.

Altercate/ऑल्टरकेट *(verb)* – विवाद करना
Don't altercate on this matter.

Altered/ऑल्टर्ड *(adj)* – परिवर्तित, बदला हुआ
This character and appearance have been completely altered.

Although/ऑल्दो *(conj.)* – यदि, यद्यपि
Although he is a high class officer he has no manners.

Altimeter/एल्टिमीटर *(noun)* – उँचाई नापने का एक प्रकार का यंत्र
The altimeter fitted in the plane showed the altitude it was flying at.

Altitude/अल्टीट्यूड *(noun)* – उँचाई, महत्त्व
He dived into the sea from the altitude of 60 metres.

Alto/अल्टो *(noun)* – स्त्री का निम्नतम और पुरुष का उच्चतम गान स्वर
Do you hear the alto it is the high singing male voice and the low tone of the women singing together.

Altogether/ऑल्टुगेदर *(adv.)* – सर्वथा, सम्पूर्ण रूप से
Altogether the plan seems reusable.

Alum/एल्यूम *(noun)* – फिटकरी

The tanners use alum in solution for dyeing and tanning.

Aluminium/एल्म्यूनियम *(noun)* – एक बहुत हल्की सफेद रंग की धातु

Aluminium is used in the manufacture of planes and window frames besides other material.

Alumnus/एल्यूमनस *(noun)* – विश्वविद्यालय या पाठशाला का विद्यार्थी

I have been an alumnus of K.M. college.

Alveary/अल्विअरी *(adj)* – मधुमक्खी का छत्ता

This alveary is situated a great height it is very difficult to get it or break it.

Alveolate/अल्विओलेट *(adj)* – मधुमक्खी के छत्ते के सदृश

This alveolate like object is full of cell like cavities may be it is an old honeycomb.

Alvine/अल्वाइन *(adj)* – पेट या तोंद सम्बन्धी

He is suffering from alvine wounds and is on high antibiotics.

Always/ऑल्वेज *(adv.)* – सदा, सर्वदा

You always get what you deserve.

Amain/एमैन *(adverb)* – बलपूर्वक, तुरन्त

The boys quickly ran away amain.

Amalgam/एमैल्गाम *(noun & verb)* – वस्तुओं का समिश्रण पारे से मिलाई हुई धातु

Don't amalgamate the various chemicals rashly it may explode.

Amaranth/एमरेन्थ *(noun)* – अम्लान रंगीन पुष्प का पौधा

This tropical plant is used as a medicine.

Amass/अमैश *(verb)* – संग्रह करना, ढेर करना

The fungus amassed overnight almost in no time.

Amative/एमेटिव *(adj.)* – प्रेमशील, श्रृंगारप्रिय, कामोत्तेजकता

During talks with her he suddenly became amative she didn't appreciate it.

Amatorial/एमेटोरियल *(adj.)*– प्रेमी–सम्बन्धी, वासनात्मक

This amatorial talk upset her.

Amatory/एमेटोरी *(adj.)* – प्रेम उत्पन्न करने वाला

He has an amatory character and has relation with many women.

Amaurosis/एमारोसिस *(noun)* – थोड़ी या पूर्ण दृष्टि–हीनता

His optical nerve was damaged and amaurosis occurred.

Amaze/एमेज *(verb)* – विस्मित करना, चकित

I was amazed at his sudden appearance after a long time.

Amazon/एमेजन *(noun)* – स्त्री योद्धा, वीरांगना

The legendary female warriors of Amazon are famous all over the world.

Amabagious/एमाबेजियस *(adj.)* – द्विअर्थी, दुविधा पूर्ण, अनेकाअर्थी

You were amabagious in your speech mainly because you presented so many alternatives and your words had more than one meaning.

Ambassador/एम्बैसडर *(noun)* – प्रतिनिधि, राजदूत

Many actors are brand ambassador of scents.

Ambassadress/एम्बैसड्रस *(verb)* – राजदूत सम्बन्धी

That lady over there in the thick of the party is an ambassadress. She is very glamorous and smart.

Amber/एम्बर *(noun)* – अम्बर, तृणमणि

Jewellers use amber to give yellow tinge to their jewellry.

Ambient/एम्बियन्ट *(adj.)*– व्यापक, चारों ओर से घेरने वाला

Boats combined create an amalgam of an ambient landscape several and visionary.

Ambiguity/एम्बिगुइटी *(noun)* – सन्देह

His dialogues are full of ambiguity always having two meanings.

Ambit/एम्बिट *(noun)* – परिधि चक्र, मण्डल

The sky has no ambit.

Ambition/एम्बिशन *(noun)* – महत्त्वाकांक्षा, अभिलाषा, लालसा

His ambition is to become a doctor.

Ambo/एम्बो *(noun)* – गिरजाघर का चबूतरा

The priest has started speaking from the ambo.

Ambrosia/एम्ब्रोसिया *(noun)* – अमृत, अद्वितीय, पीयूष, सुधा, स्वाद का पदार्थ

He is a very good cook. The food prepared by him tastes and smells of ambrosia.

Ambsace/एम्बसैस *(noun)* – गुणहीनता

It was sheer ambsace that he lost the card game.

Ambulance/एम्बुलेंस *(noun)* – चलता-फिरता फौजी अस्पताल

I'm eagerly awaiting the ambulance, my father is very sick.

Ambulant/एम्बुलेंट *(adj.)* – बाहरी रोगी

He is ambulant quite mobile on his two feet.

Ambulate/एम्बुलेट *(verb)* – इधर-उधर घूमना

He ambulated from kitchen to the garden.

Ambuscade/ऐम्बस्केड *(noun)* – छिपकर आक्रमण

He ambuscaded to attack his enemy by surprise.

Ambush/एम्बुश *(noun)* – सिपाहियों का आक्रमण, घात लगाकर आक्रमण करने के लिये छिपे रहना

Babar's army lay in ambush for surprise attack.

Ambustion/एम्बशन *(noun)* – फफोला

He suffered an ambustion as he carelessly handled the gas.

Ameliorate/एमेलिओरेट *(verb)* – सुधारना, उत्तम

The medicine ameliorated the grip of disease.

Amen/आमीन *(noun)* – ऐसा ही हो, एवमस्तु

At the end of the prayer the priest said amen.

Amenable/एमेनेब्ल *(adj.)* – उत्तरदायी, जिम्मेदार

Go and talk to him he is an amenable fellow and will respond to you.

Amend/एमेंड *(verb)* – संशोधन करना सुधारना

I shall have to amend this speech, some fool has written it.

Amenity/एम्निटी *(noun)* – सुविधा, सुख साधन

The amentity of this place is appreciable.

Amenorrhoea/एमेनेरोइया *(noun)* – स्त्रियों का मासिक धर्म बन्द होना

This amenorrhoea is not to be taken lightly let's take her at once to the hospital and consult a gyno.

Amerce/अमर्स *(verb)*– दण्ड देना, जुर्माना करना

The court has amerced him. Let us arrange lonely for the fine.

Amercement/एमर्समेंट *(noun)* – दण्ड

Amercement imposed by the court is very huge.

Amethyst/एमिथिस्ट *(noun)* – जामुनीमणी, कटैला

My watch shines in the night because it has fine particles of amethyst.

Amiable/एमिअबल *(adj.)* – सर्वप्रिय, सबका प्यारा

He is an amiable fellow.

Amid/अमिड *(prep.)* – मध्य में, बीच में

He was lost somewhere amid the huge crowd.

Amidships/एमिडशीप *(adv.&adj.)* – जहाज के बीच में

As he stood amidships he was hit by a cannon.

Amity/एमिटी *(noun)* – शुभ चिन्ता, बन्धुत्त्व, मंत्रिभाव

There is perfect amity between two friends.

Ammeter/एमीटर *(noun)* – बिजली धारा शक्ति नापने का यन्त्र

Please bring the ammeter I have to measure the current.

Ammonal/एमोनल *(noun)* – एक प्रकार का बारूद

Ammonal is the chief ingredient that terrorists use in making bombs.

Ammonia/एमोनिया *(noun)* – चूने से बनी हुई क्षार

I am making a cleaning fluid with ammonia and water.

Ammunition/एम्यूनिशन *(noun)* – गोली, बारूद, युद्ध-सामग्री

The government does not allow civilians to live near ammunition depot because it is very dangerous.

Amnesia/एम्नेसिया *(noun)* – स्मृति-हीनता

He has been suffering from amnesia for a long time.

Amoeba/एमीबा *(noun)* – एक कोशिकीय जन्तु

For reproduction purposes amoeba divides itself into two.

Amoebean/एमोबियन *(noun)* – पारी-पारी से उत्तर देने वाला

To answer in amoebean has become his habit the answers all questions in poem or song.

Amoral/एमॉरल *(adj.)* – अधर्मी, धर्मशून्य, अनैतिक

He is an amoral person not knowing what should be done and what shouldn't be.

Amorist/एमोरिस्ट *(noun)* – कामुक, प्रेम करने वाला, शृंगारी

He is a big amorist. He has written about a dozen books on love.

Amorosa/एमरोसा *(adv.&adj.)* - प्यारा, पुंश्चली
The music in the café was very amorosa.

Amorous/एमॉरस *(adj.)* - कामी, कामुक, रसिक
He is very amorous by nature having many girl friends.

Amortise/एमर्टाइज *(verb)* - ऋण चुकाना
The cost of your land has been amortised.

Amount/अमाउन्ट *(noun)* - परिमाण होना, मात्रा रकम होना
I have a large amount of money at my disposal and can buy anything I want.

Amour/अमुर *(noun)* - गुप्त प्रेम भाव या अवैध प्रेम
The amour was wounded in a sword fight.

Amourette/एमॉरेट *adj)* - छोटा प्रेम विषय या प्रेमी
Lord Krishna in his childhood was a great amourette.

Ampere/एम्पीयर *(noun)* - बिजली की धारा की नापने की इकाई
How many ampere of electricity have been used?

Amphibia/एम्फिबिया *(adj)* -उभयचर, पृथ्वी और जल दोनों जगह में रहने वाले जन्तु
Frog etc. are amphibian animals which can live on both land and water.

Amphibious/एम्फिबिअस *(adj.)* - स्थल या जल में रहने योग्य
Many snakes are amphibious.

Amphigory/एम्फिगरी *(noun)* - निरर्थक शब्द
All his work amounts to amphigory.

Amphistomous/एम्फिसटोमस *(adj)* - दुमुँहा, दोनो मुँह ओर वाला
Leech is a amphistomous creature having a sucker at each end of the body to suck blood.

Amphitheatre/एम्फीथियेटर *(noun)* - रंगभूमि
When I went to Rome I saw the famous amphitheatre there it is a round place which was built for games and athletic events.

Amphora/एम्फोरा *(noun)* - दो हत्था कलश
I saw an amphora at a museum I would have loved to drink from it.

Amply/एम्प्ली *(adv)* - पर्याप्त रूप से
The opinions of people were amply represented.

Amputate/एम्प्युटेट *(verb)* - किसी अंग को काटना
As gangrene set in the leg the doctors had to amputate it to save patient's life.

Amuck/एमक् *(adv.)* - उन्मता
The elephant ran amuck.

Amulet/एम्यलिट *(noun)* - ताबीज
I always wear an amulet given by a Sadhu.

Amuse/अम्यूज *(verb)* - विनोद करना, मन बहलाना
I was amused by the pranks played by him.

An/एन *(adj.)* - एक, कोई
I saw a hen laying an egg.

Anabaptism/एनाबैप्टिज्म *(noun)* - दुबारा, लामकरण
I am a non believer and as such I would never Anabaptism allow to be administered to me.

Anabasis/एनाबेसिस *(noun)* - फौज का आगे बढ़ना
He has gone on an unknown anabasis.

Anacathartic/एनाकाथारटिक *(noun)* - कफ निकालने वाली औषधि
If you feel like vomiting take a sip of anacathartic it will cure you.

Anaclastic/एनाक्लास्टिक *(adj)* - किरण के तिरछेपन से सम्बन्ध रखने वाला
Look at the bottom of anaclastic glass the bottom seems to spring at you.

Anaclisis/एनाक्लिसिस *(noun)* - चारपाई पर निरन्तर पड़े रहने से उत्पन्न फोड़ा
He is suffering from anaclisis for which he is seeing psychologist.

Anadem/एनाडेम *(noun)* - माला
He was offered an anadem as he entered the city.

Anaemia/एनिमिया *(noun)* - रक्तहीनता
He is suffering from anaemia. He should have checked hemoglobin.

Anaesthesia/एनसथीसिया *(noun)* - शरीर के किसी अंग की चेतना शून्यता, शल्य चिकित्सा से पूर्व दवा द्वारा संवेदनहीनता उत्पन्न करने की प्रक्रिया
His body has been made insensitive to pain by anaesthesia because he is to undergo an operation.

Anal/एनल *(adj.)* - पूँछ के नीचे का, गुदा के समीप
He had to undergo anal surgery to get rid of piles.

Analeptic/एनालेप्टिक *(adj.)* - पुष्टिकर औषधि
It is an analeptic drug, it will stimulate your mind.

Analgesia/एनलजेसिया *(noun)* - पीड़ाशून्य करने वाली दवा
Take an analgesia tablet to get relief from your pain.

Analogical/एनालोजिकल *(adj.)* – सदृश, समान

The two poems are analogical in content.

Analogy/अनैलजि *(noun)* – समानता, तुल्यता

There is a great analogy between the two brothers.

Analysable/एनालाइजेब्ल *(adj.)* – सूक्ष्म परीक्षा

This sentence is analysable.

Analyse/एनलाइज *(verb)* – सूक्ष्म परीक्षा करना, विश्लेषण करना

If you analyse this chemical properly you will know its constituent.

Analysis/एनैलसिस *(noun)* – विघटन, विभाजन

Analysis of his DNA sample must be done as soon as possible.

Analytical/एनलिटिकल *(adj.)* – विभाजन या विश्लेषण सम्बन्धी

Analytical discussion of a thing leads to its logical conclusion.

Anamnesis/एनाम्नेसिस *(noun)* – पूर्व जन्म का स्मरण, अनुस्मृति

Anamnesis occurred to him at the age of eight and he remembered many facts of his past birth.

Anarchic/एनारकिक *(adj.)* – नियम प्रतिकूल

The state was declared anarchic.

Anarchy/एनार्कि *(noun)* – अराजकता, कुशासन

Anarchy had spread all over the city.

Anathema/एनैथमा *(noun)* – ईश्वर का शाप

Casteism was anathema to her.

Anatomy/एनाटमी *(noun)* – शरीर रचना विज्ञान

Anatomy interests me greatly.

Anbury/एन्ब्यूरी – बैलों और घोड़ों की गिट्टी का एक रोग

You see this growth on this horse's back it is anbury which has to be surgically removed.

Ancestor/एन्सेस्टर *(noun)* – पुरखा, पूर्वपुरुष, पूर्वज

Our ancestor belonged to UP Kashipur.

Anchor/एन्कर *(noun)* – लंगर, विश्वास का स्थान

The ship has dropped anchor and is secured firmly in a position.

Anchorite/एन्कोराइट *(noun)* – संन्यासी, विरक्त

He is an anchorite remaining alone and talking to body.

Ancient/एन्सिएंट *(adj.)* – प्राचीन, पुराना

In ancient times there were very funny and dangerous animals.

Ancillary/एन्सिलरी *(adj.)* – मुख्य गतिविधियों में सहायक

This branch is an ancillary of the food department.

Ancon/एन्कान *(noun)* – कुहनी (केहुनी)

There is pain in my ancon.

And/एण्ड *(conj.)* – और

Love and kindness are two great virtues.

Andiron/एन्डिरॉन *(noun)* – अँगीठी के लोहे के सीकंचे

He put an andiron into the hearth for supporting fire logs.

Anecdote/एनिक्डोट *(noun)* – कथा

I'll tell you an anecdote about my brother.

Anemograph/एनेमोग्राफ *(noun)* – वायु का वेग अंकित करने का यन्त्र

The anemograph shows that a strong wind is developing.

Anemometer/एनिमॉमीटर *(noun)* – वायु की शक्ति नापने का यन्त्र

According to the anemometer the speed of the wind is 200 kms an hour.

Aneroid/एनेरोआएड *(adj.)* – एक प्रकार का निद्रव वायु, दाब मापक यन्त्र

This is an instrument called barometer or aneroid which tells us about the air pressure.

Anew/एन्यू *(adv.)*– पुनः, फिर से नये सिरे से

Now that you have served your term you must start anew.

Anfroctuous/एन्फ्रोक्टअस *(adj.)* – पेचीला, चक्करदार

Catacombs are always anfroctuous in construction.

Angel/एन्जेल *(noun)* – देवदूत, फरिश्ता, सुन्दर या अबोध मनुष्य

You have proved yourself an angel by helping me in this hour of need.

Anger/एन्गर *(noun)* – क्रुद्ध करना, कुपित करना

By his behaviour he provoked anger in me.

Angina/एन्गिना *(noun)* – गण्डमाला

Your father is holding his chest this seem angina pain. You should call a doctor at once.

Angle/एन्गल *(noun)* - कोण

A triangle has three angles.

Angler/एन्गलर *(noun)* - मछली पकड़ने वाला

He is an angler and has thousand tricks up in his sleeve so beware of him.

Anglican/एंगलिकन *(adj.)* - अंग्रेजी, इंग्लैंड के चर्च या अंग्रेजी भाषी देश के चर्च का सदस्य

This church is Anglican as this in communion with the church of England.

Angling/एन्गलिंग *(verb)* - मछली पकड़ रहा हैं

He has been angling for hours by the river side with a hook and line.

Anglo/एंग्लो *(noun)* - इंग्लैंड या ब्रिटेन से सम्बन्धित

He is an Anglo descending from British race.

Anglo-saxon/एंग्लो-सैक्सन *(noun)* - प्राचीन अँग्रेजी जाति का

Any white person speaking English chiefly north American comes under the category of Anglo Saxon.

Angrily/एंग्रिली *(adv.)* - क्रोध से with anger. *She angrily shouted at him.*

Angriness/एंग्रीनेस *(noun)* - क्रोधावस्था

In his angriness he couldn't think properly.

Angry/एंग्री *(adj.)* - क्रुद्ध, कुपित

This dog looks angry dangerous.

Anguish/एंगविश *(noun)* - शारीरिक स्थिति या जीवन के बारे में चिंता, तीव्र वेदना

He caused me emotional anguish by his scandalous remarks.

Angular/एन्गुलर *(adj.)* - कोण वाला

This house is built in an angular shape and has lots of angles in it.

Angulate/एन्गुलेट *(verb)* - कोण से अनुरूप बनाया

We angulate our body a lot of time while doing yoga.

Anil/एनिल *(noun)* - नील का पौधा और इसका रंग

I got my clothes dyed in anil blue.

Anile/एनाइल *(adj.)* - बुढ़िया के समान

He walked like an anile weak and trembling.

Aniline/एनिलाइन *(noun)* - रंगो का रासायनिक आधार

We use aniline a colourless liquid in making dyes plastic drugs.

Animadvert/एनिमाडवर्ट *(verb)* - तिरस्कार करना

He animadverted me before my friends and I felt insulted.

Animal/एनिमल *(noun)* - जन्तु, पशु

In contrast to tree animals can move.

Animalism/एनिमलिज्म *(noun)* - पाशविक प्रकृति, हैवानियत

This animalism knows no bounds.

Animality/एनिमलिटी *(noun)* - जीव-प्रदान, पाशविक प्रकृति

The animality in him is too pronounced don't go near him.

Animation/एनिमेशन *(noun)* - भरभूर जोश और उत्साह

Tom & jerry the various comics today especially historical films employ computer graphics and animation and give the images an illusion of movement of life.

Animism/एनिमिज्म *(noun)* - ब्रह्मवाद, आत्मवाद

I believe in animism i.e. all plants and inanimate objects have a soul the whole universe was organized by a supernatural power.

Animosity/एनिमॉसिटी *(noun)* - शत्रुता

I bear great animosity to this murderer, get him away from here.

Animus/एनिमस *(noun)* - द्वेष, विरोधपूर्ण भावना या इच्छा

He has great animus and will become a successful man one day.

Anise/एनीज *(noun)* - सौंफ का पौंधा

I have great liking for the aroma of anise.

Aniseed/एनिसीड *(noun)* - सौंफ का बीज

When once I was hurt in a village the local physician cured me with aniseeds.

Ankle/एंकल *(noun)* - नली

The water only came up to my ankles.

Anklet/एंकलेट *(noun)* - नूपुर, पायजेब

The American tourist wore anklets and the socks just up to her ankles.

Anaa/एन्ना *(noun)* - एक आना

Annas become obsolete currency.

Annals/एनल्ज *(noun)* - पूर्वकथा, वार्षिक

Let me consult the annals in the library. I may find something worthy.

Annalist/एनालिस्ट *(noun)* - इतिहास-लेखक
The retired professor of history was employed as an annalist by the college.

Annex/एनेक्स *(verb)* - मिलाना, लगाना
Some years back Iraq wanted to annex some territory of Kuwait claiming it as its own.

Annihilate/एनिहिलेट *(verb)* - पूरी तरह नष्ट या पराजित कर देना
During wars large chunks of territories are completely annihilated by bombarding.

Anniversary/एनिवरसरी *(noun)* - वार्षिकोत्सव
He celebrated his birth anniversary with great pomp and show.

Annodomini/एनोडोमिनी *(adv.)* - ईसा मसीह के जन्म के पश्चात् का समय
I was born on 1938 Anno Domini i.e. after the birth of Christ.

Annotate/एनटेट *(verb)* - व्याख्यात्मक टिप्पणियाँ देना
Please annotate this paragraph.

Announce/अनाउन्स *(verb)* - घोषणा करना
Ladies and gentlemen I proudly announce the engagement of my daughter Tina with Anand.

Annoy/एनॉय *(verb)* - दुःख देना
I feel annoyed please don't repeat such silly mistakes in future.

Annual/एन्युअल *(adj.)* - वार्षिक
The school is celebrating its annual sports day.

Annuitant/एन्वीटैंट *(noun)* - वार्षिक वेतन पाने वाला व्यक्ति
This farmer servant of my father is an annuitant, he gets fixed sum every year.

Annuity/एन्वीटी *(noun)* - वार्षिक वेतन या भत्ता
Each year for the whole life I'll be paying annuity to the insurance company.

Annular/एन्यूलर *(adj.)* - गोल
It is an annular object may be it is a ring of somebody.

Anodyne/एनोडाइन *(noun & adj.)* - पीड़ानाशक
Please apply some anodyne on your ankle it will relieve your pain.

Anoint/एनॉयन्ट *(verb)* - तेल लगाना, विलेपन
Before being made monarch he was anointed by a priest.

Anomaly/अनामली *(noun)* - अनियमितता, अव्यवस्था
The anomaly in his character didn't let him stick anywhere.

Anon/एनॉन *(adv.)* - शीघ्र अभी
He made a sign and anon a big crowd followed him.

Anonymous/एनॉनिमस *(noun)* - जिस पुस्तक का नाम ज्ञात न हो, अनामक ग्रंथ
This book is written by an anonymous person it is clear that writer does not want to reveal his name.

Anonymity/एनॉनिमिटी *(noun)* - अज्ञात होने की अवस्था, गुमनामी
For years she has been able to retain her anonymity.

Anosmia/एनाज्मीया *(noun)* - घ्राणशक्ति का नाश, सूँघने की शक्ति का नाश
He has lost his sense of smell may be because of the blockage of the nose caused by anosmia.

Another/अनदर *(pronoun)* - दूसरा पदार्थ या व्यक्ति
Another person is needed for help.

Anserine/एन्सराइन *(adj.)* - बत्तख के समान, मूर्ख
This egg is anserine.

Answer/आन्सर *(noun)* - उत्तर, समाधान
He answered all the questions in the paper.

Ant/एन्ट *(noun)* - चींटी
Ants are very social and hard working insects.

Antacid/एन्टासिड *(adj.)* - अम्लत्व-नाशक पदार्थ
You seem to suffer from acidity take an antacid.

Antagonism/एन्टैगनिज्म *(noun)* - बैर, शत्रुता
The English found a lot of antagonism in Indians.

Antalkali/एन्टाल्कालि *(noun)* - क्षारत्व दूर करने वाला पदार्थ या औषधि
If you want to treat alkalosis take antalkali it neutralizes alkalis.

Antarctic/एन्टार्कटिक *(adj.)* - दक्षिणी, दक्षिणी ध्रुववाली
White bears are found in the Antarctic region.

Ante/एन्टि *(noun)* - 'पूर्व' अर्थ का उपसर्ग
This is the game of poker this player has already put an ante before receiving cards.

Antecede/एन्टिसिड *(verb)* - समय से पूर्व घटित होना
A antecedes the letter B.

Antecedence/एन्टिसिडेंस *(noun)* - अगलापन, पूर्वत्व
I enjoy the privilege of antecedence. All my brothers are younger.

Antecedent/एन्टिसिडेंट *(noun)* - पूर्वगामी, पूर्वपद का
For marriage purposes we have checked the antecedents of the boy.

Antechamber/एन्टिचैम्बर *(noun)* - बाहरी दालान, उपकक्ष
Almost all the pyramids used to have a secret antechamber which led to main room or hall.

Antedate/एन्टिडेट *(verb)* - पूर्वतिथि देना, स्थिर काल से पूर्व का समय
There notes in this chapters should be antedate.

Antelope/एन्टिलोप *(noun)* - एक प्रकार का हिरन या मृग, चिकारा
Once I went to Africa there I saw impala antelope etc. gracefully running.

Antemeridian/एन्टिमिरिडियन *(adj.)* - आधी रात से दोपहर तक का समय
I'll see you tomorrow at 7 a.m. (antemeridian).

Antemundane/एन्टिमन्डेन *(adj)* - पूर्वाह्न, सुबह दोपहर होने से पूर्व
We really know nothing or very little as to what happened in antemundane period.

Anterior/एन्टिअरिअर *(adj.)* - शरीर का कोई अंग पूर्व या पिछला, पहले का
You need an anterior check up, a neurologist will be the best to consult.

Anteroom/एन्टिरूम *(noun)* - गलियारा, दालान
I waited in the anteroom to be called in the officer's mess.

Anthelion/एन्थेलियन *(noun)* - बादलों के चारों ओर आकाश का मण्डल, प्रकाश चक्र
Do you see that anthelion in the sky?

Anthem/ऐनथम *(noun)* - ईश्वर-स्तुति, भजन, देश, संगठन या पाठशाला के द्वारा अपनाया गया विशेष गान जो केवल विशेष अवसरों पर गाया जाता है
Our song of the nation i.e. National Anthem is Jan, gan, man.

Anther/एन्थर *(noun)* - परागकेशर रखने वाला फुल का भाग
You will find many insects sucking pollen at the anther.

Anthropoad/एन्थ्रोपायड *(adj.)* - केवल आकार में मनुष्य के सदृश्य
All apes and monkeys are anthropoads.

Anti/ऐन्टि *(adj & adv)* - उपसर्ग जिसका अर्थ विपरीत समान में है
I am anti dictatorship.

Antic/एन्टिक *(adj)* - अनोखा, विलक्षण
He bought an interesting antic from the bazaar of Morocco.

Antichrist/एन्टिक्राइस्ट *(noun)* - ईसा-मसीह का शत्रु, शैतान, ईशा-विरोधी
Antichrist will appear at the end of world.

Anticipate/एन्टिसिपेट *(verb)* - आशा करना, पहले से विचार करना
I don't anticipate such behaviour.

Anticyclone/एन्टिसाइक्लोन *(noun)* - प्रति चक्रवात वायु
The storm is coming we should put an anticyclone at the centre.

Antidote/एन्टिडोट *(noun)* - प्रतिविष, विषनाशक, औषधि
If a snake bites you the doctors will inject an antidote and save you.

Antilogy/एन्टिलॉजी *(noun)* - विरोधाभास
There is great antilogy between us so why talk?

Antimony/एन्टिमॅनी *(noun)* - सुरमा
In old times people used a piece of antimony to cure showing cuts.

Anti-national/एन्टी नेशनल *(adj.)* - देशद्रोही
His ideas are antinational.

Antinomy/एन्टिनोमी *(noun)* - अधिकार-विरोध
It is an antinomy that my long last friend was living in my neighbourhood and I didn't know.

Antipathetic/एन्टिपैथेटिक *(adj)* - विरुद्ध स्वभाव का
Antipathic reaction, are expected from this drug.

Antipathic/एन्टिपैथिक *(noun)* - विरूद्ध, विपरीत
I have developed deep antipathy towards my cousin. I don't know, why?

Antipathy/एन्टिपैथी *(noun)* - घृणा, अनिच्छा
I have antipathy towards her.

Antiphlogistic/एन्टिफ्लोजिस्टिक *(adj.)* - सूजन घटाने वाली
This is an antiphlogistic medicine. It will reduce your inflammation.

Antiphonal/एन्टिफोनल *(noun)* - पारी-पारी से गाया हुआ

Hymns are being sung in church in an antiphonal way.

Antiphony/एन्टिफोनी *(noun)* - प्रतिध्वनि, प्रतिगान

I daily practice antiphony in the morning.

Antipodes/एन्टिपोड्स *(pl. noun)* - प्रतिलोम

Newzealand and Australia are directly opposite one another they are called antipodes.

Antipyretic/एन्टिपायरेटिक *(adj.)* - ज्वर हटाने वाली औषधि

This is an antipyretic drug take it and your fever will come down.

Antiquarian/एन्टिक्वेरिअन *(adj.)* - प्राचीन पदार्थो का संग्रह करने वाला

He is an antiquarian studying antiques rare books etc.

Antiquated/एन्टिक्वेटड *(adj.)* - प्राचीन

This expression is no longer in use it is antiquated.

Antique/एन्टीक *(adj.)* - पुराना, प्राचीन ढंग का

Today I went to see the race of antique cars. It was fantastic.

Antiseptic/एन्टिसेप्टीक *(adj.)* - अपवित्रता-नाशक

Before operation doctors use strong antiseptics so as to kill various micro organisms.

Antisocial/एन्टिसोशल *(adj.)* - समाज विरोधी

Most of the antisocial elements have been arrested by police during a special drive.

Antitheist/एन्टिथेइस्ट *(noun)* - अनिश्वरवादी

He is an antitheist. He doesn't believe in God.

Antitheism/एन्टिथेइज्म *(noun)* - नास्तिकता

I have read many books on antitheism but none appealed to me.

Antithesis/एन्टिथेसिस *(noun)* - अर्थ के विपरीत

There is perfect antithesis between the two brothers. One is cool and other is hot tempered.

Antitoxin/एन्टिटॉक्सिन *(noun)* - विषमारक, अतिविष, रोग के विष का हटाने वाला एक तत्व

We must eat food rich in antitoxins so that they can counteract the toxins.

Antler/एन्टलर *(noun)* - बारहसिंगे की शाखादार सींग

I saw an antler in the sanctuary of South Africa. It was so thrilling.

Antonym/एन्टोनिम *(noun)* - विपरीत अर्थ का शब्द, विलोम

Cruelty is the antonym of kindness.

Antrum/एन्ट्रम *(noun)* - अस्थि कोटर

As the zoologist looked into the antrum he found something stuck into it.

Anus/एनस *(noun)* - गुदा, मलद्वार

Piles is a disease of anus.

Anvil/एन्विल *(noun)* - निहाई, स्थूणा

Blacksmiths shape iron by hammering it on the anvil.

Anxiety/एन्जाइटी *(noun)* - चिन्ता, आकुलता

He suffers from anxiety disorders and is consulting a psychiatrist.

Anxious/एन्कशस *(adj.)* - व्याकुल, चिन्तिन

I am very much anxious about my son's fate. He never succeeds anywhere

Any/एनी *(pron)* - कोई- किसी

Any of you is interested in taking part in debate.

Aorta/एओरटा *(noun)* - महाधमनी

If due to any reason aorta is cut off, the patient will at once die.

Apace/एपेस *(adv.)* - शीघ्रता, जल्दी से

I went to the accident spot apace.

Apart/अपार्ट *(adv.)* - अलग

Apart from being friends they are colleagues also.

Apartment/अपार्टमेंट *(noun)* - किसी मकान में कमरों का समूह

These city people prefer to live in apartments.

Apathetic/एपैथेटिक *(adj.)* - उदासीन, निरुत्साह

He was apathetic to her miseries.

Apathy/एपथि *(noun)* - अनिच्छा, जड़ता, उदासीनता

He developed total apathy to his friend who didn't give up his bad habits.

Apepsy/एपेप्सी *(noun)* - पाचन शक्ति की दुर्बलता

Besides other malfunctions he also suffer from apepsy.

Aperient/एपेरियन्ट *(adj.)* - मल को ढीला करने वाली औषधि

Take this aperient. It will relieve you in the morning.

Aperture/एपरचर *(noun)* – छेद, मोखा, झरी

The sun light creeping through an aperture filled the room with light.

Apetalous/एपेटैलस *(adj.)* – दलहीन

Do you see this plant it is without petals and is called apetalous.

Apex/एपेक्स *(noun)* – शिखर, चोटी

The apex court gave a landmark judgment.

Aphasia/अफेजिया *(noun)* – वाग्रोध, बोली बन्द होना, वाचाघात

He can't hear or talk because he is suffering from aphasia.

Aphelion/एफीलियन *(noun)* – अपसौर, किसी ग्रह का सूर्य से सबसे दूर का स्थान

Aphelion is getting very popular these days.

Aphorism/एफरिज़्म *(noun)* – कहावत, वचन

A bird in hand is better than two in the bush is a popular aphorism.

Aphrodisiac/ऐफ्रोडिजीऐक *(noun)* – कामोत्तेजक, कामोद्दीपक औषधि

It is believed that a rhino's horn is a great aphrodisiac.

Apiary/एपिअरी *(noun)* – मधुमक्खियों के पालने का स्थान

He must be in the apiary. He has a lot of bees there.

Apical/एपिकल *(adj.)* – शिखर-सम्बन्धी

R is an apical letter.

Apiculture/एपिकल्चर *(noun)* – मधुमक्खियों को पोसना, मधुपालन

He is an expert in apiculture.

Apiece/अपीस *(adv.)* – एक-एक करके, प्रत्येक के लिए

The trench was dug apiece.

Apocryphal/अपाक्रीफल *(adj.)* – झूठा, असत्य, संदिग्ध प्रमाण

This document is apocryphal its authenticity can't be doubled.

Apollo/अपोलो *(noun)* – यूनान के सूर्य देव

I chanced to catch an Apollo while in Europe.

Apologetic/अपालजेटिक *(adj.)* – क्षमा योग्य, प्रार्थना योग्य, क्षमायाचक, शर्मिंदा, खेदपूर्ण

I am apologetic for my rude behaviour.

Apologist/अपालजिस्ट *(noun)* – क्षमा प्रार्थना करने वाला

He is an apologist and will soon offer an apology.

Apologize/अपालजाइज *(verb)* – अपना दोष बताकर क्षमा माँगना

I apologize for having hurt you.

Apologue/ऐपलॉग *(noun)* – उपदेश पूर्ण कहानी

Children let me tell you an apologue of a can and monkey.

Apology/अपॉलजि *(noun)* – खेदसूचक क्षमा-प्रार्थना

Please accept my apology for the delay.

Apophthegm/एपॉपथेम *(noun)* – सूत्र, नीतिवचन

So I'll tell you an apophthegm live and live.

Apoplexy/एपप्लेक्सी *(noun)* – मूर्छा, मिरगी का रोग

He had a stroke of apoplexy and hence can't speak.

Apostacy/एपॉस्टैसी – स्वधर्मत्याग, अपने सिद्धान्त या दल का त्याग

His apostacy led to his ruin.

Apostate/अपोस्टेट *(noun)* – स्वधर्म-त्यागी, विश्वास

He is an apostate. He has renounced his faith

Apostle/एपॉस्ल *(noun)* – भक्त

Judas was an apostle of Christ who betrayed him.

Apostolic/एपॉस्टोलिक *(adj.)* – देवदूत सम्बन्धी

He will not change his apostolic decision.

Apothecary/एपोथिकैरी *(noun)* – दवा बेचने वाला, अत्तार

You can buy medicines from him. He is an apothecary.

Apotheosis/अपोथिओसिस *(noun)* – देवता-तुल्य, निर्माण, दैवीकरण

This is the apotheosis. You can dive from here.

Appal/अप्पल *(verb)* – डराना

He spoke appalingly bad language.

Apparel/अपरेल *(noun)* – कपड़ा, वस्त्र

The apparels of royalty used to be very costly.

Apparent/अपेरेन्ट *(adj.)* – वास्तविक जैसा आभासी

It is very apparent that he is telling a lie.

Apparition/एपरिशन *(noun)* – पिशाच, प्रेत

Suddenly in the dead of night an apparition appeared before me.

A

Appear/एपिअर *(verb)* - दुष्टिगोचर होना, जान पड़ना
It was a long voyage but ultimately the land appeared.

Appease/अपीज *(verb)* - सान्त्वना देना, मनाना
All the small animals appeased lion's demand.

Appellant/एपेलन्ट *(noun)* - पुनर्विचार की प्रार्थना करने वाला
The appellant demands that the case be reopened.

Appellation/एपलेशन *(noun)* - पदवी, उपाधि, नत्थी करना
The royal child was conferred the appellation of Prince.

Append/अपेन्ड *(verb)* - जोड़ना, लगाना, मिलाना, नत्थी करना
This piece of writing should be appended properly.

Appendix/अपेन्डिक्स *(noun)* - उण्डुक पुच्छ, परिशिष्ट, अतिरिक्त विषय जोड़ी हुई वस्तु
He usually has pain in his appendix.

Appendicitis/अपेन्डिसायटिस - आँत में एक प्रकार का फोड़ा
He has appendicitis because his appendix has swelling.

Apperception/एपर्सेप्शन *(noun)* - चित्त का आत्मज्ञान, मानसिक बोध
The psychologist put up a new apperception into his mind.

Appetence/अपेटेन्स *(noun)* - अति उत्सुक, अभिलाषा
Since long he had cherished appetency.

Appetite/एपेटाइट *(noun)* - अभिलाषा, इच्छा
I have great appetite for non-veg food.

Applaud/अप्लॉड *(verb)* - प्रशंसा करना, ताली बजाना
The show was greatly applanded by people.

Applause/एप्लॉज *(noun)* - प्रशंसा, स्तुति
He got huge applause for his acting as Shaheed Bhagat Singh.

Apple/एपल *(noun)* - सेब
I like apples a lot.

Appliance/अप्लाएन्स *(noun)* - घरेलू उपयोग का उपकरण
Electrical appliances of Bajaj are famous all over India.

Applicable/एप्लिकेबल *(adj.)* - उचित
This law is not applicable in this land.

Applicant/एप्लिकैंट *(noun)* - प्रार्थी, प्रार्थना करने वाला, आवेदक
All applicants must appear for interview at 10 a.m. in the office.

Application/एप्लिकेशन *(noun)* - प्रार्थना पत्र
I have submitted an application for leave.

Apply/अप्लाइ *(verb)* - सूचित करना, आरूढ़ होना
I have applied for several jobs.

Appoint/अप्वाइंट *(verb)* - नियुक्त करना, स्थापित करना
You are appointed as a teacher in directorate of Delhi Education Deptt. Here is your appointment letter.

Apportion/एपॉरशन *(verb)* - भाग करना, बाँटना
Let me apportion you a tough task.

Apposite/अपोजिट *(adj.)* - योग्य, संगत
It is an apposite decision taken at the right time.

Appraise/अप्रेज *(verb)* - मूल्य ठहराना
I have appraised the value of his piece of furniture.

Appreciable/अप्रीशिबल *(adj.)* - जानने योग्य, प्रशंसा करने योग्य
Your effort are appreciable.

Appreciate/एप्रिशियेट *(verb)* - गुण जानना, मान करना
I appreciate your efforts.

Apprehend/एप्रिहेन्ड *(verb)* - पकड़ना, गिरफ्तार करना
The thief was apprehended at the spot.

Apprehension/एप्रिहेन्शन *(noun)* - पकड़, बुद्धि, भय, समझ, अनुभव
I have apprehension that something will go wrong.

Apprentice/एप्रेन्टिस *(noun)* - नवसिखुआ, प्रशिक्षु
He is an apprentice learning the trade under skilled guidance.

Apprise/एप्राइज *(verb)* - सूचना देना, बतलाना
I apprised him of all the facts.

Apprize/एप्राइज *(verb)* - गुण जानना, मूल्य आँकना [archaic] put a price on.

Approach/अप्रोच *(verb)* - समीप जाना, मूल्य लगाना
I approached him boldly.

Approbate/एप्रबेट *(verb)* - अनुमोदन करना
His documents have been approbated.

Approbation/एप्रवेशन *(noun)* - अनुमोदन
His work has received a lot of approbation.

Appropriate/एप्रोप्रिएट *(adj.)* - उचित, उपयुक्त
Appropriate action has been taken against the culprit.

Approval/अप्रूवल *(noun)* - अनुमोदन, स्वीकृति
Your scheme has my approval.

Approximate/अप्रॉक्सिमेट *(adj.)* - अति समीप, लगभग, निकट
I have approximately 98% works.

Appurtenance/अपर्टनन्स *(noun)* - अनुलग्न, पूरक
A space wheel is an appurtenance in a vehicle.

Apricot/एप्रिकाट *(noun)* - खूबानी का फल
Apricot is a useful dry fruit increasing the activity of brain.

Apropos/अप्रोपो *(prep.)* - अनुरूप, अनुसार
Apropros your article in the magazine let me ask you a question.

Apse/एप्स *(noun)* - अर्ध-वृत्ताकार आला या झरोखा
You see that domed roof in the church, it is called apse.

Apt/एप्ट *(adj.)* - उचित, ठीक
I gave him an apt answer he was happy and surprised.

Aqua/एक्वा *(noun)* - तरल घोल, जल
Mix this medicine in aqua.

Aquarium/एक्वेरियम *(noun)* - जन्तुओं को पालने की पानी से भरी शीशे की टंकी
I saw an aquarium in Singapore. It was thrilling to see the huge and dangerous creatures so close.

Aquarius/अक्वेअरिअस *(noun)* - कुम्भ राशि
Do you see that large sign in the sky? It is Aquarius.

Aqueduct/एक्विडयूट *(noun)* - लहर, कुत्रिम जलमार्ग
Water in this canal is being carried through aqueduct.

Aqueous/एक्वेअस *(adj.)* - जलीय, जलयुक्त
I have bought an aqueous jar.

Aquiline/एक्विलाइन *(adj.)* - मुड़ा हुआ
Two birds have an aquline nose. May be it is an eagle.

Arabian/एरेबिअन *(noun)* - अरब देश का
He is an Arabian. It is clear from his features and complexion.

Arabic/ऐरबिक - अरब देश की भाषा
I am learning Arabic. It is an interesting language written from right to left like Urdu.

Arable/एरेब्ल *(adj.)* - जोतने-बोने योग्य भूमि
The land that I have bought is quite costly but then it is arable.

Arbiter/आरबिटर *(noun)* - मध्यस्थ
An arbiter has been appointed to solve the case between two brothers.

Arbitrary/आबिट्री *(adj.)* - स्वच्छन्द, बिना तर्क के
It is arbitrary decision. It isn't fair and I'll not abide by it.

Arbitrate/आबिट्रेट *(verb)* - पंचायत करना
I am going to arbitrate between the two parties to settle their old dispute.

Arboreal/आरबोरियल *(adj.)* - वृक्ष सम्बन्धी
Birds are arboreal creatures.

Arc/आर्क *(noun)* - चाप, कमान, वृत्तखण्ड
The gates of this building are arc shaped.

Arcade/आर्केड *(noun)* - खम्भों पर बनी हुई मेहराबें
I found him in the amusement arcade.

Arcadia/आर्केडिया *(noun)* - ग्रीक देश का पर्वतीय इलाका
He lives in Southern Greece he is an Arcadian.

Arch/आर्क *(adj.)* - प्रधान, महत्त्वपूर्ण
The arch villain of the show is Ravana in Ramlila.

Archaeology/आरकियोलॉजी - पुरातत्व
He is an archaeologist and often visits prehistoric or historic setes.

Archbishop/अर्च्बिशप *(noun)* - प्रधान, पादरी
St. Thomas was the archbishop of Conterbury.

Arch-enemy/आर्कएनेमी *noun)* - प्रधान-शत्रु, शैतान
Devil is the archenemy of human race.

Archfiend/आर्कफियेन्ड - प्रधान-भूत
Devil has been described by Christian as archfiend.

Archer/आर्चर *(noun)* - धनुष से बाण चलाने वाला
There were many fine archers in king Richard's army.

Archetype/आर्किटाइप *(noun)* – मूल रूप से आदर्श
Every man carries in his unconscious mind an archetype of his early ancestors.

Architect/आर्किटेक्ट *(noun)* – शिल्पकार
He is a renowned architect who is designing this hospital.

Archlike/आर्कलाइक *(adj.)* – मेहराब के सदृश बना हुआ *People built an archlike gate to welcome their leader.*

Archway/आर्कवे *(noun)* – मेहराब के नीचे का मार्ग
I saw an old archway in a dilapilated building.

Arctic/आर्कटिक *(adj.)* – उत्तरी
The cold is almost arctic

Ardent/आर्डेन्ट *(adj.)* – प्रचण्ड, उत्साही, तीव्र
He is an ardent lover of mine.

Ardour/आर्डर *(noun)* – उत्कण्ठा, व्यग्रता
He has great ardour to become an IAS officer.

Arduous/आरडुअस *(adj.)* – कठिन, परिश्रमी, दुष्कर
The mountain climbing proved very arduous for me.

Area/एरिया *(noun)* – क्षेत्रफल, समतल
It is an area reserved for airport.

Areca/एरिका *(noun)* – सुपारी का वृक्ष
It is an areca. Would you dare to climb it and pluck a nut.

Arefaction/अरिफैक्शन *(noun)* – सुखाने का कार्य
Arefaction has set in these plants and they are fast drying.

Arefy/एयरीफाइ *(verb)* – सुखाना
The sun will arefy clothes.

Arena/एरीना *(noun)* – अखाड़ा, रंगस्थली
In circus public sit circularly and in the middle is round shaped arena where events take place.

Arenaceous/एरिनेशस *(adj.)* – बालू के समान
This area is arenaceous full of sands and plants.

Argent/आर्जेन्ट *(adj. & noun)* – चाँदी के रंग का
This piece of writing is argent.

Argil/आरगिल *(noun)* – एल्यूमिना
The clay models are made of argil.

Argue/आर्ग्यू *(verb)* – बहस करना, दलीले पेश करना, सिद्ध करना
To argue is to completely miss the point of discussion.

Arguing/आर्ग्यूइंग *(noun)* – तर्क
The members of committee went on arguing for hours but there was no result because all had different views.

Argument/आरगुमेंट *(noun)* – तर्क-वितर्क
Heated argument were exchanged among the club members but to no avail.

Argute/आरग्यूट *(adj.)* – तीखा, कर्कश
He is an argute person.

Arid/एरिड *(adj.)* – गरमी से झुलसा हुआ
It is an arid and vast desert.

Aries/एरीज *(noun)* – मेष राशि
Your sign in Aries that is what your date of birth says and the coming times are very good for you.

Aright/एराइट *(adj.)* – ठीक
He entered the hotel turned aright.

Arise/एराइज *(verb)* – उठना
With the arise of women emancipation movement in England many countries joined it.

Arista/एरिस्टा *(noun)* – अन्न सा घास की बाल
This is a strange fly called arista. It has bristle like growth near its antenna.

Aristocracy/एरिस्टोक्रैसी *(noun)* – शिष्टजन, उच्चवर्ग
Government controlled aristocracy is out of vogue.

Aristocrat/एरिस्टोक्रैट *(noun)* – अभिजात, रईस
He is an aristocrat having lots of money and power.

Aristophanic/एरिस्टोफेनिक *(adj.)* – हँसमुख, चतुर
The aristophanic poems make us laugh.

Arithmetic/अरिथमेटिक *(noun)* – अंकगणित
He is very intelligent in Arithmetic.

Arm/आर्म *(noun)* – बाहु, भुजा, शाखा
Arms are very important limbs of human body.

Armament/अर्मामिंट *(noun)* – शक्ति, बल, युद्ध करने की सामग्री
The armament comprising of Jawans big guns anti air guns truck jeeps etc. crawled along the Mountainous area.

Armature/आर्मेचर *(noun)* – विद्युत उपकरण
The armature of this motor is burnt out, send it to the mechanic for winding.

Armistice/आर्मिस्टिस *(noun)* – युद्ध-विराम, संधि
Orders for armistice were given by the general.

Armless/आर्मलेस *(adj)* - बिना बाँह का
I saw an armless beggar.

Armlet/आर्मलेट *(noun)* - बाजूबन्द, समुद्र की शाखा
Her armlet is very beautiful.

Armorial/आर्मोरिअल *(adj.)* - कवच सम्बन्धी
The coach had armorial bearing.

Armour/आर्मर *(noun)* - कवच, अनुत्राण
The metal armour worn by soldiers in old times used to be very heavy.

Army/आर्मी *(noun)* - सैन्य, सेना
Indian army is very strong and brave.

Arose/एरोज - उठा
He arose late in the morning.

Around/एराउन्ड *(adv & prep)* - चारों ओर, बाहरी ओर
That old building must be somewhere around here.

Arouse/एराउज *(verb)* - जागृत करना, उत्तेजित करना
His behaviour aroused my anger.

Arraign/अरेन *(verb)* - दोष लगाना, कलंक लगाना
The police arraigned for charge of murder.

Arrange/अरेन्ज *(verb)* - स्थिर करना, क्रम मे रखना, व्यवस्थित करना
I have arranged everything in the room.

Arrangement/एरेन्जमेंट *(noun)* - प्रबन्ध, क्रम से स्थापन
The arrangement in the hotel was superb.

Arrant/एरैन्ट *(adj.)* - कुख्यात, अत्यन्त
What arrant stupidity!

Array/एरे *(noun)* - सजाना, सजना
The array of flowers was impressive.

Arrear/एरिअर *(pl. noun)* - बकाया, अवशेष
My arrears along with invest are worth Rs. 1 lakh which are payable by the government.

Arrest/अरेस्ट *(verb)* - बन्दी करना, गिरफ्तार करना
He was arrested by police and detained in the lock up.

Arrival/एराइवल *(noun)* - आगमन
The arrival of train created a commotion on the platform.

Arrive/एराइब *(verb)* - पा लेना, पहुँचना
The train has arrived.

Arrogance/एरोगैंस *(noun)* - गर्व
All kings used to have arrogance.

Arrogate/एरोगैट *(verb)* - किसी की वस्तु पर अन्याय से अधिकार प्रकट करना
He arrogated that he had promoted her brother.

Arrow/ऐरो *(noun)* - बाण, तीर
He shot the arrow and hit the bull's eyes.

Arse/आर्स *(noun)* - नितम्ब, चूतड़
I am going to hit his fat arse.

Arsenal/आर्सेनल *(noun)* - हथियार-घर
A suspicious man was arrested from near the military arsenal.

Arsenic/आर्सेनिक *(noun)* - संखिया, विष
Arsenic is a highly fatal chemical. It can kill you in second.

Arterial/आर्टेरिअल *(adj)* - धमनी-सम्बन्धी
The arterial system must be thoroughly understood and any defect should be soon done away with.

Arteriotomy/आरटेरिओटॉमी *(noun)* - धमनी को काटने की क्रिया
The surgeon conducted an arteriotomy to let out some blood.

Artery/आरटरी *(noun)* - धमनी
Blood must keep flowing through the arteries.

Artful/आर्टफुल *(adj.)* - चतुर, धूर्त
He is very arful at telling lies.

Arthritis/आरथराइटिस *(noun)* - जोड़ो की सूजन
I cannot bend my knees they are also painfully swollen.

Artichoke/आर्टिचोक *(noun)* - चुकन्दर, हाथी चक
Jerusalem Artichoke is a plant famous for its peculiar flower head.

Article/आर्टिकल *(noun)* - साहित्यिक लेख
I have finished writing article for the magazine.

Articular/आर्टिकुलर *(adj.)* - जोड़ सम्बन्धी, संधि
Relating to the joints of body.

Articulate/आर्टिकुलेट *(adj.)* - स्पष्ट, जुड़ा हुआ, अपने विचारों को स्पष्ट रूप से व्यक्त करने में कुशल
He is very articulate in his speech.

Articulation/आर्टिकुलेशन *(noun)* - अभिव्यतीकरण
In this music show articulation is superb.

Artificial/आर्टिफिसियल *(adj.)* - कृत्रिम, बनावटी
She is wearing artificial jewellery.

A

Artillery/आर्टिलरी *(noun)* - तोप इत्यादि चलाने वाले सैनिक

The artillery moved slowly with large calibre guns.

Artisan/आर्टिजन *(noun)* - शिल्पकार, कारीगर

A potter is an artisan.

Artist/आर्टिस्ट *(noun)* - ललित-कला मे निपुण, कलाकार

There are many fine artists in our country who either draw or paint.

Artistic/आर्टिस्टक *(adj.)* - निपुणता का, कलात्मक

This artistic background helped him to gain admission in the music academy.

Artless/आर्टलेस *(adj.)* - निष्कपट, सच्चा

He is a artless rather clumsy guy don't you suspect him on any account.

Arts/आर्ट्स *(noun)* - कला, शिल्प

Arts provide us with general knowledge and intellectual skills.

As/एज *(conj.)* - समान, जब

He is as tall as his brother.

Asafoetida/एसाफोइटिडा *(noun)* - हींग

Put a little asafoetida in dal it will make it tasty.

Asbestos/ऐस्बेसटस *(noun)* - अदह

I am wearing asbestos woven fabric it'll save me from fire.

Ascend/असेन्ड *(verb)* - सवार होना, चढ़ना, उन्नति करना

He has ascended to the post of Principal.

Ascension/असेन्शन *(noun)* - उद्‌गम, अधिरोहण, चढ़ाव

His ascension to the post of PM filled him with glory.

Ascent/असेन्ट *(noun)* - चढ़ाव या अवरोहण

The ascent to this mountain is very difficult.

Ascertain/एसर्टेन *(verb)* - निश्चय करना

I want to ascertain if I have succeeded or not.

Ascetic/एसेटिक *(noun)* - संन्यासी, तपस्वी

Saints are ascetic persons.

Ascribe/एस्क्राइव *(verb)* - आरोपण करना

He ascribed his success to his friend.

Aseptic/एसेप्टिक *(adj.)* - जो सड़ने योग्य न हो

Aseptic surgical methods are employed during operations.

Ash/ऐश *(noun)* - राख

Mountain ash is very beautiful and wonderful tress.

Ashamed/अशेम्ड *(adj.)* - संकुचित, लज्जित

I felt ashamed at having been so rude to her.

Ashen/एशेन *(adj.)* - धूसर, पीला

His face grew ashen as he looked at something in the dark.

Ashore/एशोर *(adj.)* - किनारे पर, तीर पर

I reached ashore after a long voyage.

Ashy/एशाइ *(adj.)* - धूसर

This piece of cloth looks ashy.

Asiatic/एशियाटिक *(adj.)* - एशिया-सम्बन्धी

Features of Asiatic people are different from those of Europeans.

Aside/एसाइड *(noun)* - एक ओर, दूर

He sang aside the great pop singer.

Asinine/एसिनाइन *(adj.)* - मूर्ख

He is an asinine person.

Ask/आस्क *(verb)* - पूछना, प्रार्थना करना

I asked him about his father's health.

Askew/आस्क्यू *(adj.&adv.)* - तिरछी दृष्टि से (कटाक्ष)

He looked at me askew.

Aslant/एस्लैंट *(adv.)* - तिरछी दृष्टि से

The child slipped and went aslant on the slope.

Asleep/एस्लिप *(adj.&adv.)* - निद्रा मे, सोते हुए

My father was fast asleep when I reached home.

Aslope/अस्लोप *(adj.&adv.)* - ढलान की भाँति, ढालू दशा में

The ship went aslope and then sank down.

Aspect/आस्पेक्ट *(noun)* - छवि, भाव, आकृति

I didn't pay attention to this aspect of situation.

Asperate/एस्परेट *(verb)* - रूखा करने या होने की क्रिया

I asperated the smooth surface of the stone slab.

Asperity/अस्पेरिटी *(noun)* - रूक्षता, तीव्रता, कठिनाई, कायरता

This asperity hurt me.

Asperse/एस्पर्स *(verb)* - निन्दा करना, कलंक लगाना

People aspersed her but she remained undaunted.

Aspersion/एस्पर्सन *(noun)* – निन्दा, कलंक
They cast aspersions on him but he answered all their questions fearlessly.

Asphodel/एस्फोडेल *(noun)* – एक प्रकार की कुमुदिनी
Thank you for this rare plant of asphodel.

Asphyxia/एस्फाइक्सिया *(noun)* – किसी की साँस रोक देना या दम घुटना
This man's death has been due to asphyxia.

Aspirant/ऐस्परन्ट *(adj.)* – आकांक्षी, प्रार्थी अभ्यर्थी
He is an aspirant for the job of director.

Aspirate/एस्परेट *(verb)* – एक श्वास से उच्चारण करना
Please aspirate the sound h in this word as in horse!

Aspiration/एस्परेशन *(noun)* – लालसा
My aspiration is to become an army officer.

Aspirator/एस्पीरेटर *(noun)* – वात शोषक यंत्र
Bring an aspirator to draw out the air from lungs.

Aspire/एस्पायर *(verb)* – उत्कट इच्छा करना
I aspire to be a business tycoon.

Aspirin/एस्पिरिन *(noun)* – पीड़ा-नाशक एक औषधि
Take an aspirin and your fever will come down.

Ass/ऐस *(noun)* – गर्दभ, गदहा
He is an ass by means.

Assail/एसेल *(verb)* – आक्रमण करना, चढ़ाई करना, चोट करना
A bad feeling assailed me in the morning.

Assassin/एसैसिन *(noun)* – घातक, हत्यारा
This is the assassin who shot the president.

Assault/एसॉल्ट *(noun)* – चढ़ाई, धावा, अचानक हमला
He assaulted me at a public place.

Assemble/एसेम्बल *(verb)* – एकत्रित करना
I assembled the different parts of the machinery together.

Assembly/एसेम्बली *(noun)* – मण्डली, सभा, विधानसभा
All the MLA's were asked to assemble at the assembly at 10 a.m. Sharp for voting.

Assent/असेन्ट *(noun)* – स्वीकृति देना, सहमत होना
I expressed my assent to the proposal.

Asseentient/एसेन्सियन्ट *(noun)* – स्वीकृति देने वाला
He was in an assentient mood.

Assert/एसर्ट *(verb)* – दृढ़तापूर्वक स्वीकार करना
I asserted my belief in God.

Assertive/एसरटिव *(adj.)* – निश्चित बात करने वाला
This statement was so assertive that none could doubt it.

Assess/एसेस *(verb)*– मूल्य निर्धारित करना, राय बनाना
The bank will assess the value of your property before giving you loan.

Assiduity/एसिड्यूटी *(noun)* – उद्योग, तत्परता
This assiduity for work is well known.

Assiduous/एसिडुअस *(adj.)* – परिश्रमी
His assiduous care soon cured him.

Assign/एसाइन *(verb)* – निरूपण करना, स्थिर करना
I assigned him the task of bringing money from the bank.

Asunder/एसन्डर *(adj.)* – पृथक्, भिन्न
I tore the file asunder.

Asylum/असाइलम *(noun)* – आश्रय, राजनीतिक शरण
The diplomat was granted asylum by the state.

At/एट *(prep.)* – पास, ओर में, से
I'll meet you at the railway station.

Atelier/एटेलिअर *(noun)* – चित्रालय, शिल्पशाला
Students are learning art in the atelier.

Atheism/एथेइज्म *(noun)* – ईश्वर-निन्दा, नास्तिकवाद
He believes in atheism for him there is no God.

Athirst/एथर्स्ट *(adj.)* – प्यासा, उत्सुक
He is athirst for money.

Athlete/एथलीट *(noun)* – खेलकूद प्रतियोगिताओं में भाग लने वाला
There is no dearth of good atheletes in our country.

Athwart/एथ्वार्ट *(noun)* – पार, आर-पार
The swan flew athwart the river.

Atlantic/अटलैंटिक *(noun)* – अन्ध महासागर-सम्बन्धी
Cold wind blew over the Atlantic.

Atlas/ऐटलस *(noun)* – मानचित्र की पुस्तक
Hear open this atlas and you will find all the countries and cities in it.

Atom/एटम *(noun)* – अणु, परमाणु
The present moment is so fleeting and atomic.

Atomizer/एटमाइजर *(verb)* - हाथ की पिचकारी

We use atomizer to convert any substance into fragments.

Atomy/एटमी *(noun)* - परमाणु, ठठरी

I took pity at his atomy like body.

Atone/अटोन *(verb)* - प्रायश्चित करना

I went to church to atone for my sins.

Atop/एटॉप *(prep. & adv.)* - शिखर पर, उँचाई पर

The bird sat atop the tree.

Atrophy/एट्राफी *(verb)* - योग्य आहार के बिना शरीर का क्षय होना

Atrophy of muscles is very common in an old age.

Attach/एटैच *(verb)* - बाँधना, कुर्क करना

Please find attached my biodata with the application.

Attack/एटैक *(verb)* - आक्रमण करना, धावा करना

He attacked me in open daylight.

Attain/एटेन *(verb)* - प्राप्त करना, पूर्ण करना

I succeeded to attain my goal.

Attainder/एटेन्डर *(noun)* - अपराध के कारण माल का जब्त होना

He was an attainder so his property was attached and he was executed.

Attar/एटार *(noun)* - अतर, इत्र

I have used special attar see how good it smells.

Attempt/एटेम्प्ट *(verb)* - प्रयत्न करना

He attempted to climb the mountain and succeeded.

Attend/एटेन्ड *(verb)* - उपस्थित होना, भाग लेना

I'll certainly attend the class.

Attendant/एटेन्डेन्ट *(noun)* - नौकर, अनुचर

I am attendant to the secretary.

Attender/एटेन्डर *(noun)* - सेवा करने वाला परिचर

He is an attender and regularly attends the lectures.

Attention/एटेन्सन *(noun)* - ध्यान

Don't pay any attention to him he is a fool.

Attentive/एटेन्टिव *(adj.)* - सावधान

I am attentive to you.

Attest/एटेस्ट *(verb)* - शपथ देना, अनुप्रमाणित करना

I have my document attested from a gazetted officer.

Attire/एटायर *(noun)* - वेश, वस्त्र, सजाना

He appeared in the fancy show in the attire of a king.

Attitude/एटिट्यूड *(noun)* - स्थिति, रवैया

Doesn't he behave funny? He must have same attitude problem.

Attorney/एटॉनी *(noun)* - प्रतिनिधि, मुख्तार, न्यायविद

I have hired an attorney to fight my case.

Attract/अट्रैक्ट *(verb)* - आकर्षित करना, मोहना

Full moon attracts the sea water.

Attractor/एट्रैक्टर *(noun)* - आकर्षक, मोहक, लुभावना

The hero is an attractor in the film.

Attribute/एट्रिब्यूट *(noun)* - धर्म, उपाधि, गुण

I attribute my whole success to my mother.

Attrite/एट्राइट *(verb)* - रगड़ से घिसा हुआ

His body attrited due to a long disease.

Attrition/एट्रिशन *(noun)* - रगड़, घिसावट

He travelled long through' the jungle and his body was in a condition of attrition.

Auburn/ऑबर्न *(noun)* - सुनहरा भूरा रंग

I got my hair coloured auburn.

Auction/आक्शन *(noun)* - नीलाम

He was deeply in debt so his house was auctioned.

Audacious/ऑडेशस *(adj.)* - साहसी, ढीठपन

He is an audacious fellow and will never see sense.

Audible/ऑडिबल *(adj.)* - कर्णगोचर

He has an audible and clear voice.

Audibly/ऑडिब्ली *(adv.)* - स्पष्ट रुप से, सुनने में अन्य

She spoke audibly to listeners and they understood her.

Audience/ऑडियन्स *(noun)* - सुनाई, श्रोतागण

The audience was disturbed.

Audiometer/आडिओमीटर *(noun)* - श्रवण शक्ति की परीक्षा करने का यन्त्र

Here is an audiometer whereby you can measure the sensitivity of hearing.

Audiophone/अडिओफोन *(noun)* - बहरे मनुष्यों को सुनने में सहायता देने वाला यंत्र

As he is hard of hearing he uses an audiophone.

Audit/ऑडिट *(verb)* - हिसाब की जाँच करना

Audit is going on so I can't attend to you please come tomorrow.

Audition/ऑडिशन *(noun)* - परीक्षण हेतु गायन अभिनेता का लघु प्रर्दशन

Next is my turn for audition and I'm feeling a bit nervous.

Auditive/ऑडिटिव *(adj.)* - श्रवण-सम्बन्धी

This problem is auditive.

Auditor/ऑडिटर *(noun)* - लेखा-परीक्षक

He is the auditor who is going to audit the company accounts.

Auditorial/ऑडिटोरिअल *(adj.)* - हिसाब की जाँच के सम्बन्ध का

This is an auditorial mistake.

Auditorium/ऑडिटोरिअम *(noun)* - सभा-मण्डप, सिनेमा, रंगशाला आदि

The auditorium was full of people who had come to see the famous drama.

Auditory/ऑडिटोरी *(adj.)* - श्रवण या कान सम्बन्धी

This is something that relates to auditory defect.

Augean/ऑजीअन *(adj.)* - कठिन, गन्दा, मलिन

The old place smelled and was augean.

Augur/ऑगर *(noun)* - बरमा

Take this augur it is tool for boring holes.

August/अगस्ट *(noun)* - अंग्रेजी का ८वाँ माह, प्रतापी, पूजनीय, महान

August is the 8th month of the year.

Aulic/ऑलिक *(adj.)* - राजदरबार सम्बन्धी

Sometimes I would like to see an aulic festival where there will be royal person.

Aunt/ऑन्ट *(noun)* - बुआ, मौसी, चाची

One of my aunts is a director of this company.

Aural/ऑरल *(adj.)* - श्रवण सम्बन्धी

He had aural infection.

Aureola/ऑरिओला *(noun)* - दैवी मुकुट, प्रभा मण्डल

You'll find an aureole around the head of saints.

Auric/ऑरिक *(adj.)* - सोने का

The halo around the sun is auric.

Auriferous/ऑरिफरस *(adj.)* - सुवर्ण मिश्रित

These rocks are auriferous they contain gold.

Auriform/ऑरिफार्म *(adj.)* - कान की आकृति का

I saw a tree leaf which was almost auriform like an ear.

Aurilave/ऑरिलेव *(noun)* - कान खोदनी

All ear specialists have an aurilave to clean ear.

Aurora/ऑरोरा *(noun)* - तड़का, अरुणोदय

At aurora I was half awake and saw a strange dream.

Aurum/ऑरम *(noun)* - सुवर्ण, सोना

This is an aurum necklace.

Auspicate/ऑस्पिकेट *(verb)* - भविष्य बतलाना

He auspicated his trip by going to the temple.

Auspice/ऑस्पिस *(noun)* - रक्षा, शरण में

Seeing an owl is not a good auspice.

Auspicious/ऑसपिशस *(adj.)* - अच्छे, शकुन का

It is an auspicious day.

Austere/आस्टिअर *(adj.)* - कठोर, तीखा

My father is very austere. I'm afraid of even speaking to him.

Austerity/ऑस्टेरिटी *(noun)* - कठोरता, आत्मसंयम

Many saints preach austerity.

Austral/आस्ट्रल *(adj.)* - दक्षिणी, दक्षिण का

This man seems austral in appearance, must be from Australia.

Authentic/अथेन्टिक *(adj.)* - सच्चा, यथार्थ, वास्तविक

These papers are authentic. I have shown them to a lawyer.

Authenticity/अथेन्टिसिटी *(noun)*- सत्यता, प्रामाणिकता

The authenticity of this document is beyond doubt.

Author/ऑथर *(noun)* - लेखक, प्रवर्तक

He is an author of many novels.

Authorize/ऑथराइज *(verb)* - अधिकार देना, प्रमाणित करना

I authorized him to attend the meeting on my behalf.

A

Autobiography/ऑटोबायोग्राफी *(noun)* – आत्मकथा

Almost all great men write their autobiography.

Autocracy/ऑटोक्रैसी *(noun)* – निरंकुश राज्यशासन

Autocracy is not popular these days.

Autocrat/ऑटोक्रैट *(noun)* – निरंकुश शासक

Autocrats usually meet tragic ends.

Autograph/ऑटोग्राफ *(noun)* – किसी प्रसिद्ध व्यक्ति के हस्ताक्षर

I have with me autograph of Amitabh Bachchan he has wished me and signed it.

Autogyro/ऑटोगायरो *(noun)* – एक प्रकार का वायुयान जो बिना दौड़ लगाये सीधे ऊपर को उठता है

For once I would like to sit in an autogyro which is a new kind of plane.

Automatic/ऑटोमैटिक *(adj.)* – यंत्र से चलने वाला

These days automatic devices and machines are in Vogue with little human intervention.

Automobile/ऑटोमोबाइल *(noun)* – मोटरगाड़ी

I would like to sit in a racing automobile.

Autonomous/ऑटोनामस *(adj.)* – स्वराज्य के अधीन

Judiciary is an autonomous body.

Autonomy/ऑटोनॉमी *(noun)* – स्वराज्य

People enjoy autonomy in democracy.

Autumn/ऑटम *(noun)* – पतझड़

Trees shed their leaves in autumn.

Auxiliary/अक्जिलिअरी *(adj.)* – सहायक, उपकारी

The flood victims were provided auxiliary help.

Avail/एवेल *(verb)* – सहायता देना, उपकारी होना

When the opportunity comes avail yourself of it.

Avale/एवेल *(verb)* – नीचे उतरना

I avaled from the horse.

Avarice/एवाराइस *(noun)* – लोभ, धन का लालच

He suffers from avarice for wealth.

Avenge/एवेन्ज *(verb)* – बदला लेना, दण्ड देना

I avenged myself upon him as he had dishonored me.

Avenue/एवेन्यू *(noun)* – द्वार, मार्ग

We had to walk along a long avenue before reaching the house.

Average/एवरेज *(noun)* – औसत

We calculate average in arithmetic.

Avert/एवर्ट *(verb)* – हटाना, टालना

He averted his eyes from me.

Aviary/एविअरी *(noun)* – चिड़ियाखाना, पक्षीशाला

I have built an aviary for birds.

Aviation/एवियेशन *(noun)* – विमानन

He is an expert at aviation.

Avid/एविड *(adj.)* – किसी कार्य के प्रति अति उत्साह, उत्सुक

He has an avid interest in music.

Avocation/एवोकेशन *(noun)* – व्यापार, उद्यम

Besides his hardware business his avocation is breeding dogs.

Avoid/एवॉइड *(verb)* – कुछ करने से रोकना, बच जाना

I always avoid him because he is a non-stop talker.

Avulsion/एवल्शन *(noun)* – अलगाव, तोड़फोड़

The avulsion of the tissue from its wound is not a good sign.

Await/एवेट *(verb)* – प्रतीक्षा करना, आशा करना

I'll await you here.

Awake/एवेक *(verb)* – जगाना, सचेत करना

He has long been awake.

Awaken/एवेकेन *(verb)* – जगाना

I awakened him from sleep.

Award/एवार्ड *(verb)* – अर्पण करना, देना

He was given an award for his performance in athletic events.

Aware/अवेयर *(adj.)* – सचेत, सावधान

I am aware that he is a good hero.

Away/अवे *(adj. & adv.)* – दूर, हटजा

He left his home and went far away.

Awe/ऑ *(noun)* – भय, श्रद्धायुक्त भय

I looked at the big man with awe.

Awful/ऑफुल *(adj.)* – भयंकर, डरावना

It was awful to be in such a dirty place.

Awhile/एह्वाइल *(adj.)* – क्षण भर के लिये

For awhile she was with her mother but soon she came back.

Awkward/ऑकवार्ड *(adj.)* - भद्‌दा, कुरूप, अनाड़ी

He is such an awkward fellow he never fits in any place.

Awl/ऑल *(noun)* - मोची का टेकुआ

A shoe maker sews shoes with an awl.

Awoke/अवोक - जगा

I awoke late yesterday.

Axe/एक्स *(noun)* - कुल्हाड़ी, कुठार, सूआ

Woodcutter cut wood with an axe.

Axial/एक्सिअल *(adj.)* - केन्द्र, धुरी का अक्षीय

The earth moves round the imaginary line namely axial. Which is around the axis.

Axilla/एक्सिला *(noun)* - काँख, बगल

Axilla itching is very common during summer.

Axillary/एक्जिलरी *(adj)* - काँख-सम्बन्धी

If there is an axillary growth a doctor should be consulted at once.

Axiom/ऐक्सिअम *(noun)* - सिद्धान्त, स्वयं सिद्ध

In mathematics we can't do without axioms.

Axis/एक्सिस *(noun)* - अक्ष रेखा

Our earth rotates round an imaginary line called axis

Axle/एक्सल *(noun)* - धुरा जिस पर कोई पहिया घूमता है।

Both the cart wheels are rotating on spindle like axle.

Aye/ऍ *(adv.)* - सर्वदा

Aye! We are moving ahead increase speed of your boat.

Ayes/आइज *(noun)* - किसी प्रस्ताव का समर्थन करने वाले

The passing boat asked some question I said 'Aye' i.e. answered in affirmative and rowed on.

Azure/एज्योर *(adj.)* - आकाश के समान नीला, आसमानी

She wore an azure coloured suit which looked smashing.

B

Bb

B/बी - अंग्रेजी वर्णमाला का दूसरा अक्षर the second letter of the English alphabet

(1) The seventh note in music.

(2) The second known quantity in Algebra.

Baa/बा *(verb)* - मिमियाने का शब्द

The lamb cried baa and the shepherd became alert.

Babble/बैब्ल *(verb)* - बड़बड़ाना, रहस्य या भेद खोलना

She babbled away the secret.

Babe/बेब् *(noun)* - शिशु, बच्चा

Hey babe you look special today.

Babel/बेबेल *(noun)* - कोलाहल, खलबली

I couldn't hear him clearly in that babel.

Baboon/बैबून *(noun)* - एक प्रकार का बड़ा बंदर, लंगूर

In Africa I saw herds of baboons dwelling on ground.

Baby/बेबी *(noun)* - बालक, बच्चा

Although adult he behaves like a baby.

Baccate/बैकेट *(adj.)* - जामुन या बेर की आकृति का

This seems to be the baccate that bears berries.

Bacchanal/बकैनल *(noun)* - शराबी, मधुप्रिय

Today's rave parties remind us of bacchanal parties given in honour of Bacchus the god of wine in old times.

Bachelor/बैचलर *(noun)* - अविवाहित पुरुष

People cast strange glances at bachelors.

Bacilliform/बैसिलीफॉर्म *(adj.)* - बेलन सरीखे सूक्ष्म जीवों के आकार का

These Bacilliformed objects are germs of disease.

Backbite/बैकबाइट *(verb)*- चुगली खाना

He backites in my absence.

Backbone/बैकबोन *(noun)* - रीढ़ की हड्डी, प्रधान आश्रय

I have pain in my backbone.

Background/बैकग्राउण्ड *(noun)* - चित्र में पीछे का दृश्य, पृष्ठभूमि

I have made enquiries about his background.

Backhand/बैक्हैंड *(noun)* - टेनिस में उल्टे हाथ का प्रहार, हथेली को अन्दर की तरफ रखकर किया प्रहार

Boris Becker was famous for his back hand shots.

Backing/बैकिंग *(noun)* - सहारा, सहायता, समर्थन

You have my backing go on and fight.

Backside/बैक्साइड *(noun)* - किसी पदार्थ का पिछला भाग

I am not fond of seeing the backsides of people.

Backslide/बैकस्लाइड *(verb)* - पीछे हट जाना, पतित होना, डिगना

After remaining away a long time from alcohol he backslided and took to drinking again.

Backward/बैकवर्ड *(adj.)* - पिछड़ा हुआ, पीछे

As he advanced the other man began to inch backward.

Backwards/बैकवार्ड्स *(adj.)* - पीछे की ओर

I moved backwards as the animal came forward.

Bacon/बेक्न *(noun)* - खाने योग्य सुअर का मांस

He is fond of eating bacon meat from the side or back of the pig such meat is very nourishing he says.

Bacteria/बैक्टिअरिया *(noun plural)* - वायु, जल इत्यादि के सूक्ष्म जीवाणु

Bacteria are everywhere good bacteria bad bacteria.

Bad/बैड् *(adj.)* - बुरा, दुष्ट, खराब

This is in bad condition.

Badge/बैज *(noun)* - चिह्न, लक्षण

All scouts wear a badge.

Badger/बैजर *(noun)* - बिज्जू

Beware of this animal it is badger and belongs to weasel family. Its size frightened me.

Badly/बैड्लि *(adv.)* - बुरे प्रकार से

He was badly beaten.

Baffle/बैफ्ल *(verb)* – चकरा देना, उलझन में डाल देना

I baffled the already loud sound by turning the knob.

Baft/बैफ्ट *(noun)* – मोटा सस्ता सूती कपड़ा

I have bought a piece of bafta cloth although coarse it is durable.

Bag/बैग *(noun)* – कागज या कपड़े से बनी थैली

Let us put all these things into one bag.

Bagasse/बैगेश *(noun)* – चीनी बनाने मे गन्ने की सीठी

I wonder in what way they use bagasse may be manure but it seems useless.

Baggage/बैगेज *(noun)* – यात्री की सामग्री

All my personal belongings are in this baggage.

Bagman/बैगमैन *(noun)* – व्यवसायी यात्री

He is a very successful bagman.

Bagpipe/बैगपाइप *(noun)* – मसक बाजा

He is expert at playing bagpipe.

Bail/बेल *(noun)* – जामिन, प्रतिभूति

The judge granted him bail against the security of 50,000 rupees.

Bailee/बेली *(noun)* – धरोहर जिसके पास कोई ध रोहर रखी गयी हो

I have arranged rupees 20,000 for his bail.

Bailiff/बैलिफ *(noun)* – सहकारी अमीन

Yesterday a bailiff came to my friend's house to arrest him.

Bait/बेट *(noun)* – चारा देकर ललचाना

Fisherman use a bait to catch fish.

Baize/बैज *(noun)* – मोटा ऊनी वस्त्र

Cover the billiard and card tables with baize so they do not get damp or dirty.

Bake/बैक् *(verb)* – पकाना, कड़ा करना

Biscuits are baked in the oven.

Balance-wheel/बैलन्स-ह्वील *(noun)* – घड़ी को स्थायी गति से चलाने वाला पहिया

Things are weighed in a balance.

Balancing/बैलन्सिंग *(noun)*– समतोलन, सन्तुलन

Circus people do hair raising balancing acts.

Balcony/बैल्कनि *(noun)* – छज्जा

I usually stand in my balcony and look at the sea.

Bald/बाल्ड *(adj.)* – गंजा, सिर पर बाल के बिना

He is a bald man having no hair on his head.

Balderdash/बॉल्डर्डेस *(noun)* – खुराफात, बकवास, निरर्थक बातचीत, खुराफात, बकवास

All his talk and writings are balderdash.

Baldric/बालड्रिक *(noun)* – तलवार लटकाने की पेटी

In old times soldiers wore their swords on a baldric.

Bale/बेल *(noun)* – गट्ठर

Bales of cotton paper and they were being downloaded from the truck.

Baleen/बेलीन *(noun)* – ह्वेल मछली की हड्डी

This large bone must be baleen.

Bale fire/बेल-फायर *(noun)* – चिता, होली

A strange soul of bale fire spread in some cities of a country.

Balk/बाल्क/बाक *(verb & noun)* – बाधा, रुकावट, खींचना, निराश करना

As we travelled we saw a big baulk lying in our way.

Ballad/बैलड *(noun)* – विरहा, आल्हा

The old blind man was singing a ballad.

Ballet/बैलेट *(noun)* – रंगमंच पर नाच गाना, नृत्य नाटक

In India we rarely get an opportunity to see live ballet in London and Paris you can see a lot.

Balista/बैलिस्टा *(noun)* – बड़े-बड़े पत्थर फेंकने का यन्त्र

In old time the soldiers used balista to throw big stones.

Balloon/बैलून *(noun)* – गुब्बारा

Children like balloons very much.

Ballot/बैलट *(noun)* – चुनाव के लिये प्रयुक्त टिकट

These days people cast their vote by ballot.

Balm/बाम् *(noun)* – मलहम, सुगन्धित औषधि

If you have headache you can use this balm it will be very helpful.

Balmoral/बैल्मारल *(noun)*– एक प्रकार की छोटी कुर्ती, जूते

Why not wear balmoral? It is strong walking boot.

Balsam/बाल्सम *(noun)* – गुलमेंहदी, पीड़ा हरने वाली औषधि

Balsam extracted from trees or shrubs is also of medicinal use.

Bamboo/बैम्बू *(noun)*– वंश लोचन

Bamboo is largely used in furniture.

B

Bamboozle/बैम्बूजल *(verb)* – छल करना, धोखा देना
I have been bamboozled by a fellow and thus lost a heavy amount of money.

Ban/बैन *(verb)* – प्रतिरोध करना, शाप देना
It is banned for heavy vehicles to enter this street by order magistrate.

Banana/बनाना *(noun)* – एक प्रकार का प्रसिद्ध पेड़
I daily eat two bananas in my breakfast.

Band/बैण्ड *(noun)* – चारों का समूह, बन्धन, तस्मा
I came across a band of robbers and they robbed me.

Bandog/बैन्डॉग *(noun)* – सिक्कड़ में बँधा हुआ शिकारी कुत्ता
Don't go near house. There is bandog it is very ferocious.

Bang/बैंग *(noun)* – बंदूक के धमाके जैसी आवाज करने वाली
There was a loud bang and the gun went off.

Bangle/बैंगल *(noun)* – कड़ा, चूड़ी, पहुँची
It is customary for Indian women to wear glass bangles.

Banyan/Banian/बैन्यन *(noun)* – बरगद का पेड़, बनियान
A banyan tree is very huge.

Banish/बैनिश *(verb)* – हटा देना, देश निकालना, निर्वासित करना
He was banished from his country and asked to leave it forever as an official punishment.

Banjo/बैंजो *(noun)* – बेला की तरह का एक बाजा
He plays banjo beautifully.

Banker/बैंकर *(noun)* – बैंक का स्वामी, मैनेजर
My uncle is a banker he owns a chain of banks besides being the manager of one.

Banking/बैंकिंग *(noun)* – बैंककर्मी
Some private banks offer excellent banking.

Bankrupt/बैंकरप्ट *(adj.)* – दिवालिया
My uncle was unable to pay his debts so he was declared bankrupt.

Banner/बैनर *(noun)* – दो डंडों पर लगा कपड़े का टुकड़ा जिस पर कुछ लिखा हो
The procession went on. A lot of them bearing placards and banners.

Banquet/बैंक्विट *(noun)* – विशिष्ट उत्सव
I went to the banquet hall in a marriage and ate my fill.

Bantam/बैन्टम *(noun)* – नाटा पुरुष, एक प्रकार का चूजा
My brother rears bantams.

Banter/बैन्टर *(noun)* – उपहास करना
Although I bantered my friend a lot he didn't mind it and rather bantered me in return.

Bar/बार *(noun)* – डण्डा छड़
Let us put a heavy bar across the door so that it can not open easily.

Barb/बार्ब *(noun)* – तीर के पीछे मुड़ी नोंक
Barbed wire was placed all around the school.

Barbarian/बार्बेरियन *(noun)* – असभ्य
In ancient times many kings used to be barbarian, uncultured and brutish often they gave horrible punishment to law breakers.

Barbaric/बार्बेरिक *(adj.)* – असभ्य, रूखा
People helplessly looked at the barbaric punishment given to a thief.

Barber/बार्बर *(noun)* – नाई, हजाम
I am going to the barber for a haircut.

Barbican/बार्बिकन *(noun)* – किले की रक्षा का बाहरी घेरा
In old times castles used to have barbican for defense.

Bard/बार्ड *(noun)* – भाट, कवि
Shakespeare was a bard who recited epics and wrote plays.

Bare/बेअर *(adj.)* – नंगा करना, प्रकट करना
He plays appeared bare bodied no clothes.

Bargain/बारगेन *(noun)* – सस्ता सौदा, तौलमोल
I struck a bargain with the trader and bought the blankets at almost + the price.

Barge/बार्ज *(noun)* – भारी बोझ ले जाने की बड़ी नाव
The barges ply in rivers or canals and carry loads.

Barium/बेरियम *(noun)* – एक श्वेत धातु
For a medical test I had to drink barium before X-ray.

Barker/बारकर *(noun)* – छाल उतारने वाला
He is a barker attracting the attention of passers-by for the show.

Barm/बार्म *(noun)* – शराब का फेन, खमीरा
Barm (yeast) is good for health.

Barman/बारमैन *(noun)* – वारमैन या साकी
The Barman served me the drink I ordered.

Barn/बार्न *(noun)* – खलिहान
The cattle live in barn. It is used for storage also.

B

Barometer/बैरोमीटर *(noun)* – वायु-भार मापक यन्त्र

I have a barometer at my house it is fun it gives me information about atmospheric pressure weather altitude etc.

Baronet/बैरोनेट *(noun)* – छोटा नवाब

A baronet is the lowest in British title order.

Baroque/बरॉक *(adj.)* – टेढ़ी-मेढ़ी

Baroque style in 17th – 18th century was highly ornate and extravagant.

Barouche/बारूच *(noun)* – भवन निर्माण करना, 17वीं-18वीं शताब्दी के दौरान यूरोप में प्रचलित अति अलंकृत शैली सम्बन्धित एक प्रकार की चौपहिया गाड़ी

Barouche was a popular mode of transport in old times.

Barrack/बैरक *(noun)* – सिपाहियों के रहने का स्थान

There are some military barracks where jawans live.

Barracoon/बाराकून *(noun)* – बन्दियों के रखने का बाड़ा

In old time black slaves used to be confined in barracoons.

Barrage/बैरॉज(ग) *(noun & verb)* – बाँध, किसी स्थान पर लगातार गोलियों की वर्षा

The media barraged him with questions.

Barrel/बैरल *(noun)* – पीपा

The captain of the ship ordered various barrels of rum and beer.

Barren/बैरन *(adj.)* – बाँझ, शून्य

The desert is a barren place.

Barricade/बैरीकेड *(noun)* – आड़, रोक

The town people raised a barricade to obstruct the advance of enemy forces.

Barrier/बैरियर *(noun)* – आड़, घेरा, सीमा

She was from Russia. The language barrier prevented me from talking to her.

Barring/बारिंग *(prep.)* – अतिरिक्त, को दौड़कर

Barring a few distant all relatives were invited to the birthday party.

Barter/बाटर *(verb)* – अदल-बदल का व्यापार

In ancient times when there was no currency people bartered one thing for another.

Barton/बार्टन *(noun)* – रियासत, इलाका

We have all ready lost three Pups in Borton and we do not want to lose any more.

Basalt/बैसाल्ट *(noun)* – एक प्रकार की भूरी चट्टान

Basalt is a volcanic rock.

Base/बेस *(noun)* – पेंदी, तल

The base of this statue is made of teak wood polished black.

Bash/बैश *(verb)* – कसकर घूँसा मारना

He bashed me on the head.

Bashful/बैशफुल *(adj.)* – विनीत, भीरू

He is rather bashful and can be easily embarrassed.

Basial/बेसियल *(noun)* – चुम्बन सम्बन्धी

Basial is used in cookery.

Basil/बेसिल *(noun)* – तुलसी

Basil is a very useful plant.

Basin/बेसिन *(noun)* – नदी का संग्रहण क्षेत्र

You can was your hands in the wash-basin.

Basis/बेसिस *(noun)* – मूल आधार, विचार धारा विश्वास का आधार

All our activities have some fundamental basis. This particular idea has very strong basis.

Bask/बास्क *(verb)* – किसी स्थान पर बैठकर या लेटकर गरमाहट का आनंद लेना

She was basking in the sun.

Basket/बास्किट *(noun)* – टोकरी, डलिया

Please take this basket and bring vegetables from the market.

Bass/बेस *(noun)* – गायन में सबसे नीचा सुर

As the singing went as in the church I could hear the bass in music.

Bassinet/बैशिनेट *(noun)* – बच्चों का पालना

The child was lying is a bassinet.

Bastard/बास्टार्ड *(noun)* – अविवाहित माता-पिता की संतान, नाजायज

Don't ever trust him he is a bastard.

Bastion/बैस्टियन *(noun)* – दुर्ग की रक्षा करने के लिए बना उमड़ा भाग

Heavy firing was coming from bastion.

Bat/बैट *(noun)* – चमगादड़ पक्षी, बल्ला

Thousands of bats were hanging upside down in the dark cave.

Batch/बैच *(noun)* – समुदाय, थोक, दल, टुकड़ी समूह

A batch of one thousand shirts was made ready overnight.

Bath/बाथ *(noun)* – स्नान

Pour 40 baths of water into the tank.

Batiste/बटिस्ट *(noun)* – महीन कपड़ा

I would like to have a shirt made of batiste.

B

Batman/बैटमैन *(noun)* – अधिकारी का नौकर
In British armed force an officer used to have an attendant called batman.

Baton/बेटन *(noun)* – डण्डा, इस डण्डे से मारना, छड़ी रिले दौड़ की छड़ी
The conductor moved his baton to direct the music.

Batsman/बैट्समैन *(noun)* – बल्लेबाज
Virat Kohli is a fine batsman.

Batten/बैटन *(noun & verb)* – तख्ता
He is battening upon the expense of his uncle.

Battery/बैटरी *(noun)* – तोपखाना, मारपीट, संग्रह
Charge your cell phone the battery must be running low.

Battle/बैटल *(noun)* – युद्ध, संग्राम, लड़ाई
A fierce battle between the two countries went on for a long time.

Battle-plane/बैटलप्लेन *(noun)* – युद्ध करने का बड़ा वायुयान
India bought many battleplane.

Bauble/बॉबल *(noun)* – अल्प मूल्य का आभूषण, क्रिसमस वृक्ष पर लटकाने का सजावटी गंदनुमा वस्तु
A few baubles hung on the Christmas tree looked beautiful.

Bawd/बॉड *(noun)* – कुटनी, वेश्या, स्त्रियों को बहकाकर कुकर्म करने वाली स्त्री
Arrest her! She is the bawd.

Bawdy/बॉडि *(adj.)* – अश्लील, फुहड़
He is fond of cracking bawdy jokes.

Bawl/बॉल *(verb & noun)* – चिल्लाकर बोलना, चिल्लाना, चीखना
I heard a Bawl and became nervous.

Bawn/बॉन *(noun)* – पशुशाला, बाड़ा
I have a bawn near my house where a lot of sheep graze.

Bay/बे *(noun)*– एक प्रकार का वृक्ष, खाड़ी
When I was in Calcutta I went to see bay of Bengal.

Bayonet/बेअनट *(noun)* – किरच, संगीन
The soldier stabbed the enemy with the bayonet.

Bay-window/बे-विन्डो *(noun)* – जालीदार उमड़ी हुई, खिड़की
Look out of the bay window and you'll see a man.

Be/बी *(verb)* – होना
'Be' is a symbol representing the chemical element beryllium.

Beach/बीच *(noun)* – समुद्र-तट
In Goa there are many beautiful beaches where people bathe in the sea.

Beacon/बीकॅन *(noun)* – प्रकाश-स्तम्भ, आकाशदीप
The ship saw the beacon interpreted the signal and turned left.

Beadle/बीड्ल *(noun)* – गिरजे का पदाधिकारी
He is a beadle, talk to him respectfully.

Beady/बीडी *(adj.)* – दानेदार
Look at this animal how beady and sharp are its eyes.

Beak/बीक *(noun)* – चोंच
The beak of an eagle is very different from that of a crow.

Beaker/बीकर *(noun)* – काँच का चोंचदार पात्र
We use beaker in chemistry labs.

Beam/बीम *(noun)* – धरन
You see that long square beam it is supporting the roof.

Bean/बीन *(noun)* – सेम, बोड़ा
I like beans a lot they are so tasty to eat.

Beanfeast/बीनफिस्ट *(noun)* – भृत्यों को दिया हुआ भोज
Come let us go to the beanfeast there will be a lot to eat.

Bear/बिअर *(verb)* – सहन करना
He bears himself in a dignified way.

Bear/बिअर *(noun)* – ले जाना, भालू का बच्चा
Bear is a dangerous animal.

Bearable/बिअरेबल *(adj)* – सहने योग्य, सहन करने योग्य
It is not bearable.

Beard/बिअर्ड *(noun)* – दाढ़ी
I am thinking of keeping a French cut beard this time.

Bearish/बेअरिश *(adj.)* – रीछ के समान, फूहड़
He is a bearish man tall and fat.

Bearskin/बिअरस्किन *(noun)* – भालू का चमड़ा
Cap of bearskin with black fur is worn by people in extreme cold.

Beast/बीस्ट *(noun)* – पशु, चौपाया
Lion is a big and dangerous beast.

Beat/बीट *(verb)* – पीटकर हिलाना, पीटना
The teacher beat the student as he had not done his homework.

Beatify/बिटीफाई *(verb)* - प्रसन्न करना
The church has beatified the dead man. He is in a state of bliss.

Beating/बिटिंग *(noun)* - मारपीट का दण्ड
I cannot tolerate such beating

Beatitude/बिअिट्यूड *(noun)* - मोक्ष, परम गति
He was in a state of supreme beatitude.

Belle/बेल *(noun)* - छैला, बाँका, रंगीली, सुन्दरी
That belle is my fiancée.

Beau-ideal/बो-आयडियल *(noun)* - अपूर्व सुन्दरता
Gandhi ji was a beau-ideal.

Beautiful/ब्यूटीफुल *(adj.)* - सुन्दर, आकर्षक
My girl friend is very beautiful.

Beautifully/बियूटीफली *(adv)* - सुन्दर, मनोहर, सुन्दर ढंग से
She worked beautifully.

Beaver/बिवर *(noun)* - ऊदबिलाव
The beaver has gnawed tho' the tree to make it fall.

Becalm/बीकाम *(verb)* - शान्त करना
The ship was becalmed because of lack of wind.

Became/बीकेम - हुआ
The sea became calm after sometime.

Because/बिकॉज *(conj.)* - क्योंकि, इस कारण से
You can't take the exam because you haven't come in time.

Beck/बेक *(noun)* - पहाड़ी नाला या नदी, छोटी नाली
Beck lowed through the forest.

Becoming/बिकमिंग *(adj.)* - उचित, अनुरूप
This shirt is becoming on you.

Bed/बेड *(noun)* - पलंग, शय्या
It is time for sleep. I am going to bed.

Bedaub/बेडॉब *(verb)* - रंग लगाना, रंग पोतना
The doctor bedaubed the wound with a disinfectant.

Bedazzle/बिडैजल *(verb)* - चमक से चौंधियाना
The actress bedazzled the audience with her great beauty.

Bedchamber/बेडचैम्बर *(noun)* - शयन-गृह
This way leads to the bedchamber.

Bedding/बेडिंग *(noun)* - शयन सामग्री
The bedding must be washed today.

Bed-fellow/बेड-फेलो *(noun)* - भार्या
He is my bedfellow.

Bedstead/बेडस्टीड *(noun)* - चारपाई, खटिया
Mattresses are good but I don't like the bedstead. Have it changed.

Bed-time/बेडटाइम *(noun)*- निद्रा का समय
It is bed-time now all must go to sleep.

Bee/बी *(noun)* - मधुमक्खी, भ्रमर
Honeybees are dangerous insects should you try to get their honey they will attack you.

Beech/बीच *(noun)* - एक प्रकार का जंगली विशाल वृक्ष
Mussourie forests are full of beech trees.

Beef/बीफ *(noun)* - गोमाँस
Hindus do not eat beef.

Beefy/बीफी *(adj.)* - माँसयुक्त, ठोस मांसल
He is a beefy fellow with all muscles and power.

Beehive/बीहाइव *(noun)* - मधुमक्खी का कृत्रिम घर
Bees are kept in a dome or box called beehive.

Been/बिन - हो आना, रहना होना
He has been watching TV for two hours news.

Beestings/बीस्टिंग *(plural noun)*- माँ का पहला दूध
Would you like to taste Beestings.

Beet/बीट *(noun)* - चुकन्दर
Eating beet root is good for health.

Beeves/बीव्स - गाय, बैल आदि पशु
A lot of Europeans eat beeves.

Befall/बिफाल *(verb)* - आ पड़ना, बीतना
A great misfortune befell him.

Before/बिफोर *(prep., conj. & adv.)* - आगे, पहले
Our ancestors were there before us.

Befoul/बिफॉल *(verb)* - गन्दा करना, बदनाम करना
He has befouled the whole atmosphere by his abusive language.

Befriend/बिफ्रेंड *(verb)* - मित्र बन जाना
Although you have talked ill of me I'll still befriend you.

Began/बिगेन - आरम्भ किया
He began to earn from the age of eight.

Beget/बिगेट *(verb)* - उपजाना, जन्म देना
She Beget me a son.

Begging/बेगिंग *(noun)* - याचना, प्रार्थना
Begging is something in human.

Beginner/बिगिनर *(noun)* - आरम्भ करने वाला
He is a beginner in cricket.

Begone/बिगॉन *exclamatory* - दूर हट! अलग रह! archaic go away at once! *No more talking begone!*

Begot/बिगॉट - पैदा किया
I begot a son from her.

B

Behalf/बिहाफ *(noun)* - किसी के लिए, किसी की ओर से
I am here on behalf of the director.

Behave/बिहेव *(verb)* - आचरण करना, व्यवहार करना
Will you behave yourself?

Behead/बिहेड *(verb)* - सिरकाट देना
In old times execution was often done by beheading.

Behest/बिहेस्ट *(noun)* - आज्ञा, आदेश
The troops advanced on behest of their commander.

Behold/बिहोल्ड *(verb)* - देखना
Behold! Here is my son.

Beholden/बिहोल्डन *(adj.)* - अनुगृहीत, कृतज्ञ
I am beholden to you for this favour.

Behoof/बिहूफ *(noun)* - लाभ, सुविधा, उपकार
He purchased this for his own behoof.

Behove/बिहोव *(verb)* - योग्य, उचित होना, उपयुक्त होना
It would behove you to be respectful to your elders.

Being/बिइंग *(noun)* - अस्तितव, प्रकृति, वह जिसका अस्तित्व हो, जन्तु
It is my being here that matters most.

Belated/बिलेटिड *(adj.)* - बहुत देर में आने वाला, विलंबित
I have received your belated birthday greetings.

Belay/बिले *(verb)* - लपेटकर बाँधना
Rock climbers use belay for secure footing.

Belch/बेल्च *(verb)* - ओकाना, डकारना
He belched noisily and everyone looked at him.

Beleguer/बिलिगर *(verb)* - घेर लेना
The army beleguered the town.

Belfry/बेलफ्राइ *(noun)* - घण्टाघर
Huge bells are hung in towers in belfry.

Believable/बिलिवेब्ल *(adj.)* - विश्वास के योग्य, विश्वसनीय
I find your statement believable.

Belittle/बिलिटल *(verb)* - छोटा करना, न्यून करना, महत्त्व घटाना
I belittled his importance by ignoring him.

Belladonna/बेलाडोना *(noun)* - धतूरा, अंगूरशेफ्य, कंटालिका
Belladonna is a famous homeopathy drug.

Belle/बेल *(noun)* - सुन्दरी, रूपवती स्त्री
That belle is my fiancée.

Bellicose/बेलीकोस *(adj.)* - लड़ाका, लड़ने को तत्पर
He is a very bellicose person ever ready to fight.

Belligerent/बेलिजरेंट *(adj.)* - शत्रुतापूर्ण, आक्रामक
This one is belligerent country it sure will pick up a fight with some other country.

Bell-metal/बेलमेटल *(noun)*- मिश्र धातु जिनके मेल से घण्टे बनते है
Bells are made of two metals copper and tin.

Bellow/बेलो *(verb)* - डकारना, गरजना
He bellowed in anger.

Bellows/बेलोज *(noun & plural noun)* - भाथी, धौंकनी
In old times bellows were used to blow air into the furnance.

Belly/बेली *(noun)* - पेट, उदर
My belly is only half full give me more food.

Belong/बिलांग *(verb)* - किसी की सम्पत्ति होना
I belong to Khan family and I am in my right belonging.

Beloved/बिलव्ड *(adj.)* - प्रिय, इष्ट, प्यारा
She is my beloved.

Belt/बेल्ट *(noun)* - पेटी, कमरबन्द, विशिष्ट गुणों वाला क्षेत्र
The green belt around Delhi is increasing.

Belvedere/बेल्‌विडिअर *(noun)* - दृश्य देखने का ऊँचा मंच
I stood in the belvedere and looked down on the scene pleasant.

Bemire/बिमाअर *(verb)* - कीचड़ पोतना [archaic] cover or stain with mud. *It was raining and my clothes got bemired.*

Bemoan/बिमोन *(verb)* - विलाप करना
I bemoaned the loss of my friend.

Bemuse/बिम्यूज *(verb)* - उलझन में, स्पष्ट रूप से काम करने में असमर्थ
I found him in a drunk and bemused condition.

Bend/बेन्ड *(verb)* - मोड़ना, झुकना, टेढ़ा करना
I bend the branch and plucked the fruit.

Beneath/बिनीथ *(prep.& adv.)* - नीचे, नीचे की ओर
You are beneath me in rank.

Benefaction/बेनिफैक्शन *(noun)* - धर्मदान, उपकार
The rich man gave the orphanage a big benefaction.

Benefice/बेनिफिस *(noun)* - पादरी की वृत्ति, धर्मवृत्ति
The man sitting in the benefic is our vicar.

Beneficence/बेनिफिसेंस *(noun)* - हित, दया, कृपा doing good, feeling beneficent.

Beneficiary/बेनिफिशरी *(noun)* - धर्मस्व प्राप्तकर्ता, किसी की मृत्यु के बाद धन या सम्पत्ति प्राप्त करने वाला
His father left him a lot of money in his will that makes him a beneficiary.

Benefit/बेनिफिट *(noun & verb)* - लाभ, सुविधा, प्राप्त करने वाला
I have benefited a lot from your friendship.

Benevolence/बनिवोलन्स *(noun)* - दया, कृपा, सुजनता
His benevolence earned him a lot of fame.

Benevolent/बेनिवोलेन्ट *(adj.)* - शुभचिन्तक, उदार
A benevolent person works more for charity than for profit.

Benighted/बिनाइटेड *(adj.)* - अन्धकार से आच्छादित
He is a benighted person not knowing what is moral or intellectual.

Benign/बिनाइन *(adj.)* - सौम्य या उदार, कृपालु, सुखप्रद
This tumour is not malign but benign.

Benison/बेनीजन *(noun)* - वरदान, आशीर्वाद
He has received benison from the priest.

Bent/बेन्ट - झुकाव, रुचि, मुड़ा, टेढ़ा
I saw a bent iron rod in the junkyard.

Benzene/बेनजीन *(noun)* - दाग छुड़ाने का तेल
The molecule present in benzene is the basis of most organic compounds.

Benzoin/बेनजोइन *(noun)* - लोहबान
I like the fragrant smell of benzoin.

Bequeath/बिक्वीथ *(verb)* - वसीयत द्वारा सम्पत्ति छोड़ जाना
He bequeathed all his money to a charity institution.

Bequest/बिक्वेस्ट *(noun)* - इच्छापत्र द्वारा छोड़ी हुई सम्पत्ति
The bequest of money took place when he was about to die.

Bergamot/बरगामॉट *(noun)* - नांरगी की जाति का वृक्ष
The tree bergamot bears the fruit Seville orange.

Beri-Beri/बेरी-बेरी *(noun)* - जलन्धर के प्रकार का एक रोग
Due to deficiency of vitamin B_1 my uncle was affected with Beriberi.

B

Berry/बेरी *(noun)* - एक प्रकार का बेर, सरस फल
I am fond of eating berries.

Beryl/बेरल *(noun* - हरितमणि, बिल्लौर फीरोजा
Jweller sometimes use beryl as a gemstone.

Beside/बिसाइड *(prep.)* - पास, समीप
He sat beside me in the bus.

Besides/बिसाइडज *(prep.)* - सिवाय, अतिरिक्त के साथ भी
Serve me lunch besides I would like a coffee.

Besiege/बिसीज *(verb)* - सेना की सहायता से घेर लेना
Town has been besieged by army.

Besmear/बिस्मीर *(verb)* - लेप करना पोतना, गंदा करना
He had a bullet wound and was besmeared with blood.

Besmirch/विस्मर्च *(verb)* - कीचड़ उछालना, गन्दा करना, अन्धकार करना
Even if you besmirch in public, his sound reputation will remain intact.

Bespotter/बिस्पॉटर *(verb)* - अपमानित करना
He bespattered other religion.

Bespeak/बिस्पीक *(verb)* - पहले से शर्त कर लेना
I bespeak you to reserve a seat for me in Rajdhani Express.

Besprinkle/बिस्प्रींकल *(verb)* - छिड़कना
All the wedding guests were besprinkle with fragrant scent.

Bestead/बिस्टेड *(verb)* - काम में लाना, सहायता देना
I can bestead it.

Bestir/बिस्टिर *(verb)* - चेष्टा करना
I woke up and bestirred myself.

Bestow/बिस्टो *(verb)* - प्रतिपादन करना, देना, आदर व्यक्त करने के लिए
The title was betowed on him by the parson.

Bestrew/बेरट्रियू *(verb)* - छितरना, फैलाना
Dry leaves were bestrewed all over the ground.

Bet/बेट *(verb)* - दाँव लगाना
This party team looks a good bet for victory.

Beta/बिटा *(noun)* - ग्रीक वर्णमाला का दूसरा अक्षर
As in Greek alphabet 'B' is the second letter so it is in English language.

Betake/बिटेक *(verb)* - आश्रय लेना, लगाना
I have to betake here.

Beteem/बिटीम *(verb)* - बहाना, उत्पन्न करना
She will beteem this in the drain.

Betel/बिट्ल *(noun)* - पान, ताम्बूल
Betel leave are chewed by people in Asia.

Bethink/बिथिंक *(verb)* - विचारना, सोचना, याद करना
Bethink he has not come today.

Betide/बिटाइड *(verb)* - आ पड़ना, होना
Woe betide that rascal.

Betimes/बिटाइम्ज *(adverb)* - यथासमय, शीघ्र
We must be up betimes tomorrow.

Betoken/बिटोकन *(verb)* - दरसाना, सूचना देना
Those black clouds betoken rain.

Betroth/बिट्राथ *(verb)* - वचन देना, सगाई होना, विद्रोह
She is betrothed to that gentleman.

Better/बेटर *(adj.)* - उच्चतर, श्रेष्ठतर, बेहतर
You won't find a better coffee shop than this one.

Betwixt/बिट्वीक्स्ट *(prep.&adv.)* - अन्तर में
Let this secret be hidden betwixt we two people.

Beverage/बेवरिज *(noun)* - कोई पेय पदार्थ
In beverages I like coca cola the most.

Bewail/बिवेल *(verb)* - विलाप करना
She is bewailing the loss of her husband.

Beware/बिवेअर *(verb)* - सावधान होना, सचेत होना
Beware of this dog. It is a bad tempered one.

Bewilder/बिविल्डर *(verb)* - उलझन में डालना, भरमाना
I was bewildered not to find my friend at home.

Beyond/बिऑन्ड *(prep.&adv.)* - बाहर, अतिरिक्त, परे, दूर
The city we have to reach in beyond that jungle.

Bezique/बिजीक् *(noun)* - ताश का एक प्रकार का खेल
He is an expert in the card game of bezique.

Bi/बाइ - दोहरा, दुबारा
Bi the chemical elements of bismuth.

Bias/बायस् *(noun)* - भार, पक्षपात, झुकाव
My boss is biassed against me.

Biaxial/बाइएक्सीअल *(adj.)* - दो धुरा वाला
All four wheelers are biaxial.

Bib/बिब *(noun)* - छोटा कपड़ा जो बच्चों की छाती पर फिट होते है
This child is wearing a beautiful bib round its neck.

Bible/बाइबल *(noun)* - ईसाइयों की धर्म पुस्तक
Bible is largest selling book in the world.

Bibliography/बिबलीआग्राफी *(noun)* - पुस्तक विद्या, ग्रन्थ-सूची
Most books have bibliography at the end. Telling us which books or other material have been consulted.

Bibulous/बिब्यूलस *(adj.)*
He is a bibulous man. Very fond of drinking.

Bicameral/बिकैमरल *(noun)* - दोधरा, द्विगृही
This lawyer's office is bicameral.

Bicentenary/बाइसेन्टिनरी *(adj.)* - दो सौ वर्ष पर होने वाला
Bicentenary is celebrated of many big events.

Bicephalous/बायसेफेलस *(adj.)* - दो सिर वाला
These children's bodies are joined together and only a surgeon can separate them.

Bicker/बिकर *(verb)* - बेकार की बात पर, कलह करना, वेग से बहना
He is always bickering about pocket money with his parent.

Bicuspid/बिकस्पिड *(adj.)* - दो नोकों वाला दाँत
Two of his teeth are bicuspid let us consult a dentist.

Bid/बिड *(verb)*- आज्ञा देना, घोषणा करना
At auction I'll bid for this painting.

Biddable/बिडेब्ल *(adj.)* - आज्ञा मानने वाला
He is a biddable person and will do as you say.

Bidder/बिडर *(noun)* - दाँव लगाने वाला
He is a smart bidder.

Bidding/बिडिंग - आज्ञा, आदेश
Bidding is a tricky and intelligent game.

Bide/बाइड *(verb)* - रहना, ठहरना
You can bide with me while you are in town.

Biennial/बाइएनीअल *(adj.)* - दो-दो साल में होने वाला, द्वैवार्षिक

It is a biennial plant and will die in two years.

Bier/बायर् *(noun)* - अर्थी, जनाजा

The dead body was carried on a bier to the crematorium.

Bifacial/बायफेसियल *(adj.)* - दो चेहरे वाला

A bifacial child was born to her.

Bifurcate/बाइफर्केट *(verb)* - दो भागों में विभाजित करना

This lengthy volume has been bifurcated.

Bigamist/बाइगेमिस्ट *(noun)* - द्विविवाही

He is a bigamist having two wives.

Bigamy/बाइगैमि *(noun)* - द्विपत्नीत्व

Practicing bigamy is against the law.

Bight/बाइट *(noun)* - घुमाव, झूलन

The bight was beautiful and many person bathed there.

Bigot/बिगॉट *(noun)* - हठधर्मी, कट्टर

He is a bigot it is impossible to convince him of anything other than his own belief.

Bike/बाइक *(noun)* - बाइसिकिल शब्द का छोटा रूप

I have purchased a new bike.

Bilateral/बाइलैटरल *(adj.)* - द्विपक्षीय

It is a bilateral agreement.

Bile/बाइल *(noun)* - पित्त

Bile helps digest food.

Biliary/बिलिएरी *(adj.)* - पित्त सम्बन्धी, पैत्तिक

His liver is not right so he is taking some biliary.

Billingual/बाइलिङ्ग्वल *(adj.)* - दो भाषाओं से सम्बन्धित

He is bilingual and can speak Tamil and Hindi fluently.

Bilious/बिलियस *(adj.)* - पैत्तिक, पित्तग्रस्त

He is feeling bilious may be he will vomit.

Bilateral/बाइलैटरल *(adj)* - दो अक्षरों का, द्विपक्षीय, दोतरफा

It is a bilateral agreement.

Bilk/बिल्क *(verb)* - धोखा देना, छलना, ठगना

He has bilked me of Rs. One million. I am going to lodge an FIR.

Billet/बिलेट *(noun)* - निजी आवास का भाग जब सैनिक अस्थायी रूप से टिकते है

Right now the troops are lodged in a billet soon may will move out.

Billion/बिलियन *(noun)* - एक अरब की संख्या

He has got a billion rupees i.e. thousand millions.

Billow/बिल्लो *(noun)* - तरंग, बड़ी लहर, लहराना

In the distance we could see a thick line of billows.

Billy-goat/बिलीगोट *(noun)* - बकरा

He has three Billy- goats and two she- goats.

Bimetallic/बाइमेटलिक *(adj.)* - दो धातुओं से मिलकर बना

This vase is bimetallic made of two metals copper and tin.

Bimonthly/बाइमन्थली *(adj.&adv.)* - द्वैमासिक

This magazine is bimonthly.

Binary/बायनरी *(adj.)* - दोहरा जोड़ा, युग्मक

This problem is i.e. twofold composed of two parts.

Bind/बाइण्ड *(verb)* - बाँधना, कसना

Bind the two ends of the rope together.

Binocular/बायनोक्युलर *(adj.)* - दोनों आँखों से देखने वाला दूरबीन

I looked at the distant object with a binocular.

Biogenesis/बाइओजेनिसिस *(noun)* - जीव से जीव की उत्पत्ति का सिद्धान्त

According to biogenesis a living matter given rise to another living matter.

Biography/बायोग्राफी *(noun)* - किसी व्यक्ति का जीवन-वृत्तान्त

I have read the biography of Tolstoy. It is fascinating.

Biological/बायलोजिकल *(adj.)* - जीव विज्ञान सम्बन्धी

They are his biological parents.

Biology/बायोलॉजी *(noun)* - जीव विज्ञान

I have taken biology as a subject it fascinates me to no end.

Biscope/बाइस्कोप *(noun)* - चलते-फिरते परदे पर चलचित्र

I want to see a film in bioscope.

Biplane/बाइप्लेन *(noun)* - दो पंखे वाला वायुयान

Early planes used to be called biplanes as they had one wing over the other.

Bipolar/बाइपोलर *(adj.)* - द्विध्रुवीय

He is an authority over bipolar animal life.

Birch/बर्च *(noun)* - भोजपत्र

There are a lot of birch trees in Mussourie.

B

Birdlime/बर्डलाइम *(noun)* - चिड़िया पकड़ने का लासा
People trap small birds by spreading birdlime over twigs once they sit over it they can't fly away.

Bird's eye/बर्ड्स आई *(noun)* - विशालदर्शी ऊँचे स्थान से देखा हुआ
I have taken a bird's eye view of the problem. We shall go in detail later.

Birth/बर्थ *(noun)* - जन्म, आरम्भ
My sister gave birth to a daughter.

Biscuit/बिस्किट *(noun)* - बिस्कुट
Biscuits are very popular in European countries.

Bisect/बाइसेक्ट *(verb)* - समद्विभाग करना
Now I'll bisect this circle.

Bisexual/बायसेक्सुअल *(adj.)* - द्विलिंगीय
He is bisexual by nature attracted sexually to both men and women.

Bison/बाइजन *(noun)* - जंगली साँड़
Bison is a huge north American buffalo.

Bisque/बिस्क *(noun)* - बिना पालिश किये हुए चीनी मिट्टी
I very much like to drink in bisque.

Bistoury/बिस्टॉरी *(noun)* - जर्राह की पतली छुरी
Surgeon work with a bistoury.

Bit/बिट *(noun)* - खण्ड, लगाम की मुखी, छोटा टुकड़ा
Let me have a bit of bread.

Bitch/बिच *(noun)* - सियारिन, कुतिया
I have named my bitch Sophie.

Bite/बाइट *(verb)* - कुतरना, डंक मारना, दंश
I bit a loaf of bread.

Bitter/बिटर *(adj.)* - तीता, कठोर, कड़वाहट
Bitter gourd is a bitter vegetable.

Bitumen/बिट्यूमेन *(noun)* - सड़कों या छतों पर डाला जाने वाला गाढ़ा तारकोल डामर बिटुमन
We need more bitumen for road and roof surfacing.

Bivouac/बाइवॉक *(noun)* - पड़ाव में ठहरना, पड़ाव
We stayed in bivouac camp it was so exciting and funny.

Bizzare/बिजार *(adj.)* - अनोखा, विचित्र
Yes tonight I saw a bizarre dream.

Black/ब्लैक *(adj.)* - काला, स्याह, प्रकाशरहित
Black is the opposite of white.

Black-guard/ब्लैगार्ड *(noun)* - दुराचारी, अधम
He has betrayed us. He is a blackguard.

Blackmail/ब्लैकमेल *(noun)* - डरा-धमका कर अवैध रूप से लिया गया पैसा
His grandson was kidnapped and he was subjected to blackmail.

Blackness/ब्लैकनेस *(adj.)* - कालापन
Blackness has surrounded the place.

Bladder/ब्लैडर *(noun)* - मूत्राशय
My bladder is almost bursting please show me the toilet.

Blame/ब्लेम *(verb)* - निन्दा करना, दोष लगाना
There was an accident and the blame fell on the truck driver.

Blameless/ब्लेमलेस *(adj.)* - निर्दोष
I find him blameless so he is free to go.

Blameworthy/ब्लेमवर्दी *(adj.)* - निन्दा के योग्य, कसूरवार
This fellow is blameworthy as he caused the accident.

Blanch/ब्लांच *(verb & noun)* - भय से पीला पड़ जाना
The blanched potatoes were immersed in boiling water and then peeled.

Bland/ब्लैंड *(adj.)* - नम्र, विनीत, कोमल, चिकना
He is a bland fellow lacking any features or characteristics. I have no interest in him.

Blandish/ब्लैंडिश *(verb)* - मीठे वचन से चापलूसी करना
I blandished her a lot and she became happy.

Blanket/ब्लैंकेट *(noun)* - कम्बल, धुस्सा
I bought a good quality blanket from the market.

Blare/ब्लेअर *(noun & verb)* - चिल्लाकर बोलना, गरजना
A blare of trumpets welcomed the king.

Blasphemy/ब्लासफेमी *(noun)* - ईश्वर-निन्दा करना
He talked ill of God and thus blasphemed.

Blast/ब्लास्ट *(noun)* - आँधी, भभकन, विस्फोट
Suddenly there was a bomb blast in the market.

Blatter/ब्लैटर *(verb)* - बकझक करना
The warriors attacked each other with a clatter of swords.

Blaze/ब्लेज *(noun)* - प्रभा, चमक
Captain cook was a trail blazer. He was the first to reach North pole.

Blazon/ब्लेजॉन *(verb)* - प्रचार करना, फैलाना, कुलचिह्न
He reported the incident in a blazon way.

Bleach/ब्लीच *(verb)* - धोना, सफेद करना, तिलांजित करना
This shirt has been bleached that is why it is looking so light and white.

Bleaching/ब्लीचिंग *(noun.)* - वस्त्र इत्यादि सफेद करने की कला
I have purchased a packet of bleaching powder. It is best for washing dirty white shirts.

Blear/ब्लीअर *(noun)* - मन्द करना, चौंधा देना,
I am fond of the silvery blear.

Bleb/ब्लेब *(noun)*- फफोला
Doctors have discovered a bleb on the surface of one of my cells.

Bleed/ब्लीड *(noun)* - रक्त बहाना, तरस खाना
He was bleeding profusely after the accident.

Blemish/ब्लेमिश *(noun)* - दोष, कलंक
There is a blemish on this diamond which has spoiled its appearance.

Blend/ब्लेंड *(verb)* - मिलाना
Mixing two things means blending them.

Blessed/ब्लेसेड *(adj.)* - धन्य, सुखी
Blessed are the meek for they shall also enter heaven'.

Blessing/ब्लेसिंग *(adj.)* - ईश्वर की कृपा, सौभाग्य, वरदान
I am praying for God's favour and blessings.

Blew/ब्ल्यू *(verb)* - बहा-उड़ा
Wind blew away my clothes.

Blight/ब्लाइट *(noun)* - पाला, गेरूई
The growth of this plant has been infected by blight.

Blimp/ब्लिम्प *(noun)* - एक प्रकार का छोटा हवाई जहाज
He owned a blimp and was fond of flying it.

Blind/ब्लाइण्ड *(adj.)* - अन्धा, नेत्र ज्योतिहीन हो जाना या कर देना
He is blind person he can't see anything.

Blindfold/ब्लाइन्डफोल्ड *(verb)* - आँखो पर पट्टी बाँधना
He blind folded his eyes.

Blindly/ब्लाइन्डली *(adv.)* - टटोलते हुए, बिना देखे
He obeyed me blindly.

Blindness/ब्लाइन्डनेस *(noun)* - अन्धता, अज्ञान
Blindness occurred to him because of weak eye nerve.

Blink/ब्लिंक *(verb)* - पलक मारना, मिचकाना
As he suddenly confronted bright lights he blinked his eyes.

Bliss/ब्लिस *(noun)*- परम सुख
He has been meditating long and now he is in a state of bliss.

Blister/ब्लिस्टर *(noun)* - छाला, फफोला
The sole of his feet got blisters as he walked barefooted in the desert.

Blithe/ब्लाइद् *(adj.)* - प्रसन्नवदन, आनन्दित
She is a blithe child always happy and playful.

Blizzard/ब्लिजार्ड *(noun)* - बर्फीली आँधी
We were trapped in a blizzard.

Blockade/ब्लॉकेड *(noun & verb)* - अवरोध, रोकना
There is a police blockade on the road.

Blockish/ब्लॉकिश *(adj.)* - मूर्ख, बुद्धिहीन
He is a blockish fellow.

Bloody/ब्लडी *(adj.)* - निर्दयी, हत्यारा
The dead body was too bloody.

Blossom/ब्लासम *(noun & verb)* - फूल, मंजरी, विकसित होना
The flowers blossomed on the tree.

Blot/ब्लॉट *(noun)* - दाग, धब्बा, निशान
Here is a blot on this otherwise clean page.

Blotch/ब्लॉच *(noun)* - चकत्ता, त्वचा, पौधों पर पड़ने वाला अस्थायी चकत्ता
There was rain last night and the road is covered with blotches.

Blouse/ब्लाउज *(noun)* - एक प्रकार की जनानी कुरती
She is wearing a low cut red blouse which goes well with her saree.

Blow/ब्लो *(noun)* - हवा का बहना, चलना
I gave him a blow on the chin.

Blowy /ब्लोवी *(adj.)* - हवादार
This valley is very blowy.

Bludgeon/ब्लजन् *(noun)* - लाठी या सोटे से मारना
He beat him with a bludgeon.

Blue/ब्लू *(adj.)* - नीला, आसमानी
The sky seems to be of blue colour.

Blue blood/ब्लू ब्लड *(noun)* - कुलीन व्यक्ति, अभिजात
He is a man of blue blood.

B

Blue-stone/ब्लू-स्टोन *(noun)* – तूतिया
I would like to use some blue stones on this wall.

Bluff/ब्लफ – *(noun)* झांसा देना
He bluffed me into believing that he could give me loan easily.

Bluish/ब्लूइश *(adj.)*– हल्का नीला
Your blazer has a bluish tinge. It works fantastic.

Blunder/ब्लन्डर *(noun)* – बड़ी भूल, भद्दी या मूर्खतापूर्ण भूल
I committed a blunder by delaying the loan payment.

Blunt/ब्लन्ट *(adj.)* – धारहीन, मन्द
He was hit on head with a blunt object.

Blur/ब्लर *(verb)* – धब्बा, अस्पष्ट वस्तु
My eye – sight was blurred as something hit me on the head.

Blurt/ब्लर्ट *(verb)* – बिना समझे बोल उठना
'Ah! Yes I have committed the crime he blurted out.

Bluster/ब्लटर *(verb)* – गरजना, कोलाहल करना
He gave me a blustering talk which had little effect on me.

Boa/बोआ *(noun)* – बिना जहर का भारी सर्प, अजगर
I saw a boa in jungle it was crushing its prey to death.

Boar/बॉर *(noun)* – नर सूअर
If you confront boar in the jungle it can be very dangerous.

Board/बोर्ड *(noun)* – दफ्ती, मेज
I'll need at least a dozen boards for the floor.

Boarding/बोर्डिंग – भोजन और रहने का स्थान
She liked in a boarding house.

Boast/बोस्ट *(noun & verb)* – अहंकार, गर्व
He boasted a lot about his inherited wealth.

Boat/बोट *(noun)* – नाव, नौका
I crossed the river by boat.

Boating/बोटिंग *(noun)* – नौका विहार
Let us go for boating.

Boatman/बोटमैन *(noun)* – नाविक
The boatman propelled the oars and the boat moved.

Bobby/बॉबी *(noun)* – पुलिस का सिपाही
While in U.K. a bobby stopped me and asked me some questions.

Bodice/बॉडिस *(noun)* – चोली, अंगिया, कुरती
She wore a perfectly fitting bodice.

Bog/बॉग *(noun)* – दलदल
Frogs often live in bog.

Boggle/बोगल *(verb)* – ठमकना
My mind boggled at the speed the train ran.

Bogie/बोगी *(noun)* – रेलगाड़ी का लम्बा डब्बा
There are eight bogies in this train.

Bogle/बोगल् *(noun)* – प्रेत, पिशाच
It is rumored that a bogle roams here in this forest.

Bogus/बोगस *(adj.)* – जाली, बनावट, असली या ढोंग करते हुए बनावट
This driving licence is bogus said the policeman.

Bodkin/बॉडकिन *(noun)* – लम्बा मोटा सूजा
Women fasten their hair with a bodkin.

Boil/बॉइल *(verb)* – उबाल
Water boils at 100^0 c

Boisterous/बाइस्टरस *(adj.)* – प्रचण्ड, उधमी शोरगुल मचाने वाला
Boisterous waters raged into the city.

Bold/बोल्ड *(adj.)* – शूर, साहसी, आत्मसाहसी, निडर
He is bold and will certainly succeed.

Bole/बोल *(noun)* – तना, धड़
Some years ago I engraved some letters on this bole and they are here.

Bolster/बोल्स्टर *(noun)* – मसनद
Please bring me a bolster I want to relax thoroughly.

Bolter/बोल्टर *(noun)* – दलद्रोही
Deer are the best bolters the moment you make a noise they will run and disappear.

Bomb/बम *(noun)* – बमगोला
The bomb blast killed many people.

Bombard/बामबोर्ड *(verb)* – बमवर्षा करना या आक्रमण करना
America bombarted the Taliban until surrendered.

Bomber/बॉमर *(noun)* – बमवर्षक वायुयान
Planes were largely as bombers in 2nd World War.

Bon/बॉन *(noun)* – अच्छा
Many people go to Japan to attend bon.

Bonafide/बोनाफाइड *(adj.)* – वास्तविक
It is a bonafide document and you can submit it in the court without hesitation.

Bondage/बॉन्डेज *(noun)* – दासत्व
He was held in bondage for a long time.

Bodman/बॉडमैन *(noun)* – दासी
In the court you will find lots of bondmen willing to stand surely.

Bone/बोन *(noun)* – हड्डी, अस्थि
The bones in our body are made of calcified material.

Bonfire/बॉनफायर *(noun)* – आतिशबाजी
Let us camp here and light a bonfire.

Bonny/बोनी *(adj.)* – सुन्दर, हृष्ट-पुष्ट
He is a bonny child; I would also like to have one like that.

Bonus/बोनस *(noun)* – पारितोषिक, लाभ, अतिरिक्त राशि
In this firm employees get bonus on every Diwali.

Boo/बू – असन्तोष जनक शब्द करना
She said 'Boo'! in my ear and I was started.

Booby/बूबी *(noun)* – मन्दबुद्धि, अनाड़ी, मूर्ख
No use talking to him, he is a booby.

Boodle/बूड्ल *(noun)* – नकली नोट, रिश्वत का पैसा
All money spent or won in gambling is boodle.

Boohoo/बूहू – चिल्लाकर रोने का शब्द
'Boohoo' she cried loudly as she wept over the loss of her jewellery.

Book-binder/बुक बाइन्डर *(noun)* – जिल्दसाज
My father binds books. He is a book-binder.

Book-case/बुक केस *(noun)*– पुस्तक रखने की अलमारी
I have bought a book – case just to keep books in order.

Booking/बुकिंग *(noun)* – टिकट बेचना
Booking is still open let us buy tickets for the movie.

Book-keeper/बुक कीपर *(noun)* – मुनीम, व्यापार में बही खाता रखने वाला मनुष्य
He is a book-keeper in the office.

Book-keeping/बुक कीपिंग *(noun)* – मुनीमी
The job of book-keeping is not an easy one as it involves financial dealings.

Booklet/बुकलेट *(noun)* – किसी विषय पर जानकारी देने वाली छोटे आकार की पुस्तक
I prefer booklets to books. I can finish them quickly.

Book-maker/बुकमेकर *(noun)* – पुस्तक का संकलन कर्त्ता घुड़दौड़ में लगे दाँवों का हिसाब रखने वाला व्यक्ति
A book-maker has an important place in a gambling house.

Book-mate/बुकमेट – सहाध्यायी, साथ का पढ़ने वाला
I am his book-mate, we often exchange books.

Book-post/बुकपोस्ट *(noun)* – डाक द्वारा कम कीमत पर भेजी गई पुस्तक इत्यादि
I have received a book by book-post.

Book-seller/बुकसेलर *(noun)* – पुस्तक बेचने वाला
A proprietor of a book-store you will find any book from that book-seller.

Book-worm/बुकवर्म *(noun)* – किताबों का कीड़ा
He is reading he is a book-worm.

Boom/बूम *(noun)* – समृद्धि
The firing cannons made a sound of boom-boom.

Boon/बून *(noun)* – लाभ, वरदान
His having become my partner in business was no less a boon.

Boor/बूअर *(noun)* – असभ्य, अशिक्षित
No use expecting from him fine manners he is a boor.

Boost/बूस्ट *(verb)* – संख्या, मूल्य या शक्ति में वृद्धि करना
My father having come to my help in bad times boosted my morals.

Boot/बूट *(noun)* – पूजा, सुविधा
I purchased a pair of boots.

Booth/बूथ *(noun)* – छानी, मेले की दुकान
There were a lot of booths in fair.

Boot-lace/बूट लैस *(noun)* – जूते की फीता
Will someone find my boot-laces I have to tie up shoe?

Bootless/बूटलेस *(adj.)* – बेकार, अकारथ
Ignore it. It is something bootless.

Booty/बूटी *(noun)* – लूट का माल
Let us divide the booty among ourselves before the police come.

Booze/बूज *(verb)* – अधिक मदिरा पीना
He drank a lot of booze and was out.

Borax/बोरैक्स *(noun)* – सोहागा
Here is some borax it will help us make glass.

B

B

Border/बॉर्डर *(noun)* - किनारा, छोर
The border line between India and Pakistan is very long.

Bore/बोर *(noun & verb)* - ज्वार की लहर, छेद करना
Look this place is called bore where the tide rushes up the mouth of a large river.

Borer/बोरर *(noun)* - छेदने का यन्त्र
The worm called borer has eaten into our plants as well as the rocks around.

Boring/बोरिंग *(adj.)* - विनोदहीन
He is a very boring person. You will soon get tired of him.

Born/बॉर्न *(adj.)* - पैदा हुआ
I was born in the year 1938.

Borne/बोर्न - आया हुआ
The weight was borne by him for a long distance.

Borrow/बॉरो *(verb)* - अनुकरण करना
I went to my friend to borrow some money.

Bort/बोर्ट *(noun)* - हीरे की कनी
Please get me a bort I have to cut glass.

Bosh/बॉस *(noun)* - वृथा वार्ता
Oh! He is talking bosh.

Bosky/बोस्की *(adj)* - झाड़ीदार
It is a bosky place let us rest here.

Bosom/बूजम *(noun)* - मन, भीतरी भाग
A buxom bosom adds to the beauty of a women.

Botanic/बॉटैनिक *(adj.)* - वनस्पति शास्त्र-सम्बन्धी
This problem is botanic i.e. related with plant life so go and ask a botanist about it.

Botanist/बॉटैनिस्ट *(noun)* - वनस्पति शास्त्र का पंडित
My brother is a botanist.

Botany/बॉटनी *(noun)* - वनस्पति विज्ञान
This sweater is made of merino wool the best available.

Botch/बॉच *(verb)* - पैबन्द, फोड़ा
He has botched up the plan.

Botchy/बॉची *(adj.)* - पैबन्द से भरा हुआ
No use acting upon this botchy scheme.

Both /बोथ *(adj. & prep.)* - दोनों, बराबर से
Both the brothers took up the challenge.

Bother/बॉदर *(verb)* - कष्ट देना
The problem is still bothering me.

Bottom/बॉटम *(noun)* - तल, सबसे भीतरी स्थान
The bottom of the trousers is loose I'll give it to the tailor to tighter it.

Bought/बॉट *(verb)* - खरीदा
I bought a shirt yesterday.

Boulder/बोल्डर *(noun)* - पानी से घिसा हुआ चिकना बड़ा गोला पत्थर
A boulder fell down and raced past me.

Bouncer/बाउन्सर *(noun)* - झूठा, शेखीबाज
The bouncer stopped him from entering the club because he was too drunk.

Bouncing/बाउंसिंग *(noun)* - पुष्ट, भारी
The ball hit the wall and come back bouncing.

Bound/बाउन्ड *(noun & verb)* - सीमा, किनारा, उछलना
The leopard leapt and bounded gracefully.

Boundary/बाउन्डरी *(noun)* - सीमा, मर्यादा
There is a boundary around the play ground.

Boundless/बाउन्डलेस *(adj.)* - असीम
Sportsmen have boundless energy.

Bounteous/बाउन्टिअस *(adj.)* - उदारता से
He is very bounteous, his bounty knows no limits.

Bountiful/बॉउन्टिफुल *(adj.)* - दानशील, उदार
He is bountiful person and donates generously.

Bounty/बॉउन्टी *(noun)* - उदारता
He was given a bounty by authorities for catching an escaped convict.

Bouquet/बुके *(noun)* - गुलदस्ता
She received a bouquet from her best friend.

Bourse/बुर्स *(noun)* - हाट, बाजार
When I went to France I visited bourse also.

Bout/बाउट *(noun)* - काम की पारी, बीमारी का दौरा शक्ति-परीक्षा
I had a bout of malaria.

Bovine/बोवाइन *(adj.)* - गाय, मन्दबुद्धि
A cow belongs to bovine family.

Bovril/बोवरिल *(noun)* - गोमांस का सत्व
She likes bovril.

Bow/बो *(verb)* - घुमाव, कमान
I bowed before my master.

Bowel/बावेल *(noun)* - आँत, अँतड़ी
There is something wrong my bowels are troubling me.

Bower/बावर *(noun)* - पर्णशाला, स्त्री की गुप्त कोठरी
Bower is placed in the front part of the ship.

Bowl/बाउल *(noun)* - प्याला, कटोरा
The Faqir drank from his bowl.

Bowler/बॉलर *(noun)* - गेंद फेंकने वाला
A good bowler is an asset for a winning team.

Bow-wow/बो-वो - कुत्ते की भूँक
He irritated the dog and said 'bow-wow!'

Boxing/बॉक्सिंग *(noun)* - मुक्केबाजी
I am fond of seeing boxing matches.

Boy/बॉय *(noun)* - बालक, शिशु
He is a well mannered boy.

Boyhood/बॉयहुड *(noun)* - लड़कपन
Now, your boyhood is over.

Boyish/बॉयिश *(adj.)* - लड़के के जैसा
Although mature he behaves boyish.

Brabble/ब्रैबल् *(noun)* - लड़ाई-झगड़ा
Don't brabble over petty things.

Brace/ब्रेस *(noun)* - युगल, बन्धन
She wears braces because her teeth are irregular.

Bracelet/ब्रेसलेट *(noun)* - पहुँची, कंगन, बाजू
She bought a diamond bracelet to wear on her wrist

Bracer/ब्रेसर *(noun)*- शक्ति-वर्धिनी औषधि
He needed a bracer to prepare that dangerous stunt.

Bracing/ब्रेसिंग *(adj.)* - पुष्टिकर, शक्तिवर्धक
This is a bracing drink.

Brackish/ब्रैकिश *(adj.)* - खारा
Some fish need brackish water to live in.

Bradawl/ब्रैडॉल *(noun)* - छेदने का शस्त्र
I need a bradawl to drill a hole.

Brag/ब्रैग *(noun)* - आत्मश्लाघा करना, डींग मारना, शेखी बघारना
He is a bragger. He brags all the time of his wealth, of his power, of his business ventures etc.

Braid/ब्रेड *(noun)* - गोटा, लेस
The braid she wore was made of silk and cotton woven finely into a band.

Braille/ब्रेल *(noun)* - अन्धों के लिए उभरे अक्षरों में छपी पुस्तक जिसे ढ़क कर पढ़ा जाता है
This book has been typed in Braille so that the blind can read it.

Brain/ब्रेन *(noun)* - मस्तिष्क, बुद्धि
This intellectual and nervous activities show that he has lots of brains.

Brake/ब्रेक *(noun)* - झाड़ी
He travelled a long way in brake.

Bramble/ब्रैम्बल *(noun)* - कँटीला पौधा, फाली या लाल बेरी दाली जंगली झाड़ी
The gardener is gathering blackberries from bramble.

Bran/ब्रैन *(noun)* - भूसी, चोकर
Bran is good for health.

Branch/ब्रान्च *(noun)* - शाखा, टहनी, डाल
This branch of tree is full of fruits.

Brand/ब्राण्ड *(noun)* - व्यापारिक चिह्न, तलवार
It is a levis Philippe shirts a brand name known world over.

Brandish/ब्रैण्डिश *(noun)* - घुमाना, चक्कर देना
Brandishing his sword he attacked him.

Brandy/ब्राण्डी *(noun)* - आसव, शराब
If you have cough cold you may take a little brandy that will help.

Bravado/ब्रॅवाडो *(noun)* - शेखी, धमकी
He has lot of bravado and creates impression by his boldness.

Brave/ब्रेव *(adj.)* - निडर, ईमानदार
He proved to be a brave soldier.

Bravo/ब्रावो - शाबाश वाह-वाह
Bravo cried the crowd as he hit a sixer.

Brawl/ब्रॉल *(noun & verb)* - कलह करना, विवाद करना, झड़प
Police found him indulged in a street brawl and arrested him the others ran away.

Bray/ब्रे *(noun)*- गदहे का स्वर, रेंकना
In the morning I heard a donkey's braying and woke up irritated.

Braze/ब्रेज *(verb)* - पीतल के समान रंग करना
This is a brazed joint.

Brazen/ब्रेजेन *(adj.)* - धृष्ट, पीतल का बना हुआ
Her brazen attitude irritated all in the party.

Brazier/ब्रेजिअर *(noun)* - बोरसी, ठठेरा
He works in a factory where copper joints are brazed.

Breach/ब्रीच *(noun)* - नियम, समझौते की शर्तों का उल्लंखन
To enter someone's house without permission is a breach of law.

Bread/ब्रेड *(noun)* - रोटी, जीवनवृत्ति
Bread is not native Indian food.

Breakable/ब्रेकेब्ल *(adj.)* - तोड़ने योग्य
This stick is thin and surely breakable.

Breakage/ब्रेकेज *(noun)* - टूटन
The young men who created a scene in restaurant had to pay for the breakage.

Breakdown/ब्रेकडाउन *(noun)* - वाहन या मशीन का चलते-चलते बंद हो जाना, स्वास्थ नष्ट होना
The breakdown of the car occurred at an isolated place.

Breaker/ब्रेकर *(noun)* - समुद्र की बड़ी लहर
The breaker came and almost the whole ship shook.

Breakfast/ब्रेकफास्ट *(noun)*- सुबह का नास्ता
You must not miss your breakfast as it is the first meal of the day.

Breakneck/ब्रेकनेक *(adj.)* - बहुत तेज और खतरनाक
He drove the car at breakneck speed.

Breakwater/ब्रेकवाटर *(noun)* - लहरों के आघात से सुरक्षा के लिए समुद्र के पानी में बनायी गयी दीवार
This barrier in the sea is named breakwater as it protects the coast from the force of waves.

Breast/ब्रेस्ट *(noun)* - स्तन, वक्ष-स्थल
Mammary gland are glands of a women which secrete milk for the baby after birth.

Breast-bone/ब्रेस्टबोन *(noun)* - हृदय पर की बीच की हड्डी
He was hit hard on his breast-bone.

Breath/ब्रेथ *(noun)* - मन्द पवन, जीवन, श्वास
His breath came slow.

Breathe/ब्रीद् *(verb)* - श्वास लेना, साँस
Breathing is necessary to maintain life.

Breathless/ब्रेथलेस *(adj.)* - हाँफता हुआ
I found him breathless with excitement.

Breed/ब्रीड *(verb)*- पैदा करना, जन्म देना
Insects breed like anything.

Breeder/ब्रीडर *(noun)* - प्रजनक, प्रजनन की दृष्टि से पालन करने वाला
We humans and animals are breeders if we were not so the races would have died.

Breeding/ब्रीडिंग *(noun)* - पालन, शिक्षण
See his aristocratic manners his breeding must have been high class.

Breviary/बिविअरी *(noun)* - स्तोत्र-संग्रह
Roman Catholics daily recite from breviary which contains service for each day.

Brew/ब्रियू *(verb)* - शराब बनाना, उत्पन्न करना
I would like to have a jug of brew.

Bribe/ब्राइब *(verb)* - घूस, रिश्वत
He gave me a bribe of ten thousand rupees to get his licence before due date.

Bribery/ब्राइबरी *(noun)* - घूस लेने या देने का कार्य
Bribery is very common in our country.

Brick/ब्रिक *(noun)* - ईंट
Without bricks we cannot make a house.

Bridal/ब्राइडल *(adj.)* - वैवाहिक, विवाह सम्बन्धी उत्सव
She is wearing bridal make up.

Bridegroom/ब्राइडग्रुम *(noun)* - दूल्हा, वर
The bridegroom sat on a horse.

Brief/ब्रीफ *(noun)* - संक्षिप्त या अल्पकालिक, कानूनी बहस के लिए तैयार किया गया विवरण
What I want say in brief is that you must leave tomorrow.

Brier/ब्रायर *(noun)*- गोखरू, काँटेदार झाड़ी
Be careful! It is a brier a wild rose shrub. Can you pluck a flower safely?

Brigade/ब्रिगेड *(noun)* - सैनिकों की टुकड़ी या इकाई
Brigadier commands a brigade which is a sub- division of army.

Brigadier/ब्रिगेडियर *(noun)* - छोटी पलटन का अफसर
A brigadier is high ranking office above the rank of colonel.

Bright/ब्राइट *(adj.)* - चमकीला, प्रसिद्ध, प्रदीप्त
The room was bright with light.

Brighten/ब्राइटेन *(verb)* - चमकना
I brightened light in the room switching on all the lights.

Brilliant/ब्रिलिएन्ट *(adj.)* - अति प्रकाशित, कुशाग्र
He is a brilliant student.

Brim/ब्रिम *(noun)* - प्याला, गिलास आदि का ऊपरी किनारा, कंठ, किनारा
The brim of her hat is decorated with a band of flowers.

Brimstone/ब्रिमस्टोन *(noun)* - गन्धक, गंधक तितली
I chanced to see a brimstone butterfly.

Brindle/ब्रिंडल *(adj.)* - भूरा, चितकबरा
It is a brindle coloured dog.

Brine/ब्राइन *(noun)* - खारा पानी, आँसू
I am not fond of drinking brine water.

Brinish/ब्रिनिश *(adj.)* - नमकीन
This water tastes brinish.

Brink/ब्रिन्क *(noun)* - तट
He was on the brink of bankruptcy.

Briny/ब्रिनी *(adj.)* - नमकीन
This is a briny drink and I don't like it.

Brisk/ब्रिस्क *(adj.)* - तीव्र, चपल
They set off at a brisk.

Brisket/ब्रिस्केट *(noun)* - पशु की छाती का मांस
Bring me a plate of brisket.

Bristle/ब्रिसल *(noun)* - सूअर के कड़े बाल
He has grown a bristle on his chin.

British/ब्रिटिश *(adj.)* - अंग्रेज
He is a British citizen.

Briton/ब्रिटॅन *(noun)* - ग्रेट ब्रिटेन का निवासी
My brother is a Briton.

Brittle/ब्रिटल *(adj.)* - कुरकुरा
An ice slab is brittle.

Broach/ब्रोच *(verb)* - चर्चा चलाना, जिक्र छेड़ना
I broached the bottle open.

Broad/ब्रॉड *(adj.)* - चौड़ा, स्पष्ट
In monsoon the river becomes very broad.

Broadcasting/ब्रॉडकास्ट *(noun)* - प्रसारण
Broadcasting the issue from radio is one way to solve the problem.

Broadly/ब्रॉडली *(adv.)* - मोटे तौर पर
Broadly speaking this is not a serious issue.

Brocade/ब्रोकेड *(noun)*- किमखाब जरीदार या बूटेदार कपड़ा
I would like to have a brocade saree woven with gold and silver threads.

Broccoli/ब्रॉकलि *(noun)* - फूलगोभी जैसी एक सब्जी
So far as vitamin A is concerned broccoli is far better than cabbage.

Brochure/ब्रोशर *(noun)* - एक विवरण पुस्तक
I visited the office of a building company and asked for their brochure so that I could read all detail at my home.

Broil/ब्रायल *(noun)* - झगड़ा, लड़ाई
There was a broil out somewhere.

Broke/ब्रोक *(adj.)* - तोड़ा
Give me some money I am completely broke.

Broken/ब्रोकेन *(adj.)* - टूटा हुआ, टूटा-फूटा
The foreigner spoke in broken Hindi.

Broker/ब्रोकर *(noun)* - दलाल
He is a very intelligent broker. I feel my money safe in his hands.

Bromide/ब्रोमाइड *(noun)* - एक रासायनिक मिश्रण जो औषधि में प्रयुक्त होता है
Sometimes back people used to drink bromide for sleeplessness.

Bronchus/ब्रॉन्कस *(noun)* - वायु-प्रणाली के दो प्रधान कोष्ठों में से एक
I suffer from bronchitis as my windpipe is swollen.

Bronze/ब्रॉन्ज *(noun)* - काँसा, काँसे का
India has won many bronze medal in international sport events.

Brood/ब्रूड *(noun)* - पशु या पक्षियों के एक ही बार में जने बच्चे
The hen went looking for food with her brood behind her.

Brook/ब्रुक *(noun)* - स्रोत, छोटी नदी
There are many brooks in this jungle.

Broom/ब्रूम *(noun)* - झाड़ू, बुहारी
A broom is used for cleaning the room.

Brother/ब्रदर *(noun)* - भाई
My brother is a famous sportsman.

Brow/ब्रोव *(noun)* - मस्तक, ललाट, पहाड़ों का शिखर प्रदेश
Suddenly a car came over the brow of hill.

Brown/ब्राउन *(adj.)* - भूरा
Brown colour is my favourite.

Brownie/ब्रॉवनि *(noun)* - एक प्रकार की परी
Last night I imagined I saw an elf. She was in the house of Mrs. Smith.

Brownie/ब्राउनी *(noun)* - गिरीयुक्त बड़ा चाकलेट
Bring we two prownies at is so rich in chocolate.

Brownish/ब्राउनिश *(adj.)* - कुछ भूरा
I would rather favour a brownish pair of shoes.

Browse/ब्रावजी *(verb)* - सरसरी तौर पर देखना
His favourite pastime is to browse on computer network.

Bruise/ब्रुइज*(noun)* - आघात
While fighting the robbers he received many bruises.

B

B

Bruit/ब्रट *(noun)* – सूचना, झूठी खबर
It is a bruit that he has been murdered.

Brunt/ब्रंट *(noun)* – प्रहार, चोट
I'll bear the brunt of going bankrupt.

Brushwood/ब्रशवुड *(noun)* – घनी झाड़ी
There was a lot of brushwood in the jungle.

Brusque/ब्रस्क *(adj.)* – फूहड़, असभ्य
He left me in an brusque manner.

Brutal/ब्रुटल *(adj.)* – असभ्य, क्रुर
Last night there was a brutal attack on him.

Brute/ब्रुट *(noun)* – पशु, कठोर नर, बड़े आकार का शक्तिशाली पशु
So far as manners are concerned he is a brute.

Bubble/बबल *(noun)* – बुलबुला, क्रूरतापूर्ण, निशंसतापूर्ण
The water was full of bubbles.

Buccal/बकल *(adj.)* – गाल सम्बन्धी
This is a buccal disease.

Buccaneer/बुकानिअर *(noun)* – जहाजी लुटेरा
Captain cook was a notorious buccaneer of Caribbean.

Buck/बक *(noun)* – हिरण, साबर, नर कुछ पशुओं के नर प्राणी, नर हिरण, नर खरगोश
He is to deal the cards so put the buck in front of him.

Bucket/बकेट *(noun)* – डोल, बाटली
You can bathe, the bucket is full of water.

Buckle/बकल *(noun)* – बकसुआ
I must have the buckle of my belt changed it has become loose.

Buckler/बकलर *(noun)* – छोटी ढाल, रक्षा
In old times fighters used to wear buckler on their forearm.

Buckwheat/बकव्हिट *(noun)* – मोथी नामक अन्न
Seeds of buckwheat are milled into flour and eaten during festival when ladies break their fast.

Bud/बड *(noun)* – अंकुर, कली
A bud in plant grows into a flower fruit or seed.

Budge/बज *(verb)* – सरकना, खिसकना
I won't budge an inch from my stand.

Budget/बजट *(noun)* – कोष, पूँजी
This year's budget does not suit the common man.

Buff/बफ *(noun)* – घूँसा, भैंस या बैल का चमड़ा
He is a buff on Mughal history. Ask him and he will answer any question.

Buffalo/बफलो *(noun)* – भैंस
Buffalo's milk is thicker than that of a cow.

Buffet/बुफे *(noun & verb)* – थप्पड़, घूँसा मारना
He was buffeted heavily and consequently sent to hospital.

Buffoon/बफुन *(noun)* – विदूषक भाँड, ठिठोलिया
He amuses all by his buffoonery.

Bug/बग *(noun)* – खटमल, उड़ुस
As I slept in the open I found the bugs all over me they bit like me anything.

Buggy/बग्गी *(noun)* – पालकी गाड़ी बग्घी
In old times people used to travel in buggy.

Bugle/ब्यूगल *(noun)* – विगुल, सिंगी
She has a bugle over her Kurta.

Build/बिल्ड *(verb)* – निर्माण करना, रचना करना
I am going to build my house on this plot.

Built/बिल्ट – निर्मित, बना हुआ
This lady is slightly built.

Bulge/बल्ज *(noun)* – सूजन, फूलन
Do you see that raised portion on the flat land. We are going to play on that bulge.

Bulk/बल्क *(noun)* – बोझ, परिणाम
He is a supplier in bulk.

Bull/बुल *(noun)* – साँड़
This official order has been issued by the pope.

Bullet/बुलेट *(noun)* – बन्दूक में चलाने की सीसे की गोली
He fired a bullet from his pistol and the bullet went past grazing me.

Bulletin/बुलेटिन *(noun)*– संक्षिप्त सरकारी समाचार पत्र
I just read the sports news in the bulletin.

Bullion/बुलियन *(noun)* – चाँदी या सोने की ठोस ईंट
Bullion must be a sight to see the uncoined silver and gold.

Bullock/बुलॉक *(noun)* – बरधा, बधिया किया हुआ बैल
He works hard like a bullock.

Bull's eye/बुल्स आई *(noun)* – निशाना लगाने का गोल बिन्दु
Our Silverman Vijay Kumar hit the bull's eyes with pistol in rapid firing.

Bully/बुली *(noun)* – दबंग, निर्दयी व्यक्ति
He is a school bully and intimidates weaker and smaller children.

Bulwark/बलवर्क *(noun)* – कोट, सिद्धान्त
We have created the bulwark against the enemy.

Bumper/बम्पर *(noun)* – कोई असामान्य पदार्थ
This year there was a bumper crop of wheat.

Bumpkin/बम्पकिन *(noun)* – भद्दा गँवार मनुष्य
He is a bumpkin, a simple villager.

Bunch/बन्च *(noun)* – गुच्छा, ग्रन्थि
I presented her with a bunch of flowers.

Bundle/बन्डल *(noun)* – पोटली, गठरी
He carried a bundle of sticks from the jungle.

Bung/बंग *(noun)* – पीपे की डाट
I have closed the hole with a bung.

Bunion/बुनियन *(noun)* – पैर के अँगूठे पर सुजन
I have a painful swelling near the toe the doctor said it was a bunion and that I was not to worry.

Bunk/बन्क *(noun)* – रेलगाड़ी की दीवार में लगी सोने के लिए पटरी
Last night due to lack of space I slept on a bunk.

Bunker/बन्कर *(noun)* – तलवार, बंकर, कोयला संग्रह करने का स्थान
During war soldiers live in bunkers and fight from there.

Bunt/बन्ट *(noun)* – धक्का, अनाज की बीमारी
Do you see that blown up centre in the sail it is called bunt.

Bunting/बन्टिंग *(noun)* – झण्डी बनाने का कपड़ा या रंगीन कागज
Those singing and seed eating birds finches belong to bunting family.

Buoy/बॉय *(noun)* – जहाज का मार्ग दिखलाने के लिए लंगर पर लगा पीपा
I can see a buoy let us moor there we can no longer keep afloat.

Buoyancy/बॉयोएन्सी *(noun)* – उतराव, हल्कापन
People wear buoyant jackets for water sports.

Burble/बरबल *(verb)* – कष्ट देना
He has a bad habit of burbling.

Bureau/ब्यूरो *(noun)* – दफ्तर, महकमा, सूचनाएँ उपलब्ध कराने वाली संस्था
I have purchased a bureau because I have to do a lot of writing work.

Bureaucracy/ब्यूरियोक्रेसी *(noun)* – नौकरशाही
Bureaucracy has been the misfortune of our nation.

Bureaucrat/ब्यूरॅक्रैट *(noun)* – कर्मचारी शासन-पद्वति का अनुयायी, नौकरशाह
Bureaucrats are not a popular breed.

Burette/ब्यूरेट *(noun)* – तरल पदार्थ की मात्रा नापने के लिए नली
We works with burettes in our chemistry labs.

Burgeon/बर्जन *(verb)* – उगना, निकल आना
Some plants burgeon at very fast rate.

Burgess/बर्गेस *(noun)* – नागरिक
He is a burgess and an important person in parliament.

Burglar/बरग्लर *(noun)* – सेंध मारने वाला चोर
He is a burglar has been sent many times to jail.

Burial/बरियल *(noun)* – दफन
A lot of people were present at his burial.

Burly/बर्लि *(adj.)* – पुष्ट मोटा-ताजा
He is a very burly person.

Burn/बर्न *(noun)* – जल जाना, जलन
There are many burns in this forest.

Burner/बर्नर *(noun)* – दीपक
The burner of this gas stove has become choked.

Burnish/बर्निश *(verb)* – रगड़कर चमकाना
You see these vessels they are shining because they have been burnished vigorously.

Burnt/बर्न्ट – जला हुआ
This house has been burnt to ashes.

Burrow/बरो *(noun)* – बिल खोदना, जमीन खोदना
Rats have made a burrow here.

Burst/बर्स्ट *(verb)* – फटन, धड़ाका, भीतरी दबाव से एकाएक फट जाना
He burst out in anger.

Bury/बरी *(verb)* – जमीन में दफनाना
She want to be buried in the village grave yard

Bush/बुश *(noun)* – झाड़ी, जंगल
The bushes of this mixer have to be changed they are worn out.

Business/बिजनेस *(noun)* – व्यापार, कारोबार
I run the business of export and import of clothes.

Businesslike/बिजनेसलाइक *(adj.)* – नियमपूर्वक
He is a business like efficient and practical person.

B

Buskin/बस्किन *(noun)* - घुटने तक का जूता
Many Americans still wear buskin.

Bustle/बस्ल *(verb)* - कार्य में लगना
He bustled about the kitchen making tea

Busy/बिजि *(adj.)* - कार्य में निरत, लीन
Right now I am very busy please meet me tomorrow.

Butcher/बुचर *(noun)* - कसाई
The butcher living in our street is very conscious of hygiene and is very efficient there is always a crowd of meat buyers around his shop.

Butterfly/बटरफ्लाई *(noun)* - तितली
It is right to see coloured butterflies flying or sitting on a flower. I am against catching them.

Butterine/बटरिन *(noun)* - बनावटी मक्खन, नकली मक्खन
I don't like butterine.

Buttery/बटरी *(noun)* - मक्खन के समान चिकना
Will you go to buttery and buy some food.

Buttock/बटक *(noun)* - चूतड़, नितम्ब
I feel like kicking you on buttock.

Buttony/बटनी *(adj.)* - अनेक बटनों वाला
This is a buttony coat.

Buttress/बट्रश *(noun)* - पुश्ता, आधार
This wall is buttressed by a stone wall.

Buzz/बज *(verb)* - भिनभिनाना
Flies were buzzing all around me.

By/बाइ *(prep. & adv)* - निकट में, साथ, के द्वारा
I went to Shimla by bus.

Byblow/बाइब्लो *(noun)* - दोगला बच्चा, जारज सन्तान
This child is a byblow because his father was living with another woman.

Bye/बाइ - सलाम
Bye-Bye son! Come back soon.

Byelection/बाइ-इलेक्सन *(noun)* - उपनिर्वाचन
In the byelection. The candidate of democratic party won.

Bygone/बाइगॉन *(adj.)* - बिगत, बीता हुआ
In the bygone era humans lived in caves.

By-law/बाइलॉ *(noun)* - उपनियम, उपविधि या व्यवस्था
Houses should be built according to the bylaws of corporation.

Byname/बाइनेम *(noun)* - चिढ़ाने का या अप्रधान नाम
His byname is Tinku.

Bypass/बाइपास *(verb)* - पगडण्डी, उपमार्ग
Let us try to bypass the town centre.

Byre/बायर *(noun)* - गोशाला
Cows are tied in the Byre.

Byroad/बाइरोड *(noun)* - सड़क जिस पर कम लोग चलते है
A byroad goes inside the forest.

Bystander/बाइस्टैन्डर *(noun)* - किसी घटना का मूक दर्शक
This cloth is made of bystander.

Byword/बाइवर्ड *(noun)* - कहावत, व्यक्ति या वस्तु जो किसी विशेषता का प्रतिनिधि माना जाता है
This man is a byword of honesty. A limousim is a byword for luxury.

Bywork/बाइवर्क *(noun)* - अवकाश के समय किया हुआ कार्य, उपकाम
It is my bywork.

Cc

C/सी - अंग्रेजी वर्णमाला का तीसरा अक्षर the third letter of the English alphabet.

(1) The first note in the natural major scale in music.

(2) An academic mark indicating the third highest standard.

Cabal/कैबल *(noun)* - गुप्त षड्यंत्र रचना

Cabal was a much feared organization in Russia during cold war.

Cabaret/कैबरे *(noun)* - सराय

I went to a famous cabaret I dined there as well as enjoyed the dance performance on the stage.

Cabbage/कैबिज *(noun)* - बन्दगोभी

Of all the vegetables cabbage is my favourite.

Cabin/केबिन *(noun)* - कुटी, छोटा कमरा

I am going to my cabin to sleep please don't disturb me.

Cabinet/कैबिनेट *(noun)* - छोटा कमरा, दराजवाली संदूक, मंत्रिमंडल

A wooden almirah which has various cabinets for radio TV etc.

Cable/केबल *(noun)* - मोटा, पुष्ट रस्सा

This is a cable for television. Please don't destroy it.

Cabosse/कैबूस *(noun)* - जहाज या रेल का रसोईघर

A caboose has been attached to the end of of trains in which the train crew is travelling.

Cacao/ककाव *(noun)* - कोकोआ का वृक्ष

Cacao is bean like seed, from which cacao, cacao butter and chocolates are prepared.

Cache/कैश *(noun)* - गुप्त स्थान, नशीले पदार्थ या हथियारों का

You will find this item in cache which is a hidden store of things.

Cachectic/कैकेक्टिक *(adjective)* - रोगी, रुग्ण

She seems cachectic.

Cachet/कैशे *(noun)* - मोहर

The MP's car carried a cachet.

Cachexy/कैकेक्सी *(noun)* - मस्तिष्क की रुग्णावस्था, दुर्बलता, विकृति

This chronic cachexy has weakened his body.

Cachinnate/कैकिन्नेट *(verb)* - जोरों से हँसना

Don't cachinnate here, please.

Cachou/कैशू *(noun)* - कत्था

He uses cachouto hide his bad breath.

Cackle/कैकल *(verb)* - भद्दे तरीके से हँसना

He laughed giving a cackle cry.

Cactus/कैक्टस *(noun)* - थूहर, नागफनी

I have grand collections of cactus at home.

Cad/कैड *(noun)* - अशिष्ट आचरण का मनुष्य, नीच पाजी

He is a cad having a sense of humour and behaving indecently.

Caddish/कैडिश *(noun)* - अभद्र, गँवार

I have seen caddish. It is an insect having a watery larvae which sticks to a stone.

Cadence/कैडेन्स *(noun)* - स्वर, ताल, ध्वनि

I was lost in the cadence of music.

Cadet/कैडेट *(noun)* - सैनिक छात्र, सैनिक विद्यालय का विद्यार्थी, कनिष्ठ पुत्र

I was an N.C.C. cadet.

Cadge/कैज *(verb)* - भीख माँगते फिरना, फेरी लगाना

My uncle was carrying a cadge to fields. In the cadge were sitting hooded hawks.

Cadmium/कैडमियम *(noun)* - टीन के समान एक धातु

Have you seen cadmium? It is silvery white metal resembling zink.

Cadre/काडर *(noun)* - किसी संगठन के कुछ सदस्य जो किसी विशेष उद्देश्य के लिए चुने व प्रशिक्षित किये जाते हैं

Cadre in a group of activists is a communist organization.

C

Cafe/कैफे *(noun)* – काफी गृह

A cafe suites me very well, there is light and the drink are excellent.

Cage/केज *(noun)* – पिंजरा

Do you see these caged birds? What a pity? Can a man be so cruel?

Cain/कैन *(noun)* – हत्यारा, भ्रातृहंता

These four men are responsible for caining in the public.

Cairn/केर्न *(noun)* – समाधि के ऊपर बैठाये हुए, टीला, स्तूप पत्थर

See that cairn! It is prehistoric burial.

Caisson/कैशन *(noun)* – बारूद की पेटी, गोला बारूद का बक्सा

This vessel acts as a gale across entrains of a dry look.

Caitiff/कैटिफ *(noun)* – डरपोक मनुष्य

He is caitiff and I am not ready to talk to such people.

Cajole/केजोल *(verb)* – खुशामद करना

I cajoled him into going to see a movie with me.

Cake/केक *(noun)* – मीठी रोटी

I have never asked a more sweet cake.

Calabash/कैलबाश *(noun)* – तुम्बा

Dried shell of the gourd of this fruit is used in many forms water container, tobacco pipe etc.

Calamitous/कैलामिटस *(adjective)* – अभागा, दुखद, अनर्थकर

The sudden expanding of volcano was calamitous.

Calamity/कलैमिटी *(noun)* – दु:ख, संकट

There was an earthquake and sudden calamity followed.

Calcareous/कैल्केरीअस *(adjective)* – चूना मिला हुआ, चूनेदार

This substance is calcareous and contains calcium carbonate.

Calcify/कैल्सिफाइ *(verb)* – चूने के प्रयोग से किसी वस्तु का कड़ा हो जाना या कड़ा कर देना

When you calcify it, it is jammed when it is hardened by deposition of calcium carbonate.

Calcium/कैल्सियम *(noun)* – चूने का तत्व या सार, दूध या पनीर जैसे खाद्य पदार्थों में पाया जाने वाला एक रासायनिक तत्व जो हड्डियों व दाँतों को मजबूत बनाने में सहायक होता है

Calcium is necessary for bone.

Calculate/कैल्कुलेट *(verb)* – गणना करना

I can calculate this sum easily.

Calculation/कैल्कुलेशन *(noun)* – गणना, पूर्व विचार, परिकलन

Calculation of this sum is not possible.

Calculator/कैल्कुलेटर *(noun)* – गणना करने वाला इलेक्ट्रॉनिक यंत्र

For quick calculation. There is an electronic device called calculation.

Calculus/कैल्कुलस *(noun)* – गणित की एक शाखा

My maths teacher taught calculus.

Calender/कैलेन्डर *(noun)* – जन्त्री, पंचांग

I have bought a beautiful calendar with important and events.

Calendula/कैलेन्ड्यूला *(noun)* – एक प्रकार का फूल

Calendula is a famous medicine.

Calf/काफ *(noun)* – बछड़ा

The young one of bovine family is called calf.

Calibre/कैलिबर *(noun)* – चरित्र-बल, किसी वस्तु का गुण

My company's employees are of (a) high calibre.

Calico/कैलिको *(noun)* – दरेस, छींट

I like to wear dresses made of calico cloth especially the printed ones.

Calif/कैलिफ *abbreviation* –

California is my favorite city.

Calix/कैलिक्स *(noun)* – पुष्पकोश

I love to see calix, the thing of leave that covers a flower bed.

Calk/काक *(noun&verb)* – जूते में नाल जड़ना

If a mason is not available You can yourself take same calk a water dry substance and can fill the cracks and joints.

Call/कॉल *(verb)* – नाम लेना

I called out to my friend to stop.

Call-boy/कॉल-बॉय *(noun)* - नाटक में पात्रों को बुलाने वाल लड़का

The call boy called out to cators when they had to be present is the stage.

Calligraphy/कैलिग्राफी *(noun)* - सुन्दर लिखावट की कला

If you wish to see the art of calligraphy visit the scribes near Jama Masjid.

Callisthenic/कैलिसथेनिक *(Plural noun)* - शक्ति सौन्दर्यवर्द्धक व्यायाम, शरीर की शक्ति और सुन्दरता बढ़ाने वाली

I took up callisthenic to develop grace and fitness of the body.

Callosity/कैलोसिटी *(noun)* - चमड़े का कड़ापन

This belt has callosity but cannot wrinkle.

Callous/कैलस *(adjective)* - कठोर, हृदय

This boy is simply callous.

Callow/कैलो *(adjective)* - पंखहीन, अनुभवहीन

He is a callow youth.

Callus/कैलस *(noun)* - गाँठ, रगड़ से त्वचा पर पड़ा घट्टा

I just fell down and this part has hardened callus.

Calm/काम *(adjective)* - शान्त, चुपचाप, उत्तेजनाहीन

His attitude was calm and cool.

Calmative/कामेटिव *(adjective)* - शान्ति लाने वाली

Many drugs are calmative by nature, they and calm you. You may even go to sleep.

Calmly/कामली *(adverb)* - शान्तिपूर्वक

He calmly took to my harsh call.

Calomel/कैलोमेल *(noun)* - रसकपूर

If you take calomel it may remove constipations.

Caloric/कैलोरिक *(adjective)* - थर्मल, गरम सम्बन्धी

Caloric was previously thought to be rated to heat.

Calorie/कैलोरी *(noun)* - ऊर्जा की इकाई

Don't eat fried food it has high calorie value.

Calorimeter/कैलोरीमीटर *(noun)* - गर्मी की मात्रा नापने का यन्त्र

The amount of heat generator in a chemical reaction can be measured by calorimeter.

Caluminate/कैलमिनेट *(verb)* - निन्दा करना

He caluminated me but I kept my calm.

Calumny/कलम्नी *(noun)* - मिथ्या आरोप

The calumny he made against me made me furious and I slapped him.

C

Calve/काव *(verb)* - जनना (गाय का)

The cow calved.

Calx/काक्स *(noun)* - किसी धातु का भस्म

The calx has been heated and the powder that had formed is called metallic oxide.

Calyx/कैलिक्स *(noun)* - पुटचक्र, वाह्य दलपुंज

Calyx is a ring of leaves enclosing the bud.

Cam/कैम *(noun)* - गति बदलने वाला पहिये का उभड़ा भाग

A rotating part of machine that sets in motion other part is called cam.

Cambric/केमरिक *(noun)* - महीन वस्त्र

I always like to wear lightweight cambric shirts.

Came/केम *(noun)* - आभा

You see these strips forming a panework in this leaded window pane these are called came.

Camel/कैमेल *(noun)* - ऊँट

While in desert I rode a camel and enjoyed the ride.

Camelopard/कैमेलोपार्ड *(noun)* - लकड़हरना

Camelopard is a tall and very long necked animal.

Cameo/कैमिओ *(noun)* - पत्थर में उभड़ी हुई नकाशी

I would like to buy that cameo with the portrait in the profile.

Camera/कैमरा *(noun)* - फोटो खीचनें का यंत्र

I have bought the latest digital camera with multiple devices.

Camion/कैमिअन *(noun)* - तोप ले जाने की गाड़ी

A conveyance used for transporting guns is called camion.

Camisole/कैमिसोल *(noun)* - स्त्रियों की भीतरी पोशाक

The camisole she is wearing is very colourful.

Camouflage/कैम्फ्लाज् *(noun)* - शत्रु को छलने के लिए कलापूर्ण विधि

The military men are wearing camouflaged uniform it helps them disappear in jungle.

C

Camp/कैम्प *(noun)* – शिविर

The climbers set up camp at the foot of mountain.

Campaign/कैम्पेन *(noun)* – किसी विशेष उद्देश्य से नियोजित अभियान में भाग लेना, आंदोलन करना

We campaigned for a special operation.

Comphor/कैम्फर *(noun)* – कपूर

This oil has pungent smell of camphor.

Can/कैन *abbreviation* –

He is a Canadian.

Canal/कैनल *(noun)* – नाला, नहर

Over village has a very long canal and we are fond of bathing in it. It was made by U.P. government.

Canard/कैनार्ड *(noun)* – कटिपत कथा

It is a canard that he met with an accident. I am just coming after meeting him he is all right .

Canary/कैनरी *(noun)* – पीले रंग की कैनरी चिड़िया

I have just bought a canary the bright yellow singing sweet thing. Come today and we shall hear her singing.

Cancel/कैन्सल *(verb)* – रद्द करना, निरस्त करना

The meeting has been cancelled.

Cancellation/कैनसलेशन *(noun)* – रद्द करने की क्रिया

We had to make a last minute cancellation of our air tickets to Mumbai.

Cancer/कैन्सर *(noun)* – कर्क राशि, विस्फोट

This month my cancer is strange and my financial condition will become good.

Candle/कैन्डल *(noun)* – मोमबत्ती

I love to eat candle-light dinner with my girl friend.

Candlemas/कैन्डलमास *(noun)* – कुमारी मेरी की स्मृति में दूसरी फरवरी की त्योहार

I joined candlemas last year

Candour/कैन्डर *(noun)* – सरलता, सच्चाई, निष्कपटता

I like his candour character.

Candy/कैन्डी *(noun)* – मिश्री

Children love candies a lot.

Cane/केन *(noun)* – बेंत

He was beaten with a cane as punishment.

Canister/कैनिस्टर *(noun)* – टीन का पीपा

On round or cylindrical containers called canisters.

Canker/कैन्कर *(noun)* – कीड़ी, घुन, पौधों का एक रोग

You see this damaged bark of the tree. This is caused by a destructive fungal disease called canker.

Cannon/कैनन *(noun)* – तोप

Once for a way I saw artillery, an automatic heavy gun fire that fires shells from an aircraft or tank.

Cannonade/कैननेड *(noun)* – निरन्तर गोला चलाना, गोलीबारी

There was cannonade and a heavy gun fire discharged continuously at the border.

Cannula/कैन्यूला *(noun)* – धातु की जर्राही नली

When my father was being operated upon cannula was inserted into his body.

Canny/कैनी *(adjective)* – चतुर, चालाक, सावधान

He is a canny fellow smart and shrewd in business and financial matters.

Canoe/कैनू *(noun)* – डोंगी

Once in a river in Africa I travelled in a canoe. It was great fun.

Canon/कैनन *(noun)* – गिरजाघर की डिगरी, पादरी, कानून

He is a canon Roman catholic clergy that lives like nuns and monks.

Canonical/कैनानिकल *(adjective)* – नियमानुसार की डिगरी, प्रमाणिक, धर्म वैधानिक

Please, follow canonical teaching.

Canopy/कैनपि *(noun)* – चँदवा, आच्छादन

The highest branches in the rainforest form a dense canopy.

Canorous/कैनरस *(adjective)* – सुरीला

He has got a canorous voice.

Cant/कैन्ट *(noun)* – कुभाषा, कपट की बात

The report was wonderfully free of cant.

Cantab/कैन्टब *abbreviation* – कैम्ब्रिज विश्वविद्यालय का सदस्य

Abbreviation of Cambridge university.

Cantaloup/कैन्टलूप *(noun)* - एक प्रकार का बिलायती खरबूजा

In taste I found cantaloupe better than ordinary melon.

Cantankerous/कैन्टनकेरस *(adjective)* - लड़का

He is a cantankerous fellow.

Canteen/कैन्टीन *(noun)* - जलपान गृह

I take lunch in my school canteen.

Canter/कैन्टर *(noun)* - कदम चाल, घोड़े और घुड़सवार का मध्यम गति से दौड़ना

I rode a cantering horse.

Canticle/कैन्टिकल *(noun)* - छोटा गीत

A canticle was being sung in the church.

Cantilever/कैन्टिलिवर *(noun)* - लकड़ी या धातु का लम्बा टुकड़ा जो दीवार से बाहर की तरफ निकला होता है और पुल या किसी अन्य ढाँचे को बल देता है, घोड़िया

This cantilever projecting from the wall is supporting this balcony.

Canton/कैन्टन *(noun)* - प्रदेश, भाग

Canton is a state of the Swiss confederation.

Cantonment/कैन्टॉनमेन्ट *(noun)* - छावनी

My uncle is a military officer, he stays in cantonment area which is a permanent military station.

Canvas/कैन्वस *(noun)* - तिरपाल

I use canvas for oil painting.

Canvass/कैन्वास *(verb)* - वोट माँगना, परीक्षा करना

Canvassing for election is going at full speed.

Canyon/कैन्यन *(noun)* - झरना, तीखे ढाल वाली गहरी घाटी

Grand canyon of America is worth a visit.

Cap/कैप *abbreviation* - टोपी, शिखर

I dan't have capacity for such hard work.

Capability/कैपबिलिटि *(noun)* - योग्यता

I have capability of speaking five languages.

Capable/कैपेबल *(adjective)* - कार्य करने में सक्षम या समथ

I am capable of crossing this river.

Capacious/कैपेसस *(adjective)* - विशाल

This building is quite capacious.

Capacitate/कैपेसिटेट *(verb)* - गुणयुक्त करना

He has been capacitated to become a first class lawyer.

C

Capacity/कपैसिटी *(noun)* - किसी पात्र की ग्रहणशक्ति

This glass is full of water. It has no more capacity.

Cape/केप *(noun)* - बिना बाँहों के कंधों से लटकने वाला ऊपरी वस्त्र, अंतरीप

A piece of high land that sticks out into the sea the cape of good hope.

Caper/केपर *(verb)* - उछल-कूद, कूद-फाँद, कूदना, फुदकना

She capered softly and lightly on the stage.

Capillary/कैपिलरि *(noun)* - कोशिकानली, शरीर की सबसे छोटी रुधिर वाहिनियों में से एक कोशिकानली

Very small capillaries that join the arteries and veins.

Capital/कैपिटल *(noun)* - राजधानी, मूलधन

New Delhi is the capital of India.

Capitulate/कपिट्युलेट *(verb)* - किसी शर्त पर शत्रु के अधीन हो जाना

The army capitulated before the enemy forces.

Capon/केपन् *(noun)* - बधिया किया मुर्गा, मछली, पत्र

There is our fattened capon we intend to cut it today.

Caprice/कैप्रिस *(noun)* - चपलता

As he is a man of caprice, it is difficult to deal with him.

Capricious/कैप्रिशस *(adjective)* - चपल

He is capricious and cannot be trusted.

Capricorn/कैप्रिकॉर्न *(noun)* - मकर राशि

I was born under the sign of Capricorn.

Capsicum/कैप्सिकम *(noun)* - शिमला मिर्च

I am very fond of eating capsicum.

Caprize/कैप्राइज *(verb)* - उलट देना

The boat capsized and sank into water.

Captain/कैप्टन *(noun)* - नायक, कप्तान

It is my ambition to become a captain either of a ship or of an aeroplane.

C

Captions/कैप्सन *(noun)* – अनुशीर्षक, चित्र या फोटो के नीचे लिखित सूचना

I enjoyed that Russian film simply because it had captions. The cartoon film was provided with captions.

Captious/कैप्सस *(adjective)* – दोष ढूँढ़ने वाला

He is a man of captious nature.

Captivate/कैप्टिवेट *(verb)* – मोहित करना

I found the film very captivating.

Captive/कैप्टिव *(adj)* – बन्दी, कैदी, पिंजरे में बंद

He has been captive.

Captor/कैप्टर *(noun)* – बन्दी को पकड़ने या इनाम लेने वाला

She is so beautiful as to be my captor.

Capture/कैप्चर *(verb)* – अधिकार या कब्जा करना

We captured the territories of enemy forces.

Carocole/कैरोकोल *(noun)* – घोड़े की तिरछी चाल

The horse was performing a carocole.

Carat/कैरट *(noun)* – सोने की शुद्धता की माप की इकाई कैरट

Maharaja jwellers are her favourite. She always buys in carat gold ornaments from them.

Caravan/कैरवैन *(noun)* – काफिला, कारयुक्त बड़ा वाहन जिमें आमोद यात्रा के दौरान रहने, सोने, खाने, पीने आदि का प्रबंध होता है

While in Rajasthan I came across a long colourful caravan.

Carbide/कारबाइड *(noun)* – दूसरे तत्त्वों के साथ कार्बन का यौगिक

Carbide is a compound of carbon with a metal.

Carbon/कार्बन *(noun)* – कोयला

Lots of writing problems have been solved by invention of carbon paper.

Carbonic/कार्बनिक *(adjective)* – कार्बन सम्बन्धी

Relating to carbon.

Carbuncle/कारबंकल *(noun)* – रक्तमणि

It is a carbuncle boil on year arm. You should at once consult a skin surgeon.

Card/कार्ड *(verb)* – गत्ते या प्लास्टिक का कार्ड जिस पर सूचना होती है

A sharp toothed comb to clean fibres before spinning is called card.

Cardamom/कार्डमम *(noun)* – इलायची

I like a bit of cardamom in my tea along with ginger.

Cardiac/कार्डिआक *(adjective)* – हृदय सम्बन्धी

He died of cardiac arrest.

Cardinal/कार्डिनल *(noun)* – रोमन कैथोलिक चर्च का उच्च स्तरीय पादरी

Nominated by pope, cardinal is a leading dignitary.

Cardiograph/कार्डियोग्राफ *(noun)* – एक यन्त्र

Doctors use cardiograph to measure heart activity.

Care/केअर *(noun)* – किसी की देखभाल या देखरेख

The adopled son was well taken care of.

Career/करियर *(noun)* – नौकरी या पेशा

Without career, there is no life.

Careful/केअरफुल *(adjective)* – सावधान, खबरदार

Be careful while driving lest you meet with an accident.

Careless/केअरलेस *(adjective)* – असावधानी या लापरवाही

Don't assign any important work to him he is a careless fellow.

Caress/केअरेस *(verb)* – लाड़-प्यार करना, प्रेम स्पर्श करना

I caressed her with love and affection.

Caret/कैरिट *(noun)* – काकपद

Wherever you wish to in sort in text put a mark or caret under it.

Cargo/कार्गो *(noun)* – विमान या जलपोत के द्वारा ढोया जाने वाला माल

A cargo ship is different from passenger ship.

Carking/कारकिंग *(adjective)* – कष्टकारक

He is a carking fellow.

Carl/कार्ल *(noun)* – नीच पुरुष, खेतिहर

Scottish a man; a fellow. *He is a Carl and as such I don't want to have relations with him.*

Carline/कार्लाइन *(noun)* – डाइन

A fixture of the wooden squared timber fitted in a wooden ship from end to end.

Carminative/कार्मिनेटिव *(adjective)* – बादी हटाने की दवा

Carminative is a wind relieving drug in the stomach.

Carmine/कारमाइन *(noun)* - लाल रंग

It is a carmine pigment.

Carnage/कानिज *(noun)* - संहार, सामूहिक हत्याकाण्ड

Carnage took place when Nadir Shah entered Delhi.

Carnal/कारनल *(adjective)* - दैहिक, शारीरिक

Sexual needs are regarded as carnal.

Carnation/कानेशन *(noun)* - सफेद गुलाबी या लाल सुगन्धित पुष्प

Carnation is a variety of clove.

Carnival/कारनिवल *(noun)* - आनन्द उत्सव

In south America, Rio de Jenerio the annual carnival is celebrated with much fan fare. It is a tourist attrition as well.

Carnivore/कारनिवोर *(plural noun)* - मांसभक्षी पशुओं की जाति

Lion belongs to carnivore order of mammals.

Carnivorous/कारनिवोरस *(adjective)* - मांसाहारी

Lion is a carnivorous animal.

Carol/कैरॅल *(verb)* - ईसाइयों का धार्मिक भजन जो क्रिसमस पर गाया जाता है, गीत, स्तोत्र

We sang carols happily in the streets.

Carouse/कैराउस *(verb)* - अधिक मदिरा पीना

We arranged a party shortly some other friends also joined and soon we were carousing.

Carp/कार्प *(verb)* - मीठे पानी की एक मछली

Don't carp in the morning and make my day horrible.

Carpal/कार्पल *(adjective)* - कलाई की आठ छोटी हड्डियाँ में से एक

As she fell down, she felt her carpal strained.

Carpenter/कारपेन्टर *(noun)* - बढ़ई

He is a carpenter by profession.

Carpet/कारपेट *(noun)* - कालीन, गलीचा

I bought a wall to wall carpet.

Carpus/कार्पस *(noun)* - कलाई, मणिबंध

She strained her carpus.

Carriage/कैरिज *(noun)* - परिवहन

In old times horse driven carriages were very popular.

Carrier/कैरिअर *(noun)* - यात्रियों का समान ढोने वाली कंपनी

He carried the news to me. He is a news carrier.

Carriole/कैरिओल *(noun)* - छोटी खुली गाड़ी

In old time there used to be single person driven covered carriages called carrioles.

Carry/कैरी *(verb)* - ले जाने की स्थिति संभालना, उठा रखना, किसी वस्तु या व्यक्ति को हाथों बाँहों आदि में थामकर एक स्थान से दूसरे स्थान तक ले जाना

I carried and delivered the parcel to him.

Cartilage/कार्टिलेज *(noun)* - कोमलास्थि

He is suffering from as to arthritis as the cartilage of both his knees has dried.

Cartographer/कार्टोग्राफर *(noun)* - नक्शा बनाने की कला, नक्शानवीस, मानचित्रकार

My brother is a cartographer.

Cartography/कार्टोग्राफी *(noun)* - नक्शा खींचने की कला, नक्शानवीसी

Cartography is an art.

Carton/कार्टन *(noun)* - सामान रखने का गत्ते या प्लास्टिक का डिब्बा

The new fridge I bought was enclosed in a big carton.

Cartouche/कार्टूश *(noun)* - कारतूस रखने का बक्सा

If you look at Egyptian hieroglyphs bearing the name and title of a monarch, you will usually find them enclosed in an oval or oblong cartouche.

Cartridge/काट्रिज *(noun)* - कारतूस, किसी मशीन में प्रयुक्त सामग्री को रखने का बंद पात्र, इस पुर्जे को निकाला व पुनः भरा जा सकता है

I have some space cartridges. You can keep your film spools into them.

Caruncle/कारंकल *(noun)* - मांसग्रन्थि

This fleshy outhgrawht is called caruncle.

Cascade/कैस्केड *(noun)* - छोटा झरना

There is a cascade, we can take a bath here.

Case/केस - *(noun)* घटना, स्थान

Here is a case for your spectacles. It is strong enough to protect your glasses.

C

Casement/केसमेन्ट *(noun)* – खिड़की का कब्जेदार पल्ला

Please open the window casement and you will have a nice view of the sea.

Caseous/कैसिअस *(adjective)* – पनीर के सदृश

It is cheese like medicine. It seems caseous.

Cash/कैश *(noun)* – रोकड़, नकद, नकदी

This coin seems to be cash either from China or India.

Cashier/कैशिअर *(noun)* – रोकड़िया

My father is a cashier in the bank. He handles payments and receipts.

Cashmere/कश्मीरी *(noun)* – पशमीनें का दुशाला

I am wearing a cashmere sweater. It is very warm.

Casing/केसिंग *(noun)* – ढकना

The glass pane of the window is enclosed in a metallic casing.

Casino/केसिनो *(noun)* – ऐसा स्थान जहाँ खेल-खेलकर पैसा जीता या हारा जा सकता है, जुआघर, कैसीनो

I visited a casino abroad. There a lot of gambling games were being played.

Cask/कास्क *(noun)* – पीपा

My uncle has a cask full of rum.

Casket/कासकिट *(noun)* – गहने रखने की सजावटी संदूकची

My aunt keeps all ornaments in a casket.

Casque/कास्क *(noun)* – फौजी टोपी

Soldiers used to wear a casque while going to war.

Cassia/कैशीअ *(noun)* – दालचीनी

A lot of cassia trees (cinnamon) grew in our country.

Cassock/कैसॉक *(noun)* – चोंगा

I have seen Christian clergy wearing cassocks.

Cast/कास्ट *(noun)* – किसी नाटक आदि के समस्त कलाकार

The cast of the film is impressive.

Caste/कास्ट *(noun)* – वर्ग, जाति

Casteism has been the curse of India.

Castigate/कास्टिगेट *(verb)* – ताड़ना देना, फटकारना

I was castigated by my father for bunking the school.

Cast-iron/कास्ट आयरन *(noun)* – कान्ती लोहा, ढलवा लोहा

My father deals in cast-iron business.

Castle/कासल *(noun)* – किला दुर्ग

In old times kings used to live in castles.

Castor-oil/कास्टर आयल *(noun)* – रेड़ी (अरंडी) का तेल

I took a close of castor-oil as I was suffering from constipation.

Casual/कैजुअल *(adjective)* – आकस्मिक, अचानक

He takes everything casually.

Casuist/कैसुइस्ट *(noun)* – प्रलाप

He is a casuist and as such I don't like him.

Cat/कैट *(noun)* – बिल्ली

We have a device in our cares exhaust system for converting pollutant gases into less harmful ones.

Cataclysm/कैटक्लिज्म *(noun)* – प्रलय, पानी की बाढ़

The earthquake caused cataclysm.

Catacomb/कैटकोम *(noun)* – मुर्दा रखने का, कब्रों का तहखाना

He was lost in the dark and frightening catacomb.

Catalepsy/कैटलेप्सी *(noun)* – अपस्मार, मिरगी रोग

She suffered from catalepsy and at that time she appeared dead.

Catalogue/कैटलॉग *(noun)* – वर्णक्रमानुसार सूचीपत्र

Please give your catalogue, I would like to know what you have got into your shop.

Catamaran/कैटमरैन *(noun)* – दो पाटों वाली तीव्र गति नौका

I was offered a ride in catamaran and enjoyed it.

Cataplasm/कैटाप्लाज्म *(noun)* – फोड़े आदि पर बाँधने की पुलटिस

You should apply a cataplasm on your injury.

Cataract/कैटरैक्ट *(noun)* – मोतियाबिन्द, जल का बड़ा प्रपात

You have cataract in both of your eyes. I think you should consult aneye surgeon.

Catarrh/कैटार *(noun)* – सर्दी, जुकाम

You are suffering from catarrh. Take some medicine.

Catastrophe/कैटास्ट्रॉफी *(noun)* – आकस्मिक बड़ी आपत्ति, दुर्गति

The excursive floods brought great catastrophe.

Catch/कैच *(verb)* – पकड़ना, थामना

Dravid caught a brilliant catch.

Catching/कैचिंग *(adj)* – संक्रामक, आकर्षक

It was an eye catching view.

Catchy/कैची *(adj.)* – आकर्षक छलने वाली

It is a catchy song.

Catechism/कैटकिज्म *(noun)* – ईसाई चर्च की मान्यताओं को सिखाने वाली प्रश्नोत्तरी

Principles of Christion religion are taught pen catechism.

Catechize/कैटकाइज *(verb)* – प्रश्नोत्तर विधि से पूछताछ करना

Students are instructed by using catechizing method .

Catechu/कैटिचू *(noun)* – कत्था, खैर

For tanning and dyeing a vegetable extract is used which is obtained from Indian tree acacia.

Categorical/कैटेगोरिकल *(adjective)* – सुनिश्चित, सुस्पष्ट

The answer was a categorically no.

Category/कैटगॅरी *(noun)* – समानवर्ग, व्यक्ति या वस्तुओं का वर्ग

So far as social status is concerned we belong to the same category.

Cater/केटर *(verb)* – आवश्यकताओं की पूर्ति करना

Don't worry a lot of people are here to cater to your needs.

Caterpillar/कैटरपिलर *(noun)* – कीड़ा, झिनगा

Caterpillars are beautiful to look at.

Cathectic/कैथेक्टिक *(adjective)* – रेचक, विरेचक

This powder is cathectic.

Cathedral/कथीड्रल *(noun)* – बड़ा गिरजाघर

The main church of a diocese where the bishop has his throan.

Catheter/कैथिटर *(noun)* – पेशाब कराने की नलकी

My friend could pass urine so they inserted catheter in his body through a thin opening and took out the fluid.

Catholic/कैथलिक *(adjective)* – उदारचित, सहिष्णु

My friend is of Roman catholic faiths.

Catling/कैटलिंग *(noun)* – जर्राही छुरी, नश्तर

Doctors use catling for amputation.

Catoptric/कैटोट्रिक *(adjective)* – दर्पण या प्रतिबिम्ब सम्बन्धी

In own student days we had done lots of catoptric experiments.

Cat's eye/कैट्स आई *(noun)* – लहसुनिया रत्न

My friend wears cat's eye. It suits him well.

Cattle/कैटल *(plural noun)* – गाय, मवेशी

This person has the greatest herd of cattle.

Caudal/कॉडल *(adjective)* – पूँछ का, पूच्छीय

Caudal growth in man disappeared a long time ago.

Caught/कॉट – पकड़ा

He was caught off mid wicket.

Caul/कॉल *(noun)* – रवेड़ी, शीर्षावरण, भ्रूण झिल्ली

The child has a caul of it around it in the womb.

Cauldron/काल्ड्रन *(noun)* – कड़ाही

The vegetables for the wedding guests are being cooked in a cauldron.

Cauliflower/कॉलिफ्लावर *(noun)* – फूलगोभी

I like cauliflower.

Causal/कॉजल *(adjective)* – हेतुक, कारण बताने वाला

The causal effect or rain was heavy floods.

Causility/कॉजिलिटी *(noun)* – कारणत्व

Without causility there can be no effect.

Causation/कॉजेशन *(noun)* – कारण उपस्थित करने का कार्य

The cause of his illness was being bitten by dangerous mosquitoes.

Causative/कॉजटिव *(adjective)* – कारण सूचित करने वाला, कारण वाचक, प्रेरणार्थक

The cause of his illness was being bitten by dangerous mosquitoes.

Cause/कॉज *(noun)* – ध्येय, अभिप्राय

Heavy clouds are the cause and rain its effects.

C

C

Causeless/कॉजलेस *(adj.)* – अकारण, निरुद्देश्य
This attack seems to be causeless.

Causeway/कॉजवे *(noun)* – बाँध
There is a causeway here, you can softly drive your car.

Caustic/कॉस्टिक *(adjective)* – रासायनिक क्रिया द्वारा वस्तुओं को जला देने में सक्षम, ताना भरा
Her caustic remarks upset him.

Caution/कॉशन *(noun)* – चौकस, विशेष सावधानी
Be cautious while taking that mud road.

Cautionary/कॉशनरि *(adjective)* – सचेत करने के रूप में दिया हुआ
There is a cautionary warning on the board.

Cavalier/कैवलियर *(noun)* – घुड़सवार
Cavaliers were soldiers fighting under a king.

Cavalry/कैवलरी *(noun)* – घुड़सवार लोग, घुड़सवार सेना
These are the cavalry soldiers who fought on a horseback.

Cave/केव *(noun)* – गुफा
As students we looked for caves and often went in.

Cavern/कैवर्न *(noun)* – कन्दरा, मांद
We were thrilled to explore a cavern.

Cavil/कैविल *(verb)* – बाल की खाल निकालना झूठी निन्दा करना
Women usually cavil.

Cavity/कैविटी *(noun)* – कंदरा, कोटर, गुहिका
Cavities decay a tooth.

Caw/कॉ *(noun)* – काँव-काँव करना
The crow was cawing harshly.

Cayenne/काइपन *(noun)* – बहुत तीता लाल मिर्चा
Some people have a fondness for too much chilli.

Cease/सीज *(verb)* – अन्त होना, रूकना बंद करना
When the rain ceased I stepped out of the house.

Ceaseless/सीजलेस *(adjective)* – निरन्तर, लगातार
Ceaseless rain fell and nobody could go anywhere.

Cedar/सिडार *(noun)* – देवदार का वृक्ष
I would like to have a cedar in my compound.

Cede/सीड *(verb)* – परित्याग करना
He ceded his lands to enemy forces.

Ceil/सिल *(verb)* – कमरे की ऊपरी छत बनाना
The mason is ceiling.

Ceiling/सिलिंग *(noun)* – घर की भीतरी छत
The ceiling of my room is white coloured.

Celebrate/सेलिब्रेट *(verb)* – उत्सव मनाना
We all took part in Holi celebration.

Celebrity/सेलिब्रिटी *(noun)* – कोई प्रख्यात व्यक्ति
Most film stars are celebrities.

Celerity/सिलेरिटी *(noun)* – शीघ्रता, वेग
He acted avid amazing celerity.

Celestial/सिलेस्टियल *(adjective)* – दिव्य, स्वर्गिक
One day we may begin to live on a celestial planet.

Celibacy/सेलिबेसी – कुँआरापन, शारीरिक सम्बन्धों से परहेज रखने वाला धार्मिक कारणो से ब्ह्मचर्य
Saints and faqirs often observe celibacy.

Cell/सेल *(noun)* – कोशिका, तहखाना
Prisoners are locked in cells .

Cellar/सेलर *(noun)* – भूमि के भीतर का घर, तहखाना
A stock of wine is usually kept in the cellar.

Cellular/सेल्यूलर *(adjective)* – जालीदार
Cellular phones have becomes so popular these days.

Celluloid/सेलुलाइड *(noun)* – कचकड़ा
Today we use celluloid for making toys make up material and toilet articles.

Cellulose/सेल्युलोज *(noun)* – कोशमय, वनस्पितियों की कोशिकाभित्तियों को बनाने वाला एक प्राकृतिक पदार्थ
Cellulose forms the solid framework of plants.

Cemetery/सेमट्रि *(noun)* – कब्रिस्तान
His body was buried in the cemetery.

Cense/सेंस *(verb)* – धूप देना
The grandmother burnt incense in the temple and it gave out aromatic smell.

Censer/सेन्सर *(noun)* – धूपदानी
We keep a censer in which incense is burnt.

Censor/सेन्सर *(noun)* – पुस्तक, फिल्म आदि से उन आपत्तिजनक अंशों को हटाना जो किसी की

भावनाओं को ठेस पहुँचाने की संभावना रखते हों

Censor is responsible for reaming any part of fiction or film which is objectionable to society.

Censeorious/सेन्सोरीअस *(adj)* – दोष निकालने वाला

He is very strict almost censorious.

Censorship/सेन्सरशीप – लाइसेन्स देने वाला पद

Censorship is a must even if it is a democratic country.

Censure/सेन्सर *(verb)* – निन्दा, अनुचित काम के लिए भर्त्सना करना

My father censured me over my rude behaviour.

Census/सेन्सस *(noun)* – जनगणना

Who live in a country, including information about their age job etc.

Cent/सेंट *(noun)* – एक सिक्का

I have so many cents but no dollars.

Centenarian/सेन्टनेरीअन *(noun)* – सौ वर्ष का वृद्ध पुरुष

My grandfather is a centenarian.

Centenary/सेन्टीनरी *(noun)* – शतवर्षीय समारोह

After 100 years we celebrate the centenary of many events of people.

Centennial/सेंटेनिअल *(adjective)* – सौवीं वर्षगाँठ, शताब्दी

When 100 years are complete of any event.

Center/सेंटर *(noun)* – कमर की पेटी

Ceiling fan was fixed in the center of the ceiling.

Centesimal/सेंटसिमल *(adjective)* – सौ-सौ करके गिना हुआ

These bundles are centesimal.

Centigrade/सेंटिग्रेड *(adjective)* – सौ अंशो में विभाजित

Water boils at 100°C.

Centigramme/सेंटिग्राम *(noun)* – एक ग्राम का सौवाँ भाग

One 100th part of a gram is called centigramme.

Centipede/सेंटिपीड *(noun)* – कनखजूरा

I am extremely afraid of centipedes.

Central/सेन्ट्रल *(adjective)* – प्रधान

In the crowd the heroine was of central attraction.

Centralize/सेन्ट्रलाइज *(verb)* – केन्द्र में करना

In a dictatorship power is centralized in the hands of the dictator.

Centre/सेन्टर *(noun)* – मध्य भाग

A centre forward player is the most important one.

Centrifugal/सेन्ट्रिफ्यूगल *(adjective)* – केन्द्र से हट जाने वाली

Centrifugal is the force which is tending to move away from the centre.

Centripetal/सेन्ट्रिपिटल *(adjective)* – केन्द्र की ओर जान वाली

A force which is moving towards the centre.

Centuple/सेन्ट्यूपल *(verb)* – सौगुना

100 is reduced to zero if multiplied by zero.

Century/सेन्चुरी *(noun)* – शताब्दी

Sachin has made so many centuries.

Cephalic/सेफालिक *(adjective)* – मस्तक सम्बन्धी

It is something cephalic and has nothing to do with other body parts.

Ceramics/सेरामिक्स *(adjective)* – मिट्टी से बना आग में पकाया हुआ

I bought a ceramics plate.

Cereal/सिअरिअल *(noun)* – अन्न सम्बन्धी, अन्य (चावल, गेहूँ आदि)

Cereals make carbohydrates in our body.

Cerebral/सेरिब्रल *(adjective)* – प्रधान मस्तिक सम्बन्धी, प्रमस्तिष्कीय

Cerebral part of his brain is very active.

Cerebrum/सेरिब्रम *(noun)* – मस्तिक का प्रधान भाग

Cerebrum is the main part of the brain.

Ceremonial/सेरिमोनियल *(adjective)* – विधि पूर्वक, रीति सम्बन्धी, औपचारिक, संस्कार

Marriage is a ceremonial affair.

Certain/सरटेन *(adjective)* – निस्संदेह, पक्का

I am certain that he will come.

Certainly/सरटेन्ली *(adverb)* – अवश्य, निश्चित रूप से

I'll certainly go to Shimla this summer.

C

Certificate/सर्टिफिकेट *(noun)* – प्रमाणपत्र
I have all my certificates enclosed in a file.

Certify/सर्टिफाइ *(verb)* – प्रमाण देना
It is certified that he has passed his 12th grade.

Certitude/सर्टिट्यूड *(noun)* – दृढ़, निश्चित होने का भाव
I have the certitude that he will pass the exam first class first.

Cerumen/सेरूमेन *(noun)* – कान का खूँट
The ear specialist took out a lot of cerumen from the ear.

Ceruse/सेरूज *(noun)* – सफेदा
Ceruse is the carbonate of lead.

Cervical/सरवाइकल *(adjective)* – ग्रीवा सम्बन्धी
His cervical pain has increased.

Cervine/सरवाइन *(adj.)* – हिरण के समान
Cervine is an animal resembling a deer.

Cess/सेश *(noun)* – कर लगाना
Heavy cess has been imposed on traders.

Cessation/सशेसन *(noun)* – समाप्ति
Cessation of the war brought peace.

Cession/सेशन *(noun)* – परित्याग
Cession by the defeated state ended the battle.

Chaff/चैफ *(noun)* – भूसा, हँसी उड़ाना
Chaff is mainly used on fodder.

Chaffer/चैफर *(verb)* – सौदा करना
It is the habit of ladies to chaffer.

Chagrin/शैग्रिन *(noun)* – तीव्र निराशा
She felt chagrined at having failed.

Chain/चेन *(noun)* – जंजीर, सिकड़ी
The chain of my cycle is broken.

Chair/चेयर *(noun)* – कुर्सी, सभापति
I have bought an easy chair today.

Chairman/चेयरमैन *(noun)* – सभापति
He is the chairman of our company.

Chaise/शेज *(noun)* – गाड़ी, आनन्द की सवारी
Chaise was very popular.

Chalice/चैलिस *(noun)* – प्याला
He drank from the chalice.

Chalk/चॉक *(noun)* – खड़िया मिट्टी
Teachers write with chalk on the blackboard.

Challenge/चैलेंज *(noun)* – माँग, दावा, चुनौती
He threw me a challenge for a boxing match.

Chamber/चेम्बर *(noun)* – कमरा
The meeting was held in a chamber.

Chamberlain/चैम्बरलिन *(noun)* – राज महल का प्रधान कर्मचारी
He looks after the affairs of the noble man.

Chameleon/कमीलियन *(noun)* – गिरगिट
Chameleons can change their colour according to the environments.

Chamois/केमोआयस *(noun)* – साबर, जंगली पहाड़ी हिरन
I have seen many chamois.

Champ/चैम्प *(verb)* – आवाज करते चबाना
He champed a lot while eating.

Champion/चैम्पिअन *(noun)* – वीर, योद्धा, विजेता
He is a champion into entering illegal lawsuits.

Chance/चांस *(noun)* – दैवयोग
You may succeed by chance who knows.

Chancel/चैंसल *(noun)* – गिरजाघर का पूर्वी भाग
The clergy is speaking from the chancel.

Chancellor/चान्सलर *(noun)* – कुलपति
He is our chancellor in Germany.

Chancery/चैंसरी *(noun)* – उच्च न्यायालय, दीवानी की बड़ी अदालत
Right now the case is in chancery.

Chancy/चांसी *(adj & noun)* – सन्देह जनक, अनिश्चित, जोखिम भरा
It is highly chancy that you will win this gambling game.

Chandler/चैंडलर *(noun)* – जहाज के समान बेचने वाला, मोमबत्ती बनाने एवं बेचने वाला
He is a chandler and deals in ship equipment.

Change/चेंज *(noun)* – परिवर्तन, रूपान्तर
There was a sudden change in the plan.

Changeable/चेंजेब्ल *(adjective)* – परिवर्तनशील, ढुलमुल
'Don't worry, this currency note is changeable.

Changelling/चेंजलिंग *(noun)* – बदला बच्चा
This child in a changelling.

Changing/चेंजिंग *(verb)* - बदलने वाला
The weather is changing fast.

Channel/चैनल *(noun)* - स्रोत, नाला
English channel joins two seas.

Chant/चैंट *(noun)* - गीत, भजन
People were chanting in a rhythmical and ritual way a mantra.

Chanter/चैंटर *(noun)* - वाद्ययन्त्र गायक
Scotsmen were playing on chanter.

Chanticleer/चैन्टक्लीर *(noun)* - पाला हुआ मुर्गा
In my dreams I saw fairies and chanticleer.

Chanty/शैंटी *(noun)* - मल्लाह गीत, मांझी गीत
I like chanty very much.

Chap/चैप *(noun)* - दरार, फटा होना
In winters her lips chap.

Chape/चेप *(noun)* - टोपी में का बन्द
The chape of my buckle is broken.

Chapel/चैपल *(noun)* - ईसाईयों का छोटा गिरजाघर
I prayed in a chapel.

Chaplain/चैपलेन *(noun)* - पादरी
I know a chaplain who is attached to a chapel.

Chapman/चैपमैन *(noun)* - घूम-घूमकर बेचने वाला व्यापारी, फेरीवाला
He is a poor chapmen.

Chapter/चैप्टर *(noun)* - अध्याय
I closed the chapter of my book as my mother called me.

Characterise/कैरक्टराइज *(verb)* - गुण व दोष बतलाना
Can you characterise this painting?

Characteristic/कैरेक्टरिस्टिक *(adj)* - अनोखा, विचित्र
I don't know its characteristies.

Charade/कैरेड *(noun)* - शब्द अनुमान करने की पहेली
I and my friend plagued charade and enjoyed it.

Charcoal/चारकोल *(noun)* - लकड़ी का कोयला
I drew a picture with charcoal stick of dark grey colour.

Charge/चार्ज *(verb)* - दाम माँगना
He charged me fifty rupees for carrying the luggage.

Charger/चार्जर *(noun)* - बड़ी रकाबी, बैटरी आवेशित करने का विद्युत यन्त्र
Please find my charger.

Charitable/चैरिटबल *(adj)* - धर्मात्मा, परोपकारी, दानी
This is a charitable dispensary.

Charity/चैरिटी *(noun)* - सहायतार्थ संस्था, दीन-दुखियों की सहायता करने वाली संस्था
He gives a lot in charity.

Charlatan/शार्लटन *(noun)* - जानकार होने का पाखंड करने वाला व्यक्ति, मायावी, छली
He is a charlatan and claims to possess knowledge which he doesn't have.

Charlock/चारलॉक *(noun)* - जंगली सरसों
The yellow flower of the charlock is worth seeing.

Charming/चार्मिंग *(adjective)* - रोचक, आकर्षक
He carries a magical charm with him.

Charnel-house/कारनेलहाउस *(noun* - कब्रिस्तान
I happened to see a charnel house. I was horrified to see so many corpse and bones there.

Chart/चार्ट *(noun)* - घटना या प्रगति की सूचना, रेखाचित्र
The records of Rihana have topped the chart this year.

Charter/चार्टर *(noun)* - शासन पत्र, अधिकार पत्र, किसी संगठन या व्यक्ति समुदाय के अधिकारों, विश्वासों और उद्देश्यों का लिखित दस्तावेज
Universities are created from the written charter of monarch.

Chary/चेअरि *(adjective)* - सावधान
I am chary of going to his home. Recently we had a fight.

Chase/चेज *(verb)* - किसी का पीछा करना, पीछ-पीछे भागना
The police chased the thief.

Chassis/चेसिस *(noun)* - किसी वाहन का धातु निर्मित चौखटा जिस पर अन्य पुरजे लगे होते है
The chassis of my car broke down.

Chaste/चेस्ट *(adj)* - सती, सादा, सीमित यौन सम्बन्ध
She is a chaste lady, keeping away from sex.

C

Chastise/चेस्टाइज *(verb)* – दण्ड देना, पीटना

His father chastised him for running from stool.

Chastity/चेस्टिटी *(noun)* – सतीत्व, संयम, शुचिता

Chastity is a virtue.

Chat/चैट *(noun & verb)* – बकवाद करना

Some birds are named chat which have a harsh chattering call.

Chateau /चैटेउ *(noun)* – देहात का मकान, फ्रांस में एक बड़ा महल या घर

For some time I was guest in a chateau with a French friend of mine.

Chatter/चैटर *(verb)* – वृथा की बकवाद, तेज गति से या निरर्थक किसी मामूली विषय पर बात करना

He chattered rapidly at a high pitch about small matters without stopping.

Chatty/चैटी *(adjective)* – बड़ा बकवादी

He is lively and fond of chatting.

Chauffeur/शोफर *(noun)* – दूसरों के लिए उसकी कार की नौकरी करने वाला, मोटर हाँकने वाला

I have tried a new chauffeur for my car.

Cheap/चीप *(adjective)* – सस्ता, कम कीमत

It is cheap low priced jewellery, imitated and of poor quality.

Cheapen/चीपेन *(verb)* – सस्ता करना

He cheapened the price so.

Cheat/चीट *(verb)* – छल, धूर्त

Don't get intimate with him, he is a cheat.

Check/चेक *(noun)* – एक रंगबिरंगी वर्गाकृतियों का पैटर्न

He wore a coat of check cloth.

Checker/चेकर *(noun)* – जाँच करने वाला a

There are so many checkers at metro stations.

Checkmate/चेकमेट *(noun)* – मात, शतरंज की अंतिम चाल जिसमें हार होती है

I made a move on the chess board and cried, 'checkmate'.

Cheek/चीक *(noun)* – गाल, कपोल, धृष्ट होना

He has reddish cheek.

Cheep/चीप *(noun)* – सीटी बजाना a shrill

The young bird cried 'cheep.'

Cheer/चिअर *(noun)* – खुश होना

These days in cricket matches you will usually find cheer-girls.

Cheerless/चिअरलेस *(noun)* – मन्द, उदास, खिन्नतापूर्वक

He is a sad silent cheerless fellow.

Cheerly/चिअरली *(adverb)* – प्रसन्नता से, खुशी से

He laughed cheerly.

Cheery/चिअरी *(adj)* – मगन, प्रसन्न

He is an ever smiling cheery fellow.

Cherub/चेरब – देवदूत, सुन्दर बालक

My little nephew looks like a cherup.

Chess/चेस *(noun)* – शतरंज

The two my uncle and father are busy playing chess and they would not get up till there is checkmate.

Chest/चेस्ट *(noun)* – वक्षःस्थल, सीना, पेटी, तिजोरी

There is birth mark on my chest.

Chesterfield/चेस्टरफिल्ड *(noun)* – लंबी गद्दीदार चारपाई

I have bought a chesterfield sofa.

Chestnut/चेस्टनट *(noun)* – अखरोट का फल या वृक्ष

I have a chestnut tree in my compound and I daily enjoy the roasted nuts.

Chevalier/शेवलियर *(noun)* – महाबीर, बहादुर, वीर पुरुष, घुड़सवार

Many great men have been awarded French orders of knighthood such as the legion of honour.

Chew/चिउ *(verb)* – दाँतो से चबाना, निरंतर डाँटकर झुँझला देना

We should bite small chew long so that the food digests easily.

Chic/चिक *(adjective)* – सुरुचि सम्पन्न, आकर्षक

I saw a chic young girl.

Chicane/शिकेन *(noun)* – चालाकी, दोहरा मोड़

As I looked down there has a wide chicane under me.

Chicken/चिकेन *(noun)* – मुर्गी का बच्चा

My grandmother has so many chickens.

Chide/चाइड *(verb)* – डाँटना या झिड़कना

The teacher chided me on coming late.

Chief/चीफ *(noun)* - नेता, सरदार, प्रधान पुरुष
He is the chief of our organization.

Chieftain/चीफटन *(noun)* - सेनापति, मुखिया, कबीला का सरदार
He is the chieftain of a clan.

Chiffon/शिफॉन *(noun)* - बारीक कपड़ा
My sister is fond of wearing chiffon sarees.

Chilblain/चिल्ब्लेन *(noun)* - हाथ या पैर की बिवाई, ठंड के कारण हाथ-पैर आदि पर बना दर्दीला चकत्ता
He is suffering from chilblain.

Child/चाइल्ड *(noun)* - बालक
I am fond of children.

Children/चिल्ड्रेन *(plural)* - बच्चे
Children are making a lot of noise.

Chill/चिल *(noun)* - सिहरन, ठंड,
He has been caught by chill.

Chilli/चिली *(noun)* - सूखी लाल मिर्चा
This vegetable is very chilli my mouth is burning please bring some water.

Chilly/चिलि *(adjective)* - बहुत ठण्डा और कष्टकर
It is ice all around. I am feeling chilly.

Chimera/किमीरा *(noun)* - असम्भव कल्पना
I hoped to buy a car but I found it a chimera.

Chimpanzee/चिम्पैंजी *(noun)* - अफ्रीका देश का वनमानुष
Chimpanzee are a lot of fun to see in the zoo.

China/चाइना *(noun)* - चीन देश का, चीनी
I have just bought some China crockery.

Chinese/चायनीज *(noun)* - चीन देशवासी, चीनी
He speaks Chinese well.

Chink/चिंक *(noun)* - झरोखा, दरार
He is a chink and I look down upon such people.

Chintz/चिंट *(noun)* - छींट, फूलों के प्रिंट वाला चमकीला सूती कपड़ा
Chintz is used for curtains and upholstery.

Chippy/चिप्पी *(noun)* - अरोचक
I went to a chippy to buy a fish.

Chips/चिप्स *(noun)* - भुने आलू का टुकड़ा
Many people are fond of chips.

Chirography/किइरोग्रफि *(noun)* - हाथ की लिखावट
His chirography is very good.

Chirology/किइरोलजि *(noun)* - हस्तरेखा विद्या
He is an expert in chirology.

Chiromancer/किइरोमैंसर *(noun)* - हस्तरेखा शास्त्री
I don't know any chiromancer.

Chirpy/चर्पी *(adjective)* - बकवादी
She is chirpy always talking and laughing.

Chirr/चर्र *(verb)* - चर-चर का शब्द करना
The bird mode a loud chirr sound.

Chisel/चिजल *(noun)* - छेनी, रूपानी
Carpenters use chisel for cutting wood.

Chit/चिट *(noun)* - छोटे कागज के टुकड़े पर संक्षिप्त लिखित टिप्पणी
Do you think I am going to talk to that chit of a girl.

Chitchat/चिटचैट *(noun)* - गपशप
We indulged in chitchat for a long time.

Chitty/चिटी *(noun)* - बच्चे के समान
She is sure a chitty gril.

Chivalric/शिवैलरिक *(adj)* - शिष्ट, विनीत
He is chivalric as well as handsome.

Chivalrous/शिवेलरस *(adj)* - शूर-वीर के समान
Everybody knows about his being chivalrous.

Chivalry/शिवेलरी *(noun)* - वीरता, शूरवीर के गुण
Chivalry is a custom of past now.

Chloride/क्लोराइड *(noun)* - क्लोरीन मिश्रित एक यौगिक
We daily take sodium chloride i.e., salt.

Chlorine/क्लोरीन *(noun)* - साँस घुटाने वाली एक गैस
Chlorine is a toxic chemical.

Chloroform/क्लोरोफार्म *(noun)* - बेहोश करने की एक प्रसिद्ध तरल औषधि
Before operations chloroform is given to patients so that they come unconscious thus insensitive to the pain of operation.

Chock/चॉक *(noun)* - लकड़ी का टुकड़ा
Chock is placed against a wheel to prevent it from moving.

C

Chocolate/चॉकलेट *(noun)* - कोको के बीजों से बनी भूरी मिठाई जिसे खाद्य पदार्थों को विशेष स्वाद देने के लिए भी प्रयुक्त किया जाता है, चीनी
Chocolate or chocolate drink is much liked by children as well as adults.

Choice/च्वाइस *(noun)* - चुनाव, छँटाव
I made the right choice between house work and job.

Choir/क्वाइअर *(noun)* - नाचनें वाली की मण्डली
Choir song was going on when we reached the church.

Choke/चोक *(noun)* - दम घुटना या घोंटना
Ths gas choked us.

Choler/कॉलर *(noun)* - पित्त, क्रोध
He is choleric by nature.

Cholera/कॉलरा *(noun)* - हैजा
He died of cholera.

Choleric/कॉलरिक *(adjective)* - पित्तज, क्रोधी
He has a choleric temperament.

Choose/चूज *(verb)* - चुन लेना
He chose a wrong career for himself.

Chopper/चॉपर *(noun)* - छोटी कुल्हाड़ी
He bought a chopper to kill his enemy.

Choral/कोरल *(adjective)* - गायक, मण्डली के एक साथ गाने से सम्बन्धित
Choral songs were being sung in the church.

Chord/कॉर्ड *(noun)* - वृत्त या वक्ररेखा के दो बिन्दुओं को मिलाने वाली रेखा, ताँत, चापकर्ण
The chord was struck and music rose up in harmony.

Chorion/कोरिअन *(noun)* - गर्भ की बाहरी झिल्ली
He took up research work in embryology.

Chorister/कोरिस्टर *(noun)* - गाने वाली मण्डली का सदस्य a member of a choir, especially a choir boy or choirgirl. *A beautiful chorister is leading the congregation.*

Choroid/कोरॉइड *(adjective)* - आँख की पुतली के भीतरी की झिल्ली
The pigmented vascular layer of the eyeball between the retina and the sclera is called choroid.

Chortle/कॉरटल *(verb)* - जोर से शब्द करना
He chortled when he heard the joke.

Chorus/कोरस *(noun)* - गायक दल
He sings in chorus.

Chrism/क्रिज्म *(noun)* - मलहम, पवित्र तेल
In church I was anointed with consecrated chrism.

Christ/क्राइस्ट *(noun)* - ईसा मसीह
Christ! What is that huge bloody thing.

Christian/क्रिश्चियन *(adjective)* - क्रिस्तानी
I have many Christian friends and I love all of them.

Christmas/क्रिसमस *(noun)* - ईसामसीह का जन्म दिन, बड़ा दिन
I took part in the National Christian festival which takes place on 25th December.

Chromium/क्रोमियम *(noun)* - एक धातु-विशेष
Do you know chromium a while hard metal is used in making stainless steel.

Chronic/क्रॉनिक *(adjective)* - दीर्घस्थायी पुराना
He is a chronic patient of asthma.

Chronicle/क्रानिकल *(noun)* - ऐतिहासिक घटनाओं का कालानुक्रमित लिखित ब्योरा, इतिहास, वर्णन
I went to the library to read some British Chronicle.

Chromograph/क्रोमोग्राफ *(noun)* - सूक्ष्म रीति से समय नापने का एक यन्त्र
Chronicles are recorded with the help of chronograph to help keep time accuracy.

Chronological/क्रोनोलोजिकल *(adj.)* - कालक्रम के अनुसार
A chronological record follows the order in which things occurred.

Chronology/क्रोनोलोजी *(noun)* - काल-निर्णय-विद्या
Professor consult chronology to find out in which order events followed.

Chronometer/क्रोनोमीटर *(noun)* - ठीक-ठीक समय बतलाने वाली छोटी घड़ी
Chronometer is very useful for weather specialists.

Chronometry/क्रोनोमिट्री *(noun)* - वैज्ञानिक रीति से समय की नाप
Some people study chronometry.

Chrysanthemum/क्राइसथेनमम *(noun)* – गुलादरऊदी का फूल

I am very much fond of chrysanthemum.

Chrysolite/क्राइसोलाइट *(noun)* – चन्द्रकान्त

The gemstone that I am wearing is made of chrysolite.

Chubby/चब्बी *(adjective)* – नाटा-मोटा

What a beautiful and chubby child!

Chuckle/चकल *(verb)* – मुँह बन्द करके हँसना

He chuckle at my joke.

Chucklehead/चकलहेड *(noun)* – मूर्ख मनुष्य

He is a chucklehead.

Chuckling/चकलिंग *(adj)* – मनोरंजक

It is a chuckling event.

Chum/चम *(noun)* – पुराना मित्र

You are my best chum.

Chump/चम्प *(noun)* – मूर्ख

He is a chump.

Church/चर्च *(noun)* – गिरजाघर

I go to church every Sunday as it offers public Christian worship.

Churl/चर्ल *(noun)* – देहाती

He is a churl and miserable person I avoid him.

Churn/चर्न *(noun)* – मक्खन बनाने का यंत्र

Churn the milk well and you'll get butter.

Chute/च्यूट *(noun)* – ढालू प्रणाल जिस पर वस्तुओं को सरकाया जा सकता है उन्हें उठाकर नहीं ले जाना पड़ता, वेग में जल का गिराव या उतार

Water went down the chute.

Cicatrize/सिकाट्राइज *(verb)* – सूज जाने वाले घाव का चिह्न

He has a cicatrize across his face.

Ciolar/सिओलर *(noun)* – सेब की शराब

British people drink ciolar made by fermenting apple juice.

Cigar/सिगार *(noun)* – चुरूट

Cigar is going out of fashion these days.

Cigarette/सिगरेट *(noun)* – सिगरेट कागज में लपेटा हुआ तम्बाकू

Cigarette smoking is very harmful.

Cilia/सिलिया *(plural)* – बरौनी

She has beautiful cilia.

Cilice/सिलाइस *(noun)* – भेड़-बकरी के रोवें का बना वस्त्र

In winter people wear cilice.

Cinchona/सिनकोना *(noun)* – कुनैन का पेड़

I had to eat malaria medicine cinchona for malaria fever.

Cincture/सिंक्चर *(noun)* – किनारा, कमरपेटी

I went to see a building being built. I found cinctures at either end of column shaft.

Cinder/सिन्डर *(noun)* – भस्म

We pulled out a cinder which seemed a piece of dead coal but it still had the combustible matter in it.

Cingalese/सिंगलिज *(noun & adjective)* – सीलोन का निवासी

Being a native of Ceylon.

Cinnabar/सिनाबार *(noun)* – सिंगरिफ, सिन्दूर

A married woman uses cinnabar.

Cinnamon/सिनामॅन *(noun)* – दालचीनी, दालचीनी का वृक्ष

I am fond of taste of cinnamon.

Cipher/साइफर *(noun)* – शून्य, गुप्त लिखावट

Your attainment of this year is cipher.

Circa/सर्का *(preposition)*– लगभग, चारों ओर

Born circa 150 B.C.

Circlet/सर्कलेट *(noun)* – छोटा वृत्त, मण्डल

I bought a beautiful circlet for wearing on my wrist.

Circuit/सर्किट *(noun)* – चक्कर, परिभ्रमण

The circuit of this building is about a mile.

Circuitous/सर्किटस *(adjective)* – कुटिल गतिवाला, चक्करदार

It is a circuitous way leading out of the jungle.

Circular/सर्कुलर *(adjective)* – गोल, समतल, वृत्ताकार, वर्तुलाकार

The circus animals moved in a circular path.

Circulation/सर्कुलेशन *(noun)* – परिभ्रमण, प्रचार

The circulation of this paper has gone up.

Circum/सरकम *(prep)* – चौकोर, चारों ओर

He has circumvented the difficulty.

Circumference/सरकमफरेन्स – मण्डल परिधि
Circumference stance of this dish is 5".

Circumscribe/सरकमस्क्राइब *(verb)* – घेरना, परिमित करना
He has been circumscribed for crossing the limit.

Circumsolar/सरकमसोलर *(adjective)* – सूर्य के पास या चारों ओर घूमने वाला
There are many in circumsolar stars in the galaxy.

Circumspect/सरकमस्पेक्ट *(adjective)* – सावधान
He is a very circumspect person.

Circumstance/सरकमस्टान्स *(noun)*– अवस्था
His circumstance did not allow him to pay back the loan.

Circumvent/सरकमवेंट *(verb)* – फँसाना, धोखा देना
He circumvented his opponent.

Circumvolution/सरकमवोल्यूशन *(noun)* – घुमाव
Many machines work on the basis of circumvolution.

Circus/सरकस *(noun)* – सरकस, खेल का गोल मैदान
The whole of our family went to see a circus show and we enjoyed it a lot.

Cirrus/सिरस *(noun)* – बालों के गुच्छे की आकृति का बादल
I saw a cirrus it was around a mountain peak and had streaks of lightning.

Cist/सिस्ट *(noun)* – कब्र, पत्थर का सन्दूक
I keep all my sacred utensils in a cist.

Cistern/सिस्टर्न *(noun)* – जलकुण्ड, जलाशय
I'll have to call a plumber because there is some problem with the cistern in the toilet.

Citadel/सिटाडेल *(noun)* – दुर्ग
Old forts used to have a citadel against protection from enemy.

Citation/साइटेशन *(noun)* – दृष्टांत, प्रमाण
Let me see a few citation of Mahatma Gandhis's autobiography.

Cite/साइट *(verb)* – प्रमाण देना
I will now cite a case to further strengthen my argument.

Citizen/सिटिजन *(noun)* – नागरिक
I am a citizen of India.

Citric/सिट्रिक *(adjective)* – नींबू की खटाई का
Lemon juice is citric in nature.

Citrine/सिट्रिन *(noun)* – निबुअई, पीला
I am wearing a citrine ring.

Citron/सिट्रन *(noun)* – जंभीरी नींबू, चकोतरा
This large lemon like fruit which is from citron tree will last at least a couple of days.

City/सिटी *(noun)* – नगर, शहर
I live in Patna city.

Civic/सिविक *(adjective)* – नगर या नगर से आधिकारिक रूप से सम्बन्धित नागरिक
A city or township is called civic with a local government.

Civil/सिविल *(adjective)* – जन सम्बन्धी, सभ्य
These are civil matter.

Civilization/सिविलाइजेशन *(noun)* – सभ्यता
As compared to old times, we are living in highly civilized society.

Civilize/सिवलाइज *(verb)* – सुधारना
He is a very social and civilized person.

Clack/क्लाक *(verb)* – खड़खड़ाहट, कर्कश शब्द
There was a clacking sound as the hammer hit the iron.

Claim/क्लेम *(verb)* – अपनी रकम माँगना
I claim this property to be mine.

Clamant/क्लेमेंट *(adjective)* – आवश्यक
'Please, sir, I am clamant to your attention for a second'.

Clamber/क्लाम्बर *(verb)* – कठिनता से चढ़ना
He clambered over the mountain.

Clamour/क्लेमर *(noun)* – रटन, माँग, चिल्लाहट
After the leader had spoken, there was a clamour noises in the crowd.

Clamp/क्लैम्प *(noun)* – पाहू, शिकंजा
You will find a lot of potato's and other vegetables under this clamp.

Clan/क्लान *(noun)* – जाति, दल
He is related with a monarchy clan.

Clandestine/क्लैंडेस्टाइन *(adjective)* – गूढ़ गुप्त
I don't like his clandestine ways which are of secret nature.

Clang/क्लैंग *(noun)* – झनझन का शब्द
Iron clanged against iron and there was a metallic noise.

Clank/क्लैंक *(noun)* – झनझन का शब्द
There was a clank as various machines started working.

Clannish/क्लानिश *(adjective)* – जाति का
I wanted to join their group but they acted clannish and kept me out.

Clanship/क्लानशिप *(noun)* – गोत्रत्व, सजातीयता
They are belong the same clanship.

Clansman/क्लैन्समैन *(noun)* – सजातीय व्यक्ति
We had less clansman and no women.

Clap/क्लैप *(noun)* – थप्पड़, ताली, गनोरिया, (यौन बीमारी)
Don't clap here, please.

Claptrap/क्लैपट्रैप *(noun)* – प्रसन्न करने के लिये शब्दों का प्रयोग, प्रसन्न करने हेतु ताली बजाना
Whatever you have talked so far is nothing but claptrap.

Clarence/क्लारेंस *(noun)* – चौपहिया बन्द गाड़ी
In old days Clarence was a popular mode of transport.

Clarification/कलैरिफिकेशन *(noun)* – स्पष्टीकरण
You owe me a clarification how did all this happen?

Clarify/क्लेरिफाइ *(verb)* – स्पष्ट करना, मैल हटाना
Will you please clarify your stand?

Clarity/क्लारिटी *(noun)* – स्वच्छता, सफाई
The clarity of his speech is appreciable.

Clash/क्लाश *(verb)* – झगड़ना, टकराना विरोध करना
The two cars clashed head on.

Clasp/क्लैप्स *(verb)* – बाँधना, लपेटना
He clasped my hand warmly.

Classic/क्लासिक *(adjective)* – प्रथम श्रेणी का
Some films and novels are classic. They do not fade with the passage of time.

Classify/क्लासिफाइ *(verb)* – श्रेणी में रखना
Some official documents are classified as secret or top secret.

Clatter/क्लैटर *(noun)* – झनझनाना, बकबक करना
The swords of the two warriors clattered together.

C

Clause/क्लॉज *(noun)* – कानून की उपवाक्य
There is a clause in contract that none of us can resign till this particular job is completed.

Clavicle/क्लॉविकल *(noun)* – हँसुली, हँसिया
As he fell down, he broke his clavicle.

Claw/क्लॉ *(noun)* – चंगुल, पंजा, नख
The claws of carnivorous birds are different from those of other birds.

Clay/क्ले *(noun)* – मिट्टी, कीचड़
Bricks and pottery are made out of the clay.

Claymore/क्लेमोर *(noun)* – दोधारी चौड़ी तलवार
They keep such swords in Scotland.

Clean/क्लिन *(adjective)* – निर्मल, स्वच्छ, शुद्ध
It is a clean place.

Cleanse/क्लिन्ज *(verb)* – साफ करना
She has been cleansed of her sins by a priest.

Clearance/क्लियरेंस *(noun)* – सफाई, रुकावट हटाना
Clearance sale! 30% rebate on every item.

Cleat/क्लिट *(noun)* – फन्नी, डट्टा
The cow was tied to this cleat.

Cleft/क्लेफ्ट *(noun)* – फटन, दरार
You can put your foot into that cleft and climb upwards.

Clemency/क्लेमेंसी *(noun)* – सरलता
Please sir, I plead for clemency.

Clergy/क्लर्जी *(noun)* – पादरी लोग
He is the finest speaking clergy in the church.

Clerical/कलेरिकल *(adjective)* – पादरियों का
He was offered a clerical job which he refused.

Clerk/क्लर्क *(noun)* – लेखक या मुंशी का पद
He is a clerk in an office.

Clew/क्लॉ *(noun)* – पाल का कोना
If you go into a labyrinth, don't forget to carry a clew so that you can find your way back.

C

Click/क्लिक *(noun & verb)*- खटका
She clicked her tongue as she saw the food on the table.

Client/क्लाइन्ट *(noun)* - मुवक्किल, ग्राहक
He is our best client deal with him very carefully.

Cliff/क्लिफ *(noun)* - चट्टान
Climbing cliffs is his favorites hoppy.

Climate/क्लाइमेट *(noun)* - जलवायु, ऋतु
Climate of Africa is hot.

Climax/क्लाइमेक्स *(noun)* - शिखर, चढाव
As the climax scene of the film approached, I felt very tense and my heart beat has been increased.

Climb/क्लाइम्ब *(verb)* - चढ़ना
He is a professional mountain climber.

Clime/क्लाइम *(noun)* - प्रदेश, देश, जलवायु
Summer climes in India are beautiful.

Clinic/क्लिनिक *(noun)* - चिकित्सालय
I went to doctor's clinic for a medical checkup.

Clink/क्लिंक *(noun)* - झनझन शब्द
They clinked the glasses together and drank.

Cloak/क्लोक *(noun)* - अँगरखा
I don't trust that man, he is covered in a cloak secrecy.

Clock/क्लॉक *(noun)* - घड़ी, मोजे के ऊपरी भाग पर रेशमी कढ़ाई का काम
The ornamental patterns over your stockings is beautiful.

Clod/क्लॉड *(noun)* - मूर्ख
He is a clod.

Clog/क्लॉग *(noun)* - विघ्न
The engine of the car is clogged.

Cloister/क्लायस्टर *(noun)* - मठ, विहार
He lives secluded cloister.

Close/क्लोज *(noun)* - परिणाम, अन्त
'God! I it was a close shave for me in the morning. As I was crossing the street a vehicle closely passed by me.'

Closely/क्लोजली *(adv)* - गुप्त रूप से, ध्यान लगाकर
I watched his movement closely.

Closeness/क्लोजनेस - छिपाव, समीपता
Too much closeness with anyone is unhealthy.

Closet/क्लोजेट *(noun)* - गुप्त कोठरी
I have a closet made up of teak wood.

Closure/क्लोजर *(noun)* - बन्द करने का कार्य
The closure of the shop will be at 8 p.m.

Clot/क्लॉट *(noun)* - थक्का, पिण्ड
A clot of blood blocked his artery and he died.

Clothe/क्लॉद् *(verb & noun)* - ढाँपना
I put on best of my clothes and went to the wedding.

Clotted/क्लॉटेड *(adj)* - घनीभूत
Clotted blood is a great danger.

Cloud/क्लॉउड *(noun)* - मेघ, बादल
Clouds make the sky beautiful at dawn or sunset.

Clough/क्लफ *(noun)* - कन्दरा, गुफा
The jungles was full of cloughs.

Clove/क्लोव *(noun)* - लौंग
The oil of clove has many medical uses.

Clown/क्लाउन *(noun)* - मसखरा, भाँड, असभ्य जन
All children liked the performance of clowns in the circus.

Club/क्लब *(noun)* - गदा, सफा
Club was a favourite weapon of him.

Clue/क्लू *(noun)*- विचारक्रम, सूत्र
Police found a clue and caught the gang of thieves.

Clump/क्लम्प *(noun)* - गुच्छा, जोर से पैर पटकना
The wounded animal hid itself in a clump.

Clumsily/क्लमंजिली *(adv)* - फूहड़पन से
She behaved clumsily.

Cluster/क्लस्टर *(noun)* - समूह (समुदाय), गुच्छा, भीड़
There was a cluster of ants around the piece of sweet.

Clutch/क्लच *(verb)* - पकड़ना, जकड़ना
Clutch the rope tightly, I am going to pull you up.

Clutter/क्लटर *(noun & verb)* - कोलाहल
The entire floor of the room was cluttered with a lot of broken and useless things.

Clyster/क्लाइस्टर *(noun)* - पेट में चढ़ाया जाने वाला पानी

Doctors used clysters to clean his intestines of all the excreta.

Coach/कोच *(noun)* - शिक्षक

We still remember our hockey coach of college days.

Coadjutor/कोएडजुटर *(noun)* - सहकारी, सहायक

He is a coadjutor in a church.

Coal/कोल *(noun)* - पत्थर का कोयला

It was very cold and we burnt a lot of coals to heat the room.

Coalition/कोअलिशन *(noun)* - संयोग, मेल

Our today's governments is a coalition government.

Coarse/कोअर्स *(adjective)* - सामान्य, घटिया, भद्दा

He seemed to be a country man. He was wearing coarse clothes.

Coast/कोस्ट *(noun)* - सीमा, समुद्रतट

There are some coasts very popular in European countries.

Coat/कोट *(noun)* - मर्दाना कोट, ढपना

He wore a blue coloured coat.

Coating/कोटिंग *(noun)* - रंग की तह

You have to give three coatings of paint to this room.

Coax/कोक्स *(verb)* - फुसलाना, बहलाना

I coaxed my friend into going to a movie.

Cob/कॉब *(noun)*- गोल डबल रोटी

Many Christians first pray and then eat the cob.

Cobalt/कोबाल्ट *(noun)* - गिलट के समान एक सफेद धातु

Cobalt in used in many alloys.

Cobby/कॉबी *(adjective)* - पुष्ट, तीव्र

He is strong like a cobby.

Cobra/कोब्रा *(noun)* - नाग, विषैला सर्प

We saw a cobra with its hood spread out. It looked ferocious but the snake charmer controlled it.

Cobweb/कॉबवेब *(noun)* - मकड़े का जाल, महीन जाली

The room was dirty, untidy and full of cobwebs.

Cocaine/कोकीन *(noun)* - कोकीन

Cocaine is used by many youngesters.

Coccyx/कॉक्सिक्स *(noun)* - रीढ़ की सबसे नीचे की तिकोनी हड्डी

It is the lowest small triangular bone at the end of spinal chord.

Cochlea/कॉक्लिआ *(noun)* - कान के भीतर का घोंघे के समान कोष्ठ

Inner part of the ear which responds to sound.

Cock/कॉक *(noun)* - नर चिड़िया, मुर्गा

You can see many cocks with vertical piles of hey and dung.

Cockboat/कॉकबोट *(noun)* - छोटी नाव

My cockboat has being towed by a ship as it had developed some defect.

Cockcrow/कॉकक्रो *(noun)* - अरुणोदय

He has the habit of rising at cockcrow.

Cockerel/कॉकरेल *(noun)* - छोटा मुर्गा

Our backyard is usually full of cockerel.

Cockpit/कॉकपिट *(noun)* - वायुयान में चालक कक्ष, मुर्गा लड़ने का अखाड़ा

When we were flying, I was very curious to see the cockpit but nobody was allowed there.

Cockroach/कॉकरोच *(noun)* - झींगुर

I don't know why, but when I look a cockroach I feel like vomiting.

Cockscomb/कॉक्सकम्ब *(noun)* - छैला

All male cocks have a cockscomb.

Cocksure/कॉकस्योर *(adjective)* - पूर्ण निश्चित

He was cocksure to clear the interview but then nothing worked out. He failed.

Coco/कोको *(noun)*- नारियल का पेड़

Our tropical tree is palm and it produces big nuts with water inside.

Cocoon/कॉकून *(noun)* - रेशम का कौवा

He found life so stressful that he sought the protective comfort of cocoon.

Cod/कॉड *(noun)* - कॉड नाम की समुद्री मछली

My favourite fish is cod.

Code/कोड *(noun)* - गुप्त भाषा, धर्म संहिता

While in school, we had our code words for almost everything.

C

Codger/कोजर *(noun)* – झक्की वृद्ध पुरुष

He is a codger. Many people become like that in old age.

Codicil/कोडिसिल *(noun)* – वसीयतनामे को तोड़ने का लेख

According to codicil, a part of the property will also go to deceased person's servant.

Codifier/कोडिफायर *(noun)* – कानून बनाने वाला

M.Ps are codifier.

Codify/कोडिफाइ *(verb)* – कानून बनाना

His full information has been codified.

Co-education/को-एडुकेशन *(noun)* – सहशिक्षा

For a healthy development students should study in co-educational institutes.

Coefficient/कोएफिशिअन्ट *(noun)* – गुणक

In 4xy, 4 is coefficient of xy.

Co-equal/को-इक्वल *(adjective)* – बराबरी वाला

I and my best friends are co-equals.

Coerce/कोअर्स *(verb)* – रोकना विवश करना

He coerced her into marrying him.

Coexist/को-एक्जिस्ट *(verb)* – एक ही काल में होना

In our society various members of the family coexist.

Coextensive/को-एक्सटेंसिव *(adjective)* – एक ही स्थान या समय में व्यापक

All people living today are coextensive.

Coffee/कॉफी *(noun)* – कहवा, काफी

My friend is so fond of a particular brand of coffee that he daily drinks four or five cups.

Coffer/कॉफर *(noun)* – पेटी, कोष, तिजोरी

The coffers of our government almost seem to be empty.

Coffin/कॉफिन *(noun)* – बक्सा जिसमें शव रक्खा जाता है

His dead body was placed in a coffin and carried to the crematorium.

Cog/कॉग *(noun)* – पहिये का दाँता धुरकीली

Cogs used to churn the water in medieval times.

Cogence/कोजेन्स *(noun)* – निश्चित शक्ति, विश्वस्त

He lacks cogence in this matter.

Cogent/कोजेन्ट *(adjective)* – प्रबल

His arguments were completely cogent.

Cogitate/कोगिटेट *(verb)* – ध्यान देना, विचार करना

He is given to cogitate over things.

Cognate/कॉगनेट *(adjective)* – सगोत्री

Hindi is very much cognate to Urdu.

Cognition/कॉगनिशन *(noun)* – अनुभव ज्ञान

We gain knowledge through cognition.

Cognizable/कॉग्निजेब्ल *(adj.)* – विचार के योग्य

Your argument is perfect cognizable.

Cognizance/कॉग्निजेन्स *(noun)*– ज्ञान, चेतना

Law has taken cognizance of this fact.

Cognizent/कॉग्निजेंट *(adj)* – सचेत

How was cognizant of his opponent.

Cohabit/कोहैविट *(verb)* – पति-पत्नी के समान सहवास करना

Most of the couples cohabit instead of marriage these days.

Cohesion/कोहीजन *(noun)* – संयोग, लगाव

The group acted in cohesion.

Cohesive/कोहेसिव *(adjective)* – एकता लाने वाला

This is a cohesive group of workers.

Coif/कॉइफ *(noun)* – टोपी, टोप

Nuns wear a coif which is a close cap covering top back and sides.

Coil/कॉइल *(noun)* – चक्कर, गेंडुरी

I arranged the loose threads into a coil.

Coin/कॉइन *(noun)* – मुद्रा, सिक्का

I have so many coins but no notes.

Coincide/को-इन-साइड *(verb)* – समान या अनुरूप होना, सहमत होना, ठीक-ठाक बैठना

We were together there at the same time by coincidence.

Coir/कॉइर *(noun)* – नारियल की जटा

I have some rugs and matting made of coir.

Coition/कोइशन *(noun)* – मैथुन, रति

Both the lovers indulged in coition.

Coke/कोक *(noun)* – पत्थर के कोयले को ठोस बनाना

Coke or cocaine is a dangerous drug.

Colander/कोलैंडर *(noun & verb)* – चलनी में छानना

I am in need of a colander.

Cold/कोल्ड *(adjective)* – जुकाम, सर्दी, ठंडा
I have caught cold.

Colic/कॉलिक *(noun)* – उदर-पीड़ा
I have severe colic pain, please take me to a doctor.

Collaborate/कोलेबोरेट *(verb)* – साथ-साथ काम करना
I want to collaborate you in this project.

Collapsible/कोलैप्सिब्ल *(adjective)* – सिकुड़ने या डूबने योग्य
This sofa set is collapsible it can be folded and kept in a small place.

Collapse/कोलैप्स *(noun & verb)* – क्षय, शक्ति ह्रास
The building suddenly collapsed.

Collar/कॉलर *(noun)* – माला, कण्ठा
My shirts collar is usually too dirty.

Collate/कोलेट *(verb)* – विस्तारपूर्वक तुलना करना
I worked in book binding shop and collated it.

Colleague/कलीग *(noun)* – सहायक, साथी
Many colleagues work with me in the office.

Collect/कलेक्ट *(verb)* – संग्रह करना
His job in the office was to collect mail.

Collected/कलेक्टेड *(adjective)* – शान्त
Throughout the proceeding, he remained calm and collected.

Collection/कलेक्शन *(noun)* – समूह, संग्रह
I have a big collection of newspaper photos regarding sport events.

Collective/कलेक्टिव *(adjective)* – एकीकृत
A collective effort was done to clean the old temple.

Collector/कलेक्टर *(noun)* – जिलाधीश
A tax collector collects taxes.

Collet/कॉलेट *(noun)* – नगीने की बैठकी
I have got my gem set in a beautiful collet.

Collide/कोलाइड *(verb)* – टक्कर खाना
The train collided with a truck at the railway crossing.

Collier/कोलियर *(noun)* – कोयला खोदने या ले जाने वाला
He is a collier by profession.

Collinear/कोलिनिअर *(adjective)* – एक ही रेखा में
If point A and point B are joined by a straight line, they are called collinear.

Collision/कॅलिजन *(noun)* – विरोध, टक्कर, मुठभेड़
The two ships were moving on a course of collision.

Collodion/कॉलोडिअन *(noun)* – तेजाबी रूई का चिपचिपा घोल
It is syrupy solution of nitrocellulose which if mixed with alcohol and ether is chiefly used in surgery.

Colloquy/कॅलक्वि *(noun)* – बातचीत
The colloquy between the persons did not seem to come to an end.

Collotype/कॉलोटाइप *(noun)* – फोटो का चित्र छापने की विधि
My friend uses the collotype process for making high quality prints.

Collude/कॉल्यूड *(verb)* – जाल रचना
They colluded together to form a conspiracy to kill the king.

Collusion/कॉल्यूजन *(noun)* – जाल, कपट
Both the bad characters were planning for collusion.

Collyrium/कोलिरियम *(noun)* – काजल, सुरमा
Our women use collyrium for eye colouring.

Colon/कोलोन *(noun)* – वृहदन्त्र, बड़ी आँत
Some persons develop ulcers in their colon.

Colonel/कोलोनेल *(noun)* – सैन्यदल का अध्यक्ष
My father was a colonel in the army.

Colonial/कोलोनिअल *(adjective)* – नई बस्ती का
She British had a big colonial empire.

Colonist/कोलनिस्ट *(noun)* – नई बस्ती में रहने वाला
In cities people usually live in colonies and can be called colonists.

Colonization/कोलोनाइजेशन *(noun)* – उपनिवेशन, नई बस्ती बसाने का कार्य
Britain had done the most colonization.

Colonize/कोलोनाइज *(verb)* – नई बस्ती बसाना
French, Dutch and Portuguese also tried to colonize India but the English men beat them to do it.

C

Colonnade/कॉलोनेड *(noun)* – खंभो या वृक्षों की पंक्ति
There are 12 colonnades in this hall which support the roof.

Colophony/कॉलफॅनि *(noun)* – रजन, राल
It is a kind of resin.

Coloration/कलरेशन *(noun)* – रंगने की कला का कार्य
There is something wrong with the coloration of this building, too bright colours.

Colorific/कलरिफिक *(adjective)* – दूसरे पदार्थ मे रंग लाने योग्य
This mixture of colours is rather colorific.

Colossal/कॉलाजल *(adjective)* – बड़ा दीर्घकाय
This is a colossal problem.

Colossus/कोलोसस *(noun)* – दीर्घकाय बड़ी मूर्ति
The statue of colossus was giant sized.

Colour/कलर *(noun)* – बहाना, आकृति, रंग
Almost all animals are colour blind.

Colour-bar/कलर-बार *(noun)* – गोरे मनुष्यों का सामाजिक भेद
In British rule there used to be colour-bar, there is none now.

Colouring/कलरिंग *(noun)* – रंगने का ढंग
M.F. Hussain was a master of colouring.

Colourist/कलरिस्ट *(noun)* – रंगसाज
My friend is a famous and great colourist.

Co-mate/को-मेट *(noun)* – साथी, सहचर
She is my co-mate. We live together.

Comb/कोम *(noun)* – कंघी
We should keep our combs clean.

Combat/कम्बैट *(verb)* – भिड़ना
The two forces were engaged in armed combat.

Comber/कम्बर *(noun)* – बाल सँवारने वाला
I got afraid when I saw the comber coming.

Combine/कम्बाइन *(verb)* – मिलाना
Various companies have combined to complete this project.

Combustible/कमबस्टिबल *(adj)* – ज्वलनशील उत्तेजक
This mixture is highly combustible.

Combustion/कमबसन *(noun)* – दाह, ज्वलन
Chemical combination with oxygen produces light and heat.

Comedian/कॉमीडियन *(noun)* – हँसाने वाला
Charlie Chaplin was a great comedian.

Comedy/कॉमिडी *(noun)* – सुखान्त नाटक
Most people prefer comedy to tragedy.

Comeliness/कॉमलिनेस *(noun)* – सुन्दरता
I like your comeliness.

Comely/कम्लि *(adjective)* – सुन्दर
She is a comely women.

Comer/कमअर *(noun)* – आने वाला
He is a late comer.

Comet/कॉमिट *(noun)* – पुच्छल तारा
I am so excited that tomorrow we shall see a comet. It is a bright celestial body with a long tail circling round the sun.

Comfit/कमफिट *(noun)* – मिठाई
I like comfits a lot.

Comfort/कम्फर्ट *(noun)* – सुख
I sat with comfort in the lounge.

Comic/कॉमिक *(adjective)* – हास्यकर
He had a very comic face which made us often laugh.

Coming/कमिंग *(noun)* – पहुँच
This coming Thursday.

Comity/कमिटि *(noun)* – शिष्टाचार
International comity is the need of the day.

Comma/कॉमा *(noun)* – अँग्रेजी मे छोटे विराम का चिह्न
A long sentence must be separated with commas.

Command/कमांड *(verb)* – आज्ञा देना
He is the commanding officer of this town's military.

Commandant/कमांडेंट *(noun)* – किले का अधिकारी
He is a commandant of the army.

Commander/कमान्डर *(noun)* – नायक
He is a commander in military.

Commanding/कमाडिंग *(adj)* – रोबदार
He was commanding troops in the battlefield.

Commemorate/कमेमोरेट *(verb)* – स्मरणार्थ उत्सव मनाना

Mahatma Gandhi is commemorated ejvry year on his birthday.

Commence/कमेंस *(verb)* – प्रवृत्त होना

The commonwealth games commenced at the scheduled time.

Commend/कमेंड *(verb)* – प्रशंसा करना

He was commended for his high efficiency in the office work.

Commensal/कमेंसल *(adjective)* – सहभोजी, एक ही पंगत में भोजन करने वाला

Commensal is an organism or creature living in partnership with mother.

Commensurable/कमेन्सुरेबल *(adj.)* – सदृश्य, अनुरूप सपरिमाण

Their performances are not commensurable.

Comment/कमेंट *(noun)* – टीका, समालोचना

He passed a comment on my nature which I did not like.

Commerce/कामर्स *(noun)* – वाणिज्य, व्यवसाय

Commerce between the two countries develops its relation.

Commiserate/कोमिजरेट *(verb)* – दया करना, करुणा दिखाना

I commiserated with my friend when his relative died.

Commissariat/कोमिसरियेट *(noun)* – सेना को रसद पहुँचाने का दफ्तर

Commissariat in military is an important unit.

Commessary/कॉमिसरी *(noun)* – डिप्टी, रसद भेजने वाला आफिसर

He is a commissary who has come from UK to our country.

Commissure/कोमिसर *(noun)* – दो पदार्थों का मिलन स्थान

The seam between the two bones has damaged, an operation is necessary.

Commit/कमिट *(verb)* – समर्पण करना, सौंपना

I am committed to serve the nation.

Committee/कमिटि *(noun)* – समिति

A committee appointed by a larger body does various works.

Commodious/कमोडिअस *(adjective)* – सुविधा का, उपयुक्त

It is a large and commodious room.

Commodity/कमोडिटी *(noun)* – उपयोगी वस्तु

I bought many commodities at home.

C

Common/कॉमन *(adjective)* – साधारण, सबके लिए सामान्य

We should all show common decency to one another.

Commonalty/कॉमनल्टि *(noun)* – प्रजा लोग

The commonalty does not like corrupt leader.

Commoner/कॉमनर *(noun)* – सामान्य मनुष्य

He looks glad, but he is neither an aristocrat nor a royalty, he is common like us.

Commotion/कमोशन *(noun)* – कलह, हलचल

There was great commotion in crowd over the remarks of the speaker.

Commove/कमूव *(verb)* – उत्तेजित करना

Don't commove the public.

Communal/कम्यूनल *(adjective)* – जातीय

Communal living is sharing the work and property.

Commune/कम्यून *(noun)* – संस्था, फ्रांस का एक विभाग

Commune is a communal settlement in a communist country.

Communicable/कम्यूनिकेब्ल *(adjective)* – प्रकाशित करने योग्य

I have written a article which is communicable.

Communicate/कम्यूनिकेट *(verb)* – कहना, देना

We have been communicating through letters for a long time.

Communication/कम्यूनिकेशन *(noun)* – कथन, व्यवहार

There are so many means of communication-railways, phones, computers. All of us make use of them.

Communion/कम्यूनिअन *(noun)* – साथ, सम्पर्क

An exchange of thoughts, sharing rituals, recognition and acceptance among between churches is called communion.

Communique/कम्यूनिक *(noun)* – सरकारी विज्ञप्ति

A communiqué was issued to the media by a party spokesman.

C

Communism/कम्यूनिज्म *(noun)* – साम्यवाद

I believe neither in socialism nor in democracy. I believe in communism where all property is vested in community and people give and receive according to their ability.

Community/कम्यूनिटी *(noun)* – मण्डली, समुदाय

Some people believe in community living sharing common interest and religion.

Commutator/कॉम्यूटेटर *(noun)* – बिजली की धारा का कम बदलने का यंत्र

It is a device to reverse the direction of current.

Commute/कॅम्यूट *(verb)* – अदल-बदल करना

We daily commute between our office and home.

Compact/कम्पैक्ट *(adjective)* – सट्टा, संधि

In the make up box, all the articles were compactly placed.

Companion/कम्पेनियन *(noun)* – सहचर

The railway journey was boring but luckily I found an interesting companion.

Compare/कम्पेअर *(verb)* – उपमा करना, तुलना करना

By compare, our school is for better than that one.

Comparison/कम्पीरिजन *(noun)* – उपमा, तुलना

I am comparing the two companies as to which to join.

Compass/कम्पास *(noun)* – दिशा सूचक यंत्र

In old times navigation was done with the help of compass.

Compassion/कम्पैशन *(noun)* – दया

We must have compassion for suffering of others.

Compendious/कम्पेन्डियस *(adjective)* – परिमित, संक्षिप्त सार

His lecture was brilliant it was so compendious that if gave a long explanations in very short.

Compendium/कम्पेन्डियम *(noun)* – संक्षेप, सार-संग्रह

I just bought a compendium I have so many friends to write to.

Compensation/कम्पेन्सेशन *(noun)* – हरजाना

When my friend was injured in a hockey game being played at state level, he was compensated generously. All the expenses of hospital and medicine were borne by the state.

Compensator/कम्पेनसेटर *(noun)* – क्षति चुकाने वाला

States and big companies for which the players play usually compensate for injury there.

Compete/कम्पीट *(verb)* – स्पर्धा करना, बराबरी करना

I competed in the race and won.

Compentence/कम्पीटेंस *(noun)* – योग्यता, गुण

His competence in playing the football is excellent.

Competent/कम्पिटेंट *(adjective)* – योग्य

He is competent of sitting in the civil services examination.

Competition/कम्पीटिशन *(noun)* – प्रतियोगिता

There is going to be a big sports competition and my brother in going to take part in it.

Competitive/कम्पीटिटीव *(adjective)* – स्पर्धा करने के कार्य से सम्बन्धित

He has a competitive nature always ready to competes. He wishes to prove that he is more desirable than others.

Compile/कम्पाइल *(verb)* – संग्रह करना

He is compiling a dictionary.

Complacent/कम्पलेसमेंट *(adjective)* – सन्तुष्ट

He is a complacent smug and only irritatingly satisfied with himself.

Complain/कम्प्लेन *(verb)* – शिकायत करना

I'll complain against your behaviour to the Principal.

Complaint/कम्प्लेंट *(noun)* – अभियोग

I have received so many complaints against you. What have you to say?

Complaisant/कम्प्लेसेंट *(adjective)* – अनुरोधी

He is a very complaisant person. He never minds the behaviour of others.

Complement/कम्प्लीमेंट *(noun)* – सम्पूर्णता

I gave her a complement on her performance on the stage.

Complete/कम्प्लीट *(adjective)* – पूर्ण, समाप्त

I maintain complete abstinence from alcohol.

Complex/कम्प्लेक्स *(noun)* – पेचीदा, जटिल

This is a complex machine complicate and intricate.

Complexion/कम्प्लेक्सन *(noun)* – स्वभाव, रंग-रूप

Her complexions is something to be seen to believe.

Complexity/कम्प्लेक्सिटी *(noun)* – जटिलता, पेचीदिगी

He enjoyed the complexity of modern computer.

Compliance/कमप्लायन्स *(noun)* – स्वीकृति

There is no compliance in his characteristic.

Compliant/कम्प्लायन्ट *(adjective)* – संकोची, आज्ञाकारी

My friend is very compliant. He will obey what ever is said to him.

Compliment/कम्प्लीमेंट *(noun)* – अभिनन्दन के वचन

My friend has the habit of paying compliment to everyone on some point or the other. Consequently he is very popular among people.

Comply/कम्प्लाई *(verb)* – स्वीकार करना

I'll comply with your wishers.

Component/कम्पोनेन्ट *(noun)* – साधक, अंग

A component of your machine is broken. It will take two hours to replace it.

Comport/कम्पोर्ट *(verb)* – सहमत होना, व्यवहार करना

He comports in a very peculiar way.

Compose/कम्पोज *(verb)* – टाइप बैठाना, रचना करना

His composition of music is excellent.

Composition/कम्पोजिशन *(noun)* – बनावट, साहित्यक रचना, लेख

A.R. Rehman is a great composer. His music composition won him an academy award.

Compost/कम्पोस्ट *(noun)* – यौगिक खाद

These days farmers use compost as a fertilizer.

Composure/कम्पोजर *(noun)* – शान्ति

Throughout the noise and quarrel he remained calm and composed.

Compound/कम्पाउन्ड *(noun)* – सन्धि करना, मिलाना, मिश्रित करना

The prisoners were free to move within the jail compound.

Compounder/कम्पाउन्डर *(noun)* – औषधि बनाने वाला

There are two compounder in this hospital.

Comprehend/कम्प्रीहेंड *(verb)* – समझना

I have comprehended your answer to my question sir.

Comprehensive/कम्प्रीहेंसिव *(adjective)* – समझने योग्य विस्तृत

Lecture of the professor from science academy was comprehensive.

Compress/कम्प्रेस *(verb)* – निचोड़ना, दबाना

Doctors compressed on the wound an absorbent material so as to stop bleeding.

Compromise/कम्प्रोमाइज *(noun)* – समझौता

Instead of fighting a long legal battle they compromised out of the court.

Comptroller/कम्पट्रोलर *(noun)* – हिसाब-नियन्त्रक

A comptroller is a financial officer.

Compulsion/कम्पल्सन *(noun)* – अनुरोध, दबाव

You are under no compulsion to talk to me.

Compulsive/कम्पल्सिव *(adjective)* – दबाव डालने योग्य

He is a alcoholic so it becomes compulsive irresistible for him to buy the the wine.

Compulsorily/कम्पलसरिली *(adv.)* – हठ से

It is compulsorily required by law not to drink or smoke in public.

Compulsory/कम्पलसरी *(adjective)* – अनिवार्य

It is compulsory to keep to the left while driving.

Compunction/कम्पक्सन *(noun)* – पश्चाताप

I felt great compunction for my behaviour.

Computation/कम्प्यूटेशन *(noun)* – गणना, परिकलन

He uses computer for the purpose of computation and study.

Compute/कम्प्यूट *(verb)* – गणना करना, लेख करना

He compute all his tough calculations on computer.

C

Comrade/कॉमरेड *(noun)* – मित्र, साथी

He is my comrade and we both belong to the same organization.

Con/कॉन *(verb)* – कण्ठस्थ करना, धोखा देना

He is a conman. He takes everyone into confidence and deceives him.

Conation/कॉनेशन *(noun)* – इच्छाशक्ति का प्रयत्न

He willed to go abroad and by going abroad he performed his will into action/conation.

Concave/कॉनकेव *(adjective)* – नतोदर, खोखला

A concave mirror's surface curves inside like the interior of a circle.

Conceal/कानसील *(verb)* – गुप्त रखना, छिपाना

The thief concealed the goods into a pit.

Concede/कनसीड *(verb)* – स्वीकार करना

I must concede that you are speaking the truth.

Conceivable/कन्सीवेब्ल *(adjective)* – विचारणीय

His wishes are conceivable.

Conceive/कन्सीव *(verb)* – गर्भधारण करना

She has conceived and all the members of the family are very happy.

Concentrate/कन्सेंट्रेट *(verb)* – एक केन्द्र में लाना, एकाग्र

He is concentrated on his studies.

Concentric/कन्सेंट्रिक *(adjective)* – एक केन्द्र का

He draw arcs and circles which concentric.

Concept/कन्सेप्ट *(noun)* – सामान्य विचार

I have a concept which will increase the sale of our commodity.

Concern/कन्सर्न *(noun)* – व्यापार

Nokia is big concern.

Concert/कन्सर्ट *(noun)* – योग, मेल योग, संगीत

A music concert was held in Kala Bhawan.

Concession/कन्सेशन *(noun)* – सुविधा प्रदान, छूट

The company amended 30% concession on its garments.

Conciliate/कन्सिलियेट *(verb)* – शान्त करना

I acted as a conciliator and pacified the two quarrelling friends.

Concise/कन्साइज *(adjective)* – संक्षिप्त अल्प

His information was concise and to the point.

Concision/कन्सीजन *(noun)* – खतना, मुसलमानी

Concision is the religious act of Muslim.

Conclave/कन्क्लेव *(noun)* – गुप्त बैठक या सभा, स्थान

A conclave was being held regarding the election of a pope.

Conclude/कन्क्लूड *(verb)* – समाप्त करना

The meeting was concluded on a note of harmony.

Concluding/कन्क्लूडिंग *(adj)* – अन्तिम, आखिरी

This line is concluding line.

Conclusion/कन्क्लूजन *(noun)* – समाप्ति

I have reached the right conclusion.

Conclusive/कन्क्लुसिव *(adjective)* – निर्णायक

It is conclusive that I will not sell my land.

Concomitance/कन्कमिटैंस *(noun)* – समन्वय

Now there is concomitance between the two families.

Concord/कनकॉर्ड *(noun)* – एकता

A concord was signed between the two countries.

Concourse/कॉनकोर्स *(noun)* – समूह

A big concourse gathered in the ground.

Concubinage/कन्क्यूबिनेज *(noun)* – वेश्यापन

Concubinage is when a state is given a lesser importance.

Conculate/कन्क्यूलेट *(verb)* – पैरों से कुचलना

The elephant conculate the man.

Condemn/कंडेम *(verb)* – निन्दा करना

I condemn your words.

Condensation/कन्डेन्सेशन *(noun)* – जमाव

In our [chemistry] lab, we used to convert vapour or gas into a liquid.

Condense/कन्डेन्स *(verb)* – घना करना

What I say will be condensed.

Condole/कन्डोल *(verb)* – दुःख में सहानुभूति प्रकट करना

I condoled him on his sickness.

Conduce/कन्ड्यूस *(verb)* – प्रवृत्त करना, उत्पादन करना

I conduced my friend in getting well.

Conduct/कन्डक्ट *(noun & verb)* – निर्वाह, व्यवहार, आचरण

He conducts himself gracefully.

Conduit/कन्डुइट *(noun)* – जल-प्रणाली

I bought a conduit pipe from the market.

Cone/कोन *(noun)* – शंकु

Traffic cones are usually placed on busy roads.

Coney/कोनी *(noun)* – एक प्रकार का खरगोश

They have gone out to hunt a coney.

Confection/कन्फेक्शन *(noun)* – मिठाई

I am very fond of confection.

Confideracy/कन्फिडरेसी *(noun)* – सन्धि

US is made up of confideracy.

Confer/कन्फर *(verb)* – देना, प्रतिपादन करना, सलाह करना

He was conferred the title of 'sir'.

Conference/कन्फरेंस *(noun)* – सम्मेलन

Many conferences took place in Delhi.

Confess/कन्फेस *(verb)* – स्वीकार करन

The priest heard the confession as he declared his sins to him.

Confidant/कन्फिडेंट *(noun)* – विश्वासपात्र

I always confide in my sister, she is my confidant.

Confide/कन्फाइड *(verb)* – रहस्य करना

Let me confide in you what I have gone through.

Confidence/कन्फिडेंस *(noun)* – आशा

I have full confidence in you.

Confiding/कन्फायडिंग *(adj)* – विश्वस्त

US has so many confiding agents.

Confidential/कन्फिडेंसिअल *(adjective)* – गुप्त, विश्वास

It is a confidential file, keep it in locker.

Confine/कन्फाइन *(noun & verb)* – सीमा-प्रान्त

He was confined to four walls of jail.

Confirm/कन्फर्म *(verb)* – प्रमाणित करना e

I confirmed his statement.

Confiscate/कन्फिस्केट *(verb)* – जब्त करना

His whole property was confiscated by order of magistrate.

Conflict/कन्फ्लिक्ट *(noun)* – युद्ध, विरोध

The two friends had conflict of opinion and they separated.

Conflux/कन्फलक्स *(noun)* – संगम, भीड़

At Allahabad Sangam there is a conflux of holy rivers.

Conformity/कन्फॉरमिटी *(noun)* – समानता

I live in conformity with the law of land.

Confraternity/कन्फ्रैटरनिटी *(noun)* – भाईचारा, बंधुत्व

We have formed a confraternity for a charitable purpose.

Confuse/कन्फ्यूज *(verb)* – व्याकुल करना, घबराना, भ्रमित

He is a confused man who does not know what to speak.

Confusion/कन्फ्यूजन *(noun)* – व्याकुलता

There was confusion in the entire meeting.

Confute/कन्फ्यूट *(verb)* – असिद्ध करना, झूठा सिद्ध करना

I was confuted in the meeting.

Conge/कन्ज *(noun)* – विदाई

He had to face conge.

Congeal/कन्जील *(verb)* – गाढ़ा करना

The blood flowing from his wound soon congealed.

Congener/कांजिनर *(noun)* – समान, राजनीति

Both plants are congener i.e. of the same category.

Congenial/कन्जेनिअल *(adjective)* – सहानुभूति, स्वास्थ्यकर या वंश

I find this wine very congenial.

Congenital/कन्जेनिटल *(adjective)* – जन्मजात

He cannot walk properly, it is something congenital.

Conglomerate/कन्गलोमरेट *(adj)* – एक पिण्ड

We have many corporations in India which are conglomerated by a merger of separate firms.

Conglutinate/कन्ग्लूटिनेट *(verb)* – सरेस से चिपकाना या बैठाना

These two pieces are conglutinated.

C

Congratulate/कांग्रेचुलेट *(verb)* – धन्यवाद देना, बधाई देना

I congratulated my friend on his success.

C

Congregate/कांग्रेगेट *(verb)* – एकत्रित करना

A big crowd congregated in the hall.

Congruent/कांग्रूएन्ट *(adjective)* – योग्य, अनुरूप

These two pictures are not congruent.

Conjoin/कन्जोवाइन *(verb)* – संयुक्त करना

All of us conjoined to form a meeting.

Conjugate/कन्जुगेट *(verb)* – विवाह करना, सम्भोग करना

These couples are not conjugated.

Conjunct/कन्जंक्ट *(adjective)* – संयुक्त

An adverbial clause is conjuncted to the main clause by conjunction.

Conjunctiva/कन्जक्टाइवा *(noun)* – आँख के भीतरी भाग की झिल्ली

There was some trouble with my conjunctiva so I consulted a doctor.

Conjunctive/कन्जक्टिव *(adjective)* – जोड़ने वाला

A conjunctive joins two or more sentences.

Conjuncture/कन्जक्टर *(noun)* – संयोग, घटना, अवसर

There is a conjuncture among the event of various companies.

Conjure/कन्ज्योर *(verb)* – निष्ठापूर्वक अनुरोध करना

The magician conjures up a ghost.

Connect/कनेक्ट *(verb)* – संयुक्त मिलाना

We two friends are connected together by means of chatting over computer.

Connivance/कनाइवेंस *(noun)* – उपेक्षा

It was a robbery committed with the connivance of police.

Connive/कनाइव *(verb)* – आँख मारना

We connived against the leader of the opposition group.

Connote/कॉनोट *(verb)* – अर्थ सूचित करना

The word tropics connotes heat.

Conquer/कॉन्कर *(verb)* – विजय करना

Babur conquered a state of India.

Conquest/कॉन्क्वेस्ट *(noun)* – विजय, बलपूर्वक किसी देश के अधीन करना

The conquest of Everest was a historial events.

Conscience/कॉन्-शन्स् *(noun)* – अन्तःकरण, विवेक

He is a man of high conscience.

Conscious/कॉन्-शस् *(adjective)* – सचेत

I was conscious that someone was following me.

Consecrate/कन्सिक्रेट *(verb)* – संस्कार करना

After being consecrated he was ordained a bishop's life.

Consecutive/कन्सेक्यूटिव *(adjective)* – निरन्तर

Adverbial clause of consequences shows result.

Consensus/कनसेंसस *(noun)* – एकमत, अनुकूलता

A consensus was reached in the general meeting.

Consent/कन्सेंट *(verb)* – सहमत होना

She has consent in this matter.

Consentient/कन्सेंटियन्ट *(adjective)* – एकचित

She has no consentient opinion.

Consentingly/कन्सेंटिंग्ली *(adv)* – सम्मति पूर्वक

She consentingly looked at him.

Consequent/कन्सिक्वेंट *(adjective)* – अनुयायी

His consequent efforts brough success to him.

Conservation/कन्जरवेशन *(noun)* – सुरक्षित रखने का कार्य

Conservation of wildlife and trees is a must today.

Conservative/कन्जरवेटिव *(adjective)* – स्थिति पालक, लकीर का फकीर

My granddad is very conservative. He is averse to everything new.

Conservator/कन्जरवेटर *(noun)* – रक्षक पालक

He has vowed himself to to conservative work.

Conserve/कन्जर्व *(noun)* – अचार, मुरब्बा

My father preserves most things. He protects things from harm or destruction.

Consideration/कन्सिडरेशन *(noun)* –विचार-विर्मश

After much consideration I have decided to join your party.

Considering/कन्सिडरिंग *(prep)* – समझते हुए

Considering her wishes, I took her to a fivestar hotel.

Consign/कन्साइन *(verb)* – सौंपना, देना

My consignment from Hong Cong is to arrive by the end of the month.

Consist/कन्सिस्ट *(verb)* – रहना, होना, मिलना

Tea consists of sugar milk and tea leaves.

Consolation/कन्सोलेशन *(noun)* – आश्वासन, ढाढस

My friend and many people consoled me over my loss.

Consolatory/कन्सोलेटरी *(adj)* – सान्त्वना देने की प्रवृत्ति वाला

He is a man of consolatory nature only.

Console/कन्सोल *(verb)* – ढाढस देना

I consoled to my friend for best result.

Consonance/कन्सोनैन्स *(noun)* – अविरोध

He always do his work with his consonance.

Consonant/कन्सोनैन्ट *(adj)* – अनुरूप

There are five vowels and 21 consonants in English alphabet.

Consort/कॉन्सॉर्ट *(noun)* – संगी, साथी

There are many consorts in the parl.

Conspecific/कन्सपेसिफिक *(adjective)* – एक जाति का

Apes and monkeys belong to the same conspecific.

Conspectus/कन्सपेक्टस *(noun)* – सामान्य दृश्य

The professor gave a long conspectus.

Conspicuous/कन्सपिक्यूअस *(adjective)* – प्रत्यक्ष

He was conspicuous by his absence.

Conspiracy/कन्सपिरेसी *(noun)* – कपट-प्रबन्ध

When some people plan to do something bad is called conspiracy.

Conspirator/कन्सपिरेटर *(noun)* – राजद्रोही

Cassius was the main conspirator against Cancer.

Constable/कन्सटेबल *(noun)* – पुलिस का सिपाही

A police officer of the lowest rank.

Constancy/कन्सटैन्सी *(noun)* – स्थिरता

He has the quality of constancy.

Constant/कॉन्सटैंट *(adjective)* – स्थिर

He is very constant in his work.

Constellation/कन्सटिलेशन *(noun)* – नक्षत्र मण्डल

Do you see that constellation in the sky you can locate it any time because it retains its fixed pattern these are seven stars named after a Rishi.

Constipate/कन्स्टिपेट *(verb)* – अवरोध करना

He is suffering from constipation as such he has to take a laxative.

Constituency/कन्सीच्यूएन्सि *(noun)* – निर्वाचन क्षेत्र

He is a constituency member and has great power.

Constituent/कन्सीट्यूएन्ट *(adjective)* – रचने वाला, निर्वाचक

A state is governed by its constituent it has the power to appoint or elect.

Constitute/कंस्टीट्यूट *(verb)* – नियुक्त करना, स्थापित करना, निर्माण करना

It does not constitute according to law.

Constitutive/कन्सीट्यूटिव *(adjective)* – आवश्यक, संगठन सम्बन्धी

Having the power to constitute.

Constrict/कन्सट्रिक्ट *(verb)* – दबाना

He constricted the doors bell.

Constringe/कन्सट्रियेज *(verb)* – सिकोड़ना

I constringed my clothes.

Construct/कन्सट्रक्ट *(verb)* – खींचना

My friend has constructed a huge building.

Construe/कन्सट्रयू *(verb)* – परिच्छेद करना, व्याख्या करना

My friend construed a piece of English from word to word in Hindi.

Consul/कन्सल *(noun)* – वाणिज्य दूत

If you have any problem, consult your consul.

Consult/कॅन्सल्ट *(verb)* – सूचना प्राप्त करना

At once consult a doctor for your disease.

Consumption/कन्जम्पशन *(noun)* – उपभोग

That man consumed a lot of food.

Contact/कन्टैक्ट *(noun & verb)* – सम्पर्क, संयोग, लगाव

I will contact you soon.

Contagion/कंटेजन *(noun)* – छूत का रोग

Close contact is responsible for contagion which is disease of spread by communication.

C

Contagious/कन्टेजिअस *(adjective)* – स्पर्श से रोग फैलाने वाली

People suffering from contagious disease spread this directly or indirectly.

Contain/कन्टेन *(verb)* – रखना, धरना, बराबर होना

My medicines are contained in this box very carefully.

Contaminate/कन्टैमिनेट *(verb)* – दूषित करना

Flies contaminate food.

Contemn/कण्टेम् *(verb)* – घृणा करना

I look at him with contemn.

Contemplate/कन्टेम्प्लेट *(verb)* – विचार करना, चिन्तन करना

To anticipate, to intent, to medicate. I contemplated this exercise for understanding.

Contemporaneous/कन्टैम्पोरेनियस *(adjective)* – समकालीनता

Lord Mohan's and Buddha were contemporaneous.

Contemporary/कन्टेम्पोरैरी *(adjective)* – समकालिक

Gandhiji and Vinoba Bhave were contemporaries.

Contempt/कन्टेम्प्ट *(noun)* – तिरस्कार, अनादर, अपमान

The judge said it is contempt of court and gave suitable punishment to the offender.

Contemptuous/कन्टेम्प्टयूअस *(adjective)* – घृणित, तिरस्कार युक्त

I had nothing but contempt for him.

Content/कन्टेन्ट *(adjective)* – सन्तुष्ट, प्रसन्न

I am content with my state of offers.

Contention/कन्टेन्शन *(noun)* – विवाद

A contention took place between the two friends.

Contest/कॉण्टेस्ट *(noun)* – प्रतिस्पर्धा

There was a boxing contest between the two boxers.

Context/कन्टेक्स्ट *(noun)* – प्रकरण, संदर्भ

After the event the provident said in this context that more such friendly matches will be hold.

Continence/कन्टिनेन्स *(onun)* – संयम, आत्मनियंत्रण

Continence is a must.

Continent/कन्टिनेन्ट *(noun)* – महाद्वीप

India is a big continent.

Contingency/कन्टिन्जेन्सी *(noun)* – आकस्मिक घटना

You are going to face a contingency friend but it will do you good.

Contingent/कन्टिजेन्ट *(adjective)* – संदिग्ध

A contingent of police was sent to help a larger group.

Continual/कन्टिन्यूअल *(adjective)* – सतत

He is continually late.

Continue/कन्टिन्यू *(verb)*– जारी करना

I'll continue carrying on in the same direction till I find the old temple.

Continuity/कन्टिन्यूइटी *(noun)* – निरन्तरता होने की अवस्था

The film was good but it lacked continuity.

Continuous/कन्टिन्यूअस *(adjective)* – लगातार

Yuvraj hit six sixers continuously.

Contour/कॉन्टूर *(noun)* – पर्वत, समुद्र तट आदि की परिधि की रेखा

The clay was given a definite contour and it looked beautiful.

Contraception/कन्ट्रासेप्सन *(noun)* – गर्भ अवरोध

There are so many contraceptions available in these days.

Contract/कन्ट्रैक्ट *(noun)* – संविदा

I have one year's contract with him more than I will be free.

Contradistinction/कन्ट्राडिस्टिंक्शन *(noun)* – विपक्षता

If you compare and contrast the two players, the destination will become clear.

Contrariety/कन्ट्राराइटी *(noun)* – प्रतिकूलता

There is contrariety and inconsistency between the two matches.

Contrariwise/कन्ट्रैरीवाइज *(adverb)* – विपरीत

This team is good but contrariwise the batsmen of the other team are far superior.

Contrary/कन्ट्रैरी *(adjective)* – प्रतिकूल

I am contrary to his nature. So we can't become friends.

Contrast/कन्ट्रास्ट *(noun)* - अन्तर

Black is in sharp contrast to white.

Contribute/कन्ट्रिब्यूट *(verb)* - सहायता देना

Others with Mahatma Gandhi contributed a lot to bring freedom.

Contrite/कन्ट्राइट *(adjective)* - शोकार्त

My friend has left for USA and I am feeling rather contrite.

Contrivable/कन्ट्रीवेब्ल *(adj)* - निर्माण

I am contrivable this building.

Contrivance/कन्ट्राइवेन्स *(noun)* - आविष्कार

We can contrive the problem by putting a dam over the river. This contrivance is sure going to work.

Control/कन्ट्रोल *(noun)* - निग्रह

I have full control over events.

Controllable/कन्ट्रोलेब्ल *(adj)* - वश में करने योग्य

He was not controllable.

Controller/कन्ट्रोलर *(noun)* - अध्यक्ष

He is the controller of this ship.

Controversy/कन्ट्रोवर्सी *(noun)* - प्रतिवाद

This is a controversy topic going on for a long time.

Controvert/कन्ट्रोवर्ट *(verb)* - अस्वीकार करना

I will not controvert the truth of this statement.

Contuse/कन्ट्यूज *(verb)* - कुचलना

He was contused by a car.

Conundrum/कोनन्ड्रम *(noun)* - पहेली

Delhi is a conundrum city.

Convalesce/कन्वैलेस *(verb)* - पुनः स्वस्थ होना

He has just recovered he is a convalescent.

Convection/कनवेक्शन *(noun)* - बिजली की शक्ति का एक स्थान से दूसरे स्थान का संवाहन

Convection current.

Convene/कन्विन *(verb)* - बटोरना

All you people have been called to convene in the hall.

Convenience/कन्वेनियंस *(noun)* - आराम

It is for your convenience, please.

Conventicle/कन्वेंटिकल *(noun)* - धर्मसभा

Non conformists need to hold such conventicle in old times.

Convention/कन्वेन्शन *(noun)* - सभा

It is a convention in our country to touch our elders' feet.

Conventual/कन्वेन्युअल *(adjective)* - मठ-सम्बन्धी

My sister lives in a convent. She is a nun.

Conversable/कन्वर्सेब्ल *(adj)* - वार्ता करने योग्य

It is conversable matter.

Conversant/कन्वर्सेंट *(adjective)* - परिचित

We were conversant together where he interfered.

Conversation/कन्वरसेशन *(noun)* - बातचीत

A conversation between the two leaders is going on.

Converse/कन्वर्स *(verb)* - सम्भाषण करना

I will converse with you after the office hours.

Conversion/कन्वर्सन *(noun)* - रूपान्तर

Conversion has taken place in this building.

Convert/कन्वर्ट *(verb)* - बदलना

Hydrogen and Oxygen can be converted into water.

Convex/कन्वेक्स *(adjective)* - उन्नतोदर

Convex mirrors are often used in transport vehicles.

Convey/कन्वे *(verb)* - पहुँचाना

I have conveyed your message to your friend.

Conviction/कन्विक्शन *(noun)* - दोषसिद्धि

He has been convicted to 10 years of imprisonment.

Convince/कन्विन्स *(verb)* - निश्चय कराना

I told him that one must follow the rules of the land after some argument he was convinced.

Convivial/कन्वाइवल *(adjective)* - उत्सव-सम्बन्धी

He is convivial fellow.

Convocation/कन्वोकेशन *(noun)* - समागम

He got the university award at convocation.

Convoke/कन्वोक *(verb)* - पुकारना

I convoke him.

Convolve/कन्वल्व *(verb)* - लपेटना

He convolved the roll together into a ball.

Convoy/कन्वॉय *(verb)* - सुरक्षित ले जाना

I call him to convoy this cloths.

C

Cony/कोनी *(noun)* - खरहा
I saw a cony.

Coo/कू *(noun)* - कबूतर की तरह गुटकना
She cooed into my ear and I loved it very much.

Cook/कूक *(noun)* - रसोइया
She is an expert cook and the credit goes to her for preparing some new dishes also.

Cook-house/कूक-हाउस *(noun)* - घर के बाहर की पाकशाला
Let's go to cook house to eat something.

Cool/कुल *(adjective)* - शीतल, शान्त
His behaviour was cool and unenthusiastic.

Coolie/कूली *(noun)* - मजदूर
Call that coolie he will carry our bag and baggage.

Coop/कूप *(noun)* - मुर्गी के ढाँकने की टोकरी
All poultry is confined in this rather small coop.

Cooper/कूपर *(noun)* - नाद बनाने वाला
Coopers make or repair casks and barrels.

Co-operant/को-ऑपरेंट *(adj)* - मिलकर काम करने वाला
I am with a co-operant.

Co-operate/को-आपरेट *(verb)* - साथ-साथ काम करने वाला
We both are going to co-operate to complete this mission.

Co-ordinate/को-ऑरडिनेट *(adj)* - समान पद का
We all shall co-ordinate with another so as to reach the desired result.

Coot/कूट *(noun)* - मूर्ख व्यक्ति, जल पक्षी
He is a coot a typically old eccentric person.

Copal/कोपल *(noun)* - वार्निश के प्रयोग की जाने वाली राल
Copal obtained from this tree is used to make varnish.

Coparcenary/कोपरसिनरी *(noun)* - अविभक्त जायदाद का संयुक्त उत्तराधिकारी
He is my coparcenary

Co-partner/को-पार्टनर *(noun)* - अंश भागी
We are both equal partners in this firm.

Cope/कोप *(noun)* - पादरियों का लम्बा चोंगा
He coped the crisis skilfully.

Coper/कोपर *(noun)* - घोड़ो का व्यापारी
He is the coper.

Copier/कोपिअर *(noun)* - नकल करने वाला
I am going to buy a photocopier machine.

Copious/कोपिअस *(adj)* - प्रचुर
We have capious of gold.

Copper/कॉपर *(noun)* - ताँबा
British in formal 'cop' or police office.

Copperas/कॉपरस *(noun)* - तूतिया
Copperas is blue vitriol.

Coppice/कॉपिस *(noun)* - जंगल
This areas is called coppice. Trees and stubs are out here to stimulate their growth.

Copra/कॉपरा *(noun)* - नारियल की गरी का गोला
Dry coconut copra from which oil is obtained.

Copula/कोपुला *(noun)* - बन्धनी
In grammar it connects a subject and complement.

Copulate/कोपुलेट *(verb)* - मैथुन करना
To have sexual inter course.

Copulative/कॉपुलेटिव *(adjective)* - संभोगकारी
They were found in a copulative position.

Copy/कॉपी *(noun)* - प्रतिलिपि
Will you please stop copying my notes.

Copyhold/कॉपीहोल्ड *(noun)* - पट्टा लिखाई हुई जमीन
According to manorial record, this land is copyhold.

Copying-press/कॉपिइंग प्रेस *(noun)* - प्रतिलिपि छापने का यंत्र
It is a copying-press.

Copyist/कोपिइस्ट *(noun)* - लेखक, प्रतिलिपि लेखक
He is a copyist. He imitates the art of other people.

Coquettish/कोक्वेटिश *(adj)* - चोचला दिखलाने वाली
She is a coquettish woman who is given to flirting.

Coral/कोरल *(noun)* – प्रवाल

Hard substance consists of skeletons of certain animals.

Corbel/कॉरबेल *(noun)* – ताखा

Keep these things on the corbel.

Cord/कॉर्ड *(noun)* – डोरी

The pieces of wood were tied with a cord.

Cordate/कॉडेट *(adjective)* – हृदय के आकार का

Heart shaped according [zoology] and botany.

Cordial/कॉर्डियल *(noun & adj)* – मित्रवत

He is a very cordial and polite man.

Core/कोर *(noun)* – हृदय

The core of coconut is very sweet.

Co-religionist/को-रिलिजनिस्ट *(noun)* – एक ही धर्म का अनुयायी

We both friend belong to Hindu religion.

Co-respondent/को-रिस्पॉडेन्ट *(noun)* – किसी मुकदमे में सहकारी मुद्दालेह

In this divorce case I will cite a case of person as having committed adultery with the accuser.

Coriander/कोरियन्डर *(noun)* – धनियाँ

There are many types of corianders prepared in different states of India.

Cork/कॉर्क *(noun)* – काग

The cork was so hardly pressed into the both that-it-took all our efforts to take it out.

Cormorant/कार्मरण्ट *(noun)* – पेटू मनुष्य

Cormorant is a bird worth looking at.

Corn/कॉर्न *(noun)* – दाना, पैर का गोखरू

There was a thickened skin on my too. I went to a skin surgeon and had it removerd.

Cornea/कॉरनिया *(noun)* – कनीनिका

There is nothing wrong with the cornea of your eye.

Corner/कॉरनर *(noun)* – कोना, कोण

A man was hiding in a corner he appeared a thief to me.

Cornet/कार्निट *(noun)* – एक बाजा

He plays cornet very well.

Cornice/कॉरनिस *(noun)*– दीवार का साज

The cornice of this room is beautifully decorated.

Corollary/कोरोलरी *(noun)* – अनुमान

My friend argued brilliantly and cited a corollary that followed logically from another.

Coronal/कोरोनल *(noun)* – किरीट

The coronal ceremony was held on grand scale.

Coronation/कोरोनेशन *(noun)* – राजतिलक

I had the good fortune to attend the coronation ceremony of the king.

Coronet/कोरोनेट *(noun)* – माला

At a royalty show that some lesser royalties were wearing smaller coronet.

Corporal/कॉरपोरल *(adj)* – कायिक, देह-सम्बन्धी

An NCO above corporal and below sergeant.

Corporate/कॉरपोरेट *(adjective)* – संयुक्त

The corporate office of this company is in Delhi.

Corporation/कॉरपोरेशन *(noun)* – मण्डली

Urban Development Corporation works for urban development.

Corps/कोर् *(noun)* – सेना का भाग

Subdivision of army having two or more divisions assigned to a particular work.

Corpse/कॉर्प्स *(noun)* – शव

Corpses were lying all over the battle field.

Corpulence/कॉपुलेन्स – मोटापन

He is a corpulent fat old man.

Correct/करेक्ट *(verb)* – सुधारना

My friend wrote an all correct essay.

Correlate/कोरिलेट *(noun)* – परस्पर सम्बन्धी वस्तुएँ

Establish a correlation between.

Correspond/करेस्पॉन्ड *(verb)* – पत्र-व्यवहार करना, अनुरूप होना

Each month we two friends correspond by letters.

Corridor/कॉरिडॉर *(noun)* – बरामदा

While is college, we used to spend a lot of time in the corridor.

Corroborate/कराबॅरेट *(verb)* – पुष्ट करना

I corroborated his statement in the court.

C

C

Corrode/करोड *(verb)* – धीरे-धीरे क्षय होना

The long action of water has corrode a deep gash in the rock.

Corrosion/करोजन *(noun)* – क्रम से क्षय

In this chemical reaction, corrosion will take place.

Corrosive/कोरोसिव *(adjective)* – खाने वाला

Wind and water are great corrosive agents.

Corrugate/कारूगेट *(verb)* – सिकोड़ना

The old man's face had contracted into wrinkles.

Corrupt/करप्ट *(adjective)* – भ्रष्ट

He is a very corrupt officer. He won't favour you without money.

Cortage/कॉरटेज *(noun)* – नौकर-चाकरों की श्रेणी

I joined the cortage procession of my friend.

Coryza/कॉराइजा *(noun)* – जुकाम

I have been suffering form coryza since yesterday.

Cosignatory/कोसिग्नेटरी *(noun & adj)* – दूसरे के साथ हस्ताक्षर करने वाला

Many persons and states sign a mutual treaty and other documents.

Cosmetic/कॉस्मेटिक *(noun)* – अंगराग

My friend underwent cosmetic surgery of the face. Now he looks much younger and smart.

Cosmic/कॉस्मिक *(adjective)* – जगत सम्बन्धी

Scientists have yet to know about a lot of cosmic mysteries.

Cosmogony/कॉस्मोगनी *(noun)* – विश्व की उत्पत्ति का सिद्धान्त

My friend's hobby is cosmogony.

Cosmos/कॉसमॉस *(noun)* – क्रमबद्ध संसार

A Mexican plant that bears a single dahlia-like flower.

Cost/कॉस्ट *(noun)* – मूल्य

Please tell me the cost of this diamond.

Costard/कॉस्टार्ड *(noun)* – एक प्रकार का बड़ा सेव

I didn't like the taste of this kind of costard.

Coster/कॉस्टर्ड *(noun)* – ठेले पर लादकर घूमकर फल बेचने वाला

The costar was selling fish, fruit and vegetables.

Costive/कॉस्टिव *(adjective)* – वद्धकोष्ठ, मल रोकने वाला

This man appears costive.

Costly/कॉस्टली *(adjective)* – महँगा

It is rather costly item. Haven't you something of modest price?

Costume/कॉस्ट्यूम *(noun)* – वेश

This is a special costume that belongs to 18th century.

Cot/कॉट*(noun)*– पालना, झोपड़ी

A small bed barred on side for baby or very young child.

Cote/कोट *(noun)* – बाड़ा

Pigeons live in cotes.

Co-tenant/को-टेनैंट *(noun)* – साझीदार

These two boys are co-tenant in this room.

Coterie/कोटेरी *(noun)* – सामाजिक संघ

We few friends belong to a club with commonly shared interests and tastes.

Cottage/कॉटेज *(noun)*– पर्णशाला

A monk lives in this cottage.

Cotton/कॉटन *(noun)* – सूती कपड़ा

Cotton is packed into bales and has many uses.

Couch/काउच *(noun)* – खटिया

In jungle we rolled on nature made couches.

Cough/कफ *(verb)* – खाँसना, कास

My friend kept on coughing loudly, so we took him to doctor.

Council/कौंसिल *(noun)* – विचार सभा

My friend resigned from the council due to some difference.

Counsellor/कॉउन्सेलर *(noun)* – वकील

He is a counsellor and trained to give guidance on various issues.

Countenance/काउन्टेनन्स *(noun)* – आकार

My friend has a very impressive countenance.

Counteract/काउन्टरएक्ट *(verb)* – हराना, रोकना

My friend counteracted when some absurd questions were asked from him.

Countercharge/काउन्टरचार्ज *(noun)* – नालिश

There are countercharges in this case.

Counter-claim/काउन्टर-क्लेम *(noun)*- मुकदमे में प्रतिवादी की माँग

He made a counter-claim for his lost bag and baggage.

Counterfeiter/काउन्टरफिटर *(noun)* - जालसाज

He is a counterfeiter.

Countermand/काउन्टरमांड *(verb)* - प्रतिकूल आदेश देना

It was declared that the voting was countermand.

Counterpoise/काउन्टरपॉइज *(noun)* - पसँघा

A force that neutralizes the others.

Countersign/काउन्टरसाइन *(verb)* - सांकेतिक शब्द

I didn't countersign the check.

Countless/काउन्टलेस *(adjective)* - बेगम

A lot of crowd had gathered in the ground.

Country/कन्ट्री *(noun)* - देश

A nation with its own territory currency. Government and wild territory.

Coup/कू *(noun)*- चोट

A coup is sudden violent seizure of power from a government.

Couple/कपल *(noun)* - युगल

Two people of the age are considered for marriage.

Couplet/कपलेट *(noun)* - श्लोक

Kaka Hathrasi was a master of couplets.

Courage/करेज *(noun)* - सहारा

My friend has courage to face any danger, pain or grief.

Courier/कोरिअर *(noun)* - हरकारा

There are many courier agencies operating in the city.

Course/कोर्स *(noun)* - पीछा करना

My course of commerce consists of many textbooks.

Court/कोर्ट *(noun)* - दरबार, कचहरी

In a court of law judicial cases are heard.

Courtesan/कोरटिजन *(noun)* - वेश्या, रण्डी

I met a courtesan who belonged to a rather richer and upper class.

Courtly/कर्टली *(adjective)* - सुशील

My friend moves in royal circles. His courtly behaviour is liked by all.

Courtship/कोर्टशीप *(noun)* - विवाह के निमित्त आराधना

Since my friend is courting a girl he is rather facing risky situations.

Courtyard/कोर्टयार्ड *(noun)* - घर के बाहर का सहन

Instead of open, we would rather play in our courtyard.

Covenant/कॉवनेन्ट *(noun)* - पण, सौदा

My friend is a covenant member of church. He has agreed to pay by covenant.

Coverlet/कवरलेट *(noun)* - चदरा

It is a beautiful coverlet.

Covert/कवर्ट *(adjective)* - गुप्त

It is something covert to be displayed nor to be acknowledged.

Covet/कॉवेट *(verb)* - लालच करना

I covet that piece of jewellery. I wish it were mine.

Covey/कॅवि *(noun)* - तीतरों का झुण्ड

There is a group of coveys, let's go and catch them.

Cow/कॉउ *(noun)* - गाय

The cow is a household pet animal. It is domesticated.

Cower/कॉवर *(verb)* - दबकना

There appeared a lion and the priest crouched down in great feer.

Co-worker/को-वर्कर *(noun)* - दूसरे के साथ काम करने वाला

We are friends as well as co-workers.

Crackle/क्रैकल *(verb)* - कड़ाके का शब्द करना

There is crackling sound in the jungle.

Cracknel/क्रैकनेल *(noun)* - कुरकुरा बिस्कुट

Cracknels are my favorites.

Cracksman/क्रैक्समैन *(noun)* - चोर, ठग

Police has caught a cracksman. He has looted many safes.

C

Crafty/क्राफ्टी *(adj)* – कपटी
He is a crafty fellow and not to be trusted at all.

Crambo/क्रैम्बो *(noun)* – तुकबन्दी का खेल
We are playing crambo and it is a very exciting game.

Crane/क्रेन *(noun)* – सारस
The crane is eating a fish.

Cranny/क्रैनी *(noun)* – छिद्र
He went down the narrow space and emerged at the other end.

Crashing/क्रैशिंग *(noun)* – प्रचण्ड शब्द
A violent sound is called crashing.

Crass/क्रैस *(adjective)* – अनाड़ी
He is stupid and crass, not an ounce of intelligence in him.

Crate/क्रेट *(noun)* – टोकरी
The wooden crate is ready for transportation.

Crater/क्रेटर *(noun)* – ज्वालामुखी पर्वत का मुख
The volcano has a big crater.

Crave/क्रेव *(verb)* – माँगना
My crave for her has just crossed all limits.

Craving/क्रेविंग *(noun)* – लालसा
I have no craving at all.

Craw/क्रा *(noun)* – पक्षियों का सिर या गला या पेट
A pouch in bird's throat where food is prepared for digestion.

Crawl/क्रॉल *(verb)* – रेंगना
He crawled at Guruji feet.

Creak/क्रिक *(noun & verb)* – कर्कश शब्द
The bridge creaked under our weight.

Crease/क्रिज *(noun)* – चुनन
He is an old man. His face creased all over.

Creation/क्रिएशन *(noun)* – सृष्टि निर्माण, उपाधि प्रदान
The universe is God's creation.

Creative/क्रिएटिव *(adjective)* – उत्पादक
A painting is an creative act.

Credence/क्रेडेंस *(noun)* – प्रमाण पत्र
I have given him a letter of credence.

Credent/क्रेडेंट *(adj)* – विश्वास के योग्य
He is my credent.

Credential/क्रेडेंटियल *(noun)* – विश्वास पत्र
Excuse me sir, the principal would like to see your credentials.

Credible/क्रेडिब्ल *(adjective)* – विश्वसनीय
His statement sounds credible.

Creditor/क्रेडिटर *(noun)* – महाजन
I owe a lot of money to my creditors.

Credulity/क्रेडुलिटी *(noun)* – विश्वासशीलता, सहजता
There is no credulity in him.

Creed/क्रीड *(noun)* – धर्म
Christianity is a wide spread creed.

Creek/क्रीक *(noun)* – खाड़ी
There was a creek.

Creep/क्रीप *(verb)* – रेंगना
To move very carefully and slowly so as not to be noticed.

Cremate/क्रिमेट *(verb)* – दाह करना
It is Hindu tradition to cremate the dead bodies.

Creosote/क्रेयोसोट *(noun)* – लोहबान का तेल
Prepared from various things, it is a wood preservative. Also it is a an antiseptic.

Crepitate/क्रेपिटेट *(verb)* – कड़कड़ शब्द करना
There was a crepitating sound as the wood burnt in the hearth.

Crept/क्रेप्ट – रेंगा
Past and past participle of creep.

Crest/क्रेस्ट *(noun)* – मुकुट
A plume of feathers on a helmet, fur on the head of the bird.

Crew/क्रयू *(noun)* – जत्था
A group of people working on a ship, boat aircraft. Often termed derogatory.

Crib/क्रू *(noun)* – पालना
A child's bed with barred sides.

Cricket/क्रिकेट *(noun)* – क्रिकेट, झींगुर
Cricket is a game popular throughout the world.

Cricoid/क्रिकाइड *(adj.)* – गोलाकार
My friend underwent cricoids operation of the cartilage of throat.

Crier/क्राइअर *(noun)* – पुकारने वाला
My name was called out in the court by crier.

Criminal/क्रिमिनल *(adjective)* – फौजदारी
He is a criminal and he spent 10 years in jail.

Crimp/क्रिम्प *(verb)* – तह बनाना, सिकोड़ना
She is crimping her saree.

Cripple/क्रिपल *(noun & verb)* – लगड़ा, लगड़ाकर चलना
He is a cripple and drags along the street begging.

Crisp/क्रिष्प *(adjective)* – भंगुर
These biscuits are fresh and crisp.

Critic/क्रिटिक *(noun)* – समालोचक
He is a famous film critic.

Criticism/क्रिटिसिज्म *(noun)* – समालोचना
Criticism of a work of art carries a lot of weight with public.

Critique/क्रिटिक *(noun)* – समालोचना
A critique evaluates a work of an art in a detailed and analytical way.

Croak/क्रोक *(noun)* – कौवे का काँव-काँव
There is a croak in the park.

Crocodile/क्रोकोडाइल *(noun)* – मगर
Once I saw a live crocodile in the river.

Croesus/क्रोसस *(noun)* – धनी
I specially like the yellow purple flowers of the Croesus plinth.

Croft/क्रॉफ्ट *(noun)* – छोटी खेती
A small enclosed field in Scotland typically attached to a house.

Crony/क्रॉनी *(adjective)* – परम मित्र
He is crony-unfit any fraud.

Crook/क्रूक *(noun)* – झुकाव
A hooked staff is used by shepherds, bishops.

Crooked/क्रूक्ड *(adjective)* – बदसूरत
He is a crooked and criminal person and has been jail to many times.

Croon/क्रून *(noun)* – भनभनाना
She crooned melodiously in my car.

Croquet/क्रोकेट *(noun)* – लकड़ी के गेंद और हथौड़ी से खेलने वाला खेल
A game played in a lawn in which wooden balls are used.

Crore/क्रोर् *(noun)* – एक करोड़ की संख्या
This person must have at least crore of rupees z.e. ten million or one hundred lakh.

Crotchet/क्रॉचेट *(noun)* – झक
A perverse or unfounded belief.

C

Croton/क्रॉटन *(noun)* – कोटन एक प्रकार का पौधा
A plant native to tropical and warm regions.

Crouch/क्रोच *(verb)* – झुकना, नम्रतापूर्वक पाँव पड़ना, विनय करना
All the persons crouched before the deity.

Crow/क्रो *(noun)* – कौवे
This is a crow.

Crowd/क्राउड *(noun)* – समूह, गण
Once I saw a crowd a crowd so huge and dense that one couldn't move an inch. It was a crowd of rather derogatory people.

Crown/क्राउन *(noun)* – मुकुट
Crowns are circular metal headdresses are worn by monarchs.

Crucial/क्रुसियल *(adjective)* – प्रामाणिक
Waiting for the result was a crucial moment either I will fail or I will pass.

Cruciferous/क्रुसिफरस *(adjective)* – क्रॉस से आभूषित
Plants of the cabbage family.

Crucifix/क्रुसिफिक्स *(noun)* – ईसा मसीह की मूर्ति
I wear a crucifix round my neck both as respect and love for Christ.

Cruciform/क्रुसीफॉर्म *(adjective)* – क्रास के आकार का
Many people wear ornaments in the form of cruciform.

Cruel/क्रुएल *(adjective)* – दयाहीन
Cruel people take delight in pain or suffering of others.

Cruet/क्रुएट *(noun)* – तेल रखने की ढकनेदार शीशी
A small container for the wine or water to be used in celebrations.

Cruise/क्रुइज *(verb)* – समुद्र में इधर-उधर यात्रा करना
I cruised round thinking something may be I'll find a sexual partner.

C

Crump/क्रम्प *(adj)* - ऐंठा टेढा

There was a sudden crump and all of us ran helter skelter.

Crumpet/क्रम्पेट *(noun)* - रोटी, बाटी

A thick soft cake made from yeast and eaten with butter. It is one of my favourites.

Crumple/क्रम्पल *(verb)* - पीसना

The piece of cloth was badly crimpled. It took me several efforts to smooth it out.

Crusade/क्रूसेड *(noun)* - ईसाइयों का धर्मयुद्ध

European efforts of war undertaken to recover holy land from Muslims.

Cruse/क्रूस *(noun)* - मिट्टी का बर्तन

An earthen ware pot or jar.

Crush/क्रस *(verb)* - नष्ट करना

In the accident of two cars one car was completely crushed.

Crust/क्रस्ट *(noun)* - छिलका

A layer of pastry covering a pie.

Crutch/क्रच *(noun)* - बैशाखी

I saw a lame man walking with the help of crutches. The crutch was a long stick with a crosspiece at the top.

Cryogen/क्रिग *(noun)* - हिम

A substance used to produce very low temperature.

Crypt/क्रिप्ट *(noun)* - गुफा

I visited a chapel under a church. I was rather frightened there.

Cryptography/क्राइप्टोग्राफी *(noun)* - गुप्त लेखन की विधा

Art of writing on solving codes.

Crystalline/क्राइस्टलाइन *(adjective)* - बिल्लौर के समान स्वच्छ

The water of the stream was crystal clear.

Cub/कब *(noun)* - लोमड़ी

The young one of a lion bear or fox.

Cubeb/कबेब *(noun)* - कवाबचीनी

Cubeb is shrub of pungent berries.

Cubicle/क्यूबिकल *(noun)* - छोटा शयनगृह

I share a cubicle with my room mate.

Cubiform/क्यूबिफार्म *(adjective)* - घनाकार

His office is in a cube shaped room.

Cukold/ककोल्ड *(noun)* - व्यभिचारिणी स्त्री का पति

He is a married man but a cuckold an object of laughter.

Cuckoo/ककू *(noun)* - मूर्ख, कोयल

A brown bird which lays her eggs in the nest of small song birds.

Cucumber/ककम्बर *(noun)* - खीरा

A long, green skinned fruit eaten raw in salads.

Cucurbit/ककरबिट *(noun)* - कोहड़ा

A plant of ground family-melon, pumpkin, squash.

Cuddy/कडी *(noun)* - मूर्ख मनुष्य

A cuddy, a stupid person.

Cudgel/कजेल *(noun)* - गदका

The thief beat the man with a cudgel.

Cuff/कफ *(noun)* - आस्तीन का अगला भाग

I asked my men to attach a cuff to the end part of my sleeve.

Cuisine/क्विजिन *(noun)* - पकाने की विधि

I very much like cuisine good cooked in a certain way of the century.

Culinary/कुलिनरी *(adjective)* - पाकशाला सम्बन्धी

She has great culinary stalls.

Culet/कुलेट *(noun)* - दुबारा गलाने के लिये काँच के टुकड़े

Broken glass recycled in glass making.

Culminant/कल्मिनेन्ट *(adjective)* - उच्चतम स्थान पर

As the culmination of picture arrived I began to seat.

Culminate/कल्मिनेट *(verb)* - परम कोटि को प्राप्त करना

As the debate between the two persons culminated I began to be excited.

Culpable/कलपेब्ल *(adjective)* - दोषी

He was arrested for culpable homicide.

Culprit/कल्प्रिट *(noun)* - अपराधी

The culprit was arrested by the police.

Cult/कल्ट *(noun)*- उपासना की विधि

A small religious group directed to an object or person.

Cultrate/कल्ट्रेट *(noun)* - छूरी के धार के समान बना हुआ

It is suave like cultrate.

Culture/कल्चर *(noun)* - जोताई, संस्कृति

They belong to different culture.

Cunning/कनिंग *(noun)* - चातुरी

He is a cunning fellow charming and attractive. Don't fall under his trap. He can make you do whatever he wants.

Cup-board/कप-बोर्ड *(noun)* - अलमारी

I had a storage of storing place. So I have just bought a cupboard.

Cupid/क्यूपिड *(noun)* - कामदेव, मदन

The people of Rome worship cupid.

Cupidity/क्यूपिडिटि *(noun)* - कामुकता, अति लोभ

He suffers from cupidity he needs a lot of many other possessions.

Curative/क्यूरेटिव *(adjective)* - सहायक

Many diseases these days are curative which were not in old times.

Curcuma/करक्यूमा *(noun)* - हल्दी

An Asian plant that yields turmeric and many other herbs.

Curd/कर्ड *(noun)* - दही

Curd is my favourite dish, specially when I mix sugar with it.

Curl/कर्ल *(verb)* - घुँघराला बाल

My fiancée has curly hair which I like very much.

Curnudgeon/कर्नजन *(noun)* - कृपण

He is a curnudgeon and I won't even talk to him.

Currant/क्यूरेंट *(adjective)* - दाख, सूखा अंगूर

I like currant very much.

Currency/करेंसी *(noun)* - मुद्रा

Rupee is currency of India.

Current/करेंट *(adj)* - सामान्य, वर्तमान

The current of water was too strong for me to swim.

Curricle/क्यूरिकल *(noun)* - टमटम

The curricle were very popular in 18th century.

Currier/करिअर *(noun)* - चर्मकार

A person who grooms a horse with a curry comb.

Curry//करि *(noun)* - कढ़ी, शोरबा

To groom with a curry comb.

Curse/कर्स *(noun)* - शाप

I was so angry and felt such contempt that I cursed him with all my heart.

Curt/कर्ट *(adjective)* - असभ्य ढंग से

He was rough and rude to me. He spoke in a curt way.

Curtail/कर्टेल *(verb)* - नाटका का संक्षेप करना

The powers of director were curtailed.

Curtain/कर्टेन *(noun)* - पर्दा

There was a curtain between the stage performers and audience, upside down or sideways.

Curtilage/कर्टिलेज *(noun)* - घर के बाहर का मैदान, बाग इत्यादि

A piece of land is attached to our house that has only one curtilage.

Curvature/कर्वेचर *(noun)* - घुमाव

A curved object or a curved line on paper.

Curve/कर्व *(noun)* - झुकाना, मोड़ना

He formed a curve on the paper.

Cusp/कस्प *(noun)* - शिखा

Cane shaped prominence on the surface of the tooth.

Custodial/कस्टोडियल *(adj)* - संरक्षकता-सम्बन्धी

There are so many custodial death is India.

Custom/कस्टम *(noun)* - आचार रीति

It is a custom with us that we touch the feet of our elders.

Cutaneous/क्यूटेनियस *(adjective)* - चर्म-सम्बन्धी

It is a cutaneous disease, you should have it trealed.

Cutis/क्यूटिस *(noun)* - भीतरी त्वचा

This doctor is a specialist in the true skin or dermis.

Cutlet/कटलेट *(noun)* - माँस का पकाया हुआ टुकड़ा

Nonveg cutlets are my favourites.

Cutpurse/कटपर्स *(noun)* - गिरहकट

He is a pickpocket by profession.

Cut-throat/कटथ्रोट *(noun)* - हत्यारा

He is a ruthless cut-throat person.

C

Cutting/कटिंग *(noun)* – टुकड़ा

I specially looked for a sports magazine, so that I could show the desired cutting to the teacher.

Cuvette/कवेट *(noun)* – सूखी खाई के बीच में खोदा हुआ गड्ढा

A container for holding liquid samples.

Cyanosis/सायोनोसिस *(noun)* – एक प्रकार रोग जिसमे शरीर नीला होता है

A bluish medicine was applied on my cut because I have a poor circulation of blood.

Cycloid/सायक्लायड *(noun)* – वृत्तजात

A curve on a point being rolled straight.

Cyclone/सायक्लोन *(noun)* – बवंडर

There are some such daredevils that they actually go very near cyclone for scientific study.

Cyclosis/सायक्लोसिस *(noun)* – शरीर में रुधिर का संचालन

There is no cyclosis in a dead body.

Cyclostyle/सायक्लोस्टाइल *(noun)* – हाथ की लिखावट को छापने की कला

An early device for duplicating handwriting.

Cylindrical/सिलिंड्रिकल *(adj)* – बेलन के आकार का

It is cylindrical in shape.

Cynic/सिनिक *(noun)* – निन्दाशील

My friend is a cynic.

Cynosure/सायनोस्योर *(noun)* – ध्रुवतारा

Almost all film stars are cynosures.

Cypher/सायफर *(noun)* – शून्य

Zero or cipher.

Cystic/सिस्टिक *(adjective)* – मूत्राशय-सम्बन्धी

Medicine for cyst which may be a cavity or say filled with liquid usually in gall bladder.

Dd

D/डी *(noun)* - अंग्रेजी वर्णमाला का चौथा वर्ण, आकारिक निर्माण the fourth letter of the English alphabet.

1. Denoting the fourth in a set of items, categories, sizes, etc.
2. Music the second note of the diatonic scale of C major.
3. The roman numeral for 500. [understood as half of CI, an earlier form of M.]

Dab/डैब *(noun)* - थपकी, हल्का, स्पर्श
A dab of glue is enough to stick the pages together.

Dabble/डैबल *(verb)* - किसी काम में हल्की फुल्की रुचि रखना
Riya is not serious about modelling. She only dabbles in it occasionally.

Dace/डेस *(noun)* - मीठे पानी की एक प्रकार की छोटी मछली
The dace's beautiful blue-green body sparkled in the sunlight.

Dacoit/डेकॉइट *(noun)* - डाकू
The dacoit was hiding in the bushes waiting to attack any travellers passing by.

Daft/डैफ्ट *(adjective)* - बेवकूफ, मूर्ख
Julian was scolded by his father for asking a very daft question.

Daily/डेली *(adj & adv)* - दैनिक, प्रतिदिन
The watchman was doing his daily rounds when he noticed the burglar trying to sneak into the house.

Dainty/डैन्टी *(adjective)* - भोजन विशेष, छोटा और सुन्दर
Ballet dancers are very dainty in their movements.

Dairy/डेअरि *(noun)* - दुग्धशाला, दुध, मक्खन बेचने वाली कंपनी
John's father runs a successful dairy business.

Dais/डेस् *(noun)* - चबूतरा, मंच
The professor stood on the dais while lecturing to the students.

Daisy/डेजि *(noun)* - गुलबहार
Daisies bloom in the warm summer months.

Dale/डेल *(noun)* - दर्रा, घाटी
The dale is covered with flowers in the spring.

Dally/डैली *(verb)* - खेलना, क्रीड़ा करना
She was cruelly dallying with Jack's emotions.

Dam/डैम *(noun)* - बाँध
Hoover dam is built on the Colorado River in America. There is a need to build a dam across the river.

Dame/डेम *(noun)* - गृहिणी, विशेष उपलब्धि पर किसी महिला को दी गयी उपाधि
She was awarded the title of dame due to her aristocratic connections.

Damn/डैम् *(verb)* - शाप देना
Don't damn me, please.

Damnation/डैम्नेशन *(noun)* - नरक-दण्ड
He was cursed with eternal damnation for his misdeeds.

Damned/डैम्ड *(adjective)* - नरका
The town was better known as the town of the damned because of the misdeeds of its inhabitants.

Damming/डैम्निंग *(adjective)* - शाप देने वाला
His nervousness proved to be damning against him.

Damp/डैम्प *(adjective)* - सीलनभरा
His clothes got damp after he was caught in the rain.

Damsel/डैम्जेल *(noun)* - युवती, कुमारी कन्या
The damsel smiled prettily and thanked the boy for his help.

Damson/डैमजन *(noun)* - आलूचा, आलूबुखारा
The damson tree was laden with ripe fruit.

Dance/डांस *(verb)* - नाचना, नृत्य करना
She has quickly picked up the dance steps of salsa.

Dancer/डांसर *(noun)* - नर्तकी
Jane is a professional dancer.

D

Dandelion/डैन्डेलियन *(noun)* – पीले फूल का एक प्रकार का पौधा

The field was full of yellow dandelions swaying in the breeze.

Dandiacal/डैन्डियाकल *(adjective)* – ठाट-बाटवाला

This dandiacal man is very cruel in the heart.

Dandle/डैन्डल *(verb)* – लाड़ करना

Mr. Williams was dandling his grandson and playing with him.

Dandruff/डैन्ड्रफ *(noun)* – बालों की रूसी

Dandruff is a disease where white pieces of dead skins accumulate on a person's head.

Dandy/डैन्डी *(adjective)* – छैला, बाँका

Tom is quite a dandy when it comes to his appearance.

Dane/डेन *(noun)* – डेनमार्क देश का निवासी

The famous writer of fairy tales, Hans Christian Anderson was a Dane.

Danger/डैन्जर *(noun)* – भय, संकट, खतरा

Children must be warned of the danger of playing with sharp objects.

Dangle/डैंगल *(verb)* – लटकाना, झुलाना, झूलना

The bungee jumpers were dangling from the end of the rope.

Danish/डेनिश *(noun)* – डेनमार्क की भाषा

Danish is the official language of Denmark.

Dank/डैन्क *(adjective)* – तर, गीला

The house felt dank after being shut for many months.

Dap/डैप *(verb)* – जल में थोड़ा-सा डुबाना, कूदना

He dapped the ball.

Dapper/डैपर *(adjective)* – तेज, साफ-सुथरा

Jim looked quite dapper at the wedding in the suit.

Dapple/डैपल् *(noun)* – चितकबरा होना

The sunlight dappled on the curtains creating mysterious shadows.

Dare/डेअर *(verb)* – साहस करना

How dare you challenge him for a duel?

Daring/डेअरिंग *(adjective)* – साहसी, शूरवीर, बहादुर

He is quite daring for a boy of his age.

Dark/डार्क *(adjective)* – प्रकाश का अभाव, अंधेरा

One of the bandits was a tall dark ugly looking person.

Darken/डार्केन *(verb)* – अंधेरा छा जाना

Sarah's mood darkened after hearing the bad news.

Darkish/डार्किश *(adjective)* – अंधेरे में

The rug is darkish blue in colour.

Darling/डार्लिंग *(noun)* – प्रियतम, प्रिय व्यक्ति के संबोधन के रूप में प्रयुक्त

Jane is her father's darling.

Darn/डार्न *(verb)* – रफू करना

Sarah mended the tear in the shirt by darning it before it got bigger.

Dart/डार्ट *(noun)* – बर्छी

A dart is a small pointed missile with feathers at the rear which is used in target practice.

Darter/डार्टर *(noun)* – बर्छी फेंकते रहना

The darter was catching fish with the help of its long beak.

Darwinism/डार्विनिज्म *(noun)* – विकासवाद

The followers of Darwinism refuse to accept any other theory of evolution.

Dash/डैश *(verb)* – धावा, दिखावट, पटकना, पटक देना

Why would he like to dash your hope for promotion?

Dasher/डैशर *(noun)* – मथानी

It is important to operate the dasher properly while making cream in a churn.

Dashing/डैशिंग *(adjective)* – साहसी, जोशीला, स्फूर्तिमय

Bill looked quite dashing in his new clothes.

Dastard/डेस्टर्ड *(noun)* – डरपोक मनुष्य, कायर

He was a dastard person.

Dative/डेटिव *(adjective)* – सम्प्रदान कारक

Dative case is called an indirect object.

Datum/डेटम *(noun)* – स्वीकृत तत्त्व

Datum of a place is a position from which elevations and depths are measured in surveying.

Daub/डॉब *(verb)* – लीपना-पोतना

The interior chimney hood was in silver colour with brown daub finish.

Daughter/डॉटर *(noun)* – कन्या, पुत्री
John and Kate have two daughters.

Davit/डेविट *(noun)* – क्रेन जहाज पर नाव लटकाने का यंत्र
The lifeboat was lowered into the water with the help of the davit when the ship was sinking.

Dawdle/डॉडल *(verb)* – विलम्ब करना, सुस्ती से चलना
Jack is very efficient time conscious and does not believe in dawdling.

Dawn/डॉन *(noun)* – उषाकाल, बड़े सवेरे
The rising sun appears on the horizon at dawn.

Dawning/डॉनिंग *(noun)* – तड़के, अरुणोदय का समय
I like dawning.

Daze/डेज *(verb)* – घबड़ा देना, स्तब्ध करना
To daze means unable to think in an orderly way.

Dazzle/डैजल *(verb)* – चौंधिया देना
She came under the spell of dazzle by so many lights coming on suddenly.

Deacon/डीकन *(noun)* – छोटा पादरी
Deacon is the person who oversees church charities.

Dead/डेड *(adjective)* – मृतक लोग, मृत, निर्जीव
He spoke in a cold and emotionless voice as if he were dead.

Deaden/डेडेन *(verb)* – मन्द करना, पीड़ा कम कर देना
The pain had deadened her sensitivity to the problems of others.

Deal/डील *(noun)* – व्यापारिक सौदा
I made a deal with her promising to finish homework each night in exchange for one hour of television.

Dealer/डीलर *(noun)* – व्यापारी
Jim's father is a dealer of cotton garments.

Dealing/डीलिंग *(noun)* – आचरण, सम्बन्ध, लेन-देन (व्यापार में)
Dealing with customer complaints can sometimes be challenging, but there is always a solution that can be reached.

Dean/डीन *(noun)* – गिरजाघर का अध्यक्ष, अभाव, अकाल
Mr. Harris is the dean of the college.

Dearth/डर्थ *(noun)* – दुष्काल
There is a dearth of good workers these days.

Death/डेथ *(noun)* – मरण, मृत्यु
The death of his pet dog came as a blow to Harry.

Debar/डिबार *(verb)* – निषेध करना
Having a criminal record will not debar you from doing voluntary work.

Debase/डिबेस *(verb)* – गुणवत्ता या महत्त्व कम कर देना, पदवी घटना
I admit, I did debase myself by reading her personal letter.

Debatable/डिबेटेबल *(adjective)* – विवाद योग्य
The benefits of the medicine were debatable.

Debate/डिबेट *(noun)* – झगड़ना, वाद-विवाद में भाग लेना
A debate is a discussion of the opposing sides of a specific subject.

Debauchery/डिबाचरी *(noun)* – लम्पट, व्याभिचारिता, अनैतिक
People with traditional beliefs dislike debauchery of any kind.

Debilitate/डेबिलिटेट *(verb)* – दुर्बल करना
A virus can completely debilitate your computer and potentially cause the loss of entire information.

Debility/डेबिलिटी *(noun)* – कमजोरी, दुर्बलता
In old age, people suffer from physical debility.

Debris/डेब्रिस *(noun)* – मलबा, दुर्घटना में नष्ट वस्तु के टुकड़े
The market site was littered with debris after the bomb blast.

Debt/डेट *(noun)* – उधार, कर्ज, ऋण
It is advisable to pay off one's debts on time.

Debtless/डेटलेस *(adj.)* – कर्ज से बरी
One can stay debtless if one learns to live within one's means.

Debtor/डेटर *(noun)* – देनदार, कर्जदार ऋणी
Being a debtor can be a horrible experience.

Debus/डिबस *(verb)* – मोटर गाड़ी से उतरना या सामान उतारना
The team was asked to debus from the vehicle as soon as they reached the camp.

D

Decade/डिकेड *(noun)* – दस वर्ष का समय

He ruled the movie world with his performance for more than a decade.

Decadence/डिकाडेंस *(noun)* – क्षय, नाश

The Roman Empire came to an end due to sheer decadence of their lifestyle.

Decagon/डेकागन *(noun)* – दस भुजा

The students were asked to create a model of a decagon.

Decalogue/डेकालॉग *(noun)* – ईसा मसीह के दस आदेश

There were decalogue boards behind the altar.

Decant/डिकैंट *(verb)* – पसाना, निथारना, निस्तारण करना

It is time to decant the oil into another container to preserve it.

Decapitate/डिकैपिटेट *(verb)* – सिर धड़ से अलग कर देना

Mercenaries don't hesitate to decapitate anyone caught spying.

Decease/डिसीस *(noun & verb)* – मरण, मृत्यु, मरना

Some folklore says that the spirits of the deceased are supposed to be watching over us.

Deceit/डिसीट *(noun)* – धोखाधड़ी, फर्जीवाड़ा, कपट, छल

Lying to someone is an act of deceit.

Deceive/डिसीव *(verb)* – धोखा देना

I knew she could easily deceive him.

December/दिसम्बर *(noun)* – अंग्रेजी साल का अन्तिम महीना

December comes after November.

Decency/डिसेन्सी *(noun)* – मर्यादा

You lack decency.

Decent/डिसेन्ट *(adj)* – विनीत

She has decent behaviour.

Deceptive/डिसेप्टिव *(adj)* – धोखा देने वाला

I dislike her deceptive nature.

Decadence/डेसाडेंस *(noun)* – पतन, पतनकाल

Your decadence will come soon.

Deciduous/डेसिडुअस *(adj)* – पतनशील

These are deciduous plants.

Deck/डेक *(noun & verb)* – जहाह की छत, ढाँकना

There was a big thud when I hit the deck of the ship.The ship was furnished with a deck.

Declarant/डिक्लरेंट *(noun)* – कानूनी प्रतिज्ञा करने वाला मनुष्य

A declarant is a person who signs a legal statement.

Declaration/डिक्लरेशन *(noun)* – किसी विषय में अधिकारिक घोषणा

They made the declaration in front of the whole town.

Declare/डिक्लेअर *(verb)* – सूचित करना, घोषित करना, उद्घोषणा करना, कोई बात अधिकारिक रूप से घोषित करना

The company is about to declare a final dividend on the ordinary shares.

Declension/डिक्लेन्सन *(noun)* – क्षय, अवनति, ह्रास

Sensual and carnal worship entering the gospel temple is often an evidence of spiritual declension.

Declination/डिक्लाइनेशन *(noun)* – नीचे को झुकाव

Declination the angle formed by a magnetic needle with the line pointing to the geographical North Pole.

Declivity/डिक्लिविटी *(noun)* – ढाल, उतार

Declivity of these mountain's slopes down till the sea coast.

Decoct/डिकॉक्ट *(verb)* – काढ़ा बनाना, उबालना

Please decoct by boiling if you want to extract the essence of the medicinal herb.

Decontrol/डीकन्ट्रोल *(verb)* – विनियंत्रण करना, सरकारी नियन्त्रण हटाना

The government must decontrol the sale of petrol and diesel.

Decorum/डेकोरम *(noun)* – मर्यादा, शिष्टता, शिष्टाचार

The children were strictly asked to maintain decorum of the house.

Decoy/डिकॉइ *(noun & verb)* – प्रलोभन, लुभाना, किसी को मनचाहे ढंग से फंसाना

A duck used by a hunter to try to attract other ducks is an example of a decoy. The police caught the robber by using his family as a decoy.

Decree/डिक्री *(noun)* – डिग्री, निर्णय

He was retired from government service on 31 December 2011 by a presidential decree.

Deity/डेइटी *(noun)* – ईश्वर

Krishna is worshipped as a deity by the Hindus.

Delay/डिले *(noun)* – विलम्ब करना, रोकना

Unexpected problems led to delay in timely start of the function.

Delegacy/डेलीगेसी *(noun & verb)* – प्रतिनिधि के रूप में नियुक्ति

The Chinese delegacy is in town for the seminar.

Delegate/डेलीगेट *(noun)* – प्रतिनिधि

He is a delegate representing Russia.

Delete/डिलिट *(verb)* – लिखित अंश को मिटाना

She was asked to delete all the files from the computer.

Deliberation/डिलिबरेशन *(noun)* – विस्तृत विचार-विमर्श

The matter must be given enough deliberation before a decision is reached.

Delicacies/डेलिकेसीज *(noun)* – स्वादिष्ट भोजन

That night they ate the local delicacy and stayed in a 5-star hotel - the Hotel Taj!

Delicate/डेलिकेट *(noun)* – नाजुक

The vase was very delicate and on falling broke easily.

Delicious/डिलिक्सिशस *(adjective)* – स्वादिष्ट या सुगन्धित

Mango is a delicious fruit.

Delict/डेलिक्ट *(noun)* – नियमोल्लंघन

It is an utter delict.

Delight/डिलाइट *(noun)* – अति सुखी होना, अत्यन्त प्रसन्नता

Anne took great delight in singing.

Delinquent/डेलिक्वेन्ट *(adjective)* – पाप करने वाला

The programme deals with the group of ageing delinquents.

Delirious/डिलिरीअस *(adjective)* – बेसुध, अचेत

Delirious with happiness that I am back at home after two years.

Delocalize/डिलोकेलाइज *(verb)* – केन्द्रीभूत करना

It was necessary to delocalize the sap before planting it in another nursery.

Delude/डिलूड *(verb)* – मोहित करना, किसी को भ्रमित करना

She tried to delude him into thinking that he could trust her.

Delusion/डिलूशन *(noun)* – मोह, भ्रम आभास, भ्रांति, धोखा

He suffered from the delusion that he could write well.

Demagnetize/डिमैग्नेटाइज *(verb)* – विचुम्बकित करना

Research is being done on whether it is possible to demagnetize iron.

Demagogue/डेमागॉग *(noun)* – जनसमुदाय का नेता

Demagogues played an important role in ancient Greece and Rome.

Demand/डिमाण्ड *(verb)* – प्रबल अनुरोध या ओदश

The kidnappers made a ransom demand late at night.

Demarcation/डीमार्केशन *(noun)* – किन्हीं दो वस्तुओं को पृथक् करने वाली सीमा रेखा

The demarcation between the rich and the poor was quite obvious.

Demerit/डिमेरिट *(noun)* – अवगुण

The student earned a demerit for his actions.

Demesne/डिमीन् *(noun)* – जमींदारी, भूसंपत्ति

I have demesne in my village.

Demise/डिमाइस *(noun)* – समाप्ति या विफलता

In a way, ideals of democracy led to the demise of Soviet communism.

Demolish/डिमॉलिश *(verb)* – ढाहना

It has been decided to demolish the old house to make way for a new apartment building.

Demon/डिमन् *(noun)* – दानव, राक्षस, असुर

It is usually the superstitious people who believe in demons.

Demonetize/डिमोनेटाइज *(verb)* – धातु के सिक्कों का मूल्य घटना, मुद्राकरण करना, विमुद्रीकृत

The twenty-five paise coins have been demonetized a long time ago.

Demonstrate/डिमॉन्स्ट्रेट *(verb)* – प्रमाणित करना

The teacher demonstrated the experiment to the class.

D

D

Demoralize/डिमॉरलाइज *(verb)* - उत्साह भंग करना, किसी का मनोबल गिराना

The caustic remarks by the management may demoralize the team after their defeat.

Demurrage/डिमरेज *(noun)* - माल की समय से अधिक रूकावट का हर्जाना, बिलम्ब शुल्क

Demurrage is a fine a transporter imposes on a customer for not taking delivery of goods within stipulated time.

Den/डेन *(noun)* - कन्दरा या खोह, माँद

It is dangerous to enter a lion's den.

Denaturalize/डीनैचरलाइज *(verb)* - विकृति करना, स्वाभाविक गुण बदलना

America threatened to denaturalize Ryan of citizenship for want to documents.

Dengue/डेंगू *(noun)* - लंगड़ा ज्वर, डेंगू बुखार

The health authorities are afraid of a possible dengue outbreak.

Denigrat/डेनीग्रेट *(verb)* - बदनाम करना, अलोचना करना, नीचा दिखाना

Why denigrate Jill in front of everyone if it wasn't her fault?

Denote/डिनोट *(verb)* - बतलाना, किसी बात का द्योतक होना

Use red ink to denote important points that need explanation.

Dense/डेन्स *(adjective)* - घना, गहन, बहुत सी वस्तुओं या व्यक्तियों के जुटाव वाला

The jungle is dense to the point that in places, it is almost impenetrable.

Dent/डेन्ट *(noun)* - छिद्र, गड्ढा

From a minor dent to a full scale repair, we provide the best quality repair in the city.

Denture/डेन्चर *(noun)* - कृत्रिम दाँतो की पंक्ति

Denture wearers are the most affected group along with people who have difficulties keeping their mouths clean.

Denude/डिन्यूड *(verb)* - नंगा करना, कपड़ा उतार देना

The rains washed away the soil denuding the area around the tree.

Denunciation/डिनन्सियेशन *(noun)* - किसी की तीखी सार्वजनिक भर्त्सना

The denunciation of the horrible practice resulted in everyone being relieved.

Deodorize/डियोडॅराइज *(verb)* - निर्गन्धीकरण करना, गन्धहीन करना

Room freshener was used to deodorize the room.

Decontology/डिकॉन्टोलोजी *(noun)* - धर्मशास्त्र

She is learning Decontology.

Depart/डिपार्ट *(verb)* - प्रस्थान करना, रवाना होना

They were supposed to depart at 5 o'clock to catch the train.

Depasture/डिपास्चर *(verb)* - चरने के लिए पशुओं को बाहर निकालना, रवानगी, प्रस्थान किया

It is my duty in the morning to depasture the cattle.

Depend/डिपेन्ड *(verb)* - भरोसा करना, निर्भर करना

Children depend on their parents for everything when they are young.

Depict/डिपिक्ट *(verb)* - दर्शाना, चित्रित करना

The government will take action if you depict women in a derogatory manner.

Depletion/डिप्लीशन् *(noun)* - रिक्तीकरण

The continuing depletion of the earth's natural resources could prove very dangerous.

Deplorable/डिप्लोरेबल *(adj)* - शोचनीय, निदंनीय

His actions were announced as being horribly deplorable.

Deploy/डिप्लॉइ *(verb)* - सेना या हथियारों को संभावित लड़ाई के लिए तैयार रखना

The government will deploy military to defend its frontiers.

Depolarize/डिपोलराइज *(verb)* - विद्युत धारा का क्रम हटाना

Depolarize the circuit, please.

Deponent/डिपोनेन्ट *(noun)* - गवाह, बयान देने वाला

Deponent's name, address, age and occupation should be mentioned at the head of his deposition.

Depopulate/डिपाप्युलेट *(verb)* - जनसंख्या कम करना

Countries facing a huge population explosion must come up with policies to depopulate.

Deport/डिपोर्ट *(verb)* - देश से बाहर निकालना, निर्वासन

It was considered important for one to deport oneself with dignity in the old times.

Deposit/डिपाजिट *(noun)* – धरोहर, जमा

You may also have to pay a deposit which is normally refunded at the end of your stay.

Deprave/डिप्रेव *(verb)* – कलुषित करना, बिगड़ना

To behave in such a depraved manner can only lead to disaster.

Depreciate/डिप्रीसिएट *(verb)* – एक अवधि के बाद किसी वस्तु का मूल्य घट जाना

Some assets only depreciate over time.

Depress/डिप्रेस *(verb)* – उदास करना, निपटारा करना, हताश करना

He was quite depressed after his pet died.

Deprive/डिप्राइव *(verb)* – छीन लेना, किसी को किसी से वंचित करना

She was deprived of the love of both her parents.

Depth/डेप्थ *(noun)* – गहराई

It is important to study a subject in depth to excel in it.

Deputation/डेप्युटेशन *(noun)* – नियुक्ति

The deputation performed the task on behalf of their seniors very well.

Deputy/डेप्युटि *(noun)* – प्रतिनिधि

He was recently appointed as deputy to the minister.

Deracinate/डेरासिनेट *(verb)* – जड़ से उखाड़ लेना, उन्मूलन करना

The young sap was deracinated and planted where water was in abundance.

Derby/डर्बी *(noun)* – एक प्रसिद्ध घुड़दौड़

The Derby is one of the most popular races in the world.

Derelict/डिरेलिक्ट *(adjective)* – त्यक्त, परित्यक्त, परित्याग वस्तु

The house has been in a derelict condition for a long time.

Derivation/डिराइवेशन *(noun)* – मूल शब्द की व्युत्पति

New words are derivations of old words and terms.

Derive/डिराइव *(verb)* – किसी से कुछ प्राप्त करना

Marx derived his philosophy of history from Hegel.

Derris/डेरिस *(noun)* – कीटनाशक

Derris is a woody East Indian plant whose roots are used to manufacture insecticide.

Dervish/डर्विश *(noun)* – दरवेश, फकीर

Whirling is one of the rituals practised by the Dervish fraternity.

D

Descant/डेस्कैंट *(noun)* – द्रुत उतार-चढ़ाव के साथ गाना

The angels, we could say, sang the descant to creation's chorus.

Describable/डिस्क्राइबेब्ल *(adjective)* – वर्णनीय

Happiness is a describable emotion.

Describe/डिस्क्राइब *(verb)* – व्याख्या करना

She was asked to describe her experience in a few sentences.

Description/डिस्क्रीप्सन *(noun)* – वर्णन

Thanks to the graphic facial features, the police arrested the thief in no time.

Desert/डेजर्ट *(verb)* – त्याग देना

The house was deserted when the police finally arrived.

Desert/डेजर्ट *(noun)* – निर्जन, शून्य, रेगिस्तान, मरुस्थल

Sahara is pamous desert in the world.

Deserve/डिजर्व *(verb)* – अधिकार रखना, अच्छे या बुरे फल का पात्र होना

He certainly deserved the punishment for his misdeeds.

Deshabille/डेजाबिये *(noun)* – गन्दा कपड़ा

It was not a sad thing to be caught in a state of deshabille in the old days.

Desiccate/डेसिक्केट *(verb)* – सुखाना

Please desiccate a slice of banana and put in a food dehydrator.

Desire/डिजायर *(noun)* – इच्छा, कामेच्छा, कामवासना

I confess that I have never had a burning desire to go to England.

Desirous/डिजायरस *(adj)* – इच्छुक, आकांक्षी, अभिलाषी

He is particularly desirous of visiting Andaman & Nicobar islands. Those desirous of success must work hard.

Desk/डेस्क *(noun)* – मेज

The front desk of the hotel was made of marble.

Desolate/डेसोलेट *(adjective)* – सुनसान, निर्जन और अवसादपूर्ण, एकाकी, उदास

Finally we reached a desolate place devoid of people except for some grazing sheep.

Despair/डेस्पेअर *(noun & verb)* – पूर्णनिराशा

Well, don't despair, help is at hand and we will be escorted back safely.

D

Desperate/डेसपरेट *(adjective)* – अत्यधिक निराशा के कारण दुस्साहसी

Desperate situations may lead some people to act in a risky manner.

Despise/डिस्पाइज *(verb)* – घृणा करना, तिरस्कार करना

Due to his behaviour, he was thoroughly despised by the whole society.

Despite/डिस्पाइट *(adv)* – के बावजूद

Anita was determined to do well despite her handicap.

Despond/डिस्पाण्ड *(verb)* – निराश होना

We must not despond in bad days.

Destine/डेस्टिन *(verb)* – स्थिर करना, ठहराना, नियत करना

He was destined to become an IAS officer.

Destiny/डेस्टिनी *(noun)* – भाग्य, नियति

It is his destiny to act as saviour.

Destroy/डिस्ट्रॉइ *(verb)* – नष्ट करना, किसी वस्तु को इस प्रकार हानि पहुँचाना कि वह इस्तेमाल न हो सके

The whole village was destroyed in the hurricane.

Destructibility/डिस्ट्रक्टिबिलिटि *(adj.)* – ध्वंसता

John had not calculated the power of destructibility of the hurricane while designing his house.

Destruction/डिस्ट्रक्शन *(noun)* – नाश, ध्वंस, तोड़फोड़

The complete destruction of the school in the earthquake was terrible.

Desultory/डेसल्टरी *(adjective)* – असंगत, अनियमित

They were engaging in a desultory conversation unwillingly.

Detail/डिटेल *(noun)* – एक तथ्य या सूचना, ब्योरा

Please give me the detail of his business.

Detain/डिटेन *(verb)* – किसी व्यक्ति को देरी कराना, व्यक्ति को किसी स्थान से नहीं जाने देना

He was detained at the airport for more than three hours.

Detect/डिटेक्ट *(verb)* – पता लगाना, ऐसी बात को खोज लेना जिसे जानना कठिन हो

He could detect that something was not quite right.

Detent/डिटेन्ट *(noun)* – किसी यन्त्र की गति स्थिर करने का खटका

This detent is meant to regulate motion of the machine.

Detention/डिटेन्शन *(noun)* – किसी व्यक्ति को रोकने की प्रक्रिया

Harry was sent to detention centre after school for being naughty.

Deter/डिटर *(verb)* – किसी को कोई काम करने से रोकना, संभावित दुष्परिणामों को देखते हुए

No amount of social work was going to deter her from studying to achieve her goals.

Deteriorate/डिटेरिओरेट *(verb)* – क्षय होना, बदतर होना

Jim's condition kept deteriorating even after he was treated at the hospital.

Determinant/डिटर्मिनैन्ट *(noun)* – स्थिर, निर्धारण

Y-chromosome is the determinant of the birth of a boy or girl.

Determinate/डिटरमिनेट *(adjective)* – निर्धारित

Determinate counsel of god means god determined the course of action.

Detonate/डिटोनेट *(verb)* – धड़ाका करना, बम विस्फोट होना या करना

No one was allowed to go near the place before the bomb was detonated.

Detrain/डिट्रेन *(verb)* – रेलगाड़ी से उतारना या उतरना

The whole family detrained as their plans got cancelled at the last moment.

Detriment/डेट्रिमेंट *(noun)* – हानिकारक, नुकसानदेह

The action backfired to their detriment.

Devil/डेविल *(verb)* – दानव

Some people believe that the devil exists.

Devilish/डेविलिश *(adjective)* - अति दुष्ट या उपद्रवी

He behaved in a devilish sort of way.

Devious/डीवियस *(adjective)* - दोषी

Huma acted in a devious way to get the promotion.

Devise/डिवाइज *(verb)* - उपाय या युक्ति निकालना

He devised a plan to bring them to our home quickly.

Devitalize/डिवाइटलाइज *(verb)* - निर्जीव करना

The entire team was feeling devitalized after trekking for more than six hours.

Devolution/डिवोल्यूशन *(noun)* - विकेन्द्रीकरण

The school authorities practised devolution of power to make decision making more effective.

Devolve/डिवॉल्व *(verb)* - to deliver over किसी की मृत्यु के पश्चात् उसकी संपत्ति अधिकारी को सौंपना

Devolve decision-making from central government to the people of the region.

Devote/डिवोट *(verb)* - समर्पित करना

The teacher told Mukesh to devote more time to studies in order to score better marks.

Devotion/डिवोशन *(noun)* - धर्मनिष्ठा, समर्पणभाव

Scoring high marks in exams requires a lot of devotion from the student.

Devour/डिवावर *(verb)* - भूख से मारे जल्दी-जल्दी खाना

Anil devoured food at the restaurant like he was eating after a long time.

Devout/डिवाउट *(adjective)* - अत्यधिक धार्मिक

James is a devout Christian.

Dew/ड्यू *(noun)* - तुषार, ओस

An example of dew is the liquid that drips off of blades of grass in the morning.

Dexterity/डेक्सटेरिटी *(noun)* - निपुणता

Mathews showed great dexterity in the fine arts competition.

Diabetes/डायबिटिज *(noun)* - मधुमेह

Doctors say diabetes is increasing at an alarming rate.

Diadem/डायडेम *(noun)* - मुकुट

The diadem is a symbol of adornment.

Diagonal/डायगोनल *(adjective)* - कर्ण

Do not use diagonals or right to left words.

Diagram/डाइअग्रैम *(noun)* - आकृति, रेखाचित्र

A diagram is a chart showing how all the departments within an organization are related.

Dial/डायल *(noun)* - घड़ी का गोलाकार भाग जिस पर समय की इकाइयाँ अंकित होती है

This wall clock has a very large dial.

Dialect/डायलेक्ट *(noun)* - प्रकृत भाषा, उपभाषा

I did not understand the dialect of the Bengal region.

Dialogic/डायलोजिक *(adj)* - वार्तालाप सम्बन्धी

Your dialogical statement is not appreciable.

Dialogue/डायलाग *(verb)* - बातचीत

Smith does not want to indulge in any dialogue with Jerry.

Diamantiferous/डायमन्टिफरस *(adj)* - हीरा उत्पन्न करने वाली

These mines are diamantiferous.

Diana/डायना *(noun)* - चन्द्रमा

Diana is the name of the ancient Roman goddess of moon, hunt and chastity.

Diaper/डायपर *(noun)* - बेलबूटा कढ़ा हुआ कपड़ा, अंगोछा

Diaper is an absorbent cloth worn by babies.

Diarist/डायरिष्ट *(noun)* - रोजनामचा रखने वाला

Anne Frank was a diarist.

Diarrhoea/डायरिया *(noun)* - अतिसार, दस्त की बीमारी

James missed the school trip because he was suffering from diarrhoa.

Diary/डायरी *(noun)* - रोजनामचा

Writing a diary is a good habit.

Dice/डाइस *(verb)* - पासे का खेल, वर्गाकार दाना जिस पर छ: बिंदिया होती है

The player rolled the dice on the casino table.

Dichotomy/डाइकाटामि *(noun)* - तर्क में किसी पदार्थ के दो विभाग

The dichotomy of the situation was that though he claimed to be an artist, he was unaware of Picasso's work.

D

D

Dictaphone/डिक्टाफोन *(noun)* - बोले हुए शब्दों को टाइप में लिखने का यंत्र

They recorded my speech on a dictaphone to play it at the function.

Diction/डिक्शन *(noun)* - मुहावरा

Good diction is a pre-requisite for media persons.

Dictum/डिक्टम *(noun)*- आदेश

He cited Augustine's dictum in his article.

Did/डिड - किया

past of do. *Did he go to school?*

Didactic/डिडैक्टिक *(adjective)* - उपदेशात्मक, शिक्षात्मक

The speech given at the assembly was supposed to be didactic.

Diddle/डिडल *(verb)* - बहकाना

Mom always said not to diddle away time.

Die/डाइ *(verb)* - दम निकालना, मरना

James can't stand to see anyone die.

Diehard/डाइहार्ड *(noun)* - अन्त तक विरोध करने वाला

She is a diehard fan of Tom Hanks.

Diet/डाइट *(noun)* - भोजन, खुराक

One should consume a balanced diet to stay healthy.

Difference/डिफरेंस *(noun)* - मतभेद, असहमति, विवाद

He couldn't explain the difference between the two portraits.

Different/डिफरेंट *(adjective)* - पृथक, असमान

One should understand that sex and gender are two different things.

Differentia/डिफरेंसिया *(noun)* - भेद का चिह्न

The birth spot is the differentia between the twins.

Difficult/डिफिकल्ट *(adj)* - कठिन, मुश्किल *The questions in final exam were very difficult.*

Diffidence/डिफिडेन्स *(noun)* - अविश्वास

Don't put diffidence in this matter.

Diffident/डिफिडेन्ट *(adjective)* - अविश्वस्त, आत्महीन

He is a very diffident person.

Diffract/डिफ्रेक्ट *(verb)* - टुकड़े करना

That effect is caused due to diffraction of light.

Diffuse/डिफ्यूज *(adjective)* - छितराना

Sugar diffuses in the tea on stirring.

Dig/डिग *(verb)* - गड्ढा खोदना

Please dig into your books and find the answer to this question. They went to dig the ground in search of dinosaur bones.

Dight/डाइट *(verb)* - सजाना

Please dight for the competition.

Dignify/डिग्निफाइ *(verb)* - सत्कार करना

He felt dignified in the company of leading writers.

Dignitary/डिग्निटरी *(noun)* - उच्च पद का पादरी

He is a dignitary at the office.

Dignity/डिग्निटी *(noun)* - गौरव, शान्त और गम्भीर आचरण

One should carry oneself with dignity and pride.

Digress/डायग्रेस *(verb)* - मुख्य विषय को छोड़कर भटकना

Kindly be precise and do not digress from the topic.

Dilapidate/डिलैपिडेट *(verb)* - नाश करना

For want of repairs, the house was in a dilapidated condition.

Dilate/डायलेट *(verb)* - चौड़ा करना

Capillaries were dilated to allow the excess heat to be removed by blood flow.

Dilettante/डिलेटैन्टि *(noun)* - कलानुरागी

He is a dilettante in the field of religion.

Diligence/डिलिजेन्स *(noun)* - उद्योग, कर्मठता, परिश्रम

One should show diligence towards one's work.

Dill/डिल *(noun)* - मधुरिका लता

He is such a dill that everyone takes him for granted.

Dilly-dally/डिली-डैली *(verb)* - टालमटोल करना

The government continues to dilly-dally on taking a decision on labour reforms.

Dimension/डायमेन्सन *(noun)* - लम्बाई-चौड़ाई या ऊँचाई का मापन

Dimension is the measurement of length, breadth and width.

Dimidiate/डिमिडियेट *(verb)* - भागों में विभक्त करना

He has dimidiated the property amongst his sons.

Diminish/डिमनिश *(verb)* - कम होना, छोटा होना या छोटा करना

Objects appear to diminish in size as we go farther away from them.

Diminution/डिमिन्यूशन *(noun)* - कमी

Diminution means reduction in value of an individual.

Diminutive/डिमिन्यूटिव *(adjective)* - अल्प

The meaning of diminution can be translated 'tiny', and diminutives are used frequently when speaking to small children. Harry is diminutive for Harold.

Dimity/डिमिटि *(noun)* - सूती कपड़ा

Could you buy me dimity from the market?

Dimple/डिम्पल *(noun)* - गाल की ठुड्डी की गड्ढा

Dimple is a small depression some of us get on the cheeks while laughing or talking.

Din/डिन *(noun)* - शोर-शराबा, हल्का-फुल्का

The din created by loud speakers has made our life tough.

Dingy/डिंजी *(adjective)* - गंदा और अंधेरा

That café was poorly lit, dingy and drab that we decided to come out of it immediately.

Dinner/डिनर *(noun)* - दिन का मुख्य भोजन

Let's have dinner at the restaurant tonight.

Dint/डिन्ट *(noun)* - प्रहार, प्रयत्न

He succeeded in life by dint of hard study.

Diocese/डायोसेस *(noun)* - पादरी का प्रदेश

This area is the bishop's diocese.

Dioxide/डायऑक्साइड *(noun)* - दो भाग ऑक्सीजन एवं एक भाग धातु का मेल

Carbon dioxide is used to extinguish fire.

Diphtheria/डिफ्थीरिया *(noun)* - कण्ठ का एक संक्रामक रोग

He is suffering from diphtheria.

Diplomacy/डिप्लोमेसी *(noun)* - अंतर्राष्ट्रीय कूटनीति

One should talk with diplomacy on controversial topics.

Dipper/डिपर *(noun)* - कल्छुल, सप्तऋषि, गोताखोर, जलपाख

Dipper is a bird found in and around Mexico. Truck drivers use dipper at night.

Dipterous/डिप्टरस *(adjective)* - केवल दो पंखों या पैरों वाला

The birds having two wings only are called dipterous.

Dire/डायर *(adjective)* - भयानक, गम्भीर, दारूण

There is a dire need to improve literacy in India.

Direct/डायरेक्ट *(adj & verb)* - सीधा, ठीक, प्रत्यक्ष

He was directed to report to the head quarters immediately.

Direction/डायरेक्शन *(noun)* - निर्देश

Please move in the northern direction to reach the railway station.

Director/डायरेक्टर *(noun)* - निर्देशक

She is the director of this prestigious organization.

Dirge/डर्ज *(noun)* - मर्सिया, शोकगीत

The following is a dirge in rememberance of my uncle who expired yesterday.

Dirk/डर्क *(noun)* - एक प्रकार की कटार, छूरा

Use a dirk to fight the criminal.

Disability/डिजैबिलिटी *(noun)* - अयोग्यता

He is suffering from mental and physical disability.

Disabuse/डिसएब्यूज *(verb)* - ठीक करना, झूठे विचारों से छुटकारा पाना, भ्रम निवारण

Don't disabuse innocent children.

Disadvantage/डिसएडवांटेज *(noun)* - असुविधा, हानि, नुकसान

An example of a disadvantage is a team's star player having to sit out because of an injury.

Disaffection/डिसएफेक्शन *(noun)* - घृणा, विरक्ति

She had disaffection towords her husband.

Disaffirm/डिसएफर्म *(verb)* - विरोध करना

He disaffirmed that he ever signed a contract with that party.

D

D

Disagree/डिसएग्री *(verb)* – सहमत न होना

I disagree with you on your opinion.

Disallow/डिसएलाउ *(verb)* – अस्वीकार करना

Passengers holding ordinary tickets have been disallowed to board this coach.

Disappear/डिसएपिअर *(verb)* – अदृश्य होना

Thieves disappeared from the house before the security could arrive.

Disappoint/डिसएप्वाइंट *(verb)* – नियुक्ति तोड़ना, निराश या हताश करना

Do not disappoint your parents by indulging in bad deeds.

Disapprobation/डिसएप्रोबेशन *(noun)* – अस्वीकृति

Disapprobation of smoking will not be lifted.

Disapproval/डिसएप्रुवल *(noun)* – अस्वीकृति (बुरा होने के कारण)

Our request to let us in the hostel was met with stern disapproval by the warden.

Disapprove/डिसएप्रुव *(verb)* – अस्वीकार करना, नापसंद करना

I have disapproved your leave application.

Disarm/डिसआर्म *(verb)* – हथियार ले लेना, निहत्था करना

The police disarmed the criminals.

Disarrange/डिस्अरेंज *(verb)* – क्रम हटाना, अव्यवस्थित करना

Why did you disarrange the crockery?

Disarray/डिस्अरे *(noun)* – उलट-पलट, गड़बड़

The entire house is in disarray.

Disaster/डिजास्टर *(noun)* – विनाश, तबाही

The fire was a disaster at the wedding ceremony.

Disastrous/डिजास्ट्रस *(adjective)* – नाशकारी

Dereliction of duty could prove to be disastrous for our aim.

Disband/डिस्बैंड *(verb)* – सेना भंग करना या तोड़ना

This company would be disbanded into small units for the operations.

Disbelief/डिस्बिलिफ *(noun)* – अविश्वास

She stared at the TajMahal in disbelief.

Disburden/डिस्बर्डेन *(verb)* – हल्का करना, बोझा उतारना

Please disburden yourself regarding the sale of this property.

Disburse/डिस्बर्स *(verb)* – धन देना, चुकाना, इकट्ठा किये हुए धन से पैसा देना

The college disbursed grants to all who secured more than 75 percent marks.

Discard/डिस्कार्ड *(verb)* – अलग करना

Those not scoring runs would be discarded by the selectors.

Discern/डिसर्न *(verb)* – कठिनाई से किसी वस्तु को देख या सुन पाना

I couldn't discern the difference between the shawls.

Disciple/डिस्साइपल् *(noun)* – शिष्य, चेला, अनुयायी

Seeta is a disciple of Gandhiji.

Disciplinary/डिसिप्लिनरी *(adjective)* – अनुशासन सम्बन्धी

Disciplinary action was taken against those who failed to report in time.

Discipline/डिसिप्लीन *(noun)* – अनुशासन

Discipline should be inculcated right from the time a child learns to speak.

Disclaim/डिसक्लेम *(verb)* – अस्वीकार करना, मुकरना

Due to dispute, I disclaim his ownership of the house.

Disclose/डिसक्लोज *(verb)* – किसी को कोई बात बताना या सार्वजनिक रूप से प्रकट करना

Do not disclose this information to anyone.

Discolour/डिसकलर *(verb)* – मलिन करना, रंग बिगड़ना या बिगाड़ना

The dress I bought became discoloured after the very first wash.

Discomfort/डिसकम्फोर्ट *(noun)* – पीड़ा

I feel discomfort in his peresence.

Discommode/डिसकमोड *(verb)* – कष्ट देना, सताना, परेशानी में डालना

Do not discommode the guests.

Discompose/डिसकम्पोज *(verb)* – अस्त-व्यस्त करना, अशांत कर देना

With your actions you are discomposing everybody present at the gathering.

Disconcert/डिसकन्सर्ट *(verb)* – किसी के चित्त को विक्षुब्ध कर देना

Do not disconcert the boss.

Disconnect/डिसकनेक्ट *(verb)* – पृथक् करना

Please disconnect the phone connection from my house.

Disconsent/डिसकन्सेंट *(verb)* – असहमत होना

I am disconsented with the company's performance.

Disconsolate/डिसकन्सोलेट *(adjective)* – निराश, मायूस

He was very disconsolate after he heard the loss of his court case.

Discontent/डिसकन्टेन्ट *(noun)* – असन्तोष

Restless desire for something more or different led her to high levels of discontent.

Discontinue/डिस्कन्टिन्यू *(verb)* – रोक देना या बन्द कर देना

He is discontinuing the job at the firm.

Discount/डिस्काउन्ट *(noun)* – सामान्य से कम दाम, छूट

Enjoy a 30 percent discount on this product during this Diwali festival.

Discourse/डिस्कोर्स *(noun)* – सम्भाषण, किसी विषय पर गम्भीर चर्चा

What's your discourse on this matter?

Discourteous/डिस्कर्टीअस *(adjective)* – असभ्य

One should not be discourteous to guests.

Discover/डिस्कवर *(verb)* – किसी नई बात का पता लगाना या खोज

I will discover the truth behind the robbery.

Discovery/डिस्कवरी *(noun)* – आविष्कार

The discovery of X-rays as a means to study bones was a great discovery.

Discredit/डिस्क्रेडिट *(verb)* – अपयश, बदनाम करना

They have discredited him in the market by spreading false rumours.

Discreet/डिस्क्रीट *(adj)* – विचारशील, विचारवान

Please be discreet about this information.

Discrepancy/डिस्क्रिपेन्सी *(noun)* – (दो बातों में) असंमति या अंतर

There is no discrepancy between the findings of the two projects.

Discrete/डिस्क्रीट *(adjective)* – अलग

These are discrete pages.

Discretion/डिस्क्रीशन *(noun)* – विवेक, समझ-बूझ

I will reveal this information only at your discretion.

Discriminate/डिसक्रिमिनट *(verb)* – प्रभेद करना, किसी के प्रति भेदभाव करना या रखना

One must never discriminate against people as all are equals.

D

Disdain/डिस्डेन *(noun)* – तिरस्कार करना

Her voice was choked with disdain.

Disease/डिजीज *(noun)* – रोग, व्याधि

Cancer is a disease wherein malicious tumour develops in any part of the body.

Disembark/डिसइम्बार्क *(verb)* – जलपोत या विमान पर से किनारे पर उतरना

He has disembarked from the ship.

Disembarrass/डिसइम्बैरस *(verb)* – घबड़ाहट से मुक्त करना

I disembarrass myself from this situation.

Disembroil/डिसइम्ब्रायल *(verb)* – आपत्ति से छुड़ाना, सुलझाना

He disembroiled our dispute.

Disenchant/डिसइन्चैट *(verb)* – जादू टोने के प्रभाव से छुड़ाना

He refused to promote him because he disenchanted with his performance.

Disengage/डिसइंगेज *(noun)* – अलगाना, छुड़ाना, सम्बन्ध तोड़ना

Let's disengage from this conversation before we say something we'll regret later.

Disentangle/डिसइन्टैंगल *(verb)* – सुलझाना, किसी लिपटी हुई वस्तु से किसी व्यक्ति या वस्तु को मुक्त करना

Please disentangle this knot for me.

Disfavour/डिसफेवर *(noun)* – विराग, अरुचि

He is in disfavour of the prime minister.

Disfigure/डिसफिगर *(verb)* – सौन्दर्य नष्ट करना

Don't disfigure that statue by writing something on it.

Disgorge/डिस्गॉर्ज *(verb)* – उगलना

The doctor gave an injection to help disgorge the food from the stomach.

Disgrace/डिसग्रेस *(noun)* – अपमान, निरादर

One mistake brought disgrace to the family.

D

Disguise/डिसगाइज *(verb)* – छिपाना, भेष बदलना, रूप बदलना
They disguised their faces before robbing the bank.

Disgust/डिसगस्ट *(noun)* – घृणा, गुस्सा, चिढ़
I felt disgust after hearing of the crime he had committed.

Dish/डिस *(noun)*– थाली, तश्तरी, रकाबी
I need a dish washer for my house.

Disharmonize/डिसहारमोनाइज *(verb)* – बेसुरा करना
Don't dishormonize your performance.

Disharmony/डिसहारमनी *(noun)* – बेसुरापन, लयभंग
The song is being played in disharmony.

Dishearten/डिसहार्टेन *(verb)* – उत्साह भंग करना
Don't feel disheartened as there's always a second chance.

Dishonest/डिस्आनेस्ट *(adjective)* – बेईमान, धोखेवाज
I didn't know he would turn out to be a dishonest man.

Disinclination/डिस्इनक्लानेशन *(noun)* – अरुचि
He has disinclination towards his studies.

Disinfect/डिसइन्फेक्ट *(verb)* – संक्रामक दोष दूर करना
The sanitizer will disinfect you.

Disingenuous/डिस्इन्जेन्युअस *(adj)* – कपटी, धूर्त
Don't go on his looks, he is very disingenuous.

Disinherit/डिसइन्हेरिट *(verb)* – पैतृक सम्पति से वंचित करना
The father disinherited his son from his property.

Disintegrate/डिसइन्टिग्रेट *(verb)* – विखण्डित होना, टुकड़े-टुकड़े हो जाना
In nuclear fission, the nucleus breaks into two and the process continues.

Disinter/डिसइन्टर *(verb)* – खोदना, किसी वस्तु को खोदकर बाहर निकालना
Let's not disinter past secrets.

Disinterested/डिसइन्टरेस्टेड *(adj)* – निष्पक्ष, तटस्थ
He seems absolutely disinterested in this conversation.

Disjoint/डिसज्वाइंट *(adjective)* – जोड़ पर से पृथक् करना, सम्बन्ध तोड़ना
Any disjointed effort will not achieve desired results.

Disjunct/डिसजंक्ट *(adjective)* – असम्बद्ध, पृथक् किया हुआ
There seems to be great disjunct in his work.

Dislike/डिसलाइक *(verb)* – नापसंद करना
He disliked your brother.

Dislocate/डिसलोकेट *(verb)* – अपने स्थान से हटना या हटा दिया जाना, उखड़ा जोड़, स्थान से हटाना
He fell while playing football and dislocated his elbow joint.

Dislocation/डिसलोकेशन *(noun)* – स्थान भ्रष्टता
Poor policies of the government may lead to social dislocations in the society.

Disloyal/डिस्लॉइअल *(adjective)* – बेवफा, अविश्वासी
The books he wrote about his employer were so disloyal.

Dismal/डिसमल *(adj)* – शोकयुक्त, निराशाजनक
They presented a totally dismal performance at the playground.

Dismantle/डिस्मैंटल *(verb)* – किसी वस्तु को टुकड़े-टुकड़े कर देना
Please dismantle this machine before transporting it to Mumbai.

Dismast/डिस्मास्ट *(verb)* जहाज का मस्तूल हटाना
The ship has been dismasted.

Dismember/डिस्मेम्बर *(verb)* – खण्ड-खण्ड करना
The train passed over and dismembered the body of the traveller.

Disobedience/डिस्ओबेडियन्स *(noun)* – अवज्ञाकारी, आज्ञा भंग
Gandhiji launched a Civil Disobedience Movement against British administration to make India a free nation.

Disobey/डिस्ओबे *(verb)* – आज्ञा, आदेश पालन से इनकार
Never disobey your parents or teachers.

Disoblige/डिस्ओब्लाइज *(verb)* – असन्तुष्ट करना
You are disobliging your guests.

Disorganize/डिस्ऑरगेनाइज *(verb)* - उपद्रव करना, अव्यवस्थित करना

We had to go without food or water because the authorities were so disorganized.

Disown/डिजॉन *(verb)* - त्यागना

That man disowned his daughter.

Disparage/डिस्पैरिज *(verb)* - पद घटाना, बुराई करना, निंदा करना

Don't try to pass disparaging remarks against anybody.

Disparate/डिस्परएट *(noun)* - असमान, व्यक्ति या वस्तु आचरण या गुण में बेहद भिन्न हो

A strong leader can motivate a geographically disparate team to achieve agreed goals.

Dispatch/डिस्पैच *(verb)* - किसी व्यक्ति या वस्तु को कहीं भेजना

The order was dispatched five minutes ago.

Dispel/डिस्पेल *(verb)* - (शंका आदि) को दूर कर देना

The doubts, he has, must be dispelled.

Dispensable/डिस्पेन्सेबल् *(adjective)* - अनावश्यक, अपरिहार्य

These items of my personal property are dispensable.

Dispensation/डिस्पेन्सेशन *(noun)* - वितरण, बाँटना

I look forward to an early dispensation of my request.

Dispense/डिस्पेन्स *(verb)* - बाँटना

Kindly dispense these blankets among all participants.

Dispenser/डिस्पेन्सर *(noun)* - मशनी या डिब्बा जिससे आपको अभीष्ट वस्तु मिलती है

A dispenser is a container so designed that the contents can be used in prescribed amounts.

Disperse/डिस्पर्स *(verb)* - छितराना, बिखर जाना

The police fired water cannon shots to disperse the crowd.

Dispersion/डिस्पर्सन *(noun)* - आबादी या चीजों के दूर-दूर तक फैलने की प्रक्रिया

With the help of a prism, we can observe the dispersion of light into seven colours.

Dispersive/डिस्पर्सिव *(adjective)* - फैलाने वाला

This ia a dispersive prism which disperses the rays.

Dispirit/डिस्प्रीरिट *(verb)* - उदास करना

If you keep yourself away from the meet, the participants may feel dispirited.

Displace/डिस्प्लेस *(verb)* - स्थान बदलना या स्थान छीन लेना

Some workers have been displaced from their regular duty.

Display/डिसप्ले *(verb)* - किसी वस्तु को ऐसे स्थान पर रखना कि लोग उसे देख सके

You are a public figure and your posture must display a positive attitude.

Displease/डिसप्लीज *(verb)* - अप्रसन्न करना

You should try not to displease any of your guests.

Displeasure/डिसप्लेजर *(noun)* - किसी को नाराज करना

Never be a source of displeasure to your chairman.

Disport/डिस्पोर्ट *(verb)* - आनन्द मनाना, दिल बहलाना

She disported herself thoroughly with the massage at the spa.

Disposable/डिसपोजेब्ल *(adjective)* - एक बार प्रयोग के बाद फेंकने योग्य

I would like to be served my fruit drink in a disposable glass.

Disposition/डिसपोजिशन *(noun)* - प्रवृत्ति, चरित्र

He can fight the lawsuit at his own disposition.

Dispossess/डिसपॅजेस *(verb)* - अधिकार छीन लेना, निर्वासित कर देना

These people have been dispossessed of their houses.

Dispraise/डिसप्रेज *(noun)* - निन्दा करना

Never dispraise anybody's hard work.

Disproof/डिसप्रुफ *(noun)* - खण्डन

I have no evidence or disproof of his claims.

Disproportion/डिस्प्रोपोरशन *(noun)* - अयोग्यता, विषमता

There is disproportion in the amount of water in these bottles.

Disprove/डिस्प्रूव *(verb)* - खण्डन करना, किसी बात को असत्य सिद्ध करना

I can disprove her argument.

D

D

Dispute/डिस्प्यूट *(verb)* - कलह करना

China doesn't recognize McMohan Line as a frontier between India and China.

Disqualify/डिसक्वालिफाइ *(verb)* - अयोग्य ठहराना

We will disqualify any participant who fails to match up to our standards.

Disquiet/डिसक्वायट *(verb)* - व्याकुल करना

Don't disquiet me, please.

Disregard/डिसरिगार्ड *(nout & verb)* - उपेक्षा करना, किसी बात पर ध्यान नहीं देना

His attitude reflects total disregard for her welfare.

Disrelish/डिसरेलिश *(verb)* - अरुचि करना, नफ़रत करना

There is never a time when I disrelish food.

Disrepute/डिस्‌रिप्यूट *(noun)* - अपयश

The fraud he committed has brought him great disrepute.

Disrespect/डिस्‌रिस्पेक्ट *(noun)* - अनादर, निरादर

Showing disrespect to the national flag is an offence.

Disrobe/डिसरॉब *(verb)* - वस्त्र उतारना, नंगा करना

To disrobe at this public place is an offence, police will haul you.

Disrupt/डिसरप्ट *(verb)* - बाधित करना

Your sloppy behaviour is disrupting the normal proceedings of the day.

Dissatisfied/डिससैटिस्फाइड *(adjective)* - असंतुष्ट

She is more often than not dissatisfied with her marks.

Dissatisfy/डिससैटिसफाइ *(verb)* - असन्तुष्ट करना

The poor quality of after-sales service has thoroughly dissatisfied me with the home music system.

Dissemble/डिसेम्बल *(verb)* - छिपाना

He is very cunning and always dissembles his ulterior feelings to cheat.

Disseminate/डिसेमिनेट *(verb)* - छितराना, फैलाना, प्रचार करना

Kindly disseminate the following information among all the readers.

Dissension/डिसेन्सन *(noun)* - विरोध, अनबन, झगड़ा

here has been some dissension between the family members.

Dissent/डिसेन्ट *(verb)* - मतभेद करना, सामान्य धाराण से असहमति

There were many dissenting voices over the selection of the chairman.

Disserve/डिसर्व *(verb)* - हानि पहुँचाना

Your selfish motives and other actions have been disserving this organization.

Dissimulate/डिसिम्यूलेट *(verb)* - बहाना करना

He should be open in his views and not dissimulate true feelings.

Dissipate/डिसिपेट *(verb)* - नष्ट करना, गायब हो जाना

Unnecessary discussions will only dissipate your energy.

Dissociate/डिसोसिएट *(verb)* - पृथक् करना

The company has dissociated with a few of its clients.

Dissolve/डिजॉल्व *(verb)* - गलाना, घोलना, पिघलाना, भंग करना

The President dissolved the parliament on the recommendation of the Prime Minister.

Dissonance/डिसॉनन्स *(noun)* असंगति, बेसुरापन

I dislike such dissonance.

Distance/डिस्टैंस *(noun)* - अन्तर, दो स्थानों के बीच की दूरी

Distance between Delhi and Mumbai is more than 1400 kilometres.

Distant/डिस्टैंट *(adjective)* - दूरस्थ, समय या स्थान की दृष्टि से काफी दूर

The town lay half a mile distant. He is a distant cousin of my friend.

Distemper/डिस्टेम्पर *(noun)* - पीड़ा, रोग, व्यथा, विकार

The paint made by mixing the pigment with water and a binder is called distemper. My dog is suffering from a viral infection known as canine distemper.

Distend/डिस्टेन्ड *(verb)* - अंदरूनी दबाव के कारण फूलना या फुलाना

The medical report showed the stomach to be grossly distended with a large food residue.

Distensible/डिस्टेन्सिब्ल *(adjective)*- फुलाने योग्य

This bladder is distensible.

Distinct/डिस्टिंक्ट *(adjective)* - पृथक्, अलग तरह का स्पष्ट

The twin brothers are pretty different from one another in nature.

Distinguish/डिस्टिंग्विश *(verb)* - पहचानना, भेद करना, दो वस्तुओं या व्यक्तियों में अंतर पहचानना

You must learn to distinguish between right and wrong.

Distort/डिसटोर्ट *(verb)* - शक्ल या आवाज बिगाड़ना

This photograph has been taken from one corner and presents a distorted picture of the show.

Distract/डिस्ट्रैक्ट *(verb)* - किसी व्यक्ति का किसी वस्तु से ध्यान भटकाना

Don't distract your sister from her studies by playing with her.

Distraught/डिस्ट्राट *(adjective)* - व्याकुल, विक्षिप्त

She has been very distraught about her family's well-being.

Distress/डिस्ट्रेस *(noun)* - अत्यधिक पीड़ा और कष्ट

The captain of the ship sent out distress signals upon noticing the approaching hurricane.

Distribute/डिस्ट्रिब्यूट *(verb)* - वितरण करना, बाँट देना

Kindly distribute these sweets among all children.

District/डिस्ट्रिक्ट *(noun)* - जिला

A district is a kind of administrative region.

Distrust/डिस्ट्रस्ट *(noun & verb)* - अविश्वास

Distrust politicians of all stripes.

Disuse/डिसयूज *(noun)* - अप्रचार, अनुपयोग, अव्यवहार

We have purchased a new toaster and the old one is in complete disuse now.

Ditch/डिच *(noun)* - खाई, नाला

They started digging a six feet wide ditch around the building.

Diuretic/डाइयूरेटिक *(adjective)* - मूत्रवर्धक

She has been prescribed diuretic medicines by the doctor.

Diurnal/डाइअर्नल *(adjective)* - दैनिक

This trend is diurnal.

Divagate/डिइवगेट *(verb)* - इधर-उधर भटकाना, बहकना

Don't divagate from the subject.

Dive/डाइव *(verb)* - गोता मारना, डुबकी लगाना

I am learning to dive in a swimming pool.

Diverse/डायवर्स *(adjective)* - अनेक, विविध

There is diverse variety of mugs available in the market.

Diversion/डायवर्सन *(noun)* - दिशा परिवर्तन

The construction of the mall has necessitated diversion of traffic on the roads.

Divert/डायवर्ट *(verb)* - किसी का दिशा परिवर्तन या मोड़ देना

Reading self-help books can divert your mind from silly thoughts.

Dives/डायवीज् *(noun)* - रईस मनुष्य

That man seems a dives.

Divest/डायवेस्ट *(verb)* - वस्त्रहीन करना, वंचित करना

Don't divest him of his self-earned assets.

Dividend/डिविडेन्ड *(noun)* - कंपनी के शेयर धारकों को मिलने वाला लाभांश

He has not received his dividend from the company yet.

Dividing/डिवाडिंग *(verb)* - अलगाव, बाँटना, विभाजित करना

MacMohan Line is the dividing line between India and China.

Divination/डिवाइनेशन *(noun)* - भविष्य कथन, दैविकला, शकुन

To say nothing of the later practice of using divination to determine who was or wasn't a witch. She believes in divination.

Divine/डिवाइन *(adjective)* - अपूर्व, दैविक, ईश्वरीय

Only a divine grace can help me pass this examination.

Divinely/डिवाइनली *(adverb)* - दिव्य रूप से
Some fake people name claimed to possess divinely power.

Divisibility/डिविजिबिलिटी *(noun)* - भाजकत्व
Scientists predict the divisibility of atoms into yet more smaller particles.

D

Division/डिविजन *(noun)* - खण्ड, बँटवारा, वितरण
Division of labour is central to our way of life.

Divisor/डिवाजर *(noun)* - भाजक
In the above question, 5 is the divisor.

Divorce/डायवोर्स *(noun)* - तलाक
Divorce produces insecurity among children.

Dizzily/डिजिलि *(adverb)* - चक्कर से आक्रांत होकर
After a few drinks, he was not steady and walked around dizzily.

Dizzy/डिजि *(adjective)* - जिसे चक्कर आ रहा हो, चक्कर से अक्रांत, बहुत अधिक
She felt dizzy after going on that swing.

Docile/डोसाइल *(adjective)* - विनीत
She seems to be a very docile girl.

Docker/डॉकर *(noun)* - गोदी (बंदरगाह) में काम करने वाला मजदूर
We need to employ a docker to speed up loading the materials into the ship.

Docket/डॉकेट *(noun)* - प्रमाण, दलील, सारांश
You should receive proof of purchase in the form of either a delivery docket or receipt from each of the shops you purchase from.

Doctrinaire/डॉक्ट्रिनेअर *(adjective)* - कल्पना करने वाला मनुष्य, अव्यावहारिक
Communist parties believe in the principles of doctrinaire. He is a new doctrinaire of the party.

Doctrinal/डॉक्ट्रिनल *(adj.)* - सैद्धान्तिक
They have doctrinal controversy.

Doctrine/डॉक्ट्रिन *(noun)* - सिद्धान्त, राजनीतिक दल द्वारा प्रतिपादित मत
Monroe doctrine led to the formation of the League of nations.

Document/डॉक्युमेंट *(noun)* - दस्तावेज, कागजात
All legal documents have been sent to the lawyer.

Dodder/डॉडर *(noun & verb)* - काँपना, डगमगाते हुए चलना
This machine is a dodder.

Dodge/डॉज *(verb)* - धोखा देना, बचकर निकलना, किसी से बचने के लिए तेजी से निकल जाना
At the same time they often dodge the big decisions on things they do control.

Doe/डो *(noun)* - मृगी, हिरणी, मादा खरगोश
I have seen many does and bucks in the forest.

Doer/डूअर *(adjective)* - कर्ता करने वाला मनुष्य
But prove yourselves doers of the word, and not merely hearers who delude themselves.

Doff/डॉफ् *(verb)* - उतार कर रख लेना
He doffed off his hat as a mark of respect for Don Bradman.

Dogma/डॉग्मा *(noun)* - धर्ममत, निर्धारित सिद्धान्त जिन्हें प्रश्न किये बिना स्वीकार करना पड़ता है
If necessary, you should discard any dogma and take practical steps to move ahead in life.

Dogmatic/डॉग्मेटिक *(adj)* - हठधर्मी, हठधर्मिता पर आधारित मत
I dislike a dogmatic man.

Doily/डॉयली *(noun)* - छोटा सुन्दर गमला
We need to buy doily for the house.

Doings/डूइंग्स *(noun)* - कार्यकलाप
Your doings are not beneficial to the society.

Doit/डूइट *(noun)* - हालैंड देश का छोटा सिक्का
His fraud concerned only a doit.

Dole/डोल *(noun)* - भाग्य
His dole is definitely good .

Doleful/डोलफुल् *(adjective)* - उदास या खिन्न
She looks doleful today.

Doll/डॉल *(noun)* - गुड़िया, बच्चों का खिलौना
A doll is a form of human being often used as a plaything for a child.

Dollar/डॉलर *(noun)* - अमेरिका का सिक्का
Dollar is the most acceptable currency in the world.

Dolly/डॉली *(adj)* - नादान
Dolly is a small platform with wheels to carry camera on it.

Dolorous/डोलरस *(adjective)* – कष्टकारक, शोकपूर्ण

I feel dolorous after failing in my test.

Dolour/डोलर *(noun)* – कष्ट, शोक, विषाद, क्लेश

He is in a state of dolour after his break up with his girl friend.

Dolphin/डॉलफिन *(noun)* – एक प्रकार की समुद्री मछली

Dolphins are very friendly mammals living in the sea.

Dolt/डोल्ट *(noun)* – मूर्ख मनुष्य, मंद बुद्धि मनुष्य

Sherry can't take a decision, she is a complete dolt.

Domain/डोमेन *(noun)* – प्रदेश, कार्यक्रम

Spirituality is my domain.

Dome/डोम *(noun)* – गुम्बद इमारत की गोल छत

It is claimed that there are 100,000 geodesic domes in use around the world.

Domestic/डोमेस्टिक *(adjective)* – घरेलू

Quarrels in the family are common domestic issues that need not be taken seriously all the time.

Domesticate/डोमेस्टिकेट *(verb)* – (पौधों पशुओं आदि को) घरेलू बनाना, पालतू बनाना

Trying to domesticate wild animals should be prohibited.

Domesticity/डोमेस्टिसिटी *(noun)* – पारिवारिक अभिरुचि, घरेलू चरित्र

Fights are a part of domesticity. Activities characteristically performed at home fall within the purview of domesticity laws.

Domicile/डोमिसाइल *(noun)* – गृह

Domicile is the name of the residence of your permanent home.

Domiciliary/डोमिसिलियरी *(adjective)* – गृह सम्बन्धी

This is their domiciliary matter.

Dominance/डॉमिनैन्स *(noun)* – प्रधानता, प्रभुत्व

One should avoid the use of dominance to keep co-workers happy.

Dominant/डॉमिनैंट *(adjective)* – प्रधान

His birthmark is very dominant on his face.

Dominate/डॉमिनेट *(verb)* – अधिक सशक्त और प्रभावशाली होना

There is no need for me to dominate over my workers.

Domineer/डोमिनियर *(verb)* – अत्याचार करना

The boss is such a domineering person.

Dominical/डोमिनिकल *(adjective)* – प्रभु ईसा मसीह का सम्बन्धी

These belifs are dominical.

D

Dominion/डोमिनियन *(noun)* – राज्य, उपनिवेश

Prior to independence, India was a dominion of Britain.

Don/डॉन *(verb)* – स्पेन देश की एक उपाधि ग्रहण करना, पहनना

He donned a three-piece suit for the party.

Donate/डोनेट *(verb)*– उपहार देना

Please donate blood, it may save lives.

Donation/डोनेशन *(noun)* – दान

I would like to give my old clothes in a donation drive.

Donative/डोनेटिव *(noun)* – उपहार रीति से प्राप्त, दान, उपहार

This money has been exclusively earmarked for donative purposes.

Done/डन *p.p. of do* – किया गया, समाप्त, पूर्ण

I have not done my homework.

Donee/डोनी *(noun)* – जिस व्यक्ति को दान दिया जाता है

He is the donee of this gift.

Donkey/डन्की *(noun)* – गधा

Donkeys are useful animal.

Donor/डोनर *(noun)* – दाता

He is a very gentle donor.

Don't/डॉन्ट – डूनॉट का संक्षिप्त रूप

Don't mess with the beauty products kept on the dressing table.

Doodle/डूडल *(verb)* – यूँ ही बिना ध्यान दिये रेखाएँ खींचना या चित्र बनाना

Don't doodle on the classroom walls.

Doom/डूम *(noun)* – विनाश, कयामत

The strict invigilation during examination spelled doom for many students..

Doomsday/डुम्सडे *(noun)* – प्रलय का दिन

They said 21st December 2012 would be doomsday for all living creatures on Earth.

D

Door/डोर् *(noun)* - कपाट, दरवाजा

The door handle of my drawing room is broken.

Dope/डोप *(noun)* - (गैर कानूनी) मादक द्रव्य हेरोइन एक दवा जो एथलिट की सामर्थ्य बढ़ा देती है

There will be dope-test of all athletes.

Doric/डोरिक *(adjective)* - देहाती यूनानी नगर डोरिस

Doric was the popular dialect of ancient Greek.

Dormant/डॉरमैंट *(adjective)* - कुछ समय के लिए निष्क्रिय

The volcanoes are dormant now-a-days.

Dorsal/डोरसल *(adjective)* - पृष्ठीय, किसी पशु या मछली की पीठ

Dorsal horn sensitisation reduces in line with tissue healing

Dorsum/डोरसम *(noun)* - पीठ

Dorsum is the back side of the humans or the upper part of animals.

Dose/डोज *(noun)* - दवा की खुराक

Please consume the medicine according to the dose prescribed.

Dot/डॉट *(noun)* - बिन्दु

All that the parents gave on their daughter's wedding was a dot.

Dotage/डॉटेज *(noun)* - अत्यन्त अनुराग, सठियापा

Dotage means the slowing down of mental faculties of a person.

Dotard/डोटार्ड *(noun)* - अतिवृद्ध

He has very old, weak and dotard and has to depend on others for even small things.

Dote/डोट *(verb)* - मूर्ख होना, स्नेह में डूबना

He dotes on his daughter and believes she can do no wrong.

Double/डबल *(adjective)* - दोहरा

The company has made double the profit compared to last year.

Doubt/डाउट *(verb)* - सन्देह, अनिश्चय

Please have no doubt about the instructions given.

Douceur/डूसर् *(noun)* - नजराना

He offered me douceur.

Dough/डफ *(noun)* - गूँथा हुआ गीला आटा

We need some dough for dinner tonight. Rotis were made out of soya dough.

Doughty/डाउटी *(adjective)* - शूरवीर, हिम्मती, साहसी

He is a doughty person.

Dove/डव *(noun)* - कबूतर

Many doves were seen flying around this area last year.

Dowager/डाउअजर् *(noun)* - मरे हुए व्यक्ति की संम्पति पाने वाली विधवा

I feel sorry for the dowager.

Dowdily/डाउडिली *(adv)* - गंदे ढंग से

She behaved dowdily in the party.

Dowdy/डाउडि *(adjective)* - गंदा, भद्दा, फूहड़

The dress she wore at the party looked very dowdy.

Down/डाउन *(adv)* - कछार, नीचे

Don't go down in the valley.

Downfall/डाउनफॉल *(noun)* - नाश

They had a terrible downfall in business.

Downpour/डाउनपोर् *(noun)* - मूसलाधार वर्षा

The city has been experiencing heavy downpour since morning.

Downright/डाउनराइट *(adjective)* - पूर्णतया, पूरी तरह

The rejection of application was a downright disgrace to the family.

Downstairs/डाउनस्टेअर्स *(adjective)* - सीढ़ी के नीचे पीड़ित, शोषित

Please go downstairs and meet your friend.

Down-trodden/डाउन-ट्रॉडेन *(adjective)* - पैर से कुचला हुआ

Recent government steps are addressing the concerns of the down-trodden.

Downward/डाउनवार्ड *(adjective)* - नीचे की ओर जाने वाला

The spacecraft descended downwards and splashed into the sea.

Dowry/डाउरी *(noun)* - दहेज

Asking for dowry is an offence in the eyes of the law.

Doze/डोज *(verb)* – झपकी लेना

She dozed off after immediately lunch. I would like to have a doze after this tiring day.

Dozen/डजन *(noun)* – दर्जन, बारह

I went to buy a dozen of bananas from the grocery store.

Dozer/डोजर *(noun)* – पिनक लेने वाला

A dozer is an earth moving equipment to level the surface.

Drab/ड्रैब *(noun)* – वेश्या

Don't call any woman a drab.

Drachm/ड्रेच्म *(noun)* – छोटा परिणाम

We'll need 5 drachms of water for this homeopathic medicine.

Draff/ड्राफ *(noun)* – खुद

It is draff of malt after brewing.

Draft/ड्राफ्ट *(noun)* – प्रारूप, मसौदा

Every person above 18 is compulsorily drafted into the Israeli army.

Draftsman/ड्राफ्ट्समैन *(noun)* – मसविदा बनाने वाला

We urgently require the services of a draftsman in the office.

Draggle/ड्रैगल *(verb)* – गन्दा करना

Don't draggle the clothes.

Dragnet/ड्रैग्नेट *(noun)* – मछली फँसाने का जाल, महाजाल

The police used a dragnet to catch the criminals.

Dragon/ड्रैगन *(noun)* – अजगर, अगा उगलने वाला दैत्य

A dragon is a ferocious looking mythical reptile.

Dragoon/ड्रगुन *(noun)* – घुड़सवार, सिपाही

The word dragoon originally meant infantry soldiers trained in the horse-riding.

Drain/ड्रेन *(verb)* – मोरी, पानी निकलने से सूखा कर देना

The drains of this area are overflowing.

Drake/ड्रेक *(noun)* – नर हंस

Chinese restaurants prepare a variety of drake delicacies.

Dram/ड्रैम *(noun)* – घूँट, छोटा परिमाण, ड्राम शब्द का छोटा रूप

Dram is the currency of Armenia.

Drama/ड्रामा *(noun)* – अभिनय

We have planned to enact three more dramas at this theatre this week. Let's not cause any more drama in this house.

Drank/ड्रैंक *past* – पीआ

Socrates drank the cup of poison as soon as it was offered.

Drape/ड्रेप *(verb)* – टाँकना

She went to Rekha's house and taught her how to drape a sari properly.

Draper/ड्रेपर *(noun)* – बजाज

We need to go to a draper to buy curtains for our house.

Drapery/ड्रेपरी *(noun)* – बजाज का व्यवसाय

The drapery set in this house is impeccably attractive.

Drastic/ड्रैस्टिक *(adjective)* – तीव्र, अत्यधिक और भरपूर असरदार

There has been a drastic change in her after the counselling.

Draughtsman/ड्राफ्ट्समैन *(noun)* – चित्र बनाने वाला

We need to consult a draughtsman for the designs.

Draughty/ड्राटी *(adjective)* – वायु के झोंके से पूर्ण

The weather has become very cold and draughty for anyone to venture out.

Drawback/ड्राबैक *(noun)* – कमी, असुविधा

His short height is a definite drawback in the basketball court.

Drawee/ड्रावी *(noun)* – अदाकर्ता, हुण्डी की रकम लेने वाला

He is the drawee of this bill.

Drawer/ड्रावर *(noun)* – निकालने वाला आहर्त्ता

I need a drawer to keep my belongings. He is the drawer of this cheque.

Drawl/ड्रॉल *(verb)* – धीरे-धीरे बोलना, मंद उच्चारण लम्बी स्वर धमनियों में मंद-मंद बोलने की शैली

Arun got irritated because his brother was drawling.

D

D

Drawn/ड्रान *(adjective)* – दोनों पक्ष में समान, बराबरी, अनिर्णित
Cathy was pale and drawn.

Dread/ड्रेड *(verb)* – भय
I dread the prospect of receiving thousands of emails.

Dreadnought/ड्रेडनॉट *(noun)* – किसी से न डरने वाला व्यक्ति, एक प्रकार की लड़ाई का जहाज
In 1857, the dreadnought was replaced with a larger hulk, HMS Caledonia (renamed dreadnought) which had 120 guns.

Dream/ड्रीम *(noun)* – सपना या स्वप्न
He walked around in a dream.

Drear/ड्रिअर *(adjective)* – मन्द उदास
Drear days in winter when there is no transport of any kind for going to Laddakh.

Dregs/ड्रेग्स *(noun)* – तलछट, डिब्बे में रखे गये द्रव पदार्थ की अंतिम बूँद जिसमें कूड़ा होता है
Criminals are the dregs of society.

Drench/ड्रेन्च *(verb)* – गीला करना
We got drenched in the rain because we didn't have an umbrella.

Dress/ड्रेस *(noun)* – स्त्री के कंधों से घुटने तक की पोशाक
The way she dresses is very appropriate for a formal occasion. The Anarkali dress is very popular among girls and women these days.

Drew/ड्रियू *(verb)* – खींचा
She drew the window shade to prevent strong sun rays peeping into the room.

Drib/ड्रिब *(noun)* – रिसाव, द्रव पदार्थ का बूँद-बूँद कर टपकना
A drib is a fine mist of water evaporating before it hits the ground.

Dribble/ड्रिबल *(verb)* – चूना
She dribbles the basketball very well.

Drily/ड्राइलि *(adverb)* – सूखे ढंग से
He commented drily on the text of my assignment.

Drinker/ड्रिंकर *(noun)* – पियक्कड़
A drinker destroys his own health and family.

Drinking/ड्रिकिंग *(noun)* – मदिरा-पान
He took to drinking as a way of forgetting hard blows suffered in everyday life.

Drip/ड्रिप *(verb)* – रिसना, द्रव का बूँद-बूँद टपकना
You should put a bucket underneath to catch any stray drips.

Drivel/ड्राइवल *(noun)* – निरर्थक बात
Many journalists lap up any marketing drivel for want of something more interesting to write about.

Driver/ड्राइवर *(noun)* – गाड़ी हाँकने वाला चालक
My chauffeur drives the car very slowly.

Driving/ड्राइविंग *(adjective)* – वाहन चलने का कार्य
Teachers are the driving force behind the success of their students.

Drizzle/ड्रिज्जल *(noun)* – बूँदी-बाँदी होना, फूही पड़ना, वर्षा की फुहार
Drizzle didn't allow my cloths to dry out.

Droit/ड्रायट *(noun)* – वैध अधिकार, सही
France was the first country to introduce droit de suite in 1920.

Droll/ड्रॉल *(adjective)* – विचित्र
He is a droll with a quiet tongue-in-cheek kind of humour.

Droop/ड्रूप *(verb)* – लटकना
The clothesline was drooping significantly after the clothes were hung for drying in the sun.

Drop-scene/ड्राप-सीन *(noun)* – रंगभूमि का अगला पर्दा
A drop-scene is often used in the background in plays to eliminate need of actual erection of such costly scenes.

Dropsy/ड्राप्सी *(noun)* – जलोदर
He offered me a dropsy to do his job.

Dross/ड्रास *(noun)* – तलछट, मण्डूर
The speech the chairman delivered at the farewell was rubbish and totally dross.

Drought/ड्रॉट *(noun)* – प्यास, अनावृष्टि
Gujarat is facing heavy drought this year.

Drove/ड्रोव *past tense* – झुण्ड
We drove past your house last night.

Drown/ड्रॉउन *(verb)* – डुबाकर मारना, डूबना
Michael drowned in the swimming pool.

Drowner/ड्रॉउनर *(noun)* – डुबाने वाला

Heavy load on the boat acted as a drowner into the river.

Drowse/ड्राउज *(noun)* – मन्द होना, झपकी लेना

Don't drowse in class while the teacher is teaching.

Drowsy/ड्राउजी *(adjective)* – आलसी, नींद से भरा हुआ

I was feeling incredibly drowsy after a long day at work.

Drub/ड्रब *(verb)* – बेंत से मारना पीटना

He incessantly drubbed into the pole.

Drudge/ड्रज *(verb)* – दासवृत्ति करने वाला मनुष्य, परिश्रम से काम

John was made to drudge at his previous job.

Drug/ड्रग *(noun)* – दवा या औषधि

The study of drugs results in formulation of medicines.

Druid/ड्रूइड *(noun)* – इंग्लैंड की प्राचीन जाति का पुरोहित

There lives a very famous druid near my house.

Drunk/ड्रंक *(verb)* – शराब पिये हुए

Heavy drinking or getting drunk can damage your nerves.

Dryad/ड्राइएड *(noun)* – जंगल की परी

Dryad was a nymph that lived on a tree according to Greek mythology.

Dual/डुअल *(adj)* – द्विवचन, दोनों, दोहरा

America has agreed to supply technology that has dual-use.

Dubiety/ड्यूबिटी *(noun)* – संदिग्धता, संदेह की भावना

I have dubiety on how this machine will function.

Dubious/ड्यूबिअस *(adjective)* – अस्पष्ट सन्दिग्ध

He is a very dubious man.

Dubitation/ड्यूबिटेशन *(noun)* – सन्देह

Please do not have any dubitation in your mind.

Duchess/डचेस *(noun)* – ड्यूक की सुहागिन

She is the duchess of Norfolk in England.

Duck/डक *(noun)* – बत्तख

A duck is a bird that loves swimming. Sachin returned to the pavilion out on duck.

Ducker/डकर *(noun)* – गोता लगाने वाला

Ducker is a relatively small waterfowl with a flat bill, short neck and legs, and webbed feet.

D

Ducking/डकिंग *(noun)* – गोता

The act of plumging into water is called.

Duckling/डकलिंग *(noun)* – छोटा बत्तख

We saw a duckling at the pond today.

Ductile/डक्टाइल *(adjective)* – कोमल, नमनीय, तार खींचने योग्य

This connection requires the use of ductile wires.

Ductility/डकटिलिटी *(noun)* – लचीलापन, मान लेने वाला

Not every flexible material has the property of ductility.

Dud/डड *(noun)* – व्यर्थ, बेकार

He is a complete dud, you can't really expect him to do a good job.

Dude/ड्यूड *(noun)* – छैला, दोस्त

He is quite popular among girls as a dude.

Dudgeon/डज्-जन *(noun)* – क्रोध, रोष

The manager walked out in deep dudgeon.

Duet/डुएट *(noun)* – दो आदमियों को मिलकर गाने का गीत

A duet is a song sung by two singers.

Duff/डफ *(noun)* – गूँथा हुआ आटा

We were asked to prepare a duff of the vegetables.

Dug/डग *(verb)* – खोदा

They dug into the history of the school.

Dulcet/डल्सेट *(adjective)* – मीठा, आनंदकर

Shanon can comfort anyone for her behaviour is very dulcet.

Dull/डल *(adjective)* – मन्द, जड़

All work and no play may make you a dull person.

Duly/ड्यूलि *(adverb)* – यथायोग्य, विधिवत

Please accept your payment duly sanctioned by the chief manager.

D

Dumb/डम् *(adjective)* – गूँगा

She was so dumb, she screwed her makeup.

Dummy/डमी *(noun)* – मूढ़मति, नकली, कृत्रिम

Dummy objects are used by military during firing practices.

Dump/डम्प *(noun)* – उदासीनता फेंकना, अवांछित वस्तु से पिंड छुड़ाना

This is a dumping yard for biodegradable waste.

Dumps/डम्प्स *(plural noun)* – उदासी, उदासीनता

My life is not progressing, it is totally in the dumps.

Dumpy/डम्पी *(adjective)* – नाटा-मोटा, थुलथुल

Sherry is often called dumpy because of her looks.

Dunce/डन्स *(noun)* – मूर्ख मनुष्य

People call Steve as dunce because he is slow to learn things.

Dunderhead/डन्डरहेड *(noun)* – मूर्ख

He didn't know the table manners and was acting like a dunderhead at the dining table.

Dune/ड्यून *(noun)* – किनारे पर बालू का टीला

During summers, the desert is covered with sand dunes.

Dung/डंग *(noun & verb)* – खाद, गोबर, लीद

Cow dung is used as manure by farmers.

Dungeon/डन्जन् *(noun)* – कालकोठरी

It is difficult to live in that window-less poor-lit dungeon.

Duodenum/ड्यूडेनम *(noun)* – पक्वाशय, छोटी आँत का पहला भाग

The doctors said that there was an infection in his duodenum.

Dupe/ड्यूप *(noun)* – बेवकूफ बनाना

With his smooth talks he has deceived many gullible persons.

Duplex/ड्यूप्लेक्स *(noun)* – फ्लैट या मकान जिसके दोनों मंजिलों पर कमरे सीढ़ियों द्वारा जुड़े हों

Jenny's living room is on the ground floor and bed room on the first floor in his duplex house.

Duplicate/डुप्लिकेट *(adjective)* – नकल

The stunt was played by the duplicate of Amitabh Bachchan.

Duplicity/डुप्लिसिटी *(noun)* – कपट, छल

Duplicity of documents is an offence. Duplicity is a deliberate deceptiveness in behaviour or speech.

Duramater/डुरामैटर *(noun)* – मस्तिष्क की बाहरी झिल्ली

He hurt his duramater in the accident.

During/ड्युरिंग *(preposition)* – बीच में, के दौरान

There was a bomb explosion during the ceremony.

Dust/डस्ट *(noun)* – धूल, मिट्टी

Dust particles are a major contributor in the atmospheric pollution.

Duster/डस्टर *(noun)* – झाड़न

The teacher uses a duster.

Dusty/डस्टी *(adjective)* – धूल धूसरित

The bed sheet is very dusty and needs washing.

Dutch/डच *(noun)* – हालैंड की भाषा तथा वहाँ के निवासी

Dutch culinary is very popular in Germany.

Duteous/ड्यूटिअस *(adjective)* – भक्त

Cadbury has been a very duteous servant

Dutiable/ड्यूटिएबल *(adjective)* – चुंगी लगने योग्य

All dutiable goods need to be cleared from customs department.

Dux/डक्स *(noun)* – कक्षा में सबसे प्रथम बालक

Ron is the dux of his class.

Dwindle/ड्वीन्डल *(verb)* – दुर्बल होना, क्रमिक रूप से क्षीण होते जाना

The air plane dwindled in the sky.

Dye/डाइ *(noun)* – वर्ण, रंग

Synthetic dyes are not good from environment's point of view.

Dynamic/डिनेमिक *(adjective)* – ऊर्जा तथा नाना प्रकार के विचारों से पूर्ण शक्तिमान

Only dynamic people go very far in life.

Dynastic/डाइनैस्टिक *(adj)* – राजवंश-सम्बन्धी

He asked me to correct the dynastics of the song. Dynastics are the forces that stimulate development inside a process.

Dynasty/डाइनैस्टी *(noun)* – राजवंश, वंश परंपरा

The Mughal Dynasty was very autocratic in character.

Dysentric/डिसेन्ट्रिक *(adjective)* - आमतिसार-सम्बन्धी

Doctors describe a person as dysenteric if he is suffering from inflammatory disorder of the lower intestine.

Dyspepsia/डिस्पेपशिया *(noun)* - मन्दाग्नि

The cause of most cases of functional dyspepsia is not known.

Dysphagia/डिस्फेशिया *(noun)* - निगलने में कठिनाई

Any condition that weakens or damages the muscles and nerves used for swallowing may cause dysphagia.

Dysphonia/डायफोनिया *(noun)* - मुख से शब्द निकलने में कष्ट

Spasmodic dysphonia may follow an infection of the respiratory tract, injury to the larynx or a period of excess voice use.

Dysponea/डायसपोनिया *(noun)* - श्वासकृच्छ

Dysponea is a disease associated with pulmonary problems that includes both obstructive and restrictive lung disease and difficulty in breathing.

Dysuria/डायसुरिया *(noun)* - मूत्रकृच्छ, मूत्र त्याग करने में कष्ट

In medicine, specifically urology, dysuria refers to pain in urination.

D

Ee

E/इ *(noun)* - अंग्रेजी वर्णमाला का पाँचवाँ वर्ण the fifth letter of the English alphabet.

1. Denoting the fifth in a set.
2. Music the third note of the diatonic scale of C major. *It is the fifth letter in alphabet.*

E

Each/ईच *(adj)*- एक-एक, पृथक्-पृथक्
Each battery has been kept in a separate room. They each have their own outlook.

Eager/ईगर *(adjective)* - आतुर, उत्सुक
I was so very eager to see the first show of the newly released film.

Eagle/ईगल *(noun)* - गरुड़, बाज
I once had a chance to see an eagle a bird of prey. It had powerful wings and a big hooked beak.

Eaglet/ईग्लेट *(noun)* - बाज का बच्चा
The eaglet is learning to fly.

Ean/ईन *suffix* - बच्चा जनना
Many Europeans come to visit India.

Ear/इअर *(noun)* - कान
His ear drum had been perforated. So he went to an ear specialist for surgery.

Earache/इअर्एॅक् *(noun)* - कान का दर्द
I have found earache to be one of the worst aches.

Earl/अर्ल *(noun)* - इंग्लैण्ड के सरदारों की एक पदवी
Earl is a high ranking British nobleman.

Earliness/अर्लीनेस *(noun)* - जल्दी
He is an early bird and always reaches any place the earliest.

Early/अर्ली *(adjective)* - प्रातःकाल किसी कालावधि, कार्य आदि में जल्दी (पैसा) कमाना
We ate an early dinner.

Earn/अर्न *(verb)* - प्राप्त करना
He has earned a lot of fame and money at such an early age.

Earnest/अर्नेस्ट *(adjective)* - उत्सुक, गम्भीर या दृढ़ निश्चय वाला
He is an earnest police officer, never heard a complaint against him. He has been awarded for bravery as well.

Earth/अर्थ *(noun)* - पृथ्वी
The earth shook as the earthquake came.

Earthen/अर्थेन *(adjective)* - मिट्टी का बना हुआ
I bought an earthen pot at a high price because it looked like a relic to me.

Earthling/अर्थलिंग *(noun)* - मर्त्य
This was perfectly normal earthling behaviour.

Earthly/अर्थलि *(adjective)* - सांसारिक, पार्थिव
Human life on earth is millions of years old.

Earthquake/अर्थक्वेक *(noun)* - भूकंप, भूचाल
Suddenly the earth began to tremble and many houses collapsed. It was a severe earthquake.

Earthwards - *(adverb)*
The spacecraft moved earthwards at the speed of 10,000 kmph.

Earthworks/अर्थवर्क्स *(noun)* - नींव, खुदाई, मिट्टी का बाँध
Earthworks used to be there in ancient times.

Earthworm/अर्थवर्म *(noun)* - केंचुआ
A lot of earthworms can be seen during the rainy season.

Earthy/अर्थी *(adjective)* - संसारिक, पार्थिव, स्वाभाविक
His approach to every problem is very earthy.

Ease/ईज *(verb)* - सुख
He does everything with great ease and grace.

Easement/ईजमेंट *(noun)* - परभूमावधिकार, हकशफा का कानून
He leads a life of easement.

Easeful/ईजफुल *(adj)* - शान्त, आरामतलब, आरामदेह

Life was easeful at that time.

East/ईस्ट *(adj)* - पूरब

The sun rises in the east.

Easter/ईस्टर *(noun)* - मार्च या अप्रैल के किसी रविवार को आने वाला पर्व जिसमें ईसाई लोग ईसा का पुनरुत्थान मनाते हैं

Are you going away at easter?

Easterly/ईस्टरली *(adj)* - पूर्व दिशा में

They travelled in an easterly direction.

Eastern/ईस्टर्न *(adj)* - पूर्वी

Connected with the countries of the east.

Eastward/ईस्टवार्ड *(adj)* - पूर्व दिशा की ओर

The Ganga flows eastwards.

Easy/ईजी *(adj)* - सुगम, सहज

The maths is not easy.

Eat/ईट *(verb)* - भोजन करना

Eat your dinner.

Eatable/ईटेब्ल् *(adj)* - खाद्य पदार्थ

Wheat is an eatable.

Eater/ईटर *(noun)* - किसी विशेष तरीके से खाने वाला

Tiger is a big eater.

Eating-house/ईटिंग हाउस *(noun)* - भोजनालय

I had gone to an eating house.

Eaves/ईव्स *(noun)* - ओरी

Naresh is an eavesdropper.

Ebb/ईब *(verb)* - समुद्र जल का उतरना

The crowd enthusiasm began to ebb.

Ebullience/अब्यूलिएन्स *(noun)* - प्रफुल्लित, उत्साहित, उफान, उबाऊ

There is an ebullience in the public.

Eclectic/इक्लेक्टिक *(adj)* - चुनने वाला

He is an eclectic man.

Economist/इकॉनॉमिस्ट *(noun)* - अर्थशास्त्री

He is an economist of the present times.

Ecstasy/एक्सटैसी *(noun)* - अति आनन्द की भावना

I feel ecstasy today.

Ecstatic/एक्सटैटिक *(adj)* - अति प्रसन्न

You seem in ecstatic mood today.

Eczema/एक्जिमा *(noun)* - खाज, खुजली एक प्रकार का चर्मरोग

Eczema is a skin disease.

Edacious/एडेशस *(adj)* - पेटू

The beggar seems to be an edacious man.

Edacity/इडैसिटि *(noun)* - अत्यधिक लालच

I have edacity for tasty dishes.

Eddy/एड्डी *(noun)* - भँवर

I saw an eddy in Ganga.

Eden/ईडन *(noun)* - देवलोक

The garaden of Adam and Eve is called Eden.

Edge/एज *(noun)* - किनारा, चाकू आदि की धार

He sat on the edge of the rock.

Edible/एडिबल *(noun)* - खाने योग्य

Don't worry, this fruit is edible.

Edict/इडिक्ट *(noun)* - राजा की घोषणा, फरमान

The edicts of Ashoka are famous all over the world.

Edification/एडिफिकेशन *(noun)* - मानसिक उन्नति

A video was made for edification of fresh trainees.

Edifice/एडिफिस *(noun)* - महल, भव्य भवन, बड़ी शानदार इमारत

In early times, kings made a lot of edifices.

Edition/एडिशन *(noun)* - प्रकाशन, पुस्तक का प्रकाशित रूप, संस्करण

This is the latest edition of the book.

Editor/एडिटर *(noun)* - किसी पत्र का सम्पादक

An editor's job is a tough job. He has to look after all the aspects of the magazine or the newspaper.

Educate/एड्यूकेट *(verb)* - शिक्षा प्रदान करना

He is a well educated man.

Education/एड्यूकेशन *(noun)* - शिक्षा

Education is a must for every citizen.

Educative/एड्यूकेटिब *(adj)* - शिक्षाप्रद

It is a useful educative tool.

Educator/एड्यूकेटर *(noun)* - शिक्षक

This is the view of a professional educator.

Educe/इड्यूस *(verb)* - खींचना, विकसित करना, निकाल देना

He educed the hidden talent in him.

Effable/एफबल् *(adjective)* – कथनीय

Her manner is very effable, which is what I like about her.

Efface/इफेस *(verb)* – पोछना, मिटा देना या हटा देना

Efface all the words from the blackboard.

E

Effective/इफेक्टिव *(adjective)* – प्रभावोत्पादक, क्षमताशाली

This rule is effective from today.

Effectual/इफेक्चुअल *(adjective)* – समर्थ, असर पैदा करने वाला निश्चित

The law of the land is always effectual.

Effectuate/इफेक्चुएट *(verb)* – पूर्ण करना, कार्यान्वित करना

The law has been effectuated since the 1st of this month.

Effeminacy/एफ्फेमिनैसि *(noun)* – जनानापन, नामर्दी, स्त्रीत्व

His effeminacy is not tolerable.

Effeminate/इफ्फेमिनेट *(adjective)* – डरपोक

He has an effeminate personality. People make fun of him.

Effervesce/एफरवेश *(verb)* – बुदबुदाना

Supervisors are supposed to effervesce with praise and encouragement.

Effete/इफीट् *(adjective)* – थका हुआ, कमजोर

He is an effete and thus useless for action.

Efficacious/एफिकेशस *(adjective)* – समर्थ, लाभकारी

It is an efficacious medicine.

Efficacy/एफिकसि *(noun)* – गुण, प्रभाव

There is little information on the efficacy of the new programme.

Efficient/इफिशेन्ट *(adjective)* – कार्यकुशलता

He is an efficient worker.

Effigy/ऍफिजि *(noun)* – प्रतिमा

The effigies of Ravan, Meghnath and Kumbhkaran are burnt on Dhssehra.

Effloresce/एफ्लोरेश *(noun & verb)* – फूलना

The atomic plant is at effloresce.

Effluence/एफ्लूएन्स *(noun)* – निकास प्रवाह

The effluence of sewage water could be seen clearly.

Efflux/एफ्लक्स *(noun)* – वहि:स्रवण

The efflux of rain water was very heavy.

Effort/एफर्ट *(noun)* – प्रयत्न, मानसिक या शारीरिक प्रयास

He put in great effort to clear the interview.

Effrontery/ऍफ्रण्टरि *(noun)* – धृष्ठता, गुस्ताखी

Effrontery close not pay in the end.

Effusive/एफ्यूसिव *(adj)* – अधिक परिमाण में बहाने वाला

She was effusive in her praise.

Egg/एग *(noun)* – अण्डा

This object is like an egg.

Ego/इगो *(noun)* – अहंकार, घमण्ड

She has fragile ego.

Egotistic/ईगटिस्टिक *(adj)* – अहंकारी

I dislike her egotistic behaviour.

Egress/इग्रेस *(noun)* – निर्गम, निकास

Rear seat entry and egress is better than average.

Egyptian/इजिप्शन *(noun)* – मिस्र देश का निवासी

This man seems an Egyptian.

Eh/ए *(exclamation)* – दूसरे को अपने से सहमत कराने के लिए प्रयुक्त

Did you like the files eh?

Easel/ईजल् *(noun)* – तस्वीर खींचने या रखने का ठाठ

A wooden frame used to support a picture, blackboard is called an easel.

Ejaculate/इजैक्यूलेट *(verb)* – वीर्य स्खलन करना

Don't ejaculate, control it.

Elaborate/इलैबॅरेट *(verb)* – विस्तार से वर्ण करना

Can you elaborate your idea?.

Elapse/इलैप्स *(noun)* – बीत जाना

Twenty seconds elapsed with nothing thrown.

Elasticity/इलास्टिसिटी *(noun)* – लचीलापन, प्रत्यास्थता

Rubber contains elasticity.

Elate/इलेट *(verb)* – अतिप्रसन्न, प्रफुल्लित करना

Don't try to elate me.

Elbow/एल्बो *(noun & verb)* – कोहनी

Why are you elbowing me?

Elder/एल्डर *(adj)* – आयु में बड़ा (परिवार के दो सदस्यों में)
He is my elder brother.

Eldest/एल्डेस्ट *(adj)* – आयु में सबसे बड़ा
Her eldest child is a boy.

Elect/इलेक्ट *(verb)* – मतदान द्वारा किसी प्रतिनिधि को चुन लेना
He was elected in Punjab assembly.

Electric/इलेक्ट्रिक *(adj)* – विद्युत उत्पन्न करने वाला, उत्तेजक
The atmosphere in the room was electric.

Electrification/इलेक्ट्रिफिकेशन *(noun)* – विद्युतीकरण, विद्युतीकरण करना
The electrification of the village is complete.

Electrum/इलेक्ट्रम *(noun)* – गिलट, सोना-चाँदी की धातु
Electrum is not useful for jewellery.

Elegiac/एलिजिआक *(adj)* – करुणामय
His poetry has an elegiac quality.

Elegist/एलेजिस्ट *(noun)* – शोकगीत का लेखक
Do you know any elegist in English.

Elegy/एलजी *(noun)* – शोकगीत
The elegy he recited was extremely mournful and moving.

Element/एलिमेंट *(noun)* – प्रमुख तत्त्व
There was an element of danger in that place.

Elementary/एलिमेंटरी *(adjective)* – मौलिक, सरल
It is a very elementary problem, I'll solve it right away.

Elemi/इलेमी *(noun)* – लाह
Product of certain tropical trees used in ointments and aromatherapy is called elemi.

Elephantiasis/एलिफैंटाइटिस *(noun)* – फीलपाँव
He is suffering from elephantiasis. His foot has become very large and full of wounds.

Elephantine/एलफैन्टीन *(adjective)* – हाथी का गज रूप
He is large and clumsy like an elephantine.

Elevate/एलिवेट *(verb)* – उठाना, किसी व्यक्ति या वस्तु का ऊँचा उठाना
He is a great scientist and enjoys an elevated position in the science academy.

Eleven/इलेवेन *(cardinal number)* – एकादश
There are eleven players in a cricket team.

Elicit/एलिसिट *(verb)* – किसी से सूचना तथ्य आदि निकालना
Although he was not a brilliant student still I managed to elicit an answer from him.

Eligibility/एलिजिबिलिटि *(noun)* – निर्वाहन योग्यता
His eligibility for the post cannot be questioned.

E

Eligible/एलिजिबल *(adjective)* – उपयुक्त, ग्रहण करने योग्य
Many high class young men are eligible backdoors.

Eliminate/इलिमिनेट *(verb)* – अवांछित व्यक्ति या वस्तु को हटा देना
All the anti-social elements have been eliminated from the party.

Elision/इलिसन *(noun)* – स्वर का लोप
The shortening of words or elision is quite popular.

Elite/एलीट *(noun)* – सभ्रांत वर्ग
He belongs to the group of elite people.

Elixir/इलिक्सिर *(noun)* – रसायन
Ancient people believed in elixir which could prolong life and change base metal into gold.

Elk/एल्क *(noun)* – एक प्रकार का बारहसिंघा
This kind of deer or moose is found in North America.

Ellagic/इलैजिक *(noun)* – माजूफल सम्बन्धी
An ellagic is a medicine somewhat effective against cancer.

Ellipse/इलिप्स *(noun)* – अण्डवृत
A regular oval shape.

Ellipsis/एलिप्सिस *(noun)* – अध्याहार, अर्थपूरक
It is rare for an ellipsis to happen without any linguistic antecedent.

Ellipsoid/एलिप्साइड *(noun)* – दीर्घ वृत्तज
A comparison in which an elliptical shape is described as ellipsoid.

Ellipticity/एलिप्टिसिटी *(noun)* – दीर्घवृत्तीयता
The quality of being elliptic is called ellipticity.

E

Elocution/एलोक्यूशन *(noun)* – वक्तृता व्याख्यान, श्रेष्ठ वक्तृत्व कला

He has the gift of elocution, being a leader, it makes things easy for him.

Eloquence/इलोक्वेंस *(noun)* – वाक्पटुता

His eloquence enables him to make things very clear. People love to hear him.

Eloquent/इलोक्वेंट *(adjective)* – वाक्पटु, सार्वजनिक प्रसंग में वाणी का प्रयोग करने में दक्ष

He is eloquent and always makes things very clear, never confused, never hesitating. His selection of words is excellent.

Elucidate/इल्यूसिडेट *(verb)* – व्याख्या करना make clear; explain. '*Will you please elucidate the point?*'

Elysian/एलिजिअन *(adjective)* –अति सुखकर, स्वर्गिक

It is an elysian room for us.

Elysium/एलिजिअम – स्वर्ग, बैकुंठ

An elysium is an imagenary place.

Emaciated/इमैसिएटेड *(adjective)* – कृश, दुर्बल

He is a an emaciated child, so thin and weak.

Emanate/इमनेट *(verb)* – निकलना

Water emanated from a hole in the ground.

Emancipate/इमैन्सिपेट *(verb)* – दासत्वमुक्ति, मुक्त करना

All the Negro slaves were emancipated after the civil war in America.

Emasculate/ईमैस्कुलेट *(verb)* – प्रभवहीन, नपुंसक बनाना

Many animals are emasculated by castration e.g. ox.

Embank/ऍम्बैन्क *(verb)* – बाँध बाँधना

In India many rivers cause havoc in rainy season. The government is trying to embank against those rivers.

Embark/ऍम्बार्क *(verb)* – जलपोत पर सवार होना

He embarked on the ship in time.

Embarrass/ऍम्बैरस् *(verb)* – लज्जित करना, व्याकुल करना

I felt embarrassed when they talked of my poor economic condition in front of me.

Embed/ऍम्बेड् *(verb)* – किसी वस्तु को मजबूती से बैठाना

The idea got embedded in my mind.

Embellish/ऍम्बेल्लिश् *(verb)* – सजाना

I embellished my bedroom.

Ember/ऍम्बर् *(noun)* – अंगारा

The burning coals looked like embers.

Emblazon/ऍम्ब्लेजेन *(verb)* – सुशोभित करना, अलंकरण करना, चमकना

The brand name was emblazoned on the shirt.

Emblem/ऍम्ब्लेम् *(noun)* – प्रतीक, चिह्न

The three lions are the emblem of our country.

Embodiment/ऍम्बॉडिमेन्ट् *(noun)* – अवतार, मूर्ति रूप

He seems to be living form of embodiment of vitality.

Embolism/ऍम्बॉलिज्म् *(noun)* – धमनी में रक्त संचालन का अवरोध

He was suffering from embolism.

Embower/ऍम्बावर *(verb)* – ढाँकना

His cottage was embowered by trees.

Embroider/ऍम्ब्राइडर् *(verb)* – कसीदा करना

His profession is embroidering sarees.

Embroil/ऍम्ब्राइल *(verb)* – उलझाना, आपत्ति में डालना

After embroiling himself, he cried for help.

Embryology/ऍम्ब्रिओलॅजि *(noun)* – भ्रूण-विज्ञान

His article on embryology in the medical journal was worth reading.

Emerge/इमर्ज *(verb)* – निकलना

The statue emerged slowly from the receding waters.

Emergent/इमर्जेन्ट *(adjective)* – आकस्मिक

I saw a calf emerging from its mother's body.

Emersion/इमरर्शन् *(noun)* – प्रकट होना

The emersion of a large snake from the water scared me.

Emetic/इमेटिक *(adjective)* – वमन, उबकाई

I felt emetic when I saw the rotten corpse.

Emigrant/ऍमिग्रैन्ट *(noun)* – अपना देश छोड़कर परदेश में बसने वाला

Many foreigners are now emigrants in America.

Eminence/ऍमिनेन्स *(noun)* – श्रेष्ठता
He is an eminent scientist.

Eminent/एमिनेन्ट *(adjective)* – श्रेष्ठ
He is an eminent eye specialist.

Emission/एमिशन *(noun)* – प्रवाह, उत्सर्जन
The emission of smoke from the engine upset me.

Emolument/एमॉल्युमेंट *(noun)* – पारिश्रमिक,लाभ
My emoluments are not enough to be taxable.

Emotion/इमोशन *(noun)* – भावना
I got emotional as I met my mother after a long time.

Empanel/इम्पैनल *(verb)* – सूची में नाम लिखना
Five new members have been empanelled to the expert committee.

Emperor/ऍम्परर *(noun)* – सम्राट
Ashoka was a great emperor.

Empire/ऍम्पायर *(noun)* – प्रभुत्व, एक देश द्वारा शासित देशों का समूह
The empire of Ashoka was wide spread.

Emplane/ऍम्प्लेन *(verb)* – हवाई जहाज पर सवार होना
He was late but he acted quickly and got emplaned for Londen.

Employ/एम्प्लाय् *(verb)* – नियुक्त करना
I was employed throughout the day.

Employer/एम्प्लॉअर् *(noun)* – नियुक्त करने वाला
That man over there is my employer, I drive his car.

Empress/एम्प्रेस *(noun)* – महारानी, साम्राज्ञी
There have been many famous empresses in history.

Emptier/ऍम्प्टिअर् *(adj)* – खाली करने वाला
Nothing can be emptier than an empty glass.

Emptiness/ऍम्प्टिनेश *(noun)* – शून्यता, खालीपन
Through the window of an airplane you can see vast emptiness of space.

Emulate/ऍम्युलेट *(verb)* – स्पर्धा करना
He tried to emulate a famous actor but failed.

Emulsion/इमल्शन *(noun)* – मिश्रित न होने वाले द्रवों का मिश्रण
The emulsion technique has made my house look for batter than more point.

Enable/एनेबल् *(verb)* – सामर्थ्य देना
My coaching enabled me to pass the exam with high marks.

Enact/एनैक्ट् *(verb)* – कानून बनाना
The proposal was enacted and made a law.

Enamour/इनैमर *(verb)* – मोह लेना, आसक्त करना
I was enamoured over her beauty.

Encage/ऍनकेज *(verb)* – पिंजड़े में बन्द करना, डिब्बे में रखना
Four little Australian birds were encaged in a metallic cage.

Encamp/ऍनकैम्प *(verb)* – डेरा डालना
We encamped at a safe place in jungle.

Encase/ऍनकेस *(verb)* – डिब्बे मे रखना
Please encase the sweets.

Encash/ऍनकैश *(verb)* – हुंडी
I have no money, I have to encash my cheque.

Enchain/ऍनचेन *(verb)* – कसकर बाँधना
The buffalo was taken into custody and enchained at the police station.

Enchant/ऍनचैंट *(verb)* – जादू डालना
The place is so beautiful as if it is enchanted.

Encircle/ऍनसर्कल *(verb)* – घेरना
The thief was encircled by police.

Enclose/ऍनक्लोज *(verb)* – घेरना
The tree was enclosed by herbs.

Encompass/ऍन्कम्पस् *(verb)* – घेरना
The house was encompassed by a wall.

Encore/आन्कोर् *(noun)* – संगीत सभा के अंत में दर्शकों की फरमाइश पर प्रस्तुत अतिरिक्त कार्यक्रम
Her stage performance was so nice that public demanded an encore from her.

Encounter/ऍनकाउन्टर *(noun)* – मुठभेड़, मुकाबला
I met a friend in a mall. It was a sudden encounter.

Encourage/ऍनकरेज *(verb)* – प्रोत्साहित करना, सहायता देना
I encouraged him to study hard.

Encroach/ऍनक्रोच *(verb)* – अतिक्रमण करना, सीमा को लांघना
The enemy encroached upon its neighbour territory and then there was a war.

E

Encrust/ऍनक्रस्ट *(verb)* – पपड़ी जमाना, जमना
The bread was covered with a hard crust.

Encumber/ऍनकम्बर *(verb)* – प्रतिबन्ध करना
I felt encumbered with the huge amount of homework.

Encumbrance/ऍनकम्ब्रैन्स् *(noun)* – भार
I am facing some encumbrance in executing my scheme.

E

Encyclopaedia/ऍन्साइक्लोपीडिया *(noun)* – विश्व-ज्ञानकोश
I have a set of encyclopedia at home. I can find anything in it.

Endanger/ऍन्डेन्जर् *(verb)* – व्यक्ति या वस्तु को खतरे में डालना
He endangered his life when he went very near the cubs of tiger.

Endear/ऍनडिअर *(verb)* – प्रियपात्र बनाना
I am endeared to you for the favour you have shown me.

Endeavour/ऍन्डेवर *(noun)* – प्रयास
I endeavoured to climb the mountain but failed.

Endemic/एन्डेमिक *(adjective)* – स्थानिक
Endemic a disease commonly found among people of certain area.

Ending/एन्डिंग *(noun)* – परिणाम, अंत
In the ending of film people were almost in tears.

Endmost/एण्डमोस्ट *(adjective)* – सबसे दूर का
The endmost part of the film was very exciting.

Endorse/ऍन्डॉर्स *(verb)* – घोषणा या निर्णय का सार्वजनिकतौर पर समर्थन करना
I have endorsed the document.

Endow/ऍन्डाउ *(verb)* – किसी संस्था या विद्यालय को बड़ी धन राशि दान में देना
I have endowed my property to my wife.

Endue/ऍन्ड्यू *(verb)* – धारण करना
He is endued with great ability.

Endurance/इन्ड्योरेन्स *(noun)* – सहन-शीलता
He has great endurance and can bear a lot of pain.

Endure/इन्ड्योर *(verb)* – चुपचाप पीड़ा झेलना
He endured the cancer pain for a long time.

Endways/एण्डवेज *(adverb)* – खड़े बल
The carpet covered the floor endways.

Enema/ऍनिमा *(noun)* – वस्ति
He suffered from severe constipation, so the doctor gave him enema.

Energize/ऍनर्जाइज *(verb)* – क्रियाशील करना, उत्साहित और सतर्क करना
The drink energized the boxers.

Energumen/ऍनरग्यूमेन *(noun)* – पागल
That man is energumened see how wild he is acting, if possessed.

Energy/एनर्जी *(noun)* – शक्ति, ऊर्जा
He has great energy and can work hard for a long time without rest.

Enface/एन्फेस *(verb)* – मुखाकंन करना
Enface means to write or stamp a bill on the face.

Enfeeble/ऍन्फीबल् *(verb)* – क्षीण बनाना
After the viral fever I felt very enfeebled.

Enfold/एनफोल्ड *(verb)* – लपेटना, आलिंगन करना
I enfolded the paper and made an envelope.

Enframe/ऍन्फ्रेम – चौखटे में मढ़ना
The enframed photo looked life like.

Engarland/ऍनगारलैंड – माला पहनाना
People engarlanded their leader.

Engender/ऍनजेन्डर *(verb)* – उत्पन्न करना
The issue engendered continuing political controversy.

Engineer/ऍन्जिनिअर् *(noun)* – अभियन्ता
My father was an engineer and he made many machines.

Engorge/इनगॉर्ज *(verb)* – लालज में ज्यादा खाना
His stomach was engorged with water.

Engraft/ऍन्ग्रैफ्ट *(verb)* – संयुक्त करना
Engraft as his liver was damaged only grafting another live tissue surgically could save his life.

Engrain/ऍन्ग्रेन् *(verb)* – गहरा रंग चढ़ाना
He trivialized the struggle and further engrained the long standing attitudes.

Engrave/इनग्रेव *(verb)* – धातु या पत्थर खोदना

His words were engraved in my mind for ever.

Enhance/इनहांस *(verb)* – बेहतर दिखने के लिए वस्तु में सुधार आदि पर शब्द या आकृति खोदना

As he enhanced his voice, people all over could hear him.

Enigma/एनिग्मा *(noun)* – पेचीदा

I could never understand that person, he is an enigma to me.

Enjoin/ऍन्जॉइन् *(verb)* – रोक लगाना, निषेध करना

He enjoined me to jump over the wall.

Enlighten/ऍन्लाइट्न् *(verb)* – उपदेश देना, अपेक्षित जानकारी देते हुए किसी बात की समझ को बढ़ाना

Lord Buddha enlightened many people.

Enlist/ऍन्लिस्ट *(verb)* – सेना में भर्ती होना

He got himself enlisted in the army.

Enmity/ऍन्मिटी *(noun)* – शत्रुता, विरोध

Now there is no enmity between us. Let us be friends.

Ennoble/इनोबल् *(verb)* – प्रतिष्ठा बढ़ाना

He was ennobled to the rank of general.

Ennui/आन्वी *(noun)* – मानसिक थकावट, आलस्य, उदासी

Ennui got him as he felt extremely bored.

Enormity/इनार्मिटि *(noun)* – किसी वस्तु की विशालटा प्रभाव की गंभीरता

The enormity of the crime shocked me.

Enough/एनफ *(adverb)* – प्रचुरता

Enough is enough, now please be quiet.

Enrapture/ऍनरैप्चर *(adjective)* – मंत्रमुग्ध होना

I was enraptured by the view from the hill.

Enrich/एनरिच *(verb)* – सुशोभित करना, गुणवत्ता बढ़ाना

He was further enriched as his father left him all the money and property.

Enrobe/ऍन्रोब *(verb)* – सुन्दर वस्त्र पहिनना

He was dressed in a robe.

Enroute/ऍनरूट *(adv)* – रास्ते में मार्ग द्वारा

This bus will go enroute Lady Shri Ram College, C.R. Park and Kalkaji.

Enshroud/ऍन्श्राउड् *(verb)* – लपेटना

The dead body was enshrouded for burial.

Ensign/ऍन्साइन *(noun)* – ध्वज

An ensign flew over the naval ship.

Enslave/ऍनस्लेव *(verb)* – दास बनाना

I was enslaved by her beauty.

Ensnare/इनस्नेअर *(verb)* – बन्धन में डालना, जाल में डालना

The tiger was ensnared in a trap.

Ensorcell/ऍनसॉरसेल *(verb)* – मोहित करना

I was ensorcelled by the beauty of Kashmir.

Enstamp/ऍनस्टाम्प *(verb)* – मोहर लगाना

The envelope was stamped at the post office.

Ensue/ऍनस्यू *(verb)* – कुछ घटित होना (किसी के बाद या फलस्वरूप)

Bitterness ensued as the two friends quarrelled with one another.

Ensure/एन्श्योर् *(verb)* – सुरक्षित करना सुनिश्चित करना

I will ensure that this kind of thing does not happen again.

Entente/आन्टेन्ट *(noun)* – मित्रभाव

People hope that one day there will be entente between India and Pakistan.

Entric/ऍन्टेरिक *(adjective)* – आँतो से सम्बन्धित

You are suffering from an enteric disease.

Entering/इन्टरिंग *(noun)* – प्रवेश

Your entering is prohibited here.

Enteritis/इन्टराइटिस *(noun)* – आँतो की सूजन

Enteritis medicine is given in case of inflammation of intestine.

Enterprising/एन्टरप्राइजिंग *(adjective)* – साहसी

He is an enterprising fellow and will certainly succeed.

Entertaining/ऍन्टरटेनिंग *(noun)* – मनोरंजक, दिलचस्प

An entertaining picture relieves our boredom.

Enthrone/ऍन्थ्रोन् *(verb)* – राजसिंहासन पर बैठाना, राज्याभिषेक करना

The king was enthroned with full pomp and show.

E

Enthunder/एँन्थण्डर *(verb)* – बादलों की गरज की तरह शब्द करना

The sky thundered and it began to rain heavily.

Enthusiast/एँन्थ्यूजिआस्ट *(noun)* – उत्साही

He is an enthusiast by nature. These days he is full of enthusiasm for going to USA.

Entice/एँन्टाइस *(verb)* – मोहित करना, किसी को लालच देकर कुछ करने के लिए मनाना

Being enticed by her wealth, he married an elderly women.

Entitle/एँन्टाइट्ल् *(verb)* – नाम रखना

He was entitled to this honour.

Entity/एँन्टिटी *(noun)* – अलग और स्वतंत्र अस्तित्त्व वाली वस्तु

A star is an entity.

Entoil/एँन्टाइल् – जाल में फँसाना

He entoiled a lot for his downfall.

Entomb/एँनटूम् *(verb)* – समाधि में गाड़ना

His dead body was entombed.

Entomic/एन्टॉमिक *(adj)* – कीड़े का

I purchased an entomic book.

Entomology/एँन्टामालॅजि *(noun)* – कृमि अध्ययन शास्त्र

He is studying entomology and a lot of insects in jars can be seen in his laboratory.

Entrails/एँन्ट्रेल्स *(plural noun)* – आँत

His entrails were severely damaged in an accident.

Entrammel/एँन्ट्रैम्मल *(verb)* – रोकना

On his way home, he got entrammelled with his old enemy.

Entrance/एँन्ट्रेन्स *(noun)* – द्वार

I will meet her at the entrance of hospital.

Entrant/एँन्ट्रैन्ट *(noun)* – किसी व्यवसाय में प्रवेश करने वाला व्यक्ति

All the entrants were gathered together at one place.

Entreat/एँन्ट्रीट/इन्ट्रीट् *(verb)* – प्रार्थना करना

I entreat you to please pardon me.

Entrench/एँन्ट्रन्श/इन्ट्रेन्च *(verb)* – खाई में घेरना, मोरचाबंदी करना

Congress party's firmly entrenched in power in India.

Entrust/इन्ट्रस्ट *(verb)* – किसी का किसी काम का दायित्व सौंपना

I entrusted the child to the care of the mother.

Envelop/इन्वेलप *(verb)* – लपेटना

I tore open the envelop and took out the contents.

Envelope/एन्विलोप *(noun)* – लिफाफा

A human figure appeared completely enveloped in a black dress.

Envisage/इन्विसेज *(verb)* – भविष्य में संभावित स्थिति के बारे में सोचना

I envisaged that I was flying in a plane.

Envoy/इन्वॉय *(noun)* – दूत

The envoy from U.K. met the foreign secretary.

Envy/इन्वी *(noun)* – स्पर्धा, ईर्ष्या

My envy knew no bounds when I saw that my neighbour had bought a new and costly car.

Enwrap/इनरैप *(verb)* – लपेटना

I wrapped the gift in a shining paper.

Eon/ईऑन *(noun)* – कल्प, युग, असीमित समय

It will take an eon to change it.

Ephemera/एँफेमरा *(plural noun)* – अल्पजीवी कीट

I do not like things that are ephemera.

Epicycle/एपिसाइकिल *(noun)* – छोटा वृत्त जिसका केन्द्र बड़े वृत्त की परिधि पर हो

The movement of the spring top resembles that of an epicycle.

Epidemic/एपिडेमिक *(noun)* – व्यापक रोग, महामारी

When an epidemic like cholera spreads, lots of people die.

Epidermal/एपिडरमल *(adj)*– बाह्य त्वचा सम्बन्धी

This is an epidermal infection you must consult any skin specialist.

Epigene/एपिजेन *(adjective)* – भूमितल पर बना हुआ

All trees and crops are epigene.

Epiglottis/एपिग्लॉटिस *(noun)* – घंटिका

There is some trouble with my epiglottis, I am going to a doctor.

Epilepsy/एपिलेप्सी *(noun)* – मृगी का रोग

Our neighbour has epilepsy, he often faints.

Epilogue/एपिलॉग *(noun)* – नाटक का उपसंहार

Epilogues of some books are so brilliant that they make the whole concept clear.

Epiphora/एपिफोरा *(noun)* – आँखों में आँसू इक्ट्ठा होने का रोग

For his watering eyes doctor diagnosed epiphora and prescribed a medicine.

Epistaxis/एप्सिटैक्सिस *(noun)* – बिनास फूटना

He often has epistaxis in the hot weather. He then lies down and applies ice to his nose.

Epistle/इपिस्ल *(noun)* – साहित्यिक रचना

Just out of curiosity. I bought an epistle as I wanted to know how thoughts and emotions are expressed in the form of letters.

Epistolary/एपिस्टोलरी *(adjective)* – पत्र सम्बन्धी

'Mind you, this novel is epistolary.'

Epitaph/एपिटाफ *(noun)* – स्मरण लेख, समाधि लेख

I read some beautiful epitaphs when I visited a graveyard.

Epithelium/एपिथेलियम *(noun)* – शरीर की बाह्य त्वचा

The anatomy students asked the doctors many questions about epithelium.

Epithet/एपिथेट *(noun)* – उपाधि

The epithet of a 'gentleman', suited him perfectly.

Epitome/एपिटमि *(noun)* – किसी बात का आदर्श उदाहरण

She is an epitome of beauty.

Equal/इक्वल *(adjective)* – समान

It was an equal contest between the two boxers.

Equality/इक्वलिटी *(noun)* – समानता

There is great equality of intelligence between the two brothers.

Equalize/ईक्वलाइज *(verb)* – बराबर करना

Our team scored a goal and we equalized with the rival team.

Equator/इक्वेटर *(noun)* – भूमध्य रेखा

It is very hot near the equator eg. Africa.

Equestrian/इक्वेसट्रिअन *(adjective)* – अश्वारोही

He is an equestrian champion.

Equi/इक्वि *(prefix)* – यथा

The houses of both the friends are equidistant.

Equipoise/इक्विपॉइज *(noun)* – संतुलन, पासंग

The armies of both the countries were equipoise.

Equity/इक्विटी *(noun)* – निष्पक्षता न्यायनीति

He is a man known for equity in treatment.

Era/एरा *(noun)* – युग

The era of dinosaur was over even before man evolved.

Eradicable/इरैडिकेबल् *(adj)* – निर्मूल करने योग्य

Insurance companies accept eradicable diseases while computing premiums.

Eradicate/इरैडिकेट *(verb)* – जड़ से उखाड़ना

The plan of Nazi government of Germany was to eradicate Jews.

Erase/इरेज *(verb)* – मिटाना

The pencil drawing was erased completely by an eraser.

Erect/इरेक्ट *(adjective)* – सीधा खड़ा

Some body organs become erect due to excitement.

Erectile/इरेक्टाइल *(adjective)* – सीधा होने लायक

The physician is trying to check the condition of erectile spies. Many people suffer from erectile dysfunction.

Erection/इरेक्शन *(noun)* – निर्माण करने योग्य या उसे सीधा खड़ा करने की क्रिया

Erection of Taj Mahal look 22 years.

Eremite/इरिमाइट *(noun)* – एकान्तवासी, संन्यासी

Many people become eremites.

Eristic/इरिस्टिक *(adjective)* – वाद-विवाद सम्बन्धी

His eristic arguments were rather boring.

Erode/ईरोड *(verb)* – नष्ट करना, (समुद्र, मौसम आदि का) धीरे-धीरे करना

The Fords on this coast continue to be eroded by sea. Due to public humiliation his confidence is totally eroded.

Erosion/ईरोजन *(noun)* – कटाव, अपक्षरण

Deserts have been formed as a result of erosion.

E

E

Erosive/इरोसिव *(adjective)* – कटाक्ष सम्बन्धी
Acids have erosive qualities.

Erotic/एरॉटिक *(adjective)* – कामुक, कामोत्तेजक
Many ancient temples in India display erotic postures.

Erratic/एरैटिक *(noun)* – भूगोल में हिमनद के दबाने के कारण अपने स्थान से हटी हुई चट्टान, अनिश्चित अस्थिर
The machine was defective and worked in an erratic way.

Erratum/इरेटम *(noun)* – छापने की अशुद्धि
You will find the erratum at the end of the book.

Erroneous/ए(इ)रोनियस् *(adjective)* – अशुद्ध, गलत सूचना पर आधारित
His statement is erroneous.

Error/एरर *(noun)* – दोष, गलती
There are lots of spelling errors in this article.

Erst/अर्स्ट *(adverb)* – पहले
Erstwhile many big and strange animals become extinct.

Eructate/ईरक्टेट *(noun)* – डकारना
He is eructating too much.

Erupt/इरप्ट *(verb)* – फटना
Suddenly the volcano erupted.

Erysipelas/एरिसिपिलस *(noun)* – मुँहासा नामक रोग
He is suffering from erysipelas and has gone to see a skin specialist.

Eschew/एस्च्यू *(verb)* – त्यागना, छोड़ना
He eschewed from drinking.

Escort/एस्कॉर्ट *(noun)* – अनुचर
A large escort accompanied the king.

Esculent/एस्क्युलेंट *(adjective)* – खाने योग्य, भक्षणीय
This kind of food is not esculent.

Esoteric/एसोटेरिक *(adjective)* – गोपनीय, गूढ़, रहस्यमय
This kind of meditation is esoteric.

Espial/एस्पायल *(noun)* – निरीक्षण, जासूसी
He decided to withdrwa from his point of espial.

Espionage/एस्पियनेज *(noun)* – जासूसी करने के तरीके
Russia and America were involved in a lot of espionage work against each other during the cold war.

Esplanade/एस्प्लानेड *(noun)* – टहलने का नगर का खुला मैदान
There is an esplanade road in Delhi opposite the Red Fort.

Espousal/एस्पाउजल *(noun)* – सगाई
His espousal of western ideas was not liked by village people.

Espy/एस्पी *(verb)* – ताकना
I espied a rare bird in the forests of South America.

Esquire/एस्क्वायर *(noun)* – महाशय
Noblemen training for knighthood were called esquires.

Essay/एसे *(noun)* – निबंध
He wrote a brilliant essay on 'Emancipation of Women.'

Essence/इसेंस *(noun)* – सारतत्त्व, किसी वस्तु को मूलभूत और सर्वाधिक महत्त्वपूर्ण विशेषता
The essence of this paragraph is that man is not civilized as yet.

Essential/एसेन्सियल *(adjective)* – आवश्यक fundamental; central. *It is essential that you catch today's flight.*

Estate/इस्टेट *(noun)* – जागीर, भूसंपत्ति
My father has a large estate.

Estimable/एस्टिमेब्ल *(adjective)* – आदरणीय
Mahatma Gandhi was an estimable person.

Estimate/एस्टिमेट *(noun)* – मूल्य निरूपण
At a rough estimate the government is recycling half of the paper used.

Estop/इस्टॉप *(verb)* – अपने ही कार्य से रुकावट डालना
The firm may be estopped from denying their statement.

Estrange/इस्ट्रेंज *(verb)* – दूर रखना
He has no any connation with his estranged wife.

Etcetra/एट्सेट्रा *(adv)* – इत्यादि

If you are going to the market please bring some vegetables like potato, tomato, onion, cucumber etc.

Eternity/इटरनिटी *(noun)* – अनंतकाल, पारलौकिक जीवन

We shall be loving each other till eternity.

Ethics/एथिक्स *(plural noun)* – नीतिशास्त्र

We should follow ethics strictly.

Ethnic/एथनिक *(adjective)* – जाति सम्बन्धी

Ethnic riots sometimes take place because of nationality and religious differences.

Ethology/इथॉलजि *(noun)* – आचारशास्त्र

Persons who are interested in character sticks of different people and relationships among them must study ethology.

Ethos/इथॉस *(noun)* – सामान्य प्रकृति

The ethos of Indians has always been torching the feet of elders and worshipping natural objects.

Ethyl/इथाइल *(noun)* – नशीली वस्तु का आधार

A chemical derived from ethane is called ethyl.

Etiquette/एटिकेट *(noun)* – सदाचार, शिष्टाचार

He is a man of perfect etiquette.

Eucalyptus/यूकालिप्टस *(noun)* – मेंहदी की जाति का वृक्ष

I would certainly like to have a eucalyptus tree is my garden. It is so beautiful and has so many uses.

Eugenic/यूजेनिक *(plural noun & adj)* – सुन्दर संतति उत्पन्न करने के विषय का

You should study eugenics if you want to know about controlled breeding in a population.

Eulogist/यूलोजिस्ट – प्रशंसात्मक बातें बताने वाला

He is a professional praise writer.

Eulogy/यूलॅजी *(noun)* – प्रशंसा

People often write eulogies about dead persons.

Euphonic/यूफॉनिक *(adj)* – सुरीले स्वर वाला

I like her euphonic trait.

Euphony/यूफॉनी *(noun)* – सुस्वर

There is a great euphony in her speech.

Euphorbia/यूफोर्बिया *(noun)* – कठिन शब्दों का प्रयोग करके लिखने की क्रिया

Euphorbia is a kind of tree.

Eureka/यूरेका *(exclamation as noun)* – अपूर्व आविष्कार मैने पा लिया है, प्राप्ति की घोषणा

I cried 'eureka' when I found a rare plant which I had been long searching for.

European/यूरोपियन *(noun)* – यूरोप देश का निवासी

You can see by the colour of his skin that he is a European and not an Asian.

Evacuant/इवैकुएंट *(adjective)* – रेचक औषधि

A laxative is an evacuant medicine.

Evacuate/इवैकुएट *(verb)* – लोगों को खतरनाक जगह से हटाकर सुरक्षित जगह पर ले जाना, शून्य करना

As the flood came, the villagers were evacuated.

Evade/इवेड *(verb)* – बचाना, बच निकलना

At the party he said that he was a millionaire Industrialist and had been called specially. Thus he evaded paying anything.

Evaporate/इवैपॅरेट *(verb)* – द्रव का भाप बन जाना

The water evaporated as it boiled for too long a time.

Eve/इव *(noun)* – संध्या

There are a lot of festivals on Christmas eve.

Evening/इवनिंग *(noun)* – साँझ, शाम

Most often my friend came to have tea with me in the evening or also I went to his house.

Event/इवेन्ट *(noun)* – घटना

In event of my sudden death, please call the lawyer and have my will read.

Ever/एवर *(adverb)* – किसी भी समय

'Darling, I am ever yours.'

Eversion/एवर्शन – बाहर को उलटने का कार्य

This is an act of eversion.

Evert/एवर्ट *(verb)* – बाहर को उलटना

The hyena can evert its anal pouch.

Evidence/एविडेंस *(noun)* – प्रमाण, सबूत

What is the evidence that you did not commit the crime?

E

E

Evince/इविन्स *(verb)* – दिखाना, व्यक्त करना
I evinced that I was nervous.

Evolution/इवल्यूशन *(noun)* – क्रमिक विकास उद्‌भव
The evolution of humans took bilions of years.

Evolve/इवॉल्व *(verb)* – साधारण से क्रमशः विकसित होना या करना
Creatures on the earth evolved very gradually.

Ewer/यूअर *(noun)* – घड़ा, कुम्भ
He used to drink water from an ewer.

Exact/एक्जैक्ट *(adjective)* – ठीक-ठीक, यथार्थ
What is the exact measurement of this room?

Exaggerate/ऍग्जजरेट् *(verb)* – बढ़ा-चढ़ाकर कहना
He exaggerated the facts and nobody came to know the real facts.

Examine/एक्जामिन *(verb)* – परीक्षा करना
As the police examined the case thoroughly, they came to know the culprit.

Exanimate/एक्जामिनेट *(verb)* – जाँच करना
The teacher examinate the students answersheet.

Exasperate/एक्जैस्परेट *(verb)* – क्रुद्ध करना
He was exasperated intensely by my repeated question.

Excavate/एक्सकैवेट *(verb)* – खोदना
A lot of excavation went on in Egypt when the pyramids were discovered.

Exceed/एक्सीड *(verb)* – संख्या या मात्रा विशेष से अधिक हो जाना, अधिक होना
He exceeded his time limit in speaking and thus lost marks in debate.

Excel/एक्सेल *(verb)* – श्रेष्ठ होना
You want to excel everybody.

Excellency/एक्सेलेन्सी *(noun)* – अन्य देश के प्रतिनिधि (राजदूत) आदि के लिए प्रयुक्त शब्द
His Excellency the ambassador of Britain arrived in New Delhi today.

Excellent/एक्सेलेंट *(adjective)* – उत्तम, उत्कृष्ट
He got excellent mark in English.

Exception/एक्सेप्शन *(noun)* – अपवाद
Most people exaggerate and brag about their achievements he is an exception. He a quiet and polite man.

Excise/एक्साइज *(noun)* – कुछ वस्तुओं और उत्पादन पर लगाया गया कर
The rate of excise duty on petrol has been lowered to 8 per cent.

Excision/एक्सिजन *(noun)* – उच्छेदन
The several excisions have destroyed the literary value.

Excitant/एक्साइटैन्ट *(adj.)* – उत्तेजक
The brain could become excited if chemical excitants flood into it.

Excite/एक्साइट *(verb)* – उत्तेजित करना
I was very excited to see my favorite film star in person.

Exciter/एक्साइटर *(noun)* – उत्तेजित करने वाला व्यक्ति या पदार्थ
Elections act as exciters in an atom.

Exciting/एक्साइटिंग *(adjective)* – उत्तेजक
It is always exciting to see the finals of one day cricket matches.

Exclaim/एक्सक्लेम *(verb)* – भावावेश में चिल्लाकर कुछ कहना
'An what a beautiful sea beach!' he exclaimed.

Exclusion/एक्स्क्लुजन *(noun)* – निषेध, बाहर रखना
The insurance policy contains several exclusions.

Exclusive/एक्सक्लुसिव *(adjective)* – केवल एक व्यक्ति रूप समूह के लिए
This book is for exclusive sale in USA.

Excogitate/एक्सकॉजिटेट *(verb)* – गौर से सोचना, विचारना
I excogitated cleverly and won the chess match.

Excrement/एक्सक्रिमेन्ट *(noun)* – विष्ठा, मल
In our villages excrement can be found lying extensively.

Excreta/एक्सक्रेटा *(noun)* – मल-मूत्र आदि पदार्थ
In cities in every house there is a toilet for discharging excreta.

Excruciate/एक्सक्रुसिएट *(verb)* – यातनाएँ देना, सन्ताप देना
He excruciated her to no end, ultimately she left him and ran away.

Exculpate/एक्सकल्पेट *(verb)* - निर्दोष सिद्ध करना
He was exculpated in the court.

Excursion/एक्स्कर्शन *(noun)* - पर्यटन सैर
He has gone on an excursion on his return he will visit a bird sanctuary as well.

Execrate/एक्सिक्रेट *(verb)* - शाप देना, घृणा करना
He execrated over the heinous crime.

Executive/ऍक्जिक्यूटिव *(noun)* - शासन-सम्बन्धी, प्रशासक
He is a junior executive engineer in DDA.

Executor/ऍक्जिक्यूटर *(noun)* - कार्यान्वित करने वाला, मृतक के इच्छापत्र का उत्तरसाधक
Before his death, my father had already appointed an executor.

Exemplar/एक्जेम्पलर *(noun)* - आदर्श प्रकार
It was exemplary show of fashion designing.

Exequies/ऍक्सिक्विज *(plural noun)* - अंतिम संस्कार, अन्त्येष्टि किया
When somebody dies it becomes necessary to perform exequies.

Exhale/एग्ज़हेल् *(verb)* - साँस निकलना
As he exhaled his breath, I could smell alcohol on it.

Exhilarate/एग्जिलरेट *(verb)* - हर्षित करना, प्रमुदित करना
I was exhilarated to get first position in the class.

Exhume/एक्ज्यूम *(verb)* - खोदकर भूमि से बाहर निकालना
On the orders of the judge a dead body was exhumed.

Exigent/एक्सिजेंट *(adjective)* - अतिआवश्यक
You are taking a loan from him, remember he is a very exigent person. You will have to return back all his money in time.

Exile/एक्जाइल *(noun)* - निर्वासन, देश-निष्कासन
The English exiled Bahadur Shah Zafar. He died in Burma.

Exist/एक्जिस्ट *(verb)* - जीवित रहना, अस्तित्त्व होना
Somehow or other he exists in such great poverty.

Exit/एक्जिट *(noun)* - निर्गम, बाहर निकलने का रास्ता
Sir, that is exit gate.

Exogamy/एक्सोगैमी *(noun)* - जाति के बाहर विवाह-सम्बन्ध
Clan or tribal people seldom favour exogamy.

Exorbitant/एक्जॉर्बिटैन्ट *(adj)* - अपरिमित
Despite exorbitant prices, people continue to buy onions.

Exorcist/एक्सार्सिस्ट *(noun)* - ओझा
He is an exorcist. He drives out evil spirit from a person or place.

Exorcise/एक्सॉर्साइज *(verb)* - झाड़-फूँककर प्रेत हटाना
He has exorcised the evil spirit.

Exordium/एक्जार्डियम *(noun)* - प्रस्तावना, भूमिका
The exordium of the astronomer who was speaking on black holes in sky was brilliant.

Expand/एक्सपैंड *(verb)* - बढ़ाना, फुलाना
Scientist say that our universe is ever expanding.

Expanse/एक्सपैंस *(noun)* - विस्तार, फैलाव
The expanse of sea was vast.

Expansion/एक्सपैंसन *(noun)* - वृद्धि, विस्तार देना
Expansion of the bridge was nearing completion.

Expansive/एक्सपैंसिव *(adjective)* - व्यापक, विस्तृत
During the rainy season, rivers become expansive.

Exparte/एक्सपार्टि *(adjective & adverb)*- एक तरफा, एक के पक्ष में
The law gave an exparte decision.

Expatiate/एक्सपेशिएट *(verb)* - विस्तारपूर्वक लिखना
This time he expatiated about brain surgery.

Expatriate/एक्सपैट्रियेट *(noun)* - देश से बाहर रहने वाला व्यक्ति निर्वासित व्यक्ति
He is an expatriate settled in Canada.

Expect/एक्सपेक्ट *(verb)* - आशा करना
I expect I'll be late.

Expectorate/एक्सपेक्टोरेट *(verb)* - थूकना, खखारना
He expectorated phlegm.

E

E

Expedient/एक्सपीडिएन्ट *(adj)* - उचित, स्वार्थ साधक पर नैतिक नहीं

The government decided that it was expediant not to increase taxes until after election.

Expedition/एक्सपेडिशन *(noun)* - शीघ्रता

An expedition was sent to Himalayan mountains for the study of plants.

Expense/एक्सपेन्स *(noun)* - अधिक खर्चीला

The expenses of living in a metro city are very high.

Expert/एक्सपर्ट *(noun)* - निपुण

He is an expert in flying helicopter.

Expiration/एक्सपिरेशन *(noun)* - मृत्यु

Before buying please check the expiration date of the medicine.

Expire/एक्सपायर *(verb)* - समाप्त होना

This medicine has expired.

Explain/एक्सप्लेन *(verb)* - व्याख्या करना

The teacher took us to the planetarium and explained the planetary system.

Explainer/एक्सप्लेनर *(noun)* - व्याख्या करने वाला

My English teacher is a good explainer.

Explanatory/एक्स्प्लैनेटरि *(adjective)* - स्पष्टीकरण

He was asked to submit an explanatory note to why he was absent from office for three days.

Explicate/एक्सप्लिकेट *(verb)* - व्याख्या करना, स्पष्ट करना

The professor explicated a few poems of William Blake.

Explicit/एक्सप्लिसिट *(adjective)* - स्पष्ट, स्फुट

His lecture on the properties of medicinal plants was so explicit that there was a thunderous applause.

Explode/एक्सप्लोड *(verb)* - उड़ा देना, विस्फोट होना

A bomb exploded and great damage was done.

Exploit/एक्सप्लॉयट *(verb)* - अद्‌भुत कार्य (किसी का शोषण करना)

He exploited his rich clients to no end.

Exploration/एक्सप्लोरेशन *(noun)* - अन्वेषण, जिज्ञासा

The exploration of pyramids of Egypt brought to light many strange facts.

Explosive/एक्सप्लोसिव *(adjective)* - शीघ्रदाह्य

Police found out many explosives hidden in trash boxes.

Export/एक्सपोर्ट *(verb)* - परदेश में माल भेजना

India exports high standard sugar, wheat and rice to many countries.

Expositor/एक्सपॉजिटर *(noun)* - अर्थ-प्रकाशक

He is an expositor and will explain all these theories in an explicit way.

Expostulate/एक्सपॉस्ट्यूलेट *(verb)* - तर्क करना

He expostulated against the plan of action.

Exposure/एक्सपोजर *(noun)* - प्रकाशकरण

Exposure to cold made him fall sick.

Expound/एक्सपाउन्ड *(verb)* - व्याख्या करना, समझाना

He expounded the theory lucidly.

Express/एक्सप्रेस *(verb)* - ठीक, निश्चित

He expressed his disagreement by gestures.

Expression/एक्सप्रेशन *(noun)* - कथन

The expression on his face was that of displeasure.

Expulsion/एक्स्पल्शन् *(noun)* - बहिष्कार, निर्वासन, निस्कासन

His expulsion from the class was a disciplinary action taken against him.

Expunge/एक्सपंज *(verb)* - मिटाना

His name was expunged from the club as he frequently broke its rules and regulations.

Expurgate/एक्सपर्गेट *(verb)* - परिष्कार करना

A lesson was expurgated from the textbook as it was historically untruly.

Exquisite/एक्सक्विजिट *(adjective)* - सुन्दर, उत्कृष्ट

She is a woman of exquisite beauty.

Exsect/एक्सेक्ट *(verb)* - काट डालना

You have to exsect the unruly weeds.

Extant/एक्सटैन्ट *(adjective)* - वर्तमान

Some ancient animals are still extant in some form or the other.

Extend/एक्सटेंड *(verb)* - फैलाना

He extended the offer to him to join the party.

Extensile/एक्सटेंसाइल *(adjective)* - फैलाने योग्य
The area around is extensile.

Extensive/एक्सटेंसिव *(adjective)* - चौड़ा, बड़ा
The tea shops are extensive in this area.

Extent/एक्सटेंट *(noun)* - प्रसार, फैलाना, विस्तृत करना
He can go to any extent to fulfil his ambition.

Extenuate/एक्सटेन्युएट *(verb)* - अल्प करना, शक्ति कम करना
The lawyer tried his best to extenuate the crime.

Exterior/एक्सटिरियर *(adjective)* - बाहरी रूप, बाहरी भाग
The exterior of this building is done very exquisitely.

Exterminate/एक्सटरमिनेट *(verb)* - जड़ से उखाड़ देना
The termites were exterminated from the house by spraying chemicals.

External/एक्सटरनल *(adjective)* - बाहरी
The external of this hotel is beautifully done.

Extinct/एक्सटिंक्ट *(adjective)* - अप्रचलित
Many species of plants and animals are getting fast extinct these days.

Extinguish/एक्सटिंग्विश *(verb)* - बुझाना
All the candles were extinguished as the electricity was restored.

Extirpate/एक्सटर्पेट *(verb)* - नाश करना, जड़ से उखाड़ना
All the enemy hideouts were extirpated.

Extort/एक्सटॉर्ट *(verb)* - छीनना, बलपूर्वक लेना
The mafia extorted a lot of money from shopkeepers.

Extra/एक्स्ट्रा *(adjective)* - अधिक, अतिरिक्त
All extra money he had was spent on his illness.

Extraordinarily/एक्स्ट्राऑरडिनरिलि *(adverb)* - अपूर्वता से, विलक्षणता से
He behaned extraordinarily in the court.

Extraordinary/एक्स्ट्राऑरडिनरी *(adj)* - असामान्य
He has extra-ordinary talent for writing fiction.

Extravagance/एक्स्ट्रावैगेन्स *(noun)* - अतिशय, फिजूलखर्ची
He is a reasonable man and does not indulge in extravagance.

Extravagant/एक्स्ट्रावैगेन्ट *(adjective)* - लुटाऊ मुक्तहस्त
He is not extravagant but spends money wisely.

Extreme/एक्सट्रीम *(adjective)* - यथासंभव अधिकतम, चरम
You must take extreme care when driving at night.

Extremity/एक्सट्रीमिटी *(noun)* - सीमा
There is no extremity of his anger.

Extricable/एक्स्ट्रीकेब्ल - विमुक्त करने योग्य
It is an extricable matter.

Extrinsic/एक्सट्रिंसिक *(adjective)* - बाहरी, अनावश्यक
This theory is a complex interplay of influence and extrinsic factors.

Extrude/एक्सट्रूड *(verb)* - ढकेलना
Ashes were being extruded from the volcano.
The wires being extruded from the iron rods.

Exuberance/एक्स्यूबरैंस *(noun)* - प्रचुरता, अधिक्य
They enjoyed the picnic with a youthful exuberance.

Exult/एक्जल्ट *(verb)* - अति प्रसन्न होना
Exulting in her escape, she closed the door behind her.

E

Ff

F/एफ *(noun)* - अंग्रेजी वर्णमाला का छठा वर्ण the sixth letter of the English alphabet.

1. Denoting the next after E in a set of items, categories, etc.
2. Music the fourth note of the diatonic scale of C major.

F

Fabaceous/फेबेसियस *(adj)* - सेम की तरह की

Leguminous Green-looking fabaceous plants are a good source of vitamins A, B and C.

Fabian/फेबियन *(noun)* - दीर्घसूत्री

Members of the Fabian society aim to spread socialism in a gradual way.

Fable/फेबल *(noun)* - कहानी

Children like to read fables.

Fabricate/फैब्रिकेट *(verb)* - निर्माण करना

The evidence is totally fabricated.

Fabulist/फैब्यूलिस्ट *(noun)* - मिथ्यावादी मनुष्य

Book publishers look for fabulists who can compose fables that interests children.

Fabulous/फैब्यूलस *(adjective)* - मनगढ़न्त विस्मयकारी, प्रसिद्ध

Her fabulous performances attracted everyone in the theatre.

Face/फेस *(noun)* - मुख

Face is the combination of eyes, ears, mouth and nose; Face is the part of the clock that displays the time.

Facetious/फॅसीशॅस *(adjective)* - मसखरा

It is facetious trying to be humorous when the matter is serious.

Facial/फेसियल *(noun)* - मुख-सम्बन्धी

A treatment done on your face that refreshes your skin is an example of a facial.

Facile/फेसाइल *(adjective)* - सुगम

Facile is winning a game against a team that isn't very good at that particular game.

Facilitate/फॅसिलिटेट *(verb)* - सुगम बनाना

You must facilitate to ensure that everyone's opinions are heard.

Facing/फेसिंग *(noun)* - आवरण

Facing is a name given to a piece of material sewn to the edge of a garment, such as a dress or coat, as lining or decoration.Facing is an outer layer or coating applied to a surface for protection or decoration.

Facsimile/फैक्सिमली *(noun)* - प्रतिलिपि

An exact copy that has been made of a cheque is an example of a facsimile. When you have an exact copy of a legal document, this is an example of a facsimile copy.

Fact/फैक्ट *(noun)* - तथ्य, सत्य, वास्तविकता

In fact, he has gone to Delhi today.

Faction/फैक्शन *(noun)* - दल, गुट, दलबंदी

The youngsters have formed a faction within an otherwise peaceful political party.

Factious/फैक्शस *(adjective)* - अराजक

An example of something factious is a bunch of dissatisfied elements within a class.

Factor/फैक्टर *(noun)* - गुणक, घटक, कारक

An example of factor would be eye-witness accounts to a news report about a crime. 9 is a factor of 27.

Factory/फैक्टरी *(noun)* - कारखाना

A factory is a building or group of buildings in which goods are manufactured.

Factotum/फैक्टोटम *(noun)* - विश्वस्त अनुचर या सेवक

An employee or assistant who serves in a wide range of capacities is known as factotum.

Facula/फैक्यूला *(noun)* - सूर्य पर का चमकता चिह्न

A large bright spot on the sun's photosphere is known as facula.

Fad/फैड *(noun)* - धुन

A fad is any fashion that is taken up with great enthusiasm for a brief period of time.

Fade/फेड *(verb)* – फीका पड़ना

When a colour begins to get lighter, this is an example of a time when the colour fades.

Fading/फेडिंग *(noun)* – मंद, क्षीण, म्लानता

The match had to be stopped because of fading light.

Faeces/फीसीज *(plural noun)* – विष्ठा

The body eliminates faces through rectum.

Fail/फेल *(verb)* – असफल होना

When you get only 1 question correct out of 100 on the test, this is an example of a time when you fail.

Fain/फेन *(adjective)* – प्रसन्नतापूर्वक, तैयार, उत्सुक

An example of fain is a brilliant student who is eager to study with his friend who is not as sharp.

Fainting/फेन्टिंग *(noun)* – मूर्छा या बेहोशी

She fell on the ground in dead fainting.

Faith/फेथ *(noun)* – विश्वास

Faith is belief in a person or thing that does not rest on logical proof or material evidence.

Faithful/फेथफुल *(adjective)* – सच्चा

A Muslim who adheres strictly to the tenants of the Islamic religion is faithful.

Faithless/फेथलेस *(adjective)* – अविश्वासी

How can you have faith in a person who is so faithless, treacherous and cruel?

Fake/फेक *(adjective)* – बेईमान आदमी

You are a fake person when you pretend to be sick when you aren't.

Falcate/फैल्केट *(adjective)* – हँसुए की तरह घूमा हुआ

As we moved slowly toward the deep waters in the river a big fish arched its back, showing a strongly falcate fin.

Falchion/फॉल्चन/फॉल्शन *(noun)* – कृपाण

A falchion is a short, broad sword with a curved cutting edge and a sharp point.

Falciform/फैल्सीफार्म *(adjective)* – हँसुए के आकार का

Falciform ligament is a very rare anomaly and hardly any cases are reported.

Falcon/फॉल्कन/फॉकन *(noun)* – बाज

Falcon is a high flying bird that can spot its prey on ground from 5-6 kilometres above.

Faldstool/फाल्डस्टूल *(noun)* – खेमे में रखने की छोटी तिपाई

Faldstool is a backless chair used by a bishop when officiating in any other church.

Fallacious/फैलेसस *(adjective)* – मिथ्या

When you make an argument based on a mistaken belief, then the argument would be described as fallacious.

Fallacy/फैलॅसि *(noun)* – अशुद्धि

An example of fallacy is the idea that the sun spins around the earth.

Fallibility/फैलिबिलिटी *(adjective)* – भ्रमत्व

If your analysis doesn't take all factors into consideration, you only increase your chance of fallibility.

Fallible/फैलिबॅल *(adjective)* – भ्रमकारी

We all human beings are fallible.

Falling/फॉलिंग *(noun)* – गिरने वाला पदार्थ

I saw a falling star.

Falsification/फॉल्सिफिकेशॅन *(noun)* – कूटकरण

He does deliberatey falsification of company's records.

Falsify/फाल्सीफाई *(verb)* – कपट करना

He made many attempts to falsify her statement.

Falter/फॉल्टर *(verb)* – भचकना

When facing an interview board, you must speak clearly, never falter.

Faltering/फाल्टरिंग *(adjective)* – हीनता

Try to change your faltering behaviour.

Fame/फेम *(noun)* – यश

By dint of sheer labour, he made a name and fame for himself within a short span of time.

Famulus/फैम्युलश *(noun)* – जादूगर का सहायक

A private secretary or other close attendant, especially during medieval times, was known as famulus.

Fanatic/फॅनैटिक *(noun)* – हठधमी

A fanatic is a person who has faith in a belief that is not supported by reason.

Fanaticism/फनैटिसिज्म *(noun)* – धार्मिक हठ

An example of fanaticism is following a set of rules even to the extent of killing other individuals.

F

Fancied/फैन्सिड *(adjective)* - कल्पना किया हुआ

Despite knowing the opponent was a strong side, we fancied our chances of winning by scoring quick runs.

Fanciful/फैन्सीफुल *(adjective)* - काल्पनिक

Examiners will give you marks only for knowledge, not for your fanciful writing style.

Fanion/फैनियन *(noun)* - पैमाइश करने वालों का झण्डी

Every army hoists a fanion to as evidence for a captured post or area.

Farce/फार्स *(noun)* - प्रहसन

The voting was farce since the supporters of the rival party were prevented from going near the polling booth.

Farcical/फार्सिकॅल *(adjective)* - विनोदपूर्ण

When supporters of rival party are prevented from voting, the eulogy of democracy becomes totally farcical.

Farina/फॅराइना *(noun)* - मैदा, मण्ड, माँड़ी

Farina is a wholesome meal made from different cereal grains, potatoes, nuts, etc. and eaten as a cooked cereal.

Farm/फाम *(noun)* - खेत

A farm is a place where dairy cows are raised. A farm is a place where baby fish are raised; a fish farm. Nearly 80 percent of agricultural lands is owned by state and collective farms.

Farmer/फाम(र) *(noun)* - किसान

A person who is primarily concerned with growing crops is called a farmer.

Farrago/फॅरागो *(noun)* - घालमेल, मिश्रण

There was not one reasonable balanced statement in the whole farrago.

Farrier/फैरिअर *(noun)* - नालबन्द

Make sure that your horses ' feet are regularly trimmed and shod, by a competent farrier, to prevent hoof cracks.

Farrow/फैरो *(noun)* - सूअर पालना

Piggeries have a separate farrow house for production of litters even in winter.

Fart/फाट *(verb)* - पादना

Fart is the noise that gas makes when coming from the rear. Someone who constantly complains is known as a fart.

Farthest/फाद्-इस्ट *(adjective & adverb)* - सबसे अधिक दूरी का

Within the Solar system, planet Neptune is farthest from the Earth.

Fascicle/फैसिकल *(noun)* - पुस्तिका, पुलिन्दा, गुच्छा

The part of a book published prior to publication of complete book is called fascicule.In botany, a bundle of stems, flowers, or leaves is called fascicle.

Fascinate/फैसिनेट *(verb)* - मोह लेना

With his acting ability Charlie Chaplin could fascinate a global audience for decades.

Fascism/फासिज्म *(noun)* - फासीवाद, व्यक्तिगत स्वतन्त्रता के विरुद्ध सिद्धान्तवादी

The government led by Benito Mussolini in Italy was an example of fascism.

Fast/फास्ट *(verb)* - उपवास करना

An example of fast is not eating for twelve hours before having blood drawn.

Fasten/फासॅन *(verb)* - जकड़ना

The airhostess announced to fasten seatbelt. These days traffic police will charge you if you don't fasten your seatbelt.

Fastidious/फास्टिडिअस *(adjective)*- दुस्तोषणीय

I'm normally very fastidious about citing my sources on this blog.

Fasting/फास्टिंग *(noun)* - उपवास

I keep fasting on Tuesday.

Fastness/फास्टनेस *(noun)* - स्थिरता

The colour has a smooth gloss finish whilst possessing superior light fastness. Reproduced using the latest technology, these beautiful prints have a potential light fastness of over 200 years.

Fatal/फेटॅल *(adjective)* - प्राणनाशक

The shot in the head proved fatal.

Fatalism/फेटलिज्म *(noun)* - भाग्यवाद

It's time to shake off the lazy fatalism that the poor will always side with us.

Fatalist/फेटलिस्ट *(noun)* - भाग्यवादी

He is a fatalist because he believes in fate.

Fatality/फेटलिटि *(noun)* - विपत्ति, कष्ट

Any accidental fatality to a member of the workforce is unacceptable. 9 % of motorcyclist fatalities are over the drink drive limit.

Fathom/फैदम *(noun)* - छः फुट की नाप

The engine shaft is sunk to a depth of130 fathoms. In short, scientists have not yet been able to fathom the nature of consciousness, its origins, or its role in nature.

Fatally/फेटली *(adverb)* - सांघातिक रीति से

He was fatally wounded in the racing car accident.

Fatigue/फॅटीग *(noun)* - थकावट

An example of fatigue is what you feel after you run a half marathon.

Fatiguing/फॅटिगुंइग *(adjective)* - थकाने वाला

It is very tenuous and fatiguing work.

Fatty/फैटी *(adjective)* - चर्बीदार

I saw a very fatty lady on the road.

Fatuous/फैट्यूअॅस *(adjective)* - ऊटपटांग, अनर्गल, बुद्धिहीन

There was little point continuing that fatuous discussion.

Faucet/फॉसिट *(noun)* - पीपे में लगी हुई टोंटी

Faucet is an American term for the British word tap.

Faugh/फॉ *(exclamatory)* - छिः छिः

Faugh! This place stinks.

Fault/फॉल्ट *(noun)* - अपूर्णता

It's nobody's fault, it's just one of those things.

Faultless/फॉल्टलेस *(adjective)* - निर्दोष

She was absolutely faultless at it, never ever making a mistake.

Faulty/फॉल्टी *(adjective)* - दोषयुक्त

If goods are deemed faulty they will either be repaired or replaced. Faulty wiring could cause fires or electric shocks, which may end in disaster.

Favour/फेवर *(noun)* - अनुग्रह

Please do them a favour by cleaning their home.

Favourite/फेवरिट *(adjective)* - प्रिय

My favourite colour is blue as I like it more than any other colour.

Favouritism/फेवरिटिज्म *(noun)* - पक्षपात

Favoritism is an act of giving preferential treatment to someone or something.

Fawn/फॉन *(noun & verb)* - चापलूसी

The way a young girl acts approvingly towards a boy she likes is called fawn.

Fealty/फीअॅलटि *(noun)* - निष्ठा

I will permit you to till my land for free as long as you pledge fealty to my rule.

Fear/फिअॅर *(noun)* - भय

Fear is a feeling of anxiety and worry caused by the presence or nearness of danger, evil, pain, etc.

F

Fearful/फिअरफुल *(adjective)* - भयंकर, भयानक

I am fearful of that haunted house.

Fearless/फिअरलेस *(adjective)* - निःशंक

An example of fearless is a fireman's attitude when fighting a fire.

Feasibility/फीजॅबिलिटि *(adjective)* - संभाव्यता, औचित्य

Feasibility studies indicate that the project is worthwhile and should be executed.

Feasible/फीजॅबॅल *(adjective)* - सम्भव

With deadline extended, it is now feasible to erect the plant shed.

Feast/फीस्ट *(noun)* - प्रीतिभोज, दावत

An example of a feast is a buffet-style meal.

Feat/फीट *(noun)* - वीरता का कार्य, करतब, कमाल

Sachin Tendulkar is the only cricketer to have achieved the feat of scoring one hundred international centuries.

Feather/फेदर *(noun)* - पंख

Birds of the same feathers flock together.

Feathery/फिदरी *(adjective)* - परदार

This jacket is feathery.

Feature/फिचर *(noun)* - आकृति

A feature is a distinct or outstanding part, quality, or characteristic of something.

Febrile/फीब्राइल *(adjective)* - ज्वर-सम्बन्धी

Febrile describes a person who has a fever or has something caused by a fever.

Feculent/फेक्यूलॅन्ट *(adjective)* - गन्दा

The article you have written is not original, it is rubbish and feculent.

Fecund/फीकॅन्ड *(adjective)* - उपजाऊ

A woman who can get pregnant is an example of someone who would be described as fecund.

F

Fecundate/फीकॅन्डेट *(verb)* – उपजाऊ बनाना

There are no insects to fecundate flowering plants.

Fecundity/फीकॅनडिटि *(noun)* – उपजाऊपन

The fecundity of this land is the reason for its high price.

Federal/फेडरेल *(adjective)* – संयुक्त

The constitution describes India as a unitary government with federal features.

Federate/फेडरेट *(verb)* – एक संस्था मे सम्मिलित करना

To federate means to unite various parts by common agreement under a central authority.

Federation/फेडरेशन *(noun)* – कई राज्यों का संघ

The United States is an example of federation.

Federative/फेडरेटिव *(adjective)* – सन्धि

Indian states are federative in nature.

Feeble/फीबॅल *(adjective)* – दुर्बल

The doctors made feeble attempts to revive the poor patient.

Feed/फीड *(verb)* – खिलाना

You should feed grams to horses.

Feel/फील *(verb)* – महसूस करना

An example of feel is when you run your hand over a dress.

Feeling/फीलिंग *(noun)* – स्पर्श ज्ञान

Feeling is the act of sensing that the surface of something is smooth because you touched it.

Feign/फेन *(verb)* – बहाना करना

Don't feign sickness in a feeble attempt to get your sister to mop the floor.

Felicitate/फिलिसिटेट *(verb)* – अभिनन्दन करना

I felicitate you on your marriage day.

Felicitous/फिलिसिटॅस *(adjective)* – धन्य

The author writes felicitous lines that show a genuine poetic touch.

Felicity/फिलिसिटी *(noun)* – आनन्द

Some seek their rest and happiness on earth, others eternal felicity in heaven.

Feline/फिलाइन *(adjective)* – बिल्ली के समान

A feline is an animal that belongs to the cat family.

Fell/फेल *(verb)* – गिराना, काट गिराना

When you are standing upright and then you fall down, this is an example of a situation where you fell.

Feller/फेलर *(noun)* – वृक्ष काटकर गिराने वाला

He works as a feller under a contractor.

Felony/फेलॅनि *(noun)* – महा अपराध

An example of felony is rape.

Felspar/फेलस्पार *(noun)* – एक धातु विशेष

Felspar is an ore containing silicate of iron.

Felt/फेल्ट *(noun)* – नमदा, कम्बल

We generally use felt in winter season.

Female/फिमेल *(adjective)* – स्त्री जाति

A female is a person of the sex that produces eggs and can bear young. Females are no more a weaker section.

Feminine/फेमिनिन *(adjective)* – जनाना

Sewing and cooking are examples of hobbies that were traditionally described as feminine hobbies.

Femininity/फेमिनिटी *(noun)* – स्त्रीत्व

I think she lacks feminity

Feminize/फेमिनाइज *(verb)* – स्त्री बनाना

To feminize is to make or become feminine or effeminate.

Femur/फेमर *(noun)* – जंघा पिण्डिका

The bone in your body that goes from your pelvis to your knee is known as femur.

Fen/फेन *(noun)* – दलदल

Compare with bog. Low, flat, marshy and swampy land is known as fen.

Fence – *(noun)*

An example of a fence is a two foot wooden barrier around a person's front yard.

Fencing/फेन्सिंग *(noun)* – पटेबाजी

Fencing is a popular sporting event at Olympic games.

Fenestra/फेनेस्ट्रा *(noun)* – खिड़की या छिद्र

Fenestra is a small opening in the inner wall of the middle ear.

Fennel/फेनेल *(noun)* – सोया जाति का एक शाक

Fennel is a tall herb with feathery leaves and yellow flowers whose foliage and aromatic seeds are used to flavour foods.

Feral/फेरल *(adjective)* - जंगली, वन्य

A feral is an undomesticated cat that scratches and claws if you come near it.

Ferment/फमेंट *(verb)* - खमीर उठना या उठाना

Ferment is an agent or catalyst, such as, yeast, bacterium, mould, or enzyme that cause fermentation.

Fern/फन् *(noun)* - सुन्दर महीन पत्तियों का एक पौधा

I have seen many types of fern in wet areas.

Ferocious/फॅरोशस *(adjective)* - निर्दयी

While in a zoo, you must be cautious against ferocious animals.

Ferocity/फॅरॉसिटि *(noun)* - क्रूरता

The extreme and wild nature of a storm is an example of the ferocity of the storm.

Ferriage/फेरिइज *(noun)* - नदी पार करने का भाड़ा

What is the ferriage for crossing the river?

Ferric/फेरिक *(adjective)* - लोहे का

Ferric oxide is one of the chemical compounds containing iron.

Ferrous/फेरस *(adjective)* - लोहा सम्बन्धी

Ferrous oxide is one of the chemical compounds containing iron.

Ferrule/फेरूल *(noun)* - सामी

Ferrule is a metal or plastic ring or cap put around the end of a cane, tool handle, etc. to give added strength or for tightening a joint.

Fertilize/फटिलाइज *(verb)* - उपजाऊ बनाना

To fertilize is to make the female reproductive cell fruitful by impregnating with the male gamete.Urea, phosphates and nitrates help fertilize soil for increased productivity.

Ferule/फेरूल *(noun)* - बच्चों को मारने की छड़ी

Ferule is an instrument, such as a cane, stick, or flat piece of wood, used in punishing children.

Fervency/फॅवॅन्सि *(noun)* - उत्सुकता

He has fervency in his behaviour.

Fervent/फॅवॅन्ट *(adjective)* - गरम

It is my fervent appeal to allow me 15 days leave.

Fervid/फॅविड *(adjective)* - प्रचण्ड

He is a fervid patriot and won't mind dying for the good of the motherland.

Fervour/फॅवॅर *(noun)* - उत्साह

Fervour is intense feelings or passion at a higher degree.

Fester/फेस्टर *(verb)* - सड़ना

When food is left out for days to rot, the food festers and becomes unfit for consumption.

Festival/फेस्टिवल *(noun)* - उत्सव

Deepawali is a festival of great pomp and show.

Festivity/फेस्टिविटी *(noun)* - उत्सव-काल

A week or so before Deepawali, the atmosphere acquires the look of festivity everywhere.

Fetch/फेच *(verb)* - जाकर लाना

The puppy went to fetch the stick that we had tossed.

Fetching/फेचिंग *(adjective)* - मोहक

She went for fetching a new hairstyle and a new garment.

Fete/फेट *(noun)* - त्योहार

An example of a fete is a school carnival.

Feticide/फेटिसाइड *(noun)* - भ्रूणहत्या

Cases of female feticide is on the rise in some parts of India.

Fetid/फेटिड *(adjective)* - दुर्गन्धि-युक्त

The spoiled food is an example of something that might be described as fetid.

Fettle/फेटल *(noun)* - योग्यता

Every jockey wants to keep his racing horse in fine fettle. She was in great fettle, bouncing all over the place.

Fetus/फेटस *(noun)* - भ्रूण

A baby that has been in its mother's stomach growing for 18 weeks is an example of a fetus.

Feudal/फ्यूडल *(adjective)* - जागीरदारी

Early developments were really about the maintenance of political power, essentially feudal in origin.

Fever/फीवर *(noun)* - बुखार

He was running a temperature of 103 degree fahrenheit.

Feverish/फीवॅरिश *(adjective)* - ज्वरार्त, ज्वरग्रस्त

A person who has a body temperature of 102 is an example of someone who is feverish. A crowd that is shouting and yelling because

F

their team is winning is an example of a crowd that would be described as feverish.

Fiasco/फिऐस्को *(noun)* – विशिष्ट असफलता

The party ended in a fiasco since the clown hired to entertain broke his leg and has threatened to sue the organizer.

Fiat/फाइएट – आज्ञा

It is obligatory to follow the fiat of the commissioner.

F

Fibril/फाइब्रिल *(noun)* – महीन रेशा

Electron microscope is needed to observe the fibril formation.

Fibrous/फाइब्रस *(adjective)* – रेशेदार

When this dust is inhaled it can make the lungs gradually fibrous and lead to breathing problems.

Fickle/फिकॅल *(adjective)* – अस्थिर

Children are very fickle minded and move to new toys because of their short attention span.

Fiction/फिक्सन *(noun)* – उपन्यास

Publishers are coming out with fiction that is meant for children.

Fictitious/फिक्टिशस *(adjective)* – झूठा

Many authors use fictitious names instead of their original ones.

Fiddle/फिड्ल *(noun)* – सारंगी

The space in itself plays second fiddle to the lower gallery.

Fiddler/फिड्लर *(noun)* – बजाने वाला

A person who plays violin in a folk music is known as fiddler.

Fidelity/फाइडेलिटि *(noun)* – स्वामी भक्ति

Fidelity is faithful devotion to duty or to one's obligations;

Fidget/फिडगेट *(verb)* – बेचैन या अशान्त होना

He fidgeted with his notes while lecturing.

Fie/फाइ *(interjection)* – धिक्! छी! छी!

Any exclamatory expression used to denote distaste or disapproval is known as fie.

Fiend/फीन्ड *(noun)* – पिशाच

He is so obsessed with crosswords that people call him a crossword fiend.

Fiendish/फीन्डिश *(adjective)* – क्रूर, अतिदुष्ट

Regular expressions can get quite fiendish to read at times.

Fierce/फिअॅस *(adjective)* – खूँखार, हिंसक

Fierce fighting broke out again between India and Pakistan.

Fiery/फाइअॅरि *(adjective)* – उत्सुक

He was high-spirited and had a very fiery temper, which led him at times to acts of cruelty.

Fife/फाइफ *(noun)* – एक प्रकार की छोटी बाँसुरी

A small flute with a high, piercing tone, used mainly in military bands.

Fifteen/फिफ्टीन *(cardinal number)* – पन्द्रह

Fifteen is a sum of five and ten.

Fifth/फिफ्थ *(cardinal number)* – पाँचवाँ

The sum of two and three is five.

Fight/फाइट *(verb)* – युद्ध करना

Since independence, India and Pakistan have fought four wars.

Fighter/फाइटर *(noun)* – लड़ाका

India has decided to purchase fighter jets from France.

Fighting/फाइटिंग *(noun)* – युद्ध

Do you think fighting in the dressing room will help good performance on the field?

Figment फिग्मेंट *(noun)* – कल्पित वस्तु

Novels are nothing but the figment of an author's imagination.

Figurative/फिग्युरॅटिव *(adjective)* – आलंकारिक

We haven't taken on new artists for some years, however mainly figurative artists would be considered.

Figurine/फिग्यूरीन *(noun)* – एक छोटी मूर्ति

Figurines of a goddess have also been excavated by the archaeologists.

Filament/फिलॅमॅन्ट *(noun)* – सूत, रेशा

A type of intermediate filament found in epithelial cells have been created in the laboratory.

Filature/फिलॅचॅर – *(noun)*

Filature is a reel of raw silk obtained from cocoons of silkworm.

Filch/फिल्च *(verb)* – चुराना

The thief filched the purse and ran away into hiding.

Filiform/फिलिफाम *(adjective)* – धागे की तरह

In botany, filiform is a term used to describe leaf-shapes.

Filier/फिलियर *(noun)* – भरने वाला

An item used to fill the space or time is known as filier.

Filling/फिलिंग *(adj & noun)* – संतुष्ट करने वाला, भरावन

I have got dental fillings done for rupees two thousand.

Fillip/फिलिप *(noun)* – उत्साह

The pep talk by the coach acted as a fillip to the team's sagging morale.

Filly/फिलि *(noun)* – बछेड़ी, छिनाल

He bought a lovely 3-year old filly with a view to train her for horse racing.

Filmy/फिल्मी *(adjective)* – झिटलीदार

Filmy fern grows along the banks of the river Ravi as it runs through the hills.

Filth/फिल्द *(noun)* – गन्दगी, मैल

We simply didn't expect to see such filth at the family shopping store.

Filthy/फिल्दी *(adjective)* – गन्दा

The language of these college students is pretty filthy.

Filtrate/फिल्ट्रेट *(noun)* – निभारा हुआ तरल पदार्थ

The liquid obtained after passing through the filter is known as filtrate. Is this area watered out or are you producing mud filtrate?

Fimbriate/फिम्ब्रिएट *(adjective)* – किनारीदार

The wide portion of the fallopian tube near the fimbriated extremity is known as ampulla of uterine tube.

Fin/फिन *(noun)* – मछली का सुफना

Fin is an organ attached to a fish's body that helps them in swimming under water.

Final/फाइनल *(adjective)* – अन्तिम, समापन

The final chapter of the book was quite absorbing.

Finale/फिनाले *(noun)* – वित्त, अर्थ

The grand finale will end with a fabulous firework display over the stadium.

Finance/फाइनेंस *(noun)* – धन, वित्त, इसका प्रबन्ध

Finance minister of India has imposed a severe squeeze on the Indian economy.

Finch/फिंच *(noun)* – एक प्रकार की छोटी चिड़िया

Australian finches are very engaging little birds which can provide many hours of enjoyment.

Finder/फाइन्डर *(noun)* – पता लगाने वाला

You can use the postcode finder for a wider scope.

Fine/फाइन *(noun)* – आर्थिक दंड, सुन्दर, महीन

This restaurant is renowned for fine dining, shopping and cafés.

Finery/फाइनरी *(noun)* – ठाट-बाट, अलंकार

Arrive in your own finery or choose from a wide selection of our costumes.

F

Fingering/फिंगरिंग *(noun)* – छूने का काम

The main difficulty is that for a number of instruments there is no standard fingering.

Finial/फिनियल *(noun)* – गाथिक इमारत में बना फूल

Attach a narrow wrought iron curtain rod with decorative finials to the wall.

Finical/फिनिकल *(adjective)* – तुनकमिज़ाज, अति कोमल

He is a finical person; his attitude is prone to change any moment.

Finis/फिनिश *(noun)* – अन्त

Hem lines are elegantly long with the subtle tailoring and immaculate finis to the skirt.

Finite/फाइनाइट *(adjective)* – मर्यादा युक्त

Although electricity travels fast, its speed is still finite and over a wire it is slower than in a vacuum.

Fir/फर *(noun)* – देवदार

Fir trees are extensively found in Kashmir.

First/फर्स्ट *(ordinal number)* – मुख्य, प्रधान

Put child safety first. It happened in the first half of the 20th century.

Fiscal/फिस्कल *(adjective)* – राजकर-सम्बन्धी

There is a fiscal deficit in the budget.

Fish/फिश *(noun)* – मछली

You should try not to have more than two portions of oily fish a week.

Fish-plate/फिश-प्लेट *(noun)* – रेल की पटरियों को जोड़ने की पट्टी

Fish-plates are used to strengthen railway tracks.

Fission/फिजन *(noun)* – जीव कोशिकाओं का विभाजन

Nuclear fission is what powers all modern day reactors.

Fissure/फिसर *(noun)* – दरार, फटन
Many fissures are created in the society by religious differences.

Fist/फिस्ट *(noun)*– घूँसा
He unclenched his fist to shake hands with the visitor.

Fisticuffs/फिस्टिकफ्स *(plural)* – मुक्केबाजी
Fighting with the fists is called fisticuffs.

F

Fistula/फिस्ट्युला *(noun)* – नासूर
Patients who have a fistula can usually feel it "buzzing "slightly.

Fitness/फिटनेस *(noun)* – उपयुक्तता
Running, cycling, swimming etc can all raise your body fitness.

Fitter/फिटर *(noun)* – यन्त्रों के अवययों को यथास्थान बैठाने वाला
All electrical appliances should be repaired by a qualified, registered electrical fitter.

Fittings/फिटिंग *(noun)* – आवश्यक यंत्र
This house comes with all fittings made of stainless steel.

Five/फाइव *(cardinal number)* – पाँच
Twenty divided by four is five.

Fix/फिक्स *(verb)* – स्थिर करना
Charges have been fixed in accordance with building regulations.

Fixable/फिक्सेबल *(adjective)* – स्थिर करने योग्य
All these appliances are fixable on any side of the wall.

Fixation/फिक्सेशन *(noun)* – स्थिरीकरण
Fixation of fractures is commonly used in many areas of trauma care.

Fixactive/फिक्सेक्टिव *(noun)* – स्थिर करने वाला
Some people find that using a denture fixative in the early stages gives them extra security.

Fixed/फिक्स्ड *(adjective)* – दृढ़
Fixed assets used by the charity should be briefly described, such as, make of desktop computer, or of motor vehicle.

Fixity/फिक्सिटी *(noun)* – स्थिरता
The fixity of his stave is unwavering.

Fixture/फिक्सचर *(noun)* – दृढ़ता
Provisional details of the forthcoming fixtures are listed below. It appeared to be constructed like today's plumbing fixtures.

Fizzle/फिजल *(verb)*– फूत्कार शब्द करना
Despite a hopeful beginning, Indian batting fizzled out weakly.

Flageolet/फ्लैजॅलेट *(noun)* – मुरली, शहनाई
A flageolet is a small flutelike instrument with a cylindrical mouthpiece, four finger holes, and two thumbholes.

Flagon/फ्लैगॅन *(noun)* – सुराही
A flagon is a large vessel with a handle and spout and often a lid, used for holding wine or other liquors.

Flagrant/फ्लेग्रन्ट *(adjective)* – ज्वलन्त
The draconian order issued is a flagrant misuse of bureaucratic power.

Flail/फेअल *(noun)* – मूसल
An example of a flail is a tool used to toss grain up in the air.

Flair/फ्लेअर *(noun)* – प्रवृत्ति
He possesses that natural flair for journalism without which no one will succeed in the news media.

Flam/फ्लैम *(noun)* – छल, कपट
Flam is a double drumbeat where first note is a short and the second a long one.

Flame/फ्लेम *(noun)* – अग्नि की ज्वाला
Flame is a zone of burning gases and fine suspended matter associated with rapid combustion.

Flamingo/फ्लेमिंगो *(noun)* – राजहंस
In the wild, flamingoes breed in very large numbers on salt or soda lakes.

Flange/फ्लेंज *(noun)* – निकला हुआ किनारा
I knew something was wrong when the brake drum and hub flange came off still attached to the wheel.

Flank/फ्लैंक *(noun)* – पेट, मकान का किनारा
Area between the ribs and hip of human or animal is known as flank.

Flanker/फ्लैंकर *(noun)* – गढ़, किला
Bhutia has played number eleven as open side flanker for most of the games.

Flannel/फ्लैनॅल *(noun)* – फलालीन
I saw a grey flannel suit in that shop.

Flannelette/फ्लैनलेट *(noun)* – सूती फलालीन

Flannelette is a soft cotton fabric with a nap.

Flaring/फ्लेअरिंग *(adjective)* – जगमगाता हुआ

Flaring of trousers at the bottom is no longer in fashion.

Flash/फ्लैश *(verb)* – सहसा प्रकाशित होना

The image flashed onto the screen. Rescue flashed on us the time we got caught in the storm. The cars flashed by while we were waiting.

Flashy/फ्लैशी *(adjective)* – चमकीला

I don't want anything too flashy like a Ferrari or a Bentley.

Flask/फ्लास्क *(noun)* – बोतल, कुप्पी

A thermos flask allows hot drinks to be carried.

Flat/फ्लैट *(noun)* – एक खण्ड के कमरे

High-rise flats were to be built in the inner zone.

Flattish/फ्लैटिश *(adjective)* – कुछ चिपटा

The spinners were hammered for six and fours because of bowling a flattish deliveries.

Flatulence/फ्लैटुलेंस *(noun)* – बाई, उदर-वायु

Flatulence is the expulsion of mixed gases from the body, which are the byproduct of the digestion process.

Flatus/फ्लेटस *(noun)* – अधोवायु

The medical term for mixture of gases formed as a byproduct of digestion process is known as flatus.

Flaunt/फ्लॉन्ट *(verb)* – अकड़ना

There is no justification to flaunt your wealth among the poor people.

Flavour/फ्लेवर *(noun)* – सुगन्ध

Flavoured coffees from around the world is available in this hotel.

Flax/फ्लैक्स *(noun)* – पटुआ, सन

Linen is made out of the natural fibre flax.

Flay/फ्ले *(verb)* – चमड़ा उतारना, लूटना

It is demoralizing for a person to be flayed in front of many people.

Fledge/फ्लेज *(verb)* – परदार करना

The now fledged chicks have to undertake the first migration on their own. Then the vouchers would become fully fledged shares, traded on the stock market.

Flee/फ्ली *(verb)* – भाग जाना

They were fleeing from the country in fear of persecution.

Fleece/फ्लीस *(noun & verb)* – पतला रेशा, ऊन, लूटना

You want to fleece the poor labourers.

Fleer/फ्लिअर *(verb)* – उपहास करना

Why fleer at someone who is yet to be trained for a new job?

F

Flesh/फ्लेश *(noun)* – माँस

Future generations will scarcely believe such a person like Mahatma Gandhi ever walked in flesh and blood on this Earth. Flesh is the semi solid part of vegetables which breaks up during cooking.

Fletcher/फ्लेचर *(noun)* – तीर बनाने वाला

Fletcher is a person who sells bows and arrows.

Flex/फ्लेक्स *(verb)* – लचीला होना

Exercise helps keep the muscles and joints flexed.

Flexile/फ्लेक्साइल *(adjective)* – मुलायम

Within these snow-beds the flexible fern occurs.

Flexion/फ्लेक्शन *(noun)* – घुमाव

This exercise involves the flexion and extension of the lower back.

Flexor/फ्लेक्सर *(noun)* – अंग के जोड़ को मोड़ने वाली माँसपेशी

These exercises can make only a limited contribution to strengthening the flexors.

Flexuous/फ्लेक्स्यूअस *(adjective)* – घुमौवा

Hundreds of miles of arteries and veins adjust inside the body because of their flexuous nature.

Flick/फ्लिक *(noun)* – झटका

Please flick the overdrive switch on.

Flicker/फ्लिकर *(verb)* – फड़फड़ाना

Flicker of the burning candle was finally snuffed out.

Flier/फ्लाइअॅर *(noun)* – विमानचालक उड़ने वाला

We have been distributing fliers all over the place. Bring your own kite or marvel at displays by the best fliers in the country.

Flim-flam/फ्लिम-फ्लैम *(noun)* - बकवास

He is a 'real ' person to the poor people since he doesn't have any time for all that flim flam.

Flimsy/फ्लिमजी *(adjective)* - असार

Don't come out with such flimsy reasons to stay away from the college.

Flinch/फ्लिंच *(verb)* - पीछे हटना

Never flinch from your objective in the face of any difficulties.

F

Flippancy/फ्लिपैंसी *(noun)* - वाक्-चपलता

You need to answer your absence with a little less flippancy this time.

Flippant/फ्लिपैंट *(adjective)* - छिछोरा

How can you be so flippant about shattering people's lives and dreams?

Flipper/फ्लिपर *(noun)* - मीनपक्ष

Seals use their front flippers for moving on land and hind limbs for swimming in water.

Flit/फिल्टि *(verb)* - उड़ जाना

A butterfly was flitting nearby and disturbing me during studies.

Flitter/फ्लिटर *(verb)* - फड़फड़ाहट

The flittering of the butterfly around the table was disturbing my study.

Float/फ्लोट *(verb)* - तैरना, उतराना

Helicopters have the capability to keep floating in the air without going forward.

Flocule/फ्लोक्यूल *(noun)* - ऊन का छोटा झब्बा

Flocule is a small mass of matter resembling a soft tuft of wool.

Floe/फ्लो *(noun)* - जल पर तैरता हुआ बरफ का टुकड़ा

Was the mass of ice that sank the Titanic actually an iceberg or a floe?

Flog/फ्लॉग *(verb)* - बेंत से मारना

If they are found by the police roaming suspiciously at night, they will be flogged.

Flood/फ्लड *(noun)* - नदी, बाढ़

The biblical flood brought by God upon the earth because of the wickedness of the human race.

Flooring/फ्लोरिंग *(noun)* - कमरे का फर्श

Laminated flooring has become very popular these days. Some house owners are choosing to fit laminated flooring in their homes.

Flop/फ्लॉप *(verb)* - फटफटाना

The film failed to click with the audience and flopped.

Floral/फ्लोरल *(adjective)* - पुष्प सम्बन्धी

Floral tribute was sent on behalf of all the trust.

Florescence/फ्लोरेंस *(noun)* - पुष्पन

In the laboratory, you can use x-ray florescence to determine which metals are present in the sample.

Floricultural/फ्लोरिकल्चरल *(adjective)* - फूलों की खेती से सम्बन्धित

Cultivation of flowers especially ones to be cut and sold is the business of floriculturists.

Floriculture/फ्लोरिकल्चर *(noun)* - फूलों की खेती

Floriculture is a growing commercial venture in India.

Florid/फ्लोरिड *(adjective)* - चमकीला, लाल

The initials here are crisply engraved in a very florid style.

Floridity/फ्लोरिडिटी *(adjective)* - फूलों की लाली

The complexion and dark eyes of the man seemed to glow with complete floridity.

Floriferous/फ्लोरिफरस *(adjective)* - अनेक फूलों को उत्पन्न करने वाला

Floriferous plants grow from early summer through to early winter and produce an abundance of flowers.

Florin/फ्लोरिन *(noun)* - दो शिलिंग के मूल्य का अंग्रेजी सिक्का

By 1550, the European trader had almost two thousand florins worth of debts.

Florist/फ्लोरिस्ट *(noun)* - फूल बेचने वाला, माली

Florists have a roaring business of selling flowers.

Floss/फ्लॉस *(noun)* - पौधों की बोड़ियों में के महीन रेशम के समान तन्तु

Floss between the teeth by using a gentle rocking motion.

Floatation/फ्लोटेशन *(noun)* - प्लवनशीलता, तिरने की क्रिया

Froth floatation process is used to remove impurities from extracted ore.

Flotilla/फ्लोटिला *(noun)* - नावों का बेड़ा

Flotilla leader sent off a warning signal, to warn shipping. German torpedo flotillas attacked enemy main fleet at night.

Flounder/फ्लाउन्डर *(verb)* - एक प्रकार की छोटी चिपटी मछली

The first part seldom poses any problems but people often flounder when it comes to the second.

Flourish/फ्लॅरिश *(verb)* - फलना-फूलना

Maurya Dynasty flourished during the 3rd century B.C.

Flout/फ्लॉउट *(verb)*- अपमान करना

Those who flout the law would be dealt with severely.

Flow/फ्लो *(verb)* - बहना

A dam is built across the river to restrict the flow of water.

Flower/फ्लाउअर *(noun)* - पुष्प, सार

Rafflesia is the largest known flower in the world.

Fluctuate/फ्लक्ट्युएट *(verb)* - लहराना

Sensex has been fluctuating violently in value according to bulls or bear market.

Flue/फ्लू *(noun)* - धुआँकश

A blocked flue can lead to carbon monoxide leaking into your kitchen and home. Make sure new water heaters in a bathroom are fitted to a balanced flue.

Fluent/फ्लूएन्ट *(adjective)* - धारावाही

Universities in England will admit only those students who are fluent in English.

Fluff/फ्लफ *(noun & verb)* - रोवाँ

He brushed his collar to remove the fluff.

Fluid/फ्लुइड *(noun)* - तरल पदार्थ

Fluid mechanics is an important subject in engineering studies. All fluids when compressed under high pressure become solid.

Fluke/फ्लूक *(noun)* - अनायास

You must work hard and don't depend to pass the exam by fluke. His success was largely attributed to fluke.

Flummery/फ्लमरी *(noun)* - चापलूसी, लपसी

Her flummery did not yield fruit.

Flump/फ्लम्प *(verb)* - धड़ाके से गिरना

The heavy baggage slipped from his head and flumped to the ground with a loud thud.

Flunkey/फ्लंकी *(noun)* - वर्दीधारी चपरासी

He works as a flunkey for the school manager.

Fluorine/फ्लोरिन *(noun)* - एक अधातु तत्व

Fluorine is a fluid belonging to the Halogen family.

Flurry/फ्लरी *(noun)* - हड़बड़ी

Flurry of wickets however, meant that they were reduced from 95 for 1 to 96 for 5 within a space of 3 overs.

F

Fluster/फ्लस्टर *(verb)* - घबड़ाना

Aron got a bit flustered under the glare of the camera. Flustered, excited man was talking to them.

Flute/फ्लूट *(noun)* - बाँसुरी

Flute is an Indian musical instrument.

Flutter/फ्लटर *(verb)*- व्याकुल करना

The flags flutter, the crowds cheer, and the legislatures meet to pass new constitution.

Flux/फ्लक्स *(noun)* - बहाव, स्राव

Do you want to clean the board to remove left over soldering flux?

Flying/फ्लाइंग *(adjective)* - उड़ान

He made a flying visit to the neighbours' house. He took a flying glance at the report. The flying time between Delhi and Mumbai is two and a half hours.

Foal/फोल *(noun)* - बछेड़ा

The young of a horse is known as a foal.

Fob/फॉब *(noun)* - धोखा देना

Finally release the central locking button and press the fob to check the central locking operation. Don't fob your friends off with a sham gift!

Focal/फोकल *(adjective)* - केन्द्रीय

Local centres are typically also focal points for the community life of their areas.

Focus/फोकस *(noun)* - संगम

Focus on these main issues of concern.

Fodder/फॉडर *(noun)* - चारा, भूसा

Grass and haystack are the principal fodder for cattle.

Foe/फो *(noun)* - शत्रु, बैरी

The sniper rifle is dead accurate and one shot in the head is enough to kill almost any foe. Pakistan has considered India as its foe number one since independence.

Foetus/फीटस *(noun)* - गर्भ

Last year, 40,000 female foetuses were aborted in Mumbai alone.

Foible/फॉइबॅल *(noun)* - कमी, अवगुण

Although Rita is very easy going person she does have a few foibles

Foist/फॉइस्ट *(verb)* - थोपना

Foisting unpopular policies is always resented by people.

F

Fold/फोल्ड *(verb)* - परत

The bedsheet was neatly folded.

Folder/फोल्डर *(noun)* - पुस्तिका, फाइल

Folders made of plastic have become very popular to carry important papers.

Foliage/फोलिएज *(noun)* - पत्ते

Foliage of all these trees would be collected and sent for incineration.

Foliate/फोलिएट *(adjective)* - पत्तियों से पूर्ण

Foliate designs in linear patterns, derived from Khajuraho art were on show.

Folk/फोक *(plural noun)* - जन-समूह

It is certainly a lovely place, populated by a friendly folks. one's family, especially one's parents. *I am going to my hometown to meet my parents and other folks.*

Follower/फॉलोवर *(noun)* - अनुचर

I am a devout follower of Hindu religion.

Following/फॉलोविंग *(adj.)* - निम्नलिखित

Following articles matched your search criteria.

Fondle/फॉन्डल *(verb)* - आलिंगन करना

It is indecent to fondle someone in an inappropriate way.

Foolhardy/फुलहार्डि *(adj)* - दु:साहसी,उजड्ड

It is foolhardy not to ask for discount when you can have it.

Foolish/फुलिश *(adjective)* - बुद्धिहीन

It is foolish to ignore the guidelines regarding examination.

Footing/फुटिंग *(noun)* - आधार

On a business level we are on a sound footing.

Forage/फॉरिज *(verb)* - मवेशियों का भोजन

Cattle and livestock were foraging the plains looking for food.

Foramen/फोरेमेन *(noun)* - रन्धक, रन्ध्र

Foramen are openings within the body which allow muscles, arteries, veins etc to connect with one another appropriately.

Forasmuch/फॉर-ऐज-मच *(conjunction)* - चूँकि

For as much as I know, he wouldn't come today.

Foray/फॉरे *(noun)* - चढ़ाई

The foray by the enemy forces was repulsed promptly.

Forbade/फॅबेड - रोका

The police forbade onlookers to go near the damaged bridge.

Forceps/फॉसेप्स *(plural noun)* - चिमटा

Plastic forceps are ideal for removing laboratory specimens from liquids, such as, alcohol.

Ford/फोर्ड् *(noun)*- घाट *(verb)* पार करना

Use the third ford to cross the river because water at that point is shallow.

Fore/फोर् *(adjective)* - पहले का

Before you address the audience, please come to the fore so that they can see your face.

Forecast/फोर्कास्ट *(verb)* - अन्दाज लेना, भविष्यवाणी करना

The meteorology department has forecasted a cold weather for the next 5 days.

Foreclose/फोर्क्लोज *(verb)* - मना करना, मार्ग बन्द करना

Banks have abolished the penalty imposed on customers if they foreclose their loan amount.

Forefather/फोर्फादर् *(noun)* - पितर लोग

Leo Tolstoy was the forefather of modern Russian literature.

Forefinger/फोर्फिंगर् *(noun)* - तर्जनी अगुँली

You hold a pen between your thumb and forefinger.

Forefront/फोर्फ्रंट *(noun)* - सबसे अगला भाग

Mahatma Gandhi was always in the forefront during India's freedom struggle against the British.

Forehead/फोर्हेड *(noun)* - मस्तक

The old man wiped the creased lines on his forehead with the back of his wrist and sat down.

Foreign/फॉरिन *(adjective)* - विदेशी

All foreign nationals need to report at the immigration counter.

Foreigner/फॉरिनॅर *(noun)* - अन्यदेशीय

To marry a foreigner, permission must be obtained from the home ministry.

Foreland/फोर्लैंड *(noun)* - अन्तरीय

Foreland basin near Broadway is another area where residential construction is very active.

Foreleg/फोर्लेग *(noun)* - पशु का अगला पैर

Kangaroos use both their forelegs and hind legs to run.

Foremen/फोर्मैन *(noun)* - चौधरी, प्रधान

The foreman in charge of maintenance unit is very strict.

Foremast/फोर्मास्ट *(noun)* - जहाज का अगला निचला मस्तल

The foremast of the ship usually hoists the flag of the country where it is registered.

Forenoon/फोर्नून *(noun)* - मध्याह्न के पहले का समय

Americans call the period of time between morning and noon as forenoon.

Forensic/फॉरेन्सिक *(adjective)* - अदालती

There is the wide difference between crime studies and a purely forensic procedure.

Fore-ordain/फोर्-आर्डेन *(verb)* - पहले से नियुक्त करना

He was foreordained by God to become a social leader.

Fore-reach/फोर्-रीच *(verb)* - सामने तीर चलाना, आगे बढ़ जाना

The boat headed into the wind in order to forereach the jetty before another sailing vessel coming about.

Foresee/फोर्-सी *(verb)* - सोचना

The coach could foresee a test cricketer in him, even though the trainee was just seven.

Foreshadow/फोर्शैडो *(verb)* - पहले सूचित करना

The design change in this new car foreshadows the launch of latest luxury cars in 2013.

Foreshow/फोर्शो *(verb)* - पहले से कहना

The tussle for one-upmanship foreshows the battle of titans for political supremacy.

Foresight/फोर्साइट *(noun)* - दूरदर्शिता

He had the foresight to check that his escape route was clear.

Forest/फॉरेस्ट *(noun)* - जगंल

Gir forest is the largest sanctuary for lions in India.

Forestall/फोर्स्टॉल *(verb)* - अनुमान करना

Cash transfer scheme has been vigorously launched to forestall the opposition capturing power in the forthcoming general election.

F

Forester/फॉरिस्टर *(noun)* - वनचर

Foresters are now designated as an officer under the government.

Forethought/फोर्थॉट *(noun)* - पूर्वविवेक

With a little more forethought I should have used any copper utensil.

Foreword/फोर्वर्ड *(noun)* - भूमिका

This new edition carries a foreword by the Nobel laureate.

Forfeit/फॉर्फिट् *(verb)* - जब्त करना

She forfeited another hour in bed to muck out the horse. Prize winners who do not claim their prize within seven days will automatically forfeit their right to the prize.

Forgave/फॉगेव *(verb)* - क्षमा किया

They talked over their misunderstanding and forgave each other.

Forgery/फोर्जरि *(noun)* - जालसाजी

Anyone who commits forgery in that context is guilty of a criminal offence. The local police is investigating the case of document forgery.

Forgo/फॉर्गो *(verb)* - त्याग देना

I could happily forgo the chocolate, but not the crisp and salty snacks.

Fork/फॉर्क *(noun)* - कांटा

The two-pronged fork is the ideal for eating fruits. Fork truck driver was forced to take leave off work suffering from stress.

Forlorn/फॅर्लार्न् *(adjective)* - परित्यक्त

The site has been almost entirely cleared leaving just the name of the station headquarters that looked rather forlorn.

Formality/फॉर्मैलिटि *(noun)* - यथाविधि, आचार

Board members decided to observe the formality of reappointing the current auditor in order to meet the statutory mandate.

F

Format/फॉर्मैट *(noun)* – पुस्तक का फर्मा
The pdf file format opens in adobe acrobat reader.

Formation/फॉर्मेशॅन *(noun)*– कृति
Magnetic fields play very significant role in formation of star. Vitamin D works with calcium to help control bone formation.

Formative/फॉर्मेटिव *(adjective)* – रूप देने या रचना की शक्ति
Better parental guidance is necessary during the formative years of a child.

Former/फॉर्मर् *(adjective)* – प्राचीन, पहले वाला
Sharad Pawar is the former president of BCCI.

Formica/फॉमिका *(noun)* – चींटी-सम्बन्धी
Formica is the trade name registered in the name of a company manufacturing plastic laminates.

Formidable/फॉर्मिडॅबॅल *(adjective)* – भयंकर
Australia is a formidable rival of India in the game of cricket.

Forswear/फॅर्स्वेअर *(verb)* – सौगन्ध खाना
He forswore not to break the community laws before being admitted back.

Fort/फोर्ट् *(noun)* – किला
Red fort is a historical building in Delhi.

Forte/फॉर्ट् *(noun)* – प्रधान गुण
My personal secretary is Sheila whose main forte is internet research.

Forth/फोर्थ *(noun)* – सामने, बाहर
Forth is a stack-oriented computer programming language.

Forthwith/फोर्थविथ *(adverb)* – तुरंत
You must cease to operate this programme forthwith.

Fortitude/फॉटिट्यूड *(noun)* – धैर्य
We pray to God to grant you fortitude to bear this grievous loss.

Fortnight/फॉटनाइट *(noun)* – अर्धमास
This magazine is published every fortnight, 24 issues each year.

Fortress/फॉट्रिश *(noun)* – किला, गढ़ी
The Great Wall of China was primarily built to act as a fortress against marauding Mongols.

Fortuitous/फॉट्यूइटस *(adjective)* – आकस्मिक
It was a fortuitous meeting with the manager at the station that has got me the job.

Fortuitously/फॉट्यूइटस्लि *(adv.)* – अनायास
I got could be attributed to my fortuitously meeting him at the club.

Fortieth/फॉटिथ *(noun)* – चालीसवाँ
In ascending order, fortieth comes after thirty ninth.

Forty/फॉर्टि *(cardinal number)* – चालीस
Forty is the number obtained by multiplying five with eight. Forty percent of the staff has been laid off.

Forum/फोरम *(noun)*– अदालत
The decision to hold election was decided last evening at the forum.

Forwarding/फॉर्वर्डिंग *(noun)* – माल-असबाब भेजने का कार्य
I am forwarding you details about the civil services examination.

Found/फाउन्ड *(verb)* – स्थिर करना
The physician who found the elusive particle won the Nobel Prize. She found an interesting book at the bookstore last evening.

Founder/फाउन्डर *(noun)* – ढालने वाला, संस्थापक
Raja Ram Mohun Roy was the founder of Bramho Samaj.

Foundling/फाउन्डलिंग *(noun)* – पितृहीन शिशु
The foster parents have got accustomed to foundling the infant found abandoned behind the playground two years back.

Foundry/फॉउन्ड्रि *(noun)* – ढलाई करने का कारखाना
In the brass foundry most of the work is cast from plate moulded patterns.

Fount/फाउन्ट *(noun)* – उद्गम, झरना
My idea is to reach the founts of wisdom before I turn 18.

Fourteen/फॉर्टिन *(cardinal number)* – चौदह
Fourteen is the number we get when ten is added to four.

Fourth/फोर्थ् *(ordinal number)* – चौथा
The number succeeding third is known as fourth.

Fovea/फोविया *(noun)* – शरीर में का गड्ढा

Fovea is any small cuplike depression or pit in the bone or organ in the body.

Fowl/फॉउल *(noun)* – मुर्गा

Fowl is a bird used for food. A hen is an example of fowl. Chicken is an example of fowl.

Fowler/फॉउलर *(noun)* – बहेलिया

Fowler is a person who hunts wild birds for food.

Fowling/फाउलिंग *(noun)* – पक्षिवध की कला

Fowling is a term that includes all forms of bird catching for meat, feather or any other part.

Fra/फ्रा *(noun)* – एक उपाधि

Fra friar or sometimes even fray is a title often used in the former Spanish colonies such as, the Philippines or Southwest America.

Fracas/फ्रैका *(noun)* – उपद्रव

The violent fracas between the rival factions didn't allow the function to proceed.

Fractious/फ्रैक्शॅस *(adjective)* – लड़ाका

Fractious ethnic groups say they have little in common to oppose the enemy as a cohesive unit.

Fracture/फ्रैक्चर *(noun)* – विदारण

Skull fracture can have serious complications for the normal functioning of the body.

Fragile/फ्रेजाइल *(adjective)* – मुलायम, भंगुर

Glass is a highly fragile material.

Fragment/फ्रैग्मॅन्ट *(noun)* – अंश

Fragments of asteroids keep falling in one part or the other on earth nearly every day.

Fragrance/फ्रैग्रॅन्स *(noun)* – सुगन्ध

Now you can enjoy the calming effects of this lotion's lavender fragrance.

Fragrant/फ्रैग्रॅन्ट *(adjective)* – सुगन्धित

The delicately fragrant formula is speedily absorbed and leaves you feeling fresh.

Frail/फ्रेल *(adjective)* – भंगुर, कमजोर

She was an old frail lady yet carrying heavy bundles in her hands.

Franc/फ्रैंक *(noun)* – फ्रान्स का दो पेन्स का सिक्का

Before emergence of Euro, Franc was the currency of France, Belgium and Luxemburg.

Franchise/फ्रैन्चाइज *(noun)* – विशेषाधिकार

Whether you are an industry professional or new, a franchise is the perfect business opportunity for you.

Frangible/फ्रैन्जिबॅल *(adjective)* – सहज में टूटने योग्य

These articles are frangible. Please handle with care.

Fraught/फ्रॉट *(adjective)* – परिपूर्ण

Proper care for sick and elderly remain fraught with legal uncertainty.

Fray/फ्रे *(noun)* – कलह

With five withdrawals, only two are left in fray for leadership of the party.

Frazil/फ्रेजिल *(noun)* – किसी जलाशय के तल की जमी हुई बरफ

Frazil is a name given to those tiny, round or pointed ice crystals that are formed in super cooled waters and prevented from solidifying due to turbulence.

Freckle/फ्रेकल *(noun)* – शरीर पर हल्का भूरा धब्बा

Freckles produce a sense of agedness in appearance.

Freemason/फ्रीमेसन *(noun)* – प्रेमपूर्ण

A member of a secret fraternal society named 'Free and Accepted Mason' advocating brotherly love and mutual love is known as a freemason.

Freezing/फ्रीजिंग *(adjective)* – जमाने वाला

The freezing of water is 0°C.

Freight/फ्रेट *(noun)* – मालभाड़ा

Freight carried by rail, rather than road, produces at least 80 per cent less carbon dioxide.

French/फ्रेंच *(adjective)* – फ्रान्स देश

Eiffel Tower is synonymous with the culture of French people.

Frenetic/फ्रेनेटिक *(adjective)* – पागल

Do some sincere thinking about youth force before life gets frenetic again.

Frenzy/फ्रेन्जी *(noun)* – उन्माद

Frenzy of excitement at ground since both teams were of equal standard.

Frequency/फ्रिक्वेन्सी *(noun)* - तीव्रता

Frequency of oscillations is more than nine million vibrations per second.

Fretful/फ्रेटफुल *(adjective)* - शीघ्र कुपित होने वाला

There was little for them to eat, and the non-stop wailing of children made parents very fretful.

F

Friable/फ्राइॲबॅल *(adjective)* - जल्दी से बुकनी हो जाने वाला

The property of a solid material to be broken into small pieces with little effort is known as friable.

Friar/फ्राइॲर *(noun)* - संन्यासी

These building are occupied by friars.

Friary/फ्राइॲरी *(noun)* - मठ

Friar is sometimes used in former Spanish colonies, such as, the Philippines or Southwest America as a title.

Friction/फ्रिक्शन *(noun)* - घिसाव

We can't run fast on sand desert because of very high friction. A mouse mat is normally used to reduce friction on a desk top computer.

Friday/फ्राइडे *(noun)* - शुक्रवार

Friday is the sixth day of the week and comes before Saturday.

Friendless/फ्रेंडलेस *(adjective)* - मित्रहीन

His sermon-like lectures to anyone who comes to him has left him virtually friendless.

Friendliness/फ्रेंडलिनेस *(adjective)* - मित्रत्व

Our new neighbour has become very popular because of his simplicity and friendliness.

Friendly/फ्रेंडलि *(adjective)* - दयालु

We have published many child-friendly books.

Friendship/फ्रेंडशिप *(noun)* - मित्रता

Through the group's social activities, you'd forge strong friendships which could last a lifetime. I have met many people during my holidays over the years, some of them having turned into lasting friendships.

Frigate/फ्रिगॅट *(noun)* - लड़ाई का जहाज

Indian Navy has built many frigates to defend the coastal waters of India.

Fright/फ्राइट *(noun)* - भय, शंका

Stage fright has always been a major problem with me.

Frighten/फ्राइटेन *(verb)* - डराना

Being alone, the lightning and thunder at the dead of the night frightened him no end.

Frightful/फ्राइटफुल *(adjective)* - डरावना

Frightful dreams, nonetheless they were only dreams and not a reality.

Frigid/फ्रिजिड *(adjective)* - शीत, ठण्डा

He described her nature as extremely frigid, cold, dry and devoid of any cheering influence.

Frill/फ्रिल *(noun)* - झालर

She wore an expensive frilled shirt, pleated skirt and the long multi-coloured scarf.

Fringe/फ्रिन्ज *(noun)* - किनारा

Fringe is the ornamental border consisting of loose hanging beads or threads in women's garments.

Frippery/फ्रिपॅरी *(noun)* - आडम्बर

Most Smartphone and mobiles are actually getting larger, sprouting LED or LCD screens, card readers and all sorts of other frippery. She is an intelligent lady; don't go by her cheap clothing, imitated jewellery or other fripperies.

Fritter/फ्रिटर *(verb)* - समय, धन या ऊर्जा व्यय करना

Don't fritter away time over trivial matters.

Frivol/फ्रिवल *(verb)* - आडम्बर करना, खिलवाड़ करना

Don't frivol your hard-earned money.

Frivolity/फ्रिवॉलिटी *(noun)* - निरर्थक व्यापार

Take this project seriously and don't spend time over frivolities.

Frizz/फ्रिज *(noun)* - लच्छे बनाना

Please use a conditioner to bring new shine and lustre to hair as it controls the frizz.

Frizzle/फ्रिजल *(verb)*- खदबदाना

To frizzle, you must shallow fry the food until it curls and becomes crisp fry. Ms. Frizzle with curled hair was a character in 'The Magic School Bus'.

Fro/फ्रो *(adverb)* – दूर

He is walking to and fro on the road.

Frock/फ्रॉक *(noun)* – चोगा

Frock is one of the most comfortable dresses for girls.

Frolic/फ्रॉलिक *(noun & verb)*– खेल, विहार

You can expect to see festive frolics today involving our own picnic party.

Frolicsome/फ्रॉलिकसम *(adjective)* – खिलाड़ी

Frolicsome children enjoy the thrill when it rains.

Frond/फ्रॉन्ड *(noun)* – फूलने वाली झाड़ियों में पत्तियों का अंग

Palm growers cut palm fronds, without harm to growing trees.

Front/फ्रंट *(noun)* – ललाट

The front of his house is attractively designed and decorated.

Frontage/फ्रन्टेज *(noun)* – घर का अग्रभाग

The frontage of the compound gave an appearance of a bungalow.

Frontal/फ्रंटल *(adjective)* – ललाट सम्बन्धी

The doctor detected a legion in the frontal lobe.

Frontlet/फ्रॅन्टलिट *(noun)* – मुकुट

Frontlet is an ornament or band worn on the forehead.

Froth/फ्रॉथ *(noun)* – फेन, झाग

Froth flotation process is used to segregate impurities from the mineral ore.

Frozen/फ्रोजेन – जमा हुआ

Due to very cold weather, water was frozen into ice.

Fructification/फ्रक्टिफिकेशन *(noun)* – फल उपजाने की विधि

Fructification is a name given to the structure of a fungus that is seed-bearing or spore-bearing.

Fructify/फ्रक्टिफाइ *(verb)* – उपजाऊ बनाना

Your sincere studies will let it fructify into good result.

Fructose/फ्रक्टोज *(noun)* – फलों में से निकाली हुई चीनी

Fructose is a chemical compound.

Fructuous/फ्रक्टूअस *(adjective)* – उपजाऊ

His sincere studies have been very fructuous; he passed the examination with 90 per cent marks.

Frugal/फ्रुगल *(adjective)* – कमखर्च

Frugal way would be to save up and not take out a loan.

Frugivorous/फ्रूजिवरस *(noun)* – फलाहार करने वाला

I have seen many frugivorous saints.

Fruitarian/फ्रुटेअरिअन *(noun)* – फलभोजी

It is difficult to stay energetic being just a fruitarian.

Fruiterer/फ्रुइटरर *(noun)* – फल बेचने वाला

Fruiterer is a person, mainly in England and Australia, who retails fruits and vegetables.

Fruitful/फ्रुटफुल *(adjective)*– सफल, उपजाऊ

Make your ideas attractive, focus on the benefits and how you can make life more fruitful.

Fruition/फ्रुइसन *(noun)* – सुख, स्वाद

International trade negotiations take a long time to reach fruition. The tree has begun to fruition and is likely to deliver better yield than last year.

Fruitless/फ्रुटलेस *(adjective)* – फलहीन

For one reason or the other, my five attempts to speak to him on phone remained fruitless.

Fruitlet/फ्रुटलेट *(noun)* – छोटा फल

A fruitlet is a small, yet to be fully grown fruit that is part of a multiple fruit.

Fruity/फ्रुटि *(adjective)* – फल-सम्बन्धी

My nose was filled with the smells of fruit because a number of baskets containing assorted fruits were kept in the car.

Frustrate/फ्रस्ट्रेट *(verb)* – निराश करना

Lack of money frustrated my desire to join a top ranked management school.

Frustration/फ्रस्ट्रेशन *(noun)* – पराजय, उत्साहहीनता

Try to imagine the frustration, the boredom, and the anger that this desktop computer system creates.

Frustrative/फ्रस्ट्रेटिव *(adjective)* – पराजयकारी, उत्साहहीनता करने वाला

Constant traffic jams had been terribly frustrative in our plan to reach Delhi before night.

Fry/फ्राइ *(verb & noun)* – भूनना, तलना

Young of a variety of animals, including frogs and bees, are called a fry.

Fucus/फ्यूकस *(noun)* – एक प्रकार का समुद्री सेवार

This seaweed is called fucus.

Fuddle/फॅडॅल *(verb)* – व्याकुल करना

He is so cunning; he can befuddle you any day with his ingenuity.

F

Fudge/फज *(noun)* – फज (टॉफी) अनर्थक वार्ता

This as a fudge ice cream sundae with all the chocolate toppings.

Fuel/फ्यूअल *(noun & verb)* – ईंधन, ईंधन डालना

This car takes high fuel consumption. The plane is fuelled up and ready to go.

Fugacious/फ्यूगेशस *(adjective)* – क्षणिक

In botany, fugacious is a term used to describe withering or dropping off early.

Fugitive/फ्यूजिटिव *(noun)* – चंचल, अस्थिर

The police is on the lookout for the fugitive who was released on bail three days back.

Fulcrum/फॅल्क्रॅम *(noun)* – आधार

Fulcrum is the point on which a lever is balanced when a force is exerted.

Fulgent/फल्जेंट *(adjective)* – उज्ज्वल, चमकदार

Blazing sun, blinding headlights are some of the examples of fulgent dazzle.

Fuller/फुलर *(noun)* – कपड़ा साफ करने वाला

Fuller is a worker who cleanses wool by the process of fulling.

Fulsome/फुलसम *(adjective)* – अति, बहुत, भरपूर

Her stage performance received a fulsome praise from all quarters.

Fumble/फम्बल *(verb)* – टटोलना

The ball was coming straight to him but he fumbled and dropped the catch.

Fumigate/फ्यूमिगेट *(verb)* – सुगन्धित करना

This area is fumigated every fortnight to prevent breeding of mosquitoes.

Fun/फन *(noun)*– क्रीड़ा, आन्नद

The picnic was a wholesome fun-filled pleasant trip.

Funambulist/फ्यूनैम्ब्यूलिस्ट *(noun)* – रस्सी पर चलने वाला नट

The work of a funambulist is very risky.

Fund/फण्ड *(noun)* – कोष, निधि

Funds have been earmarked to organize annual sports.

Fundament/फन्डामेन्ट *(noun)* – चूतड़

The whole fundament of this argument rested on conjecture.

Fungus/फन्गास *(noun)* – ककव, फफूँद

The discovery of penicillin has its origin in moulds.

Funicle/फ्यूनिकल *(noun)* – रज्जुका, वृन्तिका, छोटी डोरी

The little stalk that attaches a seed to the placenta is known as funicle.

Funicular/फ्यूनिक्यूलर *(adjective)* – रस्से से चलाया जाने वाला

A 4-star hotel on a hill with wonderful panoramic views and linked by funicular to the central station.

Funk/फंक *(noun)* – दुर्गन्ध

An example of funk is going to a party and feeling nervous about talking to new people.

Furbish/फॅर्बिश *(verb)* – चमकाना, माँजना, चमक लाना

The hotel had furbished all rooms with new draperies and interiors for offering stunning views out to the sea.

Furcate/फॅर्केट *(verb)* – फटे कोर का

The club has decided to furcate the entry and exit points. Entry and exit points have been furcated at the club.

Furious/फ्युऑरिॲस *(adjective)* – प्रचण्ड

He was furious at his staff for not completing the finding the important project.

Furl/फॅल *(verb)* – लपेटना, समेटना

The flag was taken down and furled properly and neatly.

Furlough/फर्लो *(noun)* – गैर हाजिरी की छुट्टी

He has rejoined duty after remaining on furlough for six months.

Furnish/फॅर्निश *(verb)* – तैयार करना

These flats are fully furnished 3 bedroom apartment with a community swimming pool.

Furniture/फॅर्निचर *(noun)* – फर्नीचर, सज्जा-सामग्री

The hotel rooms are equipped with original antique furniture.

Furor/फ्यूरॉर *(noun)* - विक्षेप, उन्माद, क्रोध

It is this photograph that caused much of the initial furor.

Furrow/फॅरो *(noun)* - हल-रेखा, लीक, नाली

Each plot of land was divided from its neighbour by a deep furrow.

Further/फॅदर *(adverb)* - आगे का

The sun lies much further from Mercury than that of earth.

Furthest/फॅर्देस्ट *(adjective)*- स्थान में सबसे दूर का

Furthest of the planets from the sun is a small icy rock of a planet.

Furtive/फॅर्टिव *(adjective)* - गुप्त, चुराया हुआ

Standing this side of the road, she gave a furtive look at the deserted shops on the opposite side of the road. Our first task as trained professional is to document what goes on in this very furtive field.

Furuncle/फ्यूरन्कल *(noun)* - जहरबाद

There may be white patches along the body side or raised furuncles on the skin.

Fuse/फ्यूज *(verb)* - गलना

Fuse wire was trimmed to up to the length of the explosive device.

Fusibility/फ्यूजिबिलिटी *(noun)* - द्रवशीलता

Fusibility of a material is the property of its melting when heat is applied.

Fusible/फ्यूजिबल् *(adjective)* - द्रवशील

Fusible metal plugs, which melt at known temperatures are placed across electric meters.

Fusiform/फ्यूजिफॉर्म *(adjective)* - सूच्याकार

Fusiform cells have been identified on the control plants.

Fusion/फ्यूजन *(noun)* - संगलन, द्रवण, गलन

Fusion reactor is like a gas burner - the fuel which is injected into the system is burnt off.

Fuss/फस *(noun)* - बतंगड़, आडम्बर

Why is this fuss over the approval of a small loan?

Fusty/फस्टि *(adjective)* - दुर्गन्धियुक्त

This is a fusty room.

Futility/फ्यूटिलिटि *(noun)* - असारता

We must now all accept the utter futility of trying to solve our border problems by war.

Future/फ्यूचर *(noun)* - भविष्य

Surf forecast websites to help you predict the future! Future of mankind will become increasingly more sophisticated but highly individualistic.

Fylfot/फिल्फॅट *(noun)* - स्वस्तिक

Fylfot is an auspicious or lucky object, especially applied to mystic science.

Gg

G/जी *(noun)* - अंग्रेजी वर्णमाला का सातवाँ वर्ण the seventh letter of the English alphabet.

1. Denoting the next after F in a set of items, categories, etc.
2. Music the fifth note in the diatonic scale of C major.

G

Gab/गैब *(noun & verb)* - गपशप, बकबक (करना)

He was gabbing about his achivements at the previous job.

Gabble/गैबल *(noun)* - बकबक

She gabbled in a panicky way during the interview and was disqualified.

Gabion/गेबियन *(noun)* - किलाबन्दी में उपयोग करने की मिट्टी भरी हुई खंचियाँ

Gabion is a part and parcel of a civil engineer's work.

Gable/गेबल *(noun)* - गृहशिखर

He tried to put a nail in the gable but failed as it was very high and hard.

Gadfly/गैड्फ्लाइ *(noun)* - गोमक्षिका, डाँस, कुकुरमाछी या दुष्ट बुद्धि वाला व्यक्ति

He is a very gadfly person beware of him.

Gaff/गैफ *(noun)* - काँटेदार बरछा या भाला

People catch fish specially big fish with gaff.

Gaffer/गैफर *(noun)* - वृद्ध पुरुष

He is a gaffer and we should respect him.

Gag/गैग *(noun)*- मुख बन्धनी

He is talking too much, they tied him up and put a gag into his mouth.

Gage/गेज *(noun)* - जमानत, प्रतिभूति, बन्धक

Here is a diamond ring, keep it as a gage all your money will be returned.

Gaggle/गैगल *(noun)* - बत्तख की तरह शब्द करना

Look at the gaggle what a beautiful scene!

Gaiety/गेइटि *(noun)* - आनन्द

I felt great gaiety as I looked at people dancing with abandon.

Gaily/गेली *(adverb)* - प्रसन्नता से

I gaily participated in the group dance.

Gainer/गेनर *(noun)* - लाभ करने वाला मनुष्य

The brown horse came out as a gainer in the race.

Gainful/गेनफुल *(adjective)* - लाभदायक

We should always try to indulge in gainful activities.

Gainings/गेनिंग्स *(plural noun)* - प्राप्ति

His gainings in the hardware business were great.

Gainsay/गेनसे *(verb)* - विरोध करना

The impact of good roads cannot be gainsaid. None could gainsay him.

Gait/गेट *(noun)* - चाल

She has a graceful gait.

Gaiter/गेटर *(noun)* - पैर ढाँकने की पट्टी

Girls usually wear gaiters in US.

Galactic/गॅलैक्टिक *(adjective)* - मंदाकिनीय

The galactic mystries are beyond man.

Galea/गेलिया *(noun)* - टोप के आकार आकृति

This plant looks like a galea.

Galipot/गैलिपॉट *(noun)* - कड़ी ताड़पीन से निकाली हुई राल

Galipots stuck to the trunk of the tree.

Gallant/गैलॅन्ट *(adjective)* - सुन्दर

He is a gallant officer.

Galley/गैलि *(noun)* - लम्बी नाव, पोत, लम्बा ट्रे

In old times criminals or slaves used to row galleys.

Galliard/गैलिआर्ड *(noun)* - एक प्रकार का नृत्य

Galliards were in fashion in old times.

Gallic/गैलिक *(adjective)* - फ्रान्स देश का

The gallic language is lovable.

Gallinaceous/गैलिनेशस *(adj)* – गृह कुक्कुट सम्बन्धी
The gallinaceous literature is very interesting.

Gallipot/गैलिपॉट *(noun)* – मरतबान, चीनी मिट्टी का छोटा प्याला
Gallipots were used by a lot of people formerly.

Gallium/गैलियम *(noun)* – एक रासायनिक तत्त्व
Gallium is a chemical element.

Gallon/गैलन *(noun)* – तीन सेर दस छटाँक तरल पदार्थ की नाप
He poured gallons of love on his beloved.

Galloon/गॅलून *(noun)* – फीता
She is very fond of galloons.

Gallop/गैलॅप *(noun)* – घोड़े की सरपट चाल
The gallop of the horses could be heard far away.

Galore/गैलोर् *(adjective)* – अधिकता
There were prizes galore.

Galoshes/गलॅशिज *(noun)* – जूता के ऊपर रबर का जूता
He wore galoshes to protect his trousers from muddy water.

Galvanic/गैल्वैनिक*(adjective)* – उत्तेजक, प्रेरक
The actor received galvanic applause from the audience.

Galvanism/गैल्वैनिज्म *(noun)* – रासायनिक क्रिया से उत्पन्न विद्युतशक्ति
Galvanism has its own place in medical science.

Galvanize/गैल्वैनाइज *(verb)* – बिजली की सहायता से धातु चढ़ाना
The adverse circumstances galvanixed him into action.

Galvanometer/गैल्वॅनॉमीटर *(noun)* – बिजली की धारा नापने का यन्त्र
Galvanometers are used in laboratories.

Gam/गैम *(noun)* – हाथीदाँत
He got hurt in his gam.

Gamble/गैम्बल *(verb)* – दाँव लगाकर जुआ खेलना
He gambles a lot for money and often loses.

Gambler/गैम्बलर *(noun)*– जुआरी
He is a gambler by habit, He does not believe in working for money.

Gambling/गैम्बलिंग *(noun)* – जुआ
Gambling is a bad habit one should never indulge in it. It can be the ruin of anyone.

Gamboge/गैम्बोज *(noun)* – गोंद के समान चिपकने वाला पीला रोगन
Gamboge is used in medicine as a purgative.

Gambole/गैम्बल *(verb)* – कलोल करना
The horse gamboled around the playground.

Gambrel roof/गैम्ब्रेल रूफ *(noun)* – दुढालू छत
Houses in China and Japan have gambrel hind of roof.

G

Game/गेम *(noun)* – खेलकूद
Last Olympic Games were held in London in 2012. athletics or sports as a lesson or activity at school *In order to be popular, you had to be good at games.*

Gamma/गामा *(noun)* – ग्रीक वर्णमाला की तीसरी अक्षर
Gamma is the third letter of the Greek alphabet.

Gammer/गैमर *(noun)* – बुढ़िया
She is a gammer. Don't mind her talk.

Gammon/गैमॅन *(noun)* – सूअर की जाँघ
He is very fond of eating gammon, pig's bottom meat.

Gamy/गेमी *(adjective)* – क्रीड़ापूर्ण
The room grew gamy as the meat cooked.

Gander/गैण्डर *(noun)* – हंस
A gander usually leads a flock.

Gang/गैंग *(noun)* – मजदूरों की टोली
The gang of bank robbers was arrested by the police.

Ganglion/गैंग्लिऑन *(noun)* – नाड़ी ग्रन्थि
The doctor diagnosed ganglion but it was benign and not cancerous.

Gangrene/गैंगरिन *(noun)* – अवसाद
Gangrene set in the wound in his leg. Ultimately doctors amputed it.

Gannet/गैनेट *(noun)* – एक प्रकार की समुद्री चिड़िया
When I had my first look at a gannet I was surprised to see how cleverly it caught the fish in the sea.

Gantry/गैन्ट्री *(noun)* – सोपानी मंच
The rocket fired into space from the gantry.

Gaol/जेल *(noun)* – बन्दीगृह
Jail was formerly written as gaol.

Gap/गैप *(noun)* – दर्रा, खाली जगह
He drove the car skilfully through the gap between two walls.

Gape/गेप *(verb)* – मुँह बाना
He stared at her with a gaping mouth.

Garage/गैरॉज *(noun)* – मोटरखाना
This house has the facility of garage.

Garb/गार्ब *(noun)* – पोशाक
In the fancy dress competition he came in the garb of a beggar.

Garbage/गार्बेज् *(noun)* – गन्दगी
I put the garbage by outside. The maid will take it away.

Gargoyle/गार्गॉइल *(noun)* – परनाला
I was amused to look at the gargoyle which had a jackal like face and water sprouted out of it.

Garish/गेरिश *(adjective)* – भड़कीला, चटकीला
His choice is weird. He wears so garish clothes.

Garland/गार्लॅण्ड *(noun)* – माला
Indian people usually garland their guests.

Garlic/गार्लिक् *(noun)* – लहसुन
Garlic is of great medicinal use. It also adds to the flavour of food.

Garner/गार्नर *(verb)* – संग्रह करना
He garnered a lot of flowers from the garden.

Garnet/गार्निट *(noun)* – रक्तमणि
He is found of wearing garnet.

Garnish/गार्निश *(verb)* – अलंकृत करना
All the food containers in the marriage feast were garnished.

Garniture/गार्निचर *(noun)* – पहिनावा, सजावट
I selected a garniture for giving as a gift.

Garret/गैरॅट *(noun)* – अटारी
He lives in a garnet as he cannot afford to pay much rent.

Garrison/गैरिसन *(noun)* – दुर्गरक्षक
The king ordered that the town should be provided with a garrison.

Garron/गेरॅन *(noun)* – छोटा घोड़ा
Here is a garron and it can pull heavy load.

Garrulity/गैरूलिटी *(noun)* – बकवाद
She always indulged in garrulity.

Garrulous/गैरूलस *(adjective)* – वाचाल
He is a garrulous old man.

Garter/गाटर *(noun)* – मोजा बाँधने का तस्मा
She regularly wears garters.

Garth/गाथ *(noun)* – मैदान
I have a garth at the back of my house.

Gasconade/गैस्कनेड *(noun)* – शेखी
Your gasconade will ruin you.

Gash/गैश *(noun)* – गहरा घाव
The gash in the forearm during fighting became infected.

Gasket/गास्किट *(noun)* – पाल इत्यादि बाँधने की डोरी
Mechanics often use gasket to seal joints.

Gasoline/गैसोलिन *(noun)* – मिट्टी के तेल से निकाला हुआ द्रव
The car needs gasoline so look out for a petrol pump.

Gasometer/गैसोमीटर *(noun)* – गैस संचित रखने का पीपा
'The petrol tanker has arrived, so open the lid of the gasometer.'

Gasp/गैस्प *(verb)* – दम लेना
He gasped with pain as he sprained his ankle.

Gastronomy/गैस्ट्रॉनॅमि *(noun)* – उदर-सेवा
He believes that gastronomy is a great way of life.

Gaud/गॉड *(noun)* – तड़क-भड़क
I dislike gaud.

Gaudy/गॉडि *(adjective)* – भड़कीला
He wears gaudy clothes.

Gaul/गॉल *(noun)* – फ्रान्स देश का प्राचीन नाम
Many labourers who worked in building pyramids lived in Gaul.

Gaunt/गॉन्ट *(adjective)* – दुर्बल
He is a gaunt old man.

Gauntlet/गॉन्टलिट *(noun)* – लोहे का दस्ताना
Gladiators wore gauntlet while fighting.

Gave/गेव - दिया

He gave his son sufficient amount of money to start business.

Gavel/गैवल *(noun)* - मुँगरी

"See, this is the gavel which the judge hits on before calling order, order".

Gawk/गॉक *(verb)* - मूर्ख या उल्लू की तरह ताकना

As she approached him, he gawked at her beauty.

Gaze/गेज *(noun & verb)* - घूरना

His gaze disturbed her.

Gazebo/गॅजीबो *(noun)* - बुर्ज या दूर का दृश्य देखने का मचान

I love living in a gazebo.

Gazette/गॅजेट *(noun)* - गजट

The news of his appointment was published in the gazette.

Gazetteer/गैजिटिअॅर *(noun)* - भूगोल-सम्बन्धी शब्दों का कोश

Look into the state gazetteer to find, this place.

Gearing/गिअरिंग *(noun)* - सामान, उपस्कर

'Get the gearing checked by some mechanic.'

Gecko/गेको *(noun)* - घरेलू छिपकली

'Look at this strange creature, it is a gecko.'

Gelatine/जेलेटीन *(noun)* - जिलेटिन, सरेस

Gelatine is used to make jelly, film for camera etc.

Gelatinous/जेलाटिनस *(adjective)* - चिपचिपा

This food is gelatinous.

Gelation/जिलेशन *(noun)* - ठण्डा करके ठोस करने का कार्य

The process of gelation takes place as you put water tray in the freezer.

Geld/गेल्ड *(verb)* - बधिया करना

An ox is a gelded animal.

Gelid/जेलिड *(adjective)* - ठण्डा

Siberia in Rusia is a gelid place.

Gem/जेम *(noun)* - मणि, रत्न

He is a gem of a person.

Gemini/जेमिनि *(noun)* - मिथुन, जुड़वा

I am a Gemini and as such I'll do well today.

Gemma/जेमा *(noun)* - पत्रकली

This gemma will fall into the earth and develop into a plant.

Gender/जेन्डर *(noun)* - लिंग

There are lot of difference between male and female gender.

Genealogy/जिनिऐलॅजि *(noun)* - वंश-परम्परा अन्वेषण करना

He is studying genealogy and willl be able to draw your family tree.

Generalissimo/जेनरेलिसिमो *(noun)* - एक पद का नाम

During war he was given the post of generalissimo.

Generality/जेनॅरैलिटि *(noun)* - सामान्यता, अधिकांश

Generality accepted him as a leader.

Generalization/जेनॅरॅलाइजेशॅन *(noun)* - सामान्य अनुमान a general steatement. *Generalization of any commodity or rule helps people.*

Generalize/जेनेरलाइज *(verb)* - विशिष्ट उदाहरणों से साधारण नियम का अनुमान करना

He generalizes a lot and his friends are quite amused by it.

Generally/जेनॅरलि *(adverb)* - बहुधा

Generally speaking leaders do not fulfil their promises.

Generalness/जेनरलनेस - सामान्यता

Generalness of his ideas appealed to people.

Generate/जेनरेट *(verb)* - उपजाना

He generates a lot of happiness wherever he goes.

Generation/जेनरेशन *(noun)* - युग, पीढ़ी

Old and young generations can never adjust with each other.

Generative/जेनरेटिव *(adjective)* - उत्पादक

All human beings are generative.

Generator/जेनरेटर *(noun)* - जन्मदाता

A generator creates electricity.

Generic/जिनेरिक *(adjective)* - जातिगत

These clothes are generic but still good.

Generosity/जेनरॉसिटि *(noun)* - उदारता

I am overwhelmed by the sheer generosity of friends and neighbours.

Genet/जिनेट *(noun)* - एक प्रकार की रोवें वाली बिल्ली
This zoo has received a genet. Let us go and see it.

Genetic/जिनेटिक *(adjective)* - उत्पत्ति-सम्बन्धी
This kind of behaiour is purely genetic.

Genetics/जिनेटिक्स *(noun)* - उत्पत्ति-विषयक शास्त्र
I find the science of genetics very interesting.

Genie/जीनी *(noun)* - पिशाच
The whole cosmos is like a genie you get whatever you want.

G

Genitive/जेनिटिव *(adjective)* - सम्बन्ध-सूचक
The genitive forms of 'I' is my and mine.

Geniture/जेनिचर *(noun)* - उत्पत्ति
I would like to know about this person's geniture.

Genius/जीनिअॅस *(noun)* - प्रतिभाशाली
He is a genius. He has got 100% marks in maths.

Genteel/जेन्टिल *(adjective)* - सुशील, सभ्य
He is a genteel person. Everybody likes him.

Gentile/जेन्टाइल *(adjective)* - यहूदी से भिन्न जाति का, नास्तिक व्यक्ति
He is gentile and firmly believes in Christianity.

Gentility/जेन्टिलिटि *(noun)* - शिष्टाचार
He has great gentility and does not believe in hurting anybody.

Gentilize/जेन्टिलाइज *(verb)* - शिष्ट बनाना
I tried to genttilize him but i failed.

Gentle/जेन्टल *(noun)* - विनीत
While fishing people generally use gentle.

Gentleman/जेन्टलमैन *(noun)* - भद्र पुरुष
He is a thorough gentleman and you can always rely on him.

Gentleness/जेन्टलनेस *(noun)* - कोमलता
You are very rude, you should cultivate gentleness.'

Gently/जेन्टली *(adv.)* - कोमलता से
He gently asked her to go away.

Genuine/जेन्यूइन *(adjective)* - यथार्थ
It is a genuine document, even the court has admitted it.

Geodesy/जीऑडिसी *(noun)* - भूमण्डल नापने का शास्त्र
He is a specialist is geodesy.

Geography/जिऑग्रफि *(noun)* - भूगोल विद्या
Geography is his favourite subject.

Geomancy/जीओमैन्सि *(noun)* - मृत्तिका-शकुन विचार
He is an expert in geomancy.

Geometry/जिआमिट्रि *(noun)* - रेखागणित
Some people find geometry very interesting.

Geonomy/जिऑनॅमि *(noun)* - प्राकृतिक भूगोल
He takes interest in reading books of geonomy.

Geophagist/जिऑफॅजिस्ट *(noun)* - मिट्टी खाने वाला
His son is geophagist.

Geophagy/जीऑफॅजि *(noun)* - मिट्टी खाने का कार्य
Geophagy has no place in civilized and cultured societies.

German/जर्मन *(noun)* - जर्मनी देश की भाषा
I am learning German these day.

Germanic/जर्मनिक *(adjective)* - जर्मनी सम्बन्धी
Germanic languages are widespread.

Germicide/जॅर्मिसाइड *(noun)* - जीवाणुनाशी
His favourite field of study is germicide.

Germinate/जर्मिनेट *(verb)* - बीज फूटना
Seeds germinate fast in rainy season.

Germination/जर्मिनेशन *(noun)* - अँखुवा फूटने का समय
Germination of these seeds has taken place and no more water is needed.

Gestation/जेस्टेशन *(noun)* - गर्भ धारण करने की स्थिति
She has great capacity for gestation.

Gesticulate/जेस्टिक्यूलेट *(verb)* - नाटक करना
He gesticulated wildly and many people came to his help.

Gesticulator/जेस्टिक्यूलेटर *(noun)* - हावभाव दिखाने वाला पुरुष
He is a greated gesticulator.

Gesture/जेस्चर् *(noun)* - चेष्टा
He gestured me to follow him.

Get-up/गेट-अप *(noun)* - बनावट

She came to the party in the get up of a princess.

Gewgaw/ग्यूगा *(noun)* - खिलौना, नुमाइशी चीज

This gewgaw is worthless and useless.

Geyser/गीजर *(noun)* - गरम पानी का झरना

There are many hidden geysers in the jungles of South America.

Ghastly/गास्ट्लि *(adjective)* - भयंकर

The ghastly accident took place on highway at 3 a.m.

Ghost/गोस्ट *(noun)* - भूत

Ghost plays important roles in the plays of Shakespeare.

Ghost-like/गोस्टलाइक *(adj)* - प्रेतवत्

The beggar's ghost like appearance frightened me.

Giant/जाइॲन्ट् *(noun)* - राक्षस

He has a giant like appearance being so tall and broad.

Gibber/जिबर् *(verb)* - बड़बड़ाना

He was so afraid that he gibbered instead of talking.

Gibbet/जिबिद् *(noun)* - फाँसी देकर मृत्यु, टिकठी

Criminals are taken to gibbet and hanged.

Gibbon/गिबॅन *(noun)* - लंगूर

Gibbons can be seen in plenty in jungles of SE Asia.

Gibe/जाइब *(noun & verb)* - हँसी करना

He made a gibe against me and I was highly irritated.

Gibus/जाइबस *(noun)* - उत्सव में पहनने की अँग्रेजी टोपी

He is fond of wearing gibus.

Giddily/गिडिलि *(adverb)* - चपलता से

He walked giddily and needed support.

Giddiness/गिडिनेस *(noun)* - चपलता, चक्कर

He suffers from giddiness and often falls down.

Gift/गिफ्ट *(noun)* - उपहार

I gave her a costly gift on her birthday.

Gimantic/जाइमैन्टिक *(adj)* - विशाल

This is a gigantic building.

Gild/गिल्ड *(verb)* - सोने का मुलम्मा करना

This is a gilded bracelet.

Gill/गिल *(noun)* - गलफड़ा, गहरी कन्दरा

All fish have gills through which the inhale oxygen.

Gilt/गिल्ट *(adjective)* - सुनहले रंग का

Many artificial jewellery is gilt edged.

Gimlet/गिम्लिट *(noun)* - छेद करने की बर्मी

We need a gimlet to bore holes in the wall to fix clothes hanger..

Ginger/जिंजर *(noun)* - अदरक

Ginger a root plant has many medicinal uses.

Gingerly/जिंजरली *(adverb)* - धीरे से

I gingerly touched the animal in the zoo.

Gingham/जिंगम *(noun)* - धारीदार सूती कपड़ा

I like to wear clothes made of gingham.

Gingival/जिनजाइवल *(adjective)* - मसूड़े का

I have bleeding gums and I need some gingival.

Ginglymus/जिंग्लाइमस *(noun)* - शरीर का कब्जे के प्रकार का जोड़

There is great pain in my ginglymus.

Girandole/जिरॅन्डोल *(noun)* - आतिशबाजी की चरखी

Please bring a girandole I have many candles to light.

Gird/गर्ड् *(verb)* - घेरना

He has a bad habit of girding and as such I dislike him.

Girder/गर्डर् *(noun)* - शहतीर

No large constructions can be done without girders.

Girdle/गर्डल् *(noun & verb)* - कमरबन्द, पेटी बाँधना

She has girdled her waist by a gorgeous belt.

Girt/गर्ट् *(noun)* - ऊपरी नाप

He has a big girt as he eats too much.

Girth/गर्थ् *(noun)* - घोड़े की साज का पेटी, घेरा

The tailor measured his girth, it was sixty inches.

Gist/जिस्ट् *(noun)* - भाव

The gist of his talk is 'never give up'.

G

Given/गिवेन *(adjective)* – दिया हुआ
Given these hints you can find the solution to the problem.

Giver/गिवर *(noun)* – दाता
God is a giver of mercy.

Giving/गिविंग *(noun)* – दान, अर्पण
Giving thanks is a good habit.

Give/गिव *(verb)* – देना
He who gives, receives.

Gizzard/गिजर्ड *(noun)* – पक्षियों तथा मछलियों का द्वितीय आमाशय
The bird was hit in gizzard.

Glabrous/ग्लैब्रश *(adjective)* – बिना रोम का
Her skin is glabrous and glowing.

Glace/ग्लेस् *(adjective)* – चमकदार सतह का
It is a glace cherry.

Glacial/ग्लेसिअल *(adjective)* – बर्फीला
The glacial mountain floated slowly on the sea.

Glaciated/ग्लेसिएटेड *(adjective)* – हिमानी से ढका हुआ
A glaciated sea is highly dangerous for ships.

Glacier/ग्लेसिअर् *(noun)* – बरफ की धीरे-धीरे सरकने वाली चट्टान
A glacier collided with the ship.

Glacis/ग्लैसिस *(noun)* – ढालुआँ किनारा
This glacis is very dangerous.

Glad/ग्लैड *(adjective)* – खुश
I am glad to see you.

Gladden/ग्लैडेन *(verb)* – खुश करना
He gladdens everybody he meets.

Glade/ग्लेड *(noun)* – वनमार्ग
Here is a glade we can fix our tents here.

Gladly/ग्लैडली *(adverb)* – खुशी से
I will gladly do what ever you say.

Gladness/ग्लैडनेस *(adjective)* – खुशी
He radiates gladness wherever he goes.

Gladstone-bag/ग्लैडस्टोनबैग *(noun)* – एक प्रकार का हल्का झोला
He is habitual of carrying a gladstone bag.

Glamour/ग्लेमर *(noun)* – जादू
The film world is a world of glamour.

Gland/ग्लैण्ड *(noun)* – ग्रंथि
Our body has many glands that secrete different substances.

Glandular/ग्लैण्ड्यूलर *(adjective)* – ग्रंथि-सम्बन्धी
This is a glandular disease.

Glare/ग्लेअर *(verb)* – घूरना
The glare of the sun was very strong.

Glaring/ग्लेअरिंग *(adj)* – देदीत्यमान
You have committed a glaring mistake.

Glass/ग्लास *(noun)* – शीशा
The screen is made of glass. The top of this dining table is made of heavy black glass.

Glaucoma/ग्लॉकोमा *(noun)* – आँख का एक रोग
He suffers from glaucoma and his eye sight is becoming dim.

Glaucous/ग्लॉकॅस *(adjective)* – हल्के नीले रंग का
This is a glaucous cloth.

Glaze/ग्लेज *(verb)* – शीशा लगाना
This house has a glazed balcony.

Glazier/ग्लेजिअर *(noun)* – खिड़कियों में शीशा जड़ने वाला
He is a glazier by profession. Call him to fix your window panes.

Glazing/ग्लेजिंग *(noun)* – खिड़कियों आदि मे काँच बैठाने का कार्य
Glazing is an art.

Gleaming/ग्लीमिंग *(adj)* – चमकने वाला
This is a brand new gleaming car.

Glean/ग्लीन *(verb)* – लवन के बाद छुटा हुआ अन्न बटोरना
He gleaned information from the library to write a new article.

Gleaning/ग्लीनिंग *(plural noun)* – बटोरने का कार्य
The act of gleaning is going on.

Glebe/ग्लेब *(noun)* – मिट्टी
His glebe has sufficient income.

Gleeful/ग्लीफुल *(adjective)* – आनन्दपूर्ण
His gleeful talk charmed her.

Gleet/ग्लिट *(noun)* – मवाद
Look at the gleet, this patient apperars to have a venereal disease.

Glen/ग्लेन *(noun)* – कंदरा

The army was attacked when it was passing through a glen.

Glib/ग्लिब *(adjective)* – चिकना

He is a glib fellow don't trust him too much.

Glimmer/ग्लिमर् *(verb)* – चमकना

The light glimmered and ultimately went out.

Glimpse/ग्लिम्प्स *(noun)* – झलक

He had only a glimpse at the report and understood everything.

Glint/ग्लिन्ट *(noun & verb)* – चमक, चमकना

A glint of light told us that the tunnel was going to end.

Glissade/ग्लिसेड *(noun)* – बरफ पर सरकना

He performed nicely with the help of glissade.

Glister/ग्लिस्टर *(verb)* – चमक

The glow worms glistered in the dark of the night.

Glitter/ग्लिटर *(verb)* – चमकना, प्रकाश फेंकना

All that glitters is not gold.

Gloaming/ग्लोमिंग *(noun)* – सन्ध्या का मन्द प्रकाश

The faint light after the sets and before it rises is called gloaming.

Gloat/ग्लोट *(verb)* – बुरी दृष्टि डालना

He was gloating at his success in the interview.

Globe/ग्लोब *(noun)* – पृथ्वी

Look at the globe and find out at what longitude India is situated.

Globular/ग्लोब्यूलर *(adjective)* – गोलाकार

The earth is globural.

Globule/ग्लोब्यूल *(noun)* – गोली

A globule of water fell down from the tree.

Gloom/ग्लूम *(noun)* – अन्धकार

He strained his eyes peering into the gloom.

Gloomy/ग्लूमी *(adjective)* – खिन्न

These rooms are cold and gloomy I want to go in warm sunlight.

Glorification/ग्लोरीफिकेसन *(noun)* – प्रशंसा

Her glorification made her a film star.

Glorious/ग्लॉरिअश *(adjective)* – तेजस्वी

This is the most glorious victory of all time.

Glossary/ग्लॉसरि *(noun)* – पारिभाषिक शब्द-कोश

Look at the glossary given at the end of the book to find out what does this word stand for.

Glossiness/ग्लॉसिनेस *(noun)* – चमक

The glass top of the table has lost its glossiness.

Glossy/ग्लॉसी *(adjective)* – चिकना

After the paint the wall has become very glossy.

Glottis/ग्लॉटिस *(noun)* – घाटी

There is something stuck in his glottis he can't speak.

G

Glower/ग्लोवर *(verb)* – तिरछी निगाह से देखना

He glowered at me and began to quarrel.

Glow-worm/ग्लो-वर्म *(noun)* – जुगनू

It is beautiful to look at glow-worm in the dark of the night.

Glucose/ग्लूकोज *(noun)* – अंगूर से निकली हुई शक्कर

Glucose is an important ingredient of diet.

Glue/ग्लू *(noun & verb)* – सरेस

The wood joints are being glued together.

Glum/ग्लम *(adjective)* – मलिनमुख

He is a glum looking fellow who rarely breaks his silence.

Glut/ग्लट *(noun)* – आधिक्य

The glut of items in the market surprised the buyers.

Gluten/ग्लूटॅन *(noun)* – लसलसा पदार्थ

Wheat possesses gluten that is why we can knead it.

Glyptography/ग्लिप्टॉग्राफी *(noun)* – रत्नों पर नक्काशी करने की विधा

He is an expert in glyptography.

Gnarl/नार्ल *(noun)* – गाँठ

Look at the gnarl, it is an old tree.

Gnarled/नार्ल्ड *(adjective)* – ऐंठा हुआ

He is a gnarled old man.

Gnat/नैट *(noun)* – मच्छर

This room is infested with gnats.

Gnathic/नैथिक *(adjective)* – दाढ़ सम्बन्धी rare

I have gnathic pain.

Gnaw/नॉ *(verb)* - कष्ट देना
The worry gnawed at him.

Gnome/नोम *(noun)* - बौना, कहावत
Children like to imagine and talk about gnomes.

Gnomic/नोमिक *(adjective)* - सूक्तिबद्ध
His gnomic talk disturbed me.

Gnostic/नॉस्टिक *(adjective)* - गूढ़वान-सम्बन्धी
He is a gnostic person maybe he will solve your problem.

Gnosticism/नास्टिसिज्म *(noun)* - ब्रह्मज्ञान का सिद्धान्त
Belief in Gnosticism was prevalent in 2nd century.

Gnu/नू *(noun)* - अफ्रीका का बारहसिंगा
Gnu can be seen in the jungles of Africa.

Go/गो *(noun)* - एक जापानी खेल
He went out to the shops she longs to go. We've a long way to go. You have to go a few miles more to reach his house.

Goad/गोड *(noun)* - अंकुश
The cowboys goaded their catlle across the field.

Goal/गोल *(noun)* - गोल, अन्त, पहुँच
Both the football teams scored a goal against each other.

Goat/गोट *(noun)* - अज, बकरा
The goats have a wonderful ability to climb rocky terrains.

Gob/गॉब *(noun)* - थूक
Don't touch it. It is a gob.

Gobbet/गॉबेट *(noun)* - छोटा टुकड़ा
This gobbet looks rotten, throw it away.

Gobble/गॉबॅल *(verb)* - शब्द करते हुए जल्दी-जल्दी खाना
He gobbled the food down as he was very hungry.

Gobbler/गॉब्लर *(noun)* - जल्दी से निगलने वाला
He is a gobbler and makes a lot of noise while eating.

Goblet/गॉब्लेट *(noun)* - कटोरा
He drank wine from a goblet.

Goblin/गॉब्लिन *(noun)* - भूत, पिशाच
Goblins often featured in early literature.

Godown/गोडाउन *(noun)* - गोदाम
Most business house maintain a godown to stock their products.

Goer/गोएर *(noun)* - जाने वाला
He is a thorough cinema goer.

Goggle/गॉगॅल *(verb)* - आँख फाड़कर देखना
He goggled at them incomplete disbelief. They were watching the circus show with their eyes goggling and their tongues hanging out.

Goggles/गॉगल्स *(noun)* - धूप का रंगीन चश्मा
People generally use goggles in summer.

Goitre/गॉइटॅर *(noun)* - गण्डमाला
People suffering from goitre are put on special medicine.

Golden/गोल्डॅन *(adjective)* - चमकीला
It is a golden opportunity, don't let it go.

Gone/गॉन *(adjective)* - बीता हुआ
They were gone a long time. The bad old days are gone. An aunt of mine, long since gone.

Gong/गॉन्ग *(noun)* - घड़ियाल
As the gong struck all the courtiers stood up to receive the king.

Goniometer/गोनिऑमीटर *(noun)* - गोनियाँ
Crystals have many faces and goniometer is used to measure the angles.

Goose/गूज *(noun)* - कलहंस
It is a flock of geese making sounds in the garden.

Gooseberry/गूजबेरी *(noun)* - करौंदा
Pick up gooseberries among the thorns.

Gopher/गॉफर् *(noun)* - एक प्रकार की गिलहरी
In US a kind of rodents is called gopher.

Gore/गोर् *(noun)* - गाढ़ा रक्त
The sight of gore sickened me.

Gorge/गॉर्ज् *(noun)* - ढालू तंग घाटी
He fell into a gorge and had to be pulled out.

Gorget/गॉर्गेट *(noun)* - गुलूबन्द
Gorgets were in fashion in early times.

Gorgon/गॉर्गन् *(noun)* - कुरूपा स्त्री
Gorgon is a frightening creature.

Gorilla/गॅरिला *(noun)* - बनमानुष
Gorillas are anthropoid creatures living in Africa.

Gormandize/गॉर्मन्डाइज *(verb)* – भुक्खड़ की तरह भोजन करना
Don't gormandize please.

Gory/गोरी *(adjective)* – रक्तरंजित, लहूलुहान
I feel horrified at such gory scenes.

Gosling/गॉस्लिंग *(noun)* – हंस का बच्चा
It is a gosling, let us play with it.

Gospel/गॉस्पॅल *(noun)* – सुसमाचार
We should study gospel if we want to know about Jesus Christ.

Gossip/गॉसिप *(noun)* – बकवाद
Almost all people are fond of gossip.

Got/गॉट *(verb)* – पाया
He got past without noticing me.

Gouge/गाउज *(verb)* – रुखानी से छेद या खाँचा काटना, निकालना
He attacked him desperately and almost gouged out his eye.

Gourmand/गुअॅमॅन्ड *(noun)* – खद्दूक
He is a gourmand and good food is his weakness.

Gout/गाउट *(noun)* – वातरोग
He is suffering from gout his uric acid is very high.

Goutiness/गाउटिनेस् *(noun)*– गठियारोग
Goutiness made him almost immobile.

Gouty/गाउटि *(adj)* – वातरोग से ग्रस्त
He is a gouty man and can't walk properly.

Governability/गॅवॅनबिलिटि *(noun)* – शासन किये जाने की योग्यता
My governability was in question I had to prove that I was a good admistrator.

Governable/गॅवॅनेबल *(adjective)* – शासनीय
It is small rebellion and therefore governable.

Governance/गॅवर्नॅन्स *(noun)* – अधिकार
There are different modes of governance all over the world.

Governess/गॅवॅनिस *(noun)* – गुरुआइन
I have at last found a good governess for my children.

Gown/गाउन *(noun)* – चोंगा
Lawyers and doctors wear gowns as required by their profession.

Grab/ग्रैब *(noun & verb)* – छीना-झपटी या छीनना
I grabbed the thief by collar.

Grabble/ग्रैबल *(verb)* – टटोलना
The officer grabbled my luggage but could find nothing objectionable.

Graceful/ग्रेसफुल *(adjective)* – सुन्दर
She is a very graceful lady.

Graceless/ग्रेसलेस *(adj.)* – दुष्ट, भ्रष्ट
She is a graceless woman.

Gracious/ग्रेशॅस *(adjective)* – दयालु
Her gracious presence enchanted all people present.

G

Gradate/ग्रॅडेट *(verb)* – सरियाना, स्तर के अनुरूप रखना
I have gradated all these books.

Gradation/ग्रॅडेशन *(noun)* – उतार-चढ़ाव
The gradation from harsh to soft tone took time.

Grade/ग्रेड *(noun)* – क्रम, कोटि, श्रेणी
He has got high grades in all subjects.

Gradient/ग्रेड्यॅन्ट *(noun)* – उतार-चढ़ाव
Be careful the gradient is very steep here.

Gradual/ग्रैड्यूअल *(adjective)* – क्रमिक
Relax, the slope is gradual here.

Graduate/ग्रैड्यूइट *(noun)* – स्नातक
He is a Delhi University graduate.

Graduation/ग्रेड्यूएशॅन *(noun)* – उपाधि प्राप्ति
He has completed his graduation from Bombay University.

Graffito/ग्रफिटो *(noun)* – खोदकर बनाया गया चित्र
The subway was covered in graffito.

Graft/ग्राफ्ट *(noun)* – कलम, घूस
Graft is spread all over our country.

Grail/ग्रेल *(noun)* – पवित्र पात्र
In early times knights used to search for grail.

Grain/ग्रेन *(noun)* – धान्यबीज
Wheat grain is our main cereal.

Gram/ग्रैम *(noun)* – ग्राम
One thousand grams make a kilogram.

Gram/ग्रैम *(noun)* – चना
Gram is a cereal rich in protein.

Grammar/ग्रैमर *(noun)* – व्याकरण
It is not easy to understand grammar of any language.

Gramophone/ग्रैमॅफोन *(noun)* – ग्रामोफोन
A gramophone or record player can be a great source of entertainment.

Granary/ग्रैनरि *(noun)* – कोठार, अन्न-भंडार
For an agricultural state, a granary is a must.

Grandee/ग्रैन्डी *(noun)* – भद्र व्यक्ति
A grandee commands respect.

Grandeur/ग्रैन्ड्यर्/ग्रैन्जॅर् *(noun)* – महत्त्व
He is a man of grandeur hence respected by all.

Grandiloquent/ग्रैन्डिलक्वॅन्ट *(adjective)* – रोब या घमण्ड से
Grandiloquent gardening is his hobby.

G

Graniferous/ग्रॅनिफेरॅस *(adjective)* – अन्न उत्पन्न करने वाला
It is a graniferous object, sow it and it will grow.

Granite/ग्रेनाइट *(noun)* – ग्रेनाइट, इमारतों में प्रयुक्त होने योग्य कड़ा पत्थर
Granite is very useful, it can be used in many ways.

Granivorous/ग्रॅनिवॅरॅस *(adjective)* – अन्न के दाने खाने वाला
A lot of people are granivorous. Their main food is cereal and not meat.

Granny/ग्रैनी *(noun)* – दादी
I love my granny she tells us a lot of nice stories.

Grant/ग्रांट *(verb)* – स्वीकृति देना
Don't worry, God will grant you your wish.

Grantable/ग्रांटेबल *(adjective)* – उपहार के योग्य
This wish of yours is not grantable.

Grantee/ग्रांटी *(noun)* – अनुदानग्राही
I was a grantee in my college days.

Granter/ग्रान्टॅर *(noun)* – दान देने वाला
God is the granter of all our wishes.

Granular/ग्रैन्यूलर् *(adjective)* – दानेदार
This is something granular, polish its surface to make it smooth.

Granule/ग्रैन्यूल *(noun)* – छोटा दाना
A granule of sand can tell us a lot if studied under a microscope.

Grape/ग्रेप *(noun)* – अंगूर
He is fond of eating black grapes.

Grapery/ग्रेपरि *(noun)* – अंगूर का बाग
I like to visit grapery in Kashmir.

Graphics/ग्रैफिक्स *(plural noun)* – लेखाचित्र कला
Graphics have done wonders in the world of cinema.

Graphite/ग्रैफॉइट *(noun)* – काला सीसा
Graphite is used in pencils to write.

Grapnel/ग्रैप्नॅल *(noun)* – अनेक धारवाला छोटा लंगर
He attacked the robber with a grapnel.

Grapple/ग्रैपॅल *(verb)* – बाँधना, हाथापाई करना
He grappled bravely with the problem.

Grass/ग्रास *(noun)* – घास
The lawn has beautiful soft grass.

Grassy/ग्रासी *(noun)* – हरा
This is a barren land with grassy patches here and there.

Grasshopper/ग्रासहॉपर *(noun)* – टिड्डा
It is a big swarm of grasshoppers and it will eat all the crop.

Grateful/ग्रेटफुल *(adjective)* – कृतज्ञ
I am grateful to you for the favour you have shown me.

Gratification/ग्रैटिफिकेशन *(noun)* – संतोष
I feel great gratification in serving the needy.

Gratify/ग्रैटिफाइ *(verb)* – प्रसन्न करना
I gratified her by calling her to dinner.

Grating/ग्रेटिंग *(adjective)* – कटु आवाज
His grating voice upset me.

Gratis/ग्रेटिस *(adverb & adjective)* – बेदाम
The gratis entry to the function insisted many people.

Gratitude/ग्रैटिट्यूड *(noun)* – कृतज्ञता
I feel great gratitude for this kindness of yours.

Gratuitous/ग्रॅट्यूइटॅस *(adjective)* – ऐच्छिक
This rude behaviour is gratuitous.

Gratuity/ग्रट्यूअटि *(noun)* – उपहार
He paid 10% the fair as gratuity to the taxi driver.

Gravely/ग्रेवली *(adverb)* – गम्भीरता से
He answered my questions gravely.

Graveness/ग्रेवनेस *(noun)* – महत्व
His graveness impressed me.

Gravel/ग्रैबेल *(noun)* – कंकड़
The path to the garden was made of gravel.

Graver/ग्रेवर *(noun)* – नक्काशी करने का औजार
His name was engraved on the stone slab by a graver.

Gravid/ग्रेविड *(adjective)* – गर्भवती
She is a gravid lady.

Gravitate/ग्रेविटेट *(verb)* – आकर्षित होना
I felt gravitated to her.

Gravitation/ग्रेविटेशन *(noun)* – आकर्षण-शक्ति
Gravitation pulls down everything to earth.

Gravy/ग्रेवी *(noun)* – मांसयूष
The gravy is very tasty.

Grayling/ग्रेलिंग *(noun)* – एक प्रकार की मछली
I would like to eat a grayling very much.

Graze/ग्रेज *(verb)* – चरना
Cows graze in fields.

Grazier/ग्रेजिअर *(noun)* – चरवाहा
He is a grazier and sells fat sheep and cattle

Grazing/ग्रेजिंग *(noun)* – चराई
This ground is good for grazing.

Grease/ग्रीज *(noun)* – चरबी
The machine is in need of grease.

Greasy/ग्रीजी *(adjective)*– चरबीदार
This potato vegetable is very greasy, I can't eat it.

Greatly/ग्रेटलि *(adverb)* – अत्यन्त
He is greatly polite.

Greaves/ग्रीव्ज *(noun)* – जंघात्राण
The warriors used to wear greaves to protect lower body doing war.

Greed/ग्रीड *(noun)* – लालच
Greed has been the ruin of many people.

Greedily/ग्रीडलि *(adverb)* – अति लोभ से
He greedily ate the food.

Greediness/ग्रीडिनिश *(noun)* – लोभ
Greediness never pays.

Greedy/ग्रीडि *(adjective)* – बहुभक्षक
He is a greedy fellow hence never satisfied.

Green/ग्रीन्स *(adjective)* – हरा, सब्जी
Major roads are marked in red, yellow or green. The girls wore red and green dresses.

Greenish/ग्रीनिस *(adjective)* – थोड़ा हरा
The greenish hue in this cloth is very attractive.

Greenness/ग्रीननेस *(noun)* – हरापन
The greenness of the valley attracted me.

Greeny/ग्रीनि *(adverb)* – हरे रंग का
I like greeny vegetables.

Gregarious/ग्रिगेअॅरिअॅस *(adjective)* – यूथचारी
He is a gregarious person.

Grew/ग्रिउ *(verb)* – बढ़ा, उगा
He grew tall very fast.

Greyish/ग्रेइश *(adjective)* – थोड़ा भूरा
He likes grayish colour clothes.

Grid/ग्रिड *(noun)* – छड़ लगा हुआ ढाँचा
He got the front of his house covered with grid.

Griddle/ग्रिडल *(noun)* – रोटी पकाने का तवा
She cooked chapattis on griddle.

Grievance/ग्रीवॅन्स *(noun)* – शिकायत
The officer patiently heard the grievance of the employee.

Grieve/ग्रीव *(verb)* – दु:ख देना
The loss in business grieved him intensely.

Grievous/ग्रीवस *(adjective)* – शोचनीय
It is a grievous matter, listen carefully.

Grill/ग्रिल *(noun)* – झँझरी
His front door was covered with a grill.

Grille/ग्रिल *(noun)* – लोहे के छड़ों की बनी हुई झँझरी
A grille encircled the whole garden.

Grim/ग्रिम *(adjective)* – डरावन, कुरूप
His grim look frightened me.

Grimalkin/ग्रिमैल्किन *(noun)* – डाइन, बुड्ढी बिल्ली
She is a grimalkin.

Grime/ग्राइम *(noun)* – जमी हुई मल या कीट
His shirt sleeves were covered with grime.

Grimy/ग्रिमि *(adj)* – गन्दा
This kitchen cloth has become grimy, wash it.

Grinder/ग्राइन्डर *(noun)* – पीसने वाला
With this set a coffee grinder comes free.

Grip/ग्रिप *(verb)* – कसकर पकड़ना
He gripped his hand firmly.

Gritty/ग्रिटि *(adjective)* – कंकड़ीला c
It is a rough and gritty road.

G

G

Grizzle/ग्रिजल *(verb)* – चिल्लाना

The child grizzled until its mother came.

Groan/ग्रोन *(verb)* – कराहना

He groaned in pain.

Groats/ग्रोट्स *(plural noun)* – भूसी निकाला हुआ अन्न

Groats can be a good source of nourishment.

Grocer/ग्रोसर *(noun)* – पंसारी

My uncle is a grocer and earns well.

Grog/ग्रॉग *(noun)* – पानी मिली हुई शराब

I want to have some grog.

Grogginess/ग्रॉगिनेस *(noun)* – पियक्कड़पन

This habitual grogginess will ruin your health.

Groggy/ग्रागि *(noun)* – पियक्कड़

He is a inferior groggy. Don't follow him.

Groin/ग्रॉइन *(noun)* – ऊरुसन्धि

The doctor prescribed him a medicine for itching in the groin.

Groom/ग्रूम *(verb)* – खरहरा करना

He was grooming the horse.

Groove/ग्रूव *(noun)* – नाली

There was a long groove along the hill.

Grope/ग्रोप *(verb)* – अन्धे की तरह खोजना

He groped for the way in dark.

Grotesque/ग्रोटस्क *(adjective)* – विचित्र

His grotesque appearance made all of us laugh.

Grotto/ग्रॉटो *(noun)* – गुफा, कंदरा

All children wanted to enter the grotto.

Ground *(verb)* –

The spices have been ground in the grinder.

Grounding/ग्राउन्डिंग *(noun)* – पूर्ण रूप की प्रारम्भिक शिक्षा

Proper grounding is necessary before you train for anything.

Groundless/ग्राउण्डलेस *(adjective)* – निराधार

These charges are groundless.

Ground-nut/ग्राउण्डनट *(noun)* – मूँगफली

I am fond of eating ground-nuts.

Groundsel/ग्राउण्डसेल *(noun)* – डेहरी

I have many groundsels in my garden.

Groundwork/ग्राउण्डवक *(noun)* – मूल आधार

Some groundwork is necessary before matter with a high official.

Grout/ग्राउट *(noun)* – मसाला

I asked the mason to fill the gap with grout.

Grove/ग्रोव *(noun)* – वृक्षवाटिका

This a beautiful mango grove.

Grovel/ग्रॉवॅल *(verb)* – उताने पड़ जाना

Some people grovel in temples before they reach their deity.

Growable/ग्रोएबल *(adj)* – उगने योग्य

This plant is not growable.

Grower/ग्रोवर *(noun)* – उपजाने वाला

He is a grower of vegetables.

Growing/ग्रोइंग *(noun)* – बढ़ने वाला

The fast growing grass had to be cut.

Grub/ग्रब *(noun)* – सूँड़ी

This is a grub crawling on the branch of the tree.

Grubble/ग्रबल *(noun)* – पैसे के लिए कुछ भी करने वाला

He is a grubble and will do anything to get many.

Grudge/ग्रज *(noun)* – दुर्भाव

Although we have quarrelled, I bear no grudge against you.

Gruff/ग्रफ *(adjective)* – कर्कश

He spoke to me in a gruff voice.

Grumble/ग्रम्बल *(verb)* – असन्तोष से बकना

He grumbled before his boss.

Grumbling/ग्रम्बलिंग *(noun)* – विवाद

By habit he is not given to grumbling.

Grumpish/ग्रम्पिश *(adjective)* – क्रोधी

He is a grumpish fellow always complaining.

Guarantee/गारण्टी *(noun)* – जमानत

I guarantee you the success of this project.

Guava/ग्वावा *(noun)* – अमरूद

Guava is a very tasty fruit.

Guerdon/गॅर्डन *(noun)* – पारितोषिक

He received a guerdon for his social work.

Guesswork/गेसवक *(noun)* – केवल कल्पना के आधार पर किया काम, अटकलबाजी

Your guesswork didn't turn out to be correct.

Guest/गेस्ट *(noun)* – अतिथि
We should entertain and respect our guests

Guidable/गाइडेबल *(adj)* – मार्ग दिखलाने योग्य
This map is not guidable for us.

Guidance/गाइडेंस *(noun)* – पथप्रदर्शक
We should give proper guidance to our children.

Guideless/गाइडलेस *(noun)* – असहाय
We had been guideless in the valley.

Guileful/गाइलफुल *(adjective)* – कपटी
He is a guileful fellow, don't mix with him.

Guileless/गाइललेस *(adjective)* – निष्कपट
He is guileless and innocent.

Guilt/गिल्ट *(noun)* – अपराध
He has a strong sense of guilt about the wrong he has done.

Guilty/गिल्टी *(adjective)* – अपराधी
He is feeling guilty over the crime he has committed.

Guise/गाइज *(noun)* – बहाना
He came to party in the guise of a king.

Guitar/गिटार *(noun)* – गिटार
He plays nice guitar.

Gular/गलर *(adjective)* – ऊपरी कण्ठ-सम्बन्धी
The gular disease of the bird in the zoo was treated by a doctor.

Gulf/गल्फ *(noun)* – खाड़ी
He fell into the gulf and hurt himself.

Gullet/गॅलिट्/गॅल्इट *(noun)* – गला
Something stuck in his gullet and a doctor had to be called.

Gully/गॅलि *(noun)* – नाली
The rain water flowed down the gully.

Gulp/गल्प *(verb)* – निगलना, गटकना
He gulped down the food.

Gummy/गमि *(adjective)* – चिपचिता, लिसलिसा
It's a gummy object and I don't like it.

Gunner/गनर *(noun)* – तोप चलाने पर नियुक्त किया हुआ पुरुष
He is a gunner in the navy.

Gunnery/गनरी *(noun)*– तोप बन्दूक की विधा
He is an expert of gunnery.

Gunny/गॅनि *(noun)* – टाट, बोरा
The stolen currency notes were found in a gunny bag.

Gush/गश *(verb)* – वेग से बहना
The blood gushed out of his wound.

Gusto/गस्टो *(noun)* – मजा, रुचि, चाव
He answered my questions with gusto.

Gusty/गस्टि *(adjective)* – झोंकेदार, झोंकीला
A gusty wind blew in the mountains.

Gut/गट *(noun)* – उदर, साहस
I do not have the guts to face him.

Gutter/गटर *(noun)* – जलमार्ग
A foul smelling water flowed in the gutter.

Guttle/गटल *(verb)* – भुक्खड़ की तरह खाना
In the party, he guttled.

Guttural/गटरल *(adjective)* – कण्ठ सम्बन्धी
He made a guttural sound before he started speaking.

Guy/गाइ *(noun)* – आदमी, लोग
That guy over there is my cousin.

Guzzle/गजल *(verb)* – लालची की तरह भोजन करना
He has guzzled down many drinks.

Guzzler/गजलर *(noun)* – लालची की तरह भोजन करने वाला
He is a guzzler of tasty food.

Gymnastic/जिम्नैस्टिक्स *(plural noun)* – व्यायाम, कसरत
She got first prize in gymnastics.

Gypsum/जिप्सम *(noun)* – खड़िया मिट्टी, जिप्सम
Gypsum is used in makina plaster of paris.

Gypsy/जिप्सी *(noun)* – कंजर जाति
She is a gypsy and will tell you your fortune.

Gyrate/जाइरेट *(verb)* – घूमना, चक्कर खाना
She gyrated to the tune of the song.

Gyre/जाइर् *(verb)* – चक्रगति
She gyred to the music.

Gype/जाइप *(noun)* – बेड़ी
The prisoner wore gype around his feet.

H/एच – अंग्रेजी वर्णमाला का आठवाँ अक्षर the eight letter of the English alphabet

1. A symbol for hydrogen in Chemistry.

Ha/हा *exclamatory* – आश्चर्य

Ha! I have finally learnt how to make a sentence.

Haberdasher/हैबरडैशर *(noun)* – बिसाती

A retail dealer in men's furnishings, such as shirts, trousers, ties, and socks is known as haberdasher.

Habergeon/हैबरजिअन *(noun)* – बिना आस्तीन का कवच

Habergeon was a sleeveless coat worn under the plated shirt during the 14th century.

Habile/ हैबिल *(adj.)* – निपुण

People would call you a habile, if you can use both hands skilfully.

Habiliment/हैबिलिमेंट *(noun)* – वस्त्र

The clothes worn in a particular profession is known as the habiliment of that profession.

Habilitate/हैबिलिटेट *(verb)* – योग्य बनाना

Get your poorly stitched dress habilitated by a draper so that it can fit you properly.

Habitable/हैबिटेबॅल *(adj.)* – निवास योग्य

Increasing volume of pollution each year is making the world less habitable to live than the previous year.

Habitant/हैबिटेन्ट *(noun)* – निवासी

Dravidians were the original habitants of India.

Habitat/हैबिटैट *(noun)* – जन्तु का प्राकृतिक वासस्थल

Forest is the natural habitat of wild animals.

Habitation/हैबिटेशन *(noun)* – निवास्थान

Wild animals prefer to live in the natural habitation of a forest.

Habitual/हैबिचुअल *(adj.)* – स्वाभाविक

Students who are habitual of getting up early for studies generally score good marks in examinations.

Habitually/ हैबिचुअली *(adj.)* – यथारीति

He habitually keeps his main entrance door closed.

Habituate/ हैबिचुएट *(verb)* – अभ्यास करना

You could harm yourself if you become habituated to self-medication.

Habituation/हैबिचुएशन *(noun)* – अभ्यस्तता

Habituation to regular use of a particular medicine reduces its efficiency on the body.

Hack/हैक *(verb)* – काटना, मारना

He hacked down the plants and saplings indiscriminately.

Hackney/हैक्नि *(noun)* – घुड़सवारी का टट्टू

In the19th century London, wealthy citizens used to sit in horse-driven hackneys to go from one place to another.

Hackneyed/हैक्निड *(adj.)* – सामान्य

To write an impressive essay, avoid using hackneyed words that have become stale with overuse.

Haddock/हैडॉक *(noun)* – एक प्रकार की समुद्री मछली

Haddock is a popular north Atlantic fish, which is usually eaten baked, roasted or fried.

Hades/हेडीज *(noun)* – पाताल

Greek mythology describes hades as a place where the spirits of the dead live.

Haematic/हीमैटिक *(adj.)* – रुधिर-युक्त

The surgeon operated upon the person to remove the haematic cyst that looked like a ball of blood.

Haematology/हीमैटॉलॅजी *(noun)* – रुधिर विधा

Doctors prescribe a number of haematological tests to determine the quality of blood of the patients.

Haematuria/हीमैट्यूरिआ *(noun)* - मूत्रनली से रुधिर का स्राव

Haematuria is a disease of the urinary tract in which blood passes along urine.

Haemoglobin/हीमोग्लोबिन *(noun)* - रक्त के कणों में के लाल परमाणु

The red colour of the blood is due to haemoglobin which contains iron.

Haemorrhage/हेमॅरिज *(noun)* - रक्त वाहिनियों से रुधिर का स्राव

Bleeding, medically known as haemorrhage is the loss of blood from the circulatory system.

Haemorrhoids/हेमराइड्स *(noun)* - खूनी बवासीर

Haemorrhoids, also known as piles are swellings that can occur in the anus and lower rectum.

Haggard/हैगॅर्ड *(adj.)* - रूक्ष आकृति का दुबला-पतला

After the marathon race, he was completely exhausted and looked haggard.

Haggle/हैगल *(verb)* - मोल-तोल करना, झगड़ना

Women are better than men at bringing down prices by haggling with sellers.

Haggler/हैगलर *(noun)* - मोलभाल करने वाला मनुष्य

He is a haggler by nature as he would haggle irrespective of the price quoted.

Hagiographer/हैजिऑग्राफर *(noun)* - धर्मग्रन्थ का लेखक

Any person who writes about the lives of the saints, especially Christian, is known as a hagiographer.

Hag-ridden/हैग-रिडेन *(adj.)* - दुःस्वप्न से ग्रस्त

After visiting a haunted house, his expressions have become fearful and hag-ridden.

Hail/हेल *(noun)* - ओला

We could not go out for picnic because of torrential rains and hail storms.

Hair/हेअर *(noun)* - बाल

I go for hair cut every month.

Hake/हेक *(noun)* - कॉड की तरह एक मछली

Hake is a fish that resembles cod and found mostly in North America.

Halberd/हैल्बॅर्ड *(noun)* - एक प्रकार का गड़ासा

Halberd was a weapon with axe at one end and spear at the other used during 15th and 16th centuries.

Halcyon/हैलॅसिअॅन *(adj.)* - रामचिरैया

Wouldn't you like to recall your halcyon days when you were happy and prosperous?

Hale/हेल *(adj.)* - स्वस्थ

If you maintain a balanced life, you would live a hale and hearty life.

Haliography/हैलिऑग्राफि *(noun)* - समुद्र का वर्णन

Old word for describing the sea. The word is no longer in use.

Halt/हाल्ट *(noun & verb)* - पड़ाव, रोकना

The police halted the march by the agitating protestors.

H

Hatting/हैटिंग *(noun)* - एक तरह की टोपी

British officers used to cover their head with a hatting made from coconut leaves to protect their head during Indian summer.

Halter/हॉल्टर *(noun)* - बागडोर या पगहा

The dog ran away after the leather halter tied around its neck broke.

Halyard/हाल्यर्ड *(noun)* - पाल-रस्सी

In boats used for sailing, the rope used to hoist the sail is called halyard.

Hamlet/हैम्लेट *(noun)* - छोटा गाँव

Since hamlets are much smaller than villages, most people know one another.

Hammock/हैमॅक *(noun)* - जहाज के कमरे की झूलन खटिया

Since canvas-made hammock is wide and light in weight, people use it as a swing after tying its both ends to branch of trees.

Hamper/हैम्पर *(noun)* - बाँस की पिटारी

Hamper is a convenient multi-purpose basket to carry food and water when going on a picnic.

Hamshackle/हैमशैकल *(verb)* - घोड़े के टाँग को उसके सिर से रस्सी बाँधना

Hamshakle is a method of tying a rope around the head and one of the legs of the domestic animals if they become violent.

Hamstring/हैमस्ट्रिंग *(noun)* - घुटने के पीछे की नस

Rafael Nadal lost in the Wimbledon tournament because his movement was severely restricted on the tennis court due to pulled hamstring.

Hand/हैंड *(noun)* – हाथ

We should wash our hands with soap before taking food. What time is it if both the small and the large hands of the watch is at two? How many hands have you employed to remove the garbage within two hours? To marry his girl friend, he met her parents asking for her hand in marriage.

Handbag/हैंडबैग *(noun)* – थैला

She bought a new handbag so that her everyday personal items could be carried decently.

Handbell/हैंडबेल *(noun)* – हाथ से बजाने की घण्टी

The peon rushed inside the cabin, when the officer pressed the handbell kept on his table.

Handbill/हैंडबिल *(noun)* – विज्ञापन पत्र

A handbill is a form of paper advertisement and typically distributed within a locality.

Hand-book/हैंडबुक *(noun)* – छोटी पुस्तक

This hand-book introduces you to the rules and regulations of this club.

Hand-cuff/हैंडकफ *(noun)* – लोहे की हथकड़ी

Thieves were hand-cuffed and taken to the police station.

Handful/हैंडफुल *(noun)* – थोड़ा-सा

Despite wide publicity, only a handful of people came to watch the game.

Handicraft/हैंडिक्राफ्ट *(noun)* – दस्तकारी

Machine-made products have very nearly displaced the handmade handicrafts.

Handiwork/हैंडिवर्क *(noun)* – हाथ से किया हुआ काम

Most carpets we see in the market are the handiwork of people living in Bhadohi in Uttar Pradesh.

Handkerchief/हैंडकरचीफ *(noun)* – दस्ती, रूमाल

Wash your hands with soap and pat it dry with a handkerchief.

Handler/हैंडलर *(noun)* – मूठ पकड़ने वाला

He is a baggage handler at the airport.

Handling/हैंडलिंग *(noun)* – व्यवहार

Every musical instrument needs careful handling.

Handloom/हैंडलूम *(noun)* – हाथ से चलाने का करधा

Fabrics made of handloom shrink when washed and dried.

Handmaid/हैंडमेड *(noun)* – दासी

Wealthy people use the services of handmaids for cooking, washing, cleaning etc.

Handmill/हैंडमिल *(noun)* – हाथ से चलाने की चक्की

These days most kitchens have a handmill to grind spices into fine powder.

Handpress/हैंडप्रेस *(noun)* – हाथ से चलाने की छापे की कल

Plastic granules can be converted into the shape of a glass with the help of a handpress.

Handrail/ हैंडरेल *(noun)* – सीढ़ी पर से चढ़ने-उतरने के सहारे का लकड़ी आदि का डँडहरा

Handrails fixed along the staircase help people climb floors easily.

Handsaw/हैंडसॉ *(noun)* – एक हाथ से चलाने की आरी

Carpenters use handsaw to cut wooden slabs to make a table.

Handsome/हैंडसम *(adj.)* – मनोहर, सुन्दर

He is a handsome person. Handsome bonuses have been given to all employees.

Handwriting/हैंडराइटिंग *(noun)* – हस्तलेख

Good handwriting will help you get good marks in examinations.

Handy/हैंडी *(adj.)* – सुलभ, पास, सुविधाजनक

Washing machines make washing clothes very handy.

Hang/हैंग *(verb)* – लटकना, लटकाना

She hanged the curtains beautifully. Hanging clothes in the sun speeds up drying.

Hangar/हैंगर *(noun)* – विमानशाला

Aircrafts are kept in the hangar for repair or when not flying.

Hanger/हैंगर *(noun)* – खूँटी

Clothes don't get crumpled or creased when hung on a hanger.

Hanger-on/हैंगरऑन *(noun)* – अनुचर

People hanging around influential people are known as hanger-on.

Hanging/हैंगिंग *(noun)* – फाँसी

Many countries have abolished the practice of hanging the criminals.

Hank/हैंक *(noun)* – लच्छा, अट्टी

In textile industry, a hank refers to a unit that is in coiled form.

H

Hanker/हैंकर *(verb)* – लालायित होना
He is always hankering for toffees and chocolates.

Hapless/हैपलेस *(adj.)* – अभागा
The batsmen hit the hapless bowler for six boundaries in an over

Happen/हैपॅन *(verb)* – घटित होना
The World Book Fair will happen every year in Delhi.

Happening/हैपनिंग *(noun)* – घटना
There is a huge crowd here. What is happening?

Happily/हैपिलि *(adj.)* – सुख से
Both of them happily went back home.

Happiness/हैपिनेस *(noun)* – सुख
Happiness is a mental state of well-being.

Harangue/हरैंग *(verb)* – जोरदार भाषण देना
Dishonest politicians harangue their honest rivals by speaking against them in public.

Harass/हैरस *(verb)* – तंग करना, सताना
Don't harass this poor fellow. God will not forgive you.

Harbinger/हार्बिंजर *(noun)* – हरकारा
Beginning of India-Pakistan cricket matches could be a harbinger of good relations between them.

Hard/हार्ड *(adj.)* – ठोस
Iron is a very hard metal that can't be easily broken.

Harden/हार्ड्न् *(verb)* – कड़ा करना
Boiling an egg hardens and solidifies its liquid material.

Hardship/हार्ड्शिप *(noun)* – कष्ट, दु:ख
In addition to pay, hardship allowance is also given to soldiers posted at Siachin.

Hare/हेअर *(noun)* – खरहा
Hare is a rabbit like animal mostly found in grassland.

Harlequin/हार्लक्विन *(noun)* – विदूषक
Harlequin is a kind of joker or clown in Italian theatres.

Harlot/हार्लट *(noun)* – वेश्या
Women who sell their bodies for money are known as harlots.

Harlotry/हॉरलट्री *(noun)* – वेश्यावृति
Harlotry is one of the oldest professions where women sell their bodies for money.

Harm/हार्म् *(noun)* – हानि
I didn't mean to cause her any harm. This oil is unlikely to do much harm to the engine. There is no harm asking her.

Harmful/हार्म्फुल *(adj.)* – हानिकारक
Ultra-violet rays are very harmful for our skin.

Harmfulness/हार्म्फुलनेस *(noun)* – सदोषता
No disease is less deadly than the other in harmfulness to the body.

Harmless/हार्म्लेस *(adj.)* – अहानिकर
You must tell jokes that are harmless to the self-esteem of a person.

Harmonious/हार्मोनियस *(adj.)* – अनुरूप
The music was very harmonious.

Harmonium/हार्मोनियम *(noun)* – हारमोनियम बाजा
Harmonium is one of the most important musical instruments to produce melodious notes.

Harmonization/हार्मनाइजेशन *(noun)* – स्वर की एकता
Harmonization of relations within communities is essential for peace to prevail in the society.

Harmonize/हार्मनाइज *(verb)* – शान्त होना
You can harmonize the area around with a soothing music.

Harmony/हार्मनि *(noun)* – अनुरूपता
Pleasing musical notes produce peace and harmony to the mind.

Harridan/हैरिडन *(noun)* – दुबली पतली जादूगरनी, डायन
Despite belonging to the same gender, women employees resent strictness of harridans.

Harrier/हैरिअर *(noun)* – एक प्रकार का बाज
Harrier is a breed of hound dog used for hunting rabbits.

Harry/हैरि *(verb)* – बर्बाद करना
By attacking the US forces persistently, Talibani forces are harassing and harrying them no end.

H

Harsh/हार्श *(adj.)* – कर्कश
Judicial courts frown upon harsh treatment by teachers to students.

Hart/हार्ट *(noun)* – लाल हरिण
More than five year old male deer are known as harts.

Harum-scarum/हेरम्-स्केरम् *(noun)* – चंचल
If you behave irresponsibly towards your family, people would call you a complete harum-scarum.

Harvest/हार्वेस्ट *(noun)* – संग्रह किया हुआ अन्न
Harvest time, when the crops are cut and processed, is a time of festivities in India.

H

Harvester/हार्वेस्टर *(noun)* – फसल काटने वाला, फसल काटने की मशीन
Harvesters are huge machines that are used these days to harvest the crops to save time and labour.

Hash/हैश *(verb)* – छोटे-छोटे टुकड़े करना
Many vegetables are hashed and cooked together to prepare the bhaji of pao-bhaji dish.

Hasp/हास्प *(noun)* – कुण्डी, कुलाबा
The door could not be locked since the hasp was not there.

Hastate/हैस्टेट *(adj.)* – बर्छी के आकार का
Look carefully, it is a hastate.

Haste/हेस्ट *(noun)* – वेग
Any work done in haste ends up as waste.

Hasten/हेस्न *(verb)* – जल्दी करना
The addition of a catalyst will speed up or hasten the chemical reaction.

Hastily/हेस्टिली *(adv.)* – तुरन्त
Seeing the dog chaging at him, he hastily retreated back to his house.

Hatch/हैच *(noun)* – छोटी खिड़की
To come out of the submarine, sailors have to use the small hatch that serves both as entry or exit point.

Hatchet/हैच्-इट *(noun)* – कुल्हाड़ी
Farmers often use a hatchet to make burrows in the field at the time of planting seeds.

Hatching/हैचिंग *(noun)* – अण्डा सेने की क्रिया
These days hatching of birds from eggs takes place in modern hatcheries.

Hate/हेट *(verb)* – घृणा करना
If you don't like another person, please try your best not to hate him.

Hateful/हेटफुल *(adj.)* – घृणित
Hateful attitude between two communities has never resolved any problem.

Hater/हेटर *(noun)* – घृणा करने वाला पुरुष
Don't carry such a cruel attitude towards others that people start calling you a hater.

Hatred/हेट्-रेड् *(noun)* – शत्रुता
Hatred or ill-feeling towards others will not let you live in peace.

Haughtily/हॉटिली *(adv.)* – गर्व से
He haughtily said no and didn't even bother to look at the poor man seeking alms.

Haughty/हॉटि *(adj.)* – घमण्डी
Haughty persons carrying an air of disdainful look are seldom liked by others.

Haulier/हॉलर *(noun)* – जहाज को हवा के रुख पर चलाने वाला
A company that transports goods, especially in Britain, is popularly called a haulier.

Haunch/हॉन्च *(noun)* – नितम्ब कूल्हा
The haunch of venison is a popular dish in Europe and America.

Hautboy/हॉटबॉय *(noun)* – झड़बेर (स्ट्राबेरी)
Hautboy is a type of strawberry found in Central Europe and Asia.

Haven/हैवेन *(noun)* – शरण-स्थान
A place to spend the night safely in a desert is as good as a haven.

Haversack/हैवरसैक *(noun)* – सिपाहियों का सामान रखने का किरमिच झोला
The kind of haversack used by soldiers has become very popular among school students to carry books and copies.

Hawk/हॉक *(verb)* – फेरी लगाना
These days hawkers use carts to hawk vegetables in the streets and lanes.

Hawker/हॉकर *(noun)* – फेरी करके माल बेचने वाला व्यापारी
These days hawkers use carts to hawk daily utility wares in the streets and lanes.

Hawk-eyed/हॉकआइड *(adj.)* – सूक्ष्म दृष्टि वाला
Hawk-eyed machines have become very popular to determine whether the ball had touched the bat or not.

Hawkish/हॉकिश *(adj.)* - बाज के सदृश

Trade unions generally resort to hawkish pronouncements against the managements.

Hawser/ हॉजर - जहाज का बड़ा रस्सा

I saw a hawser lying on the ground near the bank of the river.

Hawthorn/हॉथॉन *(noun)* - नागफनी

Hawthorn is an evergreen shrub.

Hazardous/हैजर्डस् *(adj.)* - संकटमय

All chemicals prone to catch fire or cause health problems are known as hazardous.

Hazel/हेजल् *(noun)* - जैतून के प्रकार का एक वृक्ष

Hazel is a small golden-brown coloured tree whose nuts are edible.

Hazy/हेजि *(adj.)* - अस्पष्ट

The cold winter morning was misty, foggy and hazy in which nothing could be seen clearly.

Head-ache/हेड-एक *(noun)* - सिर की पीड़ा, सिरदर्द

I couldn't come to the office because of continuous headache since last night.

Heading/हेडिंग *(noun)* - शीर्षक

The heading of this chapter is "Ways to sleep well".

Headless/हेडलेस *(adj.)* - निर्मुण्ड

This organization has remained headless ever since the chairman retired six months back.

Headlong/हेडलांग *(adv.&adj.)* - बिना विचारे

Don't recklessly headlong into doing anything without first giving sufficient thought.

Headmaster/हेडमास्टर *(noun)* - प्रधान अध्यापक

The headmaster of this school is a strict disciplinarian.

Headmost/हेडमोस्ट *(adj.)* - अगला

The ship behind which all ships follow is known as the headmost.

Headstrong/हेडस्ट्राँग *(adj.)* - हठी

He is so headstrong that he would sidestep every comfort to complete the job.

Headway/हेडवे *(noun)* - आगे की ओर बढ़ाव

Despite adequate help and support, he couldn't make any headway in finding the solution.

Heady/हेडी *(adj.)* - नशा लाने वाली

Politicians behave in a heady and arrogant way because they have power and money in their hands.

Heal/हील *(verb)* - व्याधि से मुक्त करना

The doctor's concern should be to heal sick people.

Healer/हीलर *(noun)* - पदार्थ

Anyone who can heal the sickness of mind or body is a healer.

Healing/हीलिंग *(noun & adj.)* - आरोग्यकर

A motherly healing touch is necessary to restore the sick child to health.

Healthily/हेल्दिली *(adv.)* - आरोग्य से

Children should be fed healthily so that they do well both in studies and games.

Hearing/हिअरिंग *(noun)* - सुनवाई

I couldn't understand the discussion because they conversed at a place that was out of my hearing range. Those hard of hearing are known as deaf.

Hearsay/हिअर्से *(noun)* - सुनी बात

People, especially in villages, tend to easily believe in rumours or hearsays told by elders.

Hearse/हर्स् *(noun)* - टिकठी

Hearse is a vehicle to carry the dead to hospital for post-mortem.

Heartburn/हार्ट्बर्न् *(noun)* - हृदय-वेदना

Heartburn is a burning sensation in the chest caused by eating too much of acidic food.

Heartless/हार्ट्लेस् *(adj.)* - क्रूर

In the face of heartless beating by policemen, the innocent man accepted his guilt.

Hearth/हार्थ् *(noun)* - अँगीठी

They were sitting around the hearth to protect themselves from freezing cold.

Heat/हीट *(noun)* - गरमी, ताप

Heat is a form of energy arising from the random motion of the molecules of bodies.

Heath/हीथ *(noun)* - वनभूमि

An open uncultivated land having small trees and evergreen grass is known as heath.

Heavily/हेविली *(adv.)* - भारीपन

He relied heavily on other's data to arrive at a solution.

H

H

Heaviness/हेविनेस *(noun)* - भारीपन, नीरसता, उदासी

The toys were crushed due to the heaviness of the steel box.

Heavy/हेवि *(adj.)* - भारी

Objects that sank to the bottom of the sea quickly are quite heavy by weight.

Hebetate/हेबिटेट *(verb)* - जड़ बनना या बनाना

Unless the mental faculty is exercised regularly, chances are your intellectual ability will gradually hebetate.

Hebraic/हिब्रेइक *(adj.)* - यहूदी भाषा का

Israeli people are very proud of Hebrew language, art or anything Hebraic.

Hebraist/हिब्रेइस्ट *(noun)* - यहूदी भाषा का विद्वान

Scholars of Hebrew language and literature are acknowledged as Hebraist.

Hebrew/हिब्रू *(noun)* - यहूदी

Hebrew is the official language of Israel.

Hectic/हेक्टिक *(adj.)* - अत्यधिक व्यस्त

Hectic mopping of rain water became necessary in order to make the ground playable.

Hecto/हेक्टो *prep.* - सौ का अर्थ सूचक

Hecto or hecta is a Greek word meaning one hundred.

Hedge/हेज *(noun)*-

Hedge is a line of closely spaced shrubs and small trees to form a boundary or barrier.

Hedonic/हेडोनिक *(adj.)* - सुखवादी, आनन्द

You are a hedonic if your sole aim is to seek sensual pleasure.

Hedonism/हेडोनिज्म *(noun)* - सुखवाद

Hedonism is a philosophy that propagates that real pleasure comes only from sensual sensation.

Hedonist/हेडोनिस्ट *(noun)* - आनन्दजीवी

A hedonist is a person who believes that sensual pleasure is the only real pleasure.

Heedful/हीडफुल *(adj.)* - सचेत

Unless you are heedful in the class, you would miss the main points of the lecture.

Heedless/हीडलेस *(adj.)* - असावधान

We know that heedless self-interest is bad morals for the society.

Heehaw/हीहा *(noun)* - गदहे की तरह रेंकना

The harsh unpleasant cry of a donkey is called heehaw.

Hefty/हेफ्टी *(adj.)* - बलवान

Hefty sum of money is carried in vans secured with security guards.

Height/हाइट *(noun)* - शिखर

To be eligible to apply for army, you must be at least 165 centimetres in height.

Heighten/हाइटॅन *(verb)* - ऊँचा करना

When alone, even the ticking of a wall clock heightens the perception of fear.

Heinous/हीनस् *(adj.)* - घृणित

To leave an injured person unattended is nothing short of a heinous crime.

Heiress/एअरेश् *(noun)* - राजपुत्री

Paris Hilton is the heiress to the Empire of Hilton Hotels worldwide.

Heirloom/एअॅलूम *(noun)* - जंगम द्रव्य, कुलागत वस्तु

The jewellery that has been passed down the generations is popularly known as heirloom.

Heirless/ एअरलेस *(adj.)* - लावारिस

The British government in India used to annex the properties of those Maharajas who died heirless.

Heirship/एअरशीप *(noun)* - विरासत

The state, character and priviledges of an heir is known as heirship.

Held/हेल्ड *(past & past participle)* - रोक लिया गया

The senate held a meeting of executive members and decided to start a new 4-year degree course from the next session.

Helianthus/हीलिऐन्थॅस *(noun)* - सूरजमुखी का फूल

Helianthus is used for decoration.

Helical/हेलिकल *(adj.)* - घुमौवा

The Universe is helical in appearance as if coiled one over the other.

Hell/हेल *(noun)* - पाताल

Being sent to the solitary cell in a jail is nothing short of living in hell.

Hell-cat/हेलकैट *(noun)* - कर्कशा स्त्री

Women who are spiteful and violent in nature are known in the society as hell-cats.

Helot/हेलॉट *(noun)* – प्राचीन स्पार्टा का दास

Those Spartans who were not fully free as a citizen were known as helots.

Help/हेल्प *(verb)* – सहायता

He helped me to reach Connaught Place in the shortest possible way.

Helper/ हेल्पर *(noun)* – सहायक

The carpenter needed five more helpers to make the complete set of furniture.

Helpful/हेल्पफुल *(adj.)* – उपकारक

I found his advice very helpful in passing the examination.

Helpless/हेल्पलेस *(adj.)* – असहाय

The cubs were born blind and helpless.

Helpmate/हेल्पमेट *(noun)* – पत्नी, बीबी या सहायक

My roommate is a true helpmate in all matters of study.

Helter-skelter/हेल्टर स्केल्टर *(adj. & adv)* – अव्यस्थित अवस्था में, जल्दी में

Following shooting and arson in the area, everyone started running helter-skelter to find an escape route.

Helve/हेल्व *(noun)* – किसी हथियार की मूठ

A helve is a handle attached to an axe or hammer.

Hemisphere/हेमिस्फिअर *(noun)* – गोलार्द्ध

Equator divides the earth into two halves, northern hemisphere and southern hemisphere.

Hemlock/हेमलॉक *(noun)* – धतूरा

Many allopathic medicines use hemlock as an ingredient, which otherwise is highly poisonous.

Hemp/हेम्प *(noun)* – पटुआ

Most of 50 and 100 kg bags used for packing wheat, rice and sugar are prepared from hemp.

Hempen/हेम्पेन *(adj.)* – पटुवे का बना हुआ

This is hempen bag.

Hem-stitch/हेमस्टिच *(noun)* – गोट लगाना

Skirts with hem-stitch are no longer fashionable.

Hen/हेन *(noun)* – मुर्गी

The eggs laid by a hen are very popular as a breakfast item.

Henbane/हेनबेन *(noun)* – एक जहरीला पौधा

Henbane is a poisonous plant with narcotic properties.

Henchman/हेन्चमैन *(noun)* – प्रधान सेवक

The gang leader and his henchmen creating nuisance were arrested by the police.

Hendecagon/हेन्डेकागॉन *(noun)* – ग्यारह भुज की आकृति

In geometry, a figure with eleven angles and sides is known as hendecagon.

Henpecked/हेनपेक्ड *(noun)* – भार्या-शासित

His wife bullies him so much that he no longer takes any decision and has become a true henpecked.

H

Hepta/हेप्टा *a prefix meaning* – उपसर्ग जिसका अर्थ सात होता है

Hepta is a Greek word meaning seven.

Heptad/हेप्टाड *(noun)* – सात का समुदाय

A group of seven is known as heptad.

Her/हर *(pronoun)* – उस स्त्री का

She knew I hated her. I told Salina I would wait for her at the station. The crew tried to sail her through a narrow gap.

Herbarium/हर्‌बेरिअम् *(noun)* – वनस्पतियों का संग्रह

Herbarium is a room where dry plants and herbs are stored.

Herbivorous/हर्‌बिवॅरॅस *(adj.)* – शाकाहारी

All plant-eating animals are herbivorous.

Herby/हर्बि *(adj.)* – जड़ी-वूटी से परिपूर्ण

If you want to buy herbs or herbal plants, please visit a herby dealer.

Hereabout/हिअॅरॅएबाउट *(adv.)* – आसपास

His house is hereabout Delhi railway station area.

Hereafter/हिअरआफ्टर *(adj.)* – इसके बाद

All communications intended for the director will hereafter be addressed to the secretary.

Hereby/हिअरबाइ *(adv.)* – एतद्द्वारा

The order I sent yesterday is hereby withdrawn and you are to act as if it never existed.

Hereditary/हिरेडिटरि *(adj.)* – पैतृक

The only qualification for membership is intellect; other distinctions, hereditary or acquired, do not count.

Heresy/हेरिसि *(noun)* - नास्तिकता

The practice of following unorthodox religious philosophy is known as heresy.

Heretic/हेरिटिक *(noun)* - पाखण्डी

The person who renounces the orthodox religious doctrine is known as a heretic.

Heritable/हेरिटॅबॅल *(adj.)* - वंशपरम्परा से प्राप्त होने योग्य

This property is heritable among all three children.

Heritage/हेरिटेज *(noun)* - विरासत

Taj Mahal is a world heritage site maintained by Archaelogical Survey of India.

H

Heritor/हेरिटर *(noun)* - पूर्वजों की सम्पत्ति पाने वाला

He willed his daughter as the heritor of all acquired properties after his death.

Hermit/हर्मिट् *(noun)* - संन्यासी

Away from family members, he lives a reclusive life of a hermit as if he has renounced the worldly pleasures.

Hermitage/हर्मिटेज *(noun)* - कुटी

More than 50 hermits are living in this 500 year-old hermitage.

Heroine/हीरोइन *(noun)* - नायिका

It is our moral duty to praise Rani Lakshmi Bai as heroine, who fought British forces in 1857.

Heroism/हेरोइज्म *(noun)* - पराक्रम

Perhaps this love was kindling a new heroism in him.

Heron/हेरॅन *(noun)* - सारस

Pelicans and flamingoes, geese and ducks, storks and herons, ibises and cranes, flew in from all directions.

Herpes/हर्पीज् *(noun)* - जुलपित्ती नामक रोग

Herpes is a disease badly affecting the skin and nervous system.

Herring/हेरिंग *(noun)* - एक प्रकार की पायी जाने वाली मछली

Herring is a popular edible fish mostly found in North America.

Herself/हरसेल्फ *(pronoun)* - स्वयं स्त्री का

She dressed herself with more than usual care, and came to meet visitors in her stormy beauty.

Hesitant/हेजिटैन्ट *(adj.)* - हिचकने वाला

Fearing loss of job, he looked hesitant to speak the truth in front of his employer.

Hesitation/हेजिटेशन *(noun)* - सन्देह

After slight hesitation she sat down, burying her face in her hands.

Hesitative/हेजिटेटिव *(adj.)* - शंकाशील

This college doesn't admit students who are indecisive or hesitative by nature.

Hesitator/हेजिटेटर *(noun)* - आगा-पीछा करने वाला मनुष्य

Because you don't explain your position, most people consider you a hesitator.

Hesperian/हेस्पेरिअन *(adj.)* - पाश्चात्य

It is hesperian story.

Hesperus/हेस्परस *(noun)* - सन्ध्या का तारा

In Greek mythology, Hesperus is the evening star, the planet Venus in the evening.

Heterodox/हेटरोडॉक्स *(adj.)* - नास्तिक

A person who doesn't conform to the accepted religious beliefs is known as heterodox.

Heugh/हियू *(noun)* - दर्रा

Heugh is a shaft in a coal pit through which miners and ores move between the pit and the surface outlet.

Heuristic/हियूरिस्टिक *(adj.)* - पता लगाने वाला

Heuristic method involves finding a solution by trial and error or by rules that are only loosely defined.

Hexa/हेक्सा *(combining form)* - उपसर्ग जिसका अर्थ छः होता है

Hexagon is an enclosed geometric form having six sides and angles.

Hexagon/हेक्सागन *(noun)* - षट्कोण

A geometric figure having six sides and angles is called hexagon.

Hexameter/हेक्सामीटर *(noun)* - षट्पदी

Hexameter is a verse consisting of six feet

Hey/हे *(interjection)* - आनन्द सूचक

Hey! Where had you been for such a long time?

Heyday/हेडे *(noun)* - हर्ष

During their heyday, no team could challenge the might of Brazilian football team.

Hiatus/हाइएटस *(noun)* - स्वरविच्छेद

A small difference in pitch between two musical tones is known as hiatus.

Hide/हाइड *(noun)* - खाल

Hide of cow is considered most soft and light for footwear.

Hideous/हिडिअस *(adj.)* - घिनौना, वीभत्स

They had hardly finished picnic before a hideous creature came towards them.

Hie/हाइ *(verb)* - जल्दी से भागना

Hie is an obsolete word meaning to move quickly.

Hiemal/हाइमल *(adj.)* - शीत-ऋतु सम्बन्धी

Wearing an overcoat over a coat to protect one from biting cold signals the onset of hiemal.

Hierarch/हाइअरार्क *(noun)* - प्रधान पुरोहित

Persons holding a position of authority in a church are designated hierarch.

Hierarchical/ हाइअॅरार्किकल *(adj.)* - प्रधान पुरोहित सम्बन्धी

In the hierarchical order of precedence, the prime minister stands third only behind the president and vice president of India.

Hierachy/ हायअॅरार्कि *(noun)* - पुरोहित का शासन

In the hierarchy of Army, the general is the senior-most officer.

Hiero/हाइअरो - पुरोहित-सम्बन्धी अर्थ का उपसर्ग

In ancient Greece, holy shrines and temples were known as hiero.

Higgle/हिगल *(verb)* - फेरी करके बेचना

Unless you higgle hard, the vegetable seller wouldn't lower the price.

High-born/हाइबॉर्न *(adj.)* - उच्च कुल का

This aristocratic club only admits high-born members.

High-flier/हाइफ्लायर *(noun)* - साहसी पुरुष

A British thoroughbred racing horse is known as high-flier.

High-flown/हाइ फ्लोन *(adj.)* - उन्नत

The students couldn't understand the meaning of the high-flown talk on morality delivered by the speaker.

High-handed/हाइ-हैन्डेड *(adj.)* - उद्धत

They are your employees and shouldn't be treated in a high-handed manner.

Highland/हाइलैण्ड *(noun)* - पहाड़ी प्रदेश

The mountainous northern part of Scotland is popularly known as highland.

Highly/हाइलि *(adv.)* - अति

A favourable action on my application would be highly appreciated.

High-minded/ हाइ-माइन्डेड *(adj.)* - उदारचित

He is a high-minded person and on no account would compromise on his principles.

High-priest/हाइ प्रिस्ट *(noun)* - प्रधान पुरोहित

The high-priest looked up in astonishment, as the disturbance in the church broke in on his studies.

High-sounding/हाइसाउडिंग *(adj.)* - दिखावा

The students couldn't understand the meaning of the high-sounding talk on morality delivered by the speaker.

High-spirits/हाइस्पिरिट्स *(plural noun)* - साहसी

After selection into the national team, the members were in high-spirits to do their best.

High-time/ हाइटाइम *(verb)* - उचित समय

To be retained in the team, it is high time you start making runs.

High-water/हाइवाटर *(noun)* - बाढ़ में जहाँ तक जल ऊपर होता है

At the time of high-water, fishermen are advised not to go out into the sea.

Hilarity/हिलैरिटि *(noun)* - प्रसन्नता

The attitude of hilarity can lighten the mood of any serious discussion.

Hill/हिल *(noun)* - पहाड़ी

The Aravali hills rises in the western India and merges into the plains in Delhi.

Hillock/हिलॉक *(noun)* - छोटी पहाड़ी

Hillock is a mound above the plains and lower than the hills.

Hilly/हिलि *(adj.)* - पहाड़ियों से पूर्ण

Shimla is an idyllic and hilly place surrounded by huge trees.

Hilt/हिल्ट *(noun)* - मूठ

The sword had a costly hilt decorated with rubies and turquoises.

Hindmost/हाइन्डमोस्ट *(adj.)* - सबसे पिछला

Just then the horse stepped quickly around on his hindmost feet, and looked the professor in the face.

H

Hindrance/हिन्ड्रैन्स *(noun)* - अवरोध

The hooligans were trying to create hindrance to prevent workers from going to the factory.

Hindu/हिन्ड् *(noun)* - हिन्दू

Hindu religion is one of the oldest religion in the world.

Hinny/हिनि *(noun)* - खच्चर

A hinny is an offspring of a male horse and a female donkey.

Hippodrome/हिप्पड्रोम *(noun)* - घोड़ो की दौड़ का मैदान

Hippodrome is an area where chariot race takes place.

H

Hippology/हिपलॉजी *(noun)* - अश्वविद्या

Hippology, the study of horses, helps one to learn how to breed thoroughbred racing horses.

Hippopotamus/हिपॅपॉटॅमस *(noun)* - दरियाई घोड़ा

Hippopotamus is mostly found in Africa.

Hircine/हर्साइन *(adj.)* - बकरे के समान

A strong foul smell resembling that of a goat's odour is called hircine.

Hireable/हाइअरेबल *(adj.)* - किराया के योग्य

Children below 14 years are not hireable to work in any factory.

Hireling/हायर्लिंग *(noun)* - भाड़े का आदमी

Mercenaries who fight on behalf of someone purely for money are called hirelings.

Hirer/हाइअरर *(noun)* किराये पर देना

The boss hired three more men for the job.

Hirsute/हर्स्यूट *(adj.)* - रोयेंदार, रूखा

Their hirsute chests.

Hiss/हिस *(noun)* - फुफकार

The sound made by angry snakes, cats or birds is called hiss.

Hist/हिस्ट *exclamatory* - शान्त होकर सुनो

Hist! Don't shout pere, please.

Historian/हिस्टॉरिअन *(noun)* - इतिहास लिखने वाला

Rudrangshu Mukherjee is a famous historian of India.

Historicity/हिस्टॉरिसिटि *(noun)* - ऐतिहासिक प्रवृत्ति

Historicity is the quality of being a part of recorded history as opposed to myth or legend.

Hitherto/हिदरटू *(adv.)* - यहाँ तक

Things that had hitherto seemed impossible now came true.

Hive/हाइब *(noun)* - मधुकोष

The bees live in a hive.

Hoard/होर्ड् *(noun)* - संग्रह

He rushed back to rescue his hoard of gold. an amassed store of useful information. *The police discovered a hoard of secret information about their activities.*

Hoarse/होर्स् *(adj.)* - रूक्ष

His face looked tired, and his voice hoarse with shouting commands for hours.

Hoax/होक्स *(noun)* - हँसी में छलना

The evidence has been planted as part of elaborate hoax.

Hobbledehoy/हॉब्ल्डिहॉय *(noun)* - भद्दा युवा पुरुष

That habbledehay is internally very nice fellow.

Hobgoblin/हॉब्गॉब्लिन *(noun)* - राक्षस

A small creature that tricks people or causes trouble is called hobgoblin.

Hobnob/हॉबनॉब *(verb)* - संग-साथ करना

To appear influential, he would often go to parties and hobnob with senior bureaucrats.

Hocus-pocus/होकॅस-पोकॅस *(noun)* - इन्द्रजाल

Please come to the point and not indulge in hocus pocus explanation that wastes time.

Hod/हॉड *(noun)* - मसाला ढोने की कड़ाही

These days conveyors carry bricks and mortars in building upper floors instead of hods being used on head.

Hodman/हॉडमैन *(noun)* - सुरखी चूना ढोने वाला आदमी

A hodman carries bricks and mortars on his head during building construction.

Hodge-podge/हॉज-पॉज *(noun)* - खिचड़ी

Hodge-podge is a word that describes a disorderly collection of things, items etc.

Hoe/हो *(noun)* - कुदाली

You must use a hoe to dig up earth or plants. After just two doses of the hoe in the garden, the weeds entirely disappeared.

Hog/हॉग *(noun)* - शूकर
Hog is a term given to the pig that is reared for consumption.

Hoggish/हॉगिस *(adj.)* - गन्दा
Fat-cheeked little boy and pot-bellied father displayed hoggish manners while eating at the dining table.

Hoist/हॉइस्ट *(verb)* - उठाना, फहराना
A white flag was hoisted.

Hold-all/होल्डऑल *(noun)* - बिस्तरा आदि बाँधने का बस्ता
Hold-all is a convenient carrying bag people use in packing sleeping materials during a train journey.

Holdback/होल्डबैक *(noun)* - अवरोध
Don't put a holback to views when replying to psychologist's queries.

Holdfast/होल्डफास्ट *(noun)* - काँटी
This staple pin will holdfast all papers in one place.

Holland/हालैण्ड *(noun)* - एक प्रकार का मलमल, एक देश
Cotton and linen fabric used for window and book-binding still goes by the name Holland because the manufacturing started in the country by the same name.

Hollow/हॉलो *(adj.)* - खाली, छूछा
A hollow metal tube is required. Her cheeks were hollow and there were dark circles under her eyes.

Holly/हॉलि *(noun)* - हरी रहने वाली काँटेदार झाड़ी
Holly is an evergreen, deciduous plant with white flowers and green leaves.

Holocaust/हॉलोकॉस्ट *(noun)* - सत्यानाश, पूर्ण आहुति
Holocaust is a name that surmises the slaughter of more than six million Jews by the Nazis during the Second World War.

Holster/होल्स्टर *(noun)* - खोल, कबूर, पिस्तौल रखने के लिए चमड़े का बैग
He placed the pistol back into the holster and sped away.

Holt/होल्ट *(noun)* - जंगल
Holt is a name given to an area of woodland mainly made up of grove, bushes and small trees.

Homage/होम्-एँज् *(noun)* - श्रद्धांजलि
Homage was paid by the visiting dignitary to Mahatma Gandhi, the father of the nation, at his Samadhi at Rajghat.

Homily/हॉमिलि *(noun)* - प्रवचन, धार्मिक उपदेश
Homily is a religious discourse given at a congregation for infusing morality.

Hominy/हॉमिनि *(noun)* - दलिया
Hominy is peeled and dried kernels of corn.

Homo/होमो *(noun)* - 'सदृश' अर्थ का उपसर्ग
Homo is the genus that is composed of modern humans and species closely related to them.

Homologous/हॉमोलॅगॅस *(adj.)* - तुल्य परिमाण का
The forelimbs of humans and bats are homologous in make up or structures but they are used differently.

Homonym/हॉमोनिम *(noun)* - एक ही रूप किन्तु भिन्न अर्थ वाले शब्द
Words that have the same spelling or pronunciation but different meanings are known as homonyms.

Honeymoon/हॅनिमून *(noun)* - विवाह के बाद दम्पति का आनन्द पूर्णमिलन
The young couple flew to Goa for honeymoon.

Honk/हॉन्क *(noun & verb)* - भोंपू की आवाज, जंगली बत्तख का शब्द
No honking please this is a silence zone.

Honorific/ऑनरिफिक *(adj.)* - प्रतिष्ठा सूचक
As a mark of respect, many universities offer the honorific title of doctorate to distinguished visiting dignitaries.

Hoodwink/हूडविंक *(verb)* - धोखा देना
I had been hoodwinked into buying a worthless cooker.

Hooker/हूकर *(noun)* - वारांगना, वेश्या
Hookers offer sensual pleasures to customers in return for money.

Hooligan/हूलिगॅन *(noun)* - गुण्डा
Curfew has been imposed in the city to prevent hooligans from inciting further violence.

Hopple/हॉपल *(verb & noun)* - घोड़े के पैरों को एक साथ बाँधना
Hopple is a process of strapping the foreleg and hind leg together on each side (of a horse) in order to keep the like-sided legs moving in unison.

H

Horde/हॉर्ड् *(noun)* - झुण्ड
Until they reached the palace the hordes, so eager for booty, had completely refrained from plunder and pillage.

Horizon/हॅराइजॅन *(noun)* - क्षितिज
The sun rose above the horizon.

Horizontal/हॉरिजॉन्टॅल *(adj.)* - समतल
Try to draw two lines parallel and horizontal to each other.

Hormone/हॉर्मोन *(noun)* - हार्मोन, अन्तःस्राव
The doctor has suggested hormonal treatment can reduce problem of osteoporosis.

Horner/हॉर्न्-अर् *(noun)* - तुरही या भोंपू बजाने वाला
A horner necessarily accompanies a music party to blow the horn.

Hornless/हॉर्नलेस *(adj.)* - बिना सींग का
This cow has no horn on its head.

Horology/हॉरॉलॅजि *(noun)* - घड़ी बनाने की विधा, ज्योतिष शास्त्र
Horology is the art and science of measuring time as well as of making clocks.

Horoscope/हॉरॅस्कोप *(noun)* - जन्मकुण्डली
Horoscope of both the boy and the girl is extensively matched before a marriage is settled in India.

Horrible/हॉरॅबॅल *(adj.)* - डरावना
She felt that another little while in this heated, horrible place would drive her mad.

Horribly/हॉरिब्ल् *(adj.)* - भयंकर रूप से
The news was harribly painful.

Horribleness/हॉरिब्ल्नेस *(noun)* - डरावनापन
This hotel is so filthy, it matches the horribleness to the previous one.

Horrid/हॉरिड *(adj.)* - विकट
Was she awake or was she a prey to some horrid dream?

Horrific/हॉरिफिक *(adj.)* - डराने वाला
Horrific working conditions in the mining industry is simply disgusting.

Horrify/हॉरिफाइ *(verb)* - डराना
I was horrified at the thought of being late for my interview.

Horripilation/हॉरिपिलेशॅन *(noun)* - रोमांच
This story is full of horripilation.

Horror/हॉरर् *(noun)* - अति घृणा
For the first time since the Revolution had begun, the horror of it and the meaning of it were brought home to him.

H

Horticulture/हॉर्टिकॅल्चॅर *(noun)* - बागवानी
Horticulture is the art of garden cultivation.

Hose/होज *(noun)* - होज, रबर का नल या पाइप
The firefighters were using a large hose to spray water over the building on fire.

Hosier/होजियर *(noun)* - मोजे का व्यापारी
Jockey is one of the largest manufacturer in the world engaged in trade in as a wholesale hosier.

Hospice/हॉस्पिस् *(noun)* - सराय
Hospice is a name given to homes where sick travellers can stay and get treated medically.

Hospitable/हॉस्पिटेबल् *(adj.)* - अतिथ्यकारी
If you want to learn the art of pleasant, polished and hospitable manners of treating guests, please visit a five-star hotel.

Hospital/हॉस्पिटॅल *(noun)* - अस्पताल
Hospital is a place where sick and injured are fully taken care of with medicine and surgery.

Hospitality/हॉस्पिटैलिटि *(noun)* - मेजबानी, मेहमानदारी
The poor man was received with the same hospitality by the king as that of any other rich person.

Host/होस्ट *(noun)* - आतिथेय, मेजबान समुदाय
The person you see standing there is the dinner-party host. London played host to the Summer Olympics in 2012.

Hostage/हॉस्टेज *(noun)* - प्रतिभू के रूप में शत्रु को प्रदत्त व्यक्ति
The hostages were to be released by the terrorists in exchange for five of their jailed friends.

Hostel/हॉस्टल *(noun)* - सराय
This private hostel is one of the best in the town to take care of food and lodging arrangements of students.

Hostess/होस्-टेस् *(noun)* - अतिथि-सत्कार करने वाली स्त्री
Madhuri Dixit is the hostess of today's programme. Air hostesses take care of most individual needs of the flyers.

Hostile/हॉस्टाइल *(adj.)* - विरुद्ध
A warrior had succeeded in penetrating the hostile fort of the enemy unnoticed and killed the king with a sword.

Hostility/हॉस्टिलिटि *(noun)* - विरोध
Hostility to foreign retail trade is likely to do more harm than good to Indian consumers.

Hotly/हॉटलि *(adv.)* - क्रोध से
The hotly contested election went in favour of the ruling party by a thin margin.

Hotchpotch/हॉचपॉच *(noun)* - खिचड़ी
The coalition government ruling India is a hotchpotch of many political parties.

Hotel/होटेल *(noun)* - होटल
Taj hotel is one of the best hotels in the world.

Hound/हाउन्ड *(noun)* - शिकारी कुत्ता
A hound is breed of dog mainly used for hunting in the jungles.

Houri/हूरि *(noun)* - स्वर्गकन्या
Really speaking, she is a houri on this earth.

House/हाउस *(noun)* - घर, भवन
The house which he had taken up for his residence was not a very large one.

Household/हाउसहोल्ड *(noun)* - कुटुम्ब, परिवार
The household was, to all appearance, asleep at the unusually early hour.

Houseless/हाउसलेस *(noun)* - गृहहीन
Many people are houseless in India.

Housewife/हाउसवाइफ *(noun)* - गृहिणी
She is a housewife and doesn't work in any office.

Housing/हाउसिंग *(noun)* - गृह, शरण
Housing societies are building attractive designer flats offering many options to buyers to choose.

Hovel/हॉव्-एल *(noun)* - कुटी
No bed in tent, hovel, or house was occupied; for everywhere the final packing was going on.

Hover/हॉवर *(verb)* - हवा में घूमना, बहकना
Army helicopters hovered over the area. She hovered anxiously in the background.

How/हाउ *(adv.)* - किस रूप से
How does it work? She did not know how she ought to behave. She showed me how to adjust the focus of the camera.

Howitzer/हाउइट्ज़र *(noun)* - एक प्रकार की छोटी बन्दूक
Howitzer is a short barrelled-gun armies use to fire on enemies.

Howler/हाउलर *(noun)* - भद्दी भूल
I regret my howler of throwing the banana and try to eat its skin.

Howling/हाउलिंग *(adj.)* - चिल्लाहट
If you don't stop howling, I will report to the principal

Hoyden/हॉयडन् *(noun)* - कुलटा स्त्री
This hoyden is too much dangerous.

Hub/हब *(noun)* - धुरा
Colombo is the shipping hub where ships from all countries unload and reload merchandise.

Hubbub/हबब *(noun)* - कोलाहल
It was difficult to hear in the hubbub.

Huckaback/हक्-अ-बैक् *(noun)* - तौलिया बनाने का मोटा रूखा कपड़ा
Huckaback is a strong cotton fabric used for making towels.

Huckster/हकस्टर *(noun)* - बिसाती
A huckster is a person who sells household items of daily use door-to-door.

Huddle/हडल *(verb)* - सिमट जाना
At last we reached the mouth of a ravine, and there we huddled ourselves under the streaming trees to relax.

Hue/ह्यू *(noun)* - रंग छवि
Her face took on an unhealthy hue.

Huff/हॅफ *(verb)* - शेखी करना
He was huffing under a heavy load. I was huffing and puffing to keep up with his speed.

Hull/हल *(noun)* - जहाज का पेटा
A hull is basically a foundation over which the ship construction takes place.

Hullabaloo/हॅलॅबॅलू *(noun)* - शोरगुल
In this hullabaloo of constant cross-talking, I can't lecture this class.

Human/ह्यूमन *(adj.)* - मानव, मानवीय
To forgive is the highest form of human life. It's a human error.

Humane/ह्यूमेन *(adj.)* - दयालु
Being compassionate to feelings of others is the best humane quality

Humanism/ह्यूमनिज्म *(noun)* - मनुष्य जाति की सेवा
Humanism is a reflection of respectful consideration for welfare of fellow human beings.

H

Humanity/ह्यूमनिटि *(noun)* - मानवता
Appalling crimes are being committed in Syria against humanity. No doubt our differences matter but our common humanity matters more.

Humble/हॅम्बॅल *(adj.)* - नम्र
I felt very humble when meeting her. My humble apologies for failing to attend the marriage ceremony.

Humbly/हम्बलि *(adv)* - नम्रतापूर्वक
He is very haughty but today surprisingly and very humbly he paid respect to all visitors.

Humeral/ह्यूमरल *(adj.)* - स्कन्द सम्बन्धी
Humeral means relating to humerus.

H

Humerus/ह्यूमरस *(noun)* - प्रगण्डास्थि
Humerus is a bone of the upper arm.

Humid/ह्यूमिड *(adj.)* - गीला
Due to heavy rain in this sea-resort, it has become very sultry and humid

Humidity/ह्यूमिडिटी *(noun)* - गीलापन
Humidity is a term that defines the amount of water vapour in the air.

Humility/ह्यूमिलिटि *(noun)* - दीनता
Humility is the human property of being ego-less-ness.

Humoral/ह्यूमॅरॅल *(adj.)* - त्रिदोष सम्बन्धी
Humoral imbalance causes difficulties in the body.

Humorist/ह्यूमरिस्ट *(noun)* - हँसी करने वाला मनुष्य
A humorist has the innate ability to act, speak or write in a way that gladdens the heart of everyone.

Humorous/ह्यूमरस *(adj.)* - हँसी का
Of all the books I have read, 'Bedtime Mailbox' has been the most humorous.

Humour/ह्यूमर *(noun)* - मन की भावना
His tales are full of humour. the ability to appreciate or express humour. *The inimitable brand of humour was on show.*

Hunch/हन्च *(verb)* - कूबड़
He sat with a forward bend in his body that looked almost like a hunch. He has not informed me but I have a hunch that he is coming here today.

Hung/हंग *(adj.)* - धातु का लटकाने के अर्थ में भूतकाल का रूप
Political pundits are predicting a hung parliament in the following elections.

Hungrily/हंग्रिलि *(adj.)* - भूख की अवस्था में
No sooner the food was served, the visitor attacked it hungrily as if he had not had a morsel for a few days.

Hungry/हंग्रि *(adj.)* - भूखा, दुबला
But I was not hungry any more, and did not care for food.

Hunk/हंक *(noun)* - टुकड़ा, खंड
I like a hunk of cheese with bread.

Hunting/हण्टिंग *(noun)* - आखेट
Hunting is a practice of pursuing a living wild animal for food, recreation or trade.

Huntsman/हंट्स्मैन *(noun)* - शिकारी
A huntsman is a person who pursues a living wildlife, especially animals for food, recreation or trade.

Hurdle/हॅर्ड्ल *(noun)* - बाधा, रुकावट
Hurdles are used for handling livestock, as decorative fencing and for horse-racing.

Hurl/ हर्ल *(verb)* - चक्कर देना, घूमाकर फेंकना
Javelin throwers try to hurl by hand the long spear-like object farthest in order to win the competition.

Hurley/हर्लि *(noun)* - हॉकी की छड़ी
A stick which is used in hurling is called hurley.

Hurrah/हुर्-र्-आ *exclamatory* - आनन्दसूचक अव्यय
Hurrah! Our team has won the tournament for the third time in a row.

Hurricane/हरिकेन *(noun)* - चक्रवात
Hurricane is a name given to a tropical cyclone occurring in the Caribbean and characterized by strong winds and heavy rains.

Hurry/हॅरि *(verb)* - आकुलता
It was necessary to hurry this matter to a close.

Hurtful/हटफुल *(adj.)* - घातक
His attitude of not coming up to the door to welcome his poor friend was very hurtful.

Hurtle/हर्ट्ल *(verb)* - टकराना
To enable the spacecraft escape the earth's gravitational pull, it is necessary to hurtle it at a speed more than 12 kilometres per second.

Hush/हश *(verb)* – चुप या शान्त करना
In a hushed tone he said goodbye.

Husk/हस्क *(noun)* – छिलका
Manufacturers are converting rice husk into edible oil.

Husky/हस्कि *(adj.)* – भर्राया, भारी, भूसा भरा हुआ
Because of cough and cold, her voice has become very husky.

Hussar/हूज़र् *(noun)* – घुड़सवार सिपाही
Those soldiers are called hussars.

Husting/हस्टिंग *(noun)* – चुनाव का कार्यक्रम
Husting is a physical platform, usually in America, from which public representatives air their opinion to influence the voters.

Hut/हट *(noun)* – झोंपड़ी
A hut is a single-storey dwelling unit mostly found in villages.

Hutch/हच *(noun)* – सन्दूक, खाँचा
Hutch is a box-like cage for keeping rabbits, guinea-pigs etc.

Hyaena/हाइ-ईना *(noun)*
Hyaena is a carnivorous nocturnal animal that resembles a dog and found mostly in Africa

Hybridize/हाइब्रिडाइज *(verb)* – वर्णसंकर पैदा करना
To increase yields of food crops, only option left is to cross-breed or hybridize seeds.

Hydrant/हाइड्रॅन्ट *(noun)* – पानी निकालने का बम्बा
A hydrant consists of long rubber tubes attached to water support system and located at vantage point around large buildings to extinguish fires.

Hydrate/हाइड्रेट *(verb)* – किसी पदार्थ का पानी में घोल
To hydrate the body, it is recommended to use a moisturising lotion over the exposed parts of the body while going out in the sun.

Hydraulic/हाइड्रालिक *(adj.)* – भार से चालित
To prevent accidents happening on the road, hydraulic brakes are attached in the vehicle in addition to the foot brakes.

Hydro/हाइड्रो *(noun)* – 'जल' अर्थ का उपसर्ग
A hydro is a shortened name for a place offering cure through hydrotherapy.

Hydrocele/हाइड्रोसिल *(noun)* – अण्डवृद्धि
A morbid collection of fluid in the testicle is called hydrocele.

Hydroelectric/हाइड्रोइलेक्ट्रिक *(adj.)* – जल-विद्युत
To increase the availability of power, stations generating hydroelectric power must be installed.

Hydrogen/हाइड्रोजन *(noun)* – हाइड्रोजन, उदजन
Hydrogen and oxygen when mixed produce water.

Hydrophobia/हाइड्रोफोबिया *(noun)* – जलत्रास
Hydrophobia is a disease in which the patient develops an abnormal fear of water.

Hydroplane/हाइड्रोप्लेन *(noun)* – हवाई जहाज जो जल में चलकर हवा में उड़ता है
A hydroplane is a light motorboat designed to skim over the water at high speeds with the rear part of its hull touching the water.

H

Hygiene/हाइजीन *(noun)* – स्वास्थ्य-विज्ञान
Hygiene is the art and practice for cleanliness, preservation of good health and prevention of illness.

Hygrometer/हाइग्रोमीटर *(noun)* – आर्द्रतामापी
Hygrometer is an instrument to measure humidity in the atmosphere.

Hymen/हाइमेन *(noun)* – विवाह के देवता, योनिच्छद
The god of marriage is called hymen.

Hymn/हिम *(noun)* – स्तुति
Hymn is a song which is sung in the praise of God.

Hyperbola/हाइपरबोला *(noun)* – अतिपरवलय
Hyperbola is one of the four kinds of conic section, the others being, parabola, ellipse and circle.

Hyperbole/हाइपरबोल *(noun)* – अतिशयोक्ति
Hyperbole is the use of exaggeration as rhetoric to generate strong feelings and emotional bond, such as, comparing someone knowledge to Einstein.

Hyperbolize/हाइपरबोलाइज *(verb)* – अतिशयोक्ति पूर्वक वर्णन करना
The government has chosen to hyperbolize the benefits of foreign retailers offering goods at lower prices.

Hypercritic/हाइपरक्रिटिक *(noun)* – सूक्ष्म छिद्रान्वेषी मनुष्य one
Most opposition parties play hypercritic to any government's move to bring in foreign retailers.

Hypertrophy/हाइपरट्रॅफी *(noun)* - किसी अंग की अधिक वृद्धि

Hypertrophy is the abnormal increase in the volume of an organ due to the increase in the size of cells.

Hypothecate/हाइपॉथिकेट *(verb)* - बन्धक रखना

He decided to hypothecate his property to the bank to borrow money for his son's education.

Hypothecation/हाइपॉथिकेशन *(noun)* - रेहन की क्रिया

Hypothecation is the practice where a borrower pledges a collateral as a guarantee to secure a loan.

Hypothecator/हाइपॉथिकेटर *(noun)* - रेहन रखने वाला मनुष्य

A hypothecator has signed over his personal property to the bank as security for the repayment of money borrowed.

Hypothesis/हाइपॉथिसिस *(noun)* - अनुमान

The hypothesis that particles travel faster than light is difficult to verify on the available scientific instruments.

Hypothetic/हाइपॉथेटिक *(adj.)* - माना हुआ

We have only gone as far as the Moon, it is only hypothetic to calculate the possibility of going to the Mars and come back to the Earth.

Hypothesize/हाइपॉथेसाइज *(verb)* - कल्पना करना

Since that hypothesis has been scientifically proved, there is no need for him to hypothesize again.

Hysteria/हिस्टिरिआ *(noun)* - बदहोशी

Hysteria is a state of mind characterized by unmanageable fear or emotional excesses.

Hysteric/हिस्टेरिक *(adj.)* - मूर्छा-सम्बन्धी

A person suffering from uncontrolled emotional outburst is known as a hysteric.

Ii

I/आइ *(noun)* - अंग्रेजी वर्णमाला का नौवाँ वर्ण the ninth letter of the Eglish alphabet.

1. Denoting the next after H in a set of items, categories, etc.

2. The roman numeral for one.

Iambic/आइम्बिक *adjective)* - गुरु अक्षर वाले पद से सम्बन्धित

The poem is known for its use of iambic pentameter.

Ibex/आइबेक्स *(noun)* - पर्वत का जंगली बकरा

Over those ice-covered mountains, we captured an ibex in camera.

Ibidem/इबाइडेम *(avberb)* - उसी स्थान पर

This quotation by the author is from his book on philosophy, and the next quotation, ibidem.

Ibis/आइबिस *(noun)* - सारस के प्रकार एक-एक पक्षी

We were amazed to see so many ibises, all at one place.

Ice/आइस *(noun)* - बरफ

Mom asked John to place all the ice cubes in the jug containing juice.

Ichneumon/इक्न्यूमॅन *(noun)* - एक प्रकार का नेवला

The biologist observed the larvae of ichneumon under microscope.

Ichor/आइकॉर *(noun)* - पंछा, पूयरक्त देवताओं का रक्त

The witch prophesised that a man with ichor in his blood will be the next ruler of the kingdom.

Ichthyoid/इक्थिऑइड *(adjective)* - मछली के आकर का मत्स्याभ

The aquatic animal had an ichthyoid body.

Icicle/आइसिकल *(noun)* - बरफ की लटकती नुकीली चट्टान

The icicle shaped pieces were hanging from top of the wall.

Icon/आइकॉन *(noun)* - प्रतिमा

The lovely icon on the wall was making the devotees to bow with respect and surprise.

Iconic/आइकोनिक *(adjective)* - मूर्ति-सम्बन्धी

His style soon became iconic in the world of fashion.

Iconoclast/आइक्नोक्लास्ट *(noun)* - मूर्ति तोड़ने वाला, मूर्तिभंजक

Raja Ram Mohan Roy was an iconoclast of his time as he stood against superstitions of all kind.

Icosahedron/आइकॅसहेड्रन *(noun)* - बीस फलक की ठोस आकृति

The chemistry teacher pointed to the icosahedrons figure on chart to explain the concept.

Icy/आइसि *(adjective)* - बहुत ठण्डा

The cave was dark and icy, so we could not enter it.

Idea/आइडिॲ *(noun)* - कल्पना

Backed by modern ideas, the country was able to bring necessary change in its social setup.

Ideal/आइडिॲल *(noun & adjective)* - आदर्श

The room temperature was just ideal for doctors to perform surgery.

Idealistic/आइडिअलिस्टिक *(adjective)* - आदर्शवादी

An idealistic society is hard to conceive. She is an ideal candidate for this post.

Ideality/आइडिऐलिटि *(noun)* - आदर्शत्व

Everyone wants to go with ideality when he begins some work.

Idealize/आइडिॲलाइज *(verb)* - आदर्श रूप में देखना या प्रस्तुत करना

In an idealized society, there are no crimes of any sort.

Ideally/आइडियलि *(adverb)* – आदर्श रूप में

Ideally you should exercise for 30 minutes every day. Ideally, you should take 20 mg of each tablet in the morning.

Ideate/आइडिएट *(verb)* – कल्पना करना

His aim was to ideate a theory that could be proved rationally.

Ideation/आइडिएशन *(noun)* – विचार-शक्ति

The scientist's ideation of psychological concept was too hard to believe.

Idem/आइडेम *(avberb)* – वहाँ

Marianne Elliot, Partners in revolution, 1982; idem, Wolfe Toe, 1989.

I

Identical/आइडेन्टिकल *(adjective)* – अनुरूप

Identical twins were born on July 8, to a woman in ward number 6.

Identifiable/आइडेन्टिफाएब्ल *(adj)* – पहचानने योग्य

The bodies were so charred that they were no longer identifiable.

Identification/आइडेन्टिफिकेशन *(noun)* – एकीकरण

As soon as the identification process was over, we made an exit out of the office. The police stopped the van and asked the driver to show his identification proof.

Idiocy/इडिऑसि *(noun)* – पागलपन

He was ill-famed for his idiocy.

Idiom/इडिअम *(noun)* – मुहावरा

A class on idioms was arranged for us, just a week before exams.

Idiomatic/इडिॲमैटिक *(adjective)* – मुहावरेदार

She spoke fluent, idiomatic English. After 10 years of my stay in France, I am now used to Idiomatic French.

Idiosyncrasy/इडिऑसिन्क्रॅसि *(noun)* – प्रवृत्ति की विशेषावस्था

I could no longer stand his idiosyncrasies, therefore, I left.

Idiot/इडिअॅट *(noun)* – निर्बुद्धि

What an idiot the biker was!

Idiotic/इडिऑटिक *(adjective)* – मूर्खतापूर्ण

The girl rebuked the boys for their excessive idiotic behaviour.

Idleness/आइडलनेस *(noun)* – बेकारी

He was punished for his idleness at school. Too much of an idleness can be boring enough.

Idler/आइडलर *(noun)* – निकम्मा

I knew that my best friend was the biggest idler in the world.

Idly/आइडलि *(adverb)* – आलस्य से

"What are your interests?" asked my fiancée.

Idol/आइडॅल *(noun)* – प्रतिमा

The idols were adorned with jewels before being taken out on procession.

Idolater/आइडॉलेटर् *(noun)* – मूर्तिपूजक

The things grew worse at home when I refused to be an idolater.

Idolatrous/आइडॉलट्रस *(adj)* – मूर्ति पूजन के समान

The idolatrous behaviour is seen as contempt by many societies.

Idolatry/आइडॉलट्रि *(noun)* – मूर्ति-पूजा

In Hinduism, the roots of idolatry are very deep.

Idolize/आइडॅलाइज *(verb)* – मूर्ति की भाँति पूजा करना

Don't idolize me as it would be of no use.

Idolum/आइडोलॅम *(noun)* – कल्पना

While painting, he was taking a cue from his mental idolums.

Idyll/आइडिल *(noun)* – पद्य में ग्रामीण जीवन का संक्षिप्त वर्णन

For the winter-lovers, Shimla stands out as an idyll destination.

If/इफ *(conjunction)* – मानो अगर

If you don't abide by rules, I would be forced to keep you out from this discussion.

Igloo/इग्लू *(noun)* – हिमकुटी

People living in Polar areas live in the houses called igloos.

Igneous/इग्निअस *(adjective)* – आग्नेय, अग्निमय

The area is all covered with igneous rocks.

Ignis fatuus/इग्निस फैट्युअस – *(noun)* मिथ्या प्रकाश

The path that he chose proved to be an ignis fatuus and he ended up doing nothing.

Ignite/इग्नाइट *(verb)* – आग लगाना

As the sun set, the tribal people ignited the logs of wood.

Ignition/इग्निशन *(noun)* – ज्वलन

We kept standing there, watching the ignition of industrial waste.

Ignoble/इग्नोबल *(adjective)* – नीच

His bad deeds are really ignoble for society.

Ignominious/इग्नॅमिनिअॅस *(adjective)* – घृणित, अधम

His lustful acts brought him into an ignominious situation.

Ignoramus/इग्नॅरेमॅस *(noun)* – अज्ञानी, मूर्ख पुरुष

Don't bring that ignoramus person before me.

Ignorance/इग्नॅरॅन्स *(noun)* – अज्ञान

When minister was asked about the incident, he expressed ignorance.

Ignorant/इग्नॅरॅन्ट *(adjective)* – अज्ञानी

The students were ignorant of the changes made in their curriculum.

Ignore/इग्नॉर *(verb)* – उपेक्षा करना

In spite of all the efforts he made to approach me, I kept ignoring him.

Iguana/इग्वॉना *(noun)* – पोह, एक प्रकार की छिपकली

The guide said, "Here, you will see a number of iguanas."

Iliad/इलियड *(noun)* – होमर कवि का इस नाम का महाकाव्य

Iliad by Homer is considered as one of the classic works of Greek literature.

Illation/इलेशन *(noun)* – परिणाम, निष्कर्ष

He could draw an illation from the facts that he had gathered.

Illative/इलेटिव *(adjective)* – अनुमान करने योग्य, परिणामसूचक

The nature of his work is mostly illative.

Illaudable/इलॉडबल *(adj)* – अग्रहणीय, अप्रशंसनीय

His every action and every decision was simply illaudable.

Illegality/इलिगैलिटि *(noun)* – अन्याय गैर कानूनीपन

No one could dare stop all that illegality taking place in open.

Illegally/इलीगलि *(adverb)* – अवैध (गैर कानूनी) ढंग से

Bob smuggled drugs into the country and then sold them illegally.

Illegibility/इलेजिबिलिटि *(noun)* – अस्पष्टता

Teachers were always scolding him for not paying attention to the illegibility in his written work.

Illegible/इलेजॅबॅल *(adjective)* – न पढ़े जाने योग्य

The lawyer's writing was so illegible that we could not read a single thing.

Illegitimacy/इलिजिटिमॅसि *(noun)* – हरामीपन

It was surprising that such an illegitimacy was easily overlooked by ministers.

Illegitimate/इलिजिटिमेट *(adjective)* – जारज

The boy or girl born from the parents who are not married, is called an illegitimate.

Illiberal/इलिबॅरॅल *(adjective)* – अनुदार, कड़ा अनुशासन

The policies of autocratic leaders were often illiberal and harsh.

Illicit/इलिसिट *(adjective)* – अवैध

The two were having an illicit relationship, oblivious to everyone.

Illimitable/इलिमिटेबल *(adj)* – असीम, जिसकी सीमा न की जाये

A giant with illimitable powers emerged on the scene and destroyed everything.

Illision/इलिजन *(noun)* – टक्कर

His act of illision took everyone by surprise.

Illiterate/इलिटरेट *(adjective)* – अशिक्षित, अनपढ़

A majority of people living in Indian villages are still illiterate.

Illness/इलनेस *(noun)* – बीमारी

His mental illness grew day by day.

Illumination/इल्यूमिनेशन *(noun)* – चमक

The illumination from the bright surface was directly falling in our eyes.

Illuminative/इल्यूमिनेटिव *(adjective)* – प्रकाश करने वाला

The illuminative setting was created by a group of experts.

Illumine/इल्यूमाइन *(verb)* - प्रज्वलित करना, प्रकाशित करना

In day, all the objects get illumined by the sun.

Illusion/इलूशन *(noun)* - छल, भ्रम

What he was looking at, was merely an illusion, not reality.

Illusive/इलूसिव *(adjective)* - छली, भ्रमोत्पादक

The man was trying to fool the police with his illusive looks.

Illusory/इलूसरि *(adjective)* - मायावी, भ्रमित करने वाला

The film was full of illusory scenes.

Illustrate/इलॅस्ट्रेट *(verb)* - अलंकृत करना, चित्रात्मक व्याख्या

"Could you illustrate your concept?" asked the student to his classmate.

Illustration/इलॅस्ट्रेशन *(noun)* - चित्र, स्पष्टीकरण

All the children were looking at the illustrations with surprise and interest.

Illustrative/इलॅस्ट्रेटिव *(adjective)* - दृष्टान्तयुक्त, चित्रयुक्त

He gave me a few illustrative examples for my better understanding of things.

Illustrator/इलॅस्ट्रेटॅर *(noun)* - चित्रकार

The man sitting there is a famous illustrator.

Illustrious/इलस्ट्रिअस *(adjective)* - प्रसिद्ध

When he looked back at his illustrious career, he felt good.

Imageable/इमेजिएबल *(adjective)* - चित्त में धारण करने योग्य बिम्ब निर्माण

The sheer beauty of the place is making it imageable.

Imagery/इमेजरी *(noun)* - आकृति, बिम्ब, चित्रात्मकता

The English poets have used vivid imagery to impart beauty to their work.

Imaginable/इमैजिनॅबल *(adjective)* - कल्पनीय, परिकल्पनीय

The intensity of the pain suffered by the patients is not even imaginable.

Imaginative/इमैजिनेटिव *(adjective)* - कल्पनापूर्ण

His imaginative thinking made him stand out of the crowd.

Imagine/इमैजिन *(verb)* - विचार करना, कल्पना करना

In these days of technology, it is hard to imagine a life without computers and mobiles.

Imago/इमेगो *(noun)* - कृमि की प्रौढ़ अवस्था

Imago is the final stage of insect development cycle.

Imbecile/इम्बेसाइल *(noun)* - अल्पमति

What an imbecile the person sitting on the sofa was!

Imbecility/इम्बेसिलिटि *(noun)* - शरीर या मन की दुर्बलता

The way he handled the task clearly indicated his imbecility.

Imbibe/इम्बाइब *(verb)* - पी लेना, गटक जाना

The water sprinkled quickly imbibed by the leaves.

Imbroglio/इम्ब्रोल्यो *(noun)* - बिना क्रम का ढेर

Despite of his best efforts, he soon found himself caught in an imbroglio.

Imbrue/इम्ब्रू *(verb)* - धब्बा लगना

As soon as I entered the basement, he imbrued me with colours.

Imbue/इम्ब्यू *(verb)* - दिल में बैठा देना, गहरे रंग में रंगना

His speech imbued me so much that I started clapping.

Imitable/इमिटॅबल *(adjective)* - अनुकरण करने योग्य

The singer carries a unique style that is not imitable by anyone.

Imitate/इमिटेट *(verb)* - अनुकरण करना

The actor had such a good comic sense that no one could imitate him.

Imitation/इमिटेशन *(noun)* - अनुकरण

Imitation is not everyone's cup of tea.

Imitative/इमिटेटिव *(adjective)* - अनुकरणशील

Though he denies it all the time, his style is more or less imitative.

Immaculate/इमैक्युलिट *(adjective)* - निर्मल

The saint preferred immaculate surroundings for performing meditation.

I

Immaturity/इमट्युअरिटि *(noun)* – अपरिपक्व अवस्था

The immaturity of the immune system in very young children makes them especially vulnerable.

Immeasurable/इम्मेजरेबल *(adjective)* – बहुत बड़ा

The frustration that the people were facing at office had become immeasurable.

Immediately/इमिडिएटली *(adv)* – तत्काल

The passengers asked the driver to start the bus immediately.

Immediateness/इमिडिएटनेस *(noun)* – समीपता

The boss ordered his team to show immediateness in completing the task.

Immedicable/इम्मेडिकेबॅल *(adjective)* – अचिकित्स्य

In spite of all the efforts by the surgeons, the patient remained immedicable to the drugs.

Immemorable/इम्मेमॅरेबल *(adj)* – विस्मरणीय

The violent clashes made the event only immemorable.

Immemorial/इम्मेमोरिअल् *(adjective)* – अति प्राचीन

From the times immemorial, our culture has rooted in traditions and customs.

Immense/इमेन्स *(adjective)* – अमिट extremely

The sayings of the prophet had an immense effect upon my heart.

Immensity/इमेंसिटी *(noun)* – अनन्तता

Seeing the immensity of the situation, the President cancelled his tour to Europe.

Immerge/इमॅर्ज – तरल पदार्थ में डूबना

As the water was not very cold, we decided to immerge in it.

Immerse/इमॅर्स *(verb)* – डुबाना

The holy idol of the goddess was immersed by the devotees in water.

Immersion/इमॅर्शन *(noun)* – निमज्जन

The immersion ceremony was followed by chanting of hymns.

Immethodical/इम्मेथॉडिकल *(adj)* – अव्यवस्थित

The professor dismissed the idea as being impractical and immethodical.

Immigrant/इमिग्रैण्ट *(noun)* – देशान्तर में बसने वाला

The Asian country was not willing to grant all the rights to its immigrants.

Immigrate/इमिग्रेट *(verb)* – देशान्तर में बसना या बसाना

As the country was constantly under war, many of its residents decided to immigrate to the neighbouring land.

Imminence/इमिनेन्स *(noun)* – समीपता

The imminence of a clash made the ministers avoid the rally.

Imminent/इमिनेन्ट *(adjective)* – सन्निकटता

With such a support from all the parties, a powerful change is imminent.

Immiscibility/इमिसिबिलिटि *(noun)* – अघुलनशीलता

The immiscibility of oil and water is the base of many chemical compounds.

I

Immitigable/इमिटिगॅबॅल *(adjective)* – कम न होने योग्य

The sacrifices of the martyrs remain immitigable.

Immixture/इमिक्चॅर *(noun)* – शुद्धता

There are several ways by which an immixture of substances can be separated.

Immobile/इमोबाइल *(adjective)* – स्थिर

The earthworm was crushed under leg and had turned immobile.

Immobility/इमोबिलिटि *(noun)* – निश्चलता

In an extremely old age, a person can face the immobility of joints.

Immoderate/इमॉडरिट (इमॉडरेट) *(adj)* – बेहद, अत्यधिक, अत्यन्त

As per old scriptures, it is a sin to indulge in immoderate drinking and gambling.

Immodest/इमॉडेस्ट *(adjective)* – अश्लील

His immodest behaviour was a cause of disturbance to everyone.

Immodesty/इमॉडिस्टि *(noun)* – निर्लज्जता

Client's immodesty forced the seller to put down the phone.

Immolate/इमोलेट *(verb)* – बलिदान करना

Sometimes, youngsters become so crazy in anger that they try to immolate themselves.

Immolation/इमोलेशन *(noun)* – बलिदान

Immolation is an act of cowardice and must be avoided in every situation.

Immolator/इमोलेटर *(noun)* – बलिदान देने वाला

The immolator's life could not be saved due to grave injuries.

Immoral/इमॉरॅल *(adjective)* – दुश्चरित्र

The public display of affection is considered an immoral activity by many.

Immortal/इमॉटॅल *(adjective)* – अमर

As per legends, the gods drank nectar to become immortal. His bravery on the battlefield has made him immortal in our hearts.

Immovability/इमूवबिलिटि *(noun)* – स्थिरता not able to be moved. *The immovability of the joints causes extreme pain.*

I

Immune/इम्यून *(adjective)* – आक्रमण से मुक्त

His good health is attributed to his excellent immune system.

Immunity/इम्युनिटि *(noun)* – उन्मुक्ति, प्रतिरक्षा

Immunity to malaria seems to have increased spontaneously.

Immunize/इम्यूनाइज *(verb)* – मुक्त करना

The doctor advised his patient to get immunized as soon as possible.

Immure/इम्युअॅर *(verb)* – बन्द करना

The dacoit kept the child immured for four days.

Immutability/इम्यूटॅबिलिटि *(noun)* – नित्यता

Green vegetables raise the immutability of our body.

Imp/इम्प *(noun)* – दुष्ट बालक, बाल राक्षस

The old man retorted, "Why don't you keep your imp under control?" The movie is based on the character of an imp who plays wicked all the time.

Impacable/इम्पैकेबल *(adj)* – शान्त न करने योग्य

The man is famous in office for his impacable nature.

Impact/इम्पैक्ट *(noun)* – टक्कर, परिणाम, प्रभाव

The impact was so huge that it produced a loud noise.

Impaction/इम्पैक्शन *(noun)* – टक्कर

Under the impaction of hammer, the nail got twisted.

Impairing/इम्पेअरिंग *(noun)* – क्षति

Keeping the mobile phone in close proximity to body can lead of impairing of cells.

Impalpability/इम्पैल्पेबिलिटि *(noun)* – स्पर्श-ज्ञान शून्यता

The impalpability of our soul makes it all the more difficult to understand.

Impanel/इम्पैनेल *(verb)* – निरीक्षक या पंच की सूची में दर्ज करना

A group of five judges were impanelled for the case.

Imparadise/इम्पैराडॉइज *(verb)* – आनंदविभोर कर देना

The thought of going abroad was enough to imparadise me.

Imparity/इम्पैरिटि *(noun)* – असमानता

Even in today's world, the poor are treated with imparity.

Impart/इम्पार्ट *(verb)* – प्रदान करना

As per the directions from the Principal, the teachers would be imparted technical knowledge during the training.

Impartible/इम्पार्टिबल *(adj)* – भाग न करने योग्य

According to the old theories, atoms are impartible.

Impassible/इम्पैसिबल *(adjective)* – दुःखातीत

Years of devotion have made his heart impassable.

Impassion/इम्पैशन *(verb)* – जोश दिलाना

The guidance by his mentor impassioned him so much that he took the project right away.

Impassive/इम्पैसिव *(adjective)* – भावना शून्य

His impassive attitude was ridiculed by everyone.

Impasto/इम्पेस्टो *(noun)*– रंग भरने की कला या ढंग

The beauty of the painting was aggravated by the lovely impasto work on it.

Impatience/इम्पेशन्स *(noun)* – बेसब्री

I want to work on my impatience.

Impatient/इम्पेशॅन्ट *(adjective)* – व्यग्र

Your impatient nature is the root of all the problems.

Impawn/इम्पॉन *(verb)* – बन्धक रखना

The family had to impawn its cattle to get some money.

Impayable/इम्पेएबल *(adjective)* – न देने योग्य

Whatever the man did for his country is totally impayable.

Impeccability/इम्पेकेबिलिटि *(noun)* – निर्दोषता

The impeccability of the artist's work won him many applauds.

Impendance/इम्पीडॅन्स *(noun)* – अवरोध

On the blackboard was written the formula for calculating electrical impedance.

Impendent/इम्पेन्डेंट *(adj.)* – संकटासन्न

As they were advancing into the dark, the danger was becoming more impendent.

Impending/इम्पेन्डिंग *(noun)* – आसन्न

The impending danger was the reason for the cancellation of their plans.

Impenetrable/इम्पेनिट्रेबल *(adjective)* – अथाह

The extreme darkness had made the cave totally impenetrable.

Imperative/इम्परेटिव *(adjective)* – आज्ञासूचक

The balance in ecosystem is imperative to man's existence.

Imperator/इम्परेटर *(noun)* – **सेनानायक**

Soon after king's death, his young son was declared an imperator.

Imperceptible/इम्पर्सेप्टिबॅलॅ *(adjective)* – अगोचर

Only an imperceptible change was noticed in the metabolic rate of the patient.

Impercipient/इम्पर्सिपिएन्ट *(adjective)* – अगोचर

His impercipient nature was attributed to his lack of experience in meta-physics.

Imperfect/इम्परफेक्ट *(adjective)* – अधूरा, अपूर्ण

All of us are born with imperfect minds.

Imperialism/इम्पेरियलिज्म *(noun)* – राजाधिराज का शासन

With the start of imperialism, the developed countries started expanding their territories.

Imperialize/इम्पेरियलाइज *(verb)* – राजकीय या तेजस्वी बनाना

As the time passed on, the tendency to imperialize Asia increased among the western nations.

Imperil/इम्पेरिल *(verb)* – खतरे में डालना

It was not advisable to imperil the life of the child, so he was left at home.

Impermanence/इम्पर्मानेंस *(noun)* – अस्थिरता

The impermanence of life makes the man grateful to God.

Impermanent/इम्पर्मानेंट *(adjective)* – अस्थायी

The application of wax over a surface makes it impermanent.

Impermissible/इम्पर्मिसिबल *(adjective)* – अननुज्ञेय

It was impermissible to enter without gate-pass.

Impersonate/इम्पॅर्सनेट *(verb)* – भेष बदलना

Throughout the investigation, the man impersonated as a cop.

I

Impersonation/इम्पॅर्सनेशॅन *(noun)* – भेष या व्यक्तित्व परिवर्तन

He thought that the impersonation as a saint would get him out of trouble, but it did not.

Impersonative/इम्पर्सनेटिव *(adj)* – भेष (रूप) बदलने का

There was no use him being an impersonative.

Impersonator/इम्पर्सनेटर *(noun)* – भेष बदलने वाला व्यक्ति

As an impersonator, he was a genius.

Impertinence/इम्पर्टिनेंस *(noun)* – धृष्टता

My friend was punished badly for displaying impertinence to his teachers.

Impetrate/इम्पिट्रेट *(verb)* – प्रार्थना करके प्राप्त करना

When nothing worked for him, he tried to impetrate it by prayer.

Impetration/इम्पिट्रेशन *(noun)* – प्रार्थना करने पर प्राप्त

Their impetration fell on deaf ears.

Impetuosity/इम्पिचुआसिटि *(noun)* – तीव्रता

It is better to think before taking a step, instead of behaving with impetuosity.

Impetus/इम्पिटस *(noun)* – प्रेरणा

The fear of getting public rebuke was the impetus behind quick action by the officers.

Impiety/इम्पाइअटि *(noun)* – अधर्म

In court, the peasant had to face king's impiety and cruelty.

Impinge/इम्पिन्ज *(verb)* – टकराना

It is inappropriate to impinge on someone's privacy.

Impious/इम्पायस *(adjective)* – पापी

People were surprised by his impious attitude towards them.

Impiously/इम्पायसली *(adv)* – अधर्म से

As he was behaving impiously, we left him alone.

Impiousness/इम्पाइअसनेस *(noun)* – अधर्म

It was awkward to see saint's impiousness towards his religion.

Impledge/इम्प्लेज *(verb)* – बन्धक या गिरवी रखना

At the oath ceremony, ministers impledged to take care of their responsibilities.

Impletion/इम्प्लीशन *(noun)* – भराई

It was necessary to add impletion to the boxes before they could be transferred.

Implicate/इम्प्लिकेट *(verb)* – फँसाना

As he was naïve, it was easy to implicate him.

Implication/इमप्लिकेशन *(noun)* – आशय, उलझन

"What are the implications of such a policy?"

Implicative/इमप्लिकेटिव *(adjective)* – फँसाने वाला

Nobody knew why he was giving implicative answers.

Implore/इम्प्लोर *(verb)* – प्रार्थना करना

The man without the licence implored before police to let him go.

Imploringly/इम्प्लोरिंगलि *(adverb)* – साग्रह प्रार्थना के साथ

"Don't tell it to anyone." Said the man imploringly.

Impolicy/इम्पालिसि *(noun)* – बुरी नीति

We were shocked to see the impolicy of the jury members.

Impolite/इम्पोलाइट *(adjective)* – अविनीत

"If you remain impolite to me, I shall not be able to help you", said the man to his neighbour.

Impolitic/इम्पॉलिटिक *(adjective)* – अनुचित

The minister was giving all the impolitic answers to the questions raised to him.

Imponderable/इम्पॉन्डरबॅल *(adjective)* – बहुत हल्का

The time this issue takes to settle down is imponderable.

Impone/इम्पोन *(verb)* – प्रभाव डालना

The man imponed the amount and went away immediately.

Imponent/इम्पोनेन्ट *(adj.)* – प्रभाव डालने योग्य

It was now up to the imponent as who would be relieved from paying the duty.

Import/इम्पोर्ट *(verb)* – सूचित करना, आयात करना

All the goods imported into the country are of good quality.

Importable/इम्पोर्टेबल *(adjective)* – देश में लाने योग्य

All importable goods in our country carry a special customs duty.

Importation/इम्पोर्टेशन *(noun)* – आयात, किसी देश में पहुँचाना या ले जाना, बाहर से लायी हुई चीजे

The opposition was not happy with the importation process; so they walked out.

Importance/इम्पॉर्टेन्ट *(noun)* – महत्त्व

There are people that carry high importance in our lives.

Important/इम्पार्टेन्ट *(adjective)* – प्रभावशाली

Our company has come out with some very important policies this year.

Importunate/इम्पॉर्चुनेट *(adjective)* – हठी

His importunate habits were becoming annoying for others.

Importune/इम्पॉर्चुन *(verb)* – आग्रह के साथ प्रार्थना करना

I retorted, "Don't importune me. Give me some time."

Importunity/इम्पॉर्चुनिटि *(noun)* – आग्रह

The man was always bothering us with his importunities.

Impose/इम्पोज *(verb)* – थोपना

As soon as the new rule was imposed, people started protesting.

Imposing/इम्पोजिंग *(adjective)* – रोबदार

The building looked magnificent with its imposing structure.

Imposition/इम्पोजिशन *(noun) (noun)* – लगान

Tax imposition was prevalent even in ancient times.

Impostor/इम्पॉस्टर *(noun)* – पाखण्डी

After interrogation, it was clear that he was an impostor.

Impoverish/इम्पॉवरिश *(verb)* – साधनहीन करना

The British rule impoverished Indian community to a great extent.

Impracticable/इम्प्रैक्टिकेबल *(adjective)* – दुष्कर

It is impracticable to listen to every employee and then take a decision.

Imprecate/इम्प्रिकेट *(verb)* – शाप देना

It was his nature to imprecate everyone for all his problems.

Imprecation/इम्प्रिकेशन *(noun)* – शाप

His imprecations had no affect on my mind.

Imprecatory/इम्प्रिकेटरी *(adjective)* – शापयुक्त

With time, his nature became more and more imprecatory.

Impregnation/इम्प्रिग्नेशन *(noun)* – गर्भधारण

After repeated experiments, the biologists were, finally, successful in impregnation.

Impression/इम्प्रेशन *(noun)* – प्रभाव

The interviewee was able to create good impression on everyone.

Imprimis/इम्प्राइमिस *(adv)* – सर्वप्रथम, पहले

Imprimis, he is not required here.

Imprison/इम्प्रिजन *(verb)* – कैद करना

The culprit was imprisoned for five years.

Improbability/इम्प्रोबेलिटि *(noun)* – अनहोनी

There is improbability of raining heavily this year.

Improperly/इम्प्रॉपर्लि *(adverb)* – अनुचित रीति से

Never go to an interview board improperly dressed.

Impropriety/इम्प्रॅप्राइअटि *(noun)*– असभ्यता

"Such an impropriety would not be tolerated."

Improver/इम्प्रूवर *(noun)* – व्यवसाय सीखने वाला

He has played the role of an improver very well.

Improvidence/इम्प्राविडॅन्स *(noun)* – अदूरदर्शिता

Parents were worried about their children's improvidence.

Improvisation/इम्प्राविजेशन *(noun)* – अचिन्तित रचना

Improvisation at writing has been my greatest strength.

Imprudence/इम्प्रुडेंस *(noun)* – अविवेक

She displayed her imprudence by talking angrily to his boss.

Impudence/इम्पुडेंस *(noun)* – ढिठाई

The audience were shocked to see his impudence

Impudicity/इम्प्युडिसिटि *(noun)* – अविनय

His shouting at his juniors only showed his impudicity.

Impugn/इम्प्यून *(verb)* – विपरीत बोलना

The lawyer was trying to impugn the statement given by the witness.

Impugnment/इम्प्यूनमॅन्ट *(noun)* – विरोध

The impugnment of the statement was his only motive.

Impuissance/इम्प्युसंस *(noun)* – नपुंसकता

The knight exhibited his impuissance in the battlefield.

Impulsion/इम्पल्सन *(noun)* – प्रेरणा

His impulsion made him participate in the show.

Imputation/इम्प्यूटेशन *(noun)* – दोषारोपण

He has always believed in imputation of failures to others.

Imputatively/इम्प्यूटेटिवलि *(adv)* – कलंक से

Their cause of woes has always been their boss working imputatively.

Impute/इम्प्यूट् *(verb)* – दोष लगाना

He has always imputed his awkward behaviour to laziness of his juniors.

Inability/इनएबिलिटी *(noun)* – अयोग्यता

Her inability to perform well resulted in his expulsion from dance class.

Inaccessible/इनएक्सेसिबल *(adjective)* – अप्राप्य

The presence of rugged mountains made the way to valley nearly inaccessible.

Inaccessibly/इनएक्सेसिब्ली *(adv)* – न पहुँचनते हुए

The jungle was located inaccessibly across the river.

I

Inaccuracy/इनएक्यूरेसी *(noun)* – अशुद्धता
The inaccuracy in his work irked his master.

Inaction/इनएक्सन *(noun)* – आलस्य
Police's inaction in the case has raised many eyebrows.

Inactivity/इनएक्टिविटि *(noun)* – कार्य-हीनता
The inactivity of the machines in the mill resulted in financial loss.

Inadaptability/इनएडैप्टिबिलिटि *(noun)* – प्रबन्ध हीनता
The plants with inadaptability to the changing climate die early.

Inaffable/इनएफेबल *(adjective)* – उदासीन
We could not tolerate his inaffable manners.

I

Inalterable/इनअल्टरेबल *(adjective)* – अपरिवर्तनीय
Our boss has an inalterable nature.

Inapplicable/इन्एप्लिकेबल *(adjective)* – अनुचित
This test is inapplicable to all those who are below 20 years of age.

Inapposite/इनएपोजिट *(adjective)* – अयोग्य
I was finding my presence at the party totally inapposite.

Inapprehensible/इनऐप्रिहेन्सिबल – न समझने योग्य
The matter is inapprehensible to people living outside India.

Inapt/इनऐप्ट *(adjective)* – अयोग्य
His interference in our issues is inapt.

Inaptly/इनऐप्टलि *(adverb)* – अयोग्यता से
None of us could guess why she was behaving so inaptly.

Inartistic/इन्आर्टिस्टिक *(adjective)* – फूहड़
The poet was excellent in his work, yet he thought himself to be inartistic.

Inattentive/इन्अटेन्टिव *(adjective)* – असावधान
The inattentive students were rebuked by teachers.

Inaudible/इनऑडिबल *(adjective)* – अकर्णगोचर
The music was so loud that it was almost inaudible.

Inaudibility/इनऑडिबिलिटि *(noun)* – अश्रव्यता
While constructing an auditorium, the inaudibility factor is to be taken into account.

Inaudibly/इनआडिब्लि *(adv)* – सुनाई न देते हुए
He was speaking in an inaudibly loud manner.

Inauguration/इन्आग्यूरेशन *(noun)* – उद्घाटन
MLA was present at the time of inauguration of the library.

Inauguratory/इन्आग्यूरेटरि *(adverb)* – उद्घाटन सम्बन्धी
The minister's inauguratory speech was praiseworthy.

Inborn/इनबॉर्न *(adjective)* – जन्म से
Every person carries some inborn qualities.

Inbreathe/इन्ब्रीद् *(verb)* – भीतर को श्वास लेना
While working in factory, I inbreathed some foul gas.

Inbred/इन्ब्रेड *(adjective)* – स्वाभाविक
Scientists are keen to experiment on inbred animals.

Incarnate/इन्कार्नेट *(adjective)* – शरीरधारी
Man has always believed in the incarnate forms of God.

Incarnation/इन्कार्नेशन *(noun)* – अवतार
Man believes in the incarnation of gods on earth.

Incautious/इन्कॉशस *(adjective)* – धृष्ट, अचैतन्य
His incautious nature brought much woe to his family.

Incavation/इन्कैवेशन *(noun)* – पोला छिद्र
The incavation was done by many engineers together.

Incensory/इन्सेंसरी *(noun)* – धूपदानी
The incensory was placed inside the temple premises.

Incentive/इन्सेन्टिव *(noun)* – प्रेरणा, प्रोत्साहन, प्रेरणा हेतु वस्तु
The employees were expecting huge incentives at the end of the year.

Inception/इन्सेप्शन *(noun)* – आरम्भ
The inception of the building took place in 1988.

Inceptive/इन्सेप्टिव *(adjective)* – आदि का
The project is still in its inceptive stage.

Inceptor/इन्सेप्टर *(noun)* – आरम्भ करने वाला
Many cells in body act as inceptors of signals from brain.

Incertitude/इन्सर्टिट्यूड *(noun)* - अनिर्णय

It was the incertitude of the situation that he was unable to take a decision.

Incessant/इन्सेसॅन्ट *(adjective)* - अनवरत, निरन्तर

Over the years, the country has seen an incessant growth of population.

Incestuous/इन्सेस्चुअस *(adjective)* - निकट सम्बन्धियों के साथ मैथुन से सम्बन्धित

Their incestuous relationship continued for many years.

Incidence/इन्सिडेंस *(noun)* - घटना

The incidence of crimes has increased manifold in last few years.

Incinerate/इन्सिनरेट *(verb)* - भस्म कर देना

To get rid of the excessive garbage, it was incinerated.

Incineration/इन्सिनरेशन *(noun)* - भस्मीकरण

The process of incineration continued for two days.

Incinerator/इन्सिनरेटर *(noun)* - शव भस्म करने की चिता

All the garbage was put into the incinerator.

Incise/इन्साइज *(verb)* - नक्काशी करना

The surgeons incised patient's stomach and started operating.

Incision/इन्सिजन *(noun)* - कटाव

She was quite afraid of having incision done on her belly.

Incisive/इन्साइसिव् *(adjective)* - काटने वाला

What he wanted was an incisive report of the project.

Incisor/इन्सिजर *(noun)* - आगे का काटने वाला दाँत

The incisors are meant for cutting the food bytes.

Incite/इन्साइट *(verb)* - उत्तेजित करना

The crowd was incited by its leader to assemble there.

Incivility/इन्सिविलिटी *(noun)* - असभ्यता

We were surprised to notice the incivility of his nature.

Inclemency/इनक्लेमेंसी *(noun)* - कठोरता

Our boss believes in the inclemency of punishment.

Inclement/इनक्लेमेंट *(adjective)* - प्रचण्ड

The tourists were not prepared for an inclement weather.

Inclinable/इन्क्लाइनेबल *(adjective)*- अनुकूल, झुका हुआ

I am inclinable to get up late in the morning.

Inclination/इनक्लिनेशन *(noun)* - झुकाव

The man in black trousers has inclination to the Carnatic music.

Incognito/इन्कॉग्निटो *(adjective & avberb)* - गुप्त

An incognito bar was running under the pretext of hair salon.

Incognizant/इन्कॉग्निजंट *(adjective)* - अचेत

We were surprised to know about his incognizant attitude towards marriage.

Incohesive/इन्कोहेसिव *(adj)* - असम्बद्ध

The writer took the pain of rewriting the incohesive paragraphs of the book.

Incombustibility/इनकम्बस्टिबिलिटि *(noun)* - अदाह्यता

While working on experiments ignition temperature, we came to know a lot about the incombustibility of substances.

Incombustible/इनकम्बसटिब्ल *(adjective)* - अदाह्य

We are going to make a list of incombustible substances that can be used in kitchen.

Incomer/इनकमर *(noun)* - प्रवेश करने वाला

Many writers came to India as incomers and settled here.

Incoming/इनकमिंग *(adjective)* - आने वाली

All his incoming calls were blocked by the authorities. The incoming CEO has served the previous company for 15 years.

Incomings/इनकमिंग्स *(noun)* - आमदनी

You must keep an account of all your incomings and outgoings.

Incommensurable/इन्कमेंशरेबॅल *(adj)* - अनियमित परिमाण का

The difference in their experiences makes their performances incommensurable.

Incommensurate/इन्कमेन्श्यूरेट *(adjective)* - अतुल्य

The gravity of the situation is incommensurate with the steps taken by the government.

I

Incommutable/इन्कम्यूटेबॅल *(adjective)* - अपरिवर्तनीय

The wide difference in the prices of two books makes them incommutable.

Incompatibility/इन्कम्पैटिबिलिटि *(noun)*- विभिन्नता

Incompatibility of a couple is the biggest factor responsible for a failed marriage.

Incompatible/इनकम्पैटिबल *(adjective)* - बेमेल

Their incompatible nature was always the reason behind their clashes.

Incompetence/इन्काम्पिटन्स *(noun)* - अयोग्यता

No company is willing to hire a person with incompetence to perform tasks.

Incomprehension/इन्काप्रिहेंशन *(noun)* - नासमझी

"Can I know the reason behind your incomprehension of a simple concept?" asked the manager.

I

Incomprehensive/इन्काम्प्रिहेन्सिव *(adj)*- अपूर्ण

The books recommended by teacher are incomprehensive for perfect understanding of the concept.

Incompressibility/इन्कम्प्रेसिबिलिटि *(noun)* - दबाब रोकने की शक्ति

Many uses of rubber are based on its amount of incompressibility.

Incompressible/इन्कम्प्रेसिबल *(adjective)* - दबाने योग्य

The tyres used in vehicles must not be incompressible.

Incomputable/इन्कमप्यूटेबल *(adjective)* - अगण्य

In spite of long hours spent, the problem remained incomputable.

Inconceivability/इनकन्सिवैबिलिटि *(noun)* - अकल्पनीयता

The complex nature of the machine is the reason behind its inconceivability.

Incondensable/इन्कन्डेसॅबॅल *(adj)* - द्रव से ठोस के रूप में न जमाने योग्य

Despite all efforts, the problem has remained incondensable.

Incondite/इन्कॉनडाइट *(adj)* - भद्दा

It was the incondite nature of the evidence that right judgment could not be delivered.

Inconformity/इन्कॉन्फर्मिटी *(noun)v*- असमानता

The new product failed to become popular, thanks to its inconformity to the quality standards.

Incongruent/इन्कॉन्ग्रूएण्ट *(adjective)* - अयोग्य

The two triangles shown in the diagram are incongruent.

Incongruence/इनकॉन्ग्रूएन्स *(noun)* - विरोध

The student was asked to prove the incongruence of the two triangles.

Inconsequent/इनकाूसिक्वंट *(adjective)* - अप्रस्तुत

The experiments on artificial intelligence remained inconsequent.

Inconsequential/इन्कान्सिक्वेन्शिअल *(adj)* - अयुक्त

It was known from the beginning that the experiments were going to be inconsequential.

Inconsequently/इनकन्सिक्वेंटली *(adv)* - तर्क-हीन ढंग से

They continued inconsequently, without bothering about results.

Inconsiderable/इन्कंसिडरॅबॅल *(adjective)* - कम मूल्य का

There were particles on inconsiderable size present in the atmosphere.

Inconsonant/इन्कॉन्सनॅन्ट *(adjective)* - बेसुरा

As our theories were inconsonant, we could not agree with each other.

Inconstancy/इन्कांस्टन्सि *(noun)* - चंचलता

What bothers man about life is its inconstancy.

Inconstant/इनकान्स्टंट *(adjective)* - चपल

He was trying to confuse the jury members by giving inconstant answers.

Incontaminate/इन्कॉन्टैमिनेट *(verb & noun)* - अदूषित, दूषित नहीं करना

The highest priority in this hotel is to provide incontaminate food.

Incontestable/इन्कन्टेस्टेबल *(adjective)* - निर्विवाद

The authority of the manager in financial matters is incontestable.

Incontinence/इन्कन्टिनेंस *(noun)*- असंयम

The thing that he lags in is the incontinence of emotions.

Incontinent/इन्कन्टिनॅन्ट *(adj)* - असंयत, अपवित्र

The patient had the problem of having incontinent urination.

Inconvertibility/इन्कवर्टिबिलिटि *(noun)* - न बदलने जाने योग्य स्थिति

The first problem that I faced in the foreign country was the inconvertibility of currencies.

Inconvertible/इन्कन्वर्टबल *(adj)* - अपरिवर्तनीय, न बदलने योग्य

This is an inconvertible currency.

Incorrect/इन्करेक्ट *(adj)* - अनुचित, गलत

Your opinion is incorrect.

Incorrupt/इन्करप्ट *(adjective)* - पवित्र

There are only a few countries in the world that can be called incorrupt today.

Incorruptible/इन्करप्टिबल *(adj)* - अशोधनीय

The CEO was bragging about the incorruptible nature of his employees.

Incorruption/इन्करप्शन *(noun)* - शुद्धता

Today, incorruption is the biggest call of the day.

Increasing/इन्क्रिजिंग *(adjective)* - बढ़ने वाला

The ever increasing population has posed new threats to the society.

Incredibly/इन्क्रेडिब्ली *(adv)* - अविश्वास से

The man in the movie was flying at an incredibly high speed.

Incredulity/इन्क्रेडुलिटी *(noun)* - अविश्वास

As they saw a giant bird in the sky, their eyes were wide opened with incredulity.

Incremation/इन्क्रेमेशन *(noun)* - दाह कर्म

With the setting of the sun, the incremation of the lady was over.

Increment/इन्क्रिमेंट *(noun)* - बढ़ती

I am expecting a good increment this year.

Incrimination/इन्क्रिमिनेशन *(noun)* - अभियोग

He did not know how to free her from the incrimination charges.

Incrust/इन्क्रस्ट *(verb)* - पपड़ी चढ़ाना

The pot was incrusted with a metallic alloy.

Inculcate/इन्कल्केट *(verb)* - शिक्षा देना

A good teacher inculcates good values in the minds of his students.

Incubator/इन्क्यूबेटर् *(noun)* - अंडे सेने की मशीन

During our visit to the laboratory, we were allowed to see incubators.

Inculpable/इन्कल्पेबल *(adj)* - दोष रहित

The man was declared to be inculpable and was set free.

Inculpate/इन्कल्पेट *(verb)* - दोष लगाना

It was not fair to inculpate his colleague without any concrete proof.

Inculpation/इन्कल्पेशन *(noun)* - निन्दा

His inculpation caused a stir in the film fraternity.

Inculpatory/इनकल्पटरी *(adjective)* - निन्दासूचक

An inculpatory system within the office was hard to bear.

Incumbent/इन्कम्बेंट *(noun & adj)* - वृत्तिभोगी

The help that we were offering them was seen as incumbent on us.

Incur/इनकर *(verb)* - कष्ट उठाना

The company incurred huge losses during the last fiscal year.

I

Incuriosity/इनक्यूरिऑसिटि *(noun)* - कुतुहल का अभाव

The child's incuriosity to the objects around him worried his parents.

Incurious/इन्क्यूरिअस *(adjective)* - अनुत्सुक

After observing them for a long time, it was clear that they had incurious minds.

Incursion/इन्करसन *(noun)* - चढ़ाई

The kingdom had to face a sudden incursion from the neighbouring state.

Incurve/इन्कर्व *(verb)* - भीतर मोड़ना

The bottles were incurved to give the desired shapes.

Incuse/इन्क्यूज *(verb)* - ठप्पा लगाना

All the old coins had incused designs on them.

Indecent/इन्डीसॅन्ट *(adjective)* - अश्लील

One should not tolerate any indecent behaviour at work place.

Indecision/इन्डिसिजन् *(noun)* - दुविधा

My sister's indecision delayed her engagement.

Indecisive/इन्डिसाइसिव *(adjective)* - अनिश्चित

The indecisive Cabinet Ministers could not reach any agreement.

Indeclinable/इनडिक्लाइनॅबॅल *(adjective)* - अव्यय, अविकारी

What we were taught in the class was the perfect example of indeclinable words.

I

Indecorous/इन्डेकॅरॅस *(adjective)* - अनुचित
She hated indecorous remarks from his senior.

Indecorum/इन्डिकॉरम *(noun)* - असभ्य व्यवहार
The indecorum at the award function raised a few eyebrows.

Indeed/इनडीड *(avberb)* - सचमुच
He was, indeed, a good friend of mine.

Indefectible/इन्डिफेक्टिबॅल *(adjective)* - अचूक
The company has guaranteed its products to be indefectible.

Indefensible/इन्डिफेन्सिबल *(adjective)* - अरक्षणीय
His case was an indefensible case.

Indefinite/इन्डेफिनिट *(adjective)* - अनिश्चित
The workers have gone on an indefinite strike.

Indeliberate/इन्डिलिबॅरिट *(adj)* - अविवेचित
What the employees were facing was the indeliberate result of the CEO's new plan.

Indelibility/इनडेलिबिलिटि *(noun)* - अक्षयता
The indelibility of the scars was a source of everlasting torture to her.

Indelicate/इन्डेलिकेट *(adjective)* - फूहड़
The mother was criticized for her indelicate behaviour towards her children.

Indemnification/इन्डेम्निफिकेशन *(noun)* - क्षतिपूर्ति
The process of indemnification was complete within a week.

Indemnify/इन्डेम्निफाइ *(verb)* - बदला चुकाना
Due to the pressure from victim's side, the authorities were forced to indemnify him.

Indemnity/इन्डेम्निटी *(noun)* - जमानत
We did not know whether he should be provided with indemnity or not.

Indenture/इन्डेंचर *(noun)* - इकारनामा
The two parties were given indentures of mutual agreement.

Independence/इन्डिपेंडेंस *(noun)* - आजादी
Some of the African countries got their independence very late.

Independent/इन्डिपेन्डेन्ट *(adjective)* - स्वाधीन
The social committee set up last year works as an independent body.

Indescribable/इन्डिसक्राइबॅबॅल *(adj)* - अकथनीय
The incident was so shocking that it remains indescribable for me till date.

Indestructibility/इन्डिस्ट्रक्टिबिलिटि *(noun)*- अविनाशिता
The original theory of the indestructibility of an atom was refuted by the later scientists.

Indestructible/इन्डिस्ट्रक्टिबल *(adjective)*- अविनाशी
The universe is indestructible.

Indeterminable/इनडिटरमिनेबल *(adj)* - अनिर्णेय
The insufficient data could only lead to indeterminable results.

Indeterminate/इनडिटरमिनेट *(adjective)* - अनिश्चित
The underlying cause of his cancer remained indeterminate to doctors.

Indifferent/इन्डिफरेन्ट *(adjective)* - उदासीन
The people at high positions usually have an indifferent attitude to their employees.

Indigestion/इनडाइजेशन *(noun)* - स्वदेशीय
I am suffering from indigestion from past several days.

Indigestive/इनडिजेस्टिव *(adjective)* - अपच
Cellulose is indigestive to human intestines.

Indignant/इनडिग्नॅन्ट *(adjective)* - रुष्ट, क्रुद्ध
The people were indignant over the killing of a young man.

Indignation/इन्डिग्नेशन *(noun)* - रोष, क्रोध
The residents showed their indignation over the killing incident.

Indignity/इन्डिग्निटी *(noun)* - अनादर, अपमान
No woman can tolerate any type of indignity meted out to her.

Indirect/इन्डिरेक्ट *(adjective)* - अप्रत्यक्ष
There is an indirect connection between two power grids.

Indirection/इन्डिरेक्शन *(noun)* - छलकपट
It was due to his indirection that his team members remained confused.

Indiscernible/इन्डिसॅर्नबॅल *(adjective)* - अगोचर
The presence of fog was making the scenery indiscernible.

Indiscipline/इन्डिसिप्लिन *(noun)* - अनुशासनहीनता
Principal said, "No kind of indiscipline shall be tolerated within the school premises."

Indiscrete/इन्डिस्क्रीट *(adjective)* - अभिभक्त
This novel does not have any indiscrete chapters.

Indiscretion/इन्डिस्क्रेशन *(noun)* – अविचार
Indiscretion has always been his weakness.

Indiscriminate/इन्डिस्क्रिमिनेट *(adj)*– अव्यवस्थित
He is habitual to the indiscriminate use of pills.

Indispose/इन्डिस्पोज *(verb)* – विमुख करना
Negative thinking can indispose a person of his sanity.

Indisposition/इन्डिस्पोजिशन *(noun)* – अस्वस्थता, अरुचि
My mother was admitted to hospital when she complained of indisposition.

Indisputable/इन्डिस्प्युटेबल *(adjective)* – निर्विवाद
He thought that only he was the indisputable heir to the property.

Indissolubly/इन्डिसोल्यूब्ली *(adverb)* – अविच्छेद्यता के साथ
The unions worked indissolubly to have their demands met.

Indistinguishable/इन्डिस्टिंग्विशबॅल *(adjective)* – पृथक् न किये जाने योग्य
There are animals that can change their colour to make their skin indistinguishable from their backgrounds.

Indite/इन्डाइट *(verb)* – लिखना
The writer made it a habit to indite daily.

Indivertible/इन्डायवर्टिबल *(adj)* – न हटाने योग्य
The heavy weight of the crane was making it almost indivertible.

Individual/इन्डिविजुअल *(adjective)* – अकेला
It is not possible to take care of the individual needs of all the employees.

Individually/इन्डिविड्यूअलि *(adv)* – अलग-अलग
The parents were supposed to meet the teachers individually.

Indivisibility/इन्डिविजिबिलिटि *(adj)* – अविभाज्यता
The indivisibility of atom was refuted by many scientists.

Indo/इन्डो *(combining form)* – 'भारतीय' अर्थ का उपसर्ग
The Indo-Aryans came to settle in the country.

Indocile/इन्डोसाइल *(adj)* – अविनीत या अशिक्ष्य
Her husband's indocile nature caused many problems.

Indocility/इन्डोसिलिटि *(noun)* – दुर्गमता
His indocility was a matter of concern to everyone.

Indolence/इन्डोलेंस *(noun)* – सुस्ती
His mother said, "Your indolence will not take you anywhere."

Indomitable/इन्डॉमिटेबल *(adjective)* – दुर्दमनीय
The king fortified his kingdom so well that it became indomitable by other states.

Indubitable/इन्ड्यूबिटॅबॅल *(adjective)* – निश्चित
His sincerity towards work is indubitable.

Induce/इन्ड्युस *(verb)* – बहकाना
Workers were induced to extend their working hours.

Induct/इन्डक्ट *(verb)* – प्रवेश कराना, भर्ती करना
After an initial training for six months, the soldiers were finally inducted into the army.

Inductor/इन्डक्टर *(noun)* – बिजली के यन्त्र का एक भाग
We were attending a special class on inductors and their properties.

Indulge/इन्डल्ज *(verb)* – लगना, प्रसन्न करना
After his exams were over, he indulged himself in partying day and night.

Indulgence/इन्डल्जेंस *(noun)* – आसक्ति
His indulgence into the luxuries of life took a toll of his bank balance.

Indurative/इन्ड्यूरेटिव *(adj)* – ठोस बनाने वाला
The hot weather made the soil too indurative to plough.

Industrial/इन्डस्ट्रियल *(adjective)* – उद्योग-सम्बन्धी
There are many uses of the industrial oil.

Industrious/इन्डस्ट्रियस *(adjective)* – उद्योगी
People living in mountainous areas are known to be very industrious.

Industry/इन्डस्ट्रि *(noun)* – उद्योग, परिश्रम
There has been a big boom in fishery industry this year.

Inebriety/इनीब्राइटि *(noun)* – मतवालापन, मस्ती
He was carried to his home in the state of inebriety.

Inedible/इनएडिबल *(adjective)* – न खाने योग्य
Some of the mushrooms are inedible.

Inedited/इनएडिटेड *(adj)* – अप्रकाशित, असम्पादित
The work by me remained inedited for a long time.

Ineffable/इनएफॅबल *(adjective)* – अवर्णनीय

We were thrilled to see the ineffable beauty of the nature.

Ineffably/इनएफब्लि *(adverb)* – अवर्णनीय रूप में

We were ineffably weak to say anything.

Ineffaceable/इन-इफेसबल् *(adjective)* – अमिट

The bad effects of pollution are almost ineffaceable.

Inefficacious/इनएफिकेशस् *(adjective)* – निरर्थक

The scientists' efforts had become inefficacious at that point of time.

Inefficacy/इनएफिकॅसि *(noun)* – व्यर्थता

The inefficacy of the old machines stalled the production rate.

I

Inefficiency/इन्-एफिशंशि *(noun)* – अयोग्यता

No company wants to hire people carrying inefficiency.

Inefficient/इन्-एफिशन्ट् *(adjective)* – अयोग्य

As the time passed, he came to know that his team is inefficient in delivery desired results.

Inelastic/इन्-इलैस्टिक *(adjective)* – अनम्य, चीमड़

The spring was stretched so many times that it eventually became inelastic.

Inelegance/इनएलिगॅन्स *(noun)* – सुन्दरता की कमी

The tourists were roaming about in a castle that had now acquired inelegance.

Ineloquent/इनइलोक्वेंट *(noun)* – अवाग्मी

The girl was not happy to find that her groom was ineloquent.

Ineptly/इनएप्टलि *(adverb)* – मूर्खता से

She handled the situation quiet ineptly.

Inequality/इनिक्वालिटि *(noun)* – विषमता

During my visit to the foreign country, I noticed the inequality with which poor people were treated.

Inequitable/इनइक्विटेब्ल *(adj)* – न्याय विरुद्ध

None of us was happy with the inequitable distribution of company's profit.

Inequity/इनइक्विटी *(noun)* – अन्याय

As a woman, she had to face the inequity of the justice.

Inescapable/इनेस्केपेबल *(noun)* – न भागने योग्य

The presence of heavy gases was making the balloon inescapable.

Inessential/इनएसेन्सियल *(adjective)* – अनावश्यक

After having repeated discussions, the topic is now inessential to be discussed again.

Inestimable/इनएस्टिमॅबॅल *(adjective)* – अमूल्य

Calculating the exact age of the fossils is an inestimable thing.

Inevitably/इनएविटब्लि *(adverb)* – अनिवार्य

Their end was inevitably coming.

Inexact/इनिग्जैक्ट *(adjective)* – अवश्य, अयथार्थ

The number of coins recovered from the site is still inexact.

Inexecutable/एनिक्सेक्युटेबल *(adjective)* – जो पूर्ण न किया जा सके

There was a serious glitch that had made the programme inexecutable.

Inexorably/इन्एक्सरब्लि *(adv)* – कठोरता से

Most of the time, things were going on inexorably.

Inexpectant/एन्-एक्सपेक्टैन्ट *(noun)* – निराश

It was inexpectant that he would arrive at such an odd hour.

Inexepediency/इनएक्पेडिएन्सी *(noun)* – अयोग्यता

What we were worried about was the inexpediency of the project.

Inexpendient/इनएक्पेडिएन्ट *(adjective)* – अनुचित

The proposal by the committee member seems to be inexpedient.

Inexplosive/इनएक्सप्लोसिव *(adj)* – न भभकने योग्य

It came to light that the material placed in the room was inexplosive.

Inexpressive/इनएक्सप्रेसिव *(adjective)* – वर्णन न करने योग्य

The model was not fit for acting as she had an inexpressive face.

Inextricable/इनएक्सट्रिकेबल *(adj)* – न सुलझाने योग्य

He was trying to separate the inextricable wires.

Infallible/इन्फैलिबल *(adjective)* – अमोघ

His clever mind makes him an infallible guy.

Infamize/इनफेमाइज *(verb)* – बदनाम करना

The allegation by the girl was enough to infamize the guy.

Infamy/इनफेमी *(noun)* - कलंक

To avoid facing infamy, he secluded himself from the society.

Infant/इन्फैंट *(noun)* - शिशु

He was still an infant when his mother passed away.

Infantile/इन्फैंटाइल *(adjective)* - शिशु-सम्बन्धी

The doctor got his specialization in treating infantile diseases.

Infantry/इन्फैंट्री *(noun)* - पैदल सेना

A huge infantry was prepared to take part in the war.

Infeasible/इन्फिजिबल *(adjective)* - दुष्कर

Though very useful, his plan seems to be infeasible.

Infection/इन्फेक्शन *(noun)* - संक्रामक रोग

The infection was controlled by administering a set of antibiotics.

Infelicitous/इन्फिलिसिटस् *(adjective)* - असुखकर

The patients were susceptible to the infectious disease.

Infelicity/इन्फिलिसिटि *(noun)* - अनुपयुक्तता

I had not expected such an infelicity from him.

Inferable/इन्फरेबल *(adjective)* - तर्कसाध्य, अनुमेय

The conclusion was inferable from the results of the experiment.

Inference/इन्फरेंस *(noun)* - निष्कर्ष, अनुमान

After much experimentation, the scientists, finally, reached upon an inference.

Interiority/इन्फिरिआरिटि *(noun)* - हीनता

After being rejected by all her friends, her inferiority made her live in reclusion.

Infernal/इन्फर्नल *(adjective)* - नारकीय

The place was so bad that it gave us the feeling of an infernal world.

Inferno/इन्फर्नो *(noun)* - पाताल

Before the deadly inferno could be controlled, 5 shops were already gutted in it.

Infertile/इन्फर्टाइल *(adjective)* - अनुपजाऊ

The infertile pigs were sent to the laboratory for some possible treatment.

Infinite/इन्फिनिट *(adjective)* - अपरिमित

Today, we are going to study about the infinite space that we live in.

Infinitesimal/इनफिनिटेसिमल *(adjective)* - अतिसूक्ष्म

The infinitesimal particles cannot be seen with naked eyes.

Infinitive/इनफिनिटिव *(noun)* - अपरिमित

Tomorrow, the English teacher will take class on infinitive clauses.

Infinitude/इनफिनिट्यूड *(noun)* - अपारता

The space is known for its infinitude.

Infinity/इनफिनिटि *(noun)* - अनन्तता

The amount of food required to feed all the poor in the world amounts to infinity.

Infirm/इन्फर्म *(adjective)* - दुर्बल

With time, a person becomes more and more infirm.

I

Infirmity/इन्फर्मिटि *(noun)* - दुर्बलता

In old age, people have to deal with infirmity of their bodies and mind.

Infix/इन्फिक्स *(verb)* - बैठाना

After his fracture, a rod was infixed in his leg.

Inflammation/इन्फ्लेमेशन *(noun)* - ताप, सूजन

To reduce the inflammation, he was kept on antibiotics.

Inflator/इन्फ्लेटर *(noun)* - फुलाने वाला

An inflator was used to swell the balloons.

Inflect/इन्फ्लेक्ट *(verb)* - मोड़ना

The form of the word can be changed by inflecting it with affixes.

Inflexibility/इन्फ्लेक्सिबिलिटि *(noun)* - कठोरता

The inflexibility of hours at work place is a cause of concern for many employees.

Inflexibly/इन्फ्लेक्सिब्ली *(adverb)* - दृढ़ता से

He is comfortable to work inflexibly.

Inflict/इन्फ्लिक्ट *(verb)* - दण्ड देना

The criminals inflicted grave injuries to the victim.

Infliction/इन्फ्लिक्शॅन *(noun)* - दण्ड

He had no intention to cause infliction of any kind to anyone.

Inflictor/इन्फ्लिक्टर *(noun)* - दण्ड देने वाला

After causing serious injuries to the victim, the inflictors ran away.

Inflow/इनफ्लो *(noun)*– भीतर के बहाव
Many rivers have an inflow directed from west to east direction.

Influence/इन्फ्ल्अुअंस *(noun)* – प्रभाव, असर
Teachings of Swami Vivekananda have had a great influence on me.

Infoliate/इनफोलिएट *(verb)* – पत्तियों से ढाँकना
The area was first covered with soil and then infoliated.

Inform/इनफॉर्म *(verb)* – सूचित करना
Why didn't you inform me about your ill health?

Informal/इनफॉर्मल *(adjective)* – अनौपचारिक
They decided to meet for an informal meeting.

I

Informaliity/इन्फार्मैलिटि *(noun)* – अनौपचारिकता
It was good that they gave consent to treat each other with informality.

Informatory/इन्फॉर्मेटॅरि *adjective)* – सूचना युक्त
When everyone was gone, the CEO got engaged in an informatory talk with his manager.

Infrequency/इनफ्रिक्वेंसी *(noun)* – अनित्यता
One thing for which he is known is the infrequency with which he comes to college.

Infrugal/इनफ्रुगल *(adj)* – अमितत्व्ययी
Man's infrugal ways cost him dear.

Infuriate/इनफ्यूरिएट *(verb)* – क्रुद्ध करना
He infuriated his senior by being absent from the meeting.

Infusion/इनफ्यूजन *(noun)* – काढ़ा
The hermit gave us an infusion to drink.

Ingathering/इनगैदरिंग *(noun)* – खलिहान
An ingathering of people had blocked the way.

Ingenious/इन्जीनिअस् *(adj)* – विदग्ध, प्रवीण, उम्दा
His ingenious ways have always surprised us.

Ingenuity/इन्जीन्युइटि *(noun)* – विदग्धता, पटुता
It is the ingenuity that makes a person stand out from the rest.

Ingenuous/इन्जेन्युअस *(adjective)* – मायाहीन
The cops were surprised to see how ingenuous the suspect was.

Ingestion/इन्जेशन *(noun)* – अन्तर्ग्रहण
The ingestion of food takes place in mouth cavity.

Ingestive/इनजेस्टिव *(adj)* – पेट भरने योग्य
The ingestive process in plants takes place via roots.

Ingoing/इनगोइंग *(adjective)* – भीतर प्रवेश करने वाला
The ingoing moth into the hole was injured.

Ingrain/इनग्रेन *(verb)* – डुबोना, बोरना
The moral values were ingrained in his mind since childhood.

Ingrained/इनग्रेन्ड *(adjective)* – गहरा, पक्का
The ingrained values in a person help in shaping up his personality.

Ingrate/इनग्रेट *(noun)* – कृतघ्न मनुष्य
He, being an ingrate, did not thank me for all the help that I provided.

Ingredient/इनग्रेडिएण्ट *(noun)* – अंश
I used only a few ingredients to prepare the dish.

Ingress/इनग्रेस *(noun)* – प्रवेश का अधिकार
The prevention of the ingress of the infection into the wound was the main focus of the doctors.

Ingurgitate/इन्गर्जिटेट *(adjective)* – लालच से भकोसना
His habit to ingurgitate is very bad.

Inherent/इन्हीअरन्ट *(adjective)* – स्वाभाविक
There are too many traditions that are inherent in Indian culture.

Inhospitality/इन्हॉस्पिटलिटि *(noun)* – अनादार
His inhospitality irks me.

Inimical/इनिमिकल *(adjective)* – विरोधी
Why is your behaviour so inimical all the time?

Inimitable/इनिमिटेबल *(adjective)* – अनुपम
The actor is known for his inimitable style.

Iniquitous/इनिक्विटॅस *(adjective)* – अधर्मी, पापी
When he could not be successful in other tricks, he turned iniquitous.

Iniquity/इनिक्विटी *(noun)* – दुराचार
We were not bothered by his iniquity.

Initiation/इनिसिएशन *(noun)* – दीक्षा संस्कार

On the very first day in college, we were called for an initiation session.

Initiative/इनिसिएटिव *(noun)* – सूत्रपात

Who will take the initiative now?

Initiatory/इनिसिएटरि *(adjective)* – प्रारम्भिक

The project is still in its initiatory phase.

Injudicious/इन्जुडिशस् *(adjective)* – विचारशून्य

We were not expecting such an injudicious act from him.

Injure/इनज्योर *(verb)* – हानि पहुँचाना

Two people were badly injured in the accident.

Injurious/इन्जूरिअस् *(adjective)* – हानि कारक

Thriving on too much alcohol can be injurious to one's health.

Injustice/इनजस्टिस *(noun)* – अन्याय

He had no idea how to deal with the injustice meted out to him.

Inkling/इन्कलिंग *(noun)* – संकेत

I had not the slightest inkling that she would betray me at such an hour.

Inland/इन्लैंड *(adjective & avberb)* – देश के भीतरी भाग का

We were thrilled to see a lovely inland there.

Inly/इन्लाइ *(avberb)* – हृदय में

Her inly feelings had gone strong.

Inlying/इन्लाइंग *(adjective)* – पड़ा हुआ

The inlying island was not very large.

Inmate/इन्मेट *(noun)* – निवासी

The inmates in my hospital room became life-long friends.

Inmost/इनमोस्ट *(adjective)* – अतिप्रिय

She asked, "What is your inmost desire?"

Innavigable/इन्नैविगेबल *(adj)* – अनौगम्य

The flood in the river makes it innavigable at the time of rainy season.

Innervate/इनर्वेट *(verb)* – उत्तेजित करना

The doctors were successful in innervating his legs.

Innocent/इनोसेंट *(adjective)* – निर्दोष

The lad's innocent behaviour melted down my anger.

Innocuous/इन्नोकुअस *(adjective)* – सीधा

His intentions are not as innocuous as it seems.

Innominate/इन्नामिनेट *(adj)* – बिना नाम का

I was talking to an innominate man.

Innovate/इन्नोवेट *(verb)* – नया सम्प्रदाय स्थापित करना

As the students of mechanical engineering, we were expected to innovate the existing models of machines.

Innovator/इनोवेटर *(noun)* – नयी रीति चलाने वाला

Albert Einstein was one of the best innovators of his times.

Innumerable/इन्यूमरेबल *(adjective)* – अनगिनत

I had innumerable berries in my lap.

Innutrition/इन्यूट्रिशन *(noun)* – पोषण का अभाव

The child was suffering from innutrition since his birth.

Inobservance/इन्अब्जर्वेन्स *(noun)* – ध्यानहीनता

Can't you mend your inobservance before initiating this project?

Inodorous/इन्ओडॅरॅस *(adjective)* – गन्धहीन

An inodorous gas present in the mine killed many workers.

Inofficious/इन्अफिशॅस *(noun)*– अनैतिक

He signed an inofficious will before dying.

Inoperative/इन्आपरेटिव *(adj)* – अकार्य-साधक

Half of the machines in the mill are inoperative.

Inopportune/इन्ऑपॅर्ट्यून *(adj)* – कुसमय का

I was irritated by his inopportune arrival to my office.

Inornate/इनऑरनेट *(adj)* – अविस्तृत

The building was an inornate one.

Inpouring/इनपोरिंग *(adj)* – भीतर की ओर गिरता हुआ

The inpouring water destroyed everything.

Inquietude/इनक्वाइएट्यूड *(noun)* – बेचैनी, अशान्ति

My sister complaintd of inquietude after a hectic day.

Inquire/इन्क्वायर *(verb)* – पता लगाना

The police inquired the local residents about the accident.

Inquiringly/इन्क्वायरिंगली *(adv)* - जाँचते हुए
He was asking inquiringly about the whole story.

Inquisitor/इनक्विजिटर *(noun)* - जाँच करने वाला
Everyone was annoyed by the irrelevant questions asked by the inquisitor.

Inquisitorial/इनक्विजिटोरियल *(adj)* - तहकीकात सम्बन्धी
His inquisitorial behaviour irked us too much.

Inrush/इनरश *(noun)* - भीतर की ओर तीव्र बहाव
The sudden inrush of water in the prison created frenzy everywhere.

Insalubrity/इनसैलुब्रिटी *(noun)* - अनारोग्य
His insalubrity make him leave his job.

I

Insanitary/इनसैनिटरी *(adjective)* - अस्वास्थ्यकर
Your insanitary habits put me off.

Insanity/इनसैनिटी *(noun)* - उन्माद
The old man had bouts of insanity all day.

Insatiable/इनसैटिएबल *(adjective)* - अति लोलुप
I have an insatiable hunger to learn psychiatry.

Insatiate/इनसैटिएट *(adj)* - असन्तुष्ट रहना
Desires of man can never be satiated.

Inscribable/इनस्क्राइबेब्ल *(adj)* - लिखने योग्य
The wooden block is inscribable.

Inscription/इन्सक्रिप्शन *(noun)* - लेख
King Asoka's inscriptions are etched on the pillars erected by him.

Insectarium/इन्सेक्टेरियम *(noun)* - कीड़े-मकोड़े का पालने का स्थान
It was all fun to visit the insectariums.

Insecticide/इन्सेक्टिसाइड *(noun)* - कृमिहत्या
The farmers were using excessive insecticides to prevent their crops from diseases.

Insectivorous/इन्सेक्टिवॅरॅस *(adj)* - कीट-भोजी
The insectivorous animals play a crucial role in the biological cycle.

Insectology/इन्सेक्टोलॅजि *(noun)* - कृमिशास्त्र
After passing out from school, she was looking forward to join a course on insectology.

Insecure/इन्सिक्योर *(adjective)* - असुरक्षित
We were talking about our insecure futures.

Insecurity/इन्सिक्योरिटि *(noun)* - संकट
I have no insecurities about my career.

Inseminate/इन्सेमिनेट *(verb)* - बीजारोपण करना
The goat was inseminated by a group of veterinary doctors.

Insensate/इन्सेन्सेट *(adjective)* - ज्ञानरहित
The patient's insensate limbs were showing a bit improvement.

Insensible/इन्सेन्सिबल *(adjective)* - चेतनाहीन
I met an insensible man on my way to office.

Insensitive/इन्सेन्सिटिव *(adjective)* - अचेतन
My senior's insensitive behaviou r towards me outs my mood off.

Insentient/इन्सेन्श्यन्ट् *(adjective)* - जीवरहित
The pig's insentient response was a cause of concern.

Inseverable/इन्सेवरेबल् *(adj)* - अविभेद्य
The two rocks had penetrated so deeply that they had become inseverable.

Insheathe/इनशीद् *(verb)* - मियान लगाना
The rods were insheathed inside the covering of concrete.

Inshore/इनशोर *(adjective)* - समुद्र के समीप
In this region, inshore fishing is done on a large scale.

Insight/इन्साइट *(noun)* - अन्तर्दृष्टि
In order to understand complex human behaviours, we need to develop an insight.

Insignificance/इन्सिग्नीफिकैन्स *(adj)* - तुच्छता
Let's ignore our insignificant problems as of now.

Insinuate/इन्सिन्युएट *(verb)* - धीरे-धीरे उसकाना
The dacoit was insinuated by his master to do the killing.

Insinuatingly/इनसिन्यूएटिंग्ली *(adv)* - उसकाते हुए
One of my cousins has the habit of talking insinuatingly in order to serve his means.

Insipient/इन्सिपिएण्ट *(noun)* - बुद्धिहीन
He was considered an insipient.

Insistent/इन्सिस्टेंट *(adj)* - आग्रही, हठी
Her insistent requests to do the appraisal were ignored by the authorities.

Insobriety/इन्सोब्राइटी *(noun)* - असंयम

It is dangerous to drive while in the state of insobriety.

Insolate/इन्सोलेट *(verb)* - धूप में सुखाना

During the day time, the damp clothes were insolated to ward off the moisture.

Insolence/इन्सोलेन्स *(noun)* - अविनय

Before I could tolerate more of his insolence, I left my job.

Insolent/इन्सोलेन्ट *(adjective)* - ढीठ

Her insolent answers created a bad impression on his seniors.

Insoluble/इन्सोल्युबल *(adjective)* - अघुलनशील

This is one of the insoluble riddles that I have ever come through.

Insolvable/इन्साल्वॅबॅल *(adj)* - व्याख्या न करने योग्य

The case's complexity has rendered it insolvable.

Insolvency/इन्सॉल्वन्सि *(noun)* - दिवाला

Even in the state of insolvency, my friend was looking forward to the luxuries of life.

Insolvent/इन्साल्वन्ट *(adjective)* - दिवालिया

The extravagancy turned the man into a pathetic insolvent.

Insomnia/इन्सॉम्निआ *(noun)* - अनिद्रा

This girl suffers from insomnia and depression.

Insomuch/इनसोमॅच *(avberb)* - यहाँ तक

We are addicted to the social networking sites insomuch that we feel pathetic without them.

Insouciance/इन्सूस्यॅन्स *(noun)* - असावधानी

Insouciance on part of parents can make their children become detached.

Inspect/इन्स्पेक्ट *(verb)* - परीक्षा करना

The microbiologist inspected the slide carefully.

Inspection/इन्स्पेक्शन *(noun)* - निरीक्षण

The quality manager was sent on a routine inspection to the godown.

Inspector/इन्स्पेक्टर *(noun)* - निरीक्षक

An inspector was on duty the day I joined the mill.

Inspectorial/इन्सपेक्टोरियल *(adjective)* - निरीक्षक सम्बन्धी

His inspectorial duties were assigned on the day of his joining.

Inspirator/इन्स्पिरेटर - प्रेरणा देने वाला, श्वास लेने का यन्त्र

My father has been my greatest inspirator in my life.

Inspiring/इन्सपायरिंग *(adjective)* - उत्तेजक

The children were listening to the inspiring stories narrated by their teacher.

Inspirit/इनस्पिरिट *(verb)* - साहस देना

The saint inspirited our souls.

Inspissate/इन्सपिसेट *(verb)* - गाढ़ा करना

The sugar solution was inspissated and added to the paste.

Instability/इनस्टिबिलिटी *(noun)* - अस्थिरता

The instability of the wooden stand made me fall on the ground.

Instable/इनस्टेबल *(adj)* - चंचल

A man with an instable mind was roaming on road.

Installation/इन्स्टालेशन *(noun)* - प्रतिस्थापन, अभिषेक

The installation of electric wires took a week.

Installed/इन्स्टाल्ड - स्थापित

The electrician said, "I have installed the electric meter."

Instalment/इन्स्टालमेंट *(noun)* - किस्त

We have already paid this month's instalment of house rent.

Instance/इन्सटांस *(noun)* - दृष्टान्त

It was the first instance that a child was presented as a witness to the case.

Instancy/इन्स्टॅन्सि *(noun)* - जरूरत

It was due to an instancy at office that we stayed there till midnight.

Instantly/इन्स्टैन्टलि *(adverb)* - तुरन्त, तत्काल

The student replied instantly, "I have completed the project."

Instate/इन्स्टेट *(verb)* - स्थापित करना, रखना

After intervention of authorities, the peace was instated in our area.

I

Instead/इन्स्टेड *(avberb)* – बदले में

We were hoping promotions; instead, we were given performance bonuses.

Instinct/इन्स्टिंक्ट *(noun)* – अन्तर्जात प्रवृत्ति

To seek the company of others is the human's basic instinct.

Institutor/इन्स्टिट्यूटर *(noun)* – आरम्भ करने वाला

The man in news is the institutor of Nano technology in our company.

Instructor/इन्सट्रक्टर *(noun)* – अध्यापक, गुरु

My yoga instructor has left for the U.S.A.

Instrumentality/इन्स्टुमेंटैलिटि *(noun)* – कारणत्व

The instrumentality of the protests in amending juvenile law is appreciable.

I

Instrumentally/इन्सट्रुमेंटलि *(adv)* – विधि द्वारा

He has contributed instrumentally well for the two parties.

Instrumentation/इन्सट्रुमेंटेशन *(noun)* – बाजे पर गीत का प्रबन्ध

The instrumentation of all the pieces was yet to be decided.

Insubstantial/इन्सब्स्टैन्शल *(adjective)* – अवास्तविक

This proposal seems to be an insubstantial to our company.

Insufferable/इन्सफरेबल *(adjective)* – घमण्डी

The man's saga of insufferable tortures moved me a lot.

Insufficiency/इन्सफिसिएन्सी *(noun)* – कमी

Many parts of the country still have the insufficiency of food grains.

Insufflate/इन्सफ्लेट *(verb)* – हवा भरना

An oxygen pump insufflated air into the mouth of the patient.

Insulting/इन्सल्टिंग *(adjective)* – अपमानकारी

What an insulting remark he has made!

Insuperable/इन्सपरेबल *(adjective)* – दुस्तर

The insuperable conditions forced us to leave the place.

Insupportable/इन्सपोर्ट्-एबल *(adj)* – न सहने योग्य

He was banking on an insupportable theory.

Insurable/इन्श्योरेबल् *(adj)* – बीमा कराने योग्य

The house that I purchased recently is insurable.

Insurant/इन्श्योरेन्ट *(noun)* – जीवन बीमा कराने वाला

All the insurants who had grievances gathered in the compound.

Insure/इन्श्योर *(verb)* – नाश के निवारण के लिए बीमा करना

Our company insures employees against the loss of property and life.

Insurgency/इनसरजेंसी *(noun)* – राजद्रोह

During insurgency, the government banned the use of social media sites.

Insuregent/इनसरजेंट *(adjective)* – राजद्रोही

The insurgent attacks have turned more violent recently.

Insurmountable/इनसरमाउंटेबल *(adj)* – अविजेय

We are facing insurmountable problems at our work place.

Insusceptible/इन्ससेप्टिबल *(adjective)* – विकारहीन

The Principal gave us an unsusceptible proposition.

Intaglio/इन्टैल्यो *(noun)* – नकाशी का काम

What we were looking at were the fascinating designs of intaglios.

Integral/इन्टिग्रल *(adjective)* – सम्पूर्ण

Democracy is integral to our nation.

Integrator/इन्टिग्रेटर *(noun)* – पूरक, समाकलक

In our higher classes, we were taught about integrator functions.

Integrity/इन्टेग्रिटि *(noun)* – स्थिरता

He is truly a man of integrity.

Intellection/इन्टिलेक्शन *(noun)* – विचारण, बुद्धि व्यापार

The presentation of a concept makes the intellection an easy thing.

Intellectual/इन्टेलेक्चुअल *(adjective)* – मानसिक बुद्धि सम्बन्धी

An interview tests your intellectual abilities along with the others qualities.

Intellectuality/इन्टेलेक्चुअलिटी *(noun)* – बुद्धिमानी

His intellectuality was put to test when he was asked to choose between two solutions.

Intellectually/इन्टेलेक्चुअली *(adv)* – बुद्धिमानी से

If it is to be chosen intellectually, my vote would go to my reporting manager.

Intelligibility/इन्टेलिजिबिलिटी *(noun)*– चतुराई

There are times where your intelligibility is put to test.

Intemperance/इन्टेम्परैंस *(noun)* – असंयम

His intemperance to boozing has been his biggest weakness.

Intend/इन्टेन्ड *(verb)* – इरादा करना

My sister intends to clear IAS examination this year.

Intendment/इन्टेन्डमेंट *(noun)* – अभिप्राय

The intendment of the new law was to benefit all the citizens.

Intensity/इन्टेन्सिटी *(noun)* – तीव्रता

The rainfall's intensity has decreased over the years.

Intensive/इन्टेन्सिव *(adjective)* – गहन, बलदायक

An intensive regime was suggested to him by his trainers.

Intention/इन्टेन्शन *(noun)* – आशय

He had no intention of marrying her.

Intentional/इन्टेशनल *(adjective)* – इच्छानुरूप

All his flattering was intentional.

Intently/इन्टेन्टलि *(adverb)* – निष्ठापूर्वक

We were listening to our teacher intently.

Inter/इन्टर *(verb)* – गाड़ना

After all the rituals were over, he was interred.

Interblend/इन्टर्ब्लेंड *(verb)* – परस्पर मिलाना

The painter interblended the four colours to form a unique shade.

Interbreed/इन्टर्ब्रीड *(verb)* – भिन्न जातियों के पशु का जोड़ा मिलाना

The scientists have been successful in interbreeding of species.

Intercept/इन्टर्सेप्ट *(verb)* – अवरोध करना

The criminals were intercepted to enter the office.

Interception/इन्टर्सेप्शन *(noun)* – अवरोधन

The interception of phone calls was initiated today.

Interceptive/इन्टर्सेप्टिव *(noun)* – विघ्नकारक

The interceptive phone calls were the only way cops could reach him.

Interchange/इन्टर्चेंज *(verb)* – परस्पर बदलना

Soon after the teacher ordered, the two friends interchanged their seats.

Intercolonial/इन्टर्कलोनिअल् *(adjective)* – भिन्न प्रदेशों में रहने वाला

With intercolonial discussions going on, people had to just wait and watch.

Intercommunion/इन्टर्कम्यूनियन *(noun)* – आपस का मेल

The discussions were going on to decide the place for the holy intercommunion.

Intercourse/इन्टर्कोर्स *(noun)* – बीच में होने वाली घटना, कामक्रीड़ा

It was at the end of the intercourse that the final decision was taken place.

Intercurrence/इन्टर्करेंस *(noun)* – बीच में होने वाली घटना

The intercurrence of the events was a regular thing in that area.

Intercurrent/इन्टर्करेन्ट *(adj)* – रुक-रुक कर होने वाली

The doctors were worried about the intercurrent disease that too had developed in her body.

Interdependent/इन्टर्डिपेंडेन्ट *(adj)* – परस्पर आश्रयभूत होना

It took a while for us to understand that the two factors were interdependent.

Interdiction/इन्टर्डिक्सन *(noun)* – अवरोध

The court ordered for the interdiction of illicit drugs.

Interdictory/इन्टर्डिक्टरी *(adj)* – निषेध करने वाला

The interdictory order prevented them from participating in future sacraments.

Interested/इन्टरेस्टेड *(adj)* – दिलचस्पी लेने वाला

Are you still interested in this work?

Interesting/इन्टरेस्टिंग *(adjective)* – रुचिकर

The movie was an interesting combination of action and comedy.

Interference/इन्टरफिअरेंस *(noun)* – विघ्न

His constant interference in my matters always puts me off.

I

Interferer/इन्टर्फिअरर *(noun)* – बाधा डालने वाला, दखल देने वाला
What an interferer he is!

Interfering/इन्टर्फिअरिंग *(adj)* – टाँग अड़ाने वाला
I don't like her because she is an interfering busy body.

Interfluent/इन्टर्फ्लुएन्ट *(adj)* – मध्यस्रावी
The directions in which the two rivers flow eventually makes them interfluent.

Interfuse/इन्टफ्यूज *(verb)* – परस्पर मिलाना
The writer interfused his two articles.

Intergrowth/इन्टर्ग्रोथ *(noun)* – एक साथ उत्पत्ति
The microbiologist noticed a green intergrowth in the algae.

I

Interim/इन्टरिम *(noun)* – बीच का समय
Today, the interim budget was presented in the parliament.

Interior/इन्टिरिअर *(adjective)* – भीतरी
A lovely interior made me buy this house.

Interjacent/इन्टर्जेसेंट *(adj)* – बिचला
The Interjacent Island was a place worth seeing.

Interject/इन्टर्जेक्ट *(verb)* – बीच में टोकना, बोलना
The man interjected and stopped us from any further discussion.

Interjection/इन्टर्जेक्शन *(noun)* – विस्मयादिवोधक शब्द
Lately, I am working on interjections.

Interjectional/इन्टरजेक्शनल *(adj)* – उद्गार सम्बन्धी
I was asked by my teacher to avoid using too much of interjectional words.

Interlinear/इन्टर्लिनिअर *(adjective)* – पंक्तियों के बीच में लिखा हुआ
Look at the interlinear sentences and try to understand their relation to the text.

Interlink/इन्टर्लिंक *(verb)* – कड़ियों से जोड़ना
The mechanic interlinked a series of small chains to form a long one.

Interlocution/इन्टर्लोक्यूशन *(noun)* – वार्तालाप, संवाद
The land is an interlocation between the two islands.

Intermeddle/इन्टर्मेडल *(verb)* – हस्तक्षेप करना
One of the worst habits that one can have is to intermeddle.

Intermediate/इन्टर्मीडिएट *(adjective)* – बिचवई
The best option was to stop at some intermediate place before travelling any further.

Intermediation/इन्टर्मेडिएशन *(noun)* – मध्यस्थता
It was his maturity and experience that he was chosen for intermediation.

Interment/इन्टर्मेन्ट् *(noun)* – मुर्दा गाड़ना
As the king reached there, the interment had already taken place.

Intermigration/इन्टर्माइग्रेशन *(noun)* – दो प्रदेशों के निवासी का स्थान परिवर्तन
An intermigration of the tribes resulted in mixing of their cultures.

Intermingle/इन्टर्मिंगल *(verb)* – मिलाना
As time passed on, the cultures intermingled and exchanged their traditions.

Intermission/इन्टर्मिशन *(noun)* – रुकावट
During the intermission, my friend went out for ordering some food for us.

Intermittence/इन्टर्मिटेंस – अंतर्विराम
What bothers them is the intermittence of the money inflow.

Intermittent/इन्टर्मिटेंट *(adjective)* – सविराम या अँतरिया
The intermittent flow of money does not allow him to be extravagant.

Intermix/इन्टर्मिक्स *(verb)* – आपस में मिलना या मिलाना
All the pastes were intermixed in a bowl.

Intern/इन्टर्न *(noun)* – अंतरंग डाक्टर
I am looking for a company where I can get training as an intern.

Internee/इन्टर्नि *(noun)* – नजरबन्द
Every internee was ready for his portfolio.

Internment/इन्टर्नमेंट *(noun)* – सीमित स्थान में नजरबन्दी
After finishing my internment, I am planning to settle abroad.

Internal/इन्टर्नल् *(adjective)* – आन्तरिक
The internal affairs of the company are to be kept secret.

International/इन्टर्नैश्नल् *(adjective)* – अन्तर्राष्ट्रीय
The United Nations works at an international level.

Internationalize/इन्टर्नैशनलाइज *(verb)* – अन्तर्राष्ट्रीय बनाना
There was no need to internationalize this news.

Internecine/इन्टर्नीसाइन *(adj)* – परस्पर विनाशकारी
For years, the countries were part of internecine wars.

Interosculate/इन्टर्आस्क्यूलेट *(verb)* – परस्पर मेल कराना
The biologists have made extensive researches to understand why many plants interosculate.

Interplace/इन्टर्प्लेस *(verb)* – बीच में रखना
A table was interplaced between two beds.

Interplay/इन्टर्प्ले *(noun)* – दो पदार्थों की पारस्परिक क्रिया
I am trying to understand the interplay of the musical instruments.

Interposition/इन्टर्पोजिशन् *(noun)* – व्यवधान
Doctors are working on the interposition of a chip between two valves.

Interpret/इन्टर्प्रेट् *(verb)* – मतलब बताना
What he interpreted was not very correct.

Interpretation/इन्टर्प्रिटेशन *(noun)* – व्याख्या
I am in need of an interpretation of this page.

Interpreter/इन्टर्प्रेटर *(noun)* – व्याख्या करने वाला
An interpreter was hired to translate from German into English.

Interpretress/इन्टरप्रेटेश – व्याख्या करने वाली स्त्री
She is an interpretess of German to English.

Interregnum/इन्टरेग्नम *(noun)* – राज्य का राजा से खाली रहने का काल
The news about an interregnum in the state was no surprise to me.

Interrelation/इन्टर्रिलेशन – पारस्परिक सम्बन्ध
What is the interrelation between two concepts?

Interrogate/इन्टरॅगेट *(adjective)* – प्रश्न करना
The teacher asked us to frame an interrogative sentence.

Interrogative/इन्टरॅगेटिव *(adj)* – प्रश्नार्थक
It is your interrogative gesture/remark.

Interrupt/इन्टरप्ट *(verb)* – रोकना
The way he was interrupting us again and again forced us to send him away.

Interrupted/इन्टरप्टेड *(adj)* – रुका हुआ
The execution of the programme got interrupted due to a wrong instruction.

Interrupter/इन्टरप्टर *(noun)* – विघ्न डालने वाला
I had to act as an interrupter to stop their argument.

Interruption/इन्टरप्शन *(noun)* – अवरोध
The regular interruption of the programme has spoiled my mood.

Interruptive/इन्टरप्टिव *(adj)* – विघ्न कारक
The interruptive ways of the person cost him dear.

Intersect/इन्टर्सेक्ट *(verb)* – दो टुकड़े करना
A pole was erected at the place where the roads intersected each other.

Intersection/इन्टरसेक्शन *(noun)* – कटाव
Just reach the intersection and turn left.

Interspersion/इन्टरस्पर्सन *(noun)* – छितराने का कार्य
The farmer was busy doing interspersion of the seeds in his fields.

Interstice/इन्टर्स्टिस् *(noun)* – छिद्र
The dust particles were passing easily through the interstice in door.

Interstitial/इन्टॅस्टिशॅल *(adjective)* – बीच का
The interstitial space was allowing the sun rays to enter the room.

Interwine/इन्टरवाइन *(verb)* – उलझना
As I visited the garden again, I saw that the two branches had intertwined.

Intertval/इन्टरवल *(noun)* – अवकाश
We used to chat a lot during interval time.

Intervene/इन्टर्वीन् *(verb)* – विघ्न करना
Please don't intervene in my personal affair.

I

Intervener/इन्टर्वीनर *(noun)* – बाधा डालने वाला, हस्तक्षेप करना

Despite his lack of experience, he was chosen as the intervener to settle matters.

Intervening/इन्टर्वीनिंग *(adj)* – मध्यवर्ती

In the intervening months to come, she decided to join a linguistic course.

Intervention/इन्टर्वेन्शन *(noun)* – बिचवई

In spite of the intervention by a third country, the two nations kept on fighting.

Interview/इन्टरव्यू *(noun)* – साक्षात्कार

The interview of the minister continued for two hours.

I

Intervolve/इन्टर्वॉल्व – एक में दूसरा लपेटना to roll up with each other. *The mechanic intervolved two coils.*

Interweave/इन्टर्वीव *(verb)* – मिलाना, जोड़ना

The old lady was interweaving threads of three different colours.

Intestate/इन्टेस्टेट *(adjective)* – जिसने इच्छापत्र न लिखा हो

The intestate case is still under discussion.

Intimate/इन्टिमेट *(adjective)* – आत्मीय

An intimate atmosphere was created to welcome the guests at party.

Intimate/इन्टिमेट *(verb)* – सूचना देना

I have already intimated him but he did not care.

Intimation/इन्टिमेशन – सूचना

Could you give me an intimation of how to solve the problem?

Intimidate/इन्टिमिडेट *(verb)* – डराना

His terrible mask was intimidating every one.

Into/इनटू *(preposition)* – भीतर

His entry into the room was prohibited.

Intolerable/इन्टॉलरेबल *(adj)* – न सहने योग्य

Every time I meet her, she shows an intolerable behaviour.

Intolerance/इन्टॉलरन्स *(noun)* – असहिष्णुता

The two countries are trying to lessen the intolerance to each other.

Intolerant/इन्टॉलरन्ट *(adjective)* – असहनशील

My uncle's intolerant behaviour keeps everyone annoyed.

Intoleration/इन्टालरेशन *(noun)* – असहनशीलता

Too much of an intoleration is not good for anyone.

Intomb/इन्टूम *(verb)* – कब्र में गाड़ना

Her body was intombed in the castle itself.

Intoxicant/इन्टाक्सिकॅन्ट *(noun)* – मादक

He used to stupefy his victims by using intoxicants.

Intoxicate/इन्टॉक्सिकेट *(verb)* – मतवाला करना

He gas intoxicated the girl and she fell on ground.

Intractable/इन्ट्रैक्टेबल *(adj)* – हठीला, उद्धत

That person is ill-famed for his intractable behaviour.

Intransient/इनट्रान्जिएन्ट *(noun)* – स्थिर

The final compound formed after this process is intransient.

Intrant/इन्ट्रैन्ट *(noun)* – सभा में प्रवेश करने वाला

Everyone was looking at the intrant.

Intricacy/इन्ट्रिकेसि *(noun)* – गहनता

The intricacy of the life cycle makes it more beautiful.

Introduction/इन्ट्रॅडक्शन *(noun)* – परिचय

With the introduction of new species, scientists are hoping to raise the production.

Introductive/इन्ट्रॅडक्टिव *(adj)* – प्राथमिक

The first session was only introductive.

Introspection/इन्ट्रॉस्पेक्शन *(noun)* – अन्तरावलोकन

We should spare a little time to do introspection.

Introspective/इन्ट्रॉस्पेक्टिव *(adj)* – आत्मविचार-सम्बन्धी

He was good at explaining the introspective concepts.

Introversion/इन्ट्रोवर्शन *(noun)* – अन्तर्मुखता

My master took the task of my introversion in his hands.

Introvert/इन्ट्रोवर्ट *(noun* – अन्तर्मुखी

I am quiet introvert by nature.

Intrude/इन्ट्रूड *(verb)* – टूट पड़ना

The thief intruded the house at midnight.

Intrusion/इन्ट्रूजन *(noun)* – बिना आज्ञा प्रवेश

The intrusion of the army can take place at any time.

Intrusive/इन्ट्रूसिव *(adjective)* – बिना अधिकार के प्रवेश करने वाला

He is known to be intrusive by nature.

Intuition/इन्ट्युइशन *(noun)* – सहजज्ञान

Recently, I have developed an intuition that our neighbours will leave their place.

Intuitive/इन्ट्युटिव *(adjective)* – अन्तर्ज्ञान से प्राप्त

In many people, intuitive abilities are well formed.

Intumesce/इन्ट्युमेस *(verb)* – फूल जाना

The raisins intumesced after they were placed in water.

Intwist/इनट्विस्ट *(verb)* – मिलाकर बुनना

He took two strings and intwisted them.

Inumbrate/इनम्ब्रेट *(verb)*– छाया डालना

The painter inumbrated the portion below eyes in the portrait of a lady.

Inunction/इनन्क्शन *(noun)* – मालिश करना

It was due to inunction that the burned part did not swell too much.

Inundate/इनन्डेट *(verb)* – जलमग्न कर देना

During rainy season, all the rivers got inundated.

Inurbane/इनअरबेन *(noun)* – असभ्य

The new fellow from the countryside is inurbane in his manners.

Inutile/इन्यूटिल *(adj)* – व्यर्थ

The mixer at home has become inutile.

Invade/इन्वेड *(verb)*– चढ़ाई करना

When the neighbouring country invaded, our soldiers fought back with bravery.

Invader/इन्वेडर *(noun)* – आक्रमण करने वाला

A bunch of invaders attacked from the North-West frontier.

Invaginate/इन्वैजिनेट *(verb)* – अन्तर्वलित करना

The secret letter was invaginated in a box.

Invalid/इन्वैलिड *(noun)* – बलहीन

In spite of breaking his legs, he does not consider himself an invalid.

Invalidate/इन्वैलिडेट *(verb)* – दुर्बल करना

His license was invalidated by the company.

Invalidation/इन्वैलिडेशन *(noun)* – रोगी होने से नौकरी के अयोग्य करने का कार्य

The process of invalidation took only a week.

Invaluable/इन्वैल्युअॅबॅल *(adjective)* – बहुमूल्य

I have a box of invaluable jewellery that was gifted to me by my mother.

Invar/इन्वार *(noun)* – फौलाद और गिलट की मिश्र धातु

Invar is an alloy of iron and nickel.

Invariable/इन्वरिएबल *(adj)* – सदा एक-सा, अचल

There are both variable and invariable quantities in Physics.

Invasion/इन्वेजन *(noun)* – चढ़ाई

Our country is ready to face any type of invasion.

Invasive/इन्वेसिव *(adjective)* – चढ़ाई करने वाला

The invasive intentions of the neighbouring country are well known.

Invective/इन्वेक्टिव *(noun)* – निन्दा

I want to avoid his invective talks.

Inveigle/इन्वेगल *(verb)* – ललचाना

She was able to easily inveigle men.

Invent/इन्वेंट *(verb)* – आविष्कार करना

Alva Edison invented electric bulb.

Inventive/इन्वेंटिव *(adjective)* – आविष्कार करने योग्य

With an inventive brain like him, no one could think of winning the competition.

Inventor/इन्वेन्टर *(noun)* – अविष्कारक

Our country has produced many a great inventors.

Inventory/इन्वेन्टरी *(noun)* – चल सम्पत्ति की विवरण सहित सूची

I was asked to prepare an inventory of the things to be used in shopping.

Inveracity/इन्विरैसिटि *(noun)* – असत्य

I am fed up of his inveracity.

I

Inverse/इन्वर्स *(adjective)* - उलटा

A ball from inverse direction was about to collide with another ball.

Inversion/इन्वर्सन *(noun)* - उलट-पुलट

The inversion can change the state of an object.

Invert/इन्वर्ट *(verb)* - उलटना, उलटाना

Please invert this tin full of mustart oil.

Investigate/इन्वेस्टिगेट *(verb)* - अनुसंधान करना

A private agency has been investigating the case since last one year.

Investigation/इन्वेस्टिगेशन *(noun)* - अनुसंधान

As long as investigation is going on, media is prohibited from interfering into the matters.

I

Investiture/इन्वेस्टिचर *(noun)* - प्रतिष्ठापन

The man was standing tall when his investiture going on.

Investor/इन्वेस्टर *(noun)* - धन लगाने वाला

The builder has invited many investors for his new project.

Inveterate/इन्वेटिरेट *(adjective)* - हठी

No one is able to change his inveterate truthfulness.

Invigilate/इन्विजिलेट *(verb)* - परीक्षा में विद्यार्थियों का निरीक्षण करना

In spite of the invigilation going on, students were copying from one another.

Inviolate/इन्वॉअलेट *(adjective)* - पवित्र

No one has the guts to disturb his inviolate state of mind.

Invisible/इन्विजिबल *(adjective)* - अदृश्य

An invisible gas was present in the mines.

Invitation/इनविटेशन *(noun)* - बुलावा

When I rejected his invitation, he got very angry.

Invitatory/इन्विटेटॅरि *(adj)* - न्योता सम्बन्धी

He sent me an invitatory message in mail.

Invocate/इन्वोकेट *(verb)* - स्तोत्र रूप से प्रार्थना करना

She invocated evil spires.

Involuntarily/इन्वॉलन्टरिलि *(adv)* - अनिच्छा से

They had, involuntarily, saved the boy's life.

Involuntary/इन्वॉलन्टरि *(adjective)* - इच्छारहित

We have no control over the involuntary actions of some of our organs.

Involution/इन्वॅल्यूशॅन *(noun)* - पेचीदगी

As a man grows old, involution of his organs starts taking place.

Invulnerable/इन्वॅलनॅरेबॅल *(adjective)* - अमोघ

No one can disturb his invulnerable state of mind.

Inwards/इन्वाईस *(avberb)* - आन्तरिक

As he used to practise meditation, his thought process was more inclined inwards.

Inweave/इन्वीव *(verb)* - ऐंठना

The workers at textile mill were inweaving the threads.

Inwork/इन्वर्क *(verb)* - भीतरी काम करना

The company want employees who can inwork.

Inwrap/इन्राप *(verb)* - समाप्त करना

I am about to inwrap this work.

Iodine/आइअडीन *(noun)* - औषधि में प्रयुक्त एक अँग्रेजी अधातु तत्व

Doctors advise to apply iodine solution over infections.

Ion/आइअन (आयॅन्) *(noun)* - आयन, विद्युत्शक्ति उत्पन्न करने वाला परमाणु

Exchange of ions takes place in a chemical reaction.

Irascible/इरैसिबल *(adjective)* - उत्तेजक

People with irascible nature find it hard to work with colleagues.

Ireful/आयरफुल *(adj)* - क्रोधी

I am not going to bear his ireful attitude all the time.

Irefully/आयरफुली *(adv)* - रोष से

He always behaves irefully.

Iridescent/आयरिडिसेंट *(adjective)* - रंग बदलने वाला

The party hall was glowing with iridescent lights.

Iris/आयरिश *(noun)* - इन्द्रधनुष

Iris is an important of our eyes.

Irksome/अर्कसम *(adj)* – दु:खदायी

He was making irksome remarks on the fellow passengers.

Iron/आयरन *(noun)* – लोहा

Iron vessels are still used for cooking in our country.

Irradiate/इरैडिएट *(verb)* – चमकना

Some of the cancers are treated using irradiation.

Irradiation/इरैडिएशन *(noun)* – प्रदीपन, किरणन

The cancer patient was exposed to irradiation.

Irradicate/इरैडिकेट *(verb)* – बोना, छितराना

The seeds were irradicated into the soil.

Irrational/इरैशनल *(adjective)* –अविवेकी

We need to shed our irrational attitude in order to make progress.

Irreclaimable/इरिक्लेमेबल *(adjective)* – अनुद्धार्य

They were shocked to learn that their money was irreclaimable.

Irrecognizable/इरेकॅग्नाइजॅबॅल *(adj)* – अनभिज्ञेय

He had changed so much that his face was simply irrecognizable to us.

Irreconcsilable/इरेकॅन्साइलेबॅल *(adj)* – अशाम्य

He knew from the very beginning that his nature was irreconcilable with his wife.

Irrecoverable/इरिकॅवरेबॅल *(adj)* – अपूरणीय

My mother was suffering from an irrecoverable disease.

Irredeemable/इरिडीमेबॅल *(adj)* – कभी न सुधर सकने योग्य

The accident has given him irredeemable injuries.

Irreducible/इरिड्यूसिबल *(adj)* – अखंडनीय अपरिवर्तनीय

This complex theorem is irreducible.

Irrefutable/इरेफ्यूटेबल *(adjective)* – अकाट्य

The actor has been facing some irrefutable charges.

Irregularity/इरेग्यूलैरिटि *(noun)* – अनियमितता

The Commonwealth Games saw many irregularities.

Irreligion/इरिलिजन *(noun)* – नास्तिकता

What he hates most about me is my irreligion.

Irreligious/इरिलिजस *(adjective)* – विधर्मी

People who are irreligious have to face many things in society.

Irremissible/इरिमिसिबॅल *(adjective)* – अक्षम्य

His crimes are irremissible.

Irremovable/इरिमूवेबॅल *(adjective)* – अस्थानान्तरीय

The cancer had spread to both the ovaries, thus making them irremovable.

Irrepressible/इरिप्रेसिबॅल *(adjective)* – अदम्य

His irrepressible desires was making him crazy.

Irreproachable/इरिप्रोचॅबॅल *(adj)* – निष्कलंक

This great work is irreproachable.

Irresolute/इर्‌रेजल्यूट *(adjective)* – अस्थिर

In spite of his officer's faith in him, he was irresolute of his capabilities.

Irresolution/इर्‌रेजल्यूशन *(noun)* – अदृढ़ता

The constant irresolution on his part created a wrong impression on others.

Irresolvable/इर्‌रिजॉल्वेब्‌ल् *(adjective)* – अविभाज्य करने योग्य

I have some irresolvable differences with my boss.

Irrespective/इर्‌रेस्पक्टिव *(adjective)* – पृथक्

Irrespective of what I wanted, he continued doing dilly-dally.

Irresponsible/इर्‌रेस्पान्सिबल् *(adj)* – गैर जिम्मेदारी

Both the parents had an irresponsible attitude towards their kid.

Irresponsive/इर्‌रेस्पान्सिव *(adjective)* – प्रतिवचन न देने वाला

The newly born child was displaying an irresponsive behaviour.

Irretentive/इर्‌टेन्टिव *(noun)* – न रोकने योग्य

This soil has become irretentive to hold moisture.

Irretrievable/इर्‌ट्रीवेबल *(adj)* – बिना उपाय का

The traces of the lost fossils are irretrievable.

Irreverence/इर्‌रेवरेन्स *(noun)* – अपमान

He came there with irreverence in his heart.

Irreverent/इर्‌रेवरेन्ट् *(adj)* – शक्तिहीन, अनादरकारी

It was very bad on his part to display irreverent attitude towards his elders.

I

Irreverential/इर्रेवरेन्शल *(adj)* – अपमान-सम्बन्धी
Over the years, he has become irreverential to everyone.

Irreversible/इर्रिवर्सिबल *(adjective)* – अपरिवर्तनीयता
Ageing is an irreversible process.

Irrigable/इर्रिगबॅल *(adjective)* – सींचने योग्य
A large part of India's land is irrigable.

Irrigate/इर्रिगेट *(verb)* – सींचना
The farmers use rain water to irrigate this area.

Irrigation/इर्रिगेशन *(noun)* – सिंचाई का काम
Irrigation is the main occupation of the villagers living in remote areas.

I

Irrigator/इर्रिगेटर *(noun)* – सींचने वाला मनुष्य
Large irrigators are used for supplying water to the fields.

Irritable/इर्रिटेबल *(adj)* – शीघ्र क्रुद्ध होने वाला
Would you stop doing irritable talks?

Irritably/इर्रिटेब्ली *(adverb)* – चिड़चिड़ाहट से
He said irritably, "Go away."

Irritate/इर्रिटेट *(verb)* – क्रुद्ध करना
She irritates me with her cribbing.

Irritating/इर्रिटेटिंग *(adj)* – चिढ़ाने वाला
Would you stop irritating me?

Islet/आइलेट *(noun)* – छोटा द्वीप
The water was surrounded by a number of islets.

Isometric/आइसोमेट्रिक *(adj)* – एक परिमाण का
The two triangles drawn here are isometric.

Italicize/इटैलिसाइज *(verb)* – तिरछे अक्षरों में छापना *Please italicize the important words.*

Italics/इटैलिक्स *(noun)* – छापे का अक्षर जो दाहिनें ओर झुका होता है।
Kindly note down the words that are printed in italics.

Itch/इच् *(noun)* – खुजली
The baby has developed itches on her back.

Itchiness/इचीनेस *(noun)* – खुजली
The itchiness in summers is normal.

Itchy/इची *(adjective)* – खुजली का
The powder was very itchy for my body.

Item/आइटम *(noun)* – वस्तु
Please make a list of all the items that you are going to buy.

Iterative/इटरेटिव *(adjective)* – बारम्बार दोहराने वाला
The program comprised of an iterative cycle.

Itinerancy/इटिनरैन्सि *(noun)* – दौरा, भ्रमण
In ancient times, itinerancy was a common thing among traders.

Itinerant/इटिनरन्ट *(adjective)* – घूमने वाला
A number of itinerants had gathered there.

Itinerate/इटिनरेट *(verb)* – घूमना
He had to itinerate from place to place to do the trading.

Itself/इटसेल्फ *(pronoun)* – स्वयं उसका
The dog was so crazy that it bit itself.

Ivory/आइवरी *(noun)* – हाथीदाँत
Many jewels are made from ivory.

Izard/इजर्ड *(noun)* – एक प्रकार का बारहसिंगा
The wild life sanctuary had many izards living in it.

Jj

J/जे *(noun)* – अंग्रेजी वर्णमाला का दसवाँ वर्ण the tenth of the English alphabet. *J is the tenth letter in the English alphabet.*

Jab/जैब *(noun)* – धक्का, चुभन, *(verb)* कोंचना, चुभाना

I have him a jab in his stomach. She jabbed at picture with her finger.

Jabber/जैबर *(verb)* – बड़बड़ाना

He jabbered and I failed to understand him.

Jabot/जाबो *(noun)* – किनारी, झालर

She wore a jabot which looked very attractive.

Jacinth/जैसिंथ *(noun)* – नारंगी रंग का रत्न

She wore a jacinth on her ring finger.

Jackal/जैकाल *(noun)* – सियार

Jackal is a wild dog and scavenger found in Asia and Africa.

Jackass/जैक्-ऐस् *(noun)* – मूर्ख, नर गदह

You jackass! How dare you to speak to me like that.

Jacket/जैकेट *(noun)* – जाकिट

He wore a woollen grey jacket which suited him very well.

Jacobin – *(noun)*

He was questioned for being a Jacobin.

Jaconet/जैकॅनेट *(noun)* – एक प्रकार का सूती कपड़ा

He bought two metres of jaconet for his shirt.

Jactitation/जैक्टिटेशन *(noun)* – शरीर की ऐंठन

He suffers from jactitation and is taking medicines.

Jag/जैग *(verb)* – बेंध देना, चट्टान का नुकीला भाग

A thorn jagged his skin.

Jail/जेल *(noun)* – बन्दीगृह

He was lodged in central jail.

Jalap/जैलप *(noun)* – एक प्रकार की रेचक

You can take a dose of jalap for constipation.

Jam/जैम् *(noun)* – मीठा अचार

Children like mixed fruit jams a lot.

Jangle/जैंगल *(verb)* – कर्कश शब्द करना

The bells jangled in the temple.

Janitor/जैनिटर *(noun)* – द्वारपाल, लिफ्टचालक

Janitor was appointed after careful investigation. A janitor sometimes acts as a liftman.

January/जैन्युअॅरी *(noun)* – जनवरी

Visitors to Delhi found it to be a very cold in January.

Jape/जेप *(noun)* – हँसी

I was angry because he had played a very funny jape on me.

Jar/जार *(noun)* – झगड़ा, धक्का, बर्तन

He took out some pickle from the jar.

Jargon/जार्गन *(noun)* – अनर्थक वचन, शब्दजाल

He talked a lot of political jargon which left nobody wiser.

Jasper/जैस्पर *(noun)* – एक प्रकार का रत्न

Jasper being a precious stone is put to many use.

Jaundice/जॉन्डिस *(noun)* – कामला रोग

He has been hospitalized because of advanced case of jaundice.

Jaunty/जॉन्टी *(adjective)* – बाँका, जिन्दादिल

He is a jaunty fellow and hence liked by all.

Jay/जे *(noun)* – नीलकण्ड पक्षी

Here is a jay sitting in the tree, see how beautiful it looks.

Jazz/जाज *(noun)* – शोरगुल का नाच-गाना

Jazz is my favourite music.

Jealousy/जेलॅसि *(adjective)* – डाह

Jealousy consumed her as she saw her boy friend with another girl.

Jeer/जिअर *(verb)* – उपहास करना
The crowd jeered at the speaker.

Jejune/जिजून *(adjective)* – फीका, नीरस
He is a jejune fellow and after alone.

Jelly/जेलि *(noun)* – मीठी चटनी
The dinner was followed by jelly.

Jemmy/जेमि *(noun)* – सेंध मारने की सबरी
The thieves forced open the door with a jemmy.

Jenny/जेनि *(noun)* – मादा, गधी
It is a jenny grazing over there.

Jeopardize/जेपॅडाइज *(verb)* – खतरा में डालना
He jeopardized his career by trying to bribe a clerk.

Jeopardous/जेपर्डस *(adj)* – आपत्तियुक्त
He followed a jeopardous path thereby endangering himself.

J

Jeopardy/जेपर्डि *(noun)* – शंका
The peace procese is jeopardy.

Jerk/जर्क *(noun)* – झटका
A jerk near the tree attracted his attention.

Jersey/जर्सी *(noun)* – कुर्ती
He wore a thick woollen jersey as it was bitter cold.

Jess/जेस *(noun)*– चमड़े का पतला तसमा
The hawk is wearing jesses.

Jest/जेस्ट *(noun)* – हँसी a joke. *Forget it man, I said it in jest.*

Jester/जेस्टर *(noun)* – विदूषक
There used to be court jesters in medieval times.

Jestful/जेस्टफुल *(adjective)* – ठिठोलिया
He spoke in a jestful manner.

Jestingly/जेस्टिंग्लि *(adverb)* – हँसी में
He teased her jestingly.

Jet/जेट *(noun)* – फुहारा
A jet of water drenched me.

Jetty/जेटि *(noun)* – घाट
Let us walk over the jetty, it is beautiful to be surrounded with water.

Jewel/जूऍल् *(noun)* – जवाहिर, रत्न
It is a very precious jewel and I am unable to buy it.

Jeweller/जूऍलर् *(noun)* – जौहरी
He is a jeweller by profession.

Jezebel/जेज़ॅबल *(noun)* – ढीठ स्त्री
She is a jezebel and as is out most of the nights.

Jibe/जाइब *(noun)* – ताना, हँसी
Her jibes insulted him.

Jiffy/जिफी *(noun)* – क्षण
He left in a jiffy.

Jig/जिग *(noun)* – एक प्रकार का नाच
She jigged around him in the dance hall.

Jiggle/जिगल *(verb)* – झुलाना
The forest was full of jiggling monkeys.

Jingle/जिंगल *(noun)* – टनटनाहट
The jingle of bells could be heard from far.

Jobber/जॉबर *(noun)* – छोटा कार्य करने वाला
He is a jobber, and doesn't sell in retail.

Jobbery/जॉबरी *(noun)* – दलाली
He has been accused of jobbery and an enquiry is set up against him.

Jockey/जॉकी *(noun)* – घुड़दौड़ का सवार
He is a skilful and well-known jockey.

Jocose/जोकोस *(adjective)* – खिलाड़ी
He is a jocose fellow and liked by all.

Jocular/जाक्युलॅर *(adjective)* – परिहासिक
He is a jocular character.

Jocund/जॉकन्ड *(adjective)* – प्रमुदित
He is jocund by nature.

Jogger/जॉगर *(noun)* – धीरे-धीरे चलने वाला
He is a daily jogger in the park.

Jogtrot/जॉग्ट्रॉट *(noun)* – धीमी समान गति
The horse went on a jogtrot.

Johney/जॉनी *(noun)* – ठाटदार मनुष्य
Hey Johnny! Come here and take your money.

Joinder/जाइन्डर *(noun)* – मिलाव, प्रतिशेष
The court ordered the joinder of both witnesses.

Joiner/जॉइनर *(noun)* – बढ़ई, जोड़ने वाला
He is a joiner by profession.

Joining/ज्वाइनिंग *(verb)* – संगम, जोड़ने की क्रिया
Joining army was his main aim.

Jointly/जाइन्टलि *(adverb)* – एक साथ मिलकर
We jointly stood against the injustice.

Joke/जोक *(noun)* – उपहास, चुटकुला
He cut a joke and all laughed.

Joker/जोकर *(noun)* – मसखरा, विदूषक
Children are highly amused by jokers in the circus.

Jokingly/जोकिंग्लि *(adverb)* – मसखरेपन से
I said it jokingly, please don't wind.

Jollily/जॉलिलि *(adverb)* – आनंद से
He jollily said all this.

Jolliness/जॉलिनेस् *(noun)* – प्रमोद, प्रभुदितावस्था
His jolliness is infectious.

Jonquil/जॉनक्विल *(noun)* – एक प्रकार का नरगिस
I have a few jonquils in my garden.

Jordan – *(noun)*
Jordan is a country situated in the middle-east.

Josser/जॉसर *(noun)* – मूर्ख मनुष्य
He is an old josser and talks in coherently.

Jostle/जॉसल *(verb)* – धक्का देना
The crowd jostled to reach the famous actor.

Jot/जॉट *(verb)* – संक्षेप में लिखना
He jotted down the notes.

Jotting/जॉटिंग *(noun)* – यादगार
As he read the jotting he became upset.

Jounce/जाउन्स *(verb)* – झटकारना
The ball jounced high.

Journalist/जर्नलिस्ट *(noun)* – सम्पादक
He is a journalist by profession.

Journalize/जर्नलाइज *(verb)* – पत्रिका में लिखने का कार्य करना, समाचारपत्रीय बनाना
This article has been journalized by a famous reporter. He has journalized all the events date wise.

Journey/जर्नी *(noun)* – यात्रा
He has gone on a long journey.

Jove/जोव *(noun)* – बृहस्पति नक्षत्र
By jove! You are really a tall man.

Jovian/जोविअन *(adjective)* – बृहस्पति-सम्बन्धी
A search robot will be sent for Jovian exploration.

Jowl/जॉउल *(noun)* – गाल
Some people develop jowls in old age.

Joyless/जॉयलेस *(adjective)* – उदास
He is a joyless and miserable fellow.

Joyful/जॉयफुल *(adjective)* – हर्षित
He leads a joyful life.

Jubilate /जूबिलेट – *(verb)*
It's time to senj and jubilate aloud before God.

Jubilant/जूबिलेन्ट *(adjective)* – प्रसन्न
He was jubilant after having won the race.

Jubilee/जुबिली *(noun)* – महोत्सव
He recently celebrated the silver jubilee of his marriage.

Judge/जज *(noun)* – न्यायाधीश
He has recently been appointed a judge.

J

Judgeship/जजशिप – *(noun)*
To be eligible for judegeship, a lawyer must have 10 years of practice in a law court.

Judicature /जूडिकेचर – *(noun)*
Our constitution says that the legislature is separate from the judicature.

Judicial/जुडिसियल *(adjective)* – अदालती
He has been sent to 10 days judicial custody.

Judiciary/जुडिसिअरी *(noun)* – न्यायाधीशों का समुदाय
The judiciary of a country must be impartial.

Judicious/जूडिशॅस *(adjective)* – उचित
It was a judicious division.

Jug/जग *(noun)* – जलपात्र
He has ordered a jug of juice.

Jugful/जगफुल– *(noun)*
She gave us jugful of water.

Juggins/जगिंन्स् – *(noun)*
You silly juggins, why did you listen to him?

Juggle/जॅगॅल *(verb)* – बाजीगरी करना, धोखा देना
He juggles balls faultlessly.

Juggler/जॅग्लॅर *(noun)* – मायावी
He is a barman as well as a juggler.

Jugular/जूग्यूलर *(noun)* – गरदन या कण्ठ सम्बन्धी
The murderer cut his jugular vein.

Juice/जूस *(noun)* – फल या सब्जी का रस
He is fond of fruit juice.

Juicy/जूसि *(adjective)* – रसीला

It is a cent per cent juicy drink.

Julep/जूलेप *(noun)* – शर्बत

You seem to be tired, you need a drink of julep.

July/जुलाइ *(noun)* – जुलाई

It is hot in July in Delhi.

Jumble/जम्बल *(noun)* – घालमेल

Things are in a jumble in this place, sort them out.

Jump/जम्प *(verb)* – कूदना

The cat jumped over the wall.

Jumping/जम्पिंग – *(verb)*

He is a good dancer and is called jumping jack.

J

Junction/जंक्शन *(noun)* – संगम

He was found wandering on a railway junction.

Juncture/जॅन्क्चर *(noun)* – समय

You must start doing things at this juncture.

Junior/जूनिअर् *(adjective)* – अल्पवयस्क

All juniors should gather here.

Juniority/जूनिआरिटी *(noun)* – छोटापन

Juniority or seniority matters a lot in a job.

Junket/जंकेट *(noun)* – ज्योनार

He often goes to junkets and spends a lot of money.

Junta/जन्टा *(noun)* – गुप्त मण्डली

Many countries are still ruled by military junta.

Jupiter/जुपिटर *(noun)* – बृहस्पति ग्रह

Astronomers are a lot interested in the planet Jupiter.

Jural/जूरॅल *(adjective)* – विधिक, वैधिक

It is a jural matter and advice must be sought from an expert.

Jurisprudence/जुरिस्प्रूडेन्स *(noun)* – विधिशास्त्र

Jurisprudence must be fair in delivering fair openion.

Jurist/जूरिस्ट *(noun)* – विधिशास्त्री

He is a famous jurist.

Juror/जूरर् *(noun)* – प्रमाण-पुरुष

He is a juror and a party to a many decision makings.

Just/जस्ट *(adjective)* – धार्मिक

Just a moment let me speak.

Justice/जस्टिस *(noun)* – न्याय

Justice must be done.

Justiciable/जस्टिशिअबल् *(adjective)* – न्याय-योग्य

We sijned the agreement justicable under Indian Courts.

Justiceship/जस्टिस्शिप – *(noun)*

Indian justiceship is renowned for slow but fair treatment.

Justly/जस्टली *(adverb)* – न्यायपूर्वक ठीक-ठीक

I justly believe in the action.

Justness/जस्टनेस *(noun)* – यथार्थता

The justness of the sentence is unquestionable.

Jute/जूट *(noun)* – जूट, पटुआ

Ropes among many other things are made from jute fibre.

K/के *(noun)* - अंग्रेजी वर्णमाला का ग्यारहवाँ अक्षर the eleventh letter of the English alphabet.

1. Denoting the next after J in a set of items, categories, etc.

Kail/केल *(noun)* - एक प्रकार की बन्दगोभी, करमसाग
Kail or kale is a kind of cabbage with large leaves and no compact round head.

Kaiser/कैजर *(noun)* - जर्मनी उपाधि
Kaiser was the emperor of Austria, Germany.

Kale/केल *(noun)* - बन्दगोभी
Leaves of the kale cabbage are edible.

Kaleidoscopical - *(adjective)*
The movement of dances was almost kaleidoscopical.

Kalium - *(noun)* an element. *Kalium is the Latin name for potassium.*

Kangaroo/कैन्गारू *(noun)* - कंगारू
Kangaroo is the national animal of Australia.

Kaolin/केओलिन *(noun)* - चीनी मिट्टी
Kaolin clay is used for making china and porcelain.

Keenly/किनली *(adverb)* - उत्सुकता से
He is keenly interested in Maths.

Keenness/कीननेस *(noun)* - तीखापन
She had great keenness to join dance classes.

Keener/कीनर *(noun)* - तेज, चतुर
He is keener than his brother.

Keeper/कीपर *(noun)* - रक्षक
He has employed a housekeeper.

Keeping/कीपिंग *(noun)* - रक्षा
In keeping with my dad's desire, I have taken sports as my career.

Keepsake/किपसेक *(noun)* - स्मरणार्थक चिह्न
This locket is a keepsake of my mother.

Keg/केग *(noun)* - कठरा
He is fond of keg beer.

Kemp/केम्प *(noun)* - ऊन के मोटे रेशे
Please throw this bunch of Kemp out.

Ken/केन *(noun)* - दृष्टिविषय
He has great ken of this rocky terrain.

Kennel/केनॅल *(noun)* - जलमार्ग या कुन्ताघर
The dog is sleeping in its kennel.

Kept/केप्ट - रखा, कीप क्रिया का भूतकाल का रूप
He has kept his promise.

K

Kerchief/करचीफ *(noun)* - सिर ढाँपने का चौकोर कपड़ा
He always carries a handkerchief.

Kernel/कर्नल् *(noun)* - गरी, गिरी
The kernels of most nuts are edible.

Kerosene/केरोसीन *(noun)* - मिट्टी का तेल
Kerosene stoves are still used by people who don't have cooking gas.

Kestrel/केस्ट्रल *(noun)* - बाज पक्षी
Many people living in mountains keep kestrels or pets.

Ketchup/केचअप *(noun)* - चटनी
Chilly tomato ketchups are quite popular.

Kettle/केटॅल *(noun)* - पतीली, केतली
Tea is boiling in the kettle.

Key/की *(noun)* - चाभी
I have lost my keys and I don't know how I shall open the door.

Keyhole/कीहोल *(noun)* - ताली लगाने का छिद्र
He tried to look inside through the keyhole.

Keynote/कीनोट *(noun)* - प्रधान राग
Read this keynote before you enter the conference room.

Keystone/कीस्टोन *(noun)* - प्रधान सिद्धान्त
This is the keystone to the building.

Kibble/किबल् *(verb)* – कूटना, पीसना
The meal has been kibbled into pellets.

Kibe/काइब *(noun)* – बेवाय
Her both feet are full of kibes.

Kibosh – *(noun)*
He decided to put the kibosh on the agreement.

Kid/किड *(noun)* – बकरी का बच्चा
Hey kid! Don't you mess with me, you have yet to grow.

Kiddle/किड्डल *(noun)* – मछली पकड़ने के लिये नदी लगाया बाँध
It is a kiddle here on the river with an opening to catch fish.

Kiddy/किडि *(noun)* – छोटा बच्चा
Kiddies play here.

Kier/किअर् *(noun)* – पात्र बर्तन
This is of no use, it is broken kier.

K

Kill/किल *(verb)* – मार डालना
The goat has been killed for meat.

Killer/किलर *(noun)* – हत्यारा
A serial killer is on prowl.

Killing/किलिंग *(noun)* – हत्या
Killing animals is forbidden in some religions.

Kiln/किल्न *(noun)* – आँवाँ, भट्ठा
He owns many brick kilns.

Kilo/किलो *(noun)* – मेट्रिक नाप में एक हजार के लिए उपसर्ग
Give me a kilo of potato.

Kilogram/किलोग्राम *(noun)*– एक हजार ग्राम
A kilogram of onions will cost you 30 rupees.

Kin/किन *(noun)* – नातेदार
All my kin live around here.

Kind/काइन्ड *(noun)* – किस्म, प्रकार
The kind of people you mix with are not undesirable.

Kindliness/काइनडलिनेस् *(noun)* – दयालुता
I would be much abliged for your kindliness.

Kindling/किन्डलिंग *(noun)* – आग जलाने की चैली
It is cold and dark, kindling a fire is necessary.

Kindly/काइन्डलि *(adverb)* – उपकारी, कृपा करके
He kindly asked me to have a seat.

Kindness/काइन्डनेस *(noun)* – सहानुभूति, दयालुता
Kindness is a virtue.

King/किंग *(noun)* – राजा, नरपति
He is a king and can order anything.

Kingdom/किंगडम *(noun)* – राज, साम्राज्य
The kingdom of Ashoka spread far and wide.

Kingless/किंगलेस *(adjective)* – नृपहीन
The state remained kingless for some time after the death of the king.

Kinglet/किंगलेट *(noun)* – छोटा राजा
He is merely a kinglet ruling a small state.

Kinglike/किंगलाइक *(adjective)* – राजा के सदृश
His behaviour is kinglike and rather irritating.

Kingly/किंग्लि *(adjective)* – राजकीय
He visited his kingdom to perform his kingly duties.

Kinless/किन्लेस् *(adjective)* – बिना परिवार का
He wandered into a desert and for all practical purposes a kinless person.

Kinsfolk/किन्सफोक *(plural noun)* – भाई–बन्धु
Most of his kinsfolk live abroad.

Kinship/किन्शीप *(noun)* – नातेदारी
In the very first meeting, I felt a strange kinship with her.

Kirk/कर्क *(noun)* – गिरजाघर
During my stay in UK, I will visit the kirk.

Kisser/किशर *(noun)* – चूमने वाला
He is a great kisser.

Kitchen/किचेन *(noun)* – रसोईघर
Kitchen must be kept neat and clean.

Kitchener/किचनर् *(noun)* – चूल्हों की पंक्ति
The new flats come equipped with modern kitchener.

Kloof/क्लूफ् *(noun)* – सँकरी घाटी
There are beautiful kloofs in South Africa.

Knag/नैग *(noun)* – लकड़ी की गाँठ
The trunk of this tree is full of knags.

Knap/नैप *(verb)* – शिखर
This building is made of knapped stone and flint.

Knapper/नैपर् *(noun)* – पत्थर तोड़ने वाला
He is an expert knapper capable of giving desired shape to 200 square stones.

Knapsack/नैपसैक *(noun)* - चमड़े का बैग

He is a tourist and always carries a knapsack.

Knave/नेव *(noun)* - धूर्त

He is a kvave and as such not to be trusted.

Knavery/नेवरि *(noun)* - दुष्टता, बेईमानी

Indulging in acts of knavery may land you in jail.

Knead/नीड *(verb)* - सानना

She is kneading wheat flour.

Knee/नी *(noun)* - घुटना

He has been hurt in his knee.

Knell/नेल *(noun)* - अरथी के साथ बजने वाले घण्टे का शब्द

The knell of the village bell tells us that somebody had died.

Knew/न्यू - जान लिया

I knew he wasn't a thief.

Knife/नाइफ *(noun)* - चाकू

The robber had a knife in his hand.

Knighthood/नाइट्हूड *(noun)*

He was honoured with knighthood on his birthday.

Knit/नीट *(verb)* - जोड़ना

My mother is knitting a sweater for me.

Knob/नॉब *(noun)* - गाँठ

He turned the knob and opened the door.

Knobble/नॉबल *(noun)* - छोटी गाँठ

There is a knobble on the wall.

Knotting/नॉटिंग *(noun)* - गठबन्धन

Carpets are made by knotting the yarn.

Knotty/नॉटी *(adjective)* - पेंचदार

It is a knotty rope.

Knowable/नोएबल् *(adjective)* जानने योग्य

This idea is knowable to the core.

Knowing/नोइंग *(adjective)* - ज्ञान

Today's society is too knowing too corrupt.

Known/नोन *(adjective)* - सूचित

He is a well-known person.

Knuckle/नकल *(noun)* - अँगुली का जोड़, पोर

I have pain in my knnckles.

Knurl/नर्ल *(noun)* - गाँठ

It is a knurl here and a very hard place.

Kodak/कोडैक *(noun)* - फोटो उतारने का एक यन्त्र

Kodak has caused manufacturing cameras.

Kraal/क्राल *(noun)* - बाड़ा

African villages of huts are called kraals.

Kymograph/काइमोग्राफ *(noun)* - तरंगलेखी यन्त्र

A kymograph is used for recording vibrations in circulating blood.

Ll

L/एल – *(noun)* अंग्रेजी वर्णमाला का 12वाँ अक्षर the twelfth letter of the English alphabet. *L is the Roman numeral for 50.*
1. Denoting the next after K in a set of items, categories. etc.

L

Labarum/लेबरम *(noun)* – रूमी रण-पताका
Labarum was Constantine's military symbol.

Labefaction/लैबिफैक्शन *(noun)* – नाश
His labefaction occurred soon after his business collapsed.

Label/लेबल *(noun)* – टिकट
The label on the shirt reads 'Peter England' 42.

Labial/लेबियल *(adjective)* – ओठ-सम्बन्धी
Any thing that is in some way concerned with lips is known as labial.

Laboratory/लैबॅरेंटरि *(noun)* – प्रयोगशाला
There was a cage of white mice in the science laboratory for experimental purposes.

Laborious/लेबोरियस *(adjective)* – परिश्रमी
It was a laborious job and he did it well.

Labour/लेबर *(noun)* – मेहनत, श्रमिक (वर्ग)
The labour was constantly working on the railway line.

Laboured/लेबर्ड *(adjective)* – परिश्रम-सूचक
His laboured breathing could be heard from a distance.

Labourer/लेबरर *(noun)* – कर्मकार, मजदूर
20 labourers were hired to clean the tank.

Labourite/लेबरिट *(noun)* – मजदूर दल का सदस्य
He is a labourite and will not vote for any other party.

Laburnum/लेबरनम *(noun)* – पीले फूल का एक पौधा
I have a laburnum in my garden, don't eat its fruit.

Labyrinth/लैबरिन्थ् *(noun)* – व्याकुलता
Once you enter this labyrinth underground, it will be very difficult for you to come out.

Labyrinthine/लैबरिन्थाइन *(adjective)* – पेचीला, पेचीदा, अस्पष्ट
It is labyrinthine puzzle and very difficult to solve.

Lac/लैक *(noun)* – लाख
Lac is an important ingredient of varnish.

Lacerable/लैसरेब्ल *(adj)* – चीरा लगाने योग्य
It is not lacerable.

Lacerate/लैसरेट *(verb)* – पीड़ा देना
The knife lacerated his skin.

Laceration/लैसरेशन *(noun)* – विदारण
He suffered lacerations to his face and hands.

Laches/लैचेज *(noun)* – ढिलाई
Laches resulted into refusal of his claim.

Lachrymal/लैक्रिमल *(adjective)* – अश्रु-सम्बन्धी
He has some lachrymal problem.

Lack/लैक *(noun)* – अभाव, कमी
His lack of common sense often puts him in trouble.

Lackadaisical/लैकेडेजिकल *(adj)* – व्यग्र दुःखी
His lackadaisical attitude was responsible for his failure in interview.

Lackey/लैकी *(noun)* – दास
He looks more like a lackey the master of this mansion.

Laconic/लैकोनिक *(adjective)* – छोटा
Laconic speech has become his habit.

Lactation/लैक्टेशन *(noun)* – स्तन्य-दान
Lactation process starts soon after the birth of the baby.

Lactic/लैक्टिक *(adjective)* – दुग्ध के गुण का
This is lactic powder.

Lactometer/लैक्टोमीटर *(noun)* – दूध की शुद्धता नापने का यन्त्र
A lactometer is used to find how watery is the milk.

Lade/लेड *(verb)* - भार रखना
The laden ship started its journey.

Lading/लेडिंग *(noun)* - बोझ
The labour were instructed to complete lading the ship in 6 hours.

Ladle/लैडल *(noun)* - करछुल
The guests were served soup with a ladle.

Lady/लेडी *(noun)* - गृहिणी
She is a lady and as such you should respect her.

Laggard/लैगार्ड *(adjective)* - मन्द
He is a laggard and unlikely to succeed.

Lagging/लैगिंग *(noun)* - लपेटन, परिवेष्टन
You can buy lagging from this shop.

Lagoon/लैगून *(noun)* - दलदल, समुद्र से बना झील
What a beautiful lagoon, let us go and swim.

Laid/लेड - लेटा हुआ
The table has been laid, please come for dinner.

Laird/लेअर्ड *(noun)* - जमींदार
He is a laird and as such a very rich man.

Laity/लैइटि *(noun)* - जनसामान्य
He is a lay man and doesn't know much of anything.

Lake/लेक *(noun)* - झील
Let us fish in this lake.

Lame/लेम *(adjective)* - लँगड़ा
He is a lame fellow and as such can't walk properly.

Lamentable/लैमेंटेब्ल *(adjective)* - शोचनीय
There was lamentable atmosphere in the house after the news of accident.

Lamentably/लैमेंटेब्ली *(adverb)* - शोक से
She was lamentably ignorant.

Lamentation/लैमेंटेशन *(noun)* - विलाप
The accident area presentated a scene of lamentation.

Lamenter/लैमेंटर *(noun)* - विलाप करने वाला
Look ahead, don't be a lamenter worrying about the past.

Laminate/लैमिनेट *(verb)* - तबक बनाना
He got his certificates laminated.

Lamp/लैम्प *(noun)* - दीपक
Oil lamps are still burnt in villages without electricity.

Lampoon/लैम्पून *(verb)* - आक्षेप
He was lampooned by journalists.

Lamprey/लैम्प्री *(noun)* - एक प्रकार की मछली
The fisherman caught a lamprey in his net.

Lance/लान्स् *(noun)* - बर्छी
The knight was hit by a lance.

Lancet/लाल्सेट् *(noun)* - नश्तर
His skin was pricked with a lancet.

Landau/लैन्डा *(noun)* - लण्डी गाड़ी
Royals in England used landau for travelling even in the 20th century.

Landed/लैंडेड *(adjective)* - भूमि सम्पन्न
He is inherited huge to have landed property.

Landing/लैंडिंग *(noun)* - अवतरण
The landing time of the plane has come.

Landlady/लैंडलेडी *(noun)* - जमींदारिन
She is our landlady and has come to collect rent.

Landmark/लैंडमार्क *(noun)* - सीमा चिह्न
Is there any landmark near your house whereby I can reach you easily?

Landward/लैंडवार्ड *(adjective)* - पृथ्वी की ओर
I have a house facing landwards as opposed to seawards..

Languish/लैंग्विश *(verb)* - दुर्बल होना
He is languishing in jail.

Lank/लैंक *(adjective)* - दुर्बल
He is a lank fellow.

Lantern/लैंटर्न *(noun)* - दीपक
It is very dark outside, take a lantern with you.

Lap-dog/लैपडॉग *(noun)* - छोटा कुत्ता
He is a lap-dog always obeying his wife blindly.

Lapis-lazuli/लैपिस-लैज्युलाइ *(noun)* - वैदूर्य
Lapis-lazuli rock is used in jewellery.

Lapse/लैप्स *(noun)* - अतिक्रम
He suffered from lapse of memory after the accident.

Lard/लार्ड *(noun)* - सूअर की चर्बी
The meat is being cooked in lard.

Larder/लार्डर *(noun)* - माँस रखने का भण्डार घर
All the wheat grain has been stored in the larder.

Large/लार्ज *(adjective)* - विशाल
This medicine has a large spectrum.

Largely/लार्जली *(adverb)* - विशेष करके
Largely speaking people avoid breaking social norms.

Larva/लार्वा *(noun)* - डिंभक, इल्ली
Larva is an immortive form of inseet between the stages.

Larynx/लैरिंक्स *(noun)* - हलक
Something has gone wrong with his larynx, he is unable to speak.

Lashing/लैसिंग *(noun)* - मार
Her lashing tongue didn't spare anybody.

L

Lassitude/लैसिट्यूड *(noun)* - थकावट
He is suffering from lassitude and needs rest.

Last/लास्ट *(adjective)* - अन्तिम
He came last in the race.

Lastly/लास्टली *(adverb)* - अन्त में
Lastly, I would like to thank all who have come here.

Latchet/लैचेट *(noun)* - फीता
The latchets of my shoes are worn out.

Lately/लेटली *(adverb)* - थोड़े दिन हुए
Lately he has been behaving in a strange way.

Lateral/लैटेरल *(adjective)* - बगल का
Lateral roots help plants take up water.

Latex/लैटेक्स *(noun)* - रस, दूध, दुधिया
A synthetic product resembling latex is used to make paints.

Lathe/लेद *(noun)*- खराद
Square pieces are being shaped on the lathe for making legs of the table.

Lather/लैदर् *(noun)* - साबुन का फेन
He formed a thick layer of lather on his beard before shaving.

Latin/लैटिन *(noun)* - प्राचीन रोमन सम्बन्धी, इनकी भाषा
He is a Latin American.

Latitude/लैटिट्यूड *(noun)* - चौड़ाई, स्वच्छन्दता
That city is situated at an latitude of 50° North.

Latterly/लैटरली *(adverb)* - थोड़े काल में
Latterly there has been a lot of development in sports in India.

Lattice/लैटिस *(noun)* - जाली, झँझरी
I have covered the window with a lattice.

Laudable/लाडबॅल *(adjective)* - सराहने योग्य
His stage performance was laudable.

Laudation/लाडेशन *(noun)* - स्तुति
His speech drew great laudation from audience.

Laudatory/लाडेटरी *(adjective)* - प्रशंसक
The leader was surrounded by a laudatory crowd.

Laughably/लाफेब्ली *(adverb)* - हास्यास्पद ढंग से
His actions on the stage were laughable pretensions.

Laughing-stock/लाफिंग-स्टॉक *(noun)* - हँसी का पात्र
He is a henpecked husband and as such a laughing stock among friends.

Launderer/लाउन्डरर *(noun)* - धोबी
Your clothes are dirty, get them cleaned by a launderer.

Laureate/लॉरिएट *(noun)* - प्रतिष्ठित
Tagore was a nobel laureate.

Lava/लावा *(noun)* - भूराल
Lava came out of the crater of the exploding volcano.

Lave/लेव *(verb)* - बहाना
Sea laved the rocks near the island.

Laver/लेवर *(noun)* - समुद्री शैवाल
Some people are fond of eating laver products.

Lawyer/लायर *(noun)* - वकील
As he had to appear in the court he hired a lawyer.

Lax/लैक्स *(adjective)* - शिथिल
He is lax in attitude and will not interfere with our scheme.

Layer/लेअर् *(noun)* - परत
A layer of white paint covered the walls of the room.

Lazar/लैजर् *(noun)* - रोगी

A leper used to be called lazar in old times.

Lazy/लेजी *(adjective)* - आलसी

He is a lazy fellow and will keep on delaying for hours.

Lea/ली *(noun)* - चरागाह

Let us pitch our tent here in the lea.

Leaderless/लीडरलेश *(adj)* - बिना अगुआ का

A leaderless crowd soon turns into a mob.

Leadership/लीडरशीप *(noun)* - नायकत्व

We gained freedom under the leadership of Mahatma Gandhi.

Leafage/लीफेज *(noun)* - पत्तियों का समुदाय

The leafage is very thick in this part of jungle.

Leafless/लिफलेस *(adj)* - पत्ररहित

Leafless trees have their own beauty.

Leafy/लिफी *(adjective)*- पत्तीदार

Green leafy vegetables have a lot of vitamin A.

Leaky/लीकी *(adjective)* - टपकने वाला

This is a leaky roof and droplets of water keep on trickling down.

Leal/लील *(adjective)* - ईमानदार

All these party men are leal.

Leaning/लिनिंग *(noun)* - झुकाव

This wall is not safe, a tree is leaning against it.

Leanness/लिननेस *(noun)* - दुर्बलता

Girls tend to follow the craze for leanness.

Learned/लर्नेड *(adjective)* - विद्वान

He is a highly educated and learned person.

Learning/लर्निंग *(noun)* - ज्ञान

Learning while earning is a good scheme to follow.

Lease-holder/लीजहोल्डर *(noun)*- पट्टेदार

He is a lease-holder of this property.

Least/लीस्ट *(pronoun)* - सबसे छोटा

The least you can do is to help me unpack.

Leatherette/लेदरेट *(noun)* - कृत्रिम चमड़ा

It is a belt made of leatherette.

Leathern/लेदर्न *(adjective)* - चमड़े का बना हुआ

A leathern foam covered his face.

Leathery/लेदरी *(adjective)* - चिमड़ा

This seems to be a leathery object.

Leaved/लीव्ड *(adjective)* - पर्णयुक्त

It is a brown leaved plant.

Leaven/लीवेन *(noun)* - खमीर

Leaven is added to dough to ferment and make it rise.

Leavings/लीविंग्स *(plural noun)* - जूठन

Leavings covered the entire sea beach.

Lecher/लेचर *(noun)* - लम्पट

He is a lecher, always running after women.

Lechery/लेचरी *(noun)* - कामुकता

Don't indulge into lechery in this old age.

Lecturer/लेक्चरर *(noun)* - उपदेशक

He is a lecturer in English.

Ledger/लेजर *(noun)* - लेखाबही

Here is the ledger if you want you can check it.

Leech/लीच *(noun)* - चिकित्सक

Formerly leeches were used in medicine for blood letting.

Leer/लिअर *(verb)* - कटाक्ष मारना

He leered at her as she came in wearing shorts.

Lees/लिज *(noun)* - मैल

Wine bards contain a lot of lees.

Legacy/लेगॅसि *(noun)* - उत्तरदान

He left a big legacy for his son.

Legal/लिगल *(adjective)* - कानूनी

It is a legal offence to smoke here.

Legality/लिगैलिटी *(noun)* - वैधता

Legality of this rule is in question.

Legalization/लिगलाइजेशन *(noun)* - धर्म-व्यवस्था

Legalization of something is a matter of legislature.

Leagalize/लिगलाइज *(verb)* - अधिकार देना

It has been legalized that smoking in public places is an offence.

Legally/लिगली *(adverb)* - कानूनी ढंग से

Legally speaking same rule of law applies to everyone.

Legatee/लिगेटी *(noun)* - दान पत्र पाने वाला

He is a legatee to all his father's estate.

L

Legation/लिगेशन *(noun)* – दूतकर्म

A legation has been sent to Pakistan.

Legend/लिजेंड *(noun)* – अपूर्व कहानी

There are many legends about ancient warriors.

Legendary/लेजेन्डरि *(adjective)* – कहावती

Amitabh Bachchan is a legendary figure.

Leghorn/लेग्हॉर्न *(noun)* – एक प्रकार का घरेलू मुर्गा

He is found of wearing hats made of leghorn.

Legible/लेजिबॅल *(adjective)* – पढ़ने लायक

It is a legible handwriting.

Legibly/लेजिब्ली *(adverb)* – स्पष्टता से

Try to write your notes legibly.

Legislate/लेजिस्लेट *(verb)* – कानून बनाना

The legislative body legislates.

Legitimacy/लेजिटिमैसी *(noun)* – यथार्थता, असलियत में

L

The legitimacy of this statement is doubtful.

Legume/लेम्यूम *(noun)* – शिम्ब, फली

Legume is grown as a crop.

Leguminous/लेग्यूमिनस *(adjective)* – फलीदार

Many plants are leguminous bearing seeds in pods.

Leman/लेमन *(noun)* – प्रेमिका

She is my leman.

Lemon/लेमन *(noun)* – नींबू

Would you like to have some lemon juice.

Lend/लेन्ड *(verb)* – उधार देना, उधारी

Could you lend me some money?

Lendable/लेंडेबॅल *(adjective)* – उधार देने योग्य

He doesn't have any lendable assets.

Lender/लेन्डर *(noun)* – महाजन

He is a money lender by profession.

Length/लेंग्थ *(noun)* – सीमा दूरी, लम्बाई

The length of this bridge is five km.

Lengthen/लेंग्थेन *(verb)* – बढ़ाना make or become longer. *The shadows lengthen as the sun sets.*

Lengthy/लेंग्थी *(adjective)* – लम्बा

We arrived at the conclusion after a lengthy discussion.

Leniency/लेनिएन्सी *(noun)* – दयालुता

Too much leniency with children often spoils them.

Lenient/लेनिएण्ट *(adjective)* – दयावान

He is lenient by nature.

Lenity/लेनिटि *(noun)* – दया

One of his qualities is lenity.

Lenten/लेन्टेन *(adjective)* – मितव्ययी

This food without meat is appropriate to Lent.

Lentil/लेन्टिल *(noun)* – मसूर

Lentil dal is full of proteins.

Lentisk/लेन्टिस्क *(noun)* – मस्तगी का वृक्ष

Lentisk is a mastic tree bearing gum.

Leo/लीओ *(noun)* – सिंह, शेर का बच्चा, सिंह राशि

He is a leo as he was born on 25th of July.

Leopard/लेपॅड *(noun)* – चीता

Leopards can be seen in zoo or jungles of Asia and Africa.

Leper/लेपर *(noun)* – कोढ़ी

These days there is treatment available for lepers.

Leprosy/लेप्रॅसी *(noun)* – कोढ़

Once leprosy was incurable and was deemed as a result of evil deeds in past life.

Lese-majesty/लीज़्-मैजेस्टि *(noun)* – राज-विद्रोह

Lese-majesty resulted in his being hanged on scaffold.

Lesion/लीजन *(noun)* – पीड़ा

He suffers from lesion in right arm as a result of an accident.

Less/लेस *(determine & pronoun)* – कम

The class has less students today.

Lessen/लेसन *(verb)* – कम करना

It lessened my anger when he begged pardon. Let me lessen your burden, give me those bags.

Lest/लेस्ट *(conjunction)* – कदाचित्

Don't drive rashly lest you should have an accident.

Lethal/लीथल् *(adjective)* – मृत्युकर

A lethal overdose of sleeping pills took his life.

Lethargy/लेथार्जि *(noun)* - आलस्य
He lives a lack lustre life as a result of lethargy.

Lettuce/लेटूस *(noun)* - चुकन्दर
Lettuce is an important part of salad.

Leveret/लेवरिट *(noun)* - शशक
I have caught a leveret and I'll make it a pet.

Leviable/लेविएबल *(adjective)* - कर लगाने योग्य
Octroi tax is leviable on out of state products.

Leviathan/लेवाइअथन *(noun)* - बड़ा दैत्य
Many leviathans can be seen in this part of sea.

Levity/लेबिटी *(noun)* - ओछापन
You are a highly qualified doctor and levity doesn't behove you.

Levy/लेवि *(noun)* - कर लगाना
This year the government has collected a huge levy.

Lewd/ल्यूड *(adjective)* - कामुक
His lewd remarks angered her.

Lexicon/लेक्सिकन *(noun)* - शब्द-संग्रह
This shop has a number of good lexicons.

Liability/लाइअबिलिटि *(noun)* - जवाबदेही
He is more of a liability than an asset.

Liar/लाइ-अर् *(noun)* - मिथ्यावादी
Don't believe him, he is a notorious liar.

Libel/लिइबेल् *(noun)* - अपमान-लेख
This newspaper has published a libel and a case has been filed against its editor.

Liberally/लिबरलि *(adverb)* - उदारता से
She liberally gifted all poor children.

Liberate/लिबरेट *(verb)* - मुक्त करना
Many prisoners were liberated on Independence Day.

Liberation/लिबरेशन *(noun)* - मुक्ति
Liberation was granted to many African colonies by the British government.

Liberator/लिबरेटर *(noun)* - मुक्ति देने वाला
He was seen as a liberator of persons working as bonded labourers.

Libertine/लिबर्टिन् *(noun)* - कामुक
He is a libertine and whole-heartedly enjoys life.

Librate/लाइब्रेट *(verb)* - हिलाना
Astrologers liberate the position at the time of birth to predict future.

Libration/लाइब्रेशन *(noun)* - कम्पन
Libration helps astrologers predict future of a person or thing or a country.

Lid/लिड *(noun)* - ढकना
One of the lids of the containers is missing.

Life/लाइफ *(noun)* - इच्छा से, जीवन
Compared to plants and trees, there is apparently no life in stones.

Lifelong/लाइफलांग *(adjective)* - जीवन पर्यन्त
Lifelong habits die hard.

Lifetime/लाइफटाइम *(noun)* - जीवनकाल
He didn't do even a single charitable act throughout his lifetime.

Liftable/लिफ्टेबल *(adjective)* - उठाने योग्य
Mount arteries always carry easily liftable packs.

Lightness/लाइटनेस *(noun)* - हल्कापन
The lightness of these shoes is remarkable.

Likeable/लाइकेबल *(adjective)* - पसंद के लायक
He is a likeable person welcomed by all.

Likelihood/लाइक्लिहुड *(noun)* - सम्भावना
In all likelihood, he will be arriving tomorrow.

Liken/लाइकेन *(verb)* - सदृश करना
Casteism is likened to a deadly disease.

Likeness/लाइकनेस *(noun)* - समानता
Likeness between the father and son is remarkable.

Likewise/लाइकवाइज *(adverb)* - और भी
He, likewise his brother is quarrelsome.

Limitation/लिमिटेशन *(noun)* - मियाद
Every human being has his or her limitations.

Limited/लिमिटेड *(adjective)* - सीमित
It is a private limited company and not a government concern.

Limn/लिम्न *(verb)* - चित्र रंगना
The painting was limned to attract customers.

Limner/लिम्नर *(noun)* - चित्र रंगने वाला
He is a renowned limner having painted many portraits.

Limp/लिम्प *(verb)* - लंगड़ाते हुए चलना
He walked limpingly.

L

Limpness/लिम्पनेस *(noun)* – लगड़ापन
His limpness caused him to walk slowly.

Lineage/लिनिज *(noun)* – वंश, कुल
His lineage is royal.

Lineal/लिनिअल *(adjective)* – पैतृक
The lineal crawl of ants is remarkable.

Linger/लिंगर *(verb)* – विलम्ब करना
He lingered on till he was firmly asked to leave.

Lingerer/लिंगरर *(noun)* – दीर्घसूत्री
He is a lingerer and wants go easily.

Lingering/लिंगरिंग *(adjective)* – चिरकाल का
His lingering figure caused disturbance to us.

Linguist/लिंग्विस्ट *(noun)* – भाषा प्रवीण
He is a well known linguist.

Link/लिंक *(adj)* – सम्बन्धित
Police have found his name linked to a terrorist outfit.

L

Linn/लिन *(noun)* – कन्दरा
Let's take bath in this linn.

Liny/लाइनी *(adjective)* – रेखायुक्त
It is a liny piece of paper.

Lion/लायन *(noun)* – शेर
He fought like a lion in the battle.

Lip/लिप *(noun)* – ओठ
Beautiful lips make a face attractive.

Liquefaction/लिक्विफैक्शन *(noun)* – गलाने का कार्य
Liquefaction is the process to convert gas into liquids.

Liquefier/लिक्विफायर *(noun)* – गलाने वाला
Use of liquefier is necessary to change gases into liquids.

Liquescent/लिक्वेसेंट *(adjective)* – गलाने योग्य
Ice is liquescent.

Liquidity/लिक्विडिटि *(noun)* – तरलता
How much your liquid assets are worth?

Liquidation/लिक्विडेशन *(noun)* – ऋण निस्तार
The firm went into liquidation last year.

Liquorice/लिकॅरिस *(noun)* – मुलेठी
Liquourice has a sweet taste and is used in medicine.

Listener/लिस्नर *(noun)* – सुनने वाला
I like him as he is a patient listener.

Listless/लिस्टलेस *(adjective)* – उदासीन
I found him listless and lying in bed.

Literacy/लिटरेसी *(noun)* – साक्षरता
A literacy drive has been launched in the village.

Literally/लिटरली *(adverb)* – यथाशब्द
Literally speaking, the matter is leased, no more discussion.

Litigation/लिटिगेशन *(noun)* – विवाद
No firm wishes to go into litigation.

Litigious/लिटिजियस *(adjective)* – अदालती
He is a litigious fellow always quarrelling and raising disputes.

Liturgics/लिटर्जिक्स *(plural noun)* – कर्मकाण्ड विषय
Liturgics are often performed in set places e.g. mosques or temples.

Liven/लाइवॅन *(verb)* – प्रसन्न करना
The atmosphere became livened as she sang melodiously.

Livid/लिविड *(adjective)* – नीला पड़ा हुआ
He was livid with anger.

Living/लिविंग *(noun)* – जीवन
He earns his living by working as a labourer.

Lizard/लिजर्ड *(noun)* – छिपकली, बम्हनी
I find lizards very repulsive.

Lo/लो *(exclamatory)* – अहा
Lo! here comes our esteemed guest.

Load/लोड *(noun)* – दबाव
The load is about to be moved in a truck.

Loader/लोडर *(noun)* – बोझने वाला
About fifteen persons worked round the clock as loaders to load the cargo ship.

Loan/लोन *(noun)* – ऋण
The bank gave him a loan of one lakh rupees.

Loath/लोथ *(adjective)* – अनिच्छुक
I was loath to leave the party.

Loathe/लोद *(verb)* – निन्दा करना
She loathed his presence.

Loathing/लोदिंग *(noun)* - अतिघृणा

He felt nothing but loathing for her.

Loathsome/लोदसम *(adjective)* - घृणाजनक

I find centipedes loathsome.

Labelia/लाबेलिया *(noun)* - एक फूल का पौधा

I have just bought a lobelia for my garden.

Local/लोकल *(noun)* - स्थानिक, स्थानीय

The local post office is quite near my house. It is a local infection on and can be treated in the dispensary. A local person told me your address.

Locality/लोकैलिटी *(noun)* - प्रदेश

Is there any cinema house in your locality?

Locate/लोकेट *(verb)* - स्थापन करना

I located his address with much difficulty

Location/लोकेशन *(noun)* - स्थान निर्धारण

The director was on look out for a suitable location to shoot his film.

Lockage/लॉकेज *(noun)* - नहर का बाँध

This lockage system is quite difficult to understand.

Locket/लॉकेट *(noun)* - छोटा ताला, लोलक

He wears a locket which has his wife's photo.

Lock-stitch/लॉक-स्टिच *(noun)* - दुहरी सियन

These stitches are made by a lock-stitch machine.

Lock-up/लॉक-अप *(noun)* - बन्दीगृह

He was put in lock-up for a hit and run case.

Locomotor/लोकॅमोटर *(adjective)* - गति-सम्बन्धी

Locomotor modes of all creatures are different.

Locust/लोकस्ट *(noun)* - टिड्डी

A big swarm of locust descended on the fields.

Locution/लोक्यूशन *(noun)* - वाक्शैली

His locution is unique.

Lofty/लाफ्टि *(adjective)* - ऊँचा, उन्तुंग, अहंकारी

It is a lofty building.

Loftiness/लॉफ्टिनेस *(noun)* - गर्व

His loftiness knew no bounds.

Logarithm/लॉगरिथ्म *(noun)* - घात प्रमापक लघुगणक

Logarithm simplifies calculations.

Logger/लॉगर *(noun)* - मूर्ख

He is a logger whose profession is to cut trees for timber.

Logician/लॉजिसियन *(noun)* - तार्किक

He does good reasoning, he is a fine logician.

Loiter/लॉइटर *(verb)* - देर करना

He loitered round the place.

Loiterer/लॉइटरर - आलसी

He is a loiterer and does no work.

Loitering/लॉइटरिंग *(noun)* - विलम्ब

He was found loitering and police questioned him.

Lollop/लॉलॉप *(verb)* - सुस्ती से घूमना

Some animals lollop.

Lone/लोन *(adjective)* - अकेला

He is a lone wolf, mixing with nobody.

Loneliness/लोनलिनेस *(noun)* - निर्जनता

He began to suffer as loneliness surrounded him.

Longevity/लान्विटि *(noun)* - दीर्घायु

Longevity has been a matter of study for scientists since long.

Longish/लॉन्गिश *(adjective)* - दीर्घाकार

The railway platform was quite longish.

Longitude/लाँगिट्यूड *(noun)* - लम्बाई, देशान्तर

Longitude lines are drawn on a map or globe for marking the distance of a place from Greenwich meridian.

Looker-on/लुकरऑन *(noun)* - दर्शक

The lookers-on stared at the two filthy persons in a public place.

Looking/लुकिंग *(noun)* - दिखावट

Looking down I saw a man climbing stairs.

Loom/लुम *(verb)* - अस्पष्ट रूप से देख गया

An iceberg loomed large over the ship.

Loon/लुन *(noun)* - दुर्जन

He is a loon and talks nonsense.

Loophole/लुपहोल *(noun)* - बचाव का रास्ता

Lawyers are smart enough to find loopholes in the law.

Loosely/लुजलि *(adverb)* - शिथिलता से

People avoid him as he is in the habit of talking loosely.

L

Looseness/लुजनेस *(noun)* – ढीलापन

I couldn't wear the pants because of their looseness.

Loosen/लुजेन *(verb)* – पृथक् करना

I got my trousers loosened by a tailor as they were very tight.

Lore/लोर *(noun)* – शिक्षा

Lore is an important part of any social culture.

Loser/लूजर *(noun)* – खोने वाला

He is a loser and will never amount to anything.

Lotus/लोटस *(noun)* – कमल

Lotus is regarded as sacred flower in India.

Lounger/लाउंजर *(noun)*– आलसी

I intend to buy a lounger and relax on it.

Lout/लाउट *(noun)* – ग्रामीण मनुष्य

He is a lout and sure to quarrel with you sooner or later.

L

Loutish/लाउटिश *(adjective)* – अनाड़ी

He is a loutish fellow. Don't mix with him.

Love/लव *(verb & noun)* – प्रेम करना

I love my granddaughter a lot.

Loveliness/लवलिनेस *(noun)* – सुन्दरता

Her loveliness is to be seen to be believed.

Lovely/लवलि *(adjective)* – सुन्दर

She is a lovely woman

Lowermost/लोअरमोस्ट *(adj)* – सबसे नीचे का

Our body's lowermost parts are feet.

Lowliness/लोलिनेस *(noun)* – विनय

His lowliness almost reduced him to zero.

Lowly/लोलि *(adjective)* – दर्पहीन

He is a lowly employee of the company.

Loyal/लॉयल् *(adjective)* – सच्चा

He is a loyal worker of the party.

Loyalist/लॉयलिस्ट् *(noun)* – राजभक्त

Congress loyalists keep attacking the opposition parties.

Lozenge/लोजेंज *(noun)* – समचतुर्भुज, बर्फी, मिठाई

Take this lozenge, it will melt in your mouth and soothe your throat.

Lubber/लबर *(noun)* – गँवार

He is a lubber and not smart enough to do this job.

Lucent/ल्यूसेंट *(adjective)* – प्रकाशमान्

This is a lucent piece of writing.

Lucidly/ल्यूसिडली *(adverb)* – स्पष्टता से

The tough vocabulary of the text was lucidly explained by the teacher.

Luckily/लकिलि *(adverb)* – भाग्यवश

Luckily I won the lottery.

Luckless/लकलेस *(adjective)* – भाग्यहीन

The luckless fellow passed through many difficulties in life.

Lucre/ल्यूकर *(noun)* – लाभ

He is a miser and loves to hoard lucre.

Luculent/ल्यूक्यूलेन्ट *(adjective)* – स्पष्ट

The luculent moon was a sight to see.

Lues/लूईज *(noun)* – महामारी, गरमी

He suffers from lues.

Lumbago/लम्बेगो *(noun)* – कमर का दर्द

He has been diagnosed as suffering from lumbago.

Luminary/ल्यूमिनरी *(noun)* – चन्द्रमा

He is a luminary who does a lot of inspirational talking.

Lumpish/लम्पिश *(adjective)* – भारी

It is a lumpish pointing.

Lumpishness/लम्पिशनेस *(noun)* – स्थूलता

Lumpishness is not a desirable trait.

Lunancy/ल्यूनेसी *(noun)* – उन्माद

He suffers from lunacy.

Lupine/लूपिन *(noun)* – शमीधान्य

I have received a lupine as a gift from my friend.

Lurcher/लर्चर् *(noun)* – चोर

A lurcher is a born hunter.

Lustful/लस्टफुल *(adjective)* – कामातुर

He is a lustful person, always alive and full of life.

Lustiness/लस्टिनेस *(noun)* – कामुकता

Our society does not consider lustiness a desirable trait.

Luteous/ल्यूटिअस् *(adj)* - गहरे नांरगी रंग का
He is interested in the luteous study of yellow colour.

Luxuriant/लक्जरिअंट् *(adjective)* - अत्यन्त
The plant should have luxuriant growth.

Luxuriate/लक्जरिएट *(verb)* - आनन्द मचाना
He luxuriated in a five star hotel.

Luxury/लक्जरी *(noun)* - विलासिता
He is a rich man and lives in great luxury.

Lydian/लिडिअन् *(noun)* - कोमल, जनाने ढंग का
I dislike his lydian hehaviour.

Lying/लाइंग *(adjective)* - पड़े हुए
I can see very clearly that right now you are lying.

Lymph/लिम्फ *(noun)* - शरीर में का पंछा
Lymph came out of the sore on his hand.

Lynch/लिन्च *(noun)* - अन्याय युक्त दण्ड देना
The thief was lynched by the mob.

Lynx/लिन्क्स *(noun)* - बिल्ली के कुल का जंगली पशु
We saw a lynx in the zoo.

Lyre/लायर् *(noun)* - वीणा
Ancient Greeks used to play lyre.

Lyric/लिरिक *(noun)* - वीणा का, गायन सम्बन्धी
The poet wrote a beautiful lyric.

L

Mm

M/एम *(noun)* - अंग्रेजी वर्णमाला का 13वाँ वर्ण the thirteenth letter of the English alphabet.

1. Denoting the next after L in a set of items, categories. etc.
2. The Roman numeral for 1000. *About 1M people participated in the protests.*

M

Ma/मा *(noun)* - मा
Priyanka's Ma runs her own construction business.

Ma'am/मैम *(noun)* - महोदया
Nigar ma'am is an excellent teacher.

Mab/मैब *(noun)* - परियों की रानी
Sonya played the character of Queen Mab perfectly at the carnival yesterday.

Mac/मैक *(noun)* - आ उपसर्ग
Hey there, brother Mac, could you please tell me the way to Sandy Street?

Macaque/मॅकाक *(noun)* - अफ्रीका का लंगूर
To study the habits of macaque monkeys, one needs to live close to their habitat.

Macaroni/मैकॅरोनि *(noun)* - सेवई
I remember my childhood days over a bowl full of macaroni and cheese that I often have for breakfast.

Macaronic/मैकॅरॉनिक *(adjective)* - अनेक भाषाओं का मिश्रण
English is becoming macaronic by incorporating words from other languages.

Macaroon/मकारून *(noun)* - बादाम
Strawberry macaroons are Tom's favourite evening refreshment.

Macassar-oil/मैकासर-आइल् *(noun)* - मकासर नगर का सुगन्धित तेल
Ved explained the benefits of Macassar oil at the workshop.

Macaw/मकॉ *(noun)* - तोता
Its colourful plumage characterizes the Macaw species.

Mace/मेस *(noun)* - गदा, जावित्री
The robber used a mace to attack his victim.

Machiavelli/मैकियावेली *(noun)* - धूर्त राजनीतिज्ञ
Machiavelli was a great political writer.

Machinal/मैकिनल *(adj.)* - यन्त्रवत्
Monotony is often the consequence of a machinal lifestyle.

Machinate/मैकिनेट *(verb)* - षड्यन्त्र करना
The police found out that Sandy's own brother machinated his murder.

Machination/मैकिनेशन *(noun)* - कूट प्रबन्ध
Nefertiti's political machinations brought her to control the whole of Egypt.

Machine/मशीन *(noun)* - साधन
A pulley is a simple machine.

Machinery/मशीनरी *(noun)* - यन्त्रों का समूह
Mining requires the use of some heavy machinery.

Mackerel/मैकॅरॅल *(noun)* - समुद्री मछली
Mackerel is a delicacy in some parts of the world.

Mackintosh/मैकिन्टॉश *(noun)* - बरसाती कपड़ा
Sam put his mackintosh on to shelter himself from the heavy snowfall that came suddenly.

Macrame/मॅक्रामि *(noun)* - गाँठ दी हुई झालर
Tina surprised everyone with her talent of macramé at the summer camp.

Macrocosm/मैक्रोकॉज्म *(noun)* - त्रिभुवन
Our solar system is just a small part of the macrocosm, which is a collection of several such solar systems.

Macron/मैक्रॅन *(noun)* - दीर्घचिह्न
Tina learnt the importance of macrons in her phonetics class at the university today.

Macula/मैक्यूला *(noun)* - धब्बा
Rob hurt the macula of his eyes in an accident.

Maculate/मैक्युलेट *(adjective)* - धब्बा लगाना
The maculated cloth revealed the secret behind the murder crime.

Maculation/मैक्यूलेशन *(noun)* - लांछन, धब्बा
Maculation on a leopard's body is a natural phenomenon.

Mad/मैड *(adjective)* - पागल
To challenge the authority and expecting it to bend its rules is a mad idea.

Madden/मैडेन *(verb)* - पागल होना
His love for her maddened him.

Madder/मैडर *(noun)* - छबीला
The madder plant is known for the red dye that it yields.

Mademoiselle/मैडमॅजेल *(noun)* - कुमारी
Monsieur Heathcliff requested Mademoiselle Emma for a drink in the bar.

Madhouse/मैडहाउस *(noun)* - पागलखाना
The state government employs the inmates of the Boston madhouse.

Madly/मैडली *(adverb)* - पागलपन से
Tom is madly in love with Rita.

Madness/मैडनेस *(noun)* - पागलपन
Playing with fire is an act of sheer madness.

Madrigal/मैड्रिगल *(noun)* - देहाती गीत
The Madrigal is an interesting form of music and lyrics that involves a group of people singing together or individually.

Magazine/मैग्जीन *(noun)* - शस्त्र, पत्रिका
Elle Décor is a good magazine to learn about the current trends in the market.

Mage/मेज् *(noun)* - पण्डित
Sita knew that the heavily bearded man was a mage the moment she saw him meditating in the Himalayas.

Maggot/मैगॅट *(noun)* - कृमि
The meat dish was infested with maggots.

Maggoty/मैगॉटि *(adjective)* - कीड़ों से भरा हुआ
The rice dish turned maggoty after two days.

Magi/मेजाइ *(plural noun)* - विद्वान्
Karan told her son about the Magi who brought gifts for the infant Jesus on the eve of Christmas.

Magical/मैजिकल *(adjective)* - जादू का
Preeti says that her trip to Venice was absolutely magical.

Magician/मैजिशियन *(noun)* - जादूगर
Tory invited a magician to delight the kids attending her son's birthday party.

Magnanimity/मैग्नानिमिटि *(noun)* - उदारता
Monty's donations to the children's fund reflect his magnanimity.

Magnate/मैग्नेट *(noun)* - रईस
Lalit Mohan is a business magnate in the steel industry.

Magnet/मैग्नेट *(noun)* - चुम्बक
A magnet attracts all objects made out of iron.

Magnetism/मैग्नेटिज्म *(noun)* - आकर्षणशक्ति
Leela and Sam share a strong aura of magnetism that is not easily understood by others.

Magnetization/मैग्नेटाइजेशन *(noun)* - आकर्षण संस्कार
The iron ore under the Earth's surface leads to its magnetization.

Magnifiable/मैग्निफाएबल *(adj)* - बढ़ाने योग्य
Virus and bacteria are easily magnifiable with the help of a microscope.

Magnification/मैग्निफिकेशन *(adverb)* - बृहत्तरकरण
Viruses are visible only under high magnification.

Magnificence/मैग्निफिसेंस *(noun)* - प्रताप
Nefertiti, the Egyptian queen, prided herself over the magnificence of her empire.

Magnifico/मैग्निफिको *(noun)* - रईस
The jury facilitated the illustrious magnificoes of the Bollywood industry.

Magnifier/मैग्निफायर *(noun)* - बढ़ाकर दिखलाने वाला
Biologists study microorganisms with the help of a magnifier.

Magniloquence/मैग्निलोक्वेंस *(noun)* - प्रौढ़ भाषण
The dowager Queen was known for her magniloquence throughout the kingdom.

Magpie/मैग्पाइ *(noun)* - नीलकण्ठ पक्षी
We saw a beautiful magpie at the bird sanctuary yesterday.

Mahogany/महोगनी *(noun)* - महोगनी वृक्ष
Ben ordered new mahogany wood furniture for his new office.

M

Maiden/मेडॅन *(noun)* - कुमारी कन्या

The fair maiden loved her village and never wanted to leave it.

Mailable/मेलेबॅल *(adj)* - डाक से भेजने योग्य

Betty sent all the mailable documents to Veronica as soon as possible.

Maintenance/मेन्टिनेन्स *(noun)* - जीविका

The present government of Goa has ensured strict control over the maintenance of the state.

Maize/मेज *(noun)* - मक्का

Maize forms an integral part of breakfast in the West.

Major/मेजर *(adjective)* - प्रमुख, वयस्क

Financial inadequacy is a major problem in developing nations.

Make-believe/मेक-बिलिव *(noun)* - बहाना

All the characters in the play are make-believe.

Maker/मेकर *(noun)* - रचने वाला

The maker of this chair is Sam.

M

Makeshift/मेकशिफ्ट *(adjective)* - क्षणिक

This house is a makeshift arrangement.

Makeweight/मेकवेट *(noun)* - पसँघा धड़ा

The makeweight added by the vegetable vendor was faulty.

Making/मेकिंग *(noun)* - रचना

The making of a cake requires patience and precision.

Maladjustment/मॉलएड्जस्टमेंट - बुरा प्रबन्ध

Rex is a maladjusted boy in his school.

Malady/मैलडि *(noun)* - रोग

Depression is one of the most widespread maladies in the world.

Malaise/मैलेज *(noun)* - शारीरिक क्लेश

Rita often experiences a sense of malaise at her workplace.

Malapropos/मैलऐप्रपो *(adverb)* - असमय में

He malapropos commented on his fellow colleagues.

Malcontent/मैलकन्टेन्ट *(noun)* - अतृप्त

The malcontents are the first ones to create problems in a happy environment.

Malefaction/मैलिफैक्शन *(noun)* - पाप, शाप

Unfortunately, politicians are allowed to commit crimes such as financial corruption and other such malefactions by the state apparatus.

Malefactor/मैलिफैक्टर *(noun)* - पापी

The malefactor involved in the murder is still missing.

Malefic/मॉलिफिक *(adjective)* - हानिकर

His malefic words made him exercise control over all the workers.

Maleficence/मॉलिफिसेन्स *(noun)* - अपकार

Maleficence often leads to forced agreement in a given situation.

Maleficent/मॉलिफिसेन्ट *(adjective)* - अपकारी

His maleficent eyes often led to the undoing of women.

Malevolence/मॉलेवलॅन्स *(noun)* - द्रोह

Tina's eyes reflect her malevolence towards Rob.

Malformation/मैल्फॉ:मेशन *(noun)* - बुरी बनावट

Warts are a malformation by birth and need to be removed surgically.

Malice/मैलिस *(noun)* - डाह

Rita experiences unbearable malice towards men who molested her last year and seeks revenge.

Malicious/मॅलिशस *(adjective)* - द्रोही पापाम्मा

His malicious nature is the cause of his unethical behaviour.

Malign/मॅलाइन *(verb)* - बदनाम करना, घातक

Tom's malign nature led to his dismissal from his workplace yesterday.

Malignancy/मॅलिग्नैन्सी *(noun)* - द्रोह

The biopsy revealed the nature of the malignancy.

Malignity/मॅलिग्निटि *(noun)* - ईर्ष्या

Criminals often show signs of heinous malignity.

Malignly/मॅलिग्नलि *(adverb)* - द्रोह से

All of Iago's dialogues with Othello are malignly planned.

Malison/मैलिसन *(noun)* - शाप

The onlookers screamed several malisons at the murderers.

Mall/माल *(noun)* - ठण्डी सड़क

Rob likes grocery shopping at the mall on Sundays.

Mallard/मैलॅर्ड् *(noun)* - जंगली बत्तख

Mallard is a delicacy in some parts of the world.

Mallet/मैलेट् *(noun)* - मुँगरी

She murdered her abusive husband using only a mallet.

Malodorous/मैलोडॅरॅस *(adjective)* - बदबूदार

She walked through malodorous alleys to reach the post office.

Malpractice/मैल्प्रैक्टिस *(noun)* - बुरी चाल

The doctor lost his licence to practise medicine because of his malpractice.

Malt/माल्ट *(noun)* - भिगोया हुआ जौ

Malt beer is a refreshing drink, especially during summers.

Maltreat/मैल्ट्रीट *(verb)* - गाली देना

Sam had been maltreating his wife since the day they got married.

Mammary/मैमरि *(adjective)* - स्तन-सम्बन्धी

Rita realized that her mammary tumour had spread throughout her chest area.

Mammon/मैमन *(noun)* - कुबेर

Greeks worshipped Mammon for greater wealth.

Mammoth/मैमथ *(noun & adj)* - महान्, विशालकाय

The Mammoth is an extinct animal.

Manacle/मैनॅकॅल *(noun)* - हथकड़ी

Patients who have severe mental illness are often kept in manacles.

Manage/मैनेज् *(verb)* - चलाना

She managed the entire fashion show on her own.

Manageability/मैनेजिबिलिटी *(noun)* - व्यवस्था

A person's ability to work in a stressful environment depends the manageability of various tasks.

Manageable/मैनेजेबल् *(adj)* - प्रबन्ध करने योग्य

All things are manageable once planned in an organized fashion.

Management/मैनेजमेन्ट *(noun)* - अनुशासन

The management of any company depends on its team.

Manager/मैनेजर् *(noun)* - प्रबन्धक

My Manager is a strict disciplinarian.

Manageress/मैनेजरेश *(noun)* - प्रबन्धकर्त्री

Deepika makes an intelligent and a competent mangeress.

Managerial/मैनेजीरिअल् *(adj)* - प्रबन्ध-सम्बन्धी

Preeti fulfils her managerial duties in perfect order.

Mandate/मैन्डेट *(noun)* - आदेश

All drivers are said to follow the state mandate of safe and slow driving.

Mandatory/मैन्डेटरी *(adjective)* - आज्ञा-सूचक

Mandatory rules enforced by the government ought to be followed by all the citizens on a nation. Wearing a vermillion mark on the forehead is mandatory for all married Hindu women.

Manes/मानेज/मेनीज *(plural noun)* - पितरों की आत्माएँ

Some tribes still pray to their manes hoping that they would be rid of any diseases or misfortunes.

Mangle/मैंगल *(verb)* - खण्ड-खण्ड करना

Mangles are used to dry and iron out clothes in large numbers.

Mango/मैंगो *(noun)* - आम

Mango is the king of fruits.

Mangy/मेन्जि *(adjective)* - रूखा

The mangy dog was sent to the veterinarian.

Mania/मेनिआ *(noun)* - उन्माद

Patients suffering from mania are often unable to control their anger.

Maniac/मेनिअक् *(noun)* - पागल मनुष्य

Ginger is a maniac and is very aggressive.

Manikin/मैनिकिन् *(noun)* - छोटा मनुष्य

Dicken's fictional character or Uncle Scrooge is depicted as a manikin.

Manipulation/मनिप्युलेशन *(noun)* - दस्तकारी

Rob is a manipulative boss.

Manner/मैनर *(noun)* - चाल

Clive gives orders to his team in an unstoppable manner.

Manse/मैन्स *(noun)* - पादरियों का घर

Civilians visit the manse on Sunday.

Mansion/मैन्सन *(noun)* – बड़ा भवन, हवेली, कोठी
Raman lives in a mansion in Mumbai.

Mansuetude/मैनस्विद्युड *(noun)* – सीधापन
His wife takes advantage of his mansuetude.

Mantelet/मैन्टॅलेट *(noun)* – बुरका
Tia gave the poor beggar her mantelet on Christmas eve.

Mantis/मैन्टिस *(noun)* – एक प्रकार का कीड़ा
Ned saw a Mantis on his way back home from work.

Manually/मैन्युअली *(adverb)* – हाथ से करते हुए
Some machinery ought to be operated manually.

Manufactory/मैन्युफैक्टरी *(noun)* – कारखाना
The carpenter's wife worked at the manufactory to earn a little extra.

Manufacture/मैन्युफैक्चर *(verb)* – दस्तकारी
Steel factories manufacture utensils.

Mar/मार *(verb)* – हानि करना
Spring season lasts from Mar-May.

Marasmic/मॅरैज़्मिक *(adj)* – शरीरक्षय- सम्बन्धी
Nancy felt sorry for her marasmic child.

M

Marasmus/मॅरैज्मस *(noun)* – शरीर का क्षय
Vicky's son suffers from Marasmus.

Maraud/मॅराड *(verb)* – लूटना
The invading army marauded the village.

Marcescence/मारसेसॅन्स *(noun)* – मुरझाहट
With the advent of winter, the crops in the village had started to marcescence.

Marcescent/मार्सेसॅन्ट *(noun)* – मुरझाने वाला
The China Rose had become marcescent but had not lost its beauty.

Mare/मेअर *(noun)* – घोड़ी
Ruth loved to ride her mare during vacations.

Margosa/मारगोसा *(noun)* – नीम का वृक्ष
Margosa has healing and antiseptic properties.

Marigold/मेरिगोल्ड *(noun)* – गेंदा
Marigold garlands are used to beautify the bride in Indian weddings.

Marine/मॅरीन *(adjective)* – समुद्रीय
Vinit is a botanist who specializes in marine plants.

Mariner/मैरिनर *(noun)* – नाविक
Fawaz wants to become a mariner when he grows up.

Maritime/मैरिटाइम *(adjective)* – समुद्रीय
Cindy knows all the rules of maritime sailing.

Marked/मार्क्ड *(adjective)* – चिह्नित
All the victims of the holocaust were marked on their skin.

Marker/मार्कर *(noun)* – गिनने वाला
Promotion acts as a marker of success.

Market/मार्किट *(noun)* – बाजार
I go to the market in the morning to buy fresh vegetables.

Marketable/मार्केटेबल् *(adjective)* – बिक्री के योग्य
Marketable goods often enjoy huge popularity.

Marking/मार्किंग *(noun)* – परों की रंगाई
The markings on a leopard are unique.

Marksman/मार्क्समैन *(noun)* – निशानेबाज
Sam is an excellent marksman.

Marmoreal/मार्मोरियल *(adjective)* – इसके सदृश
Rita has Marmoreal flooring in her attic.

Maroon/मैरून *(noun)* – आतिशबाजी
Ben's ancestors belonged to the Maroon community.

Marriageable/मैरिजेबल् *(adjective)* – विवाह करने योग्य
Geeta wants to be married to her lover once she attains the marriageable age.

Mars/मार्स *(noun)* – मंगल ग्रह
Mars is the fourth planet in our solar system.

Marsh/मार्श *(noun)* – दलदल
Lotus plant grows in abundance in marshlands.

Marshiness/मार्शिनेस *(noun)* – दलदली स्थिति
Tropical American land is known for its marshiness.

Marshy/मार्शि *(adj)* – दलदली
Marshy areas are usually accident prone.

Mart/मार्ट *(noun)* – हाट
Heena bought a new pair of shoes from the Mart yesterday.

Martian/मार्श्यन् *(adj)* – मंगल ग्रह का निवासी
The Martian rock was being studied by the scientists.

Martinet/मार्टिनेट *(noun)* – तीक्ष्ण शासक
George was an excellent Martinet in the American army.

Martingale/मार्टिंगेल *(noun)* - जेरबन्द
Gia fell from her horse when the Martingale broke.

Martyr/मार्टर् *(noun)* - शहीद
Shaheed Bhagat Singh was a martyr.

Masher/मैशर *(noun)* - छैला
I want to buy a potato masher.

Masked/मास्क्ड *(adjective)* - गुप्त
Both the robbers were masked in order to hide their identities.

Masker/मास्कर *(noun)* - नकाब डाले हुए
Street writers were great maskers of good literature.

Mason/मेसन *(noun)* - राजमिस्त्री
Fred's father is a mason.

Masonry/मेसन्री *(noun)* - राजगीरी
Dany says his talent lies in masonry.

Masque/मास्क *(noun)* - कठपुतली का तमाशा
Several women writers such as Aphra Behn wrote plays that were dramatized as masques in the 18th century.

Massacre/मैसॅकॅ(र्) *(noun)* - खूनखराबा
The Jallianwala massacre continues to haunt people till date.

Massage/मैसाज् *(noun)* - अंगमर्दन
A good massage is a great way to relieve stress.

Masseur/मैसॅर् *(noun)* - मालिश करने वाला मनुष्य
Michel hired a masseur for his wife after she fell from the stairs.

Massy/मैसी *(adjective)* - ठोस, भारी
I need to buy a massy bed for the kids.

Mast/मास्ट *(noun)* - मस्तूल
The sailor fixed the mast before the ship sailed.

Masterly/मास्टरली *(adjective)* - अद्वितीय
Naved's masterly act made him a popular favourite with all his superiors at his workplace.

Mastership/मास्टरशीप *(noun)* - ऐश्वर्य
A man's mastership is judged by his manners in front of his inferiors.

Mastery/मास्टरी *(noun)* - अधिकार
Fred has mastery over all of Dickens' novels.

Mastic/मैस्टिक *(noun)* - गोंद, लासा
Mastic has no side effects in the long run.

Masticable/मैस्टिकेबल *(adj)* - चबाने योग्य
This food is easily masticable.

Mastication/मास्टिकेशन *(noun)* - चबाने का कार्य
The mastication of food depends on the bacteria in the human gut.

Masticate/मास्टिकेट *(verb)* - चबाना
George's mother bit her tongue while masticating her meal.

Mastitis/मैस्टाइटिस् *(noun)* - स्तन की सूजन
Mastitis is often seen as an early symptom of cancer.

Matchable/मैचेबल *(adj)* - अनुरूप
The matchable characteristics of aquatic plants are of great importance to marine biologists.

Matchless/मैचलेस *(adjective)* - अनुपम
Cleopatra's matchless beauty is talked about even today.

Materialism/मैटीरिअलिज्म *(noun)* - जड़वाद
Materialism is a distinct characteristic of selfish individualism.

Materiality/मैटेरिअलिटि *(noun)* - भौतिकत्व
The nuclear weapons explain the materiality of the developed nations.

Materialize/मैटीरिअलाइज *(verb)* - भौतिक बनाना
The driver failed to materialize despite constant phone calls.

Maternity/मैटरनिटि *(noun)* - मातृत्व
Kareena is on her maternity leave till September.

Mathematician/मैथेमेटिशिअन *(noun)* - गणितज्ञ
Anurag was a well-known mathematician in the University of Delhi.

Mathematics/मैथेमेटिक्स *(noun)* - गणित-विद्या
Mathematics plays an important part in the study of planetary shifts in space.

Matricidal/मैट्रिसाइडल *(adj)* - मातृहत्या-सम्बन्धी
Tom is suspected to have matricidal tendencies after his mental illness.

Matricide/मैट्रिसाइड *(noun)* - मातृहत्या
Matricide is a heinous crime.

Matrimonial/मैट्रिमोनियल *(adj)* - विवाह-सम्बन्धी
Sagar got his matrimonial pictures clicked by a professional photographer.

M

Matrimony/मैट्रिमॅनि *(noun)* – विवाह-संस्कार
Guneet and Avreen are enjoying a healthy state of holy matrimony as on date.

Matting/मैटिंग *(noun)* – चटाई
Matting is a common practice in the villages of India.

Mattock/मैटॅक *(noun)* – गैंती, फावड़ा
The farmer's daughter gifted him a mattock with her first salary.

Mattress/मैट्रेस *(noun)* – गद्दा, तोशक
Prisoners are just given a mattress to sleep on in jail.

Maturate/मैच्यूरेट् *(verb)* – मवाद पड़ना, पक जाना
The soldier's wounds maturated despite the timely medication.

Maturity/मैट्युरिटि *(noun)* – परिपक्वता, सिद्धि
The farmers wait a long time for the maturity of their crops.

Maudlin/मॉडलिन *(adjective)* – भावुक
Betty is prone to sudden bouts of maudlin reactions.

M

Maund/मॉन्ड *(noun)* – मन
The Zamindar promised a maund of rice to every villager in his village.

Maunder/मॉन्डर *(verb)* – बकना
Sam is often seen maundering the streets after losing his job.

Mausoleum/मॉसोलीऑम *(noun)* – मकबरा
Shahjahan is a renowned Mughal emperor for building mausoleums in and around his territory.

Mauve/मॉव् *(noun)* – चमकीला गुलाबी रंग
Mauve is my favourite colour.

Maw/मॉ *(noun)* – उदर
The canine caught the neck of the mongoose in his maw.

Maximize/मैक्सिमाइज *(verb)* – परम संख्या तक बढ़ना
The key to a successful business is to minimize time taken and maximize profits.

Maze/मेज *(noun)* – भूलभुलैया
The maze at the theme park is the most popular form of entertainment for people in Disneyland.

Maziness/मेजिनेस *(noun)* – घबड़ाहट, व्यग्रता
The maziness of his thoughts drove people crazy.

Mead/मीड *(noun)* – मध्वासव
The men were drunk on mead.

Meagre/मीगर *(adjective)* – दुर्बल
These meagre offerings won't help the children.

Mean/मीन *(verb)* – अर्थ होना या रखना
I mean that I will see you in two hours.

Meander/मीएन्डर *(noun)* – गोमूत्रिका
The river meandered through the forest.

Meaning/मिनिंग *(noun)* – आशय
What is the meaning of this poem?

Meaningly/मिनिंग्ली *(adverb)* – अर्थ सहित
He looked at her meaningly.

Measles/मिजल्स *(noun)* – खसरा, मसूरिका
Each child must be vaccinated against measles.

Measurable/मेजॅरबॅल *(adjective)* – नापने योग्य
Please give me a measurable quantity of milk.

Measureless/मेजरलेस *(adjective)* – असीम
My love for my parents is measureless.

Measurement/मेजरमेंट *(noun)* – नाप
The designer worked on incorrect measurements.

Meat/मीट *(noun)* – मांस
The lion pounced upon the meat.

Mechanical/मिकैनिकल *(adjective)* – बुद्धिरहित
The engine being demonstrated is mechanical.

Mechanism/मेकॅनिज्म *(noun)* – यन्त्र रचना
A very complex mechanism runs this car.

Mechanization/मेकनाइजेशन *(noun)* – यन्त्रीकरण
The mechanization of the process optimized the entire process.

Meconium/मेकोनियम *(noun)* – गाढ़ा हरा पदार्थ
The meconium had a bad smell.

Meddler/मेडलर *(noun)* – विघ्न डालने वाला
He is such a meddler in everyone's business.

Medial/मीडिअल् *(adjective)* – बीच में का
The medial line was a little slanted.

Median/मीडिअन् *(adjective)* – मध्यम, मध्यस्थ
Median depth of the river is six feet.

Medical/मेडिकल *(adjective)* – चिकित्सा-सम्बन्धी
He is a medical practitioner. The boss has gone for his annual medical.

Medicaster/मेडिकास्टर - ढोंगी वैद्य
Don't go to a medicaster at any cost.

Medicinal/मेडिसिनल *(adjective)* - औषधि-सम्बन्धी
The herb has medicinal use.

Medicine/मेडिसीन *(noun)* - औषधि
The child wants to study medicine when he grows up.

Mediocre/मीडिओकर् *(adjective)* - सामान्य
His mediocre performance failed to impress the critics.

Mediocrity/मीडिऑक्रिटि *(noun)* - सामान्यता
I am tired of all the mediocrity.

Meditate/मेडिटेट *(verb)* - सोचना, मनन करना
I meditate for a few minutes every day.

Meditation/मेडिटेशन *(noun)* - चिन्तन
Meditation gives you peace.

Meditative/मेडिटेटिव *(adjective)* - ध्यानतत्पर
His stance was very meditative.

Mediterranean/मेडिटरेनियन *(adj)* - भूमध्य-सागरीय
The Mediterranean climate does not suit me.

Meed/मीड *(noun)* - इनाम
He was happy to have reserved his meed.

Meek/मीक *(adjective)* - विनीत
At times, his meek demeanour looks quite fake.

Meeting/मिटिंग *(noun)* - सभा
The meeting failed to cause any breakthrough.

Meetness/मीटनेस *(noun)* - योग्यता suitable or proper. *In spite of his meetness for the job, his profile was rejected.*

Megrim/मेग्रिम *(noun)* - झक
Snap out of your megrim.

Melancholia/मेलन्कोलिया *(noun)* - विषाद रोग
Her melancholia threatened to turn into something serious.

Melancholic/मेलन्कॉलिक *(adjective)* - विषादपूर्ण
The melancholic poem touched many a solitary hearts.

Melancholy/मेलन्कॉलि *(noun)* - उदासीनता
I wish my friend would get out of the melancholy.

Melee/मेली *(noun)* - संकुल संग्राम
I was dying to get out of the melee.

Meliferous/मेलिफरस *(adj)* - मधु उत्पन्न करने वाला
Bee is a meliferous insect.

Mellifluence/मेलिफ्लूएंस *(noun)* - मीठापन
The mellifluence of the beautiful music touched my heart.

Mellivorous/मेलिवरस *(noun)* - मधुभक्षी
Bear is a mellivorous animal.

Melodic/मिलॅडिक *(adjective)* - सुरीला
His melodic voice won him a nomination.

Melodious/मिलॅडिअस् *(adjective)* - सुरीला
The melodious music echoed in the church.

Melodist/मेलॅडिस्ट *(noun)* - गाने वाला
The melodist has done a wonderful job.

Melody/मेलॅडि *(noun)* - लय
The melody was beautiful.

Melon/मेलॅन *(noun)* - तरबूज
I love melons.

Membral/मेम्ब्रल *(adj.)* - अंग सम्बन्धी
Please collect all the membrals.

Membrane/मेम्ब्रेन *(noun)* - झिल्ली, खाल
He had hurt his tympanic membrane.

Memorize/मेमॅराइज *(verb)* - याद करना
The child has memorized the entire poem.

Memory/मेमॅरि *(noun)* - यादगार
He has a very sharp memory.

Menace/मेनेस् *(noun)* -धमकी
He is a menace to the society. You cannot menace me.

Mend/मेंड *(verb)* - मरम्मत करना
The cobbler mended my shoes.

Mendacious/मेंडेशस *(adjective)* - झूठा
He is a mendacious person.

Mendacity/मेन्डैसिटि - मिथ्यावादिता
I am tired of your mendacity.

Mendicancy/मेन्डिकॅन्सि - भिक्षावृत्ति
The family was reduced to mendicancy.

Mendicant/मेन्डिकॅन्ट *(noun)* - भिक्षुक-भिखारी
The mendicant roamed the streets.

Menial/मीनिअल् *(adjective)* - ओछा
He started his career with menial jobs.

M

Meniscus/मिनिस्कस *(noun)* – अर्द्धचन्द्राकार ताल
The meniscus was turbulent.

Mensal/मेन्सल *(adj)* – मासिक
This is a mensal occurrence.

Menses/मेन्सीज *(noun)* – आर्त्तव
She went to the doctor to consult regarding the heavy menses.

Menstruate/मेन्स्टूएट *(verb)* – रजस्वला होना
One can get stomach ache during menstruation.

Mensurable/मेन्शरेबल् *(adjective)* – नापने योग्य
The results should be mensurable.

Mensuration/मेन्सुरेशन *(noun)* – क्षेत्रमिति
He scored full marks in mensuration.

Mental/मेंटल *(adjective)* – मानसिक
The child performs mental calculations quickly.

Mention/मेंसन *(verb)* – कथन
Yes, she did mention you to me.

M

Mentioned/मेन्शन्ड *(adj p.t. of mention)* – निर्दिष्ट
I mentioned you to my boss.

Mentor/मेंटर *(noun)* – विश्वसनीय मन्त्री
I consider him as my friend and mentor.

Mercantile/म:कॅन्टाइल *(adjective)* – व्यवसायी
His mercantile interests led him to take up business studies.

Mercenary/मॅं:सिनरि *(adjective)* – स्वार्थी
The company entered India with apparent mercenary interests.

Merchandise/मॅं:चॅन्डाइज *(noun)* – व्यापारी माल
The store sold good quality merchandise.

Mercurial/मर्क्यूरिअल् *(adjective)* – चंचल
I am wary of his mercurial temper.

Mercury/मर्करी *(noun)* – पारा
There is no atmosphere on Mercury.

Mercy/मर्सी *(noun)* – दया
The government showed mercy towards the captured soldier.

Mere/मिअर *(adjective)* – मात्र
We are mere mortals, not Gods!

Meretricious/मरिट्रिशस *(adj)* – बनावटी शोभा का
The marriage party was full of meretricious people.

Merge/मर्ज *(verb)* – मिला देना
Please merge the two sentences.

Merit/मेरिट *(noun)* – श्रेष्ठता
I completed my course with a merit.

Merlin/मर्लिन *(noun)* – बाज
The two merlins were fighting for territory.

Merman/म:मैन *(noun)* – दरियाई मर्द
Mermen are mythical creatures.

Merriness/मेरिनेस *(noun)* – आनन्द
We invited our neighbours to be a part of the merriment.

Mesdames/मेडेम् *(noun)* – महाशया
Mesdames, what will you have for lunch?

Mesentery/मेसॅन्टॅरि *(noun)* – आन्त्रपेशी
The professor pointed out the mesentery to the students during dissection.

Mesmerist/मेस्मेरिस्ट *(noun)* – मूर्छित करने वाला
The mesmerist amazed the audience with his performance.

Mesmerization/मेस्मेराइजेशन *(noun)* – मूर्छित करने का कार्य
The thief claimed that he was under the effect of mesmerization when he committed the crime.

Message/मेसेज् *(noun)* – समाचार
I sent a message to all my friends to wish them a happy new year.

Messenger/मेसेन्जर् *(noun)* – दूत
The messenger handed me the envelope and rushed back.

Messieurs/Messrs/मेसॅज/मेसये *(noun)* – महाशय लोग
Messieurs, what would you like to order for lunch?

Messuage/मस्विज् *(noun)* – गृहवाटिका
The messuage was huge.

Metabolism/मेटॉबॅलिज्म *(noun)* – चयापचय
She has a high rate of metabolism.

Metabolize/मेटैबॅलाइज *(verb)* – चयापचय करना
The stomach metabolizes some types of food easily.

Metacarpus/मेटॅकार्पस *(noun)* – हाथ की हथेली
He hurt his metacarpus.

Metallic/मेटलिक *(adjective)* - धातुरूप
I like the metallic jewellery box.

Metallist/मेटलिस्ट *(noun)* - धातु कर्मकार
The metallist worked hard to shape the hard metal.

Metallography/मेटलॉग्राफि *(noun)* - धातुविद्या
She is a student of metallography.

Metallurgy/मेट्लर्जि *(noun)* - धातुशोधन
He was interested in metallurgy.

Metalogical/मेटलॉजिकल *(adj)* - न्याय-विरुद्ध
I love this metalogical discussion.

Metamorphose/मेटमॉफोज् *(verb)* - रूप बदलना
The tadpole metamorphosed into a frog.

Metamorphosis/मेटमॉफोसिस *(noun)* - रूपान्तरण
I am fascinated by the process of metamorphosis.

Metaphor/मेटॅफॅ(र) *(noun)* - रूपक
The young poet did not like using metaphors.

Metaphysical/मेटैफिजिकल *(adjective)* - आध्यात्मिक
I love metaphysical poems.

Metaphysics/मेटैफिजिक्स *(noun)* - आत्मतत्वज्ञान
He likes discussing the concepts of metaphysics.

Mete/मीट *(verb)* - सीमा
The jury meted out an appropriate punishment to the culprit.

Meteor/मीटिअॅ(र) *(noun)* - उल्कापात
I love watching meteors fall from the outer space.

Meteoroid/मीटिअरॉइड *(noun)* - उल्का के परमाणु
The students discovered a new meteoroid.

Meteorite/मीटिअॅराइट *(noun)* - उल्का
The scientists studied the meteorite.

Meteorology/मीटिअॅरॉलॅजि *(noun)* - अन्तरिक्ष विद्या
With the introduction of new satellites, there have been considerable advances in meteorology.

Meter/मीटर *(noun)* - नापने वाला
The meter was faulty.

Method/मेथॅड *(noun)* - रीति
The method to solve this mathematical problem is quite simple.

Methodical/मिथॉडिकल *(adjective)* - यथाक्रम
He is very methodical in his approach.

Methodize/मेथॅडाइज *(verb)* - व्यवस्था करना
Please methodize the slides.

Metrical/मेट्रिकल *(adjective)* - छन्दोवद्ध
The poet writes metrical poems.

Mica/माइका *(noun)* - अबरक
Little bits of mica shone through the sand.

Mice/माइस *(plural)* - चूहे
The house is infested with mice.

Microbe/माइक्रोब *(noun)* - जीवाणु
Many microbes are helpful to human beings.

Microscope/माइक्रॉस्कोप *(noun)* - खुर्दबीन
The doctors studied the sample under a microscope.

Mid/मिड *(adjective)* - बीच का
The population of this state is in the mid of the range of populations of various states of the country.

Middle/मिडॅल *(adjective)* - बिचला
The chair in the middle is slightly misaligned.

Midget/मिजिट् *(noun)* - बौना
The midget entertained the crowd.

Mien/मीन् *(noun)* - छवि, रंगढंग
We weren't comfortable with his mien.

Miff/मिफ *(verb)* - मुहाँचाही
I think I miffed him by my silence.

Migration/माइग्रेशन *(noun)* - देशान्तरगमन
The wild-beasts are about to start their annual migration.

Migratory/माइग्रेटरी *(adjective)* - घूमने वाला
Geese are migratory birds.

Mike/माइक *(noun)* - माइक्रोफोन
The mike stopped working while he was speaking.

Milch/मिल्च *(adjective)* - दूध देने वाली
This milch cow is very docile.

Mild/माइल्ड *(adjective)* - दयालु
He has very mild manners.

Mile/माइल *(noun)* - मील
I have travelled 7 miles today.

Mileage/माइलेज *(noun)* - चली हुई दूरी
The car has good mileage.

Milfoil/मिल्फॉइल *(noun)* - एक प्रकार का पौधा
The milfoil is an abundant plant.

Militancy/मिलिटंसी *(noun)* – लड़ाकापन
Militancy needs to be curbed at any cost.

Militant/मिलिटॅन्ट *(adjective)* – युद्ध में लगा हुआ
The militant organization was banned in several countries.

Militarism/मिलिटरिज्म *(noun)* – सैनिक-शासन
Confrontations are common when two neighbouring countries favour militarism.

Military/मिलिटरी *(adjective)* – फौजी
The military ways of life are very fascinating.

Militia/मिलिसिया *(noun)* – रक्षक योद्धा
Some countries consider it important to have a strong militia.

Milk/मिल्क *(noun)* – दूध
Milk is an important source of calcium for children.

Milkiness/मिल्किनेस *(noun)* – कोमलता
The milkiness of her skin got her many admirers.

Milky/मिल्कि *(adjective)* – दूधिया
The chocolate is too milky for my liking.

M

Mill/मिल *(noun)* – चक्की
The mill runs for four hours every day.

Millepede/मिलिपीड *(noun)* – गोजर
I found a millepede in my bathroom.

Millet/मिलेट् *(noun)* – बाजरा
She bought a sack of millet.

Million/मिलिअन् *(cardinal number)* – दस लाख
She needs to save 3 million dollars to buy the house she likes.

Millionaire/मिल्यनेअ(र) *(noun)* – लखपति
Her parents wanted her to marry a millionaire but she fell in love with me.

Milt/मिल्ट *(noun)* – मछली का पित्त
The fish stores its sperm in the milt.

Mimicry/मिमिक्रि *(noun)* – विडम्बना, परिहासात्मक नकल
She is very good at mimicry.

Minacious/मिनेशॅस *(adjective)* – डराने वाला
The students ran to the classroom when they saw the minacious principal coming.

Minaret/मिनारेट *(noun)* – धरहरा, कोटा मीनार
The mosque has beautiful minaret.

Mince/मिन्स *(verb)* – बनाकर बोलना, चबाकर बोलना
I went to get the meat minced.

Mind/माइन्ड *(noun)* – स्मृति-उत्सव
At times, it is prudent to follow your mind.

Minded/माइन्डेड *(adj)* – प्रवृत्त
I love to spend time with like-minded people.

Mindful/माइन्डफुल *(adjective)* – सचेत
They are very mindful of the way they speak to each other in the presence of their children.

Mine/माइन *(possessive pronoun)* – मेरा
This pencil box is mine.

Minerva/मिनर्वा *(noun)* – सरस्वती
He wanted to name her baby girl Minerva.

Mingle/मिंगल *(verb)* – एकत्र होना
The two liquids mingled well.

Miniate/मिनिएट *(verb)* – सिन्दूर से रंगना
The ladies miniated each other.

Minify/मिनिफाई *(verb)* – छोटा करना
Don't minify his contribution in your success.

Minimal/मिनिमल *(adjective)* – अतिसूक्ष्म
My expenditure on cosmetics is minimal.

Minion/मिन्यॅन *(noun)* – भृत्य
He is but a minion in the party.

Ministerial/मिनिस्टेरिअल *(adjective)* – राजकीय
The ministerial convoy has just passed this way.

Ministress/मिनिस्ट्रेस *(noun)* – प्रबन्धकर्त्री
The ministress governed her state very well.

Ministry/मिनिस्ट्री *(noun)* – मंत्रालय
The ministry approved his proposal.

Minor/माइनर *(adjective)* – छोटा
This is a minor issue.

Minotaur/मिनॅटार् *(noun)* – नरवृषभ
The movie had an excellent depiction of a minotaur.

Minster/मिन्स्टर *(noun)* – बड़ा गिरजाघर
I visit the York Minster every Sunday.

Minstrel/मिन्स्ट्रल *(noun)* – चारण, बन्दी
The minstrel was famous for his melodious voice.

Mint/मिन्ट *(noun)* – पुदीना
Mint grows very easily.

Mintage/मिन्ट्-एँज् *(noun)* - सिक्का
The mintage of coins is a complicated process.

Minute/मिनिट *(noun)* - मिनट, क्षण
It will take me 5 minutes to complete this task.

Miracle/मिरॅकॅल *(noun)* - चमत्कार
Her recovery is nothing less than a miracle.

Miraculous/मिरैक्युलस *(adjective)* - चमत्कारी
The new medicine has produced miraculous results.

Mire/मायर् *(noun)* - कीचड़
The children keep away from the mire.

Mirror/मिरर *(noun)* - दर्पण
I bought an ornate mirror for my house.

Mirth/मर्थ् *(noun)* - प्रमोद
The party was full of mirth.

Mirthless/मर्थलेस *(adj)* - आनन्दरहित
She had a mirthless face.

Misadvised/मिसएडवाइज्ड *(adjective)* - असदुपदिष्ट
Children should never be misadvised.

Misalliance/मिस्एलायंस् *(noun)* - अयोग्य वैवाहिक सम्बन्ध
Their marriage was a misalliance from the very beginning.

Misapplication/मिसअप्लिकेशन *(noun)* - कुप्रयोग
The company lost a lot of trust because of their misapplication of investor funds.

Misapprehensive/मिसएप्रिहेन्सिव *(adj)* - भ्रम-पूर्ण
You are fighting with me because of our misapprehensive interpretations of my words.

Misascribe/मिसएस्क्राइब *(verb)* - मिथ्यारोपण करना
Several works of literature are misascribed to wrong authors.

Misbecome/मिसबिकम *(verb)* - अयोग्य होना
This dress is misbecoming on you.

Misbegotten/मिसबिगॉटॅन *(adj)* - दोगला, जारज
This is a misbegotten building.

Misbehave/मिसबिहेव *(verb)* - दुराचार करना
The bus conductor was fired because he misbehaved with children.

Misbehaviour/मिसबिहेवियर *(noun)* - दुराचार
The child was reprimanded for his misbehavior.

Misbelief/मिसबिलिफ *(noun)* - मिथ्या विश्वास
The misbelief led to a wrong decision.

Miscarriage/मिस्कैरिज *(noun)* - गर्भपात
She was upset after her miscarriage.

Miscarry/मिसकैरी *(verb)* - विफल होना
She was admitted in the hospital when she miscarried.

Miscellaneous/मिसिलेन्यॅस *(adjective)* - पंचमेल
The boy had a huge collection of miscellaneous stamps.

Miscellany/मिसेलनि *(noun)* - मिश्रण
The miscellany was published by a reputed publisher.

Mischief/मिसचीफ *(noun)* - शरारत, हानि
The children's faces were full of mischief.

Mischievous/मिसचिवॅस *(adjective)* - अपकारी
The mischievous children were scolded every day.

Miscite/मिसाइट *(verb)* - मिथ्या उद्धरण देना
He miscited Shakespeare in the conference.

Misclaim/मिस्क्लेम *(verb)* - अनुचित दावा करना
He misclaimed the rights to the property.

M

Misconceive/मिस्कन्सिव *(verb)* - उलटा समझना
You misconceived what I was saying.

Misconception/मिस्कन्सेप्शन *(noun)* - भ्रान्त धारणा
I want to remove this misconception.

Miscounsel/मिस्काउन्सेल *(verb)* - बुरी सलाह देना
The lawyer miscounselled the client.

Miscount/मिस्काउन्ट *(verb)* - अशुद्ध गिनती करना
I miscounted the number of pages that I had to read.

Miscreant/मिसक्रिएण्ट *(noun)* - बदमाश, पाजी
The police caught the miscreant.

Miscreated/मिस्क्रिएटेड *(adjective)* - विकृत
The miscreated cow attracted a crowd.

Misdeem/मिसडिम *(verb)* - झूठा अनुमान करना
I have misdeemed your abilities all this while.

Misdemeanour/मिस्डिमिनर् *(noun)* - दुष्कर्म
The judge let him go with just a warning as this was his first misdemeanour.

Misdoing/मिस्डुइंग *(noun)* - कुकर्म
His mother reported his misdoing to his father.

Misdoubt/मिस्डाउट *(verb)* – आशंका
I have my misdoubts about the existence of the so-called monster.

Miser/माइजर *(noun)* – कंजूस
My uncle is a miser.

Miserable/मिजॅरबॅल *(adjective)* – दु:खी
My brother was miserable for days after losing his new ball.

Miserliness/माइजर्लिनेस् *(noun)* – कृपणता
My father was tired of his boss's miserliness.

Misfire/मिस्फायर *(verb)* – आग न पकड़ना, गोली न चलना
The rocket misfired.

Misform/मिस्फॉर्म *(verb)* – कुरूप बनाना
The misformed plans did not yield any results.

Misfortune/मिस्फॉरचुन *(noun)* – दुर्गति
We condoled him for his misfortune.

Misgiving/मिस्गिविंग *(noun)* – अविश्वास
I have my misgivings about this itinerary.

M

Misguide/मिस्गाइड *(verb)* – बहकाना
The ignorant man misguided the tourists.

Mishap/मिस्हैप *(noun)* – अनिष्ट, अनर्थ, दुर्घटना
It was nothing but a mishap.

Mishmash/मिसमैश *(noun)* – घालमेल, उपद्रव
The platter looked more like a mishmash than edible food.

Misjudge/मिस्जज *(verb)* – अन्याय करना
I misjudged the situation.

Mislead/मिसलीड *(verb)* – बहकाना, धोखा देना
Don't mislead the students.

Mislike/मिस्लाइक *(noun)* – अप्रिय होना
His mislike for her was written all across his face.

Mismanage/मिस्मैनेज् *(verb)* – बुरा प्रबन्ध करना
The event management company mismanaged the birthday party.

Misogamy/मिसॉगॅमि *(noun)* – विवाह-निन्दा
His misogamy was the reason that he never married.

Misplace/मिस्प्लेस *(verb)* – गलत जगह में रखना
I misplaced my trust in you.

Misprize/मिस्प्राइज *(verb)* – नीचा समझना
The antique dealer misprized the cutlery collection.

Misquotation/मिस्कोटेशन *(noun)* – अशुद्ध उद्धरण
The misquotation became a subject of mockery.

Misquote/मिस्कोट *(verb)* – अशुद्ध उद्धरण देना
The news channel misquoted the politician.

Misread/मिस्रीड *(verb)* – अशुद्ध पढ़ना
I misread the email and sent a wrong reply.

Misrelation/मिसरिलेशन *(noun)* – अशुद्ध वर्णन
The misrelation changed the entire message of the play.

Misreport/मिसरिपोर्ट *(verb)* – मिथ्या समाचार देना
The audit company was penalized for its misreport.

Misrule/मिसरूल *(noun)* – कुशासन
The government's misrule plunged the country into turmoil.

Miss/मिस *(noun)* – कुमारी कन्या
Miss Tate, can you please come here?

Mis-shapen/मिसशेपेन *(adjective)* – कुरूप
No one bought the mis-shapen box.

Missile/मिसाइल *(noun)* – प्रक्षेपणास्त्र
The missile was very big.

Mission/मिशन *(noun)* – लक्ष्य, शिष्टमंडल
The spies were on a mission to save the country.

Mis-spend/मिस-स्पेंड *(verb)* – अपव्यय करना
I mis-spent my life's saving on useless investments.

Mist/मिस्ट *(noun)* – कुहरा
The mist swirled across the landscape.

Mistake/मिस्टेक *(noun)* – दोष, भूल
This entire idea was a mistake.

Mistaken/मिस्टेकेन *(adjective)* – अशुद्ध
It was a case of mistaken identity.

Mister/मिस्टर *(noun)* – महाशय
Now look here Mister, you cannot get away with this.

Mistress/मिस्ट्रेस *(noun)* – प्रेमिका
The children respected the mistress.

Mistrust/मिस्ट्रस्ट *(verb)* – शंका करना
The teacher mistrusted the students.

Misusage/मिस्यूसेज् *(noun)* – दुर्व्यवहार
The public was protesting against the misusage of the victim.

Mite/माइट *(noun)* – घुन, अल्प मात्रा
The house is infested with mites.

Mitigable/मिटिगेबॅल *(adjective)* – शान्त करने योग्य
The situation is still mitigable.

Mitigant/मिटिगॅन्ट *(verb)* – मृदु करने वाला
He is a very good mitigant.

Mitigate/मिटिगेट *(verb)* – शान्त करना
He mitigated the argument between the neighbours.

Mitigation/मिटिगेशन *(noun)* – शान्ति
They had to go to the court for mitigation.

Mitigatory/मिटिगेटरी *(adjective)* – शान्त करने वाला
Their mitigatory moves were welcome.

Mix/मिक्स *(verb)* – मिलाना
Please mix this powder in the milk.

Mixture/मिक्सचर *(noun)* – मिश्रण
The mixture was very tasty and nutritious.

Mizzle/मिजॅल *(noun)* – झींसी
The mizzle at this time of the year is beneficial for the crops.

Moan/मोन *(noun)* – कराहना
The little boy moaned because of pain.

Moat/मोट *(noun)* – खाई
The moat was full of crocodiles.

Mobile/मोबाइल *(adjective)* – अस्थिर
I love the concept of mobile libraries.

Mobility/मोबिलिटि *(noun)* – चंचपता
The injury impacted his mobility.

Mobilizable/मोबिलाइजेब्ल *(adjective)* – युद्ध-कार्य के योग्य
This plan sounds mobilizable.

Mocha/मोका *(noun)* – सुन्दर कहवा
I like having a mocha with my breakfast.

Mock/मॉक *(verb)* – चिढ़ाना
The grown-up boys mocked the younger ones.

Mode/मोड *(noun)* – प्रकार
I like this mode of working.

Model/मॉड्ल् *(noun)* – प्रतिरूप
The investors were impressed by the model of the new car.

Moderate/मॉडरेट *(adjective)* – परिमित
The moderate intensity storm is expected to hit the shore today.

Moderateness/मॉडरेटनेस *(noun)* – हल्कापन
Not everyone appreciated his moderateness.

Moderation/मॉडरेशन *(noun)* – किफायत
Everything should be practised in moderation.

Moderator/मॉडरेटर *(noun)* – सभापति
The moderator did his job well.

Modern/मॉडर्न् *(adjective)* – आधुनिक
The modern mobile phones are much more sophisticated than the older ones.

Modernization/मॉडर्नाइजेशन *(noun)* – नवीनीकरण
Modernization has his benefits as well as drawbacks.

Modest/मॉडेस्ट *(adjective)* – परिमित
He is a modest player.

Modesty/मॉडेस्टि *(noun)* – विनय
I was humbled by his modesty.

Modifable/मॉडिफेब्ल *(adjective)* – परिवर्तनीय
The plan is still modifiable.

Modification/मॉडिफिकेशन *(noun)* – रूपान्तरण
The modification of the plan led to its failure.

Modulate/मॉड्युलेट् *(verb)* – आवश्यकतानुसार घटाना बढ़ाना
The new manager modulated the processes the team had been following.

Modulator/मॉड्युलेटर *(noun)* – न्यूनाधिक करने वाला
The modulator malfunctioned.

Modulus/मोड्युलस *(noun)* – मापांक
I have always found calculating the modulus tiresome.

Moist/माइस्ट् *(adjective)* – नम
The clothes were all moist in the morning.

Moisten/माइस्ट्न *(verb)* – भिगोना
The fumes moistened my eyes.

Moistness/मॉइस्टनेस् *(noun)* – तरी
The moistness of her eyes made her look as if she'd been crying.

Moisture/मॉइस्चर् *(noun)* – गीलापन
The moisture in the air encouraged moulding.

M

Molar/मोलर *(noun)* – पीसने वाला
The dentist filled the cavity in her molar.

Molasses/मोलैसेज् *(noun)* – खाँड़, गुड़, जूसी
Molasses is very useful in yeast production.

Mole/मोल *(noun)* – छछूंदर, तिल, मस्सा
I saw a mole in my garden.

Molecule/मोलेक्यूल *(noun)* – कण
It is possible to see molecules under the microscope.

Molest/मॅलेस्ट *(verb)* – कष्ट देना
The culprits who molested the girl were sentenced to the harshest punishment.

Mollification/मॉलिफिकेशन *(noun)* – शमन
He is always successful in his mollification attempts.

Mollify/मॉलिफाइ *(verb)* – मुलायम करना
The government's attempts to mollify the indignant youth backfired.

Molten/मोल्टेन *(adjective)* – गला हुआ
The molten lava flowed into the river.

M

Moment/मोमेन्ट *(noun)* – क्षण
Wait a moment! I forgot something.

Momentarily/मोमेन्टरिलि *(adverb)* – क्षण भर के लिए
I was momentarily nervous before the speech.

Momentariness/मोमेन्टरिनेस् *(noun)* – क्षणिकता
The celestial event was missed because of its momentariness.

Momentary/मोमेन्टरि *(adjective)* – अस्थायी
There was a momentary interruption in the telecast.

Momentum/मोमेन्टम् *(noun)* – गति, चाल
The vehicle's momentum kept it going for a bit.

Monachism/मानकिज्म *(noun)* – मठवाद
The ways of monachism are an interesting subject of study.

Monad/मॅनैड *(noun)* – इकाई
The number 1 is called a Monad.

Monarch/मॉनॅर्क् *(noun)* – राजा
The monarch was generous and just.

Monarchy/मॉनॅर्कि *(noun)* – साम्राज्य
A monarchy functions in a different way than a democracy.

Monastic/मनैस्टिक *(adjective)* – वैरागियों का
The monastic way of life is very difficult.

Monetary/मॉनिटरि *(adjective)* – मुद्रा-सम्बन्धी
Will there be any monetary benefit for me out of this work?

Money/मॅनि *(noun)* – धन
Everyone wants to earn money.

Mongrel/मांग्रेल *(noun)* – दोगला कुत्ता
The mongrel was dirty but cute.

Monism/मॉनिज्म *(noun)* – वेदान्त
He subscribes to the philosophy of Monism.

Monk/मॅन्क *(noun)* – उदासी, मठवासी
The monk spent his life studying theology.

Monkey/मंकी *(noun)* – बन्दर
Monkeys can be very destructive.

Monological/मॅनॅलॅजिकल *(adj.)* – भाषण– सम्बन्धी
Monological sequences depend a lot upon the acting skills of the actor.

Monophobia/मॅनोफोबिया *(noun)* – अकेले रहने का भय
She cannot stay alone because she has monophobia.

Monotonous/मॅनॅटॅनस *(adjective)* – एक लय का
I want to change my monotonous schedule.

Monsieur/मॅन्स्यो *(noun)* – महाशय
Monsieur, what would you like to order?

Monsoon/मॉन्सून *(noun)* – ऋतु-पवन
We wait eagerly for monsoon every year.

Monstrosity/मॉन्स्ट्रॉसिटि *(noun)* – राक्षसीपन
Some people show case of deformities in animals as monstrosities to earn money.

Monstrous/मॉन्सट्रॅस *(noun)* – विकट
The monstrous tree was centuries old.

Montanic/मॉन्टैनिक *(adj)* – पर्वत पूर्ण
The montanic landscape is spectacular.

Monticle/मॉन्टिकल *(noun)* – छोटी पहाड़ी
The Church stood on the monticle.

Monument/मॉन्युमेंट *(noun)* – यादगार
The monument is a popular tourist spot.

Mood/मूड *(noun)* – चित्रवृत्ति
I am in a good mood today.

Moon/मून *(noun)* – चन्द्रमा
The Moon looks exceptionally bright today.

Moonling/मूनलिंग *(noun)* – मूर्ख मनुष्य
Don't behave like a moonling.

Moor/मूर *(noun)* – बंजर भूमि
We went for a walk on the moors. The moor was actress.

Mop/मॉप *(noun)* – कूँची
The mop was very dirty and needed to be washed.

Mopish/मोपिश *(adjective)* – तेजहीन
Why are you in such a mopish mood?

Moquette/मॅकेट *(noun)* – सन
The moquette used in making this carpet is of a very good quality.

Moralist/मॉरलिस्ट *(noun)* – नीतिज्ञ
Our class teacher is a moralist.

Morality/मैरेलिटि *(noun)* – नीति विद्या
Some people need lessons in morality.

Moralization/मॉरलाजेशन *(noun)* – नीति उपदेश
Moralization of some issues is simply uncalled for.

Moralize/मॉरॅलाइज *(verb)* – धर्मोपदेश करना
The panel was attempting to moralize the crime.

Morally/मॉरली *(adverb)* – नैतिक दृष्टि से
Your argument is morally wrong.

Morbid/मॉर्बिड् *(adjective)* – अस्वस्थ, रोगी, घिनावना
Some writers enjoy writing morbid stories.

Morbose/मॉर्बोस *(adj)* – अस्वस्थ
His weight has reached the morbose levels.

Mordacious/मॉर्डेशस् *(adjective)* – तीव्र
The mordacious article hurt many egos.

Mordant/मॉर्डन्ट् *(adjective)* – चरपरा
His mordant comments earned him many enemies.

Moreover/मोरओवर *(adjective)* – सिवाय
Moreover, you also owe me a treat.

Morgue/मॉर्ग् *(noun)* – क्रोधी प्रकृति
The student felt scared when he was in the morgue.

Moribund/मॉरिबॅन्ड *(adjective)* – मरणासन्न
The moribund man asked for his lawyer.

Morning/मॉर्निंग *(noun)* – सवेरा
I like waking up early in the morning.

Moron/मॉ:रॉन *(noun)* – मंदबुद्धि
Don't brave like a moron.

Morphia/मॉर्फिआ *(noun)* – अफीम का सत्व, मार्फिया
The patient was administered morphia before the surgery.

Morrow/मॉरो *(noun)* – उत्तर दिवस, आने वाला कल
I will contact my friend the first thing morrow.

Mortalize/मॉर्टलाइज् *(verb)* – मर्त्य बनाना
The poor beggar's curse mortalized the deity.

Mortgage/मॉर्गेज् *(noun)* – गिरवी
The poor farmer offered his land as a mortgage to educate his children.

Mosque/मॉस्क *(noun)* – मसजिद (मस्जिद)
The mosque has beautiful minarets.

Mosquito/मॉस्कीटो *(noun)* – मच्छर
The mosquito buzzed around my ear all night.

Mostly/मोस्टलि *(adverb)* – अत्यन्त
The results are mostly positive.

Mot/मॉट *(noun)* – कहावत
My car failed the mot.

Mote/मोट *(noun)* – धूलिकण
The plane was no bigger than a mote.

Motely/मॉटलि *(adjective)* – विचित्र रंग का
Her motley dress didn't suit the professional working atmosphere.

Moth/मॉथ *(noun)* – कीट
The moth fluttered around the lamp.

Mother/मदर *(noun)* – माता, जननी
A mother's love is unconditional.

Motile/मोटाइल *(adjective)* – गतियोग्य
Protozoans are motile microbes.

Motion/मोशन *(noun)* – चेष्टा, व्यापार
Moving things remain in motion for a while before stopping.

M

Motive/मोटिव *(noun)* – कारण, प्रेरक
One should be focussed in working towards a motive.

Motor/मोटर *(noun)* – गाड़ी
A large capacity generator needs a powerful motor.

Motto/मोटो *(noun)* – आदर्श वाक्य
In order to be successful, everyone should have a clear motto.

Mould/मोल्ड *(noun)* – साँचा
The bakery shop near the market has lovely cake moulds.

Moulder/मोल्डर *(verb)* – सड़ना
Food was mouldering due to breakdown of refrigerator.

Mound/माउन्ड *(noun)* – ढूहा a
Soldiers hid behind the mound during attack from enemies.

Mount/माउन्ट *(verb)* – पर्वत
Stock prices mounted steadily.

Mountable/माउन्टेबल *(adjective)* – चढ़ने योग्य
He bought a set of mountable band pads.

M

Mountebank/माउन्टिबैन्क *(noun)* – नीमहकीम, कठवैद्य
The mountebank was exposed.

Mounted/माउन्टेड *(adjective)* – घुड़सवार
Mounted riders were dressed in traditional gear.

Mourn/मोर्न् *(verb)* – विलाप करना
She mourned the loss of her pet.

Mournful/मोर्न्फुल *(adjective)* – दुःखी
He played a mournful melody.

Mouse/माउस *(noun)* – चूहा, मूस
She has a pet mouse.

Mouth/माउथ *(noun)* – मुख
He filled his mouth with sweets.

Mouthless/माउथलेस् *(adjective)* – मुखहीन
The box is mouthless.

Movability/मूवेविलिटि *(noun)* – चलनशीलता
They were concerned about the movability of the display case.

Movable/मूवेबॅल *(adjective)*– चलायमान
They kept the costumes in an easily movable cupboard.

Move/मूव *(verb)* – गति, कदम
He moved left to catch the ball.

Movement/मूव्मेन्ट *(noun)* – व्यापार, चाल
The dancers' movement was reflected in the mirror.

Mower/मोअॅर *(noun)* – घास काटने का यन्त्र
He bought a new mower.

Mowing/मोइंग *(noun)* – लवन, कटाई
The mowings were kept neatly in a corner.

Muchness/मच्नेस् *(noun)* – बहुतायत
The performances appeared much of muchness.

Mucous/म्यूकस *(adjective)* – श्लेष्मल
The mucous wound took a long time to heal.

Mud/मड *(noun)* – कीचड़
The kids are playing with mud.

Muddle/मड्ल *(verb)* – गड़गड़ करना
He muddled up the piles.

Muff/मफ *(noun)* – मफ, दस्ताना
She lost her muff.

Muffler/मॅफ्ल(र) *(noun)* – गुलूबंद, मफलर
The red muffler is his favourite.

Mug/मग *(noun)* – जलपात्र
The tea mug was empty.

Mugginess/मगिनिस *(noun)* – गीलापन
It was a warm and humid, full of mugginess.

Muggy/मग्गी *(adjective)* – सूखा तथा तर
It's very muggy today.

Mulberry/मॅल्बॅरि *(noun)* – शहतूत
There is a mulberry tree in our yard.

Mulish/म्यूलिश *(adjective)* – हठी
He irritated everyone with his mulish behaviour.

Muller/मॅलॅ(र) *(noun)* – बट्टा
The cat broke my muller.

Mullock/म्यूलक *(noun)* – कूड़ा, गर्दा
Everyone avoids his mullock.

Multangular/मूल्टैंगुलर *(adjective)* अनेक कोणों वाला
He drew a multangular.

Multifarious/मल्टिफेरिअश *(adjective)* – रंगबिरंगा
The stall has a multifarious display.

Multiform/मल्टिफॉर्म् - नाना रूप का
They offer a multiform programme.

Multilateral/मल्टिलैटरल *(adjective)* - बहुभुजी
They took multilateral decision.

Multinomial/मल्टिनॉमियल *(adj & noun)* - अनेक नामों वाला
They did an exercise on multinomials.

Multiplex/मल्टिप्लेक्स *(adj)* - अनेक नामों वाला
They have a multiplex relation.

Multiplicable/मल्टिप्लिकेबॅल *(adjective)* - गुणन करने योग्य
The numbers were multiplicable.

Multiplicand/मल्टिप्लिकैंड *(noun)* - गुण्य
The multiplicand was written in blue.

Multiplication/मल्टिप्लिकेशन *(noun)* - गुणन-क्रिया
He used a calculator for multiplication.

Multiplier/मॅल्टिप्लाइअ(र) *(noun)* - गुणक
He copied the multiplier wrongly.

Multiply/मल्टिप्लाइ *(verb)* - गुणा करना
Children are learning to multiply and divide.

Multitude/मल्टिट्यूड *(noun)* - झुण्ड
A multitude of people supported the cause.

Mumble/मम्बल *(verb)* - अस्पष्ट बोलना
He only mumbled his protest.

Mummy/मॅमि *(noun)* - रक्षित मृतक शरीर
We saw Tutankhamen's mummy in the museum.

Mundane/मन्डेन *(adjective)* - संसारी
His teaching method was very mundane.

Munificence/म्यूनिफिसेन्स *(noun)* - दानशीलता
They thanked him for his munificence.

Munificient/म्यनिफिसेन्ट *(adjective)* - उदार
She is very munificent to her employees.

Muniment/म्यूनिमेंट *(noun)* - अधिकार-पत्र
He kept the muniments safely in the drawer.

Munition/म्यूनिशन *(noun)* - युद्ध-सम्बन्धी
They lost because of shortage of munitions.

Mural/म्यूरल *(noun)* - भीत सम्बन्धी
The murals on the temple walls are almost perfectly preserved.

Murderer/मर्डरर् *(noun)* - हत्यारा
He was wrongly suspected to be a murderer.

Murderous/मर्डरस् *(adjective)* - घातक
It was a murderous rage.

Mure/म्युअॅ(र) *(verb)* - बन्द करना
They were mured in because of heavy storm.

Murk/मॅर्क *(noun)* - अँधेरा
The murk was making it difficult to drive.

Murmur/मर्मर् *(noun)* - मन्द ध्वनि
The murmur of the class was very distracting.

Murrain/मरेन् *(noun)* - पशुओं की महामारी
His cow is suffering from murrain.

Murrey/मरि *(noun)* - शहतूत के रंग का
She bought a murrey scarf. He felt murrey.

Muscle/मसल *(noun)* - मांसपेशी
He pulled a muscle while running.

Museum/म्यूजिअॅम *(noun)* - अजायबघर
The museum was reopened after major renovations.

Mush/मॅश *(noun)* - गूदा a soft, wet, pulpy mass.
There was a mush outside the door.

Mushroom/मॅश्रूम *(noun)* - कुकुरमुत्ता
He loves mushrooms on his pizza.

Mushy/मॅशि *(adjective)* - गूदेदार
She gifted the baby a mushy toy.

Music/म्युजिक *(noun)* - सुर, राग
They play soothing music in the evening.

Musician/म्युजिशियन *(noun)* - संगीतज्ञ
She is a brilliant musician.

Musk/मस्क *(noun)* - कस्तूरी, मृगमद
The display showed raw musk along with the processed perfume.

Musket/मस्केट् *(noun)* - फौजी सिपाही की बन्दूक
The musket broke after it fell from the cliff.

Muslin/मस्लिन *(noun)* - मलमल, तंजेब
He hung the curd in a muslin cloth.

Muss/मॅस *(verb)* - गड़बड़ी
He mussed the sketch.

Must/मस्ट *(verb)* - होना
The seal must be broken before trying to open the can.

Mustard/मॅस्टर्ड *(noun)* – सरसों
I loved mustard in sandwich.

Musty/मस्टि *(adjective)* – सड़ा हुआ
He found a musty bread in the store room.

Mutable/म्यूटॅबॅल *(adjective)* – अस्थिर
The audience response is very mutable.

Mutation/म्यूटेशॅन *(noun)* – परिवर्तन
The mutation of the structure was too rapid.

Mute/म्यूट *(adjective)* – चुपचाप, मौन
They were so shocked that they stayed mute for a minute.

Mutilate/म्यूटिलेट *(verb)* – अंग-भंग करना injure or damage severely, typically so as to disfigure. *The doll was mutilated.*

Mutter/मटर *(verb)* – गुर्राना
He muttered his unhappiness with the arrangements.

Mutual/म्यूट्युअॅल *(adj)* – परस्पर
They had a mutual respect for each other's ritual.

M

Muzzle/मॅजॅल *(noun)* – थूथन, बन्दूक का मुँह
The child coloured crocodile's muzzle yellow!

Muzzy/मॅजि *(adjective)* – तेजहीन
He felt muzzy as he didn't get proper sleep the previous night.

My/माइ *(possess. det.)* – मेरा
My mother baked a cake for me.

Myalgia/माइएल्जिआ *(noun)* – पेशीशूल
He is taking medicines to treat myalgia.

Myalism/माइएलिज्म *(noun)* – एक प्रकार का जादू
They spent the night discussing myalism beliefs.

Myopia/माइओपिआ *(noun)* – निकटदृष्टि दोष
She suffers from myopia.

Myriad/मिरिअॅड *(noun)* – दस हजार
A myriad of colours were created by the glass work.

Myriapod/मिरिअपॉड *(noun)* – गोजर
They studied a myriapod sample in the lab today.

Myrobalan/माइरॉबॅलॅन *(noun)* – आँवला
They were asked to bring leaves of a cherry plum or myrobalan.

Myrrh/मॅर् *(noun)* – लोहबान
Ancient Egyptians were very fond of myrrh.

Myrtle/मर्टॅल *(noun)* – हिना
The gardener planted four new myrtle in the garden today.

Mysterious/मिस्टिरिअॅस *(adjective)* – गुप्त
He disappeared under mysterious circumstances.

Mystic/मिस्टिक *(noun)* – अप्रकट, गुप्त, गहन
He is self-proclaimed mystic.

Mysticism/मिस्टिसिज्म *(noun)* – गूढ़ विद्या
They discussed the popular ancient mysticism of the area.

Mystify/मिस्टिफाइ *(verb)* – घबराना
The audience was mystified by his performance.

Myth/मिथ *(noun)* – कल्पित कथा
Despite his education, he firmly believes in the Hindu myth of creation.

Mythical/मिथिकल *(adjective)* – काल्पनिक
She made a project on mythical monsters.

Mythologer/माइथोलॉजर *(noun)* – पौराणिक
He is famous mythologer.

Mythology/मिथॅलजि *(noun)* – पौराणिक कथा
Indian mythology is very vast and varied.

Mythonomy/मिथॅनमि *(noun)* – पुराण शास्त्र
I don't believe in your mythonomy.

Mythus/माइथस *(noun)* – देवताओं की काल्पनिक कथा
He narrated a mythus.

Nn

N/एन *(noun)* – अंग्रेजी वर्णमाला का 14वाँ वर्ण the fourteenth letter of the English alphabet.

1. Denoting the next after M in a set of items, categories, etc.

Nab/नैब *(verb)* – पकड़ना, बंदी बनाना
The police nabbed the thief.

Nacelle/नैसेल *(noun)* – हवाई जहाज का डिब्बा
The passengers here carried to the airship in a nacelle.

Nag/नैग *(verb)* – कष्ट देना
Disturbing nagged him day and night.

Naiad/नाइऐड *(noun)* – जल देवता
This story is a story of naiads.

Nail/नेल *(noun)* – नख, कील
He drove nail in the wall.

Naive/नेव *(adjective)* – सरल
Please forgive him, he is a naïve fellow.

Name/नेम *(noun)* – नाम
His name is famous among novelists.

Namkeen/नमकीन *(noun)* – नमकीन
Indians usually serve guests namkeen and tea as refreshment.

Nanny/नैनी *(noun)* – आया
He hired a nanny for his baby.

Nape/नेप *(noun)* – गर्दन का पिछला भाग
The hair stood on his nape as he watched the horror film.

Napery/नेपरी *(noun)* – मेजपोश
I am going to wash the napery today.

Naphtha/नेफ्था *(noun)* – शीघ्र जलने वाला खनिज तेल विशेष
Naphtha is a dangerous petroleum product.

Napkin/नैप्किन *(noun)* – नैपकिन
Please wipe your fingers on a napkin.

Napoleonic/नैपोलियोनिक *(adjective)* – प्रसिद्ध राजा नेपोलियन प्रथम के समान
It is a Napoleonic hat.

Narcissus/नारसिसॅस *(noun)* – नरगिस
I have a narcissus in my garden.

Narcosis/नारकोसिस *(noun)* – मूर्छा
He has taken a strange drug and is under narcosis.

Narcotic/नारकोटिक *(noun)* – बेहोश करने वाली दवा
He is under the influence of narcotic.

Narcotize/नारकोटाइज् *(verb)* – बेहोश करना, नशीला करना या बनाना
The robbers wanted to narcotize the family to rob with fear.

Nard/नार्ड् *(noun)* – एक पौधा (जटामासी, बालछड़)
Some Ayurvedic medicines use nards during preparation.

Narrate/नैरेट *(verb)* – वर्णन करना
He narrated the incident very clearly.

Narrative/नैरेटिव *(noun)* – कथा
It was a brilliant piece of narrative.

Narrowish/नैरोइश *(adverb)* – कुछ-कुछ सँकरा
The lane is narrowish.

Narrowly/नैरोली *(adverb)* – कष्ट से
It was a bad accident he narrowly escaped death.

Narrowness/नैरोनेस *(noun)* – संकोच
Narrowness of mind is responsible for many foolish acts.

Nasal/नेजल *(adjective)* – नासिका सम्बन्धी
He sings in a nasal voice.

Nascency/नेसेंसी *(noun)* – उत्पादन का आरम्भ
Indian space industry is 40 years old and is completely out of nascency.

Nascent/नेसेंट *(adjective)* – उगने वाला
It is a nascent bud.

Nasturtium/नैस्टर्शम् *(noun)* - एक प्रकार की रेंगने वाली या जमीन पर फैलने वाली लता

I have just purchased a nasturtium.

Nasty/नेस्टी *(adjective)* - मलिन

There was a nasty smell in the kitchen.

Natal/नेटल *(adjective)* - जन्म-सम्बन्धी

His natal sign is Gemini.

Nates/नेटीज् *(plural noun)* - चूतड़

She has well rounded nates.

Nation/नेशन *(noun)* - राष्ट्र

India is a multi-lingual and multi-cultural nation.

National/नेशनल/नैशनल *(adjective)* - राष्ट्रीय

Crimes against women have become a national issue.

Nationalism/नैशनलिज्म *(noun)* - राष्ट्रीय स्वतन्त्रता की नीति

Uncontrolled nationalism sometimes leads to dictatorship and war.

Nationalize/नैशनलाइज *(verb)* - राष्ट्रीय बनाना

Big private companies are often nationalized in socialist countries.

N

Native/नेटिव *(noun)* - देशवासी

He is a native of Australia.

Nativity/नेटिविटि *(noun)* - ईसामसीह का जन्म दिन, जन्म पत्रिका

The nativity of Jesus Christ is celebrated as festival of Christmas.

Natron/नेट्रन् *(noun)* - सज्जी-खार

Natron is a useful mineral.

Nattily/नैटिलि *(adverb)* - स्वच्छता से

She turned out at the reception dresses nattily.

Nattiness/नैटिनेश *(noun)* - स्वच्छता

She is well mannered and so is her nattiness with dress.

Natty/नैटि *(adjective)* - चालाक

Because of her fashionable style. She is known as the most natty girl in the college.

Natural/नैचुरल *(adjective)* - स्वाभाविक

Oceans, mountains, trees, rivers etc. are natural objects.

Naturalism/नैचुरलिज्म *(noun)* - प्राकृतिक नियमों के सिद्धान्त

His writings have a lot of naturalism.

Naturalist/नैचुरलिस्ट *(noun)* - पदार्थ शास्त्रज्ञ

My brother is a naturalist and studies how certain animals and plants developed into present form.

Naturalize/नैचुरलाइज *(verb)* - अभ्यस्त कराना

He is a naturalized citizen of India and not so by birth.

Naturally/नैचुरलि *(adverb)* - स्वभाव से

Naturally we don't feel at case with strangers.

Naturalness/नैचुरलनेस *(noun)* - यथार्थता

He demonstrates naturalness that many others try hard to project on the stage.

Naught/नॉट *(noun)* - शून्य

All his efforts were brought to naught.

Nausea/नॉसिया *(noun)* - मिचली, उबकाई

He had nausea in the foul smelling place.

Nauseate/नॉसिएट *(verb)* - जी मिचलाना

He felt nauseated after eating the food.

Nautical/नॉटिकल *(adjective)* - नाविक

A nautical mile covered by ship is about 2,025 yards.

Naval/नेवल *(adjective)* - नौसैनिक

He is a high ranking naval officer.

Nave/नेव *(noun)* - गिरजाघर का मध्य भाग, पहिये की नाभि

There were a lot of people present in the nave.

Navel/नेवेल *(noun)* - नाभि

She wears a diamond in her navel.

Navicular/नॅविक्युलर *(adj)* - नाव के प्रकार का

He had a navicular bone fracture in an accident.

Navigable/नैविगॅबॅल *(adjective)* - जहाज या नाव ले जाने योग्य

It is a stormy sea and not navigable at this time.

Navigate/नैविगेट *(verb)* - जहाज चलाना

The captain navigated the ship safely through ice-bergs.

Navigation/नैविगेशन *(noun)* - नौविद्या

He has finished his training in navigation.

Navigator/नैविगेटर *(noun)* – नाविक
He is an expert navigator and trusted by the captain.

Navvy/नैवि *(noun)* – भूमि खोदने वाला या नहर खोदने वाला मजदूर
A navvy is usually hired on daily wages.

Navy/नेवी *(noun)* – जहाजों का बेड़ा
The British navy is very powerful.

Nawab/नवाब *(noun)* – नवाब
He lives lavishly like a nawab.

Nay/ने *(adverb)* – नहीं
He is foolish and nay ill-mannered as well.

Neap/नीप *(noun)* – सबसे नीचे का
Trapped in a neap tide, the ship ran aground.

Near/नियर् *(adverb)* – समीप
My house is near a big super market.

Nearness/नियर्नेस् *(noun)* – समीपता
Too much nearness in any relation is not halting.

Neat/निट *(adjective)* – सुन्दर
The room was neat and clean.

Neath/निथ *(preposition)* – 'नीचे' अर्थ का यह शब्द कविता में प्रयुक्त होता है
There is a cat sitting beneath the table.

Neb/नेब *(noun)* – चोंच
The neb of a crocodile looks frightening.

Nebula/नेब्युला *(noun)* – नीहारिका
You can see the nebula shining over there in the sky.

Necessarian/नेसेसरिअन *(noun & adj)* – दैववादी
I am a staunch necessarian.

Necessary/नेसेसरी *(adjective)* – आवश्यक
It is something necessary, so do it.

Necessitate/नेसेसिटेट *(verb)* – विवश करना
He was necessitated into selling his property.

Necessitous/नेसेसिटस *(adjective)* – दीन, अकिंचन
He is a necessitous person, give him some money.

Necessity/नेसेसिटी *(noun)* – आवश्यकता
Necessity is the mother of invention.

Neck/नेक *(noun)* – ग्रीवा
She has a slim round neck.

Necrology/नेक्रोलॉजी *(noun)* – मृत्यु-लेख
His name does not appear in necrology.

Necromancy/नेक्रोमैन्सी *(noun)* – जादू
He practises black magic and is supposed to be indulged in necromancy.

Necrophagous/नेक्रोफेगस *(noun)* – शव (मुर्दा) खाने वाला
Vultures are necrophagous creature.

Necrophobia/नेक्रोफोबिया *(noun)* – मृत्यु का भय
He suffers from necrophobia.

Necrosis/नेक्रॅसिस *(noun)* – हड्डी का निर्जीव होना
The old man had an accident and died of necrosis.

Nectar/नेक्टर *(noun)* – अमृत
Bees and insects collect nectar from flowers.

Neddy/नेड्डी *(noun)* – खच्चर
He is a fine neddy and will certainly win the race.

Need/नीड *(verb)* – अभाव
If need be, I'll come to your house.

Needful/नीडफुल *(adjective)* – आवश्यक
The needful must be done urgently to help the flood victims.

Needle/नीड्ल *(noun)* – सूई
Give me a needle and some black thread I have to darn the torn pocket of my shirt.

Needless/निडलेस *(adjective)* – निरर्थक
It is needless to observe these formalities here.

Needs/नीड्स *(adverb)* – आवश्यक of necessity.
Let your needs be limited.

Needy/नीडि *(adjective)* – दरिद्र
He is needy, so let us help him.

Never/नेवर *(adverb)* – कभी नहीं
Never use such abusive language again.

Nefarious/निफेरिअश *(adjective)* – पापी
He is a nefarious fellow and had been in jail many times.

Negative/निगेटिव *(adjective)* – निषेधार्थक
Don't talk to him, he is in a negative state of mind.

Neglect/नेग्लेक्ट् *(verb)* – उपेक्षा करना
He spent a negative childhood. He neglected his studies and failed in the class.

N

Neglectful/नेग्लेक्ट्फुल *(adjective)* – ध्यान रहित
He is a neglectful parent.

Negligence/नेग्लिजेंस *(noun)* – उपेक्षा
Negligence on the part of guard cost him his job.

Negligent/नेग्लिजेंट *(adjecitive)* – असावधान
He is a negligent worker and hence cannot be relied upon.

Negligible/नेग्लिजिबल *(adj)* – उपेक्षा करने योग्य
He passed the exam with negligible margin.

Negotiable/निगोशिअब्ल् *(adj)* – बेचा-बिक्री करने योग्य
This flat is for sale and the price is negotiable.

Negro/नीग्रो *(noun)* – हब्शी
Many negroes were enslaved by European colonizers.

Negus/नीगॅस *(noun)* – नीगस
He was the negus of a big African tribe.

Neigh/ने *(noun)* – घोड़े का हिनहिनाना
The horse was disturbed and neighed as the stranger approached him.

N

Neighbour/नेबर *(noun)* – पड़ोसी
My neighbour is a nice fellow.

Nemesis/नेमिसिस *(noun)* – प्रतिशोध, दण्ड
His wife proved to be his nemesis.

Neo/निओ *(combining form)* – 'नवीन' या 'आधुनिक' अर्थ का उपसर्ग
Neoclassical paintings are a lot attractive to look at.

Neon/निऑन *(noun)* – निऑन
Neon lights are spread all over metro cities.

Neophyte/निओफाइट *(noun)* – नवदीक्षित, नया शिष्य
He is a neophyte and it will take him some time to adjust.

Neoplastic/निओप्लास्टिक *(adjective)*– नवनिर्मित या रचित
It is a neoplastic building.

Neoteric/निओटेरिक *(adjective)* – आधुनिक, नया
His neoteric views on religion are worth reading.

Nephew/नेफ्यु *(noun)* – भतीजा
This young man is my nephew.

Nephology/नेफॉलजि *(noun)* – मेघ-अध्ययन-शास्त्र
Nephology interests me a lot.

Nephritic/नेफ्रिटिक *(adjective)* – वृक्क सम्बन्धी
He has a nephritic disease, take him to a hospital.

Nepotism/नेपॉटिज्म *(noun)* – कुल पक्षपात
Almost all political leaders practise nepotism.

Neptune/नेप्ट्यून *(noun)* – समुद्र देवता
Neptune is a very distant planet.

Nerve/नर्व *(noun)* – ऊर्जा, शक्ति, बल, नस
He sure had nerve to face the challenge.

Nerveless/नर्वलेस *(adjective)* – निर्बल
He is nerveless in the face of danger.

Nervous/नर्वस् *(adjective)* – शीघ्र घबड़ा जाने वाला
He is a very nervous fellow and gets frightened easily.

Nest/नेस्ट *(noun)* – घोंसला
This large tree has many nests in its branches.

Nestle/नेसॅल *(verb)* – शरण लेना, चिपट जाना
She nestled against me.

Nestling/नेस्ट्लिंग *(noun)* – पक्षी का बच्चा, गेदा
She is a nestling and isn't ready to fly yet.

Net/नेट *(noun)* – फन्दा
Many fish were caught in the net.

Nether/नेदर *(adjective)* – नीचे
He is nether in position to many employees.

Nettle/नेटल *(noun)* – बिच्छू का पेड़
Don't touch this plant. It is a nettle.

Neural/न्युअरल *(adjective)* – तंत्रिकीय, तंत्रिका
He underwent a neural.

Neuritis/न्युअराइटिस *(noun)* – तंत्रिका शोथ
He is suffering from neuritis.

Neurosis/न्यूरॉसिस *(noun)* – एक प्रकार का पागलपन
He has neurosis and is consulting a psychologist.

Neurotic/न्यूरॉटिक *(adjective)* – नाड़ी सम्बन्धी
His neurotic behaviour upset all.

Neuter/न्यूटर *(adjective)* – नपुंसक
'It' is a neuter gender.

Neutral/न्यूट्रल *(adjective)* – उदासीन
He is a neutral person, you can go and seek his advice.

Never/नेवर *(adverb)* – कभी नहीं
Never before did he speak in such a way.

Nevertheless/नेवरदलेस *(adverb)* – तथापि, तो भी
He is foolish, nevertheless honest.

New/न्यू *(adjective)* – नया, नवीन
He has bought a new car.

News/न्यूज *(noun)* – समाचार, वार्ता
This is the latest news you are hearing.

Nexus/नेक्सस *(noun)* – बन्धन
The nexus between politicos and mafia is something highly undesirable.

Nib/निब *(noun)* – कलम की नोक
The nib of pen is broken.

Nibble/निबॅल *(verb)* – कुतरना
Rats have nibbled the piece of bread.

Nice/नाइस *(adjective)* – मनोहर
He is a nice man by nature.

Nicely/नाइसलि *(adverb)* – सुन्दरता से
The Job was nicely done.

Niceness/नाइसनेस *(noun)* – सुन्दरता
The niceness of his behaviour impressed all.

Niceties/नाइसेटिज *(noun)* – बारीकियाँ
He observed all the niceties of behaviour.

Nicety/नाइसेटि *(noun)* – सूक्ष्मता
His drawings had great nicety.

Niche/निच *(noun)* – ताखा
The golden statue was placed in a niche.

Nicknacks/निकनैक्स *(noun)* – तुच्छ पदार्थ
She is fond of wearing knickknacks.

Nicotiana/निकोटियना *(noun)* – तमाखू का
The plant of nicotiana smells fragrant at night.

Nicotine/निकोटिन *(noun)* – तमाखू का सत्व
He is addicted to nicotine.

Niddle-noddle/निडॅल-नॉडल – हिलता हुआ, झूमता हुआ, डाँवाँडोल
I don't like his niddle-noddle behaviour.

Nidification/निडिफिकेशन *(noun)* – घोंसला बनाने का कार्य
In spring birds are busy in nidification.

Niece/नीस *(noun)* – भतीजी
Meet her, she is my niece.

Nifty/निफ्टी *(adjective)* – बढ़िया, सुन्दर
It is a nifty piece of an art.

Niggard/निगर्ड् *(noun)* – कंजूस
He is a niggard, keep away from him.

Niggardliness/निगर्ड्लिनेस् *(noun)* – कृपणता
The niggardliness the government's budget angered voters.

Niggardly/निगर्ड्लि *(adjective)* – लालची
He talked to me in a very niggardly way.

Nigger/निगर् *(noun)* – हब्शी
To call a black person nigger is to insult him.

Niggle/निगल *(verb)* – तुच्छ बातों में समय नष्ट करना
She is quarrelsome and niggles her husband daily.

Night/नाइट *(noun)* – रात
It grew pitch dark at night.

Night-bird/नाइटबर्ड् *(noun)* – उल्लू
Owl keeps awake at night and hence is called a night-bird.

Night-blindness/नाइटब्लाइण्डनेस *(noun)* – रतौंधी
He suffers from night-blindness, as the night descends, he loses his vision.

Night-fall/नाइटफॉल *(noun)* – सन्ध्याकाल
It is night-fall now and he hasn't returned as yet.

Night-hawk/नाइटहॉक *(noun)* – चोर
Owl is a bird of prey and is also called night-hawk.

Nightlong/नाइटलॉन्ग *(adjective)* – रातभर
After the nightlong vigil, the police caught the culprit.

Nightsoil/नाइटसॉएॅल् *(noun)* – मल, विष्ठा
These persons collect the nightsoil.

Nigrescent/नाइग्रेसेन्ट् *(adjective)* – काला होने वाला
These negroes are nigrescent.

Nil/निल *(noun)* – नहीं
So his achievement is nil.

Nimble/निम्बल *(adjective)* – चपल
Small birds are usually very nimble.

Nimbus/निम्बस *(noun)* – प्रभामण्डल
The photos of saints have a nimbus around their heads.

Nimrod/निम्रॉड *(noun)* - शिकारी
The ancient man was a nimrod.

Nincompoop/निनकम्पुप *(noun)* - मूर्ख
What a nincompoop he is!

Nine/नाइन *(cardinal number)* - नौ
There were nine muses in Greek mythology.

Nineteen/नाइनटिन *(cardinal number)* - उन्नीस
He is only nineteen year old.

Ninety/नाइनटि *(cardinal number)* - नब्बे
Ninety is the word for the digit 90.

Ninny/निनि *(noun)* - मूर्ख मनुष्य
He is a ninny don't expect anything wise from him.

Nip/निप *(noun)* - नाखून या दाँत का कटाव
He is a nip, you can't understand his language.

Nippers/निपर्स *(noun)* - कतरनी
Please bring me a pair of nippers.

Nipple/निप्पल *(noun)* - चूचुक
The baby sucked at the nipple of her mother.

Nit/निट *(noun)* - लीख
There are many nits in her hair.

N

Nitre/नाइटर *(noun)* - शोरा
He brought a vial of nitre for some experiment.

Nitric/नाइट्रिक *(adjective)* - शोरा का
Nitric acid is used in chemical experiments.

Nitrify/नाइट्रिफाइ *(verb)* - शोरा बनाना
To nitrify means to convert ammonia into nitrates or nitrites.

Nix/निक्स *(exclamatory)* - कुछ भी नहीं
The government nixed the proposal to organise indo-pak cricket series.

No/नो *(abbreviation)* of number - कोई भी नहीं
The no.7 horse will win.

Nob/नॉब *(noun)* - सिर
I have just seen a nob near our boat.

Nobble/नॉबल *(verb)* - बेईमानी से छीन लेना
Being at an influential post, he nobbled a lot of money.

Nobility/नोबिलिटि *(noun)* - कुलीनता
He belongs to nobility and is a much respected man.

Noble/नोबल *(adjective)* - महानुभाव
He is a noble man by birth and manners.

Nock/नॉक *(noun)* - तीर के कोने का खण्ड
Every arrow has a nock at its end to fit the bow-string. *(verb)* fit to the bowstring.

Nocturnal/नाक्टर्नल *(adjective)* - रात्रि सम्बन्धी
Owl is a nocturnal bird.

Nocturne/नॉक्टर्न *(noun)* - रात्रि का दृश्य या गीत
I saw a nocturne in an art exhibition and bought it at quite a high price.

Noddle/नॉडल *(noun)* - मस्तक
There was a holo around the holy person's noddle.

Noddy/नॉडी *(noun)* - मूर्ख
Sometimes he acts noddy but otherwise is quite intelligent.

Node/नोड *(noun)* - गाँठ
New leaves are growing from the node.

Nodose/नोडोस *(adjective)* - गाँठदार
The tree was quite old and had a nodose trunk.

Nodule/नॉड्यूल *(noun)* - छोटी ग्रन्थि या गुल्म
The doctor noticed a nodule on his hand.

Noggin/नॉगिन *(noun)* - छोटा घड़ा या पात्र या प्याला
The mason finished noggin in the wooden frame.

Noise/नॉइज *(noun)* - शोरगुल
I can no longer stand this loud noise.

Noiseless/नॉइजलेस *(adjective)* - मौन
The house was noiseless as nobody lived there.

Noisily/नॉइजिलि *(adv)* - उच्च स्वर से
He noisily made his entry on the stage.

Noisy/नॉइजी *(adjective)* - कोलाहल करने वाला
It was a noisy classroom.

Nomad/नोमैड *(noun)* - बंजारा
These are nomads and won't stay here for long.

Nomadic/नोमैडिक *(adjective)* - भ्रमणकारी
He is nomadic by nature, always wandering.

Nominal/नॉमिनल *(adjective)* - नाम मात्र का
It is an outdated law and has only a nominal value.

Nominally/नॉमिनलि *(adv)* - नाम मात्र से
He was nominally in charge of the building.

Nominate/नॉमिनेट *(verb)* - किसी पद के लिए निर्दिष्ट करना
Party has nominated him as a candidate for the coming election.

Nominative/नॉमिनेटिव *(adjective)* - कर्ता कारक
He is a nominative case in grammar.

Nominee/नॉमिनि *(noun)* - नियुक्त पुरुष
He is a nominee to the leadership of the party.

Non/नॉन *(prefix)* - अ, अन्, गैर अर्थ का उपसर्ग
He is a non-believer in God. Certain species of insects have become non-existent.

Nonagon/नॅनागन् *(noun)* - रेखागणित में नव कोण की आकृति
Nonagon is a geometrical figure with nine sides and angles.

Nondescript/नानडिस्क्रिप्ट *(adjective)* - अपूर्व
He is a nondescript person, nobody takes interest in him.

Nonentity/नॉनेन्टिटि *(noun)* - अस्तित्वहीनता
People hardly notice a nonentity.

Non-existence/नान-इग्जिस्टॅन्स *(noun)* - सत्ता का न होना
Non-existence of police led to riots.

Non-plus/नॉनप्लस *(verb)* - व्याकुल करना
He became nonplussed as he saw the horrible accident.

Non-resident/ननरेजिडेन्ट *(adj)* - अपने स्थान पर न रहने वाला
There are many non-resident Indians.

Nonsense/नॉनसेन्स *(noun)* - व्यर्थ प्रलाप
What nonsense! You shouldn't have behaved like that.

Non-sequitur/नॉनसेक्विटर *(noun)* - निष्कर्ष या परिणाम जो अनुमान से नहीं निकलता है
His non-sequitur did not impress anybody.

Nonsuit/ननसूट *(verb)* - किसी मुकदमे का खारिजा
His case was declared to be nonsuited. The lack of efficient evidence resulted in nonsuit.

Noodle/नूड्ल *(noun)* - नूडल, मूर्ख
He is fond of eating noodles.

Nook/नूक *(noun)* - कोना
Many insects lived in the nooks of the deserted house.

Noon/नून *(noun)* - मध्यकाल
His much awaited call came at noon.

Noose/नूज *(noun)* - सरकने वाला फन्दा
The noose tightened around the criminal's neck.

Nor/नॉर् *(conjunction & adverb)* - न तो
He cannot use such abusive language, nor can I.

Norm/नॉर्म् *(noun)* - नमूना
He observes all norms of good behaviour.

Normal/नॉर्मल् *(adjective)* - यथाक्रम
Once his anger subsided he will behave normal.

Normalcy/नॉर्मल्सी *(noun)* - प्राकृतिक दशा
He regained normalcy of behaviour after the psychiatric treatment.

Normality/नॉर्मैलिटि *(noun)* - विधिवत्
Normality in every sphere of life is something desirable.

Normalize/नॉर्मलाइज *(verb)* - नियम बाँधना
His behaviour become normalized after a long time after accident.

Normally/नॉर्मलि *(noun)* - विधिवत्
Although angry, he behaved normally.

Norman/नॉर्मन *(noun)* - नार्मंडी देश का निवासी
He lives in Normandy and is called a Norman.

Norse/नॉर्स *(noun)* - नार्वे देश की भाषा
Ancient Norwegians spoke Norse language.

North/नॉर्थ *(noun)* - उत्तर
Delhi is situated in the north of India.

Northing/नार्दिंग *(noun)* - उत्तर की ओर जहाज की गति
By convention, everything above 80 nothing is considered as positive.

North-star/नॉर्थ्-स्टार *(noun)* - ध्रुवतारा
North-star is also called pole star.

Northward/नॉर्थवर्ड् *(adjective)* - उत्तर की ओर
The ship had hardly gone a few miles northward when a storm overtook it.

N

Northwest/नॉर्थ्वेस्ट *(noun)* - पश्चिमोत्तर

Many cities are situated in the northwest of India.

Nose/नोज *(noun)* - नाक

He has a long and prominent nose.

Nosebag/नोजबैग *(noun)* - तोबड़ा

The horse was eating from the nosebag.

Nose-ring/नोजरिंग *(noun)* - नथुनी

Most Indian women wear nose-ring.

Nosing/नोजिंग *(noun)* - सीढ़ी के डण्डे का गोल किनारा

He put his foot on the nosing.

Nostalgia/नॉस्ट्रैल्जिया *(noun)*- घर पर पड़े रहने की बीमारी

When idle he usually has nostalgia.

Nostril/नॉस्ट्रिल *(noun)* - नथुना

We breathe through our nostrils.

Nosy/नोजि *(adjective)* - कुतूहली

As he was too nosy, I asked him to mind his own business.

Not/नॉट *(adverb)* - नहीं

He does not want to go to school.

Notability/नोटेबिलिटि *(noun)* - ख्याति

He is a notability among writers.

N

Notable/नोटेबॅल *(adjective)* - प्रसिद्ध

This is the only notable part of an otherwise long speech.

Notably/नोटेब्लि *(adverb)* - प्रसिद्धि से

This guide-book is very informative, notably in the third chapter.

Notarial/नोटेरियल *(adjective)* - लिखित पत्रों को प्रमाणित करने वाले अफसर से सम्बन्धित

To perform notarial works, you must be a law graduate.

Notary/नोटरी *(noun)* - लिखित पत्रों को प्रमाणित करने वाला अफसर

This deed is to be certified by a notary.

Notation/नोटेशन *(noun)* - गणना

Look carefully at the notation of this mathematical sum.

Notch/नॉच *(noun)* - खाँच, खाँचा

There are only four notches on this belt, I need at least two more.

Noteless/नोटलेस *(adj)* - अप्रसिद्ध

It is a blank and noteless diary.

Notelet/नोटलेट *(noun)* - पुस्तिका

He sent me a notelet, inviting me on his birthday.

Notepaper/नोटपेपर *(noun)* - चिट्ठी लिखने का कागज

Please bring me pad of notepapers I have some letters to write.

Noteworthy/नोटवर्दी *(adj)* - विचार करने योग्य

It is something noteworthy that throughout the meeting he kept quiet.

Nothing/नथिंग *(pronoun)* - शून्य

There is nothing good I see in him.

Nothingness/नथिंगनेस *(noun)* - शून्यता

The nothingness of many things can be seen clearly in old age.

Noticeable/नोटिसेबॅल *(adjective)* - विचारणीय

The politeness of his behaviour was noticeable.

Notifiable/नोटिफाइअबॅल *(adj)* - सूचना देने योग्य

The fast spreading disease is modifiable and authorities must be informed about it.

Notification/नोटिफिकेशन *(noun)* - सूचना

A notification has been issued to the effect that everyone must be present in the office by 10 a.m. tomorrow.

Notify/नोटिफाइ *(verb)* - सूचना देना

All employees have been notified that no short leave will be given.

Notion/नोशन *(noun)* - कल्पना

I have a notion that we shall soon find a solution to the problem.

Notional/नोशनल *(adjective)* - मन से गढ़ा हुआ

It is only a notional problem and hence no concrete answer is available.

Notoriety/नॅटॅराइऑटि *(noun)* - कुख्याति

He soon gained notoriety as a gangster.

Notorious/नॅटोरिअस् *(adjective)* - कुख्यात

He was a notorious smuggler.

Nought/नॉट *(noun)* - शून्य

All his efforts were brought to nought because of bad luck.

Noun/नाउन *(noun)* - संज्ञा

Noun is a naming word.

Nourish/नॅरिश *(verb)* - पालना

He nourishes a grudge against me.

Nourishment/नॅरिशमेंट *(noun)* - पोषण

Proper nourishment helps children grew fast and healthy.

Novel/नॅवेल् *(noun)* – उपन्यास
He is a famous novel writer.

Novelette/नॅवलेट् *(noun)* – छोटी कहानी
I finished reading the novelette in an hour.

Novelist/नॅवेलिस्ट् *(noun)* – उपन्यास-लेखक
Charles Dickens was a famous novelist.

Novelty/नॅवेल्टि *(noun)* – कौतुक
Exploring the ancient caves was a novelty.

Novice/नॉविस *(noun)* – नवसिखिया, नवछात्र
He is a novice and as such to be pardoned for the lapse.

Noviciate/Novitiate/नॉविसिएट *(noun)* – नवशिष्यालय
Novices live in this novitiate.

Now/नाउ *(adverb)* – अभी
It is late, I should leave now.

Nowhere/नोह्वेअर *(pronoun)* – कहीं नहीं
He is nowhere to be seen.

Noxious/नॉक्सस *(adjective)* – हानिकारक
The smoke arising here is noxious.

Nozzle/नॉज़ॅल *(noun)* – फौब्बारे का अग्रभाग
The nozzle of the hose was blocked.

Nuance/नूआंस *(noun)* – भाव तथा अर्थ इत्यादि में का सूक्ष्म अन्तर
The newspaper published his views but with a nuance.

Nubile/न्यूबाइल *(adjective)* – विवाह करने योग्य
She is very nubile although quite young.

Nubility/न्यूबिलिटि *(noun)* – विवाह-योग्यता
Many lecherous employers try to take advantage of nobility of young secretaries.

Nudge/नज *(verb)* – केहुनियाकर संकेत करना
He nudged her in the crowd.

Nugatory/न्युगेटरी *(adjective)* – व्यर्थ
The committee passed a nugatory and pointless observation.

Nugget/नगेट् *(noun)* – बिना स्वच्छ किये हुए सोने का पिण्ड
He found a number of nuggets while digging the earth.

Null/नल *(adjective)* – व्यर्थ
The archaic law was declared null and void.

Numb/नॅम *(adjective)* – गति-शून्य
He became numb with grief.

Numbly/नॅम्लि *(adverb)* – स्तब्धता
He numbly nodded his head.

Numeral/न्यूमॅरॅल *(noun)* – संख्या सम्बन्धी
I understand this numeral very well.

Numeration/न्यूमॅरेशॅन *(noun)*– गिनती
Numeration requires knowledge of arithmetic.

Numeric – *(adjective)*
The list has been prepared in numeric order.

Numerical/न्यूमेरिकल *(adjective)* – संख्या-सूचक
Remember the symbol of this numerical.

Numerous/न्यूमरस *(adjective)* – बहुत
Numerous members attended the club meeting.

Numismatic/न्यूमिस्मेटिक *(adj)* – मुद्रा-सम्बन्धी
He is deeply interested in numismatics, you should show him this old coin.

Numskull/नमस्कल *(noun)* – बेवकूफ, उल्लू का पट्ठा
The numskull didn't understand me and began to quarrel.

Nuncio/नन्सियो *(noun)* – ईसाइयों के धर्माध्यक्ष का दूत
The nuncio met bishops and visited churches.

Nunnery/नॅनॅरि *(noun)* – बैरागिनियों की कुटी
She being a nun, lives over there in the nunnery.

Nuptial/नॅप्शॅल *(adjective)* – वैवाहिक
Nuptial bells rung in the church.

Nutriment/न्यूट्रिमेंट *(noun)* – पुष्टि देने वाला आहार
Fruits have lots of nutriment.

Nutrition/न्यूट्रिशन *(noun)* – आहार
The hungry man was immediately provided nutrition.

Nutritious/न्यूट्रिशस *(adjective)* – पौष्टिक
A pomegranate is a nutritious fruit.

Nutritive/न्यूट्रिटिव *(adjective)* – पुष्टिकर
The food served was high in nutritive value.

Nuzzle/नॅजॅल *(verb)* – नाक लगाना
The child nuzzled against his mother.

Nyctalopia/निक्टैलोपिया *(noun)* – रतौंधी
He suffers from nyctalopia and can't see at night.

Nymph/निम्फ *(noun)* – अप्सरा
She is almost a nymph, I love her very much.

Oo

O/ओ *(noun)* – अंग्रेजी वर्णमाला का 15वाँ वर्ण the fifteenth letter of the English alphabet.

1. Denoting the next after N in a set of items, categories, etc.
2. A human blood type lacking both the A and B antigens. *My blood group is O.*
3. Zero in a sequence of numerals, especially when spoken. *My telephone nubmer is six O triple five.*

Oaf/ओफ *(noun)* – जड़मति
He is considered an oaf among his friends.

Oak/ओक *(noun)* – सुन्दर बलूत वृक्ष
Oak trees are generally found in temperate forests.

Oaken/ओकेन *(adj)* – बलूत वृक्ष का बना हुआ
The oaken smell indicated that there was some winery around.

Oakum/ओकम *(noun)* – खण्डित रज्जु
Oakum is caulking purposes in ships.

Oar/ओर् *(noun & verb)* – नौका दण्ड
We had to oar our boats ourselves as no man was available to do the same.

Oarless/ओर्लेस् *(adj)* – बिना डाड़े का
You can't take a rowing boat out to sea of totally oarless.

O

Oarsman/ओर्स्मैन् *(noun)* – मल्लाह
A new oarsman was hired for the boat that we were going to sit in.

Oasis/ओएसिस *(noun)* – नखलिस्तान, मरूद्यान
It was pleasant to see an oasis after spending hours in desert.

Oast/ओएस्ट *(noun)* – शराब बनाने में हॉप के फल सुखाने की भट्ठी
A woman was placing hops in an oast.

Oat/ओट *(noun)* – जई
Oat plants are generally used for feeding animals.

Oath/ओथ *(noun)* – सौगन्ध
The President is going to take his oath today.

Oatmeal/ओटमिल *(noun)* – जई का दलिया, चूर्ण
Oatmeal was the primary food for the tribes living in that area.

Obduracy/आब्ड्यूरेसि *(noun)* – कठोरहृदयता
My brother's obduracy had made him unpopular in his friend circle.

Obdurate/आब्ड्युरेट *(adjective)* – दुराग्राही
The leader was so obdurate that he refused to listen to anyone.

Obeah/ओबिअ॓ *(noun)* – हब्शियों का जादू
The lady was an expert in practising obeah.

Obedience/अबीडिएन्स *(noun)* – आज्ञापालन
The student who were lacking in obedience were rusticated.

Obedient/अबीडिएन्ट *(adjective)* – आज्ञाकारी
As a student, I was quite obedient to my teachers.

Obedientiary/अबेडिएन्शरि *(noun)* – मठ का आज्ञाकरी सेवक
Two monks were made obedientiaries by their seniors.

Obeisance/ओबेसॅन्स *(noun)* – नमस्कार
Every religion teaches us the lessons of obeisance and truthfulness.

Obelisk/ऑबेलिस्क *(noun)* – सूच्याकार स्तम्भ
Beside the pyramid was standing a tall obelisk.

Obese/ओबीस *(adjective)* – स्थूलकाय
His seven year old child was quite obese.

Obesity/ओबीसिटि *(noun)* – स्थूलता
Obesity gives rise to a number of health problems.

Obey/ऑबे *(verb)* – कहना मानना
All the royal ministers were expected to obey to the command of the king.

Obfuscate/ऑब्फस्केट *(verb)* - घबरा देना, धुँधला कर देना

His action further obfuscated the situation.

Obi/ओबि *(noun)* - जादू-टोना, जापानी रूमाल

Japanese women used to wear an obi over their kimonos.

Obituarist/ओबिट्युअरिस्ट *(noun)* - मृत्युलेख लिखने वाला मनुष्य

That man has been an obituarist for many years.

Obituary/ओबिच्यूरि *(noun)* - मृत्यु-समाचार

After a day of his death, we saw his obituary in the newspaper.

Objectify/ऑबजेक्टिफाइ *(verb)* - प्रत्यक्ष रूप से उपस्थिति करना

His strength as a writer was to objectify emotions in words.

Objection/ऑब्जेक्शॅन *(noun)* - विरोध

People raised an objection to the way voting was done in our area.

Objectionable/ऑब्जेक्शनेबल् *(adjective)* - अनुचित

The movie had many objectionable scenes in it.

Objectivity/ऑब्जेक्टिविटि *(noun)* - स्थूलता

The editor said to author, "While creating this piece, you should employ objectivity."

Objectless/ऑब्जेक्टलेस *(adj)* - निष्प्रयोजन

His idea was rejected for being objectless.

Objector/ऑब्जेक्टर *(noun)* - आपत्तिकर्ता

No one had the slightest idea that the man would turn out to be an objector.

Objuration/ऑब्ज्यूरेशन *(noun)* - शपथ

The newly elected minister was undergoing the process of objuration.

Objurgation/ऑबजरगेशन *(noun)* - तिरस्कार

The party member could not bear the objurgation and left immediately.

Objurgatory/ऑबजरगेटरि *(adj)* - तिरस्कार पूर्ण

We were shocked by the objurgatory remarks that he made that day.

Oblate/ऑब्लेट *(noun)* - धर्म-कर्म में जीवन अर्पण करने वाला

The wife had no qualms about her husband being an oblate.

Obligate/ऑब्लिगेट *(verb)* - किसी कार्य के लिए मनुष्य को बाध्य करना

As per the law, the criminal was obligated to sign the documents.

Obligatory/ऑब्लिगेटरी *(adjective)* - आवश्यक

It was his obligatory duty to keep a check on the number of crimes in his area.

Oblige/ॲब्लाइज *(verb)* - विवश करना

The teacher asked to make notes and the students obliged.

Obligee/ऑब्लिजी *(noun)* - कृतज्ञ

In that case, I was an obligee and the man had to comply with my terms.

Obliging/ऑब्लाइजिंग *(adjective)* - सुशील, उपकारी

His obliging ways earned him popularity among his mentors.

Obligor/ऑब्लिगर *(noun)* - आभारी

The obligor had no choice but wait for the contract to end.

Oblique/ॲब्लीक *(adjective)* - वक्र, तिरछा

The sun rays fall obliquely on earth's surface.

Obliquely/अब्लीकलि *(adverb)* - कुटिल रीति से

The sunrays fall on earth obliquely.

Obliquity/अब्लीक्विटि *(noun)* - वक्रगति

The obliquity of the light rays determines their degree of hotness.

Obliterate/ॲब्लिटरेट *(verb)* - नष्ट करना

An entire species of turtles got obliterated after the landslide.

Obliteration/ॲब्लिटरेशन *(noun)* - लोप

The obliteration of the entire army came as a shock to the king.

Oblivious/ॲब्लिवियस *(adjective)* - भुलक्कड़

While doing work, I become oblivious of all the things happening around.

Oblong/ऑब्लॉन्ग *(adjective)* - आयताकार

The lady has an oblong face.

Obloquy/ऑब्लक्वि *(noun)* - गाली

The minister is trying to become popular by using obloquy as a tool.

Obmutescence/ऑब्म्युटेसॅन्श *(noun)* - मौन

His obmutescence was an indication that he was not interested in our discussion.

O

Obnoxious/ऑब्नॉक्शस *(adjective)* – घृणित
The obnoxious presence of the criminal in the victim's family was angering many.

Obnubilate/ऑब्न्युबिलेट *(noun)* – छिपाना
Soon, the dark clouds obnubilated the entire sky.

Obnubilation/अब्न्युबिलेशन *(noun)* – व्यग्र अवस्था
His act of obnubilation to hide his crime soon came to light.

Oboe/ओबो *(noun)* – शहनाई
As we reached the hut, some natives were playing on oboes.

Obscene/ऑब्सीन/ऑब्सीन *(adjective)* – अश्लील
I objected to the obscene remarks made by the man.

Obscurant/ऑब्स्क्युअरॅन्ट *(noun & adjective)*– सुधार का विरोधी
We did not have the slightest idea of his obscurant activities.

Obscuration/ऑब्स्क्युअरेशन *(noun)* – अँधेरा करने का कार्य
The lady's obscuration of the facts was taken in the bad light.

Obsecrate/ऑब्सिक्रेट *(verb)* – प्रार्थना करना
The man obsecrated for getting pardon.

O

Obsequies/आब्सीक्विज *(pl. noun)* – अन्त्येष्टि
Her mother's obsequies were performed in wee hours.

Obsequious/ऑब्सीक्विअॅस *(adjective)* – जीहुजूरिया, चापलूस
The employee's obsequious attitude gave him no benefits at the time of appraisals.

Observable/ऑब्ज़ॅर्वेबॅल *(adj)* – दृष्टिगोचर
Despite being very far, the island was still observable from our ship.

Observance/ऑब्ज़ॅर्वॅन्स *(noun)* – रीति
Our Principal expected from the students a thorough observance of rules.

Observant/अब्जर्वन्ट *(adjective)* – सावधान
His observant eyes were able to locate the lost keys.

Observation/ऑब्जर्वेशन *(noun)* – निरीक्षण
The mentally unstable man was kept under a strict observation.

Observationally/ऑब्जर्वेशनलि *(adv)* – विचार पूर्वक
In order to get details of an object, it is required to notice them observationally.

Observe/ऑब्जर्व *(verb)* – देखना, अवलोकन करना
I was observing the petri-dish with full concentration.

Observer/ऑब्जर्वर *(noun)* – प्रेक्षक
What a keen observer he is!

Observing/ऑब्जर्विंग *(adj)* – ध्यान से निरीक्षण करने वाला
Observing from far, he said, "The land is now not very far."

Obsess/ऑबसेस *(verb)* – कष्ट देना
He is obsessed with social media networking.

Obsession/ऑब्सेशन *(noun)* – प्रेत-बाधा
His obsession with food never seems to end.

Obsolescence/ऑब्सॅलेसॅन्स *(noun)* – अप्रचलन
The obsolescence of this technology is attributed to the new developments in the field.

Obsolescent/ऑब्सॅलेसॅन्ट *(adjective)* – अप्रचलित
The introduction of electric engine rendered the steam locomotives obsolescent.

Obsolete/ऑब्सलीट *(adjective)* – अप्रचलित
The water clocks have now become obsolete.

Obstacle/आब्स्टैकॅल *(noun)* – विघ्न
He was not deterred by the obstacles coming his way.

Obstetrics/आब्स्टेट्रिक्स *(noun)* – प्रसव-कला
My sister is keen to study obstetrics as her field of specialization.

Obstetrician/ऑब्सटेट्रिशन *(noun)* – प्रसव कराने में प्रवीण
He recommended my wife to join the hospital as a qualified obstetrician in the city.

Obstinate/ऑब्स्टिनेट *(adjective)* – हठी
Her obstinate nature did not allow her to do idol worship.

Obstreperous/ऑबस्ट्रेपरस *(adjective)* – झगड़ालू
In spite of being a jury member, he could not control his obstreperous ways.

Obstruction/ऑब्स्ट्रक्शन *(noun)* - रुकावट

Many obstructions were placed in his way, yet he did not succumb to them.

Obstructive/ॲब्सट्रक्टिव *(adj)* - प्रतिबन्धक

The path was too obstructive to drive a vehicle smoothly.

Obtain/ॲब्टेन् *(verb)* - प्रवृत्त होना

The students obtained their teacher's permission to visit the library.

Obtest/ॲबटेस्ट *(noun)* - आग्रह करना

When the thief got caught, he obtested a lot before cops.

Obtrude/ॲब्ट्रूड *(verb)* - इच्छा के विरुद्ध करना, लादना, थोपना

We were annoyed as he obtruded on us.

Obtruncate/ॲब्ट्रंकेट *(verb)* - मस्तक काटना

In a feat of anger, the villager obtruncated his brother.

Obtrusive/ॲब्ट्रूसिव *(adjective)*- बलपूर्वक प्रवेश करने वाला

We loathed him due to his obtrusive way of behaving.

Obtund/ॲब्टॅन्ड *(verb)* - निस्तेज बना देना

In summers, the monsoon rain obtunds hotness in air.

Obturate/ॲब्ट्युअरेट *(verb)* - रोकना

The rust on the surface obturated the machine from running smoothly.

Obtuse/ॲब्ट्यूस *(adjective)* - मन्द, मूढ़

The student was so obtuse that he could not get the concept even after three hours of lecture.

Obtusion/ॲब्ट्यूजन *(noun)* - भुथरा करने का कार्य

Too much of disturbance resulted in obtusion of my mind.

Obverse/आब्वर्स *(noun)* - विपरीत

The archaeologist remarked, "Look at the obverse of this coin; there is a unique symbol on it."

Obvert/ऑब्वर्ट *(verb)* - अभिमुख करना

He obverted the plank and saw a cobweb in the corner.

Obversion/ऑब्वर्सन *(noun)*- अभिमुखीकरण

The obversion of vision will help you the other aspects of the story.

Obviate/ऑब्विएट *(verb)* - हटाना, प्रतिरोध करना

She, very cleverly, obviated all the evidences related to the crime.

Obvious/ऑब्विअॅस *(adjective)* - प्रत्यक्ष

What he was trying to say was indicated from his obvious speech.

Ocarina/ॲकरीना *(noun)* - एक प्रकार का बाजा

The lovely lady in the room was playing very well on ocarina.

Occasion/ॲकेजन *(noun)* - अवसर

He knew that this was the only occasion he could convey his feelings to her.

Occasioned/अकेजन्ड् - *(adverb)*

The resignation of the CEO occasioned the company to choose the senior most person to occupy the vacant place.

Occipital/ॲक्सिपुट *(adj)* - मस्तक के पिछले भाग का

The technician took an X-ray of the patient's occipital view.

Occiput/आक्सिपॅट *(noun)* - मस्तक का पिछला भाग

The doctor examined his occiput and wrote remarks on the prescription.

Occlude/ऑक्लुड *(verb)* - रोकना

His gigantic body was occluding the light from behind.

Occlusion/ऑक्लुजन *(noun)* - रुकावट

An occlusion in her heart became the cause of her untimely death.

Occultation/ऑकल्टेशन *(noun)* - छिपाव

In astronomy, the process of occultation is used to determine the presence of asteroids.

Occultism/ऑकल्टिज्म *(noun)* - दैवी रहस्य

Occultism is related to the study of supernatural phenomena.

Occultist/ऑकलटिस्ट *(noun)* - जादूगर

The lady hired an occultist to know about her future.

Occultly/ऑकल्टली *(adverb)* - छिपी रीति से

Their occultly talk continued for hours.

Occultness/ऑकल्टनेस *(noun)* - भेद

We could not ignore the factor of occultness while discussing about astrology.

O

Occupancy/ऑक्युपॅन्सि *(noun)* – अधिकार में रखने वाला

The allotment of houses depends upon their current state of occupancy.

Occupant/ऑक्युपन्ट *(noun)*– अधिभोक्ता

The occupants of this house are out on a tour.

Occupation/आक्युपेशॅन *(noun)* – वृत्ति

His occupation with his job left him with no spare time.

Occupy/ऑक्युपाइ *(verb)* – अधिकार या भोग करना

On reaching there, we saw that the room was already occupied by a couple.

Occur/अॅकर् *(verb)* – घटित होना

When the incident occurred, the family was out of town.

Occurrence/अॅकरेंस *(noun)* – घटना

The rare occurrence of the event makes it all the more interesting.

Occurrent/अॅकरेंट *(adjective)* – घटित होने वाला

The long words are quite occurrent in this article.

Ocean/ओशॅन् *(noun)* – महासागर

The Pacific Ocean is the biggest ocean in the world.

O

Oceanic/ओशऐनिक *(adjective)* – महासागरीय

There are a number of oceanic activities that keep on taking place from time to time.

Ochlocracy/ऑक्लॉक्रसि *(noun)* – भीड़-तन्त्र

The movement to establish ochlocracy was crushed very badly.

Ochlocrat/ऑक्लॉक्रैट *(noun)* – अनियन्त्रित प्रजातन्त्र राज्य का अधिनायक

He refused to admit that he was an ochlocrat.

Ochre/ओकर् *(noun)* – एक प्रकार की मिट्‌टी

In party, a lady was wearing an ochre coloured dress.

O'clock/ओक्लॉक *(adverb)* – घड़ी में

My sister reached the airport exactly at 5o' clock in the evening.

Octad/आक्टैड *(noun)* – आठ का समुदाय

In the practical test, we were shown an octad compound and were asked to write about its properties.

Octagon/ऑक्टॅगॅन *(noun)* – अष्टभुज

It is easy to calculate area of an octagon.

Octahedron/ऑक्टहेड्रन *(noun)* – अष्टफलक ठोस आकृति

The compound that we were asked to test was an octahedron.

Octangular/ऑक्टैन्ग्युलर *(adj)* – आठ कोणों की आकृति वाला

An octangular shape is defined by the presence of eight angles.

Octant/ऑक्टन्ट *(noun)* – वृत्त का अष्टमांश

Our Mathematics teacher explained the method of calculating the area of an octant.

Octave/ऑक्टेव *(noun)* – अष्टक

Our music teacher gave us good lessons on octave.

Octavo/ऑक्टेवो *(noun)* – आठ परतों की

An octavo is the size of the pages resulting from folding a printed page into eight leaves.

Octennial/ऑक्टेनियल *(adjective)* – आठ वर्ष में होने वाला

Through our telescope, we were looking at an octennial star in the sky.

October/ऑक्टोबर *(noun)* – अंग्रेजी वर्ष का दसवाँ महीना (अक्टूबर)

My sister's birthday falls on eighteenth of October.

Octodentate/ऑक्टोडेंटेट *(noun)* – आठ दाँतों वाला

An octodentate animal was standing before us.

Octonocular/ऑक्टोनोक्यूलर *(adj)* – आठ आँखों वाला

"Have you ever seen an octonocular animal?" asked my friend.

Octopod/ऑक्टोपॉड *(noun)* – आठ पैरों वाला

Octopods are short animals with eight arms.

Octroi/अॅक्ट्राइ/अॅक्ट्वा *(noun)* – चुंगी

The truck carrying the freight had to pay an octroi before entering the neighbouring city.

Octuple/ऑक्ट्युपॅल *(adjective)* – अठगुना

In college, our octuple group was famous for giving musical performances.

Oddish/ऑडिश *(adjective)* – विचित्र

He was doing everything in an oddish way.

Oddly/ऑडलि *(adverb)* – विलक्षणता से

Of late, he is behaving in an oddly manner.

Odds/ऑड्स *(plural noun)* – विषमता, कलह

The odds on horse race are 14 to 3.

Odious/ओडिअस् *(adjective)* – घिनौना extremely

What an odious remark was passed by him!

Odium/ओडिअॅम *(noun)* – द्वेष

The recent killing of a girl has created odium among masses.

Odontalgia/ऑडॉन्टैल्जिया *(noun)* – दाँतों का दर्द

The development of plaque was giving her an odontalgia.

Odontoid/ऑडॉन्टाइड *(noun)* – दन्ताभ

He was feeling pain in his odontoid joint.

Odontology/ऑडॉन्टालजि *(noun)* – दन्तशास्त्र

His avid interest in odontology made him go abroad and do specialization in it.

Odorous/ओडॅरस *(adj)* – सुगन्धित

The fish tank was giving an odorous smell.

Odour/ओडर *(noun)* – सुगन्ध

In order to avoid the bad odour, she sprayed room freshener.

Oecology/ईकॅलॅजि *(noun)* – प्राणिशास्त्र की शाखा जिसमें प्राणियों पर वातावरण के प्रभाव का अध्ययन होता है

All the elements in an ecology should be in balance with one another.

Oedipus/ईडिपस् *(noun)* – ईडिपस

As per the legend, Oedipus was the son of Laius and Jocasta.

O'er/ओवर *(adverb & preposition)* – 'Over' का छोटा रूप

O'er that hill, he met the princess of her heart.

Oesophagus/ईसॉफॅगॅस *(noun)* – ग्रासनली

Any constriction in oesophagus does not let the food to pass to the stomach easily.

Of/ऑव *(preposition)* – का, में, पर

Of all the coaches in train, only three had passengers in them.

Off/ऑफ *(abbreviation)* – दूर

His off is not very far from his house.

Offal/ऑफॅल *(noun)* – कूड़ा

As the girl saw the man eating offal, she vomited at once.

Offence/ऑफेन्स *(noun)* – अपराध

Man's offence was too much to be given any kind of pardon.

Offenceless/ऑफेन्सलेस *(adj)* – दोष-रहित

The country was too weak and offenceless to retaliate.

Offend/ऑफेन्ड *(verb)* – कष्ट देना

By not succumbing to the demands of his master, he had offended him.

Offensiveness/ऑफेन्सिवनेस *(noun)* – अपराध, अपकार

When he could not find any other way to gather attention, he stooped to offensiveness.

Offer/ऑफर *(verb)* – प्रस्ताव

He offered me job immediately after going through my curriculum vitae.

Offerer/ऑफरर *(noun)* – प्रस्तावक

The offerer presented us with new plans.

Offering/ऑफरिंग *(noun)* – अर्पण

As soon as he entered the temple premises, we knew that he had come with some offering.

Office/ऑफिस *(noun)* – कार्यालय, दफ़्तर

Recently, we have been shifted to a brand new office.

Officer/ऑफिसर *(noun)* – अधिकारी

The officer on duty did not pay any attention to the ongoing protests.

Official/ऑफिशल *(adjective)* – अधिकार-सम्बन्धी

As per the official notice, the employees submitted their income tax forms.

Officially/ऑफिशॅलि *(adverb)* – अधिकार पूर्वक

It is now known officially that some of the projects would be kept on hold till next announcement.

Officiate/ऑफिशिएट *(verb)* – स्थानापन्न होना

The manager officiated for the time when the Director was out of the city.

Officinal/ऑफिसिनल *(adjective)* – औषधियों की जड़ीबूटियों से सम्बन्धित

We were not aware of the herb's officinal properties.

O

Officious/ऑफ़िशस *(adjective)* – धृष्ट

There was no other option but to sack him in order to get rid of his officious ways.

Offing/ऑफिंग *(noun)* – किनारे से देख पड़ता हुआ दूर का समुद्र

We were looking at a ship in the offing.

Offish/ऑफिश *(adjective)* – अलग रहने वाला

I abhorred his offish attitude towards me.

Offset/ऑफसेट *(noun)* – अंकुर, प्रतिकरण

The family of the victim was given monetary assistance as an offset against the job offer.

Offside/ऑफसाइड *(adjective & adverb)* – दूर की दिशा

The coach was explaining to him the offside rule of the game.

Offspring/ऑफस्प्रिंग *(noun)* – सन्तान

The offspring of the mammal were too small and were kept under veterinary observation.

Oft/ऑफ्ट *(adverb)* – बहुधा

It would be oft that she crossed the barrier and go across the river.

Ogive/ओजाइव *(noun)* – नुकीली कमानी की मेहराब

It was clear that some skilled craftsmen were involved in the construction of the ogive.

Ogle/ओगल *(verb)* – आँखें लड़ाना

The shabby man used to ogle the ladies waiting for the train.

Ogygian/ऑगिजिअॅन – अति प्राचीन समय का

The archeologists were working on an ogygian fossil found beneath the soil.

Oh/ओह *(exclamatory)* – ओह

The girl exclaimed, "Oh! The poor man has not eaten since yesterday."

Ohm/ओम् *(noun)* – विद्युत् प्रतिरोध की नाप

The correct answer to the question was 4 ohms.

Oil/ऑइल *(noun)* – तेल, फुलेल

The driver thought it would be better to fill the oil tank before he could run out of it.

Ointment/आइन्टमेंट *(noun)* – लेप, मलहम

Apply some ointment over the infected area.

Olden/ओल्डेन *(adjective)* – पुराने समय का

In olden days, people used to travel a lot by boats.

Oldish/ओल्डिस *(adj)* – कुछ पुराना

Retorted the manager, "This idea is a bit oldish."

Oldness/ओल्डनेस *(noun)* – बुढ़ापा

The oldness of the building is evident from its withered look.

Oldster/ओल्डस्टर *(noun)* – युवा अवस्था से अतीत

The child was too happy to see the same oldster walking down the street.

Oleaginous/ओलिऐजिनॅस *(adjective)* – चिकना

Water had almost no effect over the oleaginous wood.

Oleander/ओलिएंडर *(noun)* – करबीर

The oleanders were all boomed with lovely flowers.

Oleic/ओलिइक *(adj)* – तेल-सम्बन्धी

Oleic acid is used in the manufacture of soaps.

Olid/ऑलिड *(adj)* – दुर्गन्ध वाला

The garbage was so olid that no one of us could stand it.

Oligarch/ऑलिगार्क *(noun)* – अल्पतन्त्र का सदस्य

It was the high time that an oligarch had to be selected among the group members.

Olivary/ऑलिवरि *(adjective)* – अण्डाकार

The olivary bodies are present on medulla oblongata.

Olive/ऑलिव *(noun)* – जैतून का वृक्ष

Olives were given to the patient in order to have his speedy recovery.

Olympian/ओल्पियन *(adjective)* – श्रेष्ठ, शानदार

The prince's Olympian looks caught everybody's attention.

Omega/ओमेगा *(noun)* – यूनानी वर्णमाला का अन्तिम अक्षर

Omega is the last letter of the Greek alphabet.

Omen/ओमेन *(noun)* – शकुन

Setting out on the journey was considered a bad omen by the astrologer.

Ominous/ऑमिनॅस *(adjective)* – अशुभ

I had the ominous feeling about her going out, so I did not let her do so.

O

Omissible/ऑमिसिबल *(adj)* – छोड़ने योग्य

Before working on the project again, he got rid of all the omissible data.

Omission/ऑमिशॅन *(noun)* – चूक, भूल

The omission of data took about an hour.

Omissive/ऑमिसिव *(adj)* – छोड़ने वाला

He had no idea that he was wasting his time on the omissive details.

Omit/ऑमिट *(verb)* – छोड़ देना

As our syllabus was still pending, the teacher omitted two chapters from it.

Omni/ऑम्नि *(combining form)* – सब प्रकार से

The omnipotent gods were challenged by the demons for war.

Omnifarious/ऑम्निफेरिअस *(adj)* – सब प्रकार का

The book had omnifarious details about the growth and evolution of species.

Omnific/ऑम्निफिक *(adj)* – सर्वोत्पादक

The Almighty is considered to have omnific powers.

Omniform/ऑम्निफार्म *(noun)* – सब प्रकार के रूपवाला

Some of the microorganisms are omniform.

Omnigenous/ऑम्निजिनस *(adj)* – सब जाति का

Our database consists of omnigenous records.

Omnipotence/ऑम्निपोटेंस *(noun)* – सर्व (अनन्त) शक्ति

The demon had grown arrogant over his omnipotence.

Omnipotent/ऑम्निपोटेंट *(adj)* – सर्वशक्तिमान

The book depicted the giant to have omnipotent powers.

Omnipresence/आम्निप्रजेन्स *(noun)* – विश्वव्यापकता

Every religious text talks about the omnipresence of God.

Omnipresent/ऑम्निप्रेजेन्ट *(adjective)* – विश्वव्यापी

The priest said, "We should pay reverence to the omnipresent Almighty."

Omniscience/ऑम्निश्येन्स् *(noun)* – सर्वज्ञान

He tried to convince of his omniscience, but no one believed him.

Omniscient/ऑम्निश्येन्ट् *(adj)* – त्रिकाल दर्शी

None of our deeds is hidden from the omniscient God.

Omnivorous/ऑम्निवरस *(adjective)* – सर्वभक्षी

The birds are known to be omnivorous creatures.

Omoplate/ओमॅप्लेट *(noun)* – कन्धे पर की हड्डी

After the accident, he had to undergo surgery of his omoplate.

Onagar/ऑनगर् *(noun)* – गोरखर

Onagars are known to inhabitate in regions of northern Iran.

Once/वन्स *(adverb)* – पहले एक बार

We were allowed to talk to the Minister only once.

Oncoming/ऑनकमिंग *(adjective)* – पहुँच

The driver could not notice the oncoming bus and hence, met an accident.

One/वन *(cardinal number)* – कोई, एक

We ordered only one plate of the main course menu.

One-eyed/वन-आइड *(adj)* – काना

The story about the one-eyed man is fascinating.

Oneirocritic/ॲनाइअॅरॅक्रिटिक *(noun)* – स्वप्न का अर्थ बताने वाला

An experienced oneirocritic is called as a guest in a radio show.

Oneness/वननेस *(noun)* – एकता, अकेलापन

Only by the oneness of the nation, we can expect to thwart our enemies.

Onerous/ॲनरस *(adjective)* – कष्टसाध्य

I was pretty sure that hurdle race was going to be onerous job.

Oneself/वनसेल्फ *(pronoun)* – अपने को स्वयं

How to neglect the promises that one is making to oneself?

One-Sided/वन-साइडेड *(adj)* – पक्षपाती

The police had heard only one-sided story till then; now it was the time for the other party.

Onfall/ऑनफॉल *(noun)* – आगमन

With the onfall of summers, our literature classes were resumed.

Onflow/ऑनफ्लो *(adverb)* – आगे की ओर बहाव

Initially, the onflow was high, but later, it slowed down.

Onion/अॅन्यॅन *(noun)* - प्याज

There are many antimicrobial properties in onion.

Oniony/अॅन्यनि *(adj)* - प्याज के गन्ध का

An oniony smell was emanating from kitchen.

Onlooker/ऑनलूकर *(noun)* - दर्शक

The onlookers were just standing there, without bothering to do anything for the victims.

Onset/ऑनसेट *(noun)* - आक्रमण, प्रारंभ

With the onset of monsoons, the water-borne diseases become common.

Onslaught/ऑनस्लॉट *(noun)* - प्रबल आक्रमण

The onslaught took lives of many innocent people.

Ontological/ऑन्ट्रॅलॉजिकल *(adj)* - दार्शनिक

More research is required in the field of ontological studies.

Ontologist/ऑन्टोलॉजिस्ट *(noun)* - सत्त्व-विद्या का पण्डित

An ontologist deals with the study of metaphysics.

Ontology/ऑन्टलॅजि *(noun)* - दर्शन या सत्व विद्या

His inclination towards philosophy made him opt for a course on ontology.

O

Onus/ओनस *(noun)* - उत्तरदायित्व

As we were not ready to take the onus, another eligible person was chosen for the post.

Onward/ऑनवर्ड *(adverb)* - आगे या सामने की ओर

From that time onward, the two companies decided to work together.

Onymous/ऑनिमस् - गुमनाम नहीं (सनाम)

The site did not allow the authors to post onymous articles.

Onyx/ऑनिक्स *(noun)* - गोमेद रत्न

Onyx is used as an ornamental stone.

Oogenesis/ओअजेनिसिस *(noun)* - भ्रूण का बढ़ना

During oogenesis, female's body produces an ovum.

Oology/ओऑलजि *(noun)* - पक्षी के अण्डों का अध्ययन

I have an avid interest in oology.

Ooze/ऊज *(verb)* - रिसना, चूना, टपकना

Water was oozing out of the pore at the bottom of the pot.

Ooziness/ऊजिनेस *(noun)* - टपकन

The bark was still out of its ooziness.

Oozings/ऊजिंग्स *(noun)* - द्रव का टपकन

The oozing had stopped by then and the pore was no longer moist.

Oozy/ऊजि *(adj)* - रिसने वाला

A hole in the gum bottle had rendered it oozy.

Opacity/ओपैसिटी *(noun)* - धुँधलापन

In Photoshop, to see the underlying layer, the opacity of the upper layer needs to be decreased.

Opalescent/ओपॅलेसेन्ट *(adj)* - पोलकी रत्न का

With light shining directly over oil, its surface had turned opalescent.

Opaline/ओपलाइन *(adjective)* - दूधिया

What we were looking at was a beautiful opaline sky.

Opalize/ओपलाइज - पोलकी के सदृश बनाना

The modern infrastructure has opalized the urban cities.

Opaque/ओपेक *(adjective)* - अपारदर्शक

An opaque object does not allow light to pass through its surface.

Ope/ओप *(adjective & verb)* - खुलना

Cool breeze was coming in the room through ope window.

Openable/ओपेनेबल *(adjective)* - प्रकाशित करने योग्य

As the bottle was placed in freezer for many days, its cap was no longer openable.

Opener/ओपेनर *(noun)* - खोलने वाला

To open the soda bottles, I needed an opener.

Openly/ओपेनली *(adverb)* - दिल खोलकर

The model had no qualms to talk openly about her relationships.

Openness/ओपेननेस *(noun)* - प्रकाशता

It required a great deal of effort on leader's part to bring openness in the attitude of his workers.

Opera/ऑपरा *(noun)* - संगीत नाटक

All of us were given the passes to the Opera, but two of us could not attend it.

Opera-glass/ऑपराग्लास *(plural noun)* - नाटक देखने की दूरबीन

Sitting on rear seats, we had to put on the opera-glasses to see the happenings on the stage clearly.

Operant/ऑपरंट *(adjective)* - कार्य करने की शक्ति रखने वाला

The operant conditioning is based on the fact that the behaviour is based on the type of stimulus applied.

Operate/ऑपरेट *(verb)* - कार्य करना

As soon as the machine started operating, it developed some hitches.

Operatic/ऑपरैटिक *(adj)* - संगीत नाटक के सदृश

Their operatic performances were worth applauding.

Operative/ऑपरेटिव *(adjective)* - प्रयोजक

The machine guns were put to test during their operative phase.

Operator/ऑपरेटर *(noun)* - प्रवर्तक

The operator just put down the receiver without saying a word.

Operetta/ऑपरेटा *(noun)* - छोटा संगीत नाटक

The group members were thrilled when they were handed over the tickets of the operetta.

Operose/ऑपरोस *(adjecitve)* - अति परिश्रमी

They could not allow their operose efforts to go in vain.

Ophidion/ऑफिडिअन् *(adjective & noun)* - सर्प सम्बन्धी

The fish belonged to the ophidion genus.

Ophiology/ऑफिअलॉजि *(noun)* - सर्पविद्या

Would you like to opt for Ophiology as your field of specialization?

Ophthalmia/ऑफ्थल्मिया *(noun)* - आँख आना

The eye surgeon had many cases of opthalmia that day.

Ophthalmology/आफ्थैल्मॅलॅजि *(noun)* - नेत्र-विज्ञान

His son is keen to go abroad and study ophthalmology.

Ophthalmy/ऑफ्थैल्मि *(noun)* - आँखों की सूजन

It was due to his recurrent ophthalmy that he could not work on computer for hours.

Opine/ओपाइन *(verb)* - तर्क करना

She opined on the country's poor security system for women.

Opinion/ओपिनियन *(noun)* - अनुमान

Would you mind giving your opinion in this case?

Opium/ओपियम *(noun)* - अफीम

The illegal trading of opium from China into other Asian countries still continues.

Opossum/ऑपास्सम् *(noun)* - अमेरिका देश का एक प्रकार का चौपाया

The zoology chapter was entirely focused on the study of Opossums.

Opponency/ऑप्पोनेंसि *(noun)* - शत्रुता

The opponency, in this case, was so strong that they could not defend themselves.

Opponent/ऑपोनेंट *(noun)* - शत्रु

In the tournament, she was going to face a strong opponent.

Opportunism/ऑपर्ट्यूनिज्म *(noun)* - सुलह, सन्धि

Sometimes, it becomes necessary to employ opportunism to further one's case.

Opportunist/ऑपर्टयूनिस्ट *(noun)* - अवसरग्राही

What an opportunist he is! adjective opportunistic. *The man was too naïve to employ any opportunistic tactics.*

Opportunity/ऑपर्ट्यूनिटि *(noun)* - अवकाश, सुअवसर

An opportunity never comes twice.

Opposability/अपोजबिलिटि *(noun)* - विरोधभाव

The opposability of the human thumb makes it easy to hold objects with ease.

Opposable/ऑपेसेब्ल *(adj)* - विरोध के योग्य

Our opposable thumb has rendered us with many capabilities.

Oppose/अपोज *(verb)* - विरोध करना

When my turn came, I vehemently opposed the barbaric act.

Opposer/अपोजर *(noun)* - विरोधक

Our own team member turned out to be our opposer.

O

Opposing/अपोजिंग *(adjective)* - विरुद्ध काम करने वाला

The two opposing forces clashed and the result was disastrous.

Oppositely/ॲपोजिटलि *(adv)* - विपरीत भाव से

The two tables were placed oppositely.

Opposition/ॲपोजिशन *(noun)* - विरोध, प्रतिकूलता

The opposition is raising its voice against the recommendations proposed by the ruling party.

Oppositional/अपोजिशनल *(adjective)* - विरोधी

Their oppositional behaviour came in the way of coming out with a resolution.

Oppression/ॲप्रेशन *(noun)* - उत्पीड़न

The peasants raised their voice against the oppression of landlords.

Oppressive/ऑप्रेशिव *(adjective)* - अत्याचारी

In order to get rid of his oppressive ways, I just ran away.

Oppressor/ॲप्रेशर *(noun)* - निर्दयी

A time came when the oppressor had to succumb to the demands of the peasants.

Opprobrious/ऑप्रोब्रियस *(adjective)* - घृणित

He was staring at me with opprobrious looks.

O

Oppugn/ऑप्यून *(verb)*- विरोध करना

In spite of giving assurance about positive results, his team mates oppugned the new strategy.

Oppugnation/ऑपग्नेशन *(noun)* - विरोध

I was too timid to face the oppugnation.

Oppugner/अप्यूग्नर् *(noun)* - विरोध करने वाला

In contrast to our expectations, he turned out to be an oppugner.

Opsonic/आप्सोनिक *(adj)* - शरीर के भीतर के कृमियों पर प्रभाव डालने

An opsonic reaction became active as soon the foreign bodies entered the surface.

Opsonin/ऑपसोनिन *(noun)* - किसी रोगी के कृमियों को मारकर शरीर प्रवेश करने की

The body had not enough opsonins to fight against the attack of microorganisms.

Optative/ऑप्टेटिव *(adjective)* - इच्छा सूचक

She was talking in an optative mood that day.

Optic/अप्टिक *(adjective)* - नेत्र-सम्बन्धी

An operation needed to be done on his optic nerve.

Optical/ऑप्टिकल *(adjective)* - आँख का

The lecture was based on the use of optical devices.

Optician/ऑप्टिसियन *(noun)* - चक्षुविद्या में निपुण

I went to the optician and he advised to use glasses as soon as possible.

Optics/ऑप्टिक्स *(plural noun)* - दृष्टि-विज्ञान

Optics was a mandatory subject in our graduation course.

Optimacy/ऑप्टिमैसि *(noun)* - शिष्टजन

Her parents are searching a groom from the optimacy.

Optimist/ऑप्टिमिस्ट *(noun)* - आशावादी

He was such an optimist that even during worst period of his life, he did not get discouraged.

Option/ऑप्सन *(noun)* - रुचि

After hopping from job to job, I didn't have any options left.

Optional/ऑप्सनल *(adjective)* - ऐच्छिक

I did no preparation of the optional subject, yet passed it with flying colours.

Optophone/ॲप्टोफोन *(noun)* - अन्धों को पदार्थ दिखलाने में सहायता देने का यन्त्र

An optophone is a useful device for blind people for reading by hearing.

Opulence/ऑपुलेंस *(noun)* - ऐश्वर्य

We lived in opulence and spent extravagantly.

Opulent/ऑप्यूलेंट *(adjective)* - सम्पन्न

The child was born into an opulent family.

Or/आर् *(noun)* - अन्यथा, पहले

We were asked to write the truth-table of the logical operator 'OR'.

Oracular/ऑरेक्यूलर् *(adjective)* - देववाणी तुल्य

An oracular building was present at the centre of the city.

Oral/ओरल *(adjective)* - मौखिक

One must take care of his oral hygiene.

Orange/ऑरेंज *(adjective)* - सन्तरा

The Orange organization is based in Ireland.

Orangery/ऑरेंजरि *(noun)* – नारंगी का बगीचा
An orangery was constructed within the botanical institute.

Orant/आरैंट *(noun & adj)* – पूजक
An orant gesture indicates worship in Christianity.

Orate/ओरेट *(verb)* – व्याख्यान देना
The way he orates is quite impressive.

Orator/ऑरेटर *(noun)* – सुवक्ता
Being an orator, she was always encouraged to participate in discussions.

Oratory/ऑरेटरी *(noun)* – वक्तृत्व-शक्ति
Only priest was allowed to enter the oratory.

Orb/ऑर्ब *(noun)* – गोला
The orb present on king's crown was shimmering with light.

Orbicular/आरबीक्यूलर *(adjective)* – गोल
I could not understand what that orbicular object was.

Orbit/ऑरबिट *(noun & verb)* – ग्रहपथ
Every planet revolves in its own orbit.

Orchard/ऑर्चर्ड *(noun)* – फलों का बाग
We were fascinated by the presence of a lovely orchard near our new house.

Orchestra/ऑरकेस्ट्रा *(noun)* – वादकवृन्द
Before orchestra could begin, one of the singers fell on the stage.

Orchid/ऑर्किड् *(noun)* – रंग-बिरंगे फूलों वाले विचित्र पौधे
I am thinking of buying an orchid for my living room at my farm house.

Orchitis/ऑर्काइटिस् *(noun)* – अण्डकोष का शोथ
The man got irritated by the constant orchitis, so he consulted a sexologist.

Ordain/ऑर्डेन *(verb)* – निर्दिष्ट करना
The clergyman was ordained under the administration of a bishop.

Ordainer/ऑर्डेनर् *(noun)* – संस्थापक
The cleric was the ordainer in the holy ceremony.

Ordainment/ऑर्डेन्मेन्ट *(noun)* – आज्ञा
The ceremony of ordainment had to be interrupted in between.

Ordeal/ऑरडिअल् *(noun)* – कठिन परीक्षा
I have been facing this ordeal from a very long time.

Orderliness/ऑर्डर्लिनेस् *(noun)* – सद्व्यवहार in
The man vouched to bring orderliness in his institute.

Orderless/ऑर्डर्लेस् *(adj)* – क्रमहीन
She had no idea that she would have to teach an orderless class.

Orderly/ऑर्डर्लि *(adjective)* – क्रम के अनुसार
Everyone was impressed with the orderly way he used to do things.

Ordinance/ऑर्डिनैंस *(noun)* – अध्यादेश
The government, recently, passed an ordinance regarding vehicle parking.

Ordinarily/ऑर्डिनरिलि *(adv)* – साधारण रूप से
The Mathematics genius could solve all the problems ordinarily.

Ordinariness/ऑर्डिनरिनेस् *(noun)* – सामान्यता
We were surprised to see the ordinariness of his dress at the party.

Ordinary/ऑर्डिनरी *(adjective)* – प्रचलित
In spite of her ordinary looks, she was able to garner the attention of boys.

Ordinate/ऑर्डिनेट *(noun)* – क्रमानुसार
The class on ordinate and abscissa was an interesting one.

Ordination/ऑर्डिनेशन् *(noun)* – विधान
The man was too adamant to follow the ordination.

Ordnance/ऑर्डनैन्स *(noun)* – तोपखाना
The army ordered for a whole new ordnance.

Ordure/ऑर्ड्यूर *(noun)* – विष्ठा
The street had a stench of ordure.

Ore/ओर *(noun)* – बिना संस्कार की हुई धातु
In our Chemistry class, we learned the process of extracting iron from its ore.

Oread/ओरिड *(noun)* – पहाड़ की अप्सरा
Oread is a Greek mythological character.

Orectic/ऑरेक्टिक *(adjective)* – इच्छा-सम्बन्धी
His orectic manners clearly indicate that he had fetish for food.

Organ/आर्गन् *(noun)* – शरीर का अंग
He is dexterous at playing organ pipe.

Organdie/ऑर्गन्डी *(noun)* – अरगन्डी

She was looking pretty in her dress made of organdie.

Organic/ऑर्गैनिक *(adjective)* – जैव

The organic matter is biodegradable.

Organization/ऑर्गेनाइजेशन *(noun)* – सृष्टि संगठन

We work in an organization that works for social welfare.

Organize/ऑर्गेनाइज *(verb)* – बनाना, संगठन करना

As she saw the things scattered here and there, she started organizing them.

Orgasm/ऑर्गैज्म् *(noun)* – क्षोभ

It was not the first time that he was not able to fully enjoy the orgasm.

Orgastic/ऑर्गैस्टिक *(adjective)* – आवेग-सम्बन्धी

He could not hold his joy that he experienced during the orgastic activity.

Orgy/ऑर्जि *(noun)* – रात्रि उत्सव

Orgies are usually organized secretly.

Orient/ओरिएन्ट *(noun)* – पूर्व दिशा

The Orient is blamed for aping the West.

Oriental/ओरिएन्टल *(adjective)* – प्राचीन

O

There is no doubt about the oriental origin of the gibbons.

Orientally/ओरिएन्टली *(adverb)* – प्राचीनता से

It was clear that their mannerism was driven orientally.

Orientate/ओरिएन्टेट *(verb)* – पूरब की ओर बनाना

It was her lack of her knowledge about Indian culture that she requested me orientate her.

Origanum/ऑरिगेनम *(noun)* – एक फलवाला पौधा

The aromatic properties of Origanum are used for various purposes.

Origin/ओरिजिन *(noun)* – उद्‌गम

The origin of mankind has always remained a puzzle.

Original/ओरिजिनल *(adjective)* – मौलिक

The original species of human had a close resemblance to the modern man.

Originality/ऑरिजिनैलिटी *(noun)* – मौलिकता

The director was looking for originality in acting.

Originally/ओरिजनली *(adv)* – पहले से

Originally, there were no wireless technology in the field of communication.

Originate/ओरिजिनेट *(verb)* – प्रारम्भ होना

A few varieties of jute originated in India.

Origination/ओरिजिनेशन *(adj)* – प्रारम्भ

India is attributed to be the origination place of many spices.

Originatives/ओरिजिनेटिव्स *(adj)* – उत्पन्न करने वाला

My son is gifted with an originative mind.

Originator/ओरिजिनेटर *(noun)* – उत्पादक

Man is considered the originator of many innovations.

Orion/ओरिअन *(noun)* – मृगशिरा नक्षत्र

Orion is a constellation that can be seen during winter season.

Orison/ओरिसन *(noun)* – प्रार्थना

The devotees paid their reverence by saying an orison.

Orleans/ऑर्लिअन्स *(noun)* – एक प्रकार का बेर

Orleans is a city in France where Joan of Arc led French against England.

Orlop/ऑर्लॉप *(noun)* – जहाज की सबसे नीची छत

We saw captain sitting on an orlop.

Ornament/ऑर्नामेंट *(noun)* – अलंकार

Ornaments have been recovered from the excavation sites of Harappa civilization.

Ornamental/ऑर्नामेंटल *(adjective)* – विभूषक

The ornamental vessels have always been a part of Indian aestheticism.

Ornamentalism/ऑर्नामेंटलिज्म *(noun)* – अलंकरण

The fetish for ornamnetalism never ceases to exist.

Ornamentalist/ऑर्नामेंटलिस्ट *(noun)* – सुशोभित करने वाला

Today, I am going to meet a renowned ornamentalist from Israel.

Ornamentally/ऑर्नामेंटली *(noun)* – सजाया हुआ

The king's room was looking ornamentally beautiful.

Ornate/आर्नेट *(adjective)* - सुशोभित

The elephant was ornate with gold jewelry.

Ornithology/आर्निथॅलॅजी *(noun)* - पक्षी विद्या

Dr. Salim Ali did an excellent job in ornithology.

Orphan/ऑर्फन *(noun)* - अनाथ

The business was keen to donate money for educating orphans in his society.

Orphanage/ऑर्फनेज *(noun)* - अनाथालय

This orphanage has been blacklisted due to illegal practices carried in it.

Orphic/ऑर्फिक *(adjective)* - सुरीला

The orphic rites and rituals were common in ancient Greece.

Ort/ऑर्ट *(noun)* - जूठन

After eating he left an ort and fed it to his cat.

Orthodox/ऑर्थोडॉक्स *(adjective)* - शास्त्रानुसार सत्य धर्मावलम्बी

She belongs to an orthodox family.

Orthoepy/आर्थोएपि *(noun)* - शुद्ध उच्चारण सिखलाने की विद्या

Only a few people are interested in Orthoepy.

Orthogonal/ऑर्थोगोनल *(adjective)* - समकोणाकार

The students were asked to calculate the area of the given orthogonal shape.

Ortolan/ऑर्टलन् *(noun)* - बगेरी

A male ortolan was sitting over a tree branch.

Oscillate/ऑसिलेट *(verb)* - झूलना

The pendulum of the clock oscillates back and forth repeatedly.

Oscillation/ऑसिलेशन *(noun)* - दोलन

Electro-mechanical oscillations take place in a microphone.

Oscillating/ऑसिलेटिंग *(adj)* - इधर-उधर हिलता हुआ

The government is still oscillating over the decision to pass Jan Lokpal bill.

Oscitant/ऑसिटैंट *(adjective)* - निद्रालु

The students were usually oscitant during the boring History lecture.

Oscitate/ऑसिटेट *(verb)* - जँभाई लेना

The teacher was aghast to see that the boys in punishment were oscitating.

Oscular/ऑसक्यूलर *(adjective)* - चुम्बन का

The doctor was going to operate oscular bone.

Osculation/ऑस्क्यूलेशन *(noun)* - चुम्बन

The two were lost in their act of osculation.

Osmium/ओस्मियम *(noun)* - एक धातु

Osmium is used in applications where durability of material is required.

Ossicle/ऑसिकल *(noun)* - आस्थिक

Ossicle is a bone in man's middle ear.

Ossification/ओसिफिकेशन *(noun)* - हड्डी बनने की क्रिया

As the time progressed, the society saw an ossification of the traditional beliefs.

Ossify/ओसिफाई *(verb)* - कड़ा हो जाना

Osteoclasts are specialized cells that ossify and help in bone formation.

Ostensible/ऑस्टेन्सिबल *(adjective)* - प्रकट, प्रत्यक्ष

No one could doubt his ostensible purpose of charity.

Ostensive/ऑस्टेन्सिव *(adjective)* - स्पष्ट

Teacher's ostensive way of teaching appealed all the students.

Ostracism/आस्ट्रैसिज्म *(noun)* - देशनिकाला

The couple's ostracism from the society has raised a few eyebrows.

Ostrich/ऑस्ट्रिच *(noun)* - शुतुरमुर्ग

An ostrich lays the biggest eggs in the world.

Otalgia/ओटैल्जिआ *(noun)* - कर्णशूल

I was suffering from an otalgia.

Other/अदर *(adjective & pronoun)* - अन्य, दूसरा

The other criminal is still out of the reach.

Otherness/अदरनेस *(noun)* - परायापन

She had some sort of otherness in her and this made him fall in love with her.

Otherwise/अदरवाइज *(adverb)* - अन्यथा

Do it now, otherwise I would report it to your manager.

Otiosely/ओशिओस्लि *(adverb)* - सुस्ती से

I do not appreciate his way of living otiosely.

Otitis/ॲटाइटिस *(noun)* - कान की सूजन

Why don't you get your otitis get treated.

Otology/अॅटॅलॅजी *(noun)* – कान (के रोगों) का शास्त्र
I am going to take a course in Otology.

Otter/ऑटर *(noun)* – जलमार्जार (ऊदबिलाव)
What we were looking at was a large otter.

Otto/अॅटॅ *(noun)* – इत्र
The sweet smell of otto had an intoxicating smell on me.

Oubliette/ऊब्लिएट *(noun)* – गुप्त गुफा
The prince was hooked to a chain in the dark oubliette.

Ought/ऑट *(modal verb)* – चाहिए
You ought to carry this responsibility on your shoulders.

Our/आवर *(possession determine)* – हम लोगों का
Our culture has many flaws that need to be corrected.

Ousel/ऊज़्ल् *(noun)* – भुजंगा
An ousel resembles a blackbird.

Oust/आउस्ट *(verb)* – बाहर करना
We could no longer take his rubbish attitude, so he was ousted.

Ouster/आउस्टर *(noun)* – बेदखली
His ouster from family business came as no surprise to us.

O

Outbalance/आउटवैंलेंस *(verb)* – प्रभाव में अधिक होना
I have no idea of why the party is outbalancing the issue over other things.

Outbid/आउटबिड *(verb)* – अधिक मूल्य लगाना
The company outbid our local business to get the lucrative project.

Outbrag/आउटब्रैग *(verb)* – सुन्दरता से बढ़ना
My senior outbrags about his achievements as and when he gets the chance.

Outburn/आउटबर्न *(verb)* – तीव्रता से जलना
The flames were so high that the entire building got outburned.

Outburst/आउटबर्स्ट *(noun)* – विस्फोट
No one was amused to see her sudden outburst as soon as she had occupied her seat.

Outcaste/आउटकास्ट *(noun)* – जाति से निकाला हुआ
He was declared an outcaste after he confessed his love for the dalit woman.

Outclass/आउटक्लास *(verb)* – बढ़ जाना
She outclassed her friends in her choice of sophisticated things.

Outcry/आउटक्राई *(noun)* – पीड़ा का शब्द
After the public outcry, the case was reopened.

Outdare/आउटडेअर *(verb)* – ललकारना
She outdared her male competitors to save the child from the clutches of the leopard.

Outdistance/आउटडिस्टेंस *(verb)* – आगे बढ़ जाना
After only a mile was left, I outdistanced the person running in front of me.

Outdoor/आउटडोर् *(adjective)* – खुले मैदान का
We should encourage our children to pursue outdoor activities.

Outer/आउटर *(adjective)* – बाहरी
A line was drawn from the centre of the inner circle to the half of radius of outer one.

Outermost/आउटरमोस्ट *(adjective)* – सबसे बाहरी
The outermost region of a candle flame is the coldest.

Outfall/आउटफॉल *(noun)* – नदी का मुहाना
The tourists were allowed to have the view of the outfall.

Outfit/आउटफिट *(noun)* – (उपकरण) सामान
His outfit was apt for the occasion.

Outfitter/आउटफिटर *(noun)* – सामग्री इकट्ठा करने वाला मनुष्य
Why don't you visit a good outfitter in your area?

Outfly/आउटफ्लाई *(verb)* – उड़ने में बढ़ जाना
It was thrilling to see how the jet aircraft was able to outfly its older counterparts.

Outfool/आउटफूल *(verb)* – मूर्खता में बढ़ जाना
We were fully convinced that his outfooling himself was a thing done purposely.

Outgate/आउटगेट *(noun)* – बाहर जाने का मार्ग
We made an exit from the outgate.

Outgaze/आउटगेज *(verb)* – अधिक दूर तक देखना
The man was outgazing and keeping an eye on our every single move.

Outgive/आउटगिव *(verb)* – उदारता में बढ़ जाना
She always outgives, thanks to her philanthropic nature.

Outgoing/आउटगोइंग *(adjective)* – बाहर जाना
I wish I were a bit more outgoing.

Outgrow/आउटग्रो *(verb)* - से बढ़ जाना

My son has outgrown of his teenage clothes.

Outgrowth/आउटग्रोथ *(noun)* - अतिवृद्धि

We noticed some green outgrowths on potatoes.

Outguard/आउटगार्ड *(noun)* - दूर से रक्षा कार्य

A small outguard was positioned at about 2 kilometres from the army.

Outhouse/आउटहाउस *(noun)* - घर के बाहर का छोटा मकान

The guests had to be kept in the outhouse.

Outlaw/आउटलॉ *(noun)* - दस्यु

He being an outlaw can create problems for him.

Outlay/आउटले *(noun)* - खर्च

Kindly give me an account of the outlay on arranging tours.

Outleap/आउटलिप *(verb)* - आगे को कूदना

The deer outleapt and became invisible.

Outlet/आउटलेट *(noun)* - निकास

I forgot to close the gas outlet.

Outline/आउटलाइन *(noun)* - खाका

The teacher drew an outline of human heart and asked us to draw its parts.

Outlive/आउटलिव *(verb)* - अधिक जीना

The husband outlived her wife by several years.

Outlook/आउटलुक *(noun)* - चौकसी

You should change your negative outlook of life.

Outlying/आउटलाइंग *(adjective)* - दूर का

The doctor had no qualms about working in an outlying village.

Outmarch/आउटमार्च *(verb)* - आगे बढ़ना

We were able to outmarch the dacoits who came looking for us.

Outmeasure/आउटमेजर *(verb)* - विस्तार में बढ़ना

The imported rice outmeasured our needs.

Outmost/आउटमोस्ट *(adjective)* - सबसे बढ़कर

Pluto is the outmost planet of our solar system.

Outname/आउटनेम *(verb)* - यश में बढ़ जाना

The popularity of her novels has outnamed her failures in life.

Outness/आउटनेस *(noun)* - बाहरीपन

It is the outness of her nature that she has dozens of friends.

Outnumber/आउटनम्बर *(verb)* - संख्या में बढ़ना

The number of articles contributed by her has outnumbered the total articles written by anyone else.

Outpace/आउटपेस *(verb)* - तेज दौड़ना

My sister walks slow and can never outpace me.

Outpart/आउटपार्ट *(noun)* - केन्द्र से दूर पर का हिस्सा

Peel the outpart of the mango and throw it away.

Outplay/आउटप्ले *(verb)* - खेल में हराना

The continuous practice on her part made her outplay other girls.

Outpost/आउटपोस्ट *(noun)* - सीमा-चौकी

After some time, he was stationed at the outpost.

Outpower/आउटपॉवर *(verb)* - शक्ति में बढ़ना

In the story, the small boy overpowers the beast.

Output/आउटपुट *(noun)* - घानी

The farmers are expecting more output of grains this year.

Outrage/आउटरेज *(noun)* - उपद्रव

The delay in the murder case created an outrage in public.

Outrageous/आउट्रेजस *(adjective)* - उपद्रवी

The minister was criticized for his outrageous comment on communalism.

Outreach/आउटरीच *(verb)* - छलना

There was no doubt that our team shall outreach theirs.

Outride/आउटराइड *(verb)* - घुड़सवारी में आगे जाना

With regular practice, he could outride everyone else.

Outroot/आउटरूट *(verb & noun)* - जड़ से निकाल देना

The outroot of the dowry system requires more efforts on our part.

Outrun/आउटरन *(verb)* - निकल भागना

Can you outrun me?

O

Outset/आउटसेट *(noun)* - आरम्भ

It was clear from the outset that he was unwilling to take the case in his hand.

Outshine/आउटसाइन *(verb)* - चमकना

One of the vases in the shop was outshining others.

Outsider/आउटसाइडर *(noun)* - परदेशी

They were not willing to accept an outsider like him in their group.

Outsize/आउटसाइज *(adjective)* - सामान्य नाप से बढ़कर

His outsized body required specially tailored clothes.

Outskirt/आउटस्कर्ट *(plural noun)* - सरहद

He stopped the car on the outskirts of the city.

Outspoken/आउटस्पोकेन *(adjective)* - स्पष्ट कहा हुआ

She is always condemned for her outspoken nature.

Outspread/आउटस्प्रेड *(adjective)* - छितराया

His outspread arms showed that he wanted to hug her.

Outstanding/आउटस्टैंडिंग *(adjective)* - न चुकाया हुआ

Her performance in the exams was outstanding.

Outstep/आउटस्टेप *(verb)* - आगे को बढ़ना

Don't outstep the limits imposed on you.

Outstretch/आउटस्ट्रेच *(verb)* - फैलाना

To grab the handle, he outstretched his arm.

Outstrip/आउटस्ट्रिप *(verb)* - अतिक्रम करना

The leopard outstripped the hyena and grabbed it.

Outturn/आउटटर्न *(noun)* - तैयार माल

The outturn of the mill has exceeded the expectation.

Outvalue/आउटवैलू *(verb)* - मूल्य से हराना

That the character outvalues all other virtues in man is a fact.

Outvote/आउटवोट *(verb)* - अधिक वोट से हराना

The independent candidate surprised everyone by outvoting his rival.

Outwalk/आउटवाक् *(verb)* - अधिक तेज चलना

No matter how fast I walk, I cannot outwalk my friend.

Outwall/आउटवाल *(noun)* - घर की बाहरी दीवार

The outwall of the house badly needs a paint.

Outward/आउटवार्ड *(adjective)* - बाहरी

Don't get deceived by his outward appearance.

Outwatch/आउटवाच *(verb)* - अधिक पहरा देना

The child kept outwatching the train till it became invisible.

Outwear/आउटविअर *(verb)* - पूर्ण रूप से थका देना

The act of pushing cart outweared the man.

Outweigh/आउटवे *(verb)* - भार या महत्त्व में बढ़ना

Being a highly experienced man, his decision outweighs many others.

Outwind/आउटविंड *(verb)* - बन्धन ढीला करना

Why don't you unwind yourself a bit?

Outwit/आउटविट *(verb)* - बुद्धि द्वारा पराजित करना

It was due to his sharp mind that he outwitted everyone in the discussion round.

Outwork/आउटवर्क *(noun)* - घर के बाहर किया हुआ कार्य

The security level at the outwork is unsatisfactory.

Ova/ओवा - अण्डे

The fertilization takes place when one of the ova fuses with one or more sperms.

Oval/ओवल *(adjective)* - अण्डाकार

Her oval face makes her wear any type of makeup.

Ovarian/ओवेरियन *(adjective)* - अण्डाशय सम्बन्धी

The risk of the ovarian cancer is higher in women who smoke heavily.

Ovarious/ओवेरियस *(adj.)* - अण्डधारी

He was advised to change his ovarious diet.

Ovary/ओवरी *(noun)* - अण्डाशय

Her left ovary has a cyst.

Ovate/ओवेट *(adjective)* - अण्डाकार

Yesterday, I bought an ovate lantern.

O

Oven/ओवेन *(noun)* – चूल्हा

Why don't you purchase an oven?

Overact/ओवरएक्ट *(verb)* – आवश्यकता से अधिक काम करना

In almost every movie of hers, she has overacted.

Overalls/ओवरआल्स *(adjective)* – ऊपरी ओढ़ना या वस्त्र

The overall result of the discussion is that project should be completed by May this year.

Overawe/ओवरऑ *(verb)* – डराना

The speaker overawed the crowd by his inspiring speech.

Overbalance/ओवरबैलेंस *(verb)* – अधिक भारी होना

Being drunk, she overbalanced and fell on ground.

Overbear/ओवरबियर *(verb)* – वश में करना

The traumatic incident was too much for her to overbear.

Overbearing/ओवरबियरिंग *(adjective)* – अहंकारी

The overpowering lad badly needs a lesson.

Overblow/ओवरब्लो *(verb)* – फूलों से भरना

The musician was overblowing his flute to catch everyone's attention.

Overboard/ओवरबोर्ड *(adverb)* – जहाज की छत पर

It was due to deadly waves that he was thrown overboard.

Overbuild/ओवरबिल्ड *(verb)* – आवश्यकता से अधिक निर्माण करना

This city is overbuilt and needs a revamp.

Overburden/ओवरबर्डेन *(verb)* – अधिक लाद देना

The rearing of four children has overburdened her.

Overbusy/ओवरबिजी *(adj)* – कार्य में अतिलीन

Where are you overbusy these days?

Overcareful/ओवरकेअरफुल *(adjective)* – आवश्यकता से अधिक सावधान

Her overcareful attitude has been the subject of mockery among her colleagues.

Overcast/ओवरकास्ट *(adjective)* – मेघाच्छन

The overcast sky looks so pleasing.

Overcharge/ओवरचार्ज *(verb)* – अधिक मूल्य होना

I rebuked the seller for overcharging.

Overcoat/ओवरकोट *(noun)* – लबादा

Before setting out, don't forget to wear an overcoat.

Overcold/ओवरकोल्ड *(adj)* – बहुत ही ठण्डा

I am immune to the overcold weather.

Overcostly/ओवरकॉस्टली *(adj)* – बहुत महँगा

An average man is unable to buy overcostly things.

Overcrowd/ओवरक्राउड *(verb)* – बड़ी भीड़ जमाना

Getting in of more passengers overcrowded the bus.

Overdate/ओवरडेट *(verb)* – बाद की तारीख डालना

While signing the papers, the manager overdated them.

Overdose/ओवरडोज *(noun)* – अधिक मात्रा

Overdose of any pill can be dangerous.

Overestimate/ओवरएस्टिमेट *(verb)* – अधिक आँकना

The minister had overestimated his victory in the coming elections.

Overestimation/ओवरएस्टिमेशन *(noun)* – अधिक मूल्य निरूपण

His overestimation of the things cost him dear.

O

Overfeed/ओवरफिड *(verb)* – परिमाण से अधिक खिलाना

Overfeeding the cattle can make them ill.

Overfill/ओवरफिल *(verb)* – परिमाण से अधिक भरना

Our department is overfilled with employees.

Overgrown/ओवरग्रोन *(adj)* – अधिक बढ़ा हुआ

Farmer was busy plucking out the overgrown grass.

Overhang/ओवरहैंग *(verb)* – ऊपर लटकना

The branches of this tree are overhanging.

Overhappy/ओवरहैप्पी *(adj)* – बहुत ही प्रसन्न

What is the reason of your being overhappy?

Overhardy/ओवरहार्डी *(noun)* – अत्यधिक साहसी

The man is just pretending to be overhardy.

Overhasty/ओवरहेस्टी *(adj)* – अधिक शीघ्रता करने वाला

I have a habit of being overhasty in completing things.

Overhaul/ओवरहॉल *(verb)* – जाँचना

The driver stopped his jeep and overhauled the tyres.

Overhead/ओवरहेड *(adverb)* – सिर पर

At that time, the sun was shining overhead

Overhear/ओवरहिअर *(verb)* – छिपकर सुनना

He was overhearing to the secret conversion.

Overheat/ओवरहिट *(verb)* – अधिक गरम करना

The cylinder overheated and then exploded.

Overissue/ओवरइस्सू *(verb)* – चुकाने की शक्ति से अधिक हुंडी जारी करना

An inadvertent error in software made the bank overissue the man.

Overjoy/ओवरजॉय *(verb)* – अति प्रसन्न करना

I was overjoyed on getting through the bank exam.

Overlabour/ओवरलेबर *(verb)* – आवश्यकता से अधिक काम करना

Even overlabouring could not earn him a decent salary.

Overlavish/ओवरलैविश *(adj)* – व्ययशील

He has been living in an overlavish style.

O

Overlaying/ओवरलेयिंग – कृत्रिम ढक्कन

The skin overlaying was ruptured at many places.

Overlie/ओवरलाइ *(verb)* – ऊपर पड़ना

The cucumbers were grated and made to overlay the lower piece of bread.

Overload/ओवरलोड *(verb)* – बहुत लादना

Don't overload your taxi with the unnecessary things.

Overlong/ओवरलांग *(adjective & adverb)* – बहुत अधिक लम्बा

This overlong street bends to the right.

Overlook/ओवरलूक *(verb)* – उपेक्षा करना

All my requests to redevelop the site were overlooked.

Overlooker/ओवरलूकर *(noun)* – चौकसी रखने वाला

The company badly needs an overlooker for its godowns.

Overlord/ओवरलार्ड *(noun)* – राजाधिराज

The farmer requested his overlord to lower the rent.

Overmaster/ओवरमास्टर *(verb)* – अधीन करना

With patience and dedication, you can overmaster any difficulty.

Overmeasure/ओवरमेजर *(verb)* – अत्यधिक परिमाण

The shopkeeper was in a habit of overmeasuring the commodities.

Overmodest/ओवरमॉडेस्ट *(adj)* – अत्यधिक विनीत

There is no point in being overmodest to get the things done.

Overmuch/ओवरमच *(adv determine & pronoun)* – अत्यन्त

The man has been practising overmuch.

Overnice/ओवरनाइस *(adjective)* – नकचढ़ा

Don't try to be overnice with your boss.

Overnight/ओवरनाइट *(adverb)* – अतीत रात्रि में

Only an overnight and the government had lost its majority.

Overpass/ओवरपास *(noun)* – पार करना

As the train reached the overpass, we heard some noise.

Overpeople/ओवरपिपॅल *(verb)* – अधिक जनसंख्या से भरना

The auditorium was overpeopled and there was no vacant seats left.

Overplus/ओवरप्लस *(noun)* – वेशी

An overplus was sent by the company to its shareholders.

Overply/ओवरप्लाई *(verb)* – अत्यधिक शक्ति लगाना

His overplying has exhausted him.

Overpoise/ओवर्पॉइज *(noun)* – समतोलन से अधिक भार

The lady was overpoising her husband's new ventures to the existing ones.

Overpost/ओवरपोस्ट *(verb)*– अति शीघ्रता करना

After a heated argument, I overposted from the room.

Overpower/ओवरपॉवर *(verb)* – हराना

The king's huge army easily overpowered their enemy.

Overpraise/ओवरप्रेज *(verb)* – अतिप्रशंसा

There is no need to overpraise him for his single achievement.

Overprize/ओवरप्राइज *(verb)* – मूल्य में बढ़ जाना

The business men have the tendency to overprize their products.

Overproduction/ओवरप्रोडक्सन *(noun)* – सामग्री की माँग से अधिक पूर्ति

With the overproduction of wheat, the prices have gone down.

Overrate/ओवररेट *(verb)* – अधिक मूल्य लगाना

This movie by Shyam Bengal is overrated.

Overreach/ओवररीच *(verb)* – धोखा देना

I have no idea of why he is trying to overreach his goal.

Overrent/ओवररेंट *(verb)* – बहुत ज्यादा किराया लेना

The lady has overrented her apartment.

Override/ओवरराइड *(verb)* – कुचलना

With his power and influence, he could override any decision made by the community members.

Overrule/ओवररूल *(verb)* – रद्द करना

The judge overruled the objection raised by the lawyer.

Oversea/ओवरसी *(adverb)* – समुद्र पार

His business has seen a huge growth overseas. The overseas treaty was signed by the two countries.

Oversee/ओवरसी *(verb)* – चौकसी करना

The inspector came to oversee the quality of the manufactured goods.

Overseer/ओवरसिअर *(noun)* – निरीक्षक

He, being an overseer, was assigned the job of supervision.

Oversell/ओवरसेल *(verb)* – बहुत महँगा बेचना

He used to dupe people by overselling their shares.

Overset/ओवरसेट *(verb)* – नीचे गिरना

The son's rude behaviour has overset his mother.

Overshade/ओवरशेड *(verb)* – ढाँकना

Big leaves of the tree were overshading the plants below.

Overshadow/ओवरशैडो *(verb)* – छाया करना

The tall building has overshadowed the small house.

Overshoot/ओवरशूट *(verb)* – लक्ष्य के बाहर मारना

As she remained utterly confused, she easily overshot her destination.

Oversight/ओवरसाइट *(noun)* – भ्रम

Oversight should not be made an excuse every time.

Overskip/ओवरस्किप *(verb)* – लाँघना

My boss has the tendency to overskip anyone who is about to go up in the ladder.

Oversow/ओवरसो *(verb)* – परिमाण से अधिक बोना

In order to save space, the farmer oversowed in the field.

Overspent/ओवरस्पेंट – अधिव्यय

After shopping was done, he realized that his savings have been overspent.

Overstate/ओवरस्टेट *(verb)* – बहुत बढ़ाकर कहना

My friend has the habit of overstating any incident or happening in the company.

Overstay/ओवरस्टे *(verb)* – अधिक काल तक ठहरना

The hotel is charging more money for overstay.

Overstep/ओवरस्टेप *(verb)* – किसी कार्य में आगे बढ़ जाना

Don't overstep or I will have to do complain against you.

Overstock/ओवरस्टॉक *(verb)* – अति संग्रह करना

Most of the godowns are overstocked this year.

Oversupply/ओवरसप्लाई *(noun)* – माँग से अधिक पूर्ति

The oversupply of food grains has led the prices to go down.

Overtax/ओवरटैक्स *(verb)* – बहुत अधिक कर लगाना

In India, an average man is overtaxed.

Overtly/ओवर्टली *(adverb)* – प्रत्यक्ष रूप से

This man is prone to talk with an overtly bold way.

Overtone/ओवरटोन *(noun)* – फोटो के चित्र में गहरा रंग डालना

Overtone is a frequency that is more than the fundamental frequency.

Overtrade/ओवरट्रेड *(verb)* – पूँजी से अधिक व्यापार करना

The businessman is inclined to overtrade to get more profits.

Overturn/ओवरटर्न *(verb)* – नष्ट करना

The driver hit the pole and his car overturned.

Overvaluation/ओवरवैल्युशन *(noun)* – अधिक मूल्यांकन

Overvaluation of anything or anyone does no good, so it should be avoided.

Overvalue/ओवरवैलू *(verb)* – बहुत अधिक दाम लगाना

Don't overvalue them too much.

Overwatch/ओवरवाच *(verb)* – अधिक चौकसी करना

He was assigned the duty to overwatch the activities of his neighbours.

Overweight/ओवरवेट *(adjective)* – अधिक भारी

The overweight lady was finding it difficult to climb the stairs.

O

Overworn/ओवरवर्न *(adj)* – बहुत थका हुआ

The overworn man fainted on the road.

Overzeal/ओवरजील *(noun)* – बहुत अधिक जोश

She was overzeal to go abroad.

Ovicular/अविक्युलर *(adj)* – अण्डे से सम्बन्धित

The teacher explained the ovicular mechanism at a great length.

Ovine/ओवाइन *(adjective)* – भेड़ के समान

She was made fun due to her ovine facial features.

Oviparous/ओविपरस *(adjective)* – अण्डों से बच्चे पैदा करने वाला

Snake is an oviparous animal.

Oviposit/ओविपॉजिट *(verb)* – अण्डा देना

The hen was ovipositing at the time it was shifted to another cell.

Owing/ओइंग *(adjective)* – दातव्य

Please pay the owing amount.

Owl/आँउल *(noun)* – उल्लू

An owl is a nocturnal bird.

Own/ओन *(adjective & pronoun)* – अपना

All the property that he has rented is his own

Owner/ओनर *(noun)* – स्वामी

The owner of this building lives in Canada.

Ox /ऑक्स *(noun)* – बैल

The farmer has kept an ox that he uses as a draught animal.

Oxford/ऑक्सफोर्ड *(noun)* – इंग्लैण्ड के प्रसिद्ध विश्वविद्यालय का नगर

He preferred wearing oxford on every occasion.

Oxonian/ऑक्सोनियन *(adj)* – ऑक्सफोर्ड विश्वविद्यालय का छात्र

The Oxonian degree keeps a high value.

Oxygen/ऑक्सीजन *(noun)* – प्राणवायु

All living beings require oxygen to live.

Oxygenate/आक्सीजनेट *(verb)* – प्राणवायु से पूर्ण करना

The dying plants in room need to be oxygenated.

Oxygon/ऑक्सिगन् *(noun)* – दो न्यून-कोण का त्रिभुज

Draw an oxygon on this paper.

Oxyphonia/ऑक्सिफोनिया *(noun)* – कर्कश उच्चारण

She used to sing with an irritating oxyphonia.

Oyster/ऑइस्टर् *(noun)* – सीप, घोंघा

She is very fond of eating oysters.

Ozone/ओजोन *(noun)* – बिजली पैदा करने वाले यन्त्र से उत्पन्न हुई ठोस प्राणवायु

The ozone layer developed a hole as it got exposed to the ultra-violet rays.

Pp

P/पी *(noun)* - अंग्रेजी वर्णमाला का सोलहवाँ वर्ण the sixteenth letter of the English alphabet.

1. denoting the next after o in a set of items, categories, etc.

Pa/पा *(noun)* - बच्चों के बोली में पापा का संक्षिप्त रूप

With each pace, we were nearing the gates of the haunted house.

Pace/पेस *(noun)* - कदम, गति, विकास की गति

With each pace, we were nearing the gates of the haunted house.

Pacific/पैसिफिक *(adjective)* - शान्तिप्रिय

The pacific nature of the leaders is the reason behind justice prevailing in the State.

Pacify/पैसिफाइ *(verb)* - शान्ति स्थापित करना

Somehow we managed to pacify the angry crowd that had collected at his shop.

Pack/पैक *(noun)* - बेचा हुआ सामान, डिब्बा, समूह

The toys were rattling inside the pack noisily.

Package/पैकेज *(noun)* - डिब्बा, पुलिन्दा, प्रस्ताव का मुह

The package was nicely covered so no one could guess what was inside.

Packet/पैकेट *(noun)* - डिब्बा, पुलिन्दा

They were trying to pack all the groceries into one packet.

Packing/पैकिंग *(noun)* - डिब्बे में भरना

The instrument was covered with safe packing so it would reach safely.

Pact/पैक्ट *(noun)* - समझौता

The countries drew a pact to work towards saving and nurturing the environment.

Pad/पैड *(noun)* - सुरक्षा के लिए नीचे रखा साधन

We covered the wound with a pad so it would heal fast.

Paddle/पैडल *(noun)* - चप्पू चलाना

We were terrified when the paddles fell from our hands into the water.

Paddy/पैडी *(noun)* - धान

I like to see paddy crops in the field.

Padlock/पैडलॉक *(noun)* - ताला लगाना

Ever since the thieves struck, we have been extra careful to lock the main doors with padlocks.

Paediatrician/पैडियाट्रिसियन *(noun)* - बाल रोग विशेषज्ञ चिकित्सक

She took her baby to the paediatrician when the fever did not comedown with a tablet.

Pagan/पैगन *(noun)* - विधर्मी

The Church declared him an atheist when he told them he was a pagan.

Page/पेज *(noun)* - किताब, अखबार के पृष्ठ, सन्देश देना, परिचालक

He folded page after page though he understood nothing of what was written there.

Pageant/पेजन्ट् *(noun)* - विशेष समारोह में शोभायात्रा

The group organized pageants in the villages to educate them about the history of their country.

Pail/पेल् *(noun)* - बाल्टी, डोल

Jack and Jill went up the hill to fetch a pail of water.

Pain/पेन् *(noun)* - पीड़ा, वेदना

She was already in immense pain by the time the doctor arrived.

Painful/पेन्फुल *(adjective)* - पीड़ादायी

She was a painful character to associate with.

Painless/पेन्लेस *(adjective)* - पीड़ारहित

There is now a painless war in Iraq.

Paint/पेंट *(noun)* - रंग, रंगना

The fence required at least two coats of paint.

Painter/पेंटर *(noun)* – रंगने वाला, चित्रकार

Though he is an engineer by profession, he is also an excellent painter.

Painting/पेंटिंग *(noun)* – रंगाई

He sat in the garden all day painting the trees and birds around.

Pair/पेअर *(noun)* – जोड़ा

am in a need of a pair of shoes.

Pal/पॉल *(noun)* – साथी

Dhanya was my best pal in school.

Palace/पैलेस *(noun)* – महान्

The Buckingham Palace is indeed one of the greatest tourist attractions in UK.

Palatable/पैलेटेबल *(adjective)* – स्वादिष्ट, रुचिकर

I suggested that she should add some more salt to her curry to make it palatable.

Palate/पैलेट *(noun)* – तालु

Cleft palate is a common disability where the nose or lips do not form properly.

Palatial/पैलेसियल *(adjective)* – विशाल, भव्य, महल जैसा

She owns a palatial house in Beverly Hills.

P

Pale/पेल *(adjective)*– विवर्ण, निस्तेज, पीला चेहरा, खूँटा-खूँटी

She was pale with fever when the doctor came to see her.

Palette/पैलेट *(noun)* – रंग पट्टिका, रंग मिलाने की तश्तरी

Browns greens and blues are typical of leonardo da vinci's palette.

Pall/पाल *(noun)* – अरुचिकर हो जाना, कफन, काला आवरण

The unappealing sight of his death seemed to have been turned into a beauty thanks to the exquisiteness of the pall spread on his coffin.

Pallid/पैलिड *(adj)* – बीमारी के कारण मंद पड़ना

The pallid face of the invalid tore my heart.

Pallor/पैलर *(noun)* – बीमारी या भय से पीला पड़ना

She stood in the driveway of our garage with swollen eyes, mangled hair and an eerie pallor on her face.

Palm/पाम *(noun)* – हथेली, हाथ की सफाई, ताड़-खजूर के पेड़

The beach was lined with beautiful palms.

Palmist/पामिस्ट *(noun)* – हस्तरेखा विशेषज्ञ

Desperate to know if the astrologer's predictions were believable, we decided to take a second opinion from the palmist who lived across the street.

Palpable/पैल्पेबल् *(adjective)* – सुस्पष्ट, जिसे देखा या अनुभव किया जाये

The liver, spleen and kidneys are not palpable, said the doctor.

Palpitate/पॉल्पिटेट् *(verb)* – कँपकँपाना, धड़कन तेज होना

The air in the room seemed to palpitate with the deep fear that inflicted the children trapped there.

Palsy/पॉल्जि *(noun)* – जोड़ों में दर्द, चलने में कठिनाई

He could not finish the painting as his actions were frequently disturbed by his palsy.

Paltry/पाल्ट्रि *(adjective)* – नगण्य, तुच्छ बहुत कम

Sadly, what she received as a reward was a paltry sum in comparison to the amount her rival received.

Pamper/पैम्पर *(verb)* – अत्यधिक लाड़-प्यार

The younger sibling is always more pampered.

Pamphlet/पैम्फलेट *(noun)* – पर्चा, पुस्तिका

We had kept several pamphlets talking about the features of the product, at the counter.

Pamphleteer/पैम्फलेटियर *(noun)* – पर्चा लिखना, पर्चा-पुस्तिका से प्रचार

The people of Pamphylia are called Pamphylians, and not Pamphleteers. Pamphleteers are those who distribute or prepare pamphlets.

Pan/पैन *(noun)* – कड़ाह, कड़ाही, तसला, पलड़ा (उपसर्ग)

She made the curry in a beautiful non-stick pan.

Panacea/पैनेसिया *(noun)* – सब रोगों की दवा, रामबाण दवा

Eating chocolates is no panacea for your mental issues.

Pancake/पैनकेक *(noun)* - मैदा, दूध, अण्डा आदि मिलाकर बनाया पुआ

My aunt made chocolate and banana pancakes for tea.

Panda/पन्डा *(noun)* - मटर जैसा सफेद और काले रंग का एक जानवर

There was a time when China was the land of pandas.

Pandemonium/पैन्डिमोनियम *(noun)* - हुड़दंग, हुल्लड़, कोलाहल, अफरा-तफरी

The sisters had created such a pandemonium, their neighbours were worried.

Pander/पैन्डर *(verb)* - लोभवश - सहायता या प्रोत्साहन

He refuses to ponder to his boss's demand.

Pane/पेन *(noun)* - जंगला का एक भाग, खिड़की का शीशा

He hit a flying sixer and the next moment we heard the crash of the window pane!

Panel/पैनल *(noun)* - पल्ले का डिल्ला, पट्टी, नामित सूची a

I suggested that the architect consider a separate panel on the wall to place the telephone and other accessories.

Pang/पैंग *(noun)* - दर्द, टीस, कसक

I felt a sudden pang of guilt and pain in my heart when I heard her confession.

Panic/पैनिक *(noun)* - भगदड़, अफरा-तफरी, तहलका

People fied in panic as the fire spread.

Panorama/पैनॅरामा *(noun)* - बड़ा परिदृश्य

We were asked to climb to a certain point about 200 meters higher than our current altitude in order to get a panoramic view of the mountains.

Pansy/पैन्जि *(noun)* - फूल, पौधा, गुलबकावली जैसा फूल

The garden was blooming with pansies of all kinds and colours.

Pant/पैंट *(verb)* - हाँफना, साँस फूलना, एक वस्त्र

She came up the stairs, panting in excitement and stress, eager to see her brother waiting at the door.

Panther/पैन्थर *(noun)* - तेंदुआ

Bagheera is the name of the panther in The Jungle Book.

Panties/पैन्टिज *(plural noun)* - स्त्रियों की जांघिया

She had folded and kept her panties neatly in a pile in the drawer.

Pantomime/पैंटोमाइम *(noun)* - नकल करना, मूक अभिनय, हास्य अभिनय के नकल

The students organized a pantomime for their Annual School Day celebrations around Christmas.

Pantry/पैन्ट्री *(noun)* - रसोई, रसोई भण्डार

My father's hunger grew stronger at the mere sight of the delicious food being cooked in the pantry car next to his coach.

Pants/पैंट्स *(plural noun)* - पतलून, निकर

The kid's mother took him to the lavatory and instructed him to take off his pants on his own without her help.

Papa/पापा *(noun)* - बच्चों द्वारा प्रयुक्त पिता के लिए सम्बोधन

We wanted to wait for Papa to arrive, before we started dinner.

Papaya/पपाया *(noun)* - पपीता

The doctor advised her to stick to a papaya diet to have a detox effect.

Paper/पेपर *(noun)* - कागज, दस्तावेज, समाचार पत्र, प्रश्न

When the document did not print, I checked the printer and realized that the printing paper had finished.

Par/पार *(noun)* - अन्य के बराबर

They were late again, but that's par for the course.

Parable/पैरबल् *(noun)* - दृष्टान्त, दृष्टान्त कथा, नीति कथा

We were all asked to narrate a parable each at the storytelling session.

Parachute/पैराशूट *(noun)* - हवाई छतरी, हवाई जहाज से नीचे उतरने का साधन

We saw a parachute descending from a distance and realized it's a sky diver.

P

Parade/पैरेड *(noun)* - सैन्य-प्रशिक्षण, जुलूस

The city was lit up and the colourful parade made its way from Central Park to the farthest corner of the city where it ends.

Paradise/पैराडाइज *(noun)* - स्वर्ग, वाटिका, शान्ति स्थल

The Father said there was a place for all of us in Paradise.

Paradox/पैराडॉक्स *(noun)* - विरोधाभास, विरोधी गुण

He presented a paradoxical situation for us to evaluate, so we would know both extremes.

Paraffin/पैराफिन *(noun)* - मिट्टी तेल, कोयले आदि से प्राप्त तेल

In the candle-making class, we were taught to work with paraffin wax.

Paragon/पैरागन *(noun)* - आदर्श व्यक्ति या वस्तु

He is a paragon of excellence for all of us to follow.

Paragraph/पैराग्राफ *(noun)* - अनुच्छेद, लेख आदि का विभाजन

There were too many paragraphs in her prose. The teacher asked us to paragraph these lengthy statements to make a single story.

P

Parallel/पैरॅलल *(adjective)* - समानान्तर, समकक्ष, समतुल्य

The roads were parallel to one another and hence reached simultaneously.

Parallelogram/पैरॅलेलॅग्रैम् *(noun)* - समानान्तर चतुर्भुज

The mathematics teacher explained how to construct a parallelogram to the class.

Paralyse/पैरालाइज *(verb)* - लकवा मारना

The accident caused her to be paralysed below the waist.

Paralysis/पैरालाइसिस *(noun)* - लकवा, पक्षाघात

Her paralysis, after the accident, brought down her self esteem.

Paramilitary/पैरामिलिटरी *(adj)* - अर्द्धसैनिक बल

The government ordered the paramilitary forces to act as a last resort attack against the terrorists.

Paramount/पैरामाउन्ट *(adjective)* - अत्यधिक महत्त्वपूर्ण, सर्वोच्च

Taking over the prime minister's seat was of paramount importance to him.

Paranoia/पैरॅनीऑ/पैरानिआ *(noun)* - भ्रान्ति, मानसिक रोगी की क्षति

Post the accident, she had paranoia for a long time especially when she sat in a car.

Parapet/पैरापिट *(noun)* - मुण्डेर, दोनों ओर की नीची दीवाल

The thief hid on the parapet all night which is why he could not be caught.

Paraphernalia/पैराफर्नेलिआ *(noun)* - साज-समान, उपकरण

The photographers gathered their paraphernalia and moved to the next location.

Paraphrase/पैराफ्रेज *(verb)* - अन्वय, कथन का शब्दान्तर

The editor asked me to paraphrase the poem to suit the author's tastes. The write-up was actually a paraphrased version of a famous poem.

Parasite/पैरासाइट *(noun)* - परजीवी, दूसरे पर भोजन हेतु आश्रित

The disease is caused by single-celled parasites that multiply in the human blood stream.

Paratroops/पैराट्रूप्स *(plural noun)* - वायुयान से कूदने हेतु सैनिक

The army instructed the paratroops to be released into the building slowly.

Parcel/पार्शल *(noun)* - बँधा सामान, भेजा जाने वाला डिब्बा

I received a parcel by courier this morning.

Parch/पार्च *(verb)* - सूखना, झुलसना

The earth was parched and so were we.

Parchment/पार्चमेंट *(noun)*- लेखन-पत्र कागज के स्थान पर प्रयुक्त हेतु

The sage had written a message in a parchment.

Pardon/पार्‌डन् *(noun & verb)* - क्षमा, क्षमा करना, खेद प्रकट करना

The jury agreed in unison that the criminal should not be given pardon.

Parent/पेरेन्ट *(noun)* - माता-पिता, जिससे अन्य उत्पन्न हों वे पेड़-पौधे

All the students were asked to inform their parents about the meeting.

Parenthesis/पैरेन्थेसिस *(noun)* - वाक्यांश अलग करना, कोष्ठक

We had to memorize the parenthesis along with the formulae for the exam.

Pariah/पेरिआ *(noun)* - अछूत, चण्डाल

As I left the village, I came across a group of pariahs waiting to see me.

Parish/पैरिश *(noun)* - स्थानीय, चर्च और पादरी वाला गाँव

All the members of the parish had gathered at the Church for the baptism ritual.

Parity/पैरिटि *(noun)* - समानता, सममूल्यता

The target to achieve parity could not be reached.

Park/पार्क *(noun)* - उद्यान, सार्वजनिक उद्यान, वाहन स्थान

The kids love playing in the park every evening.

Parka/पर्का *(noun)* - टोपी सहित गरम वस्त्र

She ensured that we were all wearing our parkas before skiing.

Park/पार्क *(noun & verb)* - गाड़ी खड़ी करना, गाड़ी खड़ी करने का स्थान

We saw the parking meters and parked our car there.

Parley/पार्लि *(noun)* - सन्धि-बैठक, मैत्री सभा, सन्धिवार्ता

Unfortunately, the parley yielded little results. The ministers finally decided to hold a parley to discuss all the issues.

Parliament/पार्लियामेण्ट *(noun)* - संसद, संसद भवन

The Parliament is in a constant state of chaos in our country.

Parlour/पार्लर *(noun)* - विशेष सेवा या सामान की दुकान

We were asked to wait in the parlour for the VIP to arrive.

Parochial/पैरोकिअल *(adj)* - संकुचित, सीमित, सिकुड़ा हुआ

The parochial clergy was to be elected soon.

Parody/पैरोडी *(noun)* - किसी कृति या व्यक्ति की नकल

The children had prepared a parody of the latest movie for the Annual Day function.

Parole/पेरोल *(noun)* - अच्छे आचरण पर संक्षिप्त रिहाई

The town was living in fear ever since the news broke out of the criminal being out on parole.

Parsimony/पार्सिमनि *(noun)* - मितव्यय, कम खर्च करना

Such parsimony may help you cross this stage of financial crisis.

Parsley/पार्सलि *(noun)* - पुदीना जैसा पौधा

You may garnish the pasta with some chopped parsley.

Parsnip/पार्सनिप *(noun)* - गाजर-चुकन्दर जैसी सब्जी

We wanted Mother to make something with parsnip for dinner today.

Parson/पार्सन *(noun)* - पादरी, ईसाई पुजारी

The parson was called to fix the date of the engagement and decide the availability of the Chapel.

Part/पार्ट *(noun)* - हिस्सा, विभाग, टुकड़ा, भूमिका, अलग होना

All the parts combined make a whole.

Partial/पार्सियल *(adjective)* - आंशिक, पक्षपात, पक्षपातपूर्ण

A partial solar eclipse was visible in India.

Participate/पार्टिसिपेट *(verb)* - भाग लेना, भागीदार बनाना, सहभागी

Everybody had a chance to participate in the function.

Participle/पार्टिसिपल् *(noun)* - कृदन्त प्रत्यय, क्रिया-रूप

We were asked to identify the participle in the given sentences in the exam.

Particle/पार्टिकल *(noun)* - कण, अति लघु अंश

The tiny particles floating in the air in the room made us sneeze constantly.

Particular/पार्टिकुलर *(adjective)* - व्यक्ति विशेष से सम्बन्धित, सावधान

It was a particular child in the class that she had been talking about for the past one hour, I finally realized.

Parting/पार्टिंग *(noun)* – वियोग, अलगाव

To see the couple parting was a painful sight.

Partisan/पार्टिजन *(noun)* – पक्का हिमायती, अन्ध भक्त

Most newspaper are politically partisan.

Partition/पार्टिसन *(noun)* – विभाजन

The country's partition was the most tragic event in its history.

Partner/पार्टनर *(noun)* – भागीदार

Both the husband and wife were equal partners in their family business.

Partridge/पार्ट्रिज *(noun)* – तीतर

I was surprised to see so many partridges in the farm.

Party/पार्टि *(noun)* – दल, राजनीतिक दल, टोली

We decided to organize a surprise birthday party for our father.

Pass/पास *(noun)* – बढ़ जाना, आगे बढ़ना, गुजरना, हाथों-हाथ देना, हस्तान्तरण, दूसरे की ओर बढ़ाना, दशा में परिवर्तन, समाप्त होना, परखकर स्वीकृत, अनुमोदन, स्वीकार करना, दर्रा

The pass was closed owing to incessant snowing in the mountains.

P

Passable/पासेबल् *(adjective)* – जिसे पार किया जा सके

The last of the ten points she kept was the only passable one.

Passage/पैसिज *(noun)* – आर-पार का मार्ग, पार करने की प्रशंसा, पार गमन, गलियारा

Black Beauty was known for performing the most superior passage in the whole series.

Passbook/पासबुक *(noun)* – लेखा-पुस्तिका

My passbook was overflowing with entries, so the officer issued another one.

Passenger/पैसेन्जर *(noun)* – यात्री, दल में कामचोर व्यक्ति

The passengers beat up the eve-teaser and kicked him out of the bus.

Passing/पासिंग *(adjective)* – बहुत कम समय के लिए, गुजरने की प्रक्रिया

The band was passing by the crowd and everybody cheered.

Passion/पैशन् *(noun)* – आवेग, आवेश, तीव्र यौन-आकर्षण, उत्साह

He screamed at her passionately.

Passionate/पैशनेट् *(adjective)* – कामुकता पूर्ण, कामुक, भावावेश पूर्ण

She was very passionate about travelling.

Passive/पैसिव *(adjective)* – आवेग का अभाव, निश्चेष्टा, निष्क्रिय

We were urged to rise from our passive state and start acting!

Passport/पासपोर्ट *(noun)* – पारपत्र, विदेश यात्रा का आदेश पत्र

I showed the officer my passport so that I could board the flight fast.

Password/पासवर्ड *(noun)* – अवरोध निवारक गुप्त शब्द

I had written the password somewhere so that I do not forget it but I think I should have revealed it to my mother at least.

Past/पास्ट *(adjective)* – अतीत, भूतकाल, बीता हुआ समय

I had been waiting for the past two hours.

Pasta/पैस्टा *(noun)* – आटे, अण्डे और जल से बना एक खाद्य पदार्थ

The chef prepared the best pasta I had ever had.

Paste/पेस्ट *(noun)* – लेई, गीला आटा, मिश्रण, चिपकाना

We made a loose paste before adding coconut to it.

Pasteboard/पेस्टबोर्ड *(noun)* – कोई सूचना चिपकाने की तख्ती thin board made by pasting together sheets of paper. *The pasteboard was full, so we needed another board.*

Pastel/पैस्टेल *(noun)* – मुलायम रंगीन खड़िया, हल्का कोमल रंग

I bought her a packet of pastel colours as she loved art and colouring.

Pasteurize/पैस्ट्युराइज *(verb)* – गरम करके कीटाणु रहित करना

I have started ordering pasteurized milk.

Pastime/पास्टाइम *(noun)* – आमोद-प्रमोद, मनोरंजन का समय

Television is not the best pastime for a child.

Pastor/पास्टर *(noun)* – ईसाईयों के पुरोहित, पुजारी

We felt blessed as our neighbour was a pastor! He became the pastor of St Francis' Church shortly.

Pastry/पेस्ट्री *(noun)* – गोल-लम्बा मीठा या नमकीन खाद्य

Ma taught me how to bake the pastry-base for pie.

Pasture/पास्चर *(noun)* – चरागाह, पशुओं का चरना

The cows and buffaloes were having the time of their life in the pasture.

Pastures/पास्चर्स *(noun)* – परिस्थितियाँ

She resigned the job for pastures new.

Pasty/पेस्टी *(noun)* – चिपचिपा, चिपचिपाहट वाला

I loved the beef pasty she made for tea the other day.

Pat/पैट *(verb)* – पीठ थपथपाना, सफलता पर प्रशंसा करना

Dogs always love a pat on the head.

Patch/पैच् *(noun)* – पैबन्द, जमीन का छोटा टुकड़ा, पैबन्द लगाना

She covered the injured eye with a patch of cloth.

Patchwork/पैचवर्क *(noun)* – छोटे टुकड़े जोड़कर बनाया हुआ

She made a patchwork bag and it looked quite cool.

Patchy/पैची *(adjective)* – पैबन्द चुल, आसमान गुण या स्तर वाला

She had sewn me patchy trousers.

Patent/पैटेन्ट *(noun)* – स्पष्ट, साफ, एकत्व अधिकार, एकत्व का अधिकार लेना

She was an acclaimed scientist who had patents on six discoveries.

Paternal/पैटरनल *(adjective)* – पैतृक

His paternal instincts were aroused when he saw his child walking on the wrong track.

Paternity/पैटरनिटी *(noun)* – पितृत्व

He did not accept claims of his paternity easily.

Path/पाथ *(noun)* – मार्ग, पथ, पगडण्डी

There was a well laid out walking path in the park.

Pathetic/पैथेटिक *(adjective)* – दयनीय, कारुणिक

The pathetic state of existence of the tramp brought tears to her eyes.

Pathological/पैथलॉजिकल *(adj)* – रोग-विज्ञान से सम्बन्धित, आधारहीन

Her disease was diagnosed as pathological.

Pathology/पैथलॉजी *(noun)* – रोग-विज्ञान

The head of the pathology department is now voted to take over as the dean of the university.

Pathos/पैथॉस *(noun)* – कारुणिकता

Khalil Gibran's writings involve a lot of pathos.

Patience/पेसेंस *(noun)* – सहनशीलता, धैर्य, ताश का एक खेल

Living in those terrible conditions was testing my patience.

Patient/पेसेंट *(adjective)* – मरीज, रोगी

She has always been extremely patient with her son. She has been a patient in this hospital for the last two weeks.

Patriarch/पैट्रियार्क *(noun)* – परिवार या कबीले का मुखिया

He was the undefiable patriarch of the royal family.

Patroit/पैट्रिअट *(noun)* – देशभक्त

Shaheed Bhagat Singh was a patriot who laid down his life for the country.

Patriotic/पैट्रिअटिक *(adverb)* – देशभक्ति पूर्ण

The patriotic song that my friend sang in the School Assembly aroused tears in everyone's eyes.

Patrol/पट्रोल/पेट्रोल *(noun)* – गश्त लगाना

The patrol kept watch over the hotel that was under hijack.

Patron/पेट्रन *(noun)* – संरक्षक

My brother has been a patron of our organization for several years.

Patronage/पेट्रोनेज *(noun)* - संरक्षण और समर्थन

We thanked the president and the Trustee for their patronage to our institution.

Patronize/पेट्रनाइज *(verb)* - संरक्षक बनना, नियमित ग्राहक बनना

Though I was grateful for his contribution to our institution, I detested his patronizing attitude.

Pattern/पैटर्न *(noun)* - ढंग, उदाहरण, आदर्श

The sheriff recognized a definite pattern in the series of crimes that had been occurring in the town of late.

Paucity/पॉसिटी *(noun)* - कमी, अभाव

There was a paucity of resources in the city that is why they were demanding help from the Centre.

Paunch/पॉन्च *(noun)* - तोंद

Mother asked us to start exercising else we will soon have a paunch.

Pauper/पापर *(noun)* - कंगाल

He died a pauper.

Pause/पॉज *(noun)* - विराम

He continued playing for so minutes without a pause.

P

Pave/पेव *(verb)* - रास्ते में ईट-पत्थर लगाना, पथराव करना

It was as if the path had been paved for her to walk on.

Pavement/पेवमेंट *(noun)* - पदमार्ग, पैदल पथ

If we do not walk on the pavement, there is a risk we will get hit by a vehicle.

Pavilion/पेविलियन *(noun)* - मैदान के पास खिलाड़ियों-दर्शकों के लिए भवन

The sportsmen made their way to the pavilion to freshen up during the break.

Paw/पॉ *(noun)* - पंजा

We found paw prints in the garden, probably belonging to some wild animal.

Pawn/पॉन *(noun & verb)* - ज्यादा, मुहरा, बन्धक रखना

Moving the pawn near his bishop was the only way out for her in the game.

Pay/पे *(noun & verb)* - भुगतान देना, वेतन, वेतन देना

Today is pay-day.

Pea/पी *(noun)* - मटर

Peas masala was my favourite curry.

Peace/पीस् *(noun)*- शान्ति

I went to the mountains in search of peace.

Peaceable/पीसेब्ल् *(adj)* - शान्तिदायक, शान्तिप्रद

We should look for a peacable solution than resorting to war.

Peaceful/पीसफुल *(adjective)* - शान्त, शान्तिप्रद

Her 11th storey balcony was indeed very peaceful.

Peach/पीच *(noun)* - आड़ू, आड़ूबुखारा

We decided to try and bake a peach cake.

Peacock/पीकॉक *(noun)* - मोर, मयुर पक्षी

There were almost twenty peacocks dancing in the rain in all their glory at the zoo.

Peak/पीक *(noun)* - चोटी, शिखर, तीव्रता, पराकाष्टा

He showed in the presentation the time period when the sales of the company were at their peak.

Peal/पील *(noun)* - घंटनाद, एकाएक होने वाली घनघोर आवाज

There was a peal of bells when the priest came out of the sanctum sanctorum.

Peanut/पीनट *(noun)* - मूँगफली, अतिन्यून राशि

Having too many peanuts at a time came make you put on weight.

Pear/पेअर् *(noun)* - नाशपाती

We decided to add some pears to the dessert.

Pearl/पर्ल *(noun)* - मोती, मुक्ता, मोती के रंग का **बहुमूल्य**

He bought me a pearl necklace for our wedding anniversary.

Peasant/पेजण्ट् *(noun)* - खेतिहर, अज्ञानी व्यक्ति

The peasants were discussing a revolt against the capitalists who were trespassing into their area.

Peasantry/पेजन्ट्रि *(noun)* - किसानवर्ग

The whole peasantry was revolting against the capitalists.

Peat/पीट *(noun)* - खाद, सड़ी पत्तियों-पौधों से बना खाद

The agriculturist advised the farmers to use peat as a form of fuel.

Pebble/पेब्ल् *(noun)* - चिकना कंकड़

I love sitting quietly at the riverside, throwing an occassional pebble into the water. It was a pebble that could not be crushed.

Peck/पेक *(noun & verb)* - दो गैलन की सूखी तोल, दाना चुगना, चोंच मारना

A peck of those items would be worthless for the price I was being offered.

Peculiar/पिक्यूलिअर् *(noun)* - विशिष्ट, विलक्षण, विशेष प्रकार का

People often discuss the peculiar jurisdiction of the Archbishop of Canterbury.

Pedagogue/पेडागॉग *(noun)* - बालशिक्षक शिक्षक

The pedagogues of yore have all been laid to rest

Pedal/पेडल *(noun)* - साइकिल, नाव आदि चलाना

The bike had colourful blue pedals.

Pedantic/पेडांटिक *(adj)* - पाण्डित्य पूर्ण, पण्डितादर

It was a rather pedantic effort.

Pedestal/पेडेस्टल *(noun)* - आधार-खम्भ, मंचिका, मूर्ति का आधार

My friend asked me not to put her up on a pedestal.

Pedestrian/पिडेस्ट्रिअन् *(noun)* - पैदल यात्री, उत्साहहीन

The pedestrians had crowded around the accident site. What a pedestrian attitude she had.

Pedigree/पेडिग्री *(noun)* - वंशावली

She did not like the idea of making strays pets, so she bought a pedigree.

Peddler/पेड्लर् *(noun)* - फेरीवाला

He had been unsuccessful in big businesses and eventually became a peddler of small articles.

Pee/पी *(verb)* - पेशाब करना

She hurried to find a place to pee. The gastroenterologist asked her to pee in a bottle for a urine test.

Peek/पीक *(verb)* - झाँकना, ताक-झाँक करना

She was peeking from the corner of the tree.

Peel/पील *(noun)* - सब्जी, फल के छिलके उतारना

Could you peel the potatoes.

Peep/पीप *(verb)* - चुपके से झाँकना, धीरे से उघारना

She peeped from the hole in the wall.

Peer/पिअर् *(verb)* - समान पद या योग्यता वाला, प्रतिद्वन्द्वी

She was peering at the man who stood at a distance. To peer at someone is impolite, my mother instructed.

Peerless/पिअर्लेस *(adjective)* - अद्वितीय, अनुपम

The princess's beauty was peerless.

Peeved/पीव्ड *(adjective)* - नाराज, परेशान

She was a bit peeved at him for his carelessness.

Peevish/पीविश *(adjective)* - चिड़चिड़ा, बदमिजाज

On reviewing the conduct of the culprit, and examining his somewhat peevish and whimsical correspondence, the judge finally drew the sentence in the favour of the victim.

Peg/पेग् *(noun)* - खूँटी, मूल्यवृद्धि रोकना

The clothes, peg came off by itself a few days ago.

Pelican/पेलिकन *(noun)* - एक प्रकार का पक्षी

The zoo has several seasonal birds including pelicans.

Pellet/पेलेट *(noun)* - छर्रा, गोली, कागज का गोला

A beetle was rolling a pellet of dung up a hill.

Peil-mell/पेल-मेल *(noun)* - हड़बड़ी, अव्यवस्था

I dislike such pell-mell.

Pelt/पेल्ट *(verb)* - ढेला फेंककर या गोली से मारना

The enemies were being pelted with missiles non stop.

Pen/पेन् *(noun)* - कलम, लेखनी, लिखना

My handwriting was most beautiful when I wrote with a fountain pen.

Penal/पीनल् *(adjective)* - कानूनी दण्ड से सम्बन्धित

I was told that her crime was punishable under the penal code.

Penalty/पेनाल्टि *(noun)* - दण्ड, सजा, खेल-कूद का दण्ड

His only chance in the game was the penalty kick.

Penance/पेनैन्स *(noun)* - तपस्या

The sage was known to have been through a lot of penance to attain this state.

Pence/पेन्स *(noun)* - एक प्रकार का सिक्का

The small magnet cost just a few pence.

Pencil/पेन्सिल *(noun)* - लकड़ी में लगे पत्थर वाली लेखनी, लिखना, चित्र बनाना

She bought different kinds of pencils for her daughter's first day at school.

Pendant/पेन्डैन्ट *(noun)* - लटकन, घर आदि में नीचे लटकने वाला

I gifted her a pendant on her birthday.

Pendulum/पेंडुलम *(noun)* - लोलक, घड़ी का लगातार घूमता लोलक

She bought a grandfather clock from the antique shop with a modified pendulum.

Penetrate/पेनिट्रेट *(verb)* - प्रवेश, घुसना, आर-पार या अन्दर देखना

We tried hard to penetrate into the hole in the tree, but got stuck.

P

Penguin/पेंगुइन् *(noun)* - एक प्रकार का पक्षी

The advocates resemble penguins in their attire.

Penicillin/पेन्सिलिन *(noun)* - एक प्रकार की औषधि

We had to procure a certain dosage of penicillin as soon as possible to cure the patient.

Peninsula/पेनिन्सुला *(noun)* - प्रायद्वीप, तीन तरफ से जल से घिरा हुआ

Our geography teacher explained the concept of peninsula.

Penitent/पेनिटेंट *(adjective)* - पश्चाताप, पश्चाताप पूर्ण

What is the point of being penitent after making a mistake? She made mistakes and was penitent at the end of the whole episode.

Penitentiary/पेनिटेन्सियरी *(noun)* - कारागार

There was no other option but to send the criminal to a penitentiary institution.

Penknife/पेननाइफ *(noun)* - छोटा जेबी चाकू

I tried cutting the fruits with my penknife.

Penniless/पेनिलेस *(adjective)* - कंगाल

After the grand party, she was left penniless.

Penny/पेन्नी *(noun)* - एक प्रकार का सिक्का

We were taught by the British Academy how to exchage pennies and pounds at the Exchange Office.

Pension/पेन्सन *(noun)* - सेवा निवृत्ति के बाद का विशेष वेतन

A pension had somewhat lesser to offer than a hotel.

Pensive/पेन्सिव *(adjective)* - चिन्ता-मग्न

Don't disturb you father when he is in a pensive mood.

Pentagon/पेन्टागॅन *(noun)* - पंच भुजाकार

The geometry teacher taught us to draw a pentagon.

Penthouse/पेन्टहाउस *(noun)* - बहुमंजिला इमारत के ऊपर ऊँचा कमरा

The executive bought a plush penthouse in a posh locality downtown.

Penultimate/पेनअल्टिमेट *(adjective)* - उप-अन्त, अन्तिम के पूर्व का

The penultimate line of the chemical series was difficult to learn.

Penury/पिन्यूरी *(noun)* - दरिद्रता

Unknown to the world, she lived in a state of penury.

People/पीपल् *(plural noun)* - आम स्त्री-पुरुष, आमलोग

The people of the country were getting ready to revolt against the dictator.

Pepper/पेपर् *(noun)* - काली मिर्च, गोल मिर्च

I was growing pepper in my kitchen garden.

Peppermint/पेपरमिंट *(noun)* - पुदीने जैसे पौधे से बनी मिठी गोली

Peppermint is a nice mouthfreshner to have after dinner.

Per/पर *(preposition)* – प्रत्येक

We bought the land for Rs 3000 per square feet.

Perceive/पर्सिव *(verb)* – अनुभव करना, देखना, जानना

I perceived his comments as a criticism.

Percent/परसेंट *(adverb)* – प्रतिशत

We got 30 percent of the total distribution of the land. The land was being distributed at 30 percent of its actual landspace.

Percentage/परसेंटेज *(noun)* – प्रतिशतता

She scored a bad percentage in the internal exams.

Perceptible/परसेप्टिबल् *(adjective)* – इन्द्रियगोचर, स्पष्ट नजर आना

Only 10 percent of space lies in the perceptible limit.

Perception/परसेप्शन *(noun)* – प्रत्यक्ष ज्ञान, प्रत्यक्ष बोध

She was amazed at the level of perception of the baby.

Perceptive/परसेप्टिव *(adjective)* – सूक्ष्म दृष्टि, परखने में तेज

She was more perceptive and receptive as a student, than others.

Perch/पर्च *(noun)* – चिड़ियों का अड्डा

The bird fluttered for a while and then settled itself precariously on a perch high above.

Percolate/पर्कोलेट *(verb)* – रिसना, छनना

The liquid was percolating through the filter cloth.

Percussion/पर्कशन् *(noun)* – तालवाद्य

The percussion team was the star of the evening's performance.

Peremtory/पेरम्प्टरी *(adjective)* – शीघ्र आदेश या देश पालन की अपेक्षा

The teacher spoke in a peremptory tone.

Perennial/पेरेनिअल *(adjective)* – चिरस्थायी, बार-बार होने वाला

We were aiming at achieving perennial happiness.

Perfect/परफेक्ट *(adj)* – पूर्ण, परिपूर्ण, दोषरहित

When the batter had reached that perfect consistency, we poured it into a tin and baked it.

Perfection/परफेक्शन *(noun)* – पूर्णता, उच्चतम स्थिति या गुण

Perfection of the invention took years.

Perforate/पर्फरोट् *(verb)* – कागज में छोट-छोटे छेद करना

We placed it in a tin perforated with round holes. The paper needs to be perforated to make it easier to tear.

Perform/परफॉर्म *(verb)* – कार्य करना, निर्देशित कार्य सम्पन्न करना

She knew she had to perform in this exam.

Performance/परफॉर्मेंस *(noun)* – प्रदर्शन, कार्य पूर्ण करने की योग्यता

There was a performance scheduled for the weekend.

Perfume/परफ्यूम *(noun)* – सुगन्ध, इत्र

Her clothes smell really good because of the perfume she uses.

Perhaps/परहैप्स *(adjective)* – शायद, कदाचित्

Perhaps it was this way or perhaps it was that.

Peril/पेरिल *(noun)* – समाप्ति का संकट, गहरा संकट

She was divine, a peril indeed!

Perimeter/पेरिमिटर *(noun)* – परिमिति, आकृति की बाहरी सीमा की लम्बा

I was trying to calculate the perimeter of the circle in the paper.

Period/पिरिअड *(noun)* – निश्चित अवधि, रजस्वला का समय, पूर्ण विराम

The country was going through a period of economic prosperity.

Periodic/पिरिऑडिक *(adjective)* – निश्चित अवधि के बाद पुनरावृत्ति

The meteors appeared at periodic intervals.

Periodical/पिरिऑडिकल *(adjective)* – साप्ताहिक, मासिक पत्र, पत्रिका

She had periodical fits of depression. She had published in several periodicals.

P

Periphery/पेरिफरि *(noun)* – क्षेत्र की सीमा, किनारा

The enemies had reached the periphery of the region.

Periscope/पेरिस्कोप *(noun)* – समुद्र तल देखने का यन्त्र

Suddenly he saw a periscope rising from the water at a distance.

Perish/पेरिस *(verb)*– नष्ट होना, नष्ट कर देना, गल जाना

Thousands had perished in the fire accident.

Perjure/पर्जर् *(verb)* – सौगन्ध लेकर झूठ बोलने का अपराध

The witness perjured herself when she denied knowing the defendant.

Perk/पर्क *(verb)* – भत्ता, प्रसन्नता, प्रफुल्लित होना

She perked up as soon as she was shown a chocolate. You're in a perky mood.

Perm/पर्म *(noun)* – केश को कृत्रिम ढंग से लहरदार बनाना

The Hollywood actress's perm was back. She had her hair permed.

Permanence/परमानेंस *(noun)* – स्थायित्व, पक्का

There is no permanence to anything in this world.

P

Permanent/परमानेंट *(adj)* – स्थायी, चिरस्थायी

Nothing in this world is permanent. Her hair colour was permanent.

Permeate/परमिएट *(verb)* – फैल जाना, व्याप्त होना

A thinker once said, our thinking is permeated by our historical myths.

Permissible/परमिसिब्ल् *(adjective)* – अनुमति योग्य

The minerals in our tap water were beyond the permissible limit

Permission/पर्मिशन् *(noun)* – अनुमति

She asked for permission to leave at noon.

Permissive/पर्मिसिव् *(adjective)* – अति स्वतन्त्रता

You are lucky to have permissive parents.

Permit/पर्मिट *(verb)* – स्वीकृति देना, अनुमति देना

They were denied permit to sell alcoholic beverages.

Perpendicular/पर्पेन्डिक्युलर् *(adjective)* – लम्ब, सीधी खड़ी रेखा

The axes are perpendicular to each other.

Perpetrate/पर्पिट्रेट् *(verb)* – अपराध या गलती करना

He perpetrators of the crime will be punished.

Perpetual/पर्पेचुअल् *(adjective)* – समाप्त न होने वाला, अनन्त

She had opened a perpetual fixed deposit in the bank.

Perpetuate/पर्पेचुएट *(verb)* – बनाये रखना

The new library will perpetuate its founder's great love of learning.

Perplex/परप्लेक्स *(verb)* – हैरान कर देना

She looked perplexed when I asked her about her project.

Perquisite/परक्विजिट *(noun)* – नियमित वेतन के अतिरिक्त लाभ

Long distance calls at discount rates was one of the perquisites of the job.

Persecute/परसिक्यूट *(verb)* – सताना, मुकदमा करना, लगातार प्रश्न करना

Jews were mercilessly persecuted in the former Soviet Union.

Persevere/पर्सिविअर *(verb)* – कठिनाइयों के बाद भी कोशिश करते रहना

To persevere is the only way to success.

Persist/पर्सिस्ट् *(verb)* – लगातार करते रहना, बार-बार घटित

Though I refused to buy her a chocolate, she continued to persist.

Person/पर्सन् *(noun)* – व्यक्ति (स्त्री-पुरुष या बच्चा)

Each one of us is an individual person whose rights ought to be guarded and respected.

Personal/पर्सनल *(adjective)* – व्यक्तिगत

You have to take personal initiative to get this project done.

Personality/पर्स्नैलिटि *(noun)* – व्यक्तित्व

She had a charming personality.

Personalize/पर्सनलाइज् *(verb)* – व्यक्तिगत करना

The designer offered to get a personalized version of his product designed especially for the queen.

Personify/पर्सॅनिफाई *(verb)* – जीवन देना, मानवीकरण करना

She personified the idol.

Personnel/परसनेल *(plural noun)* – कर्मचारीगण, कार्यकर्ता वर्ग

Thousands of personnel had been employed at several points to make the fair a success.

Perspective/परसपेक्टिव *(noun)* – परिदृश्य, विस्तृत क्षेत्र का चित्र

These drawings are difficult to comprehend from a certain perspective.

Perspire/पर्स्पायर् *(verb)* – पसीना आना

She was perspiring heavily at the gym.

Persuade/पर्स्वेड् *(verb)* – मना लेना

I tried my best to persuade her about the benefits of the scheme.

Persuation/पर्स्वेजन् *(noun)* – राजी करने का प्रयास

Three foremost aids of persuasion, according to me, are humility, concentration and gusto.

Persuasive/पर्स्वेसिव् *(adj)* – विश्वास दिलाने योग्य

She was quite persuasive in her beliefs.

Pert/पर्ट *(adjective)* – उद्धत युवती

She was pert in her conduct, smart and spontaneous.

Pertain/पर्टेन *(verb)* – सम्बन्ध रखना, अपना होना

The evidence that pertains to the accident was collected and saved.

Pertinent/पर्टिनेन्ट् *(adjective)* – उपयुक्त, युक्तिसंगत

Her advice was quite pertinent to his situation.

Perturb/पर्टर्ब् *(verb)* – घबड़ा देना

She was perturbed by his carelessness as it could lead to an accident some day.

Peruse/पेरूज् *(verb)* – ध्यानपूर्वक पढ़ना

I sent the employer my project report for his perusal.

Pervade/पर्वेड् *(verb)* – सर्वत्र फैल जाना, पूर्ण व्यक्ति

Corruption is like cancer that pervades every corner of society.

Pervasive/पर्वेसिव *(adjective)* – व्याप्तिपूर्ण

The pervasive odour of garlic was irritating me.

Perverse/पर्वर्स *(adjective)* – विकृत रुचि वाला, जानबूझकर गलत व्यवहार करने वाला

He took perverse satisfaction in foiling her plans.

Perversion/परसवर्सन *(noun)* – सदाचार विमुख

His perversion was met with strong repercussions.

Pervert/पर्वर्ट *(verb)* – कदाचारी

It is an analysis that perverts the meaning of the poem.

Pessimism/पेसिमिज्म *(noun)* – निराशावादिता

Do not lie in a state of pessimism if you are unable to face your problems.

Pessimist/पेसिमिस्ट *(noun)* – निराशावादी

Do not be a pessimist and run from your problems.

Pest/पेस्ट *(noun)* – कीड़े-मकोड़े

The crop was infested with pests this season.

Pester/पेस्टर *(verb)* – सताना

Do not pester your parents for sweets when they have just had a fight.

Pesticide/पेस्टिसाइड *(noun)* – कीटनाशक

Thanks to the new pesticides, our crops were saved this year.

Pestilence/पेस्टिलेन्स *(noun)* – महामारी, छूत का रोग

The government had planned strict actions against the pestilence.

Pet/पेट *(noun)* – पालतू, दुलारा व्यक्ति

I love animals and have always wanted to own a pet.

Petal/पेटल *(noun)* – फूल की पँखुड़ी

I took out the petals of the rose and spread them in the water.

Peter/पिटर *(verb)* – शनैः शनैः समाप्त होना

The water that was gushing was now reduced to a peter.

P

Petite/पेटिट *(adjective)* - कद में छोटी, देहयष्टि आकर्षक

She had a petite figure.

Petition/पिटिशन *(noun)* - औपचारिक अर्जी, याचिका

I signed a petition in favour of the bill that was currently being discussed in the Parliament.

Petrify/पेट्रिफाइ *(verb)* - स्तब्ध रह जाना

She was petrified at the sight of the thief in the house.

Petrol/पेट्रोल *(noun)* - गैस तेल

We had to fill petrol in the car before we went on the road trip.

Petroleum/पेट्रोलीअम *(noun)* - खनिज तेल

The different countries were fighting over petroleum extraction.

Petticoat/पेटिकोट *(noun)* - स्त्रियों का अधोवस्त्र

Her petticoat seemed longer than her sari.

Petty/पेटि *(adjective)* - नगण्य, तुच्छ

The children were fighting over petty issues.

Pew/प्यू *(noun)* - लकड़ी की लम्बी कुर्सी

The VIPs were seated in the front pews while the commoners behind.

P

Phantom/फैन्टम् *(noun)* - भूत-प्रेत, भ्रान्ति-छलावा

She was paranoid and thought there was a phantom in the house.

Pharmaceutical/फार्मस्यूटिकल *(adj)* - औषधि निर्माण और वितरण

The drugs she was buying were purely for pharmaceutical use. I had to resort to pharmaceuticals as Yoga was not yielding any results.

Pharmacy/फार्मेसी *(noun)* - औषधालय, दवा-विधि का अध्ययन

I rushed to the pharmacy to buy the medicines.

Phase/फेज *(noun)* - अवस्था, चरण

We were asked to stay away from the sea when the moon's phase changes.

Pheasant/फेजन्ट् *(noun)* - बटेर

There were lots of pheasants in the jungle.

Phenomenal/फिनॉमिनल् *(adjective)* - असाधारण, चमत्कारिक

It was a phenomenal achievement to cross that border.

Phenomenon/फिनामिनन् *(noun)* - इन्द्रियगोचर, उल्लेखनीय

We decided to study the phenomenon as it was a rare occurrence.

Phew/फ्यू *(interjection)* - साँस लेने और छोड़ने की आवाज, घृणा सूचक शब्द

Phew! Finally we are there!

Phial/फाइअल् *(noun)* - काँच की छोटी शीशी

She poured the tonic into a phial and handed it over to the customer.

Philanthropy/फिलन्थ्रपि *(noun)* - दान आदि के द्वारा जरूरतमंदों की सहायता, उपकार

Bill Gates is known for being quite a philanthrope in his circle.

Philately/फिलैटिलि *(noun)* - डाक टिकट संग्रह

He had an active interest in philately.

Philology/फिललॅजि *(noun)* - भाषा विकास का अध्ययन

She decided to study philology.

Philosopher/फिलॉस्फर *(noun)* - दार्शनिक

India is known for its share of philosophers and spiritual gurus.

Philosophy/फिलॉसफि *(noun)* - दर्शन

I wanted to take up philosophy in my post graduation.

Phlegm/फ्लेग्म *(noun)* - कफ, बलगम

The doctor realized that his patient's lungs were filled with phlegm.

Phlegmatic/फ्लेग्मेटिक *(adjective)* - शान्तचित, आसानी से क्रोधित न होना

He had a phlegmatic attitude.

Phone/फोन *(noun)* - दूरभाष

I could hear different phones of music.

Phonetic/फोनेटिक *(adjective)* - ध्वनिशास्त्र, भाषा ध्वनिशास्त्र

We were trying to analyse the phonetics of the musical note.

Phoney/फोनि *(adjective)* - नकली

It was a phoney affair. He turned out to be a phoney guy.

Phosphorus/फास्फोरस *(noun)* - सहज जलने वाला पीला पदार्थ

One can modify the lights in their house and use phosphorus lamps

Photocopy/फोटोकॉपी *(noun)* - छाया प्रतिलिपि

Ever since I bought a photocopy machine, all the college students have been flocking to my shop. To photocopy her notes was the only way I could make up for the classes I missed.

Photograph/फोटोग्राफ *(noun)* - चित्र, छायाचित्र

She has lots of photographs of our school days. I wanted to take a photograph of my favourite actor with me.

Phrase/फ्रेज *(noun)* - मुहावरा

I had trouble understanding the phrases she used in her essay.

Physical/फिजिकल *(adj)* - दैहिक, शरीरिक, भौतिक

He shared a physical relationship with the girl next door.

Physician/फिजिसियन *(noun)* - चिकित्सक

We decided to approach a general physician to get a diagnosis.

Physics/फिजिक्स *(noun)* - भौतिक शास्त्र

She did a bachelors honours course in physics before going on to astronomy.

Physiognomy/फिजिऑग्नमि *(noun)* - चेहरे के नाक-नक्श का अध्ययन

His physiognomy seemed different from the actual description the witness gave.

Physiology/फिजिऑलॅजि *(noun)* - शरीर विज्ञान

We were studying the physiology of aquatic animals.

Physiotherapy/फिजिअॅथेरपि *(noun)*- व्यायाम से चिकित्सा

The doctor advised three months of physiotherapy for the patient to recover completely.

Physique/फिजिक *(noun)* - शरीर-सौष्ठव, शारीरिक गठन

His powerful physique attracted quite a few proposals.

Piano/पिआनो *(noun)* - एक वायु वाद्य

The piano was the star in the entire orchestra.

Pick/पिक *(noun & verb)* - गैंती, खोदनी, उठाना, चुनना, खुरेचना

He owned a factory that makes picks.

Picket/पिकेट् *(noun & verb)* - नोंकदार छड़ (खूँटा), धरना देना

Let's go and picket the shop.

Pickle/पिकल *(noun)* - अचार

Pickle with curd rice is a delicious combination.

Picnic/पिकनिक *(noun)* - उद्यान-भोज

The school had planned a picnic for the children. The children were excited about participating in the picnic.

Pictorial/पिक्टोरिअल *(adj)* - सचित्री, चित्रमय

The album was a pictorial description of the whole event. She bought a pictorial often sold at the newspaper shop.

Picture/पिक्चर *(noun)* - चित्र, चलचित्र

The pictures spoke for themselves.

Picturesque/पिक्चरेस्क *(adjective)* - मनोरम दृश्यावली, मनोहर प्राकृतिक दृश्य

The hill station was picturesque and a photographer's paradise.

Pie/पाइ *(noun)* - पके मांस का पुआ

I asked mother to bake an apple pie for tea.

Piece/पीस *(noun)* - टुकड़ा, अंश, हिस्सा

I asked my friend to pass me a piece of her bread to taste.

Piecemeal/पीसमिल *(adj & adv)* - खण्डित कार्य

It was a piecemeal effort she made.

Pierce/पिअर्स *(verb)* - छेदना, भेदना, बेधना

The thorn had pierced through her skin.

Piety/पाइ-इटि *(noun)* - धर्मपरायणता, श्रद्धा, धार्मिक

He impressed the gods with his piety.

Pig/पिग *(noun)* - सूअर

The pig sty had not been cleaned in weeks.

Piggery/पिगरी *(noun)* - सूअर खाना, सूअर का खोभाड़

The stench came from the piggery nearby.

Pigeon/पिजन् *(noun)* – कबूतर

Two pigeons had built a nest in my terrace.

Piggy bank/पिग्गि-बैंक *(noun)* – गोलक

I got a piggy bank as a gift on my ninth birthday.

Pigheaded/पिगहेडेड *(adjective)* – जिद्दी, अड़ियल

When I insisted stubbornly, mother asked me to stop being so pig headed.

Piglet/पिग्लेट *(noun)* – सूअर का बच्चा

The pigs in the sty had given birth to cute little piglets.

Pigment/पिग्मेंट *(noun)* – रंग, रंजक

The leaves were unique as they had different pigments. We decided to use a different combination of pigment for the rest of the painting.

Pigtail/पिग्टेल *(noun)* – गुच्छे में बँधे बाल

I like the girl with pigtails who sits at the back of the class. The pigtails were twisted and had to be repaired.

Pile/पाइल *(noun)* – ढेर, एक ऊपर एक सजाना, बल्ली

Pile is a form of deep foundation typically found in high rise buildings.

Piles/पाइल्स *(plural noun)* – बवासीर, एक प्रकार का खूनी-बादी रोग

The doctor advised the piles patient to avoid eating spicy food.

Pilgrim/पिल्ग्रिम *(noun)* – तीर्थयात्री

The facilities for pilgrims in our country need to improve dramatically. I shall pilgrim next year.

Pilgrimage/पिल्ग्रिमेज *(noun)* – तीर्थ, तीर्थ यात्रा

Mecca is one of the most crowded and famous pilgrimage points in the world. My mother shall pilgrimage after retirement.

Pill/पिल *(noun)* – दवा की गोली

The doctor prescribed sleeping pills to the insomniac.

Pillage/पिलेज *(verb)* – सैनिकों द्वारा लूटमार

A bitter pillage followed the war.

Pillar/पिलर *(noun)* – खम्भ, स्तम्भ

The pillars in the palace had been ornately designed.

Pillion/पिलियन (पिल्यॅन) *noun)* – पीछे सवारी के बैठने का स्थान

The pillion rider also needs to wear a helmet. The horse nearly threw the rider and the pillion off its back.

Pillow/पिलो *(noun)* – तकिया

He went hunting around the city for the best pillows to sleep on. Pillows add colour and style to the living room.

Pilot/पाइलट् *(noun)* – चालक, विमान चालक

Its alarming to know some of the pilots sleep over the controls during a flight. The Titanic would not have sunk if the pilots were more alert about the ice bergs.

Pimple/पिम्पल *(noun)* – फुंसी

Getting pimples may also be a sign of attaining puberty.

Pin/पिन *(noun)* – मेख, सूई सी नुकीली, नत्थी करना

The girl used a safety pin to secure her handkerchief to the uniform.

Pinafore/पिनाफोर *(noun)* – वस्त्र रक्षक ढीला वस्त्र

The children wore pinafores at nursery school.

Pincer/पिन्सर् *(noun)* – सँड़सी

I screamed when the dentist brought an instrument that looked like a pincer close to my mouth. When in danger, the crab uses its pincers as a deadly weapon.

Pinch/पिन्च *(verb)* – चुटकी, चुटकी काटना

Pinching nerves in the neck can be very painful.

Pine/पाइन *(noun)* – चीड़ का पेड़, अति दुःखी

Natural stands of scots pine can also be found in the Heathlands of southern England.

Pineapple/पाइनएपल *(noun)* – अनन्नास/अनानास

A diet based on pineapple fruit is said to work wonders for weight reduction.

Ping-pong/पिंग-पौंग *(noun)* – एक प्रकार का खेल, गेंद

The Asian teams tend to dominate Ping-Pong games at the Olympics.

Pinnacle/पिनैकल *(noun)* – पराकाष्टा

The islands are known to have a number of shallow reefs and coral pinnacles.

P

Pinpoint/पिनपॉयेन्ट्/पिनपॉइन्ट् *(adj)* – इंगित करना

The new imaging software can pinpoint the area of impact to within a few millimetres.

Pinprick/पिनप्रिक *(noun)* – सूई चुभाना, तंग करना

The tire of the bike had a small puncture much like a pinprick. Here in our little community, a pinprick on the map of the five great continents of the world.

Pint/पाइन्ट *(noun)* – एक माप

Mix extracts, pour into a clean pan and boiling until the mixture measures 2 pint.

Pioneer/पायनिअर *(noun)* – अग्रणी, अगुआ

There is an exhibition in town that explains the work of the famous Yorkshire aviation pioneer, Robert Blackburn.

Pious/पायस *(adjective)* – पवित्र, धर्मपरायण, भक्त

He was revered by many as a saint because he was so pious. The so called miracles enacted by many 'god' men in today's world need to be studied in detail before terming them as pious fraud.

Pip/पिप *(noun)* – छोटे बीज, संकेत ध्वनि, असफल होना

The fibroid detected is as miniscule as a pip of an orange.

Pipe/पाइप *(noun)* – नली, नल, नलिका, तम्बाकू

The pipe in my bathroom needs to be replaced. a *Cinema has often shown actors smoking a pipe on screen quite stylishly.*

Pipeline/पाइपलाइन *(noun)* – बड़ी नली, नलिका का प्रसार

The proposed pipeline for gas between the two countries would run below the sea. The Banzai pipeline is a surf reek break located in Hawaii.

Piper/पाइपर *(noun)* – वायुवादक

Whatever you do, at some point in time you have to pay the piper.

Piping/पाइपिंग *(noun)* – नल की लम्बाई, सीटी की ध्वनि

A frequent failure of piping in air conditioning units is a concern that needs to be addressed. One has to learn modern piping techniques to make elegant and artistic decorations on the cake.

Pirate/पाइरेट *(noun)* – जलदस्यु

The threat of pirates in the Indian Ocean has brought the South Asian countries together to weed them out.

Pisces/पिसीज् *(noun)* – मीन, मीन राशि, मछली

Pisces is a constellation lying between Aquarius and Aries.

Pistol/पिस्टॅल् *(noun)* – तमंचा

The policeman ordered the robber to throw his pistol towards the door.

Piston/पिस्टन *(noun)* – अन्य यन्त्रों को गतिशील करने वाला यन्त्र

The mechanic realized that the car was not functioning as the piston in its engine was stuck.

Pit/पिट् *(noun & verb)* – गड्ढा, खदान, गड्ढे बनाना

You should remove the pit and eat the pulp of any fruit.

Pitch/पिच *(noun)* – खेल का तैयार मैदान, तीव्रता, गिरने का स्थान, कोलतार

Applying pitch on the roof helped Anna keep her hut safe during the rains.

Pitcher/पिचर *(noun)* – घड़ा, सुराही

As the afternoon got on, the mother brought out a large pitcher of lemonade for the children playing outside.

Pitchfork/पिचफॉर्क *(noun)* – पाँचा

The police suspect that the murder was committed using the pitchfork they found lying near the body.

Piteous/पिटिअस *(adj)* – दयनीय, कारुणिक अवस्था

As the moon rose in the sky, the wolf let out a piteous cry.

Pitfall/पिटफॉल *(noun)* – संकट, अनजाना संकट

The company's new CEO has a hard task of resurrecting the firm from the recent economic pitfall.

Pith/पिथ *(noun)* – गुद्दा, महत्त्वपूर्ण अंश

The pith of the orange acts as a protective cover to the soft fruit within.

Pitiable/पिटिएबल *(adj)* – दयनीय

Mary wanted to help the man who seemed to be in a pitiable condition.

Pitiful/पिटिफुल *(adjective)* – दयाद्र, दया से भरा

The baby let out a pitiful moan on seeing his mother. Saying that you do not get time to exercise is a pitiful excuse for escaping from the punishment.

Pitiless/पिटिलेश *(adjective)* – दयाशून्य, निर्दयी

The warden at the hostel is a pitiless man.

Pittance/पिटैंस *(noun)* – छोटी रकम

Despite working hard for an entire year, he was given a pittance as salary.

Pity/पिटि *(noun)* – दया

One feels great pity for the people who have no shelter of their own.

Pivot/पिवॅट् *(noun)* – धुरी

You just need to adjust the pivot and the wheel will function effortlessly.

Pixie/पिक्सी *(noun)* – परी के समान

The farther the object, you need smaller pixie to get a clearer image.

Pizza/पिज्जा *(noun)* – सब्जियों से लदी रोटी

There are more than a dozen chains of this pizza making firm spread all across the country.

Placard/प्लैकार्ड् *(noun)* – प्रदर्शन (विरोध) हेतु तैयार नारे

The angry crowd outside the palace was holding placards against the royal family. To bring the point to the notice of the authorities, it is best to cover the topic with placards.

P

Placate/प्लैकेट् *(verb)* – शान्त करना, सन्तुष्ट करना

It is not an easy task to placate a crying toddler.

Place/प्लेस *(noun)* – स्थान, क्षेत्र, रखना

If you are searching for this place, you need to go straight and turn right at the intersection.

Placid/प्लैसिड् *(adjective)* – शान्त, उत्तेजित न होने वाला

A strong individual is always placid in his heart.

Plagiarize/प्लेजिअराइज् *(verb)* – बातों, लेखन की नकल

Imitation may be the best form of flattery but plagiarism is not appreciated by anyone.

Plague/प्लेग *(noun)* – महामारी

The best way to avoid a plague epidemic is to keep the surroundings clean.

Plain/प्लेन *(adjective)* – सीधा, साफ, स्पष्ट, समतल

I love the combination of a floral top with a plain skirt. Explaining the problem in plain words would avoid any confusion.

Plaintiff/प्लेन्टिफ *(noun)* – वादी

The plaintiff and the judge seem to be known to each other.

Plaintive/प्लेन्टिव *(adjective)* – दुःखपूर्ण, कातर

Why are you sounding so plaintive after receiving the phone call?

Plait/प्लेट *(noun)* – चोटी, बालों की चोटी बनाना

The rope has been plaited strongly around the box.

Plan/प्लान *(noun)* – योजना, विचार (किसी काम को करने के लिए)

What is your plan for the future of your children?

Plane/प्लेन *(noun)* – हवाई जहाज, रंदा

I cannot finish the varnish today as the plane is broken. The best and smoothest finish will be achieved only after we plane the surface.

Planet/प्लैनेट् *(noun)* – ग्रह

The hunt for planets outside the solar system has been on for centuries.

Plank/प्लैंक *(noun)* – पटरा

If you do not place the plank properly, the entire work will fail.

Plant/प्लांट *(noun)* – पौधा लगाना, कारखाना लगाना

Plants help maintain a balance in nature.

Plantation/प्लांटेशन *(noun)* – बाग-बगीचा, पौधा लगाना

The bride comes from a family that owns several coffee plantations.

Plaque/प्लाक *(noun)* – स्मृति-पट, दाँतों पर जमी परत

He always placed his victory plaques on the walls of his study.

Plaster/प्लास्टर *(noun)* – दीवार आदि को चिकना करना, हड्डी जोड़ने के लिए लगायी गयी औषधि पट्टिका a

Clay plaster on two walls adds a delicate contrast to concrete and redwood elements.

Plastic/प्लास्टिक *(noun)* - एक चिकना पदार्थ जिसे आसानी से मोड़ा जा सके या भिन्न आकार दिया जा सके

We need to reduce the use of plastic as much as possible to save planet earth from further poisoning.

Plate/प्लेट *(noun)* - तश्तरी, भोजन की थाली, धातु की चद्दर धातु-पट्टिका

Please clean your own plates after you have eaten your meals.

Plateau/प्लैटो *(noun)* - पठार

The Deccan plateau is one of the largest plateaus in Asia. The manager of the retail company is deeply concerned about the plateau in the sales graph over the last few months.

Platform/प्लैटफॉर्म *(noun)* - चबूतरा

A platform was raised for the political leader to address the big gathering. Many of the railway platforms are still not disabled person friendly.

Platinum/प्लैटिनम् *(noun)* - गहनों और उद्योग में प्रयुक्त एक रसायन

Platinum wedding rings are in vogue today.

Platonic/प्लैटॉनिक *(adjective)* - वासनारहित प्रेम और मैत्री

Many of the platonic ideas are so very relevant in today's world too.

Platoon/प्लाटून *(noun)* - सेना की टुकड़ी

The platoon serving in the East Coasts had highly decorated soldiers amongst them.

Plausible/प्लाजिबल् *(adjective)* - तर्कसंगत

The story narrated by the apprehended thief sounded plausible to the cops.

Play/प्ले *(verb)* - खेलना, वाद्य बजाना, अभिनय करना

She likes to play with people's emotions. Has somebody been playing with these taps?

Player/प्लेअर *(noun)* - खिलाड़ी

She got the best player's award at the Sports Day function.

Playful/प्लेफुल *(adjective)* - प्रसन्नचित, विनोदपूर्ण

Children are best in their playful age.

Playmate/प्लेमेट *(noun)* - खेल का साथी

She is my playmate and I have grown up with her.

Plaything/प्लेथिंग *(noun)* - खिलौना

The child asked her father to find her a plaything as she was bored.

Plea/प्ली *(noun)*- दलील, अपना पक्ष रखना

The criminal wanted to file a plea for mercy to save himself from the noose.

Plead/प्लीड् *(verb)* - सफाई देना, याचना करना

She pleaded self-defence.

Pleasant/प्लेजेंट् *(adjective)* - प्रसन्न कर देने वाला, रमणीय, सुखकर, मैत्रीपूर्ण

He had a pleasant nature and was easily lovable.

Please/प्लीज् *(verb)* - प्रसन्न करना

He was pleased at her social etiquettes.

Pleasure/प्लेजर *(noun)* - आनन्द

She derives great pleasure from feeding others.

Pleat/प्लीट् *(noun)* - चुनट, कपड़े की चुनट

The pleats on her skirt had to be rearranged.

Plebicite/प्लेबिसाइट *(noun)* - जनमत संग्रह

After the plebiscite, the state was left in a pathetic condition.

Pledge/प्लेज् *(noun)* - प्रतिज्ञा, वचन

The amount pledged for the child had actually increased after the advertisement.

Plenty/प्लेंटि *(pronoun)* - बहुतायत में, प्रचुरता

There was plenty of food left for the others. Food was available in plenty.

Pliable/प्लाइऍबल् *(adjective)* - लचीला

The wires were pliable and therefore could be adjusted easily.

Pliant/प्लाइअन्द् *(adjective)* - बिना टूटे आसानी से मुड़ने वाला

The tool kit was rather fancy as it even had a pliant with the plier for a sample.

Pliers/प्लाइअर्स *(plural noun)* - एक प्रकार की सँड़सी, तार आदि को काटने का औजार

I bought him a new plier for his tool kit.

Plight/प्लाइट *(noun)* - दु:ख स्थिति

You must consider the plight of the needy when you walk past them.

Plinth/प्लिंथ *(noun)* - नींव, नींव का ऊपरी भाग

When the plinth started cracking, we knew the tremors had started.

Plod/प्लॉड *(verb)* - कठिनाई से धीरे-धीरे चलना

We were plodding through the task to get the best results. After running across half the city, we were now plodding through the street near his house.

Plop/प्लॉप *(noun)* - छप-छप, छप-छपाक

The snail fell into the puddle with a plop.

Plot/प्लॉट *(noun)* - छोटा भूमिखण्ड, कथानक, कुचक्र

They had devised a sinister plot to kill the minister.

Plough/प्लाउ *(noun)* - हल, हल जोतना

The land that has been ploughed will give a better crop.

Ploy/प्लाय *(noun)* - लाभ हेतु सुनियोजित कथन

He had devised a cunning ploy to rob the bank.

P

Pluck/प्लक *(verb)* - चुनना, बिनना, हटाना

She plucked her eyebrows before setting out for the party.

Plug/प्लग *(noun)* - छिद्र बन्द करने का रबर या धातु, बिजली संचालन के लिए प्रयुक्त यन्त्र

I put the plug into the hole so it won't leak any more.

Plumb/प्लम्ब *(verb)* - सीधा करना

It was a new house so we had a lot of plumbs to fix.

Plumber/प्लम्बर *(noun)* - नल का कारीगर

The plumber came to fix the pipes in our house.

Plumb line/प्लमलाइन *(noun)*- साहुल

The leak was found to have started from the plumb below the sink.

Plume/प्लूम *(noun)* - बड़ा, पंख, पंखनुमा वस्तु

The bird's plumes were shining in the sun's rays.

Plummet/प्लमेद् *(verb)* - रस्सी की छोर पर लगाया गया वजन

The value of the shares was plummeting.

Plump/प्लम्प *(adjective)* - गोल-मटोल

I was meeting her after a long time and realized she had grown plump. She had turned plump over the years.

Plunder/प्लंडर *(verb)* - लूटपाट, लूट का सामान

The enemies had plundered the whole state. Property acquired by plundering will not yield profits for a long time.

Plunge/प्लंज *(verb)* - जबरदस्ती घुसाना

With a deep breath, he plunged into the water.

Plural/प्लुरल *(adjective)* - बहुवचन

Unfortunately, you may not have to consider the number of students appearing for the blood donation camp in plural. The teacher asked the students the list out the plural forms of the given words.

Plus/प्लस *(noun)* - जोड़ा का चिह्न (+)

When you make icing, chocolates are indeed a plus. The cheque amounts to $500,000 plus.

Plush/प्लश् *(noun)* - मखमल

Let us not live a plush life when we cannot afford it. I bought her a plush cushion to sleep on.

Pluto/प्लूटो *(noun)* - सूर्य से अति दूर एक ग्रह

Pluto is no longer considered a planet belonging to the solar system.

Plutonium/प्लूटोनियम *(noun)* - परमाणु अभिक्रिया का एक तत्त्व

Every since they discovered plutonium in the land behind his ancestral house, several government agencies have been flocking the place.

Ply/प्लाइ *(noun)* - लकड़ी की परत, ऊन की लड़ी नियमित रूप से वाहन का परिचालन

There were several layers of ply spread on the carpenter's table. The table had a four-ply structure.

Pneumatic/न्यूमेटिक *(adjective)* – हवा से भरा हुआ

We realized that the instrument he bought was not working because it was pneumatic.

Pnemonia/न्यूमोनिया *(noun)* – फेफड़े में सूजन

Unlike the earlier times, today there is a positive treatment available for pneumonia.

Poach/पोच *(verb)* – अण्डे का पकवान, जानवर चुराना

Poached egg is extremely healthy and a good option for losing weight.

Pocket/पॉकेट् *(noun)* – जेब, पृथक् क्षेत्र

I bought her a bag with several pockets so she could keep it neat and organized.

Pod/पॉड *(noun)* – फली

The friends were like peas in a pod.

Podium/पोडिअम् *(noun)* – चबूतरा

The chief guest was invited to the podium to say a few words to the audience.

Poem/पोएम *(noun)* – कविता

Her diary was full of poems.

Poet/पोएट *(noun)* – कवि

Her beauty could turn anyone into a poet.

Poetic/पोएटिक *(adjective)* – काव्यात्मक

The prose he wrote was more poetic than like prose.

Poetry/पोएट्रि *(noun)* – काल, कवित्व, कालात्मकता

She wanted to attend the poetry convention that would start soon.

Poignant/पॉइनन्ट *(adjective)* – हृदय विदारक, दहला देने वाला

It was a poignant theme to write a play on.

Point/पॉइन्ट *(noun)* – बिन्दु, नोक, नक्शे या चित्र पर स्थिति किसी की ओर इशारा करना

The spear was shining at its point so much that it would make any man shiver.

Point-blank/पॉइन्ट ब्लैंक *(adj & adv)* – बहुत समीप से

The shots were fired at point blank range.

Pointer/पॉइन्टर *(noun)* – इंगित करने के लिए छड़ी

Do not depend on the pointer too much to get your results.

Pointless/पॉइन्टलेस *(adjective)* – व्यर्थ, निरर्थक

It is pointless shedding tears before me, my father told me.

Poise/पॉइज *(noun)* – सन्तुलित रहना

He was somehow precariously poised at a 45 degree angle.

Poison/पॉइजन *(noun)* – जहर, विष

The poison was gradually spreading in the rest of his body.

Poke/पोक *(noun & verb)* – प्रहार, कोंचना, कुरेदना

He poked the stick down the hole to see how deep it was to push, to thrust.

Poker/पोकर *(noun)* – धातु की कुरेदनी, ताश का एक खेल

She took the poker out of the fire and shoved it at the boy as if to scare him away.

Polar/पोलर *(adjective)* – ध्रुव प्रदेशीय

News has been doing the rounds that the polar ice caps are melting.

Polaroid/पोलरॉइड् *(noun)* – शीघ्र तैयार चित्र का तकनीक

Father bought me a Polaroid camera this birthday.

Pole/पोल *(noun)* – ध्रुव, पोलैण्ड का निवासी

There were people from several countries in our boat, including an American, two Indians, a Chinese couple and a Pole.

Police/पॅलीस् *(noun)* – आरक्षी

Right from childhood, he has dreamt of joining the police force. The guards were asked to police the area for a few days.

Policy/पॉलिसी *(noun)* – शर्त और नियम, बीमा

The government introduced several policies in the agricultural sector this year.

Polio/पोलिओ *(noun)* – एक रोग, सन्तुलित वृद्धि का अभाव

He had polio when he was an infant.

Polish/पॉलिश *(noun)* – चमकाना, चमकाने वाला रंग, परिष्कृत साधारण

Initially I mistook his language for French but later I realized it was Polish.

P

Polite/पोलाइट *(adjective)* – विनम्र, शिष्ट

I had met her only once but she always came out as extremely polite.

Political/पॉलिटिकल *(adjective)* – राजनीतिक

That he had political ambitions was evident from the message he conveys in all his movies.

Politician/पॉलिटिसिअन *(noun)* – राजनीतिज्ञ

He made an excellent politician for the country.

Politics/पॉलिटिक्स *(plural noun)* – राजनीति

The politics of our country is beyond my understanding.

Poll/पोल *(noun)* – मतदान, जनमत सर्वेक्षण, प्राप्त मत

The results of the opinion poll were in favour of the Democrats.

Pollen/पॉलेन *(noun)* – पराग

There is a heavy concentration of pollen grains in the air here.

Pollute/पॉल्यूट *(verb)* – दूषित करना, गन्दा करना, प्रदूषण फैलाना

We were asked to get used to waste segregation and stop polluting the environment.

P

Polo/पोलो *(noun)* – चौगान, एक प्रकार का खेल

My cousin is a State level Polo player.

Poly/पॉलि *(noun)* – बहु का प्रत्यय

She had found a rare sari made of polyester fabric.

Polyandry/पॉलिएन्ड्रि *(noun)* – एक से अधिक पति

There are several instances of polyandry in our scriptures.

Polyester/पॉलिएस्टर *(noun)* – कृत्रिम, कपड़ा

She wore a lovely polyester sari for her friend's wedding.

Polygamy/पॉलिगैमि *(noun)* – बहुविवाह

In the ancient times, polygamy was actually forgiven.

Polygon/पॉलिगॅन *(noun)* – पंचकोण

I can never draw a perfect polygon.

Polytechnic/पॉलिटेक्निक *(noun)* – वैज्ञानिक तथा तकनीकि शिक्षालय

She has taken admission in civil engineering in government polytechnic.

Polythene/पालिथिन *(noun)* – एक पारदर्शी लचीली वस्तु

The poor cow died because of the polythene bag that it accidentally ate and that got stuck in its throat.

Pomp/पॉम्प *(noun)* – तड़क-भड़क, आडम्बर

The wedding will be celebrated with great pomp and show.

Pompous/पॉम्पस *(adjective)* – आडम्बरपूर्ण

He read it out in a pompous voice.

Pond/पॉन्ड *(noun)* – तालाब, ताल-तलैया

I asked the horticulturist to design a small pond for our garden.

Ponder/पॉन्डर *(verb)* – गम्भीतापूर्वक विचार

The notices were passed to all of us to ponder over.

Ponderous/पॉन्डरस *(adjective)* – नीरस, ऊबाऊ, बोझिल

He strolled about with a ponderous heavy gait.

Pony/पॉनि *(noun)* – टट्टू

The hill station had ponies at every nook and corner.

Pooh/पूह *exclamatory* – घृणा, तिरस्कार का उद्‌गार

"Pooh Pooh!" said Richard Parker, "and how could I know who did it?"

Pool/पूल *(noun)* – जलजमाव, एक खेल, संसाधन एकत्र करना

We had a pool in our ancestral house where we all learnt swimming as kids.

Poor/पूअर *(adjective)* – गरीब, निर्धन

Studies say that there are more poor people in our country than in any other country in the world.

Poorly/पूअर्लि *(adverb)* – दीनता के साथ, किसी तरह

She did poorly in the exams once again.

Pop/पॉप *(noun)* – बोतल खुलने की आवाज, तड़ाक

Michael Jackson is known as the king of pop music

Popcorn/पॉपकार्न *(noun)* – मकई का लावा

She could never imagine watching a movie without popcorn.

Pope/पोप *(noun)* – सर्वोच्च धर्म गुरु

Everyone hoped that the next pope would be a great peacemaker.

Poplin/पॉपलिन *(noun)* – चमकदार पतला सूती कपड़ा

She was prettily dressed in gray poplin, trimmed with gray velvet and a deep red sash around her trim waist.

Poppy/पॉपि *(noun)* – अफीम, खसखस

Bengalis use a lot of poppy seeds in their cooking.

Populace/पॉप्युलेस् *(noun)* – जनसाधाररण

A large proportion of the populace was against the idea of breaking down the structure.

Popular/पॉप्युलर् *(adjective)* – प्रचलित, प्रसिद्ध, प्रशंसित liked or admired by many or by a particular person or group. *She was easily the most popular girl in school.*

Populate/पॉप्युलेट *(verb)* – बस्ती बसाना

North America was largely populated by Europeans.

Population/पॉप्युलेशन *(noun)* – जनसंख्या, आबादी

The population of our country has doubled over the last few years.

Porcelain/पॉर्सिलेन *(noun)* – चीनी मिट्टी, चीनी मिट्टी की वस्तुएँ

Porcelain makes for some of the most beautiful and affordable cutlery.

Porch/पोर्च *(noun)* – प्रवेश द्वार

Every villa in the complex had a designer car porch.

Porcupine/पॉरक्युपाइन *(noun)* – शाही

The population of porcupines had reduced over the years.

Pore/पोर *(noun)* – रोमकूप, रोएँ के छिद्र, ध्यान से अध्ययन

The dermatologist advised me to wash my face frequently so the pores of my skin would not be closed.

Pork/पॉर्क *(noun)* – सूअर का माँस

Home cooked pork vindaloo was his favourite dish whenever he was at home.

Pornography/पॅर्नॅग्राफी *(noun)* – कामुक चित्र, चलचित्र, पुस्तक आदि

The government was intending to put a censor on pornography in the internet as well.

Porous/पोरस *(adjective)* – छिद्रवाला, छिद्रदार

Local limestone is extremely porous.

Porpoise/पोर्पॅस *(noun)* – सूईस, सूँस, समुद्री जीव

The island was known for an occasional sighting of the porpoise.

Porridge/पॉरिज *(noun)* – खीर, दलिया

My parents prefer having porridge for breakfast since its easy to cook.

Port/पोर्ट् *(noun)* – बन्दरगाह, द्वार, लाल शराब

Tuesday morning was a typical day at the port with all the hustle bustle and chaos of the fishermen, sailors and travellers.

Portable/पोर्टेबल *(adjective)* – हल्का सामान, आसानी से ढोया जाने वाला

I bought her a portable music player that she could take with her wherever she travels.

Porter/पोर्टर *(noun)* – कुली, सामान वाहक

The manager signalled to the porter to take the customer's luggage to his room.

Portfolio/पोर्टफोलिओ *(noun)* – चमड़े का बस्ता, निवेश, मन्त्री का विभाग

He had a portfolio in the almirah in which he keeps all his pictures and drawings.

Porthole/पोर्टहोल *(noun)* – छोटी गोल खिड़की

He clung to the frame of the porthole as the airship swung and swayed in all directions.

Portion/पोर्सन *(noun)* – हिस्सा, भाग, अंश

The dietician advised us to take only one portion of meal at a time.

Portly/पोर्टली *(adjective)* – स्थूलकाय

Men are portly and women are stout.

Portrait/पोर्ट्रेट *(noun)* – ऊपरी भाग का चित्र

I asked the painter to paint my portrait.

Portray/पोट्रे *(verb)* – पुस्तक या चित्र में दर्शाना

The actress's life was portrayed in a beautiful manner in the movie.

Pose/पोज *(verb)* – विशेष ढंग से बैठना या खड़ा होना

The teacher was dumbfound at the question the student posed.

Posh/पॉश *(adjective)* – उत्कृष्ट और महँगा

He always had a tendency to live a posh life.

Position/पोजिशन *(noun)* – स्थिति, विशेष जगह, ठिकाना

The paratroops had been given positions in such a way that the terrorists could not see where they were being attacked from.

Positive/पॉजिटिव *(adjective)* – निश्चित, रचनात्मक, पक्का

I look forward to a positive reply from you.

Possess/पॅजेस *(verb)* – स्वामित्व रखना, अधिकार में रखना

He is said to possess a huge forturne.

Possession/पॅजेशन् *(noun)* – स्वामित्व

The home team was in possession during most of the fourth quarter.

P

Possessive/पॅजेसिव *(adj)* – अधिकार में रखने को आतुर

She had a tendency to be extremely possessive of her loved ones.

Possibility/पॉसिबिलिटि *(noun)* – सम्भावना

There is a good possibility it may rain today.

Possible/पॉसिबल् *(adjective)* – सम्भव

It is not possible to finish this in two weeks.

Post/पोस्ट *(noun)* – खूँटा, ठिकाना, पद, स्थान, डाक

She had applied for an interview for the post of manager. A soldier manned the entrance post.

Postage/पोस्टेज *(noun)* – डाकटिकट, डाकव्यय

I bought a dozen postage stamps so I don't need to run to the post office every time I need one.

Postal/पोस्टल *(adjective)* – डाक से सम्बन्धित

The one postal delivery in our locality was in the morning.

Postdate/पोस्टडेट *(verb)* – बाद की तारीख

I gave her a postdated cheque.

Poster/पोस्टर *(noun)* – प्रदर्शित सूचना

The police arrested the goons for pasting posters on the wall in spite of the warning not to.

Posterity/पॅस्टेरिटि *(noun)* – भावी पीढ़ियाँ

A photographer recorded the scene for posterity.

Postgraduate/पोस्टग्रैड्युएट *(adjective)* – स्नातकोत्तर

She did her Post graduation in Applied Operation Analysis. "I am a post graduate, so I should be allowed for the seminar."

Posthumous/पॅस्ट्यूमस् *(adjective)* – मरणोपरान्त

He was given a posthumous award and title for his bravery.

Post-mortem/पोस्टमॉर्टम् *(noun)* – शव परीक्षा

They took the body from the accident site for a post mortem.

Postpone/पोस्टपोन *(verb)* – स्थगित करना

Never postpone for tomorrow the work that you can finish today.

Postscript/पोस्टस्क्रिप्ट *(noun)* – पत्र आदि के अंत में जोड़ा गया अतिरिक्त अंश, सूचना या संदेश

He had added a note as postscript in his mail saying the balance money is attached.

Postulate/पॉस्ट्युलेट *(verb)* – पहले ही मान लेना

He postulated several theories in his lifetime.

Posture/पॉस्चर *(noun)* – शरीर की मुद्रा

You must sit upright on a chair in order to have a good posture.

Pot/पॉट *(noun)* – बरतन, गमले, गोली दागना

He took a pot-shot at the bird on the fence. "What a pot he scored!"

Potable/पोटेबल् *(adjective)* – पीने योग्य

Wine and other potables were kept in a different bunker.

Potato/पोटैटो *(noun)* – आलू

Boiled potatoes with cheese and ham are a common dish Europeans eat for breakfast.

Potent/पोटेंट *(adjective)* – शक्तिशाली, गुणकारी, प्रभावशाली

The drug is extremely potent but can have extreme side effects. The boy was pleased to know he was potent.

Potential/पॅटेन्शल् *(adjective)* - संभाव्य, विकसित होने का सम्भावना

Your ideas have potential, I have to admit. He has a huge potential to become someone great when he grows up.

Pothole/पॉटहोल *(noun)* - गड्ढे, बारिस का गड्ढा

Warnings were issued as the rain had caused several pot holes on the roads.

Potter/पॉटर *(noun & verb)* - कुम्हार, भटकना

She was pottering around the whole place all day.

Potty/पॉटी *(adjective)* - छोटे बच्चे का मल त्याग पात्र

"Are you going potty?"

Pouch/पॉउच *(noun)* - थैली, पुड़िया, आँखों के नीचे लटकता त्वचा

I carried all my junk jewellery in a pouch.

Poultry/पाउल्ट्री *(noun)* - मुर्गीपालन

Most of the poultry was being culled because of the rumours of bird flu.

Pounce/पाउन्स *(verb)* - अचानक आक्रमण, दबोचना

The tiger ran after the deer and pounced on its neck.

Pound/पाउन्ड *(noun)* - ब्रिटेन की मुद्रा, चूर-चूर कर देना, धड़कना

I visited the pound down the street to buy a pet.

Pour/पोर् *(verb)* - डालना, धारा में गिराना

Pour the curry into the serving bowl.

Pout/पाउट् *(verb)* - मुँह बिचकाना

The actress tried pouting during the photo shoot but it didn't help her at all. Her pout was not really of much help.

Poverty/पावर्टि *(noun)* - गरीबी, निर्धनता

The leaders of our country dreamt of achieving a state of no poverty in the country.

Powder/पावडर *(noun)* - चूर्ण, चूरा, बारूद

Coffee beans need to be powdered to make instant coffee.

Power/पॉवर *(noun)* - शक्ति, योग्यता

The power of his love saved her.

Powerful/पॉवरफुल *(adjective)* - शक्तिशाली, योग्य, समर्थ

The ruling party is one of the most powerful we have ever had till date.

Powerless/पॉवरलेस *(adjective)* - अशक्त, अयोग्य, असमर्थ

The cat was left powerless in front of the dog.

Practicable/प्रैक्टिकेबल् *(adjective)* - व्यावहारिक, व्यवहार्य

Teachers can only be expected to do what is practicable.

Practical/प्रैक्टिकल *(adjective)* - व्यावहारिक

He gained practical experience of sailing as a deck hand.

Practice/प्रैक्टिस *(noun)* - अभ्यास

We tried putting the diet into practice but it was very difficult.

Practise/प्रैक्टिस *(verb)* - अभ्यास करना

Practise constantly to gain knowledge in maths.

Practitioner/प्रैक्टिश्नर *(noun)* - व्यवहार में लाने वाला

He has been a practitioner of Ayurvedic medicine for the last ten years.

Pragmatic/प्रैग्मेटिक *(adjective)* - व्यावहारिक, यथार्थ

He gave a pragmatic perspective to the problem at hand.

Prairie/प्रेरि *(noun)* - घास के पेड़हीन मैदान

With global warming, even the prairies were disappearing.

Praise/प्रेज *(verb)* - प्रशंसा, सराहना, स्तुति, गुणगान

She received lots of praise from her peers and teachers for being an all rounder.

Pram/प्रैम *(noun)* - बच्चा गाड़ी

He was so excited about the baby coming home, he bought five different kinds of prams.

Prance/प्रैंस *(verb)* - इठलाकर चलना

She was prancing around like a rooster in a hen house.

Prank/प्रैंक *(noun)* - शरारत, नटखटपन

The actor was known for the pranks he would play on the sets.

Prattle/प्रैटल *(verb)* - बड़बड़ाना

She prattled on till I wanted to scream. I had had enough of his mindless prattle.

Prawn/प्रॉन *(noun)* - झींगा

Prawn sandwiches are her favourite indeed.

Pray/प्रे *(verb)* - प्रार्थना, प्रार्थना करना, स्तुति करना

I have been taught from childhood to pray before I sleep at night.

Prayer/प्रेअर *(noun)* - प्रार्थना, स्तोत्र-पाठ

The doctor told us that only prayer could save her now.

Pre/प्री *prefix* - एक उपसर्ग, पूर्व

She has entered her pre-adolescent years now.

Preach/प्रीच *(verb)* - उपदेश देना

The father preached the gospel.

Preamble/प्रिएम्बल *(noun)* - प्रस्तावना, आमुख

The Preamble of our Constitution contains the Directive Principles of State Authority.

Precarious/प्रिकेरिअस *(adjective)* - खतरे में, असुरक्षित

He was standing in a precarious position, and I feared anyone could easily catch him.

P

Precaution/प्रिकॉशन *(noun)* - पूर्व से रखी जाने वाली सावधानी, पूर्व उपाय

You must take proper precautions before you go for the adventure trip.

Precede/प्रिसिड *(verb)* - पहले होना

Stone tools precede bronze tools.

Precedence/प्रिसिडेंस *(noun)* - वरीयता, प्राथमिकता

Recipients of military honour were called in order of precedence—higher ranking officers first.

Precedent/प्रिसिडेंट *(noun)* - पूर्व पीठिका, स्थापित नियम या परम्परा

The trial could set an important precedent for similar cases. The President followed historical precedent in forming the Cabinet.

Precept/प्रीसेप्ट *(noun)* - नियम, नीतिवचन

He believed and followed all the precepts of Buddhism.

Precinct/प्रीसिंक्ट *(noun)* - निर्धारित क्षेत्र

Hunting is not allowed within the precincts of the estate.

Precious/प्रेशस *(adjective)* - बहुमूल्य, अमूल्य

She has kept all her precious jewels safely in the locker.

Precipice/प्रेसिपिस *(noun)* - खड़ी चट्टान

The path had sheer rock on one side and a precipice on the other.

Precipitate/प्रेसिपिटेट *(verb)* - अचानक घट जाना, समय से पूर्व घटिन होना

The killings in the city have precipitated the worst crisis ever.

Precis/प्रेसिस *(noun)* - संक्षेपण

We were asked to present a précis before the actual presentation. His précis invited a huge applause, so I won't be surprised if his presentation was a runaway success.

Precise/प्रिसाइस् *(adjective)* - सावधानी पूर्वक कहा हुआ, सही ढंग से कहा हुआ

I want the precise details of the project that the rival company is taking up.

Preision/प्रिसिजन *(noun)* - सावधानी, संक्षिप्तता, यथार्थता

He handled it with the precision of an automated machine.

Precocious/प्रिकोशस *(adjective)* - अवस्था से पूर्व योग्यता अर्जित करना

Radhika has always been a precocious child.

Preconceived/प्रिकन्सिव्ड *(adjective)* - पहले से धारित अवधारणा

Do not enter into the experiment with any preconceived notions in your mind.

Preconception/प्रिकन्सेप्शन *(noun)* - पहले से बनी अवधारणा

He did not even try to confirm his preconceptions before he passed the news.

Predator/प्रिडेटर *(noun)* - जीव भक्षी जानवर, हिंसक जानवर

Life in the jungle follows the prey-predator format.

Predecessor/प्रिडिसेसर *(noun)* – पूर्ववर्ती, पूर्व अधिकारी, पूर्व से प्रचलित

The new manager should learn a thing or two about management from his predecessor.

Predicament/प्रिडिकमेंट् *(noun)* – अप्रिय स्थिति, परेशानी, द्विविधा

You would definitely never understand my predicament unless you were in my shoes.

Predicate/प्रेडिकेट *(noun)* – आधार पर निर्णय, भविष्यवाणी-सी घोषणा

The question was: Identify the predicate in "The child is very sleepy".

Predicative/प्रेडिकेटिव *(adjective)* – विधेयात्मक

Identify the predicative word in : Jane opened the door.

Predict/प्रिडिक्ट *(verb)* – भविष्यवाणी

Nostradamous predicted the world to come to an end in 2012.

Predictable/प्रिडिक्टेबल् *(adjective)* – जो भविष्वाण ाी करने योग्य हो

She has a predictable nature.

Predominant/प्रिडॉमिनैन्ट् *(adjective)* – अधिकार और प्रभाव में दूसरों से प्रबल

He played a predominant role in shaping the constitution of our country.

Predominance/प्रिडॉमिनैन्स *(noun)* – प्राधान्य

An interesting note was the predominance of London club players.

Predominate/प्रिडॉमिनेट *(verb)* – प्रबल होना, प्रमुखता रखना

Good predominates over evil in most of our scriptural epics.

Pre-eminent/प्रिएमिनेन्ट *(adjective)* – सर्वश्रेष्ठ

We were honoured to have a pre-eminent scholar amongst us.

Preen/प्रीन *(verb)* – आत्म सन्तुष्ट, पक्षी का पंख सँवारना

The birds were preening themselves in the sun.

Preface/प्रेफेस् *(noun)* – भूमिका, प्रस्तावना, आमुख

The preface explains how to use a dictionary.

Prefect/प्रिफेक्ट *(noun)* – छात्रों पर शासक छात्र, शासनाधिकारी

Right from primary school, I dreamt of being a prefect when I reached High School.

Prefer/प्रिफर *(verb)* – दूसरो से ज्यादा महत्त्व देना

I prefer gravy over a dry curry.

Preference/प्रिफरेंस *(noun)* – मनपसन्द, अधिक मान, कृपा दृष्टि

She has a greater preference for literature.

Preferential/प्रिफरेंसिअल *(adjective)* – प्राथमिता प्राप्त, अधिक मान

The employer was given an earful by the Chief for giving preferential treatment to his secretary.

Prefix/प्रिफिक्स *(noun)* – उपसर्ग, किसी शब्द के पूर्व जोड़ा जाने वाला

A numerical prefix implies how many places to rotate the text. I thought it agreeable to prefix your name before them in both English and Latin.

Pregnant/प्रेग्नेन्ट् *(adjective)* – गर्भवती

I gave the pregnant woman my seat as she looked very tired.

Prehistoric/प्रिहिस्टॉरिक *(adj)* – प्रागैतिहासिक

I wanted to sell of my mother's prehistoric cooker which she held on to for so long.

Prejudice/प्रेजुडिस *(noun)* – पूर्वाग्रह

Her unjust prejudice towards children with better marks was leading to a rebellious attitude developing among other children.

Preliminary/प्रिलिमिनरी *(adjective)* – प्रारम्भिक

Preliminary talks began yesterday.

Prelude/प्रिल्यूड *(noun)* – पूर्वाभास, पूर्वमंचन, पूर्वरंग

Training is a necessary prelude to employment.

Premature/प्रिमैच्यूर *(adjective)* – अवयस्क, अपूर्ण, अधूरा

A 24-year old man was suffering from premature balding.

Premeditated/प्रिमेडिटेटेड *(verb)* – पूर्वनिर्धारित

The murder was definitely premeditated.

P

Premiere/प्रॅम्येअर् *(noun)* – प्रथम प्रदर्थन

The premiere of the film was a gala event attended by the who's-who of the industry. He is organizing a special premiere of our movie specially for me.

Premise/प्रेमिस *(noun)* – तर्क सम्मत विचार

The judgment was based on the premise that men and women share equal space in society.

Premises/प्रेमिसेस *(plural noun)* – भवन, अहाता

Smoking is not allowed within the office premises.

Premium/प्रीमिअम् *(noun)* – किस्त

This month my account balance is low as I had to fill in a premium of an insurance I had applied for last year.

Premonition/प्रीमॉनिशन् *(noun)* – पूर्वाभास

I had a strong premonition that one of us would die.

Preoccupation/प्रीऑक्युपेशन् *(noun)* – कर्मरत

Post retirement men ought to find some or the other preoccupation to keep their mind busy.

Preoccupy/प्रीऑक्युपाइ *(verb)* – पूर्व से ही कर्मबद्ध

I had asked my son to study but he was preoccupied with something else.

Preparation/प्रिपेरेशन *(noun)* – तैयारी

P

Behind any successful event lies several months of preparation.

Preparatory/प्रिपेरेटरि *(adjective)* – आरम्भिक, शुरुआती

Now she has turned four, her parents wanted to send her to preparatory school.

Prepare/प्रिपेअर *(verb)* – बनाना, तैयार करना

What are you preparing for dinner tonight?

Prepay/प्रिपे *(verb)* – पूर्व भुगतान

I applied for a prepaid connection for my mobile phone.

Preposition/प्रिपोजिशन *(noun)* – कारक

We were being given a class on how to use prepositions effectively in essays.

Preposterous/प्रिपॉस्टरस *(adjective)* – तर्कहीन, मूर्खतापूर्ण

The idea she gave was more preposterous than obnoxious.

Prerequisite/प्रिरिक्विजिट *(adj)* – आवश्यक आधार

Competence is prerequisite to promotion. Crossing the age bar of 18 years is a prerequisite to vote.

Prerogative/प्रिरॅगेटिव *(noun)* – विशेषाधिकार

It was the prinicipal's prerogative to suspend a student.

Prescribe/प्रिस्क्राइब *(verb)* – नियत करना

The doctor prescribed antibiotics for her lung infection.

Prescription/प्रिस्क्रिप्शन *(noun)* – डॉक्टर का लिखा दवा का पर्चा

She took the doctor's prescription to another doctor to seek a second opinion.

Presence/प्रेजेन्स *(noun)* – उपस्थिति

Her presence was missed greatly during the family get-togethers.

Present/प्रेजेन्ट *(noun)* – वर्तमान, उपहार, विद्यामान

I thought it bad etiquette to arrive at the party without a present for the host.

Presentable/प्रेजेन्टेबल् *(adjective)* – प्रस्तुत होने, करने योग्य

I asked Ram if I was looking presentable enough for the party.

Presentation/प्रेजेन्टेशन *(noun)* – समपर्ण, मंचन, प्रस्तुति

The presentation was grand but the content was poor.

Presently/प्रेजेन्टलि *(adjective)* – अभी, कुछ देर में

The management are presently discussing the matter.

Preservation/प्रिजर्वेशन *(noun)* – रक्षा, सुरक्षा, संरक्षित

Our school taught us the importance of preservation of natural resources.

Preside/प्रिजाइड *(verb)* – अध्यक्षता करना, सभापतित्व करना, संचालन करना

The Prime Minister presided over the meeting.

Presidency/प्रेसिडेंसी *(noun)* – अध्यक्षीय, राष्ट्रपतित्व

Things were peaceful during the Eisenhower presidency.

President/प्रेसिडेंट *(noun)* - राष्ट्रपति, अध्यक्ष, सभापति, संचालक

The President likes to go for a jog every morning.

Press/प्रेस *(verb)* - समाचार संस्था, मुद्रक, दबाना

This is a pressing problem.

Pressure/प्रेसर *(noun)* - दबाव

The pressure of his fingers had relaxed.

Pressurize/प्रेसराइज *(verb)* - दबाव का प्रयोग करना

The airplane cabin is pressurized.

Prestige/प्रेस्टिज *(noun)* - प्रतिष्ठा

His work gained him international prestige.

Prestigious/प्रेस्टिजिअस *(adjective)* - लब्ध प्रतिष्ठ

He was given a prestigious award by the Prime Minister last year.

Presumably/प्रिज्यूमेब्लि *(adverb)* - अनुमानतः

Presumably, the culprit was one of the millions that died in the blast.

Presume/प्रिज्यूम *(verb)* - अनुमान करना, मानकर चलना

I presume that you would have done some preliminary research before taking on the project.

Presumption/प्रिजम्पशन *(noun)* - परिकल्पना, अवधारणा, अनुमान

He prepared a rough analysis after going through the various presumptions.

Presumptuous/प्रिजम्प्ट्युअस *(adjective)* -निर्भीक, आत्मविश्वास से पूर्ण

Your presumptuous behavior is not going too well with your friends, I can see.

Presuppose/प्रिसपोज *(verb)* - पूर्व अवधारणा, अनुमान

All your arguments presuppose that he is a rational man.

Pretence/प्रिटेंस *(noun)* - बहाना, ढोंग

He betrayed him under the pretence of friendship.

Pretend/प्रिटेंड *(verb)* - स्वाँग भरना, बहाना बनाना, ढोंग करना

I cannot pretend to say that you are wrong.

Pretension/प्रिटेंसन *(noun)* - बहानेबाजी, मिथ्या अभिमान

One of the few designers who doesn't have the pretensions to be an artist.

Pretentious/प्रिटेंसस *(adj)* - अभिमान से भरा

He talked a lot of pretentious twaddle about modern art.

Pretext/प्रिटेक्स्ट *(noun)* - बहाना

He excused himself on the pretext of a stomachache.

Pretty/प्रिटी *(adjective)* - सुन्दर, मनोरम, आकर्षक, अत्यधिक

She is a charming and pretty girl.

Prevail/प्रिवेल *(verb)* - हावी होना

We hoped that common sense would prevail.

Prevalent/प्रेवलेन्ट् *(adjective)* - प्रचलित

Smoking is becoming increasingly prevalent among younger women.

Prevent/प्रिवेंट *(verb)* - रोकना

The state took several steps to prevent the strike.

Preventable/प्रिवेंटेबल *(adjective)* - निवारण योग्य

It is sad that preventable diseases kill half of our population.

Prevention/प्रिवेंशन *(noun)* - रोकथाम, निवारण

Prevention is better than cure.

Preventive/प्रिवेंटिव *(adjective)* - रोकने वाला

They accused the police of failing to take enough preventive measures.

Preview/प्रिव्यू *(noun)* - पूर्व दर्शन, पूर्व समीक्षा

They were releasing previews of the forthcoming movie before show in the movie hall.

Previous/प्रिवियस *(adjective)* - पूर्वता, पूर्ववर्ती, पिछला

She had two children from a previous marriage.

Prey/प्रे *(noun)* - शिकार, शिकार करना

The muggers recognized their prey.

Price/प्राइस *(noun)* - मूल्य, दाम

Rice is sold at a lower price in the kirana store near my house.

Prick/प्रिक *(verb)* – चुभाना

She gave a prick and the ball burst.

Prickle/प्रिकल *(noun)* – काँटा

A hedgehog is covered with prickles.

Prickly/प्रिकलि *(adjective)* – काँटेदार

I had a prickly sensation in my foot.

Pride/प्राइड *(noun)* – अभिमान, गर्व, अहंकार, अहं

She felt a sense of pride rising in her when she saw her project report.

Priest/प्रिस्ट *(noun)* – पुरोहित, पुजारी

He became a priest after dropping out of school.

Prim/प्रिम *(adjective)* – अतिव्यावहारिक

The new teacher was prim and proper in her attire.

Primafacie/प्राइमाफेसी *(adj & adv)* – प्रथम दृष्टि में

Primafacie evidence showed the culprit trying to flee from the scene of crime.

Primary/प्राइमरी *(adjective)* – प्रारम्भिक, मूलभूत

Your health is primary to dieting.

Prime/प्राइम *(adjective)* – मूलभूत, महत्त्वपूर्ण, उत्कृष्ट

Political stability was of prime concern.

P

Primer/प्राइमर *(noun)* – प्रथम, रंगने के पूर्व का रंग

I put a coating of primer on the walls before applying the paint.

Primitive/प्रिमिटिव *(adjective)* – आदिम

All credits go to primitive man for discovering fire, for all the technological development that followed.

Primrose/प्रिमरोज *(noun)* – पीले रंग का एक जंगली फूल

She had primroses in her garden, in full bloom.

Prince/प्रिंस *(noun)* – राजकुमार

The kingdom rejoiced as the prince was born.

Principal/प्रिंसिपल *(adjective)* – प्रधान, प्रमुख, प्राचार्य, प्रधानाचाय

Their principal concern is of winning the election. Nowadays they have even introduced a loan on the principal amount.

Principle/प्रिंसिपल *(noun)* – सिद्धान्त

He is known for being a man of principle.

Print/प्रिंट *(verb)* – मुद्रण, मुद्रित

This news should not be printed.

Prior/प्रायर *(adjective)* – पहले का, पहले से

The promotion came prior to his taking on the project. Prior to joining the new job and marriage, he had been convicted and had spent a few years in jail.

Priority/प्रायरिटी *(noun)* – प्रमुखता

She gave priority to her home over her job.

Prison/प्रिजन *(noun)* – कारागार

She was born in a prison. He was imprisoned for his crime.

Prisoner/प्रिजनर *(noun)* – बन्दी

The princess was kept prisoner in a tower far far away.

Pristine/प्रिस्टाइन *(adjective)* – मूल दशा में

At the hill station, we saw nature in its pristine glory.

Privacy/प्राइवैसि *(noun)* – एकान्त, एकान्तता, हस्तक्षेप विहीन

The employer instructed the secretary not to disturb him as he wanted some privacy for the next few hours.

Private/प्राइवेट *(adjective)* – निजी, व्यक्तिगत, गुप्त

The actor was known for being a very private person.

Privatize/प्राइवेटाइज *(verb)* – निजीकरण

Several public sector organizations are being privatized these days.

Privilege/प्रिविलेज् *(noun)* – विशेष सुविधा

Shareholders have several privileges in the company.

Privy/प्रिवि *(adjective)* – गोपनीय

His wife was privy to his official confidential information.

Prize/प्राइज *(noun)* – पुरस्कार

The winners were awarded a prize of Rs 2000.

Pro/प्रो *(preposition)* – वास्ते, नियमित

Those who were against and pro the motion were grouped separately.

Probability/प्रॉबबिलिटि *(noun)* – सम्भावना

There is a probability she may take voluntary retirement from her service.

Probable/प्रोबेबल *(adjective)* – सम्भावित, अपेक्षित

War seemed probable in 1938. Chances of her promotion are highly probable.

Probation/प्रोबेशन *(noun)* – परिवीक्षा

He was kept under probation until his crime was proved.

Probationary/प्रोबेशनरी *(adjective)* – परिवीक्षा में शामिल

She joined the bank as a probationary officer.

Probe/प्रोब *(noun)* – जाँच, खोज, अन्वेषण

The probe helped to bring out the shrapnel stuck deep in his shoulder.

Problem/प्रॉब्लम *(noun)* – समस्या

We need an urgent solution for the problem at hand.

Procedure/प्रॅसीड्योर *(noun)* – औपचारिक प्रक्रिया

Stick to the procedure and you will surely arrive at the solution.

Proceed/प्रोसीड् *(verb)* – जारी रखना, बढ़ना, आगे बढ़ना

Please proceed with your work without a break.

Proceedings/प्रोसीडिंग् *(plural noun)* – कानूनी कारवाई

The monkey perched up on the tree watched the fishermen below and their proceedings.

Proceeds/प्रोसिड्स *(plural noun)* – राशि, लाभ, आय

The proceeds of the show will go to charity.

Process/प्रॉसेस *(verb)* – प्रणाली, प्रक्रिया

Leaves and plants follow the process of photosynthesis to breathe and live.

Procession/प्रॅसेशन *(noun)* – जुलूस, जुलूस निकालना

Processions should be forbidden during peak traffic hours.

Proclaim/प्रक्लेम *(verb)* – पोषण करना

He was proclaimed king.

Procrastinate/प्रोक्रैस्टिनेट *(verb)* – टाल-मटोल

You should stop procrastinating and start acting.

Procure/प्रक्योर् *(verb)* – प्राप्त करना

The minister asked the pimp to procure a woman for him the following night.

Procurement/प्रक्योरमेन्ट् *(noun)* – प्राप्ति, सरकारी खरीद

He was waiting for his procurement to arrive.

Prod/प्रॉड *(verb)* – कोंचना, छेड़ना

Her ceaseless prodding got on his nerves.

Prodigal/प्रॉडिगल *(adjective)* – व्ययी

His prodigal habits will lead him to his own doom.

Prodigious/प्रॅडिजॅस *(adj)* – अनोखा, विशाल

He seemed to have a prodigious amount of energy.

Prodigy/प्रॅडिजी *(noun)* – विलक्षण प्रतिभा

The child was growing into a prodigy.

Produce/प्रोड्यूस *(verb)* – उत्पन्न करना, पैदा करना, उत्पादन करना

The yield produced a huge profit this year.

Producer/प्रोड्सर *(noun)* – उत्पादक, निर्माता

They are producers of high quality wine.

Product/प्रोड्क्ट *(noun)* – पैदावार, उपज, उत्पादन

Try to get the best products at the lowest price.

Production/प्रोड्क्शन *(noun)* – पैदावार, उपज, उत्पादन

Production and manufacture at the factory had reduced by at least three times ever since the company went bankrupt.

Productive/प्रोड्क्टिव *(adjective)* – उपज देने वाला, लाभकारी, परिणाम देने वाला

The crop has been highly productive ever since we started using the new fertilizers.

Productivity/प्रोड्क्टिविटि *(noun)* – उपजाऊपन, उत्पादकता, उत्पादनशक्ति

Productivity had increased five times this year.

P

Profane/प्रोफेन *(adjective)* – विधर्मी, सांसारिक काम में रमा

I encouraged her to listen to more sacred and profane music.

Profess/प्रोफेस *(verb)* – दावा करना, घोषित करना

She professes peace but her actions prove otherwise.

Profession/प्रोफेशन *(noun)* – जीविका, पेशा, व्यवसाय

She has taken up stitching for a profession.

Professional/प्रोफेशनल *(adjective)* – व्यासायिक

The event was attended by several professionals such as doctors, engineers, lawyers, and the like.

Professor/प्रोफेसर *(noun)* – आचार्य

She works as a professor of English literature at the university now.

Proficient/प्रॅफिशॅन्ट *(adjective)* – कुशल, दक्ष, प्रवीण, निपुण

She is proficient in Spanish language.

Proficiency/प्रॅफिशॅन्सि *(noun)* – कुशलता, दक्षता, प्रवीणता, निपुणता

She has established her proficiency in the language.

P

Profile/प्रोफाइल *(noun)* – पार्श्व का दृश्य, रूपरेखा, वर्णन

She asked the photographer to click a side profile.

Profit/प्रॉफिट *(noun)* – लाभ, फायदा, लाभ पाना

The company had made a profit of US$ 200,000000 this year.

Profitable/प्रॉफिटेबल *(adjective)* – लाभप्रद, लाभदायक

Drug manufacturing the most profitable business in the US.

Profound/प्रोफाउन्ड *(adjective)* – गहरा, गम्भीर

The book was indeed profound.

Profundity/प्रोफन्डिटी *(noun)* – गहराई, गम्भीता

The profundity of this book had baffled.

Profuse/प्रोफ्यूज *(adjective)* – प्रचुर, अत्यधिक

He was bleeding profusely by the time the doctor arrived.

Profusion/प्रोफ्यूजन *(noun)* – प्रचुरता, अधिकता

We came across a delightful river with a profusion of flowers growing along its banks.

Progeny/प्रॉजिनि *(noun)*– बच्चे, संतान

They set aside funds for the welfare of their progeny.

Programme/प्रोग्रैम् *(noun)* – कार्यक्रम, योजना, कर्म में उत्प्रेरित

He was admitted to a new programme at the university.

Progress/प्रोग्रेस *(noun)* – प्रगति, विकास, उन्नति

The road was too rough to make any progress in the car.

Progression/प्रोग्रेसन *(noun)* – क्रम, शृंखला, विकास क्रम में

Both the drugs slow the progression of the virus.

Progressive/प्रोग्रेसिव *(adjective)* – प्रगतिशील, विकासमान

He has been experiencing a progressive decline in popularity in the last few months.

Prohibit/प्रोहिबिट *(verb)* – प्रतिबन्ध लगाना, निषेध करना

She was prohibited from leaving the country till a judgement was passed.

Prohibitive/प्रोहिबिटिव *(adjective)* – निषेधात्मक, प्रतिबन्धकारी

Prohibitive regulations were set up for the welfare of the animals.

Project/प्रोजेक्ट *(noun)* – परियोजना, योजना, शोध कार्य

The children were working on a community clean-up project.

Projectile/प्रोजेक्टाइल *(noun)* – प्रक्षेपास्त्र

At the museum we saw an ancient enormous artillery gun used to fire a huge projectile.

Projection/प्रोजेक्शन *(noun)* – भाव स्थिति का आकलन, प्रदर्शन

The meeting involved a presentation on the company's sales projections for the next year.

Projector/प्रोजेक्टर *(noun)* – प्रक्षेपक

My colleague showed me how to use the projector for the presentation scheduled for the next day.

Proletariat/प्रोलेटरिऑट *(noun)* – श्रमजीवी वर्ग, सर्वहारा वर्ग

Karl Marx's philosophy led to a war between the bourgeoisie and the proletariat.

Proliferate/प्रॅलिफरेट *(verb)* – प्रजनन एवं वृद्धि करना

A certain section of the population fears that nuclear weapons might proliferate.

Prolific/प्रॅलिफिक *(adjective)* – उर्वर, प्रचुर मात्रा में सृजन, उत्पादन

Closer planting will give you a more prolific crop.

Prologue/प्रोलॉग *(noun)* – मंगलाचरण, प्रस्तावना, भूमिका

The prologue of the book was written in the form of a newspaper account.

Prolong/प्रोलांग *(verb)* – विस्तृत अवधि तक, समय बढ़ाना

We should not prolong the appointment with the doctor any more. The foreign military aid was prolonging the war.

Prominent/प्रॉमिनेन्ट *(adjective)* – महत्त्वपूर्ण, प्रसिद्ध, प्रमुख

We had to invite a prominent personality as a chief guest for the event.

Promiscuous/प्रोमिस्क्युअस *(adj)* – व्यभिचारी

She is promiscuous by nature.

Promise/प्रॉमिस *(verb)* – वचन, प्रतिज्ञा, वचन देना

I promise never to hurt you again.

Promote/प्रॅमोट *(verb)* – बढ़ावा देना, समर्थन देना

He wishes to promote this appeal. The boss announced that he will promote the boy in a month's time.

Promotion/प्रॅमोशन *(noun)* – प्रचार, प्रसार, पदोन्नति

The actors were present for the promotion of their movie. We need to keep an amount separately for promotions.

Prompt/प्रॉम्प्ट *(verb)* – सील, बिना बिलम्ब, प्रेरित करना, प्रोत्साहित करना, नेपथ्य से सहायता

I wonder what prompted her to reply so caustically.

Promulgate/प्रॅमल्गेट *(verb)* – लागू करना, औपचारिक घोषणा करना

The decree was promulgated across the town.

Prone/प्रोन *(adjective)* – पीड़ित होने की प्रबल सम्भावना

She has always been prone to accidents.

Prong/प्रॉन्ग *(noun)* – कांटा, शूल

I think she will need to use prongs here.

Pronoun/प्रोनाउन *(noun)*– सर्वनाम

Translate this sentence and underline any pronouns it might contain.

Pronounce/प्रोनाउन्स *(verb)* – उच्चारण करना, घोषणा करना

The kid can now pronounce some basic words. How do you pronounce your surname.

Pronunciation/प्रनन्सिएशन *(noun)* – उच्चारण, उच्चारण शैली

She is good at writing but her pronunciation is really bad.

Proof/प्रुफ *(noun)* – प्रमाण, सुरक्षा देने वाला

I cannot believe all this without seeing any proof.

Prop/प्रॉप *(noun)* – टेक लगाना, पर्दा, पोशाक

This was supposed to be an important prop for tonight's show.

Propaganda/प्रॉपगैन्डा *(noun)* – प्रचार, दुष्प्रचार

The people opposed such shocking propaganda by the leaders.

Propogate/प्रॉपगेट *(verb)* – फैलाना प्रसारित करना, प्रजनन करना

The new species could propagate without the drug.

Propel/प्रॅपेल *(verb)* – धकेलना, धक्का, उत्प्रेरक

Be careful not to propel the decision into the opposite direction.

Propensity/प्रॅपेन्सिटि *(noun)* – कुछ करने की प्रवृति (प्राय: अनुचित)

He had a propensity for violence.

Proper/प्रॉपर *(adjective)* – उचित

He is exhibiting proper depression tendencies.

Property/प्रॉपर्टी *(noun)* – सम्पति, जायदाद, भूमि, भवन, गुण

Do not eye another's property. He owns atleast four properties across the country.

Prophecy/प्रॉफेसि *(noun)* – भविष्यवाणी
The Mayan prophesy dictates that the Earth will perish in less than a month from today.

Prophet/प्रॉफेट *(noun)* – सिद्ध, भविष्यवक्ता
They read the teachings of the Prophet every morning.

Prophetic/प्रॉफेटिक *(adjective)* – भविष्य सूचक
Sometimes she seems so prophetic.

Propitiate/प्रॅपिशिएट *(verb)* – क्रोध शान्त करना, मना लेना
The tribes believed their dance would propitiate their gods.

Proponent/प्रॅपोनेन्ट *(noun)* – जन्मदाता विचारक, समर्थक विचारक
He is the proponent of this principle.

Proportion/प्रॅपोर्शन *(noun)* – मात्रा में, मात्रा, अनुपात, आकार
Take only in proportion to what others should take. A large proportion of the earth's surface is coverred by Sea.

Proportional/प्रॅपोर्शनल *(adjective)* – समुचित अनुपात में
Keep the weights on one side, proportional to the weight of goods required.

P

Proportionate/प्रपोर्शनेट *(adjective)* – समानुपाती
If the bricks are placed proportionate to the height, they will hold on for a longer period of time.

Proposal/प्रॅपोज़ॅल *(noun)* – प्रस्ताव
There have been many proposals for this construction site in the past few months.

Propose/प्रपोज *(noun* – प्रस्ताव रखना
I propose we meet after you complete your exams.

Proposition/प्रॉपॅजिशन *(noun)* – सुझाव, अर्थ
This proposition needs to be proved using the right formula.

Propound/प्रॅपाउण्ड *(verb)* – सिद्धन्त प्रस्तुत करना
He wishes to propound a new plan of action.

Proprietor/प्रोप्राइटर *(noun)* – स्वामी, मालिक, व्यवस्थापक
I wish to have a meeting with the proprietor.

Propriety/प्रोप्राइटी *(noun)* – औचित्य, मर्यादा
She believes in maintaining propriety

Propulson/प्रोपल्सन *(noun)* – उत्तेजक बल, प्रणोदित बल
The right amount of propulsion will help the rocket take off into the sky.

Prosaic/प्रोजेइक *(adjective)* – गद्यात्मक
That poet had a prosaic style of writing.

Prose/प्रोज *(noun)* – गद्य
He loved speaking in prose.

Prosecute/प्रॉसिक्यूट *(verb)* – अभियोग चलाना, कानूनी कारवाई
Trespassers will be legally prosecuted.

Prosecution/प्रॉसिक्यूशन *(noun)* – अभियोग, अभियोग की प्रक्रिया
Your prosecution shows selfish motives.

Prospect/प्रॉस्पेक्ट *(noun)* – प्राप्ति की सम्भावना, प्रत्याशी
What are her prospects at winning tournament.

Prospective/प्रॉस्पेक्टिव *(adj)* – भावी, सम्भावित
He looks like a prospective son-in-law.

Prospectus/प्रॉस्पेक्टस *(noun)*– विवरणिका, सूचना
The application form will be provided along with the college prospectus.

Prosper/प्रॉस्पर *(verb)* – समृद्धि, समृद्धि प्राप्त करना, फलना-फूलना
I want you to prosper beyond anyone's imagination.

Prosperity/प्रॉस्परिटि *(noun)* – समृद्धि, वैभव
Wishing you prosperity and happiness as you embark upon the journey.

Prosperous/प्रॉस्परस *(adjective)* – समृद्धि की ओर अग्रसर
It is a joy to see him become so prosperous today.

Protagonist/प्रॅटैगॉनिस्ट् *(noun)* – नायक, मुख्य पात्र
You can never guess who the actual protagonist turns out to be.

Protect/प्रॅटेक्ट *(verb)* – सुरक्षा देना, रक्षा करना
Wear woollens to protect yourself from the harsh winds.

Protection/प्रॅटेक्शन *(noun)* – रक्षा, सुरक्षा
She left me under their protection.

Protective/प्रॅटेक्टिव *(adjective)* – सुरक्षा देने वाला
I feel very protective of her.

Protector/प्रॅटेक्टर *(noun)* – रक्षा देने वाला व्यक्ति
I have always seen my father as my protector.

Protein/प्रोटीन *(noun)* – वसा, एक पौष्टिक तत्व
You should include less proteins and more carbohydrate in your diet for the next few months.

Protest/प्रोटेस्ट *(noun)* – विरोध, प्रतिवाद करना, असहमति जताना
The streets are filled with people who want to protest against the new law.

Protestant/प्रॅटेस्टॅन्ट *(noun)* – ईसाई धर्म का एक विभाजन
The protestant Christians of this town have always been a tolerant group.

Protocol/प्रोटॅकॉल *(noun)* – व्यवस्था नियम, नियम की व्यवस्था
I cannot breach the protocol followed in such situations.

Prototype/प्रोटॅटाइप *(noun)* – आदिम रूप का नमूना
Bacteria is considered to be a prototype to all animal forms.

Protracted/प्रोट्रैक्टेड *(adjective)* – दीर्घकालिक
They just ended a much protracted divorce.

Protrude/प्रॅट्रूड *(verb)* – बाहर निकला हुआ
The broken long protruded out of the top floor window.

Proud/प्राउड *(adjective)* – घमण्डी, गौरवान्वित
He made us all proud of him today.

Prove/प्रूव *(verb)* – प्रमाधा, प्रमाणित करना
I will believe only if you can prove this.

Proven/प्रूवन *(verb & adjective)* – प्रमाणित, सिद्ध, जाँच द्वारा परखा हुआ
He will be treated as a convict until proven otherwise.

Proverb/प्रॉवर्ब *(noun)*– कहावत, लोकोक्ति
"Making hay while the sun shines" is a very popular proverb.

Proverbial/प्रॉवर्बिअल *(adjective)* – कहावत की बात, लोकयुक्ति के आधार पर
This feels like the proverbial catch-22 situation.

Provide/प्रॅवाइड *(verb)* – उपलब्ध करना
Please provide me with the raw materials.

Provided/प्रवाडेड *(conjunction)* – यदि, इस शर्त पर
She agreed to go and work abrouad provided (that) her family could go with her.

Providence/प्रॉविडेंस *(noun)* – विधाता का विधान, ईश्वरीय नियम
I certainly believe providence to be the reason for his success.

Provident/प्रॉविडेंट *(adjective)* – भविष्य के प्रति जागरूक
He prefers to invest in provident funds.

Providential/प्रॉविडेंसियल *(adjective)* – सौभाग्य-पूर्ण
Your appearing in the morning seems to be providential.

Province/प्रॉविंस *(noun)* – प्रदेश, प्रान्त
I do not recognize which province he belongs to.

Provincial/प्रॉविंसियल *(adjective)*– प्रादेशिक, प्रान्तीय, प्रदेशीय
This battalion belongs to the provincial army.

Provision/प्रॉविजन *(noun)* – उपलब्ध कराने की क्षमता
Please make the necessary provisions for their stay.

Provisional/प्रॉविजनल *(adjective)* – अस्थायी, कामचलाऊ
This is just a provisional certificate and you will get the final document soon.

Proviso/प्रॅवाइजॅ *(noun)* – शर्त, प्रतिबन्ध, प्रतिबन्ध के शर्त
This has been clearly mentioned in the proviso, I sent in the morning.

Provocation/प्रॉवॅकेशन *(noun)* – उत्तेजित करने की क्रिया, छोड़-छाड़
You should never hit children, even under extreme provocation.

Provocative/प्रॉवॅकेटिव *(adjective)* - उत्तेजक

Everyone avoids the provocative neighbour on the street.

Provoke/प्रॅवोक *(verb)* - उकसाना

Do not provoke unnecessarily or the dog will bite you.

Prow/प्राउ *(noun)* - मथनी

The prow was the last bit to be seen slowly drowning into the waters.

Prowess/प्राउएस् *(noun)* - पराक्रम, योग्यता

He not only plays the piano, but his prowess is also in writing stories.

Proximity/प्रॉक्सिमिटी *(noun)* - समीपता, निकटता

The rumbling sound assured us that the vehicle was in our proximity.

Proxy/प्रॉक्सि *(noun)* - प्रतिनिधित्व, दूसरे का मुख बनना

John would like to give proxy for his father William.

Prude/प्रूड *(noun)* - अतिपाखण्डपूर्ण, विनीत स्त्री, कपटी

She is a prude.

Prudent/प्रुडेन्ट *(adjective)* - विवेकपूर्ण

He is a prudent and miserly fellow.

P

Prune/प्रून *(noun & verb)* - सूखा आलू-बुखारा, पौधे काँटना

She stared at the giant prunes strewn all over the backyard.

Pry/प्राइ *(verb)* - हस्तक्षेप, ताक-झाँक, खोलना, विलगाना

I do not intend to pry, but if ever you need anything please let me know.

Psalm/साम् *(noun)* - भजन, कीर्तन, स्तोत्र-पाठ

We have to memorize five psalms for the function on Sunday.

Pseudo/स्यूडॅ *(pref.)* - छद्म, नकली

I fired him as he was a pseudo at work. I will not stand to tolerate any pseudo workers at my firm.

Pseudonym/स्यूडॅनिम *(noun)* - छद्मनाम, उपनाम

Many letters are sent to the editors under pseudonyms.

Psych/साइक् *(verb)* - आत्मविश्वास कम कर देना

His confidence sometimes looks like a plan to psych the opponent before the duel.

Psyche/साइकि *(noun)* - मानस, चित्र

Tom loves to study the psyche of his fellow team mates.

Psychiatry/साइकाइअट्रि *(noun)* - मनोरोग अध्ययन और चिकित्सा

Psychiatry is a never ending study.

Psychiatrist/साइकिअट्रिस्ट *(noun)* - मनोरोग चिकित्सक

Please show her to a good psychiatrist soon.

Psychic/साइकिक *(adjective)* - पारलौकिक

Ever since she has been meditating, she has become increasingly psychic.

Psychoanalysis/साइकोएनालिसिस *(noun)* - मनोविश्लेषण

The company policies call for a psychoanalysis of each new recruit.

Psychology/साइकोलॉजी *(noun)* - मनोविज्ञान

A parent always understands the psychology of the child.

Psychopath/साइकोपैथ *(noun)* - मनोचिकित्सा शास्त्र

The police declared the man a psychopath and warned his friends to be careful around him.

Psychatherapy/साइकोथिरैपी *(noun)* - मनोचिकित्सा

She has trained in psychotherapy treatment under the guidance of this professor.

Pub/पब *(noun)* - शराब खाना

He often heads to the nearest pub after work.

Puberty/प्यूबर्टि *(noun)* - यौवन का आरम्भ (स्त्रियों में)

Most of the female chimpanzees seem to have crossed their puberty years.

Public/पब्लिक *(adjective)* - जनता

This is her first public performance in two years.

Publication/पब्लिकेशन *(noun)* - प्रकाशन

Which publication house have you approached?

Publicity/पब्लिसिटी *(noun)* – प्रचार

There has been a lot of publicity for this film.

Publicize/पब्लिसाइज *(verb)* – प्रचार करना

Be careful not to publicize the issue any further.

Publish/पब्लिश *(verb)* – प्रकाशित करना

How many copies have been published so far?

Pucker/पकर *(verb)* – सिकन पड़ना, सिकन डालना

The child puckered under his mother's angry eyes.

Pudding/पुडिंग *(noun)* – खीर

My favourite dessert is chocolate pudding.

Puddle/पड्ल *(noun)* – जलजमाव

The children loved sailing their paper boats in the puddle.

Puff/पफ् *(noun)* – धुएँ या भाप की फूँक, कश लेना

The man huffed and puffed as he walked up the alley.

Puffin/पफिन *(noun)* – एक पक्षी

My friend sent me this photograph of a beautiful puffin stuttering around in their yard.

Puke/प्यूक *(verb & noun)* – उल्टी करना

This stench makes me want to puke.

Pull/पुल *(verb)* – खींचना, घसीटना

Try pulling the door knob towards you.

Pulley/पुलि *(noun)* – घिरनी

I can haul this rock to the upper landing with the pulley.

Pulp/पल्प *(noun)* – गूदा, निकृष्ट साहित्य

The pulp is kept out in the sun to harden up.

Pulpit/पुल्पिट *(noun)* – चर्च का मंच

The churchgoers waited patiently for the Bishop to step on to the pulpit.

Pulsate/पल्सेट *(verb)* – फैलना-सिकुड़ना, धड़कना

The doctor exclaimed that the body still pulsated feebly.

Pulse/पल्स *(noun)* – नाड़ी, धड़कन, दाल

Pulses are a rich source of proteins in our diet.

Pulverize/पल्वराइज *(verb)* – चूर करना, पीस देना

The aliens pulverised the entire building into a huge heap of rubble.

Pump/पम्प *(noun)* – निकालने-भरने का यन्त्र, एक प्रकार का जूता

He refused to come jogging with us as he couldn't find his pumps.

Pumpkin/पम्पकिन *(noun)* – कद्दू

We have a pumpkin farm in the backyard.

Pun/पन *(noun)* – श्लेष, द्वै-अर्थक

He loves to include pun in his speech.

Punch/पंच *(verb)*– घूँसा मारना, छेद करना

He punched the air when he heard the good news.

Punctual/पंक्चुअल *(adjective)* – नियत समय पर

She believes in being punctual to the last second.

Punctuate/पंकचुएट *(verb)* – विरामचिह्न लगाना

His rhythmic snoring seemed to punctuate the silence of the night.

Punctuation/पंकचुएशन *(noun)* – विरामचिह्न

I wish you re-write this sentence by changing the punctuation marks.

Puncture/पंक्चर *(noun)* – छिद्र करना, आत्मविश्वास तोड़ना

Where can I get my punctured tyre mended?

Pungent/पंजेण्ट *(adjective)* – तीखा, तिक्त

The kitchen had a pungent smell of rotten eggs.

Punish/पनिश *(verb)* – दण्ड देना

His father would certainly punish him today.

Punishable/पनिशेबल *(adjective)* – दण्डनीय

Littering the streets is a punishable offence.

Punishment/पनिशमेंट *(noun)* – दण्ड

He deserves the harshest punishment possible for this crime.

Punitive/प्यूनिटिव *(adjective)* – दण्ड विषयक

This is such a punitive remark from you.

Punk/पंक *(noun)* – तीव्र संगीत

My Parents loved punk during their college days.

Puny/प्यूनि *(adjective)* – दुर्बल

I am not affected by your puny threats.

Pupil/प्यूपिल *(noun)* – शिष्य, विद्यार्थी, पुतली

The teacher observed the pupil sleeping in the last row.

Puppet/पपेट *(noun)* – कठपुतली

The charlatan pretended to belong to the puppet show party.

Puppetry/पपेट्रि *(noun)* – कठपुतली का खेल करना

She is holding a workshop on traditional puppetry this Saturday.

Puppy/पपि *(noun)* – पिल्ला

The children promised to take good care of the puppy.

Purchase/परचेज *(noun & verb)* – खरीद, खरीदना, खरीदी वस्तु

The captain ordered a purchase as the wind changed course.

Pure/प्योर *(adjective)* – शुद्ध

She was dressed in pure white.

Purge/पर्ज *(verb)* – शुद्ध करना, स्वच्छ करना

I wish to purge myself of this emotional baggage.

P

Purify/प्योरिफाइ *(verb)* – शुद्ध करना, साफ करना

Camphor is considered to purify the surroundings.

Purification/प्योयरिफिकेशन *(noun)* – शोधन, शुद्धीकरण

The temple prienst demanded a purification ceremony.

Puritan/प्यूरिटन *(noun)* – नैतिकतावादी

The puritans always were a bane to the church.

Purity/प्योरिटी *(noun)* – शुद्धि

The goldsmith rubbed the ring on his stone to check for its purity.

Purl/पर्ल *(adjective)* – उल्टी सिलाई

The new sewing machine has facilities of doing the purl stitch.

Purple/पर्पल *(noun)* – बैंगनी रंग का

The sky turned a dark shade of purple in the setting sun.

Purpose/पर्पस् *(noun)* – प्रयोजन, उद्देश्य

What is the purpose of studying all night if you end up sleeping during the exam.

Purr/परर् *(verb)* – घुरघुराहट

The cat purred contentedly as she lazed around in the winter sun.

Purse/पर्स *(noun)* – बटुआ, उपलब्ध धन, होठ सिकोड़ना

The lady let out a scream as the thief ran off with her purse.

Pursue/पर्स्यू *(verb)* – पीछा करना, जारी रखना

Do not try to pursue him or you might get hurt.

Pursuit/पर्स्यूट *(noun)* – पुरुषार्थ, खोज, पाने की चेष्टा धन्धा

The police gave pursuit to the escaping convicts.

Purview/पर्व्यू *(noun)* – सीमा

What is the purview of this brand on the market?

Push/पुश् *(verb)* – ढकेलना, ठेलना, आक्रमण

Push the table back into the corner.

Pushy/पुशि *(adjective)* – महत्त्वाकांक्षी, बिल्ली

No one likes the pushy kid in her class.

Put/पुट *(verb)* – रखना

Please put the books back in the right order.

Putrefy/प्यूट्रिफाइ *(verb)* – सड़ना, सड़ाना

The abandoned flat had a putrefied odour to it.

Putty/पटि *(noun)* – धुरकिली, जोड़ने का मसाला

The architect suggested using the latest brand of putty instead of the usual brand.

Puzzle/पजल *(noun & verb)* – पहेली, चकरा देना

Do not try to puzzle me with your riddled speech.

Puzzled/पजल्ड *(adjective)* – घबड़ाया हुआ

He looked puzzled as the police asked him to show his licence.

Pygmy/पिग्मि *(noun)* – बौना

Consider yourself lucky that you were not caught by the indigenous pygmy clan in the jungle.

Pyjamas/पाइजामज *(pl noun)* – पायजामा, सलवार

Whatever I may forget, I can never forget to carry my pyjamas during any trip.

Pylon/पाइलॅन *(noun)* – ऊँचा खम्भा

The electrician needed a pylon to carry all the cables.

Pyramid/पिरामिड *(noun)* – त्रिकोणीय स्तम्भ

Who built the pyramids in Egypt is still a mystery waiting to be solved.

Pyre/पायर *(noun)* – चिता

Matt was inconsolable as he lit his father's pyre.

Python/पाइथॅन *(noun)* – अजगर

The highlight of our safari trip was a python we found lying on the side of the road.

P

Qq

Q/क्यू *(noun)* - अंग्रेजी वर्णमाला का सत्रहवाँ वर्ण the seventeenth letter of the English alphabet.

1. denoting the next after P in a set of items, categories, etc.

Q-boat/क्यू-बोट *(noun)* - व्यवसायी पोत का रूप धारण किये लड़ाकू पोत

Germany had used q-boats to chase boats and ships of allied forces.

Qua/क्वे *(conjunction)* - योग्यता से या योग्यता के रूप में

Equity holders qua members must attend the meeting called by the mompany.

Quack/क्वैक *(noun)* - कुवैद्य, बत्तख की बोली

Ducks make the sound of quack, quack!

Quackery/क्वैकरी *(noun)* - चिकित्सा का ढोंग या अभ्यास

Quackery is the cause of many deaths.

Quackish/क्वैकिश *(adjective)* - बुरे वैद्य के समान

Quackish treatment leads to medical complications.

Quadragesimal/क्वाड्राजेसिमल *(adj)* - चालीस दिन का व्रत

During lent, many Christians observe fast to repent for wrong doing they may have commiteed.

Q

Quadrangle/क्वाड्रैंगल *(noun)* - चतुर्भुज क्षेत्र

He has a quadrangle courtyard at the back of his house.

Quadrangular/क्वाड्रैंगुलर *(adjective)* - चतुष्कोण

Quadrangular teams were playing against one another in a big playground.

Quadrant/क्वाड्रैंट *(noun)* - वृत्त का चतुर्थ भाग, इस प्रकार का यन्त्र जो कोण नापने में काम आता है

A quadrant is used for measuring angles.

Quadrate/क्वाड्रेट *(noun)* - चतुर्भुज

This plot seems quadrate.

Quadrennial/क्वाड्रेनियल *(adjective)* - प्रत्येक चौथे वर्ष होने वाला

The term of my computer course is quadrennial.

Quadrilateral/क्वाड्रिलैटेरल *(noun)* - चतुर्भुज क्षेत्र

I want to buy a quadrilateral plot.

Quadrumanous/क्वाड्रुमेनस *(adjective)* - चतुर्भुजी

This figure seems quadrumanous.

Quadruple/क्वाड्रुपल *(adjective)* - चतुर्गुण

Four teams formed a quadruple alliance.

Quadruplicate/क्वाड्रुप्लिकेट *(verb)* - चतुर्गुण करना

Please quadruplicate this document.

Quag/क्वैग *(noun)* - दलदल

The animal fell in a quag.

Quagmire/क्वैगमायर *(noun)* - धँसाव

His downfall was to get trapped in the quagmire of dirty politics.

Quail/क्वेल *(noun)* - साहस छोड़ना

While in jungle, he shot some quails.

Quaint/क्वेंट *(adjective)* - पुराने ढंग का

It is a quaint little piece of art.

Quake/क्वेक *(verb)* - काँपना

His legs quaked with fear as a violent crowd confronted him.

Qualifiable/क्वालिफाइएबल *(adj)* - अनुकूल करने योग्य

Qualifiable speeds for 100 metres race have been announced.

Qualified/क्वालिफाइड *(adjective)* - योग्य

He is fully qualified for this job.

Qualifier/क्वालिफाइअर् *(noun)* - योग्य बनने या बनाने वाला

He was the sixth and the last qualifier for one-mile race.

Qualitative/क्वालिटेटिव *(adjective)* - जाति स्वभाव

The difference is qualitative and not quantitive.

Quality/क्वालिटि *(noun)* – विशेषता, गुण

Although rude, he has many qualities.

Quandary/क्वान्डेरी *(noun)* – व्याकुलता

He was in a quandary as he found no place in the hostel.

Quantitative/क्वान्टिटेटिव *(adjective)* – परिमाण सम्बन्धी

It is not the qualitative but the quantitative value of these things that counts.

Quantity/क्वांटिटी *(noun)* – परिमाण

Our success depends upon the quantity of goods that we produce.

Quarrel/क्वॅरल् *(noun)* – कलह, विवाद

He picked up a quarrel with his neighbour.

Quarry/क्वैरी *(noun)* – खदान

The mining mafia is extracting lots of minerals from illegally dug quarries.

Quart/क्वार्ट *(noun)* – चौथाई गैलन

I bought two quarts of milk.

Quarterage/क्वार्टरेज *(noun)* – भुगतान

The quarterage sum is only rupees tour thousand.

Quarterly/क्वार्टर्लि *(adjective)* – त्रैमासिक

The installments are quarterly payable.

Quartern/क्वाटर्न *(noun)* – पाइन्ट का चौथाई भाग

He drank a quarter of beer.

Quartz – *(noun)*

Quartz watches are quite popular.

Quasi/क्वेसाइ (क्वाजी) *(comb. form)* – जो जैसा लगे वैसा वस्तुत: हो न अर्थात्

Think this statement is quasi scientific.

Quaternary/क्वाटर्नरि *(adjective)* – चार भाग का

He is a quaternary officer.

Quaternion/क्वाटरनियन *(noun)* – चतुष्क

Quaternion is a theory in identities in algebra.

Quatrain/क्वाट्रेन *(noun)* – चतुष्पदी श्लोक

It is a poem in quatrain.

Quatre-foil/क्वाट्रफायल (कैटर्फ़ॅइल्) *(noun)* – इमारत में चौपतिया छिद्र

The flowers were arranged in quatre-foil.

Quaver/क्वेवर *(verb)* – काँपना

He quavered as he ran.

Quean/क्वीन *(noun)* – वेश्या, पतुरिया

She is a quean and as such not worth talking to.

Queasiness/क्वीजिनेस *(noun)* – सुकुमारता

Queasiness overwhelmed me and I threw up.

Queasy/क्वीजि *(adjective)* – रोगी होने वाला

The smell is the kitchen was queasy.

Queer/क्विअर *(adjective)* – विचित्र, झक्की

His face was a queer pink colour.

Quench/क्वेंच *(verb)* – बुझाना, दबाना

He quenched his thirst by drinking a few glasses of water.

Quenelle/क्वेनेल *(noun)* – पीसा हुआ माँस का लोंदा

Quenelle is being cooked.

Querist/क्वेरिस्ट *(noun)* – प्रश्न पूछने वाला

Here is a querist for you to answer.

Quern/क्वर्न *(noun)* – जाँता, चक्की

Querns may still be in use in villages.

Querulous/क्वेर्युलस *(adjective)* – सर्वदा शिकायत करने वाला, विलापी

She became querulous as her husband rebuked her.

Quest/क्वेस्ट *(noun)* – खोज

Quest for pyramids had begun in early twentieth century.

Questionable/क्वेस्चनेब्ल *(adjective)* – संदिग्ध अनिश्चित

Your behaviour is questionable.

Questionnaire/क्वेस्चनेअर *(noun)* – उत्तर देने के लिए प्रश्नों का समूह

Kindly fill this questionnaire, a survey is going on.

Quibble/क्विब्ल् *(noun)* – वाक्छल, वक्रोक्ति

Quibble started after his talk to the press.

Quick/क्विक *(adjective)* – सजीव, फुर्तीला

He is a quick fellow and acts immediately.

Quicken/क्विकेन *(verb)* – सचेत करना

As she approached me, my heart beat quickened.

Quick-eyed/क्विकआइड *(adj)* – तीव्र दृष्टिवाला

Crow is a quick-eyed bird.

Quicklime/क्विकलाइम *(noun)* – बिना बुझाया हुआ चुना
Quicklime is obtained from limestone.

Quickly/क्विकली *(adjective)* – झटपट
He quickly jumped into water to save her from drowning.

Quicksand/क्विकसैंड *(noun)* – कछारी बालू
He was pulled out timely from being sucked into quicksand.

Quickset/क्विकसेट *(noun)* – हरी वनस्पति
Quickset was thick and nobody could enter.

Quick-silver/क्विकसिल्वर *(noun)* – पारा
His moods change rapidly like quick-silver.

Quick-witted/क्विकविटेड *(adjective)* – हाजिर दिमाग वाला
Birbal was a quick-witted courtier of Akbar.

Quid/क्विड *(noun)* – अशर्फी
He used to save one quid every day.

Quiddity/क्विडिटी *(noun)* – तत्त्व, पाखण्ड
Quiddity of a person hardly changes.

Quiscent/क्विसेंट *(adjective)* – निश्चल, स्थिर
He is quiescent these days, recovering from illness.

Quiet/क्वायट *(adjective)* – शान्ति, आनन्द
I like this quiet place.

Q

Quietus/क्वाइ-ईटस् *(noun)* – अन्तिम निर्णय
The man is dead, we have to find the quietus.

Quinate/क्विनेट *(noun)* – पंचपतिया
Easter of quinic acid is known as quinate.

Quince/क्विंस *(noun)* – शरीफा
Quince a fruit, grows on shrubs in Asia and is used for flavouring.

Quinine/क्विनाइन *(noun)* – कुनेन की दवा
Quinine used to be taken against malaria.

Quin-quennium/क्विन-क्वेनियम *(noun)* – पाँच वर्ष की अवधि
It is a quin-quennium course of computer training.

Quinsy/क्विन्सी *(noun)* – कण्ठमाला
He had pain in throat as he suffered from quinsy.

Quintal/क्विंटल *(noun)* – एक सौ किलोग्राम का वजन
He purchased a quintal of wheat grain.

Quintessential/क्विन्टेसेन्शल *(adj)* – सारयुक्त
She is a quintessential of beauty.

Quintet/क्विंटेट *(noun)* – पंचक
The band was played by a quintet.

Quintuple/क्विंट्युपल *(adj)* – पंचगुना
Ten is the quintuple of two.

Quintuplicate/क्विंट्युप्लिकेट *(verb)* – पाँच तह करना
You need to have quintuplicate. Copies of this document.

Quintuply/क्विंट्युप्लाई *(adverb)* – पंचगुने रूप में
The companie's profits quintuplied last year.

Quip/क्विप *(noun)* – ताना
A quip is usually on his lips.

Quirk/क्वर्क *(noun)* – व्यवहार में छल
A quirk of fate destroyed his career.

Quit/क्विट *(verb)* – त्यागना
He has quit smoking.

Quite/क्वाइट *(adverb)* – सर्वथा
You are quite right in saying this.

Quittable/क्विटेबल *(adj.)* – खाली करने लायक
This assignment is not quittable.

Quitter/क्विटर *(noun)* – छोड़ने वाला
He is a quitter and never stays in one job.

Quits/क्विट्स *(adjective)* – चुकती
We are quits now, there should be no longer any grudge.

Quiver/क्विवर *(noun)* – तरकस
All archers carry quivers on their back.

Quivevingly/क्विविंगली *(adverb)* – काँपते हुए
He quiveringly told us about her horror dream.

Quivive/क्विवाइव *(noun)* – सचेत
Every soldier has to be very quivive on border.

Quixotic/क्विकसॉटिक *(adjective)* – अद्भूत, विलक्षण
His quixotic behaviour amused her.

Quixotism/क्विकसॉटिज्म *(noun)* – विवेकहीन विलक्षण विचार
Sometimes his quixotism is very upsetting.

Quixotry/क्विक्सॅट्रि *(noun)* – विवेकहीन कल्पना
We are tired of his quixotry in seaching for clean hotels.

Quiz/क्विज *(noun)* – पहेली, मसखरा, झक्की आदमी
Can you solve this quiz?

Quizzically/क्विजिकली *(adv)* – ठिठोलियापन से
He answered all my questions quizzically.

Quod/क्वॉड् *(noun)* – जेल
He spent five years in quod.

Quoin/कॅइन् *(noun)* – इमारत का बाहरी कोना
Most building in the hills were made with coloured quoins.

Quoit/क्वॅइट *(noun)* – लोहे का चक्र जो निशाने पर फेंका जाता है
He won a many prizes in the game of quoit.

Quota/क्वोटा *(noun)* – अंश, भाग
There is only 30 p.c. quota fixed for the export of these goods.

Quotable/क्वोटेब्ल् *(adjective)* – उद्धरण योग्य
There are many quotable words in his speech. It is a quotable quote.

Quotation/क्वोटेशन् *(noun)* – किसी पदार्थ का प्रचलित मूल्य
Let us buy this book of famous quotations.

Quote/क्वोट *(verb)* – पहले कही या लिखी गयी बात को सही से दोहराना
He quoted Gandhiji many times in his speech.

Quotient/क्वोशन्ट *(noun)* – भजनफल, भागफल
Four divided by two has the quotient two.

Q

Rr

R/आर *(noun)* - अंग्रेजी वर्णमाला का 18वाँ वर्ण the eighteenth letter of the English alphabet.

1. denoting the next after Q in a set of items, categories, etc.

Rabbi/रैबाइ *(noun)* - यहूदियों का धर्मगुरु, यहूदी विद्वान

There was a Rabbi among the rebels who were against anti-abortion laws in Ireland.

Rabbit/रैबिट् *(noun)* - खरगोश, शशक

There were cute little rabbits running around on the farm.

Rabble/रैब्ल् *(noun)* - भीड़

A rabble of uncouth young men greeted the minister outside the court.

Rabid/रैबिड *(adjective)* - अनातंक रोग से पीड़ित, उग्र, प्रचण्ड

She is a rabid feminist, known for her scathing remarks to the ministers and politicians.

Race/रेस *(noun)* - दौड़, प्रतियोगिता, आपाथापी, घुड़दौड़

People of all races, colour and creed are welcome to our country.

Racial/रेसियल *(adjective)* - जाति, मानव प्रजाति, नस्ल, आनुवांशिक, जातिगत, जातीय

Racial minority is a one of the reasons why the Blacks are still suffering today.

Racism/रेसिज्म *(noun)* - जातिवाद

We were taught theories of racism in Sociology class today.

Rack/रैक *(noun)* - खण्डदार खुला अलमारी, तबाह होना (लापरवाही से) हल्ला

The horse's rack had everyone smiling.

Racket/रैकेट *(noun)* - अवैध ढंग से पैसा बनाने का काम

The rackets are out and the players are ready!

Radar/रडार *(noun)* - रेडियो तरंग वाला एक उपकरण

The ship was frantically sending radar messages hoping someone will respond.

Radial/रेडिअल *(adjective)* - किरणों की तरह क्रम में रखी हुई

Four mosaics having a radial arrangement were placed on a mat.

Radiant/रेडिएण्ट *(adjective)* - चमकदार, प्रकाश करने वाला

We met a radiant sage at the hermitage in the forest today.

Radiate/रेडिएट *(verb)* - चमकना, स्पष्ट अभिव्यक्ति

The stars radiate energy.

Radiation/रेडिएशन *(noun)* - विकिरण, हानिकारक तरंग बिखेरना

The boy suffering from cancer has been exposed to high level radiation.

Radical/रैडिकल *(adjective)* - आमूल, मूलभूत, आधार से

We need a radical transformation of the existing legal system.

Radio/रेडिओ *(noun)* - रेडियो

Radio stations were demanding the eviction of the RJ from the Big Brother show.

Radioactive/रेडियोएक्टिव *(adjective)* - परमाणु की हानिकारक किरणें निकलना

The water was radioactive.

Radiography/रेडियोग्राफी *(noun)* - एक्सरे द्वारा चित्र लेने की प्रक्रिया

He worked in the radiography department of the hospital.

Radish/रैडिश *(noun)* - मूली

There were radishes of all kinds in the farm.

Radium/रेडियम *(noun)* - एक प्रकार का धातु

Radium was used on clocks to make dials.

Radius/रेडियस *(noun)* - त्रिज्या की लम्बाई, गोलाकार क्षेत्र

The radius of a circle is half its circumference.

Raffle/रैफल *(noun)* – कुछ बेंच कर सद्कार्य हेतु धन एकत्रित करना

I bought a raffle ticket at the mall.

Raft/रैफ्ट *(noun)* – लकड़ी का बेड़ा, रबड़ की हवा भरी नाव

Pi was stranded on a raft in the middle of the sea for 200 days.

Rafter/रैफ्टर *(noun)* – शहतीर

The rafters above the bed were falling off.

Rag/रैग *(noun)* – पुराना कपड़ा, चिथड़ा, लत्ता, मजाक से तंग करना

I wiped my hands on a rag after cleaning the walls.

Rage/रेज *(noun)* – अतिशय क्रोध

He was trembling with rage.

Ragged/रैगड् *(adjective)* – फटा-पुराना वस्त्र, कटा-पिटा

The tramp wore ragged clothes on his body and a radiant smile on his face.

Raid/रेड *(noun)* – धावा

A bombing raid was carried out in the desert.

Rail/रेल *(verb)* – छड़, पटरी, गाली देना

She railed at the police inefficacy in the high profile murder case.

Railing/रेलिंग *(noun)* – घेरा

The thief jumped over the railing and escaped.

Railway/रेलवे *(noun)*– पटरी का मार्ग

The railway tracks badly needed maintenance.

Rain/रेन *(noun)* – बर्षा, बौछार

I love dancing in the rain.

Rainbow/रेनबो *(noun)* – इन्द्रधनुष

There was a beautiful rainbow visible from my window.

Rainy/रेनी *(adjective)* – बरसाती

It is going to be a rainy month now.

Raise/रेज *(verb)* – उठाना, उभारना, एकत्र करना, सम्मुख रहना, फसल उगाना, लालन-पालन करना

Raise the curtain rod a bit higher.

Raisin/रेजिन *(noun)* – किशमिश

I bought raisins for the cake.

Rake/रेक *(noun)* – पाँचा, समतल करना, उखाड़ना

He is known for being a merry Restoration rake.

Rally/रैली *(verb)* – एकत्रित होना, एकत्रित करना

I've been rallied throughout high school for my funny hair.

Ram/रैम *(noun)* – भेड़ा

There were scores of rams on the farm.

Ramble/रैम्बल *(verb)* – भ्रमण करना, बहक जाना, विषयान्तर करना

I wanted a vacation where I can ramble aimlessly among trees in the woods.

Ramification/रैमिफिकेशन् *(noun)* – जटिलता, विषमता

His angiogram showed a ramification of the right coronary artery.

Ramp/रैम्प *(noun)* – ढलान

They had built a wheelchair ramp to make the hospital disabled-friendly.

Rampage/रैम्पेज *(verb)* – रूक्षता का व्यवहार कना *(noun)* क्रोध का उन्माद

The protestors rampaged around the whole city.

Rampant/रैम्पैंट *(adjective)* – उच्छृंखला, अनियंत्रित

Corruption is rampant in our country.

Ramshackle/रैम्शैक्ल् *(adjective)* – जर्जर

I was shocked to see the ramshackle cottage, he lived in.

Ranch/रैंच *(noun)* – खेती-बाड़ी

She has been living in a ranch for several years now.

Rancid/रैंसिड *(adjective)* – बासी, खट्टा

We could smell the rancid meat from outside.

Rancour/रैंकर *(noun)* – वैमनस्य

He spoke without rancour.

Random/रैंडम *(adjective)* – क्रमहीन

It was evident from the result that she had made a random decision.

Range/रेंज *(noun)* – एक ही प्रकार की विभिन्न वस्तुएँ, सीमा क्षेत्र, मार करने की अधिकतम दूरी, अँगीठी

The cost for this house will range between Rs 25 lakh to Rs 35 lakh.

Rangefinder/रेंजफाइन्डर *(noun)* – गोली आदि का पता लगाने वाला

She bought a new fancy rangefinder to be attached to her camera.

Rank/रैंक *(adjective)* - पद-स्तर, श्रेणी, बदबूदार
There were clumps of rank grass in her garden.

Rankle/रैंकल *(verb)* - दूषित करना, निरंतर कष्ट देना
His mannerisms still rankle.

Ransack/रैन्सैक *(verb)* - खोज-बीन, तोड़-फोड़
The thieves had ransacked every house in the whole village.

Ransom/रैंसम *(noun)* - फिरौती
The kidnappers had demanded a ransom of Rs 15 lakh.

Rant/रैंट *(verb)* - प्रलाप करना
The politician was ranting about the opposition's demonstrations outside his house.

Rap/रैप *(noun)* - छोटा टुकड़ा, खटखटाहट
He doesn't care a rap.

Rapacious/रपेशस् *(adjective)* - अति लोभी
Rapacious landlords are ruling the countryside to this day.

Rape/रेप *(verb)* - बलात्कार करना
There were rape seeds in the nursery.

Rapid/रैपिड *(adjective)* - शीघ्रगामी, तेजी से बार-बार
The rapid economic decline of the country brought huge changes in its people's lifestyles.

Rapids/रैपिड्स् *(noun)* - नदी की तीव्र धारा, झरना, प्रपात, क्षिप्रिका
The raft was stuck in one of the rapids.

Rapport/रैपार्ट् *(noun)* - घनिष्टता
I share a good rapport with my colleagues and employer.

Rapt/रैप्ट *(adjective)* - तन्मय
The therapist had a rapt teenage audience at his introduction speech.

Rapture/रैप्चर *(noun)* - आनन्द-विह्वल, अत्यधिक आनंद
My daughter listened to my stories with rapture.

Rare/रेअर *(adjective)* - विरला
The bird is rarely seen during this time of the year.

Rarefied/रेअरिफायड *(adjective)* - कम वायु दबाव
Trudging uphill in rarefied air can turn out to be the most difficult task.

Raring/रेअरिंग *(adjective)* - आतुर
She was raring to go.

Rarity/रेअरिटी *(noun)* - दुर्लभता
Honesty and integrity are a rarity in people today.

Rascal/रॉस्कल *(noun)* - नटखट, बेईमान
Dennis is such a rascal!

Rash/रैश *(adjective)* - फोड़े-फुन्सी, अविवेकी, जल्दीबाज
Please refrain from making a rash assumption.

Rasher/रैशर *(noun)* - सूअर के माँस का टुकड़ा
She placed two rashers on his plate.

Rasp/रैस्प *(noun)* - मोटी रेती, किरकिराहट, कर्कश ध्वनि
She tried rubbing on the table with a rasp.

Raspberry/राज्बेरि *(noun)* - रसवरी
I bought a kilo of raspberries from the fruit market.

Rat/रैट *(noun)* - चूहा
There has been a rat menace in the colony of late.

Rate/रेट *(verb)* - मूल्य, कीमत, दर, मूल्यांकन
She berated her daughter for forgetting her values.

Rather/रैदर *(adverb)* - किसी हद तक, काफी हद तक
Would you like chocolate or would you rather stick to a sugar-free sweet?

Ratify/रैटिफाई *(verb)* - संपुष्टि करना
Both the parties have to ratify the treaty in a few days.

Rating/रेटिंग *(noun)* - श्रेणी, श्रेणी में विभाजन
The company retained its five star rating.

Ratio/रेसियों *(noun)* - अनुपात
The sex ratio in the state has dipped in favour of males.

Ration/रैशन *(noun)* - राशन
The bread ration had reduced during battle times.

Rational/रैशनल *(adjective)* – बौद्धिक

There has to be a rational explanation to your action.

Rationalism/रैशनलिज्म *(noun)* – बुद्धिवाद

Scientific rationalism has its own limitations.

Rationalise/रैशनलाइज *(verb)* – तर्कसम्मत करना

You cannot rationalize your urge to eat sweets.

Rattle/रैटल *(verb)* – खड़खड़ाहट

The tiles on the roof were rattling in the strong wind.

Ravage/रैवेज *(verb)* – उजाड़ना

The town was ravaged by the tornado.

Rave/रेव *(noun)* – प्रलाप

The raves were bending under the weight of the load.

Raven/रैवेन *(noun)* – काला कौवा

The farm had more ravens than common crows.

Ravenous/रैवेनस *(adjective)* – भुक्खड़

He had a ravenous appetite.

Ravine/रैविन *(noun)* – खड्ड

The car plunged into the deep ravine.

Ravishing/रैविशिंग *(adjective)* – मनमोहक

She was a ravishing beauty.

Ray/रे *(noun)* – किरण, एक मछली

The marine researcher died when he was bitten by a ray.

Raze/रेज *(verb)* – पूर्णत: नष्ट कर देना

Villages were razed to the ground.

Razor/रेजर *(noun)* – उस्तरा

I bought an electric razor from the shop.

Reach/रिच *(verb)* – पहुँचना

I tried to reach up to the loft to take out the suitcase.

React/रिएक्ट *(verb)* – प्रतिक्रिया दिखाना या व्यक्त करना

She reacted angrily at the news of the break up.

Reaction/रिएक्शन *(noun)* – प्रतिक्रिया

My immediate reaction was to throw something at him.

Reactor/रिएक्टर *(noun)* – प्रतिक्रिया कराने का यन्त्र

The nuclear reactor is under threat.

Read/रिड *(verb)* – पढ़ना

It is the best story she had ever read.

Reader/रिडर *(noun)* – पाठक, आचार्य

She is a voracious reader.

Readership/रिडरशीप *(noun)* – आचार्य का पद, पाठकों की संख्या

The readership of the daily had gone down.

Reading/रिडिंग *(noun)* – पढ़ने की क्रिया, वाचन, माप

It was time for reading the will.

Ready/रेडी *(adjective)* – तैयार, उपलब्ध

Get ready for the party quickly.

Real/रिअल *(noun)* – वास्तविक, यथार्थ

This is a real silk.

Realism/रिअलिज्म *(noun)* – यथार्थवाद

Try and ground yourself in realism instead of getting deluded.

Reality/रिअलिटी *(noun)* – वास्तविकता

Try and face the reality now.

Realize/रिअलाइज *(verb)* – स्वीकार करना, उगाही करना, अनुभूति करना

He realized his mistake when I pointed out.

Really/रिअलि *(adverb)* – वस्तुत:, निस्सन्देह

The pie is really good.

Realm/रेल्म *(noun)* – राज्य, क्षेत्र

He was banished from the realm.

Ream/रीम *(noun)* – 20 जिस्ते कागज की गड्डी

She bought several reams of paper for her business.

Raep/रीप *(verb)* – फल पाना, फसल काटना

We've been reaping a rich crop this year.

Reappear/रिअपिअर *(verb)* – फिर से दिखना

Where did you just reappear from?

Rear/रिअर *(noun)* – पिछला, पिछला हिस्सा, पालन-पोषण करना

I will be waiting at the rear side of the building.

Rearrange/रिअरेंज *(verb)* – क्रम परिवर्तित कर सजाना

I was in a mood to rearrange our furniture.

Reason/रिजन *(noun)* – कारण, हेतु, तर्क

She didn't give a reason for her decision.

Reasonable/रिजनेबल् *(adj)* – विवेक, विवेकपूर्ण
It is only reasonable to allow him to present his side of the argument.

Reassure/रिअश्योर् *(verb)* – आश्वासन देना, निश्चिंत करना
She gave me a reassuring smile.

Rebate/रिबेट *(noun)* – छूट
Rebates will be given in the first year alone.

Rebel/रिबेल *(noun)* – विद्रोही
She has been a rebel ever since her teenage days.

Rebellion/रिबेलिअन *(noun)* – विद्रोह
The army took the rebellion to the streets to rebel against the ruling government.

Rebound/रिबाउण्ड *(verb)* – टकरा कर लौटना
The ball hit the post and rebounded right on to his face.

Rebuff/रिबफ *(verb)* – दो टूक जवाब
She rebuffed my offer in no mean terms.

Rebuild/रिबिल्ड *(verb)* – पुनर्निमार्ण
The house will be rebuilt in the same way.

Rebuke/रिब्यूक *(verb)* – डॉट-फटकार करना
She was rebuked for sporting the wrong look at the theme party.

Recall/रिकॉल् *(verb)* – याद करना, वापस बुलाना
I do recall meeting your friends long back.

Recapitulate/रिकैपिट्यूलेट *(verb)* – मुख्य बिन्दु दोहराना
He was trying to recapitulate his arguments before stepping into the courtroom.

R

Recede/रिसिड *(verb)* – पीछे हटना, वापस लौटना
The sea had receded after the tsunami.

Receipt/रिसीद् *(noun)* – रसीद, प्राप्ति-स्वीकृति
I requested the shopkeeper to give a receipt of the commodities bought.

Receive/रिसिव *(verb)* – पाना, प्राप्त करना
She received an advance of Rs 10,000 for her project.

Receiver/रिसिवर *(noun)* – चोंगा, प्राप्तकर्ता
Did you check the receiver before mailing the courier?

Recent/रिसेंट *(adjective)* – हाल-फिलहाल का
She is the most recent employee to have joined the company.

Receptackle/रिसेप्टेकल् *(noun)* – थैला, सन्दूक
We got the food packed in the receptacle.

Reception/रिसेप्शन *(noun)* – स्वागत, स्वागत कक्ष, स्वागत समारोह
She received a warm reception at the event.

Receptive/रिसेप्टिव *(adjective)* – ग्रहणशील
My appraisal says I am quite receptive to criticism.

Recess/रिसेस *(noun)* – मध्यावकाश
The table has a recess in its base.

Recession/रिसेसन *(noun)* – मन्दी
It was IT that was least affected in the recession.

Recipe/रेसपि *(noun)* – निर्देश, नुस्खा
I learnt the typical South Indian recipe for pancakes.

Recipient/रेसिपिएण्ट *(noun)* – पाने वाला
She was the recipient of my gift.

Reciprocal/रेसिप्रोकल *(adjective)* – पारस्परिक
I was hoping for some reciprocal action from him.

Recital/रिसाइटल *(noun)* – पाठ
I bought passes for the sitar recital this weekend.

Reckless/रेक्लेस् *(adjective)* – लापरवाह
He was a reckless driver.

Reckon/रेकॅन् *(verb)* – गणना करना, समझना
Her bank balance was reckoned to be around 5 crore.

Reckoning/रेकनिंग *(noun)* – गिनती, हिसाब, गिनती में
By my reckoning, we are at least 5 miles away.

Reclaim/रिक्लेम *(verb)* – पुनः अधिकार जताना
You must reclaim your lost money.

Recline/रिक्लाइन *(verb)* – आराम के साथ (सहारा लेते हुए), बैठना या लेटना
She was reclining on her beach chair.

Recluse/रेक्लूज *(noun)* – संत, एकांतवासी
The actress became a recluse after the death of her husband.

Recognition/रिकॅग्निशन *(noun)* – पहचान, मान्यता पाना
He has been working towards a recognition from his workplace.

Recognize/रिकॉग्नाइज *(verb)* – पहचानना, मान्यता देना, स्वीकृति देना
I recognized her at the market.

Recoil/रिकॉइल् *(verb)* – लपेटा जाना, पीछे हटना
She recoiled at the memories of that accident.

Recollect/रिकलेक्ट *(verb)* – याद करना, स्मृति में लाना
I do recollect certain episodes of that drama.

Recollection/रिकलेक्शन *(noun)* – याद करने की क्रिया, अनुस्मरण
To my recollection, he has never given a reason to complain.

Recommend/रिकमेंड *(verb)* – अनुशंसा करना
She recommended me for the post.

Recompense/रिकमपेन्स *(verb)* – पुरस्कृत करना, हर्जाना देना, क्षतिपूर्ति करना
Victims should be recompensed by their culprits.

Reconcile/रेकनसाइल *(verb)* – विवाद हल करना, सामंजस्य बैठाना, मेल कराना
The two warring actors had reconciled.

Recondition/रिकन्डिशन *(verb)* – फिर से ठीक करवाना, पुनः कार्य के योग्य बनाना
The car needs to be reconditioned.

Reconnaissance/रिकॅनिसन्स *(noun)* – पता लगाना, टोह लेना
The plan was shot down while on a reconnaissance mission over enemy territory.

Reconsider/रिकन्सिडर *(verb)* – फिर से विचार करना
Would you like to reconsider your decision?

Reconstruct/रिकनस्ट्रक्ट *(verb)* – फिर से निर्मित करना
The ship was being reconstructed.

Record/रेकॅर्ड *(noun)* – अभिलेख, विवरण
They had a record of the proceedings of the court.

Recorder/रिकॉर्डर *(noun)* – रिकार्ड करने की मशीन
I bought a recorder from the market.

Recount/रिकाउन्ट *(verb)* – यादकर बताना
The police asked her to recount the sequence of events.

Recoup/रिकूप *(verb)* – क्षतिपूर्ति
The companies are trying to recoup the money they lost in the recession.

Recourse/रिकोर्स *(noun)* – अन्य स्रोत
A surgery may be the only recourse.

Recover/रिकवर *(verb)* – शान्त होना, धन या स्वास्थ्य वापस पाना
She has recovered well from her trauma.

Recovery/रिकवरी *(noun)* – पुनः प्राप्ति, वसूली, स्वास्थ्य लाभ
I phoned a recovery vehicle to come and help immediately.

Recreation/रिक्रिएशन *(noun)* – मन बहलाव, मनोरंजन
There are few options for recreation here.

Recruit/रिक्रूट *(verb)* – रंगरूट
Our toughest soldiers are recruited from the desert.

Rectangle/रेक्टैंगल *(noun)* – आयताकार
She bought me a curio that was a rectangular marble piece.

Rectify/रेक्टिफाइ *(verb)* – सुधारना, परिशोधन
Statements made now cannot be rectified later.

Rector/रेक्टर *(noun)* – पुरोहित, अध्यक्ष
He is a rector at the parish nearby.

Rectum/रेक्टम *(noun)* – मलाशय
The doctor broke the news to the patient that he had been diagnosed with rectum cancer.

Recuperate/रिक्यूपरेट *(verb)* – स्वास्थ्य लाभ
She is still recuperating from her illness.

Recur/रेकर *(verb)* – बार-बार होना
This phenomenon has been seen to be recurring in her body ever few years.

Recurrence/रेकरेंस *(noun)* – पुनरावृत्ति
The recurrence of this phenomenon can be a source of worry.

Recycle/रिसाइकल् *(verb)* – गलाकर ढालना, पुनश्चक्रण
Water recycling is a good option to follow in our future.

Red/रेड *(adjective)* – लाल
She was bright red with embarrassment as soon as she saw her boyfriend entering the show.

Redden/रेडेन *(verb)* – लाल करना, लाल होना
She was reddened and tanned after the whole week she spent at the beach.

Redeem/रिडीम् *(verb)* – गुणों की क्षतिपूर्ति
It was a disappointing competition redeemed only by the exceptional performance of the winner.

Redemption/रिडेम्पशन *(noun)* – उद्धार
The terms of redemption were not very attractive.

Red-handed/रेड-हैंडेड *(adjective)* – रंगे हाथ
We hatched a plan to catch the thief red-handed.

Redistribute/रिडिस्ट्रिब्यूट *(verb)* – पुनर्वितरण
The products were redistributed among the teammates.

Redouble/रिडबल *(verb)* – दोगुना करना
I thought it was over, but it was back redoubled!

Redress/रिड्रेस *(verb)* – सुधारना
The onus was on the government now to set policies to redress racist issues.

Reduce/रिड्यूस *(verb)* – घटाना
They reduced the workforce by 10,000.

Reduction/रिडक्शन *(noun)* – कटौती
Talks on arms reduction have resumed.

R

Redundent/रिडन्डेन्ट *(adjective)* – निष्क्रिय, अनुपयोगी, निरर्थक, पालतू
Microsoft Windows 2 is redundant.

Reed/रीड *(noun)* – सरकंडा, नई, बाँसुरी
Reeds had grown and spread all around the pond.

Reef/रीफ *(noun)* – पाल का हिस्सा, समुद्री चट्टान
The coral reef of the Australian coast is endangered.

Reek/रीक् *(verb)* – दुर्गन्ध, तीव्र दुर्गन्ध
He was reeking, so I knew where he was coming from.

Reel/रील *(noun & verb)* – चरखी, लिपटा धागा, लिपटे चलचित्र, चक्कर खाना, डगमगाकर चलना
I bought a cotton reel from the thread shop.

Refectory/रिफेक्टरी *(noun)* – भोजनालय, संस्था का भोजनालय
The monk took his bowl of gruel and made his way towards the refectory.

Refer/रेफर *(verb)* – उल्लेख, उद्धृत करना
She never referred to him again.

Referee/रेफरी *(noun)* – निर्णायक
The referee showed the red card at the player.

Reference/रेफरेंस *(noun)* – सन्दर्भ कथन, सन्दर्भ सूची
Please use the Chicago style of reference in the Bibliography.

Referendum/रेफरेन्डम *(noun)* – जनमत संग्रह
The parliament was discussing a referendum.

Refill/रिफिल *(verb)* – फिर से भरना
Could you please refill my glass?

Refine/रिफाइन *(verb)* – शुद्ध करना, शुद्धीकरण, सुधारना
Please refine the liquid twice before consuming it.

Refinement/रिफाइन्मेंट *(noun)* – शोधन, परिष्कार, परिशोधन
The model has electric windows and other refinement.

Refit/रिफिट *(verb)* – मरम्मत करना, ठीक करना
I'm taking up a contract to refit the factory equipment.

Reflect/रिफ्लेक्ट *(verb)* – परावर्तित करना
The light was reflected off the box's surface.

Reflection/रिफ्लेक्शन *(noun)* – परावर्तन, प्रतिविम्ब
The teacher showed us how reflection of light occurs.

Reflective/रिफ्लेक्टिव *(adj)* – विचारशील, परावर्तनीय
She bought some reflective clothing.

Reflex/रिफ्लेक्स *(noun)* – सहज क्रिया, सहज प्रतिक्रिया
I thought you would have basic reflexes.

Reform/रिफॉर्म *(verb)* – सुधार, सुधार लाना, परिवर्तन
We need to reform this society.

Reformation/रिफॉर्मेशन *(noun)* – सुधार की प्रक्रिया
The philosopher is responsible for the Reformation that has taken the society by surprise.

Refrain/रिफ्रेन *(verb)* - आत्मनियन्त्रण, स्थायी-टेक, स्फूर्ति लाना

Please refrain from taking a hasty decision.

Refresh/रिफ्रेश *(verb)* - तरो-ताजा करना, ताजगी लाना

The old lady brought out some lemonade to refresh the spirits of the construction workers. He refreshed his memory by going through his class notes.

Refreshing/रिफ्रेशिंग *(adjective)* - स्फूर्तिदायक, ताजगी लाने वाला

A refreshing shower helps out tremendously on a hot sweaty day.

Refreshment/रिफ्रेशमेंट *(noun)* - जलपान, अल्पाहार, ताजगी

The refreshments at the party were delicious.

Refrigerate /रेफ्रिजरेट *(verb)* - शीतल-ताजा रखना

Please refrigerate the chicken until further use.

Refrigerator/रेफ्रिजरेटर *(noun)* - शीत-यन्त्र

Cold meat straight from the refrigerator should not be put into a hot pan.

Refuge/रिफ्यूज *(noun)* - सुरक्षित स्थान, शरण स्थल

A number of people took refuge from the storm in their basements. Refuges are necessary to provide safety for pedestrians.

Refugee/रिफ्यूजी *(noun)* - शरणार्थी

A large percentage of refugees suffer from depression.

Refund/रिफण्ड *(verb)* - लौटाना, धन वापस करना

Customers will be refunded if the device is found faulty.

Refusal/रिफ्यूजल *(noun)* - अस्वीकृति, इनकार, अस्वीकृत करना

My request for more chocolate was met with outright refusal.

Refuse/रिफ्यूज *(verb)* - अस्वीकार करना, नकारना

The dessert was too good to refuse.

Refute/रिफ्यूट *(verb)* - खण्डन करना, गलत प्रमाणित करना

He refutes any hint that he behaved badly.

Regain/रिगेन *(verb)* - पुनः पाना, दोबारा प्राप्त करना, खोया हुआ स्थान, धन प्राप्त करना

She regained her strength after a week of rest.

Regal/रिगल *(adjective)* - राजसी, राज्योचित

The regal gesture of the queen left the commoners in awe.

Regale/रिगेल *(verb)* - कथा, चुटकुला से मनोरंजन

The sailor regaled the boys with stories of his old days.

Regard/रिगार्ड *(verb)* - मानना, समझना, सम्मान देना

She regards herself as a dog lover.

Regency/रिजेन्सी *(noun)* - संरक्षक पद, संरक्षण का अधिकार

The wealth of the kingdom was restored during his regency.

Regenerate/रेजेनरेट्/रिजेनरिट *(verb)* - पुनः शक्ति संचार करना, पुनर्जीवित करना

Salamanders are remarkable for their ability to regenerate limbs.

Regent/रिजेन्ट *(noun)* - संरक्षक

The regent represented the King of Denmark as sovereign of Iceland until the country became a republic.

Regime/रेजिम *(noun)* - शासन

Hitler's regime showed early signs of army fascism.

Regimen/रेजिमेन *(noun)* - आहार-व्यायाम निदेश, हिदायतें

The new regimen will surely make her lose weight.

Regiment/रेजिमेंट *(noun)* - सैन्यदल

The British army has an armoured regiment.

Region/रीजन *(noun)* - क्षेत्र

The river flows downstream along the northern region of the city.

Regional/रीजनल *(adjective)* - क्षेत्रीय

His accent has a regional.

Register/रजिस्टर *(noun)* - पंजी, पंजिका, पंजीकरण, सूचीबद्ध करना

The teacher always carried her attendance register.

Registrar/रजिस्ट्रार *(noun)* - प्रशासक, पंजीकरण-अधिकारी

The Commissioner is the Registrar of Births and Deaths in some corporations.

Registration/रजिस्ट्रेशन *(noun)* - पंजीकरण

The newly-married couples are eager for their marriage registration.

Registry/रजिस्ट्री *(noun)* - पंजीकृत, पंजीकरण की प्रक्रिया

Windows maintains a hefty registry of files.

Regret/रिग्रेट *(verb)* - दु:ख प्रकट करना, खेद प्रकट करना, खेद, अनुताप, उदासी, खिन्नता

I regret not reaching the venue on time.

Regular/रेगुलर *(adjective)* - नियमित, व्यवस्थित, सामान्य

The plants in the lawn were placed at regular intervals.

Regulate/रेगुलेट *(verb)* - व्यवस्थित, नियन्त्रित

The green button regulates the tension in the sewing machine.

Regulation/रेगुलेशन *(noun)* - नियम, नियमन, व्यवस्था

The new regulations were too tough.

Rehabilitate/रिहैबिलिटेट *(verb)* - पुनः स्वास्थ्य लाभ, जीवन सामान्य करना

The sensible doctor successfully rehabilitated the alcoholic.

Rehearse/रिहर्स *(verb)* - अभ्यास करना, दुहराना

The dance troupe rehearsed their act many times.

Reign/रेन *(verb)* - राज्य-काल, शासन

The cruel king reigned for decades.

R

Reimburse/रिइम्बर्स *(verb)* - पुनर्भुगतान करना, प्रतिपूर्ति करना

My company reimburses my travel expenses.

Rein/रेन *(noun)* - राज, बागडोर, नियन्त्रण

The new rider pulled the reins too hard.

Reindeer/रेनडियर *(noun)* - बड़ा हिरन

The herd of reindeers grazed on the sparse grasses.

Reinforce/रिइनफोर्स *(verb)* - अतिरिक्त शक्ति देना, अतिरिक्त सेना भेजना

After the threat, the government reinforced the security at crowded places.

Reinstate/रिइनस्टेट *(verb)* - पुनः पद देना, पूर्व अवस्था में लाना

The law and order situation was reinstated with some tough actions.

Reiterate/रिइटरेट *(verb)* - बार-बार दुहराना, जोर देकर कहना

The principal reiterated her points regarding importance of discipline.

Reject/रिजेक्ट *(verb)* - अस्वीकार, अस्वीकार करना

The manufactured goods were rejected by the inspection department.

Rejoice/रिज्वॉयस *(verb)* - हर्ष प्रदर्शित करना, उल्लास दिखाना

The children rejoiced upon hearing about the unexpected holidays.

Rejuvenate/रिजुविनेट *(verb)* - पुनर्नवा, पुनः युवा होना, तरुणाई पाना

The morning walks have rejuvenated me.

Relapse/रिलैप्स *(verb)* - पुनर्पतन, सुधरने के बाद बिगड़ना

The conditions of the patient relapsed.

Relate/रिलेट *(verb)* - वर्णन करना, विवरण देना

The child related the details of the family vacations to all his friends.

Relation/रिलेशन *(noun)* - सम्बन्ध, नातेदार, सम्बन्धी, रिश्तेदारी

The relation between them demanded respect.

Relationship/रिलेशनशीप *(noun)* - सम्बन्धी

The relationship between hard work and success cannot be denied.

Relative/रिलेटिव *(adjective)* - सम्बन्धी, नातेदार, रिश्तेदार

He admired his elder brother for his relative success in the sad economic environment.

Relax/रिलैक्स *(verb)* - विश्राम करना, शिथिलता लाना, नरमी

Her face relaxed and broke into a smile.

Relay/रिले *(verb)* - संकेत या संदेश को (प्राप्त कर) आगे भेजना

Instructions were relayed to us by phone.

Release/रिलिज *(verb)* - मुक्त करना, छोड़ देना, खोल देना

The policeman released the little pickpocket.

Relegate/रेलिगेट *(verb)* - पीछे ढकेल देना, निम्न पद देना

The general relegated the officer.

Relent/रिलेण्ट *(verb)* – नरम पड़ना, दया दिखाना

The teacher relented when the student told her the reason.

Relentless/रिलेण्टलेस *(adjective)* – बिना सुस्ताए, लगातार, अनवरत

The relentless winds damaged the seaside houses.

Relevant/रेलिवन्ट् *(adjective)* – प्रासंगिक, सम्बद्ध, संगत युक्त

The audience asked all the relevant questions.

Reliable/रिलाइअबल् *(adj.)* – विश्वनीय, भरोसेमन्द

My car is pretty reliable.

Reliance/रिलायन्स *(noun)* – विश्वास, विश्वसनीयता

It was a question of reliance.

Relic/रेलिक *(noun)* – स्मृति-अवशेष, स्मृति-शेष, अवशेष

The archaeologists were thrilled to find the relic.

Relief/रिलिफ *(noun)* – राहत, आराम महसूस करना, नक्कासी का उभार

She felt some relief after taking the painkillers.

Relieve/रिलिव *(verb)* – चिन्ता-मुक्ति, कार्यभार से निवृत्ति, चिन्तामुक्त

The morning guard relieved the night guard late today.

Religion/रिलिजन *(noun)* – धर्म, ईश्वर में आस्था

There are many religions in the world.

Religious/रिलिजियस *(adj)* – धार्मिक, धर्मपरायण

This is a congregation of religious people.

Relequish/रेलिक्विश *(verb)* – त्याग देना, अधिकार छोड़ना

I relinquished my claim on the property.

Relish/रेलिश *(noun)* – रसास्वाद, आस्वाद, अत्यन्त आनन्द

I wish the relish lasts forever.

Relive/रिलिव *(verb)* – पुनः अनुभव करना, दुहराना

I relived my college life during the reunion.

Reluctant/रिलक्टैंट *(adjective)* – अनिच्छुक, चाहत की कमी

I took my reluctant dog to the vet.

Rely/रिलाइ *(verb)* – विश्वास करना, निर्भर रहना

I rely upon you for quality work.

Remain/रिमेन *(verb)* – बाकी रहना, बने रहना

She remained in her seat even after all the students had left.

Remainder/रिमेन्डर *(noun)* – बचा हुआ, शेष

She calculated the remainder wrong.

Remains/रिमेंस *(plural noun)* – अवशेष, मृत शरीर, बचा भाग

The remains of the fight still make me angry.

Remand/रिमान्ड *(verb)* – हवालात में डालना, भेजना

The court remanded the suspect.

Remark/रिमार्क *(verb)* – टिप्पणी

He remarked about the quality of the thesis.

Remedy/रेमिडि *(noun)* – उपचार, दवा, चिकित्सा

It was an effective remedy.

Remember/रिमेम्बर *(verb)* – याद रखना, याद करना, स्मरण में रखना

Do you remember our first meeting?

Remembrance/रिमेम्ब्रैन्स *(noun)* – स्मृति चिह्न, निशानी, स्मरण

Please keep this ring as a remembrance of our relationship.

Remind/रिमाइन्ड *(verb)* – स्मरण दिलाना, याद दिलाना

It was good of you to remind me of this association.

Reminder/रिमाइन्डर *(noun)* – स्मरण-पत्र

Did you get a reminder from the company?

Reminiscent/रेमिनिसेंट *(adj)* – स्मरण कराने वाला

Your voice is reminiscent of someone I knew.

Remiss/रिमिस *(adjective)* – काहिल, लापरवाह, कामचोर

It would be remiss of me not to convey this information to students.

Remission/रिमिसन *(noun)* – माफी, क्षमा, दण्ड कम करना

The poor family was glad to have received a remission.

Remit/रेमिट *(verb)* – ऋण या सजा माफ करना, डाक से धन भेजना

Will God remit my sin?

Remittance/रेमिटैंस *(noun)* – रुपये भेजने की क्रिया

Have you received the notification about the remittance?

Remnant/रेमनन्ट *(noun)* - अवशेष, शेष
These few trees are the remnant of a huge forest.

Remonstrate/रिमॉन्सट्रेट *(verb)* - प्रतिवाद करना, विरोध करना
The students remonstrated against the new rules.

Remorse/रिमोर्स *(noun)* - पश्चाताप
I was touched by his genuine feelings of remorse.

Remote/रिमोट *(adjective)* - दूर का, दूर से
The remote village didn't have any electricity supply.

Remove/रिमुव *(verb)* - हटाना
The guard was removed after he was found sleeping.

Remunerate/रिम्यूनरेट *(verb)* - पारिश्रमिक देना
The company promised to remunerate him well for his services.

Remuneration/रिम्यूनरेशन *(noun)* - पारिश्रमिक
Diana agreed to work overtime if her firm promised to pay her extra remuneration.

Renaissance/रिनेसन्स् *(noun)* - पुनर्जागरण
Shakespeare and Ben Jonson are writers that belonged to the Renaissance age.

Render/रेन्डर *(verb)* - करना, देना, हिसाब भेजना, प्रदर्शित करना
Sheela wished to be adequately paid for the services rendered by her.

R

Rendezvous/रेन्डवू *(noun)* - निश्चित मिलन-स्थली, संगम
Sameer had a secret randezvous with Deeya.

Renew/रिन्यू *(verb)* - नवीकरण, नवीनीकरण
The sisters renewed their love and affection for each other after the fight.

Renounce/रिनाउन्स *(verb)* - त्यागना, अधिकार त्याग, संन्यास
The priest renounced all his worldly possessions for a life of piety.

Renovate/रिनोवेट *(verb)* - पुन: उद्धार, पुनरुद्धार
The old house was renovated last month.

Renown/रिनॉउन *(noun)* - यश पाना, प्रसिद्धि पाना
Dancers of great renown were present at the party last night.

Renowned/रिनाउन्ड् *(adjective)* - यशस्वी, प्रसिद्ध
Vineet is renowned the world over for his talent of tap dancing.

Rent/रेंट *(noun)* - किराया, भाड़ा, भाड़े पर लगाना
Fiona was ready to pay the exorbitant monthly rent for the seaside apartment.

Renunciation/रिनन्सिएशन *(noun)* - त्याग देना
The promise to celibacy demands the renunciation of marriage.

Reorganize/रिऑरगनाइज *(verb)* - पुनर्गठन, पुन: संगठित करना
The General reorganized the ranks to suit the interest of the army.

Repair/रिपेअर *(verb)* - मरम्मत करना
Cindy repaired her bike for the new year at college.

Repartee/रिपार्टी *(noun)* - श्लेष, व्यंग्यपूर्ण चतुर उत्तर
Seema is popular all over the college campus for the witty repartee.

Repast/रिपास्ट *(noun)* - भोज
We had a sumptuous repast during the morning celebration.

Repatriate/रिपैट्रिएट *(verb)* - स्वदेश वापस भेजना
After the war ended, trucks were repatriating the enemy soldires to their country.

Repay/रिपे *(verb)* - वापस लौटाना
Fiona repaid her car loan in just about six months time.

Repeal/रिपील *(verb)* - रद्द करना
The law was repealed after the mass murder.

Repeat/रिपीट *(verb)* - दुहराना
Ben decided to repeat himself in order to get his point through to the audience at the workshop.

Repel/रिपेल *(verb)* - पीछे धकेल देना, घृणा
Oil and water repel each other.

Repent/रिपेंट *(verb)* - पछताना, पश्चाताप करना
It is futile to repent one's actions after the damage has been done.

Repentance/रिपेंटैंस *(noun)* - पछतावा, पश्चाताप
The capacity of repentance is impossible in the heart of an egotist.

Repercussion/रिपरकसन *(noun)* - परिणाम, प्रभाव, प्रतिक्रिया
The political agenda can have multiple repercussions.

Repertoire/रेपरट्वार *(noun)* – अभिनय संग्रह, रंग पटल

Jim is renowned all over the city for his performances and impeccable repertoire.

Repetition/रेपिटिशन *(noun)* – दुहराई हुई, पुनरावृत्ति, प्रतिकृति

Any concept can be learned and internalized by the process of repetition.

Replace/रिप्लेस *(verb)* – स्थानापन्न होना, स्थान ग्रहण करना

We will replace any goods that are damaged.

Replacement/रिप्लेसमेंट *(noun)* – स्थानापन्न

Ted found a suitable replacement for his secretary who has gone on a maternity leave.

Replay/पिप्ले *(verb)* – फिर से खेलना, फिर से चलाना

Danny requested his wife to replay the song on the recorder at the party.

Replenish/रिप्लेनिश *(verb)* – परिपूर्ण कर देना, हरा-भरा कर देना

Europe turns to India in order to replenish all their resources.

Replete/रिप्लीट *(adjective)* – परिपूर्ण, भरा-पूरा, ठसाठस भरा

Our trip to Egypt was replete with incidents that reminded us of the yester years.

Replica/रेप्लिका *(noun)* – प्रतिकृति, समान आकृति, नकल, दूसरे जैसा

The museum of Madame Tussaud has on display exact replicas of famous personalities from all over the world.

Reply/रिप्लाइ *(verb)* – उत्तर देना

I hope my mother replied to the Principal's letter.

Report/रिपोर्ट् *(verb)* – विवरण, विवरण देना, जानकारी देना

All the new cadets reported their daily schedules to the manager on duty.

Repose/रिपोज *(verb)* – आराम करना, लेटना, आस्था रखना

Tina succumbed to her fate of loneliness with quiet repose.

Represent/रिप्रेजेंट *(verb)* – प्रतिनिधित्व करना, वर्णन करना

Dan surprised the judge when he chose to represent the guilty party.

Representation/रिप्रेजेंटेशन *(noun)* – प्रतिनिधित्व

The theatre group was present at the court for representation purpose only.

Representative/रिप्रेजेंटेटिव *(adjective)* – प्रतिनिधि

Anna Hazare is a proper representative of the working class in India.

Repress/रिप्रेश *(verb)* – दबाना, कुचलना, दमन करना

Celibacy demands the repressing of all sexual desires.

Reprieve/रिप्रीव् *(verb)* – सजा रोकना, सजा निरस्त करना, परेशानी से थोड़ी राहत देना

The new policy allowed the punishment of all wrong doers to be reprieved.

Reprimand/रेप्रिमैन्ड *(noun)* – फटकारना, भर्त्सना करना

To reprimand is to teach control and manners.

Reprisal/रिप्राइजल *(noun)* – प्रतिशोध, बदला

The British government was shocked by the Indian reprisal.

Reproach/रिप्रोच *(verb)* – असफलता, भूल जाने के लिए फटकार, धिक्कार, उलाहना भरा

Tina was strongly reproached by her mother for her indecent behaviour.

Reproachful/रिप्रोचफुल *(adjective)* – उलाहना पूर्ण, निन्दात्मक

Tia was reproachful of her husband's behaviour towards her relatives.

Reproduce/रिप्रोड्यूस *(verb)* – दुबारा करना, दुबारा बना देना, नकल प्रति तैयार करना, पुनः उत्पादन की प्रक्रिया

The play was to reproduce in the original art form.

Reproof/रिप्रूफ *(noun)* – भर्त्सना, दोष निकालना, निन्दा

Tim strongly disapproved of his public reproof by his boss.

Reprove/रिप्रूव *(verb)* – कड़ी भर्त्सना, कड़ी निन्दा

Tina was strongly reproved by her husband at the party last night.

Reptile/रेप्टाइल *(noun)* – सरीसृप, रेंगने वाले जीव

Lizard is a reptile.

Republic/रिपब्लिक् *(noun)* – गणतन्त्र

He was unanimously elected President of the Republic of Kenya.

Republican/रिपब्लिकन् *(adjective)* - गणतन्त्र राज्यीय, गणतन्त्र समर्थक

Every nation ought to have democratic as well as republican attributes.

Repudiate/रिप्यूडिएट *(verb)* - नकारना, अस्वीकार करना

Tina repudiated the gender sensitization policies of the firm that she was working with.

Repugnant/रिपग्नैंट *(adj)* - अरुचिकर, जुगुप्सा

Domestic violence is a repugnant act.

Repulse/रिपल्स *(verb)* - पीछे ढकेलना, हमले को निष्फल करना, घृणा उत्पन्न करना

Ned's repulsive behaviour was the main cause of his banishment from the Sunday meet group.

Repulsion/रिपल्सन *(noun)* - अत्यधिक घृणा, अरुचि, प्रतिकर्षण

The estranged husband and wife shared a mutual feeling of repulsion towards each other.

Repulsive/रिपल्सिव *(adj)* - घृणास्पद, प्रतिकर्षक

A repulsive odour emanated from the cupboard.

Reputable/रिप्यूटेबल् *(adj)* - प्रतिष्ठित, ख्याति प्राप्त

The company can bank upon its reputable owners.

Reputation/रिप्यूटेशन *(noun)* - ख्याति, प्रसिद्धि, प्रतिष्ठा

The company's reputation depends upon its employees as well as its employers.

R

Repute/रिप्यूट *(noun)* - ख्याति, नाम, प्रतिष्ठा

Lack of public safety can lead to a bad repute for the government.

Reputed/रिप्यूटेड *(adj)* - यशस्वी, लब्धप्रतिष्ठ, नामी, ख्याति प्राप्त

He's reputed to be the highest paid sportsman in the world.

Request/रिक्वेस्ट *(noun)* - निवेदन, अनुरोध, प्रार्थना

Tim's plea to his father regarding the mowing down of their family home was more of a humble request.

Require/रिक्वायर *(verb)* - निर्भरता, आवश्यक, जरूरत होना

The orphanage required a great amount of donation to provide proper education for its inmates.

Requisite/रेक्विजिट *(adj)* - आवश्यक, जरूरी

The divorce proceedings will not be forwarded until the requisite fee is paid.

Requisition/रेक्विजिशन *(noun)* - सामान की माँग

Heidi was required to make various requisitions to hire the office area.

Rescue/रेस्क्यू *(verb)* - मुक्त कराना, छुड़ाना

The stray dogs were rescued by the shopkeepers.

Research/रिसर्चर *(noun)* - अन्वेषण, अनुसंधान

Field work is an important part of any scientific research.

Researcher/रिसर्चर *(noun)* - अन्वेषण, अनुसंधान कर्ता

Tim is employed as a researcher at the University of California.

Resemble/रिजेम्बल *(verb)* - एकसा, समान, सदृश होना

John greatly resembles his grandfather.

Resemblance/रिजेम्ब्लेंस *(noun)* - समानता, सादृश्यता

The resemblance between Tim and his father is uncanny.

Resent/रिजेंट *(verb)* - नाराज होना, बुरा मानना, क्रोध उपजना

Sam resents having betrayed his girlfriend for another woman.

Resentment/रिजेंटमेंट *(noun)* - मनोमालिन्य, रोष, नाराजगी

The resentment that Gill has towards her estranged husband is very visible.

Reservation/रिजर्वेशन *(noun)* - आरक्षण

Tim made reservations in a popular restaurant to surprise his wife on her birthday.

Reserve/रिजर्व *(verb)* - बचाकर, संचित, अतिरिक्त शक्ति

Tina believes in reserving her money for the rainy day.

Reserved/रिजर्व्ड् *(adjective)* - आरक्षित, अल्पभाषी

Tina's reserved nature is her only drawback.

Reservoir/रिजरवायर *(noun)* - जलाशय

Fiona's mother is a reservoir of information where their family history is concerned.

Reshuffle/रिशफल *(verb)* – फेंटना, पत्ते फेंटना, फेर बदल करना

Coach Ned decided to reshuffle the team for better productivity.

Reside/रिजाइड *(verb)* – निवास करना, रहना

The family has been residing in the same locality for over five decades now.

Residence/रेजिडेंस *(noun)* – निवास, निवास स्थान

The company owner needed a residence in the city to open an office.

Resident/रेजिडेंट *(noun)* – निवासी

American residents are investing in property in india.

Residential/रेजिडेंसियल *(adjective)* – आवासीय

John was given a residential apartment by his company upon relocation to another city.

Residue/रेजिड्यू *(noun)* – अवशेष, बचा हुआ भाग

The washing powder left a white residue on the clothes.

Resign/रिजाइन *(verb)* – त्याग, पद-त्याग करना

Tina's improper behaviour with her co-workers forced her to resign from her job.

Resignation/रेजिग्नेशन *(noun)* – त्याग-पत्र

Fiona made her resignation public after being accused of being unethical.

Resilient/रिजिलिअन्ट *(adj)* – सहने में समर्थ, सहनशील

She won accolades all over campus for her resilient behaviour and forbearance.

Resist/रिजिस्ट *(verb)* – प्रतिरोध, सबलता से रोकना, विरोध करना

She strongly resisted his favours.

Resistance/रिजिस्टन्स *(noun)* – प्रतिरोधक क्षमता, सहनशीलता

The boys showed resistance when confronted by the school authorities.

Resistant/रिजिस्टन्ट *(adj)* – प्रतिरोधक

This watch is water-resistant.

Resolute/रेजोल्यूट *(adjective)* – दृढ़निश्चयी, कृतसंकल्प, संकल्पवान

Nina's resolute behaviour is her greatest strength.

Resolution/रेजल्यूशन *(noun)* – दृढ़ता, निश्चय, संकल्पबद्ध

Tina listed her New Year resolutions on a piece of paper.

Resolve/रिजॉल्व *(verb)* – दृढ़ निश्चय, पक्का इरादा, पारित प्रस्ताव

The medicine is said to resolve my problem in a month.

Resonant/रेजनॅन्ट *(adjective)* – गूंज, गूंजित, अनुगूँज की ध्वनि

His resonant voice charmed the ladies.

Resonance/रेजनन्स *(noun)* – अनुगूँज, निनाद, प्रतिध्वनित

The audience was mighty impressed with the resonance of the speaker's voice.

Resort/रिजॉर्ट *(noun)* – सैरगाह स्थल, आश्रय

The bride and groom decided to book the entire resort for their honeymoon.

Resound/रिजाउन्ड *(verb)* – गूँजना, प्रतिध्वनित

The palace resounded with a distinct echo of the yester year charm that the place once enjoyed.

Resource/रिसोर्स *(noun)* – स्रोत, संसाधन, सम्पदा, युक्ति

Sheena wanted to take full advantage of her estranged husband's resources even after their divorce.

Respect/रिस्पेक्ट *(noun)* – आदर, आदर भाव, आदर भावना, आदर देना

We should respect our elders.

Respectable/रिस्पेक्टेबल् *(adjective)* – आदरणीय, सम्मानीय, सम्मान योग्य

Ria wanted to be married into a respectable family.

Respectful/रिस्पेक्टफुल *(adjective)* – आदरपूर्ण

Children should be taught to be respectful of elders.

Respective/रिस्पेक्टिव *(adj)* – क्रमशः अपना-अपना

All the candidates were requested to talk about their respective personal lives as part of the interview process.

Respiration/रेस्पिरेशन *(noun)* – श्वास, श्वास लेने की क्रिया

The doctors decided to monitor the patient's respiration for a day or so.

Respire/रेस्पायर *(verb)* – श्वास लेना, साँस लेना

Plants respire throughout the day.

Respite/रेस्पाइट *(noun)* – राहत, आराम

The prisoners of war sought respite from the Pakistan government.

Resplendent/रेस्प्लेन्डेन्ट *(adjective)* – चमकता-दमकता, भव्य

The peacock's resplendent plumage is a sight to behold.

Respond/रिस्पॉन्ड् *(verb)* – उत्तर देना, प्रतिक्रिया दिखाना

The court responded to her pleas.

Response/रिस्पॉन्स् *(noun)* – उत्तर, अनुक्रिया, प्रतिक्रिया

It is impossible to elicit a positive response from an intolerant person.

Responsibility/रिस्पॉन्सिबिलिटि *(noun)* – उत्तरदायित्व

It is the responsibility of children to take care of their parents.

Responsible/रिस्पॉन्सिबल् *(adjective)* – उत्तरदायी, जबावदेह

Diana relies a lot on her responsible son.

Responsive/रिस्पान्सिव् *(adjective)* – रुचि लेन वाला, अनुकूल, उत्तरदावी

A well defined organization is responsive to any misdemeanours in society.

Rest/रेस्ट *(noun)* – विश्राम, आराम, स्थिर, शेष, सहारा

He was unable to convince the rest of the group.

Restaurant/रेस्टरान्ट *(noun)* – भोजनालय

He made reservations at the restaurant for lunch.

Restitution/रेस्टीट्यूशन *(noun)* – खोई या चुराई हुई वस्तु की उसके मालिक को वापसी

Restitution of the documents was vital for the reputation of the institution.

Restive/रेस्टिव *(adjective)* – बैचैन, नियन्त्रण से बाहर

A restive wife causes strife.

Restless/रेस्टलेस *(adj)* – अधीर, बेचैन

She was feeling rather restless after lunch.

Restoration/रेस्टोरेशन् *(noun)* – पुनर्स्थापना, पुर्नरचना

Restoration is definitely needed in our building.

Restore/रिस्टोर *(verb)* – पुरानी स्थिति पर, वापसी

The government restored peace in the war struck area.

Restrain/रिस्ट्रेन *(verb)* – रोकना, नियन्त्रित करना, नियन्त्रण में रहना

The child had to be restained from walking out of the house.

Restrict/रिस्ट्रिक्ट *(verb)* – रोकना, सीमित करना, सीमा में रखना

Entry to the museum was restricted.

Result/रिजल्ट *(noun)* – फल, परिणाम

His poverty was result of his carelessness.

Resume/रिज्यूम *(verb)* – पुनः कार्यारम्भ, फिर से शुरू करना

We shall resume our work after a short break.

Resurgent/रिसर्जेन्ट *(adjective)* – उत्साह के साथ उठना, पुनः सक्रियता

Resurgent communalism is a result of intolerant religious factions of society.

Resurrect/रिजरेक्ट *(verb)* – फिर से प्रयोग में लाना, पुनर्जीवन

The mummy was resurrected from his sarcophagus.

Resuscitate/रिससिटेट *(verb)* – चेतना में लाना

The man tried to resuscitate his wife using his mouth to blow air directly into her mouth.

Retailer/रिटेलर *(noun)* – फुटकर विक्रेता, खुदरा बेंचने वाला

My brother is a retailer of sports goods.

Retain/रिटेन *(verb)* – रखना, अधिकार में रखना

Katherine decided to retain her mother's jewellery.

Retaliate/रिटैलिएट *(verb)* – प्रत्याक्रमण, प्रतिकार करना

Tina retaliated violently to her husband's accusations.

Retaliation/रिटैलिएशन *(noun)* – बदले की कार्रवाई, प्रतिकार का प्रयास

The terrorist group said that the shooting was in retaliation for the murder of one of its member.

Retard/रिटार्ड *(verb)* – विकास में रुकावट, बाधा, बाधित

Bad weather conditions retard the growth of plants.

Retarded/रिटार्डेड *(adj)* – मन्दबुद्धि, अर्द्धविकसित

The progress of the Indian economy is retarded owing to slow implementation of laws.

R

Retention/रिटेंशन *(noun)* - स्वामित्व बनाये रखना, अधिकार रखना स्मृति में रखने की शक्ति, याददास्त

The state government ordered the retention of all landed property even after the buyout by the multinational company.

Rethink/रिथिंक *(verb)* - पुनर्विचार, पुनःचिन्तन

I am rethinking my decision of buying a sedan car.

Reticent/रेटिसेंट *(adjective)* - अल्पभाषी

His reticence adds to his charming personality.

Retina/रेटिना *(noun)* - पुतली, दृष्टिपटल

The optician informed her that her blurred vision was a result of her torn retina.

Retinue/रेटिन्यू *(noun)* - परिजन, मातहत

The judge always travels with his retinue of lawyers.

Retire/रिटायर *(verb)* - अवकाश प्राप्त, सोने जाना, निवृत्त, सेवा निवृत्त होना

My father retired from job last year.

Retirement/रिटायरमेंट *(noun)* - सेवानिवृत्ति के पश्चात

He was given a farewell party post retirement by his office people.

Retort/रिटॉर्ट् *(verb)* - मुहँतोड़ जवाब देना, समुचित प्रत्युत्तर देना

She retorted to her sister's accusatory tone.

Retouch/रिटच *(verb)* - लघु संशोधन करना

The marble sculptures needed a retouch before being reinstalled to the hotel lobby.

Retrace/रिट्रेस *(verb)* - वापसी, लौटना, दूसरे का मार्ग खोलना

She retraced her footsteps to get out of the jungle safely.

Retract/रिट्रैक्ट *(verb)* - समेटना, पलटना, मुकरना draw or be drawn back or back in. *The snail retracted into its shell on being disturbed.*

Retreat/रिट्रिट *(verb)* - पीछे हटना, वापस लौटना

The lion retreated back to his cave after having ravished his prey.

Retrench/रिट्रेंच *(verb)* - खर्च कम करना, कर्मचारी हटाना, कटौती करना

Several people lost their jobs because their companies retrenched.

Retrenchment/रिट्रेंचमेंट *(noun)* - कटौती करना, छँटनी करना

Numerous companies were forced to undergo retrenchment following the global economic slowdown.

Retribution/रिट्रिव्यूशन *(noun)* - प्रतिफल, बदला, प्रतिकार

The thieves were pelted to death by the public as retribution for their heinous crime.

Retrieve/रिट्रीव *(verb)* - वापस पाना, दोबारा पाना, खोज निकालना

The emperor sent his general to retrieve his imperial sword.

Retrograde/रिट्रोग्रेड *(adjective)* - अधोगामी, अवनति की ओर

To act negatively would be a retrograde step.

Retrospect/रिट्रॉस्पेक्ट *(noun)* - सिंहावलोकन, स्मृति फलक पर देखना

In retrospect, war can be considered a mass murder.

Retrospective/रिट्रॉस्पेक्टिव *(adjective)* - विगत तिथि से, अतीत में झाँकना

His paintings were retrospective in nature.

Return/रिटर्न *(verb)* - लौटना, लौटने की क्रिया

He promised to return after his project.

Reunion/रियूनियन *(noun)* - पुनर्मिलन

All classmates decided to meet at the school reunion.

Reunite/रियूनाइट *(verb)* - पुनः मिल जाना

The refugee camp ensured that all refugees were reunited with their family members.

Revalue/रिवैल्यू *(verb)* - पुनर्मूल्यांकन करना

He revalued his property before the final sell off.

Reveal/रिविल *(noun)* - प्रकट करना, रहस्य खोलना

Jesus revealed his presence to his followers on the 40th day.

Revel/रेवेल *(verb)* - मौज, आमोद-प्रमोद, शोरगुल-प्रमोद समारोह

They revelled themselves eating and dancing at the picnic yesterday.

Revelry/रेवलरि *(noun)* - रंगरलियाँ, गुलछर्रे

Carnival ensures a night of revelry and joy.

R

Revelation/रेवलेशन *(noun)* - प्रकटन, रहस्योद्घाटन
Suddenly, he had a revelation that life was not just about monetary benefits, but also about love and brotherhood.

Revenge/रिवेंज *(noun)* - प्रतिशोध
Revenge is a vice that ought to be avoided under all circumstances.

Revenue/रेवेन्यू *(noun)* - राजस्व
The government body in villages is responsible for collecting revenue from the villages every year.

Reverberate/रिवरवरेट *(verb)* - गूँजना, अनुगूँज
Diana's screaming reverberated through the entire hall and took everyone by surprise.

Revere/रिवीअर् *(verb)* - आदर, श्रद्धा रखना
Good teachers are always revered by their students.

Reverence/रेवरेंस *(noun)* - श्रद्धा
Everybody stood up as the retired teacher entered the classroom as a mark of reverence.

Reverend/रेवरेंड *(adjective)* - श्रद्धेय
The reverend jury members were requested to attend the court hearing.

Reverent/रेवरेंट *(adjective)* - श्रद्धालु
The students were taught the importance of being reverent in class today.

Reverie/रेवरि *(noun)* - दिवास्वप्न
Leela pinched Tim on the arm in order to snap him out of his reverie.

Reversal/रिवर्सल *(noun)* - विपरीत, विपरीत, पृष्ठ भाग, पलटना
The judge ordered a reversal of the court proceedings in order to ensure justice.

Revert/रिवर्ट *(verb)* - पूर्वदशा में आना, पुरानी आदत पकड़ना
The teacher reverted back with the results within a day.

Review/रिव्यू *(noun)* - सर्वेक्षण, समीक्षा, निरीक्षण
The government plans to review certain laws for the betterment of the society.

Reviewer/रिव्यूअर *(noun)* - समीक्षक, सर्वेक्षक
The student hired two reviewers to review her paper.

Revile/रिवाइल *(verb)* - गाली देना, कटु शब्द कहना
The teacher reviled the student who had abused his classmate.

Revise/रिवाइज *(verb)* - संशोधन, पुनर्निरीक्षण
I want to read the revised version of this play.

Revision/रिविजन *(noun)* - पुनर्पाठ, संशोधन, पुन: देखना
Preeti is a travel editor who heads the revisions team.

Revival/रिवाइवल *(noun)* - नवजागरण, पुनर्जीवन, पुनरुत्थान
The Celtic revival is a defining moment in the history of English Literature.

Revive/रिवाइव *(verb)* - पहले-सी शक्ति पाना, पुन: स्फूर्ति पाना, पुनर्जीवित करना
The doctor managed to revive the patient by injecting coramin.

Revoke/रिवोक *(verb)* - रद्द करना, वापस लेना
I am revoking all your powers.

Revolt/रिवोल्ट *(verb)* - विद्रोह करना
The Indian Army revolted on realizing what the British troops had done.

Revolting/रिवोल्टिंग *(adj)* - अरुचिकर, विद्रोह जगाने वाला
The filth strewn all over the house was a revolting sight.

Revolution/रिवोल्यूशन *(noun)* - विद्रोह, क्रान्ति
The Marxist leaders demanded a revolution to change the existing order.

Revolutionary/रिवोल्यूशनरी *(adj)* - क्रान्तिकारी, विद्रोही
His revolutionary spirit can land him into trouble with the authorities.

Revolutionize/रिवोल्यूशनाइज *(verb)* - विद्रोह जगाना, क्रान्ति उत्पन्न करना
Liberal thinking leads to a revolutionized society.

Revolve/रिवॉल्व *(verb)* - गोल घूमना, चक्कर खाना, परिक्रमा करना
The earth revolves around its own axis.

Revolver/रिवॉल्वर *(noun)* - तमंचा
Sam carries a licensed revolver for his personal safety.

Revulsion/रिवल्सन *(noun)* - घृणा, जुगुप्सा
Gia felt a sense of revulsion after meeting her sister's husband.

Reward/रिवार्ड *(noun)* - पुरस्कार, पारितोषिक
A reward acts as motivation to perform better.

Rewarding/रिवार्डिंग *(adj)*– पुरस्कार, पारितोषिक
Sid's rewarding work brought him laurels at his workplace.

Rewind/रिवाइन्ड *(verb)* – विडियो कैसेट या टेप को पीछे करना या उल्टा घुमाना
Please rewind the tape at the end of the film.

Rewrite/रिराइट *(verb)* – किसी बात को दो बार लिखना (भिन्न रूप से या बेहतर तरीके से)
Mandy was asked to rewrite the essay by his teacher.

Rhetoric/रेटरिक *(noun)* – शब्द-पटुता, शब्दालंकार, शब्दाडम्बर
Rhetoric and prosody is an essential subject in literature.

Rheumatic/रूमेटिक *(adjective)* – गठिया, गठिया से सम्बन्धित
Sid's rheumatic legs made it tough for him to run swiftly.

Rheumatism/रूमेटिज्म *(noun)* – गठिया
Rheumatism is an affliction of the bones.

Rhinoceros/राइनॅसरस *(noun)* – गैंडा
Rhinoceros is one of the endangered species.

Rhombus/रॉम्बस *(noun)* – समचतुर्भुज
Tom learned about geometrical shapes such as the rhombus today.

Rhyme/राइम *(noun)* – तुक, तुकान्त कविता, तुक मिलना
It is easier to remember songs that have words that rhyme.

Rhythm/रिद्म् *(noun)* – लय, ताल
Tim's tutor realized that his pupil's music was in perfect rhythm and that he was nothing short of a prodigy.

Rib/रिब *(noun)* – पसली
Eve is said to have been created from Adam's rib.

Ribbon/रिबन *(noun)* – फीता
Sia ties a pretty red ribbon to her plait.

Rice/राइस *(noun)* – चावल
Rice is the staple food in India.

Rich/रिच *(adjective)* – धनी, बहुलतापूर्ण, ऊर्वर
Tom's rich relative offered to finance his university education.

Riches/रिचेज *(plural noun)* – धन-दौलत, सम्पति
He lost all his riches due to his incompetence and misdemeanour.

Rickety/रिकेटी *(adjective)* – जर्जर, डाँवाँडोल
The rickety bullock cart was unable to pull through the course of the entire journey.

Ricochet/रिकॅचेट *(verb)* – टकराकर वापस लौटना
The ball ricocheted across the room due to the forceful impact of the thump.

Rid/रिड *(verb)* – पिंड छुड़ाना, पीछा छुड़ाना
Tina wished to be rid of all her financial troubles by Christmas.

Riddance/रिडेंस *(noun)* – छुटकारा, राहत
Doing away with meaningless superstitions is good riddance.

Ridden/रिडेन – वशीभूत
Nightmares are often ridden with mental imbalance.

Riddle/रिडल *(noun)* – पहेली, बुझौवल
This is complex riddle.

Ride/राइड *(verb)* – सवारी, झूला पर चढ़ना, बैठना
He rides his bicycle to work.

Rider/राइडर *(noun)* – सवार
She is an expert rider.

Ridge/रिज *(noun)* – पहाड़ का लम्बा तंग ऊँचा भाग
I am going to the ridge.

Ridicule/रिडिक्यूल् *(noun & verb)* – खिल्ली उड़ना, उपहास
Your ridicule doesn't help anyone.

Ridiculous/रिडिक्यूलस *(adj)* – हास्यास्पद, बेतुका
Your ridiculous idea spoilt everything.

Rife/राइफ *(adj)* – छितराया हुआ
The rife violence was a cause of worry.

Rifle/राइफल *(noun)* – बन्दूक
The hunter carried a rifle on his shoulder.

Rift/रिफ्ट *(noun)* – फटन, दरार, मतभेद, मनमुटाव
The rift in the rock was dangerous.

Rig/रिग *(verb)* – धांधली (अपने अनुकूल परिणाम के लिए किसी गतिविधि को अनुचित रूप से प्रभावित करना)
He rigged the records to his benefit.

Rigging/रिगिंग *(noun)* – जहाज के रस्से पाल इत्यादि
The rigging was old and needed to be replaced.

Right/राइट *(adjective)* – सही, उचित, अधिकार, सही दशा में, दाहिना
She says that my views are right.

Righteous/राइट्यस् *(adjective)* – नैतिक, नैतिक रूप से सही
I sometimes find your righteous approach tiresome.

Rightful/राइटफुल *(adjective)* – यथोचित्
You are the rightful owner of the estate.

Rightfully/राइटफुली *(adverb)* – उचित तौर पर
This estate is rightfully yours.

Rigid/रिजिड *(adjective)* – कड़ा, अड़ियल, न मुड़ने वाला
You have a rigid personality.

Rigidity/रिजिडिटि *(noun)* – कठोरता, दृढ़ता
Your rigidity will cause problems for you in your life.

Rigmarole/रिग्मरोल् *(noun)* – अनर्थक कथा, बिना अर्थ की बातचीत
When will this rigmarole end!

Rigour/रिगर *(noun)* – कड़ाई, संयम
The rigour lasted only a few minutes.

Rigorous/रिगरस *(adjective)* – कष्टसाध्य, श्रमसाध्य
He hurt his back while doing some rigorous exercise.

R

Rim/रिम *(noun)* – पहिया का घेरा
The rim of the spectacle was bent.

Rind/रिन्ड *(noun)* – छिलका
Some people consume the rind of an orange.

Ring/रिंग *(noun)* – अँगूठी, छल्ला, घेरा, अखाड़ा, नाथना, बजना, बजाना, गूँजना, बजने की ध्वनि
He gave her a ring.

Rinse/रिन्स *(verb)* – खंगालना
Please rinse this bottle properly.

Riot/राइअट् *(noun)* – दंगा, बलवा
The riots went out of control.

Rip/रिप *(verb)* – चीरना, काटना
The bully ripped the toy away from the child.

Ripe/राइप *(adjective)* – पका, पूर्ण विकसित
The fruit was ripe.

Ripen/राइपेन *(verb)* – पकना, पकाना
The fruits ripen by February.

Ripple/रिप्ल् *(noun)* – तरंग, तरंगाचित
Ripple look beautiful on the surface of water.

Rise/राइज *(verb)* – उठना, वृद्धि, चढ़ाव, जगना, उन्नति, स्रोत
He rose up the corporate ladder.

Risk/रिस्क *(noun)* – जोखिम, खतरा
This investment is a huge risk.

Rite/राइट *(noun)* – अनुष्ठान, संस्कार
They left as soon as all the rites completed.

Ritual/रिचुअल *(noun)* – कर्मकाण्ड, अनुष्ठान
Hindu marriages involve many rituals.

Rival/राइव्ल् *(noun)* – प्रतिद्वन्द्वी
The two rivals fought a bitter battle.

Rivalry/राइवलरि *(noun)* – प्रतिद्वन्द्विता
There was a lot of rivalry between the sisters.

River/रिवर *(noun)* – नदी
The river has carved a passage for itself across the centuries.

Rivet/रिवेट *(noun)* – कील, आँख गड़ाना
Watch out for the rivet.

Rivulet/रिव्युलेट् *(noun)* – छोटी धारा
Several rivulet flow into the river.

Road/रोड *(noun)* – सड़क, मार्ग
The road was wide and smooth.

Roam/रोम् *(verb)* – घूमना, निरुद्देश्य घूमना
He roamed all across the world when he was young.

Roar/रोर् *(noun)* – दहाड़, गर्जन, दहाड़ना, गरजना
The lion's roar could be heard miles away.

Roast/रोस्ट् *(verb)* – सेंकना, भूनना
Please roast the meat.

Rob/रॉब *(verb)* – लूटना, डाका डालना
She robbed the man at gunpoint.

Robbery/रॉबरी *(noun)* – डकैती, लूट
The police were able to crack the case of robbery.

Robe/रोब *(noun)* – लबादा, ढीला बाहरी वस्त्र
She wore a beautiful robe over her dress.

Robin/रॉबिन *(noun)* - लाल छाती वाली गाने वाली एक छोटी चिड़िया, एक पक्षी
Robins flitted around in the sky.

Robot/रोबोट् *(noun)* - मशीनी मानव, यन्त्र मानव
My sister gifted me a robot for my birthday.

Robust/रोबस्ट *(adjective)* - तगड़ा, हृस्ट-पुष्ट
The robust laptop didn't need any repairs for many years.

Rock/रॉक *(noun & verb)* - चट्टान, डुलाना, हिलना, तेज संगीत
The rock from moon was placed in a museum.

Rocket/रॉकेट *(noun & verb)* - अग्निबाण, तीव्र वेग से बढ़ना
We saw the rocket launch.

Rod/रॉड *(noun)* - छड़, छड़ी, (लकड़ी या धातु की)
Rods of iron were used to give strength to the structure.

Rodent/रोडेन्ट् *(noun)* - कुतरने वाले जीव
I don't think rodents make good pets.

Roe/रो *(noun)* - मछली का अण्डा (जो खाये जाते हैं)
Roe is a delicacy in many parts of the world.

Rogue/रोग् *(noun)* - दुष्ट, दुर्जन, खतरनाक a
He is such a rogue.

Role/रोल *(noun)* - भूमिका
Can you tell me more about your role in the movie?

Roll/रोल *(noun & verb)* - लपेटा, लपेटी वस्तु, लुढ़कना
The ship rolled towards the port.

Roller/रोलर *(noun)* - बेलन, बेलना, तरंग, लहर
Use a roller to roll the cotton.

Romance/रोमैंस *(noun)* - रोमांचक अनुभव, रोमांचकारी घटना, प्रेम कथा
I know several romances.

Romantic/रोमैन्टिक *(adj)* - प्रेम-विषयक, रूमानी
This is a romantic poem.

Romp/रॉम्प *(verb)* - खेलना, खिलवाड़ करना, उछलना-कूदना
The children romped around.

Roof/रूफ *(noun)* - छत
The ladder almost touched the roof.

Rook/रूक् *(noun)* - कौवे की प्रजाति, शतरंज का हाथी
A rook was making a lot of noise around the tree.

Room/रूम *(noun)* - कमरा, स्थान
There was no room to move.

Roomy/रूमि *(adjective)* - लम्बा-चौड़ा
This is a roomy house.

Roost/रूस्ट - *(noun)* बसेरा, अड्डा
These waters are risky because of the tidal race.

Rooster/रूस्टर *(noun)* - मुर्गा
I bought a rooster yesterday.

Root/रूट *(noun & verb)* - जड़, शोर, स्रोत, स्थिर करना, जमा देना
The antelopes rooted around.

Rope/रोप् *(noun)* - रस्सी
The rope was very strong.

Rosary/रोजरी *(noun)* - सुमिरनी, जपमाला
I love the sound of rosary.

Rose/रोज *(noun)* - गुलाब
I planted a rose in my garden.

Rostrum/रोस्ट्रम *(noun)* - चबूतरा
The rostrum had been set up well.

Rosy/रोजी *(adjective)* - गुलाबी, स्वस्थ
She is very proud of her rosy cheeks.

Rot/रॉट *(verb)* - सड़ना
The vegetables had started rotting.

Rota/रोटा *(noun)* - कार्य-सूची
No one seems to be following the rota.

Rotate/रोटेट *(verb)* - धूरी पर घूमना
The ball rotated for quite some time.

Rote/रोट *(noun)* - रट्टा मारना, रटना
I am trying to break out of my rote.

Rotor/रोटर *(noun)* - धूरी पर घूमने वाला
The rotor needs cleaning.

Rotten/रॉटन *(adjective)* - सड़ा-गला
The tomato is rotten.

Rotund/रोटण्ड *(adjective)* - गोल-मटोल
The rotund man went to the dietician for advice.

Rouble/रूबल *(noun)* - रूस की मुद्रा
This costs 100 Roubles.

R

Rouge/रूज *(noun)* – लाली
She applied rouge with perfection.

Rough/रफ *(adjective)* – खुरदरा, आरम्भिक, कर्णकटु, रूक्ष
The rough terrain is making the ride uncomfortable.

Roughly/रफली *(adverb)* – रूक्ष व्यवहार
He was punished for handling the patient roughly.

Roughage/रफेज *(noun)* – पाचक अंश
You need to increase the amount of roughage in your diet.

Roughen/रफन *(verb)* – खुरदुरा करना, रूखा बनाना
The ride roughened as the quality of the roads went down.

Roulette/रूलेट *(noun)* – जुए का एक खेल
She was delighted to have won the roulette.

Round/राउन्ड *(adjective)* – गोल, चारों ओर, घूमते हुए, फेरा, बारी, दौरा, गोली दागना, अनुमोदन
I liked the round logo better than the square one.

Roundabout/राउन्डएबाउट *(noun)* – चक्करदार
There was an accident on the roundabout.

Rouse/राउज *(verb)* – नींद से जागना, प्रेरित होना, क्रोधित करना
The noise of the boxes falling roused the sleeping family.

Rout/राउट *(noun)* – पूर्णहार
The rout was intercepted by the enemy.

R

Route/रूट *noun)* – रास्ता, मार्ग
What route should I take to the railway station?

Routine/रूटीन *(noun)* – दिनचर्या, विकरणी
I finished my daily routine well in time.

Rove/रोव *(verb)* – मटरगस्ती करना
She roves around the world.

Row/राउ *(noun)* – पंक्ति, कतार
I sat in the third row.

Royal/रॉयल *(adjective)* – राजकीय, राजषी
The royal family travelled to the hills for vacations.

Rub/रब *(verb)* – रगड़ना
He rubbed her back to ease her backache.

Rubber/रबर *(noun)* – चिपकाउ स्राव, मिटाने वाला पदार्थ
This unusual dress is made of rubber.

Rubbish/रबिश *(noun)* – कूड़ा-कचरा, रद्दी
There was rubbish everywhere.

Rubble/रब्ल् *(noun)* – मलवा
Some people rummaged through the rubble.

Ruby/रूबि *(noun)* – माणिक्य, गहरा लाल रंग
I like wearing rubies.

Rucksack/रकसैक *(noun)* – पीठ का थैला
My rucksack is too heavy.

Rudder/रडर *(noun)* – पतवार
The rudder can be used to decide the direction of the boat.

Ruddy/रडि *(adjective)* – लालिमा, लालिमापूर्ण
She has a ruddy complexion.

Rude/रूड *(adjective)* – रूखा, उग्र
His rude language made him very unpleasant to work with.

Rudiments/रूडिमेंट्स *(noun)* – आधारभूत सिद्धान्त, आरम्भिक
You don't even seem to know the rudiments.

Rudimentary/रूडिमेंटरि *(adj)* – प्रारम्भिक, अविकसित
It is important to follow the rudimentary practices.

Ruffian/रफिअन *(noun)* – गुण्डा, बदमाश
The ruffian turned out to be the king in disguise.

Rug/रग *(noun)* – कालीन, कम्बल
The rug had gathered dust.

Rugged/रगेड् *(adjective)* – ऊबड़-खाबड़
The terrain is rugged.

Ruin/रूइन *(noun)* – तबाह, बरबाद, तबाह करना, बरबाद करना
No one knows what led to the ruin of the civilization.

Ruinous/रूइनस *(adjective)* – बरबाद करने वाला
His ruinous tendencies are bound to land him in trouble.

Rule/रूल *(noun)* – नियम, आदत, शासन, रेखा खींचना
The new rule wasn't acceptable to the students.

Ruler/रूलर *(noun)* - शासक, पैमाना

The ruler of this country is tough but just.

Ruling/रूलिंग *(noun)* - अधिकारिक आदेश, प्रभावशाली

The court issued the ruling without any delay.

Rum/रम *(noun)* - गन्ने की शराब, अजीब, अनोखा

He drank rum with water.

Rumble/रम्बल *(verb)* - धड़धड़ाना, धड़धड़ाते हुए चलना

The thunder rumbled throughout the night.

Ruminate/रूमिनेट *(verb)* - चिन्तन करना

I would like to ruminate over this matter for some time.

Rummage/रमेज *(verb)* - ढूँढ़ने के लिए चीजों को छितराना

They rummaged through the cabinets.

Rumour/रूमर *(noun)*- उड़ती खबर, अफवाह

Rumour has it that they are going to marry soon.

Run/रन *(verb)* - दौड़ना, चालू करना, बहना, दौड़, दौड़ की संख्या

The thief ran as soon as he saw the police.

Rung/रंग *(noun)* - सीढ़ी का डंडा, जिस पर पैर रखते हैं

The rung broke as I was climbing up the ladder.

Runner/रनर *(noun)* - धावक

He is a fast runner.

Running/रनिंग *(noun)* - दौड़ना, धावन

The running in the race today was exceptional.

Runny/रनि *(adjective)* - सामान्य स्तर पर आशा से अधिक तरल

The cake batter is too runny.

Runway/रनवे *(noun)* - पथ

A deer strolled on to the runway.

Rupee/रूपी *(noun)* - भरतीय मुद्रा

I spent Rupees 300 on this dress.

Rupture/रप्चर *(verb)*- सम्बन्ध-विच्छेद

She had to be operated upon immediately when her appendix ruptured.

Rural/रूरल *(adjective)* - ग्रामीण

I am very fascinated by the rural lifestyle.

Ruse/रूज *(noun)* - धोखा, छल

The ruse was very clever.

Rush/रश *(noun)* - तालाब आदि के पास उगने वाला एक प्रकार का पौधा

This basket is made of rush.

Russet/रसद् *(adjective)* - गेरूआ रंग का

The russet dress is my favourite.

Rust/रस्ट *(noun)* - जंग (लोहे आदि में लगने वाला), मोरचा

The rust made the rod unusable.

Rustic/रस्टिक *(adjective)* - देहाती, ग्रामीण

He had a rustic home.

Rustle/रसल *(verb)* - सरसराहट

Her dress rustled in the wind.

Ss

S/एस - अंग्रेजी वर्णमाला का 19वाँ वर्ण the nineteenth letter of the English alphabet.

1. Any object shaped like S.
2. Roman numeral for 70 or 70,000.

Sabbath/सैबथ *(noun)* - प्रार्थना, विश्राम, प्रार्थना दिवस

I will visit my grandmother on Sabbath.

Sable/सेबल *(noun)* - रोएँदार खाल

I believe I saw a sable take a flight at dawn.

Sabotage/सैबॅटाज् *(verb)* - तोड़-फोड़, क्षतिग्रस्त करना

The athlete who had sabotaged the practice session was suspended.

Sabre/सेबर *(noun)* - तेग, तलवार

Even though the sabre was old, it was still sharp.

Saccharin/सैकरिन *(noun)* - अति मीठी टिकिया

She added saccharin to her porridge.

Sachet/साशे *(noun)* - पुड़िया, लिफाफा

Companies use sachets to promote their consumer products.

Sack/सैक *(noun)* - बोरा, बोरी

The social workers gathered the garbage in sacks.

S

Sacrament/सैक्रमेंट *(noun)* - शुद्धीकरण संस्कार (ईसाई धर्म में)

During the sacrament, everyone's face was lit with joy.

Sacred/सैक्रेड *(adjective)* - पवित्र, पावन

All sacred objects were collected from the antique dealer and installed in the temple.

Sacrifice/सेक्रिफाइस *(noun)* - उत्सर्ग, त्याग, बलिदान

She offered all her jewellery as a sacrifice for her husband's health.

Sacrilege/सैक्रिलेज् *(noun)* - अपवित्र करना, अपमान

He was punished severely for the sacrilege he had committed.

Sad/सैड *(adjective)* - उदास

She felt very sad when her cousin had to go back home after vacations.

Sadden/सैडेन *(verb)* - उदास कर देना

The news of the delay in his parents arrival saddened him.

Sadness/सैडनेस *(noun)* - उदासी

However hard she tried, she couldn't explain the sadness in her heart.

Saddle/सैड्ल *(noun)* - जीन

The saddle was made of pure leather.

Safari/सफारी *(noun)* - वन्य पशु दर्शन या आखेट के लिए सैर

The science students were very excited about going on a safari.

Safe/सेफ *(adjective)* - सुरक्षित, निरापद, तिजोरी

He believed that he was at a safe place.

Safeguard/सेफगार्ड *(noun)* - बचाव, सुरक्षा

Construction of the new fence around the house prove to be an effective safeguard.

Safe-keeping/सेफकीपिंग *(noun)* - देख-भाल, संरक्षण

My father left his car with his brother for safe-keeping.

Safety/सेफ्टि *(noun)* - सुरक्षा

They stayed indoors for safety.

Safety net - *(noun)*

It was fortunate that the trapeze artist fell on the safety net.

Saffron/सैफ्रन् *(noun)* - केसर, जाफरानी

The flavour of the saffron overwhelmed the other flavours of the dish.

Sag/सैग *(verb)* - धँसना

The roof of the house sagged dangerously.

Saga /सागा *(noun)* – बहुत लम्बी कहानी

I was touched by the sheer courage of the hero of the medical saga.

Sage/सेज *(noun)* – एक प्रकार की सुगंधित वनस्पति

I love the fragrance of sage.

Sagittarius/सैगिटेरियस *(noun)* – धनुर्धारी, धनु राशि

The students tried but weren't able to locate Sagittarius.

Sail/सेल *(noun)* – पाल, पाल के सहारे, समुद्री यात्रा

The boat could be identified easily by its bright sails.

Sailor/सेलर *(noun)* – नाविक

The actress was smitten by the handsome sailor.

Saint/सेंट *(noun)* – सन्त, धर्मात्मा

There is no doubt that he was a saint.

Sake/सेक *(noun)* – चावल की बनी हुई जापानी मदिरा

The boss shamed his company by getting drunk on Sake.

Salad/सैलड् *(noun)* – खीरा, प्याज आदि का मिश्रित खाद्य

Her diet consisted mostly of salads.

Salary/सैलरि *(noun)* – वेतन

The employees were overjoyed to receive bonus with their salary.

Sale/सेल *(noun)* – बिक्री

The family is very happy with the sale of the flat.

Saleable/सेलेब्ल *(adjective)* – विक्री हेतु, बिकाऊ

The mirror was very old but saleable.

Salesman/सेल्समैन *(noun)* – पुरुष बिक्रेता

The door-to-door salesman managed do good business.

Salesmanship/सेल्समैनशीप *(noun)* – बिक्रय कला

The experienced businessman delivered a valuable lecture on salesmanship.

Saleswoman/सेल्सवुमन *(noun)* – बिक्री करने वाली स्त्री

The saleswoman made a very strong sales pitch to sell her product.

Salient/सेलिएन्ट *(adjective)* – प्रमुख

Her shapely nose was the salient feature of her face.

Saline/सेलाइन *(adjective)* – रासायनिक नमक वाला, नमकीन

The saline solution tasted horrible.

Saliva/सलाइवा *(noun)* – लार

He swallowed his own saliva because he was thirsty.

Sallow/सैलो *(adjective)* – पीला तथा अस्वस्थ

The student's sallow skin was a reminder of her long illness.

Salmon/सैमन *(noun)* – एक मछली, रोहू सी मछली

I enjoyed watching the salmon jump.

Saloon/सैलून *(noun)* – कमरा, बैठका

They entered the saloon expecting splendour.

Salt/साल्ट *(noun)* – नमक, लवण

I added salt to my bland salad.

Salty/साल्टी *(adjective)* – नमकीन

The fish was salty.

Salubrious/सल्यूब्रिअस *(adjective)* – स्वास्थवर्धक

My mother's salubrious potion has always worked for me.

Salutary/सैल्यूटरी *(adjective)* – हितकर, अच्छा प्रभाव डालने वाला

The salutary interview will prove to be very helpful for the new gradates.

Salute/सैलूट *(noun)* – अभिवादन, सलाम

The children offered salutes to everyone who passed them that day.

Salvage/सैल्वेज् *(verb)* – नष्ट हुए से आंशिक बचाव

The rescue team salvaged the precious jewel just before the ship sank.

Salvation/सैल्वेशन् *(noun)* – मुक्ति, मोक्ष

My grandfather prays for salvation every day.

Same/सेम *(adj)* – एक तरह का, वही, वैसा ही, उसी तरह का

The twins had the same taste in food.

Sample/सैम्पल् *(noun)* – नमूना

The artist showcased a sample of his work.

Sanatorium/सैनटोरिअम *(noun)* – स्वास्थ्य केन्द्र, पागलखाना

The family sent the woman to a sanatorium to recover.

S

Sanctify/सैंक्टिफाइ *(verb)* – पवित्र करना

The priests sanctified the piece of land.

Sanctimonious/सैंक्टिमोनिअस *(adj)* – पाखण्डी

Her sanctimonious attitude is the reason why no one wants to talk to her.

Sanction/सैंक्शन *(noun)* – अनुमति, अनुज्ञप्ति, दण्ड

The community imposed sanctions against the family for disobeying the law.

Sanctity/सैंक्टिटी *(noun)* – पवित्रता

No one can question his sanctity.

Sanctuary/सैंक्ट्युअरि *(noun)* – शरणस्थान, अभयारण्य

Even though the criminal was in the sanctuary, he never felt secure.

Sand/सैंड *(noun)* – बालू, रेत

The sand sparkled in the sun.

Sandpaper/सैंडपेपर *(noun)* – सरेस

It was good that I had the sandpaper handy.

Sandstone/सैंडस्टोन *(noun)* – बलुआ पत्थर

The spectacular formations of sandstone mesmerized the onlookers.

Sandy/सैंडि *(adjective)* – रेतीला, बालू से भरा

The sandy beach was abandoned during the day.

Sandal/सैंडल *(noun)* – चप्पल

I prefer sandals over the other types of footwear.

Sandwich/सैंडविच *(noun)* – ब्रेड के दो टुकड़े जिनके बीच में खाद्य वस्तु हो

One sandwich is enough for me.

Sane/सेन *(adjective)* – विवेकपूर्ण, स्वस्थचित्त

The lawyer proved in the court that the accused was a sane person.

Sanguine/सैंग्विन *(adjective)* – विश्वासयुक्त, आशावान

The naughty boy remained sanguine even when he was on his way to the principal's office.

Sanitary/सैनिटरी *(adjective)* – स्वच्छ, स्वस्थकर

The sanitary conditions of the market were horrible.

Sanitation/सैनिटेशन *(noun)* – सफाई–व्यवस्था

At last, the department woke up to the sanitation.

Sanity/सैनिटी *(noun)* – उत्तेजना रहित, मानसिक सन्तुलन

I was thankful of my sanity through the tough times.

Sap/सैप *(noun)* – रस, रस निचोड़ना, दुर्बल करना

The sap of the tree was sweet.

Sapling/सैपलिंग *(noun)* – पौधा, कलम

The sapling looked healthy.

Sapphire/सैफायर *(noun)* – नीलमणि

The large sapphire on her engagement finger confused everyone.

Sarcasm/सरकाज्म *(noun)* – कटाक्ष

His sarcasm irritated me during our fight.

Sardine/सार्डिन *(noun)* – छोटी मछली

The preserved sardines tasted nice.

Sash/सैश *(noun)* – कमरबन्द

She wore her sash with pride.

Satan/सेटन *(noun)* – शैतान

The family was accused of worshipping Satan.

Satanic/सेटैनिक *(adjective)* – शैतान सा, दुष्टतापूर्ण

His satanic ideas were rejected by his friends.

Satchel/सैचल *(noun)* – बस्ता

He picked his satchel reluctantly and started walking towards the school.

Satellite/सैटलाइट *(noun)* – उपग्रह

The satellite was visible to naked eyes on clear nights.

Satiate/सैटिएट *(verb)* – तृप्त करना, अघा जाना

The generous helping satiated the poor man's hunger.

Satin/सैटिन *(noun)* – साटन

he planned to wear satin for the awards ceremony.

Satire/सैटायर *(noun)* – व्यंग्य, व्यंग्य रचना

The satire managed to move many people.

Satisfaction/सैटिस्फैक्शन *(noun)* – सन्तोष

Satisfaction made his life peaceful.

Satisfactory/सैटिस्फैक्टरी *(adj)* – सन्तोषजनक

His work was satisfactory.

Satisfy/सैटिस्फाई *(verb)* – सन्तुष्ट करना

The quality of the student's work satisfied the teachers.

Saturate/सैच्युरेट *(verb)* – संतृप्त होना, संतृप्त करना

The sponge was saturated and therefore left a trail of water when used for wiping.

Saturday/सैटरडे *(noun)* – शनिवार

I promise I will complete the work by this Saturday.

Saturn/सैटर्न *(noun)* – शनि

Saturn has several rings of different colours.

Satyr/सैटर *(noun)* – अर्द्धमानव देवता

The image of the Satyr frightened my son.

Sauce/सॉस *(noun)* – चटनी

He ate pizza with sauce.

Saucepan/सॉसपैन *(noun)* – डेकची

My saucepan broke when it fell from the stove.

Saucer/सॉसर *(noun)* – तश्तरी

The saucer looked more beautiful than the cup.

Sauna/सौना *(noun)* – भाप-स्नान

I enjoyed being in the sauna.

Saunter/सॉन्टर *(verb)* – चहलकदमी, चहलकदमी करना

The doctor leisurely sauntered through the wards

Sausage/सॉसेज *(noun)* – लंगोचा

The sausages were excellently cooked.

Savage/सैवेज *(adjective)* – जंगली, असभ्य

The savage eyes of the accused convinced the jury that he could have committed the crime.

Save/सेव *(preposition & conjunction)* – बचाना, सुरक्षित रखना

I'm saving up for a new bike.

Saving/सेविंग *(noun)* – बचत

The saving proved to be timely.

Saviour/सेव्यर् *(noun)* – रक्षक, मुक्तिदाता

My boss proved to be my saviour when I made a mistake in the presentation.

Savour/सेवर *(verb & noun)* – सुगन्ध, रस-स्वाद

I savoured cardamom-flavoured cookies.

Savoury/सेवरि *(adjective)* – नमकीन भोजन

I prefer savoury dishes to sweet ones.

Saw/सॉ *(noun)* – आरा

I saw several animals in the zoo.

Saxophone/सैक्सॅफोन *(noun)* – एक बाजा

He played saxophone like an expert.

Say/से *(verb)* – कहना, दुहराना

Please do as I say.

Saying/सेइंग *(noun)* – लोकोक्ति, कहावत

The little girl is well versed with many common sayings.

Scab/स्कैब *(noun)* – घाव की पपड़ी

The little boy kept scratching his scab.

Scabbard/स्कैबर्ड् *(noun)* – म्यान

The museum had only the scabbard, not the sword.

Scabies/स्केबिज *(noun)* – खाज, खुजली

He had a bad case of scabies.

Scaffold/स्कैफॉल्ड् *(noun)* – फाँसी का फन्दा

The crowd was relieved when the execution was called off and the scaffold dismantled.

Scald/स्कॉल्ड *(noun & verb)* – जला अंग, झुलसाना

The hot water scalded my hand.

Scale/स्केल *(noun)* – माप, सरगम, स्वर क्रम, कवच, तराजू, तुला के पल्ले

The vegetable vendor's scale didn't give correct results.

Scalp/स्कॉल्प *(noun)* – सिर की खाल

His hair had thinned so much that his scalp was visible through them.

Scalpel/स्कैल्पेल् *(noun)* – नस्तर

I was petrified by the sight of the surgeon holding the scalpel.

Scam/स्कैम *(noun)* – घोटाला

The rich businessman lost a lot of respect after the scam came to light.

Scamp/स्कैम्प *(noun)* – शरारती

The teacher scolded the scamp after he was caught trying to jump the school gate.

Scamper/स्कैम्पर *(verb)* – चौकड़ी भरना

The children scampered away as soon as the gate of the haunted house opened.

Scan/स्कैन *(verb)* – निरीक्षण, परीक्षण करना

My brother scanned the store and saw the laptop he would like to buy.

Scandal/स्कैन्डल *(noun)* - अफवाह

The coalgate scam was a scandal that people talked about for months.

Scant/स्कैन्ट *(adjective)* - अल्प, अपर्याप्त

The scant food barely satisfied anyone's hunger.

Scanty/स्कैन्टी *(adjective)* - अल्प मात्रा में

The beggar's scanty clothes hardly protected him from cold.

Scapegoat/स्केपगोट *(noun)* - बलि का बकरा

The employee was made a scapegoat when the scam came to light.

Scar/स्कार *(noun)* - दाग, निशान

Even though the burn had healed, the scars would take some time to go.

Scarce/स्केअर्स *(adjective)* - बिरला

The scarce vegetables worried everyone.

Scarcely/स्केअर्सलि *(adj)* - बहुत ही कम, मुश्किल से

There was scarcely a car on sight.

Scare/स्केअर *(verb)* - भयभीत करना, डराना

The old man scared the children with his stories of ghosts.

Scarecrow/स्केअरक्रो *(noun)* - बिजूका, चिड़ियों को डराने का पुतला

The scarecrow looked like a man from a distance.

Scarf/स्कार्फ *(verb)* - बल्ले के छोरों को जोड़ना

I scarfed the strip of leather.

Scarlet/स्कारलेट *(noun)* - सिन्दूरी

Her scarlet dress complemented her fair complexion.

S

Scathing/स्केदिंग् *(adjective)* - कठोर

His mother-in-law often gave him scathing looks.

Scatter/स्कैटर *(verb)* - तितर-बितर, बिखेरना

The decorators scattered the rose petals on the carpet.

Scavenge/स्केवेंज *(verb)* - कूड़े-कबाड़ में ढूँढ़ना

The hungry dog scavenged for food in the garbage.

Scenario/शेनारिओ *(noun)* - दृश्यावली पटकथा

The scenario the writer had presented interested the publisher.

Scenery/सीनरि *(noun)* - दृश्य, मंच सज्जा

The scenery took my breath away.

Scenic/सेनिक/सीनिक *(adjective)* - सुरम्य

I am so glad we took the long but scenic route to the desert.

Scent/सेंट *(noun)* - सुगन्ध

The scent of the roses attracted bees to the garden.

Sceptic/स्केप्टिक *(noun)* - संशयवादी

I am a sceptic by nature.

Sceptre/सेप्टर *(noun)* - राजचिह्न

The king carried a beautifully ornated sceptre.

Schedule/शेड्यूल् *(noun)* - कार्य-सूची, समय-सारणी

The secretary couldn't find even one empty slot in the boss's schedule.

Scheme/स्कीम *(noun)* - योजना

We were interested in the scheme as it seemed to offer considerable profit.

Schizophrenia/सिजोफ्रेनिआ *(noun)* - भ्रम से पीड़ित

Several members of his family were suffering from Schizophrenia.

Scholar/स्कॉलर *(noun)* - विद्यार्थी, विद्वान

The students were highly impressed by the knowledge of the history scholar.

Scholarly/स्कॉलर्लि *(adjective)* - पाण्डित्यपूर्ण

The boy's scholarly approach to everything has enabled him to learn a lot from life.

Scholarship/स्कॉलर्शिप *(noun)* - छात्रवृत्ति, विद्वता

The learned man has a series of scholarships to his credit.

Scholastic/स्कॉलैस्टिक *(adjective)* - पण्डिताऊ, शैक्षिक

The organization's concerns were mostly scholastic.

School/स्कूल *(noun)* - विद्यालय, पाठशाला

Their children are still at school.

Science/साइंस *(noun)* - विज्ञान

The young scientist revealed that she had become interested in science when she was very young.

Scientist/साइंटिस्ट *(noun)* – वैज्ञानिक

The scientist changed the world by his new discovery.

Scientifie/साइंटिफिक *(adjective)* – विज्ञान से सम्बन्धित

We need to be more scientific in agriculture production.

Scissors/सिजर्स *(plural noun)* – कैंची

The children's mother took the scissors away from them.

Scoff/स्कॉफ *(verb)* – ताना मारना, खिल्ली उड़ाना

His friends scoffed at his new hairstyle.

Scold/स्कोल्ड *(verb)* – डाँटना, फटकारना

My mother often scolds me for not studying.

Scone/स्कोन *(noun)* – एक नरम खाद्य

I had a scone with my tea.

Scoop/स्कूप *(noun)* – कलछी, बेलचा, खबर

The ice-cream vendor used the scoop with perfection.

Scooter/स्कूटर *(noun)* – दो चक्के की छोटी गाड़ी

He loved his new scooter.

Scope/स्कोप *(noun)* – क्षेत्र, व्याप्ति, गुंजाइश

This topic is beyond the scope of this discussion.

Scorch/स्कॉर्च *(verb)* – किसी वस्तु को झुलसाना

The extreme heat scorched all the leaves of the tree.

Score/स्कोर *(noun)* – प्राप्त अंक, कोड़ी, बीस की संख्या

Everyone was eagerly watching the score.

Scorn/स्कार्न् *(noun)* – घृणा, तिरस्कार, घृणा दिखाना

No one could ignore the persistent scorn she expressed throughout the party.

Scorpio/स्कॉर्पिओ *(noun)* – वृश्चिक राशि

I have many good friends whose zodiac sign is Scorpio.

Scorpion/स्कॉर्पिअन *(noun)* – बिच्छू

A poisonous scorpion was hiding in the bathroom.

Scot-free/स्कॉटफ्री *(adj.)* – बिना दण्ड पाये

He went scot-free even though he had committed the crime.

Scoundrel/स्काउन्ड्रल *(noun)* – दुष्ट, घृणित व्यक्ति

The scoundrel ran away after cheating all of his neighbours.

Scour/स्काउर् *(verb)* – माँजना, रगड़कर चमकना

I watched with amazement as the man scoured age-old dust off the antique tray.

Scourge/स्कर्ज *(noun)* – कोड़ा

I can't imagine from where he found the old scourge.

Scout/स्काउट *(noun)* – बालचर, भेदिया

People were amazed to see the scouts on the streets.

Scowl/स्काउल् *(noun)* – त्योरी, बल पड़ना

The teacher's scowl made him think that he had said something wrong.

Scrabble/स्क्रैब्ल् *(verb)* – खुरचना, टटोलना

She scrabbled inside her purse for money.

Scraggy/स्क्रैगि *(adjective)* – मरियल

The little boy was scraggy as compared to the rest of his classmates.

Scramble/स्क्रैम्बल *(verb)* – रेंगना, छीना-झपटी

All of them scrambled out of the room as soon as the angry teacher looked at them.

Scrap/स्क्रैप *(noun)* – कतरन, टुकड़ा, झगड़ा

The scraps were delivered to the merchant.

Scrape/स्क्रेप *(verb)* – घिसकर चिकनाना, खरोचना

The cupboard was scraped across the room.

Scratch/स्क्रैच *(verb)* – कुरेदना, खुरचना, नोचना

I scratched my skin with the hard wooden board.

Scrawl/स्क्रॉल *(verb)* – जल्दी में लिखना

The students scrawled the notes as the professor spoke.

Scream/स्क्रीम् *(verb)* – चीखना

My mother screamed when she saw the fat rat.

Screech/स्क्रीच् *(noun)* – कर्कश, चीख

The screech startled me out of my sleep.

Screen/स्क्रीन् *(noun)* – परदा, ओट

The screen effectively divided the huge room into two.

Screw/स्क्रू *(noun & verb)* – पेंच, पेंच से कसना

The screws held the dilapidated cupboard together.

Scribble/स्क्रिब्ल *(verb)* - जल्दीबाजी में लिखा हुआ

I like to scribble important information when I am talking on the phone. .

Scribbe/स्क्राइब *(noun)* - मुंशी, लिपिक

The scribe maintained the records very diligently.

Scrip/स्क्रिप *(noun)* - पावती

The shareholders were pleasantly surprised to receive the scrip.

Script/स्क्रिप्ट *(noun)* - लिपि, मुद्रण, पटकथा

Hindi has a script different from English.

Scriptures/स्क्रिप्चर्स *(noun)* - धर्मग्रन्थ

My mother likes to read scriptures of all religions.

Scroll/स्क्रोल् *(noun)* - लिखने या रंगसाजी के लिए लिपटे हुए कागज का मुट्‌ठा

The scroll was so fragile that it looked as if it will crumble at the slightest touch.

Scrub/स्क्रब *(noun)* - साफ करना, झाड़-झंखाड़

The scrub was vast and deserted.

Scruff/स्क्रफ *(noun)* - गर्दन का पिछला भाग

The magician held the rabbit by its scruff.

Scruple/स्क्रप्ल *(noun)* - धर्मभीरुता

He has no scruples against stealing.

Scrupulous/स्क्रूप्युलस *(adjective)* - अति सावधान या ब्योरों पर अधिक ध्यान देने वाला

I need a very scrupulous person for this job.

Scrutinize/स्क्रूटिनाइज् *(verb)* - जाँच करना

You need to scrutinize all evidences thoroughly before the court case.

S

Scrutiny/स्क्रूटिनि *(noun)* - जाँच

There was no cheating in the examination hall because of the scrutiny.

Scuffle/स्कफ्ल *(noun)* - हाथापाई

I came running out of my room when I heard the scuffle.

Scull/स्कल *(noun)* - चप्पू, नौका-दौड़

The rower felt so weak that he wasn't even able to hold the sculls.

Scullery/स्कलरि *(noun)* - वर्तन माँजने का स्थान

The maid worked in the scullery after clearing the table.

Sculptor/स्कल्पटर *(noun)* - मूर्तिकार

I couldn't believe I was meeting the famous sculptor in person.

Sculpture/स्कल्प्चर् *(noun)* - मूर्तिकला

The sculpture was true to life.

Scum/स्कम् *(noun)* - झाग, फेन

They cleared the scum off the surface of the lake.

Scurrilous/स्करिलस् *(adjective)* - अभद्र, अपमान जनक

When I joined my job, my father warned me of scurrilous colleagues.

Scurry/स्करि *(verb)* - छोटे-छोटे तेज कदमों से आगे बढ़ना

The little man scurried to take cover as soon as the rain started.

Scurvy/स्कर्वि *(noun)* - एक प्रकार का रक्त रोग

Many people are suffering from scurvy and they don't even know it.

Scuttle/स्कट्ल *(noun)* - टोकरा, छेद करना, असफल करना, भागना

Mother noticed just in time that the scuttle was almost empty.

Scythe/साइद् *(noun & verb)* - हँसिया, हँसिया से काटना

The old scythe was rusty and blunt.

Sea/सी *(noun)* - समुद्र

The sunset at the sea was mesmerizing.

Seal/सील *(noun)* - मोहर, मुहर बन्द करना, समुद्री पशु

The young seal was barely able to swim.

Seam/सीम *(noun)* - सिलाई, सीवन

I was about to leave for office when I noticed that my dress was torn at the seam.

Search/सर्च *(verb)* - खोज

I searched through my bag to find my keys.

Searchlight/सर्चलाइट *(noun)* - खोजी प्रकाश

The rescue services were using searchlights to look for the ship.

Season/सीजन *(noun)* - ऋतु, मौसम

This is not the season for mango trees to produce fruit.

Seasonal/सीजनल *(adjective)* - मौसमी

Apple is a seasonal fruit.

Seasoned/सीजन्ड *(adjective)* - अनुभवी

She has become a seasoned lawyer over time.

Seat/सीट *(noun)* - आसन, सभा, बैठना

It was uncomfortable sitting there because the seats were hard.

Secede/सीसिड *(verb)* - अलग होना

After giving it a good thought, I seceded my membership in the union.

Seclude/सिक्लूड *(verb)* - स्वतन्त्र हो जाना

The family secluded themselves from everyone.

Secluded/सिक्लूडेड् *(adjective)* - एकान्त, निर्जन

Not many people enter the secluded part of the forest.

Second/सेकंड *(noun)* - पल, दूसरा, समर्थन

He was up and ready to go in seconds.

Secondary/सेकंडरि *(adjective)* - माध्यमिक

Studies were secondary to the tennis player.

Secrecy/सीक्रेसि *(noun)* - छिपाव, गोपनीयता

I can't understand the secrecy around this issue

Secret/सीक्रेट *(adjective)* - गोपनीय, रहस्यमय, भेद, गूढ़

I formed a secret society with my friends when I was young.

Secretive/सिक्रीटिव् *(adjective)* - गोपनीय

The actress was very secretive about her real identity.

Sect/सेक्ट *(noun)* - पंथ, सम्प्रदाय, मत

A sect has often broken away from a larger group.

Sectarian/सेक्टेरिअन् *(adjective)* - साम्प्रदायिक

They passed a sectarian judgment for the man's sins.

Section/सेक्शन *(noun)* - अंश, टुकड़ा, हिस्सा, खण्ड, परिच्छेद

You need to fill all sections of the form

Sector/सेक्टर *(noun)* - क्षेत्र अंचल, युद्धस्थल

Our sector mostly has apartments.

Secular/सेक्युलर *(adjective)* - धर्मनिरपेक्ष

India is a secular country.

Secure/सिक्योर् *(adjective)* - सुरक्षित, निश्चिंत

The door was secured properly.

Security/सिक्यूरिटि *(noun)* - सुरक्षा, प्रतिभूति, जमानत

Security made him very generous.

Sedate/सिडेट *(adjective)* - सौम्य, नींद हेतु दवा

The sedate Congressman had a huge fan following.

Sedative/सिडेटिव *(noun)* - नींद या आराम की औषधि

The sedative properties of the medicine kept me from taking it during office hours.

Sediment/सेडिमेंट *(noun)* - बहाकर लाये गये टुकड़े

The sediment was a proof of the dirtiness of water.

Sedimentary/सेडिमेंटरि *(adjective)* - टुकड़े-टुकड़े में जमा

The sedimentary rock formations were breathtaking.

Sedition/सिडिशन *(noun)* - राजद्रोह

Even though he was punished for sedition, his speech inspired many.

Seduce/सिड्यूस *(verb)* - प्रलोभन देना

Special affers seduce customers into spending their money.

Seduction/सिडक्शन *(noun)* - प्रलोभन देकर राजी करना

Several people fell prey to her seduction.

Seductive/सिडक्टिव *(adjective)* - प्रलोभनपूर्ण

People often tell her that she has a very seductive voice.

Seductiveness/सिडक्टिवनेस *(noun)* - प्रलोभन देने की कला/क्रिया

People often compliment her on the seductiveness of her eyes.

See/सी *(noun & verb)* - देखना

The see was surrounded by dense forest.

Seed/सीड *(noun)* - बीज, कारण, उद्गम

The seed sprouted almost immediately.

Seedy/सीडी *(adjective)* – बीज से भरा हुआ, मैला, अस्वस्थ

The place looked very seedy.

Seek/सीक *(verb)* – प्राप्त करने का प्रयत्न, खोजना

I seek a good friend in you.

Seem/सीम *(verb)* – प्रतीत होना

He made it seem so simple.

Seemly/सीमली *(adjective)* – उपयुक्त

Her dress was quite seemly.

Seep/सीप *(verb)* – टपकना, रिसना

Water seeped in through the concrete.

Seer/सीअर *(noun)* – मनीषी, भविष्यद्रष्टा

The seer foretold that the businessman would do very well.

See-saw/सी-सा *(noun)* – एक झूला, ढेंकी

My nephew was desperate to go to the see-saw but there was no other child to play with him.

Seethe/सीद् *(verb)* – खौलकर बुदबुदाना

I seethed the vegetables so that they could be cooked in a short time.

Segment/सेग्मेंट *(noun)* – टुकड़ा, हिस्सा, खण्ड, फांक

That segment of the crowd is much more disciplined than this segment.

Segregate/सेग्रिगेट *(verb)* – छाँटना, पृथक् करना

The teacher segregated the children into two groups based on their heights.

Segregation/सेग्रिशन *(noun)* – अलग-अलग करना

The teacher does not believe in any kind of segregation.

S

Seismic/साइज्मिक *(adjective)* – भूकम्प से सम्बन्धित

The geologists predicted heavy seismic activities during the day.

Seize/सीज *(verb)* – छीनना, कब्जा में लेना

The thugs seized my uncle's property.

Seizure/सीजर *(noun)* – जब्ती, मिरगी का दौरा

They called the police after the unauthorized seizure.

Seldom/सेल्डम *(adverb)* – कभी-कभार, यदा-कदा

I seldom visit the city park.

Select/सिलेक्ट *(verb)* – चुनना, पसन्द करना

The teacher selected the tallest students for the dance.

Selection/सिलेक्शन *(noun)* – चुनाव, चयन, चुने हुए

Even though the selection appeared random, it had an unseen logic to it.

Selective/सिलेक्टिव *(adjective)* – चयनित, पसंदीदा

The film star claims that he is very selective about his roles.

Self/सेल्फ *(noun)* – आत्म, स्वत्व, स्वार्थ, स्वयं

He doesn't understand the concept of self.

Self-centred/सेल्फसेंटर्ड *(adjective)* – आराम-केन्द्रित

The man was very self-centred.

Self-conscious/सेल्फकॉन्सस् *(adj)* – आत्मचेतन

The self-conscious student forgot his lines during the play.

Self-control/सेल्फकन्ट्रोल *(noun)* – आत्म नियन्त्रण

Everyone commended his self-control in the face of loss.

Self-defence/सेल्फडिफेंस *(noun)* – आत्मरक्षा

The crime was committed in self-defence.

Selfish/सेल्फिश *(adjective)* – स्वार्थी

His actions appeared selfish to the others.

Selfishly/सेल्फिश्लि *(adverb)* – स्वार्थवश

He selfishly ate all the food.

Selfless/सेल्फलेस *(adjective)* – नि:स्वार्थ

No one can question a mother's selfless love.

Selfmade/सेल्फमेड *(adjective)* – आत्मनिर्भर

My father is a self-made man.

Self-respect/सेल्फरिस्पेक्ट *(noun)* – आत्मसम्मान, आत्म गौरव

The matter became a question of self-respect for her.

Self-sufficient/सेल्फसफिश्यन्द् *(adj)* – स्वयं में पूर्ण

The island dwellers were self-sufficient in their agricultural needs.

Self-willed/सेल्फविल्ड *(adjective)* – जिद्दी

At times, he regretted his self-willed attitude.

Sell/सेल *(verb)* – बेंचना

I sold my painting for good money.

Seller/सेलर *(noun)* – विक्रेता

The vegetable seller lived a honest life.

Selvage/सेल्वेज *(noun)* – सिला, किनारी

The selvage of the fabric was very ornate.

Semantic/सिमैंटिक *(adjective)* – शब्द शास्त्र

I have never understood the semantic behind the usage of some words.

Semblance/सेम्ब्लन्स *(noun)* – सादृश्य

The friendship they shared had the semblance of love.

Semi/सेमि *(pref.)* – अर्द्ध, आंशिक

The boy and his father lived in a semi-decorated house.

Semicolon/सेमिकोलन *(noun)* – अर्द्ध विराम का चिह्न

I asked the teacher to explain me the usage of a semi-colon.

Semifinal/सेमिफाइनल *(noun)* – अन्त के पूर्व

The semifinal match was very exciting.

Seminar/सेमिनार *(noun)* – विचार गोष्ठी, गोष्ठी

Some very relevant topics were covered in the seminar.

Senate/सिनेट *(noun)* – सदन, शासीनिकाय

The senate is meeting tonight to discuss the bilateral ties between the two countries.

Send/सेंड *(verb)* – भेजना

I requested my father to send me some books.

Senior/सीनिअर *(adjective)* – वरिष्ठ, ज्येष्ठ

Show respect to senior people.

Seniority/सीनिऑरिटि *(noun)* – वरीयता, वरिष्ठता

He never took advantage of his seniority.

Sensation/सेंसेशन *(noun)* – अनुभूति उत्पादक सनसनी

I had a sensation of pain in my arm.

Sense/सेंस *(noun)* – ज्ञान, ज्ञानेन्द्रिय, बोध

Dogs have a powerful sense of smell.

Senseless/सेंसलेस *(adjective)* – बेहोश, अचेत, मूर्खतापूर्ण

The drunkard lay senseless on the footpath.

Sensibility/सेंसिबिलिटि *(noun)* – भावुकता, संवेदना, संवेदनशीलता

The artist had the sensibility to judge a good work of art.

Sensible/सेंसिब्ल *(adj)* – विवेकी, विवेकपूर्ण wise

My father is a very sensible man.

Sensitive/सेंसिटिव *(adjective)* – भावुक

The blind man is very sensitive to the changes in the intensity of light.

Sensual/सेंसुअल *(adjective)* – दैहिक आनन्द, भोग-विलास

The artist was very proud of his sensual paintings.

Sensuous/सेंसुअस *(adjective)* – इन्द्रियजनित, इन्द्रिय सम्बन्धी

The movie was very sensuous.

Sentence/सेन्टेंस *(noun)* – वाक्य

The child has started talking in complete sentences.

Sentiment/सेंटिमेंट *(noun)* – भावुकता, संवेदना

I express my sentiments very openly.

Sentimental/सेंटिमेंटल *(adjective)* – भावुक, संवेदनशील

The sentimental actress started crying for real during the scene.

Sentinel/सेंटिनल *(noun)* – पहरेदार

The sentinel came running to announce the approach of the enemy.

Sentry/सेन्ट्रि *(noun)* – पहरेदार, संतरी

The sentry was doing his job well.

Separable/सेपरेब्ल *(adjective)* – अलग करने योग्य

The hair-dryer has separable attachments.

Separate/सेपरेट *(adjective)* – अलग या पृथक् करना

Both friends run separate businesses.

Separation/सेपरेशन *(noun)* – विभाजन, पृथक्करण, बँटवारा

Their separation was very traumatic for their children.

September/सेप्टेम्बर *(noun)* – सितम्बर

My niece was born in September.

Septic/सेप्टिक *(adjective)* – विषाक्त

The septic wound needed to be treated immediately.

Sepulchre/सेपल्कर् *(noun)* – समाधि

The children were scared to go near the Sepulchre.

Sequel/सीक्वेल *(noun)* – परिणाम, उत्तरकथा

I loved the movie so much that I was desperately waiting for the sequel.

Sequence/सीक्वेन्स् *(noun)* – क्रमबद्ध, संबद्ध, संवद्धता

The piano sequence in the musical left everyone in awe.

Seraph/सेरफ *(noun)* – स्वर्गीय दूत

The seraphs floating around in her dream made a beautiful picture.

Serene/सिरीन् *(adjective)*– शान्त, गम्भीर

The serene look on the saint's face was worth noticing.

Serenely/सिरीन्लि *(adverb)* – शान्ति से

My mother listened to my problem serenely before giving me advice.

Serf/सर्फ *(noun)* – दास

In earlier times serfs were made to work without wages.

Sergeant/सर्जेंट *(noun)* – एक पद नाम

The sergeant ordered his platoon to gather in the grounds for a warm-up.

Serial/सीरिअल *(adjective)* – क्रमबद्ध, क्रमवार, धारा, वाहिक

The class was asked to stand according to their serial numbers.

Series/सीरीज *(noun)* – शृंखला, शृंखलाबद्ध, श्रेणीबद्ध, विद्युतधारा

The kidnapper was caught with the series of banknotes that had been marked out by the police.

S

Serious/सीरिअस *(adjective)* – गम्भीर, विचारमग्न

Are you serious about starting your own business?.

Seriously/सीरिअस्लि *(adverb)* – गम्भीरता से

We need to think seriously about the problem of beggars in our country.

Sermon/सर्मन *(noun)* – उपदेश, प्रवचन

During the Sunday church service the sermon lasts for over an hour.

Sermonise/सर्मनाइज *(verb)* – भाषण झाड़ना

Nowadays children feel that every time their parents tell them something, they are sermonizing

Serpent/सर्पेंट *(noun)* – साँप

There is a serpent in the tree trunk.

Serpentine/सर्पेंटाइन *(adjective)* – कुण्डलीनुमा मुड़ा हुआ

Many people suffer from motion sickness while travelling to the hills due to the serpentine roads.

Serrated/सेरेटेड *(adjective)* – दाँतेदार आरी जैसे दाँत वाला

The serrated blade of the knife was very sharp.

Servant/सर्वेंट *(noun)* – नौकर, कर्मचारी

Guru Nanak looked upon himself as a servant of God.

Serve/सर्व *(verb)* – सेवा करना, नौकरी करना, लेन-देन करना, तामील करना, आराम करना

To serve the poor is the service of God.

Service/सर्विस *(noun)* – नौकरी, सेवा

He was in government service for 21 years.

Serviette/सर्विएट *(noun)* – खाने के समय प्रयुक्त नैपकिन

I asked the waiter for a serviette.

Servile/सर्वाइल *(adjective)* – दासोचित

Sam has a servile attitude when interacting with his boss.

Sesame/सेसमि *(noun)* – तिल

My uncle grows sesame in his fields.

Session/सेशन *(noun)* – सत्र

I had a session with the dietician today.

Set/सेट *(verb)* – रखना, तैयार करना, गाड़ना, स्थापित करना, समूह, समुच्चय

The stage was set for the play.

Settee/सेटी *(noun)* – आराम कुर्सी

Most of the guests preferred to sit on the settee.

Setting/सेटिंग *(noun)* – मंचसज्जा, सुसज्जित

The author used the town of his birth as the setting.

Settle/सेटल *(noun)* – समझौता द्वारा निर्णय करना, स्थिर होना, धँसना

The settle has broken down because of disrepair.

Settlement/सेटलमेंट *(noun)* – समझौता, निपटारा, बस्ती, उपनिवेश

The settlement was taking a long time.

Settler/सेटलर *(noun)* – नया बसने वाला

The settlers soon began to cultivate crops.

Seven/सेवेन *(cardinal number)* – सात

There were seven children in the balcony.

Seventh/सेवेन्थ *(ordinal number)* – सातवाँ

He stood seventh in the queue.

Seventeen/सेवेन्टीन *(noun)* – सत्रह

There were a total of seventeen pigeons in the tree.

Seventy/सेवेन्टि *(cardinal number)* – सत्तर

The class had 70 students.

Sever/सेवर *(verb)* – विभाजित करना, कटना

The workmen severed the ropes.

Several/सेवरल *(pronoun)* – अनेक

Several of the guests left very early.

Severe/सिविअर *(adjective)* – तीव्र, कठोर, प्रचण्ड

I had a severe headache.

Sew/सियू *(verb)* – सीना, सिलाई

I sewed the torn rim of my skirt.

Sewing/सियूंग *(noun)* – सिलाई करना

My mom loves sewing.

Sewage/सिवेज *(noun)* – मल-नाली

The smell of the sewage made it difficult to stand there.

Sewer/सिवर *(noun)* – भूमिगत नाला

The road was dug up because the sewer was being laid.

Sex/सेक्स *(noun)* – लिंग, सम्भोग

The lion cub belonged to female sex.

Sexism/सेक्सिज्म *(noun)* – लिंगवाद

Sexism isn't healthy in workplaces.

Sexual/सेक्सुअल *(adjective)* – यौन विषयक

The photographer was working on a documentary about the sexual behaviour of tigers.

Shabby/शैबि *(noun)* – जीर्ण-शीर्ण, फटेहाल, कमीना

The shabby man roamed around in the streets late at night.

Shack/शैक *(noun)* – फूहड़, झोपड़ी

We were glad to find the shack when we got lost in the forest.

Shackle/शैकल *(noun)* – बेड़ी, हथकड़ी

The man in the shackles was very menacing.

Shade/शेड *(noun)* – छाया

The shade was such a relief in the blazing sun.

Shadow/शैडो *(noun)* – साया, परछाई, छाया

The dog chased its shadow.

Shadowy/शैडोवि *(adj)* – धुँधला, अस्पष्ट

A shadowy figure was coming towards me.

Shady/शेडि *(adjective)* – छायादार, अवैध

Let us move to a shady part of the park.

Shaft/शैफ्ट *(noun)* – भाले आदि का डण्डा

He was hit by the shaft of the spear.

Shaggy /शैगि *(adjective)* – उलझे बाल, मैल-कुचैले बाल

The dog had shaggy hair.

Shake/शेक *(verb)* – थरथराना, हिलना, हिलाना

The entire building shook with the impact.

Shaky/शेकि *(adjective)* – अस्थिर, हिलता हुआ, कमजोर

The shaky man narrated his horrible tale of fear.

Shall/शैल *(modal verb)* – सहायक क्रिया

I shall get the work done

Shallow/शैलो *(adjective)* – छिछला सतही, छिछोरा

The lake was shallow but dangerous.

Sham/शैम *(noun)* – स्वाँग भरना

His love was just a sham.

Shambles/सैम्बल्ज् *(noun)* – अव्यवस्थित

No one wanted to visit the shambles.

Shame/शेम *(noun)* – लज्जा, शर्म

He experienced a lot of shame when he was caught cheating.

Shameful/शेमफुल *(adjective)* – शर्मनाक, लज्जाजनक

Her actions were seen as shameful by her relatives.

Shameless/शेमलेस *(adjective)* – बेशर्म, निर्लज्ज

The thief was absolutely shameless even when he was caught by the police.

Shampoo/शैम्पू *(noun)* – बालों को धोने का तरल पदार्थ

I prefer using a herbal shampoo.

Shape/शेप *(noun)* – आकृति, निर्धारित करना

I could see the shape of a man behind the curtains.

Shapeless/शेपलेस *(adjective)* – आकृतिहीन

The dress is decidedly shapeless.

Shapely/शेपली *(adjective)*– आकर्षक आकृति

It is important for a model to have a shapely body.

Share/शेअर *(noun)* – हिस्सेदारी, भाग, हिस्सा

Everyone was happy with their share in the property.

Shavings/शेविंग्स *(noun)*– कतरन

My friend collected pencil shavings.

Shawl/शॉल *(noun)* – ऊनी चादर

I loved her pashmina shawl.

She/शी *(pronoun)* – स्त्री वाचक 'वह'

Ruby is the only daughter of her parents, and she is her father's favourite.

Sheaf/शीफ् *(noun)* – धान का पूल, गट्ठर

The farmer's wife carried the sheaf of wheat on her head.

Shear/शिअर *(verb)* – ऊन काटना, भेंड़ का बाल काटना

The men sheared the unwilling sheep.

Shears/शिअर्स *(plural noun)* – घास, पौधे काटने की कैंची

S

The shears were very sharp and dangerous.

Sheath/शीथ् *(noun)* – म्यान, आवरण, निषेध

The sheath was very ornate.

Sheathe/शीद् *(verb)* – म्यान में रखना

The warrior sheathed the sword.

Shed/शेड *(noun)* – छतदार, जानवरों की झोपड़ी गिराना, उतारना, छुटकारा पाना

The tractor rolled out of the shed.

Sheen/शीन *(noun)* – चमक, तड़क-भड़क

The new car had a beautiful sheen.

Sheep/शीप *(noun)* – भेंड़

I love to see the sheep on the rolling green hills.

Sheepish/शीपिश् *(adjective)* – भेड़ के सदृश, लज्जालू, डरपोक

The boy was caught because he was acting sheepish.

Sheer/शिअर *(adjective)* – पूरा का पूरा, बारीक

He owed his success to sheer hard work.

Sheet/शीट *(noun)* – चादर, (कपड़ा, शीशा, कागज, लोहा)

The sailor desperately pulled the sheet.

Shelf/शेल्फ *(noun)* – खाना, टाँड़, कगार

All my books are displayed on the shelf.

Shell/शेल *(noun)* – कोश, छिलका, आवरण, सीप, सीपी

Some children were collecting shells on the beach.

Shelter/शेल्टर *(noun)* – शरणस्थली

The storm shelter proved to be very helpful when the tornado hit.

Shelve/शेल्व *(verb)* – स्थगित करना

Our project was shelved after the product manager declared that the product will not sell.

Shepherd/शेफर्ड *(noun)* – गड़ेरिया

The shepherd sat near the sheep and played his flute.

Sheriff/शेरिफ *(noun)* – शासकीय पद

The sheriff ordered the men to be arrested immediately.

Shield/शील्ड *(noun)* – कवच, ढाल, खेल का पुरस्कार, रक्षक

His shield protected him from the enemy's sword.

Shift/शिफ्ट *(verb)* – खिसकना, खिसकाना, बदलाव, पाली

The passengers shifted themselves slightly to accommodate the old man.

Shifty/शिफ्टी *(adjective)* – अविश्वनीय

I did not trust the man because he looked shifty.

Shilling/शिलिंग *(noun)* – ब्रिटेन का सिक्का

The child had a huge collection of Shillings.

Shimmer/शिमर *(verb)* – झिलमिल करना, झिलमिलाना

The water shimmered in the sun.

Shin/शिन *(noun)* – टाँग

Her dressed came down to the middle of her shins.

Shine/शाइन *(verb)* – चमकना, चमकाना, श्रेष्ठ या यशस्वी होना

Her eyes seemed to shine with excitement.

Shingle/शिंगल *(noun)* – कंकड़ों का ढेर (समुद्र तट पर)

Several shingles fell from the roof.

Ship/शिप *(noun)* – जहाज, पोत

The ship was huge but didn't have enough lifeboats.

Shipmate/शिपमेट *(noun)* – सहनाविक

The young sailor got along well with his shipmates.

Shipment/शिपमेंट *(noun)* – जहाज पर लादा जाने वाला माल

The shipment has happened an hour back.

Shipshape/शिपशेप *(adjective)* – सुव्यवस्थित, साफ

The shipshape cabin was such a relief.

Shipwreck/शिपरेक *(noun)* – जहाज का टूटना, डूबना

The shipwreck happened miles from the shore.

Shipyard/शिपयार्ड *(noun)* – जहाज बनाने का कारखाना

The shipyard was full so we had to move ahead.

Shirk/शर्क *(verb)* – कठिन या अप्रिय काम से जी चुराना

Only irresponsible people shirk their responsibilities.

Shirker/शर्कर *(noun)* – कामचोर

The shirker got scolded by his boss regularly.

Shirt/शर्ट *(noun)* – कमीज

The pattern of his shirt was very tropical.

Shiver/शिवर *(verb)* – काँपना, ठिठुरना

I shivered because of fear.

Shoal/शोल *(noun)* – मछलियों का झुंड

The shoal was getting bigger and bigger.

Shock/शॉक *(noun)* – आघात, आघात पहुँचाना

The shock is a very effective arrangement.

Shoddy/शॉडी *(noun)* – घटिया, रद्दी

The sticking was very shoddy.

Shoe/शू *(noun)* – जूता

He likes leather shoes.

Shoelace/शूलेस *(noun)* – जूते का फीता

His shoelaces had come undone.

Shoot/शूट *(noun & verb)* – गोली चलाना, गोली मारना, अंकुर, शिकार

He shot the dummy thrice.

Shop/शॉप *(noun)* – दुकान

The shop is closed today.

Shopping/शॉपिंग *(noun)* – खरीदारी

Shopping is my favourite activity.

Shore/शोर *(noun)* – तट, किनारा

Workers were worried because the shore had started splintering.

Short/शॉर्ट *(adjective)* – छोटा, नाटा, संक्षिप्त, कम, अचानक

We took the short journey to home.

Shortage/शॉर्टेज *(noun)* – अभाव

The shortage of water caused a lot of worry amongst the residents.

Shorten/शार्टेन *(verb)* – छोटा करना

The orator shortened his speech as the time was running out.

Shortly/शॉर्टली *(adverb)* – शीघ्र

I will be there shortly.

Shorts/शार्ट्स् *(plural noun)* – जांघिया, निकर

No one was allowed to wear shorts at the workplace.

Shot/शॉट *(adjective)* – गोली की आवाज woven

The shot fabric brought out the beauty of the dress.

Should/शुड *(modal verb)* – क्रिया रूप

You should make a schedule for your studies.

Shoulder/शोल्डर *(noun)* – कंधा, स्कंध, भार उठाना

My shoulder started aching when I lifted the heavy suitcase.

Shout/शाउट *(verb)* - चीखना, पुकारना

The teacher shouted at the students.

Shove/शोव *(verb)* - धकेलना

The girl shoved her friend away.

Shovel/शॅवॅल *(noun)* - बेलचा

They bought a shovel to prepare for the winters.

Show/शो *(noun & verb)* - दिखाना, प्रदर्शन, कार्यक्रम

He showed the film in his home theatre.

Shower/शॉवर *(noun)* - बौछार, फुहारा-स्नान

The meteor shower was a spectacular sight.

Shred/श्रेड *(noun)* - धज्जी, धज्जियाँ उड़ाना

The shred was too small to be used as a patch.

Shrewd/श्रूड *(adjective)* - चतुर, समझदार, सयाना

Her shrewd observations were very helpful for the company.

Shriek/श्रीक *(verb)* - चीख मारना, चीख

She shrieked when she saw the shadow.

Shrill/श्रिल *(adjective)* - तीखी, कर्णभेदी ध्वनि

Stop the shrill sound immediately.

Shrimp/श्रिम्प *(noun)* - झींगा मछली

The shrimps swam away.

Shrine/श्राइन *(noun)* - समाधि

The shrine received millions of visitors each year.

Shrink/श्रिंक *(verb)* - सिकुड़न, सिकुड़ना

The t-shirt shrank considerably after the first wash.

S

Shrivel/श्रिवेल *(verb)* - झुर्री, शिकन, कुम्हलाना

The long exposure to water shrivelled her hands.

Shroud/श्राउड् *(noun)* - कफन

The holy man was wrapped in a saffron shroud.

Shrub/श्रब *(noun)* - झाड़ी, झाड़-झंखाड

The thorny shrub had to be removed.

Shrug/श्रग् *(verb)* - कंधे झटकाना

He shrugged away the opinions of his subordinates.

Shudder/शडर *(verb)* - हिलना, काँपना, भय से काँपना

I shudder at the memory of those tough times.

Shuffle/शफल *(verb)* - घिसते हुए चलना

The lazy boy shuffled away.

Shun/शन् *(verb)* - बचना

I shunned his views on traditional education.

Shunt/शन्ट *(verb)* - मार्ग बदलना, दुरस्थ करना

The extra carriages were shunted to another route.

Shut/शट *(verb)* - बन्द करना

I shut the door as it was very windy outside.

Shutter/शटर *(noun)* - दुकान का लोहे का दरवाजा

The shutter was opened by the helper.

Shuttle/शट्ल *(noun)* - जाना-आना, फेरा करना

The shuttle from the office to the train station isn't running today.

Shy/शाइ *(noun & verb)* - संकोची, झेंपू, हया से भरा

He shied his shoe at the rat. His shy missed its target.

Sibling/सिब्लिंग *(noun)* - सहोदर

I have one sibling.

Sick/सिक *(adj)* - स्वस्थ नहीं, बीमार

Half of my staff were sick.

Sicken/सिकेन *(verb)* - ऊबना, ऊबा देना

The stench in the abandoned house sickened me.

Sickle/सिकल *(noun)* - हंसिया

We needed to buy a new sickle as the old one was broken.

Sickly/सिक्ली *(adjective)* - दुर्बल, अस्वस्थ रहने वाला

She was a sickly child.

Sickness/सिक्नेस् *(noun)* - बीमारी

Doctors are yet to diagnose my aunt's sickness.

Side/साइड *(noun)* - बगल, पार्श्व, भुजाएँ, पक्ष, दल

Please move to the other side.

Sidle/सिड्ल् *(verb)* - दबकर चलना

She sidled up to her to surprise her.

Siege/सीज *(noun)* – घेराबन्दी
The siege was successful after seven days.

Sieve/सिव *(noun)* – चलनी, छाननी
I bought a new sieve today.

Sift/सिफ्ट *(verb)* – चालना, छानना
He sifted the beach sand to look for small snails.

Sigh/साइ *(verb)* – आह भरना, ठण्डी साँस खींचना
She repressed a sigh at the sight.

Sight/साइट *(noun)* – दृश्य, दृष्टि, देखना
Her sight is perfect.

Signal/सिग्नल *(adjective)* – चेतावनी, संकेत से सूचना, संकेत के उपकरण
The article describes the signal historical events of the city.

Signature/सिग्नेचर *(noun)* – हस्ताक्षर
The papers were cancelled as her signatures were missing.

Significance/सिग्निफिकॅन्स *(noun)* – महत्त्व, तात्पर्य
The significance of her contribution was recognized by everyone.

Significant/सिग्निफिकॅन्ट *(adjective)* – महत्त्वपूर्ण, अर्थवान
She gave her a significant glance.

Signify/सिग्निफाइ *(verb)* – अर्थ रखना, महत्त्व रखना
The gathering signified the importance of the event.

Silence/साइलेंस *(noun & verb)* – चुप्पी, मौन, मौन कर देना
She likes to study in silence.

Silent/साइलेंट *(adjective)* – चुप, मौन, मूक, अल्पभाषी
They presented a silent act.

Silhoutte/सिलुएॅट *(noun)* – छायाचित्र, परछाई का चित्र
She identified them from their silhouette only.

Silicon/सिलिकॉन *(noun)* – एक रसायन
She presented a paper on the different uses of silicon.

Silk/सिल्क *(noun)* – रेशम, रेशमी वस्त्र
Silk fibre is quite expensive.

Silky/सिल्कि *(adjective)* – रेशमी
The fabric was silky soft.

Sill/सिल *(noun)* – जंगला का कोण
She kept the flowers on the window sill.

Silver/सिल्वर *(noun)* – चाँदी, चाँदी के सामान, रजत पदक
She gifted her friend a silver pendant.

Similar/सिमिलर *(adjective)* – समान, समतुल्य
She bought similar gifts for all the kids.

Similarity/सिमिलैरिटी *(noun)* – सादृश्यता, समानता
They were asked to list the similarities.

Simile/सिमिलि *(noun)* – उपमा, उपमा-अलंकार
He used too many similes in his essay.

Simmer/सिमर *(verb)* – उबलता हुआ
The soup smelled wonderful after it started simmering.

Simple/सिम्पल *(adjective)* – साधारण, सादा, सहज, सरल
She taught them simple calculations.

Simplicity/सिम्पलिसिटि *(noun)* – सादगी, सहजता
Everyone was impressed by his simplicity.

Simplify/सिम्पलिफाइ *(verb)* – सरल करना
She simplified the problem for him.

Simulate/सिम्युलेट *(verb)* – नकल करना, स्वांग करना
They were asked to simulate the experiment.

Simultaneous/सिमल्टेनिअस् *(adjective)* – एक ही समय में
Both of them were burning crackers in simultaneous interval.

Sin/सिन *(noun)* – पाप, गम्भीर अपराध
Immortality is considered a sin.

Sinful/सिनफुल *(adjective)* – पापयुक्त
His actions were sinful.

Sinfully/सिनफुल्लि *(adverb)* – पापमय
It was sinfully delicious.

Sinfulness/सिनफुलनेस *(noun)* – पापकर्म
The sinfulness of their act is unforgiveable.

Since/सिन्स *(preposition)* – के बाद से
They have been fighting since morning.

Sincere/सिन्सिअर *(adjective)* – सच्चा, निष्कपट
Their sincere work won them the first prize.

Sincerity/सिन्सिअरिटि *(noun)* – निश्च्छलता, यथार्थता
Her sincerity was recognized by the administration.

Sing/सिंग *(verb)* – गाना, चहचहाना
All gathered to hear her sing.

Singer/सिंगर *(noun)* – गायक, गायिका
She's my favourite singer.

Singe/सिन्ज *(verb)* – झुलसना, झुलसाना
He singed his hair in the lab.

Single/सिंग्ल *(adjective)* – एक, अकेला
He didn't eat a single cookie.

Singly/सिन्ग्लि *(adverb)* – अकेले
The teacher talked to each student singly.

Singular/सिंगुलर *(adjective)* – एक वचन, असाधारण
He is a singular performer.

Sinister/सिनिस्टर *(adjective)* – अनर्थकारी
He acted out his sinister ideas. There is another more sinister possibility.

Sink/सिन्क *(noun & verb)* – डूबना, धंसान, क्षीण होना, बर्तन या हाथ धोने का स्थान
The sink broke yesterday.

Sinner/सिनर् – *(noun)* पाप करने वाला
He was termed a sinner by the society.

Sinus/साइनस *(noun)* – नाक से जुड़ा खाली स्थान
His sinus troubles him in the winters.

S

Sip/सिप *(verb)* – चुस्की, घूँट
He sipped the tea slowly.

Siphon/साइफन *(noun)* – खंगालना, निकास नली से दूसरे में लाना
It worked as a siphon.

Sir/सर *(noun)* – महाशय, महोदय, श्रीमान्
They all call him 'sir'.

Siren/साइरन *(noun)* – भोंपू-भोंपू की आवाज
The siren woke him up.

Sissy/सिसि *(noun)* – स्त्री स्वभाव वाला
He was angry when they called him sissy.

Sister/सिस्टर *(noun)* – बहन, अस्पताल की सेविका
He has two sisters.

Sister in law/सिस्टर इन लॉ *(noun)* – साली, ननद
He hates his sister-in-law.

Sit/सिट *(verb)* – बैठना
He sat down immediately after the race.

Site/साइट *(noun)* – स्थान, स्थल, भवन-निर्माण स्थल
This is the site for proposed metro station.

Sitting/सिटिंग *(noun)* – बैठक
He was bored in the sitting.

Situate/सिचुएट *(verb)* – स्थित होना, स्थिति
He situated the new comers in perfect roles.

Situation/सिच्युएशन *(noun)* – स्थिति, हालत
He got caught in a bad situation.

Six/सिक्स *(cardinal number)* – छः
I have six pens in my bag.

Sixteen/सिक्सटीन *(cardinal number)* – सोलह
She has won 16 races so far.

Sixty/सिक्स्टि *(cardinal number)* – साठ
There are 60 chairs in that room.

Size/साइज *(noun)* – वस्तु का आकार (छोटी व बड़ी)
Russia is six times the size of India.

Sizzle/सिजल *(verb)* – कड़कड़, कड़कड़ाहट
The meat is sizzling on the grill.

Sizzling/सिजलिंग *(adjective)* – उत्तेजना, सनसनी
She heard the sizzling sound.

Skate/स्केट *(noun)* – चक्के वाले जूते, चक्के पर चलना
I cooked skate last night.

Skeleton/स्केलिटन् *(noun)* – कंकाल, ढाँचा, रूपरेखा
I saw skeletons of dinosaurs in the museum.

Sketch/स्केच *(noun)* – रेखाचित्र, खाका
He drew an impressive sketch of the couple.

Skewer/स्क्यूअर *(noun)* – सीक, सेंका कबाब
She poked him with a skewer. My little niece likes skewer.

Ski/स्की *(noun)* – फिसलने की पट्टी

My brother gifted me a new pair of skis.

Skid/स्किड *(verb)* – फिसलना

He skidded on the ice.

Skill/स्किल *(noun)* – कुशलता, निपुणता

She has the skill to drive heavy trucks. She skilled him in carpentry.

Skim/स्किम *(verb)* – मलाई निकालना

He skimmed the milk.

Skimp/स्किम्प *(verb)* – कम खर्च में प्रबन्ध

They skimped the farewell lunch.

Skin/स्किन *(noun)* – चमड़ा, त्वचा, चर्म

She used moisturizer to soften her dry skin.

Skip/स्किप *(noun)* – बीच में छोड़ना, उछलना, कूद जाना, चूक जाना

The skip needed to be emptied.

Skipper/स्किपर *(noun)* – अगुआ, नेता, संचालक

The skipper is down with fever. She knows how to skipper small yatchs.

Skirmish/स्करमिश *(noun)* – भिड़ंत, मुठभेड़, कटु विवाद

The skirmishes were tiring and fruitless. They skirmished with the king's army.

Skirt/स्कर्ट *(noun)* – घघरा, लहंगा

She wore a black skirt.

Skittle/स्किटल *(noun)* – एक प्रकार का खेल

He didn't win even a single game of skittles.

Skulk/स्कल्क *(verb)* – छिपकर चलना

The spy skulked around the colony. The skulk only came out at night.

Skull/स्कल *(noun)* – खोपड़ी, कपाल

I bought a model of a skull.

Sky/स्काइ *(noun)* – आकाश, आसमान

The sky is clear today.

Skyline/स्काइलाइन *(noun)* – क्षितिज

It's a beautiful skyline.

Slab/स्लैब *(noun)* – पटिया, पटरी

The slab fell down and broke.

Slack/स्लैक *(noun)* – ढीला, ढीला ढाला, मन्दा, सुस्त

He cleaned the slack off the floor.

Slacken/स्लैकेन *(verb)* – ढीला, मन्दा या सुस्त होना

The children slackened their pace to let others catch up.

Slacks/स्लैक्स *(noun)* – पतलून, ढीला अधोवस्त्र

She had outgrown her pair of slacks.

Slake/स्लेक *(verb)* – प्यास बुझाना

The athletes slaked their thirst after the long run.

Slam/स्लैम *(noun)* – धमाके से, धमाकेदार जीत

He won the slam.

Slander/स्लैंडर *(noun)* – झूठी निन्दा, दोषारोपरण, बदनाम करना

He sued the company for slander. He slandered the government.

Slang/स्लैंग *(noun)*– केवल बोलचाल में प्रयुक्त शब्द

He has learned the language but still faces problem with local slang.

Slant/स्लैंट *(verb)* – तिरछा, ढालुआ, तोड़-मरोड़कर पेश करना

The building slanted dangerously.

Slap/स्लैप *(verb)* – थप्पड़, थप्पड़ मारना

The older child slapped the younger one.

Slapdash/स्लैपडैश *(adj & adv)* – लापरवाही का काम

It was a slapdashed project.

Slapstick/स्लैपस्टिक *(noun)* – दोहरी पट्टी

He enjoys slapstick humour.

Slash/स्लैश *(verb)* – छपाक से काटना, चर्र से चीरना

The tiger slashed the sheet with its claws.

Slat/स्लैट *(noun)* – पट्टी

The slats were left piled up on the wet floor.

Slate/स्लेट *(noun)* – तख्ती

The slate formed spectacular scenery in the hills.

Slaughter/स्लॉटर *(noun & verb)* – हत्या, काट देना

The slaughter was a grisly sight to see.

Slave/स्लेव *(noun)* – गुलाम, दास

She was a slave to fitness.

Slavish/स्लैविश *(adjective)* – नकल

The slavish writer churned out manuscript after manuscript of unsuccessful writing.

Slay/स्ले *(verb)* – काट देना, हत्या करना

The criminal slayed the victim mercilessly.

Sleazy/स्लीजि *(adjective)* – गन्दी जगह

His sleazy actions are bound to land him in trouble one day.

Sledge/स्लेज *(noun)* – बर्फ पर चलने वाली गाड़ी

My father bought me a new sledge. I sledged down the snow-covered hill.

Sledge-hammer/स्लेज हैमर *(noun)* – लम्बे हत्थे वाला बड़ा और भारी हथौड़ा

The sledge-hammer was too heavy for me to carry.

Sleek/स्लीक *(adjective)* – चिकना-चुपड़ा, देखने में स्वस्थ्य

She has sleek hair.

Sleep/स्लीप *(noun)* – नींद, निद्रा

I went to sleep really late in the night.

Sleepless/स्लीपलेस *(adjective)* – निद्रारहित

I spent many sleepless nights worrying about my exam results.

Sleeper/स्लीपर *(noun)* – तख्ती, सोने के लिए तख्ती

The sleeper was very comfortable.

Sleepy/स्लीपि *(adjective)* – निद्राग्रस्त, नींद से भरा

I am very sleepy.

Sleet/स्लीट *(noun)* – बर्फीली वर्षा

The sleet made the roads slippery. It sleeted in the morning.

S

Sleeve/स्लीव *(noun)* – आस्तीन, बाँह

The sleeves of his pullover were too tight.

Sleigh/स्ले *(noun)* – बर्फगाड़ी

I enjoyed sleigh ride in Kashmir.

Slender/स्लेन्डर *(adjective)* – छरहरा, पतला-लम्बा

The athletic girl was very slender.

Slice/स्लाइस *(noun)* – फाँका, कतरा, हिस्सा

I would love to have a slice of cake.

Slick/स्लिक *(adjective)* – दक्षता, निपुणता, फिसलाऊ

His slick operating the computer impressed the interviewer.

Slide/स्लाइड *(noun & verb)* – फिसलना, खिसकना, काँच की पट्टी

Children slid down the slides.

Slight/स्लाइट *(adjective)* – छरहरा, हल्का, मामूली, उपेक्षा

Even a slight drop in the temperature now will make it uncomfortably cold.

Slim/स्लिम *(adjective)* – दुबला-पतला

The slim girl looked like a model.

Slime/स्लाइम *(noun)* – कीचड़ कींचड़ में लिप्त

The porridge was covered with slime and had a horrible smell.

Sling/स्लिंग *(noun)* – जख्मी हाथ, कलाई आदि को सहारा देने के लिए प्रयुक्त पट्टी

A good sling is enough to make him happy.

Slink/स्लिंक *(verb)* – लुक-छिपकर आना जाना

The thief slinked through the kitchen door and headed towards the safe.

Slip/स्लिप *(noun)* – कागज का छोटा टुकड़ा, परची

He gave the waiter a slip, instructing him to bring the surprise birthday cake.

Slipper/स्लिपर *(noun)* – चप्पल, चट्टी

I don't mind wearing my slippers even when I am stepping out.

Slippery/स्लिपरि *(adjective)* – फिसलन भरा

The surface was slippery because of the rain.

Slipshod/स्लिपसॉड *(adjective)* – फूहड़

She had a slipshod way of working.

Slit/स्लिट *(noun)* – चीरा, दरार, चीर देना

The slit was getting longer by the minute.

Slither/स्लिदर *(verb)* – फिसल जाना, फिसलते हुए चलना

The snake slithered around in the enclosure.

Slob/स्लॉब *(noun)* – आलसी

He was such a slob when it came to keeping his workplace clean.

Slog/स्लॉग *(verb)* – कठिन या उबाऊ काम को लम्बे समय तक करना

I slogged the entire last year.

Slogan/स्लोगन *(noun)* – नारा

The brand had a catchy slogan.

Slop/स्लॉप *(noun)* – छलक जाना, रसोई या स्नान का गन्दा पानी

The slop was so dirty by the end of the day that it had to be discarded.

Slope/स्लोप *(noun & verb)* – ढलान, ढलुआ बनाना
The skiers skied down the slope.

Sloppy/स्लॉपि *(adjective)* – गीला, अतिभावुक
The sloppy curry was tasteless.

Slot/स्लॉट *(noun)* – खाँचा, खाका, कार्यक्रम, सूची
The curious child followed the slot.

Sloth/स्लॉथ *(noun)* – सुस्ती, आलस्य
He is such a sloth when it comes to work.

Slovenly/स्लॅवन्लि *(adjective)* – लापरवाह
Her slovenly hair needed washing.

Slow/स्लो *(adjective)* – धीमा, सुस्त
My car was stuck behind the slow bullock cart.

Sludge/स्लज *(noun)* – गाढ़ा कीचड़
The sludge spoiled the entire scenery.

Slug/स्लग *(verb)* – घोंघा-सा
The wrestler slugged the opponent. The slug made him fall down.

Sluggish/स्लगिश *(adjective)* – सुस्ती, सुस्त
The sluggish movement of the traffic was very frustrating.

Slum/स्लम *(noun)* – घनी गन्दी बस्ती
Several plans were formulated for the betterment of the slum dwellers.

Slumber/स्लम्बर *(noun)* – सोना, निद्रा
The deep slumber refreshed me. The woodcutter slumbered beneath the tree he was planning to cut.

Slump/स्लम्प *(verb)* – धम से बैठना, मन्दी
Don't slump. Sit straight.

Slur/स्लर *(verb)* – अस्पष्ट उच्चारण
He slurred under anaesthesia.

Slurp/स्लर्प *(verb)* – आवाज करते हुए कुछ पीना
He slurped his tea.

Slush/स्लश *(noun)* – पिघलता बर्फ, भावुकता
The slush made walking around very inconvenient. watery mud. *His trousers got dirty when he walked through the slush.*

Slut/स्लट *(noun)* – फूहड़ स्त्री, बदतमीज औरत
She played the role of a slut in the movie.

Sly/स्लाइ *(adjective)* – चालाकी, छल
She is a sly woman.

Smack/स्मैक *(noun)* – थप्पड़, थप्पड़ मारना, नशीला पदार्थ
His smack is in urgent need of repair.

Small/स्माल *(adjective)* – नन्हा, छोटा, मामूली
When I was small we lived in a big old house.

Smallpox/स्मॉलपॉक्स *(noun)* – चेचक, शीतला
They claim that smallpox has been eradicated.

Smart/स्मार्ट *(adjective)* – आकर्षक, साफ-सुथरा, बना-ठना
Her room is smart.

Smash/स्मैश *(verb)* – तोड़ना, पटककर तोड़ना, हरा देना
The mirror smashed into a hundred pieces.

Smattering/स्मैटरिंग *(noun)* – किसी वस्तु की छोटी मात्रा
A smattering of raindrops was enough to make the children happy.

Smear/स्मिअर *(verb)* – पोतना, धब्बा लगाना
The smear didn't go away even after getting the dress dry-cleaned.

Smell/स्मेल *(noun)* – सूँघना, गन्ध आना
She lost her sense of smell in the accident.

Smelt/स्मेल्ट *(noun)* – पिघलाना, गलाना
The smelt quickly swam away.

Smile/स्माइल *(noun & verb)* – मुस्कान, मुस्काना
They smiled at each other.

Smirk/स्मर्क *(verb)* – व्यंग्यात्मक हँसी हँसना
He smirked at our low marks.

Smith/स्मिथ *(noun)* – लोहार
The smith repaired the spade.

Smock/स्मॉक *(noun)* – ढीला आराम देह वस्त्र
She wore a blue smock.

Smooth/स्मुद *(adjective)* – चिकना, महीन, मधुर, प्रवाहमय
The smooth batter will rise beautifully when baked.

Smother/स्मॅदर *(verb)* – दम घोंटकर मारना,
The thief tried to smother the servant but failed.

Smoulder/स्मोल्डर *(verb)* – सुलगना
The coal smouldered for a long time.

Smudge/स्मज *(noun & verb)* - धब्बा लगाना

We could see the low smudge of the mountain during winter nights.

Smug/स्मग *(adjective)* - सुन्दर आकृति का, अपने में प्रसन्न

The student's smug attitude irritated everyone else.

Smuggle/स्मगल *(verb)* - तस्करी करना

The smugglers smuggled many paintings and artifacts out of the country.

Snack/स्नैक *(noun)* - हल्का नास्ता

We just had snacks at the party.

Snag/स्नैग *(noun)* - छिपा हुआ, अप्रत्याशित रुकावट

The snag tasted stale.

Snail/स्नेल *(noun)* - घोंघा

I saw several snails in my garden.

Snake/स्नेक *(noun)* - साँप, सर्प

My brother was excited to see the snake in the zoo.

Snap/स्नैप *(verb)* - फोटो खींचना, टूट जाना

The stick snapped.

Snare/स्नेअर *(noun)* - जाल, फन्दा, चूहेदानी

The snare failed to catch anything.

Snarl/स्नार्ल *(verb)* - गुर्राना

The dog snarled at me.

Snatch/स्नैच *(verb)* - झपट लेना

The child snatched my pencil.

Sneak/स्नीक *(verb)* - गल्तियाँ बताना, चोरी से घुसना

She sneaked into the house late at night.

S

Sneer/स्निअर *(noun & verb)* - मुँह बिचकाना, उपहास करना

Her sneer was quite unnecessary. The senior sneered at the juniors.

Sneeze/स्निज *(verb)* - छींकना

He sneezed loudly. His loud sneeze alarmed the entire class.

Snide/स्नाइड *(adjective)* - अप्रिय बातें कहना

This is no time for making snide remarks.

Sniff/स्निफ *(verb)* - सूँघना

My friend sniffed the air.

Sniffle/स्निफल *(verb)* - सों-सों करना

He was sniffling by the time he reached home.

Snigger/स्निगर *(noun)* - ही-ही करना, खी-खी करना

The girls didn't know that everyone could hear their sniggers.

Snip/स्निप *(verb)* - कैंची से काटना

The barber snipped the locks off.

Snipe/स्नाइप *(noun)* - एक प्रकार की दलदल की चिड़िया

I saw a snipe near the pond.

Snippet/स्निपट *(noun)* - छोटा-सा सूचना-अंश

This is a snippet from the story she wrote.

Snivel/स्निवल *(verb)* - खीझना

She snivelled after the fall.

Snob/स्नॉब *(noun)* - दंभी

At times, you sound like a snob.

Snooker/स्नूकर *(noun)* - एक खेल

She is a good player of snooker.

Snoop/स्नूप *(verb)* - ताक-झाँक

The detective snooped around the crime scene for clues.

Snooty/स्नूटी *(adjective)* - दंभी

She is such a snooty employer.

Snooze/स्नूज *(noun)*- झपकी, झपकी लेना

I took a snooze in the afternoon. She snoozed in the class.

Snore/स्नोर *(noun & verb)* - खर्राटा, खर्राटा भरना

His snores made it difficult for me to sleep. She snores at times.

Snorkel/स्नोरकेल *(noun)* - एक उपकरण

He forgot to carry his snorkel.

Snort/स्नार्ट *(noun)* - फुफकारना

He laughed with a snort.

Snot/स्नॉट *(noun)* - नाक का कफ

Please wipe the snot off your nose.

Snout/स्नाउट *(noun)* - थुथून

The alligator hurt its snout

Snow/स्नो *(noun)* - बर्फ, हिम, हिमपात

Pure white sheet of snow covered the landscape.

Snub/स्नब *(verb)* - अवज्ञापूर्ण

She snubbed me in the party.

Snuff/स्नफ *(verb)* – सूँघनी, मोमबत्ती बुझाना
Please snuff the candles.

Snug/स्नग *(adj)* – हल्का गरम और आरामदेह
Adjust the safety belt to give a snugfit.

Snuggle/स्नग्ल *(verb)* – छाती से चिपकाकर सोना
The puppies snuggled together to keep warm.

So/सो *(adverb & conj.)* – ऐसा, इतना, अतः, इसालिए
She thanked me so much.

Soak/सोक *(verb)* – तरबतर
I soaked my clothes overnight.

Soap/सोप *(noun)* – साबुन
I ran to the market as I had run out of soap.

Soar/सोर *(verb)* – मँडराना
The eagle soared through the sky.

Sob/सॉब *(verb)* – सिसकी, सिसकना, सिसकी लेना
The little girl sobbed when she thought she was lost. His sobs were heard by some men passing by.

Sober/सोबर *(adjective)* – संयत, सन्तुलित
The drunk was sober today.

Sobriety/सॅब्राइटि *(noun)* – संयत, गम्भीरता
Everyone was curious about his sobriety.

Soccer/सॉकर *(noun)* – गेंद का खेल
The game of soccer was very exciting.

Sociable/सोशएबल/सोशॅबॅल *(adj)* – सामाजिक, मिलनसार
She is a sociable person.

Social/सोशल *(adjective)* – सामाजिक
This is a social gathering.

Socialism/सोशलिज्म *(noun)* – समाजबाद
He believed in socialism.

Society/सोसाइटी *(noun)* – समाज, समिति, संगठन
They were very protective about their society.

Sociology/सोशिऑलजि *(noun)* – समाजशास्त्र
He took up sociology in college.

Sock/सॉक *(noun)* – मोजा
The sock was torn.

Socket/सॉकेट *(noun)* – छिद्रदार विद्युत उपकरण
The socket was too tight for the shaft.

Soda/सोडा *(noun)* – क्षार
I want to have a soda with my pizza.

Sofa/सोफा *(noun)* – आराम कुर्सी
She sat on the sofa.

Soften/सॉफ्टेन *(verb)* – नरम बनाना
My mom softened the dough.

Software/सॉफ्टवेअर *(noun)* – जिसे उपकरण पर देखा जाना जाए
Software are usually very expensive.

Softy/सॉफ्टी *(noun)* – नरम, कमजोर
I want to eat a softy after dinner.

Soggy/सॉगी *(adjective)* – गीला, दलदली
The bread was soggy.

Soil/सॉइल *(noun)* – मिट्टी
The soil was very fertile.

Sojourn/सॅजर्न *(noun)* – अस्थायी निवास
I loved my little sojourn to the hills.

Solace/सॅलेस् *(noun)* – सान्त्वना
Her solace really helped me in my grief.

Solar/सोलर *(adjective)* – सौर, सूर्य से सम्बन्धित
Solar energy is green energy.

Solder/सोल्डर *(noun)* – टाँका लगाना
The electrician forgot to bring the solder with himself. The electrician soldered two ends of the wire together.

Soldier/सोल्जर *(noun)* – सिपाही
The soldier was very brave.

Sole/सोल *(noun)* – तलुआ, तल्ला, एक मछली, अकेला
His soles hurt after the long run.

Solemn/सॉलेम *(adjective)* – सौम्य, गम्भीर
The funeral was a solemn procession.

Solemnity/सॉलेम्निटी *(noun)* – सौम्यता, गम्भीरता
Her solemnity was noticed by everyone.

Solemnize/सॉलेम्नाइज *(verb)* – विधिवत संस्कार करना
Their marriage was solemnized in a church.

Solicit/सॉलिसिट *(verb)* – माँगना
I solicited his advice.

S

Solicitor/सॉलिसिटर *(noun)* - वकील
They called a solicitor for advice.

Solicitous/सॉलिसिटस *(adjective)* - उत्कंठित
She was very solicitous about his situation.

Solicitude/सलिसिट्यूड *(noun)*- उत्कण्ठा, उत्सुकता
His solicitude was very evident.

Solid/सॉलिड *(noun)* - ठोस, पक्का, पुष्ट
He had a solid body.

Solidarity/सॉलिडैरिटि *(noun)* - एकात्मकता
Their solidarity was quite evident.

Solidify/सॉलिडिफाइ *(verb)* - ठोस करना, पक्का करना
The liquid solidified under certain conditions.

Soliloquy/सॅलिलॅक्वि *(noun)* - स्वगत भाषण
The soliloquy was very touching.

Solitary/सॉलिटरि *(adjective)* - अकेला, सुनसान
She was a solitary person.

Solitude/सॉलिट्यूड *(noun)* - एकान्त, अकेलापन
He loved his solitude.

Solo/सोलो *(noun)* - एकल, संगीत-रचना
His solo was touching.

Soluble/सॉल्युब्ल *(adjective)* - घुलनशील
The substance was soluble.

Solution/सॅल्यूशन *(noun)* - हल, समाधान निकालना
Can you tell me the solution to this problem?

Solve/सॉल्व *(verb)* - हल करना, समाधान निकालना
I was able to solve the puzzle.

Sombre/सॉम्बर *(adjective)* - धुँधला, निराशाजनक
The movie was very sombre.

S

Some/सम् *(adj & pron. & adv.)* - कुछ, थोड़ा
Some people were talking.

Somebody/सम्बॉडि *(pronoun)* - कोई व्यक्ति, एक आदमी
Somebody needs to do this work.

Someday/सम्डे *(adverb)* - एक दिन, किसी दिन
I will do this someday.

Somehow/समहाउ *(adverb)* - किसी तरह in some
I will complete this somehow.

Somersault/समरसाल्ट *(noun)* - हवा में कलैया खाना, कलाबाजी
The somersault was perfect.

Something/सम्थिंग *(pronoun)* - कुछ
Something is moving upstairs.

Sometime/सम्टाइम *(adverb)* - कभी
I will do this sometime.

Somewhat/समह्वाट *(adverb)* - कुछ-कुछ, किसी तरह
I find this somewhat disturbing.

Somewhere/समहूवेअर *(adverb)* - कहीं
I am going somewhere.

Somnolent/सॉम्नॅलेन्ट *(adjective)* - निद्रा लाने वाला, नींद से भरा
I was somnolent after the sleepless night.

Son/सन *(noun)* - पुत्र
They are very proud of their son.

Sonata/सॅनाटा *(noun)* - एक प्रकार का संगीत
The audience enjoyed the sonata.

Song/सांग *(noun)* - गीत, गाना
The song was very beautifully composed.

Sonic/सोनिक *(adjective)* - ध्वनि सम्बन्धी
The sonic waves carried the sound far.

Son-in-law/सन इन लॉ *(noun)* - दामाद
She invited her daughter and son-in-law for dinner.

Sonnet/सॉनेट *(noun)* - कविता का प्रकार
The sonnets were beautifully written.

Soon/सून *(adverb)* - तत्क्षण, तत्काल, तुरन्त
I will work on this soon.

Soot/सूट *(noun)* - कालिख
The young boy was covered with soot.

Soothe/सूद *(verb)* - शान्त करना, शमन करना
His mom's hand on his head soothed his headache.

Sooty/सूटि *(adjective)* - कालिख से भरा
The sooty chimney needed to be cleaned.

Sop/सॉप *(noun)* - घूस, मँहगाई
It was a sop for the cop.

Sophisticated/सफिस्टिकेटेड *(adj)* - परिष्कृत, जटिल
It was a sophisticated piece of machinery.

Soppy/सॉपी *(adjective)* – अतिभावुक

Her soppy behaviour often irritated her friends.

Soprano/सॅप्रानो *(noun)* – पंचम सुर

The soprano's voice was very soothing.

Sorcerer/सोर्सरर् *(noun)* – जादूगर, जादू-टोना करने वाला

Everyone thought that he was a sorcerer.

Sordid/सॉर्डिड *(adjective)* – फटेहाल, गन्दा

It was a sordid affair.

Sore/सोर् *(adjective)* – दुखने वाला, दर्दीला, क्रोधित

I have a sore throat.

Sorrow/सॉरो *(noun)* – व्यथा, उदासी

His sorrow was written all over his face.

Sorry/सॉरि *(adjective)* – शोकाकुल, खिन्न, उदास, दुःखद

I was sorry for her.

Sort/सार्ट *(noun & verb)* – वर्ग, विशेष प्रकार, छाँटना

He is the sort of person who plays to win.

SOS/एसओएस *(noun)* – संकट सन्देश

The ship sent out an SOS.

Soul/सोल *(noun)* – आत्मा

The solitude appealed to my soul.

Soulful/सोल्फुल *(adjective)* – भावपूर्ण

His soulful voice mesmerized the audience.

Sound/साउन्ड *(noun)* – ध्वनि, स्वस्थ, ध्वनि उत्पन्न करना

I love visiting the sound when I want to be alone.

Soundproof/साउन्डप्रुफ *(adj)* – ध्वनि निरोधक

The room is soundproof.

Soup/सूप *(noun)* – शोरबा, झोल

The soup was very tasty.

Sour/सावर *(adjective)* – खट्टा

The sour orange was very difficult to eat.

Source/सोर्स *(noun)* – उद्गम, स्रोत

He was a source of inspiration for many youngsters.

South/साउथ *(noun)* – दक्षिण

There is a park towards the south.

Southwards/साउथवर्ड्स *(adverb)* – दक्षिण की ओर

The train was southwards bound. The colony stood southwards to the park.

Southern/साउदर्न *(adjective)* – दक्षिणी

The southern hemisphere has more water.

Souvenir/सूवनिर् *(noun)* – स्मारिका

She kept the ticket as a souvenir.

Sovereign/सॅव्रेन *(noun)* – सम्प्रभुत्ता, प्रभुसत्ता, सत्तासम्पन्न

He was a well-loved sovereign.

Sow/सो *(verb)* – बीज बोना

They sowed tomato seeds.

Spa/स्पा *(noun)* – खनिज जल वाला झरना

I would love to visit a spa.

Space/स्पेस *(noun)* – जगह, स्थान, अन्तरिक्ष, आकाश

The space was empty for a long time.

Spacecraft/स्पेसक्राप्ट *(noun)* – अन्तरिक्ष यान

The spacecraft started its journey today.

Spaceman/स्पेसमैन *(noun)* – अन्तरिक्ष यात्री

The spaceman described his adventures.

Spacious/स्पेशस *(adjective)* – लम्बा-चौड़ा

They had a spacious house.

Spade/स्पेड *(noun)* – कुदाल, फावड़ा

The spade was broken.

Spadework/स्पेडवर्क *(noun)* – श्रमसाध्य कार्य

Do some spadework before the presentation.

Spaghetti/स्पेगेटि *(plural noun)* – एक पश्चिमी भोजन

I love spaghetti.

Span/स्पैन *(noun)* – बीता, अवधि, दूरी, आर-पार

The span was broken.

Spank/स्पैंक *(verb)* – थप्पड़ मारना, थप्पड़

His mother spanked him. He still remembered the spanking.

Spanner/स्पैनर *(noun)* – एक उपकरण

The spanner was missing from his toolkit.

Spare/स्पेअर *(adjective)* – अतिरिक्त, खाली
The spare tyre was flat.

Spark/स्पार्क *(noun)* – चिंगारी
He was the spark of the party. They sparked together.

Sparkle/स्पार्कल *(verb)* – झिलमिलाना, चिंगारी फेंकना
The stage sparkled.

Sparrow/स्पैरो *(noun)* – गौरैया
Sparrows chirped outside my house.

Sparse/स्पार्स *(adjective)* – छितराया हुआ, बिखरा हुआ
He had sparse hair on his head.

Spartan/स्पार्टन *(noun)* – सादा और कठोर
I ate a Spartan after lunch.

Spasm/स्पैज्म *(noun)* – मरोड़, ऐंठन, दौरा
His body went into spasms during the fit.

Spate/स्पेट *(noun)* – बाढ़, अचानक वृद्धि
Children were overwhelmed with a spate of tests.

Spatial/स्पेशल् *(adjective)* – स्थानिक
I find the spatial discussions very interesting.

Spatter/स्पैटर *(verb)* – छिड़कन
The child spattered the table with milk.

Spawn/स्पॉन *(verb)* – अण्डे देना, मछली के अण्डे
The frog spawned in the pond.

Speak/स्पीक् *(verb)* – बोलना
I was glad I heard him speak.

S

Spear/स्पिअर *(noun)* – भाला, बरछी
The ancient spear was very valuable

Spearhead/स्पिअरहेड *(noun)* – अभियान का नेतृत्व
Archaeologists found several spearheads on the site of the ancient battle.

Special/स्पेशल *(adjective)* – विशिष्ट, असाधारण
The special occasion deserves to be celebrated.

Speciality/स्पेशिअल्टि *(noun)* – विशेषता, कौशल
Chicken curry was the chef's speciality.

Specialize/स्पेशलाइज *(verb)* – विशेषज्ञता प्राप्ता करना
I specialize in growing flowering plants.

Species/स्पीशीज् *(noun)* – जाति, किस्म
New species are being discovered every day.

Specific/स्पेसिफिक *(adjective)* – निश्चित, निर्दिष्ट, निर्धारित
Her instructions were quite specific.

Specification/स्पेसिफिकेशन *(noun)* – विस्तृत सूचना
I have brought the specifications of design for the meeting.

Specify/स्पेसिफाइ *(verb)* – निश्चित उल्लेख, विस्तृत उल्लेख
They specified their choice of the dish clearly.

Specimen/स्पेसिमेन *(noun)* – नमूना
He is a fine specimen of human species.

Speck/स्पेक *(noun)* – धूल कण
Don't worry it is just a speck. The child specked the wall with paint.

Spectacle/स्पेक्टकल *(noun)* – दर्शनीय दृश्य, भव्य, तमाशा
The ballet was a spectacle.

Spectacles/स्पेक्टकल्स *(plural noun)* – चश्मा, ऐनक
The spectacles suited him very well.

Spectacular/स्पक्टैक्युलर *(adjective)* – शानदार
The spectacular firework show is about to begin.

Spectator/स्पेक्टेटर *(noun)* – दर्शक
The spectators applauded his performance.

Spectre/स्पेक्टर *(noun)* – भूत, पिशाच (बेताल)
The spectre floated around in the old building.

Spectrum/स्पेक्ट्रम *(noun)* – कार्यक्रम, रंगक्रम, रंग-पट्टी
The whole spectrum of colours was visible in the rainbow.

Speculate/स्पेक्युलेट *(verb)* – अन्दाजा करना, सट्टा लगाना
The team was speculating the change.

Speculation/स्पेक्युलेशन *(noun)* – अन्दाज, अटकलबाजी, सट्टेबाजी
His speculation proved to be accurate.

Speech/स्पीच *(noun)* - वाणी, भाषण
The child developed speech very early.

Speechless/स्पीचलेस *(adjective)* - अवाक रह जाना, बोल न पाना
The teacher's response left me speechless.

Speed/स्पीड *(noun)* - गति, चाल, रफ्तार
They were moving at a high speed.

Speedy/स्पीडि *(adjective)* - द्रुतगामी, शीघ्र
That was a speedy recovery.

Spell/स्पेल *(noun)* - छोटी समयावधि, दौर
There was a short spell of silence.

Spellbound/स्पेलबाउंड *(verb)* - मन्त्रमुग्ध, मोहित
The little girl left the crowd spellbound with her poetry.

Spend/स्पेंड *(verb)* - खर्च करना
He spends a lot of money in buying clothes.

Spendthrift/स्पेंडथ्रिफ्ट *(noun)* - फिजूलखर्च
She was a spendthrift.

Spew/स्पिउ *(verb)* - तेज प्रवाह से बहना या प्रवाहित करना
The volcano spewed ash.

Sphere/स्फिअर *(noun)* - क्षेत्र, कार्यक्षेत्र, गोल
The sphere of light became bigger by the day.

Spherical/स्फेरिकल *(adjective)* - गोलीय, गोलाकार
The scientists discovered a spherical asteroid heading towards the comet.

Sphinx/स्फिंक्स *(noun)* - सिंह के धड़ की मानव मूर्ति
The Sphinx is located near the pyramids.

Spice/स्पाइस *(noun & verb)* - मसाला, उत्तेजना, छौंकना
The dish had all the spices in the correct proportion.

Spider/स्पाइडर *(noun)* - मकड़ा
I am afraid of spiders.

Spike/स्पाइक *(noun)* - नोक, नुकिला भाग
The colourful spikes made the garden beautiful.

Spill/स्पिल *(noun & verb)* - छलकना, जलाने का टुकड़ा
The campers used a spill to light a fire.

Spin/स्पिन *(verb)* - चक्कर खाना, चक्कर खिलाना
All planets spin on their axes.

Spinach/स्पिनैक् *(noun)* - पालक
Spinach is good for health.

Spinal/स्पाइनल *(adjective)* - रीढ़ सम्बन्धी
Her spinal injury took a long time to heal.

Spine/स्पाइन *(noun)* - रीढ़ की हड्डी
It is important to sit with your spine in the correct position.

Spinster/स्पिन्स्टर *(noun)* - अविवाहित महिला
The spinster didn't want to get married.

Spiral/स्पाइरल *(adjective)* - घुमावदार, कुण्डलीनुमा
The spiral staircase was very risky.

Spire/स्पार *(noun)* - मीनार
The snail had a beautiful spire.

Spirit/स्पिरिट *(noun)* - आत्मा, चित्र, प्रेतात्मा, भूत, उत्साह
People say his spirit still haunts the building.

Spiritual/स्पिरिचुअल *(adjective)* - आध्यात्मिक
My sister enjoys spiritual discussions.

Spit/स्पिट *(noun & verb)* - थूक, पीक, थूकना, मांस भूनने का सीकंचा
The spit was too hot to touch.

Spite/स्पाइट *(noun)* - दोष, दुर्भावना
She let go of her spite against her opponent.

Spiteful/स्पाइटफुल *(adjective)* - द्वेषी
She is very spiteful.

Splash/स्प्लैश *(verb)* - छपाका, छपछपाना, छींटा, धब्बा
Children splashed around in water.

Splashdown/स्प्लैशडाउन *(noun)* - समूह में उतरना
The splashdown was successful and the crew were all fine.

Splatter/स्प्लैटर *(verb)* - छिड़कना, उछालना
The child splattered the glue over the sheet.

Splay/स्प्ले *(verb)* - फैलाना
They splayed the dummy's arms.

S

Spleen/स्प्लीन *(noun)* - प्लीहा, तिल्ली

I had a pain in my spleen.

Splendid/स्प्लेन्डिड *(adjective)* - भव्य, शानदार

The valley was a splendid sight.

Splendour/स्प्लेंडर *(noun)* - भव्य, शानदार, वैभवपूर्ण

The audience were blinded by all the splendour.

Splice/स्प्लाइस *(verb)* - टुकड़े जोड़ना

The sailors spliced the rope ends.

Splint/स्प्लिंट *(noun)* - खपची

He had to get a splint for his broken arm.

Splinter/स्प्लिन्टर *(noun)* - लकड़ी, धातु या कांच के छोटे नुकीले टुकड़े

A splinter pierced my skin. The blow splintered the log of wood.

Split/स्प्लिट *(verb)* - विभाजित, विभाजन करना, चीरना, पकड़ना

The cell split into two.

Spoil/स्पॉइल् *(verb)* - बिगाड़ना, खराब करना, बेकार करना

Our holiday was spoilt by bad weather.

Sprit/स्प्रिट *(noun)* – गैस *The sprit broke in the rough weather.*

Spoke/स्पोक *(noun)* - पहिए की तीली या आरा

The spokes of the wheel were broken.

Spokesman/स्पोक्समैन *(noun)* - प्रवक्ता

He was born to be a spokesman.

Sponge/स्पंज *(noun)* - समुद्री जीव, सोखना, छिद्रदार

The wreck was covered with sponges.

Spongy/स्पंजी *(adjective)* - छिद्रदार, रसीला

The creature had a spongy feel to it.

Sponsor/स्पॉन्सर *(noun)* - प्रायोजक, प्रवर्तक, खर्चवाहक

The sponsors wanted their product to be featured at a prominent place.

Spontaneous/स्पॉन्टेनिअस *(adjective)* - स्वतः, अनियोजित सहज

His spontaneous help was well appreciated.

Spooky/स्पूकि *(adjective)* - डरावना

The spooky mansion has always been an attraction for the children.

Spoon/स्पून *(noun)* - चम्मच, चमचा

The man used a spoon to eat rice.

Spoonful/स्पूनफुल *(noun)* - चम्मचभर

The child ate only a spoonful of rice.

Sporadic/स्पैरेडिक *(adjective)* - कभी-कभार, कहीं-कहीं

The city was under curfew because of reports of sporadic violence.

Sport/स्पोर्ट *(noun)* - खेल, जी बहलाना, उदारता दिखाना

I love sports.

Sportsmen/स्पोर्ट्समैन *(noun)* - खिलाड़ी

The sportsmen gathered to discuss the improvements in the stadium.

Sporty/स्पोर्टि *(adjective)*- आकर्षक, खेल-कूद में रुचि रखने वाला

The athlete was sporty even when he was a child.

Spot/स्पॉट *(noun)* - चित्ती, किसी सतह पर छोटा गोल निशान

The spots on one cheetah were darker than the spots on the others.

Spotless/स्पॉटलेस *(adjective)* - बेदाग, दागहीन

His spotless white shirt was visible amongst the crowd.

Spotlight/स्पॉटलाइट *(noun)* - केन्द्रित प्रकाश

She couldn't believe it when the spotlight fell on her.

Spouse/स्पाउज *(noun)* - पति या पत्नी

He introduced his spouse in the party.

Spout/स्पाउट *(noun)* - चायदानी आदि की नली या टोटी

The spout of the kettle was dirty.

Sprain/स्प्रेन *(verb)* - मोच, मोच आना

I sprained my arm. The sprain in my arm was very painful.

Sprawl/स्प्रॉल *(verb)* - पसर कर बैठना

My father scolded me when he found my friends sprawled all over the drawing room.

S

Spray/स्प्रे *(noun)* – फुहारा सा छिड़काव, फुहारा देना

The sprays were weighed down by the flowers.

Spread/स्प्रेड *(verb)* – हाथ-पैर फैलाकर बैठना या लेटना

The spilt milk spread out all over the floor.

Spree/स्प्री *(noun & verb)* – रंगरलिया (मनाना)

I went on a shopping spree after receiving my salary. I spreed with rest of the participants.

Sprightly/स्प्राइटलि *(adjective)* – प्रसन्नचित्त, जिन्दादिल

She is a sprightly young girl.

Spring/स्प्रिंग *(verb)* – कमानी, झरना, लोच, बसंत, उछलना

The cat sprung forwards on the mouse.

Springy/स्प्रिंगि *(adjective)* – लचीला

The springy couch was very comfortable to sit on.

Sprinkle/स्प्रिंकल *(verb)* – छिटकाव, छिड़कना

I sprinkled salt over my salad.

Sprint/स्प्रिंट *(verb)* – तेज दौड़

He sprinted through the market to catch the rickshaw.

Sprout/स्प्राउट *(verb)* – अंकुरित होना, अँखुआना

My tamarind plant sprouted branches.

Spur/स्पर *(noun)* – घुड़सवार का एँड़ (काँटा) उत्प्रेरक, प्रेरणा, प्रेरणा स्रोत

The rider fell down from the horse and broke the spur.

Spurious/स्पुरिअस *(adjective)* – जाली, नकली

The text claimed to be ancient was of spurious origin.

Spurn/स्पर्न *(verb)* – तिरस्कार करना, ठुकराना

She spurned his attention.

Spurt/स्पर्ट *(verb)* – अचानक फूटना, फुहारा छोड़ना

The water gushed forwards in a spurt.

Spy/स्पाइ *(noun)* – भेदिया, गुप्तचर, जासूस

The spy kept an eye on the suspect.

Squabble/स्क्वाब्ल *(noun)* – तू-तू मैं-मैं

The noise of their squabble disturbed the neighbours. They squabbled frequently.

Squad/स्क्वॉड् *(noun)* – दल, दस्ता, टुकड़ी

The squad worked together as a good team.

Squadron/स्क्वाड्रन *(noun)* – दल, दस्ता

The squadron performed a spectacular stunt.

Squalid/स्क्वालिड *(adjective)* – गन्दा, घिनौना

The squalid shop hardly ever got any customers.

Squall/स्क्वाल *(noun)* – वायु का झोंका, बर्फीली आँधी

The squall lasted only for about half an hour.

Squalor/स्क्वालर *(noun)* – गन्दगी

I am tired of your squalor.

Squander/स्क्वान्डर *(verb)* – अपव्यय करना

He squandered his father's money.

Square/स्क्वेअर *(noun)* – वर्ग, वर्गाकार, ईमानदार, सन्तोषप्रद, सीधा

The child drew a square on the paper.

Squash/स्क्वैश *(noun)* – कुचलना, एक शरबत, एक खेल

I don't like squash much.

Squat/स्क्वाट *(verb)* – उकडूँ, बैठना, कब्जा करना, ठिगना

The homeless people squatted on the pavement.

Squawk/स्क्वाक *(verb)* – पक्षी का कलख, बत्तख की आवाज

The parrot squawked.

Squeak/स्क्विक *(noun & verb)* – चूँ-चूँ, चूँ-चूँ करना, चरमराना

I didn't hear a squeak out of them.

Squeal/स्क्विल *(noun & verb)* – किलकारी, किलकारी मारना

The squeal rang through the hall.

Squeeze/स्क्विज *(verb)* – कसकर दबाने की क्रिया

I squeezed the water out of the sponge.

Squib/स्क्विब *(noun)* – फुलझड़ी, पलीता

My nephew didn't find the squib exciting.

Squid/स्क्विड *(noun)* – समुद्री जीव

The squid swam away quickly.

Squiggle/स्क्विगल *(noun)* – टेढ़ी-मेढ़ी रेखा

The little girl squiggled on the paper.

S

Squint/स्क्विंट *(verb)* - अधखुली आँखों से देखना, भेंगापन

He squinted in the sun.

Squire/स्क्वायर *(noun)* - जमींदार

The squire walked with a lot of poise.

Squirm/स्क्वर्म *(verb)* - ऐंठना, छटपटाना

The man squirmed in pain. The squirm proved that he was in a great pain.

Squirrel/स्क्विर्ल् *(noun)* - गिलहरी

The squirrel was running up and down the tree.

Squirt/स्क्वर्ट *(verb)* - पिचकारी मारना

The water squirted out of the pipe suddenly.

Stab/स्टैब *(verb)* - चाकू भोंकना, घोंपना, विश्वासघात करना

I stabbed the pumpkin with the knife.

Stable/स्टेबल *(adj. & noun)* - स्थिर, हठ, स्थिर चित, अस्तबल

The scaffolding was very stable.

Stability/स्टेबिलिटि *(noun)* - स्थिरता, दृढ़ता

You can be sure of the programme's stability.

Stack/स्टैक *(noun & verb)* - अंबार, एक के ऊपर एक सजा हुआ ढेर लगाना, चिमनी

The clothes were all arranged in a stack.

Stadium/स्टेडियम *(noun)* - खेल का घिरा मैदान

The stadium was being prepared for the games.

Staff/स्टाफ *(noun)* - कर्मचारी, सेना अधिकारी, डण्डा, लाठी

The construction workers had run out of staff.

Stag/स्टैग *(noun)* - हिरण

The stag was a magnificent creature.

Stage/स्टेज *(noun)* - मंच, रंगमंच, अवस्था, मंजिल, पड़ाव

We have reached the second stage in the building project.

Stagger/स्टैगर *(verb)* - लड़खड़ाना, डगमगाना, धक्का पहुँचाना

The drunk man staggered across the street.

Stagnant/स्टैग्नन्ट *(adjective)* - ठहरा हुआ, गतिहीन

The stagnant water needed to be drained.

Stagnate/स्टैग्नेट *(verb)* - ठहर जाना, उन्नति-अवरोध

The decisions have stagnated our growth in the company.

Staid/स्टेड *(adjective)* - नीरस

The staid gentleman didn't have too many friends.

Stain/स्टेन *(verb)* - धब्बा, दाग, दाग पड़ना, दाग लगाना

The turmeric stained my white dress.

Stair/स्टेअर *(noun)* - सीढ़ी

The child climbed down the stairs carefully.

Staircase/स्टेअरकेस *(noun)* - सीढ़ियाँ, सीढ़ी

The staircase was antique and beautifully ornate.

Stake/स्टेक *(noun)* - खूँटा, खम्भा, दाँव, नियोजित धन

I used a stake to support my tomato plant.

Stale/स्टेल *(adjective)* - बासी, घिसा-पिटा

The potatoes were stale.

Stalemate/स्टेलमेट *(noun)* - गतिरोध, बराबर की बाजी

The experienced player soon placed the opponent in a stalemate.

Stalk/स्टॉक *(noun & verb)* - डण्ठल, डण्डी, पीछा करना, अकड़ना

The stalk was still strong even though the plant had shed all its leaves.

Stall/स्टॉल *(noun & verb)* - छोटी दुकान, टाल देना

The stall was selling some interesting bags.

Stallion/स्टैलिअन् *(noun)* - वयस्क घोड़ा

The magnificent stallion trotted around the field.

Stamina/स्टैमिना *(noun)* - दम-खम, शक्ति

The athlete was asked to work on his stamina.

Stammer/स्टैमर *(verb)* - हकलाना

She stammered while addressing the public. She went to the speech therapist to consult regarding her stammer.

S

Stamp/स्टाम्प *(noun & verb)* - टिकट , पैर पटकना, पैर पटक कर चलना, छापना, मोहर लगाना, छल, दबाना

The horse stamped the ground.

Stampede/स्टैम्पीड *(noun & verb)* - भगदड़, भगदड़ मचाना

Several people were injured in the stampede.

Stance/स्टैंस *(noun)* - मुद्रा, अंदाज, खड़े होने का तरीका

He copied my stance.

Stand/स्टैंड *(verb)* - खड़ा होना, खड़ा रहना, खड़ा करना, खड़ा होने का निश्चित स्थान

They stand in the queue every day.

Standard/स्टैन्डर्ड *(noun)* - स्तर, स्तरीय, औसत, मान्य, नियमित

He met all the requirements demanded by a standard.

Standardise/स्टैंडर्डाइज *(verb)* - मानक बनाना

The company standardized its processes.

Standing/स्टैंडिंग *(noun)* - स्थिति, स्तर, स्थायी

He has a standing in the community.

Standpoint/स्टैंडपाइन्ट *(noun)* - दृष्टिकोण, आधार

I understand your standpoint.

Standstill/स्टैन्ड्-स्टिल *(noun)* - रुकावट, गतिरोध

Due to an accident the traffic came to a standstill.

Stanza/स्टैंजा *(noun)* - काव्य-पंक्तियों की इकाई, पद

The third stanza of the poem was the most powerful.

Staple/स्टेप्ल *(noun & verb)* - बाँधना, बाँधने का तार

We need to buy more staples.

Star/स्टार *(noun)* - तारा, श्रेष्ठ, तारा चिह्न

Many stars were visible in the pollution-free sky.

Starry/स्टारि *(adjective)* - तारों भरा

The starry sky was treat for the eyes.

Starboard/स्टारबोर्ड *(noun)* - दाहिना भाग

The starboard looked clear.

Starch/स्टार्च *(noun)* - आलू चावल और डबल रोटी में पाया जाने वाला श्वेत पदार्थ, माड़ी लगाना

I am off starch for some time.

Stardom/स्टारडम *(noun)* - उच्च का दर्जा

He was largely unaffected by stardom.

Stare/स्टेअर *(verb)* - घूरना, टकटकी लगाकर देखना

If you stare at someone, you may offend them.

Stark/स्टार्क *(adjective)* - कड़ा, कठोर

The stark boat was much older than the other more ornate ones.

Starling/स्टार्लिंग *(noun)* - सारिका

The starling sang throughout the day.

Start/स्टार्ट *(noun & verb)* - आरम्भ, शुरुआत

The Start did not lead to any conclusions.

Starter/स्टार्टर *(noun)* - आरम्भ करने वाला, पहला दौर

I was full after eating the starters.

Startle/स्टार्टल *(verb)* - चिहुँकना, चौंकना, चौंका देना

You startled me.

Starve/स्टार्व *(verb)* - भूखा रहना, भूखा रखना

It is a shame that many poor people still starve to death every year.

State/स्टेट *(noun)* - अवस्था, दशा, स्थिति, राज्य, प्रदेश, व्यक्त करना, विचार कर कहना

He was in a very shocked state.

Stately/स्टेटली *(adjective)* - राजसी, वैभवशाली

Everyone was in awe of her stately figure.

Statement/स्टेटमेंट *(noun)* - कथन, पंक्ति, व्योरा

The witness gave his statement to the police.

Stateroom/स्टेटरूम *(noun)* - विशेष कमरा

The stateroom was prepared for the meeting.

Statesman/स्टेट्समैन *(noun)* - राजकीय पुरुष, राजनेता

The statesman addressed the crowd and pacified them.

Static/स्टेटिक *(adjective)* - गतिहीन, थमा हुआ

His career had been static for a really long time.

Station/स्टेशन *(noun)* - ठहराव, केन्द्र

The station was crowded.

Stationary/स्टेशनरी *(adjective)* – स्थिर, अचल, गतिहीन

The turtle was stationary for a long time.

Stationer/स्टेशनर *(noun)* – लेखन-सामग्री विक्रेता

The stationer was well stocked.

Stationery/स्टेशनरि *(noun)* – लेखन-सामग्री

I love buying stationery.

Statistics/स्टैटिस्टिक्स *(noun)* – आँकड़ा, सांख्यिकी

Statistics say that the number of boys in the country is much larger than the number of girls.

Statistical/स्टैटिस्टिकल *(adjective)* – आँकड़े से सम्बन्धित, सांख्यिकी से सम्बन्धित

The statistical analysis of the situation revealed some interesting developments.

Statue/स्टैचू *(noun)* – प्रतिमा, मूर्ति

The statue had stood there for centuries.

Stature/स्टेचर *(noun)* – योग्यता, सामाजिक वाद, कद

He was of a tall stature.

Status/स्टेटस *(noun)* – प्रतिष्ठा, पद, उच्चता

He was very much aware of his status while talking to the others.

Status symbol /स्टेटस सिम्बल *(noun)* – वैभव का प्रतीक

The expensive watch was a status symbol.

Status quo /स्टेटस को *(noun)* – यथास्थिति

The status quo is very volatile.

S

Statute/स्टैट्यूट *(noun)* – संविधि, अधिनियम

The statute helped restore law and order in the city.

Statutory/स्टैट्यूटरि *(adjective)* – नियमित, निर्धारित, कानूनी

The statutory warning is displayed at the beginning of the movies at times.

Staunch/स्टॉन्च *(adjective)* – निष्ठावान, दृढ़निश्चयी

He was a staunch supporter of Gandhian views.

Stay/स्टे *(noun)* – स्थगित करना, ठहरना, निश्चित स्थिति में

The stay needed to be tightened.

Stead/स्टेड *(noun)* – स्थान विशेष पर

The vice-principal was appointed in the principal's stead.

Steadfast/स्टेडफास्ट *(adjective)* – जिद्दी, अटल, पक्का

He was steadfast in his views.

Steadfastness/स्टेडफास्टनेस *(noun)* – जिद्दीपन, अकड़पन, अक्खड़पन

His steadfastness bordered on stubbornness.

Steady/स्टेडि *(adjective)* – समानगति से, नियमित, सन्तुलित, संयमित

They had a steady relationship.

Steak/स्टेक *(noun)* – टिक्की, टिक्का, मोटा टुकड़ा

He liked his steak well done.

Steal/स्टील *(verb)* – चोरी करना

The thieves stole the diamond.

Stealth/स्टेल्थ *(noun)* – गुप्तरूप से, चोरी-चुपके

He used stealth to win the game.

Stealthily/स्टेल्थिलि *(adverb)* – चोरी-चुपके से

He approached the base stealthily.

Steam/स्टीम *(noun)* – भाप, भाप निकलना

Steam was coming out of the boiling water.

Steamy/स्टीमि *(adjective)* – भापयुक्त, कामुकता पूर्ण

I love steamy hot soup.

Steel/स्टील *(noun)* – इस्पात

The utensils were made of steel.

Steep/स्टीप *(verb)* – खड़ा, कठिन, अनुचित

I steeped the sponge in soap and wiped the slab.

Steeple/स्टीप्ल *(noun)* – मीनार

Beautiful ringing of the bell issued from the steeple.

Steer/स्टीअर *(noun & verb)* – परिचालन, परिचालित करना, चलाना

The cart was being pulled by two steers.

Stem/स्टेम *(noun & verb)* – डण्ठल, डण्डी, तना, रोकना, बाँधना

I tried to stem the growth of weeds in my garden.

Stench/स्टेन्च *(noun)* - बदबू

The stench was getting stronger by the hour.

Stencil/स्टेन्सिल *(noun)* - छापने के लिए कटा प्रारूप

The child used a stencil to label the chart.

Stenographer/स्टेनोग्राफर *(noun)* - आशुलिपिक

The stenographer took notes during the meeting.

Step/स्टेप *(noun)* - कदम, डग भरना, चरण, सीपान

She walked in small steps.

Stereo/स्टेरिऑ *(noun)* - ध्वनि यन्त्र

The stereo was very pleasant on the ears.

Stereotype/स्टेरिऑटाइप *(noun)* - रूढ़ि, परम्पराबद्ध

One should not judge based on stereotypes.

Sterile/स्टेराइल *(adjective)* - बाँझ, नपुंसक, अनुर्वर, बंजर

The sterile seeds were thrown away.

Sterility/स्टेरिलिटि *(noun)* - बाँझपन, बंध्यापन

He was ashamed of his sterility.

Sterilize/स्टेरिलाइज *(verb)* - बाँझपन, बंध्या बनाना, जीवाणुहीन बनाना

They sterilized the milk before packing it.

Sterling/स्टर्लिंग *(noun)* - ब्रिटिश मुद्रा, खरा, विश्वसनीय

I paid in Sterlings for this gift. The toy turned out to be a sterling gift.

Stern/स्टर्न *(noun)* - सख्त, कठोर, गम्भीर, पिछला भाग

The crew tied the stern of the boat to the pontoon.

Stethoscope/स्टेथॉस्कोप *(noun)* - चिकित्सक का यन्त्र विशेष

The child started crying as soon as the doctor put on the stethoscope.

Stew /स्ट्यू *(noun)* - दमपुख्त, तालाब, पोखर

The stew was full of fish.

Steward/स्टिवार्ड *(noun)* - कारिन्दा, भण्डारी

The steward did his job well.

Stick/स्टिक *(noun)* - छड़ी, खेलों में प्रयुक्त छड़ी, चुभाना, चिपकना, चिपकाना, कायम रहना

My nephew gathered sticks and used them in his games.

Sticker/स्टिकर *(noun)* - चिपकने वाला लेबल

I love collecting stickers.

Stickler/स्टिकलर *(noun)* - अपेक्षित व्यवहार चाहने वाला

He was such a stickler for propriety.

Sticky/स्टिकि *(adjective)* - चिपचिपा, गन्दा

The sticky substance was difficult to wash off with soap.

Stiff/स्टिफ *(adjective)* - सख्त, कड़ा न मुड़ने वाला, दुस्साहाय, रूखा

Her stiff back made it difficult for her to move.

Stiffness/स्टिफनेस *(noun)* - कड़ापन, रूखड़ापन

His stiffness is his strength as well as his weakness.

Stiffen/स्टिफन *(verb)* - कड़ा या सख्त होना

The body stiffened by the hour.

Stifle/स्टिफल *(noun & verb)* - दमन करना, दबा देना, बुझाना

The dog hurt his stifle.

Stigma/स्टिग्मा *(noun)* - लांछन, दाग, कलंक

The children hadn't been taught how to write the symbol of stigma yet.

Still/स्टिल *(noun)* - शान्त, निश्चेष्ट, अब तक, तब भी

The still needed to be sterilized.

Stillborn/स्टिलबॉर्न *(adjective)* - मृत नवजात

A stillborn plot to assassinate the President.

Stilt/ स्टिल्ट *(adjective)* - खम्भा, ऊँचा बाँस, मदारी का बाँस

The stilted conversation yielded no results.

Stimulant/स्टिम्युलन्ट *(noun)* - उत्तेजक, प्रेरक, भेषज, उद्दीपक

The athlete was accused of taking a stimulant just before the race.

Stimulate/स्टिम्युलेट *(verb)* - प्रेरित कर, उत्तेजित करना

Their discussion stimulated the revolution.

Stimulus/स्टिम्युलस *(noun)* - उद्दीपक, प्रेरक, प्रेरणा

The change in the intensity of light was a stimulus for the pupil.

Sting/स्टिंग *(noun & verb)* - डंक, डंक मारना, टीस, टीसना

The sting of a scorpion is located in its tail.

Stingy/स्टिन्ज़ि *(adjective)* - नीच, कृषण, लोभी

He is so stingy that he doesn't ever dine outside.

Stink/स्टिंक *(verb)* - दुगन्ध, दुर्गन्ध देना

The rotten tomatoes in the refrigerator has started to stink.

Stint/स्टिंट *(noun)* - अवधि

They claimed that they sighted a stint.

Stipend/स्टाइपेंड *(noun)* - निर्धारित राशि, शुल्क, वेतन

He says the reason he can't afford a better establishment is because he doesn't get a good stipend in his current job.

Stipulate/स्टिप्युलेट *(verb)* - अन्दाजा करना

All clauses of the agreement were stipulated in the deed.

Stir/स्टर *(noun)* - चम्मच आदि से किसी तरल पदार्थ को चलाना, बिलोड़ना

She stirred her coffee with a teaspoon.

Stirrup/स्टिरप *(noun)* - रकाब

After getting off the horse, the rider lost his balance for a moment, so he grasped the stirrup to gain control.

Stitch/स्टिच *(noun & verb)* - टाँका, सिलना, टाँका लगाना, सिलाई करना

The stitch of this dress seems fine.

Stock/स्टॉक *(noun)* - भण्डार, माल, पशुधन, वंशधन, कुंदा, कलम-पौध, भण्डार में होना

The stock available in the warehouse has been below mark for the past few weeks.

Stockbroker/स्टॉकब्रोकर *(noun)* - दलाल

It is worth wondering why during any natural disaster activity of stockbrokers increases manifold.

Stocking/स्टॉकिंग *(noun)* - लम्बा मोजा

A fine pair of stockings with a skirt is what some woman prefer to wear when stepping out for a formal meeting.

Stocky/स्टॉकि *(adjective)* - नाटा परन्तु गठीला

I would describe the accused as being a middle-aged man with a stocky figure.

Stoke/स्टोक *(verb)* - झोंकना, बढ़ावा देना

Stoke the fire well so that it keeps us warm all night in this freezing temperature.

Stolid/स्टॉलिड *(adjective)* - भावशून्य

The man seemed to be having a stolid appearance.

Stomach/स्टमक *(noun & verb)* - आमाशय, पेट, सहन करना

It takes about two hours for the stomach to digest a full meal.

Stomp/स्टॉम्प *(verb)* - भारी कदमों से चलना

After being disobeyed his wife, he stomped about the room in anger.

Stone/स्टोन *(noun)* - पत्थर, पत्थर का टुकड़ा, गुठली

Protesters were dispersed just when they started throwing stones at the advancing troop of policemen.

Stonemason/स्टोनमेशन *(noun)* - मिस्त्री, संगतराश

After losing his job as an architect, the last that I heard about him was that he was working as a stonemason somewhere.

Stony/स्टोनि *(adjective)* - पथरीला, कठोर हृदय

The ground here is generally stony.

Stool/स्टूल *(noun)* - तिपायी

The envelope was lying on a small stool in a corner of the room.

Stoop/स्टूप *(noun)* - झुकना, झुकाव

The stoop in front of that house is lined with pots of freshly bloomed purple orchids.

Stop/स्टॉप *(verb)* - ठहरना, ठहराव, रोकना, रुका हुआ, गतिहीन

"Stop this evil practice!" cried the tribal leader.

Stopgap/स्टॉपगैप *(noun)* - कामचलाऊ

Shifting into that attic room was just a stopgap arrangement till we found something better.

Stoppage/स्टॉपेज *(noun)* - ठहराव, बाधा, विराम, विराम स्थल

Agitated at the lack of heed paid by the management to their demands, the workers called for work stoppage.

Stopper/स्टॉपर *(noun)* - डाट

The stopper was broken and the bottle was lying in a pool of the spilled ketchup.

Stopwatch/स्टॉपवाच *(noun)*- विराम घड़ी

Jim won the race with a record time of 56.65 seconds, strictly by the stopwatch.

Store/स्टोर *(noun & verb)* - भण्डार, गोदाम, भण्डार गृह, गोदाम में रखना

The store of cereals is fast depleting and we need an urgent refill.

Storey/स्टोरी *(noun)* - तल्ला, मंजिल

Three storeys of that building are dedicated to car parking.

Stork/स्टॉर्क *(noun)* - सारस, लकलक

Well, we didn't come across any tigers in the jungle safari, but definitely saw a stork.

Storm/स्टॉर्म *(noun)* - तूफान, आँधी, वेगवान

There was a storm last evening.

Story/स्टोरी *(noun)* - कथा, कहानी, घटना का वर्णन

The manuscript has a good story line.

Stout/स्टाउट *(adjective)* - मजबूत, शक्तिशाली

He had a stout figure.

Stove/स्टोव *(noun)* - अँगीठी, चूल्हा

I guess all that we did to stave off the worse all this while was not enough.

Stow/स्टो *(verb)* - माल सजाना

Stow the oars away in a dry place when on shore.

Strafe/स्ट्राफ *(verb)* - गोलियों से हमला

Strafe the jungle on the territorial border so that we are sure none of the militants have survived.

Straggle/स्ट्रैग्ल *(verb)* - पिछड़ जाना, भटक जाना

We straggled slowly ahead in the march against inflation.

Straight/स्ट्रेट *(adjective)* - सीधा, सरल, व्यवस्थित, ईमानदार

The queue went straight ahead at the bus stop.

Straightforward/स्ट्रेटफॉरवार्ड *(adj)* - स्पष्टवादी, सीधा-सादा

It was a straightforward question.

Strain/स्ट्रेन *(noun)* - तनाव, परिश्रम, थकान, तान, शैली

This strain of bacteria is multi-drug resistant.

Strait/स्ट्रेट् *(noun)* - जल-संयोजी, जल-डमरूमध्य

The Palk Strait lies between India and Sri Lanka.

Straitened/स्ट्रेटेंड *(adjective)* - तंगहाली

After losing his job, his means were straitened.

Strand/स्ट्रैंड *(noun)* - कपास, ऊन आदि का एक अकेला तार या धागा

There was a loose strand of rope that needed to be tied in.

Strange/स्ट्रेंज *(adjective)* - अनोखा, निराला

It was a strange incident.

Stranger/स्ट्रेंजर *(noun)* - अनजाना

He is a stranger to me.

Strangle/स्ट्रैंग्ल *(verb)* - दम घोंटना

Based on prima facie evidence, the police said he had been strangled to death.

Strangulation/स्ट्रैंग्युलेशन *(noun)* - दम घोंटना

There were strangulation marks on his neck.

Strap/स्ट्रैप *(noun)* - फीता, पट्टा, पट्टी बाँधना

A pair of leather straps kept the shoe fastened.

Strategic/स्ट्रेटेजिक *(adjective)* - व्यूह, व्यूह सम्बन्धी

This measure is part of our strategic planning.

Strategy/स्ट्रेटेजि *(noun)* - व्यूह, व्यूह रचना

We must have a plausible strategy in place for our firm for the next ten years.

Straw/स्ट्रॉ *(noun)* - भूसा, पुआल, सूखी घास

There was a heap of straw kept in the backyard.

Strawberry/स्ट्रॉबेरि *(noun)* - झरबेरी

Strawberries are often used in desserts.

Stray/स्ट्रे *(verb)* - पथहीन, भटका हुआ, छिट-पुट

The man strayed away from his companions in the jungle.

Streak/स्ट्रीक *(noun)* - लगातार चलती अवधि, धारी, परत

The streak of red on the rock was an evidence of recent violence.

S

Streaky/स्ट्रीकि *(adjective)* – धारीदार

The streaky animal was difficult to spot.

Stream/स्ट्रीम *(noun)* – नदी, प्रवाह

The stream merged into the river.

Streamline/स्ट्रीमलाइन *(verb)* – प्रभावशाली व्यवस्था करना

The engineers streamlined the boat.

Street/स्ट्रीट *(noun)* – सड़क, गली

I walked down the street to reach the café.

Strength/स्ट्रेंग्थ *(noun)* – शक्ति, बल, गुण

They tested the wrestler's strength before letting him fight the professional.

Strengthen/स्ट्रेंग्थेन *(verb)* – शक्तिवर्धक, ताकतवर होना

Unity strengthened their small country.

Strenuous/स्ट्रेन्युअस *(adjective)* – श्रमसाध्य

Strenuous exercise left him feeling drained.

Stress/स्ट्रेस *(noun)* – दबाव, तनाव

The rope gave way to the stress.

Stressful/स्ट्रेसफुल *(adj)* – तनाव बढ़ाने वाला

This is a stressful exercise.

Stretch/स्ट्रेच *(verb)* – लहराना, खींचकर बड़ा करना, तानना, अंगड़ाई लेना, फैलकर सोना, फैलाव

They stretched the rope to as far as it could go.

Stretcher/स्ट्रेचर *(noun)* – मरीजवाहक

The stretchers came in very handy when the ambulance crashed into a tree.

S

Strew/स्ट्रियू *(verb)* – विखेरना

The little girls strewed flower petals across the road.

Striken/स्ट्रिकेन *(adj.)* – आक्रान्त, पीड़ित

People were stricken with grief at the news of the mishap. His stricken face told a different story.

Strict/स्ट्रिक्ट *(adjective)* – कठोर, सख्त

The strict principal scolded the students.

Stride/स्ट्राइड *(noun)* – डग, कदम

She strided across the floor.

Strife/स्ट्राइफ *(noun)* – झगड़ा, अनबन

The strife left them stressed.

Strike/स्ट्राइक *(verb)* – मारना, प्रहार करना, हड़ताल, हड़ताल करना

We watched him strike the ball across the stadium.

Striker/स्ट्राइकर *(noun)* – गोल करने वाला, हड़ताली

The team was relying upon the striker to help them win.

Striking/स्ट्राइकिंग *(adjective)* – विशिष्ट, आकर्षक

The striking building was an identifying feature of the city's skyline.

String/स्ट्रिंग *(noun)* – डोरी, फीता, तार

The string broke and the basket fell.

Stringent/स्ट्रिन्जेन्ट *(adjective)* – सख्त, कड़ा

His stringent action made the students work harder.

Strip/स्ट्रिप *(noun)* – धारी, धज्जी, पट्टी, आवरण

The children decorated the room with colourful strips of paper.

Stripe/स्ट्राइप *(noun)* – धारी, रंगीन

The stripes were visible from a distance.

Strive/स्ट्राइव *(verb)* – प्रयत्न करना, प्रयास करना, संघर्ष करना

We saw them strive to bring about the change.

Stroke/स्ट्रोक *(noun)* – मार, निशान, रंग की लकीर, प्रहार, पक्षाघात

The clock's strokes were quite alarming.

Stroll/स्ट्रॉल *(verb)* – टहलना, सैर

I strolled through the park.

Strong/स्ट्रांग *(adjective)* – शक्तिशाली, हृष्ट-पुष्ट, टिकाऊ, तीव्र

He is a strong man.

Stronghold/स्ट्रांगहोल्ड *(noun)* – प्रभाव क्षेत्र

The palace was a stronghold of the kingdom.

Structure/स्ट्रकचर *(noun)* – बनावट, रचना, ढाँचा, संरचना

The structure of the organization was difficult to understand.

Structural/स्ट्रकचरल *(adjective)* – संरचनात्मक

The building had a structural weakness.

Struggle/स्ट्रगल *(verb)* – संघर्ष, जूझना
The captives struggled against the ropes.

Strum/स्ट्रम *(verb)*– बजाना
The guitarist strummed along with the music. The strum was not unpleasant.

Strut/स्ट्रट *(noun & verb)* – अकड़ की चाल, अकड़कर चलना
The strut was the most reliable part of the structure.

Stub/स्टब *(noun)* – घिसने या जलने के बाद बचा छोटा हिस्सा
The stub of the pencil was of no use to the child.

Stubble/स्टब्ल *(noun)* – फसल की खूँटी, जड़
The stubble was attacked by parasites.

Stubborn/स्टबॅर्न *(adjective)*– जिद्दी, अड़ियल
He was a stubborn man.

Stubby/स्टबि *(adjective)* – ठूँठ
She wriggled her stubby fingers. He emptied the stubby in no time.

Stud/स्टड *(noun)* – बढ़िया नस्ल के घोड़े या अन्य पशु के प्रजनन के लिए प्रयुक्त स्थान
The stud produced some excellent racehorses.

Student/स्ट्यूडेन्ट *(noun)* – विद्यार्थी, छात्र
He has been a student for 30 years now.

Studio/स्ट्यूडिऑ *(noun)* – चित्रांकन या प्रसारण का कमरा
His studio was his home.

Studious/स्ट्यूडिअस *(adjective)* – अध्ययनशील, परिश्रमी
He is a studious boy but he also enjoys sports a lot.

Study/स्टडि *(noun)* – अध्ययन, परीक्षण
The man devoted a lot of time to studies.

Stuff/स्टफ *(noun & verb)* – सामग्री, भरना, तुच्छ पदार्थ, भकोसना
The scientists were trying to determine the stuff of which the alien craft was made.

Stuffing/स्टफिंग *(noun)* – पूर्ति या भराव की वस्तु
The stuffing was too rich for my taste.

Stuffy/स्टफि *(adjective)* – रुचिहीन
The stuffy room made me feel sick.

Stumble/स्टम्बल *(verb)* – ठोकर खाना, लड़खड़ाना
He stumbled towards his home.

Stump/स्टम्प *(noun)* – पेड़ का ठूँठ भाग
Several stumps rose from the ground.

Stumpy/स्टम्पि *(adjective)* – छोटा और मोटा
The dog has a stumpy tail.

Stun/स्टन *(verb)* – बेहोश करना, हक्का-बक्का करना
She was stunned after falling from her bed.

Stunning/स्टनिंग *(adjective)* – चकित करने वाला
Our hotel room has a stunning view of the lake.

Stunt/स्टन्ट *(noun & verb)* – कलाबाजी, करतब, कठिन कमाल, वृद्धि रोकना
My brother likes to perform stunts on his bike.

Stupefy/स्टुपिफाइ *(verb)* – मति मंद करना
She was stupefied after the ride on the roller coaster.

Stupenduous/स्ट्यूपेन्डस *(adjective)* – विस्मयकारी
The kids gave a stupendous performance on the occasion of diwali.

Stupid/स्टुपिड *(adjective)* – मूर्ख, नासमझ
It was stupid of him to try and finish the whole cake at once.

Stupidity/स्टुपिडिटी *(noun)* – मूर्खता, गलती
His stupidity made him lose the race.

Stupor/स्ट्यूपर् *(noun)* – अर्द्धबेहोशी
After the 14 hour-long journey, all of us were in a stupor.

Sturdy/स्टर्डि *(adjective)* – ठोस, स्वस्थ, सुदृढ़
My father gifted me a sturdy study table on my birthday.

Stutter/स्टटर *(verb)* – हकलाना
He often stutters when he is afraid.

Sty/स्टाइ *(noun)* – सूअर-बाड़ा, गन्दा स्थान
She visits the pig in the sty daily.

Style/स्टाइल *(noun)* – शैली, आकृति, प्रचलित विशिष्ट शैली
The Roman style of architecture fascinates me.

Stylish/स्टाइलिश *(adjective)* – सजीला
She prepared a stylish bouquet of flowers.

Stylus/स्टाइलश *(noun)* – ग्रामोफोन की सूई
On my grandmother's birthday, I replaced the stylus of her gramophone.

Suave/स्वेव *(adjective)* – शिष्ट
The Hatter in Alice and the Wonderland was very suave and entertaining.

Sub/सब *(noun)* – उप
We are going to take the sub ride to see the underwater features of Grand Cayman next month.

Subconscious/सबकांशस *(adjective)* – अवचेतन मन
She took a subconscious decision to teach in a village.

Subcontinent/सबकंटिनेन्ट *(noun)* – उपमहादेश
He visits the Indian subcontinent every year.

Subdivide/सबडिवाइड *(verb)* – उपविभाजित
The term syllabus was subdivided into three sections.

Subdue/सब्ड्यू *(verb)* – नियन्त्रित करना, हराना, शान्त करना
It took a long time for the police to subdue the crowd protesting against the price hike.

Subject/सबजेक्ट *(noun)* – विषय, कर्ता, प्रजा
Many believe it is cruel to use animals as test subjects for different new treatments.

Subjective/सबजेक्टिव *(adjective)* – व्यक्तिगत
His review of the book was very subjective.

S

Subjudice/सबज्युडिस *(adjective)* – न्यायालय में, विचाराधीन
The media could not provide much about the murder case as it was still sudjudiced.

Sabjugate/सबजुगेट *(verb)* – नियन्त्रण में लाना
Alexander the Great subjugated many states in a relatively short time.

Sublet/सबलेट *(verb)* – किरायेदार द्वारा किराये पर देना
She is subletting the second floor of the house as she doesn't need so much space.

Sublime/सब्लाइम *(adjective)* – उदात्त, लोकोत्तर
The experience of successfully scaling a high mountain is sublime.

Submarine/सबमेरिन *(noun)* – पनडुब्बी
I built a model submarine for my science project.

Submerge/सब्मर्ज *(verb)* – पानी के अन्दर
The legendary city of Dwarka is believed to have been submerged after Lord Krishna's death.

Submission/सब्मिशन् *(noun)* – सहिष्णुता, परवशता, प्रस्तुतीकरण, हार की स्वीकृति
The labour were forced into submission and made to end the strike.

Submissive/सब्मिसिव *(adjective)* – विनम्र, मिलनसार
The hotel staff is very submissive.

Submit/सब्मिट *(verb)* – प्रस्तुत करना
They submitted to the demands of the workers.

Subnormal/सब्नॉर्मल *(adjective)* – सामान्य से नीचे
We learnt the function of subnormal in our computer class today.

Subordinate/सबॉर्डिनेट *(adjective)* – कनिष्ठ, मातहत, अधीनस्थ
The subordinate counsellors handled the meeting very well.

Subscribe/सब्सक्राइब *(verb)* – ग्राहक बनना, आवेदन देना, समर्थन देना
I subscribe to two food magazines.

Subsequent/सब्सिक्वेंट *(adjective)* – बाद का, परवर्ती
He won the first round but could not participate in subsequent rounds due to a minor injury.

Subsequently/सबसिक्वेंटलि *(adverb)* – बाद में
Many wanted to cancel the picnic but they subsequently changed their mind.

Subservient/सबसर्विएन्ट *(adjective)* – सम्मान देते हुए, कम महत्त्वपूर्ण
The new domestic help is very subservient.

Subside/सब्साइड *(verb)* – शान्त होना, बँट जाना
The comic act made even the sulkiest child to subside to laughter.

Subsidiary/सब्सिडियरी *(adjective)* - पूरक, अन्य से नियंत्रित, सहायक

The subsidiary groups meet every month to get directives for the coming months.

Subsidy/सबसिडि *(noun)* - आर्थिक सहायता

The Indian government provides subsidy on railway service.

Subsidize/सब्सिडाइज *(verb)* - आर्थिक सहायता देना

Our school provides us subsidized food in the canteen.

Subsist/सब्सिस्ट *(verb)* - जारी रहना, अस्तित्व बनाये रहना

She subsists by giving dance lessons after her classes.

Subsistence/सब्सिस्टेंस *(noun)* - जीविका, जीविकोपार्जन

Despite the subsistence provided, there was a shortage of medicines at the camp.

Substance/सब्स्टैन्स *(noun)* - सारतत्व, अर्थ

The toxic substance from the factory is polluting the river.

Substandard/सब्स्टैण्डर्ड *(adjective)* - सामान्य से नीचे, मानदण्ड से नीचे

The food is usually good at the mess but it was substandard last night.

Substantial/सबटैंन्शल् *(adjective)* - कीमती, मूल्यवान, महत्त्वपूर्ण

We collected a substantial amount in the annual bake sale.

Substantiate/सब्स्टैंन्शिएट *(verb)* - प्रमाणित करना, सिद्ध करना, सबूत देना

She substantiated her report with facts and figure from multiple cases.

Substitute/सब्स्ट्यिूट *(noun)* - स्थानापन्न, दूसरे की जगह पर

The class was given to a substitute till the teacher got back from her leave.

Substitution/सबस्टिट्यूशन *(noun)* - स्थानापन्न, बदलाव

The substitution of the LPG with natural gas would be cheap and environment-friendly.

Subterranean/सब्टर्रानिअन् *(adj)* - भूमिगत

Earthquakes and volcanoes are caused by subterranean movements and pressures.

Subtitle/सबटाइटल *(noun)* - उपशीर्षक, उपनाम

We could not really enjoy the French movie that we saw last week as the subtitles were not in sync.

Subtle/सट्ल *(adjective)* - सूक्ष्म

There is a subtle taste of saffron in the dish.

Subtlety/सट्ल्टि *(noun)* - सूक्ष्मता से, चतुराई से

She has mastered the subtleties of this crochet design.

Subtract/सबट्रैक्ट *(verb)* - घटाना

She subtracted the fancy envelopes to save money for the return gifts.

Subtraction/सबट्रैक्शन *(noun)* - घटाव

I got all the answers right in the subtraction exercise.

Suburb/सबर्ब *(noun)* - उपनगर

I am searching for a flat in the suburbs.

Suburban/सबर्बन *(adjective)* - उपनगरीय, बाहरी बस्तियों से सम्बन्धित

The suburban locations often have better residential facilities.

Subversive/सबवर्सिव *(adjective)* - विनाशक

The writer's article against the government was taken as subversive material.

Subvert/सबवर्ट *(verb)* - समाप्त करने की चेष्टा, विश्वासघात करना

Teenagers often try to subvert their parents' authority.

S

Subway/सबवे *(noun)* - सुरंग-पथ, भूमिगत पथ, उपपथ

The authorites made a subway to help pedestrians cross the busy road.

Succeed/सक्सीड *(verb)* - सफल होना, परवर्ती होना, बाद में होना

Work hard to succeed in life.

Success/सक्सेस *(noun)* - सफलता

The soft drink is a huge success all over the world.

Successful/सक्सेसफुल *(adjective)* - सफल

She is a successful entrepreneur.

Succession/सक्सेसन *(noun)* - उत्तराधिकार, अनुक्रम, अनवरतता

I was so hungry that I ate three bananas in succession.

Successive/सक्सेसिव *(adjective)* - क्रमिक, बाद के

The team was happy at winning three successive tournaments.

Successor/सक्सेसर *(noun)* - उत्तराधिकारी

The captain finally named his successor.

Succint/सक्सिंक्ट *(adjective)* - संक्षिप्त और स्पष्ट

I will always keep your succinct words in mind.

Succumb/सकम *(verb)* - झुक जाना, हार मानना, मर जाना

The government succumbed to the pressure of the business community.

Such/सच *(det.)* - ऐसा

People think they can get away with any crime, but such people should be punished severely.

Suck/सक *(verb)* - चूसना

Many children suck their thumbs.

Suction/सक्शन *(noun)* - चूसने वाला चूषक, चुसाव

Suction helped clear the drain.

Sudden/सडेन *(adjective)* - अचानक

He felt a sudden pain in his leg.

Suds/सड्ज *(plural noun)* - झाग, फेन

The child played with the suds.

Sue/सू *(verb)* - मुकदमा करना

He stole my patent so I am going to sue him.

Suede/स्वेड *(noun)* - मुलायम चमड़ा या कपड़ा

The rain muddied my nice new boots made of suede.

Suffer/सफर *(verb)* - कष्ट उठाना, भुगतना

The farmers might suffer some losses but no one will starve.

Suffering/सफरिंग *(noun)* - पीड़ा, वेदना

Painkilling drugs were not enough to relieve her suffering.

Suffice/सफाइस *(verb)* - पर्याप्त होना

They thought that two meals a day would suffice an old man.

Sufficient/सफिसिएन्ट *(adjective & det.)* - पर्याप्त, जरूरत के बराबर

We have sufficient funds for this trip.

Suffix/सफिक्स *(noun)* - प्रत्यय

He used the suffix incorrectly.

Suffocate/सफोकेट *(verb)* - दम घुटना, घुटने से मरना

Because of faulty respirator the patient suffocated to death.

Suffocation/सफोकेशन *(noun)* - घुटन

Because of the suffocation in the crowded carriage, several people felt sick.

Suffrage/सफ्रेज *(noun)* - मतदान का अधिकार

I am going to practise my suffrage this year.

Sugar/सुगर *(noun)* - चीनी, शक्कर

She added sugar to her tea.

Sugary/सुगरी *(adjective)* - भरपूर मिठास

He eats too much sugary food.

Suggest/सजेस्ट *(verb)* - सुझाव देना

There is strong evidence to suggest that she is telling the truth.

Suggestion/सजेशन *(noun)* - सुझाव

We like your suggestion.

Suicide/सूइसाइड *(noun)* - आत्महत्या

Several charities work towards preventing suicides.

Suicidal/सूइसाइडल *(adjective)* - आत्महत्या जैसा

The psychologist cured the man's suicidal tendencies.

Suitable /सूटेबल *(adjective)* - अनुकूल, उचित, उपयुक्त

This is a suitable dress for the occasion.

Suitcase/सूटकेस *(noun)* - बक्सा

He dragged his heavy suitcase across the railway station.

Suite/सूइट *(noun)* - जोड़ा कमरा

We booked a suite for the family.

Suitor/सुटर *(noun)* - प्रार्थी, विवाहयोग्य

She had a long queue of suitors to choose from.

S

Sulk/सल्क *(verb)* - उदासीन (उद्विग्न) होना

The child sulked when his mom scolded him.

Sulky/सल्कि *(adjective)* - चिड़चिड़ा

She doesn't have too many friends because of her sulky nature.

Sullen/सलेन *(adjective)* - उदास, चिड़चिड़ा

She is in a sullen mood again.

Sulphur/सल्फर *(noun)* - गन्धक

The bottle containing sulphur fell and broke.

Sultry/सल्ट्रि *(adjective)* - उमस भरा

The sultry weather makes me want to bathe again and again.

Sum/सम *(noun)* - धनराशि, योग, मुख्यतः

Please pay me the entire sum.

Summary/समरि *(noun)* - सारांश, संक्षिप्त

The summary of our discussion will reach you in a minute.

Summarize/समराइज *(verb)* - सारांश प्रस्तुत करना

Please summarize your speech.

Summer/समर *(noun)* - गरमी, ग्रीष्म

The summer was old and unstable.

Summon/समन् *(verb)* - उपस्थित होने का आदेश

The witness was summoned by the court.

Sumptuous/सम्पचुअस *(adjective)* - भव्य, शानदार, कीमती

He organized a sumptuous meal for his guests.

Sun/सन *(noun)* - सूर्य

The sun was hidden behind a blanket of fog.

Sunny/सन्नि *(adjective)* - चमकीली, प्रसन्न

The sunny morning was a welcome change from the foggy days.

Sunblind/सनब्लाइंड *(noun)* - झिलमिली

The sunblinds made the room dark.

Sunburn/सनबर्न *(noun)* - तापित, धूप-झुलस

The sunburn was very painful. I sunburnt myself.

Sunlit/सनलिट *(adjective)* - धूप से भरा, प्रकाशित

Violet valleys and the sunlit ridges.

Sunrise/सनराइज *(noun)* - सूर्योदय

I saw a beautiful sunrise today.

Sunset/सनसेट *(noun)* - सूर्यास्त

The sunset was spectacular today.

Suntroke/सनस्ट्रोक *(noun)* - लू, लू की लपट

Sunstroke can be a dangerous to life.

Sunday/सन्डे *(noun)* - रविवार

This Sunday, I will spend the time with my family.

Sundry/सन्ड्रि *(adjective)* - फुटकर, विविध

They bough sundry stuff from the store.

Super/सुपर *(adjective)* - असाधारण

You just gave me a super idea.

Superannuate/सुपर्आन्युएॅट् *(verb)* - सेवानिवृत्त

My father superannuated 12 years ago.

Superannuation/सुपर्आन्युशन् *(noun)* - सेवानिवृत्ति

The pension from superannuation is a helpful scheme.

Superb/सुपर्ब *(adjective)* - श्रेष्ठ, सर्वोत्तम

The superb food was very difficult to resist.

Supercilious/सुपरसिलिअस *(adj)* - घमण्डी, दंभी

Her supercilious attitude does not go down too well with her friends.

Superficial/सुपरफिसिअल *(adjective)* - सतही, छिछला

The burns were just superficial.

Superfluity/सुपरफ्लुइटि *(noun)* - अधिक

Superfluity is not recommended in the current economic scenario.

Superfluous/सुपरफ्लुअस *(adjective)* - सतही, अतिसामान्य

The superfluous kindness appeared fake.

Superimpose/सुपरइम्पोज *(verb)* - किसी पदार्थ के ऊपर रखने की क्रिया, अध्यारोपण

I superimposed the transparent sheet of printed paper over the painted wall.

Supritend/सुपरिन्टेंड *(verb)* - प्रबन्ध, निरीक्षण, नियन्त्रण करना

She superintends the girls' hostel.

Superitendent/सुपरिन्टेंडेंट *(noun)* - अधीक्षक, संचालक

Everyone ran to their seats as soon as they heard the superintendent arriving.

Superior/सुपिरिअर *(adjective)* - उच्च, श्रेष्ठ, वरिष्ठ

He is superior to us in rank.

Superiority/सुपिरिअरिटी *(noun)* – उच्चता, श्रेष्ठता, वरिष्ठता

He often made his superiority clear.

Superlative/सुपरलेटिव *(adjective)* – अन्यतम, उच्चतम, सर्वश्रेष्ठ

His superlative power of speech was very evident. "Best" is the superlative of "Good".

Supermarket/सुपरमार्केट *(noun)* – एक भवन में सीमित बाजार

I went to the supermarket to buy groceries.

Supernatural/सुपरनेचुरल *(adjective)* – अलौकिक

People claimed that they felt a supernatural force in the house.

Supersede/सुपरसिड *(verb)* – किसी का पद पाना, पद स्थापना

The director's instructions superseded the ones issued by the HR department.

Supersonic/सुपरसॉनिक *(adjective)* – तीव्रध्वनि एवं गति

The jet moved at a supersonic speed.

Superstar/सुपरस्टार *(noun)* – अतिप्रसिद्ध

He enjoyed being the superstar.

Superstition/सुपरस्टिशन *(noun)* – अन्धविश्वास

Our society is plagued by superstitions.

Superstitious/सुपरस्टिशस *(adj)* – अन्धविश्वासी

She is a superstitious girl.

Supervise/सुपरवाइज *(verb)* – निगरानी करना

I supervised the arrangements for the party.

Supervisor/सुपरवाइजर *(noun)* – निरीक्षक

I was the supervisor of the party arrangements.

Supper/सपर *(noun)* – रात्रि भोजन

I go for a walk after the supper.

Supplant/सप्लान्ट *(verb)* – स्थानापन्न करना

The boss supplanted the instructions issued by the manager.

Supple/सपल *(adjective)* – लचीला, सुरम्य

She had a supple body. He suppled the iron rod.

Supplement/सप्लिमेंट *(noun)* – अनुपूरक, परिशिष्ट

The sugar supplement made the sugar-free dessert edible.

Supplementary/सप्लिमेंटरी *(adjective)* – पूरक

She took some supplementary diets to help her recover.

Supply/सप्लाई *(adj)* – आपूर्ति, आपूर्ति करना

The farmer supplies eggs to the surrounding villages.

Support/सपोर्ट *(verb)* – समर्थन, सहायता, थामना, संभालना, भरण-पोषण करना

He supports himself well on the stick.

Supporter/सपोर्टर *(noun)* – समर्थक, सहायक

The team had many supporters.

Supportive/सपोर्टिव *(adj)* – सहायता जनक

Her family was very supportive of her decision to go back to studies.

Suppose/सपोज *(verb)* – मानना, कल्पना करना, अटकल करना

I suppose that you lead a busy life.

Supposition/सपोजिशन *(noun)* – अनुमान, अटकल

The supposition became invalid when the assumption proved to be incorrect.

Suppress/सप्रेश *(verb)* – दबाना, कुचलना, गुप्त रखना

The police suppressed the protests.

Supreme/सुप्रीम *(adjective)* – सर्वोच्च, सर्वश्रेष्ठ

The President's word is supreme in some countries.

Supremacy/सुप्रेमैसि (स्युप्रेमॅसि) *(noun)* – शासन, श्रेष्ठता, उच्चता

No one could question her supremacy.

Supreme Being/सुप्रीम बिइंग *(adjective)* – ब्रह्म, ईश्वर

There are several schools of thoughts regarding the Supreme being.

Surcharge/सरचार्ज *(noun)* – अतिरिक्त कर

There were many surcharges apart from the regular ones.

Sure/शूअर् *(adjective)* – निश्चित, आश्वस्त, अचूक

She is very sure of herself.

Surely/शूअर्लि *(adverb)* – निश्चित रूप से

She treaded the red carpet surely.

Surety/शूअर्टि *(noun)* – जमानत, जमानती

He stood as a surety for his friend.

Surf/सर्फ *(noun)* – फेन

The surf was tossed high in the air as the waves became steeper.

Surfing/सर्फिंग *(noun)* – खोजना, खेलना

I enjoy surfing.

Surface/सर्फेस *(noun)* – सतह, बाहरी परत, ऊपरी हिस्सा, सतह पर आना, सतह पर लाना

The surface of the sphere was smooth.

Surfeit/सर्फिट *(noun)* – पूर्ण आहार, अधिकता

The surfeit of her emotions disgusted me after a point.

Surge/सर्ज *(noun)* – लहराना, लहर-सदृश

The surge uprooted the tree.

Surgeon/सर्जन *(noun)* – शल्यचिकित्सक

He was a respected surgeon.

Surgery/सर्जरी *(noun)* – शल्यचिकित्सक

He was undergoing surgery for the stones in his kidney.

Surly/सर्लि *(adjective)* – उजड्ड, अक्खड़

People stayed away from him because of his surly temper.

Surmise/सर्माइज *(verb)* – अन्दाजा लगाना, अनुमान करना

I surmise that they don't care for the cause.

Surmount/सरमाउंट *(verb)* – कठिनाइयों पर विजय पाना, बाधा पार करना

He surmounted his bad finances to become a doctor.

Surname /सरनेम *(noun)* – कुलनाम, उपनाम

My surname says a lot about my heritage.

Surpass/सरपास *(verb)* – आगे निकलना, मात देना

You surpass me in intelligence.

Surplus/सरप्लस *(noun)* – अतिरिक्त, ज्यादा

The company didn't know what to do with the surplus.

Surprise/सरप्राइज *(noun & verb)* – आश्चर्य, आश्चर्यजनक

I was surprised to see all my friends at my place.

Surrender/सरेंडर *(verb)* – समर्पण, परित्याग करना

The terrorists surrendered before the army.

Surrogate/सरोगेट *(noun)* – स्थानापन्न, एवज में

She acted as a surrogate to the child's mother.

Surround/सराउन्ड *(verb)* – चारों ओर से घिरा/घेरना

They surrounded their leader eagerly.

Surroundings/सराउन्डिंग्स *(plural noun)* – आस-पास, पास-पड़ोस

I was happy with my surroundings.

Surveillance/सर्वेलन्स *(noun)* – निगरानी

She was put under surveillance.

Survey/सर्वे *(verb)* – सर्वेक्षण

The police surveyed the crime scene thoroughly.

Surveyor/सर्वेअर *(noun)* – सर्वेक्षक

The surveyor did a good job.

Survival/सर्वाइवल *(noun)* – जीवित रहना, अस्तित्व में रहना

Doctors raised serious doubts on her survival.

Survive/सर्वाइव *(verb)* – बचना, अस्तित्व में होना

Gandhi ji's philosophy will survive for a long time.

Susceptible/ससेप्टिबल *(adj)* – शीघ्र प्रभावित, सरलता से प्रभावित

The hut was susceptible to tornadoes.

Suspect/सस्पेक्ट *(noun & verb)* – सन्देह करना, संदिग्ध व्यक्ति

I suspect that what you are telling me is your own story, not your friend's.

Suspend/सस्पेंड *(verb)* – स्थगित करना, कार्य से रोकना

I suspended my work to take a break.

Suspense/सस्पेंस *(noun)* – दुविधा, आसमंजस, अनिश्चय

I couldn't stand the suspense any longer.

Suspension/सस्पेंशन *(noun)* – निलंबन, स्थगन, अधर में

The suspension was cancelled at the last moment.

Suspicion/सस्पिशन *(noun)* – सन्देह, शक

She was arrested on suspicion of murder.

Suspicious/सस्पिशस *(adjective)* – सन्देहास्पद, शक के घेरे में, शंका

The police arrested him for his suspicious activities.

Sustain/सस्टेन *(verb)* – सहजाना, बचा रहना, अस्तित्व बनाये रखना

The rope sustained the sails well.

Sustenance/सस्टिनन्स् *(noun)* – पोषण, आहार, अड़े रहने की शक्ति

Everyone needs sustenance to survive.

Swab/स्वॉब *(noun & verb)* – मुलायम कपड़ा, रूई से पोंछना

They cleaned the wound with a swab.

Swagger/स्वैगर *(verb)* – इठलाना, इतराना, अकड़कर चलना

He swaggered through the party, acting snooty and snobbish.

Swallow/स्वॉलो *(noun & verb)* – निगलना, लीलना, फिरगिजी या अबाबील पक्षी

The swallows were welcome visitors in our city.

Swamp/स्वॉम्प *(noun)* – दलदल

I squelched my way through the swamp.

Swampy/स्वॉम्पी *(adjective)* – दलदली, दलदल से भरा

The swampy ground was dangerous in foggy conditions.

Swan/स्वान *(noun)* – हंस

Several beautiful swans lived near the lake. The young man swanned through the streets.

Swarm/स्वार्म *(noun)* – झुण्ड

A swarm of locusts descended upon the fields.

S

Swat/स्वैट *(verb)* – चपटी चीज से मारना

I swatted the fly.

Swathe/स्वेथ *(verb)* – पट्टी बाँधना, लपेटना

She swathed the baby to protect it from chill.

Sway/स्वे *(verb)* – डोलना, झूलना, शासन, प्रभाव

The trees swayed in the gentle breeze.

Swear/स्वेअर *(verb)* – शपथ लेना, कोसना, श्रापना

The spy swore that she would lay down her life before being caught.

Swear-word/स्वेअरवर्ड *(noun)* – अपशब्द, गाली

You should not use swear-words.

Sweat/स्वेट *(noun)* – पसीना, पसीना बहाना

I hate the smell of sweat.

Sweaty/स्वेटि *(adjective)* – पसीने से लथपथ

She was sweaty after the exercise.

Sweater/स्वेटर *(noun)* – ऊनी वस्त्र

I bought a new pullover from the store.

Sweeper/स्वीपर *(noun)* – सफाई करने वाला, बहारने वाला, मेहतर

The sweeper worked hard to keep the school clean.

Sweeping/स्वीपिंग *(adjective)* – व्यापक, सामान्य, बहाले जाने वाला

She gestured with sweeping movements of her arms.

Sweet/स्वीट *(adjective)* – मीठा, रोचक, सुन्दर, आकर्षक, मधुर, मिठाई, मीठा भोजन

I love sweet porridge.

Sweeten/स्वीटेन *(verb)* – मीठा करना, मना लेना, ठण्डा करना

She sweetened the tea.

Swell/स्वेल *(verb)* – फूलना, फुलाना, बढ़ जाना

Her injured leg swelled up.

Swelling/स्वेलिंग *(noun)* – सूजन

He cold-pressed the swelling on his injured leg.

Swelter/स्वेल्टर *(verb)* – उमस, कड़ी गरमी

All of us sweltered in the sun. The swelter was getting very difficult to deal with.

Swerve/स्वर्व *(verb)* – अचानक दिशा बदलना, तीव्र गति

The speeding vehicle swerved to the right.

Swift/स्विफ्ट *(adjective)* – तेज, शीघ्र, तीव्र, द्रुत

I spied a swift movement from the corner of my eye.

Swig/स्विग *(verb)* – जल्दी से, तेजी से

He quickly swigged his drink and left.

Swill/स्विल *(verb)* – पानी डालना, बहाना, ज्यादा पीना

She swilled the curry out into the sink.

Swim/स्विम *(verb)* – तैरना, उतराना

I swam the length of the swimming pool.

Swimmer/स्विमर *(noun)* – तैराक

She is a brilliant swimmer.

Swindle/स्विंडल *(verb)* – ठगना, ऐंठ लेना, ठगी
The company swindled the customers' funds.

Swine/स्वाइन *(noun)* – सूअर
The swine grew very fat.

Swing/स्विंग *(verb)* – झूला, झूलना, झुलाना, झूमना
The father swung the child around.

Swipe/स्वाइप *(verb)* – तीव्र गति से घुमाकर मारना
The cricketer swiped the ball.

Swirl/स्वर्ल *(verb)* – गेंद की भाँति चक्कर खाते हुए
The dancers swirled gracefully.

Swish/स्विश *(verb)* – सरसराना, सरसराहट
She swished across the hall.

Switch/स्विच *(noun)* – विद्युत परिचालन यन्त्र, परिवर्तन, परिवर्तक
I could hear sparking in the switch.

Swivel/स्विवल *(noun)* – घुमाऊ, घूमना
The canon could swivel to change directions.
The dancer swivelled for one whole minute.

Swoon/स्वून *(verb)* – मूर्छित होना, अचेत होना
She swooned upon receiving his letter.

Sword/सोर्ड् *(noun)* – तलवार, कटार
The warrior drew the sword and entered the fight.

Swot/स्वॉट *(noun & verb)* – खूब पढ़ना, पढ़ाकू, परिश्रमी छात्र
He swotted for days.

Sycophant/सिकफैन्ट् *(noun)* – चापलूस, चाटूकार
The sycophant wasn't really liked much.

Syllable/सिलेबल *(noun)* – मात्रा, एक ध्वनि के वर्ण-समूह
She pronounced each syllable clearly.

Syllabus/सिलेबस *(noun)* – पाठ्यक्रम
The teacher followed the syllabus closely.

Symbol/सिम्बल *(noun)* – प्रतीक, प्रतीक चिह्न, चिह्न, निशान
A white dove is a symbol of peace.

Symbolic/सिम्बलिक *(adj.)* – प्रतीकात्मक, लाक्षणिक
She often uses symbolic images in her writings.

Symbolism/सिम्बलिज्म *(noun)* – प्रतीकवाद
The imparting of a symbolic meaning of an object or action is called symbolism.

Symmetrical/सिमेट्रिकल *(adjective)* – एक सा, समान और एक सा
Symmetrical designs are out of fashion as of now.

Symmetry/सिमेट्रि *(noun)* – समानता
He was very particular about the symmetry of things.

Sympathetic/सिम्पथेटिक *(adj)* – सहानुभूतिपूर्ण, सहृदयता से भरा
His sympathetic feelings did not appeal to everyone.

Sympathy/सिम्पथि *(noun)* – संवेदना, सहानुभूति
My sympathies are with you.

Symphony/सिम्फनि *(noun)* – लिपिबद्ध स्वर, स्वर संगति, सुरीलापल
The symphony was beautifully composed.

Symposium/सिम्पोजियम *(noun)* – विचार-गोष्ठी, वैचारिक सम्मेलन
The symposium turned out to be an interesting event.

Symptom/सिम्पटम *(noun)* – लक्षण, रोग के लक्षण
She showed all symptoms of a viral infection.

Synagogue/सिनगॉग *(noun)* – प्रार्थना भवन
There was a huge crowd outside the synagogue.

Synchronize/सिन्क्रनाइज *(verb)* – एक साथ बजाना, चलाना या करना
Please synchronize your steps with the rest of the troop.

Synchronous/सिन्क्रनस *(adjective)* – साथ घटित होने वाला, समकालिक
I cannot attend both the synchronous events.

Syndicate/सिंडिकेट *(noun)* – व्यवसायी संघ, सदन, परिषद्
The syndicate's cause was to spread peace and tolerance amongst people.

Syndrome/सिन्ड्रोम *(noun)* – लक्षण, एक ही विशेषता
She suffers from Down's Syndrome.

Synonym/सिननिम *(noun)* – पर्यायवाची शब्द
"Help" is a synonym for "aid".

S

Synonymous/सिननिमस *(adj)* – समानार्थी शब्द

Her name was synonymous with success.

Synopsis/सिनॉपसिस *(noun)* – शोध का प्रारूप, सारांश

The synopsis was too long.

Syntax/सिन्टैक्स *(noun)* – वाक्य रचना

The grammatical and due arrangement of words in a sentence is called syntax.

Synthesis/सिन्थेसिस *(noun)* – संयोजन, संश्लेषण, सम्मिलित

This school of philosophy was a result of the synthesis of various thoughts.

Synthetic/सिन्थेटिक *(adjective)* – कृत्रिम

Synthetic fibres are often used to make clothes.

Syringe/सिरिन्ज *(noun)* – प्लास्टिक या काँच से बनी सूई से युक्त एक नली

The syringe needed to be sterilized.

Syrup/सिरप *(noun)* – शीरा, चाशनी, मीठा घोल

The syrup was too sweet.

System/सिस्टम *(noun)* – प्रणाली

The entire system failed when a small fault was introduced during the testing.

Tt

T/टी *(noun)* - अंग्रेजी वर्णमाला का बीसवाँ वर्ण the twentieth letter of the English alphabet.

1. Denoting the next after S in a set of items, categories, etc.

Tab/टैब *(noun)* - पहचान चिह्न, कुंजी पटल की सारणी

The can will opened only if you pull the tab.

Table/टेबल *(noun)* - मेज, तालिका, सारिणी, सामने रखना

The newest addition to our house is the fancy dining table.

Tablecloth/टेबलक्लॉथ *(noun)* - मेजपोश

I bought a bright and flowery tablecloth for our new dining table.

Tablespoon/टेबलस्पून *(noun)* - बड़ी चम्मच

You need to add exactly a tablespoon of milk in the batter.

Tabletennis/टेबलटेनिस *(noun)* - गेंद का एक खेल

Being a state level table tennis champion helped her get a seat in the best college.

Tableau/टैब्लो *(noun)* - नाटकीय, झाँकी, प्रभावशाली दृश्य

The movie was a tableau of a warrior's life.

Tablet/टैब्लेट *(noun)* - गोली, अंकित पट्टी

They put up a marble tablet in the memory of his father.

Tabloid/टैब्लाइड *(noun)* - लोकप्रिय

The news of the actress's breakup was fodder for all the tabloids in town.

Taboo/टैबू *(noun)* - निषिद्ध वस्तु, वर्जित कार्य

There was a time in our country when widow remarriage was considered a taboo.

Tabular/टैब्यूलर *(adjective)* - सारिणी, तालिका

We were asked to arrange all the information in a tabular form.

Tabulate/टैब्युलेट *(verb)* - सारिणी या तालिका में क्रमबद्ध करना

Tabulating all the data would be an efficient way of recording it.

Tacit/टैसिट *(adjective)* - मौन, अनकहा, उपलक्षित

The boss gave a tacit approval to his employee's plan.

Taciturn/टैसिटर्न *(adjective)* - चुप्पा, अल्पभाषी

A taciturn man, he replied to my queries in monosyllables.

Tack/टैक *(noun)* - सामान्य प्रवृत्ति, चपटी कील

She straightened the tack and sat upright on the horse.

Tackle/टैकल *(noun)* - एक यन्त्र

I had to buy better fishing tackle to go for the competition.

Tact/टैक्ट *(noun)* - व्यवहार कुशलता

You must use your tact while dealing with such issues.

Tactic/टैक्टिक *(noun)* - दाँव-पेंच, युक्ति, चाल

The teacher knew the student was using some tactic to achieve something.

Tadpole/टैडपोल *(noun)* - मेढक का बच्चा

The pond needed urgent cleaning as I could easily spot the tadpoles and the weeds.

Tag/टैग *(noun & verb)* - नत्थी, पूर्जा नत्थी करना, शब्द जोड़ना

As soon as we reached the park the children ran and started playing tag.

Tail/टेल *(noun)* - पूँछ, दूम, पिछला भाग

When she went to demand her rights in the property, his sons told her that the estate was in tail.

Tailor/टेलर *(noun)* - दर्जी, अनुकूलता

I searched and searched and finally found a good tailor to stitch his shirts.

Taint/टेंट *(noun)* - दूषित वस्तु का दूषकारी प्रभाव, छूत, दूषित

The government could not shake off the taint of corruption.

Take/टेक *(verb)* - लेना, ले जाना, स्वीकार करना, सहन करना

We took over the enemy fortress in no time.

Takings/टेकिंग्स *(noun)* - दुकान, थिएटर आदि को माल टिकट आदि बेचने से हुई आमदनी

He knew he would have to analyse the takings of his department thoroughly before giving the presentation.

Talcum-powder/टैल्कम-पाउडर *(noun)* - मुलायम, सुगन्धित, महीन

The talcum powder she uses was quite visible over her clothes.

Tale/टेल *(noun)* - कहानी, किस्सा, अफवाह

She spun a tale around the whole incident that she could boast to her friends about.

Talent/टैलेंट *(noun)* - प्रतिभा, आन्तरिक योग्यता

Both her children have a talent for cooking and music right from childhood.

Talismant/टैलिस्मन *(noun)* - कवच, तावीज

The Tantric gave the woman a talisman to be hung around her neck for the next ten days till her desire was fulfilled.

Talk/टॉक *(noun & verb)* - बातचीत, वार्ता, बातचीत करना, बोलना, चर्चा, अफवाह, भाषण

We were forbidden from talking inside the seminar hall.

Talkative/टॉकेटिव *(adjective)* - बातूनी, बक-बक करने वाला

Her daughter was more talkative than her.

Tall/टॉल *(adjective)* - औसत से अधिक लम्बा

Her daughter was taller than her father.

T

Tallow/टैलो *(noun)* - चरबी

The butcher was trying to break the lump of tallow in half.

Tally/टैलि *(noun & verb)* - मेल, मेल खाना, मेल कराना

Their tally was exact with the list.

Talon/टैलॅन *(noun)* - पंजा, चंगुल, पकड़

The bird dug its talons into the skin of the prey.

Tamarind/टैमरिन्ड *(noun)* - इमली

Add tamarind extract to the cooked lentil to make the sambhar perfect.

Tame/टेम *(adj. & verb)* - पालतू, घरेलू, पालतू बनाना

The pigeon in my balcony was quite tame.

Tamper/टैम्पर *(verb)* - छेड़छाड़ करना, बिना अधिकार बदलना

I warned my brother not to tamper with my project. She used the tamper to flatten the ground coffee.

Tan/टैन *(noun)* - प्रभावित त्वचा, चर्म शोधन

She bought a tan dress for the party.

Tanner/टैनर *(noun)* - चर्म शोधक

He sold his leather piece to the tanner.

Tannery/टैनरि *(noun)* - चर्म शोधन स्थान

He arrived at the tannery early today.

Tang/टैंग *(noun)* - तीखा स्वाद या गन्ध

She could smell the salty tang of the sea.

Tangent/टैन्जेन्ट *(noun)* - स्पर्श रेखा, विषय-व्यवहार बदलना

The teacher showed how to draw a tangent to three given lines.

Tangible/टैन्जिब्ल् *(adjective)* - स्पष्ट, निश्चित, वास्तविक

Just because emotions are not tangible does not mean they are insignificant.

Tangle/टैंग्ल *(verb)* - उलझा हुआ, उलझन, उलझाना

The ropes were too tangled to undo.

Tank/टैंक *(noun)* - हौज, बड़ा पात्र

We ran to switch off the motor when we saw the tank overflowing.

Tantalize/टैंटलाइज *(verb)* - ललचाना, तरसाना

The stripper tantalized her customers at the bar.

Tantamount/टैंटामाउंट *(adjective)* - तुल्य, समतुल्य, बराबर

His statement was tantamount to an admission of guilt.

Tantrum/टैन्ट्रम *(noun)* - आवेश, क्रोध, झोंक में आना

The mother lost her temper when the child threw tantrums in the movie hall.

Tap/टैप *(noun & verb)* - नल, टोटी, सुनने का उपकरण, चीरा लगाना, थपकी, थपथपाना, खटखटाना

The water wouldn't stop as the washer was broken.

Tape/टेप *(noun)* – पट्टी, पट्टी पर अंकित करना, चिपकाना

When the vase cracked, I applied tape on it temporarily till I could get a better adhesive.

Taper/टेपर *(verb)* – संकरा होता जाना

The spire tapers towards the end.

Tapestry/टैपिस्ट्रि *(noun)* – कपड़े पर ऊन से बिनावट

Huge tapestries hung on the wall.

Tar/टार *(noun)* – तारकोल

The newly spread tar on the road was making it impossible for vehicles to pass.

Tardy/टार्डि *(adjective)* – धीमी मंद गति से, सुस्त

Mother asked me why I have been so tardy with my appointment with the dentist.

Target/टार्गेट *(noun)* – लक्ष्य, निशाना, उद्देश्य, लक्ष्य बनाना

He's a good sportsman who has never missed his target in the game.

Tariff/टैरिफ *(noun)* – दर की सूची, शुल्कदर

India is trying to do away with tariff on items such as electronics.

Tarmac/टार्मैक *(noun)* – पक्की सड़क

The plane was waiting on the tarmac. The airport had a new runway where new tarmac had been applied.

Tarnish/टार्निश *(verb)* – दागदार बनाना, धब्बा लगाना

The old statue of Buddha had tarnished over the years.

Tarpaulin/टार्पालिन *(noun)* – तिरपाल

The storm blew away the tarpaulin on the terrace.

Tarry/टैरि *(adjective)* – ज्यादा देर ठहरना, आने-जाने में बिलंब

The road was still a bit tarry, so we didn't risk driving on it.

Tart/टार्ट *(noun)* – खट्टा, कटु-व्यंग्यात्मक, एक खाद्य

I am making tarts for tea today.

Task/टास्क *(noun)* – काम, दिया गया काम

He was given the task of breaking the news to the patient's family.

Taskmaster/टास्कमास्टर *(noun)* – कठोर अधिकारी

Your new boss is known for being a hard taskmaster.

Tassel/टैसल *(noun)* – फूँदना, झब्बा

On his body, the cord and the tassel hung loosely in the wind.

Taste/टेस्ट *(noun)* – स्वाद, चखने की शक्ति, चखना, स्वाद लेना

She loved the tangy taste of the curry put on display.

Tasteless/टेस्टलेस *(adjective)* – स्वादहीन

He gave a rather tasteless remark about her performance.

Tasty/टेस्टि *(adjective)* – स्वादिष्ट

The snacks were tasty at the party.

Tattered/टैटर्ड *(adjective)* – फटा-पुराना, चिथड़ा

I saw a tattered old man begging outside the temple.

Tattoo/टैटू *(verb)* – गोदना

The couple had tattooed their names on each other's arms.

Taunt/टान्ट् *(noun)* – ताना, ताना मारना

Her taunts fell on deaf ears this time.

Taurus/टॉरस *(noun)* – वृष राशि

The boy was born under the Taurus constellation.

Taut/टॉट *(adjective)* – तना हुआ, खींचा हुआ

Her nerves were taut with anxiety.

Tavern/टैवर्न *(noun)* – सराय

I'll meet you in the evening over a drink at the tavern 200.

Tawdry/टॉड्रि *(adjective)* – भड़कीला, कुत्सित

She wore some tawdry costume at the party.

Tax/टैक्स *(noun)* – कर, माँग, बोझ

It was time to file our tax returns.

Taxable/टैक्सेब्ल *(adjective)* – कर योग्य

The gain from an option is taxable as soon as the shares are acquired.

Taxing/टैक्सिंग *(adjective)* – थकाने वाला

The whole trip was quite taxing to the nerves.

Taxation/टैक्सेशन *(noun)* – कर पद्धति

We had a class on taxation scheduled for this evening.

Taxi/टैक्सि *(noun)* – भाड़े की गाड़ी, जहाज के पहिए पर चलना

I took an airport taxi and rushed to catch my flight.

Tea/टी *(noun)* – चाय, चायपत्ती

She makes tea really well.

Teach/टीच *(verb)* – अध्यापन करना

It takes a knack of dealing with children, to be able to teach well.

Teacher/टीचर *(noun)* – शिक्षक, अध्यापक

I had the best teacher in the school to give me maths tuitions.

Teak/टीक *(noun)* – सागौन

I bought some teak furniture for my guest room.

Team/टीम *(noun)* – दल

The team had to use a unique strategy this time to win.

Teamwork/टीमवर्क *(noun)* – संगठित प्रयत्न

Nothing succeeds like teamwork.

Tear/टीअर *(noun & verb)* – आँसू, चीरना, फाड़ना, खोंच

I could make out from her tears that there was something deeply disturbing on her mind.

Tearful/टीअरफुल *(adjective)* – अश्रुपुरित

She stood tearful at the station as the train passed by.

Tease/टीज *(verb)* – छेड़ना, चिढ़ाना

The young girl bashfully asked the boy to stop teasing her in front of her friends.

Technical/टेक्निकल *(adjective)* – तकनीकी

One needs technical knowledge of the product before sitting for an exam.

Technician/टेक्निशन *(noun)* – दक्ष, विशेषज्ञ

We need to recruit a new lab technician.

Technique/टेक्निक *(noun)* – तकनीक

She used a special technique of mixing the icing with the cream and the batter and then frosting the cake.

Technology/टेक्नॅलॅजि *(noun)* – प्रायोगिक विज्ञान

The information technology boom was the greatest leap in industrial development our country could take.

Teddybear/टेडिबियर *(noun)* – खिलौनों वाला भालू

I still have the teddy bear I used to sleep with as a baby.

Tedious/टीडिअस् *(adjective)* – कठिन ऊबाऊ कार्य

I had a long tedious day at work today.

Teem/टीम *(verb)* – बड़ी संख्या में उत्पन्न करना, उड़ेलना, भरपूर होना

The hall was teeming with people of all castes, regions and race.

Teenager/टीनेजर *(noun)* – युवा होते लड़के-लड़कियाँ

She has turned 13 and is now a teenager.

Teens/टीन्स *(plural noun)* – किशोरावस्था

Smoking and drugs are most common among teens today.

Teethe/टीद् *(verb)* – दाँत निकलना

She has been feeling a lot of pain ever since she teethed.

Teetotaller/टिटोटलर *(noun)* – जिसने कभी शराब नहीं पिया हो/पीता हो

Though he was a drunkard five years back, he is now a teetotaller.

Telecast/टेलिकास्ट *(noun)* – प्रसारित करना

They were showing a live telecast of the royal wedding.

Telecommunication/टेलिकम्युनिकेशन *(noun)* – दूर-संचार

She joined BSNL as a telecommunication engineer.

Telegram/टेलिग्राम *(noun)* – तार

She rushed to her hometown as soon as she got the telegram about her grandmother's demise.

Telegraph/टेलिग्राफ *(noun)* – तार भेजने का उपकरण

If only there was a telegraph service on the ship, help would have reached on time and the passengers would have survived the wreck.

Telepathy/टेलिपैथी *(noun)* – अन्तः संवेदन, अन्तः बोध

I was alarmed at the telepathy, as she called just when I was thinking of her.

Telephone/टेलिफोन *(noun)* – दूरभाष

Did you get the message on telephone or internet?

Telescope/टेलिस्कोप *(noun)* – दूरबीन

He took out his toy telescope and tried to see if he could spy on the girl next door.

Television/टेलिविजन *(noun)* – दूरदर्शन

We bought a new television transmitter for our audio visual system.

Telex/टेलेक्स *(noun)* – दूर-संदेश

The telex system is finally being phased out after nearly 30 years.

Tell/टेल *(verb)* – कहना, बताना, सुनाना

Abu Hureyra is a tell, exacavated near the Euphrates valley in Syria.

Temper/टेम्पर *(noun)* – मनोदशा, क्रोधी स्वभाव

He is known for his short temper.

Temperament/टेम्परामेंट *(noun)* – स्वभाव

He was known for his temperament in his social circle.

Temperance/टेम्परेंस *(noun)* – संयम

I was overwhelmed when I saw a reformed alcoholic, rejoicing in the joys of temperance.

Temperate/टेम्परेट *(adjective)* – संयमी, समशीतोष्ण, सहज (जलवायु)

We are now in the temperate region.

Temperature/टेम्परेचर *(noun)* – तापमान

He has been running a temperature for the last two days.

Tempest/टेम्पेस्ट *(noun)* – तूफान, अति उत्तेजित

The ship caught in the tempest never made it to the shore.

Template/टेम्पलेट *(noun)* – साँचा

The boss asked me to follow the template that he had mailed me for the presentation.

Temple/टेम्पल *(noun)* – मन्दिर, कनपटी

A new temple had come up down the street.

Tempo/टेम्पो *(noun)* – रफ्तार, ताल-लय

The crowd was up on its feet as soon as he increased the tempo.

Temporal/टेम्पोरल *(adjective)* – सांसारिक

Specific acts are related to a spatial and temporal context.

Temporary/टेम्पॅररि *(adjective)* – अस्थायी

Everything in life is temporary, the wise sage said. He joined on a temporary contract and is on probation now.

Tempt/टेम्प्ट *(verb)* – प्रलोभन देना

Do not tempt me with sweets as I'm trying to lose weight.

Temptation/टेम्पटेशन *(noun)* – प्रलोभन

The first rule for losing weight is to stop fighting your temptations.

Ten/टेन *(cardinal number)* – दस

There were ten children in a row.

Tenth/टेन्थ *(number)* – दसवाँ

I was talking to the tenth child in the row.

Tenacious/टिनेशस् *(adjective)* – दृढ़ संकल्प का

I had to face a persistent and tenacious interviewer once.

Tenant/टेनन्ट् *(noun)* – किरायेदार

The new tenants in our house are a nice family.

Tend/टेंड *(verb)* – रखवाली करना, सेवा-शुश्रूषा करना, प्रवृत्त होना, विशेष दिशा की ओर

We were given the responsibility to tend wounded soldiers.

Tendency/टेन्डेन्सी *(noun)* – प्रकृति, झुकाव, रूझान

She has a tendency to go off track during her lectures.

Tender/टेंडर *(verb)* – कोमल, संवेदनशील, सदय, ठेका

She tendered her resignation this evening.

Tendon/टेंडन *(noun)* – हड्डी और माँसपेशी जोड़ने वाले नस

He damaged a tendon in his leg in the games.

Tendril/टेंड्रिल *(noun)* – लताओं में पतले धागे या सूत का अंश (जिसके सहारे वही दीवार आदि पर चढ़ती है)

A plant uses tendrils to fasten itself to wall.

Tenement/टेनिमेंट *(noun)* – अहाता, चाल

He gazed at the tenements across the wall, dreaming of having a roof above his head some day.

Tenet/टेनेट *(noun)* – मत, सिद्धान्त, धारणा

Increasing intrusion of scientists has challenged some of the basic tenets of aboriginal life.

Tennis/टेनिस *(noun)* – एक खेल

Leander Paes is one of our country's best tennis players.

Tenor/टेनर *(noun)* – दस्तूर, दिशा, स्वभाव, स्वर
His tenor could not be matched.

Tense/टेन्स *(noun)* – तनावग्रस्त, बेचैन, काल
In English class today, the teacher taught us the application of tenses.

Tension/टेन्शन् *(noun)* – तनाव
I have noticed that she has been under some sort of tension for the last few days.

Tent/टेन्ट *(noun)* – तंबू, खेमा, शिविर
As soon as we reached the farm, we took out and fixed our tents.

Tentacle/टेन्टकल् *(noun)* – कीड़ों के सूँड़
The jelly fish seemed to be coming nearer with its tentacles almost touching me.

Tentative/टेन्टेटिव *(adjective)* – अनिश्चित, अंतरिम
The college administration has released the tentative timetable for the exams.

Tenuous/टेनुअस *(adjective)* – नाजुक जोड़, कमजोर तर्क
She was holding on to life by a tenuous thread.

Tenure/टेन्युर् *(noun)* – कार्यकाल, अवधि
Lack of security of tenure has led to more unemployment among the youth.

Tepid/टेपिड *(adjective)* – गुनगुना
He hates the tepid bath water.

Term/टर्म *(noun)* – पद, पदबंध, शब्द, अवधि
She used some difficult words to comprehend terms in her lecture.

Terminal/टर्मिनल *(adjective)* – अन्त, आखिरी, मरणांतक लाइलाज
I was waiting for her at the bus terminal.

T

Terminate/टर्मिनेट *(verb)* – समाप्त करना
The journey was terminated halfway because of the bomb threat in the area.

Terminology/टर्मिनॅलॅजि *(noun)* – शब्दावली
The terminology the lecturer used in the class was beyond the comprehension of the students.

Terminus/टर्मिनस *(noun)* – अन्तिम स्टेशन
There was a huge traffic jam at the railway terminus.

Termite/टर्माइट *(noun)* – दीमक
All our furniture was being eaten up by termites.

Terracotta/टेराकोटा *(noun)* – पथरी मिट्टी के बरतन या मूर्ति
She works in a boutique where they make terracotta items.

Terrestrial/टेरेस्ट्रिअल *(adjective)* – थलचर
I gave the teacher a list of terrestrial birds, just as she had asked.

Terrible/टेरिब्ल *(adjective)* – संगीन, गम्भीर, भयानक
She came from the room with a grim face and revealed the terrible news of the death of her parents.

Terrier/टेरिअर *(noun)* – छोटे नस्ल का कुत्ता
I spotted a fox terrier at the kennel the other day.

Terrific/टेरिफिक *(adjective)* – विशाल, श्रेष्ठ, भयानक
Listening to songs in our speakers has a terrific effect.

Terrify/टेरिफाई *(verb)* – भयभीत करना
Children were terrified of going to the Dark House.

Territory/टेरिटरि *(noun)* – सीमा
The Congress Party ruled most of the territories in India.

Terror/टेरर *(noun)* – भय, आतंक
Hitler was a terror the world had to live with for a long long time.

Terrorism/टेररिज्म *(noun)* – आतंकवाद
Terrorism is an evil our world has been facing for a long time now.

Terrorist/टेररिस्ट *(noun)* – आतंकवादी
Three terrorists were caught in the recent bomb attacks.

Terse/टर्स *(adjective)* – कठिन, रूखा
She explained her role to the subordinates in a rather terse manner.

Tertiary/टरशरि *(adjective)* – तीसरे क्रम या दर्जे का
Tertiary education follows secondary education.

Test/टेस्ट *(noun)* – जाँच परीक्षण, परीक्षण
We had to break the test to know what the body composition of the sea urchin was like.

Testament/टेस्टामेंट *(noun)* - प्रमाण

She wrote a testament giving all rights to her property to her husband, before she died.

Testify/टेस्टिफाइ *(verb)* - गवाही देना

Bill Clinton was the only President in the USA to have testified for an embarrassing case.

Testimonial/टेस्टिमोनिअल *(noun)* - संस्तुति प्रमाण पत्र

She didn't expect him to give testimonials on her skill.

Tetanus/टेटनस *(noun)* - धनुषटंकार

We had to get a tetanus vaccination done before the disease spreads.

Tether/टेदर् *(noun)* - पशुओं को बाँधा गया पगहा (रस्सी) आदि

The cow was pulling at the string, trying to break the tether to which it was tied.

Text/टेक्स्ट *(noun)* - मूल पाठ

There were more than a thousand words of text to study and analyse.

Textile/टेक्सटाइल *(noun)* - वस्त्र, बुना हुआ वस्त्र

She has been into textile business for quite some time now.

Texture/टेक्सचर *(noun)* - रंग-आस्वाद

The dress had a rough texture making it itchy when you wear.

Than/दैन *(conjunction & preposition)* - तुलना हेतु प्रयुक्त

She is a better athlete than I.

Thatch/थैच *(noun)* - छप्पर, फूस की छत

Thatch roofs are a common sight in houses in South India.

Thaw/थॉ *(verb)* - पिघलना

It was time to thaw the ice.

The/द *(det.)* - निश्चित सूचक शब्द

The river was flowing in the wrong territory, apparently.

Theatre/थीएॅटर् *(noun)* - रंगशाला, नाट्यशाला

I got a list of movies running at the theatre nearby.

Theft/थेफ्ट *(noun)* - चोरी

There has been a theft in my neighbourhood.

Their/देअर *(possessive det.)* - उनका

The principal read out their accomplishments at the end of his speech.

Them/देम *(pronoun)* - वे

We saw them at the party.

Theme/थीम *(noun)* - सार, विषय वस्तु

The theme of their speech was world peace.

Then/देन *(adverb)* - तब

Back then, there were no cars, only horse carriages.

Thence/देन्स *(adverb)* - वहाँ से

We flew to Norway and thence to Denmark.

Thenceforward/देन्सफॉरवार्ड *(adverb)* - उस समय के बाद

With a significant nod of the head, he left the scene, and thenceforward, the world was a happy place to live in.

Theology/थिऑलजि *(noun)* - धार्मिक विश्वास

She wanted to do her post graduate studies in theology.

Theorem/थिअॅरम *(noun)* - प्रमेय, साध्य

He proved the theorem he postulated.

Theoretical/थिअरेटिकल *(adjective)* - सैद्धान्तिक

After scoring well in the practical exam, it was now time to prepare for the theoretical exam.

Theory/थिअरि *(noun)* - सिद्धान्त

She postulated a theory and was asked to prove it.

Therapeutic/थेरप्यूटिक *(adjective)* - स्वास्थ और चिकित्सा सम्बन्धी

The spa treatment had a therapeutic effect on her.

T

There/देअर *(adverb)* - वहाँ

We were asked to sit there.

Thereabouts/देअरएबाउट्स *(adverb)* - लगभग

Thereabouts lay the haunted house.

Thereby/देअरबाइ *(adverb)* - इस तरह

She knocked the jug, thereby staining the tablecloth.

Thereupon/देअरअपॉन *(adverb)* - फलस्वरूप

Thereupon the whole class gave a standing ovation to their favourite professor.

Therm/थर्म *(noun)* - ऊष्मा की इकाई

1 therm of gas produces 100,000 B.T.U.

Thermal/थर्मल *(adjective)* - ऊष्मा से सम्बन्धित

The scientists were working on discovering a new source of bio-thermal energy.

Thermometer/थर्मामीटर *(noun)* - तापमान मापक यन्त्र

The thermometer showed that she was running a temperature of 107.

Thermostat/थर्मस्टैट *(noun)* - ताप नियन्त्रक

Turn down the thermostat, its getting hot!

Thesaurus/थीसॉरॅस *(noun)* - पर्यायवाची शब्दकोश

I had to repeatedly refer to the thesaurus to be able to get synonyms for the words.

These/दिज - ये

These chocolates are mine.

Thesis/थीसिस *(noun)* - सिद्धान्त, शोध-प्रबन्ध

Now that you've presented the thesis, kindly explain the antithesis and the synthesis.

They/दे *(pronoun)* - वे

They had gathered at the ground for a demonstration.

Thick/थिक *(adjective)* - मोटा, घना, काफी

I had to get a thick board that wouldn't fall off easily.

Thickness/थिकनेस *(noun)* - मोटाई

The thickness of her hair was every hair stylists' dream.

Thick-skinned/थिक-स्किन्ड *(adj)* - अपमान से अप्रभावित

Your words would have no effect on this thick-skinned man.

T

Thicket/थिकेट *(noun)* - झाड़ी, झुरमुट

The voice seemed to be coming from the thicket at a distance.

Thief/थिफ *(noun)* - चोर

We ran and caught the thief.

Thigh/थाइ *(noun)* - जाँघ

He had cut a deep wound in his thigh that needed urgent treatment.

Thimble/थिम्बल *(noun)* - अंगुस्ताना, अँगुलित्राण

She could not stitch unless she had her thimble replaced.

Thin/थिन *(adjective)* - पतला, दुबला, महीन, कमजोर

I gave her a thin book to read.

Thin-skinned/थिनस्किन्ड *(adjective)* - अपमान से शीघ्र प्रभावित

He is too thin-skinned to survive the competition.

Thing/थिंग *(noun)* - वस्तु, परिस्थिति, शर्त

The sword had a black thing on it.

Think/थिंक *(verb)* - विचारना, सोचना, धारणा बनाना

She thought good of him.

Thinker/थिंकर *(noun)* - विचारक

Paul Brunton is a famous thinker.

Thinking/थिंकिग *(adjective)* - विचार, सोचने की क्रिया, सोच

I thought he is a thinking man. She told me I need to change my thinking and consider a different perspective.

Third/थर्ड *(ordinal number)* - तृतीय, तिहाई

Look at the third boy in the row.

Third-rate/थर्डरेट *(adjective)* - घटिया किस्म का

The sun glasses you bought were a third rate commodity.

Thirst/थर्स्ट *(noun)* - प्यास, जिज्ञासा

We were dying of thirst in the desert.

Thirsty/थर्स्टि *(adjective)* - प्यासा

I felt sad for the thirsty plants.

Thirteen/थर्टीन् *(cardinal number)* - तेरह

There were thirteen children in the room.

Thirty/थर्टि *(cardinal number)* - तीस

At least thirty people died in the bomb blast.

Thirtieth/थर्टियथ *(number)* - तीसवाँ

Yesterday was his thirtieth birthday.

This/दिस *(pronoun & det.)* - यह

This is the tree I was talking about.

Thistle/थिसल *(noun)* - गोखरू

Thistles were growing in abundance in her garden.

Thistledown/थिस्लडाउन *(noun)* - गोखरू के बीज

Like a ball of thistledown, it kissed the sea.

Thorax/थोरैक्स - वक्ष, छाती, कीट के शरीर का मध्य भाग

Thorax is a part of body between the neck and the stomach.

Thorn/थॉर्न *(noun)* - काँटा

The thorn in the plant pierced into my skin.

Thorny/थॉर्नि *(adjective)* - काँटेदार

We had to cut and remove the thorny bush that was growing in the garden.

Thorough/थॉरो *(adjective)* - सभी प्रकार से

She was thoroughly ready for the exam.

Thoroughbred/थॉरोब्रेड *(adjective)* - असली नस्ल का

One look at the horse and I knew it was a thoroughbred.

Thorughfare/थॉरोफेअर *(noun)* - आम रास्ता

It was a busy thoroughfare.

Those/दोज - वे, उन

Those were the people who should have been punished.

Thought/थाट - विचार, चिन्तन

You spend too much time in thought.

Thousand/थाउजैन्ड *(cardinal number)* - हजार

I received a thousand rupees as prize.

Thrash/थ्रैश *(verb)* - पीटना

I will thrash him if he behaves like this again.

Thread/थ्रेड *(noun)* - धागा, तारा, सूत, सूई में तारा डालना

The thread on the fabric was standing up.

Threat/थ्रेट *(noun)* - आशंका, खतरा

We received a threat call this evening and immediately informed the police.

Threaten/थ्रेटेन *(verb)* - धमकी देना

The kidnappers threatened to kill the boy if their ransom was not paid.

Three/थ्री *(cardinal number)* - तीन

Three men made their way on a horse towards Jerusalem.

Thresh/थ्रेस *(verb)* - कूट-पीटकर अनाज निकालना, दँवनी

I found a new technique for threshing.

Threshold/थ्रेसोल्ड *(noun)* - देहरी, द्वार, प्रवेश-निकास मार्ग

She stood at the threshold, waiting for everyone to come out of their shock of seeing her.

Thrice/थ्राइस *(adverb)* - तीन बार

Shake the bottle thrice before consuming the medicine.

Thrift/थ्रिफ्ट *(noun)* - कमखर्च

Save money and be thrift.

Thrill/थ्रिल *(noun)* - पुलक, रोमांच

She felt the thrill rising and adrenaline pumping her blood as the rollercoaster started.

Thrive /थ्राइव *(verb)* - फलना-फूलना

Virus thrives on garbage.

Throat/थ्रोट *(noun)* - गला, कंठ

She has been having severe throat pain for the last four days.

Throb/थ्राब *(verb)* - धड़कन, धड़कना, स्पंदन

I could feel my heart throbbing through my veins.

Throes/थ्रोज *(plural noun)* - प्रसव वेदना, व्यथा, वेदना

He convulsed in his death throes.

Throne/थ्रोन *(noun)* - सिंहासन, राजगद्दी

The prince would be the heir to the throne. The prince was throned on June 25th.

Throng/थ्राँग *(noun)* - भीड़

He made his way through the throng of people. A crowd thronged the station.

Throttle/थ्रॉटेल *(noun)* - गला घोंटना

The devices were at full throttle.

Through/थ्रू *(preposition & adverb)* - आर-पार

The sword went right through his heart.

Throw/थ्रो *(verb)* - फेंकना, फेंकने की दूरी

She threw the newspaper into the window.

Thrush/थ्रश *(noun)* - सारिका, गायिका पक्षी

The patient called the sad looking doctor a singing thrush.

Thrust/थ्रस्ट *(verb)* - धकेलना, घुसेड़ना, आगे की

She thrust her hand into his box and it got stuck there!

Thud/थड *(noun)* - धम की आवाज, धब-धब

I heard a thud from somewhere downstairs, around midnight.

Thug/थग *(noun)* - आक्रामक, हिंसात्मक, अपराधी

The thugs were convicted without much delay.

Thumb/थम्ब *(noun)* - अँगूठा

She broke her thumb in the accident.

Thump/थम्प *(verb)* - टोकना, खटखटाना, आघात

My heart was thumping so loud I thought everyone would hear.

Thunder/थंडर *(noun & verb)* - कड़क, गरज, कड़कना, गरजना

There was thunder and lightning all night.

Thunderbolt/थंडरबोल्ट *(noun)* - बिजली, वज्र

The news hit her like a thunderbolt.

Thunderstorm/थंडरस्टॉर्म *(noun)* - गरजता तूफान

The town was struck by a thunderstorm.

Thunderstruck/थंडरस्ट्रक *(adjective)* - हक्का-बक्का, जड़, हो जाना

They stood thunderstruck when they heard the news.

Thursday/थर्जडे *(noun)* - गुरुवार

I look forward to our Thursday-parties.

Thus/दस *(adverb)* - इस प्रकार, इसलिए

She killed him, thus landing up in jail.

Thwart/थ्वार्ट *(verb)* - निष्फल करना, बाधा डालना

Their plans were thwarted by the teacher who had always an eye on them.

Tick/टिक *(noun)* - टिक-टिक

The sound of the clock ticking was actually comforting.

T

Ticket/टिकेट *(noun)* - यात्रा का, दर्शन का अनुमति पत्रक

She ran to get the tickets before the movie starts.

Tickle/टिकल *(noun & verb)* - गुदगुदी, चुनचुनी, गुदगुदाना

She tickled me so badly I was rolling on the floor.

Tidal/टाइडल *(adjective)* - ज्वार-भाटा सम्बन्धी

The river here is not tidal.

Tide/टाइड *(noun)* - ज्वार-भाटा

We were asked to stay away from the beach as the tide was higher than usual.

Tiding/टाइडिंग *(singular noun)* - समाचार

If the tiding ever reached her, there would be nothing to save her from dishonour.

Tidy/टाइडि *(adjective)* - सुव्यवस्थित

She keeps her cupboard quite neat and tidy.

Tie/टाइ *(verb)* - बन्ध, फीता, गला बन्ध, बाँधना

The thief tied the hands of the lady with a string.

Tier/टीयर *(noun)*- ऊँचे-नीचे खाने में सोने की व्यवस्था, स्तर

We were travelling on a three-tier AC compartment.

Tiff/टिफ *(noun)* - दोस्ताना झगड़ा

The couple were caught in a tiff.

Tiger/टाइगर *(noun)* - बाघ

The number of tigers in the country has dwindled.

Tight/टाइट *(adjective)* - कसा हुआ, चुस्त, तंग, दृढ़, सख्त

Her shawl was twisted into a tight knot.

Tighten/टाइटन *(verb)* - कस देना

The noose was tightened around the neck of the culprit.

Tight-fisted/टाइटफिस्टेड *(adjective)* - हाथ दाब लेना, कम खर्च

He is extremely tight-fisted with his finances.

Tight-lipped/टाइटलिप्ड *(adjective)* - होठ सी लेना, कम बोलना

Everyone was instructed to be tight-lipped about the incident.

Tights/टाइट्स *(plural noun)* - चुस्त कपड़े

She wore tights under her skirt.

Tigress/टाइग्रेस *(noun)* - बाघिन, शेरनी

The tigress roared at the trembling goat.

Tile/टाइल *(noun)* - पत्थर का खपड़ा या पट्टी

She was using vitrified tiles for her house.

Till/टिल *(prep. noun & verb)* - तब तक, दराज, हल जोतना

There were long queues at the till.

Tiller/टिलर *(noun)* – पतवार का डण्डा

The tiller was swinging with the ship completely out of control.

Tilt/टिल्ट *(verb)* – झुकना, झुकाना, तिरछी

The windows tilted slightly.

Timber/टिम्बर *(noun)* – इमारती लकड़ी

They had a timber plantation in their estate.

Time/टाइम *(noun)* – समय, काल, अवधि

He dreamt of travelling through space and time.

Timeless/टाइमलेस *(adjective)* – समय से अप्रभावित

Some of Kishore Kumar's songs are timeless melodies.

Timely/टाइमलि *(adjective)* – समय पर

Thanks to the doctor's timely arrival, her father was saved.

Timid/टिमिड *(adjective)* – कायर, भीरु

She was rather timid when she was new to the city.

Timorous/टिमॅरस *(adjective)* – कायर और भ्रान्त

A timorous voice spoke from the last bench.

Tin/टिन *(noun)* – डिब्बा

She bought a tinplate for some lab work.

Tinge/टिन्ज *(noun & verb)* – हल्का रंग, आभा, झलक, हल्का रंग देना

The pink-tinged cloud was a picture worth being framed.

Tingle/टिंगल *(noun & verb)* – झुनझुनी, सनसनाहट महसूस करना

She was tingled all over with joy. A tingle went down my spine at the mere thought of going to that house.

Tinker/टिंकर *(noun)* – अकुशल कारीगर

I met a tinker once in one of my trips.

Tinkle/टिंकल *(verb)* – घण्टा ध्वनि

The tinkling of the cycle bells seemed too loud in this quite town.

Tinsel/टिंसेल *(noun)* – सजावटी धागा, पट्टी

I decorated her room with tinsels and party lights.

Tint/टिंट *(noun)* – रंग की आभा, झलक

The sky had a grey tint to it.

Tiny/टाइनि *(adjective)* – नन्हा, लघु

A tiny little insect was nibbling at my feet.

Tip/टिप *(noun & verb)* – नोक, उलट देना, झुकाना, इनाम देना, सूचना

What we saw before us was just the tip of the ice berg.

Tipsy/टिप्सि *(adjective)* – सरूर में

I asked the others to ignore her as she is tipsy.

Tiptoe/टिप्टो *(verb)* – पंजों के बल चलना

We tip-toed through the hall and stealthily entered the kitchen.

Tirade/टिरेड *(noun)* – उत्तेजक भाषण

As soon as I entered, I was welcomed with a tirade of complaints.

Tire/टायर *(verb)* – थक जाना, ऊब जाना

I was tired of hearing her complaints everyday.

Tiresome/टायरसम *(adjective)* – ऊबाऊ, कष्टकर

Her tantrums were indeed getting quite tiresome.

Tissue/टिशू *(noun)* – ऊतक, कागज का रूमाल

She had a tear in the tissue near her elbow.

Tit/टिट *(noun)* – एक छोटी चिड़िया

There was a tit mouse in the attic.

Titbit/टिटबिट *(noun)* – चटपटे आहार का टुकड़ा

The little mouse was hunting around for titbits.

Title/टाइटल *(noun)* – नाम, शीर्षक, उपाधि, पदवी, अधिकार

The title of the book had to be mentioned in bold caps.

Title-page/टाइटलपेज *(noun)* – मुखपृष्ठ

The author had unreasonable demands for even the title page.

To/टू *(preposition)* – तक, वहाँ तक

We were on the way to the station when the accident happened.

Toad/टोड *(noun)* – मेढक

A rather big toad jumped in front of our vehicle.

Toadstool/टोडस्टूल *(noun)* – कुकुरमुत्ता,

Learn to distinguish between a mushroom and a toadstool.

Toast/टोस्ट *(noun)* - सेंकना, सेंकी हुई दोहरी रोटी, शुभकामना घूँट

I like toast and tea in the morning.

Tobacco/टॅबैको *(noun)* - तम्बाकू

There is too much tobacco in this particular brand of cigars.

Tobacconist/टॅबैकोनिस्ट *(noun)* - तम्बाकू बेंचने वाला

He worked as a tobacconist for 15 years down the road.

Today/टुडे *(adverb)* - आज

The effect of the radiation that spread 50 years ago continues even today.

Toddle/टॉडल *(verb)* - छोटे बच्चे का चलना

The baby has started toddling.

Toe/टो *(noun)* - पैर की अँगुली

She had sharp toe nails.

Toffee/टॉफी *(noun)* - एक मिठाई

She was planning to make toffees for Christmas.

Together/टुगेदर *(adverb)* - साथ में, सम्मिश्रण

My parents have been together for 35 years now.

Toil/टॉयल *(verb)* - श्रम, कड़ा परिश्रम

He has been toiling away at the farm for days now.

Toilet/टॉयलेट *(noun)* - शौचालय

The public toilet was in desperate need for maintenance.

Token/टोकन *(noun)* - सिक्के जैसा साक्ष्य

She was given a bonus as a token of appreciation for her hard work.

T

Tolerate/टॉलरेट *(verb)* - सहन करना

I will not tolerate this disobedience any more.

Tolerance/टॉलरन्स *(noun)* - सहनशक्ति, सहिष्णुता

Gandhiji is known for his great level of tolerance.

Tolerant/टॉलरन्ट *(adjective)* - सहिष्णु

We must learn to be tolerant of others.

Toll/टॉल *(noun)* - मार्ग कर, मृतको की संख्या, लय में

The toll for this road was increased twice in the last few months.

Tomato/टमैटो *(noun)* - टमाटर

I like tomato sandwiches better than onion.

Tomb/टम्ब *(noun)* - समाधि

The Taj Mahal is the greatest tomb of love.

Tomboy/टॉम्बॉय *(noun)* - लड़कानुमा लड़की

She grew up as a tomboy but transformed into a lovely lady later.

Tombstone/टूमस्टोन *(noun)* - समाधि लेख

Her tombstone mentioned her name differently, I noticed.

Tommorow/टुमॉरो *(adverb)* - अगला दिन

The dress will be delivered tomorrow.

Ton/टन *(noun)* - तोल की एक माप

I have got tones of homework to do.

Tone/टोन *(noun)* - स्वर-शैली, स्वभाव, आभा

They were talking in hushed tones.

Toneless/टोनलेस *(adjective)* - नीरस, फीका, निर्जीव

I wonder why he is singing in a toneless voice.

Tongs/टॉग्स *(plural noun)* - चिमटा, सँड़सी

She moved the barbecue away from the fire with the tongs.

Tongue/टंग *(noun)* - जीभ, भाषा, बोली, बोलने की शैली

The ox has a really long tongue that reaches almost till its eyes.

Tonic/टॉनिक *(noun)* - स्फूर्तिदायक

You should take this tonic as it will give you energy.

Tonight/टुनाइट *(adverb)* - आज की रात या शाम

Let's go for a drink tonight.

Tonnage/टनेज *(noun)* - कुल भार

Trucks carry more tonnage than tractors.

Tonne/टन *(noun)* - माप की इकाई

Six tonnes of iron were being transported.

Tonsil/टॉन्सिल *(noun)* - गले की ग्रन्थि, गलसुआ

He had to have his tonsils taken out.

Tonsure/टॉन्सर *(noun)* - मुडन

At this rate, he'll soon have a tonsure like a monk.

Too/टू *(adverb)* - भी, इसके अतिरिक्त, अधिक

I'm sorry, you're too late.

Tool/टूल *(noun)* - औजार

I bought him a tool kit for his birthday.

Toot/टूट *(noun & verb)* - भोंपू, सीटी, भोंपू बजाना

I could hear the toot of the school bus from down the street.

Tooth/टूथ *(noun)* - दाँत, दाँतनुमा

My one tooth was broken in an accident.

Toothache/टूथ-ऍक *(noun)* - दाँत का दर्द

She has been having a toothache for the last few days now.

Top/टॉप *(noun)* - चोटी, शिखर, पराकाष्ठा, लट्टू, ऊपरी भाग, ऊपरी वस्त्र, ऊँचा, सर्वोपरि

The top was her favourite toy throughout her childhood.

Topaz/टोपाज *(noun)* - पुखराज

She has been wearing a topaz ring for the last few years now.

Topic/टॉपिक *(noun)* - विषय, विचार, प्रकरण, वार्ता

What exactly is the topic of discussion here?

Topical/टॉपिकल *(adjective)* - सामयिक

One of my favorite topical affairs programme was We The People.

Topography/टॅपॅग्राफि *(noun)* - स्थान की आकृति, स्थान का विवरण

I could see the topography change as the train went from the North to the South.

Topple/टॉपल *(verb)* - गिराना, लुढ़कना, लुढ़काना

I laughed at the story of Humpty Dumpty toppling off the wall.

Topsy-turvy/टाप्सिटर्वि *(adjective & adverb)* - अव्यवस्थित, उल्टा-पुल्टा

Why is the whole house topsy-turvy today?

Torch/टॉर्च *(noun)* - प्रकाश यन्त्र, मशाल, आग लगाना

I took the torch when I left her house last night as it was really dark outside.

Torment/टॉरमेंट *(noun)* - सताना, वेदना, यातना

She has been the chief cause of my torment.

Tornado/टॉर्नेडो *(noun)* - बवंडर, तूफान, समुद्री तूफान

The entire state was devastated by the twin tornadoes that struck yesterday.

Torpedo/टॉर्पीडो *(noun)* - एक प्रकार की मछली

The torpedo attack was started by the US first.

Torrent/टॉरेंट *(noun)* - बौछार

It was pouring in torrents in the neighbouring state.

Torrid/टॉरिड *(adjective)* - गरम और सूखा, तीव्र

The torrid heat of the desert was getting to me.

Torso/टॉर्सो *(noun)* - धड़

His torso was visible in the night.

Tortoise/टॉर्टस (टार्टिज) *(noun)* - कछुआ

The zoo kept different kinds of tortoise.

Tortuous/टार्ट्युअस *(adjective)* - चक्करदार, वक्र, टेढ़ा-मेढ़ा

The route is remote and tortuous.

Torture/टॉर्चर *(noun)* - यन्त्रणा, कष्ट देना

The prisoners have been through immense torture.

Toss/टॉस *(verb)* - उछालना, झटका देना

She tossed her bag on to the sofa.

Total/टोटल *(adjective)* - समग्र, पूर्ण, सब

The total figure amounts to $5,000.

Totalitarian/टोटलिटेरियन *(adjective)* - एक का पूर्ण अधिकार

The country was experiencing a totalitarian regime.

Totter/टॉटर *(verb)* - लड़खड़ाना, डगमगाना

The old lady came tottering towards the train.

Touch/टच *(verb)* - छूना, स्पर्श करना

The child was glad when his feet touched the ground.

Touching/टचिंग *(adjective)* - मर्मस्पर्शी, कारुणिक

The scene was indeed touching. preposition concerning. *Several discoveries touching the lost traditions of the Andamanese tribes, have been made.*

Touchy/टचि *(adjective)* - तुनुक मिजाज

He is a touchy guy when it comes to his race.

Tough/टफ *(adjective)* - कड़ा, कठिन, दुर्भाग्यपूर्ण

The bread you made was too tough.

Tour/टूर *(noun)* - दौरा, यात्रा, यात्रा करना

Guided tours may limit your scope for discovering unknown places.

Tourism/टूरिज्म *(noun)* – पर्यटन

The movie has promoted tourism in the state.

Tourist/टूरिस्ट *(noun)* – पर्यटक

Tourists receive a lot of special attention in this restaurant.

Tournament/टूर्नामेंट *(noun)* – खेल प्रतियोगिता

The tournament was organized to improve the relations between the two countries.

Tow/टो *(noun & verb)* – खींचकर ले जाना, खिंचाई करना

The tow was ready for spinning.

Towards/टुवार्ड्स *(preposition)* – की ओर

We drove towards the beach.

Towel/टॉवेल *(noun)* – तौलिया

There were clean and fresh towels in the cupboard.

Tower/टॉवर *(noun)* – मीनार, ऊँचा

The bell on the church tower rang non-stop.

Town/टाउन *(noun)* – नगर

There were seven towns in the province.

Town hall/टाउन हॉल *(noun)* – नगर भवन

The protestors gathered at the town hall to conduct their demonstration.

Toxic/टॉक्सिक *(adjective)* – विषाक्त, जहरीला

There have been reports of toxic water in certain areas.

Toxin/टॉक्सिन *(noun)* – नशा उपजाने वाला, बीमार करने वाला

The doctor could clearly spot harmful toxins in the patient's bloodstream.

T

Toy/टॉय *(noun)* – खिलौना, गम्भीरताहीन

She had a room overflowing with toys.

Trace/ट्रेस *(noun & verb)* – अवशेष, चिह्न, थोड़ी मात्रा, खोज निकालना

The traces were wearing off and the horse was revolting too.

Track/ट्रैक *(verb)* – चिह्न, पदचिह्न, लीक, दिशा, पटरी

He was trying to track the canoe up the rapids.

Tract/ट्रैक्ट *(noun)* – भूभाग, बड़ा क्षेत्र, नलिका

I read out the tract we received from the Church.

Traction/ट्रैक्शन *(noun)* – खींचना, खींचने की शक्ति

There was a primitive vehicle used for animal traction at the museum.

Tractor/ट्रैक्टर *(noun)* – खेत जोतने वाली गाड़ी

She worked in a factory that manufactures tractors.

Trade/ट्रेड *(noun)* – व्यापार, लेन-देन, व्यवसाय, पेशा

All kinds of trade between the two countries have been stopped.

Trademark/ट्रेडमार्क *(noun)* – व्यावसायिक चिह्न

The invention got the trademark of the company.

Tradition/ट्रेडिशन *(noun)* – परम्परा

Traditions were made by man and therefore are liable to be changed.

Traditional/ट्रेडिशनल *(adjective)* – पारंपरिक

The traditional festivities of Onam were all set to begin.

Traffic/ट्रैफिक *(noun)* – यातायात, वाहन-संचालन, अवैध व्यापार

The traffic was being diverted to let the VIPs pass.

Tragedy/ट्रेजिडि *(noun)* – दुःखद, दुःखान्त, त्रासदी

The family was struck by a tragedy three years ago.

Trail/ट्रेल *(noun)* – पीछा करना, पदचिह्न, अवशेष

The police found a trail of blood at the site of crime.

Trailer/ट्रेलर *(noun)* – साथ खींची जाने वाली गाड़ी, लघु अंश

He has been living in a trailer for the last few months.

Train/ट्रेन *(noun & verb)* – रेलगाड़ी, कतार, पंक्तिबद्ध, ताँता, सिलसिला, प्रशिक्षण देना, सिखाना

The students were being trained to become good professionals.

Trainer/ट्रेनर *(noun)* – प्रशिक्षक

He enrolled at the farm as a horse trainer.

Training/ट्रेनिंग *(noun)* – प्रशिक्षण

She is undergoing rigorous training for the event.

Trait/ट्रेट *(noun)* – विशेष गुण

She did show instances of self denigration typical to her family trait.

Tram/ट्राम *(noun)* – पटरी पर चलने वाली गाड़ी

There have been terror attack threats to the local trams.

Tramp/ट्रैम्प *(verb)* – धब-धब करते चलना, लम्बी पद यात्रा

The little girl was tramping around the whole house.

Trample/ट्रैम्प्ल *(verb)* – रौंदना, कुचलना

The child trampled all over the ants on the doorway.

Trance/ट्रैन्स *(noun)* – बेहोशी, समाधि, गहन ध्यान, मग्न

The patient entered into a state of trance as directed by the hypnotist.

Tranquil/ट्रैन्क्विल *(adjective)* – शान्त, प्रशान्त, निस्तब्ध

The sea was as tranquil as a sleeping baby.

Tranquillity/ट्रैन्क्विलिटी *(noun)* – शान्ति, स्तिब्धता

We went to the monastery in the hills seeking tranquility and peace of mind. We went to the monastery in the hills seeking tranquillity and peace of mind.

Trans/ट्रैन्स *(prefix)* – उस पार का

Their transatlantic journey had just begun.

Transact/ट्रैन्जैक्ट *(verb)* – कारोबार करना, सौदा करना

Be careful while transacting on the phone.

Transaction/ट्रैन्जैक्शन *(noun)* – कारोबार, सौदा करना

Transactions on the phone are extremely risk prone.

Transcend/ट्रांसेन्ड *(verb)* – सीमा से ऊपर जाना

The monk had transcended the limits of phenomenal life.

Transcendent/ट्रांसेन्डेन्ट *(adjective)* – उत्कृष्ट, अति उत्तम

Philosophy is about the search for a transcendent level of knowledge.

Transcription/ट्रांसक्रिप्शन *(noun)* – प्रतिलेखन, अभिलेख

They produced a complete transcription of the journal.

Transfer/ट्रांसफर *(verb)* – स्थानान्तरण, हस्तान्तरण

Your money is being transferred from the headquarters to the home branch.

Transfix/ट्रांसफिक्स *(verb)* – स्तंभित

He was transfixed with the sorrow in her eyes.

Transform/ट्रान्सफॉर्म *(verb)* – परिवर्तित होना, परिवर्तित करना, रूपान्तरित

We have learnt that energy can be transformed to light. Your transformation needs rules to be implemented.

Transfusion/ट्रांसफ्यूजन *(noun)* – खून चढ़ाना

Blood transfusion was the only option she had for a treatment.

Transgress/ट्रांसग्रेस *(verb)* – उल्लंघन करना

You will be punished if you transgress the rules I have laid out for this house.

Transient/ट्रांजिएण्ट *(adjective)* –अस्थिर, कुछ समय के लिए

Fame is transient, so don't hold on to it.

Transistor/ट्रांजिस्टर *(noun)* – ध्वनि प्रसारक यन्त्र

The mechanical professor explained how to fix a transistor connection.

Transit/ट्रांजिट *(noun)* – गमन, गति

His instrument was damaged in transit.

Transition/ट्रांजिशन *(noun)* – संक्रमण

The girl has been through a phase of transition and has come out way more mature and sensible than she was.

Transitive/ट्रांजिटिव *(adjective)* – सकर्मक

The English Grammar teacher explained the significance and application of transitive verbs in language.

Translate/ट्रांसलेट *(verb)* – अनुवाद

She works as a translator at the Embassy.

Translucent/ट्रांसल्यूसेंट *(adjective)* – पारभासी, अर्ध-पारदर्शक

She kept a translucent sheet of cloth over the window.

Transmission/ट्रांसमिशन *(noun)* – प्रसारण

The transmission of the virus is facilitated by the rains.

Transmit/ट्रांसमिट *(verb)* – प्रसारित करना

The sages of ancient Indian transmitted their knowledge to their students who in turn went to on to transmit it down the generations.

Transparent/ट्रांसपैरेन्ट *(adjective)* – पारदर्शी
There was a transparent sheet on the table.

Transparency/ट्रांसपैरेन्सी *(noun)* – पारदर्शिता
The masses were seeking transparency from the government.

Transplant/ट्रांसप्लांट *(verb)* – दूसरी जगह पौधा हटाना, प्रतिरोपण
The club was transplanted from its current location to the erstwhile community centre.

Transport/ट्रांसपोर्ट *(verb)* – ढोना, ले जाना, दूरस्थ भेजना, परिवहन
Arrangements were being made to transport the criminal to the jail in the outskirts of the city.

Transpose/ट्रांसपोज *(verb)* – स्थान परिवर्तित करना
You will realize the truth of the situation only if you and the opposing party were transposed.

Transverse/ट्रांसवर्स *(adjective)* – आड़ा, तिरछा
From the transverse hall, the stairway ascends.

Trap/ट्रैप *(noun)* – फँसाना, पकड़ना, फन्दा
There have been sightings of trap in the mines here.

Trapese/ट्रैपीज *(noun)* – कलाबाजी का झूला
The trapeze artist is my favourite sight at the circus.

Trash/ट्रैश *(noun)* – रद्दी, बेकार
The trash was accumulating and the garbage van was late.

Trauma/ट्रॉमा *(noun)* – आघात, सदमा, चिन्ता
She has been through the trauma of losing her parents.

T

Travail/ट्रैवेल *(noun)* – अप्रिय अनुभव
The woman in travails was really loud. The travails of life sometimes lead to happy endings.

Travel/ट्रैवल *(verb)* – यात्रा, यात्रा करना, चलना
I will be travelling across the country next month.

Traveller/ट्रैवलर *(noun)* – यात्री
I made friends with random travellers during my journey.

Traverse/ट्रैवर्स *(verb)* – तानना
He traversed the hills and the forests.

Travesty/ट्रैवेस्टि *(noun)* – नकल, तमाशा
A travesty of the trial will not be dealt with benignly. By travestying the situations of his family in the play, he has distanced himself from them even more.

Trawl/ट्रॉल *(verb)*– छान डालना, खंगाल डालना
The boat was out in the sea trawling for big fish.

Tray/ट्रे *(noun)* – तश्तरी, किश्ती, खाद्य व पेय पदार्थों को ले जाने के लिए प्रयुक्त बर्तन
The girl brought a tray of tea to be served to the guests.

Treacherous/ट्रेचरस *(adjective)* – विश्वासघाती, धोखेबाज
The treacherous minister was banished from the kingdom.

Treachery/ट्रेचरि *(noun)* – विश्वासघात, धोखा
The king accused the minister of indulging in treachery.

Treacle/ट्रीकल *(noun)* – शीरा, राब, अतिभावुक
I bought some treacle syrup from the grocer's and stored it in my larder.

Tread/ट्रेड *(verb)* – कुछ पर से चलना, कुचलना, मार्ग बनाना
Tread carefully on the path as its pebbled and may hurt your tender feet.

Treadle/ट्रेडल *(noun)* – पायदान
I made a treadle for him to complete his school project. He was treadling the machine made for his school project.

Treason/ट्रेजन *(noun)* – विश्वासघात
The party leader was arrested on charges of treason and corruption.

Treasure/ट्रेजर *(noun)* – कोष, खजाना, मूल्यवान वस्तु अतिप्रिय
Legend says that there is a pirate's treasure down in the wreck.

Treasurer/ट्रेजरर *(noun)* – खजांची, कोषाध्यक्ष कोषपाल
He has been working as the party's treasurer for five years now.

Treasury/ट्रेज़रि *(noun)* – कोष, राजकोष, कोषागार, सरकारी खजाना
The party leader wondered how he would tell the party that the treasury was almost empty.

Treat/ट्रीट *(verb)* – विशेष व्यवहार, समझना, मानना, दावत
You must learn to treat your elders with respect.

Treatise/ट्रीटिस् *(noun)* – ग्रन्थ, शोध ग्रन्थ, उत्तम ग्रन्थ
She wrote a treatise on Indian political theory.

Treatment/ट्रीटमेंट *(noun)* – चिकित्सा, समाधान, व्यवहार
The bill declared equal treatment for men and women in the issue of remarriage.

Treaty/ट्रीटि *(noun)* – सन्धि, सुलह, सन्धि-पत्र
The two countries signed a treaty regarding the distribution of oil.

Treble /ट्रेब्ल *(noun)* – तिगुना करना, उच्च स्तर
The boy had a brilliant treble that got everybody's notice.

Tree/ट्री *(noun)* – पेड़, वृक्ष
We had different kinds of trees in our garden.

Trek/ट्रेक *(noun)* – लम्बी यात्रा
She is planning a trek up the mountains for sometime end of the month. We've been trekking for five hours now.

Tremble/ट्रेम्बल *(verb)* – काँपना, कँपकँपी, उदिग्नता
She was trembling with fever.

Tremendous/ट्रेमेन्डस *(adjective)* – विशाल, भयंकर आकार वाला
Scaling that peak was a tremendous achievement by the team.

Tremor/ट्रेमर *(noun)* – कँपकँपी, कंप, उत्तेजित तरंग
Tremors have been felt in the nearby areas of the epicentre.

Tremulous/ट्रेम्युलस *(adjective)* – उत्तेजना या आशंका से काँपना
She gave a tremulous smile.

Trench/ट्रेन्च *(noun)* – खाई
The car was parked at the tip of the trench.

Trend/ट्रेन्ड *(noun)* – झुकाव, प्रचलन, प्रचलित
A trend towards part time jobs has begun in the East.

Trepidation/ट्रेपिडेशन *(noun)* – आशंका, घबड़ाहट
There was trepidation in the air about the impending blow.

Trespass/ट्रेस्पास *(verb)* – अनधिकार प्रवेश
There was a board outside the boundary wall stating that trespassers will be prosecuted.

Tresses/ट्रेसेस *(noun)* – लट, महिला के लम्बे बाल
Many men have been victims of the charm of her eyes, her long tresses.

Tri/ट्राइ *(prefix)* – तीन
Today's experiment was using tri-chloroethylene.

Trial/ट्रायल *(noun)* – मुकदमा, साक्ष्य की जाँच, परीक्षण, परख
The trial for her case is scheduled sometime early next month.

Triangle/ट्राइऐंगल *(noun)* – त्रिकोण, त्रिकोण की आकृति
The teacher taught us equilateral triangles today.

Tribe/ट्राइब *(noun)* – जनजाति
Relief has been sent to the tribes on the island affected by the tsunami.

Tribal/ट्राइबल *(adjective)* – जनजातीय
There was tribal jewellery exhibited at the fair.

Tribulation/ट्रिब्युलेशन *(noun)* – विपत्ति
They have been through trials and tribulations all their life.

Tribunal/ट्रिब्यूनल *(noun)* – विशेष न्यायालय
The case of the insurance claim was taken to the tribunal.

Tributary/ट्रिब्यूटरी *(noun)* – सहायक नदी
The tributary was as big as the river itself.

Tribute/ट्रिब्यूट *(noun)* – श्रद्धांजलि, प्रशंसा
His victory was a tribute to his persistence.

Trick/ट्रिक *(noun)* – चाल, छल-कपट, दाँव-पेच
The magician performed a trick of the light.

Trickery/ट्रिकरि *(noun)* – छल, धोखा
His trickery cannot escape the eyes of the warden.

Trickle/ट्रिकल *(verb)* – बूँद-बूँद टपकना
Water was trickling from the roof.

Tricky/ट्रिकि *(adjective)* – जटिल, कपटपूर्ण

The question was tricky and needed careful analysis.

Tricycle/ट्राइसिकल *(noun)* – तीन पहिया साइकिल

I asked the little girl to first be confident of riding a tricycle before moving on to a grown-up's cycle. She has caught on to tricycling big time!

Trident/ट्राइडेन्ट *(noun)* – त्रिशूल

The trident stood proudly on the mast of the pirate ship.

Trifle/ट्राइफल *(noun)* – तुच्छ, नगण्य

Don't trouble mother with such trifles when she is working.

Trigger/ट्रिगर *(noun)* – बन्दूक का घोड़ा, यन्त्र को चालू करने का पुर्जा

The thief's finger was on the trigger, all set to shoot.

Trigonometry/ट्रिगॅनॅमेट्रि *(noun)* – त्रिकोणमिति

Trigonometry is one of my favourite topics in mathematics.

Trillion/ट्रिल्यन् *(cardinal number)* – एक लाख करोड़

The fraud was of a whopping six trillion dollars.

Trilogy/ट्राइलॅजि (ट्रिलॅजि) *(noun)* – तीन का समूह

The Lord of the Rings trilogy is one of Hollywood's best made movies.

Trim/ट्रिम *(verb)* – काट-छाँट करना, संवारना, सुव्यवस्थित

I will pay you to trim the hedges.

T

Trinity/ट्रिनिटि *(noun)* – त्रिकक, तीन वस्तुओं का समूह, ब्रह्म, विष्णु और महेश

We were taught many stories about the Holy Trinity.

Trio/ट्रायो *(noun)* – तीन समूह

The trio set out to try their luck in the jungle.

Trip/ट्रिप *(verb)* – लड़खड़ाना, पतन, भेद खोलना, भूल करना

She tripped and fell flat on her face.

Triple/ट्रिपल *(adjective)* – तीन, त्रिपक्षीय, तिगुना

Having eggs ensure triple benefits.

Triplet/ट्रिप्लेट *(noun)* – तीन, तीन का समूह, तीन बच्चे

We never knew Mary was one of triplets.

Tripod/ट्राइपॉड *(noun)* – तीन टाँगों वाला

She set the camera on the tripod and waited.

Trite/ट्राइट *(adjective)* – घिसा-पिटा, मौलिकताहीन

I couldn't read through the trite story.

Triumph/ट्राइअम्फ *(noun)* – विजय, सफलता, जीत

He has led his side to many a triumphs.

Triumphant/ट्राइअम्फन्ट *(adjective)* – विजयी

We heard their triumphant shouts for a mile around.

Trivia/ट्रिविआ *(plural noun)* – तुच्छ, महत्त्वहीन

Do not waste time on such trivia.

Trivial/ट्रिविअल *(adj)* – नगण्य, तुच्छ

It is a trivial matter.

Trolley/ट्रालि *(noun)* – हाथगाड़ी

Take the luggage on this trolley to the train.

Trombone/ट्रॉम्बोन *(noun)* – तुरही

She couldn't stand her son playing the trombone at night.

Troop/ट्रूप *(noun)* – सेना दल

Lead this troop safely.

Trophy/ट्रॉफि *(noun)* – विजयोपहार, विजय प्रतीक

She needs an entire room to exhibit all her trophies.

Tropic/ट्रॉपिक *(adjective)* – समशीतोष्ण क्षेत्र

This plant exhibits tropic behaviour against the sun.

Trot/ट्रॉट *(noun)* – दुलकी

Do not get into an argument with that trot.

Trouble/ट्रबल *(noun)* – चिन्ता, परेशानी, कठिनाई

I blame you for all out troubles.

Trough/ट्रफ *(noun)* – नाद, मन्दी का दौर

Plant the seeds in a trough and place it on the window sill.

Trounce/ट्राउन्स *(verb)* – हराना, हराकर बाहर करना

He will never forget this trounce.

Trousers/ट्राउजर्स *(plural noun)* – पतलून

He walked in completely drenched in shirt and trousers.

Trousseau/ट्रूसो *(noun)*- दुल्हन का सामान

Have you finalized your wedding trousseau?

Trout/ट्राउट*(noun)*- कतला, मछली का एक प्रकार

Let us serve them trout this evening. This is your night to go fishing for trout.

Trowel/ट्रावेल *(noun)* - करनी

The mason used his trowel to flatten the mud.

Truant/ट्रूअन्ट *(noun)* - पलायनवादी, भगोड़ा

He may be a truant so keep an eye on him. You will be punished for being truant all week.

Truce/ट्रूस *(noun)* - शान्ति, युद्धविराम

The king offered a truce in order to avoid a war.

Truck/ट्रक *(noun)* - खुली गाड़ी, खुला डिब्बा, ठेला गाड़ी

This truck is over-loaded.

Trudge/ट्रज *(verb)* - थकावट के कारण धीरे-धीरे चलना, धीमी गति

He trudged up the steep path. I cannot trudge any further.

True/ट्रू *(adjective)* - सच्चा, वास्तविक

This is a true story.

Truly/ट्रूलि *(adverb)* - सच ही

This is a truly beautiful scene.

Trumpet/ट्रम्पेट *(noun)* - तुरही

Go out and practise your trumpet someplace else.

Truncate/ट्रंकेट *(verb)* - सिरा छोटा करना

The long scene needs to be truncated to fit into the film.

Truncheon/ट्रंशन *(noun)* - हथियार रूपी छड़ी

The robber stared at the police's truncheon.

Trundle/ट्रंडल *(verb)* - लुढ़कना, लुढ़काना

The drunk trundle out of the bar every night. Stop trundling or you will lose balance and fall on the road.

Trunk/ट्रंक *(noun)* - तना, धडा, वक्सा, सूँड़

This tree has the softest trunk in the world.

Trust/ट्रस्ट *(noun & verb)* - विश्वास, भरोसा, न्यास, सौंपना

I trust your decision.

Trustee/ट्रस्टी *(noun)* - न्यासी

He was selected into the board of trustees on account of hard work.

Trusting/ट्रस्टिंग *(adjective)* - विश्वासी

His trusting nature will harm him in the long run.

Trustworthy/ट्रस्टवर्दि *(adjective)* - विश्वास योग्य

He is a trustworthy employee.

Truth/ट्रूथ *(noun)* - सत्य

I want to hear the whole truth.

Truthful/ट्रूथफुल *(adjective)* - सत्यवादी

This is an example of a truthful man.

Try/ट्राइ *(verb)* - प्रयत्न या कोशिश करना, परखना

Did you try out each and every shirt?

Tryst/ट्राइस्ट *(noun)* - मिलनस्थल

There were rumours of their trysts. She asked him to arrange a tryst next week.

Tub/टब *(noun)* - नाद

Pour the water into the tub.

Tube/ट्यूब *(noun)* - नली

The doctor passed a tube into the patient's throat.

Tuber/ट्यूबर *(noun)* - कन्द

He has been advised to stay off any tuber.

Tuberous/ट्यूबरस *(adjective)* - कन्द वाला

You can identify this root by its tuberous appearance.

Tuberculosis/ट्यूबरक्यूलोसिस *(noun)* - यक्ष्मा, क्षयरोग

Tuberculosis was considered to be incurable till the last century.

Tuck/टक *(verb)* - सुरक्षित स्थान पर रखना, समेटना, लपेटना

Her mother tucked her to bed every night and read her a story.

Tuesday/ट्यूजडे *(noun)*- मंगलवार

They hold a market here every Tuesday.

Tug/टग *(verb)* - प्रयत्न से खींचना

Please stop tugging at the other end.

Tugged/टग्ड *(p.t. of tug)* - झटका दिया

The little girl tugged at her pigtails nervously.

Tuition/ट्युशन *(noun)* – शिक्षण, अध्यापन

She wants to take tuitions in mathematics.

Tulip/ट्यूलिप *(noun)* – फूल का एक प्रकार

I suggest you gift her a bunch of tulips.

Tumble/टम्बल *(verb)* – लुढ़कना, गिरना

The clown tumbled down from the staircase.

Tumbler/टम्ब्लर *(noun)* – गिलास

The giant drinks milk from that huge tumbler.

Tumour/ट्यूमर *(noun)* – गाँठ, घाव, रसौली

She was shocked to discover a tumour in her stomach.

Tumult/ट्यूमल्ट *(noun)* – हंगामा, उत्पात, शोर-शराबा

The shouting was growing really tumult with each passing minute.

Tumultuous/ट्यूमल्ट्युअस *(adjective)* – उत्पाती, कोलाहलपूर्ण

She always gets her way by being tumultuous with her demands.

Tuna/ट्यूना *(noun)* – समुद्री मछली

She loves tuna sandwiches.

Tune/ट्यून *(noun)* – धुन, राग, स्वर-संगीत

This was a truly haunting tune.

Tuneful/ट्यूनफुल *(adjective)* – मधुर

Can you please repeat the tuneful melody?

Tunic/ट्यूनिक *(noun)* – चोंगा, लबादा

I loved the colour of her tunic.

Tunnel/टनल *(noun)* – सुरंग, सुरंग खोदना

This is the longest tunnel in the country.

Turban/टर्बन *(noun)* – पगड़ी, साफा

She thinks she knows the man wearing the blue turban.

Turbine/टर्बाइन *(noun)* – एक यन्त्र

The deafening roar of the turbines could be heard for miles.

Turbulent/टर्ब्युलेंट *(adjective)* – अव्यवस्थित, अशान्त

The sea turned turbulent within a matter of minutes.

Turf/टर्फ *(noun)* – घास, गोबर या कृत्रिम मैदान

The architect has designated a small patch of turf in the front of the house.

Turkey/टर्की *(noun)*– एक पक्षी

Have you seen the turkey at the zoo?

Turmoil/टर्मॉइल *(noun)* – तूफानी अस्त-व्यस्तता

I could sense he was in a great turmoil within.

Turn/टर्न *(verb)* – मोड़ना, मुड़ना, घूमना, घुमाना, क्रम, बारी

Please turn your face away from the bonfire.

Turnip/टर्निप *(noun)* – शलजम

The rabbit loves chewing on turnip leaves.

Turpentine/टर्पेन्टाइन *(noun)* – तारपीन, तारपीन का तेल

Just apply oil of turpentine and the scar will heal quickly.

Turquoise/टरक्वाइज *(noun)* – फिरोजा, फिरोजी रंग

Her turquoise gown was the talk of the evening.

Turret/टरेट *(noun)* – कंगूरा, बुर्ज

The turret of the medieval era castle was stinking due to neglect.

Turtle/टर्टल *(noun)* – कछुआ

You can see the migratory turtles on the beach next month.

Tusk/टस्क *(noun)* – दाँत, हाथी दाँत

The tusk itself weighed nearly 2 kilos.

Tussel/टसल *(noun)* – संघर्ष, हाथापाई

Freedom always comes after a tussle. The teacher suspended the students who participated in the tussle.

Tutor/ट्यूटर *(noun)* – निजी शिक्षक

He will be your tutor for this semester.

Tutorial/ट्यूटोरिअल *(noun)* – शिक्षकीय

He attends tutorial classes after work.

Tweak/ट्वीक *(verb)* – झटके से खींचना, चिकोटी काटना

The nail will come off if you tweak it.

Tweed/ट्वीड *(noun)* – खुरदरी-सी सतह वाला मोटा गरम कपड़ा

I love wearing my father's tweed coat during winters.

Tweezers/ट्वीजर्स *(plural noun)* – चिमटा, चिमटी

The lab assistant used the tweezers to pick the tiny particles from the bowl.

T

Twelve/ट्वेल्व *(cardinal number)* - बारह

There were twelve packets arranged on the bed.

Twelfth/ट्वेल्फ्थ *(number)* - बारहवाँ

Which is the twelfth alphabet in Latin?

Twenty/ट्वेन्टि *(cardinal number)* - बीस

I wish to buy twenty books for the class.

Twentieth/ट्वेन्टिअथ *(number)* - बीसवाँ

This is his twentieth attempt so far.

Twice/ट्वाइस *(adverb)* - दुगुना

Playing with the kids was twice the fun.

Twiddle/ट्विडल *(verb)* - बेचैनी में कुछ करना

The boy twiddled his way through the crowded market.

Twig/ट्विग *(noun)* - टहनी

They saw many dry twigs lying below the tree.

Twilight/ट्वाइलाइट *(noun)* - संध्या का प्रकाश, गोधूलि, झुटपुटा

The twilight gave the entire hill an eerie glow.

Twin/ट्विन *(noun)* - जुड़वा

You two look like twins.

Twinge/ट्विन्ज *(noun)* - टीस, हूक

The boy twinged as the doctor took an injection.

Twinkle/ट्विंकल *(verb)* - टिमटिमाना, चमकना, चमक

I could detect a twinkle in his eyes.

Twirl/ट्विर्ल *(verb)* - चक्कर खिलाना, घुमाना

The girl twirled and her skirt formed a neat circle around her. She always ends her signature with a twirl.

Twist/ट्विस्ट *(verb)* - ऐंठना, लपेटना, बटना, मरोड़ना, ऐंठन, मरोड़

The woman twisted the towel to drain the water.

Twitch/ट्विच *(verb)* - फड़कन, फड़कना, खिंचाव

The boy's arm twitched as the lighted matchstick fell on his palm.

Twitter/ट्विटर *(verb)* - चहचहाना, चहकना, चहचहाहट

I woke up hearing the twittering of birds on my window sill.

Two/टू *(cardinal number)* - दो

There were two eggs in the basket.

Tycoon/टाइकून *(noun)* - व्यावसायिक बादशाह, पूँजीपति

He recognized the man to be a business tycoon.

Type/टाइप *(noun)* - जाति, प्रारूप, नमूना, प्रकार, मुद्रण के अक्षर

The scientists have never see this type of organism till date.

Typhoid/टाइफाइड *(noun)* - एक प्रकार का ज्वर

The student missed his examinations as he was suffering from typhoid.

Typhoon/टाइफून *(noun)* - तूफान

We expect the typhoon to hit the coast before tomorrow noon.

Typical/टिपिकल *(adjective)* - नमूना, विशेष प्रकार का, विशेष लक्षणों वाला, प्रतिनिधि लक्षण

Feigning innocence is typical of her.

Typify/टिपिफाइ *(verb)* - प्रतीकात्मक, प्रतीक लक्षण

Snow will typify the winter season in this land.

Tyranny/टिरॅनि (टिरैनि) *(noun)* - तानाशाही, प्रजा का उत्पीड़न

Our country ruled under tyranny during the last decade.

Tyrannical/टिरैनिकल *(adjective)* - अत्याचार पूर्ण

The government formed by Talibans was believed to be tyrannical in nature.

Tyrant/टाइरैंट *(noun)* - तानाशाह, अत्याचारी

He will always be known as a tyrant in this country.

Tyre/टायर *(noun)* - पहिए का बाहरी खोल

The cycle wobbled as the tyre moved on the rocky surface.

Uu

U/यू - अंग्रेजी वर्णमाला का इक्कीसवाँ वर्ण the fifth Vowel and the twenty first letter of the English alphabet.

Udder/अडर *(noun)* - थन, थान
Udder is an organ shaped like a bag that produces milk and hangs underneath the body of a cow, goat etc.

Ugly/अग्लि *(adjective)* - कुरूप
She has an ugly face.

Ulcer/अल्सर *(noun)* - फोड़ा, घाव
Harish is suffering from stomach ulcer.

Ulterior/अल्टिरिअर *(adjective)* - परोक्ष, परवर्ती, घातक
Sachin claims he just wants to help Aman but I suspect he has an ulterior motive.

Ultimate/अल्टिमेट *(adjective)* - चरम, परम
Infidelity is considered the ultimate betrayal.

Ultimatum/अल्टिमेटम *(noun)* - चेतावनी
Shweta has given Sachin an ultimatum – she could either stop seeing him and come back to him.

Ultra/अल्ट्रा *(noun)* - परा, सूक्ष्म
Ultra violet rays can darken our skin when exposed to the sun.

Ultrasonic/अल्ट्रासॉनिक *(adjective)* - परा ध्वनि से सम्बन्धित, पराश्रव्य
At normal condition our ears can't hear ultrasonic sound.

U

Ultrasound/अल्ट्रासाउण्ड *(noun)* - अन्त:चित्र का तकनीक
Doctors use ultrasound to monitor ovaries to see if they're responding to the treatment.

Umbilical cord/अम्बिलकल कॉर्ड *(noun)* - नाल, जनमोती नाल, मातृ सम्पर्क नाल
He asked the doctor if he could cut his wife's umbilical cord.

Umbrage/अम्बरेज *(noun)* - अपमानित
She'll take umbrage if she isn't invited to the wedding.

Umbrella/अम्ब्रेला *(noun)* - छाता, छतरी
Gauri used to carry her umbrella while walking to school.

Umpire/अम्पायर *(noun)* - संचालक, नियन्त्रक
Umpires play a significant part in a cricket match.

Umpteen/अम्पटीन - अनेक, लम्बा
She has told this story upteen times.

Unable/अनेबल *(adjective)* - असमर्थ, अयोग्य
My father is unable to get to town without a car.

Unacceptable/अनएक्सेप्टबॅल *(adj)* - अस्वीकार्य
The coach told the players that defeat was unacceptable.

Unaccompanied/अनएकम्पनिड *(adj)* - बिना साथी
The baby stayed home unaccompanied.

Unanimous/यूनैनिमस *(adjective)* - एकमत, सर्वसम्मति से
The owner of the house wants a unanimous decision.

Unanimity/यूनॅनिमिटि *(noun)* - सर्वसम्मत
People always look for unanimity.

Unanimously/यूनैनिमसली *(adv)* - सर्वसम्मति से
The Parliament unanimously approved the bill.

Unarmed/अॅन्-आर्म्ड *(adjective)* - बिना हथियार, नि:शस्त्र, शस्त्रहीन
Unarmed peasants were shot down in the valley.

Unashamed/अॅनशेम्ड *(adj)* - बेशर्म, बिना संकोच के
He is a sinner and an unashamed man.

Unassuming/अनॅस्यूमिंग *(adj)* - अहंकाररहित, विनम्र
Unassuming to a fault, Vinay is unassuming about the value of his work.

Unattached/अनटैच्ड *(adj)* - अविवाहित, असम्बद्ध
He is unattached to his office.

Unattended/अनॅटेन्डिड *(adj)* - बिना देखभाल के
He dashed out leaving the bar unattended.

Unauthorised/अनआथराइज्ड *(adjective)* - अवैध, अनधिकृत
The employees go for an unauthorized strike.

Unavoidable/अनएवायडेबल *(adjective)* - जिससे बचा न जा सके, टाला न जा सके
According to eye witness the accident was unavoidable.

Unaware/अनवेअर *(adjective)* - अनजान, अनभिज्ञ
Unaware of the danger they entered the room.

Unawares/अनवेअर्स *(adv)* - अनजाने में, औचक में
Rain caught the family unawares.

Unbalanced/अनबैलंस्ड *(adj)* - असंतुलित
A man who had gone unbalanced is very difficult to manage.

Unbearable/अन्बेयरेबल *(adjective)* - असह्य
Raju suffers an unbearable degree of sentimentality.

Unbelievable/अनबिलिवेबल *(adj)* - अविश्वसनीय
The matter is unbelievable to many.

Unborn/अनबॉर्न *(adjective)* - अजन्मा
Please do something good for unborn generations.

Unbreakable/अनब्रेकेबल *(adjective)* - अटूट
Raju gifted her unbreakable plastic dinnerware.

Unbroken/अनब्रोकेन *(adjective)* - अटूट, बाधारहित, बिना टूटे
Fortunately the other lens is unbroken.

Unburden/अनबर्डेन *(verb)* - भारहीन, भाररहित, हल्का
She unburdened the family from giving her economical support.

Uncalled-for/ॲनकॉल्ड-फॉर *(adj)* - बिन बुलाये
Ramesh is not interested in uncalled-for suggestions.

Uncanny/अनकैनी *(adj)* - आन्तरिक विचित्रता, असामान्य
The new born baby had uncanny shapes as of monstrous creatures.

Uncertain/अन्सर्टेन *(adjective)* - अनिश्चित
He is facing an uncertain recollection of events.

Uncharacteristic/अनकैरेक्टरिस्टिक *(adj)*-अस्वाभाविक
The prize goes to a book uncharacteristic of its author.

Uncle/अंकल *(noun)* - चाचा, काका, मामा, फूफा, मौसा
Sachin loves his uncle very much.

Uncomfortable/अन्कम्फॅटेबॅल *(adj)* - अस्थिर-चित, बेचैन
We spent an uncomfortable day in the hot sun.

Uncommon/ॲन्कॉमॅन *(adjective)* - असामान्य
Frost and floods are uncommon during these months in many countries.

Uncompromising/अन्कम्प्रोमाइजिंग *(adj)* - हठी
The minister of state took an uncompromising stance in the peace talks.

Unconcerned/अनकर्न्सन्ड *(adjective)* - उदासीन, रुचिहीन, बिना परवाह
He seemed unconcerned during the entire process of negotiation.

Unconditional/अनकन्डिशनल *(adj)* - बिना शर्त
Police want unconditional surrender of the criminals.

Unconscious/अनकांशस *(adjective)* - अचेत, बेहोश, बेसुध, सुध-बुधहीन
He is lying unconscious on the floor.

Uncontrollable/अनकंट्रोलॅबॅल *(adj)* - अनियन्त्रित जो नियन्त्रित न हो
He is facing uncontrollable pain.

Unconventional/अनकन्वेंशनल *(adj)* - अपारम्परिक, परम्परा से अलग
People look at her unconventional dress and hair style.

Uncountable/अनकाउन्टॅबॅल *(adjective)* - अगणित, अनेक, अनगिनत
There are uncountable people present in the meeting.

Uncouth/अनकूथ *(adjective)* - असभ्य, अपरिष्कृत
Don't behave like an untutored and uncouth human being.

Uncover/अनकवर *(verb)* - उघाड़ना, भेद खोलना, प्रत्यक्ष करना
Summer uncovers bright clothes in nature.

Undecided/अनडिसाइडेड *(adjective)* - अनिर्णित, जिस पर निर्णय न हुआ हो

Our position on this bill is still undecided which affects the case significantly.

Undeniable/ॲन्डिनाइॲबॅल *(adj)* - अखण्डनीय

There are undeniable consequences to their actions.

Under/अण्डर *(preposition)* - नीचे, आच्छन्न, दबा हुआ

A book is lying under the table.

Undercover/अण्डरकवर *(adjective & adverb)*- छिपकर, छिपा हुआ, गुप्त रूप से

Police want an undercover operation to catch the culprits.

Undercurrent/अण्डरकरेंट *(noun)* - जल के तल के नीचे की धारा, गुप्त प्रभाव

The undercurrent of the river is very strong.

Undercut/अण्डरकट *(verb)* - कम दाम पर बेचना, नीचे प्रहार करना

The local exporter will actually undercut the foreign dealer by very nearly the whole difference.

Underdog/अण्डरडॉग *(noun)* - जिसे श्रेष्ठ न माना जाए

Our sympathies were always with the underdog.

Underdone/अण्डरडन *(adjective)* - अधपका of

The old lady served us underdone rice and burnt bread.

Underestimate/अंडरएस्टिमेट *(verb)* - कम करके आँकना

Don't underestimate the value of this land, you could get more than what you think. You should not underestimate his capabilities.

U

Undergo/अण्डरगो *(verb)* - सहना, भुगतना

Suddenly his behaviour undergoes a strange change.

Undergraduate/अण्डरग्रेजुएट *(noun)* - स्नातक पूर्व, स्नातक से नीचे

Only undergraduate students can apply for the post.

Underground/अण्डरग्राउण्ड *(adj & adv)* - भूमिगत

Underground caverns.

Undergrowth/अण्डरग्रोथ *(noun)* - निम्नविकास, घास-पात

The ferny undergrowth covers the road to the temple.

Underhand/अण्डरहैण्ड *(adj)* - गुप्त बेईमानी से

Anurag achieved success in business by underhand methods.

Underlie/अण्डरलाइ *(verb)* - के नीचे पड़ा होना

The mobile underlies the bed.

Underline/अण्डरलाइन *(verb)* - रेखांकित करना, महत्त्व देना

The teacher advises the students to underline the important sentences.

Undermine/अण्डरमाइन *(verb)* - महत्त्व घटाना, क्षीण करना, जड़ खोदना

Our confidence in the team has undermined by their recent defeat.

Underneath/अण्डरनिथ *(preposition & adverb)* - तल में नीचे

The floor underneath the table.

Underpay/अण्डरपे *(verb)* - वेतन कम देना

The labourers have been underpaid since the inception of the factory.

Underplay/अण्डरप्ले *(verb)*- कम कर देना

The experienced actor underplayed his role brilliantly.

Underprivileged/अण्डरप्रिविलेज्ड *(adjective)*- कम अधिकार वाले

The church brought gifts to the underprivileged children of the neighbourhood.

Underrate/अण्डररेट *(verb)* - कम आँकना

She underrated the work that went into the renovation.

Underscore/अण्डरस्कोर *(verb)* - रेखांकित करना

His gesture underscored his words.

Undersigned/अण्डरसाइन्ड *(adj)* - अधोहस्ताक्षरी

He has to bear the responsibility as the undersigned person.

Understand/अण्डरस्टैंड *(verb)* - समझना

I understand what he means; She understands French. You don't need to explain-I understand.

Understandable/अंडरस्टैंडॅबॅल *(adj)* - समझने योग्य

The students weren't getting the simple and understandable lesson.

Understatement/अण्डरस्टेटमेंट *(noun)* - बात हल्की करना

To say that he is pleased, is an understatement.

Understudy/अण्डरस्टडि *(noun & verb)* - स्थानापन्न अध्येता

He understudied the role of the most experienced actor of their troupe.

Undertake/अण्डरटेक *(verb)* - भार लेना, बीड़ा उठाना

The social worker undertakes the responsibity of opening an English medium school in the village.

Undertaking/अण्डरटेकिंग *(noun)* - वचन

The youth organisation is preparing for great undertakings.

Undertaker/अण्डरटेकर *(noun)* - अन्त्येष्टि का प्रबंधक

The oldest undertaker is suffering from some grave diseases and there is a little time left in him.

Undertone/अण्डरटोन *(noun)* - मंद स्वर

The doctor spoke in undertones.

Underwater/अण्डरवाटर *(adjective & adverb)* - जलमग्न

Many ships get wrecked after colliding underwater rocks.

Underwear/अण्डरवियर *(noun)* - जांघिया

Always wear good quality underwears.

Underweight/अण्डरवेट *(adj)* - कम वजन

He is underweight to his age.

Underworld/अण्डरवर्ल्ड *(noun)* - छिपा हुआ, अपराधलोक

The Underworld is notorious for demanding money from celebrities and kill innocent people for ransom.

Underwrite/अण्डरराइट *(verb)* - बीमा करना, जिम्मा लेना

The insurance companies underwrite all the damage caused by the devastating fire.

Undesirable/ॲन्डिजाइअरॅबॅल *(adj)* - अवांक्षित

It is important to separate the undesirable impurities in steel.

Undivided/अन्डिवाडिड *(adjective)* - अविभाजित

All the three brothers keep an undivided interest in the property.

Undo/अन्डू *(verb)* - खोलना

The child requests to undo the shoelace.

Undoubted/अनडाउटिड *(adjective)* - असंदिग्ध

The schoolmaster is the undoubted judge of the entire village.

Undress/अन्ड्रेस *(verb)* - वस्त्र उतारना

The mother requests the child not to undress in front of everybody.

Undue/अन्ड्यू *(adjective)* - उचित से अधिक, अनुचित

Please don't show undue excitement in that matter.

Undulate/अन्ड्यूलेट *(verb)* - लहराना

The crops undulate pleasantly in the country side.

Unearth/अन्अर्थ *(verb)* - खोज निकालना

The police unearthed the town to capture the criminals. searching. *The CBI unearthed a plot to kill the Prime Minister.*

Unearthly/अन्अर्थलि *(adjective)* - अलौकिक

He somehow believes in unearthly love which is quite strange for others.

Uneasy/ॲन्ईजी *(adjective)* - बेचैन

The shy girl is feeling uneasy in the crowded marriage reception.

Uneconomical/अन्इकोनॉमिकल *(adj)* - खर्चीला, अलाभकर

The main issue is whether a firm would ever operate in the uneconomical region.

Uneducated/ॲन्एड्यूकेटिड *(adjective)* - अशिक्षित

Only an uneducated person behaves like this.

Unemployed/अनइम्प्लाइड *(adjective)* - बेरोजगार

The unemployed workers marched on the capital city.

Unemployment/अनइम्प्लाइमेन्ट *(noun)* - बेरोजगारी

Unemployment is considered as serious social evil in alomost all countries in the world.

Unending/अन्एन्डिंग *(adjective)* - अन्तहीन

I am tired of his unending demands.

U

Unequal/अनईक्वॅल *(adjective)* – असमान

The proposed human resource is unequal to the project.

Unequivocal/अनइक्विवॅकॅल *(adjective)* – स्पष्ट, एकार्थक

It is not very difficult to understand the plain and unequivocal language of the presentation.

Unerring/अन्एरिंग *(adjective)* – अचूक

He is believed to be an unerring shooter.

Unethical/अनएथिकल *(adjective)* – अनैतिक

Many social organisations fight to remove unethical business practices.

Uneven/अनईवन *(adjective)* – असमतल

An uneven colour.

Uneventful/अनइवेंटफुल *(adjective)* – घटनारहित

The journey was pleasant and uneventful.

Unexpected/अन्एक्सपेक्टेड *(adj)* – अप्रत्याशित

He was shocked after hearing the unexpected news.

Unexplained/अनएक्सप्लेन्ड *(adjective)* – अस्पष्ट

It is not possible to accomplish the task with some unexplained process.

Unfair/अनफेअर *(adjective)* – अन्यायपूर्ण

It was an unfair trial.

Unfaithful/अनफेथफुल *(adjective)* – अविश्वासी

She is suffering for his unfaithful lover. Her husband was unfaithful.

Unfamiliar/अन्फैमिल्यर *(adjective)* – अपरिचित

His name is unfamiliar to the most of the people of this country.

Unfashionable/ॲन्फैशनॅबॅल *(adjective)* – अप्रचलित

He wears unfashionable clothes.

U

Unfasten/अन्फासॅन *(verb)* – खोलना

The airhostess requests the passengers to unfasten their belts.

Unfavourable/ॲनॅफेवॅरॅबॅल *(adjective)* – प्रतिकूल

He will suffer for his unfavourable comments.

Unfit/अनफिट *(adjective)* – अयोग्य

The manager thinks all the project members are unfit for the new challenging project.

Unfold/अनफोल्ड *(verb)* – खोलना, रहस्य बताना

He unfolded the report to have a comprehensible idea.

Unforeseen/अन्फोर्सीन *(adjective)* – अदृश्य

The poor people are preparing to face the unforeseen circumstances.

Unforgettable/ॲन्फर्गेटॅबॅल *(adj)* – अविस्मरणीय

Rajesh has recorded all the unforgettable moments of his baby's life on video.

Unforgiving/अन्फॉर्गिविंग *(adjective)* – क्षमाहीन

His mother is surely an unforgiving old woman.

Unfortunate/अन्फॉरट्यूनेट *(adjective)* – दुर्भाग्यपूर्ण

An unfortunate night for all concerned.

Unfounded/ॲन्फाउन्डेड *(adjective)* – निराधार

He has been facing unfounded suspicion from various people.

Ungainly/ॲन्गेन्लि *(adjective)* – अभद्र

What an ungainly creature a giraffe is!

Ungratful/ॲन्ग्रेटफुल *(adjective)* – कृतघ्न

He left behind all his possession to some ungrateful heirs.

Unguarded/अन्गार्डेड *(adjective)* – असुरक्षित

The unguarded queen of Mysore was open to attack.

Unhappy/अनहैप्पि *(adjective)* – अप्रसन्न

After the argument all the members lapsed into an unhappy silence.

Unhealthy/ॲन्हेल्दि *(adjective)* – अस्वस्थ

He seems to be unhealthy. He frequently takes an unhealthy diet of fast foods.

Unheard/ॲन्हर्ड *(adjective)* – अनसुना

The teacher will ask questions from the chapters which is unheard to all the students.

Unicorn/यूनिकॉर्न *(noun)* – एकसिंहा

He always dreams of riding a unicorn.

Unidentified/ॲनॅआइडेन्टिफाइड *(adj)* – अनपहचाना

The prosecutor is talking about an unidentified witness.

Uniform/यूनिफॉर्म *(adjective)* – एकरूपता, वर्दी

We are passing through a street of uniform tall white buildings.

Unify/यूनिफाइ *(verb)* – एकीकरण करना

We should unify our resources.

Unilateral/यूनिलैटॅरॅल *(adjective)* – एकपक्षीय, एकतरफा, एकात्मक

A unilateral decision was taken.

Union/यूनियन *(noun)* - संघ

There is strength in union.

Unique/यूनिक *(adjective)* - अजूबा, विचित्र, असामान्य

We have seen a unique copy of an ancient manuscript; He spoke with a unique accent.

Unison/यूनिसॅन *(noun)* - एक स्वर से

The army is marching in unison.

Unit/यूनिट *(noun)* - इकाई

The word is a basic linguistic unit.

Unite/यूनाइट *(verb)* - संयुक्त करना

Unless we unite, our enemies will defeat us.

Universal/यूनिवॅर्सल *(adjective)* - सार्वभौमिक

Universal experience; The movie opened to universal acclaim.

Universe/यूनिवॅर्स *(noun)* - विश्व, ब्रह्माण्ड

They wish to study the evolution of the universe.

University/यूनिवॅर्सिटी *(noun)* - विश्वद्यालय

His daughter is a university professor.

Unjust/अॅन्जस्ट *(adjective)* - अन्यायपूर्ण

He used unjust methods to earn material gain.

Unkempt/अनकेम्प्ट *(adjective)* - मैला-कुचैला

wild unkempt hair.

Unkind/अॅन्काइन्ड *(adjective)* - निर्दयी

The teacher made a thoughtless and unkind remark of the students.

Unknown/अॅन्नोन *(noun)* - अज्ञात

An unknown island; an unknown amount; an unknown poet.

Unlawful/अॅन्लॉफुल *(adjective)* - अवैध

People are engaged in unlawful banking practices.

Unleaded/अॅन्लेडिड *(adjective)* - बिना शीशे का

They use unleaded petrol.

Unless/अॅन्लेस *(conjunction)* - जब तक नहीं

The new rules shall not have effect unless they have been approved.

Unlike/अन्लाइक *(preposition)* - असमान

He is very friendly, unlike his father.

Unlikely/अॅन्लाइकलि *(adjective)* - असंभावित

It is unlikely to question the legislation.

Unlimited/अॅन्लिमिटेड *(adjective)* - असीमित

He wants a internet connection with unlimited downloading.

Unload/अॅन्लोड *(verb)* - उतारना, निकालना

The manager ordered the labourers to unload the truck.

Unlock/अॅन्लॉक *(verb)* - ताला खोलना, खोलना

She quickly unlocked the door.

Unlucky/अॅन्लॅकि *(adjective)* - अभागा

The unlucky prisoner was put in prison again.

Unmarried/अॅन्मैरिड *(adjective)* - अविवाहित

He invited only unmarried men and women to the function.

Unmistakable/अॅन्मिस्टेकॅबॅल *(adj)* - सुस्पष्ट

His guide's opposition to slavery was unmistakable.

Unnatural/अॅन्नैचुरल *(adjective)* - अप्राकृतिक

His unnatural behaviour is dangerous to the society.

Unnecessary/अॅन्नेसेसॅरि *(adjective)* - अनावश्यक

Remove the unnecessary stuff from the car.

Unnerve/अॅन्नॅर्व *(verb)* - हिम्मत जबाब देना

The incident shouldn't unnerve him at all.

Unnoticed/अॅन्नोटिस्ड *(adj)* - अनदेखा, अलक्षित

He has crossed the road unnoticed.

Unobtrusive/अॅन्ब्ट्रूसिव *(adjective)* - कठिनाई से दिखने वाला

He is living an unobtrusive life of self-denial.

Unofficial/अन्ऑफिशॅल *(adjective)* - अन-अधिकारिक, गैर सरकारी

He announced an unofficial declaration to the members.

Unpack/अॅन्पैक *(verb)* - सामान खोलना

The child's mother unpacks the birthday presents.

Unpaid/अॅन्पेड *(adjective)* - बिना अदायगी

He notices the unpaid bill.

Unpleasant/अॅन्प्लेजॅन्ट *(adjective)* - अप्रिय

She can't tolerate his unpleasant personality.

Unplug/अॅन्प्लग *(verb)* - सम्बन्ध-विच्छेद, विद्युत-विच्छेद

She unplugged the hair drier after using it.

U

Unpopular/ॲन्पाप्यूलॅर *(adj)* – अप्रसिद्ध, अनचाहा
The country is ready to wage an unpopular war.

Unprecedented/अनप्रेसिडेंटेड *(adj)* – अभूतपूर्व, अघटित
Our generation is witnessing an unprecedented expansion in population and industry.

Unpredictable/ॲन्प्रिडिक्टॅबॅल *(adj)* – जिसकी भविष्यवाणी न हो सके
His sudden outburst is completely unpredictable.

Unprepared/ॲन्प्रिपेअॅड *(adj)* – तैयार नहीं होना
He is unprepared for today's exam.

Unpretentious/ॲन्प्रिटेन्शॅस *(adjective)* – अहंकार रहित, विनम्र
His quiet unpretentious demeanour attracts all.

Unprofessional/ॲन्प्रॅफेशनल *(adj)* – अव्यावसायिक
His unprofessional behabviour surprises all.

Unprovoked/ॲन्प्रॅवोक्ड *(adj)* – बिना भड़काये
The army is not prepared for the unprovoked and dastardly attack.

Unqualified/ॲन्क्वॉलिफाइड *(adj)* – मान्यताहीन, योग्यताविहीन
Raj is unqualified for the post applied for.

Unquestionable/ॲन्क्वेस्चॅनॅबॅल *(adj)* – निर्विवाद, निस्संदेह
He upholds his unquestionable authority.

Unravel/अनरैवल *(verb)* – सुलझाना
His old grandmother asks him to unravel the thread.

Unreal/ॲन्रिअॅल *(adjective)* – अवास्तविक
She is desirous of unreal success.

Unreasonable/ॲन्रीजनॅबॅल *(adjective)* – अनुचित
The young man's unreasonable attitude distracts all from the goal.

Unreliable/ॲन्रिलाइअबल *(adj)* – अविश्वसनीय
People consider our generation unreliable.

Unremitting/ॲन्रिमिटिंग *(adjective)* – निरन्तर
We couldn't go out for picnic because of unremitting rain.

Unrest/ॲन्रेस्ट *(noun)* – अशान्ति
I feel a bit unrest today.

Unripe/ॲन्राइप *(adjective)* – कच्चा
The vendor is ready to sell unripe fruits to the customers.

Unrivalled/ॲन्राइवल्ड *(adj)* – अद्वितीय, प्रतिद्वन्द्वी विहीन
Her unrivalled mastery of art suppresses all others.

Unroll/ॲन्रोल *(verb)* – खोलना
The activist unrolls the banner before the followers.

Unruly/ॲन्रूलि *(adjective)* – बेकाबू, उपद्रवी
The teachers find his attitude unruly.

Unsafe/ॲन्सेफ *(adjective)* – असुरक्षित
People think their fortune was increasingly unsafe.

Unsaid/ॲन्सेड *(adjective)* – अनकहा
Many things left unsaid.

Unsatisfactory/ॲन्सैटिस्फैक्टरी *(adj)* –असन्तोषप्रद
Life is becoming increasingly unsatisfactory.

Unsavoury/ॲन्सेवरि *(adjective)* – आक्रामक, अनचाहा स्वाद
I cannot eat such unsavoury food.

Unscathed/ॲन्स्केद्ड *(adj)* – बिना घायल हुए
The young man survived unscathed.

Unscrew/ॲन्स्क्रू *(verb)* – पेंच खोलना
He is asked to unscrew the outlet plate.

Unscrupulous/अनस्क्रुप्युलस *(adj)* – कपटी
Unscrupulous politicians are destroying our country.

Unsettle/ॲन्सेटॅल *(verb)* – अस्थिर करना
Don't unsettle them.

Unshaven/अनशेवेन *(adjective)* – बिना दाढ़ी बनाये
The young man looked unshaven but energetic.

Unsightly/ॲन्साइटलि *(adjective)* – घिनावना, घृणित, नहीं देखने योग्य
There were unsightly seenes on the road last night.

Unskilled/ॲन्स्किल्ड *(adjective)* – अकुशल
He is unskilled in the art of rhetoric.

Unsound/अन्साउण्ड *(adj)* – अस्वस्थ, कमजोर
The new organization is based on an unsound foundation.

Unspeakable/अॅन्स्पीकेबॅल *(adj)* - अकथनीय

He can't express unspeakable happiness in words. Never dare to utter the unspeakable name of the witch.

Unstable/अॅन्स्टेबॅल *(adjective)* - अस्थिर

We are witnessing the worst unstable political conditions of the country.

Unsteady/अॅन्स्टेडी *(adj)* - अस्थिर, हिलने वाला

His hand was unsteady as he poured the wine.

Unsuccessful/अॅन्सक्सेसफुल *(adjective)* - असफल

Ramesh was unsuccessful in his first attempt.

Unsuitable/अन्सूटेबल *(adjective)* - अनुपयुक्त

The college authority forms new rules unsuitable to students.

Unsure/अन्श्यूर *(adjective)* - अनिश्चित

His father thinks him to be a very unsure young man.

Unsuspecting/अॅन्सस्पेक्टिंग *(adj)* - संदेह से परे

The politicians are deceiving the unsuspecting public.

Untamed/अॅन्टेम्ड *(adjective)* - न दबने वाला

The man is fond of the untamed wilderness.

Untangle/अॅन्टैंगल *(verb)* - सुलझाना

Untangle the thread.

Unthinkable/अॅन्थिंकॅबॅल *(adjective)* - कल्पनातीत, विचार से परे

The unthinkable usually remains the unmentionable.

Unthinking/अॅन्थिंकिंग *(adjective)* - विचारहीन, अविचारी

The unthinking activities of the young prince will bring the doomsday to the kingdom soon.

Untidy/अॅन्टाइडि *(adjective)* - गन्दा, तितर-बितर, अव्यवस्थित

He lives in an untidy living room.

Untie/अॅन्टाइ *(verb)* - खोलना

The people untied the prisoner.

Until/अॅन्टिल *(preposition & conjunction)* - तक

He sleeps until it gets light.

Untimely/अॅन्टाइम्लि *(adjective)* - कुसमय

He makes an untimely remark. Alcohol brought him to an untimely end.

Unto/अॅन्टु *(preposition)* - तब तक

The Lord said unto Moses.

Untold/अनटोल्ड *(adjective)* - अनकहा

Thieves caused untold damage to the family.

Untouchable/अन्टचेबल *(adjective)* - अछूत

He is untouchable for the critics.

Untoward/अनटुवार्ड *(adjective)* - अप्रत्याशित

They made a place for themselves under the most untoward conditions.

Untrue/अनट्रू *(adjective)* - असभ्य

The statement was simply untrue.

Untruth/अनट्रूथ *(noun)* - असत्य, झूठा

Don't tell me a untruth story to save your life.

Unused/अॅन्यूज्ड *(adjective)* - अप्रयुक्त, अनुभवहीन

He has seen an unused envelope.

Unusual/अॅन्यूजुअल *(adjective)* - असामान्य

Nuclear families are no longer unusual.

Unutterable/अॅन्अटरेब्ल *(adjective)* - अकथनीय

The small girl can't describe the unutterable incident.

Unveil/अॅन्वेल *(verb)* - परदा हटाना, घूँघट उठाना

Women are not allowed to unveil themselves in public in Islamic societies.

Unwanted/अॅन्वांटेड *(adjective)* - अनचाहा

The family is scared of unwanted guests.

Unwelcome/अॅन्वेलकम *(adjective)* - अवांछित

He is unwelcome in the function.

Unwell/अॅन्वेल *(adjective)* - अस्वस्थ

He is severely unwell.

Unwieldy/अॅन्वील्डि *(adjective)* - बोझिल

The person almost dropped the unwieldy parcel.

Unvilling/अॅन्विलिंग *(adjective)* - अनिच्छुक

She is unwilling the do the homework.

Unwind/अॅन्वाइन्ड *(verb)* - लपेट खोलना

Unwind a ball of yarn.

Unwitting/अॅन्विटिंग *(adjective)* - अनजाना

He is going to encounter an unwitting accomplice.

Unwrap/अॅन्रैप *(verb)* - खोलना, अनाकृत करना

Let's unwrap the gifts!

Up/अप *(adverb)* - ऊपर, पूरी तरह, उठना
I am up and about here.

Upbeat/ऑप्बिट *(noun)* - प्रसन्न और उत्साहित
His wishes are considered upbeat.

Upbraid/ऑप्ब्रेड *(verb)* - झिड़कना, डाँटना
The president upbraided the minister for his irresponsible behaviour.

Upbringing/ऑप्ब्रिंगिंग *(noun)* - पालन-पोषण
His behaviour reflects his upbringing.

Update/ऑप्डेट *(verb)* - अद्यतन करना
We updated the bedroom in the old house.

Upgrade/ऑप्ग्रेड *(verb)* - स्तर बढ़ाना
The teacher upgraded the most brilliant student to the next class.

Upheaval/ऑप्हीवल *(noun)* - उथल-पुथल
The industrial revolution was a period of great upheaval in the world.

Uphill/ऑप्हिल *(adverb)* - कठिन
He moves uphill.

Uphold/ऑप्होल्ड *(verb)* - अनुमोदन करना
He upholds the conditions put forward by the suffering family; The man is trying to uphold the family tradition.

Upholster/ऑप्होल्स्टर *(verb)* - गद्दा लगाना
There are many chair companies that import all types of upholstery, frames.

Upholstery/ऑप्होल्स्टरि *(noun)* - गद्दा
The family is doing the business of importing upholstery for many decades.

Upkeep/ऑप्कीप *(noun)* - रख-रखाव
His upkeep of maintaining the museum is commendable.

Upland/ऑप्लैंड *(noun)* - ऊच्चभूमि, ऊँचासी
Upland agriculture may bring good result.

Uplifting/ऑप्लिफ्टिंग *(noun)* - ऊपर खींचना
The uplifting of the clouds revealed the blue of a summer sky.

Upon/ऑपॉन *(preposition)* - पर, किसी पर
The man balanced upon one leg well.

Upper/अपर *(adjective)* - ऊपरी
The small tree is located in the upper centre of the picture.

Uppermost/अपरमोस्ट *(adjective)* - सबसे ऊपर
Please bring me the uppermost book in the pile.

Upright/ऑप्राइट *(adjective)* - सीधा, ईमानदार
He is a man of upright nature.

Uprising/ऑप्राइजिंग *(noun)* - विद्रोह
The security has been stepped up since the recent uprising in the city.

Uproar/ऑप्रोर *(noun)* - हंगामा
There is a sudden uproar in the city due to a terrorist threat.

Uproot/ऑप्रूट *(verb)* - उखाड़ना, जड़ से उखाड़ना
Uproot the vine that has spread all over the garden.

Upset/ऑप्सेट *(verb)* - गड़बड़ी करना, हड़बडी़ होना
The hostile talks upset the peaceful situation in the room.

Upshot/ऑप्शॉट *(noun)* - निष्कर्ष
The recent incidents are the upshot of various happenings occurred two decades ago.

Upside-down/ऑप्साइड-डाउन *(adj & adv)* - उलटा-पुलटा
The box was lying on the floor upside down.

Upstairs/ऑप्स्टेअर्स *(adverb)* - ऊपरी मंजिल
The younger son lives upstairs.

Upstart/ऑप्स्टार्ट *(noun)* - नवधनाढ्य
The man who was so poor one year back is considered an upstart in the city.

Upstream/ऑप्स्ट्रीम *(adj & adv)* - प्रतिकूल दिशा में
He went upstream to look at a sure-enough fish wheel.

Uptake/ऑप्टेक *(noun)* - उद्ग्रहण
The machine makes paper napkins with a greater uptake of liquids.

Uptight/ऑप्टाइट *(adjective)* - भयभीत, आशंकित
For some unknown reasons these animals are more laid back than their uptight counterparts.

Up-to-date/ऑप्-टू-डेट *(adj)* - आधुनिक, अद्यतन
People are discussing an up-to-date issue of the magazine.

Upward/ऑप्वार्ड *(adverb)* - ऊपर की ओर
The cards are faced upward. The team moves upward.

Urban/अर्बन *(adjective)* – नागरी, नगरीय, शहरी

The urban property owners behvave very rudely to students.

Urbane/अर्बेन *(noun)* – सुसभ्य

The director maintained an urbane tone in his letters.

Urchin/अर्चिन *(noun)* – गन्दा, नटखट

The urchin makes the family members' life very difficult with his mischievous deeds.

Urge/अर्ज *(verb)* – सुझाव देना, प्रेरणा देना

Father urged me to finish my studies. The leader urges the team members to wind up things quickly.

Urgent/अर्जन्ट् *(adjective)* – अति आवश्यक

The old bridge requires an urgent need of repair.

Urine/यूरिन *(noun)* – मूत्र

There was blood in her urine.

Urn/अर्न *(noun)* – पात्र, अस्थि कलश

The son kept his father's ashes in an urn.

Us/अस *(pronoun)* – हम, हमें

Give the football to us.

Usage/यूजेज *(noun)* – प्रयोग, व्यवहार

The Police warned against the usage of narcotic drugs.

Use/यूज *(verb)* – उपयोग, उपयोग करना

Don't use illegal drugs.

Used/यूज्ड *(adjective)* – पुरानी, प्रयोग में लायी हुई, अभ्यस्त

He bought a used car.

Used to/यूज्ड टु – आदी, आदत, करने की आदत

I am telling you, you'll get used to the idea.

Useful/यूजफुल *(adjective)* – उपयोगी

The servant is useful to the owner.

Useless/यूजलेस *(adjective)* – अनुपयोगी, बेकार

He is useless in an emergency.

User/यूजर *(noun)* – उपभोक्ता

The user exploits his employee.

Usher/अॅशर् *(noun)* – उपयोक्ता

The usher is doing his job properly in the marriage reception.

Usual/यूजुअल *(adjective)* – सामान्य, अधिकतर होने वाला

Mother knows the child's usual bedtime.

Usurp/यूजर्प *(verb)* – हड़प लेना, हड़पना

He usurped my rights.

Usury/यूजरी *(noun)* – सूदखोरी

Usuries are done by very rich persons.

Utensil/यूटेन्सिल *(noun)* – बरतन, रसोई के वर्तन

Use of utensils should be minimum.

Utilitarian/यूटिलिटेरिअन *(adj)* – उपयोगितावाद

She prefers utilitarian steel tables.

Utility/यूटिलिटी *(noun)* – उपयोगिता, उपयोग

The utility of a computer is known to all people in today's era.

Utilize/यूटिलाइज *(verb)* – प्रयुक्त, उपयोग करना, सदुपयोग

Do you know how do you utilize this tool?

Utmost/अटमोस्ट *(adjective)* – परम, सर्वाधिक

He endures to the utmost measure of human endurance. She tried her utmost.

Utopia/यूटोपिया *(noun)* – कल्पना जगत्, काल्पनिक श्रेष्ठ स्थान

Some people still think India to be a Utopia.

Utter/अटर *(adjective & verb)* – पूरा, निरा, कहना, बोलना, उच्चारण करना

His behaviour shows utter nonsense.

Utterance/अॅटॅरॅन्स *(noun)* – अभिव्यक्ति, कथन, उद्‌गार

The sudden utterance of the speech of the political leader disturbs the peaceful environment of the school.

U-turn/यू-टर्न *(noun)* – पीछे मुड़ना, छोड़कर हट जाना

He takes a U-turn as he has mistaken the road to be the right one.

V/वी *(noun)* – अंग्रेजी वर्णमाला का 22वाँ वर्ण the twenty second letter of the English alphabet.

1. Denoting the next after U in a set of items, categories, etc. V-*shaped sweaters are quite popular during winter.*
2. The Roman numeral for five. *He is a student of class V.*
3. Denoting an internal combustion engine with a number of cylinders arranged in two rows at an angle to each other. *A V-engine is an internal combustion engine used to convert fuel into energy to run motor car.*

Vacancy/वेकेन्सि *(noun)* – शून्यता, रिक्त स्थान

There is a vacancy for a DTP operator in our office.

Vacant/वैकेन्ट *(adjective)* – रिक्त

Nearly half of the offices are still vacant.

Vacate/वैकेट *(verb)* – खाली करना, परित्याग करना

Hotel room must be vacated by noon on the last day of the month.

Vaccinate/वैक्सिनेट *(verb)* – शीतला का टीका लगाना

All the children of this school were vaccinated against tuberculosis.

Vaccinia/वैक्सिनिया *(noun)* – चौपायों का विस्फोटक रोग

The virus that causes small pox is known as vaccinia.

Vacillate/वैसिलेट *(verb)* – डगमगाना

He vacillated between teaching and writing.

Vacuity/वैकुइटि *(noun)* – खालीपन

He spoke on the subject of frivolity or vacuity in modern day literature.

Vacuole/वैकुओल *(noun)* – गर्त

The small cavity developed in nervous tissue as the result of disease is known as vacuole.

V

Vacuous/वैक्युअस *(adjective)* – खाली

The vacuous smile he gave out was quite inappropriate at such a serious discussion session.

Vagabond/वैगाबांड *(noun)* – आवारा, फालतू आदमी

He is a vagabond, here today, there tomorrow.

Vagary/वैगरि *(noun)* – मनजौज

Vagaries of nature are difficult to predict and hard to control.

Vagina/वजाइना *(noun)* – योनि, संगम-पथ

Vagina is the passage in the body of a woman or female animal between the outer sex organs and womb.

Vagrancy/वेग्रन्सि *(noun)* – आवारापन, आपन

Drug abuse may lead to descent into vagrancy.

Vagrant/वेग्रन्ट *(noun)* – घुमक्कड़

A person without a settled home or regular work who wanders from place to place and lives by begging is known as a vagrant.

Vague/वेग *(adjective)* – अस्थिर

There are many patients who suffer from vague symptoms. She has been very vague about her life and activities.

Vale/वेल *(noun)* – घाटी

The Vale of Glamorgan as a poetic term is popular all over the literary world.

Valentine/वैलेन्टाइन *(noun)* – प्रेमी, प्रेमिका, प्रेम-पत्र

Radha is my valentine, I send her a card but without putting my name on it.

Valetudinarian/वैलेट्यूडिनेरियन *(noun)* – रोगी

People suffering from poor health are commonly known as valetudinarian.

Valiance/वैलिअन्स *(noun)* – पराक्रम

He always demonstrates great courage and valiance in all battles.

Valid/वैलिड *(adjective)* – प्रबल

The article carried a valid criticism just below the story.

Valley/वैलि *(noun)* - घाटी

There are many valleys between the mountains in Himachal Pradesh.

Valorous/वैलरस *(adjective)* - साहसी

The medal was awarded to the Colonel for his valorous act in the battle area.

Valuable/वाल्युएँबल (वैल्यूअॅबॅल) *(adj)* - मूल्यवान

She bought a valuable antique in London. I respect my time as highly valuable.

Value/वैल्यू *(noun)* - सारता, मूल्य

The value of products seldom remains constant. At Rs.1000/- it is good value for this mobile phone.

Valve/वैल्व *(noun)* - कपाट

This valve will shut off the flow from the boiler when the water is hot enough.

Vampire/वैम्पायर *(noun)* - प्रेत

In TV serials, we see that vampires have long pointed sharp teeth. The members who oppose money spent on welfare measures are no less than a blood sucking vampire.

Vanadium/वैनेडियम *(noun)* - चाँदी जैसा एक धातुतत्त्व

Vanadium is a soft poisonous silver-grey metal that is added to some type of steel to make it stronger.

Vanguard/वैनगार्ड *(noun)* - सेनामुख

Vanguards have reported sighting enemy forces near the border.

Vanish/वैनिश *(verb)* - लुप्त हो जाना

The ship vanished into the sea without a trace. The environment is under threat since large trees are vanishing due to rising temperature.

Vanishing Point/वैनिशिंग पॉइंट *(noun)* - अदृश्य होने वाला

The rates of interest have dwindled to vanishing point.

Vantage/वैन्टेज *(noun)* - सुविधा

From my vantage point, I could see the whole of Delhi.

Vaporable/वेपरेब्ल *(adjective)* - वाष्प में बदलने योग्य

Water is vaporable liquid.

Varicosity/वैरिकोसिटि *(noun)* - शिरा की सूजन

Following the accident, he has been diagnosed as suffering from varicosity due to poor circulation of blood in the leg.

Varied/वैरिड *(adjective)* - बदला हुआ

His bio data reflects a long and varied career.

Variety/वेराइटी *(noun)* - परिवर्तन

It's the variety that makes my job so enjoyable.

Variform/वैरिफॉर्म *(adj)* - विभिन्न आकार का

India has a variform of languages. Variform education is necessary to succeed in present day competitive world.

Variola/वेराइअॅला *(noun)* - चेचक

In 18th century, smallpox was known as variola.

Varlet/वारलेट *(noun)* - सेवक

Dishonest people go by the name of varlet.

Varletry/वारलेट्रि *(noun)* - भीड़-भक्कड़

Practice of varletry was fairly in vogue about a century ago.

Varnish/वार्निश् *(noun)* - रोगन, चमक

The cupboard was coated with several coats of varnish.

Vary/वैरि *(verb)* - पलटना

The properties here vary in size and price.

Vascular/वैस्कुलर *(adjective)* - वाहक नलियों से सम्बन्धित

Overweight and lack of physical activity have started affecting his vascular system.

Vasculum/वैस्क्युलम *(noun)* - बटुआ

Vasculum is a metallic container botanists use to collect plants.

Vase/वेस *(noun)* - बर्तन

Porcelain vases containing cut flowers make drawing rooms a showpiece.

Vaseline/वेसलिन *(noun)* – मिट्टी के तेल से निकाला गया तैलीय पदार्थ

The doors glide open as if their rails have been vaselined.

Vassal/वैसल *(noun)* – प्रजा

Macedonia was a vassal state of the Ottoman Empire.

Vast/वास्ट *(adjective)* – विशाल

Tired of walking we decided to rest at a vast plain full of orchards. India is a vast country in terms of area and population.

Vastitude/वास्टिट्यूड *(noun)* – विशालता

Many neighbouring countries are fearful due to Chinese assertiveness and vastitude.

Vastly/वास्ट्लि *(adverb)* – विपुलता से

He vastly exaggerated the inconveniences he faced during training.

Vaticinate/वैटिसिनेट *(verb)* – भविष्य कहना

The lady spent much of her time vaticinating on learned political panels.

Vaulter/वॉल्टर *(noun)* – कूदने वाला

He is the only vaulter who could jump over twenty feet in the first attempt.

Vegetable/वेजिटेब्ल *(noun)* – शाक

Cauliflower, cabbage, potato, turnip, and bean are vegetables.

Vegetal/वेजिटल *(adjective)* – वनस्पति-सम्बन्धी

A vegetal aroma was coming out strongly when cooking was under way.

Vegetarian/वेजिटेरिअन *(noun)* – शाकाहारी

I would like to order a vegetarian lunch today. We decided to go to a vegetarian restaurant.

V

Vegetate/वेजिटेट *(verb)* – उत्पन्न होना, नीरस जीवन बिताना

If left alone, he would become inactive, sit in front of a TV and vegetate.

Vehicle/वीइकल *(noun)* – वाहन, गाड़ी, साधन

Mercedes has launched a new series of premium passenger vehicles in India. Heavy vehicles are not allowed to enter the city limit during day time.

Velarium/विलेरियम *(noun)* – छत के नीचे तानी हुई चाँदनी

Velariums are still used overhead to protect tennis courts from vagaries of weather.

Velleity/वेलेइटी *(noun)* – इच्छा

The outlandish speech angered me, but I chose to remain a velleity.

Velocity/विलॉसिटि *(noun)* – गति

There are high-tech machines to increase the velocity of the emitted particles. The rocket blasted off with an incredible velocity.

Velvet/वेल्वेट *(noun)* – मखमल

The armchair we bought is covered in velvet.

Venal/वीनल *(adjective)*– घूसखोर, उत्कोची

The customs officers at air and seaports are notoriously venal.

Vend/वेन्ड *(verb)* – बेचना

There was a woman vending cakes and panties at the cinema hall.

Vender/वेन्डर *(noun)* – बेंचने वाला, ठेले पर सामान बेंचने वाला

We buy vegetables from the vendor, he comes here each evening.

Vendee/वेन्डी *(noun)* – खरीददार

The real estate developer invited all vendees to lunch and showed them their flats.

Vendue/वेनड्यू *(noun)* – नीलाम द्वारा बिक्री

Dutch used to call sale by auction as vendue during 18th century.

Venerability/वेनरेबिलिटि *(noun)* – आदर

He is known for great wisdom and, therefore, his venerability is not in doubt.

Venereal/विनीरिअल *(adjective)* – मैथुन-सम्बन्धी

There has been a steady increase in venereal infection in South Africa.

Venery/वेनरि *(noun)* – शिकार

All but a few of them engaged in venery.

Vengeance/वेन्जिएन्स *(noun)* – बदला

In the ensuing election, voters are ready to wreak vengeance on all politicians.

Venial/वीनिअल *(adjective)* - क्षम्य

Everything they have disclosed up to now can be seen as venial.

Venter/वेन्टर *(noun)* - गर्भाशय

The underside of the belly of animal is known as venter.

Ventiduct/वेन्टिडक्ट *(noun)* - वायु मार्ग

The ventiduct of the air conditioner is not working.

Ventricle/वेन्ट्रिकल *(noun)* - प्रवेश

Each of the two main chambers of the heart, left and right, that pump blood to the body are called a ventricle.

Ventricular/वेन्ट्रिक्यूलर *(adj)* - कोष्ठक सम्बन्धी

An x-ray was done to determine the ventricular positioning of the heart.

Verdancy/वरडैन्सी *(noun)* - हरापन

We stayed for a few hours enjoying the alluring verdancy of the hills in Kodaikanal.

Verderer/वर्डरर *(noun)* - जंगलों का रक्षक

The verderer arrested the poachers who were trying to kill elephants for their tusk.

Verdict/वर्डिक्ट *(noun)* - न्याय

The jury returned a verdict of not guilty.

Verdure/वर्ड्योर *(noun)* - हरियाली से ढँका हुआ

Fresh green colour of lush vegetation is called verdure.

Verifiable/वेरिफाइएबल *(adj)* - प्रमाणित करने योग्य

This matter is verifiable.

Verily/वेरिलि *(adverb)* - अवश्य

Verily, what these people are doing is nothing but madness.

Veritable/वेरिटेबल *(adjective)* - सत्य

The meal that followed was a veritable feast.

Vermicelli/वर्मिसेलि *(plural noun)* - सेवई

Fine wheat flower converted into long thin threads is known as vermicelli.

Vermicide/वर्मिसाइड *(noun)* - कीड़ा मारने वाला पदार्थ

Vermicides are used to kill worms in sewerage lines.

Vermicular/वर्मिक्युलर *(adj)* - कीड़े के समान

Medical tests confirmed some vermicular movement in his stomach.

Vermilion/वर्मिलिअन *(noun)* - सिन्दूर

Married Indian women put vermilion on their head between the partings of hair. They coated the outer portion of their house using vermillion coloured paint.

Vermination/वर्मिनेशन *(noun)* - कीड़े की संख्या बढ़ने की क्रिया

Vermination in this area must be curbed.

Vernacular/वर्नाकुलर *(noun)* - प्राकृत

He writes in the vernacular to reach a larger audience. When talking to the gardener, I used the gardening vernacular.

Vernal/वर्नल *(adjective)* - वासन्तिक

The vernal freshness of the land was very alluring.

Vernier/वर्नियर *(noun)* - अंको में अंकित, एक स्केल (वर्नियर)

Vernier calliper is used to make small measurements in the laboratory.

Versant/वर्सन्ट *(noun)* - परिचित, ढाल

We came down the mountain by using the low gradient eastern versant.

Versify/वर्सिफाइ *(verb)* - कविता बनाना

It was never suggested that Wordsworth should simply versify Coleridge's ideas.

Version/वर्सन *(noun)* - वर्णन, कथन

The revised version of the paper was produced for a later meeting.

Versus/वर्सस *(preposition)* - विपरीत, के विरुद्ध

England versus Australia cricket test match starts today. The company is weighing up the pros and cons of organic versus inorganic produce.

Vertebra/वर्टिब्रा *(noun)* - पृष्ठवंश

The needle was inserted between two of the vertebrae.

Vertical/वर्टिकल *(adjective)* - लम्बरूप

The y-axis is at right angle to the x-axis. Don't move, please keep your back in vertical position.

Vertiginous/वर्टिजिनस *(adjective)* – घूमता हुआ

We encountered a vertiginous drop to the valleys below.

Vertigo/वर्टिगो *(noun)* – चक्कर

Be warned that looking down from the mountain can bring about vertigo leading to fall.

Vertu/वर्टू *(noun)* – कला की विशिष्टता

Literary speaking, the good qualities inherent in a person or thing is referred as vertu.

Verve/वर्व *(noun)* – उत्साह

Shakira sings with supreme verve and flexibility.

Very/वेरी *(adverb)* – सच्चा, ठीक

A very large amount of money was deposited yesterday. He decided to donate his very own car.

Vesical/वेसिकल *(adjective)* – मूत्राशय सम्बन्धी

The tests confirm that his vesical artery is functioning properly.

Vesicant/वेसिकैंट *(adjective)* – फफोला उत्पन्न करने वाला लेप

Rubbing hands on a stone may be vesicant. Even dilute hydrochloric acid is a vesicant; you must wear hand gloves for protection.

Vessel/वेसल *(noun)* – पात्र, नाव

Titanic was the largest sea-going passenger vessel during 1910s.

Vestal/वेस्टल *(adjective)* – पवित्र

Romans even today go to vestal temple to seek blessings of Goddess Vesta.

Vestiary/वेस्टिअरि *(adjective)* – अँगरखा

Gender equality demands one to stay away from vestiary. Vestiary is a place similar to a vestibule to keep coats and hats.

Veteran/वेटरन *(noun)* – अभ्यासवृद्ध

Sachin Tendulkar is a veteran Indian cricketer.

Veterinary/वेटरिनरि *(adj)* – पशुचिकित्सा सम्बन्धी

There are not enough veterinary doctors to take care of animals in India.

Vex/वेक्स *(verb)* – पीड़ा देना

Food security is proving to be a vexed issue defying solution at World Trade Organisation meetings. Price rise is the most vexing questions for policymakers.

Vexatious/वेक्सेशस *(adjective)* – दुःखदायी

Her behaviour is vexatious to others.

Vexing/वेक्सिंग *(adjective)* – सन्तापकर

Solution to India-Pakistan border issues is a vexing problem.

Via/वाया *(preposition)* – मार्ग से

We came to India via Bangladesh. Many people buy a home with a mortgage via a housing society. We have a file sent via electronic mail.

Viaticum/वियाटिकम *(noun)* – यात्रा सामग्री

Viaticum is an occasion when Christian people eat and drink in memory of last Supper Jesus had with his disciples.

Vibrancy/वाइब्रंसि *(noun)* – कम्पन

During Christmas time you will find the whole city flirting with vibrancy.

Vibrant/वायब्रैंट *(adjective)* – काँपने वाला

We went around the vibrant cosmopolitan city. The huge ball room was decorated in vibrant blues and greens.

Vibrissa/वाइब्रिस्सा *(noun)* – गलमुच्छा

Vibrissae is one of the characteristics to differentiate animals into kinds. There are many birds that make use of their characteristic of vibrissae to survive.

Viceregal/वाइसरिगल *(adjective)* – राज-प्रतिनिधि सम्बन्धी

The viceregal carriage moved out drawn with eight horses.

Vicious/विशस *(adjective)* – दुराचारी

As a result of vicious assault, the person had to be hospitalized with multiple fracture. The dog was vicious and likely to bite.

Victor/विक्टर *(noun)* – विजयी

The president congratulated the victors.

Victorious/विक्टोरिअस *(adjective)* – जयप्राप्त

The victorious team was accorded a red carpet welcome on arrival at the airport.

Victual/विट्ल *(verb)* – रसद जुटाना

Meat, chicken, fish and other savoury victuals were served at the party.

Vide/वाइड *(verb)* – देखो

Vide your comments I have to state the following.

Videlicet/वाइडिलिसेट *(adverb)* – अर्थात्

Instead of 'videlicet', people are better aware of its short form 'viz'.

Vie/वाइ *(verb)* – स्पर्धा करना

Both finalists are vying with each other to win the trophy.

Vigneron/विनेरॉन *(noun)* – अंगूर की खेती करने वाला

He is the most trusted vigneron for suppling grapes to wine manufacturers.

Vignette/विग्नेट *(noun)* – छोटा

The function was organized to witness the classic vignette of embassy life.

Vigour/विगर *(noun)* – शक्ति

His physique reflected a sign of vigour and health. He set about executing the new task with vigour.

Village/विलेज *(noun)* – गाँव

The coastal areas in Kerala consist essentially of pretty fishing villages. A Olympic village was built for participants to live comfortably.

Vim/विम *(noun)* – बल

You should go out and play the game with vim, vigour and energy.

Vindicable/विन्डिकेब्ल *(adj)* – समर्थन करने योग्य

More sober views expressed by respectable citizens were vindicable of proper action taken by police.

Vindicator/विन्डिकेटर *(noun)* – रक्षक

Immediate action taken by police was vindicator of its seriousness to arrest the criminals.

Vindictive/विन्डिक्टिव *(adj)* – बदला लेने वाला

The barrage of criticism was both vindictive and personalized.

Vinegar/विनेगर *(noun)* – सिरका

Most pickles served at hotels and restaurants are made with the help of vinegar.

Viol/वाइअल *(noun)* – एक प्रकार की वायलिन

Shaped like a violin, early type of musical instrument that produced similar kind of music was known as viol.

Violate/वाइअॅलेट *(verb)* – तोड़ना

Those who violate the agreement, would be punished.

Violet/वायलेट *(noun)* – बैंगनी रंग

Violet is a small garden plant that grows in spring with purple or white flowers. She came dressed in violet.

Violin/वायलिन *(noun)* – सारंगी, बेला, चिकारा

Violin is one of the most popular musical instruments.

Viper/वाइपर *(noun)* – सर्प, साँप

Russel viper is one of the most deadly snakes in the world.

Virgate/वर्गेट *(noun)* – डण्डे के आकार का

He purchased in the suburban area a land measuring a virgate for constructing farmhouse.

Virgo/वर्गो *(noun)* – कन्या राशि

Virgo is a large constellation of bright stars, largest of which is Spica.

Virility/विरिलिटि *(noun)* – मनुषत्व, पुरुषत्व

This club lays great importance on a man's virility.

Virtuosity/वर्चुऑसिटी *(noun)* – ललित कला के प्रेमी

The auditorium vibrated with high performance of considerable virtuosity.

Virtuous/वर्चुअस *(adjective)* – सदाचारी

She considered herself virtuous because she neither drank nor smoked.

Virulence/विर्युलेंस *(noun)* – प्रचण्डता

The virulence of influenza is causing concern among medical fraternity.

Virus/वाइरस *(noun)* - विषैला तत्त्व

The tests have confirmed existence of hepatitis B virus in the sample.

Visage/विसेज *(noun)* - चेहरा

The candidate selected for this position has an elegant, angular visage. There was lurking sadness behind his visage of cheerfulness.

Viscera/विसरा *(plural noun)* - आँत

The large organs inside the body, such as the heart, lungs and stomach are known as viscera.

Viscous/विस्कस *(adjective)* - चिपचिपा

Diesel is more viscous than petrol or kerosene.

Viscus/विस्कस - आँत

The viscus has been sent for medical examination.

Visibility/विजिबिलिटि *(noun)* - प्रत्यक्षता

A reduction in police presence helped improve visibility of people on the streets. All trains are running slow because the visibility, because of fog, is down to 15 yards.

Visible/विजिबल् *(adjective)* - दृष्टिगोचर

The temple spire is clearly visible from miles away. Silhouette of a man hiding behind the bush was visible even in that dark night.

Vision/विजन *(noun)* - दृष्टि, नजर, परिकल्पना

She has a defective vision.

Visit/विजिट *(verb)* - देखने जाना, मिलना

He went to visit his grandmother. He went out to visit Qutub Minar in Delhi with his friends.

V

Visor/वाइजर *(noun)* - घूँघट

He purchased a plastic safety helmet with a transparent visor.

Vista/विस्टा *(noun)* - तरुपंक्ति

The telescope allowed us to see the vista of bright stars.

Visual/विजुअल *(adjective)* - नेत्रीय

You should have a visual perception of the landscape before shooting the film.

Vital/वाइटल *(adjective)* - अति आवश्यक

It is vital that the system is regularly checked. Her vital organs were showing signs of improvement.

Vitamin/विटामिन *(noun)* - खाद्योज

Most people generally don't get all the vitamins they need from a regular diet.

Viticulture/विटिकल्चर *(noun)* - अंगूर की खेती

The study of grape cultivation is known as viticulture.

Vitreous/विट्रिअस *(adjective)* - काँचमय

A coarse-grained rock with much grey vitreous quartz was available for sale at a premium. This dinner-set is made of vitreous china.

Vitriol/विट्रिओल *(noun)* - निन्दा के योग्य

It was as if his words were spraying vitriol right in front of her.

Vituperate/विट्युपरेट *(verb)* - रोचक

For no fault of hers, she was at the centre of vituperative sarcasm.

Vivacious/वाइवेशस *(adjective)* - उत्साह

We were amused with the vivaciousness of a little girl jumping all over the park.

Vivacity/वाइवैसिटि *(noun)* - प्रफुल्लता

He was struck by her vivacity, sense of humour and charm.

Viva-voce/वाइवा-वॅवि *(adj)* - मौखिक, जबानी

The viva voce examination has been scheduled for today itself. We had better discuss this viva voce.

Vivarium/विवेरिअम *(noun)* - जीवशाला

In most zoological parks, at least one vivarium is built to keep animals under observation, when required.

Viviparous/विविपेरस *(adjective)* - सजीव बच्चा देने वाली

Animals that produce live babies from their body rather than eggs are known as viviparous.

Vixen/विक्सन *(noun)* - मादा लोमड़ी, कर्कशा औरत

She is a kind of outrageous little shaven-headed vixen who is always ready to get into a tiff with anyone.

Vogue/वोग *(noun)* – प्रचलित, व्यवहार

Child-centred education is quite in vogue these days.

Voice/वॉइस *(noun)* – वाणी, ध्वनि

She raised her voice so that everyone present in the hall could hear her speech. The soprano is in good voice.

Volition/वॉलिशन *(noun)* – इच्छा

She went to the carnival on her own volition.

Voltage/वोल्टेज *(noun)* – विद्युत शक्ति, वोल्टों की नाप

Electric trains are powered by high voltage traction wires.

Volubility/वाल्युबिलिटि *(noun)* – वाचालता

Her legendary volubility deserted her at the time of making first public speech.

Volume/वॉल्यूम *(noun)* – पुस्तक, अलग भाग

We have published a biography of Rabindranath Tagore in three volumes.

Voluptuous/वॅलप्ट्युअस *(adjective)* – विषयी, भोगी

We bought long curtains for our bedroom in voluptuous crimson red.

Volution/वल्यूशन *(noun)* – घुमौवा माला

A single turn of a spiral or coil is defined as a volution.

Volvulus/वॅल्व्युलस *(noun)* – आँतों का ऐंठन

The doctor advised surgery for caecal volvulus.

Vomit/वॅमिट *(verb)* – वमन द्वारा निकला हुआ पदार्थ

She used to vomit every time she took solid food. The newspaper press vomited fold after fold of paper.

Vowel/वॉवेल *(noun)* – स्वर

He spoke with deep-vowelled German accent. In the English alphabet there are five vowels, namely, A, E, I, O and U.

Vowelled/वॉवेल्ड *(adjective)* – स्वरपूर्ण

A man with heavy vowelled voice came to the restaurant.

Voyage/वॉयेज *(noun)* – समुद्रयात्रा

He has decided to go on a voyage to Spain. He spent substantial part of his life voyaging along the Latin American coast.

Vulcan/वल्कन *(noun)* – अग्नि देवता

In Roman mythology, Vulcan is a name given to the God of fire.

Vulgarian/वल्गेरियन *(noun)* – असभ्य व्यवहार वाला धनी मनुष्य

Due to enormous ancestral wealth coming his way, he has become a sort of jumped-up vulgarian.

Vulpine/वल्पाइन *(adjective)* – धूर्त

She gave a vulpine smile while plotting next course of action.

W/डब्ल्यू *(noun)* – अंग्रेजी वर्णमाला का 23वाँ वर्ण the twenty third letter of the English alphabet.

1. Denoting the next after V in a set of items, categories, etc.

Waddle/वैडल *(verb)* – डगमगाते चलना, हंस के समान चलना

Two geese have waddled across the road.

Wade/वेड *(verb)* – पानी में हेलकर चलना

He waded through the knee-deep water.

Wafer/वेफर *(noun)* – मालपुआ (पतली रोटी)

We purchased a wafer packet with a layer of chocolate.

Waft/वैफ्ट *(verb)* – तैरने वाला पदार्थ

The smell of stale food wafted out from the kitchen. A waft of roasting chicken was coming out from the kitchen.

Wag/वैग *(verb)* – हिलाना

The dog was wagging its tail.

Wages/वेजेज *(noun)* – मजदूरी, वेतन

The factory workers were struggling to get better wages.

Waggery/वैगरि *(noun)* – ठिठोली

You can expect such pranks and waggery only from the older boys.

Waggish/वैगिश *(adjective)* – मसखरा

Don't try out waggish tales on every occasion.

Wagonette/वैगनेट *(noun)* – आमने-सामने की गद्दी की चौपहिया हल्की गाड़ी

Wagonettes are hardly in use today, they have given way to modern sleek cars.

Wagtail/वैग्टेल *(noun)* – खंजन पक्षी

Wagtails are found wagging up and down over rivers only in Siberia.

Waif/वेफ *(noun)* – फेंका हुआ बालक

She is foster-mother to various waifs who have nowhere to go.

Wail/वेल *(noun)* – विलाप करना

Harish let out a wail as soon as lights went out. The wail of air siren made them a worried lot.

Wainscot/वेन्स्कॉट *(noun)* – दीवार से लकड़ी की पट्टियों का जड़ाव

It has been decided to wainscot the interior to a height of 6 feet.

Waist/वेस्ट *(noun)* – कमर

He put his arm around her waist.

Waken/वेकन *(verb)* – जगाना

She wakened the child and dressed him.

Waking/वेकिंग *(noun)* – जागृत अवस्था

I was in waking state when all were asleep.

Wall/वाल *(noun)* – दीवार

It was difficult to jump over the garden wall. We entered the drawing room having tapestries on the walls.

Walled/वाल्ड *(adjective)* – दीवार से घिरा हुआ

One doorway has been completely walled up.

Wall-eyed/वाल-आइड *(adjective)* – कंजी आँख वाला

Pikeperch is a wall-eyed fish.

Wall-flower/वाल-फ्लाउअर *(noun)* – एक प्रकार का फूल

Wall-flower is a garden plant with yellow, orange or red flowers.

Wallet/वैलेट *(noun)* – झोला

He took out money from his wallet.

Wallop/वॉलॅप *(verb)* – कोड़ा मारना

He walloped the back of her head with a flexible stick.

Walnut/वाल्नट *(noun)* - अखरोट

Walnut is a good source of high quality protein.

Wan/वैन *(adjective)* - पीला

He was disappointed when she gave him a wan smile.

Wander/वान्डर *(verb)* - घूमना

He wandered aimlessly around the park. The child was found wandering in the streets all alone.

Wane/वेन *(verb)* - कम होना

Confidence in dollar has waned considerably around the world markets.

Wang/वैंग *(noun)* - दाद की हड्डी

His wang is broken in the accident.

Want/वान्ट *(verb)* - कमी

We want to go to the beach party. I want to speak to her immediately.

Wanted/वान्टेड *(adjective)* - इच्छित, जिसकी खोज हो

He is wanted by the police in connection with robberies.

Wanton/वॉन्टॅन *(adj)* - लम्पट, मर्यादाहीन, चंचल

Properties were destroyed due to sheer wanton vandalism.

Warble/वार्बल *(verb)* - कूकना

Birds were warbling in the trees. He warbled in an implausible baritone voice.

Warbler/वार्बलर *(noun)* - गाने वाला

These are a few warblers that catch insects with the help of their melodious songs.

Ward/वार्ड *(noun)* - 'दिशा' सूचक प्रत्यय

Hospitals designate different wards for different diseases.

Warden/वार्ड्न *(noun)* - संरक्षक

The warden came down heavily on the boys creating nuisance in the hostel.

Warder/वार्ड्र् *(noun)* - पहरेदार

Warders have been cautioned to be in a state of high alert in the face of intelligence reports.

Ware/वेअर *(noun)* - सौदा, पण्य, द्रव्य

These are the cooking wares recently excavated from this area. These wares are of Italian make.

Warehouse/वेअरहाउस *(noun)* - गोदाम

Before sending to the distributors, we sent all our products from the factory to our warehouse.

Wares/वेअर्स *(noun)* - माल-असबाव

All aluminum wares were on display.

Warily/वेअरिलि *(adverb)* - सावधानी से

He walk warily down the street, afraid of being caught.

Wariness/वेअरिनेस *(noun)* - सावधानी

I seldom use computer at night because of my mother's wariness. They had all regarded her presence with wariness.

Warlock/वारलॉक *(noun)* - जादूगर

Stay away from him, he is a warlock.

Warner/वार्नर *(noun)* - सावधान करने वाला

He acted like a warner that police were searching for him.

Warning/वार्निंग *(noun)* - चेतावनी, प्रबोधन

The police issued a warning about fake Rs 100 notes.

Warren/वॅरिन (वॉरन) *(noun)* - खरहों के पालने का बाड़ा

At the end of this lane is a warren of narrow gas-lit streets.

Warrior/वॉरिअर *(noun)* - योद्धा

Warriors have been decorated with medals recently.

Warship/वॉर्शिप *(noun)* - युद्ध का जहाज

Indian Navy has more than 100 warships.

Wary/वेअरि *(adjective)* - होशियार

I am quite wary of going to that place again.

Wasp/वास्प *(noun)* - बर्रे

Wasp is a yellow and black flying insect that can sting.

Wastage/वेस्टेज *(noun)* - क्षय से हानि

This is a sheer wastage of natural resources. The government is trying to cut wastage of food grains by 20 per cent.

We/वी *(pronoun)* – हम लोग

Nobody knows kids better than we teachers do. May we have a drink now? We should eat as well-balanced a diet as possible.

Weak/वीक *(adjective)* – दुर्बल

He was recovering from flu, and was very weak.

Weal/वील *(noun)* – सुख

He slapped her cheek and a bright red weal sprang up on it.

Wealth/वेल्थ *(noun)* – ऐश्वर्य

Many industrialists use their wealth to bribe officials. Many people buy bungalows and cars to display their wealth.

Weasel/वीजल *(noun)* – नकुल

Siberian weasels have stormed the city.

Wednesday/वेनेज्डे *(noun)* – बुधवार

We are going on a picnic next Wednesday. Parents-teachers meeting is held the first Wednesday of each month.

Wee/वी *(adjective)* – छोटा

The lyrics of the song are a wee bit too sweet and sentimental.

Weeds/वीड्स *(noun)* – विधवा का शोक-वस्त्र, घास

The garden was overgrown with weeds.

Week/वीक *(noun)* – सप्ताह

The training programme lasts twenty six weeks. She has dance classes twice a week.

Ween/वीन *(verb)* – विचारना

Don't ween too much on the matter.

Weep/वीप *(verb)* – रोना

He wept over his poor result. A grieving son wept over the body of his father. A young woman is weeping her lost lord.

W

Weir/वेअर *(noun)* – नदी का बाँध

The government has built a weir on the western side of the river to prevent flood water entering the city.

Welkin/वेल्किन *(noun)* – आकाश

The crew made the welkin ring with their hurrahs.

Well/वेल *(adverb)* – हितकर

The whole team played very well. They lived well and were generous with their money.

Wellington/वेलिंगटन *(noun)* – जूता

Wellington boots are hardly used these days.

Welsh/वेल्श *(verb)* – ऋण दिये बिना भाग जाना

I am not in the habit of welshing on my promises.

Wen/वेन *(noun)* – माँस की गाँठ

A sebaceous cyst is generally known as a wen.

Wench/वेंच *(noun)* – दुष्टा स्त्री

In the new film about Shaley, she plays the token buxom wench.

Wend/वेंड *(verb)* – जाना

He wended his way home through bylanes and not straight.

Went/वेंट *(verb)* – गया

We went to a party last night.

Wept/वेप्ट *(verb)* – रोया

He literally wept on seeing the poor workmanship.

Wet/वेट *(adjective)* – भींगा हुआ

He followed the leader, slipping on the wet rock in the process. We had nothing for protection on that wet, windy evening.

Wetness/वेटनेस *(noun)* – गीलापन, भींगा होना

The child caught cold due to wetness of his body.

What/ह्वाट *(pronoun)* – क्या

What's the time? What did you say?

Wheat/ह्वीट *(noun)* – गेहूँ

Wheat is a staple food in India.

Wheaten/ह्वीटेन *(adjective)* – गेहूँ का बना हुआ

The content of these packets are wheaten products.

Wheedle/ह्वीवडल *(verb)* – फुसलाना

He had wheedled us into employing his sister.

Wheen/ह्वीन *(noun)* – थोड़ा-सा

She carried a when of small changes.

Wheeze/ह्वीज *(verb)* – कष्ट से साँस लेने का शब्द

The sickness often leaves her wheezing. The engine of the motor car coughed, wheezed, and came to a standstill.

Whelk/ह्वेल्क *(noun)* – दिदोरा

Only a few whelks are edible.

Whelp/ह्वेल्फ *(noun)* – पिल्ला

The lioness was suckling her whelps.

When/ह्वेन *(interrogative adverb)* – जबकि

When are you reaching? When can you make it to the station, the train is about to depart?

Whence/ह्वेन्स *(interrogative adverb)* – कहाँ से

The Andes Mountains, whence the ore is procured. Whence does our Parliament derive this power?

Whenever/ह्वेनएवर *(conjunction)* – जब कभी

You can seek help whenever you need it. The springs in the chair creak whenever I change my position.

Where/ह्वेअर *(interrogative adverb)* – कहाँ

Where are we going? Where does the argument lead?

Wherewithal/ह्वेअरविदल *(noun)* – जिस किसी के साथ

They lacked the wherewithal to pay the dues.

Wherry/ह्वेरि *(noun)* – छिछली नाव

We enjoyed a short sea trip on a wherry.

Whether/ह्वेदर *(conjunction)* – हो न हो

She appeared undecided whether to go or stay at home. I'll see whether she's at home.

Whew/ह्यू *(exclamatory)* – आश्चर्यसूचक अव्यय

Whew—and I thought it was a serious matter!

Whey/ह्वे *(noun)* – मट्ठा

Whey is very good for health if taken in the morning or afternoon.

Which/ह्विच – कौन

Which way is the wind blowing? It was a crisis for which he was completely unprepared.

Whiff/ह्विफ *(noun & verb)* – फूँक, फूत्कार, फूँकना

I caught a whiff of Lakme perfume.

Whilst/ह्वाइलस्ट *(adverb)* – जब तक

The captain was in the pool whilst other players were toying in the field.

Whimper/ह्विम्पर *(verb)* – ठुनकना, धीमा शब्द करना

Being alone, the child in a bed nearby began to whimper. Her first appearance on the stage ended with a whimper rather than a bang.

Whimsey/ह्विमजी *(noun)* – लहर, जोश

The movie we watched was an awkward blend of whimsy and moralizing. The stone carvings and whimsies.

Whinny/ह्विन्नि *(verb)* – प्रसन्नता से हिनहिनाना

The horse whinnied and tossed his head happily.

Whippy/ह्विपि *(adjective)* – लम्बा एवं लचीला

This stick is whippy.

Whisky/ह्विस्कि *(noun)* – जव से बनी हुई मदिरा

Bottles of whisky were ordered for the party.

Whisper/ह्विस्पर *(verb)* – कानाफूसी करना

She was whispering in his ear. be rumoured. *It was whispered that he would soon join the opposition party.*

Whither/ह्विदर *(interrogative adverb)* – जिधर

They asked people whither they would emigrate. Whither modern architecture.

Whittle/ह्विटल *(verb)* – जेब की छोटी छुरी

He was sitting at the door, whittling a piece of wood with a knife.

Whiz/ह्विज *(verb)* – सनसनाहट का शब्द

The missiles whizzed past us. The weeks whizzed by and the time arrived to go back to hostel.

Who/हू *(pronoun)* – किसने

I wonder who that letter was from. Aron plays the cat who caught the mouse.

Whoa/ह्वो *(exclamatory)* – ठहरो!

Whoa! That's a huge bargain.

Whop/ह्वॉप *(verb)* – एकाएक गिराव

Tony whopped him on the nose. The loud whop of the helicopter echoed in the still air.

Whopper/ह्वॉपर *(noun)* – अति विलक्षण पदार्थ

The novel is nearly 2000 page whopper.

Whoso/हूसो *(pronoun)* – जो कोई

The word whoso is an archaic word.

Wicked/विकेड *(adjective)* – पापी

There is no dearth of wicked and unscrupulous politicians.

Wicker/विकर *(noun)* – कमाची

We went to the market looking to buy a set of wicker chairs.

Wide/वाइड *(adjective)* – चौड़ा

At last we reached a wide road. This page measures 15 cm long by 12 cm wide.

Width/विड्थ *(noun)* – विस्तार

The cricket pitch was about seven feet in width.

Wig/विग *(noun)* – कृत्रिम केश

She wore an auburn coloured wig.

Wigeon/विजन *(noun)* – एक प्रकार का बत्तख

Penelope and Americana ducks are two prominent species of wigeon.

Wiggle/विगल *(verb)* – शरीर को आगे पीछे घुमाना

My teeth were wiggling about due to fear. The dancer tantalizingly wiggled her hips.

Wile/वाइल *(noun)* – कपट

He is a wily politician. She could be neither driven nor wiled into flaunting her physical assets.

Will/विल *(modal verb)* – गा, गी, गे

You will regret it as you become older. I will succeed, come what may.

Willy-nilly/विलि-निलि *(adverb)* – अनिच्छापूर्वक

The management has been forced to accept labour union's terms willy-nilly.

W

Windbag/विन्डवैग *(noun)* – निरर्थक शब्द बोलने वाला मनुष्य

You can discount 90 percent of anything that windbag says.

Winder/विन्डर *(verb)* – ओसाना

The farmer is windering.

Windling/विन्डलिंग *(noun)* – घुमौवा

The windings of the stream pass through the valleys of that mountain.

Window/विन्डो *(noun)* – झरोखा, खिड़की

Thieves smashed a window and took all jewellary and cash.

Windpipe/विन्डपाइप *(noun)* – वायुप्रणाली

Something has got stuck in his windpipe.

Wind-up/विन्डअप *(noun)* – परिणाम

Surely this was a wind-up.

Wine/वाइन *(noun)* – सुरा

They decided to celebrate the success by opening a bottle of red wine. He ordered a glass of seine wine of France.

Winsome/विनसम *(adjective)* – मनोहर

She fell for his winsome behaviour.

Wire/वायर *(noun)* – तार

We purchased a coil of aluminum wire. We have decided to wire our compound to prevent animals from getting near our house.

Wise/वाइज *(noun)* – चतुर

It would only be wise to discuss the matter with the director.

Wish/विश *(verb)* – आकांक्षा, इच्छा करना

Every one wished for peaceful election.

Wit/विट *(noun & verb)* – बुद्धि, चातुरी, अवगत होना

She needed all her wits to figure out the way back. I had the wit to realize that the only way out was up.

Witch/विच *(noun)* – डाइन

Witches are popularly depicted as wearing a black cloak and pointed hat casting spell on unsuspecting people.

Withal/विदल *(adverb)* – साथ-साथ

She gave him a grateful smile, but rueful withal. They sat with little to nourish themselves withal but vile water.

Wither/विदर *(verb)* – सुखा देना

The grass had withered to an unappealing brown.

Within/विदिन *(preposition)* - बीच में

The fire spread fast within the building. All illegal buildings within the green belt have been demolished.

Without/विदाउट *(preposition)* - बाहर

She went to England without him.

Witness/विटनेस *(noun)* - प्रमाण

I was a witness in a murder case.

Witticism/विटिसिज्म *(noun)* - हँसी

His witticism was remarkable and harmless.

Wive/वाइव - विवाह करना

He has two wives.

Woe/वो *(noun)* - दु:ख, शोक, शाप

To add to automobile company's woes, customers have been spending less.

Wold/वोल्ड *(noun)* - खुला मैदान

There are many Wolds in England that have hardly ever been cultivated.

Wolf/वुल्फ *(noun)* - भेड़िया, हुँड़ार

Tasmanian and Maned wolves are an endangered species.

Woman/वुमन *(noun)* - औरत, नारी

The court was composed of seven women and five men.

Won/वन् *(adjective)* - जीत लिया

India had won five medals at the London Olympic Games in 2012.

Wonder/वन्डर *(noun)* - आश्चर्य

She observed the intricacy of the woodwork with the wonder of a child.

Wondrous/वन्डरस *(adjective)* - आश्चर्यजनक

Mumbai is a wondrous city. (adverb) wonderfully. *She is grown into a wondrous pretty.*

Wood/वुड *(noun)* - चाल-ठाल

We use only best quality woods in furniture making.

Worry/वरि *(verb)* - चिन्तित होना

I began to worry whether I had done the right thing. She was worried about his soldier son in the war.

Worst/वर्स्ट *(adjective)* - सबसे बुरा

The speech was the worst he had ever made. At least 25,000 people died in Bhopal's worst industrial accident.

Worsted/वर्स्टेड *(noun)* - सुलझाया हुआ ऊन

He came to the party wearing a worsted three-piece suit.

Wort/वर्ट *(noun)* - एक प्रकार की वनस्पति

The manufactures add yeast to the wort for production of malted liquor.

Wound/वुण्ड *(noun)* - घाव

She slipped and suffered chest wounds.

Wove/वोव *(verb)* - धुना हुआ

He wove a story to escape punishment.

Woven/वोवेन *(verb)* - बुना हुआ

He came again with woven stories to convince us about his sincerity.

Wow/वॉऊ *(interj.)* - आश्चर्यसूचक अव्यय

'Wow!' she cried enthusiastically! Your speech was a real wow.

Wraith/रेथ *(noun)* - भूत, प्रेत

Constant chest pains had reduced his father to a wraith.

Wrangle/रैंगल *(noun)* - लड़ाई, झगड़ा

The compensation was held up due to an insurance wrangle.

Wrap/रैप *(verb)* - लपेटना, ढाँकना

She wrapped up the marriage gifts attractively. She wrapped herself with a pashmina shawl.

Wrath/रॉथ *(noun)* - क्रोध, गुस्सा

The students faced the wrath of the professor for bunking the class.

Wreak/रीक *(verb)* - बदला लेना, नुकसान करना

The environmental damage wreaked by years of industrial pollution.

Wreath/रीद *(noun)* - माला, हार

The visiting president laid a wreath at the Mahatma Gandhi's Samadhi at Rajghat.

Wreathe/रीद *(verb)* - लपेटना, लिपटाना

She sits wreathed in smoke. Should I once more wreathe my arms about Anita's waist?

Wreck/रेक *(noun)* – पोतभंग

A naval ship brought ashore the survivors of the wreck. Another ship was dispatched for salvaging of treasure from wrecks.

Wrest/रेस्ट *(verb)* – छीन लेना

She tried to wrest her arm from robber's hold. They wanted to wrest control of their lives from irresponsible bureaucracy.

Wrestle/रेस्लॅ *(verb)* – कुश्ती लड़ना

A shot rang out as the policeman wrestled with the gunman. The security guards wrestled the ruffians to the ground.

Wretch/रेच *(noun)* – अभागा

Can the poor wretch's corpse tell us anything about his death? Ungrateful wretches of the society.

Wriggle/रिगल *(verb)* – छटपटाना

She kicked and wriggled to free herself from his hold. She wriggled to come out of her tight dress.

Wright/राइट *(noun)* – कारीगर, बढ़ई

Carpenters in Scotland are usually called a wright.

Wring/रिंग *(verb)* – निचोड़ना, मरोड़ना

She wrung the cloth out in the tub. extract in this way. *She wrung out the excess water from the cloths.*

Wrinkle/रिंकल *(noun)* – झुर्री

She ironed out the wrinkles from her shirt.

Wrist/रिस्ट *(noun)* – कलाई

She fell down and sprained her wrist. The parts have elastic wrists and ankles.

Writ/रिट *(noun)* – कानूनी दस्तावेज, आज्ञापत्र

The reinstated employee issued a writ for libel against the applicants. You have business here which is out of my writ and competence.

Wrong/रॉंग *(adj.)* – अशुद्ध

That is the wrong answer.

Wrote/रोट *(verb)* – लिखा

He wrote the article last night.

Wroth/रॉथ *(adjective)* – अति क्रुद्ध

The professor is majestically wroth with the students.

Wrung/रंग *(verb)* – ऐंठा हुआ

The confession wrung by the police was rejected in the court.

Wye/वाइ *(noun)* – बैशाखी

Wye is the river which forms part of the border between Wales and England.

Wynd/वाइन्ड *(noun)* – पतली गली

Fleet Street is a wynd where leading newspapers have offices.

X/एक्स *(noun)* - अंग्रेजी वर्णमाला का 24वाँ वर्ण the twenty fourth letter of the English alphabet.

1. Denoting the next after W in a set of items, categories, etc.
2. Denoting an unknown or unspecified person or thing. *In mathematics we use the symbol 'X' to denote an unknown number quantity.*

Xangti/जैन्ग्टि *(noun)* - चीन देश के पुराणों में ईश्वर का नाम
Xangti is the name of God.

Xanthic/जैन्थिक *(adj.)* - चमड़े के रंग के पीला पड़ जाने की क्रिया
Yellow coloured products are also known as xanthic.

Xanthium/जैन्थियम *(noun)* - गेंदा के समान एक फूल
Xanthium is a small flower.

Xanthoma/जैन्थोमा *(noun)* - पीले रंग की रचना
People who are suffering from Xanthoma should take proper care and consult doctor immediately.

Xanthophyll/जैन्थोफिल *(noun)* - पीत
Xanthophyll is a natural pigment that causes leaves to turn yellow.

Xanthosis/जैन्थॅसिस *(noun)* - पीले रंग की रचना
Xanthosis makes skin colour yellow.

Xanthous/जैन्थस *(adjective)* - पीत, पीले रंग का
Xanthous is a shade of colour that looks like the colour of egg yolk.

Xenarthral/जेनाथ्रल *(noun)* - पीठ के रीढ़ के सदृश जुटा हुआ
Xenarthral is a strange looking mammal largely due to its odd shaped vertebrae.

Xenial/जेनियल *(adjective)* - आतिथेय सम्बन्धी
His xenial attitude attracts all.

Xenogamy/जेनोगैमि *(noun)* - वृक्षों में गर्भधारण की क्रिया
Xenogamy is a process of fertilization of flower.

Xenogenesis/जेनोजेनेसिस *(noun)* - माता-पिता से भिन्न सन्तति की उत्पत्ति
Xenogenesis is a name given to those plants that can produce hydrogen cyanide.

Xenomania/जेनोमैनिया *(noun)* - परदेशी वस्तुओं पर उत्कट प्रेम
I do not suffer from xenomania.

Xenon/जेनन *(noun)* - एक धातु विशेष
Xenon is a gas used in manufacturing specialised electric lamps.

Xerophilous/जेरोफायलस *(adj)* - सूखा चाहने वाला
To stay in a desert you need to be Xerophilous.

Xerophyle/जेरोफायल *(noun)* - सूखी भूमि का पौधा
Xerophyle grows in desert.

Xerophytic/जेरोफायटिक *(adj)* - सूखी स्थिति के योग्य
Cacti are xerophytic plants.

Xerostomia/जेरॉस्टोमिया *(noun)* - मुख सूखने का रोग
In hot summer days people normally suffer from xerostomia.

Xerotes/जेरॉटस *(noun)* - शरीर का सूखापन
In xerotes condition fishes die in rivers.

X-ray/एक्स-रे *(noun)* - अदृश्य किरण जो भीतर की तस्वीर खींचे
X-ray eyes are required to see what is going in the godown of the merchant.

Xylem/जाइलम *(noun)* - वनस्पति का लकड़ी का भाग
Xylem tissue is responsible for passing water and nutrients from roots to the whole tree.

Xylocarp/जाइलोकार्प *(noun)* - कड़ी लकड़ी के समान फल
Xylocarp is a coconut like fruit that some people eat.

Xylograph/जाइलोग्राफ *(noun)* - लकड़ी पर खुदाई का काम
Xylograph should be avoided as it reduces the life of three.

Xylographic/जाइलोग्राफिक *(noun)* - लकड़ी की नक्काशी से सम्बन्धित
Xylographic art was practised widely in older times.

Xylol/जाइलॉल *(noun)* - लकड़ी से निकाला गया तेल
Xylol is used as solvent in washing powder.

Y/वाइ *(noun)* - अंग्रेजी वर्णमाला का 25वाँ वर्ण the twenty fifth letter of the alphabet.

1. Denoting the next after X in a set of items, categories, etc.
2. Denoting an unknown or unspecified person or thing.
3. The second unknown quantity in an algebraic expression, usually the dependent variable. denoting the secondary or vertical axis in a system of coordinates. *Vertical axis in co-ordinate geometry is known as 'Y' axis.*

Yacca/याका *(noun)* - एक प्रकार का सर्वदा हरा रहने वाला वृक्ष

Yacca looks very pretty during summer.

Yahoo/याहू *(noun)* - जंगली असभ्य मनुष्य

People hate yahoo.

Yak/याक *(noun)* - याक, सुरागाय, चमर

In Tibet yak is domesticated.

Yam/यैम *(noun)* - अरुई

Have you ever tested yam? People say it is very tasty.

Yank/यैन्क *(noun & verb)* - झटका, झटके से खींचना

Naresh yanked at my arm. She gave a yank to the rope.

Yap/यैप *(verb)* - कुत्ते की तरह भौंकना

The puppies yapped.

Yapok/यापक *(noun)* - एक चौपाया जीव

Yapok is generally found in tropical America.

Yardarm/यारडर्म *(noun)* - पाल के डण्डे का सिरा

People are resting and enjoying the evening sitting in the yardarm.

Yare/येअर *(adjective)* - उत्सुक

Don't be in hurry, move yare.

Yarn/यार्न *(noun)* - सूत, तन्तु

She uses sharp yarn to sew. Her yarn was hesitant.

Yarrow/यैरो *(noun)* - एक प्रकार का पौधा

Yarrow is a very useful medicine for many diseases.

Yataghan/यॉटगैन *(noun)* - कटार

Don't allow children to use the yatoghan.

Yaup/याउप *(verb)* - बच्चे की तरह चिल्लाना

Please don't yaup.

Yaw/या *(verb)* - विचलना, विचलन

The yawing motion of the ship.

Yawl/यावल *(noun)* - मछली पकड़ने की नाव

Many yawls are lying in the vacant space of the ship.

Yawn/यॉन *(verb)* - उबासी लेना

The cute child yawned during the long performance.

Yaws/यॉज *(plural noun)* - एक बीमारी

Yaws is considered a very dangerous disease by doctors.

Yea/ये *(noun)* - हाँ

Yea, I will surely meet you in the function.

Yean/यीन *(verb)* - ब्याना

The goat yeaned two yeanlings.

Year/यीअर *(noun)* - वर्ष

Our planet earth takes a year to complete one revolution around the sun.

Yearn/यर्न *(verb)* - इच्छा करना

He yearned for a cigarette badly.

Yeast/यीस्ट *(noun)* - खमीर, यीस्ट

Have you ever seen yeast through microscope? Yeast is used as food supplement.

Yell/येल *(noun)* - चीत्कार

He uttered a yell of pain.

Yellow/येलो *(adjective)* - सुनहला

My mother wants to know the reason for the yellow tinge on my teeth.

Yen/येन *(noun)* - शिलिंग मूल्य का सिक्का

Yen is of the highly rated currencies in the world.

Yeoman/योमॅन *(noun)* - किसान

Yeomen are very respectable persons in society.

Yes/येस (यस) *(exclamatory)* - हाँ, हूँ

Yes! I will do the job for you.

Yesterday/यस्टरडे *(noun)* - गत दिवस

Yesterday's solutions are not good enough.

Yew/यू *(noun)* - हरा रहने वाला वृक्ष

Never dare to try the fruit of yew tree.

Yiddish/यिडिश *(noun)* - परदेशी यहूदियों का भाषा

The Yiddish language is almost no longer in use now a days.

Yoke/योक *(noun)* - जूआ

Experienced farmers know well how to use a yoke properly. The small oxen pair can only plough yoke of land each day.

Yokel/योकल *(noun)* - अज्ञानी

The yokel behaved very rudely with the woman.

Yolk/योक *(noun)* - पीतक, जरदी

It is very good for health to have yoke every day as breakfast.

Yon/यॉन *(adjective)* - सामने का

He asks me what is my yon place.

Yonder/यॉन्डॅर *(adverb)* - वहाँ, उधर

Ramesh visited the yonder valley last year.

You/यू *(pronoun)* - तुम लोग

I love you are listening?

Younker/यंकर *(noun)* - लड़का

He is proud to be a younker.

Yowl/याउल *(noun)* - भौंकना

The old lady's yowl filled the hallway.

Yucca/यका *(noun)* - कुमुदनी के प्रकार की वनस्पति

Yucca is native to warm regions like US and Mexico.

Yuck/यक *(exclamatory)* - छि:, गंदा, घिनौना

Yuck, that's really gross! The environment of the restaurant is yuck to me.

Yurt/यर्ट *(noun)* - ध्रुवदेश के निवासियों के रहने का खेमा

Yurt is normally used in Mongolia and Turkey.

Z z

Z जेड *(noun)* – अंग्रेजी वर्णमाला का 26वाँ वर्ण the twenty sixth letter of the English alphabet.

1. Denoting the next after Y in a set of items, categories, etc.
2. The third unknown quantity in an algebraic expression. denoting the third axis in a three dimensional system of coordinates. *Third unknown quantity in the co-ordinate geometry.*

Zabrus/जैब्रस *(noun)* – एक प्रकार का बड़ा झींगुर या गुबरैला

Have seen a Zabrus

Zadkiel/जैड्किअल *(noun)* – इस नाम का प्रसिद्ध ज्योतिष पंचांग

I have no knowledge of Zadkiel almanac.

Zaffre/जैफर *(noun)* – एक प्रकार का खनिज विशेष

In today's world zaffre is rarely used.

Zarf/जार्फ *(noun)* – कहवा पीने का सुन्दर पात्र

Rajesh is very fond of having his morning coffee in a zarf.

Zebu/जीब्यू *(noun)* – पलुआ साँड़

Zebu is rarely found to see in India now a days.

Zephyr/जेफायर *(noun)* – पश्चिमी वायु

The zephyr was cooled by the river.

Zeppelin/जेपेलिन *(noun)* – बेलन के आकार का हवाई जहाज

Zeppelin aircraft were used by German Forces during First World War.

Zero/जीरो *(cardinal number)* – शून्य

The number zero was invented in India.

Zeus/ज्यूस *(noun)* – ग्रीस देश-निवासियों का सबसे बड़ा देवता

The state of Zeus at Olympic is one of the seven wonders of the world.

Zither/जिथर *(noun)* – एक प्रकार का सितार

I have a desire to listen to the music of zither once in my life time.

Zizania/जिजैनिया *(noun)* – एक प्रकार की सेवार

People from different parts of the world are still using zizania.

Zoetrope/जोइट्रप *(noun)* – एक प्रकार जिसमें तस्वीर चलती देख पड़ती है

Collection of zoetrope is found in many renowned museums in the world.

Zonal/जोनल *(adjective)* – कटिबन्धों से सम्बन्धित

Krish will reach the zonal frontier tomorrow. The Railway department has ordered to divide the east wing in zonal division.

Zonula/जोन्युला *(noun)* – छोटी मेंखला

The zonal is divided into many zonulas.

Zoo/जू *(noun)* – पशु वाटिका

Kamal's parents and children visited the zoo yesterday.

Zooide/जूआइड *(noun)* – जीवित प्राणि की आकृति का

Research is going on to find out the advantages and disadvantages of development of zooid.

Zoolatry/जूलेट्री *(noun)* – पशु पूजा

The tradition of zoolatry is still in practice in many countries.

Zoology/जूलॉजि *(noun)* – जीव विज्ञान

Patrick is doing his research in Zoology.

Zoomorphism/जूमॉरफिज्म *(noun)* – देवता या मनुष्य को पशु रूप में दिखाने की कला

The concept of Zoomorphism reflects the conducts and behaviour of some societies.

Zoophyte/जूफाइट *(noun)* – जन्तु तथा उद्भिज दोनों का गुण रखने वाला तत्त्व

The life cycle of zoophytes is being telecast in many documentaries in discovery channel.

Zopilote/जोपाइलोट *(noun)* – अमेरिका देश का छोटा गिद्ध

People could see Zopilote in many American Zoos.

Zoroastrian/जोरोस्ट्रियन *(adj)* – पारसी धर्म का अनुयायी

Zoroastrians live in many countries in the world and their population is recognisable in those countries.

Zoster/जॉस्टर *(noun)* – एक प्रकार का चर्म रोग
People suffering from zoster have to take proper medication.

Zulu/जूलू *(noun)* – दक्षिणी अफ्रीका की एक जाति
Zulu people are said to be very adventurous.

Zwieback/स्वीबैक *(noun)* – एक प्रकार का मीठा बिस्कुट
American people like to have zwieback in their breakfast.

Zygomatic/जिगॅमैटिक *(adj.)* – गाल की हड्डी का
The zygomatic bone is very delicate, it needs proper care.

Zymogen/जाइमॅजेन *(noun)* – उफान लाने वाला पदार्थ
Scientists use various methods to convert zymogen into enzymes.

Zymoid/जाइमॉइड *(adjective)* – उफान के सदृश
You won't be able to see zymoid with normal eyes.

Zymotic/जाइमॅटिक *(adjective)* – उफान सम्बन्धी
Sachin is now recovering from Cancer, but doctor has advised him to be careful of zymotic diseases.

Zymurgy/जाइमर्जि *(noun)* – आसव बनाने का रसायन
Mr. Sharma's younger daughter is very much interested in studying zymurgy.

Appendix-1/परिशिष्ट–1
Means of Transport
यातायात के साधन

Aeroplane	एयरोप्लेन	हवाई जहाज
Airbus	एअरबस	हवाई गाड़ी
Airship	एअरशीप	हवाईजहाज
Aircraft	एअरक्राफ्ट	विमान
Ambulance	एम्बुलेंस	मरीज वाहक
Auto rickshaw	ऑटो रिक्शा	ऑटो
Bike	बाइक	साइकिल (मोटर साइकिल)
Boat	बोट	नाव
Bus	बस	बस
Ballon	बैलून	गुब्बारा
Bomber plane	बम्बर प्लेन	बमवर्षक विमान
Bullock cart	बुलॉक कार्ट	बैलगाड़ी
Bicycle	बाइसिकल	साइकिल
Cart	कार्ट	गाड़ी
Car	कार	कार
Cycle rickshaw	साइकिल रिक्शा	रिक्शा
Camel cart	कैमेल कार्ट	ऊँटगाड़ी
Double decker bus	डबल डेकर बस	दो मंजिला बस
Engine	इंजिन	इंजन
Fire engine	फायर इन्जिन	अग्निशमक
Fighter plane	फाइटर प्लेन	लड़ाकू विमान
Helicopter	हेलिकॉप्टर	हेलिकॉप्टर
Jeep	जीप	जीप
Motor bike	मोटरबाइक	मोटर बाइक
Motor	मोटर	मोटर गाड़ी
Motor cycle	मोटर साइकिल	मोटर साइकिल
Moped	मोपेड	मोपेड
Metro rail	मेट्रो रेल	भूमिगत रेल
Parachute	पैराशूट	पैराशूट
Pram	प्राम	शिशुगाड़ी

Plane	प्लेन	विमान
Rail	रेल	पटरी
Railway	रेलवे	पटरी मार्ग
Roller	रॉलर	मार्ग बेलन
Rocket	रॉकेट	अन्तरिक्षयान
Rickshaw	रिक्शा	रिक्शा
Ship	शीप	जहाज
Scooter	स्कूटर	स्कूटर
Scooty	स्कुटी	स्कुटी
Space craft	स्पेस क्राफ्ट	अन्तरिक्ष यान
Shuttle	शटल	दो स्थानों के बीच की गाड़ी
Satellite	सेटेलाइट	उपग्रह
Tram	ट्राम	ट्राम
Trolley	ट्रॉली	ट्रॉली
Track	ट्रैक	मार्ग
Train	ट्रेन	रेलगाड़ी
Tyre	टायर	चक्का
Tonga	टाँगा	तांगा
Tractor	ट्रैक्टर	खेत जोतने की गाड़ी
Truck	ट्रक	मालवाहक, ट्रक, माल ढोने वाली गाड़ी
Tempo	टेम्पो	टेम्पो
Tricycle	ट्रॉइसिकल	तीन पहिया साइकिल
Tank	टैंक	युद्ध की गाड़ी
Tanker	टैंकर	तरल वाहक
Van	वान	वान
Wheel	ह्विल	चक्का
Yatch	याच	नाव
Brake	ब्रेक	ब्रेक
Pedal	पैडल	पायडिल
Pump	पम्प	पम्प
Rim	रिम	चक्का

Appendix-2/परिशिष्ट–2
Travel and Transport
यात्रा और यातायात के शब्द

Accelerator	एक्सिलेरेटर	गतिउत्पादक यन्त्र
Axle	एक्सल	धूरा, धुरी
Brake	ब्रेक	गति नियन्त्रक
Bonnet	बॉनेट	बॉनेट
Battery	बैटरी	बैटरी
Bumper	बम्पर	बम्पर
Booking-office	बुकिंग ऑफिस	टिकट घर
Carrier	केरियर	सामान ठोने का जगह
Carburattor	कारब्यूरेटर	कारबोरेटर
Crossroad	क्रॉसरोड्स	चौराहा
Clutch	कल्च	क्लच
Compartment	कम्पार्टमेंट	डिब्बा
Coach	कोच	विलासी डिब्बा
Footboard	फुटबोर्ड	पायदान
Freight	फ्रेट	भाड़ा
Guard	गार्ड	गाड़ी रक्षक
Gear	गिअर	गेअर
Helmet	हेलमेट	शिरस्त्राण
Horn	हॉर्न	भोंपू
Harness	हार्नेश	नियन्त्रित करना
Hub-cap	हब–कैप	सायकिल के चलने का एक यन्त्र
Headlight	हेडलाइट	अग्रप्रकाश
Hand brake	हैंड ब्रेक	हस्त नियंत्रक
Jack	जैक	गाड़ी उठाने वाला
Level crossing	लेवल क्रॉसिंग	लाइन पार करने का स्थान
Left turn	लेफ्ट टर्न	बायें मुड़ना
Luggage rack	लगेज रैक	सामान स्टैंड
Lever	लिवर	लिवर
Light	लाइट	बत्ती

Mudguard	मडगार्ड	कींच से बचाने वाला
Milo meter	मायलोमीटर	दूरी सूचक निर्देशक
Number plate	नम्बर प्लेट	गाड़ी संख्या पट्टिका
No parking	नो पार्किंग	गाड़ी खड़ी करना प्रतिबंधित
Passenger	पैसेंजर	यात्री
Plateform	प्लेटफॉर्म	यात्री स्थान
Parking place	पार्किंग प्लेस	गाड़ी खड़ी करने का स्थान
Pedal	पैडल	पायडिल
Pump	पम्प	पम्प
Rear mirror	रीअर मिरर	पृष्ठदर्शक
Right turn	राइट टर्न	दाहिने मुड़ना
Refreshment room	रिफ्रेशमेंट रूम	अल्पाहार कक्ष
Sleeper car	स्लिपर	शयनयान
Station	स्टेशन	विराम-स्थान
Stand	स्टैंड	विराम-स्थान
Signal	सिग्नल	निर्देशिका
Speed limit	स्पीड लिमिट	गतिसीमा
Speed braker	स्पीड ब्रेकर	गतिनियन्त्रक
Steering wheel	स्टियरिंग ह्वील	गाड़ी नियंत्रक
Sparking plug	स्पार्किंग प्लग	विद्युत संचालक
Speedo-meter	स्पीडोमीटर	गतिसूचक
Tyre	टायर	चक्का
Tool bag	टूल बैग	औजार का थैला
Traffic light	ट्रैफिक लाइट	नियन्त्रक बत्ती
Traffic sign	ट्रैफिक साइन	नियन्त्रक चिह्न
Traffic police	ट्रैफिक	यातायात पुलिस आरक्षी
Waggon	वैगन	मालडिब्बा
Wind screen	विन्ड स्क्रीन	वायु नियन्त्रक
Wind wiper	विन्ड वायपर	पोंछने वाला
Wheel brake	ह्विल ब्रेक	चक्का नियन्त्रक
Wheel	ह्विल	चक्का
Zigzag	जिग्जैग	घुमावदार

Appendix-3/परिशिष्ट–3
Animal Sound
जानवरों की आवाजें

Cry	क्राई	चिल्लााना, रोना
Bark	बर्क	भूँकना
Neigh	नाइ	हिनहिनाना
Howl	हाउल	फें करना, हुआँ-हुआँ करना
Yowl	यॉल	भूँकना
Wail	वेल	रोना, कलपना
Ululu	उलुलु	हुलकना
Whine	ह्वाइन	हेंकरना
Blat	ब्लैट	भेंकरना
Bleat	ब्लीट	मिमियाना
Moo	मू	हेंकरना
Low	लो	रंभाना
Squeak	स्क्वीक	चूँ-चूँ करना
Squeal	स्क्वील	चीं-चीं करना
Grunt	ग्रन्ट	गुर्राना, बुरबुराना
Hiss	हिस	फुफकारना, फुसकरना
Blow	ब्लो	पीं-पीं बजना
Rattle	रॉटल	खड़खड़ाना, खड़खड़ाहट
Bay	बे	साँय-साँय करना
Yap	याप	केंकियाना
Yelp	येल्प	कें-कें करना
Yip	यिप	हेंकरना
Whinny	ह्विन्नी	हिनहिनाहट
Whieker	ह्विकर	खी-खी करना
Snort	स्नॉर्ट	घुँ-घुँ करना
Bray	ब्रे	रेंकना
Mew	मियू	म्याऊँ करना
Miau	मिआऊँ	म्याऊँ करना
Purr	पर्र्	पड़पड़ाना
Roar	रोर	गीजना

Bellow	बेलो	डकरना
Trumpet	ट्रम्पेट	चिघाड़ना
Growl	ग्रॉल	गुर्राना
Snarl	स्नार्ल	घुघुआना
Yarr	यर्र्	कोंकिचाना
Troat	ट्रॉट	हिरनी सा कामोत्तेजक आवाज
Bell	बेल	घंटी की आवाज
Chirp	चर्प	चहचहाना
Sing	सिंग	गाना
Trill	ट्रिल	टिहकारी भरना
Call	कॉल	पुकारना
Chip	चिप	चिहुकना
Chirrup	चर्प	चहचहाना
Chirr	चर्र्	चहचहाना
Chitter	चिटर	किटकिटाना
Twitter	ट्विटर	चहचहाना
Tweet	ट्विट	चहकना
Cheep	चीप	चींचीं करना
Chuck	चक	चहकना
Churr	चउर	चहचहाना
Chatter	चैटर	कटकटना
Coo	कू	गुटरू गूँ करना
Curr	कर्र्	करकराना
Whistle	ह्विस्टल	सीटी सी आवाज करना
Pipe	पाइप	बाँसुरी सी आवाज
Crow	क्रो	कुकड़ूँ कूँ करना
Cock-a-doodle	कॉक-ए-डूडल	कुकड़ूँ कूँ
Cluck	क्लक	कूँ-कूँ करना
Cackle	कैकल	कूँ-कूँ करना
Chuckle	चकल	चिहकना
Gabble	गैबल	गिलगिलाना
Quack	कैक	कों-कों करना
Gobble	गोबल	गिलगिलाना, भकोसना
Hiss	हिस	फुफकारना
Clang	क्लैंग	सीत्कार भरना

Honk	हॉन्क	बुबुआना
Scream	स्क्रीम	चीखना
Screech	स्क्रीच	चिल्लाना
Squawk	स्क्वीक	कोलाहल
Squall	स्क्वैल	चिल्लाहट
Hoot	हूट	बुड़कना
Tuwhit	टुहिट	टिहकारी भरना
Tuwhoo	टुहू	टहकना
Whoop	हूप	फटाक करना
Boom	बूम	भड़ाम करना
Crock	क्रॉक	टर्र-टर्र करना
Caw	कॉ	काँव-काँव करना
Plunk	पलंक	पुटपुटाना
Croank	क्रोंक	कूँ-कूँ करना
Buzz	बज	भनभनाना
Hum	हम	गुनगुनाना
Drone	ड्रून	मसकबाजे सी आवाज
Stridulate	स्ट्रिडुकेट	कर्कश आवाज, चिल्लाहट
Creak	क्रीक	चर्र-चर्र करना
Crick	क्रिक	करकराना
Bellow	बेलो	हकरना, गरजना
Whir	ह्वर	किर्न-घिर्न करना
Whir	ह्वर्र	घिर्न-घिर्न करना
Whirl	ह्वर्ल	गलगलाना
Clulk	क्लक	कुक-कुक करना
Hoot	हूट	बुबुआना
Whiff	ह्विफ	फुत्कार करना, फू-फू करना

Appendix-4/परिशिष्ट–4
Sound of Objects
वस्तु की आवाजें

Aeroplane zoom	एअरोप्लेनन्स	जूम हवाई जहाज गरजते हुए उड़ते हैं
Bells ring	बेल्स रिंग	घंटी टनटनाती हैं
Boots creak	बूट्स क्रीक	जूते चरमराते हैं
Bugles blow	बगल्स ब्लो	बिगुल बजाता है
Coins gingle	क्वायन्स	सिक्के जिंगल खनकते हैं
Clocks tick	क्लॉक्स	घड़िया टिक खड़खड़ाती है
Clouds thunder	क्लाउड्स थंडर	बादल गरजते हैं
Dishes rattle	डिशेज रैटल	थालियाँ खड़खड़ाती हैं
Fire crachles	फायर क्रैकल्स	अग्नि पटपटाती है
Guns boom	गन्स बुम	बन्दूकें गरजती है
Steam hiss	स्टीम हिस	भाप फदफदाता है
Engines whistle	इन्जिन ह्विस्ल्स	गाड़ियाँ सीटी देती हैं
Cooker whistle	कूकर ह्विस्ल्स	कूकर सीटी देती है
Feet patter	फीट पैटर	पाँव पटपटाते हैं
Hinges creak	हिन्जेस क्रीक	कब्जे चरमराते हैं
Hands clap	हैन्डस क्लैप	हाथ ताली बजाती है
Hoofs clatter	हुफ्स क्लैटर	खुर खटपटाते हैं
Dry leaves clatter	ड्राइ लिव्ज क्लैटर	सूखे पत्ते खड़खड़ाते हैं
Leaves rustle	लिव्ज रस्ल	पत्तियाँ सरसराती हैं
Metals ring	मेटल्स रिंग	धातु टनटनाते हैं
Raindrops patter	रेनड्रॉप्स पैटर	वर्षा की बूँदें पटपटाती हैं
Rifles report	रायफल्स रिपोर्ट	रायफल धमाके करते हैं
Shoes creak	सूज क्रीक	जूते चरमराते हैं
Weapons clatter	विपन्स क्लैटर	हथियार खड़खड़ाते हैं
Wind howl	विन्ड हाउस	हवा हू-हूकर बहती है
Wind whistle	विन्ड ह्विसल	हवा सनसनाती है
Spinning wheels whirr	स्पिनिंग ह्विल्स ह्वर्र	चरखा घरघराता है

Appendix-5/परिशिष्ट–5
Professionals
पेशेवर

Announcer	एनाउन्सर	उदघोषक
Auctioneer	ऑक्शनियर	नीलामी करने वाला
Acrobat	एक्रोबैट	नट
Artist	आर्टिस्ट	कलाकार
Artisan	आर्टिजन	कारीगर, शिल्पकार
Astrologer	एस्ट्रोलोजर	ज्योतिषी
Agent	एजेन्ट	प्रतिनिधि, कारिन्दा
Author	ऑथर	लेखक
Advocate	एडवोकेट	वकील
Barber	बारबर	हजाम, नाई
Blacksmith	ब्लैक स्मिथ	लोहार
Butcher	बुचर	कसाई
Butler	बटलर	भण्डारी
Boatman	बोटमैन	नाविक, मल्लाह
Brasier	ब्रेसिलर	ठठेरा
Baker	बेकर	नानबाई
Broker	ब्रोकर	दलाल
Binder	बाइन्डर	जिल्दसाइज
Barrister	बैरिस्टर	वकील
Beggar	बेगर	भिखारी
Betel-seller	बिटल सेलर	तमोली
Bookseller	बुक सेलर	पुस्तक विक्रेता
Carrier	कैरियर	सामान ठोने वाला
Clerk	कर्ल्क	किएनी
Cobbler	कॉबलर	मोची
Chemist	केमिस्ट	दवा विक्रेता
Cashier	कैशियर	खजांची, रोकड़िया
Cook	कुक	रसोइया
Coolie	कुली	कुली, मोटिया
Carder	कार्डर	धुनिया

Contractor	कॉन्ट्रैक्टर	ठीकेदार
Compositer	कम्पोजिटर	प्रेस में शब्द बिठाने वाला, कम्पोजिटर
Coachman	कोचमैन	कोचवान
Confectioner	कन्फेक्सनर	हलवाई
Cleaner	क्लिनर	खलासी, सफाई करने वाला
Constable	कांस्टेबल	सिपाही
Counsellor	काउन्सेलर	सन्मतिदाता
Conductor	कन्डक्टर	गाड़ी नियन्त्रक
Carpenter	कारपेन्टर	बढ़ई
Compounder	कम्पाउन्डर	डाक्टर का सहायक
Chanffeur	शोफर	कार चालक
Cartman	कार्टमैन	गाड़ीवान
Dentist	डेन्टिस्ट	दाँत-निर्माता
Doctor	डाक्टर	चिकित्सक
Dramatist	ड्रेमेस्टि	नाटककार
Draper	ड्रेपर	जबाज
Dancer	डांसर	नर्तका, नर्तकी
Druggist	ड्रगिस्ट	दवा-विक्रेता
Draftsman	ड्राफ्ट्समैन	चित्र बनाने वाला
Dyer	डायर	रंगरेज
Brummer	ब्रमर	तबला वादक, तबलवी
Decorator	डेकोरेटर	सज्जाकार
Docker	डॉकर	गोदी-मजदूर
Engineer	इन्जिनियर	अभियन्ता
Engraver	इन्ग्रवेर	नक्काशी करने वाला
Enchanter	इन्चैन्टर	जादूगर
Enchantress	इन्चैन्ट्रेस	जादूगरनी
Editor	एडिटर	सम्पादक
Enameller	इनामेलर	मीनाकार
Examiner	एक्जामिनर	परीक्षक
Employee	इम्पलाई	नौकरी-पेशा कला, कर्मचारी
Fisherman	फिशमैन	मछुआरा
Farmer	फारमर	किसान
Fireman	फायरमैन	अग्निशमक

Fitter	फिटर	यन्त्र संयोजक
Foreman	फोरमैन	प्रधान कर्मचारी
Gardener	गार्डेनर	माली
Goldsmith	गोल्ड स्मिथ	सोनार
Greem grosser	ग्रीन ग्रोसर	सब्जी विक्रेता
Hawker	हॉकर	फेरीवाला
Inkman	इंकमैन	रोशनाई वाला
Inn-keeper	इनकीपर	धर्मशाला वाला
Inspector	इन्सेपेक्टर	निरीक्षक
Janitor	जैनीटर	द्वारपाल
Jeweller	ज्वेलर	जौहरी
Judge	जज	न्यायाधीश
Lawyer	लायर	वकील
Mason	मेसन	राजमिस्त्री
Milkman	मिल्कमैन	ग्वाला
Middleman	मिड्लमैन	दलाल
Magician	मैजिसियन	जादूगर
Minor	माइनर	खनिक
Mechanic	मेकेनिक	यान्त्रिक
Musician	म्यूजिशियन	गायक, संगीतज्ञ
Merchant	मरचेंट	सौदा व्यापार
Midwife	मिडवाइफ	दाई
Messenger	मेसेन्जर	दूत, धावक
Manager	मैनेजर	प्रबंधक
Milkmaid	मिल्कमेड	अहीरिन, ग्वालिन
Newsreader	न्यूजरीडर	समाचार वाचक
Newspaper vandor	न्यूजपेपर वेन्डर	अखबार वाला
Nurse	नर्स	नर्स, धाय, दाई
Novelist	नोवेलिस्ट	उपन्यासकार
Nun	नन	भिक्षुणी
Oilman	वायलमैन	तेली
Operator	ऑपरेटर	मशीन चालक
Order-supplier	ऑर्डर सप्लायर	आदेश आपूरक
Orderly	ऑर्डरली	अर्दली
Potter	पॉटर	ठठेरा, कुम्हार

Pupil	पुपिल	शिष्य, छात्र
Printer	प्रिंटर	मुद्रक
Publisher	पब्लिशर	प्रकाशक
Priest	प्रिस्ट	पादरी
Painter	पेंटर	चित्रकार
Postman	पोस्टमैन	डाकिया
Photographer	फोटोग्राफर	तस्वीर उतारने वाला
Proprietor	प्रोप्राइटर	मालिक
Proprietress	प्रोप्राइट्रेस	मालकिन
Pleader	प्लीडर	वकील
Procurer	प्रोक्यूरर	कुटना
Player	प्लेयर	खिलाड़ी
Policeman	पुलिसमैन	सिपाही
Packer	पैकर	सामान बाँधने वाला
Pager	पेजर	दूत
Pawner	पावनर	बंधक रखने वाला
Peddler	पेडलर	फेरी वाला
Perfumer	परक्यूमर	इत्र बेचने वाला
Repairer	रिपेअरर	मरम्मत करने वाला
Retailer	रिटेलर	खुदरा विक्रेता
Sculptor	स्कल्पटर	मूर्तिकार, संगतराश
Seedsman	सीड्समैन	बीज बिक्रेता
Sailor	सेलर	मांझी, नाविक
Sweeper	स्वीपर	मेहतर, मंगी
Surgeon	सर्जन	शल्य-चिकित्सक
Sanitary inspector	सैनिटरी इन्सिपेक्टर	निरीक्षक
Shopkeeper	शॉपकीपर	दुकानदार
Salesman	सेल्समैन	विक्रेता
Shoemaker	शूमेकर	मोची
Student	स्टुडेंट	छात्र
Scientist	साइन्टिस्ट	वैज्ञानिक
Soldier	सोल्डर	सैनिक
Teacher	टीचर	शिक्षक

Tailor	टेलर	दर्जी
Ticket collector	टिकट कलक्टर	टिकट जमाकर्ता
Tabla player	टबला प्लेयर	तबला वादक, तबलची
Treasurer	ट्रेजरर	खजांची
Turner	टर्नर	खरादने वाला
Trainer	ट्रेनर	प्रशिक्षक
Typist	टाइपिस्ट	टंकक
Vegetable seller	वेजिटेब्ल सेलर	सब्जी विक्रेता
Washerman	वाशर मैन	धोबी
Weaver	वीवर	बुनकर
Waiter	वेटर	बेयरा

Appendix-6/परिशिष्ट–6

Cereals/अनाज/उपज/अन्न

Grain/	ग्रेन–अन्न, दाना, अनाज	
Pea	पी	मटर
Pigeon pea	पिजिअन पी	अरहर
Field pea	फिल्ड पी	गोल मटर
Pulse	पल्स	दाल, दलहन
Gram	ग्राम	चना
Phaseolies mungo	फेजलीज मंगो	उड़द
Coffee	कॉफी	कहवा
Cluster bean	कलस्टर बीन	ज्वार
Wheat	ह्विट	गेहूँ
Paddy	पैडी	धान
Rice	राइस	चावल
Millet	माइलेट	बाजरा
Oat	ओट	जई
Barley	बार्ली	जौ
Great millet	ग्रेट माइलेट	ज्वार, चोलम
Sesame	सिसेम	तिल
Pear millet	पर्ल माइलेट	बाजरा
Poppy	पॉपी	पोस्ता दाना
Corn	कॉर्न	मकई
Corn ear	कॉर्न ईअर	मकई के बाल
Maize	मेज	मकई
Lentil	लेंटिल	मसूर
Kidney bean	किडनी बीन	मूँग
Buck wheat	बक ह्विट	मेथी
Mustard	मस्टर्ड	तोरी, राई, सरसों
White mustard	ह्वाइट मस्टर्ड	सफेद सरसों
Castor seed	कस्टर सीड	रेंड़ी

Appendix-7/परिशिष्ट–7

Eatables/खाद्य पदार्थ

Rice	राइस	चावल
Flour	फ्लोर	आटा
Arrowroot	एरोरूट	अरारूट
Pickle	पिकल	अचार
Grain	ग्रेन	अनाज
Comfit	कमफिट	इलायचीदाना
Curry	करी	शोरबा, रसा
Coffee	कॉफी	कहवा
Meat	मीट	मांस
Mutton	मटन	बकरे का मांस
Minced meat	माइसिड मीट	कीमा
Beaf	बीफ	गाय का मांस
Pork	पोर्क	सूअर का मांस
Kulfi	कुल्फी	कुल्फी
Ice-cream	आइसक्रीम	आइसक्रीम
Butter	बटर	मक्खन
Clarified butter	क्लैरिफायड	घी बटर
Ghee	घी	घी
Cheese	चीज	पनीर
Sweets	स्वीट्स	मिठाईयाँ
Confectionary	कंफेक्सनरी	मिठाईयाँ
Pulse	पल्स	दाल
Fried	फ्रायड	भूना हुआ
Cooked	कुक्ड	पकाया हुआ
Sauce	सॉस	चटनी
Tomato sauce	टोमैटो सॉस	टमाटर की चटनी
Bread	ब्रेड	रोटी
Sliced bread	स्लाइस ब्रेड	पावरोटी
Chapati	चपाती	चपाती
Beaten paddy	बिटेन पैडी	चिउड़ा
Beaten rice	बिटेन राइस	चिउड़ा

Baked grain	बेकड ग्रेन	भूजा
Tea	टी	चाय
Broth	ब्रॉथ	रस, शोरबा
Vegetable	बेजटेब्ल	सब्जी
Fruit	फ्रुट्स	फल
Salad	सलाद	सलाद
Gruel	ग्रुएल	दलिया, माँड़
Oil	आयल	तेल
Refined oil	रिफाइन्ड आयल	फैटरहित तेल
Curd	कर्ड	दही
Milk	मिल्क	दूध
Vinegar	वाइनेगर	सिरका
Semolina	सेमोलिना	सूजी
Tomato ketchup	टोमैटो केचप	टमाटर की चटनी
Loaf	लोफ	फूली हुई रोटी
Bun	बन	गोल फूला हुआ रोटी
Biscuit	बिस्कुट	बिस्कुट
Baked corn	बेक्ड कार्न	भुट्टा
Corn flake	कॉर्न फ्लेक	कुटा हुआ मकई
Whey	ह्वे	मट्ठा
Cream	क्रीम	मलाई
Sugar	सुगर	चीनी
Sugar candy	सुगर कैंडी	मिश्री
Murabba	मुरब्बा	मुरब्बा
Papar	पापड़	पापड़
Mixture	मिक्सचर	मसालेदार भूना हुआ दाना
Maida	मैदा	मैदा
Syrup	सिरप	मीठा रस
Sorbet	शर्बत	शरबत
Treacle	ट्रिकल	चाशनी
Wine	वाइन	शराब
Beer	बिअर	बिअर
Whisky	ह्विस्की	ह्विस्की
Honey	हनी	शहद, मधु
Drinks	ड्रिंक्स	पेय
Cold-drinks	कोल्ड ड्रिंक्स	शीतल पेय
Mathari	मठरी	मठरी

Puri	पुरी	पुड़ी
Pua	पुआ	पुआ
Breakfast	ब्रेकफास्ट	नास्ता
Lunch	लंच	दिन का भोजन
Snax	स्नैक्स	हल्का नास्ता
Luncheon	लंचिअन	हल्का नास्ता
Dinner	डिनर	रात का भोजन, भोज
Supper	सपर	रात का भोजन
Feast	फीस्ट	भोज
Food	फुड	भोजन
Chew	चिउ	चबाना
Swallow	स्वैलो	निगलना
Digest	डायजेस्ट	पचाना
Vomit	वोमिट	उगलना
Jelly	जेली	जेली
Jam	जैम	जैम
Pizza	पिज्जा	पिज्जा
Toast	टोस्ट	टोस्ट
Sausage	सौसेज	सॉसेज
Hamburger	हैम्बरगर	हैम्बरगर
Egg	एग	अण्डा
Cake	केक	केक
Pancake	पैनकेक	पैनकेक
Soup	सूप	सूप
Dessert	डेजर्ट	मीठा पकवान
Pie	पाइ	अदौरी, तिलौरी
Chicken	चिकेन	मुर्गा
Fish	फिश	मछली
Honey	हनी	शहद
Maeggrone	मारजेरिन	सेवई
Samosa	समोसा	समोसा
Noodle	नूडल	नमकीन पेठा
Toffee	टॉफी	टॉफी
Chocolet	चॉकलेट	चॉकलेट
Pudding	पुडिंग	खीर
Chips	चिप्स	चिप्स
Croquette	क्रोक्वेट	आलूचप

Appendix-8/परिशिष्ट–8

Spices/मसाले

Vitriol	विटरियोल	तूतिया
Musk	मस्क	कस्तुरी
Nigella	नाइजेला	कलौंजी
Salt	साल्ट	नमक
Coriander	कोरिएण्डर	धनिया
Cinnamon	सिनामॉन	दालचीनी
Cassia	कैसिया	तेजपात
Basil	बेसिल	तुलसी
Niger	नायगर	तिल
Cumin seed	क्यूमिन सीड	जीरा
Mace	मैस	जावित्री
Nutmeg	नटमेग	जायफल
Chirota	चिराटा	चिरैता
Sandal	सैंडल	चंदन
Menthol	मेन्थॉल	पोदीना
Indian madder	इन्डियन मैडर	मजीठ
Gall nut	गॉलनट	माजूफल
Red pepper	रेड पिपर	लाल मिर्च
Chili	चिली	मिर्च
Licorice	लिकोराइस	मुलैठी
Black pepper	ब्लैक पिपर	गोल मिर्च
Pseudo-alum	स्यूडो एलम	फिटकिरी
Saffron	सेफ्रॉन	केसर
Cocain	कोकीन	कोकीन
Feast	ईष्ट	खमीर
Aloe	एलो	मुसब्बर
Parsley	पार्सलि	अजवाइन खुरासानी
Caraway	कारावे	अजवाइन
Thymol	थायमल	अजवाइन का सत
Ginger	जिंजर	अदरख
Linseed	लिनसीड	अतली

Phyllanthus embhica	फाइलेथंस इम्बिलंक	आँवला
Cardamom	कारडामॉम	इलाइची (छोटी)
Catechu	कैटेचु	काथ
Camphor	कैम्फर	कपूर
Nitre	नाइटर	शोरा
Opium	ओपिअम	अफीम
Cubeb	क्यूबेब	कबाबचीनी
Ruddle	रडल	गेरू
Copper sulphate	कॉपर सल्फेट	तूतिया
Bitumen	बिटुमेन	राल
Soapnut	सोपनट	रीठा
Benzoin	बेन्जोयाइन	लोहबान
Arsenic	आर्सेनिक	संखिया
Alkali	अलकलि	सज्जीखार
Litharge	लिथार्ज	सफेदा
Sago	सैगो	साबूदाना
Cinnabar	सिनाबार	सिंगरिफ
Betel-nut	बिटलनट	सुपारी
Vinegar	वाइनेगर	सिरका
Albaster	एलबास्टर	सेतखली
Dry ginger	ड्राइ जिंजर	सोंठ
Borex	बोरैक्स	सोहागा
Turmeric	टरमेरिक	हल्दी
Myrobalan	मायरोबलान	हर्रे
Asafoctida	एसफोएटिडा	हींग
Curcuma	करक्यूमा	हल्दी
Clove	क्लोव	लवंग
Mado saffron	मैडो सेफरॉन	शरत केसर
Pistil	पिस्टिल	केसर
Origanum	ऑरिगेनम	शिकाकाई

Appendix-9/परिशिष्ट–9

Fruits/फल

Apple	एप्ल	सेव
Pine apple	पाइनएप्ल	अनानास
Stone apple	स्टोन एप्ल	बेल
Crab apple	क्रैब एप्ल	जंगली सेव
Custard apple	कस्टर्ड एप्ल	शरीफा
Melon	मेलन	तरबूज
Water melon	वाटरमेलन	खरबूजा
Musk melon	मस्क मेलन	फूट
Cucumber	ककम्बर	खीरा, ककड़ी
Berry	बेरी	बैर
Black berry	ब्लैक बेरी	जामुन
Sweet berry	स्वीटबेरी	लसलसा
Mul berry	मलबेरी	शहतूत
Rose berry	रोजबेरी	गुलाब जामुन
Nut	नट	कड़े छिलके का फल
Betel nut	बिटलनट	सुपारी
Chest nut	चेस्ट नट	अखरोट
Cashew nut	कैशियू नट	काजू
Ground nut	ग्राउण्ड नट	बादाम
Water nut	वाटरनट	सिंघाड़ा
Coconut	कोकोनेट	नारियल
Kernel	करनेल	कड़े फल का खाने योग्य बाग
Pomegranate	पॉमग्रेनेट	अनार
Grapes	ग्रेप्स	अंगूर
Fig	फिग	अंजीर
Mango	मैंगो	आम
Sugar cane	सुगरकेन	ईख
Jack fruit	जैकफ्रुट	कटहल
Currant	क्यूरेंट	किशमिश
Plantain	प्लेंटेन	केला
Banana	बनाना	केला
Guava	ग्वावा	अमरूद
Date	डेट	खजूर
Apricot	एप्रिकॉट	खूबानी
Carrot	कैरॉट	गाजर

Euryle forex	यूराइल फोरेक्स मखाना	
Sweet potato	स्वीट पोटैटो	शकरकन्द
Lichi	लिची	लिची
Cifrus fruit	साइट्रस फ्रुट	खट्टे-रसीले फल
Orange	ऑरेंज	नारंगी
Mausambi	मौसमी	मौसमी
Lemon	लेमन	नींबू
Pear	पीअर	नाशपाती
Peach	पीच	सतालू
Papaya	पपाया	पपीता
Mountain papaya	माउन्टेन पपाया	पहाड़ी पपीता
Pistalhio	पिस्टैचियो	पिस्ता
Plum	प्लम	बेर
Almond	आल्मन	बादाम
Yam	याम	रतालू
Stone	स्टोन	गुठली
Pulp	पल्प	गुदा
Skin	स्किन	छिलका
Juice	जूस	रस
Sap	सैप	रस
Seed	सीड	बीज
Sapling	सैप्लिंग	कलम
Plant	प्लांट	पौधा
Gerom	जर्म	अंकुर
Graft	ग्राफ्ट	कलम
Bud	बड	कली
Rind	रिंड	छिलका
Fibre	फायबर	रेशा
Cherry	चेरी	चेरी
Sour cherry	सावर चेरी	खट्टी चेरी
Sopodilla	सैपोडिला	चीकू
Sugar beet	सुगर बीट	चुकन्दर
Gravia	ग्राविया	फालसा
Raspberries	रैस्पबेरीज	रसीलेबेर
Kivi fruit	किवीफ्रुट	किवीफल
Strawberry	स्ट्रॉबेरी	स्ट्रॉबेरी
Jambu	जैम्बु	जैम्बु

Appendix-10/परिशिष्ट–10

Flowers/फूल

Oleander	ओलिएण्डर	कनेर
Lotus	लोटस	कमल
Lily	लिलि	कमलिनी, कुमुदनी
Pandanus	पैन्डेनस	केतकी, केवड़ा
Chrysanthemum	क्राइसथेंमम	गुलदाऊदी
Touch-me-not	टचमी नॉट	गुल मेंहदी
Daisy	डेजी	गुलबहार
Marogold	मेरीगोल्ड	गेंदा
Jasmine	जेस्मिन	चमेली
Magnolia	मैग्नोलिया	चम्पा
Amaranthus	एमरैन्थस	चौलाई
Prickly amaranthus	प्रिकली एमरैन्थस	कटीली चौलाई
Belladona	बेलाडोना	धतूरा
Narassus	नारसिसस	नरगिस
Cactus	कैक्टस	नागफनी, सेहुड़
Prickly pear	प्रिकली पिअर	नागफनी, कटीले फूल
Cobra flower	कोबरा फ्लावर	नागफनी, नागमिका
Lilac	लाइलैक	बकाइन
Pyrus malus	पायरस मेलस	वंगूगोशा
Violet	वायलेट	बनफशा
Sweet violet	स्वीट वायलेट	सुगन्धित बनफशा
Mogra	मोगरा	बेला
Allamanoa	एलामानोआ	एलामानोआ
Periwinkle	पेरिविंकल	पेरिविंकल
Balsam	बाल्सम	गुलहजारा
Creeper	क्रीपर	लता
Rose	रोज	गुलाब, चुवती
Ivory	आइवरी	दूधिया फूल
Cosmos	कॉसमॉस	कॉसमॉस
Blue bell	ब्लूबेल	ब्लूबेल
Dog flower	डॉग फ्लावर	कुत्ता फूल
Petunia	पिटुनिया	पिटुनिया
Platonica	प्लेटोनिका	दसबजिया

Agastya	अगस्त्य	अगस्त्य
Kanak	कनक	कनक
Aparajita	अपराजिता	अपराजिता
Shami	शमी	शमी
Poppy	पॉपी	अफीम
Desert blue bell	डेजर्ट ब्लूबेल	जंगली ब्लूबेल
Pensy	पैंजी	पैंजी
Dahlia	डालिया	डालिया
Zinnia	जिनिया	जिनिया
Carnation	कारनेशन	कारनेशन
Blue carnation	ब्लू कारनेशन	नीला कारनेशन
Morning glory	मार्निंग ग्लोरी	आभा
Night queen	नाइट क्विन	रात की रानी
Rajnigandha	रजनीगंधा	रजनीगंधा
Hibiscus	हिबिसकस	हिबिसकस
Tulip	ट्यूलिप	ट्यूलिप
Gandhraj	गंधराज	गंधराज
Mountain lotus	माउन्टेन लोटस	इन्द्रकमल
10 O' clock	टेन ओ क्लॉक	दसबजिया
4 O' clock	फोर ओ क्लॉक	चरबजिया
Root	रूट	जड़
Stem	स्टेम	तना
Leaf	लिफ	पत्ता
Branch	ब्रांच	डाली
Hair root	हेअर रूट	महीन रेशा
Flower	फ्लावर	फूल
Fruit	फ्रूट	फल
Seed	सीड	बीज
Sapling	सैप्लिंग	बीचड़ा
Plantation	प्लांटेशन	रोपना
Grafting	ग्राफ्टिंग	एक में दूसरा पौधा जोड़ना
Seedling	सिडलिंग	बीचड़ा
Harsingoor	हरसिंगार	हरसिंगार
Kamini	कामिनी	कामिनी
Rakhi	राखी	राखी (कौरव-पांडव)
Shivling	शिवलिंग	शिवलिंग
Kachnar	कचनार	कचनार

Appendix-11/परिशिष्ट–11
Vegetables/सब्जियाँ

Bulbous	बलबस	कन्द
Ginger	जिंजर	अदरक
Potato	पोटैटो	आलू
Tomato	टोमैटो	टमाटर
Tamarind	टेमरिंड	इमली
Cucumber	ककम्बर	खीरा, ककड़ी
Jack fruit	जैक फ्रुट	कटहल
Pumpkin	पम्पकिन	कोहड़ा
Gourd	गावर्ड	कद्दू
Carambola	कैरमबोला	कमरख
Bitter gourd	बिटर गावर्ड	करेला
Jhigune	झिंगुनी	झिंगुनी
Ghiya	घिया	घिया
Red pumpkin gourd	रेड पम्पकिन गोवर्ड	काशीफल
Mushroom	मशरूम	कुकुरमुत्ता
Banana	बनाना	केला
Cucurbit gourd	ककरबिट गावर्ड	फूट, कोहड़ा
Lime	लाइम	नींबू
Carrot	कैरॉट	गाजर
Knol khol	नोलखोल	गाँठ गोभी
Cabbage	कैबेज	बन्द गोभी
Cauliflower	कावलीफ्लावर	फूलगोभी
Luffa	लुफा	तुरई, तोरी
Snake gourd	स्नेक गावर्ड	चिचड़ी
Luffa gourd	लुफा गावर्ड	चिकनी चुरई, तोरी
Pinus geradiana	पायनस जेराडियाना	चिलगोजा
Sapodilla	सैपोडिला	चीकू
Beetroot	बीटरूट	चुकन्दर
Sugar beet	सुगर बीट	चुकन्दर
Yam	याम	रतालु
Coriandor	कोरिएण्डर	धनिया

Papaya	पपाया	पपीता
Trichosanths dioica	ट्रिकोसेन्थस डियोइका	परवल
Parval	परवल	परवल
Brassica campestrice	ब्रासिका केम्पेस्ट्राइस	पत्तागोभी
Spinch	स्पिनैच	पालक
Mint	मिन्ट	पुदीना
Onion	ओनियन	प्यास
Brinjal	ब्रिंजल	बैगन
Lady finger	लेडीफिंगर	भिण्डी
Pea	पी	मटर
Nightshade	नाइटशेड	मकोय
Chilli	चिली	मिर्च
Raddish	रैडिश	मूली
Turnip	टरनिप	शलजम
Bean	बीन	सेम
Lettuce	लेट्यूस	सलाद
Green leaves	ग्रीन लिव्स	साग
Garlic	गारलिक	लहसुन

Appendix-12/परिशिष्ट–12

Birds/पक्षी

Swallow	स्वैलो	अबाबील
Owl	आउल	उल्लू
Woodpecker	वुडपेकर	कठफोड़वा
Pigeon	पिजन	कबुतर
Cockatoo	कोकाटू	काकतुआ
Crow	क्रो	कौवा
Raven	रैवेन	डोमकौवा
Cuckoo	ककू	कोयल
Nightingale	नाइटिंगेल	बुलबुल
Stanglin	स्टारलिंग	सारिका
Mynah	मैना	मैना
Eagle	ईगल	गरूड़
Lark	लार्क	लवा
Kite	काइट	चील
Skylark	स्काईलार्क	बाज
Vulture	वल्चर	गिद्ध
Sparrow	स्पैरो	गोरैया
Bat	बैट	चमगादड़
Thrush	थ्रश	सारिका
Falcon	फैल्कॉन	बाज
Bulbul	बुलबुल	बुलबुल
Partridge	पार्ट्रिज	तीतर
Magpie	मैजपी	नीलकंठ
Dove	डोव	पैन्डुक
Drake	ड्रोक	बत्तख
Duck	डक	बत्तख
Duckling	डकलिंग	बत्तख का बच्चा
Weaverbird	विवरवर्ड	बयाँ
Quail	क्वेल	बटेर
Hawk	हॉक	बाज, मुसैचा
Fowl	फॉल	मुर्ग
Cock	कॉक	मुर्गा
Hen	हेन	मुर्गी
Chicken	चिकेन	मुर्गी का बच्चा
Peacock	पीकॉक	मोर

Peahen	पीहेन	मोरनी
Ostrich	ऑस्ट्रिच	शुतुरमुर्ग
Crane	क्रेन	सारस
Parrot	पैरोट	तोता
Macaw	मकाव	हीरामन तोता
Swan	स्वान	हंस
Stork	स्टॉर्क	सारस, बगुला
Golden oriole	गोल्डेन ओरियोल	सुनहला पक्षी
Swift	स्विफ्ट	उड़नछू
Painter bird	पेन्टर बर्ड	चित्रकार पक्षी
Albatross	अल्बट्रॉस	अल्बाट्रॉस
Condor	कॉन्डर	कॉन्डर
Humming bird	हम्मिंग बर्ड	गाने वाला पक्षी
Kiwi	किवी	किवी
Hornbill	हॉर्नबिल	लम्बे चोंच वाला पक्षी
Goose	गूज	हंसिनी
Gander	गैंडर	हंस
Gosling	गॉस्लिंग	हंस का बच्चा
Flamingo	फ्लेमिंगो	फ्लेमिंगो
Turkey	टर्की	टर्की
Canary	कैनरी	कैनरी
Dragon	ड्रेगन	ड्रेगन
Toucan	टॉकन	मोटे चोंच वाला पक्षी
Kingfisher	किंगफिशर	टिटहरी
Penguin	पेन्गुइन	पेन्गुइन
Pelican	पेलिकन	पेलिकन
Hoopoe	हूपो	मथबन्हनी
Emu	इमू	इमू
Puffin	पफिन	पफिन
Robin	रॉबिन	रॉबिन
Gold finch	गोल्डफिंच	गोल्डफिंच
Wing	विंग	डैना
Feather	फिदर	पैख
Claw	क्ला	पंजर
Beak	बिक	चोंच
Bill	बिल	चोंच
Nest	नेस्ट	घोंसला

Appendix-13/परिशिष्ट–13

Animals/जानवर

Antelop	एन्टिलोप	बारहसिंगा
Ape	एप	लंगूर
Ass	आस	गदहा
Beast	बीस्ट	पशु
Bitch	बिच	कुतिया
Boar	बोअर	जंगली सूअर
Bear	बिअर	भालू
Buffallow	बुफैलो	भैंस
He-buffallow	ही–बुफैलो	भैंसा
Bull	बुल	साँड़
Bison	बायसन	जंगली बैल
Cat	कैट	बिल्ली
Cattle	कैटल	मवेशी
Kitten	किटन	बिल्ली का बच्चा
Claw	क्ला	पैजा
Chimpanzee	चिम्पैंजी	बनमानुष
Colt	कोल्ट	बछड़ा
Cow	काउ	गाय
Calf	काफ	बछड़ा
She calf	शी काफ	बछिया
Chipmon	चिप्मान	गिलहरी
Camel	कैमल	ऊँट
Deer	डिअर	हिरण, मृग
Dog	डॉग	कुत्ता
Bull-dog	बुलडॉग	मुँह काला कुत्ता
Ewe	इयू	भेड़ी
Elephant	एलिफैंट	हाथी
Filly	फिली	बछेड़ी
Fox	फॉक्स	लोमड़ी
Fawn	फॉन	हिरण का बच्चा
Foal	फोल	फोल

Giraffe	जिर्राफ	जिर्राफ
Guinea-pig	गिनी पिग	एक पूँछहीन वाला जानवर
Goat	गोट	बकरी
He-goat	ही–गोट	बकरा
She-goat	शी–गोट	बकरी
Hound	हाउंड	शिकारी कुत्ता
Hind	हिन्ड	बारहसिंगी
Heifer	हीफर	बछिया
Hyena	हायना	लकड़बग्घा
Horn	हॉर्न	सींग
Hare	हेअर	खरगोश
Hoop	हूप	खुर
Hog	हॉग	सुअर
Pig	पिग	सुअर
Swine	स्वाइन	सुअरी
Hanster	हैंस्टर	चूहा सा जानवर, हैंस्टर
Jackal	जैकाल	सियार
Jaguar	जगुआर	अमेरिकन चीता, जगुआर
Kid	किड	बकरी का बच्चा, बच्चा जानवर
Koala bear	कोयला बीअर	भालू जाति का छोटा भालू
Kangaroo	कंगारू	कंगारू
Lion	लायन	शेर
Lioness	लायनेस	शेरिनी
Leo	लियो	शेर का बच्चा
Lamb	लैम्ब	मेमना
Leopard	लेपर्ड	तेंदुआ
Moose	मुज	डालिदार सींगो वाला हिरण
Mole	मोल	छछुन्दर
Mouse	माउस	चूहा
Mice	माइस	चूहे
Musk deer	मस्क डिअर	कस्तूरी मृग
Mule	म्यूल	खच्चर
Mare	मेअर	घोड़ी
Monkey	मंकी	बन्दर
Mongoose	मोन्गुज	नेवला

Orangutan	ओरंगुटन	बनमानुष
Ox	ऑक्स	बैल
Oxen	ऑक्सेन	बैलों की जोड़ी
Oxyx	ऑक्सिक्स	आक्सिक्स
Otter	ओटर	जलमार्जर, ऊदबिलाव
Poreupone	पॉर्क्यूपाइन	साही
Paw	पॉ	पंजा
Panther	पैन्थर	चीता
Pony	पोनी	टट्टू
Puppy pup	पपी पप	पिल्ला, छोटा कुत्ता
Porporise	पोरपोआयज	सुईंस
Polar bear	पोलर बिअर	ध्रुवीय भालू
Panda	पंडा	पंडा, चीनी नाटा भालू
Pointer	पोआयन्टर	शिकारी कुत्ता
Piglet	पिगलेट	छोटा सुअर
Pigling	पिग्लिंग	सुअर का बच्चा
Rabbit	रैबिट	खरगोश
Reindeer	रेइन्डियर	मृग
Doe	डो	मृगी
Rhinoceros	रीनोसॉर्स	रीनो
Ram	रैम	भेंड़
Swine	स्वाइन	सुअरी
Spaniel	स्पैनियल	झबरा कुत्ता
Stag	स्टैग	बारहसिंगा
Sheep	शीप	भेंड़
Mammoth	मेमॉथ	ऐरावत हाथी
Billy-goat	बिल्ली गोट	बकरा
Tusker	टस्कर	बड़ा हाथी
Hedgehog	हेजहॉग	जंगली चूहा
Cub	कब	जंगली जानवर के बच्चे
Catling	कैअलिंग	बिल्ली का बच्चा
Gibbon	गिबॉन	बन्दर का प्रकार
Gorilla	गोरिल्ला	बनमानुष का प्रकार
Frog	फ्रॉग	मेढक
Tadpole	टैडपोल	मेढक का बच्चा

Appendix-14/परिशिष्ट – 14
Reptiles and Insects
सरीसृप एवं कीड़े

Raptiles	रेप्टाइल्स	सरीसृप, रेंगने वाले जानवर
Raptileen	रेप्टायलिन	सरीसृप सम्बन्धी
Saurian	सॉरियन	सॉरियन
Dragon	ड्रेगॉन	चीनी दैत्य
Dinosaur	डायनोसोर	डायनोसोर
Ichthyosaur	इचथायोसोर	इचथाओसोर
Snake	स्नेक	साँप
Cobra	कोबरा	नाग
Boa	बोआ	अजगर
Python	पायथन	अजगर
Serpent	सर्पेंट	साँप
Ophidian	ओफिडियन	सर्प सम्बन्धी
Eel	ईल	सर्प सी मछली
Viper	वाइपर	जहरी साँप
Crocodile	क्रोकोडायल	मगरमच्छ
Alligator	एलिगेटर	घड़ियाल
Turtle	टरटल	कछुआ
Newt	न्यूट	गोह
Tortoise	टोरट्वाएज	कछुआ
Terrapin	टेरापिन	कछुआ
Lizard	लिजार्ड	छिपकली
Chameleon	चेमेलियन	गिरगिट
Eft	इफ्ट	इफ्ट
Geeko	गेको	घरेलू छिपकली
Horned	हार्नेड	सिंगदार मेढक
Iguana	इगुआना	छिपकली का एक प्रकार
Gila monster	गिला मॉनस्टर	गिला मॉनस्टर
Slough	सल्फ	केंचुली
Insects	इन्सेक्ट्स	कीड़े
Bug	बग	खटमल

Centipede	सेन्टिपेड	गोजर
Earwig	इअरविग	कनगोजर
Millipede	मिलिपेड	गोजर
Nit	निट	लीख
Maggot	मेजॉट	कृमि
Maggoty	मेगॉटी	कीड़ों से भरा हुआ
Blight	ब्लाइट	पौधों का कीड़ा
Pest	पेस्ट	पौधे का कीड़ा
Vermin	वरमिन	अन्न का कीड़ा
Louse	लाउस	जूँ
Leech	लीच	जोंक
Flea	फ्ली	देहिक
Bedbug	बेड्बग	खटमल
Bee	बी	मधुमक्खी
Honeybee	हनी	बी मधुमक्खी
Queen bee	क्वीन बी	रानी मधुमक्खी
Drone	ड्रॉन	नर मधुमक्खी
Wasp	वास्प	बर्रे
Ant	एण्ट	चींटी
White ant	ह्वाइट एण्ट	दीमक
Teronite	टरमाइट	दीमक
Grass hopper	ग्रास हॉपर	टिड्डा, फतिंगा
Pismire	पिसमायर	पिसमायर
Spider	स्पाइडर	मकड़ा
Scorpion	स्कॉरपियन	बिच्छू
Fly	फ्लाई	मक्खी
Fire fly	फायर फ्लाइ	जुगनूँ
Mosquito	मॉस्क्विटो	मच्छर
Butterfly	बटरफ्लाइ	तितली
Moth	मॉथ	कपड़े का कीड़ा
Beetle	बीटल	गोबरैला
Weevil	विविल	पौधा खाने वाला झींगुर
Locust	लोकस्ट	टिड्डे
Cricket	क्रिकेट	झींगुर
Cockroach	कॉक्रोच	तिलचट्टा

Pupa	प्यूपा	तीसरी अवस्था का कीड़ा
Chrysalis	क्राइसेलिस	तितली, कीड़े की पहली अवस्था
Aurelia	एउरेलिया	सुनहरे रंग का कीड़ा
Nymph	निम्फ	मत्स्य कन्या
Larva	लार्वा	मच्छर का अण्डा
Grub	ग्रब	कीड़ा, कोआ
Oyster	वायस्टर	सीप
Bivalve	बाइवॉल्ब	द्विकोशिय
Clam	क्लैम	क्लैम
Mussel	मसेल	मसेल
Mollusk	मोलुस्क	मोलुस्क
Snail	स्नेल	घोंघा
Slug	स्लग	स्लग
Whelk	ह्वेल्क	ह्वेल्क
Univalve	यूनिवॉल्व	एककोषीय
Scallop	स्कैलॉप	स्कैलैप
Lobster	लोबस्टर	केंकड़ा
Shrimp	श्रृम्प	श्रृम्प
Crab	क्रेब	केकड़ा
Dolphin	डॉलफिन	डालफिन
Porporise	पॉरपोअएज	सुईंस
Seal	सील	सील मछली
Sea-lion	सीलायन	सागरीय शेर
Walrus	वालरस	दरियाई घोड़ा
Whale	ह्वेल	ह्वेल
Conch	कोंच	शंख
Worm	वर्म	बीमारी के कीड़े
Angleworm	एंगलवर्म	केंचुआ
Earthworm	अर्थवर्म	केंचुआ
Tapeworm	टेपवर्म	फीताकृमि
Leech	लीच	जोंक
Roundworm	राउन्डवर्म	राउन्डवर्म
Flatworm	फ्लैटवर्म	फ्लैटवर्म
Silkworm	सिल्क वर्म	रेशम का कीड़ा

Appendix-15/परिशिष्ट–15
Relations/सम्बन्ध और रिश्ते

Guest	गेस्ट	अतिथि, यजमान
Teacher	टीचर	अध्यापक, गुरु
Mother	मदर	माता
Tenant	टिनैंट	किरायेदार
Mistress	मिस्ट्रेस	उप-पत्नी
Preceptor	प्रिसैप्टर	गुरु
Customer	कस्टमर	ग्राहक
Uncle	अंकल	चाला
Aunt	ऑन्ट	चाची
Disciple	डिसाइपल	चेला
Land lord	लैंड लॉर्ड	जमींदार
Sister in law	सिस्टर-इन-लॉ	साली, जेठानी, देवरानी, ननद
Adopted daughter	ऐडॉप्टिड डॉटर	दत्तक कन्या
Adopted son	ऐडॉप्टिड सन	दत्तक पुत्र
Grand father	ग्रैण्ड फादर	दादा
Grand mother	ग्रैण्ड मदर	दादी
Son in law	सन इन लॉ	दामाद
Friend	फ्रैंड	दोस्त, मित्र
Maternal grand father	मैट्रनल ग्रैण्ड	फादर नाना
Maternal grand mother	मैट्रनल ग्रैण्ड मदर	नानी
Husband	हसबैंड	पति
Wife	वाइफ	पत्नी
Daughter in law	डॉटर इन ला	पतोहू, बहू
Father	फादर	पिता
Son	सन	बेटा
Daughter	डॉटर	बेटी
Lover	लवर	प्रेमी
Brother	ब्रदर	भाई
Sister	सिस्टर	बहन
Brother in law	ब्रदर इन लॉ	बहनोई
Nephew	नेफ्यू	भतीजा, भांजा

Niece	नीस	भतीजी, भांजी
Maternal uncle	मैटर्नल अंकल	मामा
Maternal aunt	मैटर्नल ऑन्ट	मामी
Client	क्लाइंट	मुवक्किल
Mother's sister	मदर्स सिस्टर	मौसी
Keep	कीप	रखैल
Patient	पेशेंट	रोगी
Heir	एयर	वारिस
Pupil	प्यूपिल	शिष्य
Own	ऑन	सगा
Father in law	फादर इन लॉ	ससुर
Mother in law	मदर इन लॉ	सास
Relative	रिलेटिव	सम्बन्धी
Step daughter	स्टेप-डॉटर	सौतेली कन्या
Step son	स्टेप सन	सौतेला पुत्र
Step father	स्टेप फादर	सौतेला पिता
Step sister	स्टेप सिस्टर	सौतेली बहन
Step brother	स्टेप ब्रदर	सौतेला भाई

Appendix-16/परिशिष्ट–16

Colours/रंग

White	ह्वाइट	सफेद
Milky white	मिल्की ह्वाइट	दुधिया सफेद
Sea green	सी ग्रीन	हल्का हरा
Parrot green	पैरॉट ग्रीन	गहरा हरा
Sky blue	स्काई ब्लू	हलका नीला
Navy blue	नेवी ब्लू	गहरा नीला
Royal blue	रॉयल ब्लू	मद्धिम नीला
Blue	ब्लू	नीला
Green	ग्रीन	हरा
Bottle green	बोट्ल ग्रीन	गहरा हरा
Yellow	येलो	पीला
Mustard	मस्टर्ड	पीला
Off white	ऑफ ह्वाइट	गाढ़ा सफेद
Silver white	सिल्वर ह्वाइट	चाँदी से धवल
Golden	गोल्डेन	सुनहरा
Orange	ऑरेंज	संतरा, नारंगी रंग
Black	ब्लैक	काला
Cream	क्रीम	गाढ़ा सफेद
Gray	ग्रे	भूरा
Grayish	ग्रेयिश	भूरा सा
Greenish	ग्रीनिश	हरा सा
Whitish	ह्वाइटिश	सफेद सा
Bluish	ब्लूयिश	नीला सा
Yellowish	येलोयिश	पीला सा
Blackish	ब्लैकिश	काला सा
Red	रेड	लाल
Reddish	रेडिश	लाल सा
Purple	परपल	बैंगनी
Violet	वायलेट	बैंगनी
Maroon	मारून	गाढ़ा नीला

Lemon	लेमन	हल्का पीला
Brick red	ब्रिक रेड	सूर्ख लाल
Scarlet	स्कार्लेट	गहरा गुलाबी
Pink	पिंक	गुलाबी
Brown	ब्राउन	भूरा
Dark brown	डार्क ब्राउन	गहरा भूरा
Light brown	लाइट ब्राउन	हल्का भूरा
Chocolate	चॉकलेट	कत्थई
Saffron	सेफ्रॉन	केसरिया
Pale	पेल	पीला
Mauve	मॉव	चमकीला गुलाबी
Natural	नेचुरल	प्राकृतिक
Artificial	आर्टिफिसल	बनावटी, कृत्रिम
Mixed	मिक्सड	मिश्रित
Matabi	मटाबी	मटमैला
Gold bulsh	गोल्डबल्श	सुनहरा पीला
Skin colour	स्कीन कलर	चमड़ी सा हल्का भूरा रंग
Coffee colour	कॉफी कलर	गहरा भूरा रंग
Snow white	स्नो ह्वाइट	बर्फ सा श्वेत
Baby pink	बेबी पिंक	हल्का गुलाबी
Crimson	क्रिमसन	गहरा लाल
Blood red	ब्लड रेड	रक्तिम
Paint	पेंट	उड़ा हुआ रंगा
Copper	कॉपर	ताँबे सा भूरा
Jet black	जेट ब्लैक	गहरा काला

Appendix-17/परिशिष्ट–17
Household Articles
घेरलू सामान

Almirah	अलमिरा	अल्मारी
Ash	एश	राख
Attache	एटैची	एटैची
Ash-tray	एशट्रे	राख झाड़ने का बर्तन
Bed	बेड	बिछावन
Bed-sheet	बेड सीट	चादर
Bucket	बकेट	बाल्टी
Brush	ब्रश	ब्रश
Bottle	बोटल	बोतल, शीशी
Broom	ब्रूम	झाड़ू
Bolster	बोल्स्टर	मसनद, तकिया
Box	बॉक्स	बक्शा
Bowl	बॉउल	कटोरा
Balance	बैलेंस	तराजू
Basket	बास्केट	टोकरी
Blanket	ब्लैंकेट	कम्बल
Bundle	बंडल	गट्ठर
Bale	बेल	गाँठ, गट्ठर
Button	बटन	बटन
Cover	कवर	खोल
Cot	कॉट	चारपाई
Chair	चेअर	कुर्सी
Comb	कम्ब	कंघी
Canister	कैनिस्टर	कनस्तर
Cauldron	कॉलड्रॉन	कड़ाही
Cylander	सिलेंडर	सिलेंडर
Cinder	सिंडर	अंगार, राख
Casket	कास्केट	शृंगारदान
Candle	कैंडल	मोमबत्ती
Calender	कैलेंडर	पंचांग, तिथि-पत्र
Cup	कप	कप
Chandelier	शैनडिलियर	झाड़-फानूस

Container	कन्टेनर	बर्तन
Dish	डिश	थाली
Door-mat	डोर-मैट	पाँवदान
Electric lamp	इलेक्ट्रिक लैम्प	बिजली का दीप
Earthen lamp	अर्थेन लैम्प	दीया
Earthen pot	अर्थेन पॉट	मिट्टी का बर्तन
Earthen vessel	अर्थेन वेसल	मिट्टी का बड़ा बर्तन
Electric stove	इलेक्ट्रिक स्टोव	बिजली का चूल्हा
Flagon	फ्लगन	सुराही
Flower vase	फ्लावर वेस	फूलदान
Flower pot	फ्लावर पॉट	गमला
Funnel	फनेल	कीप
Fork	फॉर्क	काँटा
Fuel	फुएल	जलावन
Grate	ग्रेट	चूल्हे आदि की जाली
Hearth	हर्थ	अंगीठी, बड़ा चूल्हा
Harp	हार्प	बाजा
Hardware	हार्थवेअर	लोहे के सामान
Hubble-bubble	डबल-बबल	हुक्का
Ice	आइस	बर्फ
Ice-cream	आइस क्रीम	क्रीमयुक्त बर्फ
Ice-tray	आइस ट्रे	बर्फ का ट्रे
Ice-pot	आइस पॉट	बर्फ का बर्तन
Ice-box	आइस बॉक्स	बर्फ की पेटी
Ice-cube	आइस क्यूब	चौकोर बर्फ
Iron	आयरन	इस्त्री, प्रेस
Jar	जार	मर्तबान, गगरा, बड़ा बर्तन
Knit yarn	निट यार्न	बुनाई का धागा
Knitting needle	निटिंग नीड्ल	सलाई
Key	की	चाभी
Lamp	लैम्प	बत्ती
Lantern	लैन्टर्न	लालटेन
Lock	लॉक	ताला
Ladle	लैड्ल	करछुल
Mace	मैस	मुगदर
Mirror	मिरर	ऐनक
Mirror stand	मिरर स्टैंड	ऐनक रखने का उपकरण

Mat	मैट	चटाई
Match	मैच	माचिस
Match box	मैच बॉक्स	माचिस की डिबिया
Match stick	मैच स्टिक	माचिस की तीली
Mortar	मोरटार	खरल
Mosquito net	मॉस्क्विटो नेट	मच्छरदानी
Mosquito spray	मॉस्क्विटो स्प्रे	मच्छरमार छिड़काव
Mosquito coil	मॉस्क्विटो क्वायल	मच्छर अगरबत्ती
Needle	नीड्ल	सूई
Needle box	नीड्ल बाक्स	सूई की पेटी
Nut cracker	नट क्रेकर	सरौता
Nail-cutter	नेल कटर	नाखून काटने वाला
Nail sharpner	नेल शार्पेनर	नाखून चिकना करने वाला
Nail file	नेल फाइल	नाखून की रेती
Nail paint	नेल पैंट	नाखून का रंग
Oil	ऑयल	तेल
Oven	ओवेन	चूल्हा, तन्दूर
Pincers	पिंसर्स	चिमटा
Pencil	पेन्सिल	पेन्सिल
Pen	पेन	कलम
Pencil cutter	पेन्सिल कटर	पेन्सिल छिलने वाला
Perambulator	पेरैम्बुलेटर	शिशु-गाड़ी
Plate	प्लेट	थाली
Powder	पावडर	पावडर
Palanquin	पैलेंक्विन	पलंग, पालकी
Pestle	पेसल	मूसल
Pastry-board	पेस्ट्री-बोर्ड	चकला
Pillow	पिलो	तकिया
Pillow cover	पिलो कवर	तकिया का खोल
Rolling pin	रॉलिंग पिन	बेलन
Rope	रोप	रस्सी
Rack	रैक	सामान रखने के लिए फर्निचर
Spittoon	स्पिटून	पीकदान
Safe	सेफ	तिजोरी
Sack	सैक	बोरा
String	स्ट्रिंग	रस्सी
Soap	सोप	साबुन

Soap case	सोप केस	साबुनदानी
Soap cake	सोप केक	साबुन की टिकिया
Sieve	सीव	चलनी
Spoon	स्पून	चम्मच
Spoon stand	स्पून स्टैंड	चम्मच धारक
Stove	स्टोव	चूल्हा (लोहे या पीतल का)
Stick	स्टिक	छड़ी
Swing	स्विंग	झूला
Saucer	सॉसर	तश्तरी, छोटा प्लेट
Sundry	सनड्राइ	फुटकर वस्तुएँ
Sprayer	स्प्रेअर	छिड़कने वाला
Tooth paste	टूथपेस्ट	दाँतों का मंजन
Tooth powder	टूथपाउडर	दंतपाउडर
Tooth prick	टूथपिक	दाँत खोदनी
Table	टेबल	मेज
Tablet	टेबलेट	टिकिया
Table cloth	टेबल क्लाथ	मेज पोश
Table spoon	टेबल स्पून	बड़ा चम्मच
Table mat	टेबल मैट	भोजन वस्त्र
Thread	थ्रेड	कपड़ा, धागा
Tap	टैप	नल
Tray	ट्रे	सामान ढोने का बड़ा बर्तन
Thimble	थिम्बल	अंगुश्ताना
Tong	टांग	चिमटा
Taper	टैपर	छोटी मोमबत्ती
Tapestry	टैपेस्ट्री	खोल
Tassel	टैसल	रेशमी गुच्छा, फुंदना
Tankard	टैंकार्ड	चषक, जल ढोने का बड़ा बर्तन
Umbrella	अम्ब्रेला	छाता
Utensils	यूटेन्सिल्स	बर्तन
Vase	वेस	बर्तन
Wardrobe	वार्डरोब	वस्त्रधारक
Wire	वायर	तार
Wick	विक	बत्ती, बतिहर
Wool	वुल	ऊन

Appendix-18/परिशिष्ट–18
Jewels/गहने और आभूषण

Chain	चेन	कड़ी, कड़ीदार हार
Coral	कोरल	मूँगा
Cat's eye	कैट्स आई	लहसूनिया पत्थर
Crown	क्रॉन	मुकुट
Clip	क्लिप	चिमटा जैसा पकड़ने वाला
Hair clip	हेअर क्लिप	बालों का क्लिप
Pin	पिन	नुकीला पहनने का गहना
Nose pin	नोज पिन	लवंग, नाक गहना
Ear pin	इअर पिन	कान का लवंग जैसा गहना
Ring	रिंग	अँगूठी, छल्ला
Ear ring	इअर रिंग	कान का गोल गहना
Nose ring	नोज रिंग	नथिया
Toe ring	टो रिंग	पाँव की अँगुलियों का छल्ला
Sari pin	साड़ी पिन	साड़ी का काँटा
Sari clip	साड़ी क्लिप	साड़ी को पकड़ने वाला गहना
Broach	ब्रूच	साड़ी का काँटा
Tops	टॉप्स	कर्णफूल, कान का फूलदार गहना
Bangle	बैंगल	चूड़ी
Jewellery	ज्वेलरी	आभूषण, जवाहिरात
Head locket	हेड लॉकेट	माँग टीका
Ear stud	इअर स्टड	कान का तल्ला
Nose stud	नोज स्टड	नाक का तल्ला
Bracelet	ब्रैसलेट	कंगन, कड़ा
Wristlet	रिस्टलेट	तोड़ा, पहुँची
Belt	बेल्ट	कमरबन्द
Anklet	एंकलेट	पायजेब
Armlet	आर्मलेट	बाजूबंद
Neckless	नेकलेस	गले का हार
Garland	गारलैंड	माला
Tiara	टिआरा	माँग टीका, मुकुट

Diamond	डायमण्ड	हीरा
Mother of pearl	मदर ऑफ पर्ल	सीप
Pearl	पर्ल	मोती
Ruby	रूबी	माणिक
Quartz	क्वार्टज	बिल्लौर
Torquois	टरकॉयज	फीरोजा
Opal	ओपल	दूधिया पत्थर
Zircon	जिरकॉन	गोमेद
Gold	गोल्ड	सोना
Silver	सिल्वर	चाँदी
Bronze	ब्राँज	ताँबा
Sapphire	सेफायर	नीलम
Emerald	इमरॉल्ड	पन्ना
Topaz	टोपाज	पुखराज

Appendix-19/परिशिष्ट–19
Musical Instruments
वाद्य-यंत्र

Veena	वीणा	वीणा
Sitar	सितार	सितार
Sarod	सरोद	सरोद
Ektara	एकतारा	एकतारा
Mridang	मृदंग	मृदंग
Corch	कोंच	शंख
Tabor	टेबर	तबला
Tomtom	टॉमटॉम	ढोलक
Drum	ड्रम	ढोल, नगाड़ा
Clorionet	क्लेरियोनेट	शहनाई
Guitar	गिटार	गिटार
Harp	हार्प	चंग, सारंगी
Symbol	सिम्बल	करताल, छैना
Tambourine	टैम्बरीन	डफ, डफली
Bugle	बगल	बिगुल, सिंघा, तुरही
Jew's harp	जिउज हार्प	मुरचंग
Flute	फ्लूट	बाँसुरी
Piano	पियानो	पियानो
Violin	वायलिन	वायलिन
Bagpipe	बैगपाइप	मशक
Bell	बेल	घंटी
Dumet	डमेट	डुगडुगी
String instrument	स्ट्रिंग इन्स्ट्रूमेंट	तारवाद्य
Brass	ब्रास	ताम्बे के वायुवाद्य
Woodwind instrument	वुडविंड इन्स्ट्रूमेंट	लकड़ी के वायु वाद्य
Jazz instrument	जाज इन्स्ट्रूमेंट	जाज के सेट
Percussion	परक्यूशन	पीटकर बजाने वाले वाद्य
Bango	बैंगो	बैंगो
Congo	कौंगो	कौंगो
Timpani	टिम्पानी	टिम्पानी

Bass drum	बास ड्रम	बड़ा ढोल
Drum stick	ड्रम स्टिक	ढोल बजाने का डंडा
Keyboard	की बोर्ड	पटरी युक्त बोर्ड
Reed	रीड	पटरी
Saxophone	सेक्सोफोन	एक मोटी आवाज का पीतल का बाजा
Acoustic guitar	एकॉस्टिक गिटार	गिटार का एक प्रकार
Electric guitar	इलेक्ट्रिक गिटार	गिटार का एक प्रकार
Drum kit	ड्रम किट	ढोलों का समूह
Triangle	ट्रिंगल	तिकोना बाजा
Bassoon	बैसुन	बैसुन
Piccolo	पिकोलो	पिकोलो
Tuba	ट्यूबा	ट्यूबा
French horn	फ्रेंच हॉर्न	फ्रेंच हॉर्न
Trombone	ट्रॉम्बॉन	ट्राम्बॉन
Trumpet	ट्रम्पेट	तुरही
Viola	वायला	बेला या वायलिन का एक प्रकार
Xylophone	जाइलोफोन	जाइलोफोन
Banjo	बेंजो	बेंजो
Harmonica	हारमोनिका	माउथ आरगन
Mouth organ	माउथ ऑरगन	मुँह से बजाने का बाजा
Harmonium	हारमोनियम	हारमोनियम
Whistle	ह्विसल	सीटी
Bell	बेल	घंटी

Appendix-20/परिशिष्ट–20

Classified Vocabulury (वर्गीकृत शब्दावली)

Parts of Body

शरीर के अंग

Ring finger	रिंग फिंगर	अनामिका
Toe	टो	अँगुली पैर की
Finger	फिंगर	अँगुली हाथ की
Thumb	थम	अँगूठा
Eye	आई	आँख
Intestine	इन्टेस्टाइन	आँत, अंतड़ी
Cartilage	कार्टिलिज	उपास्थि
Lip	लिप	ओंठ
Heel	हील	एड़ी
Shoulder	शोल्डर	कंधा
Temple	टैम्पल	कनपटी
Waist	वेस्ट	कमर
Eardrum	ईयरड्रम	कर्णपटल
Wrist	रिस्ट	कलाई
Ear	ईयर	कान
Little finger	लिटिल फिंगर	छोटी अँगुली
Armpit	आर्मपिट	काँख, बगल
Elbow	एल्बो	कोहनी
Skull	स्कल	खोपड़ी
Neck	नैक	गर्दन, ग्रीवा
Womb	वूम	गर्भाशय
Uterus	यूटेरस	गर्भाशय
Whiskers	व्हिस्कर्स	गालमुच्छ
Throat	थ्रोट	गला
Cheeks	चीक्स	गाल
Anus	ऐनस	गुदा
Kidney	किडनी	गुर्दा, वृक्क
Lap	लैप	गोद

Knee	नी	घुटना
Skin	स्किन	चमड़ा
Nipple	निप्पल	चूचुक
Rump	रम्प	चूतड़
Face	फेस	चेहरा
Chest	चैस्ट	छाती पुरुष की
Breast	ब्रैस्ट	छाती स्त्री की
Stomach	स्टोमक	आमाशय
Jaw	जॉ	जबड़ा
Thigh	थाइ	जाँघ
Liver	लिवर	जिगर
Tongue	टंग	जीभ
Bun	बन	जूड़ा बालो का
Ankle	ऐंकल	टखना
Joint	जाएंट	जोड़
Chin	चिन	ठुड्डी
Index finger	इंडैक्स फिंगर	तर्जनी
Sole	सोल	तलवा
Palate	पैलेट	तालू
Snout	स्नाउट	थूथन
Molar teeth	मोलर टीथ	चबाने वाला दाँत
Beard	बिअर्ड	दाढ़ी
Tooth	टूथ	दाँत
Brain	ब्रेन	दिमाग
Artery	आर्टरी	धमनी
Nail	नेल	नाखून
Nostril	नॉस्ट्रिल	नथुना
Vein	वेन	नस
Nose	नोज	नाक
Pulse	पल्स	नाड़ी
Navel	नेवल	नाभि
Gullet	गलेट	निगल नली
Eyelid	आइलिड	पलक
Rib	रिब	पसली
Spleen	स्प्लिन	प्लीहा

Calf	काफ	पिंडली
Bile	बाइल	पित्ति
Back	बैक	पीठ
Belly	बैली	पेट बाहरी
Abdomen	ऐब्डोमेन	पेट
Eyeball	आइबॉल	पुतली आँख की
Muscle	मस्ल	मांसपेशी
Foot	फुट	पैर
Lung	लंग	फेफड़ा
Armpit	आर्मपिट	बगल
Eyelash	आइलैश	बरौनी
Hair	हेयर	बाल, रोंवा
Arm	आर्म	बाँह
Vagina	वजिना	भग, योनि
Glans clitoris	गलैन्स क्लिटोरिस	भगनास
Embryo	एम्ब्रयो	भ्रूण
Eyebrow	आइब्रो	भौंह, भृकुटि
Middle finger	मिड्ल फिंगर	मध्यमिक
Gum	गम	मसूड़ा
Brain	ब्रेन	मस्तिष्क
Fist	फिस्ट	मुट्ठी
Mouth	माउथ	मुख
Urinary bladder	यूरिनरी ब्लेडर	मूत्राशय
Moustache	मास्टेच	मूँछ
Nerve	नर्व	रग
Pore	पोर	रोमकूप
Forehead	फोरहेड	ललाट
Saliva	सेलिवा	लार
Penis	पेनिस	लिंग
Blood	ब्लड	लहू, रक्त, खून
Trunk	ट्रंक	मध्य धड़
Bone	बोन	हड्डी
Palm	पाम	हथेली
Collar bone	कालर बोन	हसुली की हड्डी
Heart	हॉर्ट	हृदय

Ailments & Body Conditions
रोग और शारीरिक दशाएँ

Pericardium	पेरीकार्डियम	हृदयावरण
Acidity	एसिडिटी	अम्ल पित्त, गैस
Diarrhoea	डायरिया	अतिसार
Hernia	हर्निया	आँत उतरना
Tears	टिअर्स	आँसू
Eczema	एग्जिमा	उकवत
Yawn	यॉन	उबासी
Stature	स्टैचर	कद
Vomit	वौमिट	कै करना
Indigestion	इंडाइजैशन	बदहजमी
Blind	ब्लाइंड	अन्धा
Jaundice	जॉन्डिस	कामला, पीलिया
Typhus	टाइफस	काला ज्वर
Bronchitis	ब्रॉनकाइटिस	कास
One eyed	वन आइड	काना
Hunchback	हन्चबैक	कुबड़ा
Leprosy	लेप्रोसी	कोढ़, कुष्ठ
Constipation	कांस्टिपेशन	कब्ज
Worm	वर्म	कृमि
Measles	मीजल्स	खसरा
Scabies	स्कैबीज	खाज
Cough	कफ	खाँसी
Itch	इच	खुजली
Anaemia	एनेमिया	खून की कमी
Bleeding	ब्लीडिंग	खून का बहना
Rheumatism	रूमेटिज्म	रूठिया
Abortion	एबॉर्शन	गर्भपात
Syphilis	सिफलिस	गरमी
Sore throat	सोर थ्रोट	गलदाह
Hoarseness	होर्सनैस	गला बैठना
Tonsil	टॉन्सिल	गलसुआ

Tumour	ट्यूमर	गाँठ
Gland	ग्लैंड	गिल्टी
Dumb	डम	गूँगा
Bald	बॉल्ड	गंजा
Wound	वून्ड	घाव
Giddiness	गिडीनैस	चक्कर आने की स्थिति
Obesity	ओबेसिटी	चर्बी बढ़ना
Hurt	हर्ट	चोट
Sneezing	स्नीजिंग	छींकना
Cancer	कैंसर	जहरबाद
Dropsy	ड्राप्सी	जलोदर
Coryza	कोरिजा	जुकाम
Ague	ऐग्यू	शीतज्वर
Yawning	यॉनिंग	जंभाई
Fever	फीवर	ज्वर, बुखार
Chill	चिल	ठंड
Belching	वैल्चिंग	डकार
Health	हैल्थ	तन्दरुस्ती
Spittle	स्पिटल	थूक
Asthma	एस्थमा	दमा
Pain	पेन	दर्द
Headache	हैडेक	दर्द सिर का
Stomachache	स्टमकएक	दर्द पेट का
Loose stool	लूज स्टूल	दस्त
Motion	मोशन	दस्त
Ring worm	रिंगवर्म	दाद
Lean	लीन	दुबला
Psychosis	साइकोसिस	दुस्साध्य उन्माद
Long- sightedness	लांग साइटिडनैस	दूरदृष्टि
Bronchitis	ब्रानकाइटिस	श्वासनली शोथ
Epistaxis	एपिसटैक्सिस	नकसीर
Sprain	स्प्रेन	मोच
Narcolepsy	नार्कोलैप्सी	निद्रा रोग
Sleep	स्लीप	नींद
Insomnia	इन्सोम्निया	नींद न आना

Stone	स्टोन	पथरी
Sweat	स्वैट	पसीना
Mad	मैड	पागल
Lunacy	ल्यूनेसी	पागलपन, उन्माद
Pus	पस	पीव
Dysentery	डाइसेंट्री	पेचिश
Leucorrhoea	लिकोरिया	प्रदर
Thirst	थर्स्ट	प्यास
Plague	प्लेग	प्लेग, महामारी
Pimple	पिम्पल	फुंसी, मुहांसा
Boil	बॉयल	फोड़ा
Phlegm	फ्लेग	बलगम, कफ
Piles	पाइल्स	बवासीर
Diabetes	डायबिटीज	मधुमेह
Sore	सोर	वृण
Dwarff	डवार्फ	बौना
Fistula	फिस्टुला	भगन्दर
Lack of appetite	लैक ऑप एपिटाइट	मन्दाग्नि
Griping	ग्राइपिंग	मरोड़
Wart	वॉर्ट	मस्सा
Epilepsy	एपिलैप्सी	मिरगी
Acne	एक्नि	मुंहासे का रोग
Urine	यूरिन	मूत्र
Cataract	कैटेरेक्ट	मोतियाबिन्द
Typhoid	टायफायड	मोतीझरा
Hepatitis	हेपाटिटिस	यकृत शोध
Sun stroke	सनस्ट्रोक	लू लगना
Stool	स्टूल	विष्टा
Tuberculosis	ट्यूबर कुलोसिस	राजयक्ष्मा
Disease	डिजीज	रोग
Lame	लेम	लंगड़ा
Dengue	डेंगू	लंगड़ा बुखार
Influenza	इन्फ्लुएन्जा	शीतज्वर
Small pox	स्माल पॉक्स	शीतला
Leucoderma	ल्यूकोडेर्मा	श्वेत कुष्ठ

Breath	ब्रेथ	साँस
Swelling	स्वैलिंग	सूजन
Albino	एल्बिनो	सूरजमुखी
Gonorrhoea	गोनोरिया	सूजाक
Hiccup	हिक्कप	हिचकी
Cholera	कॉलरा	हैजा
Pericarditis	पैरिकार्डिटिस	हृदय झिल्ली शोध
Consumption	कनसम्पशन	क्षय
Anorexia	ऐनोरेक्सिया	अरुचि

Dress
वेशभूषा

Lining	लाइनिंग	अस्तर
Sleeve	स्लीव	आस्तीन
Bodice	बॉडिस	चोली, अंगिया
Hat	हैट	अंग्रेजी टोपी
Wool	वूल	ऊन
Cloth	क्लॉथ	कपड़ा
Belt	बैल्ट	कमरबन्द
Shirt	शर्ट	कमीज
Shirting	शर्टिंग	कमीज का कपड़ा
Blanket	ब्लैंकेट	कम्बल
Cap	कैप	टोपी
Cashmere	कैश्मीर	कश्मीरा
Diaper brocade	डिआपर ब्रोकेड	कामदानी
Border	बॉर्डर	किनारा
Canvas	कैनवास	किरमिच
Coat	कोट	कोट
Suit	सूट	कोट-पतलून
Mattress	मैट्रेस	गद्दा
Suspenders	सस्पैंडर्स	गैलिस
Muffler	मफलर	गुलूबन्द
Skirt	स्कर्ट	घाघरा

Veil	वेल	घूँघट
Sheet	शीट	चादर
Chints	चिंट्स	छींट
Socks	सॉक्स	छोटा मोजा
Damask	डैमस्क	रेशमी वस्त्र
Gauze	गॉज	जाली
Underwear	अंडरवियर	जांघिया
Drill	ड्रिल	जीन
Pocket	पॉकेट	जेब
Trimming	ट्रिमिंग	झालर
Cap	कैप	टोपी
Scarf	स्कार्फ	दुपट्टा
Laces	लेसिस	तसमे
Thread	थ्रैड	तागा
Towel	टॉवेल	तौलिया
Gloves	ग्लव्स	दस्ताने
Shawl	शॉल	दुशाला
Lace	लेस	पट्टा
Trousers	ट्राउजर्स	पतलून
Pyjama	पाजामा	पाजामा
Jacket	जैकेट	फतुही
Flannel	फ्लैनेल	फलालीन
Tape	टेप	फीता
Button	बटन	बटन
Overcoat	ओवरकोट	बड़ा कोट
Velvet	वेल्वेट	मखमल
Border	बॉर्डर	मगजी
Linen	लिनेन	मलमल
Stockings	स्टॉकिंस	मोजे
Oil-cloth	आइल क्लॉथ	मोमजामा
Quilt	क्विल्ट	रजाई
Darning	डार्निंग	रफू
Cotton	कॉटन	रूई
Handker chief	हैंडकर-चीफ	रूमाल
Silk	सिल्क	रेशम

Gown	गाउन	चोगा
Long cloth	लांग क्लाथ	लट्ठा
Long skirt	लांग स्कर्ट	लहंगा
Uniform	यूनिफार्म	वर्दी
Satin	सैटेन	साटन
Turban	टर्बन	साफा
Yarn	यार्न	सूत
Bright colour	ब्राइट कलर	चटख रंग
Light colour	लाइट कलर	हल्का रंग

Appendix-21/परिशिष्ट–21
Antonyms/विपरीतार्थक शब्द

Above	ऊपर	**Below**	नीचे
Aceept	स्वीकारना	**Deny**	नकारना
Acquire	कमाना	**Lose**	गंवाना
Ancient	प्राचीन	**Modern**	नवीन
Agree	सहमत होना	**Differ**	असहमति होना
Alive	जीवित	**Dead**	मृत
Admire	प्रशंसा	**Despise**	निन्दा
Big	बड़ा	**Small**	छोटा
Blunt	कुंद	**Sharp**	तेज
Bold	साहसी	**Timid**	कायर
Bright	चमकीला	**Dim**	धुंधला
Broad	चौड़ा	**Narrow**	पतला
Civilised	सभ्य	**Savage**	असभ्य
Care	देखभाल	**Neglect**	लापरवाही
Clean	साफ	**Dirty**	गंदा
Confess	स्वीकारना	**Deny**	इनकार करना
Cool	ठंडा	**Warm**	गर्म
Cruel	क्रूर	**Kind**	दयालु
Domestic	पालतू	**Wild**	जंगली
Difficult	कठिन	**Easy**	आसान
Danger	खतरा	**Safety**	सुरक्षा
Dark	अंधेरा	**Bright**	उजाला
Death	मृत्यु	**Birth**	जन्म
Debit	उधार	**Credit**	जमा
Early	जल्दी	**Late**	बिलम्ब
Earn	कमाना	**Spend**	खर्च करना
Empty	खाली	**Full**	भरा हुआ
Enjoy	मौज मनाना	**Suffer**	तकलीफ रहना
Freedom	स्वतंत्रता	**Slavery**	गुलामी
Fierce	निर्दय	**Gentle**	नम्र
False	झूठ	**True**	सच
Fine	महीन	**Coarse**	मोटा
Foolish	मूर्ख	**Wise**	बुद्धिमान

Fresh	ताजा	**Stale**	बासी
Fear	भय	**Courage**	साहस
Guilty	दोषी	**Innocent**	निर्दोष
Gain	लाभ	**Loss**	हानि
Good	अच्छा	**Bad**	बुरा
Handsome	सुन्दर	**Ugly**	कुरूप
High	ऊँचा	**Low**	नीचा
Humble	विनम्र	**Proud**	घमंडी
Honour	सम्मान	**Dishonour**	अपमान
Joy	हर्ष	**Sorrow**	विषाद
Knowledge	ज्ञान	**Ignorance**	अज्ञान
Lie	झूठ	**Truth**	सच
Little	थोड़ा	**Much**	ज्यादा
Masculine	पुल्लिंग	**Feminine**	स्त्रीलिंग
Make	बनाना	**Break**	तोड़ना
Natural	प्राकृतिक	**Artificial**	कृत्रिम
Noise	शोर	**Silence**	मौन
Oral	मौखिक	**Written**	लिखित
Permanent	स्थायी	**Temporary**	अस्थायी
Presence	उपस्थिति	**Absence**	अनुपस्थिति
Profit	लाभ	**Loss**	हानि
Prose	गद्य	**Poetry**	काव्य
Quick	तेज	**Slow**	धीमा
Receive	पाना	**Give**	देना
Reject	अस्वीकार	**Accept**	स्वीकार
Ripe	पका	**Raw**	कच्चा
Rough	खुरदुरा	**Smooth**	चिकना
Remember	याद करना	**Forgot**	भूल जाना
Rich	धनी	**Poor**	गरीब
Superior	बढ़िया	**Interior**	घटिया
Thick	मोटा	**Thin**	दुबला
Tragedy	दु:खान्त	**Comedy**	सुखान्त
Universal	सर्वजनीय	**Particular**	व्यक्तिगत
Victory	विजय	**Defeat**	हार
Weak	कमजोर	**Strong**	मजबूत
Wisdom	बुद्धिमान	**Folly**	मूर्खता
Youth	युवा	**Aged**	अधेड़

Appendix-22/परिशिष्ट–22
Synonyms /समानार्थक शब्द

Aid	सहायता	Assistance, help, relief, support
Apology	क्षमायाचना	Pardon, excuse, regret, amends
Adversity	मुसीबत	Misery, calamity, misfortune
Ability	योग्यता	Capacity, capability, skill, talent
Anger	क्रोध	Fury, rage, wrath
Answer	उत्तर	Reply, response, respond
Attack	आक्रमण	Onslaught, assault, aggression, invasion
Actual	वास्तविक	Current, real, effectual
Bane	शाप	Curse, scourge, mischief, harm
Barbarous	असभ्य	Cruel, uncivilized, savage, illiterate
Bear	सहन करना	Tolerate, endure
Belief	आस्था	Confidence, faith, trust, credence
Beautiful	सुन्दर	Gratifying, delighting, lovely, charming
Brave	साहसी	Fearless, courageous, bold, valiant
Busy	व्यस्त	Engaged, occupied, preoccupied, employed
Capture	पकड़ना	Arrest, apprehend, seize, nab
Clever	चालाक	Ingenious, skilful
Confess	दोष स्वीकारना	Avow, acknowledge, own, admit
Coquer	जीतना	Vanquish, overcome, win, triumph
Crown	ताज	Skull, dignity, tiara
Convict	अपराधी	Prisoner, criminal, captive
Command	आदेश	Control, order, restrain
Cunning	धूर्त	Strewed, witty, sly, crafty
Decide	निर्णय लेना	Determine, settle, fix, finalize
Decent	शानदार	Proper, modest, tolerable
Defeat	पराजय	Frustrate, foil, reject
Delightful	आनन्ददायक	Enjoyable, pleasing, charming, alluring
Desolate	निर्जन	Lonely, forlorn, barren, solitary
Despise	घृणा करना	Disdain, dislike, hate, scorn
Destroy	नष्ट करना	Demolish, devastate, ruin, ravage
Devotee	भक्त	Worshipper, votary, disciple

Disaster	बरबादी	Misfortune, calamity, tragedy
Discover	अन्वेषण	Find, reveal, disclose, discern
Dispute	विवाद	Controversy, argument, quarrel
Distribute	वितरण	Scatter, divide, classify
Divine	स्वर्गिक	Celestial, godlike, holy
Doubt	सन्देह	Hesitate, suspense, uncertainly
Dull	मूर्ख	Blunt, stupid, boring
Earnest	गम्भीर	Solemn, serious, determined
Effert	प्रयत्न	Endeavour, attempt, venture, trial
Enemy	शत्रु	Adversary, opponent, foe, antagonist
Enoronous	विशाल	Huge, tremendous, stupendous
Enthusiasm	उत्साह	Force, spirit, zest, fervour
Eternal	अनन्त	Immortal, everlasting, endless
Fade	धुंधला	Vanish, dim, pale, languish
Fatal	घातक	Deadly , lethal, fateful, mortal
Fierce	भयंकर	Savage, ferocious, aggressive
Forbod	प्रतिबंधित	Ban, prohibit, check
Fury	रोष	Rage, excitement, anger
Gloom	निराशा	Dejection, shadow, darkness
Glory	कीर्ति	Fame, pride, splendor
Grief	दुःख	Sorrow, distress, tribulation
Hard	कठिन	Rough, difficult, solid, firm
Haven	शरण	Refuge, protection, settler
Holy	पवित्र	Godly, pious, blessed, saintly
Hope	आशा	Desire, anticipation, expectation
Horror	भय	Terror, dread, disgust
Humble	विनम्र	Modest, meek, submissive
Ideal	आदर्श	Model, example, perfect, paragon
Idle	आलसी	Unemployed, inactive, futile, useless
Immortal	अमर	Divine, everlasting, eternal
Industrious	परिश्रमी	Hardworking, assiduous, diligent
Infinite	अनन्त	Limitless, boundless, endless, timeless
Jealous	ईर्ष्यालु	Envious, suspicious
Kill	मारना	Assassinate, murder, behead
Lack	कमी	Shortage, deficiency, need, want

Lazy	आलसी	Indolent, sluggish, slothful
Lusture	चमक	Shining, brilliance, brightness
Marvel	आश्चर्य	Surprise, wonder, miracle
Mourn	शोक	Bewail, aggrieve, lament, bemoan
Naughty	शरारती	Mischievous, troublesome, disobedient
Obstacle	बाधा	Barrier, hindrance, obstruction
Obvious	स्पष्ट	Plain, manifest, evident, clear
Outlaw	अपराधी	Criminal, bandit, fugitive
Outstanding	विशिष्ट	Eminent, prominent, exceptional
Overcome	विजय	Conquer, overthrow, surmount
Pain	दुःख	Suffering, misery, distress
Peak	चोटी	Apex, top, summit, pinnacle
Pledge	प्रतिज्ञा	Security, promise, vow, oath
Pray	प्रार्थना	Beg, request, revere
Precious	मूल्यवान	Priceless, costly, invaluable, dear
Pressure	दबाव	Force, urgency, affection
Prevent	रोकना	Restrain, hinder, check, stop
Proficient	कुशल	Skilful, expert, adept
Prominent	प्रसिद्ध	Distinguished, notable, eminent
Protect	रक्षा करना	Guard, defend, save, shield
Quarrel	झगड़ा	Controversy, dispute, wrangle
Question	प्रश्न	Inquiry, interrogation, doubt
Regard	सम्मान	Respect, esteem, worship
Soothe	शान्ति देना	Console, comfort, assuage
Splendid	शानदार	Glorious, magnificent, gorgeous
State	बासी	Musty, tasteless, decayed, insipid
Struggle	संघर्ष	Try, endeavour, fight, strive
Understanding	समझ	Insight, perception, comprehension
Unique	विचित्र	Matchless, singular, unequalled
Vice	पाप	Wickedness, sin, degradation
Victory	विजय	Success, conquer, triumph, win
View	दृश्य	Sight, scene, display
Vigour	शक्ति	Energy, force, power
Wisdom	बुद्धिमान	Prudence, intelligence, foresight
Wretched	दुःखी	Unfortunate, miserable, deplorable

Appendix-23/परिशिष्ट–23
One word Substitute
अनेक शब्दों के बदले एक शब्द

Alien	विदेशी नागरिक	A citizen of another country
Ambassador	राजदूत	An official person sent to another country
Antidote	विषहर	A medicine to counter the effect of a disease
Antiseptic	घाव नियन्त्रक	A medicine which prevents decay
Antibiotic	जीवाणुनाशक	A medicine which destroys bacteria
Atheist	नास्तिक	A man who does not believe in God
Audience	श्रोता	A group of listeners
Bigot	कट्टरपंथी	A person who holds strongly to an opion
Biography	आत्मकथा	Life story of a person written by somebody else
Bankrupt	दीवालिया	A person who is incapable of paying his debts
Cosmetics	प्रसाधन	The things used to increase physical beauty
Credible	विश्वसनीय	That can be believed
Deaf	बहरा	One who is incapable of listening a sound
Democracy	प्रजातन्त्र	A government by the people
Drought	सूखा	Lack of rain
Edible	खाने योग्य	Fit to eat or consume
Eligible	योग्य	Fit to be chosen
Epidemic	महामारी	A disease which spreads over a large area
Export	निर्यात	Things sent to another country
Fatal	घातक	Which may cause death
Foreigner	विदेशी	A person of another country
Glutton	पेटू	An over eating person
Honorary	अवैतनिक	An office without pay or emolument
Ignorant	अनभिज्ञ	A person who lacks in knowledge
Illegal	अवैधानिक	Contrary to law

Invincible	अजेय	That which cannot be conquered
Inavdible	आश्रव्य	That which cannot be heared
Inedible	अखाद्य	A thing unfit for eating
Inflammable	प्रज्वलनशील	That which catches fire easily
Illigible	अपठनीय	Which cannot be read
Illiterate	अनपढ़	A person who can neither read not write
Indelible	अमिट	Which cannot be effaced
Invincible	अजेय	He who can not be defeated
Laboratory	प्रयोगशाला	A place where experiments are performed
Library	पुस्तकालय	A place where various books are kept
Optimist	आशावादी	One who looks at the bright side of things
Orphan	अनाथ	A child whose parents are dead
Patriot	देशभक्त	One who has great love for his country
Pedestrian	पदयात्री	One travels on foot
Pilgrim	तीर्थयात्री	One who goes on a journey to a holy place
Spokesman	प्रवक्ता	A person who speaks on behalf
Theist	आस्तिक	One who believes in God
Vegetarian	शाकाहारी	One who lives on vegetative food
Widow	विधवा	A woman whose husband is dead
Zoo	चिड़ियाघर	A place where animals are kept

Appendix-24/परिशिष्ट–24
Homophones Pairs of Words
श्रुतिसम भिन्नार्थक शब्द

Accede	सहमत होना	**Exceed**	अधिक होना
Accept	स्वीकार करना	**Except**	सिवाय
Adapt	समायोजित होना	**Adept**	प्रवीण
Affect	प्रभाव होना	**Effect**	प्रभाव
Alien	विदेशी	**Align**	सीध में रहना
All ready	सब तैयार	**Already**	पहले से ही
Altar	वेदी	**Alter**	बदलना
Amiable	मधुर	**Amicable**	मैत्रीपूर्ण
Artist	कलाकार	**Artiste**	पेशेवर कलाकार
Ascent	चढ़ाई	**Assent**	स्वीकृति
Berth	सीट	**Birth**	जन्म
Beside	निकट पास में	**Besides**	के अतिरिक्त
Bonne	अच्छा	**Bone**	अस्थि
Chase	पीछा करना	**Chess**	शतरंज
Chaste	पवित्र	**Chest**	छाती
Chord	वाद्ययन्त्र का तार	**Cord**	डोरी
Check	रोकना, जाँच करना	**Cheque**	धनादेश
Cite	उदाहरण देना	**Site**	स्थान
Coarse	मोटा, भद्दा	**Course**	पाठ्यक्रम
Complement	पूरक	**Compliment**	सम्मान, शुभकामनाएँ
Confidant	विश्वासपात्र	**Confident**	आश्वस्त
Corps	सेना की शाखा	**Corpse**	मानक शव
Deference	सम्मान	**Difference**	अन्तर
Deprecate	असहमति	**Depreciate**	कम करके आँकना
Decent	विनीत, शानदार	**Descent**	नीचे उतरना
Die	मरना	**Dye**	रंगना
Draught	हवा का झोंका	**Drought**	सूखा
Dual	दोहरा	**Duel**	द्वन्द्व युद्ध
Egoist	स्वार्थी	**Egotist**	अहंकारी
Eligible	योग्य	**Illegible**	अपठनीय
Eminent	प्रसिद्ध	**Imminent**	शीघ्र घटित होने वाली

Ensure	सुनिश्चित करना	**Insure**	बीमा करना
Expense	व्यय	**Expanse**	विस्तार
Fair	मेला	**Fare**	किराया
Feat	साहसिक कार्य	**Feet**	पैर
Flea	पिस्सू	**Flee**	भाग जाना
Gaol	जेल	**Goal**	लक्ष्य
Groan	कराहना	**Grown**	प्रौढ़
Human	मानव	**Humane**	सहृदय
Idle	आलसी	**Idol**	मूर्ति
Incite	उकसाना	**Insight**	अन्तर्दृष्टि
Jealous	ईर्ष्यालु	**Zealous**	उत्साही
Lessen	कम करना	**Lesson**	पाठ
Lose	खोना, गंवाना	**Loose**	ढीला
Marry	विवाह करना	**Merry**	प्रसन्नता
Meter	मीटर, यन्त्र	**Metre**	इकाई
Miner	खनिज खोदने वाला	**Minor**	लघु, पुच्छ
Need	आवश्यकता	**Knead**	गूँथना
Peace	शान्ति	**Piece**	टुकड़ा
Pray	प्रार्थना करना	**Prey**	शिकार
Rage	तीव्र क्रोध	**Raise**	उठाना
Rest	विश्राम	**Wrest**	ऐंठना
Root	जड़	**Route**	मार्ग
Sale	बिक्री	**Sell**	बेचना
Siege	घेरा डालना	**Seize**	जब्त कर लेना
Storey	मंजिल	**Story**	कहानी
Soar	उड़ना	**Sore**	पीड़ा युक्त
Soar	खट्टा	**Shore**	समुद्र तट
Stationary	स्थिर	**Stationery**	लेखन साम्रगी
Tail	पूँछ	**Tale**	कहानी
Taste	स्वाद	**Test**	परीक्षण
Troop	सेना की टुकड़ी	**Troupe**	मण्डली
Umpire	निर्णायक	**Empire**	साम्राज्य
Urban	नगरीय	**Urbane**	सुसंस्कृत
Vacation	छुट्टी	**Vocation**	व्यवसाय
Vale	घाटी	**Veil**	घूँघट
Vain	व्यर्थ	**Vein**	नस
Waste	बर्बाद करना	**Waist**	कमर

Appendix-25/परिशिष्ट–25

Designations/कुछ पदनाम

Chairman & Managing Director	अध्यक्ष एवं प्रबन्ध निदेशक
Executive Director	कार्यपालक निदेशक
General Manager	महाप्रबन्धक
Joint-general Manger	संयुक्त महाप्रबन्धक
Deputy General Manager	उपमहाप्रबन्धक
Secretary	सचिव
Manager	प्रबन्धक
Chief Manager	मुख्य प्रबन्धक
Branch Manager	शाखा प्रबन्धक
Divisional Manager	मण्डल प्रबन्धक
Chief Officer	मुख्य अधिकारी
Accountant	लेखाकार
Security Officer	सुरक्षा अधिकारी
Medical Mfficer	चिकित्साधिकारी
Law Officer	विधि अधिकारी
Investigation Officer	जाँच अधिकारी
Head Clerk	प्रधानलिपिक
Translator	अनुवादक
Typist	टंकण
Cashier	खजांची
Bill Collector	बिल संग्राहक
Publication	प्रकाशन
Publisher	प्रकाशक
Publishing	प्रकाशन व्यवसाय
Author	पुस्तक लेखक/रचयिता
Writer	लेखक
Editor	सम्पादक
News Editor	समाचार सम्पादक
Chief Sub-editor	मुख्य उप-सम्पादक
Sub Editor	उप-सम्पादक
Proof Reader	लेख त्रुटि शोधक
Printer	मुद्रक
Superintendent of Police	पुलिस अधीक्षक

Appendix-26/परिशिष्ट–26

Occupation/व्यवसाय

News-agent–अखबार वाला
Professor–अध्यापक
Milkmaid–अहिरिन
Milkman–अहीर
Engineer–इंजीनियर
Butcher–कसाई
Artist–कारीगर
Farmer–किसान
Book-seller–किताब फरोश
Coolie–कुली
Coachman–कोचवान
Banker–कोठीवाल
Treasurer–खजांची
Turner–खरादने वाला
Retailer–खुदरा विक्रेता
Perfumer–गन्धी
Coachman–गाड़ीवान
Author–ग्रन्थकार
Postman–चिट्ठीरसाँ
Surgeon–जर्राह
Sailor–जहाजी
Magician–जादूगर
Book-binder–जिल्दसाज
Weaver–जुलाहा
Shoe-maker–जूता बनाने वाला
Jeweller–जौहरी
Compositor–टाइप बैठाने वाला
Brasier–ठठेरा
Contractor–ठीकेदार
Doctor–डाक्टर
Drummer–तबलची

Betel-seller–तमोली
Oil-man–तेली
Sorcerer–तान्त्रिक
Tailor–दर्जी
Broker–दलाल
Druggist–दवा विक्रेता
Midwife–दाई
Dentist–दाँत बनाने वाला
Shopkeeper–दुकानदार
Nurse–धाय
Carder–धुनियाँ
Washerwoman–धोबिन
Washerman–धोबी
Baker–नानबाई
Waterman–पनभरा
Examiner–परीक्षक
Watchman–पहरेदार
Publisher–प्रकाशक
Manager–प्रबन्धकर्ता
Hawker–फेरी वाला
Photographer–फोटो वाला
Carpenter–बढ़ई
Draper–बजाज
Barrister–बारिस्टर
Seeds-man – बीच-विक्रेता
Beggar–भिक्षुक
Parcher–भूँजा
Butler–भंडारी
Fisherman–मछुवा
Repairer–मरम्त करने वाला
Boatman–मल्लाह

Proprietor–मालिक
Gardener–माली
Enamellet–मीनाकार
Agent–मुनीम
Printer–मुद्रक
Clerk–मुंशी
Sweeper–मेहतर
Cobbler–मोचो
Grocer–मोदी
Writer–लेखक
Chemist–रसायनी
Cook–रसोइयादार
Cashier–रोकड़िया
Inkman–रोशनाई वाला
Painter–रंगसाज
Dyer–रंगरेज
Carrier–लादने वाला
Writer–लेखक
Blacksmith–लोहार
Pleader–वकील
Physician–वैद्य
Teacher–शिक्षक
Groom–साईस
Vaccinator–सीतला छापने वाला
Glazier–सिकलीगर
Goldsmith–सोनार
Sculptor–संगतराश
Editor–सम्पादक
Barber–हज्जाम
Confectioner–हलवाई

Appendix-27/परिशिष्ट–27
English and Hindi Equivalents of terms used in Indian Constitution
भारतीय गणतन्त्र के संविधान में प्रयुक्त अंग्रेजी और हिन्दी के पारिभाषिक शब्द

Abandonment	परित्यजन
Abandonment	परित्याग
Abridgement	न्यूनन
Abrogate	निराकरण करना
Access	प्रवेश
Accession	प्रवेशन
Account	लेखा
Accretion	प्रोद्भवन
Accrue	प्राप्त होना
Accrued	उपार्जित
Accrued	प्रोद्भूत
Accusation	अभियोग
Accused	अभियुक्त
Acquisition	अर्जन अर्जी
Act	अधिनियम
Acting	कार्यकारी
Actionable wrong	अभियोज्य दोष
Ad hoc	तदर्थ
Adaptation	अनुकूलन
Additional Judge	अतिरिक्त न्यायाधीश
Additional Judge	अपर-न्यायाधीश
Addressed	सम्बोधित
Adherence	अनुशक्ति
Adjourn	अवधिदान
Administered	प्रशासित
Administration	प्रशासन
Administrative	प्रशासनीय
Administrative functions	प्रशासनीय कृत्य
Admiralty	नावाधिकरण
Admiralty	नौकाधिकरण
Admissible	ग्राह्य
Adoption	दत्तक ग्रहण
Adoption	दत्तक स्वीकरण
Adult suffrage	वयस्क मताधिकार
Adulteration	अपमिश्रण
Advance	अग्रिम धन
Advance	पेशगी
Advice	मन्त्रणा
Advice	सलाह
Advice, Instruction	उपदेश
Advise	मन्त्रणा देना
Advisory Council	मन्त्रणा परिषद्
Advocate	अधिवक्ता
Advocate General	महाधिवक्ता
Affect prejudicially	प्रतिकूल असर डालना
Affect prejudicially	प्रतिकूल प्रभाव डालना
Affirmation	प्रतिज्ञान
Agency	अभिकरण
Agent	अभिकर्त्ता
Agreement	करार
Agreement	चुकती

Air Force	विमान बल
Air navigation	विमान परिवहन
Air traffic	विमान यातायात
Airway	वायु-पथ
Alienate	अन्य-संक्रामण
Alienation	अन्य-संक्रामण
Alienation	परकीकरण
Aliens	अन्यदेशीय
Allegation	अभिकथन
Allegation	आरोप
Allegiance	निष्ठा
Allocation	बटवारा
Allot	वंटन
Allotment	बाँट
Allowance	भत्ता
Amendment	संशोधन
Amnesty	सर्वक्षमा
Amount	राशि
Annual	वार्षिक
Annual financial statement	वार्षिक वित्त विवरण
Annuities	वार्षिकी
Annulment	रद्द करना
Appeal	अपील
Appear	उपस्थित होना
Appended	संरक्षक संलग्न
Application	लागू होना
Application exercise	प्रयोग
Appointment	नियुक्ति
Appropriation	विनियोग
Appropriation bill	विनियोग विधेयक
Approval	अनुमोदन
Arbitration	मध्यस्थ निर्णय
Arbitrator	मध्यस्थ
Arbitrator Tribunal	मध्यस्थ न्यायाधिकरण
Area	क्षेत्र
Armed forces	सशस्त्र बल
Arrest	प्रग्रहण
Article	अनुच्छेद
As the case may be	यथास्थिति
Assemble	समवेत होना
Assembly	सभा
Assent	अनुमति
Assessment	निर्धारण
Assign, Entrust	सौंपना
Association	संस्था
Assurances of transfer of property	संपत्ति हस्तांतरण पत्र
Attachment	कुर्की
Attorney General	महान्यायवादा
Audit	लेखा परीक्षा
Auditor General	महालेखापरीक्षक
Authentication	प्रमाणीकरण
Authorised	प्राधिकृत
Authority	प्राधिकरण
Authority	प्राधिकारी
Autonomy	स्वायत्तता
Auxiliary	सहायक
Award	पंचाज्ञा
Bail	जामिन
Bank	बैंक
Banking	महाजनी
Bankruptcy, insolvency	दिवाला
Bar	रुकावट
Bet	पण लगाना
Betting	पण क्रिया

Bicameral	द्विगृही
Bill	बिल
Bill	विधेयक
Bill of exchange	विनिमय पत्र
Bill of Indemnity	क्षतिपूर्ति बिल
Bill of indemuity	परिहार विधेयक
Board	बोर्ड
Body	निकाय
Body, Corporate	निगम निकाय
Borrowing	उधार ग्रहण
Broadcasting	प्रसारण
Business	कारबार
Business	कार्य
Bye-election	उपनिर्वाचन
Bye-law	उपविधि
Calculation	गणना
Callings	आजीविका
Callings tax	आजीविका कर
Camp	शिविर
Candidate	अभ्यर्थी
Candidate	उम्मीदवार
Cantonment	छावनी
Capital	पूँजी
Capital	मूलधन
Capital value	मुलधन मुल्य
Capitation tax	प्रतिव्यक्ति कर
Casting vote	निर्णायक मत
Cattle pound	काँजी हौस
Cattle pound	पशु अवरोध
Cause	वाद
Cause of action	वादमूल
Census	जनगणना
Central Intelligence	केन्द्रीय गुप्तवार्ता
Bureau	विभाग
Certificate	प्रमाण पत्र
Certiorarl	उत्प्रेषण लेख
Cess	उपकर
Charge	अभियुक्ति
Charge	दोषारोप
Charge	भार
Charities	दातव्य
Cheque	चेक
Chief	मुख्य
Chief Commissioner	मुख्य आयुक्त
Chief Election Commissioner	मुख्य निर्वाचन आयुक्त
Chief Judge	मुख्य न्यायाधीश
Chief Justice	मुख्य न्यायाधिपति
Chief Minister	मुख्यमन्त्री
Citizenship	नागरिकता
Civil	असैनिक
Civil	दीवानी
Civil	व्यवहार
Civil Court	दीवानी अदालत
Civil power	असैनिक शक्ति
Claim	दावा
Clarification	स्पष्टीकरण
Clause	खण्ड
Code	संहिता
Colonization	उपनिवेशन
Commerce	वाणिज्य
Commercial	वाणिज्य सम्बन्धी
Commercial Tax	व्यापार कर
Commission	आयोग
Commissioner	आयुक्त
Common good	सार्वजनिक व्यवस्था

Common seal	सामान्य मुहर
Common seal	सार्वजनिक अभिसूचना
Communicate	संचार करना
Communication	संचार
Community	लोक समाज
Community	समुदाय
Commute	लघुकरण
Company	कम्पनी
Company	समवाय
Compensation	प्रतिकर
Competent	क्षमताशाली
Competent	सक्षम
Complaint	फरियाद
Computation	संगणना
Concurrence	सहमति
Concurrent list	समवर्ती सूची
Condition	शर्त
Condition of service	सेवा की शर्त
Conference	सम्मेलन
Conscience	अन्त:करण
Consent	सम्मति
Consideration	विचार
Consolidated Fund	संचित निधि
Constituency	निर्वाचन क्षेत्र
Constituent Assembly	संविधान सभा
Constitution	संविधान
Construe	अर्थ-दण्ड
Consul	वाणिज्यदूत
Consultation	परामर्श
Consumption	उपभोग
Contact	सम्पर्क
Contempt	अवमान
Contempt of Court	न्यायालय अवमान
Context	प्रसंग
Contingency Fund	आकस्मिकता निधि
Contract	संविदा
Contravention	उल्लंघन
Contravention	प्रतिकूलता
Contribution	अंशदान
Control	नियन्त्रण
Controller & Auditor General	नियन्त्रक महालेखा परीक्षक
Controversy	वाद प्रतिवाद
Convention	अभिसमय
Convicted	अभिशस्त
Convicted	दोष-प्रमाणित
Convicted	सिद्ध दोष
Conviction	अभिशस्ति
Conviction	दोष सिद्धि
Co-operative society	समवाय संस्था
Co-operative Society	सहकारी संस्था
Copy	प्रतिकृति
Copy	प्रतिलिपि
Corporation	निगम
Corporation sole	एकल निगम
Corporation tax	निगम कर
Corrupt	भ्रष्ट
Cost	खर्च
Cost	परिव्यय
Cost	लागत
Council	परिषद्
Council of Ministers	मन्त्रि परिषद्
Council of States	राज्य परिषद्
Countervailing duties	प्रति शुल्क
Court	न्यायालय
Court Martial	सेना न्यायालय

Court of Appeal अपील न्यायालय
Court of Appeal पुनर्विचार न्यायालय
Court of record अभिलेख न्यायालय
Court of Wards प्रतिपालक अधिकरण
Credit पत
Crime, offence अपराध
Criminal अपराधी
Criminal आपराधिक
Criminal दंड सम्बन्धी
Criminal Court दंड न्यायालय
Criminal Law दंड विधि
Current प्रचलित
Custody अभिरक्षा
Custody कावल
Custom आचार
Custom रूढ़ि
Custom duty बहि:शुल्क
Custom duty सीमा शुल्क
Customs duty शुल्क सीमान्त
Dealing व्यवहार
Dealings लेना-देना
Death duty मरण शुल्क
Debate वाद-विवाद
Debenture ऋणपत्र
Debt ऋण
Decision विनिश्चय
Declaration घोषणा
Decree आज्ञप्ति
Decree डिक्री
Dedicate समर्पण
Deed विलेख
Defamation Validity मानहानि मान्यता
Defence प्रतिरक्षा

Deliberate पर्यालोचन
Delimitation परिसीमन
Demand अभियाचना
Demand माँग
Demarcation सीमांकन
Demobilization सैन्य वियोजन
Deprive वियुक्त करना
Deprive वंचित करना
Deputy Chairman उपसभापति
Deputy Commissioner उपायुक्त
Deputy Speaker उपाध्यक्ष
Derogation अल्पीकरण
Descent उद्भव
Design रूपांकन
Detrimental अहितकारी
Diplomacy राजनय
Direct election प्रत्यक्ष निर्वाचन
Direction निर्देश
Disability निर्योग्यता
Discharge निर्वहन
Disciplinary अनुशासन-सम्बन्धी
Discipline अनुशासन
Discover प्रकट करना
Discretion स्वविवेक
Discrimination विभेद
Discussion चर्चा
Dismiss पदच्युत करना
Dispersion विसर्जन
Dispute विवाद
Disqualification अनर्हता
Disqualification अनर्हीकरण
Dissent विमति
Dissolution विघटन

Distribution वितरण
Distribution विभाजन
District जिला
District Board जिलागण
District Board जिला मंडली
District Council जिला परिषद्
District Court जिला न्यायालय
District Fund जिला निधि
District Magistrate जिलाधीश
Dividend लाभांश
Divorce विवाह-विच्छेद
Document दस्तावेज
Document लेक्ष्य
Domicile अधिवास
Domiciled अधिवासी
Due, Payable देय
Dullness मतिमान्द्य
During the pleasure of the President राष्ट्रपति प्रसाद पर्यन्त
During good behaviour सदाचरण पर्यन्त
Duty कर्तव्य
Duty शुल्क
Economic आर्थिक
Efficiency of administration प्रशासन कार्यपटुता
Efficiency of administration प्रशासन कार्यक्षमता
Elected चुने हुए
Elected निर्वाचित
Election निर्वाचन
Election Commissioner निर्वाचन आयुक्त
Election Tribunal निर्वाचन अधिकरण
Electoral rolls निर्वाचक गण
Electoral rolls निर्वाचक नामावली
Eligibility पात्रता
Eligible पात्र
Emergency आपात
Emergent आपाती
Emigration उत्प्रवास
Emolument उपलब्धि
Employer's liability नियोजक उत्तरवादिता
Employer's Liability नियोजक दात्व्य
Employment उपायोजन
Employment नौकरी
Employment सेवा नियोजन
Employment tax नौकरी कर
Enactment अधिनियमन
Encumbered estate भारग्रस्त संपदा
Endorsed अंकित
Endorsed पृष्ठांकित
Endorsement अंकन
Endorsement पृष्ठांकन
Endowment धर्मस्व
Engagement वचन बन्ध
Engineering यन्त्र शास्त्र
Enquiry परिप्रश्न
Enterprise उद्यम
Entitled हक्क
Entitled हक्क होना
Entrust न्यस्त करना
Entry दाखिला
Entry प्रविष्टि
Equal protection of law विधियों का समान संरक्षण
Equality समता
Establish स्थापित करना

Establishment	संस्थापन
Establishment	स्थापना
Estate	सम्पदा
Estate duty	सम्पदा शुल्क
Estimate	आकलन
Estimate	आँक
Estimate	प्राक्कलन
Evidence	साक्ष्य
Excess profit	अतिरिक्त लाभ
Excise duty	उत्पादन शुल्क
Exclude	अण्वर्जन करना
Exclusion	अपवर्जन
Exclusive jurisdiction	अनन्य क्षेत्राधिकार
Executive	कार्यपालिका
Executive power	कार्यपालिका शक्ति
Exempt	मुक्त
Exercise	अनुष्ठान
Ex-officio	पदेन
Expenditure	व्यय
Explanation	स्पष्टीकारण
Explosive	विस्फोटक
Export	निर्यात
Export duty	निर्यात शुल्क
Export Tax	निर्यात कर
Extent	विस्तार
External affairs	वैदेशिक कार्य
Extradition	प्रत्यर्पण
Extraterritorial operation	राज्य क्षेत्रातीत प्रवत्तन
Factory	कारखाना
Faith	धर्म
Faith	श्रद्धा
Fare	किराया
Fare	भाड़ा
Federal Court	फेडरल न्यायालय
Fees	फीस
Finance	वित्त
Finance bill	वित्त विधेयक
Finance Commission	वित्तायोग
Financial	वित्तीय
Financial obligation	वित्तीय भार
Financial statement	वित्तीय विवरण
Fined	जुर्माना किया
First reading	प्रथम पठन
Fishery	मीन क्षेत्र
Fleet	निर्वाचन (करना)
Forbid	निषेध
Forbidden	निषिद्ध
Forces	बल
Foreign affairs	विदेशीय कार्य
Foreign exchange	विदेशीय विनिमय
Form	प्रपत्र
Form	फारम
Form	रूप
Formula	सूत्र
Formulated	सूत्रित
Freedom	आजादी
Freedom	स्वतंत्रता
Freedom	स्वातंत्र्य
Freedom of speech	वाक्स्वातंत्र्य
Freight	वस्तु भाड़ा
Frontiers	सीमान्त
Function	कृत्य
Fund	निधि
Future market	वायदा-बाजार
Gambling	जुआ

Gambling	द्यूत
Gazette	गजट
General election	साधारण निर्वाचन
Govern	शासन करना
Governance	शासन
Governing body	शासी निकाय
Government	सरकार
Government of India	भारत सरकार
Governor	राज्यपाल
Grant	अनुदान
Grants-in-aid	सहायक अनुदान
Gratuity	उपदान
Guarantee	प्रत्याभूति
Guidance	मार्ग प्रदर्शन
Habeous Corpus	बन्दी प्रत्यक्षीकरण
Handicraft	दस्तकारी
Handicraft	हस्त शिल्प
Hazardous	संकटमय
Headman	मुखिया
High Court	उच्च न्यायालय
Honorarium	मानेदय
Illegal	अवैध
Illegal practice	अवैधाचरण
Immunity	उन्मुक्ति
Impeachment	महाभियोग
Implement	परिपालन
Import duty	आयात शुल्क
Impose	आरोपण करना
Impose	लगाना
Imprisoament	कारावास
Imprisonment	कैद
Improvement Trust	सुधार प्रन्यास
Incapacity	असमर्थता
Incidental	प्रासंगिक
Incidental, Ancillary	आनुषंगिक
Income Tax	आयकर
Incompetency	अक्षमता
Incompetent	अक्षम
Incorporation	निगमन
Incumbent of an office	पदधारी
Indebtedness	ऋणग्रस्तता
Indirect election	परोक्ष निर्वाचन
Industry	उद्योग
Ineligibility	अपात्रता
Ineligible	अपात्र
Infant	शिशु
Infectious	सांक्रामिक
Influence	प्रभाव
Inheritance	दाय
Injury	क्षति
Inland waterway	अन्तर्देशीय जलपथ
Inoperative	अप्रवृत्त
Inquire	जाँच करना
Inspection	पर्यवेक्षण
Institution	संस्था
Instruction	अनुदेश
Instruction, Education	शिक्षा
Instructions	हिदायतें
Instrument	लिखित
Insurance	बीमा
Intercourse	समागम
Interest	वृद्धि
Interest	सूद
International	अन्तर्राष्ट्रीय
Interpretation	निर्वचन
Intestacy	इच्छा पत्रहीनत्व

Intestacy	निर्वसीयता
Intestate	इच्छा पत्रहीन
Intestate	निर्वसीयत
Introduction	पुर:स्थापना
Invalid	अमान्य
Invalidity pension	असमर्थता निवृत्ति वेतन
Investigation	अनुसंधान
Involved	अन्तर्ग्रस्त
Involvement	अन्तर्ग्रसन
Irregularity	अनियमितता
Irrelevant	विसंगत
Issue	वाद-पद
Joint-family	अवभिक्त कुटुम्ब
Joint-family	अविभक्त परिवार
Judge	न्यायाधीश
Judgment	निर्णय
Judicial power	न्यायिक शक्ति
Judicial proceeding	न्यायिक कार्यरीति
Judicial proceeding	न्यायिक कार्यवाही
Judicial stamp	न्यायिक मुद्रांक
Judiciary	न्यायपालिका
Jurisdiction	क्षेत्राधिकार
Justice	न्यायाधिपति
Labour	श्रम
Labour Union	श्रमिक संघ
Land records	भू-अभिलेख
Land revenue	भू-राजस्व
Lapse	व्यपयत होना
Laws of Nations	राष्ट्रों की विधि
Legal	कानून सम्बन्धी
Legal	विधि सम्बन्धी
Legal tender	विधि मान्य
Legislation	विधान
Legislative	विधान मण्डल
Legislative Assembly	विधान सभा
Legislative Council	विधान परिषद्
Legislative power	विधायिनी शक्ति
Levy	आरोपण
Levy	उगाहना
Levy	उद्ग्रहण
Liability	उत्तरवादिता
Liability	दायित्व
Libel	अपमान लेख
Liberty	स्वाधीनता
Licence	अनुज्ञप्ति
License	लाइसेन्स
Lieutenant, Governor	उपराज्यपाल
Limitation	परिसीमा
Livelihood	जीविका
Living-wage	निर्वाह मजूरी
Loan	उधार
Local area	स्थानीय क्षेत्र
Local Authority	स्थानीय प्राधिकारी
Local Board	स्थानीय मण्डली
Local body	स्थानीय निकाय
Local Government	स्थानीय शासन
Lok Sabha	लोकसभा
Lunacy	उन्माद
Lunatic	उन्मत्त
Magistrate's Court	दंडाधिकारी न्यायालय
Maintain	पोषण करना
Maintain	बनाये रखना
Maintenance	पोषण
Major	वयस्क
Majority	बहुमत
Mandamus	परमादेश

Manufacture	निर्माण
Maritime shipping	समुद्र नौवहन
Mark	चिह्न
Maternity relief	प्रसूति साहाय्य
Maternity relief	प्रसूति सहायता
Means of Communications	संचार साधन
Memo	ज्ञापक
Memorandum	ज्ञापन
Memorial	स्मारक
Mental deficiency	मनोवैकल्य
Mental weakness	मनोदौर्बल्य
Merchant marine	वणिक पोत
Migration	प्रव्रजन
Military	सैनिक
Mineral	खनिज
Mineral resources	खनिज सम्पत
Minister	मन्त्री
Minor	अवयस्क
Minority	अल्पसंख्यक वर्ग
Misbehaviour	कदाचार
Modification	रूपभेद
Money	धन
Money lender	साहूकारी
Money lending	सांसर्गिक
Money-bill	धन विधेयक
Morality	सदाचार
Mortgage	बन्धक
Motion	प्रस्ताव
Motion for consideration	विचारार्थ प्रस्ताव
Motion of confidence	विश्वास प्रस्ताव
Motion of no-confidence	अविश्वास प्रस्ताव

Municipal area	नगर क्षेत्र
Municipal Committee	नगर समिति
Municipal Corporation	नगर निगम
Municipal tramway	नगर ट्रामवे
Municipality	नगर पालिका
Nation	राष्ट्र
National highway	राष्ट्रीय राजपथ
Naturalization	देशीयकरण
Naval	नौसेना सम्बन्धी
Navigation	नौ-परिवहन
Nomination	नाम निदर्शन
Nomination	मनोनयन
Notice in writing	लिखित सूचना
Notification	अधिसूचना
Obligation	आभार
Occupation	उपजीविका
Occupation	धंधा
Octroi	चुंगी
Office	पद
Officer	पदाधिकारी
Official residence	पदावास
Opinion	अभिप्राय
Opinion	राय
Order	आदेश
Order	व्यवस्था
Order-in-Council	पदिषद् आदेश
Ordinance	अध्यादेश
Own	स्वामी होना
Owner	स्वामी
Ownership, Royalty	स्वामित्व
Pardon	क्षमा
Parliament	संसद
Partnership	भागिता

Party	पक्ष
Passed	पारित
Passport	पार पत्र
Patent	एकस्व
Pay, Salary	वेतन
Peace	शान्ति
Pecuniary Jurisdiction	आर्थिक क्षेत्राधिकार
Penalty	शास्ति
Pending	लम्बमान
Pending	लम्बित
Pension	निवृत्ति वेतन
People	लोक
Permit	अनुज्ञा
Permit	परमिट
Perpetual succession	शाश्वत उत्तराधिकार
Perquisite	परिलब्धि
Person	व्यक्ति
Personal law	स्वीय विधि
Petition	अर्थ करना
Petition	याचिका
Piracy	जलदस्युता
Plead	वकालत करना
Pleader	वकील
Police	आरक्षक
Police force	आरक्षक बल
Police Station	थाना
Police Station Officer	थानेदार
Policy of insurance	बीमा पत्र
Port quarantine	पत्तन निरोध
Possession	कब्जा
Post	जगह
Post	पद
Power	शक्ति

Preamble	प्रस्तावना
Preference	अधिमान
Prejudice	प्रतिकूल प्रभाव
Preside	अध्यासीन होना
Preside	पीठासीन होना
President	राष्ट्रपति
Presiding officer	अधिष्ठाता
Presiding Officer	पीठासीन पदाधिकारी
Prevention	निरोध
Preventive detention	निवारक निरोध
Previous consent	पूर्व सम्मति
Previous sanction	पूर्व मंजूरी
Prime Minister	प्रधानमन्त्री
Prison	कारागार
Prison	जेल
Prisoner	काराबन्दी
Prisoner	कैदी
Privilege	विशेषाधिकार
Procedure	प्रक्रिया
Process	आदेशिका
Proclamation	उद्घोषणा
Proclamation of emergency	आपातकाल उद्घोषणा
Production	उत्पादन
Profession	पेशा
Profession	वृत्ति
Profession Tax	वृत्ति कर
Profit	लाभ
Prohibited	प्रतिषिद्ध
Prohibition	प्रतिषेध
Promissory note	प्रामिसरी नोट
Promissory note	वचन पत्र
Promulgation	प्रख्यापन

Propagate	प्रचार करना
Proportional representation	अनुपाती-प्रतिनिधित्व
Proposal	प्रस्थापना
Prorogue	सत्रावसान
Prosecution	अभियुक्ति
Prosecution	अभियोजन
Provided	परन्तु
Provident Fund	भविष्य निधि
Province	प्रान्त
Provision	उपबन्ध
Proxy	प्रतिपत्री
Public debt	राष्ट्र ऋण
Public demand	सरकारी अभियाचना
च्नइसपब कमउंदक	सार्वजनिक कल्याण
Public health	लोक स्वास्थ्य
Public notification	लोक अधिसूचना
Public notification	सार्वजनिक अभियाचना
Public order	साहूकार
Public Service Commission	लोक सेवा आयोग
Public Services	लोक सेवाएँ
Publication	प्रकाशन
Punish	दंड देना
Purporting to be done	कर्तुमभिप्रेत
Qualification	अर्हता
Question of law	विधि प्रश्न
Quo warranto	अधिकार-पृच्छा
Quorum	गणपूर्ति
Railway	रेल
Ratification	अनुसमर्थन
Receipt	प्राप्ति
Receipt	रसीद
Receipt (Paper)	पावती
Record	अभिलेख
Record of rights	अधिकार अभिलेख
Recruitment	भर्ती
Recurring	आवर्त्तक
Redemption	विमोचन
Redemption charges	विमोचन भार
Reference	निर्देश
Reformatory	सुधारालय
Regional Commissioner	प्रादेशिक आयुक्त
Regional Council	प्रादेशिक परिषद्
Regional Fund	प्रादेशिक निधि
Register	पंजी
Registered	निबद्ध
Registered	पंजीबद्ध
Registration	निबन्धन
Registration	पंजीबन्धन
Registration	पंजीयन
Regulate	विनियमन करना
Regulation	विनियम
Relevancy	सुसंगति
Relevant	सुसंगत
Remedy	उपचार
Reminder	अनुस्मारक
Remission	परिहार
Removal	हटाना
Remuneration	पारिश्रमिक
Rent	लगान
Repeal	निरसन
Report	प्रतिवेदन
Representation	प्रतिनिधित्व
Representative	प्रतिनिधि
Reprieve	प्रविलम्बन

Republic	लोकतंत्रात्मक गणराज्य	Scheduled tribe	अनुसूचित-जनजाति
Repugnance	विरोध	Seal	मुद्रा
Repugnancy	विरोध	Second reading	द्वितीय पठन
Repugnant	विरुद्ध	Security	प्रतिभूति
Requisition	अधिग्रहण	Select Committee	प्रवर समिति
Research	गवेषणा	Self Governmen	स्थानीय स्वशासन
Research	शोध, शोधना	Sentence	दंडादेश
Reservation	रक्षण	Service	सेवा
Reserved forest	रक्षित वन	Service charges	सेवा भार
Resignation	पदत्याग	Session	सत्र
Resolution	संकल्प	Sessions Court	सत्र न्यायालय
Respite	विराम	Share	अंश
Restriction	निर्गन्धन	Sheriff	शेरीफ
Retire	निवृत्त होना	Single transferable vote	एकल संक्रमणीय मत
Retirement	निवृत्ति	Sinking Fund	निक्षेप निधि
Return	विवरणी	Sitting	उपवेशन
Revenue	राजस्व	Sitting	बैठक
Revenue Court	राजस्व न्यायालय	Slander	अपमान-वचन
Review	पुनर्विलोकन	Social custom	सामाजिक रूढ़ि
Revision	पुनर्निरीक्षण	Social insurance	सामाजिक बीमा
Revoke	प्रतिसंहरण	Social service	सामाजिक मुद्रा
Reward	पारितोषिक	Sovereign	प्रभु
Right	अधिकार	Sovereign democratic	सम्पूर्ण प्रभुत्व सम्पन्न
Rule	नियम	Sovereignty	प्रभुता
Rule of the road	पथ कर	Speaker	अध्यक्ष
Ruler	शासक	Staff	कर्मचारी वृन्द
Safeguard	परित्राण	Stamp duty	मुद्रांक शुल्क
Safeguard	रक्षाकवच	Standing Committee	स्थायी समिति
Sales tax	विक्रय कर	Standing Orders	स्थायी करना
Sanction	मंजूरी	State	राज्य
Schedule	अनुसूची	State Fund	राज्य निधि
Scheduled area	अनुसूचित-क्षेत्र	State-list	राज्य सूची
Scheduled caste	अनुसूचित जाति	Sub-division	उपविभाग

Subject अधीन
Subject विषय
Subject matter वाद-विषय
Subordinate Court अधीन-न्यायालय
Subordinate Officer अधीन-अधिकारी
Succession उत्तराधिकार
Succession duty उत्तराधिकार शुल्क
Successor उत्तराधिकारी
Suffrage मताधिकार
Summoned आहूत
Summons आह्वान
Superintendence अधीक्षण
Superintendent अधीक्षक
Supplementary अनुपूरक
Supplementary grant अनुपूरक अनुदान
Supreme Command सर्वोच्च समादेश
Supreme Court उच्चतम न्यायालय
Surcharge अधिभार
Suspension निलम्बन
Tax कर
Technical training शिल्पी प्रशिक्षण
Tenant किसान
Tenure पदावधि
Term निबंधन
Terminal Tax सीमाकर
Territorial Charges प्रादेशिक भार
Territorial jurisdiction प्रादेशिक क्षेत्राधिकार
Territorial waters जल प्रांगण
Territory राज्य क्षेत्र
Third reading तृतीय-पठन
Tidal water ज्वार जल
To arrest बन्दी करना
To charge भारित करना
To initiate उपक्रमण करना
To introduce पुरःस्थापन करना
To suspend निलम्बन करना
Toll पथ नियम
Trade व्यापार
Trade association व्यापार संघ
Trade mark व्यापार चिह्न
Trade union कार्मिक संघ
Trademark पण्य चिह्न
Traffic यातायात
Traffic in human beings मानवी पण्य
Training प्रशिक्षण
Tram car ट्रामगाड़ी
Tramway ट्राम
Tranquillity प्रशान्ति
Transfer स्थानान्तरण
Transfer हस्तांतरण
Transition संक्रमण
Transport परिवहन
Transportation निर्वासन
Treasure trove निखात निधि
Treaty सन्धि
Tribal area जनजाति क्षेत्र
Tribal Council जनजाति परिषद्
Tribe जनजाति
Tribunal अधिकरण
Tribunal न्यायाधिकरण
Triennial त्रैवार्षिक
Trust न्यास
Typewriting टंगण
Undischarged अनुन्मुक्त
Undue influence अयुक्त प्रभाव

Unemployment	बेकारी
Union	संघ
Union List	संघ-सूची
Unit	अंग
Unit	एकक
Unit	एकांश
Unsound mind	विकृत चित्त
Unsoundness of mind	चित्त विकृति
Vacancy	रिक्तता
Vacancy	रिक्त स्थान
Vacancy	रिक्ति
Vagrancy	आवारागर्दी
Vice President	उपराष्ट्रपति
Village Council	ग्राम परिषद्
Violation	अतिक्रमण
Vocation	व्यवसाय
Void	शून्य
Vote	मत
Voter	मतदाता
Votes on accounts	लेखानुदान
Voting	मतदान
Wage	मजूरी
Want of confidence	विश्वास का अभाव
Warrant	अधिपत्र
Will	इच्छा पत्र
Will	वसीयत
Winding up	समापन
Writ	लेख
Writ of prohibition	प्रतिषेध लेख

Appendix-28/परिशिष्ट–28
Terms used in Government Notifications
शासकीय शब्दावली

A fee in cash	नकद फीस
A vain Tuberculosis test	पक्षियों की यक्ष्मा परीक्षा
Abate	शांत होना
Abatement	घटना (घटाया जाना)
Abatement of rent	लगान में कमी
Abbreviated	संक्षिप्त
Abduction, Kidnapping	अपहरण
Abetment	दुरुत्साहन
Abide by	पालन करना
Abnormal, Irregular	नियम विरुद्ध
Abolition	उन्मूलन
Above par	अधिक मूल्य पर
Above standard	प्रमाण से ऊपर
Absconder	भगोड़ा
Absconding	फरार
Absentee statement	अनुपस्थिति विवरणपत्र
Absolute order	अबाधित करना
Absorption	खपत
Abstract	उपसंक्षेप
Abstract book	उपसंक्षेप पुस्तक
Abstract of cost	परिव्यय उपसंक्षेप
Abutment	तोरणाधार
Academy	विद्यापरिषद्
Acceleration	वेगवृद्धिकर
Access	पहुँच
Accessories	सहायक वस्तुएँ
Accessory, Subsidiary	सहायक
Accord	एकमत्य
Account	लेखा (गणना)
Accountant	कणनाध्यक्ष
Accountant General	महालेखाकार
Accounts officer	गणनाधिकारी
Accoutrement	आकल्प (सज्जा)
Accrual increment	संभूत वेतन वृद्धि
Accusation	अभियोग (दोषण)
Accused	अभियुक्त
Acknowledgment	प्राप्ति स्वीकार
Acknowledgment due	पावती-पावनी
Acknowledgment, Receipt	पावती
Acknowledgment, Sanction, Approval	स्वीकृति
Acoustics	ध्वनि शास्त्र
Acquisition	अधिगमन

Acquisition	प्राप्ति
Acquittal	दोष मुक्ति
Acquittance roll	निष्क्रयवर्ति, (वेतन चिट्ठा)
Acreage	एकड़ों में क्षेत्रफल
Act	अधिनियम
Act	विधान
Acting appointment	कार्यवाह नियुक्ति
Actinomycosis	अंशुक वकीय (रोग)
Active allowance	सक्रिय भत्ता
Actual travelling allowance	वास्तविक यात्रा व्यय
Actuals	वास्तविक आँकड़े
Acute angle	न्यूनकोण
Ad Hoc	एतदर्थ
Ad valorem	मूल्यानुसार
Addendum	क्षप (क)
Addendum	जोड़पत्र
Additional	उपाधिक
Additional entry	अतिरिक्त प्रविष्टि
Additional grant	अतिरिक्त अनुदान
Adequate	यथोचित
Adhesive stamp	श्लेष्क मुद्रांक
Adjacent	समीपस्थ (आसन्न)
Adjournment	स्थगन
Adjudication	दिवालिया ठहराना
Adjudication	न्यायिक निर्णय
Adjustment	समाधान
Administration	प्रशासन
Administrative	प्रशासकीय
Administrative bond	प्रशासकीय प्रतिज्ञापत्र
Administrative department	प्रशासकीय विभाग
Administrator	प्रशासक
Administrator General	महा प्रबंधक
Admissibility in evidence	साक्ष्य में ग्राहिता
Admissible	ग्राह्य
Admission board	प्रवेश परिषद्
Admitted for hearing	सुनवाई के लिए स्वीकृत
Admonition	डाँट-फटकार
Adoption deed	दत्तक पत्र
Adulteration	मिलावट
Adumbrated	छायांकित
Advance, Taqavi-advance.	अग्र ऋण
Advice of Credit Transfer	नाम संक्रम सूचना
Advisory officer	मंत्रणा अधिकारी
Advocate	अधिवक्ता
Advocate General	महाअधिवक्ता
Affect	प्रभावित करना
Affected	ग्रस्त (प्रभावित)
Affidavit	शपथ पत्र
Affiliation	संबद्धता

Affinity	रुझान
Affirmation	प्रतिज्ञा, प्रतिज्ञान
Affirmative	स्वीकारात्मक
Aflux	बहाव
Against	विरुद्ध
Age limit	वयस प्रतिबंध
Agenda	कार्यावली
Agent	अभिकर्ता
Aggregate	योग
Aggregate	सकल
Agreement for service	सेवानियम पत्र
Agricultural	कृषि विषयक
Agricultural implements	कृषि उपकरण
Agricultural lease	कृषि पट्टा
Agriculturists Loan Act	कृषक ऋण एक्ट
Aide-de-camp	परिधिस्थ
Air force	हवाई बेड़ा
Air gun	वायुसंचालित बन्दूक
Air-force	नभ-सेना
Alienatipn	हस्तांतरण
Alien's branch	विदेशी शाखा
Alignment	पंक्ति
Alignment	पंक्तिकरण
Alimony	दारा-भूति
Alimony pendentilite	विचारकालिक दाराभृति
Allegation, Imposition	आरोप
Allocation	नियतन
Allocation	विभाजन
Allocation of fund	रुपये का बँटवारा
Allotment	दिष्टि
Allotment	निर्दिष्ट भाग
Allowance	भत्ता
Alluvial	नदमट (कछार)
Alluvion	कछार
Amalgamation, Coordination	एकीकरण
Amendment Act	संशोधक विधान
Ammunition	गोला-गारूद
Ammunition	गोली
Amnesty	राजक्षमा
Amortization	ऋणशोधन (किश्तों में)
Amphistome worm	द्विमुखी कृमि
Anachronism	कालव्यतिक्रम (तारीख की गलती)
Analysis	विश्लेषण
Analyst	विश्लेषक
Ancestral property	पैतृक संपत्ति
Anchor bolt	लंगर
Angle of repose	विश्रामकोण
Animal Husbandry Department	पशुपालन विभाग
Ankle, Ring	कड़ा

Annexure	नत्थी
Annotated	सटीक
Annuling	अभिशून्यन
Annulled	निरर्थक किया हुआ (मंसूख किया हुआ)
Annulment of Marriage	विवाह का रद्द किया जाना
Anomalous	अनैयमिक
Anomaly	अनियम
Anonymous	अनामक
Ante	पूर्व
Antecedent, precedent	पूर्व दृष्टांत
Anthrax	विसहारिया
Anticipated	प्रत्याशित
Anticipated excess and savings	प्रत्याशित अधिक व्यय और बचत
Anticipation	प्रत्याशा
Anticipator	प्रत्याशिक
Antidote	विषमार
Anti-inflatory	मुद्रास्फीतिरोधक
Antiquities	प्राचीन अवशेष
Anti-rabies treatmerit	जलांतक चिकित्सा
Antiseptic fluid	सड़न रोक रस
Apathy	उदासीनता
Aperture	छेद
Apex	सिरा (चोटी)
Apparatus	यन्त्र-कलाप
Apparatus (as a whole)	यन्त्रजाल (यन्त्र कलाप)
Apparatus (for a particular experiment)	यन्त्रजात
Appeal	अपील
Appear	उपस्थित होना
Appearance	उपस्थिति
Appearance slips	न्यायालय उपस्थितिपत्र
Appellant	अपीलकर्ता
Appellate	अपीली
Appendix	परिशिष्ट
Appliance	यन्त्र (औजार)
Applicant	प्रार्थी
Apportionment	संविभाग
Appraisement	कनकत
Appreciation	अधिमूल्यन
Apprehend	बन्दी करना
Apprehension	बन्दीकरण
Apprentice	शिक्ष्यमाण
Appropriate	उपयुक्त
Appropriation	पर्यादान
Approval	अनुमति
Approved candidate	स्वीकृत उम्मीदवार
Approved service	अनुमोदित सेवा
Approver	राजसाक्षी
Approximate	उपसन्न

Approximate areas	लगभग क्षेत्रफल
Apron	पिटवा
Aquaduct	जलनियन्त्रक पुल
Arbitration	पंचायत
Arbitration, Tribunal	पंचमंडल
Arbitrator	पंच (मध्यस्थ)
Arboriculture	वृक्षरोपण विद्या
Arcade	छत्ता
Archaeological department	पुरातत्त्व विभाग
Architect	स्थपति
Architecture	वास्तु विद्या (स्थापत्य)
Argument	तर्क
Armed guard	सशस्त्र रक्षकगण
Armourer	आयुधक
Armourer	आयुधकार
Arrear claims	अवशिष्ट के प्राप्य
Arrears	अवशिष्ट
Arrows	सूजा
Art gallery	कलादीर्घा
Arterial road	नगर योजक सड़क
Artery	धमनी
Article, Bench	अधिकरण
Artisan	शिल्पकार
Arts college	साहित्यादि विद्यालय
Asbestos	अदह
Ashman	राखिया
Asphalt	डामर
Assault	आक्रमण
Assess	आँकना
Assessment, Assess	कर निर्धारण
Assets	परिसम्पत (संपत्ति)
Assets (as opposed to liability)	आदेय
Assignee	अभिहस्तांकिती
Assignee	सुपुर्दगी लेने वाला
Assignment (of land)	अभिहस्तांकन (बेंची)
Assignment (of Property)	संकल्प
Asstt. Inspector General	सहायक महानिरीक्षक
Asstt. Supdt. fo Police	सहायक पुलिस अधीक्षक
Assumed rent	माना हुआ लगान
Assurance	आश्वासन
Asterisk	तारा चिह्न
At a discount	बट्टे पर (से)
At a premium	बढ़ती पर (से)
At your earliest convenience, As early as possible	यथाशीघ्र
Athletic	खेल-कूद
Attach (Legal Term)	कुड़क करना
Attendant	परिचर
Attendant	परिचारक
Attestation	साक्षीकरण

Attested साक्षीकृत

Auction घोष विक्रय (नीलाम)

Audit लेखा परीक्षा

Audit objection लेखा परीक्षा आपत्ति

Audit officer लेखा परीक्षा अधि कारी

Audit report गणना परीक्षा विवरण

Auditor लेखा परीक्षक

Auditor General लेखा महापरीक्षक

Auditorium सभाभवन

Auger बरमा

Aural education कर्ण शिक्षा

Authentic आप्त (प्रामाणिक)

Authentication of power of attorney दत्तक ग्रहण का अधिकारपत्र

Authorise अधिकृत

Authorised agent प्राधिकृत अभिकर्ता

Authority प्राधिकारी वर्ग

Authority of consideration विचाराधिकार

Authority, Officer अधिकारी

Authrax बिसहरिया

Automatic स्वयंचल

Automatically स्वत:

Available उपलब्ध

Average औसत

Average emoluments औसत परिलाभ

Average pay माध्य वेतन

Award पंच निर्णय

Axis अक्षधुरी

Axis of a cone शंकुकक्ष

Bacteriological examination कीटाणु परीक्षा

Bail bond, Security bond प्रतिभू पत्र

Bailable प्रतिभाव्य

Bailment निक्षेपण

Ballast गिट्टी

Ballot गुप्तमत

Balustrade कटहरा

Bamboo measuring rod गट्ठा

Ban प्रतिबन्ध

Bank अधिकोष (धनागार)

Bank draft बैंक की हुंडी

Banquet जेवनार

Bar (as in efficiency bar), Bolt, Latch अर्गल

Bar Association, Bar अभिभाषक संघ

Bar Council अभिभाषक परिषद्

Bar-fetters डंडा बेड़ी

Barometer वायुभार मापक

Barrack योधागार

Barrack सहतावारिक

Barred by limitation अवधि बाधित

Barren ऊसर

Barrister, Advocate, Lawyer	विधि वक्ता
Barrow	हाथ गाड़ी (ठेला)
Base line	आधार-रेखा
Basement	नींव
Basic coupon	मूलकूपन
Batch	जत्था
Battalion	बटालियन
Batten	पुश्तीवान
Bay window	निकासा
Bayonet	संगीन
Bearing, (Direction)	दिक स्थिति
Beet (Patrolling), Patrol	गश्त
Belief	विश्वास
Bellows	भस्त्रका
Below par	अंकित मूल्य से कम
Bench mark	स्तरांक
Bench of magistrates	अधिकरणिक वर्ग
Beneficiary	हिताधिकारी
Benevolent trust	पर हितकारी प्रन्यास
Benevolent trust	हितकारी ट्रस्ट
Berth	दूला (नौशय्या)
Beyond time	समय के बाहर
Bib cock, Cock stop	टोंटी
Biennial	द्विवर्षीय
Biennial	द्विवार्षिक
Bifurcation	द्विविभाजन
Bilious fever (horse)	पैत्तिक ज्वर (अश्व)
Bill	विधेयक
Bill of lading	वहन पत्र
Bit, Bit-Head, Bit-Rims	लगाम (दहाना)
Biting	डाँस
Bitumen	राल
Black quarter	लँगड़िया
Blight	तुषार
Blue fringe	झालर (नीली)
Blue Vitriol	नीला थोथा (तूतिया)
Bluk	थोक
Board of revenue	माल बोर्ड
Boiler	पिठर (बायलर)
Boiler	भबका
Bond	प्रतिज्ञापत्र
Bond	बंध (बमस्सुक)
Bond of indemnity	क्षतिपूरक बंध
Bone marrow	अस्थि-मज्जा
Bonus	लाभांश
Book craft	गत्ताकारी
Book transfer	पुस्त संक्रम
Books of reference	संदर्भ ग्रन्थ
Bots & warble	उदरकीट का विरु
Bottle-neck	संर्कीणनिगम मार्ग

Bottle-neck	संकेत लिपिक
Boulders	महाशिला
Brace	अढ़वाल (कसनी)
Bracket	दीवारगीर
Brake speed	रुद्गति
Branch depot	शाखाकोठार
Branded portion	दग्ध भाग
Branding Gertificate	गग्धांकन प्रमाणपत्र
Breach of law	विधि भंग
Breach of peace	शांति-भंग
Breach of rule	नियम भंजन
Breast wall	आवक्ष भित्ति
Breeder	ढोर पालक
Breeding operation	पशु प्रर्वधन क्रिया
Bressummer	सरदल
Brick	इष्टिका
Buck ammunition	छर्रा
Budget	आयति
Budget	आयव्ययक (बजट)
Budget manual	आयव्ययक सारसंग्रह
Bulletin	बुलेटिन
Bullet-proof	गोली रोक
Bullion	सोना-चाँदी
Bully	गुंडा
Bundle Lifter	बस्ताबरदार
Burden of proof	प्रमाण भार
Bureau	कार्य पीठ
Burglar Alarm	चोर घंटी
Burglary	सेंध लगाना
Business statement	कार्यविवरण पत्र
By order of the Court	न्यायालय की आज्ञा से
By virtue of	कारण से
Bye-laws	उपनियम
Cable Crossing	तार काट
Cable jointers	तार जोड़
Cadet	बालबीर (सेनाछात्र)
Cadre	मूल रचना
Calamity, Distress	विपत्ति
Calculation	गणना
Calendar month	पंचांग मास
Calendar year	पत्री वर्ष
Calibre	क्षमता
Calibre	छिद्र व्यास
Calling for the record	कागजात तलब करना
Camp	शिविर
Camp equipage	निवेश संभार
Camp equipment	निवेश सज्जा
Canal irrigation	नहर की सिंचाई
Cancellation	विलापन
Cancelled	रद्द किया गया
Cancelling officer	रद्द करने वाला
Cantonment Act	छावनी कानून
Cap	फौजी टोपी

Capital sentence	प्राणदण्ड
Capital, Cash	पूँजी परिव्यय
Capitalized	पूँजीकृत
Capitation charges	प्रतिव्यक्ति प्रभार
Carbine bucket	कड़ाबीन आधार
Care (attention)	प्रणिधि
Care (regard)	अवेक्षा
Care Protection	संरक्षा
Cargo	नौभार
Cash balance	रोकड़ बाकी
Cash book	रोकड़ बही
Cash chest	रोकड़ की पेटी
Cash Outlay	नगदी लगान
Cash payment	नकद भुगतान
Cash rents	नकदी लगान
Castration	बधिया करना
Casual (As in casual prisoner)	इकबारा
Casual Leave	आकस्मिक छुट्टी
Catchment	पोषक क्षेत्र
Category	श्रेणी
Cattle Breeding farm	पशुओं की नसलकशी का फार्म
Cattle house	काजी हाउस
Cattle killer	पशुवध यन्त्र
Cattle prioplasmose, or Red water	लालमूत्र रोग
Caution	सतर्कता
Caveat	उच्चदारी (इत्तलानामा)
Caveat	सावधान
Ceased	समाप्त
Cellular	कोष्ठीय
Censure	निन्दा
Census	जनगणना
Central division	केन्द्रीय विवरणपत्र
Central Excise & Salt	केन्द्रीय उत्पादकर और नमक
Central Record Office	केन्दीय अभिलेखालय
Central Revenue Stamp	केन्द्रीय राजस्व मुद्रांक
Centrifugal	केन्द्रायग
Centripetal	केन्द्राभि
Certified extract	प्रमाणित अवतरण
Cess	अतिरिक्त कर
Cess	उपकर
Chain (measuring)	जरीब
Character of rainfall	वर्षा की दशा
Character-roll	चरित्रवर्ति (चरित्रावली)
Charge	अभियोग
Charge	प्रभार
Charge certificate	कार्यभार प्रमाणपत्र
Charge of office	पदभार
Charge sheet	अभियोग फलक
Charge, Expenditure	व्यय

Chargeable	देय
Charter party	जहाज का किराया नाम
Check against fraud	धोखादेही से बचाने की रोकथाम
Check of discount	बट्टे की जाँच पड़ताल
Check of stamp register	स्टाम्प रजिस्टरों की जाँच-पड़ताल
Cheque	धनादेश
Chevron, Badge, Stripe	बिल्ला
Chief Commissioner	मुख्य आयुक्त
Chief controlling revenue authority	मुख्य नियन्त्रक राजस्व प्राधिकारी
Chief Justice	मुख्य न्यायाधीश
Chord	जीवा
Chronological order	ऐतिहासिक क्रम
Circle	हलका
Circle officer	चक्राधिकारी
Circular (letter)	परिपत्र
Cistern	हौज (टंकी)
Citation	उपस्थिति के लिए सफीना
Citations	नजीर का हवाला
Civil	नागरिक (दीवानी)
Civil employee	असैनिक कर्मचारी
Civil list	अधिकारवर्ग सूची
Claim	अधियाचन (दावा)
Claimant	अधियाचक
Claimant	दावेदार
Clamp	सिकिजा
Classification	वर्गीकरण
Clause	वाक्य खण्ड
Cleaner	परिमार्जक
Cleaning losses	फटकन
Cleaning register	सफाई का रजिस्टर
Clearing agent	चेक चुकाई एजेन्ट
Clearing office	चेक चुकाई कार्यलय
Clemency	राजदया
Client	मुवक्किल
Clinical	रोग विषयक
Clinically affected	प्रत्यक्ष रोगग्रस्त
Closing balance	अंतिम शेष
Coat of arms	कुल चिह्न
Coccidiosis	बदरावण रोग
Code	संहिता
Codicil	क्रोड़पत्र
Co-efficient	बारद्योतक
Coercion	अनुचित दबाव
Cognate	सगोत्र
Cognizable	अनुसंधेय
Cognizable	हस्तक्षेप्य
Coinage	टंकन
Collaboration	सहयोग
Collateral agreement	अतिरिक्त नियमपत्र

Collecting government	समाहरणकारी सरकार
Collection	समाहरण
Collective subscription	सामूहिक चन्दा
Collector	समाहर्ता
Colonial service	उपनिवेशी सेवा
Combination	मवषय
Combustion	दहन
Combustion chamber	दहनागार
Command	समादेश
Commandant	समादेशक
Commanded area	अधिक्षेत्र
Commander	सेनापति
Commemoration volume	स्मारक ग्रन्थ
Commencement	आरंभ
Commencement and transitory	आरंभ और क्षणिक
Comment	आलोचना
Commercial	वाणिज्य सम्बन्धी
Commercial department	वाणिज्य विभाग
Commission	आयोग
Commission of inquiry	जाँच आयोग
Commissioner	आयुक्त
Commitment	समर्पण (कारागार भेजना)
Committal	सौंप
Committee	समिति
Common contingent charges	सामान्य प्रासंगिक व्यय
Commutation	पलटा करना
Commutation	संराशिदान
Commutation of pension	पेंशन का संराशिकरण
Commuted value	संराशि
Compass (pair of)	परकार
Compassionate	दवामूलक
Compassionate Gratuity	अनुग्रह-धन
Compensation	प्रतिकर (क्षतिपूर्ति)
Compensatory allowance	प्रतिकर भत्ता
Competency	योग्यता
Competent	योग्य (समर्थ)
Competent authority	शक्त प्राधिकारी
Competent court	समर्थ न्यायालय
Competitive examination	प्रतियोगिता परीक्षा
Compilation	संकलन
Compilation of statistics	आँकड़े का संकलन
Complainant	अभियोक्ता
Complainant	अभियोगी
Complaint	परिदेवना
Completion	समापन
Compliance	पालनादेश
Component parts	अवयव
Composition deed	निपटारा पत्र

Compoundable offences	समाधेय अपराध
Compounder, Mixer	मिश्रक
Compression	संपीड़न
Compulsory retirement	अनिवार्य निवृत्ति
Computation of fees	शुल्क गणना
Computer	गणनाकार
Concentration camp	कारा शिविर
Concessions	रियायतें
Concurrence	सहमति
Concurrent	समकालिक
Concurrent	सहवर्ति (संगामी)
Concurrent judgment	एकमत निर्णय
Condemned	फाँसी का (कैदी)
Condition	दशा
Condition	शर्त
Condition of qualifying service	योग्यकारी सेवा की शर्त
Condition of service	नौकरी की शर्त
Conditional long settlements	सोपाधिक दीर्घकालीन बन्दोबस्त
Conditional Order	औपाधिक आदेश
Conditional release	सोपाधिक मुक्ति
Conditional sale	सप्रतिबन्धक विक्रय
Condonation	क्षमा
Conduct	आचरण
Conduction	संवाहन
Conduit	बम्बा (पटी हुई नाली)
Cone	शंकु
Confederacy	प्रसंधि
Confederacy	राजसंघ
Confidential	गोप्य
Confinement	बंधन (कैद)
Confirmation	पक्का करना
Confiscation	राजसात्करण
Confiscation, Forfeiture	जब्ती
Conformity	अनुरूपता
Conjugal right	वैवाहिक अधिकार
Connivance	गजनिमीजिका
Conscription	अनिवार्य भर्ती
Consecutive	निरंतर
Consequential	पारिणामिक
Consignee	परेषणी
Consignment	प्रेषण
Consignment	सौंप पत्र
Consistent	संगत
Consolidated	एकस्थीकृत
Consolidated forecast	एकीकृत पूर्वानुमान
Consolidated pay	एकीकृत वेतन
Consolidation	एकस्थीकरण
Consolidation of holdings	चकबंदी
Consolidation Officer	चकबंदी अधिकारी

Consolidator	चकबंदीकर्ता
Constable	रक्षी (तिलंगा)
Constitution	संविधान
Consultation	संमन्त्रण
Consumer	उपभोक्ता
Contact	सम्पर्क
Contagious disease	संक्रामक रोग
Contempt of Court	न्यायालय अपमान
Content	अंतर्वस्तु
Context	प्रसंग
Contingencies	आकस्मिक व्यय
Contingency	प्रासंगिक व्यय
Contingent	प्रासंगिक
Contingent Reserve	आकस्मिक घृतदल
Continuous active service	अविरत सक्रिय सेवा
Continuous service	अविरत सेवा
Contraband	व्यासिद्ध (विनिषिद्ध)
Contract	ठेका
Contract allowance	नियत भत्ता
Contract of sale	नियमबद्ध विक्रय
Contractual relation	संविद्‌जनित सम्बन्ध
Contribution	अंश दान
Control over expenditure	व्यय पर नियन्त्रण
Controller of stamps	मुद्रांक नियन्त्रक
Controlling Officer	नियन्त्रक अधिकारी
Convener	संयोजक
Conventionally	प्रथानुसार
Conversion	पलट
Conveyance	सवारी
Conveyance	हस्तांतरण पत्र
Convict	आधर्षित
Conviction	आधर्षण
Co-operation	सहकारिता (सहयोग)
Co-operative	सहकारी
Co-operative societies	सहकारी समितियाँ
Co-ordinate	आसजन
Co-owner	सहस्वामी
Co-parcener	अंशी
Copy stamped papers	प्रतिलिपि मुद्रित पत्र
Copying Department	प्रतिलिपि विभाग
Copyist	प्रतिलिपिक
Corbel	भारधारक बढ़ाव
Cornice	सीका (कगार)
Coroner	अपमृत्यु-मीमांसक
Corporal punishment	शारीरिक दण्ड
Corpuscles	अणु-कण
Correction	शोधन (सुधार)
Correction slip	शुद्धि पर्ची
Corrigendum	शुद्धिपत्र
Corrosive sublimate	रसकपूर

Corrugated	नालीदार
Corruption	भ्रष्टाचार
Cost outstanding	गैर वसूल लागत
Cost realized	वसूल लागत
Co-tenant	सहकृषक
Cotton balls	कपास का गोला
Council of State	राज्य परषिद्
Council, Board	परिषद्
Counsel	मंत्रण
Counter affidavit	प्रतिशपथ पत्र
Counter balance	बराबर करना
Counter claim	मुकाबिल दावा
Counter signature	प्रतिहस्ताक्षर
Counterfoil	प्रतिपर्ण (मुसन्ना)
Counterpart	प्रतिरूप
Counterpart, Copy	प्रतिलिपि (मुसन्ना)
Course of law	विधि प्रक्रम
Courses of training	शिक्षण पाठचर्या
Court fee label	न्याय शुल्क चिप्पी
Court fees	न्याय शुल्क
Court fees act	न्याय शुल्क विधान
Court of law	न्यायालय
Covenant	संविदा
Covenanty	पारस्परिक संविदा
Cover	आवरक
Cover	छद (आवरण)
Cover glass preparation	काचावृत रचनाएँ
Covering farm	गाभिन फार्म
Covering return	गाभिन विवरण पत्र
Creamery	मक्खन-मलाई शाला
Creation (of post)	पद स्थापन
Creative	रचनात्मक
Credit	ऋण (उधार)
Credit	जमा
Credit	साख
Credit advice	जमा की सूचना
Crest	शिखर
Crime police	अपराध रोधक पुलिस
Crime, Offence	अपराध
Criminal conspiracy	आपराधिक षड्यन्त्र
Criminal offence	दंडअपराध
Criminal procedure	जाब्ता फौजदारी
Criminal Procedure Code	दंड विधि संग्रह
Crop prospects	फसल की प्रत्याशा
Cropped area	बोया हुआ क्षेत्रफल
Cross examination	जिरह
Cross examination	प्रतिपरीक्षा
Cross mark	कर्तनी चिह्न
Cross objection	प्रति आपत्ति
Cross objection	प्रत्याक्षेप
Cross, bar, fetter	कैंची, डंडा, बेड़ी
Crossing	चतुष्पथ
Crosssection	अनुप्रस्थ छेद

Crown of an arc तोरण शीर्ष

Crown post शिखर खण्ड

Cube घन

Cube-root घनमूल

Culinarv पाक विषयक

Culpable दंडनीय (अपराध)

Cultivator कृषक

Culturable waste कृषि योग्य बंजर

Culture medium पोषक माध्यम

Curative measure रोगहर उपाय

Current चालू

Current duty चालू कर्तव्य

Current fallow वर्तमान पड़ती

Curve वक्र

Cusecs प्रतिसेकंड घनफुट

Custodian of museum संग्रहालय संरक्षक

Custody संरक्षण

Custody & Supply of forms फार्मों का संरक्षण और दिया जाना

Custody of stamp स्टाम्प का संरक्षण

Custody of wills रिक्थपत्रों का संरक्षण

Cut, Deduction कटौती

Cutaneous चर्मीय

Cyclostyle साइक्लोस्टाइल

Cylinder बेलन

D. O. letter अर्ध सरकारी पत्र

Dacoity बटमारी

Daily labour return श्रमिकों का दैनिक नकशा

Dairy दुग्धशाला

Dairy farm डेरी फार्म

Dak डाक

Dam संवर (बाँध)

Damage हरजाना

Damages suit क्षतिपूर्ति का वाद

Data दी हुई बात

Date of institution दायर करने की तारीख

Day scholar. अनावासिक छात्र

De jure विधानतः

De Novp नये सिरे से

Deal thoroughly पूरी तरह उपचार करना

Debenture ऋणपत्र

Debit विकलन

Debit advice नाम की सूचना

Debit and Credit नाम और जमा

Decay क्षय

Decentralization विकेन्द्रीकरण

Decentralization committee विकेन्द्रीकरण (समिति)

Decided निर्णीत

Decimal fraction दशमलव भिन्न

Decision, Finding, Judgment निर्णय

Declaration of trust प्रन्यास घोषणा

Declaratory decree	अधिकार घोषक न्यायपत्र
Decorations	सैनिक चिह्न
Decree	डिग्री
Decree	न्याय पत्र
Decree absolute	अंतिम डिगरी
Decree nisi	प्रतिबन्धित न्यायपत्र
Decree-holder	न्याय पत्रग्राही (डिगरीदार)
Deed (Sale, Lease)	विक्रयपत्र, पट्टा
Deed of agreement	नियम पत्र
Deed of gift	दानपत्र
Defalcation	व्ययहरण
Defamation, Contempt	मानहानि
Default	अनुपस्थान
Default	दोष
Defence	उत्तर पक्ष
Defence	प्रतिरक्षा
Defence Department	प्रतिरक्षा विभाग
Defence witness	प्रतिवाद साक्षी
Defendant	प्रतिवादी
Deferred pay	आस्थगित वेतन
Delegation	प्रत्यायुक्ति
Delegation	शिष्टमडण्ल
Deletion	अपमार्जन
Delinquent	दोषी (अपराधी)
Delivered	समर्पित
Demand, Requisition	माँग
Demi-official	अर्धसरकारी
Demodectic scabies	खुजली
Denaturalised	स्वभाव विकृत
Denial of execution	निष्पादन की इन्कारी
Denomination	मूल्यवान
Departmental	वैभागिक
Departmental account	वैभागिक लेखा
Deportation	निर्वासन (देश निकाला)
Depose	राजच्युत करना
Depose	शपथपूर्वक साक्ष्य देना
Deposit	उपनिधान
Deposit	धरोहर
Deposition	सशपथ कथन
Deposition	साक्षी का बयान
Depreciation	अवलूल्यन
Deputation	अभिप्रेषण
Deputation	प्रतिनियुक्ति (प्रतिनिधि मण्डल)
Deputation (duty) allowance	प्रतिनियुक्ति भत्ता
Depute	प्रत्यायुक्त
Derogatory	लाघवकारक
Descriptive roll	वर्णनवर्ति
Deserter	दलत्यागी

Design	परिकल्पना
Designate	मनोनीत
Designation	पदनाम, ओहदा
Designed	परिकल्पित
Designer	परिकल्पक
Despatch Rider	डाक सवार
Despatcher	संप्रेषक
Detailed bill	ब्योरेवार बिल
Detention	अवरोध
Detenue	अवरुद्ध
Development minister	विकास मन्त्री
Deviate	रास्ते से हटना
Devolution	अवक्रमण
Diary	दैनंदिनी (दिन पंजी)
Diet money	भोजन व्यय
Difference of opinion	मतभेद
Digest	संक्षिप्त संग्रह
Direct charge	प्रत्यक्ष व्यय
Direct supervision	सीधी देखभाल
Direction	निर्देश
Directory	निर्देशिनी
Disability leave	अशक्तता छुट्टी
Disappearance	लोप
Disbursement, Distribution	वितरण
Disbursing authority	भुगतान प्राधिकारी
Disbursing officer	भुगतानकारी अधिकारी
Discharge of duties	कर्तव्य पालन
Discharge of water	निकासी
Discharged	अभियोग मुक्त
Discharged	कार्यत्यक्त
Discharged	दोष मुक्त
Disciplinary action	अनुशासनात्मक कार्यवाही
Disciplinary action	अनुशासन की कार्यवाही
Discipline	अनुशासन
Disciplined	अनुशासित
Disclaimer	दावा छोड़ने वाला
Discount	बट्टा
Discredited document	अमान्य लेख
Discredited document	रद्द किया हुआ लेखपत्र
Discrepancy	असंगति
Discrepancy	भिन्नता
Discrepancy memo	कमी का स्मृतिपत्र
Discretion	विवेक
Discretional registration	विवेकाधीन रजिस्टरी
Disinfectant	कीटाणु नाशक
Disinfectant	रोगाणु नाशक
Disinherit	दाय वंचित करना
Dismiss, Weed out, Set side	खारिज करना
Dismissal	पदच्यूति

Dismissed summarily	सरसरी तौर पर खारिज
Display	प्रदर्शन
Disposal	निवर्तन
Disposed off	निबटाया
Disputed	विवादास्पद
Disqualification	अयोग्यता
Dissolution of partnership	साझाभंग पत्र
Distemper	दीवार पकड़ रंग
Distinguishing letter	विभेदक अक्षर
Distrain	कुड़क कराना
Distress warrant	अभिहरण अधिपत्र
Distributory	रजबहा
Diversity factor	भंदगुणक
Division of holdings	जोत का बँटवारा
Divisional canal Officer	नहर डिविजन अधिकारी
Document	लेखपत्र (लेख्य)
Documentary	लेख्यात्मक
Domicile	स्थायी निवास
Dotted line	विन्दु रेखा
Double shift system	द्विपारी प्रथा
Dourine Act	उपदंश कानून
Draft	आलेख (नक्शा)
Draft	पांडुलेख (मसविदा)
Draftsman	आलेखक
Drainage	जलोत्सारण
Dress	वेष, वस्त्र
Dress regulation	वेष नियमावली
Drought	अनावृष्टि
Dryage	सूख
Ductility	नरमी (तार खींचे जाने की क्षमता)
Dues	प्राप्य
Duly	यथावत्
Duly approved	यथाविधि स्वीकृति
Duly stamped	यथोचित टिकट लगा हुआ
Duplicate	दुहरा
Dust-proof	धूलरोक
Duty	शुल्क
Duty allowance	कर्तव्य भत्ता
Duty of transfer	हस्तांतरण शुल्क
Duty on counterpart or duplicate	प्रतिलिपि पर शुल्क
Duty on release	अधिकार त्यागपत्र
Dying declaration	मरणासन्न कथन
Dynamics	गतिशास्त्र
Earmark	निर्दिष्ट करना
Earnest money	सत्यकार (बयाना)
East coast fever	पूर्वतटीय ज्वर
Eaves	अलोनी
Ebony	आबनूस
Eccentric	उत्केन्द्र
Ectozoa	बहिर्परजीवी
Effective capacity	वास्तविक क्षमता

Effective span	कारगर चौड़ाई
Efficiency bar	प्रगुणता अर्गल
Egress	निष्कास
Ejectment	निर्मुक्ति (बेदखली)
Ejectment	बेदखली
Election Campaign	चुनाव आन्दोलन
Electrical equipment	विद्युत् सज्जा
Electrical installation	विद्युत् प्रतिष्ठापन
Electrician	वैद्युतिक
Eligibility	पात्रता
Eligibility	वरणीयता
Eligible	योग्य पात्र
Eliptic and curved figures	अंडाकार क्षेत्र तथा वक्र क्षेत्र
Ellipse	अण्डवृत्त
Embankment	पंकार (बंध)
Embezzlement	अपहार
Embezzlement	गबन
Embezzlement	छल (हरण, गबन)
Emergency	आकस्मिक
Emergency	संकटकाल (आपत्, विपत्ति)
Emergency	संकट कालीन
Emergency (Police)	संकट (पुलिस)
Emoluments	परिलाभ
Emulsion	दूधा
Enactment	विधायन (कानून)
Enactment	विधिकरण, विधि निर्माण
En-camera trial	गुप्त अक्ष विचार
Encamping ground	निवेश स्थल
Encampment	निवेशन (छावनी)
Encasing	कोष
Enclosure	अनुपत्र
Enclosure	अंतर्गतपत्र
Encroachment	जमीन बढ़ाना
Encroachment	प्रत्यधिकार
Encroachment	सीमा-भंजन
Encumbered	ऋणग्रस्त
Endorsement	पृष्ठ लेख
Endorsement	पृष्ठांकन
Endorsement, Approval	अनुमोदन
Endowment	अग्रहार-दान
Energy	शक्ति
Enfacement	बिगाड़ना
Enhancement	वृद्धि
Enrolment	नाम निवेश
Entozoa	अंतर्परजीवी
Entry	प्रविष्टि
Epidemic	व्यापक संक्रामक रोग (मनुष्य)
Epidemic disease	महामारी
Epizootic	व्यापक संक्रामक रोग (पशु)
Equilibrium	समतोल

Equipage	संभार
Equipment	सज्जा
Equipment catalogue	सज्जा सूची
Equipment table	सज्जा सारणी
Equity	न्यायता
Errata list	अशुद्धि-सूची
Erratic	अनिश्चित
Escape (for surplus water)	परिवाह
Escapee	अपसृत
Escheat	अस्वाभाविक धन
Escheat	साजसात् किया माल
Escort	गारद
Escort	रक्षक वर्ग
Establishing	सिद्ध करना
Establishment	स्थापना
Estimate	आगणन
Estopped	उत्तर रोध
Evasion of registration	सकपट रजिस्ट्री को बचा लेना
Evidence	साक्ष्य
Evolution	उद्विकास
Excepted	वर्जित
Exception	अपवाद
Excessive	अत्यधिक
Exchange	विनिमय
Exchange deed	विनिमय पत्र
Exchange instrument	विनिमयकरण पत्र
Exchange of compensation allowance	विनिमय क्षतिपूरक भत्ता
Excise department	आबकारी विभाग
Excise duty	उत्पाद कर
Excreta	पुरीप (विष्ठा)
Executable	निर्वर्तन योग्य
Executed document	लिखा-पढ़ा गया लेखपत्र
Execution	तामील
Execution	फाँसी
Execution (as of decree)	निष्पादन
Executive	निर्वाही
Executor	इच्छापत्र साधक
Executor of will	रिक्थ साधक
Exemplify	उदाहुत करना
Exemption	मुक्ति (छूट)
Ex-gratia relief	अनुग्रह रूप सहायता
Exhaust	तली
Exhibit	प्रदर्शित वस्तु
Ex-officio	पद कारणात्
Ex-officio	पदेन
Ex-officio Sub-Registrar	पदकारणात् उपपंजीयक
Ex-officio vendor	देन विक्रेता
Exoneration	छुटकारा
Exparte	एकपक्षीय
Experimental	प्रयोगात्मक
Expert	विशेषज्ञ

Explanatory supplement	व्याख्यानात्मक अनुपूरक
Export	निर्यात
Exposure	खुला रखना
Express	आशु
Express letter	आशुपत्र
Ex-proprietary	गतस्वामित्व
Ex-tenant	भूतपूर्व असामी
Extension	अवधि वद्धि
Extension of leave	छुट्टी बढ़ाना
Extension of load	भार-वृद्धि
Extortion	बलात ग्रहण
Extract	अवतरण (उद्धरण)
Extract	उद्धरण
Extradition	विदेशी अपराधी का प्रत्यर्पण
Extraneous duties	अतिरिक्त कर्तव्य
Extraordinary leave	असाधारण छुट्टी
Extremist	उग्रवादी
Exudation	स्राव
Eye and hook	तुकमा और हुक
Factor	गुणक
Faculty	शाखा
Faecal discharge	मलत्याग
Fair copy	विशुद्ध प्रतिलिपि
Family arrangement	पारितोषिक व्यवस्थापन
Famine-code	दुर्भिक्ष संहिता
Famine-duty	दुर्भिक्ष कर्तव्य
Farcy	जहरबाद
Fatigue	दलेल
Federation, Union	संघ
Feeder	पोषक
Fellowship	परिषद्यता
Fenestra	गवाक्ष
Ferries	घाट
Ferries Act	घाट विधान
Ferrule	छल्ला
Fertiliser, manure	खाद
Fetter	गेड़ी
Fibrin	रक्त तन्तु
Field-book	खसरा
Figures, Statistics	आँकड़े
File	नत्थी (मिसिल, नस्ती)
File register	नस्ती पंजी
Filing of document	मुकदम में कागजात दाखिल करना
Fillet	फीता
Finality	पूर्णता (अंतिमता)
Finally disposed of (decided)	अंतिम रूप से निर्णीत
Finance Minister	अर्थमन्त्री
Financial hand book	अर्थ पुस्तिका
Fine	अर्थदण्ड
Finger Print	अँगुली छाप
Finial	कलश (शिखर)
Fire brigade	दमकल

Fire service दमकल भृत्या

Fire-brick. अग्नि-इष्टिका

Fireman, Fire-extin अग्नि प्रशामक

Fire-place अलाव

Fire-proof safe. अग्नि सुरक्षित तिजोरी

First aid प्रथमोपचार

First Information Report प्रारंभिक सूचना रपट

Fiscal राजस्व विषयक

Fish ladder मत्स्यारौह सीढ़ी

Fish plate मत्स्य पट्टिका

Fitness certificate काय्र योग्यता प्रमाणपत्र

Fitness certificate निरोगिता प्रमाणपत्र

Fitness for further advance अधिकतम उन्नति के लिए योग्यता

Fixed deposit स्थिर जमा

Fixed for hearing सुनवाई के लिए नियत की गयी

Fixed point duty एक स्थानीय चौराहा ड्यूटी

Flag staff पताका दंड

Flake पापड़ (पपड़ी)

Flange अग्रीव

Flat charge समान प्रभार

Fleas पिस्सू

Floating debt अल्पकाल ऋण

Florescence बसन्त (ऋतुराज)

Fluctuation उतार-चढ़ाव

Flush उद्धावन

Flush latrine धवनी

Fly-proof मक्खी रोक

Focus नाभि

Folio पर्ण

For consideration विचारार्थ

Forced labour बेगार

Forecast पूर्वानुमान

Foreclosure of mortgage बंधक मोक्षण प्रतिरोध

Foreign currency विदेशी मुद्रा

Foreigner पर राष्ट्रिक

Foreman of the Jury जूरी पंच

Foremost अग्रतम (प्रमुख)

Fore-noon पूर्वाह्न

Forensic न्यायालय सम्बन्धी

Forfeit जब्त करना

Forfeiture अपहरण

Forgery कूटकरण (बाल कल्पना)

Forgery कूट रचना

Form रूपपत्र (फार्म)

Forma pauperis. अकिंचनता का मद

Formal यथाचार

Formal (superficial) ऊपरिक

Formal warning यथानियम चेतावनी

Formula सूत्र

Forthcoming आगामी

Forwarded प्रेषित

Foundry	संघानी
Framing of issues	विवाद प्रश्नों को स्थिर करना
Fraud	कपट (कूट, छल, धोखा)
Freight	अनुतर
Frequency	वारंवारता
Frontis piece	मुखचित्र
Fugitive criminal	पलायित दोषी
Fulcrum	आलंब (टक)
Full Bench	न्यायाधीश गण
Full particulars	सारा वृत्तान्त
Function	कृत्य
Function	पद कर्तव्य
Functus officio	समाप्ताधिकार
Fund	निधि
Fundamental	आधारभूत
Fundamental	मौलिक
Fundamental guide book	मौलिक पथप्रदर्शनी
Fundamental rule	मौलिक नियम
Furnish security	जमानत दाखिल करना
Furniture	उपस्कर
Fuse	दहन वर्ति
Gallery	दीर्घा
Gallows	वधस्थान
Galvanized	जस्ता चढ़ी
Gauge	आमान
Gazette	राजपत्र (गजट)
Gazetted Officer	राजपत्रित अधिकारी
General Provident fund	सामान्य पूर्वोपायी कोष
General rules	सामान्य नियम
General Rules, Civil	दीवानी के सामान्य नियम
Generating station	विद्युत उत्पादन संस्थान
Generator	जनित्र (जनक)
Geological survey	भूगर्भ अनुदर्शन
Girder	गार्टर
Girth	तंग
Glue	सरेस
Good behaviour	सदाचार
Good Faith	सद्भाव
Goods	भंडक (माल)
Governed	शासित
Government order	सरकारी आज्ञा
Government pleader	सरकारी अधिवक्ता
Government pleader	सरकारी अभिभावक
Government, Crown	सरकार
Governor	राज्यपाल
Gradation	कोर्ट साहिब
Gradation list	कोटिक्रम
Grand total	पूर्णयोग
Grant	अनुदान
Grant-in-aid	सहायक अनुदान
Graph	विन्दुरेख

Gratification परितोष

Gratings जाली (झँझरी)

Gratuity सेवोपहार

Gravel रोड़ा (कंकड़)

Gravity गुरुत्व

Gravity canal ढाल चालित नहर

Grease free चर्बी रहित

Gridiron तवा (लपरी)

Grind-stone सान

Gross load सकल भार

Gross negligence भारी प्रमाद

Gross salary सकल वेतन

Ground water supplied पाताल जलपुंज

Grounds of appeal अपील के आधार

Group गुट (समूह)

Group leader टोली नायक

Groyne जलतोड़

Guarantee letter सुरक्षापत्र

Guards & Escorts गादद और कमान

Guilty दोषी (दोष प्राप्त)

Gunpowder बारूद

Guts, Water course गूल

Gymnasium व्यायामशाला

Habitual offender आभ्यासिक अपराधी

Half-margin अर्धोपान्त

Halt निवेशन

Halting (allowance) निवेशन (भत्ता)

Hand grenade हथगोला

Hand slip हथचिट्ट

Hand writing हस्तलिपि

Harness काठी

Hasp कुन्दा कब्जा

Head and Sub-head शीर्षक और उपशीर्षक

Head of account लेखा शीर्षक

Head of the department विभागाध्यक्ष

Head Regulator शीर्षस्तर नियामक

Head rope शिररज्जु

Head works उद्गम कार्यजात

Headquarter मुख्य स्थान

Headquarters मुख्यालय

Headway प्रगति

Health certificate स्वास्थ्य प्रमाणपत्र

Hearing सुनवाई

Heel file एड़ी जोड़ा

Helmet शिरस्त्राण

Hereditary पारंपरीय (पैतृक)

Heritage, Inheritance दाय (बपौती)

High Court उच्च न्यायालय

High flood level महाप्लवस्तर चिह्न

Higher authority उच्च अधिकारी

Highway राजमार्ग

Hindu reversioner हिन्दू उत्तरभोगी

Hindu widow's हिन्दू विधवा का

Hip rafter	शीर्ष शहतीर
Hire purchase	भाड़ाक्रय
His Excellency	महामान्य (महामहिम)
History sheet	अपराध वृत्त
Holding cost	रोक रखने की लागत
Home guard	होमगार्ड
Homogeneous	सजातीय (समाधान)
Honorarium	मानदेय
Honorary	अवैतनिक
Horse power	अश्व-शक्ति
Horse stallion	बीजाश्व (घुड़साँड़)
Hot-pursuit	तीव्र अनुधावन
House rent allowance	मकान किराया भत्ता
human resources department	नियुक्ति विभाग
Humane cattle killer	अनिर्दय पशुवध-यन्त्र
Hundi, Stamp	हुंडी मुद्रांक
Hydraulic	जल चालित
Hydro	जल
Hydro-electric grid	जल विद्युत तारजाल
Hypotenuse	कर्ण
Hypothecation	आड
Hypothesis	कल्पना
Identical	अनन्य
Identification	पहचान
Identification mark	चिह्न
Illegal	अवैध
Illegible copy	दुर्वचनीय कापी
Illustrated, Illustrate	उदाहृत
Imminent	प्रत्यासन्न
Immoral traffic	अनैतिक पण
Immovable property	अचल सम्पत्ति
Immovable property	स्थावर सम्पत्ति
Impersonation, False personation	छद्मव्यक्तिता
Impervious	अप्रवेश्य
Implement, Tools	उपकरण
Implementation	कार्यान्वयन
Import	आयात
Impound	निरोध करना
Impounded documents	जब्त किये हुए लेख पत्र
Impressed stamp	मुद्रांकित स्टाम्प
Impression	छाप
Impression (copy)	निवेश
Imprest	अग्रधन
Improved	सुधरा हुआ
In Camera	कक्षस्थ (गुप्त)
In compliance with	पालन करते हुए
In consequence	परिणामस्वरूप
In due course	यथासमय
In furtherance of a common cause	सार्वजनिक हितोन्नति
In moderate excess	कुछवाजिबी अधिक
In pursuit of	अनुशीलन

In supersession of.	अकारण करते हुए
In toto	बिलकुल
Inadequate	अपर्याप्त
Inadmissible claims	अग्राह्य दावा
Inaugural	प्रतिष्ठापनिक
Incidence	आपात
Incidental charge	आनुषंगिक व्यय
Inclined	झूका
Incognizable	अहस्तक्षेप्य
Income-tax	आयकर
Increment	वेतन वृद्धि
Incumbency	पद धारणा
Indemnification	तावान देना
Indemnity bond	क्षतिपूरक प्रतिज्ञापत्र
Indemnity bond	हानिपूरक नियमपत्र
Indemnity, Compensation	क्षतिपूर्ति
Index	अनुक्रमणिका
Indian Arms Act	भारतीय शस्त्र विधान
Indian Army Act	भारतीय सेना विधान
Indian Civil Service	भारतीय जनपद भृत्या
Indian Divorce Act	भारतीय विवाह विच्छेद विधान
Indian Evidence Act	भारतीय साक्ष्य विधान
Indian Penal Code	भारतीय दण्ड संहिता
Indian Succession Act	भारतीय उत्तराधिकार विधान
Indicator	देशित
Indigent	निर्धन
Indiscriminate	अविवेकी, अविवेकपूर्ण
Indivisible transaction	अविभाज्य लेन-देन
Indoor patient	भरती रोगी
Inducement	प्रेरणा (प्रलोभन)
Industrialization	औद्योगीकरण
Industry, Labour	परिश्रम
Inefficiency	अप्रगुणता
Inertia	जड़ता
Infanticide	शिशुवध
Infantry	पदाति
Infections, Jaundice of the dogs	कुत्ते का संक्रामक पाण्डुरोग
Inferior staff	अवर कर्मचारी वर्ग
Infinitesimal	अत्यन्त छोटा
Infirm	अशक्त
Infirmary	आतुरालय
Infirmity	असमर्थता
Inflation	मुद्रास्फीति
Influence line	प्रभाव रेखा
Infra	नीचे
Infringement	भंग करना
Infringement, Contravention	उल्लंघन
Ingredient	अंश (घटक द्रव्य)
Ingress, Inlets	प्रवेश (द्वार)
Initial pay	आरंभिक वेतन
Initialled	लघुहस्ताक्षरित

Injunction	निषेधाज्ञा
Injured stamp	क्षत मुद्रांक
Injury	आघात
Injury to records	कागजात का नुकसान
Inoculation, Comments, Notes	टीका
Inscription	शिलालेख
Insemination	गर्भाधान
Insertion	अंतर्न्यास
Insignificant	तुच्छ
Inspection	निरीक्षण
Inspection fee	निरीक्षण शुल्क
Inspector General	महानिरीक्षक
Inspector General of Prisons	महाकारानिरीक्षक
Inspectorate of stamp	स्टाम्प निरीक्षणाधिकारी वर्ग
Installation	प्रतिष्ठापन
Institute	ज्ञानमन्दिर (ज्ञानालय)
Instruction	अनुदेश
Instrument (in writing)	करणपत्र
Instrument of dowery	दहेहकारणपत्र
Instrument of furthep charge	अधिक भार का कारण पत्र
Instrument of gift	प्रदान पत्र
Instrument of Settlement	व्यवस्थापत्र
Instruments creating interest	स्वार्थोत्पादक करणपत्र
Insulation layer	विसंवाहकस्तर
Insulator	विसंवाहक
Intangible property	अमूर्त सम्पत्ति
Integrity	सत्यशीलता
Intensity	प्रगाढ़ता
Intercourse	संसर्ग
Interest-free	बेब्याज
Interim	अंतर्कालीन (अंतरिम)
Interim	मध्यवर्ती
Interim stay	मध्वर्ती स्थगन
Interlination	पंक्तिमध्य लेख
Inter-lineation	लाइन के बीच में लिखना
Intermediary, Intermediate	अंत:स्थायी
Intermediate	माध्यमिक
Intermediate forecast	बीच का पूर्वानुमान
Intermittent cultivation	अतिरिक्त खेती
Interpolating	कोई शब्द छल से लिख देना
Interpretation	व्याख्या
Interrogation, Inquiry	प्रच्छना
Interval	अंतराल
Intimation	सूचना
Intoxicating drug	मादक द्रव्य
Intrados	महराब
Intramural	भित्ति भीतर
Introduction	पुरः स्थापना

Inventory	सूची
Inverse rate	प्रतीप दर
Investigation	अनुसंधान
Investment	रुपये का लगाना
Invidious	द्वेषजनक
Invoice	बीजक
Ipso facto	स्वत: सिद्ध
Irksome	अप्रिय (थकाऊ)
Irrecoverable	अप्रतिलक्ष्य
Irregularity	अनियमता
Irrelevant	असंगत
Isometric	चित्रसम (प्रक्षेप)
Issue Price	निर्गम मूल्य
Issue, Code	जारी करना
Issues	निर्गमन
Item	मद
Jail premises.	कारोपान्त
Jailor	कारापाल
Jambs	छिद्र पक्ष
Jet	नाल (टोंटी)
Job	काम (ठेके का)
Joining time	कार्यग्रहण अवधि
Joint family property	अविभक्त परिवार सम्पत्ति
Joint holding	अविभक्त जोत
Joist	धरणी
Judgment writer	निर्णय लेखक
Judgment-debtor	निर्णीत ऋणी
Judicature	न्यायाधिकार
Judicial	न्याय सम्बन्धी
Judicial authority	न्यायालयिक प्राधिकारी
Judicial Department	न्याय विभाग
Judicial investigation	न्यायिक विचारण
Judicial proceeding	न्यायिक कार्यवाही
Judiciary	न्यायाधिकारी वर्ग
Junction	संगम
Jurisdiction	अधिकार क्षेत्र
Jurisdiction Act	विचाराधिकार विधान
Justice of the peace	शांति-रक्षा दण्डनायक
Justice of the Peace	शांति रक्षा आधिकरणिक
Juvenile offender	अल्पवयस्क अपराधी
Juvenile offender	किशोर अपराधी
King post	खड़ा लम्ब
Kink	अलपेट
Lack, Want	अभाव
Land record manual	भूअभिलेख सार संग्रह
Land Improvement loan	भूमि सुधारार्थ ऋण
Land Improvement Loans Act	भूमि सुधार ऋण विधान
Land record	भू लेखा
Land record clerk	भूअभिलेख लेखक
Land record department	भू लेखा विभाग

Land revenue	भू राजस्व
Land revenue	मालगुजारी
Landed property, Estate	भूसम्पत्ति
Landlord	भूस्वामी
Lapse	अतिवृत्त
Lapsed	कालातीत
Larder	खाद्य सामग्री भण्डार
Lathe	कुन्द
Lathe	खराद
Lawful assembly	विधि अनुकूल सभा
Lay out	समहिति
Lease	पट्टा
Lease hold	पट्टे की भूमि
Leases	पट्टे
Leave preparatory to retirement	निवृत्ति पूर्व छुट्टी
Leave salary	छुट्टी वेतन
Leaves of door	द्वारपट
Ledger	बहीखाता
Legal	वैधिक
Legal practitioner	विध्युपजीवी अभिभाषक
Legal Rememberancer	वैध उद्बोधक
Legatee	रिक्थी
Legislative assembly	व्यवस्थापिका सभा
Legislative department	व्यवस्थापिका विभाग
Legitimate	न्याय्य
Legitimate (as in legitimate child)	औरस
Legitimate dues	न्यायोचित दातव्य
Lessee	पट्टेदार
Lessor	पट्टा करने वाला
Letter of administration	उत्तराधिकार (विरासत) का प्रमाणपत्र
Letter of administration	प्रबंधाधिकार पत्र
Letter of credit	प्रत्ययपत्र
Letters patent appeal	राजदया अपील
Letting	जमीन का उठाना
Levelling staff	स्तरमापक दण्ड
Levy	लगान उगाहना
Liability	दायित्व
Liable	उत्तरदायी
Licence	अनुज्ञा-पत्र
Licencing authorities	अनुज्ञा पत्र दायक
Licensee	अनुज्ञाधारी
Lien	ग्रहणाधिकार
Lien suspended	स्थगित ग्रहणाधिकार
Lieutenant Governor	उपराज्यपाल
Life-tenure	आजीवन पट्टा
Lightning conductor	तड़ित संवाहक
Limitation	अवधि
Linear	लकीरी
Link	कड़ी
Lintel	पटीरन

Liquidation	अपाकरण (दिवाला)
Listing of cases	मुकदमों को सूचीगत करना
Litigation	विवाद
Live stock	पशुधन
lndent	माँग पत्र
lnquest	मृत्यु विचारणा
Loaded	भारित
Lobby	सभाकक्ष
Lobby, Chaupal	चौपार (डेवढ़ी)
Local	स्थानिक (स्थानीय)
Local allowance	स्थानीय भत्ता
Local bodies	स्थानीय निकाय
Local cess	स्थानीय कर
Local depot	स्थानीय कोठार
Local funds	स्थानीय संस्थाकोष
Local government	स्थानीय सरकार
Lock-up	हवालात
Locus standi	स्थानाधिकार
Locust	टिड्डी
Logarithm	छेदा
Long section	अन्वायाम काट
Longitude	देशांतर (लंबान)
Loose cotton	खुली हुई रूई
Louvre	झिलमिली
Lower	अधस्तन
Lump	पिंड
Lump sum	एकराशि
Lump-sum	पिंडराशि
Lunatic criminal	विक्षिप्त दोषी
Lymphatic glands	लसीका ग्रन्थि
Magazine	शस्त्रागार
Maggot	कोट (कृषि)
Magistrate	अधिकरणिक
Magistrate	दंडनायक
Main wall (Jail ward), Baton, Bludgeon	डंडा
Maintenance	अनुपालन
Maintenance	रखरखाव
maintenance	जीवन निर्वाह
Maintenance officer	रखरखाव निरीक्षक
Maintenance officer	रखरखाव अधिकारी
Major	वयस्क
Major head	बड़ा शीर्षक
Majority	बहुमत
Make restoration, Compensate	टोटा भरना
Malignant growth	रोगज वृद्धि
Manager	प्रबंधक
Mandatory	आदेशात्मक
Manifesto	घोषणापत्र
Manual (books)	सार-संग्रह
Manual of Irrigation Order	सिंचाई आदेश सारसंग्रह
Manual of orders	आज्ञासार संग्रह
Manufacturing process	निर्माण क्रिया

Manufiicture	निर्माण
Margin	उपात
Marginal	औपान्तिक
Marginal heading	उपांत शीर्षक (पार्श्व शीर्षक)
Marginally noted	उपांत लिखित
Marine Officer	समुद्री अधिकारी
Maritime policy	समुद्री पालिसी
Market	विपणी (आपण)
Marketable security	क्रयविक्रय योग्य सरकारी हुण्डी
Marriage (Dissolution of)	विवाह भंग
Marriage certificate	विवाह प्रमाणपत्र
Mask	मुखावरण
Mason	राज
Masonry	राजगीरी
Master of ship	पोतपति
Material change	मुख्य परिवर्तन
Material injustice	वास्तविक अन्याय
Maternity hospital	प्रसूति चिकित्सालय
Maternity leave	प्रसूति छुट्टी
Matrimonial reader	विवाह विषयक पेशकार
Matron	मातृका
Mature	प्रौढ़ (परिपक्व)
Maturity	परिपक्वता
Maximum demand indicatory	अधिकतम माँग-सूचक
Mean	माध्य (औसत)
Measurement book	नाप पुस्तक
Medical leave	चिकित्सकीय छुट्टी
Medium pressure	मध्यम भार
Member (Roof)	अंग
Memo of appearance	उपस्थिति का स्मृतिपत्र
Memorandum	स्मृतिपत्र
Memorialist, Applicant	आवेदक
Mensuration	क्षेत्रमिति
Mercy petition	दया की अभ्यर्थना
Merger	समावेश
Mesh	जाल (जालि का छेद)
Mesne profit	अपलाभ (जरे वासलात)
Metalled (Road)	पक्की (सड़क)
Meteorological observatory	अंतरिक्ष विज्ञान मान-मन्दिर
Meter	मापक (मीटर)
Meter reader	मीटर वाचक
Microscopical examination	सुक्ष्मदर्शकीय परीक्षा
Military officer	सैनिक अधिकारी
Military service	सैनिक सेवा
Military stores	सैनिक कोषागार
Miniature	सूक्ष्माकार (लघुचित्र)
Minister of food	खाद्य मन्त्री
Minor	अल्पवयस्क

Minute book	कार्यवाही का रजिस्टर
Minutes	कार्यवाही
Misappropriation	अपाहरण
Misbehaviour	अविनय
Miscarriage	गर्भपात
Miscarriage of Justice	न्याय वैफल्य
Miscellaneous	प्रकीर्ण (विविध)
Mis-description	अशुद्ध वर्णन
Mitigation	शमन (न्यूनीकरण)
Mobile squad	गश्ती दस्ता
Modification, Amendment	संशोधन
Modified grant	संशोधित अनुदान
Modulus	माप
Moiety fees	अल्पशुल्क
Moment of inertia	जड़ता प्रवृत्ति
Momentum	झोंक
Monetary allotment	आर्थिक दिष्टि
Monopoly	एकाधिकार
Monthly abstract	मासिक उपसंक्षेप
Monthly return	मासिक विवरणपत्र
Morbid material	विकृत कायिक पदार्थ
Mortgage	बंधक
Mortgage	रेहन बन्धक
Mortgage bond	बंधक पत्र
Mortgagee	बन्धक ग्राही
Mortgagor	बन्धक कर्ता
Mould	खाँचा
Mound	टीला
Mounted police	घुड़सवार पुलिस
Movable property, Movable effect	चल सम्पत्ति
Mud mortar	गारा
Mufti	साधारण वेष
Multifarious (suit)	अनेकार्थ (वाद)
Multifarious suit	बहुविधवाद
Municipality	नगरपालिका
Muster	गिनती (हाजिरी)
Muster-roll	गिनती की किताब
Mutation register	दाखिल खारिज रजिस्टर
Mutatis Mutandis	आवश्यक परिवर्तनों सहित
My Lord	धर्म–मूर्ति
Narrative	वृत्तान्त
National Service	राष्ट्रीय सेवा
Nationalization	राष्ट्रीयकरण
Native of India	भारतवासी
Naturalization	देशीकरण (नागरिकीकरण)
Nature of the case	मुकदमे का प्रकार
Naval Force	नाविक सेना
Navigation	नौचालन
Negative	ऋणात्मक
Negligence	असावधानी

Net	शुद्ध
Net assets	वास्तविक सम्पत्ति
Net emoluments	शुद्ध परिलाभ
Net profit	शुद्ध लाभ
Neutral axis	क्लीवाक्ष
New fallow	नई परती
Nomenclature	नामकरण
Nominal roll	नाम सूची
Non Judicial	न्यायालयेत्तर
Non Judicial Stamp	न्यायेतर स्टाम्प
Non-commissioned officer	अनायुक्त अधिकारी
Non-compliance	न पालन करना
Non-contract	अनियत
Non-food crops	अखाद्य फसल
Non-gazetted (officer)	अराजपत्रित (अधि कारी)
Non-labouring	अपरिश्रमी
Non-occupancy tenant	गैरदखिलकारी असामी
Non-official	अनाधिकारिक
Non-porous	असोख
Non-recurring expenditure	अनावर्ती व्यय
Non-residential	अनावासिक
Non-scheduled	अपरिगणित
Non-testamentary	असम्बन्धित इच्छापत्र
Normal	साधारण

Normal, General	सामान्य
Northern India	उत्तरी भारत
Notary public	लेख्यप्रमाणक
Notch	दान्ता
Noter and Drafter	टिप्पणी लेखक तथा पाण्डु लेखक
Notes and orders	टीपें और आज्ञाएँ
Notification, Communique	विज्ञप्ति
Nozzle	नाक (टोंटी)
Nuisance	कंटक (बाधा)
Null and void	निष्प्रभाव और निरर्थक
Numbered	संख्यात
Numerator, Share	अंश
Nursery	पौधशाला
Oath of allegiance	राज्य निष्ठा शपथ
Object	उद्देश्य
Objection	आपत्ति
Objection (statement)	अवक्षेपण (विवरण पत्र)
Objector	आपत्तिकर्ता
Obligation instrument	दायरा का करणपत्र
Obligation of residence	निवास प्रतिबंध
Oblique	तिर्यक्
Oblong	आयत (याताकार)
Obscure	अस्पष्ट (अप्रसिद्ध)
Observation	आलोचन

Obsolete stamp	अप्रचिलत स्टाम्प
Occupancy right	भोगोधिकार (दखीलकारी)
Occupancy tenant	दखील असामी
Occupation	वृत्ति, पेशा
Occupiers' rate	किरायेदार की दर
Octroi duty	चुंगीकर
Odd	विषम
Offer	उपदान
Officer under training	शिक्षणाधीन अधि कारी
Officer on special duty	विशेष कार्याधिकारी
Official	कर्मचारी
Official Assignee	सरकारी अधिहस्तांकिती
Official trustee	सरकी प्रन्यासी
Officiating appointment	स्थानापन्न नियुक्ति
Officiating, Substitute	स्थानापन्न
Offset piece	गुनिया
Old fallow	पुरानी परती
On parole	संगर-बद्ध
On special duty	विशेष कार्यार्थ
Ooze	चूना (टपकना)
Opening balance	आरंभिक
Operator	चालक
Opposite party	प्रतिपक्ष
Opposite party	विपक्ष
Option	रुचि
Option, Alternative	विकल्प
Oral evidence	मौखिक साक्ष्य
Orbit	अक्षिकप
Orbit	कक्ष (ग्रहपथ)
Order book	आज्ञा पुस्तक
Order file	आज्ञा नस्ती
Order sheet	आज्ञा फलक
Order-book	आदेश-पंजी
Ordinance (law)	अध्यादेश
Ordinate, Grade	कोटि
Organisation	संगठन
Organisation	संघटन
Organiser	आयोजक
Organiser	संघटनकर्ता
Oriental	पूर्वी
Original	मूल
Original award	आरंभिक निर्णय
Outlay	लागत
Outlet	निकास
Outpost (Police)	चौकी
Oval or rounded creature	वर्तुलाकार जीव
Overcharge	अधिक व्यय
Overcharge, Surcharge	अधिभार
Overhead charges	उपरिव्यय
Overpayment	अधिक भुगतान

Overseas pay	समुद्र पार का वेतन
Overseer	अवेक्षक
Overstay	अत्वस्थान
Overtime	समयोत्तर (काम)
P. T. Instructor	व्यायाम शिक्षक
P.W. (Prosecution witness)	अभियोग साक्षी
Painter	रंजक
Panel (architecture)	दिलाहा
Pantographer	प्रतिलिपिक यन्त्र
Pantry	खाद्य कोष्ठ
Par	समता
Para	अनुच्छेद
Parallel	समान्तर
Parapet	कमरकोटा (मुँडेर)
Paraphernalia	सामान
Parcel	पोट्टलिका (पार्सल)
Park	उद्यान
Parlour	बैठक (बरोठा)
Parole	संगर
Part performance, Part supply	आंशिक पूर्ति
Part time	अंश कालिक
Part-heard	सुना भाग
Particular	विशिष्ट (सविशेष)
Particular, Statement	विवरण
Parties	उभयपक्ष
Passage (voyage by sea)	संयात्रा
Pass-book	ग्राहक-पुस्तिका (पासबुक)
Passport	पारपत्र
Patch repairs	थोप चेप मरम्मत
Patent medicine	एकस्व भेषज
Pathological specimens	रोग विषयक नमूने
Pathology	रोगशास्त्र
Patron, Custodian	संरक्षक
Pattern	प्रतिमान
Pauper appeal.	अकिंचन अपील
Pauper suit.	अकिंचन वाद
Pawn, Pledge	आधि (गिरवी)
Pay	वेतन
Pay account	वेतन लेखा
Payment	भुगतान
Peace	शांति
Pebble	रोड़ी (छान)
Pecuniary, Monetary	आर्थिक
Pedestrian	पदिक
Penal	दंड विषयक
Penalty	डाँड़
Pencil	अंकनी
Pendant, Hanger	लटकन (झूमका)
Pendency	लम्बमानता
Pending	अम्बमान
Penology	दंडशास्त्र
Pension	निवृत्ति वेतन
Pensioner	निवृत्ति वेतनी

Perforator	वेधनी
Perimeter	परिमाप
Period of limitation	अवधिताकाल
Periodical	सामयिक
Permanent advance	स्थायी अग्रधन
Permanent alimony	स्थायी दाराभूति
Permanent post	स्थायी पद
Permanent tenure holder	स्थायी भू भुक्तिधारी
Permanently settled	स्थायी बन्दोबस्ती
Permissible	अनुज्ञेय
Permit	अनुमतिपत्र
Perpetration, Delinquency	अपराध (बुरा काम)
Perpetual allowance	शाश्वत भत्ता
Personal appearance	व्यक्तिगत उपस्थिति
Personal law	स्वधर्म शास्त्र
Personal ledger	वैयक्तिक प्रपंजी
Personal pay	वैयक्तिक वेतन
Pertain	सम्बन्ध रखना
Petition	अभ्यर्थना (याचिका)
Petitioner	अभ्यर्थी
Petty contingent expenditure	क्षुद्र प्रासंगिक व्यय
Petty establishment	लघु स्थापना
Physical assets	भौतिक परिसम्पत्
Piece work	ठेके का काम
Pier	पाया (संभा)
Pile bridge	भूमि प्रविष्ट पुल
Pilot scheme	पथदर्शक योजना
Pivot	चूल (जिस पर कोई वस्तु घूमे)
Plaint	वाद, अर्जीदावा
Plaint	वादपत्र (अर्जी दावा)
Plaintiff	वादी
Plan	मानचित्र
Plane	समतल
Plant and machinery	स्थिर यन्त्र और मशीनें
Plate	पट्टिका
Pleader	अभिभाषक
Plinth	पीठभू (कुर्सी)
Plumb (mason)	संबक
Plumber	सीसागर
Plus & minus memo	धन तथा ऋण का स्मृति पत्र
Polygon	बहुभुज
Pool	पल्वल (पोखर)
Portable	सुवहनीय
Positive	धनात्मक
Post	रास्ता
Post, Rank	पद (ओहदा)
Posting	तैनाती
Post-mortem	शवपरीक्षा
Postscript	अनुलेख

Posture	मुद्रा (आसन)
Post-war	युद्धोत्तर
Power	अधिकार
Power of attorney	अभिकर्तापत्र
Power of attorney	प्रतिनिधि पत्र
Power-vested	संप्राप्त अधिकार
Preamble, Introduction	प्रस्तावना
Precaution	पूर्वोपाय
Precedence	पूर्वता (आदिता)
Pre-censorship	पूर्वदोष वेंचन
Predecessor-in-title	स्वत्वाधिकार पूर्ववर्ती
Predication	उपाधि प्राप्ति
Pre-emption, Right of pre-emption	पूर्वक्रयाधिकार (हकशफा)
Preference	अधिमान
Prejudice	पक्षपात
Preliminary	प्रारंभिक
Premises	गृहोपान्त
Preponderance	प्रधान
Prescribed	नियत
Prescribed	विहित (निर्धारित)
Prescribed form	नियत फारम
Presented, Submitted	प्रस्तुत
Preservation	परिरक्षा
Presiding officer	निर्वाचनाध्यक्ष
Presumptive (pay)	अनुमानिक (वेतन)

Preventive	निवारक
Prima facie	पहली दृष्टि में
Prima facie	प्रामि दृष्टि सिद्ध
Primary unit	प्राथमिक इकाई
Prime mover	प्रधान प्रेरक
Principal money	मूलधन
Principal rafter	मुख्य धरणी
Priority	आदिता (पूर्वता)
Privilege	विशेषाधिकार
Privilege leave	रियायती छुट्टी
Privy Council	प्रिवी कौंसिल
Prize bonds	पारितोषिक प्रतिज्ञापत्र
Probate	इच्छापत्र की प्रमाणित प्रतिलिपि
Probation	परीक्षण
Probationer	परीक्ष्यमाण
Procedure	कार्य पद्धति
Procedure	कार्यविधि
Procedure	प्रक्रम
Procedure	विधि
Proceedings, Action	कार्यवाही
Process	रीति
Process fees	आह्वान शुल्क
Process server	आदेश पत्र वाहक
Proclamation, Declaration	घोषणा
Procuress	दूती (संचारिका)
Production	उत्पादन
Production (as a document)	प्रस्तुति

Profession	वृत्त (व्यवसाय)
Proficient	प्रवीण
Pro-forma	नियमानुरूप
Proforma respondent	यथानियम उत्तरवादी
Proforma-defendant	गौण प्रतिवादी
Proforma-respondent	गौण उत्तरवादी
Progressive pay	वर्धमान वेतन
Prohibition	निषेध
Prohibition	मद्यनिषेध
Project, Scheme	योजना
Projection	प्रक्षेपण
Promotion	पदोन्नति
Pronote	बचन पत्र
Pronote	रुक्का
Propaganda	प्रचार
Proportion	अनुपात
Proportion	समानुपात
Proportionate	आनुपातिक
Proposition statement	प्रस्तावित नकशा
Proposition statement	प्रस्तावित विवरण
Proprietor	स्वामी
Propulsion charges	चालान-व्यय
Pro-rata	अनुपातत:
Prosecute	अभियोग (चलान)
Prosecuting inspector	कोषस्थीकरण
Prosecution	अभियोग
Prosecution	अभियोग पक्ष
Prospective	भावी
Protected land	सुरक्षित भूमि
Protection	रक्षा
Protector of emigrants	उत्प्रवासी संरक्षक
Pro-vice-chancellor	प्रति उपकुलपति
Provident	दूरदर्शी
Provident fund	पूर्वापायी कोष
Provision (Budget)	व्यवस्था
Provision, Instructions (law)	आदेश
Provisional	अस्थायी
Provisional substantive	अस्थायी मूल
Proviso	प्रतिबन्धात्मक वाक्य खण्ड
Proxy, Locum tenens	प्रतिपुरुष
Public Prosecution	सरकार-चालित मुकदमा
Public affairs	सार्वजनिक मामले
Public conveyance	किराये की गाड़ी
Public debt	सार्वजनिक ऋण
Public Officer	सार्वजनिक अधिकारी
Public safety	जन-सुरक्षा
Public servant	जन-सेवक
Public utility	सार्वजनकि उपयोगिता
Public works Department	सार्वजनिक निर्माण विभाग

Publicity	प्रकाशना (प्रख्यापना)
Punishment, Penalty	दंड
Purview	अधिकार सीमा
Pyramid (ancient world)	सूची
Quadrant	पाद
Quadratic equation	वर्ग समीकरण
Quadrennial	चौसाला
Quantity, Volume	परिमाण
Quarantine	स्पर्शवर्जन
Quarantine leave	स्पर्शवर्जन छुट्टी
Quarterly statement	त्रैमासिक विवरण
Quasi-permanent	अर्थ स्थायी
Questionnaire	प्रश्नावली
Quinquennial	पंचवर्षीय
Rafter	कड़ी (धरणी)
Railings, Rack	करघटा
Rain gauge	वर्षामापक
Rake	पाँचा
Random	अव्यवस्था
Rank	आस्पद (पदवी)
Rank and file	साधारण सैनिक वर्ग
Ratchet	कुत्ता
Rate of exchange	विनिमय दर
Raw material	कच्चा माल
Realization	उगाही (वसूली)
Re-appropriation	पुनः पर्यादान
Re-armament	पुनः शस्त्रीकरण
Rebate	अवहार (छूट)
Recall from leave	छुट्टी से वापस बुलाना
Receipt book	रसीद बही
Receipt register	प्राप्ति पंजी
Receiver	प्रतिग्राहक
Receptacle	भाजन (आधान)
Recess	विश्राम (छुट्टी)
Recess, Vacation	अवकाश
Recipient	आदाता
Reciprocity	पारस्परिकता
Recognised agent	मान्यता प्राप्त अभिकर्ता
Recognition	मान्यता
Recognizance	मुचलका
Reconnaissance	पूर्वानुदर्शन
Re-constitution	पुनः रचना
Record	अभिलेख
Record of service	सेवाभिलेख
Record operation	अभिलेख संशोधन
Record-in-charge	अभिलेखाधिकृत
Record-keeper	अभिलेख पाल
Recovery	प्रतिलब्धि
Recruitment	भरती
Rectification of error	अशुद्धि शोधन
Rector	अधिष्ठाता

Recurring	आवर्ती
Redemption	विमोचन
Redemption of mortgage	बंधकमोचन
Reduction	पदावनति
Re-employed	पुनर्नियुक्त
Re-employment	पुनर्नियक्ति
Re-establishment, Re-instatement	पुनः स्थापन
Reference	अभ्युद्देश
Reflection	प्रतिकाश
Reflector	प्रतिकाशक
Refresher's course	नवीकर कोर्स
Refugee	शरणार्थी
Refund	रुपये की वापसी
Region	प्रदेश
Regional	प्रादेशिक
Register	पंजी
Register of duty	ड्यूटी का रजिस्टर
Registered	पंजीयित
Registrar	पंजीयक
Registration	पंजीयन
Regulation	आनियम (नियमन)
Regulator	नियामक
Reinforcement	अधिक बलन
Rejoinder	प्रत्युत्तर
Relaxation	शिथिलता
Relaxation	शिथिलीकरण
Relaxation	शैथिल्य
Relaxed	शिथिलीकृत
Relief (Carving)	उभार
Relinquishment	परित्याग दस्तबरदारी
Relinquishment of land	भूमि का अधिकारत्याग
Relinquishment, Abandonment, Surrender	त्याग
Remain at large	अबन्धित आज्ञा
Remarks	अभ्युक्ति (कैफियत)
Reminder	अनुस्मारक
Reminder	स्मारकपत्र
Remission	छूट
Remittance	विप्रेषित धनराशि
Remuneration	पारिश्रमिक
Renewal	नवीकरण
Renort	प्रतिवेदन
Renovation	पुनर्नवीकरण
Rent statement	किराये का नक्शा
Rent statement	लगान का नकशा
Rental	मालियत जमाबन्दी
Re-organisation	पुनः संगठन
Repatriation	स्वदेशार्पण
Repeal	मंसूखी
Repeal	विखंडन करना
Replacement	प्रतिस्थापन
Report	रपट
Report	विवरण प्रतिवेदन

Representation	आवेदन पत्र
Representative	प्रतिनिधि
Representative fraction	नमना
Repugnant	विपरीत
Requisition	अपेक्षण
Re-registration	पुनः पंजीयन
Rescue Home	तारण गृह
Reserve	रक्षित
Reservists	धृतदल रक्षिगण
Reservoir	जलाशय (टंकी, हौज)
Residence, Quarter	आवास
Resident	आवासिक
Residue	अवशेष
Resignation	त्यागपत्र
Resistance	प्रतिरोध
Res-Judicata	प्राङ्‌गन्याय
Resolution	संकल्प
Resolution, Proposal	प्रस्ताव
Respondent	उत्तरदायी
Respondent and Co-respondent	उत्तरवादी और सहोत्तरवादी
Restitution	यथापूर्व कर देना
Restraint by Court	न्यायालय द्वारा रोक
Resumption	पुनर्ग्रहण
Resumption	प्रत्यादान
Retainer	आयुधपाल
Retardation	वेगक्षय
Retention	प्रतिधारण
Retirement	निवृत्ति
Re-totalling	पुनर्योग
Retrenchment	छटनी
Retrograde (Motion)	वक्र (पीछे को, उलटा)
Retrospective effect	पूर्व प्रभाव
Return	प्रबंधक विवरण पत्र
Return (Statistics)	विवरण पत्र
Returning	प्रतिदान
Revenue	माल
Revenue	राजस्व
Revenue administration report	माल विभाग की रिपोर्ट
Revenue administrator	माल प्रशासक
Revenue Establishment	मालस्थापना
Revenue stamp	माल का स्टाम्प
Reverend	परम पूज्य
Reverend	पूज्य
Reversion	प्रत्यावर्तन
Review	पुनर्दर्शन
Review	पुनरवलोकन
Review of judgment	निर्णय का पुनर्निरीक्षण
Revised	संशोधित
Revised estimate	संशोधित आगणन
Revision	पुनरावृत्ति

Revision of scale of pay	वेतन क्रम का संशोधन
Revision Officer	संशोधक अधिकारी
Revocation of licence	अनुज्ञप्ति खण्डन
Revocation, Cancellation	निरसन (मंसूखी)
Revoke	निरस्त करना
Rib of an arc	डाट का पार्श्व
Ribands (of decorations & medals), Sash and banner	मानचित्र
Rinderpest	बेदन
Rolled (steel)	पीड़ित
Rotten	पूतिक
Rule of proportion	समानुपात नियम
Ruling	व्यवस्था (नजीर)
Run off, Gradient	ढाल
Runner	धावक (हरकारा)
Running statement	चलता विवरण
Rupture	फटाव
Rural	ग्राम्य
Rust	मंडूर (जंग)
Saddle	पर्याण
Safety factor	अरिष्ठ गुणक
Sale certificate	विक्रय प्रमाणपत्र
Sale proposal	विक्री का प्रस्ताव
Sanctioned estimate	स्वीकृत आगणन
Sanctioned grant	स्वीकृत अनुदान
Satchel	खलीता
Satisfactory	संतोषजनक
Savings	संचय
Scabbard	मियान
Scale of pay	वेतन क्रम
Scale prescribed	निर्धारित वेतन क्रम
Scarbutic	खुजीला
Scene of outbreak	रोग फैलाने का स्थान
Schedule	अनुसूची
Schedule of rates	दरअनुसूची
Scheduled	परिगणित
Scrap	छीलन
Script	लिपि
Scrum	चर्भसार (पन्छा)
Scrutiny	सूक्ष्म परीक्षा
Sculpture	मूर्तिकर्म
Seal	मुहर
Secant	छेदिका
Secret service Charges	गुप्त सेवा व्यय
Secretary	सचिव
Secretary of state	राजमन्त्री
Section	उपविभाग
Section	धारा
Section (Cross & long)	काट (खाड़ी और खंबानी)
Sector (Radius Vector)	ओरी कोल
Security	सरकारी ऋण पत्र
Security	अरिष्ठि

Security (of a person) Bail order	प्रतिभू
Security, Bail, Surety	प्रतिभूति
Sedition	राजद्रोह
Segment	कट्टा
Segregation	अलगाव
Seizure, Attachment	कुड़की
Select committee	प्रवर समिति
Selection	वरण
Selection post	चुनावपद
Self-explanatory	स्वतः व्याख्यात्मक
Seniority	ज्येष्ठता
Sentencing authority	दंड आज्ञा देने वाले प्राधिकारी
Sentry	प्रहरी
Serial	क्रमिक
Serpentine	सर्पीली (सँपेनी)
Served	तामील किया गया
Service roll	सेवावर्ति
Service-book	सेवा पुस्तिका
Service-rules	सेवा नियमावली
Servitude	दंडात्मक श्रम
Sessions	दौरा
Sessions House	दौरा न्यायगृह
Sessions Judge	दौराजज
Sessions trial	दौरा अदालत में मुकदमा
Set aside	पराकृत (करना)
Set off	घटोत्तरी
Settlement	भूव्यवस्था
Settlement	व्यवस्थान
Settlement, revocation of	व्यवस्था खण्डन पत्र
Severality	संपत्ति का पृथक् पूर्ण अधिकार
Sewer	गंदा नाला
Sextant	षटक
Shade	रंगमान (रंग)
Shaft	दंड (धुरा)
Shank	बारंग (डंडी)
Share warrant	अंशाधिपत्र
Sharp curve, Hairpin	तंग मोड़
Shingle	कंकड़ी (छोटी-छोटी)
Shrivelled grain	पतला अनाज
Side wall	पार्श्व भित्ति
Sieve test	छलनी परीक्षा
Sight	बन्दूक की मक्खी
Silt	चहला (कीचड़)
Silt	पंककिट्ट
Sink	मलकूप
Sinking fund	ऋण चुकाव कोष
Site	आस्थान
Site plan	स्थल चित्र
Sizarship	फीसमाफी
Skeleton form	रूप (ढाँचा)
Skilled labour	प्रवीण श्रम

Sliding scale	चढ़ता
Slip book	पर्चीपुस्त
Small Causes Court	अल्पवाद न्यायालय
Small Causes Court	लघुवाद न्यायालय
Smuggling	चौर्यपण
Soil classifier	भूमि वर्गीकारक
Solitary confinement, Dungeon	कालकाठरी
Solution (chemistry)	घोल
Solution (Math)	सुलझान
Space	आकाश (रिताई)
Space Science	अंतरिक्ष विद्या
Spare	फालतू
Special duty	विशेष कार्य
Special messenger	विशेष दूत
Special pay	विशेष वेतन
Special prosecuting officer	विशेष अभियोग अधिकारी
Specific	आपेक्षिक
Specific	निर्दिष्ट
Specific area	विशिष्ट क्षेत्र
Specific performance	विशिष्ट अनुष्ठान
Specification	ब्यौरा
Speculative reference	अनुमानित अभ्युद्देश
Speed limit	गति सीमा
Spelling	अक्षरोटी
Sphere	गोला
Spill way	जल निर्गमन मार्ग
Splinter	छिपटी (खपच्ची)
Sport	आखेट (खेल)
Spring level	स्रोतस्तर
Spur	काँटा (ठोकर)
Square	चौक (चबूतरा, बाजार, कचहरी)
Stabilization	स्थिरीकरण
Stable	गोष्ठ
Stable gear	सामान अस्तबल
Staff	कर्मचारी वर्ग
Stamp defalcation	स्टाम्प व्यवहरण
Stamp duty	स्टाम्प शुल्क
Stamp vendor	स्टाम्प विक्रेता
Standard	प्रमाण
Standard at work	कार्यस्तर
Standard of work	कार्यसमिति
Standard, Bonafide	प्रामाणिक
Standardization	प्रामणिक करना
Standing counsel	स्थायी वकील
Standing Order	स्थायी आदेश
Statement	वर्णन
Statement of expenditure	व्यय विवरण
Station	संस्थान
Station officer	थानेदार (बड़े)
Stationary	स्थिर
Stationed	संस्थापित

Stationery	लेखन सामग्री
Statistics	संख्याशास्त्र
Statistical assistant	संख्या शास्त्रीय सहायक
Statuary	वैधानिक
Statuary Responsibility	वैधानिक उत्तरदायित्व
Statute	कानून-व्यवस्था
Statutory form	विधिविहित फार्म
Stave	पटरी (पाया)
Stay application	स्थगन प्रार्थनापत्र
Stay of suit	वाद स्थगन
Stay order	स्थगन आज्ञा
Stear	पिचक
Stencil	निकृन्त (स्टेन्सिल)
Stenographer	संकेन्द्र
Stimulus	प्रोत्साहन
Stipendiary	वैतनिक
Stirrup	रकाब
Stock	निचय
Stock-in-hand	वर्तमान स्टाक
Storage	संचयन
Storage losses	संचयन में माल की हानियाँ
Storeman	भांडागारिक
Strain	आतान
Stream gauging observation	प्रवाहमान ईक्षण
Stretcher	तानक
Strong room	दृढ़ कोष्ठ
Strut	रोक
Stud buck	बीज छाग
Stud ram	बीजाज
Study-leave	अध्ययन-छुट्टी
Sub-committee	उपसमिति
Sub-division	उपभाग
Sub-head	उपशीर्षक
Sub-Inspector	थानेदार
Submerged	जलमग्न
Submission	उपस्थापन
Subordinate	अधीनस्थ
Subordinate Veterinary service	अधीनस्थ पशुचिकित्सा सेवा
Sub-paragraph	उप अनुच्छेद
Sub-proprietor	उपस्वामी
Subscription for the loan	कर्जे में दिया गया रुपया
Sub-section	उपधारा
Subsequent proceeding	बाद की कार्यवाही
Subsidiary rule	सहायक नियम
Subsistance grant	निर्वाह अनुदान
Subsistence	उपजीवन (निर्वाह)
Subsistence allowance	निर्वाह भत्ता
Substitution application	प्रतिस्थानी बनने के लिए प्रार्थनापत्र
Substantive	स्वनिष्ठित
Substantive pay	मूल वेतन
Substantive post	मूलपद
Sub-station	उपसंस्थान

Subtraction	घटाव
Sub-voucher	उप प्रमाणक
Succession	अनुक्रम (परम्परा)
Succession certificate	उत्तराधिकार प्रमाणपत्र
Successor	उत्तराधिकारी
Suction	चूसण
Suffix	प्रत्यय
Suit	वाद (नालिश)
Suit for maintenance	रोटी कपड़े का दावा
Suit of easement	सुखाधिकार का वाद
Suit Valuation Act	वादमूल्य विधान
Suit, case	वाद
Suits clerk	दायरा क्लर्क
Suits for guardianship	संरक्षतावाद
Summary Judgement	सरसरी निर्णय
Summon dasti	हाथ समन
Summons	आह्वान पत्र
Summons	सम्मन
Superannuation	पचपन साला
Superannuation (date of)	पचपन साले की तारीख
Superior staff	प्रवर स्थापना
Supervisor	पर्यवेक्षक
Supplemental deed	पूरक लेख्य
Supplementary	अनुपूरक
Supporating lesion	मवाद पड़ा हुआ घाव
Supra	ऊपर
Surgeon	शल्यवैद्य (सर्जन)
Surplus	अतिरेक (वचत)
Surrender of lease	पट्टा समर्पण पत्र
Surveillance, Revision	निगरानी
Survey	अनुदर्शन (जाँच)
Survey and Settlement	भूमाप और भूव्यवस्था
Survey instructor	भूमाक शिक्षक
Survey sheet	भूमाप फलक
Suspect, Suspected	संदिग्ध
Suspend	स्थगित करना
Suspense	उचन्त (अवर्गित)
Suspension	निलंबन
Suspension	प्रलंबन
Suspension	स्थगन
Switch-board	पिजापट्ट
Sword knot	असिग्रन्थि
Symptoms	लक्षण
Syphon	निनाल
Syringe	पिचकारी
Table	सारिणी
Tack	बिरंजी
Tag	नस्या (टग)
Taking up execution proceedings	इजरा की कार्रवाई करना
Tallow	पीट्ट (चरबी)
Tariff	मांडकशुल्क

Tariff, Customs-duty.	आयात-निर्यात कर
Tarpaulin	तरपल (तिरपाल)
Taxing Judge	करनिर्धारक जज
Tear-smoke squad	अश्रु-धूम टुकड़ी
Technical	औद्योगिक
Technical	प्राविधिक
Technical pay	विशेष विषयक वेतन
Technical sanction	प्राविधिक स्वीकृति
Technique	प्रविधि
Telephone	दूरभाष (टेलीफोन)
Temporary post	अस्थायी पद
Tenancy	कब्जा आराजी
Tenancy	भूमि अधिकार
Tenant at will	कच्चा काश्तकार
Tenant-in-chief	असली काश्तकार
Tender	निविदा (टेंडर)
Tenement	भवन भाग (घर)
Tensile	तन्य
Tension	आतति (तनाव)
Tenure in perpetuity	पट्टा इस्तमरारी
Tenure in severality	पट्टीदारी
Tenure of post	सार्वधिक पद
Tenure, Land tenure	मिल्कियत अमीन
Term of Sentence	दंड विधि
Terminal	आवधिक
Terminal	सीमांकित
Terminal tax	सीमाकर
Termination, Abolition	समाप्ति
Territorial application	प्रादेशिक ढंग पर लागू होना
Testator	इच्छापत्र कर्ता
Tetanus	धनुर्वाद
The charge should be debited to the head	प्रभार शीर्षक पर डाला जाये
Theorem	प्रमेय (साध्य)
Theory	सिद्धान्त
Thermometer	तापमापक
Thorax	वक्षस्थल
Tillage, Holdings	जोत
Time barred	समय सार्गल
Time Scale	कालक्रम
Time scale of pay	वेतन कालक्रम
Time table	समय विभाग
Time-barred	कालतिरोहित
Time-keeper	समय लेखक
Title	स्वत्वाधिकार
Title-deed	आगमपत्र
To be recouped from time to time	समय-समय पर पूरा किया जाय
To cover	गाभिन करना (या कराना)
To defend the case	मुकदम की पैरवी करना
To execute decree	डिग्री इजरा करना
To serve notice on	पर नोटिस तामील करना

Toe wall	अंगुष्ठ भित्ति
Token	प्रतीक
Topography	पृष्ठ विवरण
Torch	चोरबत्ती
Torsion	मरोड़ (ऐंठन)
Totalling register	योग पंजी
Tour programme	दौरा का प्रोग्राम
Tracer	अनुचित्रक
Tracings	अनुरेखण
Tract	भूमि खण्ड
Trade mark	व्यापार चिह्न
Trade pay	व्यवसाय वेतन
Traffic Police	व्यवस्था पुलिस
Traffic, Communication	यातायात
Training	उपशिक्षा
Transaction	पणायन (लेनदेन)
Transaction	व्यवहार (लेनदेन)
Transcription	प्रतिलेखन
Transfer	बदली
Transfer	स्थानान्तरण
Transfer charge	हस्तांतरहण व्यय
Transfer of control	नियन्त्रण परिवर्तन
Transfer of share	अंश हस्तांतरण
Transfer, Transit	संक्रम
Transferee	क्रेता
Transformation	रूपान्तर
Transformer	रूपपरिवर्तक
Transition	संक्रमण
Transitory	क्षणिक
Transmission	पारेषण
Transmit	पारप्रेषण
Transport	वाहन
Trans-shipment	नावन्तरण
Trapezium (with only two sides parallel)	समलम्ब चतुर्भुज
Trapezoid (with no sides parallel)	असलम्ब चतुर्भुज
Travelling allowance	यात्रा भत्ता
Tread of steps	सीढ़ी
Treasure vault	खजाना
Treasury, bill	सरकार द्वारा जारी की हुई हुंडी
Trial court	विचार न्यायालय
Tribe	जनजाति
Tripod	त्रिपाद
Troops	फौज, फौजी दस्ते
Troops	सेना
Truncheon	लाठी
Trust endowment	प्रन्यास वृत्तिदान
Trust property	प्रन्यास सम्पत्ति
Tube well	नलकूप
Tubercular	क्षय रोग सम्बन्धी
Tuberculin test	यक्ष्मा परीक्षा
Tumour	फोड़ा
Turban	कुलाह
Turbine	परीवर्त
Turbine mistri	वरीवत मिस्त्री

Turn down collar	लौटकालर
Turn over	पूर्ण बिक्री
Turner	कुन्दकार
Turpitude	हीनता
Type writing	मुद्रलेखन
Typist	मुद्रलेखक
Unclaimed	अस्वामिक
Unclaimed documeat	अस्वामिक लेखपत्र
Unclassified	अवगीकृत
Uncurrent coin	अप्रचलित मुद्रा
Under consideration	विचाराधीन
Under cultivation	काश्त में
Under section	धारा के अधीन
Under the auspices	तत्वावधान में
Under-secretary	अनुसविच
Undertaking	समारम्भ
Undertrial prisoner	विचाराधीन बन्दी
Undertrial prisoner	हवालाती
Unexpired	शेष
Unhealthiness	अस्वास्थ्यकरदा
Uniform	इकसार
Uniform	एक सार (वर्दी)
Uniform	गणवेश
Uniform	वर्दी
Uniform procedure	समान कार्यविधि
Unlawful assembly	अवैध समुदाय
Unmanageable	असाध्य
Unnatural	अस्वाभाविक
Unproductive	अनुत्पादक
Unserviceable	निकम्मा
Unskilled	अप्रवीण
Unsound	अस्वस्थ
Unwholesome	अस्वास्थ्यकर
Up-to-date	आतिथि
Urban	शहरी
Urgent	आत्ययिक
Urgent slip	आत्ययिक पर्ची
Vacancy	रिक्त स्थान
Vacancy	रिक्ति
Vaccinal lymph	वैक्सीन लसीका
Vaccine	मसूरी, मसूरी लाल
Vaccine depot	वैक्सीन भण्डार
Vacuum	शून्यक (रिक्त)
Vagrancy	आवारगर्दी
Vagrant	आवारागर्द
Validity	वैधता
Valuation	मालीयत्त
Value	मूल्य
Variation	घटबढ़
Various	विभिन्न
Vault	गुंबज
Velocity	वेग
Ventilation	वायु संचार
Ventilation	संवातन

Ventricle	हृदय संपुट
Verbal	मौखिक
Verification	जाँच
Verification	सत्यापन (जाँच)
Verification, Authentication, Certification	प्रमाणीकरण
Vernacular Department	देशी भाषा विभाग
Versus	प्रति (बनाम)
Vertex	शीर्ष
Vesting	प्रदान
Veteran	ज्ञान वृद्ध
Veterinary Assistant Surgeon	पशुचिकित्सा सहायक सर्जन
Veterinary College	पशुविज्ञान महाविद्यालय
Veto	निषेधाधिकार
Viaduct	सेतु
Vice versa	विलामत:
Vicinity	पड़ोस
Vide	देखिए
Vigil	जागरण
Vigilance	चौकसी
Vigilant control	जागर नियन्त्रण
Village defence society	ग्राम रक्षा समिति
Violate	तोड़ना (भंग करना)
Violence	हिंसा
Violent	झगड़ालू
Virulent	प्रचंड
Visa	दृष्टांत
Viscosity	संलग्नशीलता
Visitation	भेंट
Visitor, Inspector	निरीक्षक
Visitors' book	निरीक्षण पुस्तक
Visual signalling Section	द्राष्टिक संकेत उप. विभाग
Viva voce	मौखिक परीक्षा
Vocation	व्यवसाय
Vocational	व्यावसायिक
Void	शून्य
Volatile	बाप्प शील
Volley	बौछार
Volume	आयतन (खंड)
Volume, Bay (division of roof)	खंड
Voluntary contribution	स्वेच्छापूर्ण चंदा
Voted allotment	मतदत्त दिष्टि
Voucher	प्रमाणक
Wage	भृति
Wage earner	मजदूर
Wage earning scheme	भृति अर्जन योजना
Waive the recovery	वसूली छोड़ देना
Walking stick gun	बन्दूकदार छड़ी
Waqf	वक्फ
Warder	वार्डर
Warder reserve	धृतवार्डर

Warning	चेतावनी
Warrant	अधिपत्र
Warrant for goods	माल अधिपत्र
Warrant of arrest	आसेध
Warrant of commitment	सुपुर्दगी का अधिपत्र
Warrant of precedence	पूर्वता अधिपत्र
Warrant-officer	अधिपत्र-अधिकारी
Watch & ward (Police)	चौकी पुलिस
Water carrier	भिश्ती
Water closet	संडास
Water proof	बरसाती
Water-logged land	चोपे की भूमि
Wear and tear	टूट-फूट
Wedge	फन्नी
Weeding	निराई
Weeding	निर्दान (निराई)
Weeding label	निर्दान चिप्पी
Weeding list	निर्दान सूची
Weeding slip	निर्दान पर्ची
Weeviling	घुन लगना
Weighment	बोझ
Weir, Barrage	बाँध

Welder	संधाता
Welding	पिघलाकर जोड़ना
Welfare centre	कल्याण-केन्द्र
Well boring	कूट वेधन
Whistle	सीटी
Whole	सम्पूर्ण
Wholesale price	थोक भाव
Will	रिक्थ (वसीयत)
Wireless operator	बेतार तार चालक
With retrospective effect	पूर्व प्रभाव सहित
Withdrawal	वापसी
Withdrawal of amount	निकाली हुई धनराशि
Withhold	रोकना
Witness	साक्षी
Workman	कामगर
Workshop	कर्मशाला
Writ	आज्ञापत्र (फरमाना)
Write-off	बट्टे खाते डालना
Written statement	लिखित उत्तरवाद
Yield	उपज
Yield	दावा छोड़ देना
Yours truly, Yours sincerely, faithfully	भवन्निष्ठ

Appendix-29/परिशिष्ट–29

Terms defined in English and their Hindi Equivalents in the Indian Constitution

भारतीय गणतन्त्र के संविधान में प्रयुक्त अंग्रेजी के पारिभाषिक शब्दों और पदों के हिन्दी समानार्थक शब्द व पद

Abandonment	परित्यजन, परित्याग
Abridgement	न्यूनन
Abrogate	निराकरण
Access	प्रवेश
Account	लेखा, गणना
Accrue	प्रापण, प्रोद्भवन
Accrued	प्राप्त, प्रोद्भूत उपार्जित
Accusation	अभियोग
Accused	अभियुक्त
Acquisition	अर्जन
Act	अधिनियम
Acting	कार्यकारी
Actionable wrong	अभियोज्य दोष
Adaptation	अनुकूलन
Addressed	सम्बोधित
Adherence	अनुषक्ति
Ad hoc	तदर्थ
Adjourn	स्थगन, स्थापित करना, अवधिदाब, कालदान
Administer	प्रशासन करना
Administration	प्रशासित
Administrative	प्रशासन
Administrative function	प्रशासकीय
Admiralty	नौसेना प्रमुख
Admissible	स्वीकार्य
Adoption	ग्राह्य
Adulteration	दत्तक ग्रहण, दत्तक स्वीकरण
Adulteration	अपमिश्रण
Adult suffrage	वयस्क मताधिकार
Advance	अग्रिम धन, पेशगी
Advice	मन्त्रणा, उपदेश, सलाह
Advise	मन्त्रणा देना
Advisory Council	मन्त्रणा परिषद्
Advocate	अधिवक्ता
Advocate General	महाधिवक्ता
Affect prejudicially	प्रतिकूल प्रभाव डालना
Affirmation	प्रतिज्ञान
Agency	अभिकरण
Agent	अभिकर्त्ता
Agreement	करार
Air Force	विमान बल
Air navigation	विमान परिवहन
Air traffic	विमान यातायात
Air ways	वायु पथ
Alien	अन्यदेशीय
Alienate	अन्य संक्रामण करना
Alienation	अन्य संक्रामण, परकीयकरण
Allegation	अभिकथन, आरोप
Allegiance	निष्ठा
Allocation	बँटवारा
Allot	बाँट लगाना

Allotment	बाँट
Allowances	भत्ता
Amendment	संशोधन
Amnesty	सर्वक्षमा
Amount	राशि
Annual	वार्षिक
Annual financial statement	वार्षिक वित्त-विवरण
Annuity	वार्षिकी
Annulment	रद्द करना
Appeal	अपील
Appear	उपस्थित होना
Appended	संलग्न
Application	प्रयुक्ति, लागू होना, आवेदन पत्र
Appointment	नियुक्ति
Appropriation	विनियोग
Appropriation bill	विनियोग-विधेयक
Approve	अनुमोदन करना
Approval	अनुमोदन
Arbitral Tribunal	मध्यस्थ न्यायाधीशकरण
Arbitration	मध्यस्थ निर्णय
Arbitrator	मध्यस्थ
Area	क्षेत्र
Armed Forces	सशस्त्र बल
Arrest	बन्दी करना
Article	अनुच्छेद
Assemble	समवेत होना, सम्मिलित होना
Assembly	सभा
Assent	अनुमति
Assessment	निर्धारण
Assignment	सौंपना
Association	संस्था
Assurance of property	संपत्ति हस्तांतरण पत्र
As the case may	यथास्थिति, यथाप्रसंग
Attach	कुर्की
Attorney General	महा-न्यायवादी
Audit	लेखा परीक्षा
Auditor-General	महालेखा परीक्षक
Authentication	प्रमाणीकरण
Authorize	प्राधिकृत करना
Authority	प्राधिकारी
Autonomous	स्वायत्त
Autonomy	स्वायत्तता
Award	पंचाज्ञा
Bail	प्रतिभू, जमानत
Ballot	मतपत्र
Bank	बैंक
Banking	महाजनी
Bankruptcy	दिवाला
Bar	रुकावट
Benefit	हित
Betting	पण लगाना, पण क्रिया
Bicameral	दोघरा, द्विगृही
Bill	विधेयक, बिल
Bill of exchange	विनिमय पत्र
Bill of indemnity	परिहार-विधेयक, क्षतिपूर्ति बिल
Bill of lading	वहन पत्र
Board	परिषद्
Body	निकाय
Body, Corporate	निगमनिकाय
Body governing	शासीनिकाय
Borrowing	उधार ग्रहण
Boundary	सीमा
Broadcasting	प्रसारण
Business	कारबार
Bye-election	उपनिर्वाचन

Bye-law उपनियम
Calling आजीविका
Camp शिविर
Candidate अभ्यर्थी, उम्मीदवार
Cantonment छावनी
Capacity सामर्थ्य
Capital मूलधन, पूँजी
Capital Value मूलधन-मूल्य
Capitation tax प्रतिव्यक्ति कर
Carriage परिवहन
Casting vote निर्णायक मत
Cattle pound पशु अवरोध, कांजीहौस
Cause वाद
Cause of Action वादमूलक
Census जनगणना
Central Bureau of Intelligence केन्द्रीय जाँच ब्यूरो विभाग
Certificate प्रमाण पत्र
Certiorari उत्प्रेषण-लेख
Cess उपकर
Chairman सभापति
Charge दोषारोप, अभियुक्ति
Charge भार, भारित करना
Charity पूर्त, दातव्य
Charitable and endowments दातव्य तथा धार्मिक धर्मस्व
Charitable institution दातव्य संस्था
Cheque चेक
Chief मुख्य
Chief Commissioner मुख्य आयुक्त
Chief Election-Commissioner मुख्य निर्वाचन आयुक्त
Chief Judge मुख्य न्यायाधीश
Chief Justice मुख्य न्यायाधिपति
Chief Minister मुख्यमन्त्री
Citizenship नागरिकता
Civil व्यवहारिक, असैनिक
Civil Court दीवानी अदालत
Civil power असैनिक शक्ति
Claim दावा
Clarification स्पष्टीकरण
Clause खण्ड
Code संहिता
Coinage टंकण
Colonization उपनिवेशन
Commerce वाणिज्य
Commercial वाणिज्य सम्बन्धी
Commission आयोग
Commissioner आयुक्त
Committee समिति
Committee, Select प्रवर समिति
Committee, Standing स्थायी समिति
Common good सार्वजनिक कल्याण
Common Seal सामान्य मुद्रा, सामान्य मुहर
Communicate संचार करना
Communication, Means of संचार साधन
Community लोकसमाज समुदाय
Commute लघुकरण
Company कम्पनी
Compensation प्रतिकर
Competent सक्षम
Complaint फरियाद
Comptroller and Auditor General नियंत्रक महालेखा परीक्षक
Compute संगणना
Concurrence सहमति
Concurrent list समवर्ती सूची

Condition	शर्त
Conditions of service	सेवा की शर्तें
Conference	सम्मेलन
Confidence, want of	विश्वास का अभाव
Conscience	अन्तःकरण
Consent	सम्मति
Consent, Previous	पूर्व सम्मति
Consequential	आनुषंगिक
Consideration	विचार
Consolidated Fund	संचित निधि
Constituency	निर्वाचन क्षेत्र
Constituency, territorial	प्रादेशिक निर्वाचन क्षेत्र
Constituent Assembly	संविधान सभा
Constitution	संविधान
Consul	वाणिज्य-दूत
Consultation	परामर्श
Construe	अर्थ करना
Consumption	उपभाग
Contact	सम्पर्क
Contagious	सांसर्गिक
Contempt	अवमान
Contempt of Court	न्यायालय अवमान
Context	संदर्भ, प्रसंग
Contingency-Fund	आकस्मिकता निधि
Contract	संविदा
Contravention	प्रतिकूलता, उल्लंघन
Contribution	अर्थदान
Control	नियंत्रण
Controversy	प्रतिवाद
Convention	प्रथा, परम्परा
Conveyance	सम्पत्ति हस्तांतरण
Convicted	दोषसिद्ध, अभिशस्त, दोष प्रमाणित
Conviction	दोषसिद्धि, अभिशस्ति
Co-operative	सहकारी संस्था
Copy	प्रतिलिपि, प्रतिकृति
Copyright	प्रकाशनाधिकार
Corporation	निगम
Corporation, Sole	एकल निगम
Corporation Tax	निगम-कर
Corresponding	तत्स्थानी
Corrupt	भ्रष्ट
Cost	परिव्यय, खर्च, लागत
Council	परिषद्
Council of Ministers	मन्त्रिपरिषद्
Council of State	राज्यपरिषद्
Council Regional	प्रादेशिक परिषद्
Council, Tribal	जनजाति-परिषद्
Countervailing duty	प्रति शुल्क
Court	न्यायालय
Court of Appeal	पुनर्विचार न्यायालय
Court, Civil	दीवानी अदालत
Court, District	जिला न्यायालय
Court, High	उच्च-न्यायालय
Court, Magistrate	दंडाधिकारी न्यायालय
Court, Martial	सेना न्यायालय
Court of Wards	प्रतिपालक अधिकरण
Court, Revenue	राजस्व न्यायालय
Court, Sessions	सत्र न्यायालय
Court, Subordinate	अधीन न्यायालय
Court, Supreme	उच्चतम न्यायालय
Credit	प्रत्यय, साख, पत्त
Crime	अपराध
Criminal	अपराधी, आपराधिक, दण्ड सम्बन्धी
Criminal Law	दण्ड-विधि
Currency	प्रचलित मुद्रा
Custody	अभिरक्षा
Custom duty	सीमा शुल्क

Customs duty	शुल्क, सीमान्त
Custom	रूढ़ि, आचार
Dealing	व्यवहार, लेना-देना
Debate	वाद-विवाद
Debenture	ऋण-पत्र
Debt	ऋण
Decision	विनिश्चय
Declaration	घोषणा
Decree	आज्ञप्ति, डिगरी
Dedicate	समर्पण
Deed	विलेख
Detamation	मानहानि
Defence	प्रतिरक्षा
Deliberation	पर्यालोचन
Demand	माँग, अभियाचना
Demarcation	सीमांकन
Demobilisation	सैन्य-वियोजन
Deprive	वंचित करना
Deputy Chairman	उपसभापति
Deputy Commissioner	उपायुक्त
Deputy Speaker	उपाध्यक्ष
Descent	उद्‌भव
Derogation	अल्पीकरण
Design	रूपांकरण
Detrimental	अहितकारी
Diplomacy	राजनय
Direction	निर्देश
Disability	निर्योग्यता
Discharge	निर्वहन
Discipline	अनुशासन
Disciplinary	अनुशासन सम्बन्धी
Discovery	अन्वेषण, खोज
Discretion	स्वविवेक
Discrimination	विभेद
Discussion	चर्चा
Dismiss	पदच्युत करना
Disperse	विसर्जन करना
Dispute	विवाद
Disqualification	अनर्हता
Disqualify	अयोग्य ठहराना
Dissent	विमति
Dissolution	विघटन
Distribution	वितरण, विभाजन
District	जिला
District Board	जिला परिषद्
District Council	जिलापरिषद्
District Fund	जिलानिधि
Dividend	लाभांश
Divorce	विवाह-विच्छेद
Documents	लेख्य, दस्तावेज
Domicile	अधिवास
Domiciled	अधिवासी
Dullness	प्रतिमान्द्य
During good behaviour	सदाचारपर्यन्त
During the pleasure of the President	राष्ट्रपति-प्रसाद पर्यन्त
Duty	शुल्क, कर्तव्य
Duty, Custom	सीमा-शुल्क
Duty, Death	मरण शुल्क
Duly, Estate	सम्पत्ति शुल्क
Duty, Excise	उत्पादन शुल्क
Duty, Export	निर्यात शुल्क
Duty, Import	आयात शुल्क
Duty, Stamp	मुद्रांक शुल्क
Duty, Succession	उत्तराधिकार शुल्क
Economic	आर्थिक
Education	शिक्षा
Efficiency of administration	प्रशासन कार्य क्षमता
Elect	निर्वाचित करना
Elected	निर्वाचित चुने हुए

Election	निर्वाचन
Election Commissioner	निर्वाचन आयुक्त
Election, Direct	प्रत्यक्ष निर्वाचन
Election, General	साधारण निर्वाचन
Election, Indirect	परोक्ष निर्वाचन
Election Tribunal	निर्वाचन अधिकरण
Electoral roll	निर्वाचन नामवली
Eligibility	पात्रता
Eligible	पात्र होना
Emergency	आपात
Emergent	आपाती
Emigration	उत्प्रवास
Emoluments	उपलब्धियाँ
Employer's liability	नियोजक दात्व्य, नियोजक उत्तरवादिता
Enact	अधिनियम
Encumbered estate	भारग्रस्त सम्पदा
Endorse	पृष्ठांकन
Endorsed	पृष्ठांकित
Endowment	धर्मस्व
Engagements	वचनबद्ध
Engineering	यन्त्र शास्त्र
Enterprise	उद्यम
Entitled	हक्क होना
Entrust	सौंपना
Entry	प्रविष्टि, दाखला
Equality	समता
Equal protection of laws	विधियों का समान संरक्षण
Escheat	राजगामी
Establishment	स्थापना, संस्थापन, स्थापना करना
Estates	संपदा
Estimates	आँक, प्राक्कलन
Evidence	साक्ष्य
Excess profit	अतिरिक्त लाभ
Exclude	अपवर्जन करना
Exclusion	अपवर्जन
Exclusive jurisdiction	अनन्य क्षेत्राधिकार
Executive	कार्यपालिका
Executive power	कार्यपालिका शक्ति
Exempt	मुक्त
Exercise	प्रयोग, अनुष्ठान
Ex-officio	पदेन
Expenditure	व्यय
Explanation	व्याख्या, स्पष्टीकरण
Explosives	विस्फोटक
Export	निर्यात
Extent	विस्तार
External Affairs	वैदेशिक कार्य
Extradition	प्रत्यर्पण
Extra territorial operations	राज्य क्षेत्रातीत प्रवर्तन
Factory	कारखाना
Faith	धर्म-श्रद्धा
Fare	भाड़ा, किराया
Finance Bill	देय शुल्क
Finance	वित्त
Financial bill	वित्त विधेयक
Financial Commission	वित्तायोग
Financial	वित्तीय
Financial obligation	वित्तीय भार
Finance statement	वित्तीय विवरण
Fine	अर्थदण्ड
Fishery	मीन क्षेत्र, मीन पण्य
Forbid	निषेध
Forbidden	निषिद्ध
Forces	बल
Foreign affairs	विदेशीय कार्य

Foreign exchange	विदेशीय विनिमय
Form	रूप, प्रपत्र, फारम
Formula	सूत्र
Formulated	सूत्रित
For the time being	तत्समय
Freedom	स्वतंत्रता, स्वातंत्र्य, आजादी
Freight	वस्तु भाड़ा
Frontiers	सीमान्त
Function	कृत्य
Function, Administrative	प्रशासकीय कृत्य
Fund	निधि
Fund sinking	निक्षेप निधि
Future market	वायदा बाजार
Gambling	द्यूत, जुआ
Gaztte	सूचना-पत्र, राजपत्र
General election	साधारण निर्वाचन
Govern	शासन करना
Governance	शासन
Government	सरकार, शासन
Government of State	राज्य की सरकार
Government of India	भारत सरकार
Governor	राज्यपाल
Grant	अनुदान
Grant-in-aid	सहायक अनुदान
Gratuity	उपदान
Guarantee	प्रत्याभूति
Guardian	संरक्षक
Guidance	मार्ग प्रदर्शन
Habeas Corpus	बन्दी प्रत्यक्षीकरण
Handicrafts	हस्तशिल्प, दस्तकारी
Hazardous	संकटमय
Headman	मुखिया
High Court	उच्च न्यायालय
Honorarium	मानदेय
House	सदन
House of People	लोकसभा
Illegal	अवैध
Illegal practice	अवैधाचरण
Immunity	उन्मुक्ति
Impeachment	महाभियोग
Implementing	परिपालन
Impose	आरोपण लगाना
Imprisonment	कारावास, कैद
Improvement Trust	सुधार प्रन्यास
Incapacity	असमर्थता
Incidental	प्रासंगिक
Incompetency	अक्षमता
Incompetent	अक्षम
Incorporation	निगमन
Incumbent of an office	पदधारी
Indebtedness	ऋणग्रस्तता
Industry	उद्योग
Ineligibility	अपात्रता
Ineligible	अपात्र
Infectious	सांक्रामिक
Inheritance	दाय
Initiate	उपक्रमण करना, दीक्षा देना
Injury	क्षति
Inland waterways	अन्तर्देशीय जलपथ
Inoperative	अप्रवृत्त
Inquiry	परिप्रश्न, जाँच
Insolvency	दिवाला
Inspection	पर्यवेक्षण
Institution	संस्था
Instruction	शिक्षा, अनुदेश, हिदायत

Instrument संविदा, विलेख, उपकरण, साधन
Insurance बीमा
Intercourse समागम
Interest ब्याज, सूद
International अन्तर्राष्ट्रीय
Interpretation निर्वचन, व्याख्या
Intestacy इच्छापत्र-हीनत्व, निर्वसीयत
Intestate इच्छापत्र-हीनत्व, निर्वसीयता
Introduce पुरःस्थापन करना
Introduction पुरःस्थापना
Invalid अमान्य, असमर्थ
Invalidity pension असमर्थता निवृत्ति वेतन
Investigation अनुसंधान
Involve अन्तर्ग्रस्त
Involved अन्तर्ग्रस्त
Irregularity अनियमितता
Issue बाद-पद
Joint family अवभिक्त कुटुम्ब, अविभक्त परिवार
Judge न्यायाधीश
Judge, Additional अतिरिक्त न्यायाधीश
Judgement निर्णय
Judicial power न्यायिक शक्ति
Judicial proceeding न्यायिक कार्यवाही, न्यायिक कार्यरीति
Judicial stamp न्यायिक मुद्रांक
Judiciary न्यायपालिका
Jurisdiction क्षेत्राधिकार
Justice, Chief मुख्य न्यायाधीश
Labour श्रम
Labour union श्रमिक संघ
Land records भू-अभिलेख
Land revenue भू-राजस्व
Land tenures भू-धृति
Law विधि
Law of Nations राष्ट्रों की विधि
Legal विधि सम्बन्धी
Legislation विधान
Legislative power विधायिनी शक्ति
Legislative Assembly विधान सभा
Legislative Legislature विधान परिषद्
Legislature विधान-मण्डल
Letters of credit प्रत्ययपत्र
Levy आरोपण, उद्ग्रहण, उगाहना
Liability दायित्व
Libel अपमान लेख
Liberty स्वाधीनता
Licence अनुज्ञप्ति, लाइसेन्स
Lieutenant Governor उप राज्यपाल
Limitation परिसीमा
List सूची
List, Concurrent समवर्ती सूची
List, State राज्य सूची
List, Union संघ सूची
Livelihood जीविका
Loan उधार, ऋण
Local area स्थानीय क्षेत्र
Local authorities स्थानीय प्राधिकारी
Local Board स्थानीय मण्डली
Local body स्थानीय निकाय
Local Government स्थानीय शासन
Local Self Government स्थानीय स्वशासन
Lock up बन्दीखाना
Maintain पोषण, बनाये रखना
Maintenance पोषण

Major	वयस्क
Majority	बहुमत
Mandamus	परमादेश
Manufacture	निर्माण
Maritime shipping	समुद्र-नौवहन
Maternity relief	प्रसूति सहायता, प्रसूति साहाय्य
Member	सदस्य
Memo	ज्ञाप, स्मृति पत्र
Memorandum	ज्ञापन
Memorial	स्मारक
Mental deficiency	मनोवैकल्प
Mental weakness	मनोदौर्वल्य
Merchandise marks	पण्य-चिह्न
Merchant Ship	वणिक-पोत
Migration	प्रव्रजन
Mind, unsound	विकृतचित्त
Mineral	खनिज
Mineral resources	खनिज-सम्पत्
Minor	अवयस्क
Minority	अल्पसंख्यक वर्ग
Misbehaviour	कदाचार
Modification	रूपभेद
Money bill	धन-विधेयक
Morality	सदाचार
Motion of confidence	विश्वास-प्रस्ताव
Motion of no-confidence	अविश्वास-प्रस्ताव
Municipal area	नगर-क्षेत्र
Municipal Committee	नगर-समिति
Municipal Corporation	नगरनिगम
National highways	राष्ट्रीय राजपथ
Naturalization	देशीयकरण
Naval	नौसेना-सम्बन्धी
Navigation	नौ-परिवहन
Newspaper	समाचार-पत्र
Nominate	नामनिर्देशन, मनोनयन
Notice in writing	लिखित सूचना
Obligation	अधिसूचना
Occupation	आभार
Official residence	उपजीविका, धंधा
Officer	पदाधिकारी
Official residence	पदावास
Opinion	अभिप्राय, राय
Order in Council	परिषद्-आदेश
Order, Standing	स्थायी आदेश
Ordinance	अध्यादेश
Organization	संघटन
Owner	स्वामी
Parliament	संसद
Partnership	भागिता
Pass	पारण, आदेश, परिचयपत्र
Passed	पारित
Passport	पारपत्र
Patent	एकस्व
Pecuniary jurisdiction	आर्थिक क्षेत्राधिकार
Penalty	शास्ति, दण्ड
Pending	रुका हुआ
Pension	निवृत्ति वेतन
Permission	अनुज्ञा
Perpetual succession	शाश्वत उत्तराधिकार
Perquisite	परिलब्धि
Personal law	स्वीय विधि
Piracy	जल-दस्युता
Plead	वकालत करना
Police	आरक्षक, पुलिस
Police Force	आरक्षक बल
Policy of insurance	बीमा-पत्र
Port-quarantine	पत्तन-निरोधा

Possession	स्ववश, कब्जा
Preamble	प्रस्तावना
Preference	अधिमान
Prejudice	प्रतिकूल प्रभाव
Preside	पीठासीन होना, सभापतित्व करना
President	राष्ट्रपति
Presiding Officer	पीठाधीश
Preventive detention	निवारक निरोध
Prisoner	बन्दी, कैदी
Privileges	विशेषाधिकार
Process	आदेशिका
Proclamation	उद्घोषणा
Proclamation of emergency	आपतकाल उद्घोषण
Prohibited	प्रतिषिद्ध
Prohibition	प्रतिषेध, निषेध
Promulgation	प्रख्यापन
Proportional representation	अनुपाती प्रतिनिधित्व
Proposal	प्रस्ताव
Prorogue	सत्रावसान
Provided	परन्तु
Proxy	प्रतिपत्री
Publication	प्रकाशन
Public debt	राष्ट्र-ऋण
Public demand	सार्वजनिक अभियाचना
Public health	लोक-स्वास्थ्य
Public notification	सार्वजनिक अधिसूचना, लोक-अधिसूचना
Public order	सार्वजनिक व्यवस्था
Public Service Commission	लोक सेवा आयोग
Public service	लोक सेवा
Qualification	अर्हता

Quarantine	निरोधा
Question of Law	विधि प्रश्न
Quorum	गणपूर्ति
Quo warranto	अधिकारपृच्छा
Ratification	अनुसमर्थन
Reading first	प्रथम वाचन
Receipt (paper)	पावती रसीद
Recommend	सिफारिश करना
Recommendation	सिफारिश
Records, Court of	अभिलेख न्यायालय
Record of rights	अधिकाराभिलेख
Recruitment	भर्ती
Recurring	आवर्तक
Redemption charges	विमोचन भार
Reference	निर्देश
Reformatory	सुधारालय
Refundable to	लौटाई जाने वाली
Regional Commissioners	प्रादेशिक आयुक्त
Regional Councils	प्रादेशिक परिषद्
Regional Fund	प्रादेशिक निधि
Registered	पंजीबद्ध, निबद्ध
Registration	पंजीयन, पंजी-बन्धन, निबन्धन
Regulation	विनिमय
Relevancy	सुसंगति
Relevant	सुसंगत
Remission	परिहार
Remuneration	पारिश्रमिक
Repeal	निरसन
Representation	प्रतिनिधित्व
Representative	प्रतिनिधि
Repreive	प्रविलम्बन करना
Repugnancy	विरोध
Repugnant	विरुद्ध

Requisition अधिग्रहण
Reservation रक्षण
Reserved forest रक्षित वन
Respite विराम
Restriction निबन्धन
Retire निवृत्त होना
Retirement निवृत्ति
Review पुनर्विलोकन
Revoke प्रतिसंहरण
Reward पारितोषिक
Rule of the road पथ-नियम
Ruler शासक
Safeguard रक्षा
Sale विक्रय
Sanction, previous पूर्व मंजूरी
Savings बचत
Security प्रतिभूति
Sentence दण्डादेश
Service charges सेवा भार
Session सत्र
Single transferable vote एकल संक्रमणीय मत
Sinking Fund निक्षेप निधि
Slander अपमान वचन
Social custom सामाजिक रूढ़ि
Social insurance सामाजिक बीमा
Social service सामजिक सेवा
Sovereign प्रभु
Sovereign Democratic Republic सम्पूर्ण प्रभुत्व-संपन्न लोकतन्त्रात्मक गणतन्त्र
Speaker अध्यक्ष
Speech, Freedom of वाक्स्वातन्त्र्य
Staff कर्मचारी-वृन्द
Stamp duties मुद्रांक-शुल्क
Standing orders स्थायी आदेश
State Funds राज्य-निधि
Stock exchange श्रेष्ठि-चत्वर
Subject matter वाद-विषय
Subordinate officer अधीन अधिकारी
Succession उत्तराधिकार
Successor उत्तराधिकारी
Sue व्यवहार लाना
Suffrage मताधिकार
Suit, Civil दीवानी मुकदमा
Summon आह्वान
Superintendence अधीक्षण
Supplementary grant अनुपूरक अनुदान
Supreme Command सर्वोच्च समादेश
Suspend निलम्बन
Tax, Callings आजीविका कर
Tax, Capitation प्रतिव्यक्ति कर
Tax, Corporation निगम कर
Tax, Employment नौकरी कर
Tax, Entertainment मनोरंजन कर
Tax, Export निर्यात कर
Tax, Profession वृत्तिकर
Tax, Income आयकर
Tax, Sale विक्रयकर
Tax, Terminal सीमा कर
Tax, Commercial व्यापार कर
Technical training शिल्पी प्रशिक्षण
Tenant किसान
Tender, Legal विधि मान्य
Tenure पदाविधि
Term अवधि
Territorial charges प्रादेशिक भार
Territorial Jurisdiction प्रादेशिक क्षेत्राधिकार
Territorial waters जल-प्रांगण
Territory राज्य-क्षेत्र
Tidal waters वेला-जी, ज्वार-जी

Tolls	पथ-कर
Trade marks	व्यापार चिह्न
Trade Union	कार्मिक-संघ
Traffic	यातायात
Traffic (human)	मानव-पणन
Training	प्रशिक्षण
Transfer	स्थानान्तरण, हस्तान्तरण
Transition	संक्रमण
Transport	परिवहन
Transportation	निर्वासन
Treasure troves	निखात निधि
Treaty	ंधि
Tribal area	जनजाति क्षेत्र
Tribe	जनजाति
Tribunal	न्यायाधिकरण
Triennial	त्रैवार्षिक
Trust	न्यास
Undischarged	अनुन्मुक्त
Unemployment	बेकारी
Union	संघ
Unity	एकता
Unsoundness of mind	चित्त-विकृति
Vacancy	रिक्ति, रिक्तता
Vagrancy	अवारागर्दी
Validity	मान्यता
Vice-President	उप-राष्ट्रपति
Village Council	ग्राम-परिषद्
Violation	अतिक्रमण
Vocation	व्यवसाय
Vote, Casting	निर्णायक-मत
Voter	मतदाता, वोटदाता
Votes on account	लेखानुदान
Votes of credit	प्रत्ययानुदान
Wage	मजूरी
Wage, Living	निर्वाह मजूरी
Warrant	अधिपत्र
Will	इच्छा-पत्र, बिल, वसीयत
Winding up	समापन
Writ	लेख

Appendix-30/परिशिष्ट–30

Prefixes (उपसर्ग)

English Prefixes

A—signifies in, on, asleep, abroad, ashore, aside, away ; away from, far away: arise, awake, avert, abide, ago; in intensive meaning : athirst, afresh, aweary.

Al—all : altogether : almighty.

Be—identical with the meaning of by in the senses (1) adding intensive force to transitive verb : bedaub, besmear. (2) making intransitive verbs transitive : become. (3) when prefixed to transitive verbs, it changes the object of the transi¬tive relation : bethink, becalm, bespeak. (4) in the privative meaning : behead. (5) in conver¬ting nouns into transitive verbs : befriend. (6) in converting adjec¬tives into transitive verbs : bedim, becalm. (7) in forming adverbs and prepositions from nouns: beside, because. By—by, by the side of: bypath, bystander.

Em— form of en before p or b: if the sense of 'to make' enlighten, embitter.

For—through, completely, away, oppo¬site : forbear, forgive, forswear, forget, forbid.

Fore—in advance of : foretell, foresight.

Forth—forward: /forthcoming. Fro—from, away: /reward.

Gain—against: gainsay.

In—into, in : inside, insight, incision.

Mis—in the sense of wrong, mistake, mislead.

Off—of Offspring, offshoot. Out-t-beyond : outbreak, outside; denoting excess; outrun, outbid, outshine. Over—above, beyond : overhang, overflow, overhold, overdo.

Un—not : unnatural, untrue, unbro¬ken in sense of reversal : unloose, undress; against back : untie, undo, unwind.

Under—lower, below, beneath : under¬sell, underwear,' underlie, under-ground.

With—from, back, against : withdraw, withhold, withstand.

Appendix-31/परिशिष्ट–31

Suffixes (प्रत्यय)

English Suffixes

संज्ञा के अर्थ

-ard$_r$ —*art*—to form nouns, one who; *drunkard,* braggart.

-dom—dominion, state or jurisdiction : martyrdom, kingdom, freedom.

-er—male agent : painter, gardener.

-hood—state or rank, nature: man-*hood;* likeli*hood,* false*hood*, neigh-bour*hood.*

-head—rank: godhead,

-kin—diminutive: napkin, lamb*kin,*

-let—diminutive: eyelet, streamlet.

-ling—diminutive: duckling, codling,

-ledge, lock—state: knowledge, wedlock.

-ness—state of: mildness, redness.

-ock—diminutive: *bullock,*

-ow—diminutive: shadow.

-red—state: kindred.

-ship, -skip, -sc condition : counsel*ship,* land*skip,* land*scape.*

-ster—(one who), agent : spinster, huckster.

-ther—agent or instrument : *feather, father.*

-wright—a workman : wheelwright.

-y—state or quality, place of; smithy, dirty.

विशेषण के अर्थ

-fast—firm : steadfast.

-fold—repetition : manifold, twofold.

-ish—in sense of (1) like : *childish,* waspish (2) designating nationalities : *English* (3) joined to adjectives with weakened effect; yellow-*ish, sweetish.*

-less—without : shoeless, fearless.

-ly—like, in manner of: manly, silently.

-some—same, full of : gladsome, frolicsome.

-wise—manner or position : lengthwise.

क्रियापद के प्रत्यय

-worth—worth : stalworth.

-ate—to make : variegate, captivate, invalidate.

-en, -er—to make of: broaden, lighten, hinder, potter.

-el, -le—turning into frequentative verbs: grovel, nipple.

-fy (Fr.)—to make : clarify, mollify.

-ize (Gr.)–to make: patronize, monopolize, dogmatize, philosophize, Christianize.

Latin and Greek Suffixes

क्रियापद के प्रत्यय

-able, -ible—able to : eatable, receivable, legible.

-aceous—distinguished by: herbaceous.

-age—collective sense: parsonage, assemblage.

-ary, -ier, -eer, -er—place or profession: seminary, parliamentary, *-ary, -ier, -eer, -er*—place or profession: seminary, parlia-

mentary, grenad. *ier,* engineer, painter, falconer.

-*ee*—object of acquisition: examinee.

-*ery, -ry*—an art, collective: cookery poultry.

—*ferous*—producing: cupriferous.

-*ic* (Gr.)—art or science: Physic.

-*ic*—belonging to: metallic, sulphuric.

-*icle*—diminutive: particle.

-*ism* (Gr.)—state or doctrine: *egoism* barbarism, spiritualism.

-*ist* (Gr.)—agent: artist.

-*ive*—that which is operative: explosive, pensive.

-*scle*—diminutive : corpuscle.

-*ment—state* of: concealment, pavement.

-*sque*—like: picturesque.

-*tery*—condition: mastery.

-*five*—able to: sensitive.

-*tory, -sory*—place: dormitory, illusory.

-*ose, -ous*—full of: bellicose, glorious.

Appendix-32/परिशिष्ट–32
Weights and Measures
भार, तौल तथा माप

अंग्रेजी चालू तौल
(Avoirdupois Weight)

27.32 grains make 1 dram.
16 drams ... 1 ounce.
16 ounces. ... 1 pound (1b.)
28 pounds ... 1 quarter (qr.)
4 quarters ... 1 hundred weight (cwt)

अंग्रेजी जौहरियों की तौल सोना, चाँदी और मणियों के लिए
(Troy Weight)

4 grains make 1 carat.
24 grains ... 1 penny weight (dwt).
20 dwts. ... 1 ounce troy
12 ounces troy ... 1 pound troy
25 lbs. ... 1 quarter.
100 lbs. ... 1 cwt.
20 cwts 1 Ton of gold or silver

सूखी औषधियों की अंग्रेजी तौल
(ApothecariesWeight (Dry)

20 grains make 1 scruple.
3 scruples ... 1 drachm.
8 drachms ... 1 ounce.
12 ounces. ... 1 pound (lb.)

तरल औषधायों की अंग्रेजी तौल
(Apothecaries Fluid Measure)

60 minims (drops) make 1 dra fluid
8 dra fluid ... 1 fluid ounce.
16 ounces make ... 1 pint.
8 pints ...1 gallon.

भूमि के क्षेत्रफल का माप या वर्ग परिमाण
(Measurement of Area)

144 sq. inches = 1 sq. foot.
1296 sq. inches = 9 sq. ft. = 1 sq. yd.

काल या समय माप
(Measurement of Time)

60 seconds = 1 minute.
60 minutes = 1 hour.
24 hours = 1 day.
7 days = 1 week.
28 days = 1 Lunar Month.
28 to 31 days = 1 Calender Month.
12 Calender Months = 1 Year.
365 ¼ days = 1 Common Year.
366 days = 1 Leap Year.

भारतीय लम्बाई का परिमाप
(Indian Measurement of Length)

72 बिन्दु या 3 लम्बे जव = 1 इंच
9 इंच = 1 बित्ता (Span) या बालिश्त
2 बित्ता या 18 इंच = 1 हाथ
2 हाथ = 1 गज

भारतीय भूमि या धरती की लम्बाई नापने का परिमाण
(Indian Measurement of Area)

22 गज या चार पोप या लाठा = 1 जरीब या चेन
1 जरीब = 100 कड़ी (Links)

भारतीय काल या समय परिमाण

(Indian Measurement of Time)

60 अनुपल = 1 विपल

60 विपल = 1 पल या 24 सेंकड

60 पल = 1 घड़ी या दण्ड या 24 मिनट

2।। घड़ी = 1 घण्टा

7।। घड़ी = 1 पहर (प्रहर)

8 पहर या 60 घड़ी = 1 दिन (दिवस)

1 चन्द्र मास = 29 दिन, 31 घड़ी, 50 पल और 7 विपल

7 दिन = 1 सप्ताह

15 दिन = 1 पक्ष या पाख

30 दिन = 1 मास या महीना

12 मास = 1 युग

100 वर्ष = 1 शताब्दी या सदी

भारतीय काल या समय परिमाण

12 units = 1 dozen या 12 इकाई = 1 दर्जन

12 dozen = 1 gross या 12 इकाई = 1 ग्रोस

20 units = kori या 12 इकाई = 1 कोड़ी

20 sheets of paper = quire

या 20 ताव कागज = 1 दस्ता या जिस्ता

20 qrires of paper = 1 ream

या 20 दस्ता = 1 रीम

10 reams of paper = 1 gattha

या 20 रीम = 1 गट्ठा

परिवर्तन सारिणी—बीच वाले कालम में मोटे अक्षरों में छपे अंक मीट्रिक या ब्रिटिश पैमाने के हैं। अतः 1 मीटर = 1.09 गज या 1 गज = 0.91 मीटर।

मीटर		गज	लीटर		पिन्ट्स	किग्रा		पाउंड
0.91	1	1.09	0.28	½	0.88	0.11	¼	0.55
1.83	2	2.19	0.57	1	1.76	0.23	½	1.10
2.74	3	3.28	1.14	2	3.52	0.45	1	2.20
3.66	4	4.37	1.70	3	5.28	0.68	1	3.31
4.57	5	4.47	2.27	4	7.04	0.91	2	4.41
			2.84	5	8.80	2.27	5	11.02
						2.72	6	13.23
						3.17	7	15.47
कि.मी		**मील**	**सें.ग्रे.**		**फा.हाईट**	**लिटर**		**गैलन**
1.61	1	0.62	−18	0	32	4.55	1	0.22
3.22	2	1.24	−14	6	43	6.82	1½	0.33
4.83	3	1.86	−11	12	54	9.09	2	0.44
6.44	4	2.48	−4	24	75	11.36	2½	0.55
8.05	5	3.11	0	32	90	13.64	3	0.66
9.65	6	3.73	2	36	97	15.91	3½	0.77
11.26	7	4.35	9	48	118	18.18	4	0.88
12.87	8	4.97	16	60	140	20.46	4½	0.99
14.48	9	5.59	22	72	162	22.73	5	1.10
			29	84	183	27.28	6	1.32
			36	96	205	31.82	7	1.54
			38	100	212	36.37	8	1.76
						40.91	9	1.98

Appendix-33/परिशिष्ट–33

Roman Numerals/रोमन अंक प्रणाली

1	एक	I
2	दो	II
3	तीन	I I I
4	चार	IV
5	पाँच	V
6	छः	VI
7	सात	VII
8	आठ	VIII
9	नौ	I X
10	दस	X
11	ग्यारह	XI
12	बारह	XII
13	तेरह	XIII
14	चौदह	XIV
15	पन्द्रह	XV
16	सोलह	XVI
17	सत्रह	XVII
18	अठारह	XVIII
19	उन्नीस	XIX
20	बीस	XX
21	इक्कीस	XXI
22	बाइस	XXII
23	तेइस	XXIII
24	चौबीस	XXIV
25	पच्चीस	XXV
26	छब्बीस	XXVI
27	सत्ताइस	XXVII
28	अट्ठाइस	XXVIII
29	उन्तीस	XXIX
30	तीस	XXX
31	इक्तीस	XXXI
32	बत्तीस	XXXII
33	तैंतीस	XXXIII
34	चौंतीस	XXXIV
35	पैंतीस	XXXV
36	छत्तीस	XXXVI
37	सैंतीस	XXXVII
38	अड़तीस	XXXVIII
39	उन्तालिस	XXXIX
40	चालीस	XL
41	इकतालिस	XLI
42	बयालिस	XLII
43	तैतालिस	XLIII
44	चौवालिस	XLIV
45	पैंतालिस	XLV
46	छियालिस	XLVI
47	सैंतालिस	XLVII
48	अड़तालिस	XLVIII
49	उन्चास	XLIX
50	पचास	L
51	इक्यावन	LI
52	बावन	LII
53	तिपन	LIII
54	चौवन	LIV
55	पचपन	LV
56	छप्पन	LVI
57	सत्तावन	LVII
58	अट्ठावन	LVIII
59	उनसठ	LIX
60	साठ	LX
61	एकसठ	LXI

62	बासठ	LXII
63	तिरसठ	LXIII
64	चौंसठ	LXIV
65	पैंसठ	LXV
66	छाछठ	LXVI
67	सड़सठ	LXVII
68	अड़सठ	LXVIII
69	उनहत्तर	LXIX
70	सत्तर	LXX
71	इकहत्तर	LXXI
72	बहत्तर	LXXII
73	तिहत्तर	LXXIII
74	चौहत्तर	LXXIV
75	पचहत्तर	LXXV
76	छिहत्तर	LXXVI
77	सतहत्तर	LXXVII
78	अठहत्तर	LXXIII
79	उन्यासी	LXXIX
80	अस्सी	LXXX
81	एक्यासी	LXXXI
82	बयासी	LXXXII
83	तिरासी	LXXXIII
84	चौरासी	LXXXIV
85	पचासी	LXXXV
86	छियासी	LXXXVI
87	सत्तासी	LXXXVII
88	अट्ठासी	LXXXVIII
89	नवासी	LXXXIX
90	नब्बे	XC
91	एक्यानबे	XCI
92	बानवे	XCII
93	तिरानवे	XCIII
94	चौरानबे	XCIV
95	पंचानबे	XCV
96	छियानवे	XCVI
97	सत्तानबे	XCVII
98	अट्ठानवे	XCVIII
99	निन्यानवे	XCIX
100	सौ	C
200	दो सौ	CC
300	तीन सौ	CCC
400	चार सौ	CD
500	पाँच सौ	D
600	छः सौ	DC
700	सात सौ	DCC
800	आठ सौ	DCCC
900	नौ सौ	CM
1000	एक हजार	M
2000	दो हजार	MM
3000	पाँच हजार	MMM

CAREER & BUSINESS MANAGEMENT

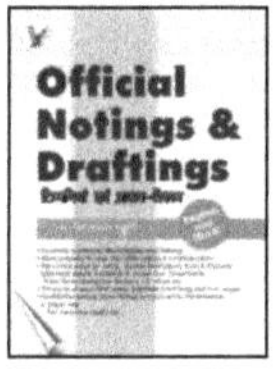

CONCISE DICTIONARIES

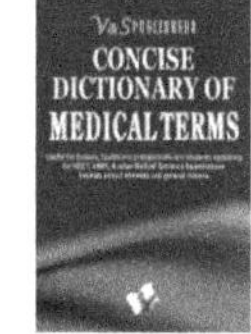

www.ingramcontent.com/pod-product-compliance
Lightning Source LLC
Chambersburg PA
CBHW060420100426
42812CB00030B/3244/J

* 9 7 8 9 3 5 0 5 7 1 4 2 2 *